Mastering
Autodesk® Revit® MEP 2015

Mastering
Autodesk® Revit® MEP 2015

Don Bokmiller

Simon Whitbread

Dan Morrison

AUTODESK.
Official Press

Senior Acquisitions Editor: Willem Knibbe

Development Editor: Susan Herman

Technical Editor: Steve Stafford

Production Editor: Rebecca Anderson

Copy Editor: Judy Flynn

Editorial Manager: Pete Gaughan

Vice President and Executive Group Publisher: Richard Swadley

Associate Publisher: Chris Webb

Book Designers: Maureen Forys, Happenstance Type-O-Rama; Judy Fung

Proofreader: Sarah Kaikini, Word One New York

Indexer: Ted Laux

Project Coordinator, Cover: Lauren Buroker

Cover Designer: Wiley

Cover Image: © iStock.com/bluecmu

ISBN: 978-1-118-87115-7
ISBN: 978-1-118-93251-3 (ebk.)
ISBN: 978-1-118-87132-4 (ebk.)

Library of Congress Control Number: 2014931960

10 9 8 7 6 5 4 3 2 1

Dear Reader,

Thank you for choosing *Mastering Autodesk Revit MEP 2015*. This book is part of a family of premium-quality Sybex books, all of which are written by outstanding authors who combine practical experience with a gift for teaching.

Sybex was founded in 1976. More than 30 years later, we're still committed to producing consistently exceptional books. With each of our titles, we're working hard to set a new standard for the industry. From the paper we print on, to the authors we work with, our goal is to bring you the best books available.

I hope you see all that reflected in these pages. I'd be very interested to hear your comments and get your feedback on how we're doing. Feel free to let me know what you think about this or any other Sybex book by sending me an email at `contactus@wiley.com`. If you think you've found a technical error in this book, please visit `http://sybex.custhelp.com`. Customer feedback is critical to our efforts at Sybex.

Best regards,

Chris Webb
Associate Publisher, Sybex

To my wife, family, friends, and coworkers, with much gratitude.

—Don Bokmiller

To my wife and daughter for all their support, all the time, thank you.

—Simon Whitbread

To my wife and children, family, friends, and fellow "Reviteers," thank you for all your support.

—Dan Morrison

Acknowledgments

This is my favorite part of the book to write, where I get to thank my darling wife, Shelley. Thanks also to my family for your kindness and encouragement.

I have had the great opportunity to work with many wonderful people who have influenced my career and provided wisdom, guidance, and friendship. I want to thank my friends and colleagues at Clark Nexsen, where I have been given the opportunity to grow and learn in a terrific working environment, which I could never take for granted. Thanks Johan, Jeff, Creighton, Freddy, Cheryl, Kat, and Larry. Thank you to all the great people I've met at the Revit Technology Conference events and those I've had the opportunity to work with at Autodesk University, especially Joel and Jarrod. Peer-networking is such a great way to learn and develop new ideas. Thank you also to Phil and Adam at Read|Thomas.

I cannot bypass the opportunity to thank all the incredible people at Sybex. Thank you, Willem, for once again keeping things moving. Thank you, Susan, Becca, and Judy for being such great editors. I'm sure there are many others who have worked hard to bring this book together. Thank you, all!

Thank you, Simon. I truly enjoy working with you on these books. Thanks also for your friendship. Thank you, Dan, for coming on board and providing your wisdom and experience. Thank you, Steve, for doing the dirty work of the technical edit. Your input has proven invaluable. It has been my pleasure to work with you all.

—Don Bokmiller

To my wife, Carole, and daughter, Jess, thank you both for your continued support over the past year while I have been working on this and other projects; it doesn't come anywhere near the thanks due for all your hard work and patience during the time I have been either working away from home or writing late into the night. The support from you both over the years has helped me achieve so much—what else can I say but thank you and I love you.

On the move… Again! I've been able to broaden my skills back in the United Kingdom and as I write this, I am settling into a new role, with Autodesk, providing BIM and Revit support to Enterprise clients. Life is never dull. Thank you also to everyone at Sybex who helped to get this edition moving. It seems unfair to single out any one person; suffice it to say that without you, there would be no book.

Finally, a special thanks to Don Bokmiller. What? You came back for more? You wanted to collaborate…again? With Dan now on board, and Steve who doesn't get enough credit, it's been a pleasure. THIS time we have a great team; let's keep it going!

—Simon Whitbread

To my wonderful wife, Rachel, thank you for your understanding, patience, and support over the last year and for all the time we have known each other. Without you I would not be where I am and would not have achieved what I have. To my beautiful children, I love you. Each of you is more important to me than you know.

I would also like to thank those who have been a big part of my journey with Revit MEP. There have been too many over the years to name them all, but the group of us that had worked together until recently was as good a team as I have ever been a part of: Matt, Graham, Eoin, and Lee, thank you so much for all the help you have given me. Thank you as well to all the fantastic people I have met through the West Australian Revit Users Group and the Revit Technology Conference events. These events are great forums for learning and mixing up new ideas. I must also thank those at BPi, particularly the rest of the VDC team, Levi, Tenae and Chris, for giving me a fantastic opportunity to continue to grow and learn at the cutting edge of what we do.

Thank you also to everyone at Sybex, from Willem who first gave me the chance to be a part of the book, to editors Pete, Susan, and Becca and all the rest of the team.

A special thanks to Simon, who recommended me to become a part of the authoring team, and to Don, who for some unknown reason actually listened to him and agreed, and to Steve, who did his best to remove my errors in the technical edit. I do look forward to working with you all in the future.

—Dan Morrison

About the Authors

Don Bokmiller is a design technologist at Clark Nexsen, an architecture and engineering firm in Norfolk, Virginia. He has worked in the AE design industry since 1996, when he started out as a CAD technician in the electrical department. As the company grew, he eventually became one of a few CAD managers, while also participating as an electrical designer on several projects. When Revit Systems came along, he participated in the Autodesk Beta program and has continued to do so for each release. His current position is to optimize the company's use of Revit. He currently works under the direction of the technical director, tying the software user experience directly to the software, hardware, and network administrators. Don has also worked as an application specialist, supporting clients of various sizes and various company structures on their use of Revit MEP. He has taught classes and given presentations to local engineering organizations. Don is an Autodesk User Group International (AUGI) member and has presented at Autodesk University and the Revit Technology Conference North America.

Simon Whitbread, Revit and CAD implementation specialist, started using Revit at release 5.1. He has over 30 years of experience in the building services and architectural industries. Since the early 1990s, he has been involved in developing and managing CAD and IT systems. He moved to New Zealand in 2002, where he led the implementation of Revit Architecture at Jasmax, one of New Zealand's leading architectural practices. More recently he has been providing implementation, support, and training services for AutoCAD and the Revit suite of programs to companies in Australia, Dubai, Indonesia, New Zealand, Singapore, the United States. Now living back in the United Kingdom, Simon enjoys spending time with his family, is a frequent speaker at Autodesk University and Revit Technology Conference (RTC) events, and is a member of AUGI, Twitter, and that odd Facebook thingy.

Dan Morrison is VDC engineer at BPi - BGC POS International, in Perth, Australia. With over 20 years' experience as a Mechanical Engineer, designer, and modeler, he started at AECOM (then Bassett Consulting Engineers) in Sydney in 2000. He was transferred to Perth in 2003 to build up the West Australian team and was part of the growth of that office from just 5 to 100 people, including introducing Revit MEP to the company in 2006. Daniel became an implementation and development leader for AECOM in the Australia and New Zealand region. In 2013 it became time to move on to new adventures and Daniel became VDC engineer at BPi, a joint venture between BGC and POSCO E&C, where his role includes using various BIM tools to help the collaboration between all members of the design and construction teams. Daniel is an Autodesk Beta tester for Revit and Navisworks, is an active member of the AUGI Forum and Revitforum.org, and has presented at the Revit Technology Conference (RTC) AUS event, BIM Day Out (Perth), and various other seminars, conferences, panel discussions, and industry events.

Contents at a Glance

Contents

Introduction

Welcome to *Mastering Autodesk® Revit® MEP 2015*. We have worked diligently to bring you a book that takes you through the core features and functionality of Revit MEP 2015 from both the design and documentation perspectives.

Revit MEP started out as Revit Systems in 2006, and in just a few years, it started on a fast-track development pace to bring it up to speed with the Revit Architecture and Revit Structure platforms. The 2015 release of Revit MEP provides platform improvements along with MEP-specific features that make this a very exciting edition. When Revit Systems was first released, it was primarily to allow MEP engineers to join the move toward building information modeling (BIM) that was being taken on by architects and structural engineers. The features and functionality were, in the opinion of most, limited to provide a complete MEP project. The development team has been listening to the needs of users and has delivered tools and features in this release that have been desired by many from the beginning. We now have new methods for calculating pressure drop and adding images to schedules, new MEP content, tapped duct and pipe flow tags, and many other new features.

The primary focus of this book is, of course, on the MEP disciplines, but there is plenty of information that applies to Revit in general. The idea behind the format is to take you through the major points of the design process and requirements for completing a building design and project submittal. This book focuses on building engineering, but it may also be helpful for other types of engineering projects, such as process piping design or any others that require a combination of data and model components.

The book is written in five parts, the first of which covers general functionality that is useful for all disciplines. You will find suggestions throughout the book for including features and components in your project templates. The first part does not cover every pick and click available in the software; it approaches the use of Revit from a best-practices standpoint, which we hope will inspire you to think about ways to make Revit MEP 2015 work best for you. Any topics not covered were not omitted to imply that they are unimportant but simply because you can find information about these features in the documentation provided by Autodesk and in Revit MEP 2015 Help.

The next three parts of the book are MEP specific and have been written to cover the key design areas of each individual discipline (mechanical, electrical, and plumbing). Again, we focus on best practices by relating our professional experience with not only the software but also the design industry. In an effort to tie it all together, the fifth part of the book contains information on how to optimize your Revit experience by learning the tools and features available for creating the various components that make up an MEP model.

Who Should Buy This Book

This book is intended for readers who are at least somewhat familiar with Revit MEP. It is not intended to be a "how-to" book by simply explaining picks and clicks; it is more for readers who are looking to find ideas on how to make the software work for them. Engineers, designers, modelers, and CAD technicians will all find useful information related to their workflows. If you are looking to move further with your Revit MEP implementation, you should find this book to be a useful resource. Even if you know the topics discussed in this book, we hope you will be inspired to think of new ways to improve your Revit MEP experience.

What's Inside

Here is a glance at what's in each chapter:

Part 1: General Project Setup

Chapter 1: Exploring the User Interface The ribbon interface is designed for optimal workflow. In this chapter, you will discover the features of the user interface that allow you to work efficiently. Some new features in Revit MEP 2015 improve the user interface dramatically.

Chapter 2: Creating an Effective Project Template The key to success with Revit projects is to have a good template file. Chapter 2 takes you through the major areas of a template file, offering ideas for settings that will make starting a project as simple and efficient as possible.

Chapter 3: Worksets and Worksharing This chapter guides you through the process of setting up a project file in a multiuser environment. The features of a worksharing-enabled file are explained in a manner that promotes ideas for project workflow efficiency.

Chapter 4: Project Collaboration Revit has many features that make project collaboration easy to manage. In this chapter, you will learn about ways to use the power of Revit MEP to coordinate your design and documents with other members of the project team.

Chapter 5: Multiplatform Interoperability: Working with 2D and 3D Data This chapter provides best-use techniques for importing non-Revit data into your projects. You will learn about the data types available and how to use them effectively in your Revit project files.

Chapter 6: Parameters Parameters are the intelligence within a BIM project. This chapter explores how parameters can be used in both projects and families for applying computable data to your Revit models. The creation of shared parameters and their use is also covered.

Chapter 7: Schedules The best way to extract the data contained in your Revit project model is to use the power of schedules. In this chapter, you will learn about the tools available for scheduling model components and how to use schedules to manage data within your projects. The panel schedule template feature is also covered in this chapter.

Part 2: Mechanical Design

Chapter 8: HVAC Cooling and Heating Load Analysis Mechanical design must start with understanding how your building will perform in different weather conditions and climates. In Chapter 8, you will learn that properly produced building loads can ensure that the mechanical design has been sized for maximum efficiency, saving energy and money while reducing the impact on the environment.

Chapter 9: Creating Logical Systems In this chapter, you will learn how to set up logical systems and how each system is affected by the type you assign it. From mechanical systems to fire-protection systems, all have a certain role to play in BIM.

Chapter 10: Mechanical Systems and Ductwork Understanding how to route ductwork successfully can lead to error reduction and better coordination. In Chapter 10, you will learn how to locate mechanical equipment and how to use the proper routing methods for ductwork.

Chapter 11: Mechanical Piping Routing mechanical piping can be a daunting task. In this chapter, you will learn how to route and coordinate your piping and how, through these techniques, you can speed up production and take full advantage of what Revit MEP 2015 has to offer.

Part 3: Electrical Design

Chapter 12: Lighting In this chapter, you will learn how to place lighting fixtures into your projects, including site lighting. The use of lighting switches is also discussed, along with the relationship between lighting fixtures and the spaces they occupy. This chapter also covers the basics for using Revit MEP for lighting analysis.

Chapter 13: Power and Communications In this chapter, the basics for placing power and communication devices into a model are covered. You will also learn how to place electrical equipment and connections for use in distribution systems. Conduit and cable tray modeling tools are also explored in this chapter.

Chapter 14: Circuiting and Panels Creating systems for your electrical components is just as important as it is for mechanical components. In this chapter, you will learn how to set up your projects to your standards for wiring, create circuits within your model, and create Panel schedules to report the loads. The tools for load classification and demand factors are also covered in this chapter.

Part 4: Plumbing

Chapter 15: Plumbing (Domestic, Sanitary, and Other) In this chapter, you will learn how to modify plumbing fixture families and create custom systems to speed up plumbing design. You will also learn how to use the Copy/Monitor features in ways never discussed before.

Chapter 16: Fire Protection Fire-protection systems protect buildings and lives. You will learn how to lay out a fire pump system and assemble components to help in your design process. You will learn how to coordinate with other disciplines and how to enter into the BIM arena effectively through the use of Revit MEP 2015.

Part 5: Managing Content

Chapter 17: Solid Modeling The foundation for custom content creation is having the ability to create the forms required to build component families. In this chapter, you will learn how to use the tools available in Revit MEP to create model geometry. You will also learn how to make geometry parametric, increasing its usability.

Chapter 18: Creating Symbols and Annotations Because so much of MEP design information is conveyed with schematic symbols, it is important to have the symbols and annotative objects commonly used for projects. Revit MEP has the tools needed to create schematic symbols for use in component families or directly in projects. In this chapter, you will learn how to use these tools and how to create constraints within families for display of the symbols in your projects.

Chapter 19: Creating Equipment Equipment families are an important component of a Revit model because of the space they occupy within a building. In this chapter, you will learn how to use solid modeling tools to create equipment. You will also learn how to add connectors for systems and how to create clearance spaces for coordination with other model elements.

Chapter 20: Creating Lighting Fixtures Lighting fixture families are special because they can hold photometric data that allow for lighting analysis directly in your Revit model. This chapter covers how to create lighting fixture families and add the data needed for analysis. You will also learn how lighting fixture families can be represented in project model views using detail components, linework, and annotation within the family file.

Chapter 21: Creating Devices This chapter examines the process for creating MEP system devices and how to use annotations to represent them on construction documents. In this chapter, you will also learn how parameters can be used to control and manage symbol visibility.

Chapter 22: Details Although creating a model with computable data is the primary reason for using Revit MEP, you do not want to model every minute detail of the design. The tools for creating detail drawings of your design are examined in this chapter.

You will also learn how to use existing CAD details along with strategies for creating a library of Revit details.

Chapter 23: Sheets When it comes time to submit a project, you need to have a set of coordinated construction documents. In this chapter, you will learn the ways you can create and manage your project sheets. You will also learn about how you can print and export your project sheets for submittal or coordination with clients.

The Mastering Series

The Mastering series from Sybex provides outstanding instruction for readers with intermediate and advanced skills in the form of top-notch training and development for those already working in their field and clear, serious education for those aspiring to become pros. Every Mastering book includes the following:

- Real-World Scenarios, ranging from case studies to interviews, that show how the tool, technique, or knowledge presented is applied in actual practice
- Skill-based instruction with chapters organized around real tasks rather than abstract concepts or subjects
- Self-review test questions so you can be certain you're equipped to do the job right

How to Contact the Authors

We welcome feedback from you about this book or about books you'd like to see from us in the future. You can write to us at the following email addresses:

Don Bokmiller: `dbokmiller@verizon.net`

Simon Whitbread: `simonwhitbread@outlook.com`

Daniel Morrison: `mozdan11@bigpond.com`

For more information about our work, visit our websites:

Don Bokmiller: `www.linkedin.com/pub/don-bokmiller/8/642/182`

Simon Whitbread: `www.uk.linkedin.com/in/simonwhitbread`

Daniel Morrison: `www.linkedin.com/pub/daniel-morrison/35/14a/a10`

For More Information

Sybex strives to keep you supplied with the latest tools and information you need for your work. Please check the website at `www.sybex.com/go/masteringrevitmep2015`, where we'll post additional content and updates that supplement this book if the need arises.

Part 1

General Project Setup

Chapter 1

Exploring the User Interface

The Autodesk® Revit® MEP 2015 software is similar to the majority of the software produced by Autodesk in that it utilizes a ribbon interface. This allows for not just ease of access to the tools needed for mechanical, electrical, and plumbing (MEP) design and modeling but also a familiarity between those different software packages, making the transition between them easier.

Although this book is titled *Mastering Autodesk Revit MEP 2015*, having a good knowledge of where tools are located and how to access the commands easily is the best way to efficiently use Revit MEP 2015, hence this chapter on the user interface. Improvements and changes have been made to the user interface for this version through the addition of tools in contextual tabs and improved functionality.

The ribbon-style interface works well in Revit because it allows many of the tools to be organized in one area of the interface, which gives you more screen real estate for viewing the model. Although the user interface is customizable, you are limited in the amount of customization and number of features that you can change. At first this may seem a bit restrictive, but as with any software, with familiarity comes an increased proficiency.

Some features have been added to improve workflow and efficiency, and typical workflow features that were previously accessed through buttons in the interface are now available as part of the interface itself.

In 2012, Autodesk introduced Autodesk® Revit® which combined all the features of the Autodesk® Revit® Architecture, Autodesk® Revit® Structure, and Autodesk® Revit® MEP platforms. This version is available to those who purchase the Building Design Suites packages released by Autodesk and gives users the option to deploy/install either each separate version of Revit or the all-inclusive one, giving them all the available Revit tools in one box. Knowing your way around the Revit MEP 2015 user interface is the first step to reaping the benefits of utilizing a building information modeling (BIM) solution for your building projects.

In this chapter, you will learn to do the following:

- Navigate the ribbon interface
- Utilize user interface features
- Use settings and menus

The Ribbon

If you are familiar with the Revit MEP user interface prior to the 2010 version, transitioning to the ribbon-style interface may indeed take some getting used to. Once you understand the way that the ribbon is set up and how you can customize it to better suit your workflow, you will see that it is an optimal interface for a BIM and design application. If you are transitioning from an earlier ribbon interface, you will inevitably notice some changes to the location and order of the tabs and the introduction of additional tabs/commands.

Using Tabs

The ribbon portion of the user interface consists of several tabs, each organized by panels that relate to the topic of the tab. Each panel contains one or more buttons for the relevant features available in Revit MEP 2015. You can access a tab by simply clicking the name at the top of the ribbon. Although each tab is designed to provide a unique set of tools, some of the features of Revit are repeated on different tabs. Depending on your screen resolution, some of the buttons on the panels may become compressed to fit on your screen. The panels and tools for each tab are described here (not all panels are shown for each tab):

Systems The Systems tab, shown in Figure 1.1, is the main tab for MEP modeling tools. Formerly the Home tab, this tab has been renamed to allow for continuity between Autodesk Revit MEP and Autodesk Revit. The tab is divided into panels that are specific to each of the main disciplines. The Systems tab is where you can find the tools to build an MEP model. Each of the discipline panels has a small arrow in the lower-right corner that provides quick access to the MEP settings dialog box for that discipline.

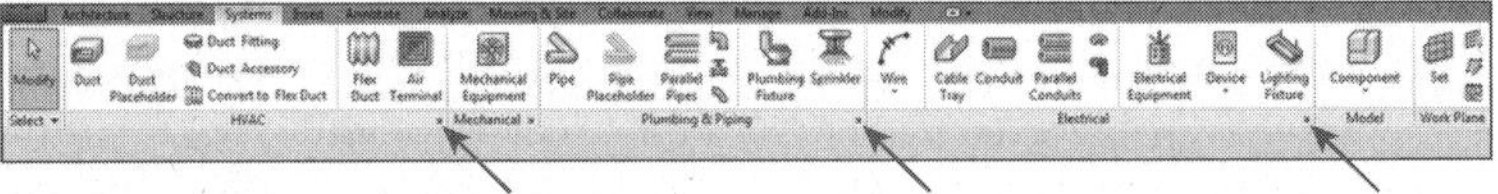

Figure 1.1
The Systems tab

Architecture and Structure There will always be a need for creating architectural elements in a Revit MEP model, whether this is purely during a Copy/Monitor operation or if you are building an as-built model and have no architect to work with. This tab features most of the architectural tools required for this. From the Build panel with the basic architect's tools to openings, grids, and rooms, these are all available on the Architecture tab. Note that access to Color Schemes and Area And Volume Computations is available by clicking the down arrow on the Room & Area panel, as shown in Figure 1.2.

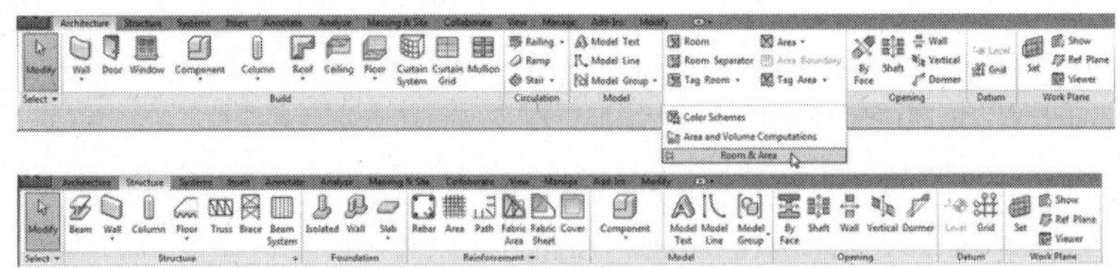

Figure 1.2
The Architecture and Structure tabs

The Structure tab contains tools for modeling structural elements as well as some common tools for grids and reference planes. Both of these tabs are available if you install Revit as part of a Building Design Suite package.

Insert Whether you want to link another Revit project file, overlay Design Web Format (DWF) markup, or insert 2D elements from another file, the Insert tab contains all these tools and more for bringing other files or objects into your Revit projects, as shown in Figure 1.3. The tab is organized by panels for linking and importing files, and it also contains tools for loading Revit families. The small arrow at the lower right of the Import panel is for accessing the Import Line Weights dialog box, where you can associate imported computer-aided design (CAD) color numbers to a Revit line weight, as indicated in Figure 1.4. The Insert tab also contains the Autodesk Seek panel, which provides a search window for content available on the Autodesk Seek website.

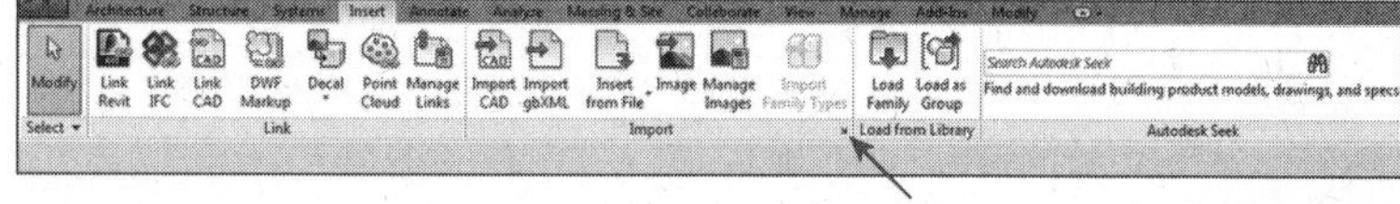

FIGURE 1.3
The Insert tab

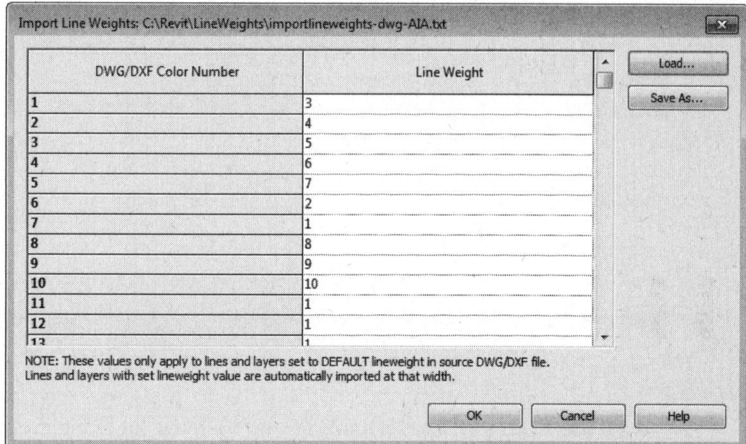

FIGURE 1.4
Import Line Weights dialog box

New to Revit 2015 is the Link IFC button, which allows you to link an IFC file directly from the user interface.

Annotate On the Annotate tab, you can find the tools needed to add annotations to your model views along with drafting tools for creating details. The Dimension and Tag panels can be extended by clicking the arrow next to the panel name, which reveals the tools for establishing dimension settings and determining the default tags to be used upon initial placement, as shown in Figure 1.5. The Symbol button is used for placing annotation families onto views or sheets. The small arrow at the lower-right corner of the Text panel provides access to the Type Properties dialog box for creating or modifying text styles, as shown in Figure 1.6.

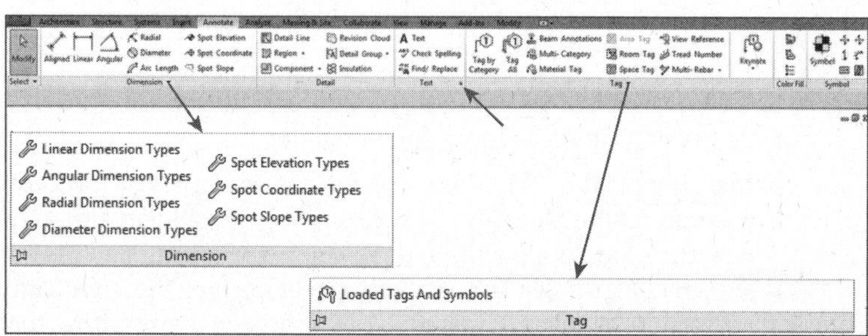

FIGURE 1.5
The Annotate tab

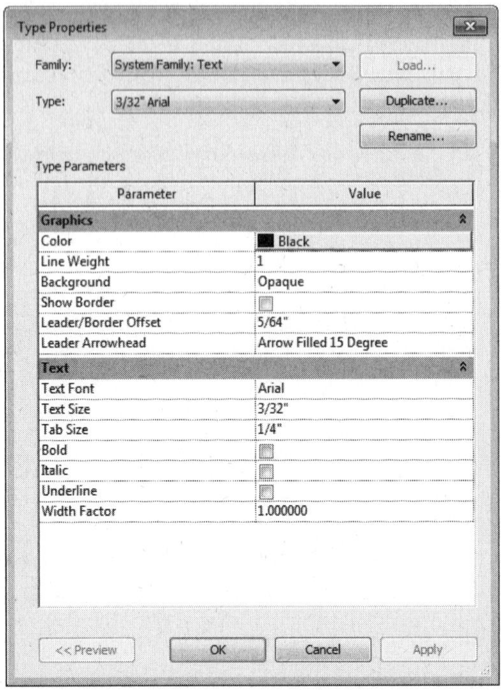

FIGURE 1.6 Text Type Properties dialog box

Analyze Tools for model analysis and systems checking are located on the Analyze tab. Other tools on this tab allow you to add color to your ductwork and piping based on defined criteria. The Spaces & Zones panel contains the tools for placing Space objects and space separator lines. The Check Systems panel contains tools for checking MEP systems to ensure proper connectivity and valid system assignments of components. Note that access to the Color Schemes and Area And Volume Computations options is available by clicking the down arrow on the Spaces & Zones panel, as shown in Figure 1.7, while building and space properties, as shown in Figure 1.8, can be accessed from the arrow on the Reports & Schedules panel.

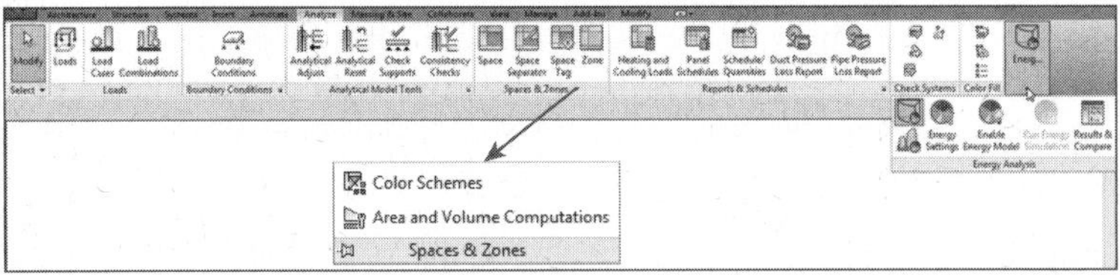

FIGURE 1.7 The Analyze tab

Tools on the Energy Analysis panel allow for choosing a mass model or the building components to establish an energy analysis model.

Massing & Site The Massing & Site tab combines the conceptual tools used for creating masses and the Modeling By Face objects. It provides MEP users with access to site tools, including topography, site and parking components, and building pads or foundations, as shown in Figure 1.9. The Site Settings dialog box, shown in Figure 1.10, for adjusting contour separation and site cut material, can be accessed by clicking the arrow on the Model Site panel.

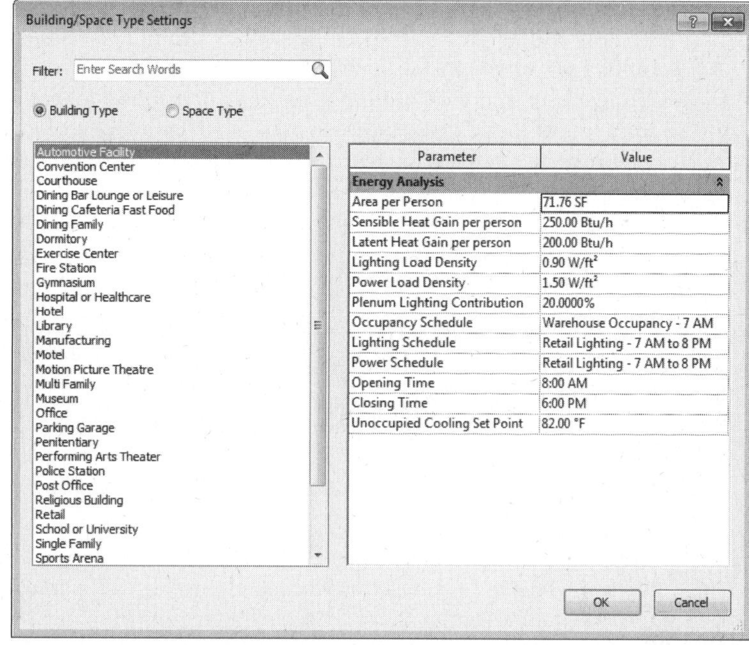

FIGURE 1.8
Building/Space Type Settings dialog box

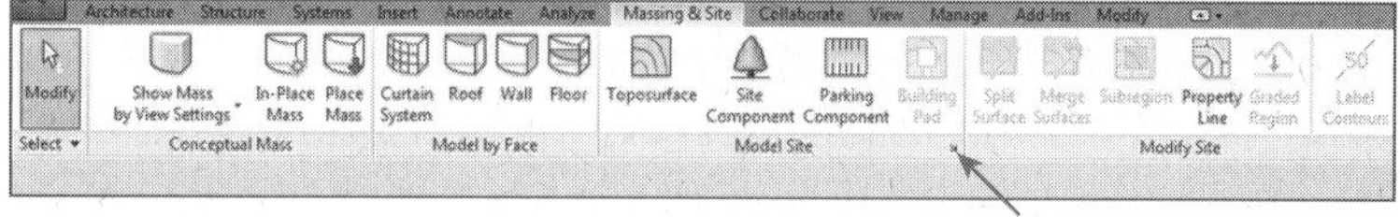

FIGURE 1.9
The Massing & Site tab

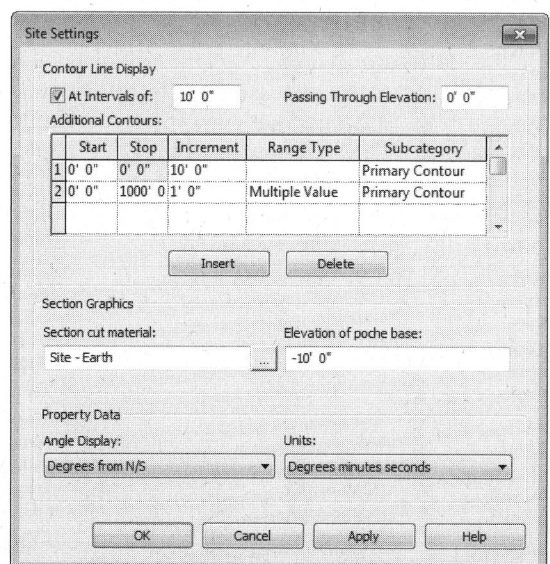

FIGURE 1.10
Site Settings

Collaborate You need tools that allow you to keep your model coordinated with other disciplines and work within a multiuser environment. These tools can be found on the Collaborate tab. The Manage Collaboration panel has a drop-down list for setting the current workset, and the Coordinate panel contains tools for copying and monitoring objects from linked files. The Coordinate panel also has a tool for locating face-hosted elements that have lost their association to their host. You can check for clashes between model objects by using the Interference Check tool on the Coordinate tab. The Editing Requests button on the Synchronize panel allows you to see any requests that have been made to modify elements you are borrowing or own. You also have the option to connect to a Revit server accelerator by clicking the arrow, as shown in Figure 1.11.

FIGURE 1.11
The Collaborate tab

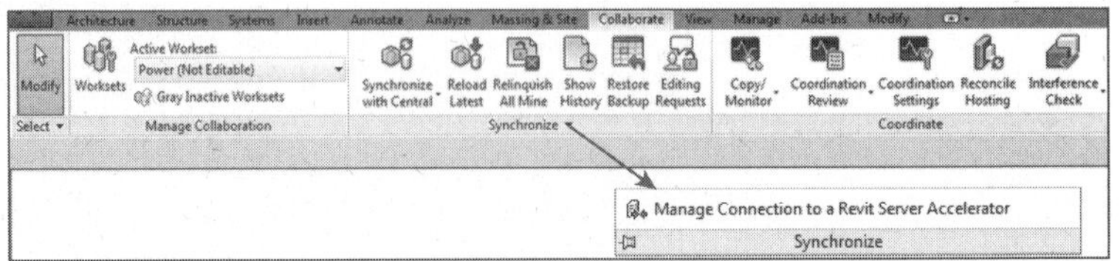

View Figure 1.12 shows the View tab; here you can use the tools to create different types of views. This tab also has tools for managing the views you have open in the drawing area. On the Graphics panel, there are tools for creating view templates and filters. The arrow on the base of this panel accesses the Graphic Display Options dialog box, shown in Figure 1.13. The Sheet Composition panel has tools for creating sheets as well as adding match lines or revisions. The User Interface button allows you to toggle the visibility of key user-interface features including the Properties palette, System Browser, and Project Browser.

FIGURE 1.12
The View tab

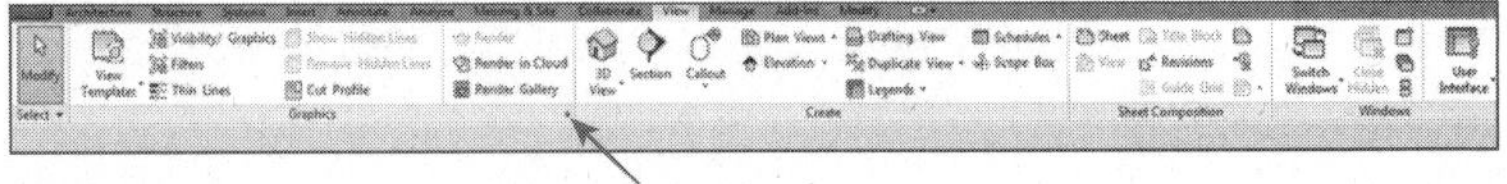

Manage On the Manage tab, you can find the tools needed to establish project settings. The Inquiry panel has tools that can be used to locate specific objects in your project model, and to display any warnings associated with your project. Along with the settings that can be accessed from the tools on the Settings panel, the Additional Settings button is a drop-down list of even more options. The MEP Settings button is located on the Settings panel. This is where you can establish settings related to MEP components and system behavior. The Selection panel, as indicated in Figure 1.14, has tools that allow the user to save, load, and edit a selection set of objects for use in a filter list.

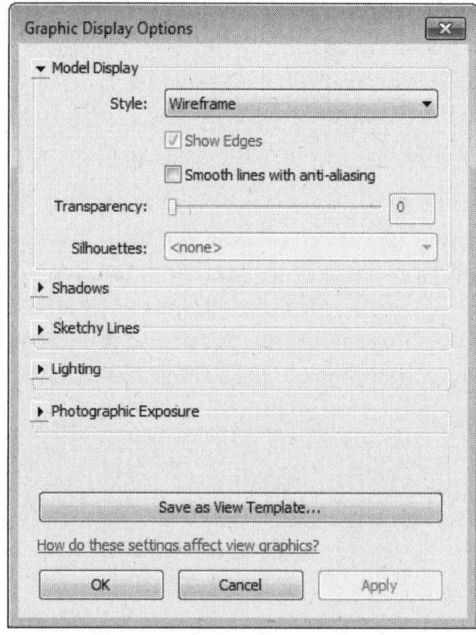

FIGURE 1.13
Graphic Display Options

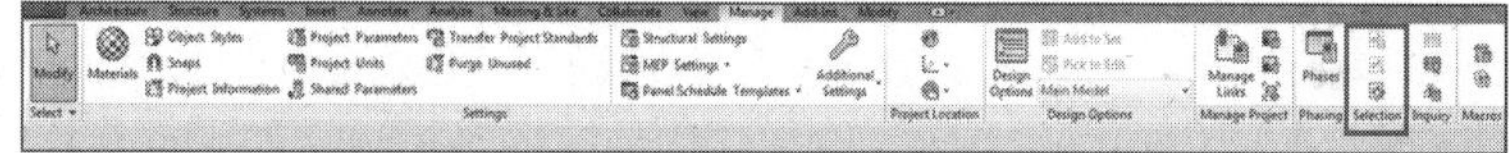

FIGURE 1.14
The Manage tab

Modify The Modify tab, as shown in Figure 1.15, is located at the end of the tabs by default so that it is closer to the center of the user interface, for easy access. The Modify tab has the tools needed to make changes to components or linework in your project views. The tools on the Modify panel have been arranged with the more commonly used tools that have larger buttons. Some of the tools that have multiple-use options have a separate button for each use, such as the Mirror, Split, and Trim/Extend tools. The tools for creating groups, assemblies, or parts are located on the Create panel.

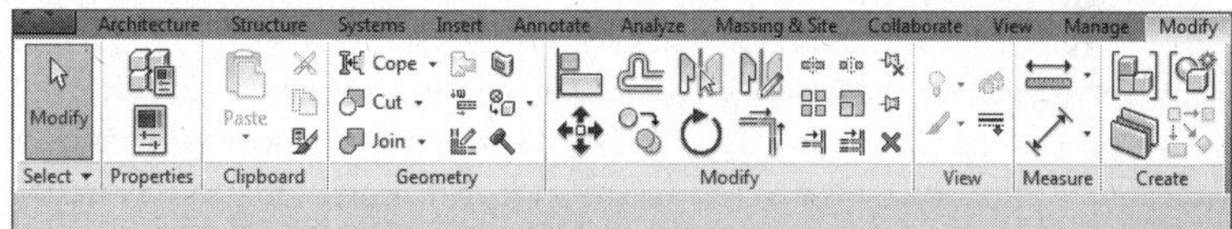

FIGURE 1.15
The Modify tab

Add-Ins The Add-Ins tab appears on your ribbon as the next-to-last tab by default. This tab contains a BIM 360 panel with tools for use in the Autodesk® 360 environment and requires you to sign into an Autodesk account. If you have installed any external applications, the buttons or other features provided appear on the tab as configured. Some third-party applications create an additional tab on the ribbon.

The Modify button appears in the Select panel on every tab. This button allows you to exit from any active command, giving you an alternative to using the Esc key multiple times or selecting another tool. Another feature of this panel is the drop-down that contains options for selection in the drawing area. These options also appear as icons on the status bar. Figure 1.16 shows the various selection options available. Notice that you can select elements by clicking anywhere on the element by using the Select Elements By Face option. However, this option does not work when a view is set to Wireframe.

FIGURE 1.16
Selection settings

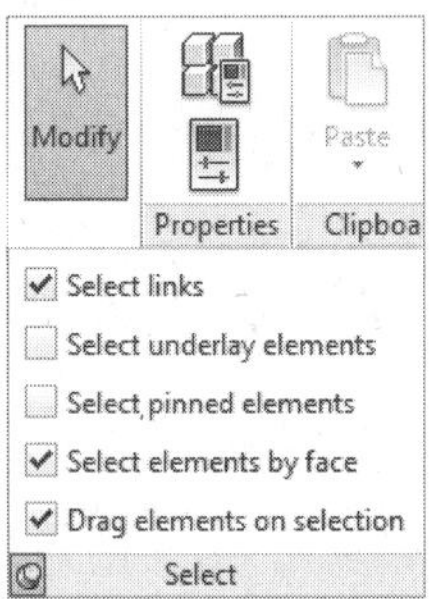

You may need to experiment with combinations of these settings to achieve the results that suit your workflow. Note that if you deselect the Select Underlay Elements check box, you cannot select non-MEP components such as doors, walls, or windows that may exist in your model.

Using Contextual Tabs

In addition to the tabs provided by default on the ribbon, other tabs appear when you select objects in your project. These contextual tabs contain tools specific to modifying the selected object. Contextual tabs appear in the location of the Modify tab and are identified by their green color and a name that applies to the selected object. A contextual tab for a selected object is an extension of the Modify tab, which is why the base Modify tab is so compact compared to the other tabs. This allows for the selection-specific tools to appear on the right side of the Modify tab. The top of Figure 1.17 shows the contextual tab for an electrical distribution board selected in the model of a project. The standard tools on the Modify tab are available to the left but are not shown in this figure.

When you select an object in the model that is part of a system, an additional contextual tab appears with tools for editing the system. These tabs are completely separate from the standard Modify tab and contain only tools for system editing. If you select an object on a system, the system tab appears along with the contextual Modify tab, as shown at the bottom of Figure 1.17. However, if you select an entire system, only the system tab appears. The panels and buttons on contextual tabs cannot be removed or rearranged on the ribbon. The buttons cannot be added to the Quick Access toolbar.

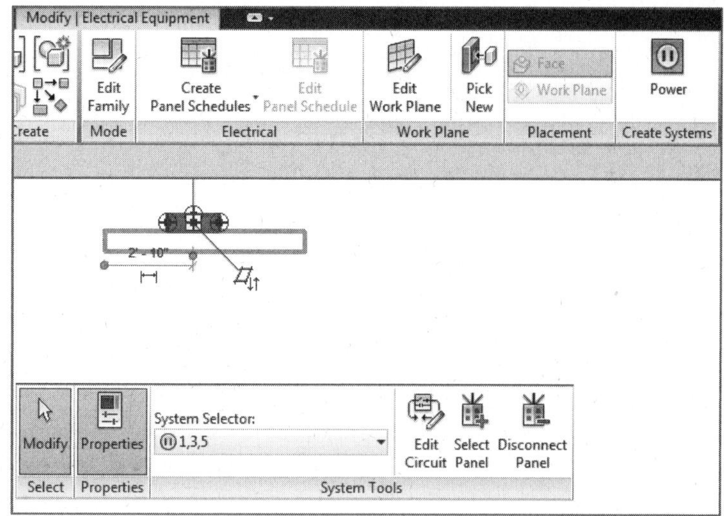

FIGURE 1.17 Contextual tab for an electrical distribution board (top), and contextual tab for an electrical system (bottom)

Using Family Editor Tabs

The tabs in the Family Editor environment differ from those in the project file environment. When you open a family file, the tabs on the ribbon contain some familiar tools, but many of them are specific to the creation and modification of family components. The tabs available in the Family Editor environment are as follows:

Create The Create tab in the Family Editor environment, shown in Figure 1.18, contains tools for creating solid geometry and lines, adding system connectors, and creating and managing references.

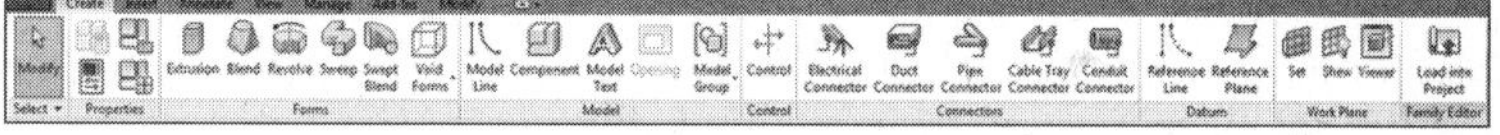

FIGURE 1.18 The Family Editor—Create tab

Insert Figure 1.19 shows the Insert tab in the Family Editor; this environment contains tools for bringing other files into your family file. The tools for linking are visible but disabled because importing is the only available method for bringing a CAD file into a Revit family file. The arrow on the Import panel accesses the same dialog box as in the project environment and can be seen earlier in Figure 1.4.

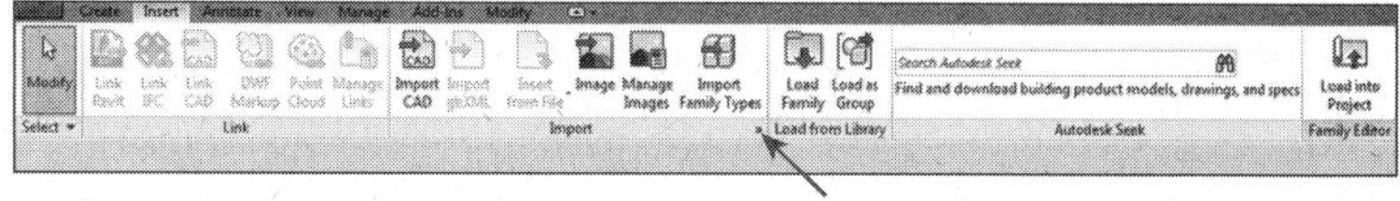

FIGURE 1.19 The Family Editor—Insert tab

Annotate On the Annotate tab within the Family Editor environment, you will find the types of annotation tools that can be used in a family file. The Dimension panel can be expanded to establish dimension styles within the family file, as shown in Figure 1.20. Text styles, as indicated previously in Figure 1.6, can be accessed from the arrow on the Text panel.

FIGURE 1.20
The Family Editor—Annotate tab

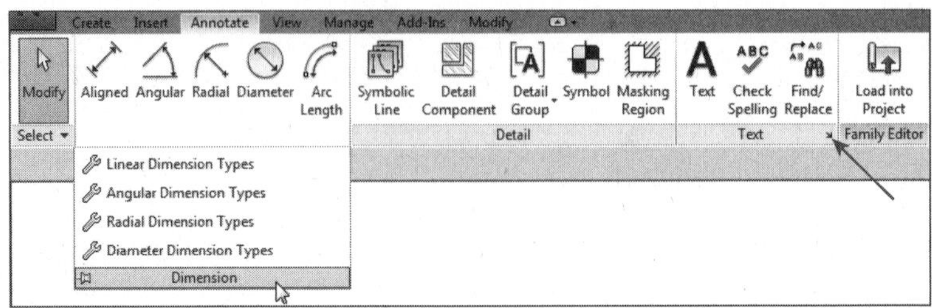

View The View tab in the Family Editor environment, as shown in Figure 1.21, is limited to tools for managing the family views. Section views can be created and camera positions can also be established for 3D views.

FIGURE 1.21
The Family Editor—View tab

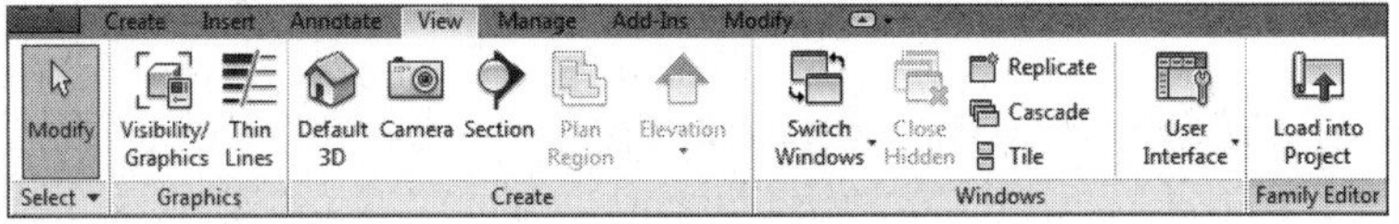

Manage In the Family Editor environment, the Manage tab, shown in Figure 1.22, is populated with tools for establishing settings within the family file. The MEP Settings button allows you to establish load classifications and demand factors, while the Additional Settings button drops down for access to general settings.

FIGURE 1.22
The Family Editor—Manage tab

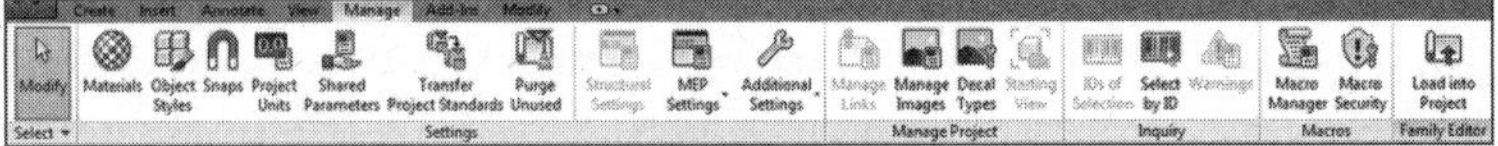

Modify The Modify tab in the Family Editor environment, as shown in Figure 1.23, is nearly the same as the one found in the project file environment. The main difference is that there is no View panel and the Geometry and Create panels have fewer tools. This tab is also compact, allowing for a contextual tab when objects within the family are selected.

FIGURE 1.23
The Family Editor—Modify tab

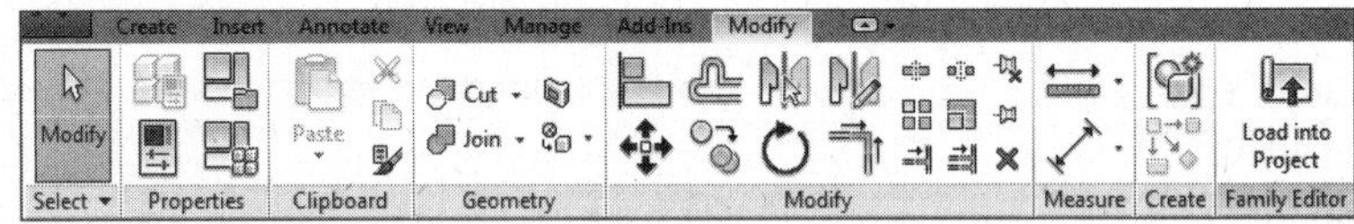

Add-Ins The Add-Ins tab also appears in the Family Editor environment, with the same BIM 360 panel as in the project file environment. The Load Into Project button is available on each tab in the Family Editor environment. This allows you to load the family into another open file at any time.

Customizing the Ribbon

You can customize the ribbon interface to better suit your workflow. For example, you can rearrange the order of the tabs by holding down the Ctrl key and clicking a tab name to drag it to a new location.

You can move panels on a tab to different locations on the tab by clicking a panel name and dragging it to a new location. Figure 1.24 shows the Mechanical panel being dragged from its location on the Systems tab. The panels to the right slide over to fill in the space left by the moved panel.

FIGURE 1.24
Moving a tab panel

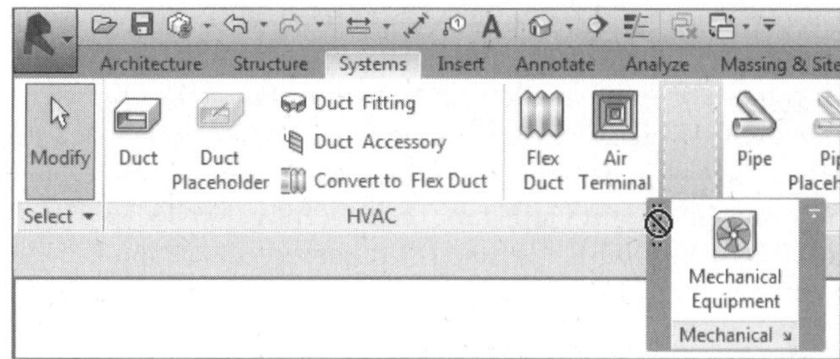

You cannot move a panel from one tab to another, however. If you attempt to drop a panel onto another tab, it returns to its original location on its original tab.

You can remove panels from a tab and place them in another location on your screen. You can dock floating panels together by dragging one panel over the other, and you can move the docked panels as a group by clicking and dragging the gray grip that appears when you hover your mouse pointer over a floating panel. If you use dual monitors, you can even drag a panel to the second monitor. The panel's new position is maintained when you restart the software, but the panel does not appear until a file is opened. Keep in mind that moving tools to another screen may actually hinder your workflow, your efficiency, and possibly the stability of the program itself.

BACK TO NORMAL

You can return a floating panel to its default location by clicking the small icon in the upper-right corner of the panel.

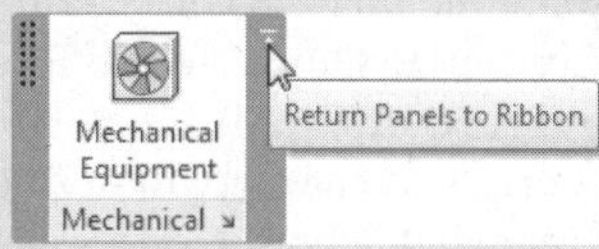

If you want to return the entire ribbon interface to its default settings, you can do so by browsing to `%USERPROFILE%\AppData\Roaming\Autodesk\Revit\Autodesk Revit 2015`, deleting the `UIState.dat` file, and then reopening the application. Deleting this file also removes any customization done to the Quick Access toolbar.

You can control the visibility of the ribbon tabs by clicking the small button to the right of the tabs. This button cycles through the different display options. You can also click the small arrow next to the button to display and select a specific option, as shown in Figure 1.25.

FIGURE 1.25
Ribbon visibility

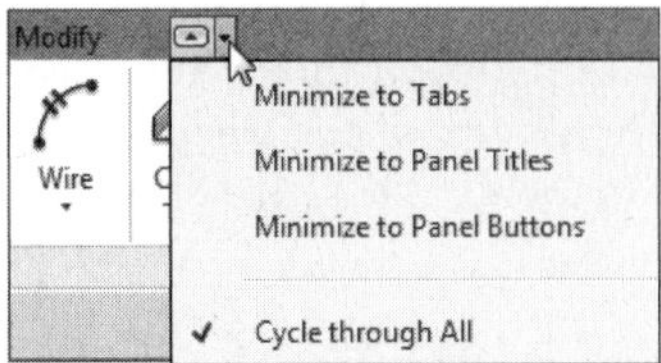

You can establish the switching behavior of the tabs on the ribbon to determine which tab is displayed when you exit a tool or command. When you click a tool, the contextual Modify tab for that tool appears. The interface stays on the Modify tab when you exit the tool, or you can set it to return to the previous tab. These settings are located on the User Interface tab of the Options dialog box, which is discussed later in this chapter.

Quick Access Toolbar

As you are working, you may find yourself taking extra steps to switch tabs in order to access the desired tools. Figure 1.26 shows the Quick Access toolbar (QAT) as a place where you can put frequently used tools for instant access.

FIGURE 1.26
Quick Access toolbar

You can add tools from any of the standard tabs to the QAT simply by right-clicking that tool's button or drop-down and selecting the Add To Quick Access Toolbar option. The tool will be placed at the end of the QAT. To manage the tools available on the QAT, you can click the small arrow button to access the customization menu, shown in Figure 1.27. Each button on the QAT is listed, and removing the check mark next to it turns off its visibility in the QAT.

The option at the bottom of the list allows you to set the location of the QAT either above or below the ribbon. Setting it below the ribbon moves it closer to the drawing area for easier access. If you add several buttons to the QAT, you may want to move it below the ribbon so that it does not crowd out the filename on the title bar.

Clicking the Customize Quick Access Toolbar option in the drop-down menu opens the dialog box shown in Figure 1.28. In this dialog box, you can change the order of the buttons as they appear from left to right, create separator lines, or delete buttons.

You can also right-click a button on the QAT for quick options such as removing the button, adding a separator line, or accessing the customization dialog box.

FIGURE 1.27
Quick Access toolbar customization menu

FIGURE 1.28
Customize Quick Access Toolbar dialog box

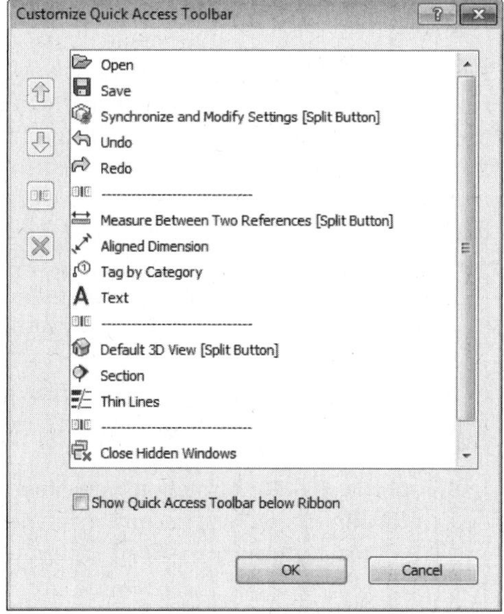

Additional User Interface Features

The Revit MEP 2015 user interface is full of features designed to help you design and model efficiently. Some items are new, some have been modified, and some are the same as they have always been. The title bar at the top of the screen still informs you of what file you are in and what view is currently active in the drawing area.

Options Bar

Despite the functionality of the ribbon with its contextual tabs, the Options Bar, shown in Figure 1.29, is still an important part of the user interface. This should be the first place you look when a tool or object in the project is selected. Although the number of options that appear may be limited for each command you use, they are important to the task in which you are engaging. When placing round duct, for example, pay close attention to the Diameter and Offset options to ensure proper location.

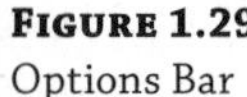

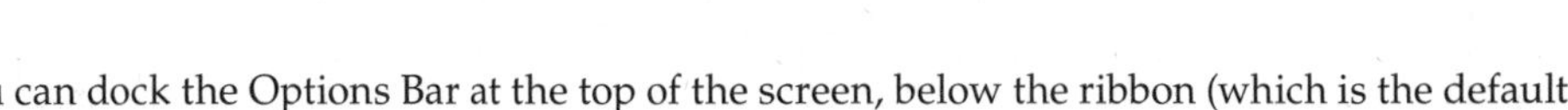

FIGURE 1.29
Options Bar

You can dock the Options Bar at the top of the screen, below the ribbon (which is the default location), or at the bottom of the screen, just above the status bar. Right-click the Options Bar to change its docked position.

Properties Palette

The Properties palette is a dialog box that can stay open all the time and allows you to access the properties of items in your project. This feature reduces the number of mouse clicks necessary to access the properties of a model object or project component. You can dock the Properties palette to the sides of the screen or at the top of the drawing area just below the Options Bar, or it can float. If you dock the Properties palette to the same side of the screen as the Project Browser, there are two options for how they can be displayed. You can either show both, split in the docked space as seen in Figure 1.30, or have them both occupy the same docked space, depending on how you drag them to the docked space. A gray box appears to indicate whether they will split or share the space.

When the Properties palette and Project Browser are sharing the same docked space, you can access either one by the tabs that appear at the bottom. To remove either one from the shared docked space, click and drag its tab away from the dock.

If you do not have the Properties palette turned on, you can access it by clicking the Properties button located on the Modify tab or the contextual Modify tab of a selected object, or you can right-click anywhere in the drawing area. The Properties palette remains on until you close it.

When no object is selected in the model or in a drafting view, the Properties palette displays the properties of the current view in the drawing area. You can select a view in the Project Browser to view its properties in the Properties palette.

The top section of the Properties palette contains the Type Selector when an object is selected or a tool is chosen for placing an object. When an object is selected, you can switch to the properties of the current view by using the drop-down list located just below the Type Selector, as shown in Figure 1.31.

FIGURE 1.30
Project Browser and Properties palette docked together

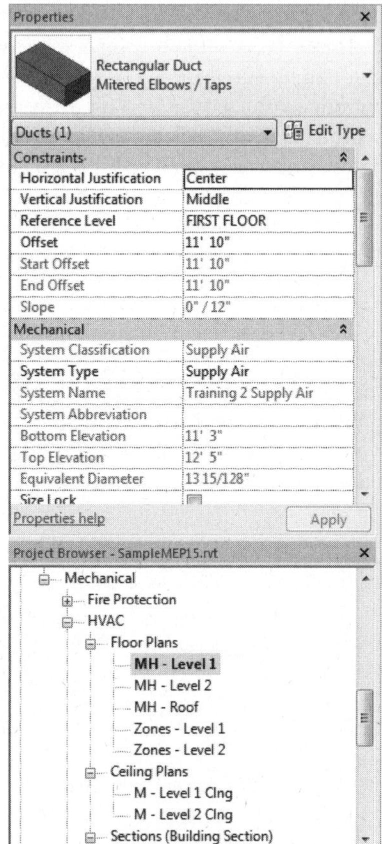

FIGURE 1.31
Properties palette

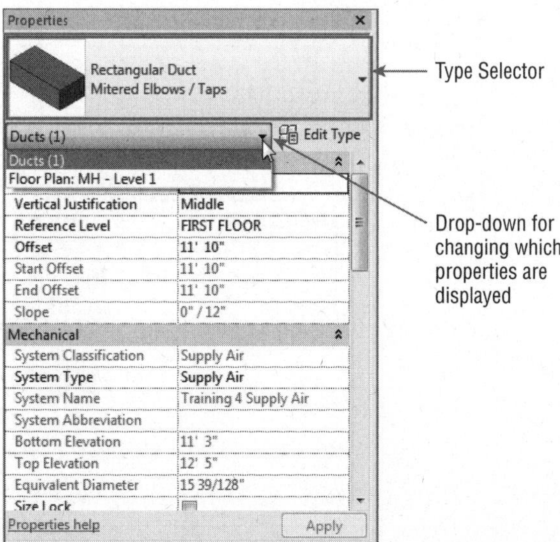

The properties shown in the Properties palette are instance properties. You can click the Edit Type button to display the Type Properties dialog box for a selected item or view. When you're viewing the instance properties of an object or view, the scroll bar on the right side of the palette holds its position when you move your mouse pointer away from the palette. The scroll bar remains in position even when other items are selected in the model.

When you make a change to a parameter in the Properties palette, you can click the Apply button at the bottom-right corner of the palette to set the change. Alternatively, you can simply move your mouse pointer away from the palette and the change will be applied.

View Control Bar

The View Control Bar is often overlooked, but it contains tools that are important to the display of the contents in the drawing area.

The Visual Styles button provides access to the Graphic Display Options dialog box, shown in Figure 1.32. This dialog box has settings to control the visual display of the view. These include Model Display, Shadows, Sketchy Lines, Lighting, Photographic Exposure, and the ability to save these settings as a view template. If you are working in a 3D view, the dialog box also has a Background setting.

FIGURE 1.32
Graphic Display Options dialog box

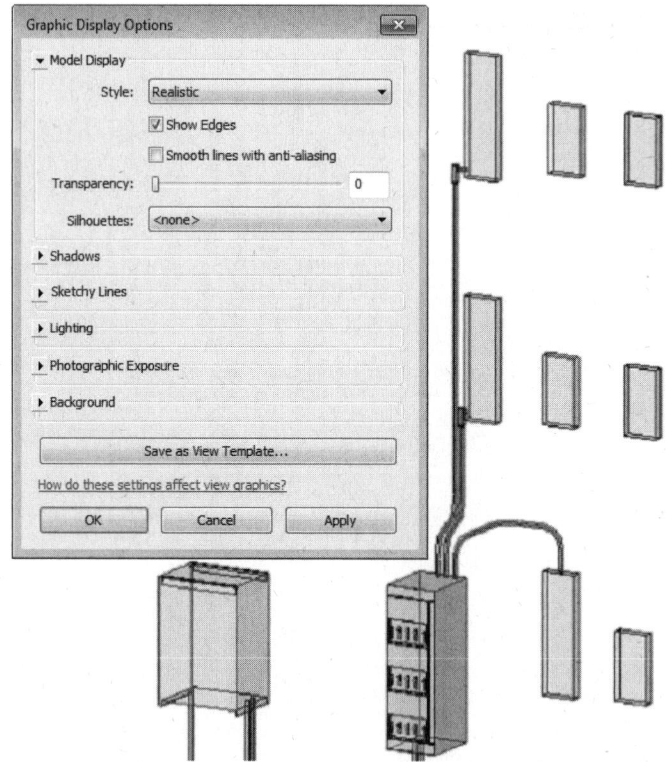

The View Control Bar, shown in Figure 1.33, essentially remains the same as the previous version, with the options for scale, level of detail, visual style, sun path, shadows, rendering, view crop, and crop region visible. The ability to save and lock the orientation of a 3D view also remains the same. When a 3D view is locked, you can tag items in the view. You can zoom and pan in a locked view, but you cannot orbit the model.

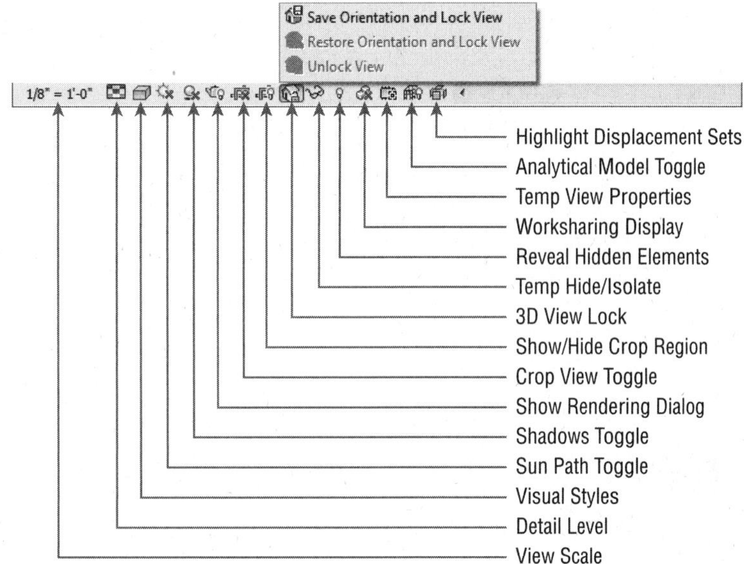

FIGURE 1.33
View Control Bar and Lock 3D view options

When you unlock a view, any tags applied in the view are not displayed until it is returned to its saved orientation.

The Temporary Hide/Isolate, Reveal Hidden Elements, and Worksharing Display tools remain the same from the previous release. The Temporary View Properties button allows you to temporarily override the properties of a view or temporarily apply a view template to the view. This enables you to change visibility settings without having to duplicate the view. Figure 1.34 shows the options available with this setting. When the setting is activated, a border appears around the drawing area.

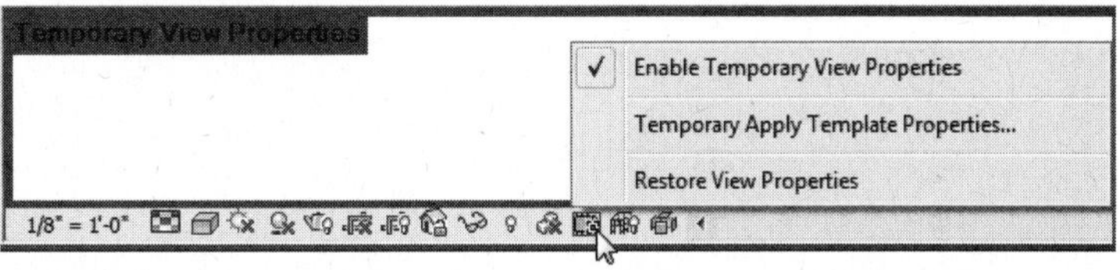

FIGURE 1.34
The Temporary View Properties setting applied to a view

The Show Analytical Model button allows you to toggle the visibility of the analytical model on and off. The last button changes the view so that any displacement sets are highlighted, as shown in Figure 1.35.

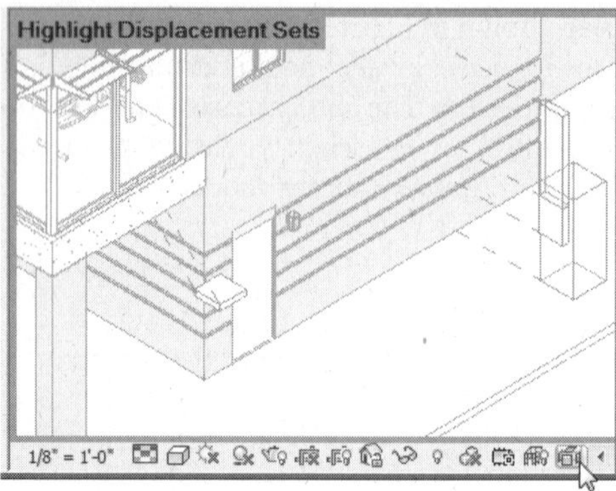

FIGURE 1.35
Displacement sets highlighted in a 3D view

When your project has worksets, worksharing display can be useful for collaboration on a project and can save you time by helping you avoid trying to make changes to objects that are not editable. The Worksharing Display Settings option on the View Control Bar provides a menu from which you can access the Worksharing Display Settings dialog box, where you can establish the colors used for the various options of worksharing display. You can apply colors to worksets based on who owns them, whether they are up to date, or simply by their name. Figure 1.36 shows the dialog box and settings for worksets colored by their name. Notice that, in the Show Color column, you can choose to show a workset's color in the view by selecting its check box.

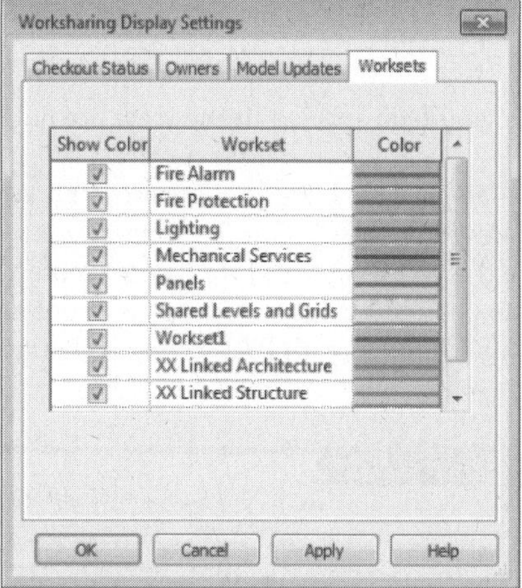

FIGURE 1.36
Worksharing Display Settings dialog box

When you choose an option for worksharing display, a box appears in the upper-left corner of the drawing area, indicating the option being displayed, as shown in Figure 1.37 (colors are labeled for the black-and-white image). These settings take precedence over any view filters that may be applied to the view. If you override the graphics of a category in the view, only the changes to line weight are applied (color overrides are not displayed).

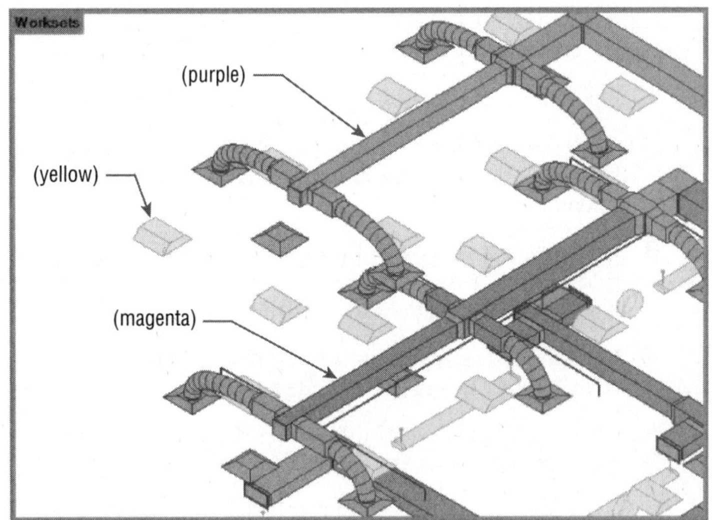

FIGURE 1.37 3D view with work-sharing display activated

To turn the sun path on or off in a view, you use the Sun Path toggle on the View Control Bar, as shown in Figure 1.38. The Sun Settings option takes you to a dialog box where you can define the type of solar study performed, the project location, and the time of day.

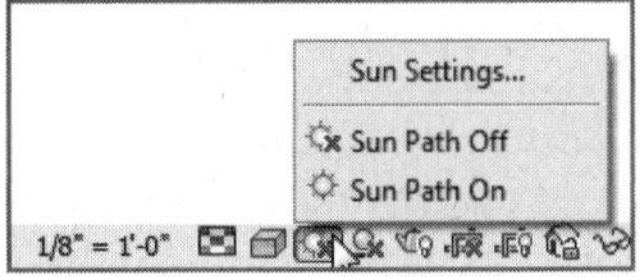

FIGURE 1.38 Sun path visual display options

In the Visual Styles button menu shown in Figure 1.39, the Ray Trace option gives you a fully rendered view. In both this option and in Realistic mode, any rich photorealistic content (RPC) objects display correctly.

FIGURE 1.39 Visual styles

Take some time to explore the visual styles by completing the following exercise. If you do not have Hardware Acceleration turned on, you can do so by clicking the Options button on the application menu and choosing the Graphics tab. You must do this prior to opening the file. If activating Hardware Acceleration causes problems because of your video driver, you can choose not to activate it and skip step 5:

1. Open the `Ch1_Project.rvt` file found at `www.sybex.com/go/masteringrevitmep2015`.
2. Click the Visual Styles button on the View Control Bar, and select Shaded. Zoom, pan, and orbit the view, and make note of the variations in color based on the model orientation.
3. Click the Visual Styles button and select Graphic Display Options. In the dialog box that appears, deselect the Show Edges radio box and set Transparency to 50%; then click Apply. Notice the change to the view. Change Transparency back to 0% and click OK.
4. Click the Visual Styles button and change the style to Consistent Colors. Notice that the colors remain a consistent shade when you zoom, pan, and orbit the view.
5. Click the Visual Styles button and change the style to Realistic. Notice that the render material defined for the objects is now displayed.
6. Click the Visual Styles button and change the style to Ray Trace. Notice that the performance considerably slows, but the image should be more like a rendered image.
7. Click any object in the model. If you do not already have the Properties palette active, click the Properties button on the Properties panel of the contextual tab. Take some time to become familiar with the behavior of the Properties palette.

Status Bar

The status bar for Revit MEP 2015 not only reports information about a selected item and shows prompts with instructions for multilevel commands, it also has an active workset indicator and design options indicator. The selection options that are available on the Selection panel of the ribbon also show up on the status bar as icons, as shown in Figure 1.40.

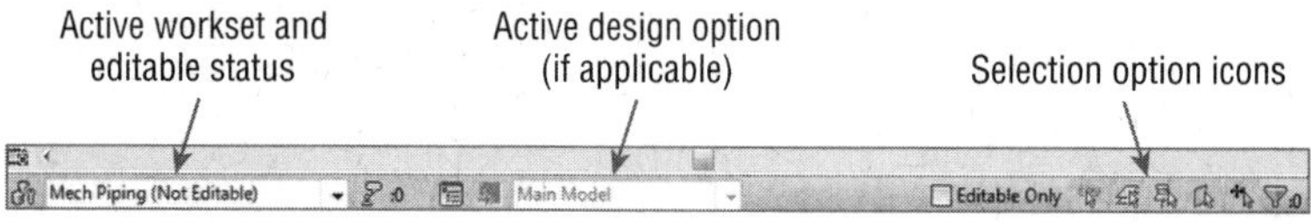

FIGURE 1.40
Status bar

You can access the Worksets dialog box by clicking the Worksets button next to the active workset window. You can switch between active worksets by clicking the window and selecting the desired workset. These are the same tools as found on the Collaborate tab, but having them on the status bar eliminates the need to switch tabs on the ribbon to access them. This also eliminates the need to add the tools to the Quick Access toolbar. The Design Options window displays the active design option, and you can access the Design Options dialog box by clicking the button.

The Editable Only check box is for filtering a selection by only those objects that are editable in a worksharing environment. You can access any editing requests, as shown in Figure 1.41, by clicking the small button next to the active workset indicator. This opens the Editing Request dialog box, which displays any pending requests by others to borrow elements. This dialog box also displays any requests made by you to other users. Next to the button is an indicator that shows the number of requests that are currently pending.

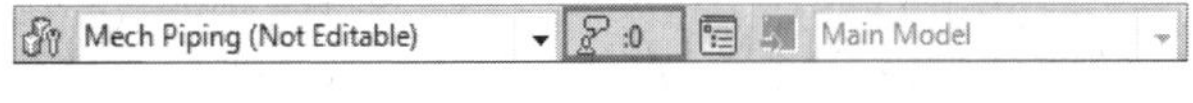

FIGURE 1.41
Workset editing requests

When a user places a request to edit an element that you own or are borrowing, you receive a notification dialog box of the request. The request remains in a list of pending requests until action is taken. You can view the list at any time by clicking the Editing Requests button on the Collaborate tab of the ribbon.

Info Center

The Info Center is the portion of the title bar that gives you quick access to the Help menu or information about Revit MEP 2015. The search window allows you to search for information about a topic, as indicated in Figure 1.42.

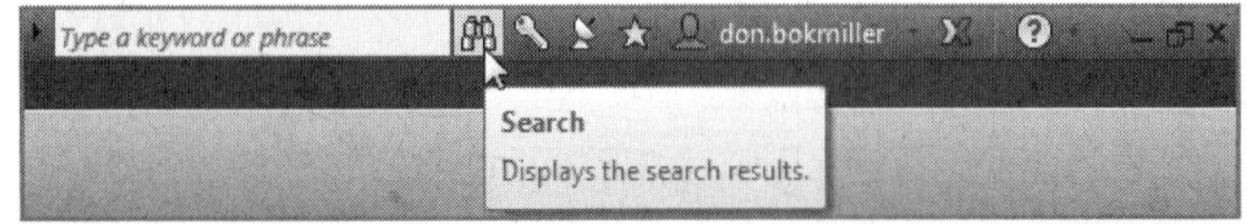

FIGURE 1.42
Info Center

You can easily access the Subscription Center by clicking the key icon. Any topics found in the search window or listed in the Subscription Center panel can be added to your Favorites list by clicking the star icon to the right of the topic. Clicking the star icon on the Info Center lists all your favorite topics. The Help menu is displayed by clicking the question mark icon. Revit 2015 has a web-based Help menu. You can access additional information by clicking the arrow next to the Help icon, as shown in Figure 1.43.

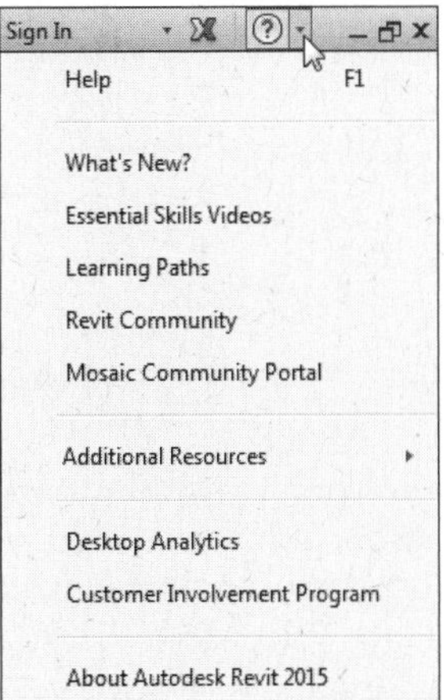

FIGURE 1.43
Additional Help options

You can sign into an Autodesk account by clicking the Sign In icon next to the Favorites star icon.

The Communication Center button is the one with the satellite dish on it. The Communication Center provides information about product updates and announcements.

Exchange Apps

Figure 1.44 shows the button for the Autodesk Exchange App store. This takes the user to a website where applications written for the Revit platform are listed. These are applications, either free or available for purchase, that can be loaded into Revit to provide enhanced performance and additional functionality.

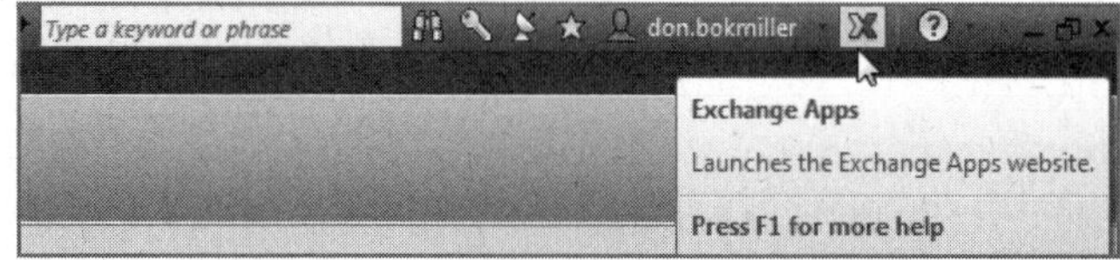

FIGURE 1.44 Accessing Exchange apps

User Interface Control

Many components of the Revit MEP 2015 user interface can be turned on or off for workflow efficiency or to maximize screen real estate. The User Interface button, located at the far right of the View tab, allows you to select which user interface components are visible, as shown in Figure 1.45.

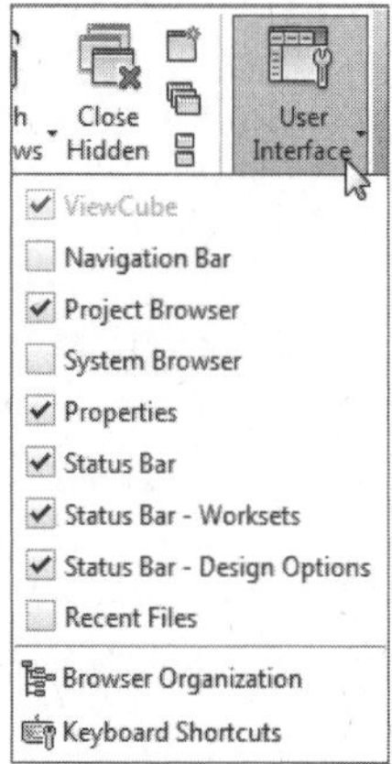

FIGURE 1.45 User Interface button options

The User Interface button provides not only a way to display or remove interface components for more screen real estate but also a way to access the Recent Files screen, which cannot be accessed from the Switch Windows drop-down button until it has been activated by using the User Interface button.

Menus and Settings

The menus within Revit MEP 2015 offer access to many tools for user interface settings. Context menus, available by right-clicking an item, also contain various tools based on the selected item.

The application menu includes options for exporting, printing, opening, and saving files. This menu also has an Options button for accessing settings that establish the behavior of the interface as well as the location of directories and files used for working on projects. You access the application menu by clicking the Revit logo button in the upper-left corner of the user interface. The Options button is located in the lower-right corner of the menu, as shown in Figure 1.46.

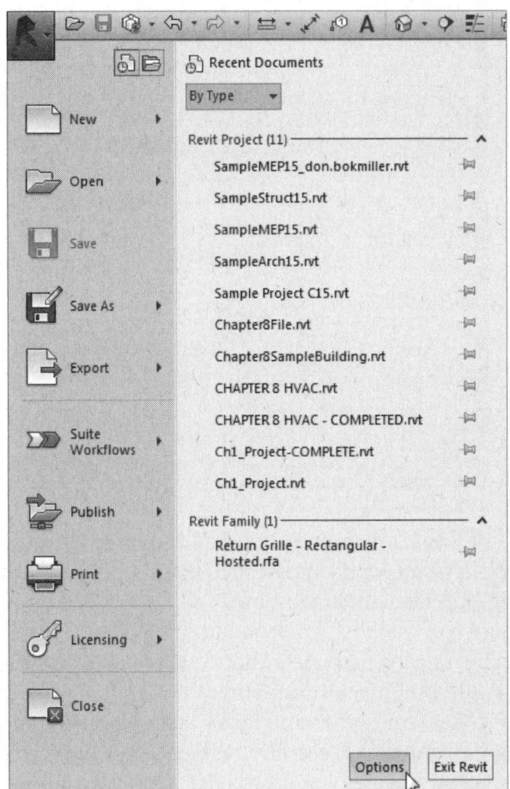

FIGURE 1.46
Application menu

The Options dialog box has several tabs for different settings within Revit MEP 2015. The General section, as shown in Figure 1.47, contains a slider that allows you to control how frequently your file updates when you're working in a worksharing environment and utilizing the Model Updates option of the worksharing display features.

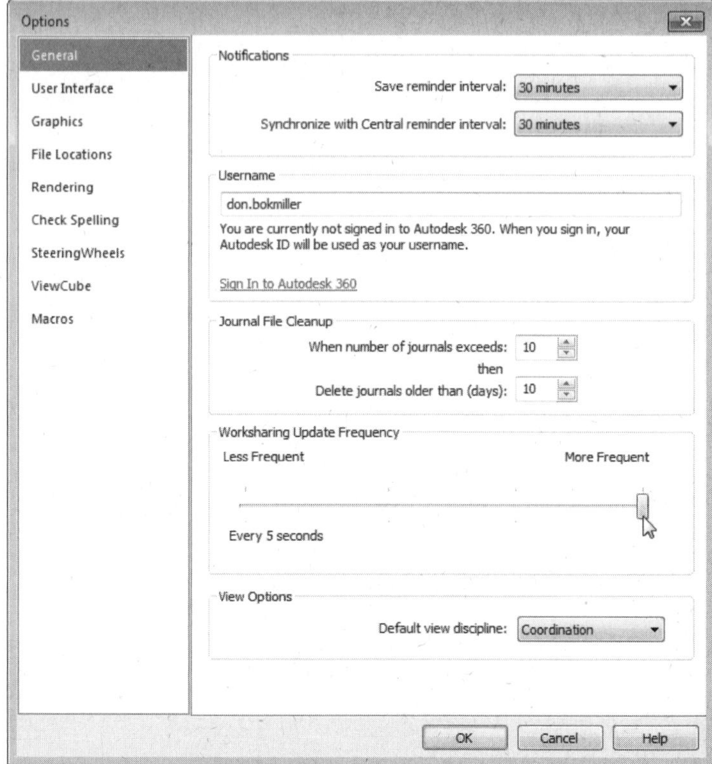

FIGURE 1.47 Options dialog box—General section

The General section is also where you define your username for Revit MEP 2015. This is important for worksharing because Revit uses this name to identify you for editing requests, workset ownership, and element borrowing.

This is also where you establish your default view discipline. This is important because it assigns this discipline to each new view that you create, unless the view is defined by a view template that has a different discipline setting.

The User Interface section, shown in Figure 1.48, is where you can set some general behavior for the interface. For example, you can choose between a light gray or dark gray theme for the interface from the Active Theme drop-down list. This tab is also where you determine which ribbon tabs and tools are available.

The Tab Switching Behavior section in this screen is where you define how the ribbon tabs behave after an action is completed. There are settings for the behavior in both the project environment and the Family Editor. The check box for displaying a contextual tab on a selection allows you to have the ribbon tab switch immediately to the contextual tab when an object is selected. If that check box is not selected, the contextual tab still appears on the ribbon, but it does not automatically become the active tab.

In addition, you can define the level of information provided by tooltips from the Tooltip Assistance drop-down menu, shown in Figure 1.49. If you are still learning the functions of different tools within Revit MEP 2015, you may want to set this option to High so that you receive detailed descriptions of how tools work when you hover over them with your mouse pointer. If you find that the tooltips interfere with your workflow, you can set this option to Minimal or None.

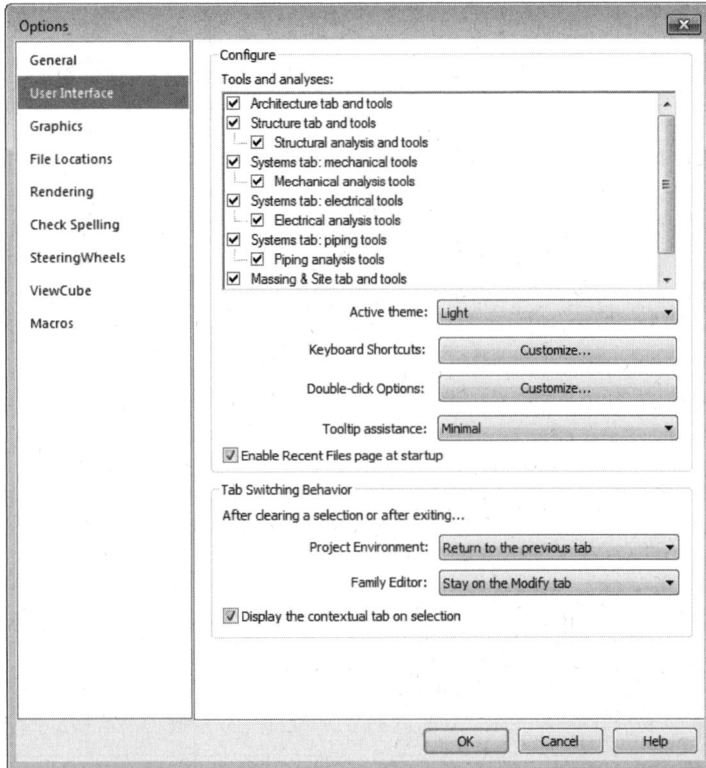

FIGURE 1.48 User Interface section of the Options dialog box

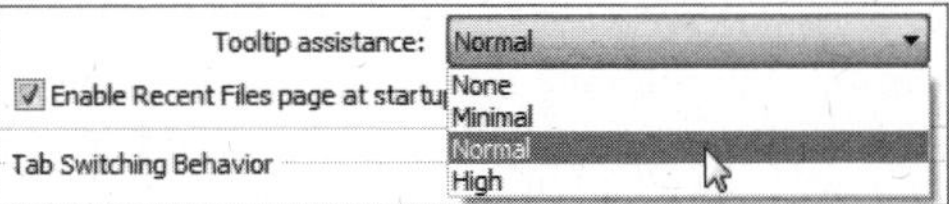

FIGURE 1.49 Tooltip assistance

Keyboard Shortcuts

On the User Interface tab of the Options dialog box is a button that enables you to customize your keyboard shortcuts. Clicking this button activates the Keyboard Shortcuts dialog box. In this dialog box, you can filter the commands to make the list easier to manage and edit. You can even filter by specific tabs or menus, as shown in Figure 1.50.

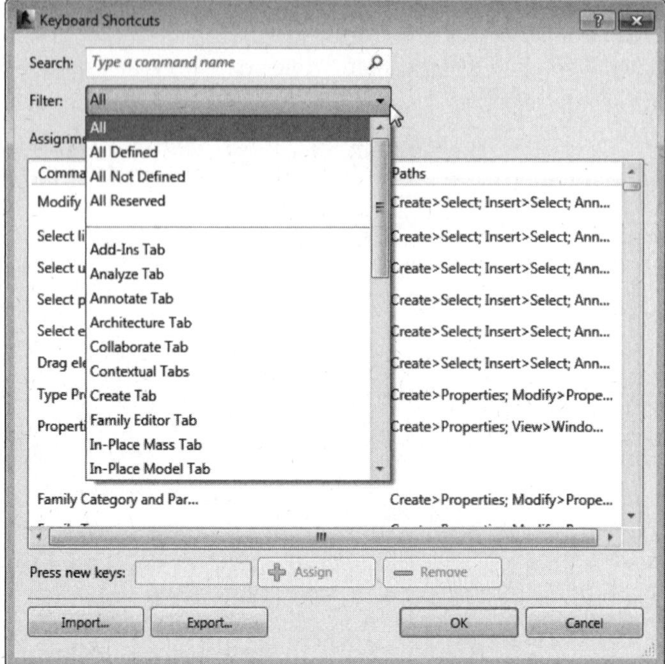

FIGURE 1.50 Filter options for the Keyboard Shortcuts list

SHORTCUT ACCESS

You can access the Keyboard Shortcuts dialog box by clicking the User Interface button on the View tab. There is even a keyboard shortcut for the Keyboard Shortcuts dialog box: KS.

You can sort the list in ascending or descending alphabetical order by clicking the desired column. Once you have located a command for which you want to create a keyboard shortcut, you can select the command to activate the Press New Keys text box at the bottom of the dialog box. Input the desired keys that will activate the command. You can input up to five characters for a keyboard shortcut. Reserved keys cannot be used for keyboard shortcuts; you can find the reserved keys by using the filter in the Keyboard Shortcuts dialog box. Click the Assign button to apply the shortcut to the selected command.

You can create multiple shortcuts for a single tool, and you can use the same shortcut keys for multiple tools. When you create a shortcut that is used for multiple tools, you must use the status bar to determine which tool to use when working in your project. When you type the shortcut, the first matching command is displayed on the status bar. You can use the arrow keys on your keyboard to cycle through available commands for the shortcut. Once the desired command is displayed on the status bar, you can activate it by pressing the spacebar. You can remove a keyboard shortcut from a command by selecting the specific shortcut and clicking the Remove button, as shown in Figure 1.51.

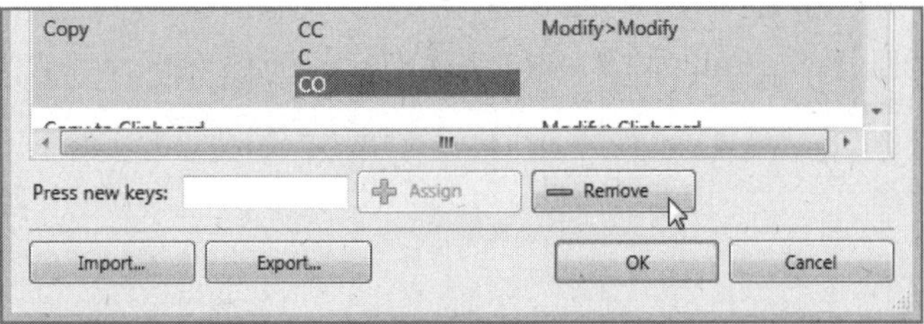

FIGURE 1.51 Removing a keyboard shortcut

You can export your keyboard shortcut settings by clicking the Export button at the bottom of the Keyboard Shortcuts dialog box. This saves your settings as an XML file that can be edited in a spreadsheet program. Using a spreadsheet is another way to manage and share your keyboard shortcuts. The XML file can then be imported into Revit by using the Import button, allowing you to set a standard for keyboard shortcuts in a multiuser work environment.

WHAT DO I TYPE?

With Tooltip Assistance set to at least Minimal, you can see the keyboard shortcut for a tool by hovering your mouse pointer over it. The keyboard shortcut is shown in parentheses next to the name of the tool.

 **Real World Scenario**

COMMON SHORTCUTS

Clark is responsible for teaching a Revit MEP 2015 class. He has established keyboard shortcuts that fit his workflow best and allow for efficient use of the software. Because he is so familiar with these shortcuts, he wants to share them with his students so that they will all be using the same ones during class.

Clark exports his shortcut settings to a file, which he imports into Revit MEP 2015 on the computers in the classroom. Prior to importing the custom settings, he exported the default settings so that they can be used later if necessary. During class he notes that the settings provided are preferred, but each student can further customize them if doing so results in improved efficiency.

Graphics

The Graphics section, shown in Figure 1.52, of the Options dialog box allows you to set the Selection, Pre-Selection, and Alert colors used in the drawing area. The drawing area's background color can be inverted if you are more comfortable using a black background. Settings for temporary dimensions are also available to make them more readable. You can set the background for temporary dimensions to Transparent or Opaque.

FIGURE 1.52 Graphics section of the Options dialog box

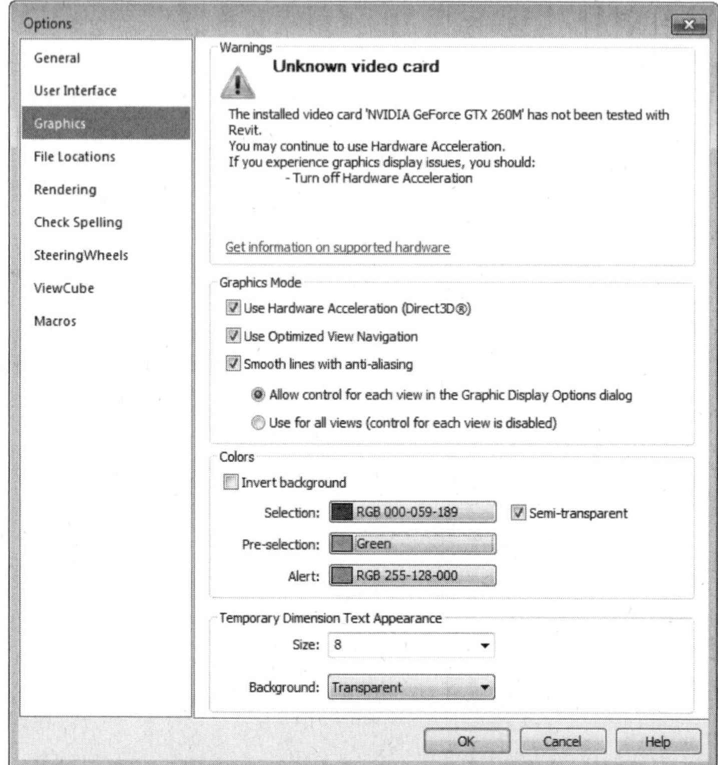

If you are experiencing graphics issues, you may need to change the Graphics Mode settings. Hardware acceleration works best when you are using an Autodesk-certified video driver. Certified and recommended drivers are available for download from here:

```
http://usa.autodesk.com/adsk/servlet/syscert?id=18844534&siteID=123112
```

Settings for the appearance and behavior of the SteeringWheels® and ViewCube® features can be found in their respective sections in the Options dialog box.

Context Menus

Although the ribbon interface is designed for efficient workflow, context menus can be the easiest, most effective way to access settings or make changes to components of your Revit projects. A *context menu* is one that appears when you right-click in open space in the drawing area, on an item in the Project Browser, or on an object in the drawing area. Right-clicking in open space in the drawing area activates a context menu that includes the Repeat and Recent Commands tools. The last command used can be activated by pressing the Enter key or by clicking the Repeat option on the context menu. The Recent Commands option displays a list of recently used commands for easy access during repetitive work. Figure 1.53 shows a context menu and the recent commands used during a working session. The Recent Commands list displays the last five commands used.

FIGURE 1.53
Context menu showing recent commands

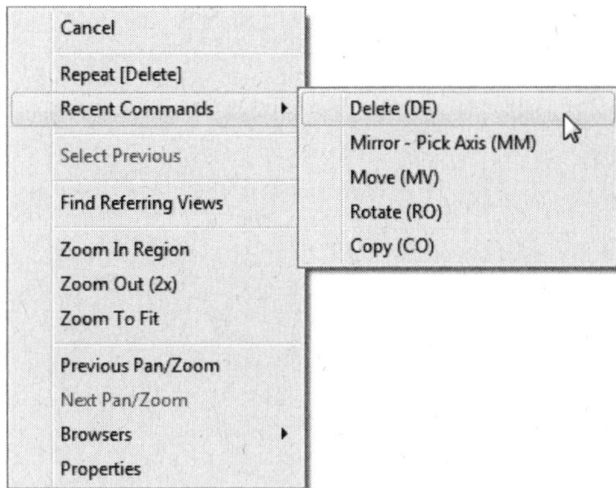

The options displayed on a context menu depend on the object selected when the menu is accessed. One nice feature of Revit MEP 2015 is the ability to define the selection set when the Select All Instances option is chosen. Figure 1.54 shows that you have the option to select only the objects in the active view or to select them throughout the entire project. This makes the Select All Instances feature much more useful because you don't have to worry about objects that should not be selected being inadvertently included in the selection set.

FIGURE 1.54
Selection set options

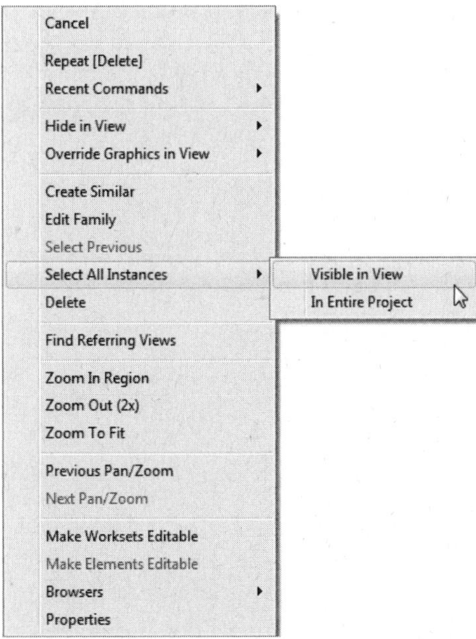

There is no longer a View Properties or Element Properties option in the context menus (as in versions prior to Revit MEP 2011) because of the addition of the Properties palette. The Properties option at the bottom of a context menu allows you to toggle the Properties palette on or off.

You can also right-click an element in the Project Browser to access a context menu. Right-clicking a view activates a menu with options for applying or creating a view template from that view. You can also save the view to a new file, as shown in Figure 1.55.

FIGURE 1.55
Context menu for a view selected in the Project Browser

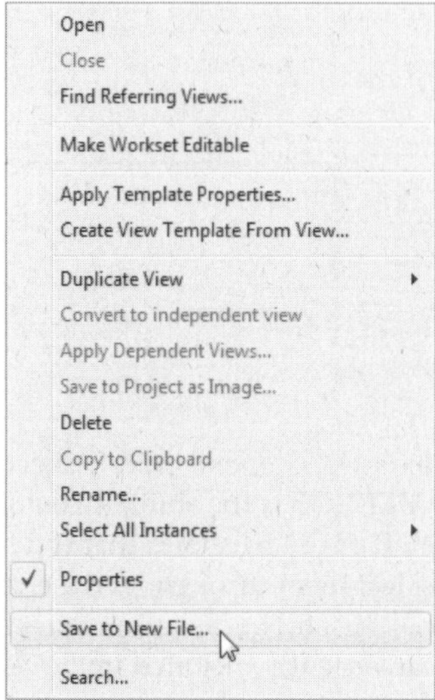

When you right-click a family in the Project Browser, you get a context menu with options to edit, rename, or reload the family. You can right-click a family type in the Project Browser to access its type properties or to select the instances in the project without having to locate one of the instances in the model, as shown in Figure 1.56.

FIGURE 1.56
Context menu for a selected family type

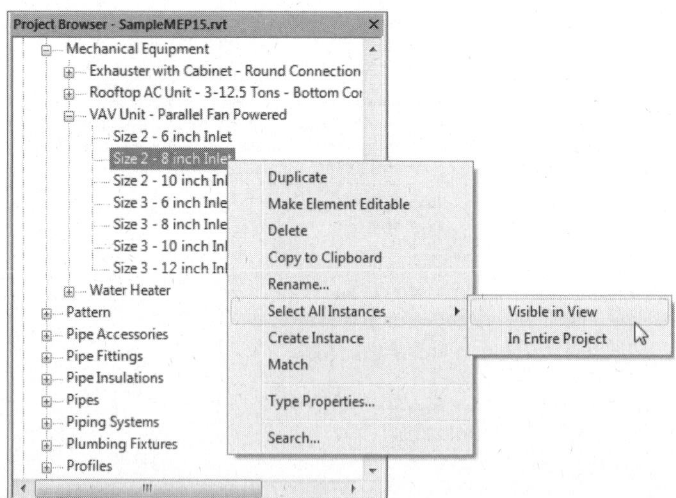

You can also use a context menu to manage linked files through the Project Browser. Figure 1.57 shows the options available on a context menu when a linked Revit file is selected in the Project Browser.

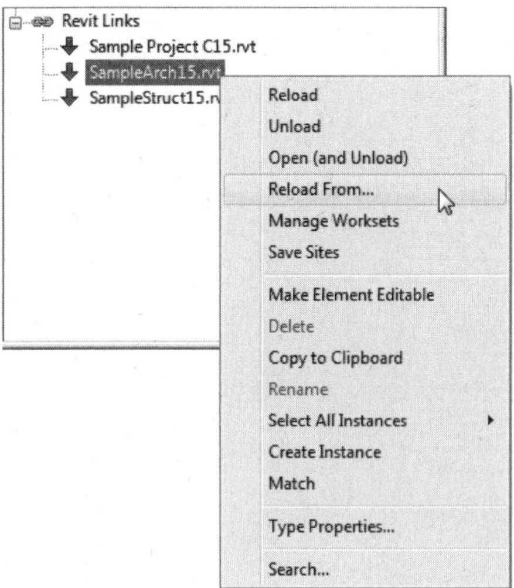

FIGURE 1.57 Context menu for a linked file in the Project Browser

The Bottom Line

Navigate the ribbon interface. The ribbon is an efficient user interface style that works well in Revit. The ability to house numerous tools in a single area of the interface allows for maximum screen real estate for the drawing area.

> **Master It** Along with the standard tabs available on the ribbon interface, contextual tabs are available while you're working on a project. Explain what a contextual tab is and how it may differ throughout your workflow.

Utilize user interface features. Many features are available in the Revit MEP 2015 user interface that allow for quick access to tools and settings. The use of keyboard shortcuts can also improve workflow efficiency.

> **Master It** To enhance workflow efficiency, it is important to know how to access features of the user interface. What tool can be used to activate or remove user interface features?

Use settings and menus. Establishing settings for your user interface is another way to create a working environment that is the most efficient and effective for your use of Revit MEP 2015.

> **Master It** The use of keyboard shortcuts has been part of design and drafting software for a long time. The ability to customize the shortcuts to best suit your workflow is key to improved efficiency. How can the settings for keyboard shortcuts be accessed? How can modified keyboard settings be reset?

Chapter 2

Creating an Effective Project Template

A lot of work goes into putting together a building design project. Not only must you coordinate the design intent, you must also coordinate the means to communicate it. Anyone interested in saving time and money to achieve the goals required by a project immediately begins to ask how they can simplify or automate the numerous tasks.

Project templates are the cornerstone to improving efficiency when you're working on an Autodesk® Revit® MEP 2015 project. Revit for MEP is a design and documentation tool, and those who are paid to do design work should not have to spend time on anything other than achieving their design goals. A well-developed project template lets you focus more on design without having to spend time developing and defining settings or standards each time a task is required, because they are already created for you.

The first consideration for creating a Revit project template should be the requirements for the delivery of the design. There is no need for certain settings or features in a template if they are not used on a project-by-project basis. Some clients may have certain standards that require a unique template altogether. Because project templates are the culmination of company or client standards, they should be managed by one person or a small group of people, with input required from the leads of each discipline. Project templates are fluid documents that require updates, so allowing global access to them makes them difficult to manage. However, input as to what should be included in a template can be made by anyone who works on projects and understands the need for features or functionality.

Revit MEP 2015 comes with template files that can be used for starting a project right away. You may choose to use these templates for a project or as a starting point for building your own template.

Whatever their use, project templates are the starting points that allow you to work seamlessly without breaking the momentum of collaboration and coordination efforts of your projects. The goal of creating a template is not to include every single item or standard that you use but to determine what is most often needed.

The creation of templates is usually assigned to the most Revit-savvy people in a company. If you are new to Revit, consider reading this chapter from an informational standpoint or skipping it altogether and coming back to it when you have developed a better understanding of Revit terminology, concepts, and best practices.

In this chapter, you will learn to do the following:

- Set up views and visibility
- Establish project settings
- Define preloaded content and its behavior
- Create sheet standards

Understanding Templates

The reason for setting standards is so that project documents look the same within a construction document set and so that different sets of documents appear to have come from the same place. Some companies care more about how their drawings look than others, but uniformity should exist regardless. This applies not only to the content that makes up a model but also to the organization of model views, the naming of views and schedules, and the overall drafting conventions used.

Once it has been determined how views should be displayed for each type and each discipline, you can establish those settings in your project template so that each project begins from the same starting point. Because every project is unique in some way, it is possible to modify the default settings as needed, but that does not eliminate the need for baseline settings.

You want to be able to begin working on a project without having to spend time setting up how the project appears in your views. Having preset views and visibility settings increases productivity on your projects by eliminating the need to do repetitive tasks just to get started.

There is no right or wrong way to create a template. Choosing one way over another is just a matter of preference. As you go through this chapter, we will do our best to give you multiple ideas of how to do things.

Determining the Number and Types of Views Needed

From a production standpoint, the purpose of a project template is to eliminate or reduce the need for repetitive tasks, such as setting the scale of a view or turning off the visibility of certain model objects each time a new view is created. The ability to create a view and begin working without spending time setting it up can help reduce the time it takes to complete a project. It is also helpful in reducing drafting errors and maintaining a consistent look among construction documents.

We know that certain elements should be displayed in certain types of views and that some elements should be displayed differently depending on the type of view. For example, you may want to show plumbing fixtures as halftone in a mechanical heating, ventilation, and air-conditioning (HVAC) plan but display them normally in a plumbing plan.

The way that objects are displayed by default is set up in the object styles of a project. We'll discuss object styles later in this chapter. The way that a view displays the model and specific objects within the model is controlled by the properties of the view.

When you select a view in the Project Browser, its properties are displayed in the Properties palette; if you are not using the Properties palette, you can right-click a view and select Properties.

ACCESS TO VIEW PROPERTIES

One useful feature of the Project Browser is that it allows you to access the properties of your views (and any other element in the project) without having to open them in the drawing area. Parameters can be changed on many views without taking the time to open each view; just hold down Ctrl and select the views that you want to modify at once.

Some properties of a view are the result of the type of view that has been created. View types include floor plans, reflected ceiling plans, sections, elevations, and 3D views. These are all views used for displaying the model. There are also drafting and detail views that are used for displaying 2D details or diagrams. Some detail views are a combination of model display and detail components.

When building a project template, you should consider what types of views will be necessary. As with any component of a template, there is no need to create every type of view imaginable just because it might be used. Choose to create only those views that you know will be used on nearly every project. Otherwise, you might end up creating more work for each project by having to clean out all the unused items. The types of views you create also depend on your workflow for a Revit project. If all the design disciplines share a common Revit model, you want to have the views that each discipline requires. Obviously, if you create a separate project file for each discipline, there is no need for all the discipline views in each template. However, managing multiple templates can be time-consuming and inconsistent standards could be created among them.

Setting the Number of Levels

Another important consideration is the number of levels to include in a template. A view should be created for each level, so it is important to decide on how many to start a project with. If you work primarily on two- or three-story buildings, it may be best to have only three or four levels established in your template, including one for the roof. More levels can be added to a project as needed. The architect typically determines the number of levels, so it is possible to not include any levels in your template and copy/monitor the architectural levels after the project file has been created. However, you must have levels in your template if you want to create views.

Working with Plan Types

Views should be created in your template for each type of view to be used. These are generally determined by the Sub-Discipline property of the views. Whether your template is single-discipline or multidiscipline, a floor plan should be created at each level for each subdiscipline type.

When creating reflected ceiling plan views, it is a good idea to create only one ceiling plan view for each level. This promotes coordination among disciplines because everyone will be viewing the same ceiling plan and because all components of the model that occupy the ceiling can be made visible. Because this type of view does not belong to any one specific discipline, you may want to assign it to the Coordination discipline to distinguish it as unique.

Reflected ceiling plan views that are needed for construction documents can be created for the specific discipline that requires them after the project has been created.

Creating a Working View

A useful type of view to create is typically called a *working view*. This type of view is the same as the views that will be used on construction documents, but the settings are different so that more or less of the model can be seen. Working views also allow for different graphic representations without having to constantly change back and forth within the view that goes on a sheet. For example, ductwork plans are typically shown in Hidden Line style, which can be difficult to navigate because of performance. A working view can be created that is set to Wireframe, which is easily navigable, and the modeling can be done there.

One thing to note about using working views is that it may cause problems with keeping your project coordinated. If you are used to working in this type of view during the course of a project, you may place tags, dimensions, or other annotation elements in the working views, which will not show up in the view that actually gets placed on a sheet. To avoid this kind of problem, you may want to consider disabling tags in the working views. This way, whenever the designers attempt to tag an object, the tag won't be visible, reminding them that they are trying to tag in the wrong view.

Working and Documentation Views

Working views are not required by Revit but they can be a useful way of ensuring that the view settings used for printing views aren't changed unwittingly by a user. It is important to get a grasp of this workflow and realize that working views do not get placed on sheets and do not have annotation objects such as tags and dimensions. In contrast, *documentation views* should not change in respect to scale, shading, level of detail, and visibility of objects.

One trick to differentiating the two views is to set your documentation views to black only while using filters to display working views in full color. Or, if you are using color in deliverables, color could still be used to a greater extent in your working views. So you can keep track of which system a duct or pipework belongs to, for example, chilled water pipework flow and return could be a different color in a working view, whereas they would be the same color in a sheet view.

Alternatively, you could use a naming convention to differentiate, or you could add an extra view-related parameter that would then be added to your Project Browser view filter. Views would then be filtered by use and discipline. Keep in mind that the use of working views is optional and there are no specific working views with out-of-the-box templates.

Choosing Display Settings for Views

Once you have established the types and number of views to include in your template, you can set the properties that determine the display characteristics of the view. These settings will be the default, or *baseline*, settings because the need to change them occurs regularly while you're working in a project. In fact, the need is so common that a set of tools is available on the View Control Bar of the user interface for quick access to changing the settings. It may not seem necessary to set these properties because they can be easily changed, but it is good to start with the best options for these settings.

You can choose the default settings by editing these parameters:

- View Scale
- Detail Level
- Visual Style

For the most part, model plan views are set to 1/8″ = 1′-0″ (1:100 mm) scale and are displayed at Medium detail with a Hidden Line visual style. Consider using the Shaded visual style with the Show Edges option at a Fine level of detail for 3D views. This gives the viewer a better sense of the model and will display any pipes or conduit in full 3D.

When you're creating views that will include piping, setting the detail level to Fine enables you to see the actual pipe, pipe fittings, and accessories instead of their single-line representation. Many users prefer to model their piping systems in Fine detail because it is easier to see where connections are made and to discern differences in pipe sizes. For piping plans that are set to Fine detail, the Visual Style option should be set to Wireframe, because this will help improve performance when zooming or panning in the view. The visual style should be set to Hidden Line when these views are printed so that it can be easily determined which pipes are crossing.

You may also want to edit the following parameters:

- Underlay
- Underlay Orientation
- Phase properties

You can use the Underlay and Underlay Orientation parameters to display other levels of the model as an underlay to the current view. Doing so causes the underlay to appear as halftone, while any detail or annotation graphics are displayed normally. You can choose which level to underlay by using the Underlay parameter, while the Underlay Orientation parameter determines how the model is being viewed. Any level of the model can be used in any other view. Although these are useful settings for seeing how things line up in your model, it is not necessary to set an underlay in your default view settings.

Phase properties of a view are important when working in phased projects. They add another level of visibility that can cause frustration if not set properly. Although these are instance parameters, they really should be used to determine the types of views you create. If you do a lot of renovation work, it is good to have default existing and demolition phase views in your template. Items placed into your model will take on the phase of view in which they are placed. Another option is to have a template that is phase ready, for remodeling projects, and another one that is not, for your new construction projects.

Plan views have type parameters only for setting what family to use for callout tags within the view and for setting what reference label is used when other callouts reference the view. Drafting views have the same type parameters as well as one for the section tag. Once you have determined what families will be used for your sections and callouts, you can assign them to the appropriate views.

Section and elevation model views have a unique parameter: You can set a threshold that prevents Revit from displaying annotations in views using a scale coarser than the threshold. Revit uses the *words* finer and *coarser* to distinguish between view scales. For example 1/8″ = 1′-0″ (1:100) is coarser than 1/2″ = 1′-0″ (1:20). This eliminates the need for controlling the visibility of these markers with Visibility/Graphic Overrides settings. Figure 2.1 shows the parameter for hiding a section view marker at a specified scale.

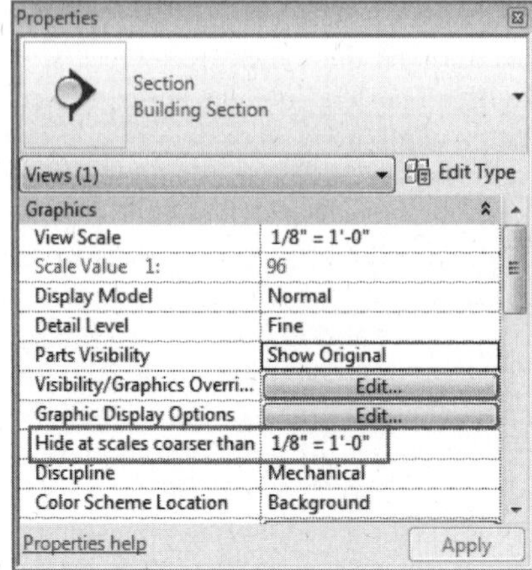

FIGURE 2.1 Parameter for hiding a section view

Visibility Settings for Template Views

There are many parameters for view properties that can be set by default. It is best to keep things simple by setting the most common parameters that will determine the general style of the view. Visibility settings are the most important to any view because you want to see what you expect to see in a particular type of plan. It can be frustrating and time-consuming to have to turn off unwanted model elements every time you open or create a new view.

There are two primary areas of visibility control within a view: the View Range settings, which determine the field of view when you're looking at the model, and the Visibility/Graphics Overrides settings, which allow for turning categories of elements on or off as well as other aspects of their appearance. Setting default values for these parameters is a key element of a good project template. Because working in a Revit project is a collaborative exercise, it is good to have the objects in your views appear as expected and not to have objects showing up from other disciplines as they are placed in the model. For example, in a plumbing floor plan, you would want to use the Halftone check box under Visibility/Graphics Overrides for mechanical equipment and turn off all ducts, air terminals, fire-protection elements, and so on. The pipe visibility can be controlled with filters, so you can turn off the mechanical pipe systems. The end result is a plumbing plan displaying only the elements that are relevant to the plumbing discipline, with all others either turned off or displayed in halftone.

VIEW RANGE

There are two parts to View Range: Primary Range and View Depth. The primary range consists of the top, bottom, and cut plane of a view. For a floor plan, Top defines the elevation from which the model is being viewed. Bottom is the extent to which the model is being viewed from the Top setting. In other words, it is how far you are looking. Cut Plane refers to an imaginary plane that cuts through the architectural and structural elements. The portions of these elements in a floor plan view that are above the cut plane elevation are not visible.

For a ceiling plan\view (also called a reflected ceiling plan), the view is the other way around. Essentially it is as if you are looking up from the cut plane to the top of the view.

The View Depth setting can be used to extend the range of view beyond the top or bottom. However, any elements that fall within that range will not react to any overrides assigned to their category in the view. In other words, if you override the color of pipes to be blue in a view, only pipes that are between the Top and Bottom settings of the view range will be blue. Any pipes that fit within the range of the View Depth setting are displayed with the style assigned to the <Beyond> Line style, which can also be adjusted per view. Of course, you can manually override elements by using graphic overrides or the Linework tool under the Modify tab after they have been created.

Although you may have levels established in your template, there is no way of knowing what their actual dimensions will be until the building is modeled. However, there is a way to set default View Range settings that ensures that the initial view of the model will correctly show the building elements. For example, to establish a view range that ensures visibility of objects for a first-floor plan view, follow these steps:

1. For plan views, choose View Properties ➤ View Range and set Top to Level Above with an Offset setting of **0′-0″** (**0** mm).
2. Set Cut Plane to **4′-0″** (**1200** mm).
3. Set Bottom and View Depth to Associated Level with an Offset setting of **0′-0″** (**0** mm).

Adjustments may be required, depending on the construction of the building, but these settings are a good starting point because they will display all the visible model components from floor to floor. Because the Cut Plane setting is what determines the visible architectural and structural components, you don't need to worry that the actual floor object of the level above will interfere with visibility.

Figure 2.2 shows the View Range dialog box with the settings described in the previous steps for a first-floor plan view.

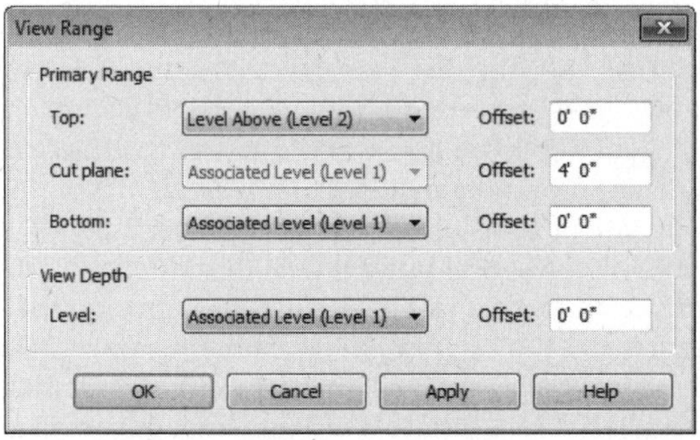

FIGURE 2.2 Typical View Range settings for a plan view

For a ceiling plan view, do the following:

1. Set Top to Level Above with an Offset setting of **0′-0″** (**0** mm).
2. Set Cut Plane to **4′-0″** (**1200** mm).

   You may choose a higher Cut Plane value if you do not want to see items such as doors or windows in your ceiling plans. The Bottom setting is irrelevant in a ceiling plan because it is always behind your field of view.

3. Set View Depth to Level Above with an Offset of **0′-0″** (**0** mm).

These settings ensure that, for your ceiling plans, you see all visible model elements from the cut plane up to the top of the view range. So, if there are ceilings with varied elevations on a level, they are all displayed, and any items you want to see above the ceiling for coordination are also visible.

Visibility/Graphics Overrides

In the Visibility/Graphics Overrides settings of a view, you can not only can you turn components on or off, you can also change their color, linetype, or transparency. Items that might ordinarily appear with normal lines can be set to Halftone. You can apply settings to the subcategories of components as well.

One of the ideas behind establishing default visibility settings is that you do not want certain items showing up in specific views. For example, lighting fixtures are typically shown on a separate plan from receptacles and power devices, but because all of these components are being placed into one model, they show up in every view (depending on the View Range settings) unless they are turned off.

It is a good practice to make a list of all model components that you would like to see in a particular type of plan, and then turn off all others. If you are not quite sure about some components, it is best to leave them on because seeing items encourages coordination, whereas not seeing them may lead to a design conflict in the model. Be sure to check the necessary disciplines from the Filter list pull-down in the upper-left corner of the Visibility/Graphic Overrides dialog box (see Figure 2.3).

Annotation components are specific to the view in which they are placed, so it is not crucial to set up default visibility for them. After all, it is not likely that you will be placing air terminal tags in your lighting plan, for example, so there is no need to turn them off. In fact, if the air terminals are turned off from the Model Categories tab for the lighting plan, Revit can't display air terminals tags. Tags appear only when the model element is visible. However, there are some annotation categories that you may want to adjust, such as setting the Space Tags category to Halftone. Many families contain nested annotations, so you should also check the subcategories of Generic Annotations to set any necessary visibility.

If your workflow consists of using linked files from other disciplines or consultants, those links will react to whatever visibility settings you apply to the view. This usually works well when a project begins, but as the model is more fully developed, you will find that you are constantly managing the visibility of the linked files in views. Consider linking files into your template that will act as placeholders for the actual project files to be linked. Doing so lets you establish default visibility settings for the links, reducing time spent managing visibility after the project is in design.

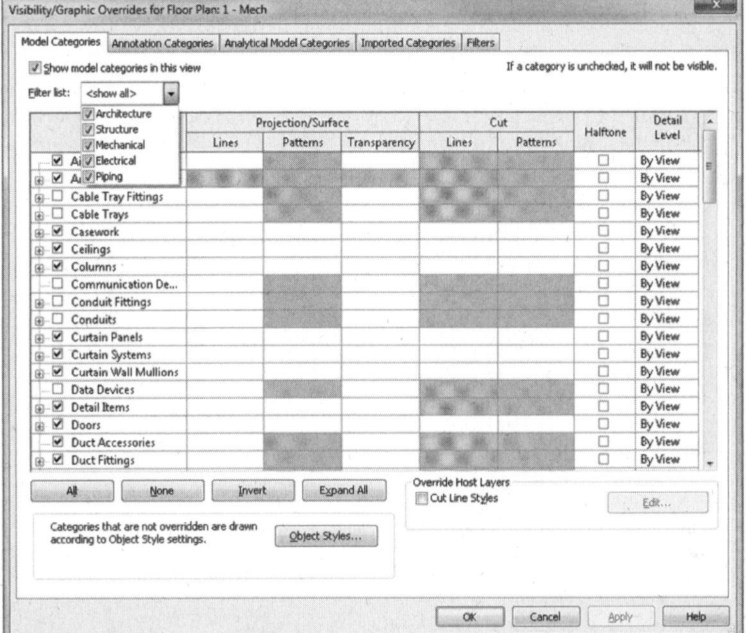

FIGURE 2.3 Visibility/ Graphics Overrides

PLACEHOLDER LINKS

Having linked files in your project template is a useful feature for not only visibility but also model positioning. If the Auto – Origin To Origin positioning option is used for a placeholder link, then the file used to replace it will also be positioned at its origin. Placeholder links can be very small files. In fact, they do not need to contain any information at all. When a project is set up, all that is needed is to use the Reload From option to replace the placeholder link with the actual model file.

Worksharing cannot be enabled in a Revit template (RTE) file, so if you want to establish default worksets and visibility settings for them, you need to create a Revit project (RVT) file that is to be used as a project template. The file can then be copied to establish the central file for a new project.

This scenario requires careful management of the file because of the nature of a worksharing environment. Some companies have written applications to make it easy for their users to set up a project this way without damaging or misplacing the project "template" file. You should set up your template this way only if you are absolutely certain that personnel who have extensive Revit experience will manage it.

For more information on worksharing, see Chapter 3, "Worksets and Worksharing."

VIEW FILTERS

View filters let you document your project and separate domestic hot water from the hydronic supply, for example. One of the systems needs to appear on the plumbing sheets, the other on the mechanical sheets; without filters, you can't do that.

To set up view filters, you can go to the View tab and click Filters. Another way to access filters is to type **VG** in any floor plan to access Visibility/Graphics Overrides. Next, select the Filters tab and click Edit/New to open the Filters dialog box, shown in Figure 2.4. This dialog box lists the names of several filters that are in Revit by default. Think of accessing filters through Visibility/Graphics Overrides as a back door because both paths get you to the same place. However, remember that Visibility/Graphics Overrides changes are per view, and because changes to Filters are project-wide, accessing Filters through Visibility/Graphics Overrides may be confusing.

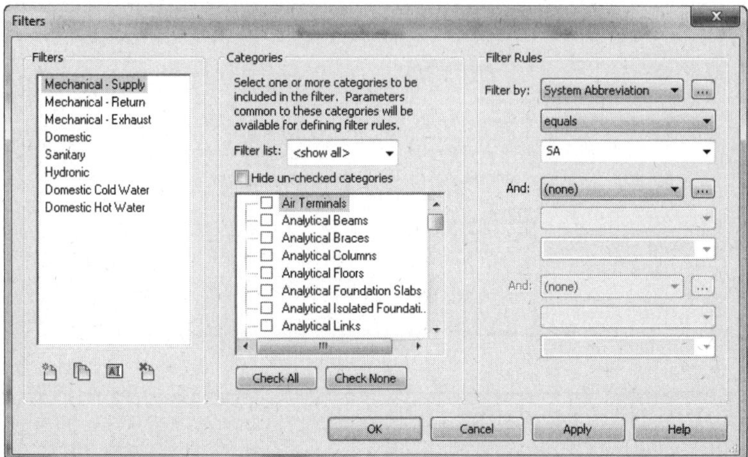

FIGURE 2.4
Creating view filters

Notice that categories have different elements selected. These are the items you want the filter to affect. Next, notice under Filter Rules that, by default, System Classification is selected. Because of the large number of filters that are normally created for a project, you should change the Filter By setting from System Classification to System Abbreviation. This helps to identify and separate your systems properly. If you try to use the default System Classification setting, soon you will find its limitations. The mechanical supply air system rule is set to Filter By - "System Classification" with a rule - "to contain" and value "supply". This may not be a problem for small projects, but for larger ones with multiple supply systems, it won't work. This limitation is especially obvious for the piping systems, where distinguishing between all the supply and return systems is critical. System Abbreviation has the necessary flexibility to allow for distinguishing hundreds of systems. To create new system filters, the easiest method is to select an existing system filter and then click the Duplicate icon. Once the system filter is duplicated, make sure the proper category elements are selected and then rename the filter rule to the name by which you want to filter.

To apply these filters to your views, you can go to the View tab on the ribbon and then select Visibility/Graphics. Next, select the Filters tab (see Figure 2.5).

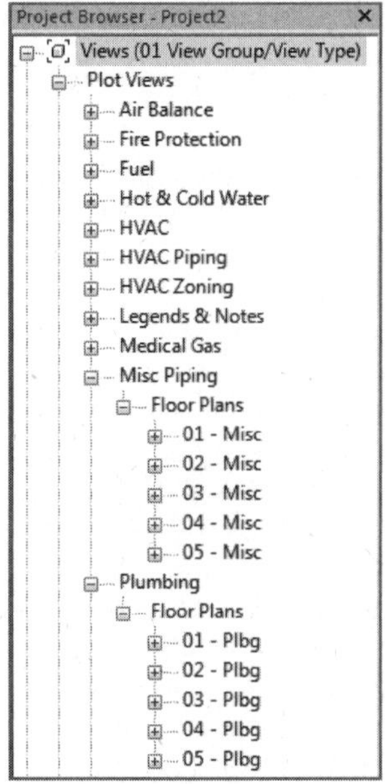

FIGURE 2.5
Applying view filters

On the Filters tab, click Add. This brings up the filters that you have created, so select the filters that apply to your project. Once the filters are loaded, you can turn the filters on and off and adjust line weights, colors, and patterns. It might be a good idea to test whether your filters are working properly by turning them off one at a time and ensuring that the appropriate elements are turned off in the view.

Mastering filter options will give you the ability to create your models with the standards that your office has developed over years of producing CAD drawings.

Prior to the introduction of duct and pipe systems as system families in Revit MEP 2012, filters were also used to control the color and the linetype of pipes and ducts. Some companies may still choose to do it this way, but the main benefit of using the duct and pipe systems is that the color and linetype are set globally instead of per view. This benefit is most obvious when you start creating additional views such as sections and callouts and you need to keep adding the filters to get the colors of the systems. Since Revit MEP 2012, the proposed workflow is to control color and linetype with duct and pipe systems, and use filters to control the visibilities of elements.

New in Revit 2014 was the ability to create a selection filter. Selection filters allow you to apply a filter only to selected items instead of an entire object category.

Visibility Settings Shortcut: View Templates

Revit allows you to create view templates within your project templates to expedite the process of establishing the visibility settings of your views. View templates enable you to define preset properties of view types that can be applied to any view in one simple step. These are not just visibility properties; you can also set any of the main properties of a view.

You can create a view template by clicking the View Templates button on the View tab of the ribbon and then selecting the Manage View Templates option. On the left side of the dialog box is a list of view templates that exist. You can sort the list by view type by using the drop-down list in the upper-left corner. The right side of the dialog box lists the commonly used view parameters. Here, you can set the default values for these parameters to establish the view template.

There are also Edit buttons for the various tabs within the Visibility/Graphics Overrides dialog box. The Graphic Display Options have been separated into Model Display, Shadows, and Lighting settings. Any project parameters that you create that apply to views will also be available for editing.

The buttons in the lower-left corner of the dialog box are for duplicating, renaming, or deleting a view template. There is no button to create a new template, so you must duplicate an existing one before you can begin. In fact, if no view templates exist in your file, you cannot access the View Templates dialog box from the ribbon. To work around this, you can click the Create Template From Current View button, which will use the current view settings to create a view template and give you access to the Manage View Templates dialog box.

A more common method for creating a view template is first to create a view and then to establish its desired properties, including the visibility settings. This is a preferable method because you can see what the view will look like as you make adjustments to the properties. Creating a view template this way in your project template requires you to load a model temporarily to be used as the visual reference. Once you have the properties of a view established, you can right-click the view in the Project Browser and create a view template based on that view. You can also use the View Templates button on the View tab and select the Create Template From Current View option, as shown in Figure 2.6.

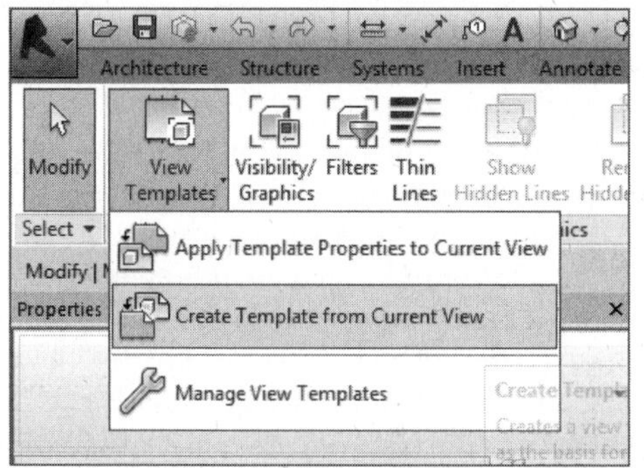

FIGURE 2.6
View Templates button

View templates are useful while creating your project template, but they are also useful after the project has been created. Revit gives us the ability to assign a view template to any given set of views, and those views update if the view template is changed. You can also apply any view template to any view, especially newly created ones, and quickly have the desired settings. When you work on a large project that has many levels or many dependent views, having view templates can save a significant amount of time.

In the View Templates dialog box, there is a check box next to each property that you can use to determine whether the settings of the template for that property will be applied to the view. This enables you to apply only the desired portions of a view template if necessary. By applying a view template to a view, if the Visibility/Graphics Check box is selected, you will no longer be able to control Visibility/Graphics Overrides from the Visibility/Graphics Overrides dialog box;

instead, you will be controlling multiple view settings at once from Manage View Templates. This applies to all settings that are controlled by the view template.

Schedule Views

Preset schedules in a project template are another feature that can increase productivity and coordination. This topic is included here because, by displaying the data within the components that make up the model, schedule views are actually views of the model components.

Schedule views can be saved as their own project file that can be loaded into a project as needed, so it is not necessary to have every schedule that you might use in your project template. The types of schedules you should include are ones that you know will be in every project. If you are going to create a schedule in your template, you must use parameters that are available in the template file. The parameters will be available either because they exist in components that are loaded into your template or because they are set up as project parameters. This is most easily achieved by using shared parameters because it is important that the parameters in your content are the same as those in the schedule. Careful consideration should be taken as to what parameters need to be in the template prior to setting up a schedule. For more information on creating schedules, see Chapter 7, "Schedules." For more about creating and managing parameters, see Chapter 6, "Parameters."

Some types of schedules can be included in your template; this can be useful for managing the project. Consider adding a View List schedule to your template. This enables you to quickly see information about your views to determine whether you have all the views required for a project or whether a view has not yet been placed onto a sheet. This also is a good way to change the parameters of your views without having to locate them in the Project Browser. Figure 2.7 shows a small sample of a View List schedule as it would look in a project file. Much more information can be added to a View List schedule, including any custom parameters that you create for views.

FIGURE 2.7
Sample View List schedule

VIEW LIST					
View Name	Title on Sheet	Sheet Number	Sheet Name	Scale Value 1:	Detail Level
E-Site	ELECTRICAL SITE PLAN	E2	ELECTRICAL SITE PLAN	120	Medium
EL - Level 1	FIRST FLOOR - LIGHTING	E3	FIRST FLOOR PLAN - LIGHTING	96	Coarse
EL - Level 2	SECOND FLOOR - LIGHTING	E4	SECOND FLOOR PLAN - LIGHTING	96	Medium
EP - Level 1	FIRST FLOOR - POWER	E5	FIRST FLOOR PLAN - POWER	96	Fine
EP - Level 2	SECOND FLOOR - POWER	E6	SECOND FLOOR PLAN - POWER	96	Medium
ISO DIAGRAM	DOMESTIC WATER ISO DIAGRAM	P4	DIAGRAMS AND DETAILS	96	Medium
MH - Level 1	FIRST FLOOR PLAN - HVAC	M2	FIRST FLOOR PLAN - HVAC	96	Medium
P - Level 1	FIRST FLOOR PLAN - PLUMBING	P2	FIRST FLOOR PLAN - PLUMBING	96	Medium
P - Level 2	SECOND FLOOR PLAN - PLUMBING	P3	SECOND FLOOR PLAN - PLUMBING	96	Fine
Riser Diagram	POWER RISER DIAGRAM	E8	DIAGRAMS AND DETAILS	48	Fine
SANITARY ISO	SANITARY ISO DIAGRAM	P4	DIAGRAMS AND DETAILS	96	Medium
Zones - Level 1				96	Medium
Zones - Level 2				96	Medium

Other types of schedules you should consider for your template are those that are used for quality assurance or analysis or schedule keys for applying values to parameters. These other types of schedules are often Space schedules, because spaces hold much of the analytical information. Even if you do not use Revit for energy or engineering analysis, there is a type of Space schedule that can be useful for managing names and numbers.

The ability of Revit to generate spaces automatically is a great feature; however, it will generate spaces where there is no room object in the linked model. It can be tedious and time-consuming to search through a large floor plan looking for spaces that should not be in the model. When these spaces are found in a plan view, deleting them removes them only from the model and not from the project. A simple Space schedule can be used to find all the spaces that should not exist and gives you the ability to delete all of them from the project with one click.

Figure 2.8 shows a sample Space schedule that reports the room name and room number of each space. The blank rows indicate spaces that have been placed where there is no room object. These rows can be highlighted in the schedule and removed from the project by clicking the Delete button on the ribbon. If you do energy analysis with the Revit model, those spaces will be needed. However, for energy analysis it is recommended to set up another project because in most cases the architectural model will need to be altered in ways that are unacceptable for a typical documentation model. For the documentation model, those "blank" spaces are simply polluting the model and will create more work if you use the Tag All command.

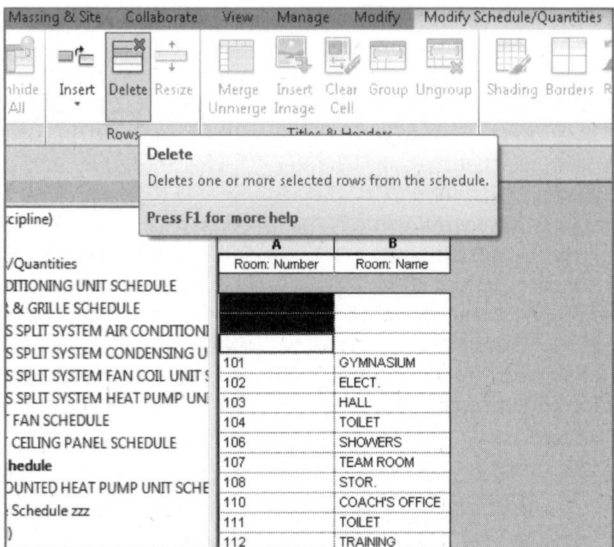

FIGURE 2.8
Space schedule

If you are using the Panel Schedule feature within Revit MEP 2015, you can create templates for panel schedules and store them in your project template. Click the Panel Schedule Templates button on the Manage tab, and select Manage Templates. In the dialog box is a list of any templates in your file. You can create a new one by clicking the Duplicate button at the bottom of the dialog box. See Chapter 7 for more information on creating and editing panel schedule templates.

You likely will end up with an extensive list of schedules, most of which are not going to be used for all of your projects. This is the case with all mechanical equipment and accessory schedules. In addition, certain organizations may require you to build a separate schedule for their projects (for example, the U.S. Department of Veterans Affairs or the U.S. Army Corps of Engineers). Instead of cluttering your template with all those schedules, you may want to consider creating a project that contains all of your company schedules or multiple projects based on major clients. Designers can then use the Insert View From File tool or just copy and paste only the needed schedules for their projects. The same method can be applied to details, using a single Revit project to store all of your details.

Establishing Project Settings

Many settings can be preset in a project template to make it easier to begin a project. Some settings relate to how system families behave, while others determine things such as how objects print or what text looks like. There are also settings for values that Revit uses in calculations. Having these set properly in your project template ensures that when you begin a project, you will see the model and data correctly and according to your standards.

Object Styles

The Object Styles settings within Revit determine how elements will be displayed by default (globally for the entire project) if no overrides are applied to them in a view (locally). You can set the defaults for model and annotation components as well as for the layers of any linked or imported CAD files (assuming you load dummy placeholder files). These settings can be applied to subcategories as well.

Even though the Visibility/Graphics Overrides settings are often used in views, it is important to set the standards for how elements display. The need for overrides comes from having several types of an element within one category. For example, plumbing fixtures may need to appear in halftone on the HVAC views and black in the plumbing views. This can be achieved by selecting the Halftone check box for plumbing fixtures on the Model Categories tab. However, if you need to do something similar for plumbing and mechanical equipment, you will find that there is no such thing as plumbing equipment in Revit. To be able to use halftone for the plumbing equipment in your HVAC views, you can create filters that are looking at a parameter within the mechanical equipment families (something like a Yes/No parameter called Is Plumbing Equipment). You could also use subcategories for this by creating subcategories in your mechanical equipment families for HVAC, plumbing, and so on, but you would need to ensure that all of your families are set up correctly for this to work. Possibly the easiest way to filter by trade within a single model would be to use worksets, but this is not what worksets were set up for, and care needs to be taken whenever worksets are involved.

Prior to Revit MEP 2012, filters were used to separate the way pipes and ducts are displayed. But in Revit MEP 2012, Autodesk introduced system families called pipe systems and duct systems, which allowed us to control color and linetype globally for the project. The reason you need to know about this change and when it happened is that if your company has active projects in multiple versions of Revit, most likely you will need to consider managing multiple templates as well as training your users how to use the different methods.

You can access the Object Styles settings for your template from the Manage tab of the ribbon. The Object Styles dialog box lists all the model, annotation, and imported categories on separate tabs for easy access. These are the types of settings you can apply to a category:

Line Weight Projection line weight is the thickness of the lines of an object if it falls within the view range and is not cut by the cut plane.

Cut Line Cut line weight is the thickness of the lines of an object that is cut by the cut plane. Keep in mind that the cut plane does not apply to MEP objects and affects only architectural and structural elements, which is why the column is grayed out for MEP categories. Also worth mentioning is that walls that are less than 6′-0″ (2,000 mm) high will not show as "cut"; they are shown in your plan from above, regardless of the location of the cut plane. Architects generally use a lighter line weight for walls that are not full height, floor to floor, so Revit somewhat arbitrarily decides that walls 6′ or shorter will not use the cut line weight. Walls that have a top constraint, such as the level above the cut plane, but use a negative offset to reduce their height will use the cut line weight.

Line Color This setting is for establishing the default color of objects within a category.

Line Pattern This setting determines what type of line will be used for objects in a category. This setting does not utilize a line style but rather applies a line pattern directly to the objects.

Material You can apply a material to a model category. This is primarily for rendering purposes, but it can also be useful for material takeoffs; however, the material applies to the entire category, so you cannot establish unique materials for different types of pipes or ducts by using this setting.

With duct and pipe systems as system families, you can define properties for specific engineering systems and apply graphic overrides for unique display of the components that make up the system. The display of these systems is not established in the Object Styles dialog box but rather in the type properties of the system families, as shown in Figure 2.9.

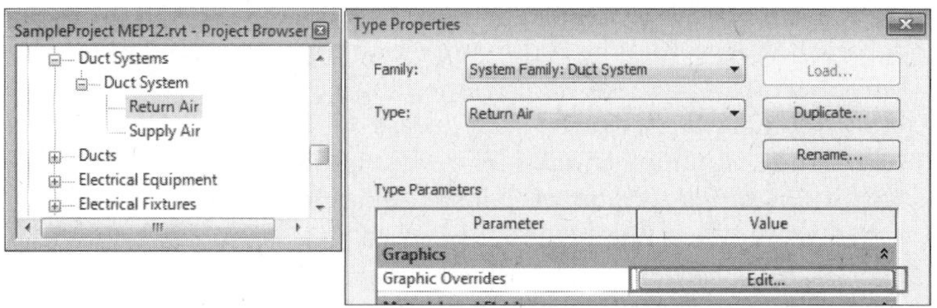

FIGURE 2.9 Duct system graphic overrides

The display of the new placeholder categories can be defined in the Object Styles dialog box, along with the lining and insulation categories that have been added for both pipes and ducts.

Drafting Line Settings

In the same way that the Object Styles settings define how model, annotation, and imported objects are displayed and printed, it is necessary in a template file to define the various line styles that will be used for any drafting or detailing that may be done in your projects. A line style is defined by its weight, color, and pattern. You can create different combinations of these settings to define lines that are used for specific drafting purposes or that match your standards.

LINE WEIGHTS

The first settings to consider when creating line styles are the available line weights in your template file. You can access the Line Weights settings by clicking the Additional Settings button on the Manage tab of the ribbon.

With Revit, you can establish 16 line weights. Typically, line weight 1 is the thinnest line, and line weight 16 is the thickest. The Line Weights dialog box has three tabs that give you access to the settings for lines, depending on what type of view or to what objects the line weights are applied. The first tab is for model objects. Model line weights are dependent on the scale of the view in which they appear. You can define a thickness for each of the 16 line weights as they appear in a specific view scale. This gives you the freedom to show lines that are usually very thick as much thinner when the view scale is larger. Figure 2.10 shows the Model Line Weights tab of the Line Weights dialog box. Notice that line weight 14 is half as thick in a 1/16″ scale view as it is in a 1/8″ scale view. This keeps items from printing as blobs in larger scale views without having to adjust the line weights of objects manually using Visibility/Graphics Overrides.

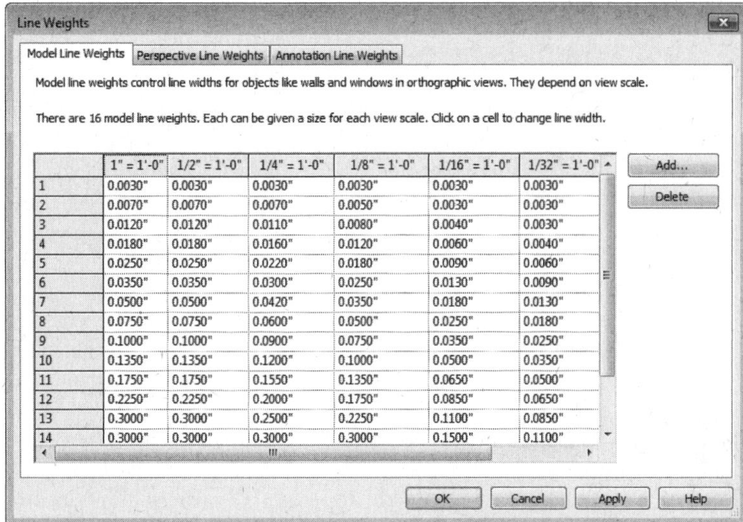

	1" = 1'-0"	1/2" = 1'-0"	1/4" = 1'-0"	1/8" = 1'-0"	1/16" = 1'-0"	1/32" = 1'-0"
1	0.0030"	0.0030"	0.0030"	0.0030"	0.0030"	0.0030"
2	0.0070"	0.0070"	0.0070"	0.0050"	0.0030"	0.0030"
3	0.0120"	0.0120"	0.0110"	0.0080"	0.0040"	0.0030"
4	0.0180"	0.0180"	0.0160"	0.0120"	0.0060"	0.0040"
5	0.0250"	0.0250"	0.0220"	0.0180"	0.0090"	0.0060"
6	0.0350"	0.0350"	0.0300"	0.0250"	0.0130"	0.0090"
7	0.0500"	0.0500"	0.0420"	0.0350"	0.0180"	0.0130"
8	0.0750"	0.0750"	0.0600"	0.0500"	0.0250"	0.0180"
9	0.1000"	0.1000"	0.0900"	0.0750"	0.0350"	0.0250"
10	0.1350"	0.1350"	0.1200"	0.1000"	0.0500"	0.0350"
11	0.1750"	0.1750"	0.1550"	0.1350"	0.0650"	0.0500"
12	0.2250"	0.2250"	0.2000"	0.1750"	0.0850"	0.0650"
13	0.3000"	0.3000"	0.2500"	0.2250"	0.1100"	0.0850"
14	0.3000"	0.3000"	0.3000"	0.3000"	0.1500"	0.1100"

FIGURE 2.10
Model Line Weights tab

You can add or delete view scales for line weight settings by using the buttons on the right side of the dialog box.

The Perspective Line Weights tab lists the thickness settings for the 16 line weights as they would appear in a perspective view. These settings do not apply to the default 3D view types but only to views that are generated from an explicit camera position. There is only one setting for each line weight because perspective views don't have a view scale parameter.

The Annotation Line Weights tab is used for defining the thickness of annotation objects. These settings are also independent of view scale. Another way to think of this is that the settings you apply determine how thick the lines will print. This is the easiest place to start when establishing your line weights for your template. Most people use only about six or seven different line weights, so it is not necessary to come up with a thickness for all 16 line weight options.

Once you have established the settings for your line weights on the Annotation Line Weights tab, you can then apply the same settings to the Model Line Weights and Perspective Line Weights tabs. For the Model Line Weights tab, you will need to decide how to reduce the thickness of your heavier line weights at larger scales. The line weights that you define will be available for use in your template and subsequent project files for setting object styles or overriding the visibility of categories in views.

Customizing line weights doesn't come without consequences. If you are relying on downloading content from manufacturers or online resources, the line weights might not appear consistently. Also, customizing the line weights may affect the people who receive your file. When working with Revit, you should always consider the rule, "Just because you can doesn't mean you should." If you are just starting with Revit, we recommend trying to use line weights out of the box to see how well they work for you first.

Fill Pattern Line Weights

If you are using fill patterns as a visual indicator of differences between items (for example, lining thickness in ductwork), it is worth noting that the thickness of the lines within the pattern will be the same as the item itself, so if your ductwork is to be shown with a thick line, the pattern will be thick as well. However, if you change the thickness of the item with a graphic override, this will not affect the pattern. The workaround if you do want a thin-lined pattern on the ductwork is to set the duct with a thin line weight via Object Styles, then change the duct line weight in each view/view template to be thicker.

Line Colors

The next consideration for a line style is the color of the lines. The main thing to remember when setting the color for objects or for lines is that the color has no bearing on how thick the lines will print. You can have a red line with a line weight of 3 next to a blue line with a line weight of 3 and they will both print the same thickness.

Color can be useful for distinguishing systems or objects in a crowded engineering plan or detail. If you have a set of standards for the color of specific types of components, you can set the color for line styles that you create to represent those objects in the same way as you would set the color for model objects in the Object Styles settings. Be aware that using colors in Revit may cause printing issues. If your print settings are set to print color, then all colored lines and objects will print as expected. However, if you are printing to a black-and-white printer and your settings are set to grayscale, any colored objects or lines will print at the grayscale equivalent of that color, which could produce unexpected results. This relates to managing your print settings, but it is important to consider when deciding to apply colors to line and object styles. If your practice is to print with black lines, colors won't affect your output.

Line Patterns

The final consideration for creating a line style is the pattern of the lines. To access the line patterns available in a Revit file, click the Additional Settings button on the Manage tab and select Line Patterns. Revit line patterns consist of dashes, dots, and spaces.

Text in a Line Pattern

It is not possible to include text in a line pattern in Revit. Since we are using a database, there are other ways that this information can be represented and still maintain the look of a CAD drawing. One of the most commonly used tools for this feature is tags. You can place a tag as many times as required along a line that represents something such as a pipe or wire. Although the tags must be placed individually, they will move with the object, can be spaced to suit the layout, and will be removed when the object is deleted.

The line patterns in Revit are independent from the view scale in which they are drawn, and there is no setting to apply a scale to an individual line. Therefore, you may need to create multiple line patterns for the same kind of line at different scales, if this is important to you. This will allow for various lengths of the dashes, and the spaces between dashes and dots, as needed to display the line pattern properly. In Figure 2.11, you can see in the Line Patterns dialog box that additional center line patterns have been created at 1/4″, 3⁄8″, and 5⁄8″ scales to be used in different view scales. Keep in mind that if you take the route of creating line patterns for the various scales, it may become cumbersome to manage them as views and change their scales. Line patterns for pipes and ducts should be controlled globally using duct and pipe systems, not per view, even though you can control them per view with filters. So, ask yourself whether it is worth it. If it is, consider defining line patterns for the most common scales you use: 1/2″, 1/4″, 1⁄8″.

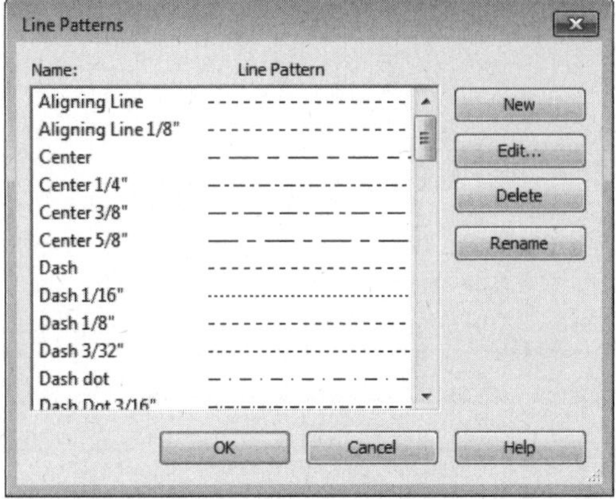

FIGURE 2.11
Line Patterns dialog box

You can modify the settings for a line pattern by clicking the Edit button on the right side of the dialog box. In the Line Pattern Properties dialog box, you will see the components that make up the line pattern. In the Type column, you can select a dash, dot, or space. Spaces can be used only after a dot or a dash. In the Value column, you assign the length of the dashes or spaces. Dots have a static length value that cannot be changed. You can enter up to 20 of these components, and when you reach the point where the pattern repeats, you are finished.

Variations of a line pattern for different view scales can be made by first looking at the settings for a line pattern. Figure 2.12 shows the settings for a Dash Dot Dot line pattern that is used in 1⁄8″ scale views. To create the same pattern for use in 1/4″ scale views, you would click the New button on the right side of the Line Patterns dialog box, give the pattern a name such as **Dash Dot Dot 1/4″**, and then put in the dashes and dots with values that are double of those in the Dash Dot Dot 1⁄8″ pattern.

It is good practice to test your line patterns as you create them. You can do so by creating a drafting view and drawing some parallel lines. As you create new patterns, you can assign them to the lines to see how the variations appear and make adjustments to dash or space values as necessary. Figure 2.13 shows the multiple variations of a centerline pattern. The variations you create do not have to match the view scales. You can create variations that slightly modify the lengths of dashes and spaces so that the line pattern is more usable in certain situations. The 3⁄8″ and 5⁄8″ patterns in Figure 2.13 are examples of line patterns that may be used at any view scale, depending on the length of the line.

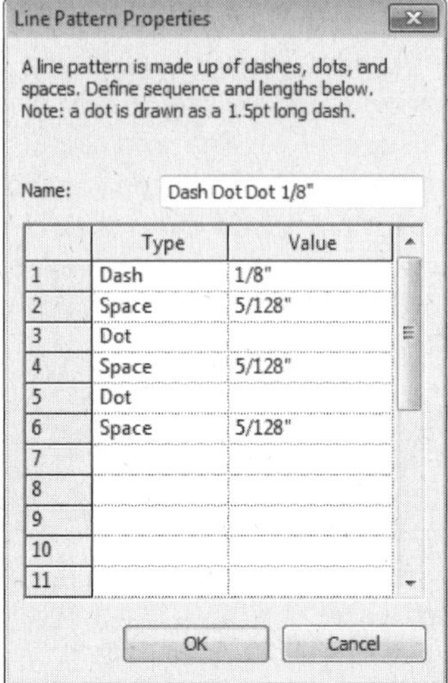

FIGURE 2.12 Line Pattern Properties dialog box

FIGURE 2.13 Line pattern variations

LINE STYLES

With line weights and patterns defined in your template file, you can create line styles that can be used for model or detail lines in your projects. Line styles are separate from object styles because they apply only to lines created by using the Detail Lines and Model Lines tools or when you're creating the boundary of a region. The line patterns (not line styles) you create will appear under the Lines category on the Model Categories tab of the Visibility/Graphics Overrides dialog box when you're changing the appearance of a view. You can access the Line Styles and Line Patterns settings by clicking the Additional Settings button under the Manage tab. Revit comes with some line styles that are coded into the program and cannot be removed or renamed, although you can change the settings for these lines. Figure 2.14 shows these lines and their default settings.

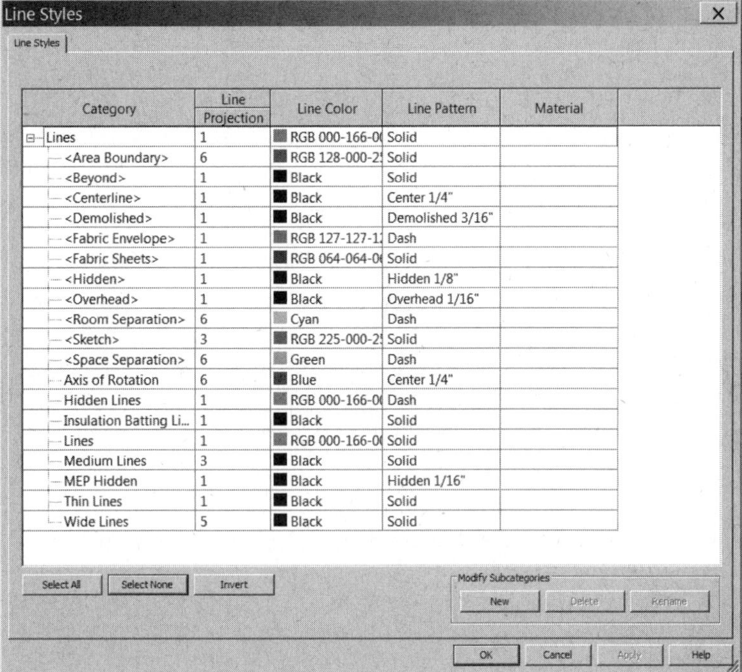

FIGURE 2.14
Line Styles dialog box

To create a line style, simply click the New button under Modify Subcategories at the lower-right side of the dialog box and enter a name. You can then assign a weight, color, and pattern to the line style. In some cases, it is useful to create line styles that match line patterns you have created to ensure consistency between model objects and drafting items. For example, if you create a line pattern that will be used for a domestic hot-water pipe, you may want to create a line style called Domestic Hot Water that uses that pattern. That way, the domestic hot-water pipe in your model can be given the pattern using a filter, and your diagrams and details can use the Domestic Hot Water linetype that matches. Otherwise, you would have to override each line in your diagram to the appropriate pattern.

You should consider using consistent naming conventions for your line styles. There are a number of popular alternatives; here are a couple for your reference: *<Line Weight>* – *<Line Color>* – *<Line Pattern>* (for example, 01 – Black – Center) groups all of the 01 line weights together; *<Line Pattern>* – *<Line Color>* – *<Line Weight>* (for example, Continuous – Black – 01) groups all of the linetypes together. The grouping of line styles is mostly important when you're creating details. It is very inefficient to scroll from top to bottom on a pull-down with over 50 line styles all the time. Based on your workflow and company standards, you should select the method that is most efficient for you.

Line styles are useful, and having a good set of line styles can save time when drafting in a project. You can change a line from one style to another by using the Type Selector that appears in the Properties palette when you select a line. This is useful for creating details, because you can draw all the linework with the most common line style and then easily change any lines that need to be different.

Export Settings

To share your project with consultants, it is often necessary to export your Revit views to CAD. Once you establish line weights and styles, it is a good time to consider your settings for exporting views. This task can be a bit tedious and time-consuming, but the settings you define can be saved and used anytime. The settings you establish for exporting do not need to be applied to your template, but it is a good idea during your template creation to consider your export settings.

You can access the Export settings from the application menu, as shown in Figure 2.15. You can create settings for various types of CAD file formats and also for IFC export.

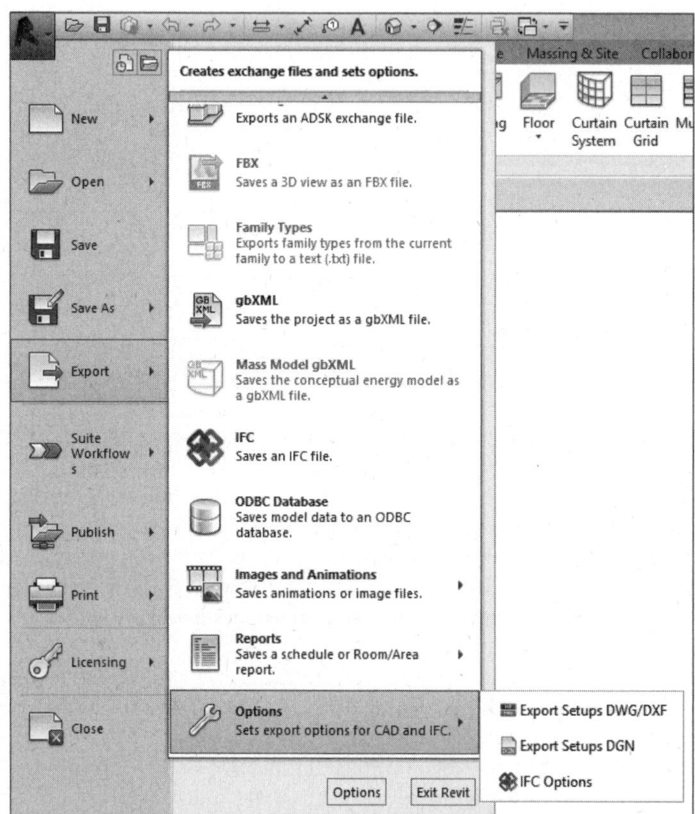

FIGURE 2.15 Export settings

IFC

Just as with CAD programs, there is a need for a standard file type that can be read by any BIM application. Industry Foundation Classes (IFC) files can be shared by BIM applications with the goal of being a seamless translation of data from one application to another. For more information on IFC, visit `www.buildingsmart.com/bim`.

When you click the Export Setups DWG/DXF option, a dialog box opens with options for defining Revit categories and styles in Autodesk® AutoCAD® software. This dialog box shows tabs across the top that are organized for specific settings. The buttons in the lower-left corner can be used to create a new setup or to manage existing setups. Creating these setups in your template makes them available to all of your projects.

The Layers tab is where you can assign Revit categories and subcategories to layers within the exported DWG file. Alongside the list of categories are columns that allow you to assign an associated AutoCAD layer name and color ID to each category and subcategory. The color ID is as it is defined in AutoCAD: 1 is for red, 2 is for yellow, and so on. There are also columns for assigning layers and colors to objects that are cut by the cut plane of a view. The Layer Modifiers column allows you to assign modifiers to the layer names depending on the category being exported. Clicking a cell in the column reveals the Add/Edit button for that category. Click the button to apply modifiers, as shown in Figure 2.16. Modifiers are useful for adding information to layer names, such as EXST or DEMO for existing and demolished work, respectively.

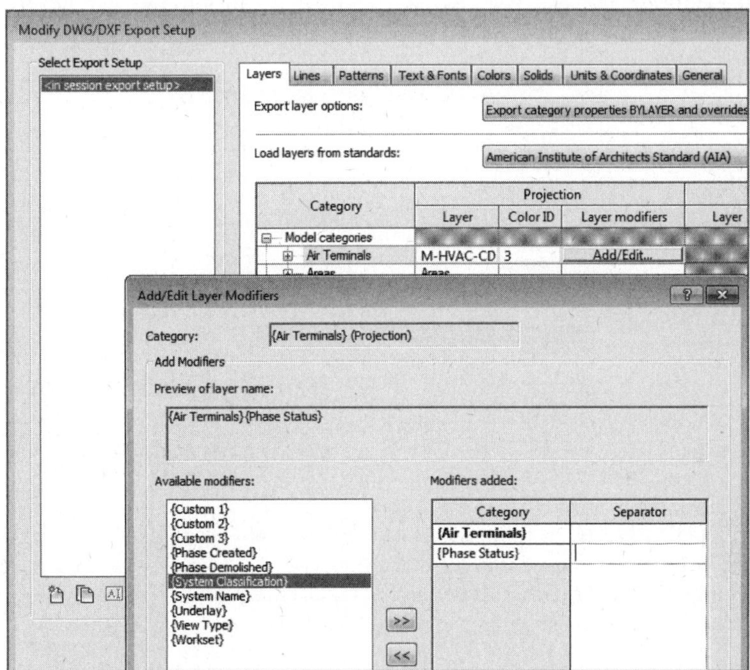

FIGURE 2.16
Adding a layer modifier to a Revit category

The Export Layer Options drop-down list has options for BYLAYER and how overrides are exported, as shown in Figure 2.17.

Layers | Lines | Patterns | Text & Fonts | Colors | Solids | Units & Coordinates | General

Export layer options: Export category properties BYLAYER and overrides BYENTITY

Export category properties BYLAYER and overrides BYENTITY
Export all properties BYLAYER, but do not export overrides
Export all properties BYLAYER, and create new layers for overrides

Load layers from standards:

FIGURE 2.17
Export layer properties

You can choose an industry standard for export settings from the drop-down list over the columns, as shown in Figure 2.18.

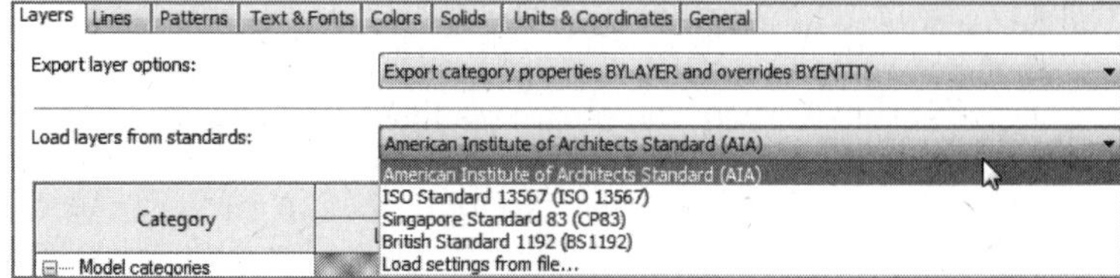

FIGURE 2.18 Layering standards

The Lines tab allows you to associate Revit line styles with linetypes within a specified linetype file. You can browse to any linetype file by using the ellipsis button. Once you have selected a linetype file, you can associate Revit line styles by clicking in the Linetypes In DWG column and choosing a linetype, as shown in Figure 2.19. If no linetype is chosen, one is automatically created on export. Notice that there is a drop-down list for the Set linetype scale behavior near the top of the tab.

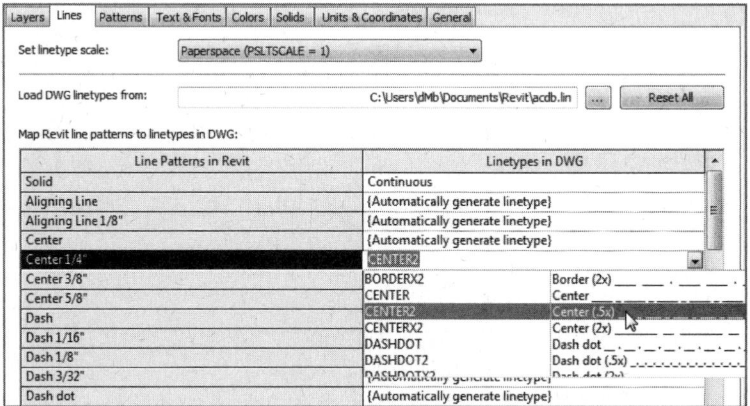

FIGURE 2.19 Selecting a linetype for a Revit line style

The Patterns tab is for associating Revit fill patterns to hatch patterns in the exported DWG file. The same process for associating linetypes with line styles is used. The Text & Fonts tab is for mapping text in Revit to text in the exported drawing file. Formatting options are available in the drop-down list at the top of the tab, shown in Figure 2.20.

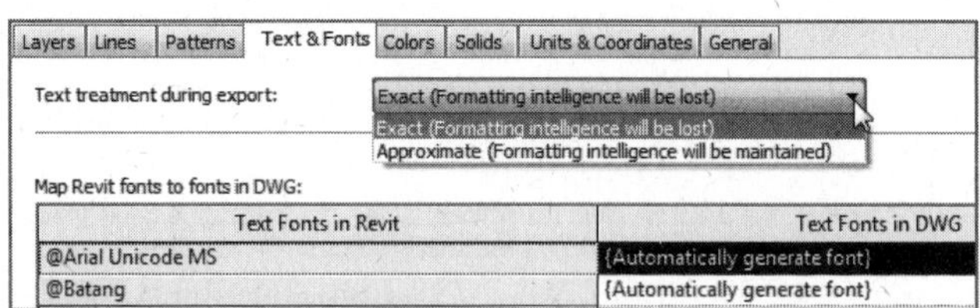

FIGURE 2.20 Text & Fonts properties

The Colors tab lets you choose between two color options, as shown in Figure 2.21.

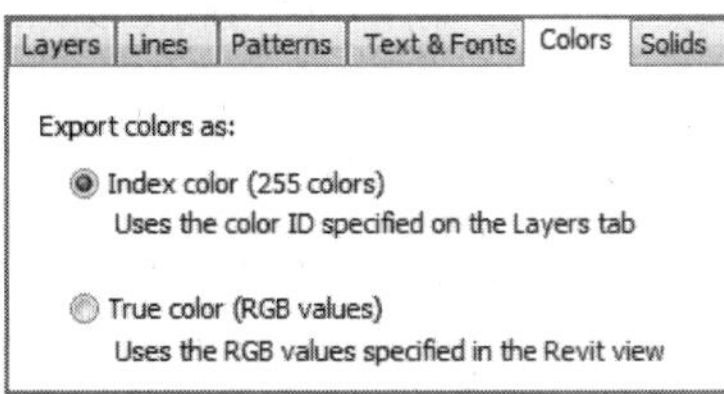

FIGURE 2.21
Color options

The Solids tab is for determining how solid objects will be exported to the DWG file. This applies only when exporting a 3D view. The drawing units and coordinate system can be set on the Units & Coordinates tab. The General tab has settings for room and area boundaries along with an option to define which layers will not be plottable. From here you can also decide the version of the exported DWG file and whether linked files are going to be acting like X-refs or inserted blocks after the export. From Revit 2014 we have had the ability to hide objects such as scope boxes, reference planes, and unreferenced view tags, as shown in Figure 2.22.

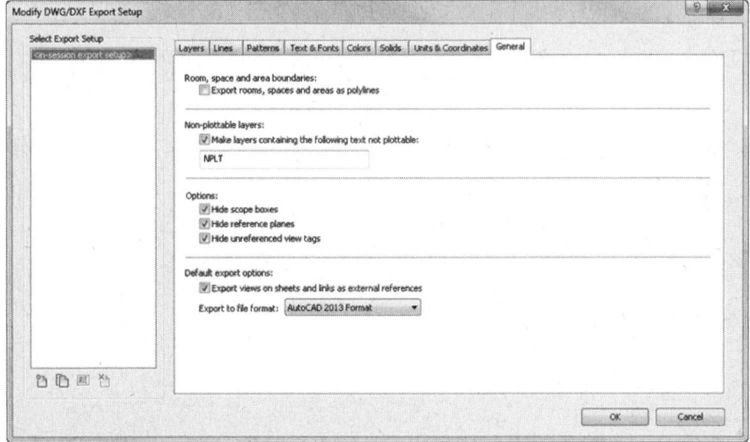

FIGURE 2.22
General options

Once you have established export settings, they can be used in other projects by using the Transfer Project Standards feature and transferring DWG/DXF Export Setup Settings. Consider creating these settings in a separate file and transferring them into your projects or templates as needed. This gives you a single file location to manage any changes or updates.

The process for creating export settings for DGN files has been greatly enhanced in Revit; instead of Layer selection, you have Levels. Possibly the biggest option here is the ability to specify a "seed" file, giving the translation process more accuracy and definition—this could be provided by your collaborating partner. File formats supported are DGN v7 and v8.

Annotation Styles

The goal of most Revit projects is to create a set of coordinated construction documents. Annotation that is consistent from drawing to drawing and from discipline to discipline is a major part of that coordination. One of the benefits of using computers to do drafting is that it makes it easier to apply drafting standards. In the days of manual drawing, there was no guarantee that one person's lettering would look exactly like another's. Some may argue that you still don't have that guarantee by using computers. That is why it is important to establish your annotation standards in your Revit project template.

TEXT

The various text styles that you need can be created as types. There is no dialog box for text settings, so to create the styles you want, you should start by accessing the properties of the default type and duplicating them for each type. This is done by clicking the small arrow located on the Text panel of the Annotate tab, shown in Figure 2.23.

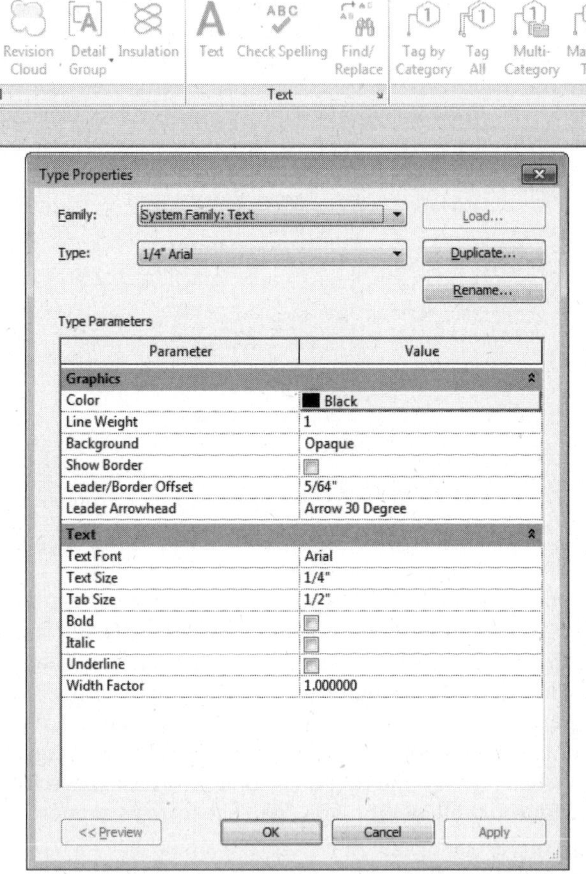

FIGURE 2.23 Accessing the type properties of the text system family

To create a new text type, duplicate an existing type and provide a name for your creation. It is a common practice to name text types by using the size and name of the font applied to the type. The type properties allow you to set the behavior and general appearance of the text type. Another common naming convention is to indicate what the type is going to be used for—Normal Notes, Bold Heading, Standard Heading, and so forth.

It is important to understand how Revit handles text types before choosing how to set up your text family types. Each text family type that is created is unique to the file in which it was created. Figure 2.24 shows an example of a text type called STYLE 1 that was created in a project and a text type called STYLE 1 that was created in an annotation family. When the annotation family is used in the project, the text within the annotation family maintains its settings as defined in the family file. It does not take on the settings for STYLE 1 as they are defined in the project, even though both family types have the same name.

FIGURE 2.24
Text types with the same name

The easiest way to manage this behavior is to use the default font, which is Arial. Although this may be a deviation from your normal CAD standards, it provides a huge return in time savings. If you choose to use a different font, you will have to change the text and labels in every family or detail that you bring into your Revit project in order to maintain consistency in your construction documents. This includes all the preloaded content that comes with your Revit installation. One thing to consider is the font style of tags. By default, all tags in Revit use the Arial font. If that font doesn't comply with your company standards, you would have to go through all tags and modify them.

For all of your future family needs, you may want to consider creating family templates that can contain your company standards to avoid having text types with the same name, as Figure 2.24 shows.

By setting the properties of a text style, you can create several variations of text for use in your projects. Remember that these are type properties, so you will need to create a new text type for each variation in settings. The most common types are based on text height, background, and leader arrowhead style. You can also create types based on other properties, which are usually variations of your standard text types. For example, you can create a standard 3⁄32″ (2.4 mm) Arial text type for normal use and then create another type that is 3⁄32″ (2.4 mm) Arial and underlined for use where underlined text is required. This will save you time in having to edit text to make it underlined by giving you the option to switch from one type to the other. Although the Underline option is available as a Type and Instance parameter, you could create some confusion. For example, if you create text called 3/32″ (2.4 mm) Arial – Underlined, you can place the text and it will be underlined. But you would also have the option to highlight the text and deselect Underline from the ribbon, and you have text that is using the underline text style but is not underlined. This applies to Bold and Italic as well. So maybe those are best managed per instance instead of per text type.

The Show Border and Leader/Border Offset parameters allow you to create a text type that has a border automatically placed around the text that is offset a certain distance from the text. Even if you do not show the border, the Leader/Border Offset parameter determines the distance between where the leader starts and the text. The thickness of the leader and the border are determined by the Line Weight parameter. The Color parameter determines the color of not only the text, but also the border and leader. Figure 2.25 shows some sample text types, the names of which are based on the settings used for each type.

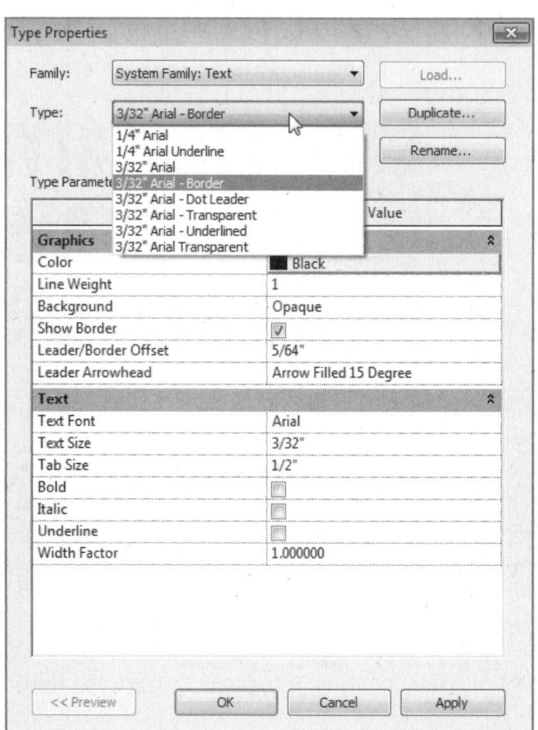

FIGURE 2.25
Sample text types

ARROWHEAD STYLES

One of the key considerations for setting the text standards in your template is the type of arrowhead your text types will use. You can modify the look of arrowhead types to suit your needs if necessary. You can find the settings for arrowheads by clicking the Additional Settings button on the Manage tab and selecting Arrowheads. Arrowheads are a Revit system family, and although you can create different types, the Arrow Style parameter determines the shape of the arrowhead. You cannot create your own arrow styles.

By adjusting the settings, you can control the size of an arrowhead type. The Tick Size parameter controls the overall length of the arrowhead, while Arrow Width Angle determines the angle of the arrow from its point, which ultimately sets the width of the arrow. The dimension styles you establish can use these same arrowhead styles.

DIMENSION STYLES

Dimension styles are another key factor in creating consistently annotated construction documents. To establish the settings for your dimension styles, click on the Dimension panel of the Annotate tab, as highlighted in Figure 2.26. Each type of dimension can have its own unique settings. If you do not use dimensions very often in your projects, you may want to consider leaving the default settings. When the need arises to show dimensions, you could establish the settings or transfer the dimension settings from a file in which they have already been established, such as a linked consultant's file or a previous project.

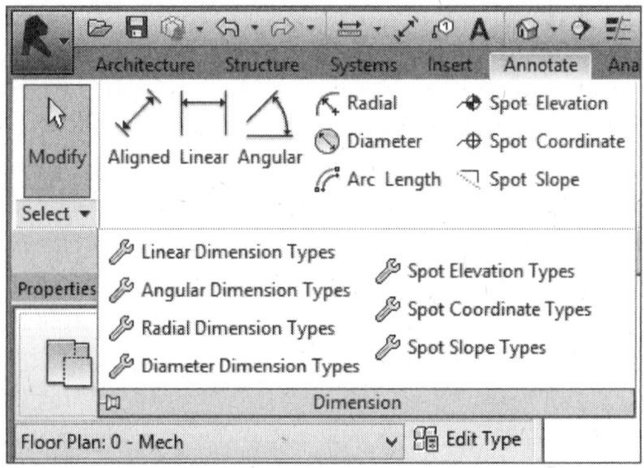

FIGURE 2.26 Accessing dimension settings

TRANSFER PROJECT STANDARDS

The Transfer Project Standards feature of Revit can be useful and save you time on your projects, but you should use it with caution. If you find that you are using this feature often on projects, you should consider establishing the settings you are transferring in your template to reduce the need for transferring.

Another option is to transfer only the particular standards that are needed, not every single one. Deselect those that are not required or you could find your project filling up with duplicate families named, for example, Round Elbow1 or additional subcategories that are not required.

The Transfer Project Standards utility transfers all types of a particular standard. For example, you can't transfer only one text style. The workaround is to use Copy and Paste across files, which is not available for all standards (cable tray settings, pipe segments, and so forth). Where Copy and Paste are not options, consider revising and possibly removing the types that you don't need right after the transfer, in order to keep your project clean.

Each dimension style is a system family, and you can create types within that family in the same way that text types are created. Dimension styles have more parameters than text, however. Many of these parameters are for controlling how the graphics of the dimension will display. One of the key parameters in determining a dimension family type is the Dimension String Type parameter. This defines how the dimension will behave when a string of dimensions is placed. You have options for creating a continuous, baseline, or ordinate dimension string. If you use all or some of these types, you will need to create a separate dimension type for each one.

The Tick Mark parameter determines which arrowhead style is used. When editing this parameter, a drop-down list indicates all the arrowhead styles defined in the file. The line weight of the dimension can be controlled independently from the line weight of the tick mark by setting the parameters for each. The line weight for tick marks in dimensions should match the line weight for leader arrowheads in your text types for consistency. Because of their relatively small size, using a heavy line weight may cause your arrowheads to look like blobs, so choose wisely. The Interior Tick Mark parameter is available only when you have set the dimension tick mark to an arrow type. This determines the style of arrowhead to be used when adjacent dimension lines are too close together to fit the default tick marks.

Other parameters control the lengths of witness line components and gaps and also the text used in the dimension style. Some of the settings for text within a dimension style are the same as those in a text style, such as font and text height. The Read Convention parameter allows you to set the direction in which the text will be read for vertically oriented dimensions. With the Units Format parameter, you can set the rounding accuracy of dimension types independently from the default project settings.

Beginning with Revit 2014 you have had the ability to assign alternate units. This allows companies to display their dimensions in imperial and metric units at the same time. Since that edition, we also have more control over the Equality dimensions' appearance.

Project Units

Whether you are creating a template with metric or imperial units, you will need to establish which units of measurement are used and their precision. These settings will determine the default reporting of data, not only in views but also in schedules and parameters. They do not affect the accuracy of calculations. Click the Project Units button located on the Manage tab to access the settings for units.

You can set the default units for any graphical or engineering measurements. Figure 2.27 shows the Project Units dialog box. The drop-down list at the top contains the different discipline-specific groups of units, with the Common option containing units that are used by all regardless of discipline.

Clicking the button in the Format column next to a unit activates the Format dialog box for that unit. Here you have a drop-down list for the options for that unit type. Once you have chosen a unit of measurement, you can determine the precision by selecting a Rounding option. The rounding increment will display to the right of the drop-down as an example of the option chosen. If you are using a decimal measurement, you can select Custom from the Rounding drop-down and designate the rounding increment manually. The Unit Symbol drop-down offers the option of displaying the measurement unit next to the value if desired. Check boxes in the bottom half of the dialog box enable you to suppress zeros or spaces, or to group digits depending on the type of unit you are formatting. When you click OK to finish formatting a unit type, you will see a sample in the button in the Format column next to the unit.

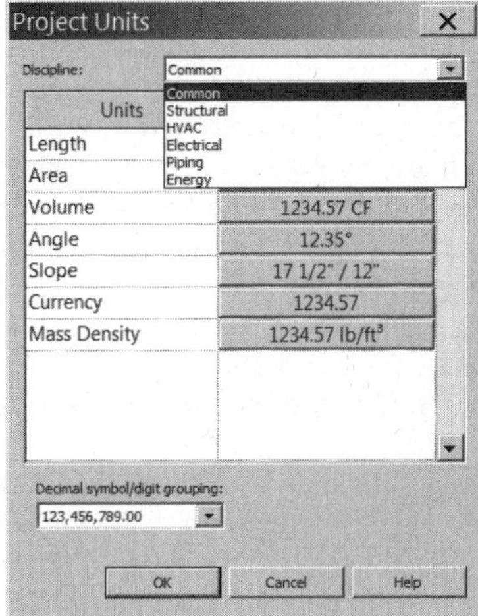

FIGURE 2.27 Project Units dialog box

Setting the precision of certain unit types does not affect the availability of model elements, but it may cause nonsensical results to be shown in tags. For example, if you set the rounding of the Pipe Size unit to the nearest inch, then when you go to tag a pipe in the model that is less than 1/2″ in size, the pipe size tag will show 0″ (as shown in Figure 2-28). It also establishes the default units and rounding globally for the entire project. Certain elements can override those global settings; schedules are one example.

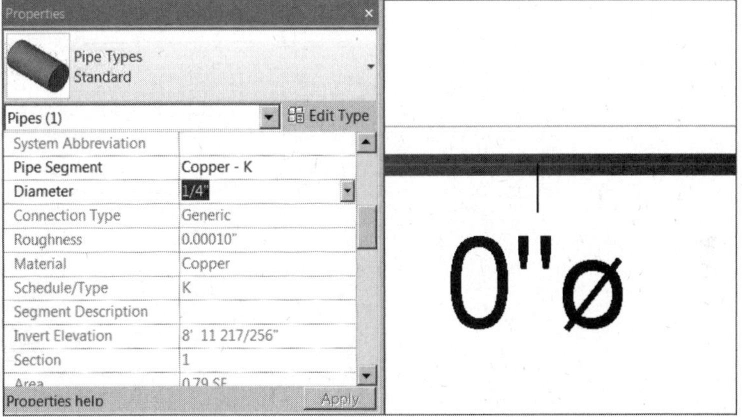

FIGURE 2.28 Pipe size tag showing 0″

Project Phases

Although each project is different, you may want to establish phases in your project template if you are required to use them on many of your projects. The most common use of phasing is for renovation projects in which the existing portion of the project is modeled. Phasing can be difficult to manage, so having the settings established in your template can be beneficial.

Click the Phases button on the Manage tab to access the settings for phases in your template. The Phasing dialog box has three tabs for setting up the phases and their behavior. The Project

Phases tab is where you establish what phases exist in your file. Revit starts each file with an Existing phase and a New Construction phase by default.

You can add phases by using the buttons on the upper-right side of the dialog box, inserting new phases before or after the phase selected in the list. The list of phases starts from the earliest and ends with the latest. So if you were to insert a Demolition phase between Existing and New Construction, you could either select New Construction and use the Insert Before button or select Existing and use the Insert After button. The order of phases is important because when views are set up, you will establish what phase they belong to. Any items placed into the model will be part of the phase that is set for the view in which they are placed.

During the course of a project, it may be decided that a phase is no longer necessary. You can use the Combine With buttons at the right side of the dialog box to transfer the items from one phase to another.

The Phase Filters tab of the dialog box lists the different viewing options that can be applied to any view in order to display items from various phases, as shown in Figure 2.29.

The filter names describe what will be shown in the view to which they are applied. The New, Existing, Demolished, and Temporary columns define how the items that belong to the phases will be displayed. If you create a custom phase, the New column controls how the items are displayed in a view set to that phase. Any items placed in a phase prior to that are considered existing phases. When you demolish an item, you can assign the phase in which the demolition occurs; otherwise, the item is considered to be demolished in the phase that is applied to the view in which you are working. You can create custom settings by using the New button at the bottom of the dialog box to create a new filter. It is a good practice to name a filter so that it is evident what will be shown when the filter is applied to a view.

FIGURE 2.29
Phasing dialog box

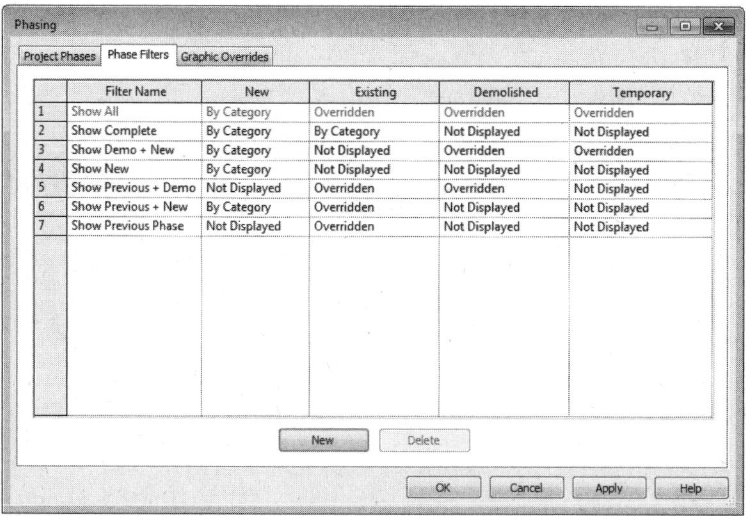

	Filter Name	New	Existing	Demolished	Temporary
1	Show All	By Category	Overridden	Overridden	Overridden
2	Show Complete	By Category	By Category	Not Displayed	Not Displayed
3	Show Demo + New	By Category	Not Displayed	Overridden	Overridden
4	Show New	By Category	Not Displayed	Not Displayed	Not Displayed
5	Show Previous + Demo	Not Displayed	Overridden	Overridden	Not Displayed
6	Show Previous + New	By Category	Overridden	Not Displayed	Not Displayed
7	Show Previous Phase	Not Displayed	Overridden	Not Displayed	Not Displayed

The options for the display of a phase are defined on the Graphic Overrides tab of the Phasing dialog box. Overrides to each phase status will affect only the objects when they are shown via a phase filter. They do not override the object styles defined in your project in views in which the objects are created. In other words, if you apply an override to the existing status, the overrides will not apply when you are working in an existing view, only when the existing phase is displayed in a view of another phase.

Figure 2.30 shows two pipes in a view that is set to the New Construction phase. The pipe on the bottom is modeled in a view that is set to the Existing phase. The Phasing dialog box shows the overrides for existing items. Notice in the properties of the view that the Phase Filter property applied to the view is Show Previous + New. These settings result in the existing pipe being displayed as dashed and halftone in the New Construction view.

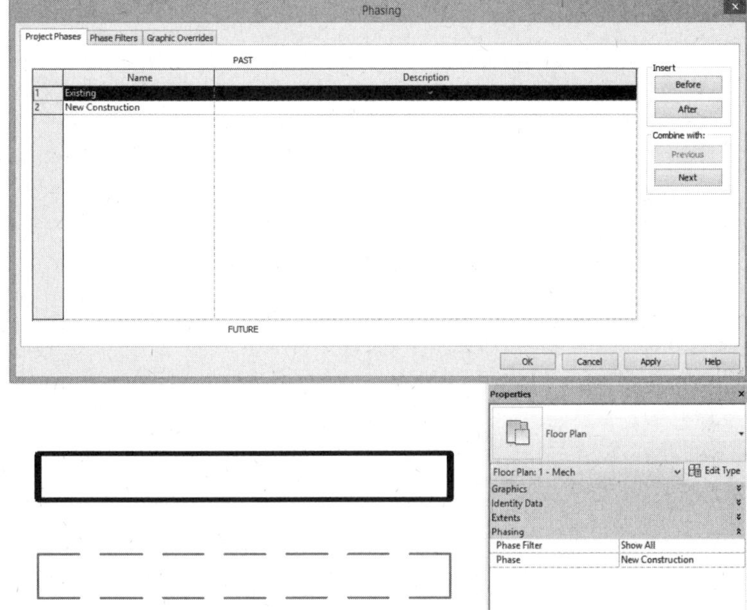

FIGURE 2.30 Existing and new pipes shown to demonstrate phase display

If you establish phases in your template file, it is helpful to create views for each phase with the proper Phase and Phase Filter properties to maintain consistency throughout the project and to ensure expected results when modeling.

Usually the engineers match whatever phasing customizations the architect has for a particular project. One place where you should check whether your phases are matching the architectural phases when you are setting up a project is in the Type Properties dialog box of the linked architectural background, under Phase Mapping (see Figure 2.31).

When you have a project that involves phases, some planning and consideration can go a long way. Many companies are getting remodeling projects that they have completed in the past using AutoCAD. Even though those companies have moved to Revit, they still should ask themselves what they would gain by doing the project in Revit. If you need to redraw the existing project in Revit, and the demolition will be an ongoing process, doing the job in AutoCAD may not be a bad idea after all. Whenever you demolish a duct or a pipe, Revit produces a message that the element needs to be disconnected, as shown in Figure 2.32. Aside from the annoying fact that you need to respond to this message every time you demolish an element, those elements will become disconnected, and therefore making any further changes to them is much more time-consuming.

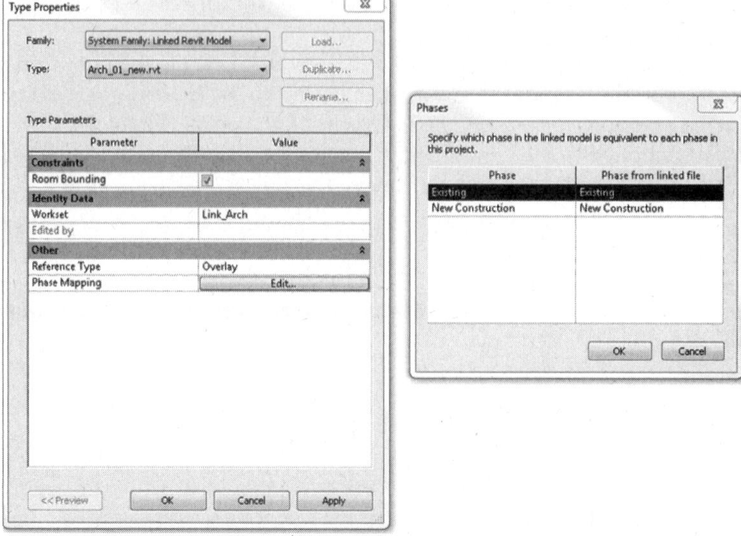

FIGURE 2.31 Phase mapping of linked files

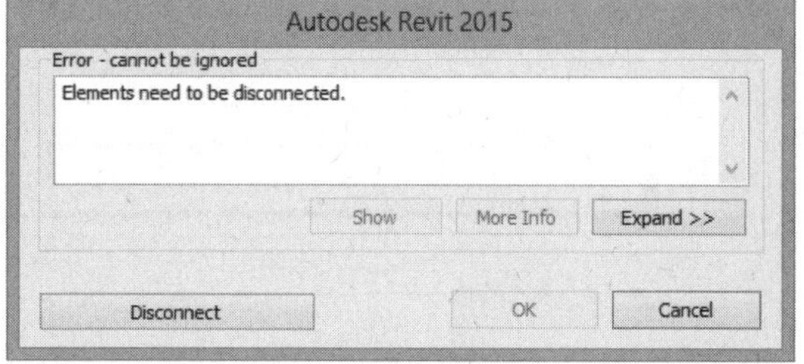

FIGURE 2.32 Warning that appears when you are demolishing connected elements like pipes and ducts

Another option you can consider is a hybrid project between AutoCAD and Revit. You can do all existing and demo plans in AutoCAD and all new construction in Revit. You can link the DWGs into Revit and still document the entire project in Revit. This would certainly help your project's bottom line.

Defining Preloaded Content and Its Behavior

There are three types of families that enable you to create content: annotation families, component families, and system families.

Annotation families are 2D symbols and text families used for sections, callouts, elevations, and tags. They are also used for creating standard symbols that are shown instead of the 3D geometry. Refer to Chapter 21, "Creating Devices," for more information on using annotations in families.

Component families are generally created separate from the project and loaded in as required. Although they can be created "in place," this is not recommended for most MEP families.

System families include ducts, pipes, cable trays, and even text. They cannot be loaded into the project, and you can make new types only by duplicating the existing types and adjusting the settings in the Type Properties dialog box. There are only predefined profiles in Revit for system families; for example, you can only have a rectangular, round, or oval duct, and any other shape will need to be a component family and won't act as a duct.

When you begin a project by using a template file, you want to be able to start modeling right away, without taking the time to load components and set up system families up front or having to stop periodically during the design and modeling process. Determining what content is loaded or defined in the template gives you more time to focus on the model and design decisions and ensures consistency of standards across projects.

Annotation Families

Loading annotation families is especially important for consistent standards when working in a project that is shared by multiple disciplines. Even if you are creating a template for just one discipline, there are many annotations that are used on every project and should be included in your template.

> **COMPANY STANDARDS VS. PROJECT STANDARDS**
>
> In some cases, you may be required to use specific text styles, dimensions, view titles, and so forth to comply with the project display requirements. Using the Transfer Project Standards command will take care of most things you need. However, it can also create a big problem if the names of text styles exist in both projects. In that case, you will end up with duplicate items, or the items in your project will be used instead. To save yourself this headache, a popular trick is to add your company abbreviation in front of all system family styles, such as text, view titles, and so on. This helps you distinguish between your company standards and the project standards.

The symbols used for sections, callouts, and elevations should all be defined in your template file. To set up these standards, click the Additional Settings button on the Manage tab. For section tags, you can define what annotation family is used for the head of the section as well as the tail. There is also a setting for how the section tag will appear when broken by using the Gaps In Segments grip on a section line. These settings apply to the section tag system family. You can then create different types of sections by defining what section tag is used in the type properties of a section.

Elevation marks are created in a similar fashion. You first define the different types within the elevation tag system family by indicating which annotation symbol is used and then applying the elevation tag types to their respective elevation mark types within the elevation system family. For callout tags, you can define what annotation is used and also the radius of the corners of the callout box that is drawn around a room or area of the model. The type properties of a callout define the callout tag and label to use when a callout references another view.

View titles are another type of annotation that should be defined in your template to match your drafting standards. To create custom viewport types, you first need to establish the annotation family to be used as a view title. These annotations do not require a line for the title line because title lines are part of the viewport system family and are generated automatically when the viewport is placed on a sheet. You also do not need to include a callout tag within the view title annotation because the tag to be used is defined in the type properties of a view. When creating the label that will be the view title, be sure to extend the limits of the label to accommodate a string of text; otherwise, your view titles will become multiple lines with only a few words. You can load several annotations into your template file to create multiple types of viewports.

To access the properties of a viewport, you need to place one on a sheet. You can then click the viewport and access its type properties. There, you can duplicate the selected type and give it a descriptive name. In the type properties of a viewport, you can define the annotation used for the title as well as the color, line weight, and pattern of the title line. There are also options for displaying the title or the title line, giving you the ability to create viewport types that do not display a title.

Another type of annotation to consider for your template is any tag that is commonly used. Pipe and duct size tags, wire tags, and equipment tags should all be loaded into their respective templates or into a template shared by MEP disciplines. In some cases, you may have more than one tag for a category, such as a pipe size tag and a pipe invert elevation tag. For categories with multiple tags, it is helpful when working in a project to have the default tag set. Click the small arrow on the Tag panel of the Annotate tab, and select Loaded Tags to access the Tags dialog box. In the Tags dialog box, you can define which tag to use by default for each category. You can change this at any time during the project, but it is nice to start with the most commonly used option.

General annotations such as graphic scales or north arrows should also be included in your project template. You may choose to include a north arrow in your view title annotation, but keeping it separate gives you the freedom to rotate and place it anywhere on a sheet.

The same annotation families that are used in your model components can also be loaded into your template for creating legends. Legend components are limited in their placement options, so it may be easier to use annotation symbols; however, this method also results in having numerous annotation families loaded into your project that are there only for the legend view.

If you use a generic tag for plan notes, it should be loaded into your template. If you use the keynoting feature within Revit, you should have a keynote tag loaded as well as a keynote data file location defined. You access the Keynoting settings by clicking the small arrow on the Tags panel of the Annotate tab. In this dialog box, you can browse to the keynote data file to be used and set the path options. You can also define the numbering method to either display the specification section number and text from the data file or use the By Sheet option, which numbers the notes sequentially as they are placed. Make sure to assign the appropriate leader for each loaded tag (and each tag's type) in the project template so your users don't have to do it later.

Component Families

The types of component families that you load into your project template really depend on the discipline for which you are creating the template. If your template is used for a single MEP discipline, there is no need for components that are used by other disciplines, unless you use those types of components regularly in your projects.

Too Much of a Good Thing

It may be tempting to load your entire component library into your project template so that you would never have to pause what you are doing to load a family. Another reason may be so that you are certain the proper content is loaded. Although this may seem logical, with proper training on how to load families, it is not really necessary. Having an entire library of components in your template will greatly increase the size of the file and will result in every one of your projects starting at that size, not to mention that most of that content will be unused.

The most effective use of preloaded components is to have components loaded that are used on every, or nearly every, project. The following are examples of the types of components to consider for each discipline:

Mechanical Projects with HVAC systems will require air terminals and some type of distribution equipment. Consider loading an air terminal family for each type of air system into your template. Even if the types of air terminals used for the project end up being different from those in the template, at least you will have something to start with for preliminary design. The same is true for equipment. Load an equipment family that you most commonly use. Figure 2.33 shows an example of components loaded into a template for HVAC systems. Load any duct and pipe fittings that you will use to define pipe types or to be used in special situations where the default needs to be replaced. You should also set up the duct and pipe system families you will require.

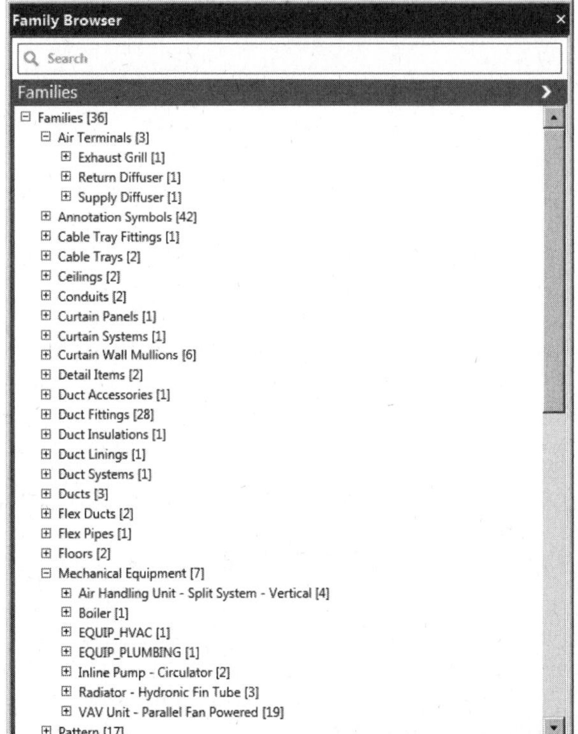

FIGURE 2.33
Sample HVAC components in a template

Electrical Projects with lighting, power, and communications systems require fixtures and receptacles along with distribution equipment. Having the common types of these components that you use on every project loaded into your template will make it easy to begin laying out a preliminary design while decisions are being made for specific object types. The components used in a preliminary layout can easily be changed to the specified components after a decision is made. Figure 2.34 shows some examples of components loaded into a template for an electrical system design.

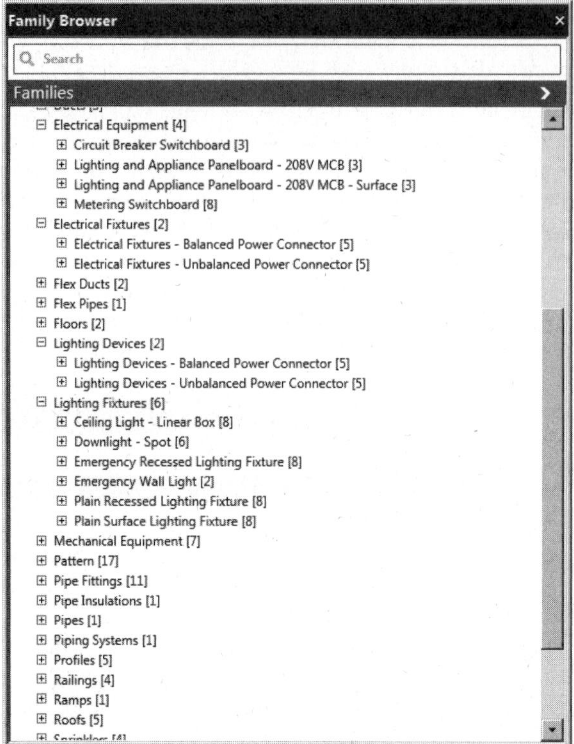

FIGURE 2.34 Sample electrical components in a template

Plumbing The types of plumbing components you load into your project depend on your workflow and how you coordinate with the architectural model. If you work in an environment in which the architects typically show the plumbing fixtures, you do not need to have plumbing fixtures loaded into your template. It is important to have the fittings you will use to define pipe types loaded into the project. Sometimes you need to swap fittings out, so having additional ones loaded can save time.

One item that is useful is a plumbing fixture connector, which acts as a plumbing fixture and provides a connection point for piping. If there are valves or other types of components that you use regularly, they should be loaded into your template. You should also set up the piping system families you will require. Figure 2.35 shows some examples of plumbing components loaded into a template.

The basic idea is to keep it simple. Your template will be a fluid document that changes as your needs change or as you discover new requirements. If you find that you have to load a particular component on many projects, you should consider adding that component to your project template file.

Other components that you need in your template are all of the duct, pipe, cable tray, and conduit fittings that will be used by their respective system families. You also need your company titleblock, company logo, and company stamps.

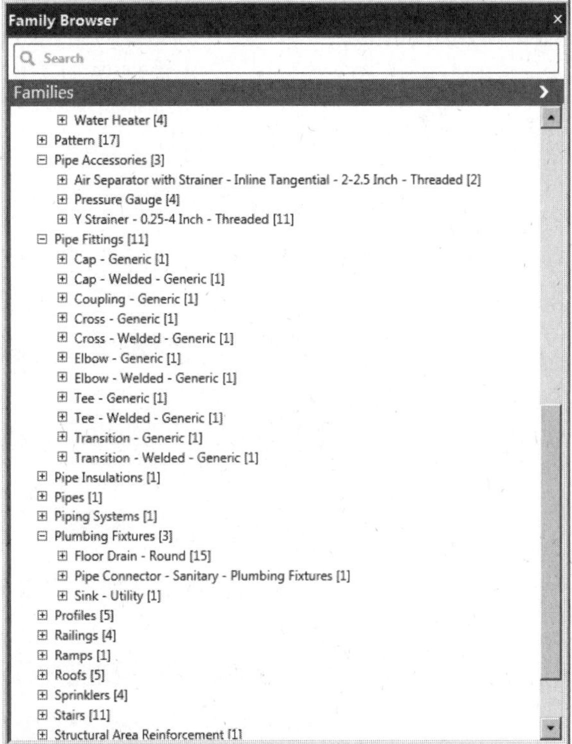

FIGURE 2.35
Sample plumbing components in a template

System Families

Along with having components preloaded into your project, it is important to define your system families. This will establish the default behavior for any types of system families that you define. If you start your template from scratch without using another template as a basis for your file, you will need to attempt to draw a duct, pipe, cable tray, or conduit before the system family will appear in the Family Browser.

Once you have the desired system family in the Family Browser, you can right-click it to access its properties. The properties for MEP system families are primarily the same for each system. The idea is that you need to define what types of fittings are used. You can create variations of a system family to utilize different fittings. System family types should be named descriptively to indicate their use. Additional fittings can be added at any time to create new family types, but it is best to start with the basics for your project template.

An MEP system family (duct systems, pipe systems, conduits, and cable trays) will not be usable without fittings defined. To establish the fittings for a system family, right-click the family in the Project Browser. You can use the Duplicate button to create a new type of system family. In the Type Properties dialog box, you will see a button for editing the routing preferences. Using this, you can enter the Routing Preferences dialog box, which will give you options for assigning fitting component families to the system family. The fitting components you have loaded into your project will be available in the drop-down of the Fitting parameter for each specific type of fitting. You can add as many of each type of fitting as you want and place them in order, even give them size ranges. For pipe only, you can also specify different pipe segment types. This is useful, for instance, with chilled-water pipe, which would usually be copper up until a certain size and then carbon steel above that size. Figure 2.36 shows an example of the pipe routing settings for the pipe system family.

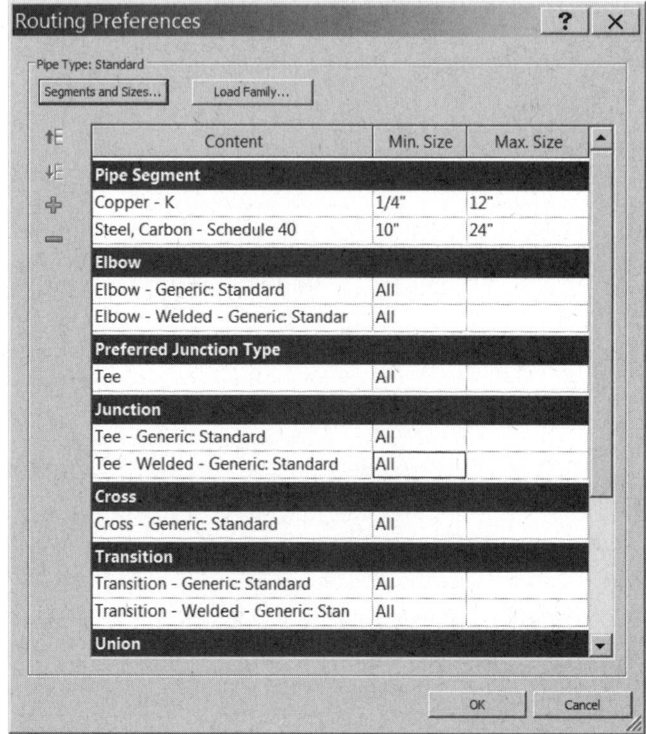

FIGURE 2.36
Routing Preferences for pipes

There are also duct and pipe system families available that define duct and piping systems within your project. The properties of a duct or piping system allow you to control the graphical display of components that belong to the system. This is independent of the Object Styles settings for the components. However, view filter settings take precedence over the graphical settings for these systems, so if you use a filter to turn a supply duct blue, for example, it will be blue regardless of the settings defined in the supply duct system family. The dialog box will also give you an option for a fabrication service if required, and you can also determine whether calculations are performed within the system, as shown in Figure 2.37. For pipe systems, you can also choose the fluid type and temperature, which can be important if pressure drop is being calculated.

Now that we have covered the importance of settings in your project template, you can practice setting the properties of both views and model objects by completing the following exercise:

1. Open the `Ch2_Template Settings.rte` Revit project template file at `www.sybex.com/go/masteringrevitmep2015`.

   First you'll set up the phases for each view, starting with the view to show new work.

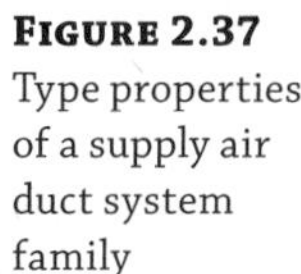

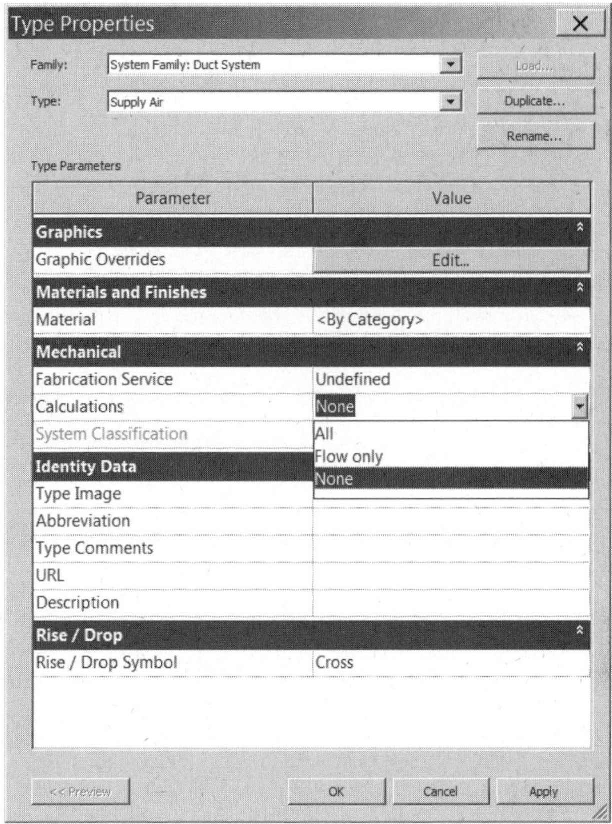

FIGURE 2.37 Type properties of a supply air duct system family

2. Access the properties of the 1 – Mech floor plan view. Set the Sub-Discipline parameter to HVAC. Set the Phase Filter parameter to Show Previous + New. Note that the phase for this view is set to New Construction.

3. Click the Edit button in the View Range parameters. Set Top to Level Above, and set Offset to **0′-0″** (**0** mm). Verify that the Cut Plane setting is at **4′-0″** (**1200** mm), and that the Bottom setting is at Associated Level (Level 1) with an Offset setting of **0′-0″** (**0** mm). Click OK.

4. Click the Apply button in the Properties palette to apply the changes.

   Now you are going to set up the view for showing existing services.

5. Access the properties of the 1 – Mech Existing floor plan view. Apply all of the same settings as in steps 2 and 3, except set the Phase Filter parameter to Show All. Click the Apply button in the Properties palette. Note that the phase for this view is set to Existing.

   Then onto the rest of the settings required.

6. Open the 1 – Mech view, and access Visibility/Graphics Overrides. On the Annotation Categories tab, set Grids to Halftone. Click OK.

7. Click the Object Styles button on the Manage tab. Set the Projection Line Weight parameter for the Ducts category to **5**. Set Line Color for Ducts to Blue. Click OK.
8. In the Project Browser, expand Families and then expand Ducts. Right-click Standard under Rectangular Duct, and select Properties. Click the Duplicate button in the Type Properties dialog box. Name the new duct type **Mitered Elbows – Taps**, and click OK. In the Type Properties dialog box, select Routing Preferences. Then add it to the Elbow parameter Rectangular Elbow – Mitered: Standard and move this to the top of the list. Verify that the Preferred Junction Type parameter is set to Tap.
9. Choose settings for each of the fitting types from the available items in the drop-down list for each parameter. The Multi Shape Transition Oval To Round parameter can be left as None. Click OK to exit the Type Properties of the duct family.
10. Use the Save As command to save the template in a location that you can access. Close the file.

    Now you are going to test how the template works.
11. Click the arrow next to New on the application menu, and select Project. In the New Project dialog box, click Browse to find the location where you saved the file in step 10. Verify that Project is selected and click OK.
12. Open the 1 – Mech Existing view. Click the Duct button on the Home tab. If the Properties palette is not visible, click the Properties button on the ribbon. Click the drop-down at the top of the Properties palette, and set the duct type to Rectangular Duct Mitered Elbows – Taps. Draw a duct from left to right in the view, and then change direction to draw a duct toward the bottom of the screen, creating a 90-degree bend. Notice that the duct is blue and that a mitered elbow fitting is used.
13. Open the 1 – Mech view. Notice that the ductwork drawn in step 12 is displayed as halftone, which is because it was modeled in an existing view and is therefore existing ductwork. Click the Duct button on the Home tab, and draw ductwork in the 1 – Mech view. Notice that the ductwork is blue because it is new ductwork drawn in a New Construction phase view.
14. Click the Grid button on the Architect tab, and draw a grid across the view. Notice that the grid line and bubble are halftone.
15. Open the 1 – Mech Existing view. Notice that the ductwork drawn in the 1 – Mech view does not appear in this view. However, notice that the grid drawn in the 1 – Mech view does appear in this view.

MEP Settings

You can use another group of settings to establish standards in your project template. The MEP settings of a Revit project file are used to determine some of the graphical representations of systems as well as the available sizes and materials of system families used. Click the MEP Settings button on the Manage tab to access the settings for a discipline. You can also access this from the Routing Preferences dialog box of either the duct family or the pipe family. The settings you establish may determine the type of template you are creating. Some of the standards defined for the MEP settings may be unique to a project type or client's requirements, which would result in a unique template for those settings.

Mechanical Settings In the Mechanical Settings dialog box, you can establish the display of hidden-line graphics and also define values used in calculations. The left side of the dialog box lists all the settings. When you select a setting from the list, the options will appear in the right side of the dialog box. You can choose to include or exclude certain duct or pipe sizes for each type of pipe or duct. In Figure 2.38, the odd duct sizes have been excluded from use in projects and by Revit when ductwork is sized.

Be aware that the options you choose for pipe settings will apply to all plumbing and mechanical piping, so you may have to experiment with different settings to achieve the desired results for both disciplines. This is another reason for creating separate template files for each discipline.

With the sloped pipe functionality in Revit MEP, it is important to define the available slopes within your projects. In the Slopes section of the Mechanical Settings dialog box, you can define any slope values that will be used in your projects, as shown in Figure 2.39.

A feature that was new to Revit 2014 was the ability to use specific angles for pipe, duct, conduit, and cable tray fittings. Configuring this setting properly ensures that your design is using industry standard fittings, which are cheaper than any custom fittings (see Figure 2.40).

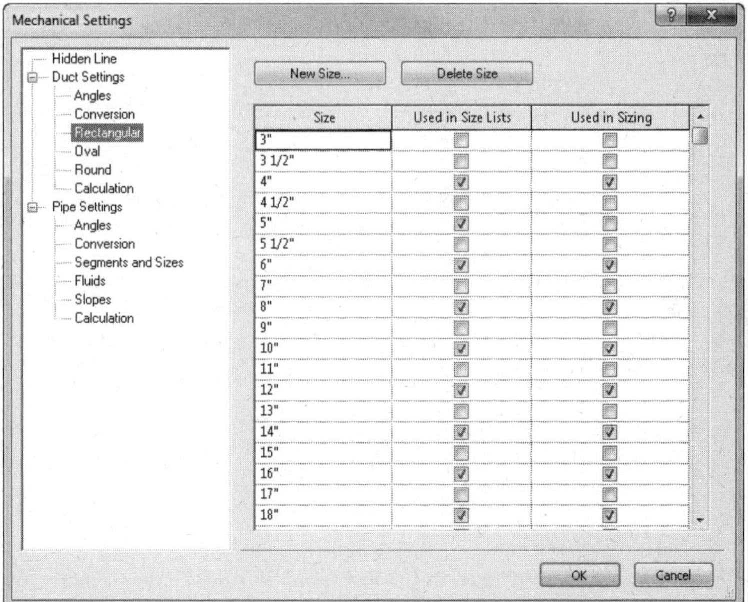

FIGURE 2.38
Mechanical Settings dialog box

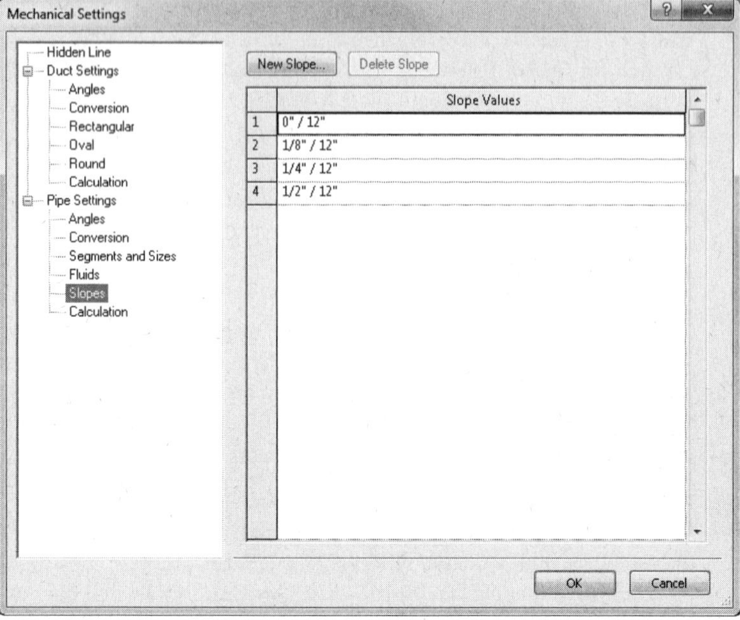

FIGURE 2.39 Slope settings for a project

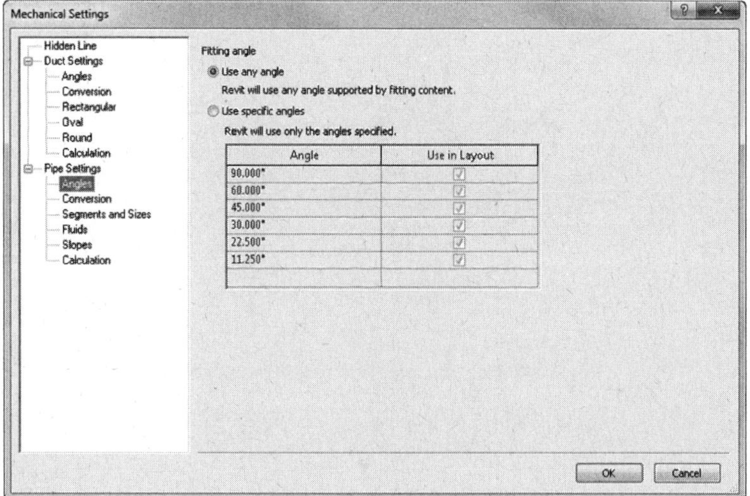

FIGURE 2.40 Fitting angles

Electrical Settings In the Electrical Settings dialog box, the options you choose define the graphical representation of items such as tick marks or circuit names. Here you can also define voltages and the behavior of distribution systems. There are settings for conduit and cable tray displays and sizes as well. There is also the ability to designate the label to be used for spares and spaces in panel schedules, as shown in Figure 2.41. You can also merge multi-pole circuits into a single cell. These settings are applied to all panel schedules in your projects.

There are also MEP settings for load classifications and demand factors as well as building/space type settings. All of these should be established in your template to the extent that they are used in your projects.

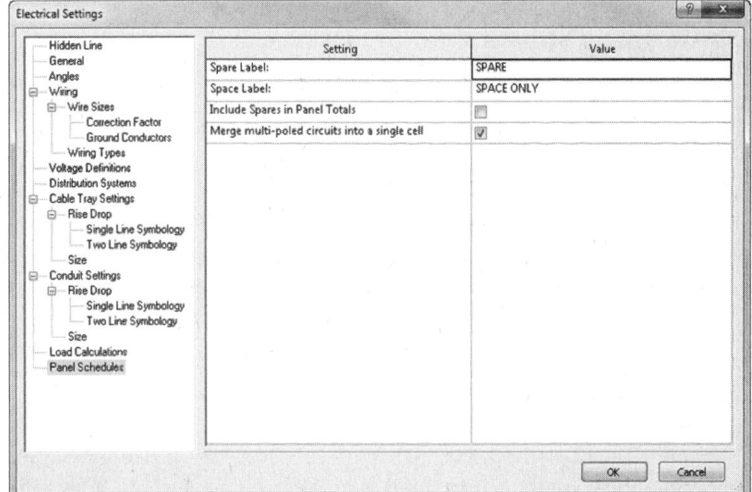

FIGURE 2.41
Panel schedule settings

Creating Sheet Standards

Drawing sheets are a key element of your project template. Because these are often the delivered product, it is important that they are put together in a consistent manner. The ability to easily manage the information included in your sheet views is one of the benefits of establishing sheet standards in a project template.

Titleblocks

The sheet border of a construction document is called many things by many people and organizations. In this chapter and throughout this book, the graphics and information that make up the border of a construction document, or sheet, are referred to as a *titleblock*.

If you generally work as a consultant to the primary design discipline, you might not need a titleblock family for your template. In this type of environment, you would normally acquire the titleblock from the primary design discipline and load it into your project file(s).

If you work in the project's primary design discipline and have a titleblock that is unique to your standards, it should be included in your project template. You can have multiple titleblocks loaded into your template. Your clients may require their own standards for a titleblock. This is another reason that you might create multiple templates. If you incorporate all the titleblocks that you work with into one template, it is possible that the wrong one could be applied to a sheet. This is not to say that you need a separate template file for each variation of titleblock.

For example, if you have a company standard titleblock that comes in two sizes, including both sizes in your template would be reasonable. When a project begins and the size of the sheets is determined, the unused titleblock should be removed to avoid confusion or to make sure it's not mistakenly being used.

For more information on the creation of titleblocks and how to include the desired information within them, see Chapter 23, "Sheets."

Defining Sheets

You know that some types of sheets will be included in every project that you do. These sheets can be created in your template file to ensure that they are properly set up for each project. Any views that are required for these sheets can also be applied to the them. So when a project has begun, any modeling done in the views will be shown on the sheets, streamlining the process of creating construction documents.

Having multiple titleblocks in your template can complicate this slightly. Unless you want to set up each type of sheet with each available titleblock, it is best to use the most commonly used titleblock for your preset sheets. If the project requires a different titleblock, the default one can be switched by using the Type Selector.

Preset Sheets

With preset sheets, you can establish consistent locations of sheet-specific items such as plan notes, key plans, and graphic scales. Preset detail sheets give you a place to put drafting and detail views as they are loaded or created. General notes or legends that are used on every project can already be in place when a project begins.

Having a set of sheets is also useful for determining how views will be organized and how many sheets will be required for a project. Once a project begins, you can print the sheets to create a mock-up set, sometimes referred to as a *cartoon set*, to better determine the number of sheets that need to be added to or removed from the project as well as how the building model will fit onto plan view sheets. With this available at the start of a project, decisions can be made early on to increase efficiency and improve workflow.

As with any element or standard you create in your project template(s), it is important to recognize how much is needed on a project-by-project basis. Consult with the people who work on projects daily to determine the types of things they would like to have in their projects from the start to improve their workflow.

Placeholder Sheets

Placeholder sheets are a Revit feature that allow you to create a list of sheets without them being physically created (in the Project Browser) yet. They are typically used to host information from other disciplines such as sheet name and number in order to create a complete sheet list within the project. Placeholder sheets can be created through a Sheet List schedule by inserting a data row. When you are creating a regular sheet from the View tab with the Sheet command, placeholder sheets will be listed in the bottom portion, and you can select one or more of them and convert them to regular sheets on which you can place views. Placeholder sheets can be created in the template, but they can't have views on them unless they are converted into regular sheets.

Understanding the Project Browser Organization

Keeping your project organized within the Project Browser in Revit goes a long way toward efficiency in your workflow. Consistency makes working on several projects at once easier. You always want to know where to find specific types of views and also what a view is by its name.

The first area of organization in the Project Browser consists of the views within the project. When transitioning from a traditional CAD program, it can be difficult at first to comprehend that each view is not a separate file. The views are created to determine how you are looking at the model. Views have many properties that determine their appearance and the discipline or system to which they belong. You can organize your views based on any of these properties to group like views together. Figure 2.42 shows the types of view organizations available by default. You access this dialog box by right-clicking the Views heading in the Project Browser and selecting Browser Configuration.

FIGURE 2.42
Default view organization types

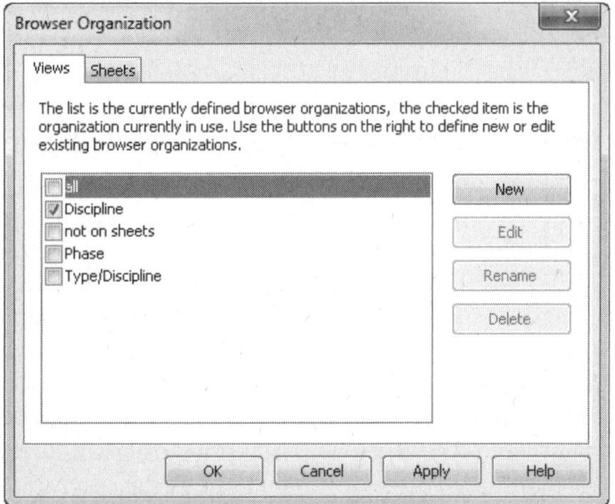

Notice that the organization of views in the Project Browser is a system family. This means that you can create additional browser configuration types by selecting New, and you can rename, edit, or delete the default types—except for the type All, which cannot be changed, or deleted—and then changing how the views are grouped and listed.

When you click the Edit button for the Folders parameter in the Type Properties dialog box, you can modify how the views are organized and listed in the Project Browser. Via the Filters tab you can choose up to three filters, and then with the Grouping And Sorting tab you can choose up to six levels for grouping (three in Revit MEP 2013 and prior) for your views and one sorting option. Each grouping option is determined by a view property. Once a property is chosen, you can select another level of grouping by using a different property, and then you can choose another level if necessary. When all the grouping options have been established, you can select the sorting option for the views. Thus, creating grouping options is similar to creating a folder structure for files, and the sorting option determines how the views are listed in the folder.

You can organize views in any number of ways. Figure 2.43 demonstrates a method that adds numbers in front of the browser organization name. This way, you have better control over the sorting.

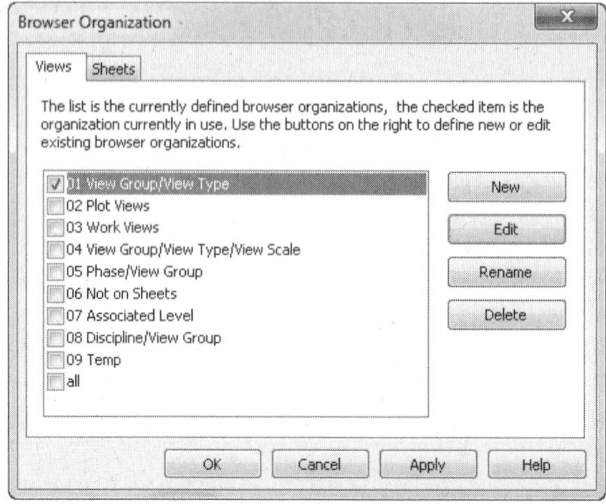

FIGURE 2.43 Sample browser organizations

Determining Which Views Are Grouped Together

Every view within a project belongs to a design discipline. The Discipline property of a view is the most common property used for the first level of grouping. Revit 2015 has six disciplines to select from: Architectural, Structural, Mechanical, Electrical, Plumbing, and Coordination. When any MEP discipline is applied to a view, the architectural and structural model components are displayed in a sort of halftone and transparent mode. The objects are still in front of the object you are trying to select, and you still need to hide them or change the view mode in order to select anything. The Architectural and Structural disciplines display the model differently and are generally used when you want to view linked files as originally intended, while the Coordination and Architectural disciplines are great for viewing all disciplines together.

The Sub-Discipline parameter can be used as the second level of grouping to further distinguish views used for fire protection, plumbing, or other types of engineering systems. This parameter exists in the default templates that can be installed with Revit. If you choose to create a template or project without starting with one of the default templates, you have to create a parameter for this type of use.

You can also create a project parameter for your views. If you create a project parameter for your own company discipline structure, you can then have, for example, both Wet Fire (sprinkler systems) and Dry Fire (detectors) come under the same primary grouping even though they would usually come under Plumbing and Electrical, respectively. Using a Sub-Discipline type parameter makes it possible to separate views into their specific engineering systems. You can have all your electrical views listed under the Electrical discipline, but that may make it difficult to find views you want quickly. Having a second-level grouping that puts all the lighting, power, communications, and other systems views in their own groups creates a more organized environment in the Project Browser.

The Family And Type property of a view is another commonly used level of grouping. This is what defines your views as plan views, sections, elevations, 3D views, or ceiling plans. When you begin to annotate your views to place them on construction documents, it is important to place the annotation in the views that will be used on your sheets, so being able to easily locate the proper view for annotation is important. Each grouping option can be set to utilize all the characters of the parameter value or only a specific number of leading characters.

Another popular method is to separate the views by Plot and Work for their first level and again by another parameter for the subdisciplines (see Figure 2.44). This can be done through the creation of two custom parameters, in this case View Group and View Type. What you name the parameters is really not important as long as it makes sense to you. This method has more flexibility because you can create additional first-level groups and not be limited to the six disciplines using the Discipline parameter.

You can also use filters to not show any views that are on sheets in the views section of your project browser. These views would then have to be accessed via the Sheets section. However, this will not work when using dependent views unless the parent view is also on a sheet. Another use of the filters is to create a browser for only one discipline so you can remove all other disciplines except that which is being worked. This is discussed in more detail in the section "Sheet Organization" later in this chapter.

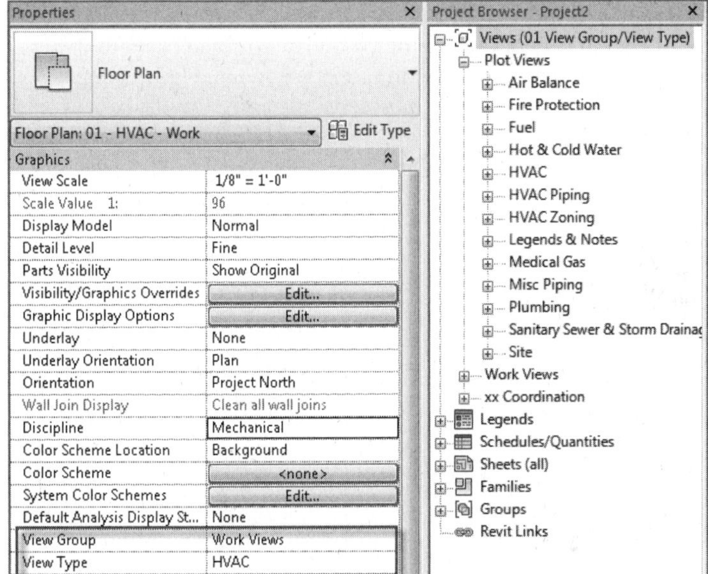

FIGURE 2.44 Using the custom parameters View Group and View Type for browser organization

Sorting Views within Groups

Once you have established what types of views will be grouped together, you can determine how the views will be sorted in their respective groups. View Name is most often used, because ultimately you have to find the view you are looking for in the Project Browser. Views can be sorted in either ascending or descending order, alphabetically or numerically.

Figure 2.45 shows the setup of a view organization that utilizes the Discipline, Sub-Discipline, and Family And Type properties as a grouping structure, with the views sorted by View Name. Notice how the views are shown in the Project Browser because of this organization.

Schedule views and legends are organized separately from model views. The only control you have over how they are listed is by your naming convention because they will be listed alphabetically. The sheets used in your project are the only other project element that you can sort and group in the Project Browser. Sheet organization options are discussed in the next section.

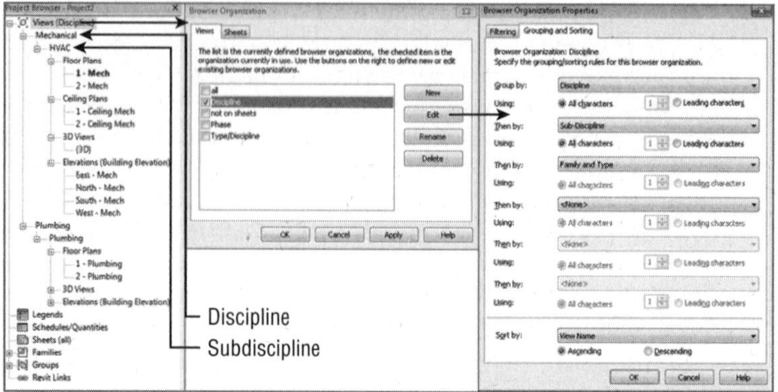

FIGURE 2.45
Sample view organization structure

Another way of organizing your views instead of spelling out *Level 1* at the end of the name is to use numbers at the beginning, as shown in Figure 2.46.

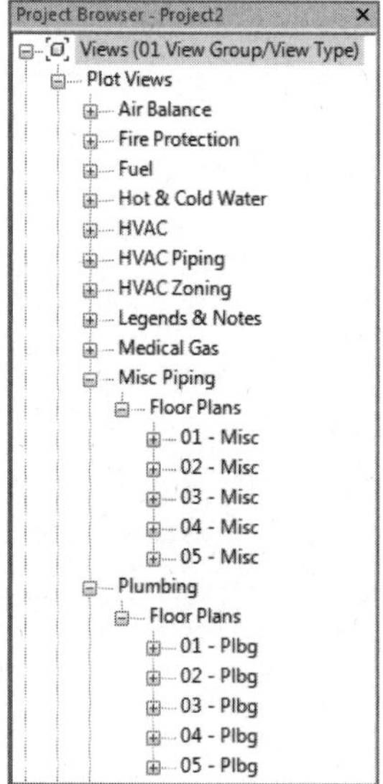

FIGURE 2.46
Sample view organization structure

Sheet Organization

Whether you are creating a single-discipline template or one for use by multiple disciplines, it is important to establish the organization of your drawing sheets to make sheet management consistent from project to project.

Setting up sheet organization is similar to setting up the organization of views. You can set up the Browser Organization for the Sheets system family with different types to organize your sheets in any manner desired. To access this system family, right-click Sheets in the Project Browser and select Properties. Use the New button in the type properties of the system family to create a new organization method. It is helpful to name the type based on how it organizes the sheets so that what the type is used for is clear to all users. Once you have created a new family type, you can click the Edit button of the Folders parameter to set the organization settings. Figure 2.47 shows a sample of the settings for an organization type that is based on the discipline of sheets. In this example, the sheets are numbered using a discipline prefix and then organized by the first character in order to group each discipline's sheets together.

Additional parameters can be applied to sheets that can be used as a basis for organization. These parameters can be included as project parameters in your template so that when a new sheet is created, it will have the parameters applied to it. If you create a drawing list that appears on your construction documents, you can use these parameters to organize the order of the list, which may not always match the order in the Project Browser. For more information on creating a drawing list or adding parameters, see Chapter 6 and Chapter 7.

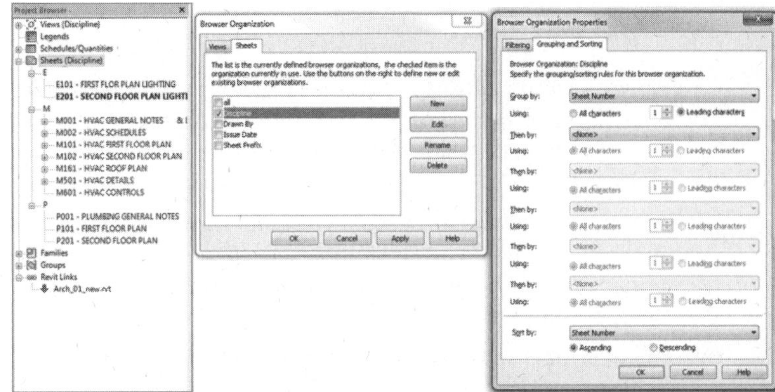

FIGURE 2.47 Sample sheet organization settings

> **TIPS FOR MANAGING TEMPLATES**
>
> The management of a project template is an ongoing process. As standards are developed and enhanced, new workflows are discovered and new clients are acquired. Thus, the need for template maintenance grows. Here are some items for consideration when managing your templates:
>
> **Be Careful When Transferring Project Standards** Once a standard has been developed in an actual project, the easiest way to establish it in a template is to use the Transfer Project Standards feature of Revit. This is a powerful but potentially dangerous tool. When you use it, be sure that you transfer only the standards required; otherwise, you may overwrite standards in your template with ones that are specific to a project.
>
> **Use Purge Unused Cautiously** The Purge Unused command is another powerful but potentially dangerous tool, especially when used while working on a project template. After all, nearly everything in a template file is "unused." Exercise extreme caution when using this tool in a template file. Some items such as text styles can be removed only with this tool, so its use is sometimes required.
>
> **Keep It Simple** It can be tempting to include anything and everything in your project template(s). More often than not, this will cause more work than it saves. Along with the potential for the wrong types of components being used in the model, there will be a lot of
>
> *continues*

(continued)

work cleaning up unwanted or unneeded items. Having to weed through a bunch of components just to find the one you want will hamper your productivity.

Keep It Safe It is usually best to limit access to your project templates. The more people who have access to project templates, the more potential for project templates to be lost or damaged. Keep an updated archive of your templates in a secure location so that when the time comes, you can replace it with minimal interruption of work.

The Bottom Line

Set up views and visibility. The settings for views are crucial to being able to visualize the design and model being created and edited in a project. Establishing the default behavior for views and visibility of objects can increase not only the efficiency of working on a project but also the accuracy of design.

Master It The properties of a view determine how objects and the model will appear in the view. Along with Visibility/Graphics Overrides, what other view property determines whether items are visible in that view? For a floor plan view, describe all components of this property.

Establish project settings. Many project settings can be established in a Revit template to determine the display of objects in views and on construction documents. There are also settings that define the makeup of the project itself.

Master It Phase settings for a project are very important for defining what portions of a building design occur in certain phases. Explain why having phases established in a template might require a separate template file for phased projects.

Define preloaded content and its behavior. The more items you have available for immediate use when a project begins, the more your focus can be on design decisions and less on loading required items. In a multiuser environment, preloaded content ensures that improper variations, which can cause inconsistencies in the project documentation, do not occur.

Master It Having system family types defined in your template is just as important as having the appropriate components loaded. Explain why certain component families are required in order to create and define MEP system family types.

Create sheet standards. As with other template elements, standards for sheets are a useful component to have established.

Master It Having a predefined organization for drawing sheets in your template will ensure consistency from one project to the next. True or false: You must have all the required sheets for any project built into your template in order for them to be organized properly. Explain.

Chapter 3

Worksets and Worksharing

The Autodesk® Revit® MEP 2015 platform enables users to design and model complex buildings and engineering systems. Usually this is a team effort, so it is important to fully understand how a Revit MEP project file can be set up in a way that allows for multiple designers and engineers to work on these systems at the same time. Unlike traditional CAD solutions that require many files to represent the design intent, the entire mechanical, electrical, plumbing, and fire-protection systems can be modeled in one Revit MEP file. Doing so requires careful setup of the project file in the early stages of the design.

Harnessing the power of Revit MEP to create a single model containing all the MEP systems can result in quick and easy collaboration and coordination. The same is true for any Revit project file that requires more than one person working on the same model at the same time. Activating worksharing allows the user to create central and local files in which all users' changes are accounted for and ensures that these changes can be coordinated as they occur. This empowers the team to make design decisions early in the design process. It also enables you to control how entire systems are displayed in views and ultimately in construction documents.

To take advantage of the functionality created by enabling worksharing, you need to know how the features work and how to manage them to best suit your company workflow and standards.

In this chapter, you will learn to do the following:

- Create a central file by activating worksharing and dividing the model into worksets
- Allow multiple users to work on the same dataset utilizing local files
- Work with and manage worksets
- Control the visibility of worksets

Understanding Central Files

It can be difficult to grasp the idea that several users can work in the same file at the same time. When worksharing has been enabled in a Revit MEP file, the file is "transformed" into a *central file*. This file is the repository for the model and all of its associated components. In truth, each user will not be working in this specific file but rather in a copy of this file that communicates the actions and model changes of the user back to the central file. A copy of a central file is called a *local file*. These local files can be created in two ways:

- By opening the central file from the Open dialog box (ensuring that the Create Local File check box is selected).
- By copying and pasting the central file to a folder that is connected to the location of the central file via a networked solution. When the copied file is opened for the first time, Revit warns the user that saving the file will make it into a local-file copy of the central file.

A typical practice for working with a central file is to store it in a job folder on a network, with the local copies residing on the hard drives of the users' workstations. This prevents the users from having to work across the network while designing and modifying the model. This workflow reduces network traffic because the data transfer occurs only when the local file is synchronized with the central file.

Dangers of Opening a Central File

Once multiple users have begun work on the Revit project, the central file should not be opened by any user. If the central file is open, edits made by users working in local files will prevent the person working in the central file from saving their work, unless they save that file as a local file and then sync with central like everyone else. Avoid opening the central file unless absolutely necessary—in other words, for situations such as relocation and regular auditing. Whenever this is done, however, all other users must have relinquished control of any worksets that they are using.

This workflow can be achieved regardless of the number of users. Each user works in their respective local file, saving changes to the design and periodically synchronizing those changes with the central file. So the big question is, How do several users all work in one file at the same time? One analogy to explain the workflow is a jigsaw puzzle (albeit a puzzle to which you can add and remove pieces while still retaining a whole). You could dump the pieces onto a table, gather your friends or family, and begin work on the puzzle. Each person could scoop up a handful of the pieces (local file) and work to put the puzzle (central file) together.

We could also use a library to explain the workflow. The central file is the library itself, the sections could be worksets, and the books in the library would be the elements in a workset. If a section of the library is closed because, say, the owners are taking inventory, then only they have access. Everyone can see the books/elements, but they are not available for borrowing.

The local file contains everything, like a filing system, and it is from here that users can borrow books/elements or perform an inventory and check out a section/workset. The next sections explain the workflow in more detail.

Creating a Central File

Like most data files on a computer, Revit project files can be accessed by only one user at a time. To allow for multiple users, the project file must be made into a central file. This process starts when worksharing is enabled for a project. Any user can enable worksharing, and it needs to be done only once—by whoever is setting up the project. To enable worksharing, click the Worksets button on the Collaborate tab.

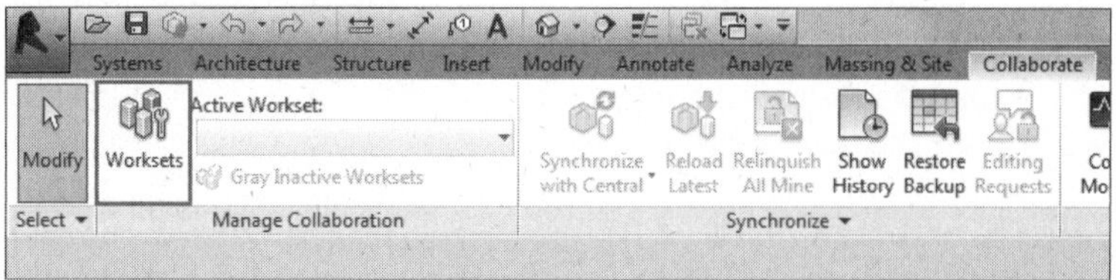

This can be done at any stage of a project, but it is best to do so as early as possible. The later you do this, the more work is required because you have to assign elements to specific worksets after they have already been placed.

Worksets represent the division of a model into four groups:

- User-Created
- Families
- Project Standards
- Views

Each group contains a number of worksets, depending on the makeup of the Revit project. Each view of the model, component, and project standard (things such as settings and types) has its own unique workset. Every family that is loaded into the project is also assigned its own unique workset. This partitioning is done by Revit automatically when worksharing is enabled, to keep users from modifying or changing the properties of the same elements at the same time. The User-Created category allows you to create your own set(s) of model components in order to control access to those components as a group or to control their visibility.

For example, if you are working on a project that will contain the elements from multiple disciplines, you may decide to create worksets that correspond to those disciplines. In other words, there would be a workset for all the electrical components, one for the mechanical components, one for plumbing, and so on. However, the real world often dictates that multiple designers and drafters will be working on a project, so it may be necessary to divide the model into more-specific categories based on the roles of the people assigned to the project. Perhaps one person will be working on the HVAC systems while another works on the mechanical piping. Likewise, a designer may be doing the lighting as another develops the power systems. In this type of scenario, it is wise to use worksets to divide the model into these categories to allow for control of these specific systems.

Figure 3.1 shows the dialog box that appears the first time you click the Worksets button in a project. This dialog box informs you that you are about to enable worksharing, and it contains some important information.

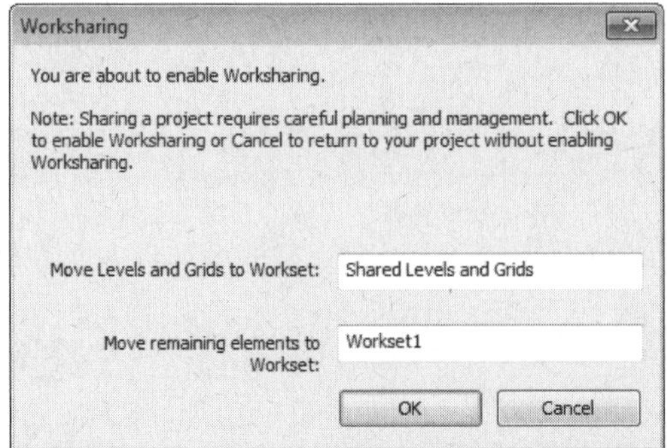

FIGURE 3.1 Worksharing dialog box

ENABLING WORKSHARING

The emphasis on this first dialog box cannot be stressed enough. It warns that you are in the process of enabling worksharing. This does require careful planning and management. In other words, once you have enabled worksharing for a project, it will always be enabled. Thus, the file will always behave as a central file—that is, of course, unless you open the central file by using the Detach option and follow it up with Discard Worksets. The significance of this warning is that if you do not need multiple users working on the file at the same time, then enabling worksharing is not necessary. At this point, there are several points of view regarding how to proceed. One is that all project files, regardless of how many people are working on the project, should be enabled for worksharing. This method means that all projects can be accessed in the same way and users always work on a local file. The benefits of this are as follows:

- The user has a separate place to design prior to sharing the file with the project team.
- There is less network traffic.
- There is more than one location for backup files.
- Users, especially those who are new to the software, have less to think about.
- There is less reliance on users renaming files.

This dialog box also indicates the worksets to which the components in the model will be assigned (if any worksets exist when you click the Worksets button). So if you have already begun to build the model and later decide to enable worksharing, Revit will place all the model components into two default worksets. Revit puts any levels and column grids into a workset called Shared Levels and Grids. This is done because these types of elements are typically used by all disciplines and are typically visible in all model views. Everything else that exists in the model is placed into a workset called Workset1. You can rename these default worksets to something more appropriate to meet your project needs. However, it is recommended that you do not rename Workset1 because it cannot be deleted. You should, however, create your own worksets and move the objects to the appropriate one. If you enable worksharing in a file that contains no model, the default worksets will still be created; they will just be empty.

When you click OK in this dialog box, Revit creates worksets for each view, project standard, and family that are in the project file. If a model exists, Revit assigns each component to the default workset. Once worksharing has been enabled, you have access to the Worksets dialog box, shown in Figure 3.2.

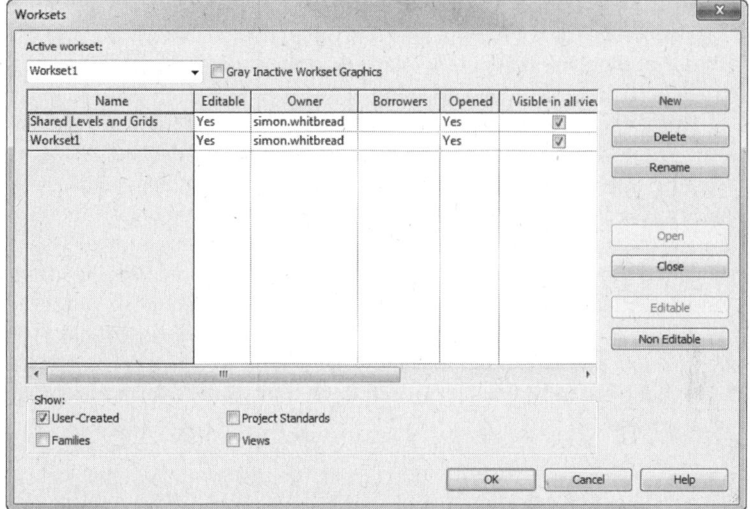

FIGURE 3.2 The Worksets dialog box

The first thing to notice is the drop-down list in the upper-left corner of the dialog box. This indicates which workset is active. When a workset is active, any components that are placed into the model are part of that workset. This is similar to more-traditional CAD systems; when lines are drawn, they are on the layer that is set as the current layer. The Name column of the dialog box lists all the worksets in the project, depending on which category is being shown. The check boxes below the columns allow you to switch between the categories of worksets you are viewing. This keeps you from having to view the entire list of worksets at one time.

The Editable column in the dialog box has two options: Yes or No. When a workset is set to Editable (Yes), the user has what is known as *ownership* of that workset. Having ownership of a workset means that you are the only person who can modify the model elements that belong to that workset. Ownership can be taken only by the user; it cannot be assigned by someone else. If a workset is set to Non Editable (No), it does not mean that the workset cannot be edited. It simply means that nobody owns that particular workset, so anybody working in the model can modify elements that belong to that workset.

You will notice that, by default, the user who first enables worksharing and creates a central file is the owner of the default worksets. That user must save the file before being able to relinquish ownership of those worksets. This is a critical step when a central file is created, because the goal is to allow multiple users to access the model.

Next is the Owner column. Notice in Figure 3.3 that there are several owners of worksets, yet only two are marked as Editable. These are worksets in a local file reflecting the changes made by user simon.whitbread; the action of making a workset *editable* means the person who performed the action is the owner. There cannot be two owners of a workset.

The next column in the Worksets dialog box is the Borrowers column. This displays the username of anyone who has worked on elements in the model that belong to that particular workset. As you can see in Figure 3.3, the username DBokmiller is listed in the Borrowers column for the workset M-570 HVAC because that user modified a model element or elements in that workset, while user Dan_Morrison made the workset P-520 Drainage editable and is therefore the owner.

Also notice the three dots after Dan_Morrison (...) for the workset P-520 Drainage; this indicates that there are multiple borrowers in the same workset. You can see who those borrowers are by left-clicking in the right side of the Borrowers column.

This is the core functionality of worksharing. At all times, Revit is keeping track of who is manipulating the model and on what parts of the model they are working. The central file is keeping track of the work done in the local files. Two users cannot borrow the same model element at the same time; this is how multiple users can work on the same model simultaneously. If you select a model element such as a light fixture and another user has already selected and modified that light fixture, Revit will warn you with a dialog box that you cannot modify that model element until the other user relinquishes control of it. You will learn more about this workflow later in the chapter. Going back to the (expanding) jigsaw puzzle analogy, if you were to pick up a puzzle piece to place it somewhere, no other person at the table could do anything with that piece until you let go of it. Revit lists all the usernames of anyone borrowing elements on a workset.

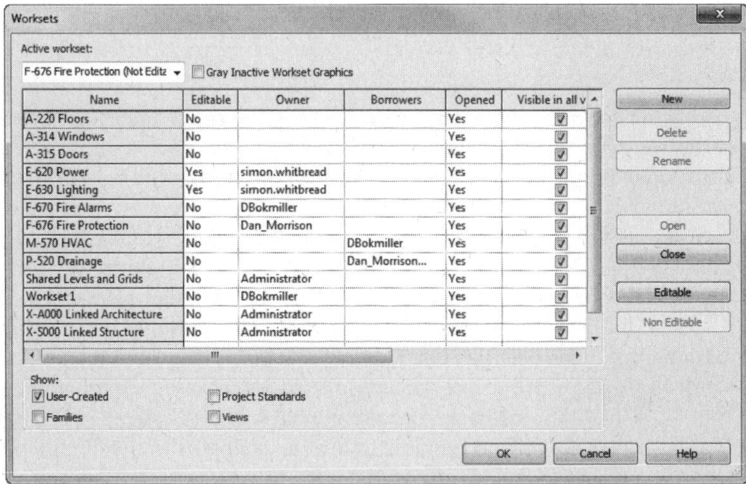

FIGURE 3.3 Usernames displayed in the Borrowers column of the Worksets dialog box

The next column of the dialog box indicates whether a workset is open. If a workset is not open, Revit will not display its elements in any view of the project. When you open a Revit project that has worksharing enabled, you have the option in the Open dialog box to set which worksets will be open with the file. This can save file-opening time and improve file performance. For example, you could choose not to open the Lighting workset if you are working only on the plumbing systems and have no need to coordinate with the lighting portion of the model at that time. This may help with model regeneration time and improve your productivity.

The last column of the dialog box is the Visible In All Views column, which allows you to control the visibility of the worksets. You will see that when you create a workset, you can determine whether it is visible in all views.

Creating a New Workset

To create a new workset, click the New button in the upper-right corner of the Worksets dialog box. This displays the New Workset dialog box, which allows you to name your new workset, as indicated in Figure 3.4.

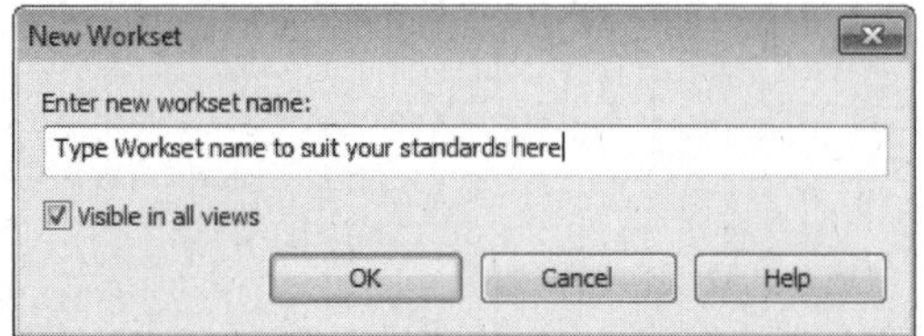

FIGURE 3.4 New Workset dialog box

This dialog box has a check box allowing you to set the default visibility of the workset in your model views. When you give the new workset a name and click OK, it is added to the list of User-Created worksets. Whoever creates a workset is the owner of that workset by default. Once you have created the worksets necessary for your project and you click OK in the Worksets dialog box, you must save the file to complete the creation of a central file. Revit will warn you with a dialog box if you attempt to relinquish your control of the worksets prior to saving the file as a central file.

After enabling worksharing and establishing your worksets, click the Save button to create the central file. Because this is the first time you have saved the file as a central file, the message box shown in Figure 3.5 is displayed.

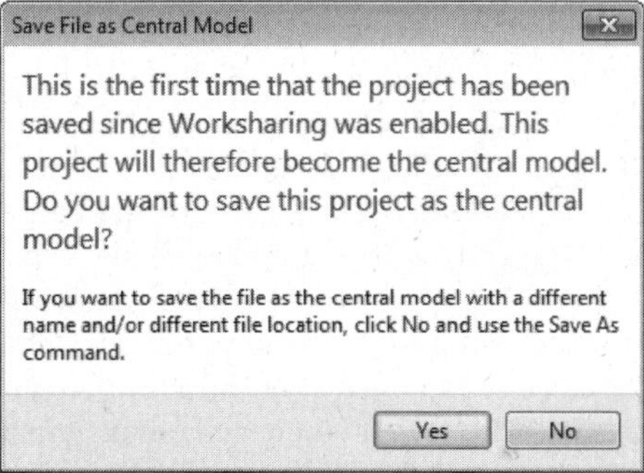

FIGURE 3.5 Save File As Central Model

If, however, you want to change the name of the central file, use the Save As option. For example, some companies use one naming convention for nonworkset projects and another for those with worksets enabled. In the former, the project is named with a project number (`12345-HVAC.rvt`) and then, after worksharing has been enabled, the name is changed via the Save As process to contain the word *Worksets* or the letters *WS* (`12345-HVAC-Worksets.rvt` or `12345-HVAC-WS.rvt`). Because this file has just had worksharing enabled, clicking the Options button shows you that this file is being saved as a central file, and the Make This A Central Model After Save check box is grayed out, as shown in Figure 3.6.

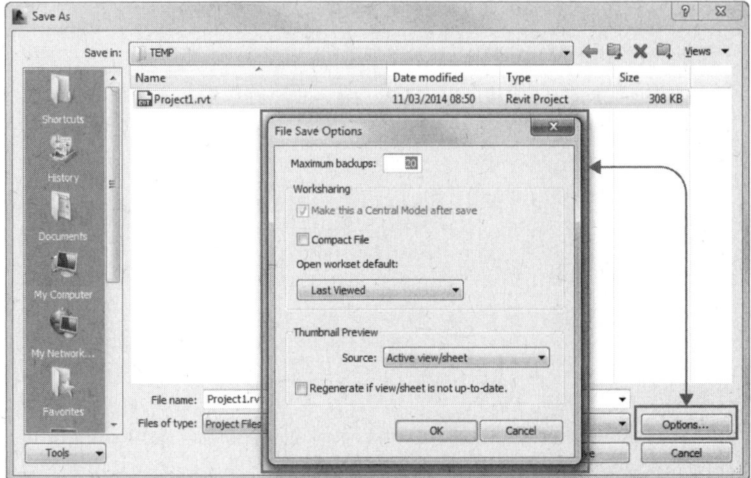

FIGURE 3.6 Options for saving a file after enabling worksharing

Once your file has been made into a central file, a backup folder is automatically created. This folder contains data files that will allow you to restore a backup version of your project if you should ever need to roll it back to an earlier date or time. Having several users on a project who are saving frequently can limit how far back in time you can go to restore your project. Therefore, it is recommended that you archive your project file at intervals logical to the submittal of the project. It is also worth pointing out the difference between the nonworkset backups, which are copies of the old file before saving. If your project is 50 MB and you have 20 backups, you now have a project taking up approximately 1 GB of storage. However, with a worksharing-enabled project, this becomes less of an issue because the backups are recorded as the *changes* to the original file, and although they can be more in number, less actual data is represented because there is no need to have complete duplicates.

The first thing you should do after the file is saved is click the Relinquish All Mine button on the Collaborate tab. This releases ownership of all worksets and borrowed elements. The file should then be saved again so the central file is in a state where no user has ownership of any worksets. A more efficient way to achieve the same result is to use the Sync And Modify Settings option; here Revit saves the local file, synchronizes, and saves the local file again—in one action. However, if you have a central file open, you will notice that the Save button is inactive. To save a central file when you have it open, you must click the Synchronize With Central button on the Collaborate tab. This saves the file and creates a backup folder of the project. Once the central file has been saved, it should be closed before any more work is done on the project file. From this point on, all work should be done in the local files of the project. In summary, follow this basic procedure:

1. Save the file correctly.
2. Enable worksets.
3. Save the file again to commit changes.
4. Synchronize to relinquish ownership of everything.
5. Close the file.

The project is now ready for users to create local files and begin work.

Best Practice for Naming Central Files

Regardless of your company file-naming standards, it is a good idea to put the word *worksets*—or an equivalent designation—somewhere in the name of your central file. Because the central file is so important, you want to identify it clearly in your project folder structure. Using this naming convention will also help confirm that the correct file is being shared with consultants.

To summarize, these are the steps to create a central file for a brand-new project:

1. Choose New ➢ Project from the application menu.
2. Click OK in the New Project dialog box or click Browse to choose a different template.
3. Click the Worksets button on the Collaborate tab.
4. Verify that the worksets Shared Levels and Grids and Workset1 appear in the Worksharing dialog box, and then click OK.
5. Create any additional worksets needed for your project in the Worksets dialog box.
6. Click OK. You will be asked whether you want to make one of your User-Created worksets the current workset. You can choose to do so, but it has no effect on the file creation.
7. Save your file to the desired location. Your file will be saved as a central file. You are the owner of all of the worksets until you relinquish them.
8. After you have saved your file, click the Relinquish All Mine button on the Collaborate tab. The Save button is no longer active, so you must use the Sync And Modify Settings button to save your changes.

Working with Local Files

Now that the central file has been created, each person who will work on the project must create a local-file copy of the project. This local file can reside on the users' local workstations or on the network, although local C: drives are generally the best location. The important thing is that the local-file copies must be connected to the central file via the network so they can be synchronized and so Revit can keep track of borrowing of elements.

Creating a Local File

The Create New Local option in the Open dialog box shown in Figure 3.7 is selected by default when you attempt to open a central file.

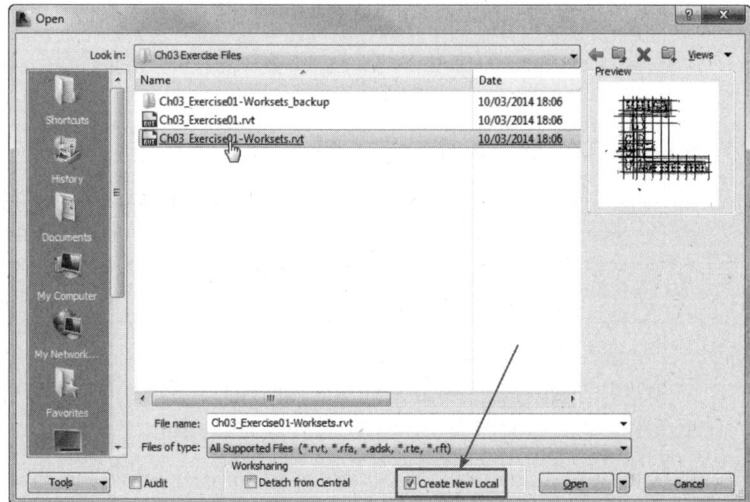

FIGURE 3.7
The Revit MEP 2015 Open dialog box

The Create New Local option can prevent users from accidentally opening the central file by automatically creating a local file when they click Open. This is the easiest way to create a local file. Using this method creates a local-file copy of the central file in the folder specified in your Revit settings. The filename will be the same as the central file, with *_username* added to the end. Figure 3.8 shows the File Locations tab of the Options dialog box indicating the destination folder for project files, while Figure 3.9 shows the local file saved to the destination folder.

Utilities are available that automate the creation of a local file, and many companies are developing their own routines that conform to their specific standards, such as file naming and project folder structure. If you do not have such a utility, another way to create a local copy of a central file is simply to browse to its location and copy/paste it to the desired location by using Windows Explorer (see Figure 3.9). Once you have placed the local copy, it is important to rename the file, removing the word *central* from the filename (if used) to avoid confusion. Having your username in the filename helps to keep track of who owns the local files. If you use this method when you open the copied file, you will receive a warning dialog box stating that the central file has moved or has been copied and that saving the file will make it a local file—which is the intent. Click Close on this warning, shown in Figure 3.10, and you will have a local file after you save.

One thing worth stressing is that users should *not* use Windows Explorer to *open* a project file. Although this has almost become the *de rigueur* way of opening other CAD files (or, for that matter, any format file), you can land in trouble if you use this method when opening a Revit central file. Invariably, users forget to use Save As to create a local file, and when they select Synchronize With Central a few hours later, there is the potential to overwrite any changes made when others have synchronized *their* local files.

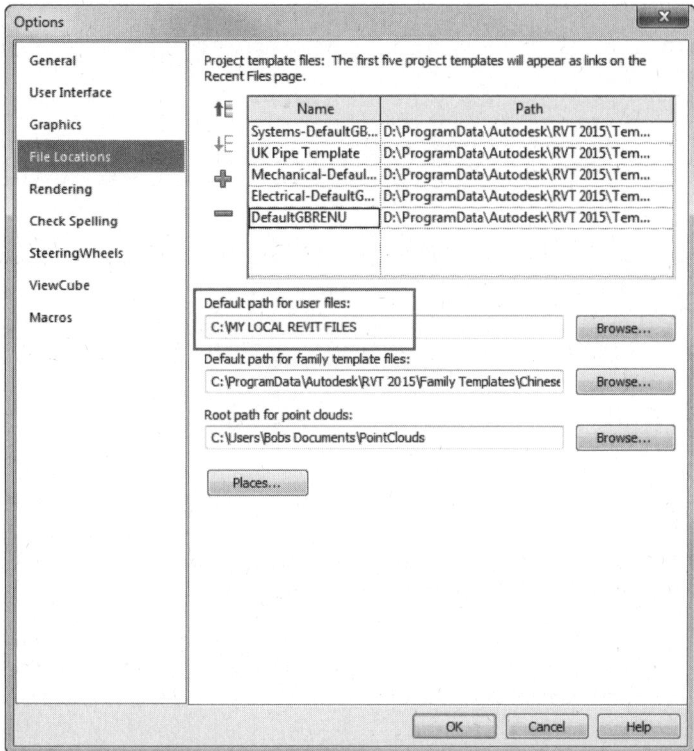

FIGURE 3.8 Options dialog box

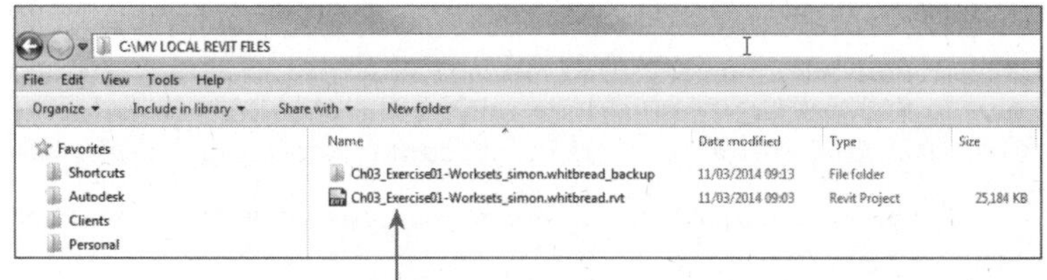

FIGURE 3.9 File saved to destination folder

Synchronizing a Local File with the Central File

The Revit software itself is in constant communication with the central file and all the local-file copies in order to maintain coordination of the model elements. As you are working in the model, it is aware of the elements over which you have control. You have two ways of saving your work. The first is to save your local file by simply clicking the Save button or selecting Save from the application menu. When these changes are saved, they are saved to your local file only. This gives you the freedom to save at frequent intervals without accessing the central file. This also allows for a more efficient workflow, because minor changes and reworking of the design can be finalized before pushing them out to the entire design team.

FIGURE 3.10
Copied Central Model warning

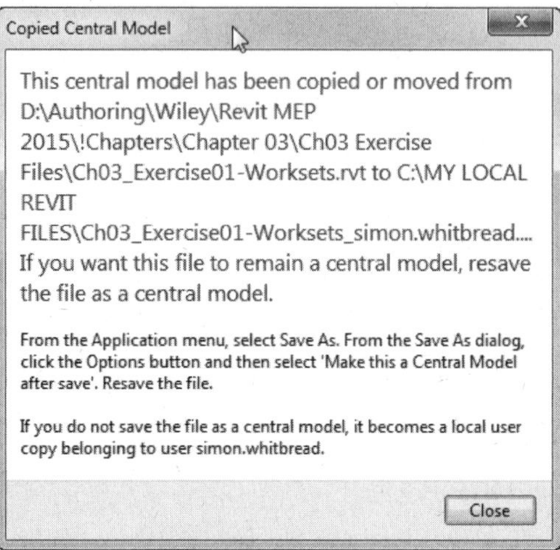

The second method for saving changes is to synchronize with the central file. There are two parts to the Synchronize With Central button:

- Synchronize Now synchronizes with the central file and relinquishes control of any borrowed elements. User-Created worksets—and their objects—are not relinquished at this point if the user is the current owner. This means the objects you own remain in your control.
- Synchronize And Modify Settings gives you additional options. Synchronizing occurs, and the user also has the option to relinquish control of any type of workset element, save the local file, and add a comment to the central file. This could be a note to other users or a reminder that the project was issued at a particular date and time. Additionally, you have the Compact Central Model option. This should be treated as a maintenance process and used when you can work in the central file while no one else is accessing it.

The Synchronize commands are on the Collaborate tab, shown here, and the Quick Access toolbar (QAT).

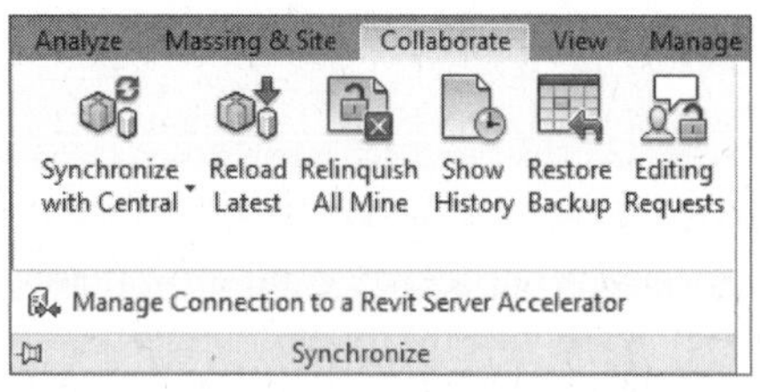

Clicking any of these buttons saves any changes made in the local file to the central file. The Synchronize command also updates the local file with any changes that have been synchronized to the central file by other users. Thus, when you click Synchronize, you are updating your local file to the most current status of the project. Another very important thing happens when you synchronize with the central file: Any items that you are borrowing in the model are relinquished when you synchronize. If you need to relinquish your control over items in the project but are not yet ready to save your changes, you can do so by saving your local copy and then clicking the Relinquish All Mine button on the Collaborate tab. If, however, these objects have been changed in any way, the only method for relinquishing control is using the Synchronize With Central option.

Synchronizing and relinquishing will become a regular part of your daily workflow when the project gets rolling. You should be aware of some important occurrences in this workflow. If two or more users try to synchronize with the central file at the same time, Revit will synchronize them in the order in which the synchronize actions occur. So whoever hits the button first will have their changes saved first. While the central file is being updated, other users who have attempted to synchronize may see a dialog box with a message that the central file is currently busy. They can cancel their attempt to synchronize or wait until the central file is available. Clicking the Cancel button means that no synchronization will occur. If they wait, the synchronization will happen as soon as the central file becomes available.

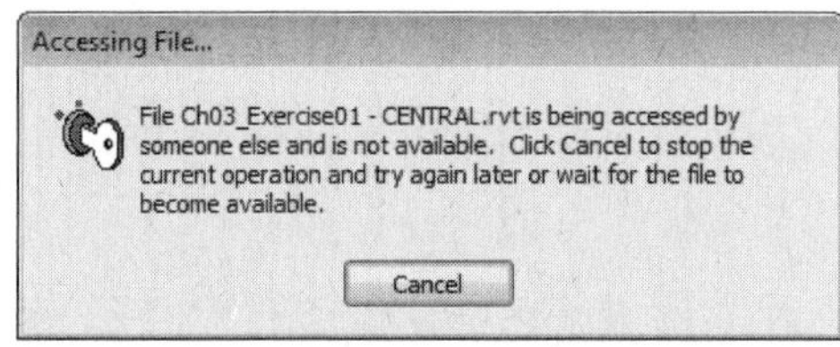

Local files can be deleted and new ones created at any time. It is recommended that you create a new local file every day as you begin work. This limits the number of warning and error messages that are saved to the central file and ensures that you start your Revit session with an updated copy of the central file. If you do not choose to make a new local file each day, it is important to update your local file with any changes that other users may have made while you were gone. You can do this by selecting Reload Latest from the Collaborate tab. When another user synchronizes with the central file, keep in mind that your file will not update with those changes automatically. You must either synchronize your file or reload the latest version of the central file.

When you start working on a project and want to create a new local file, you can browse to the location of the central file and open it with the Create New Local option selected. If you already have a local file for the project, a dialog box will appear with options for creating the new local file, as shown in Figure 3.11.

Depending on the changes made since the last time you worked on the file, your local file could become irreconcilable with the central file. Therefore, it is a good practice to create a new local file each day.

When the time comes to end your session of Revit MEP, it is best to synchronize your local file with the central file. If you forget or you choose not to by closing the program, you will see a dialog box with options for closing your session of Revit MEP. Figure 3.12 shows these options for closing a local file that has not been saved or synchronized with the central file.

FIGURE 3.11 New local-file creation options when a local file already exists

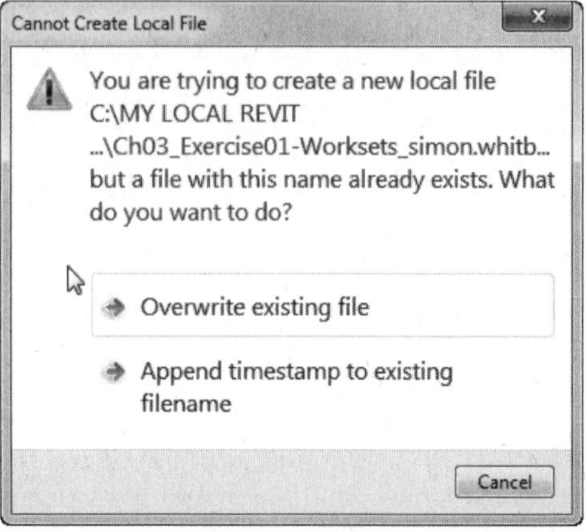

FIGURE 3.12 Ending Revit MEP session options

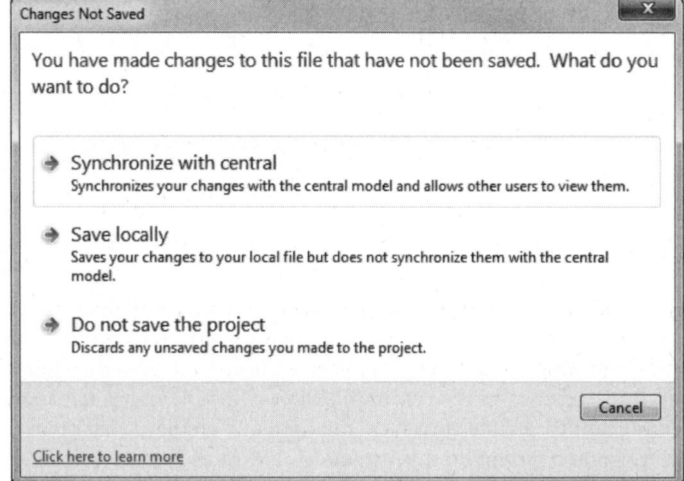

Clicking the Cancel button in this dialog box will return you to your session of Revit MEP. Clicking the Synchronize With Central option will open a dialog box with settings for your synchronization, as shown in Figure 3.13.

Notice in Figure 3.13 that you have the option to save your local file before and after it is synchronized with the central file. There is also a setting to control whether you will relinquish any worksets or borrowed elements.

If you click the Save Locally option in the dialog box shown in Figure 3.12, another dialog box appears with your options for relinquishing any borrowed elements or owned worksets, as seen in Figure 3.14.

You can choose to relinquish any items even though your changes are saved only to your local file and not the central file, or you can choose to keep ownership of the items. Keeping ownership prevents others from editing those items even after you close your Revit session.

Selecting the third option, Do Not Save The Project, in the dialog box shown in Figure 3.12 will also open a dialog box, this time specifying that you are about to close a project without saving, and that any changes will be lost. The options provided are identical to those in Figure 3.14 for relinquishing control of worksets and borrowed elements. So, even if you open the file to make changes that you don't intend to keep, be aware that you may affect others' use of the model by borrowing elements. It is important to relinquish worksets and borrowed elements when you are closing your Revit MEP session to allow others to work without running into the obstacle of not being able to edit an element because you have ownership.

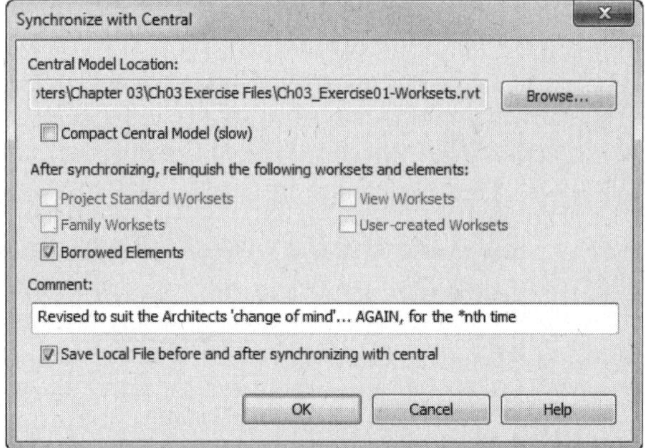

FIGURE 3.13 Synchronization settings

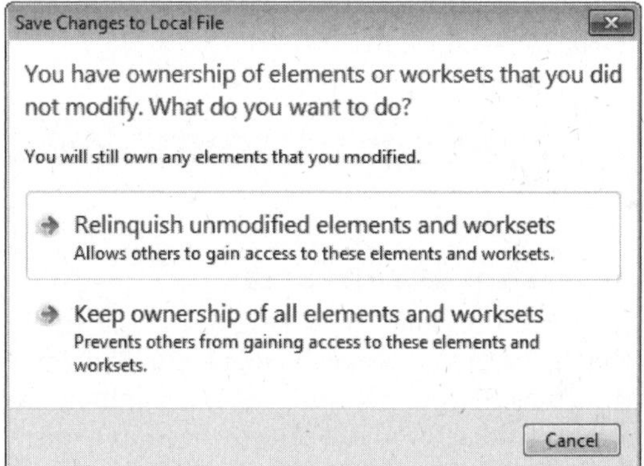

FIGURE 3.14 Save Changes To Local File dialog box

Managing and Using the Power of Worksets

Any work done in a local file transfers to the central file when synchronized. This is also true for worksets. When the central file is created, you may not know what worksets will be necessary, so they may be created in the local file and will appear in the central file after synchronization.

To make a model element part of a workset, either that workset has to be set as the active workset or you can change the element after placing it. (This is not necessarily the best workflow, because you then have to remember to make the change.) You do not need to be the owner of a workset to place a model element in it.

You do not have to access the Worksets dialog box to set a workset as active. The Workset panel of the Collaborate tab contains a drop-down list of all the worksets in the project. The workset visible in the drop-down window is the one that is set as the active workset. Remember that the words *Not Editable* next to the workset do not mean that changes cannot be made to the workset; they simply indicate that the workset is not owned by you.

With the ribbon-based user interface, it can be cumbersome to switch to the Collaborate tab each time you want to set a workset as the active workset or check to confirm that the correct workset is active before placing an element in the model. Therefore, the current workset drop-down list is available on the status bar, so it is visible at all times. You can also add the Workset drop-down to the QAT if you choose, as shown in Figure 3.15.

FIGURE 3.15 Synchronization settings

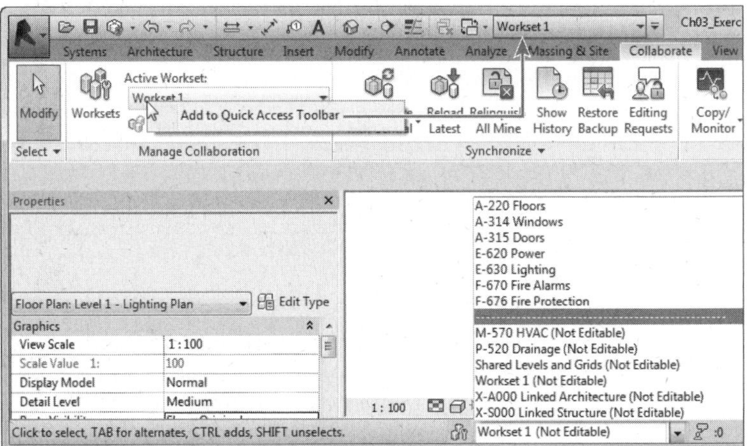

Taking Ownership of Worksets

There are two primary reasons for making a workset editable. When you make it editable, no other user can edit any model elements that are in that workset.

First, if you are concerned that someone else might inadvertently move or edit an element that is part of your workset, you can take ownership of the workset. However, this scenario can be detrimental to the efficiency of the team if other users need to make changes. There are other alternatives to protecting elements in a model, such as pinning them in place.

A second reason for workset ownership is to protect a group of elements such as a system or area of the model from changes while design decisions are being made. This most commonly occurs when you have to work on the project offline, such as when meeting with a client.

To take ownership of a workset, all you have to do is open the Worksets dialog box and change the value to Yes in the Editable column. It is best to synchronize your local file with the central file after taking ownership of a workset. Additionally, you can use the right-click context menu to choose Make Workset Editable when you select the element.

Real World Scenario

USING WORKSET OWNERSHIP AWAY FROM THE OFFICE

Roberta is an electrical designer working for an engineering firm that is consulting with an architect in another state. She is nearing her project deadline, and the client is ready to decide on some of the proposed lighting options. While Roberta is meeting with the architect and client, she wants to make sure that no unnecessary work is done to the lighting model because she will most likely bring back a new design that would make those changes obsolete. So, she takes ownership of the Lighting workset and then takes a copy of the project with her on her laptop.

During the next two days, Roberta makes several modifications to the lighting design while the client and architect provide input. When Roberta returns to her office, she connects her laptop to her network, opens her local file, and synchronizes her changes with the central file. Because she had ownership of that workset and has confined her design work to only that workset, no other work could be done to the lighting design, and her changes made remotely are now part of the central file.

Although this workflow does work, all users in this project need to be aware of the process. None of the views, annotations, or sheets associated with Roberta's workset should be amended because this would cause Roberta's work to be irreconcilable. Unfortunately, this scenario is fairly common and usually ends in heartache for everyone concerned.

A far better, and safer, workflow would be for Roberta to use remote desktop access and connect to her workstation back in the office, or she could work on her laptop but use a VPN connection. This way, she can stay connected to the rest of the project team and carry on with her design.

Working with Model Elements and Their Worksets

When a workset is set to be the active workset, any component placed into the model will be part of that workset. Annotative elements such as text, tags, or dimensions do not become part of a User-Created workset but rather the workset of the model view in which they are drawn. Each project view, including sheet views, has its own workset. When you are working in a view, adding annotation or detailing, you remain the borrower of those objects, but do not become a borrower of the actual view until you alter something already assigned to that view's workset. Other users can annotate objects in the same view, but the reality is that most workflows would make this difficult unless the view was a multiservice one that had several engineers providing input to the design. They cannot, however, change the properties of that view until your changes are synchronized.

OH NO I'M NOT!

Users often forget to select the Views, Project Standards, and Families check boxes when looking at the Worksets dialog box to see whether they are borrowing an element. Approached by fellow workers who cannot access items in the project, they insist that because the User-Created list of worksets is clear, there must be a problem with the software!

The User-Created worksets are ours to manage. The Views, Families, and Project Standards worksets are managed by Revit. They are created automatically for us and we cannot delete them; we can only choose to make them editable. Deleting a family or view will remove its workset from the project.

To delete a User-Created workset, you must first take ownership of it. You can do so only if no other users are borrowing elements on that workset. You also have to close the Worksets dialog box after taking ownership before you can delete the workset. You can then reopen the Worksets dialog box, select the workset from the list, and click the Delete button on the right side of the dialog box. If you are deleting a workset that contains elements, a dialog box presents options for those elements. As shown in Figure 3.16, you can either delete the elements from the model or move them to another workset.

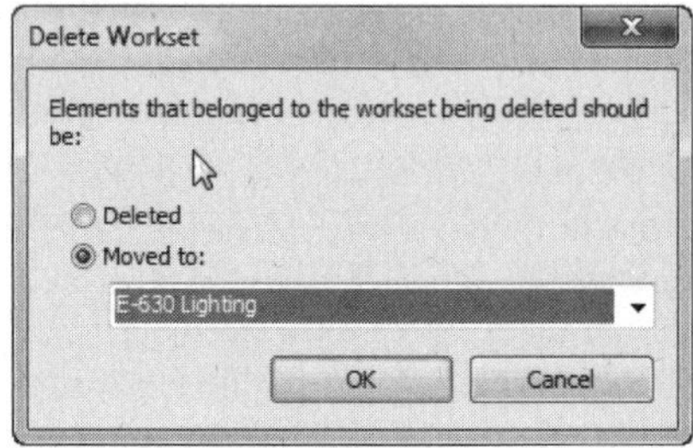

FIGURE 3.16 Options for deleting a workset

If another user owns the workset into which you are trying to move your elements, you will need to have that user relinquish ownership of the workset before you can move your items to it.

When you place your cursor over an object in the model, a cursor tooltip lists information about that object, as shown in Figure 3.17. When worksharing has been enabled in a project, the first item in the tooltip is the name of the workset to which the object belongs (unless design options are in use, in which case that information will be first).

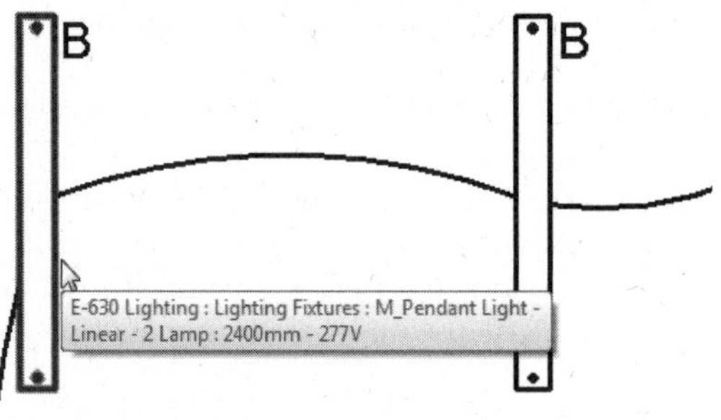

FIGURE 3.17 Model object information in the cursor tooltip

This is the easiest way to determine the workset to which the object belongs. This information can also be found in the properties of a model object or project component. The Workset parameter of an object is an instance parameter listed under the Identity Data group. If you need to change the workset of an object, you can edit the setting for the parameter in the Properties palette.

> **SELECTING MODEL ELEMENTS**
>
> Clicking an element to select it does not mean that you are borrowing that element. You must modify it in some way—by changing one of its properties, by moving it, or by making the element editable—before you can borrow it.

Apart from directly editing an object to make it editable, there are two other ways to make it editable. Select an object and you will see the Make Element Editable symbol appear, as shown in Figure 3.18; clicking this symbol gives you control of the object.

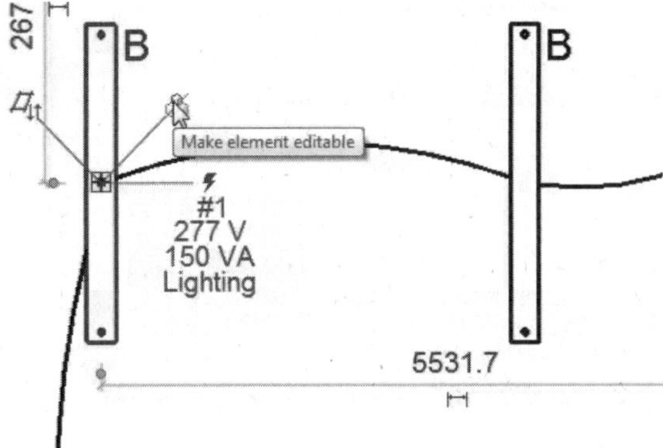

FIGURE 3.18 Make Element Editable symbol

The alternative is to select one or more objects and right-click. This gives you the option to make either the object(s) or the entire worksets editable, as shown in Figure 3.19.

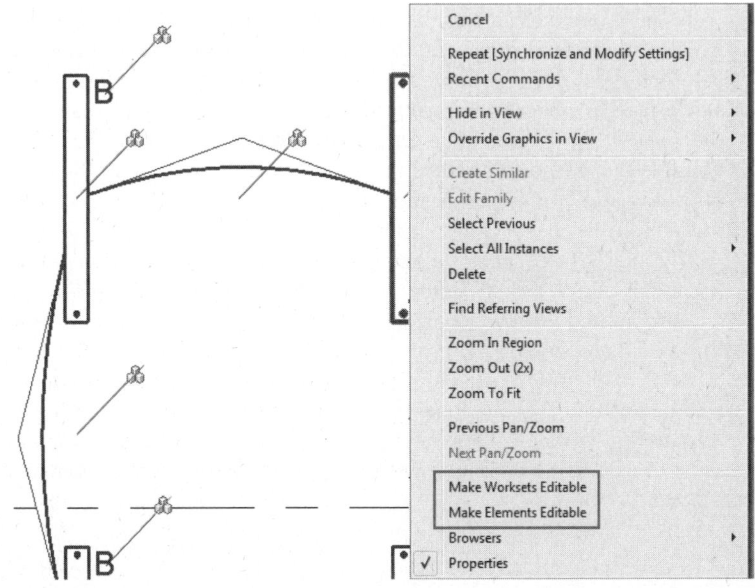

FIGURE 3.19 Make Worksets Editable and Make Elements Editable options

You can change an object's workset either by first borrowing the items in the model or by just selecting those elements. In either case, the Workset parameter is available, and you can change its value by selecting from the drop-down list of workset names, as shown in Figure 3.20.

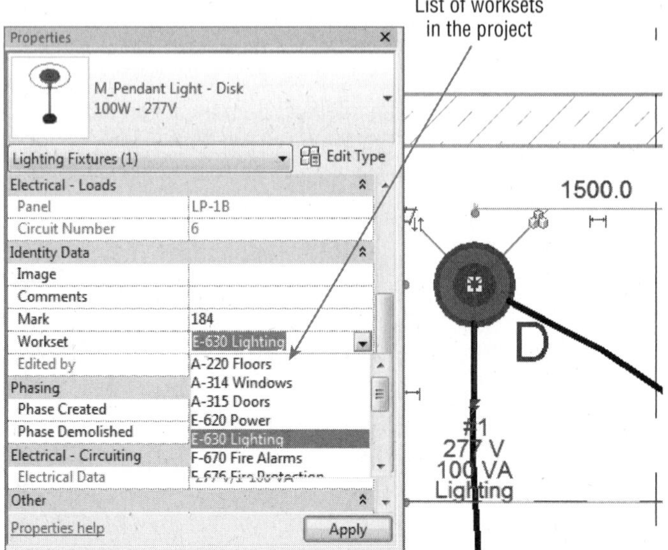

FIGURE 3.20 The Workset parameter in the properties of a model object

You can change the workset of multiple items by selecting them all and then accessing the Workset parameter in the Properties palette. Keep in mind that nobody else will be able to edit items on that workset that you own until you relinquish your ownership, even if they are not items on which you are working.

As mentioned earlier, each model component has its own workset. So say you select a family item in the model and you then select the Edit Family option from the Modify tab. After you load the family back into the project, a dialog box notifies you that the family is not editable and asks whether you would like to make it editable. This will give you ownership of the workset for that family. Because this does not occur until you load the family back in, it is possible that two or more users could edit a family but only the first one to load it back into the project would gain access to the workset; therefore, only that user's changes would occur in the project.

If you are the owner of a workset and want to release your ownership, you can do so by accessing the Worksets dialog box and changing the editable value from Yes to No. If it is a User-Created workset that you are releasing, you will remain the borrower of any items that you have modified on that workset until you synchronize with the central file. If you attempt to use the Workset dialog box to release your ownership of a family workset, you will be notified that the local file must be synchronized with the central file in order to release that workset. This method, however, may not work efficiently in all cases, and the most thorough and reliable way of reconciling these differences is to use Synchronize And Modify Settings.

> **UNDO, UNDO, ... *UNDO!***
>
> We tend to rely on the good-old Undo button to clean up our messes, but beware: The Undo function will have no effect on workset ownership or borrowing of elements. Once you own a workset or borrow an element, it is yours until you release it. Additionally, should you delete objects such as views or families from the Project Browser without first making their workset editable, the Undo history is reset. Just as you would when opening and unloading a linked file, you should take extreme care when deleting anything.

Controlling Visibility and Worksets

One of the key advantages to using Revit for project design is that it enables you to visualize the model. You can also use visibility settings to define how your views will appear on construction documents. With the model divided into worksets that denote the engineering systems, you can harness this power to help you design more efficiently by using working views. A *working view* is one that may show more or less model information than would be represented on a construction document.

The first feature of visibility control is simply turning items on or off. This applies not only to model categories but also to worksets. When worksharing has been enabled in a project, an additional tab, Worksets, appears in the Visibility/Graphic Overrides dialog box, as shown in Figure 3.21.

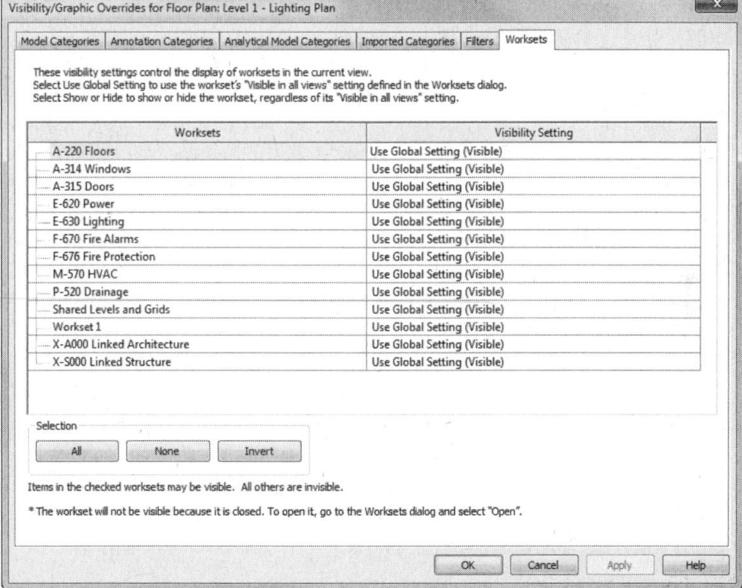

FIGURE 3.21 Visibility/Graphic Overrides dialog box

This tab of the dialog box provides a list of the User-Created worksets in the project and enables you to set the visibility behavior of the worksets in the current view.

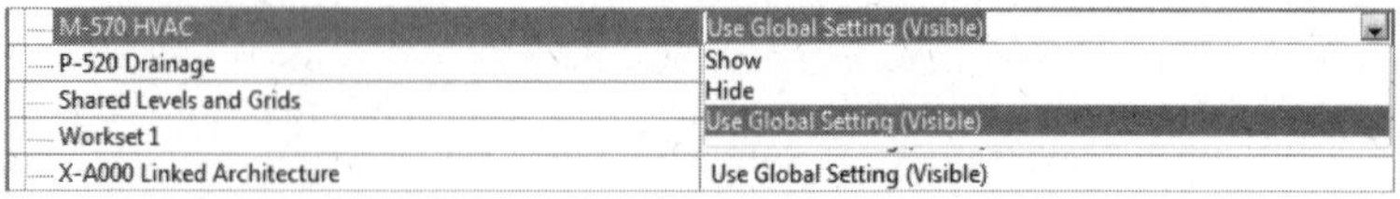

M-570 HVAC	Use Global Setting (Visible)
P-520 Drainage	Show
Shared Levels and Grids	Hide
Workset 1	Use Global Setting (Visible)
X-A000 Linked Architecture	Use Global Setting (Visible)

There are three options for workset visibility in a view:

- When you hide a workset, none of the items assigned to that workset are visible in the view, even if the categories of the individual items are set to Visible. The visibility settings for the workset take precedence over the settings for model categories.
- The Use Global Setting option means that the visibility of the workset is determined by the Visible In All Views setting established when the workset was created or the status of that setting in the Worksets dialog box. The status is shown in parentheses.
- The Show option is an override of Use Global Setting, which could be set to Not Visible. Using Show displays the elements assigned to this workset regardless of what the global setting requires. If an element does not appear, other factors (such as filters, design options, or individual graphic overrides) may be determining visibility.

When setting up your project worksets, it is important to consider this functionality. Thinking about what types of systems or groups of model components might need to be turned on or off will help you determine what worksets to create. Doing so early will save time from having to do it later, when the model contains many components that would have to be modified, and will make controlling visibility easier from the start.

Although this workflow is a valid one, consider that in any office you may have a mixture of workset-enabled projects and others that just come in the standard file format. Some users may even be using the Revit LT version of the platform, where worksharing cannot be enabled. While worksets can be added to view templates, they cannot be added into your project-template file because worksets cannot exist in a project template. This means that you cannot create a standard view template to carry through all your projects. The alternative would be to use filters that *can* be applied in the template file and can cover most, if not all, of your needs for view control.

Another way to control a workset's visibility is to determine whether the workset will be opened when the project is opened. In the Open dialog box, you can click the arrow button next to the Open button to access options indicating which worksets to open with the file. Figure 3.22 shows the options.

Selecting the All option will open all the User-Created worksets when the file opens. This does not mean that all the worksets will be visible in every view; it just means that the worksets are open, or loaded into the project. Selecting the Editable option will open (load) all worksets that are editable (owned) by you. If another user has ownership of a workset, it will not be opened with this option. The Last Viewed option is the default.

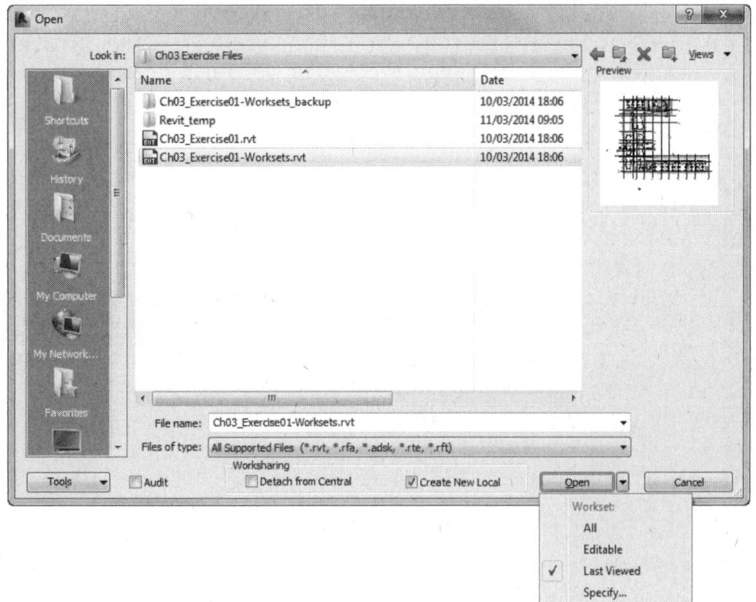

FIGURE 3.22 Workset options in the Open dialog box

FILE LINKS ON THE RECENT FILES SCREEN

Whatever option you choose from the Open dialog box will be applied to the thumbnail link of the file on the Recent Files screen. Using the link opens your file with the Last Viewed workset settings applied. However, as with using Windows Explorer to open a file, using the Recent Files screen is not a recommended workflow with workset projects; it is a best practice to always use the Open dialog box. You could be opening an old local file or even the central file itself— both of which can cause problems, not just for yourself, but also for everyone else on your project team.

The final option for opening (loading) worksets in a file is the Specify option. This allows you to choose which worksets will be open when the file is opened. Selecting this option opens the dialog box shown in Figure 3.23, where you can choose the worksets to open.

This is a powerful option because it can greatly improve the file-opening time and overall performance of your model. If you need to work on a system in the model and do not need to see other systems, you can choose not to open their respective worksets, decreasing the amount of time for view regeneration and limiting the number of behind-the-scenes calculations that are occurring when you work on your design. If you decide later that you want to see the items on a workset that you did not open when you opened the file, you can open the workset via the Worksets dialog box. When you select the Visibility/Graphic Overrides dialog box for a view, unopened worksets will appear in the list with an asterisk next to them, as shown in Figure 3.24. So if you are not seeing a workset that is set to be visible, you can quickly see that it is not visible because it is not open.

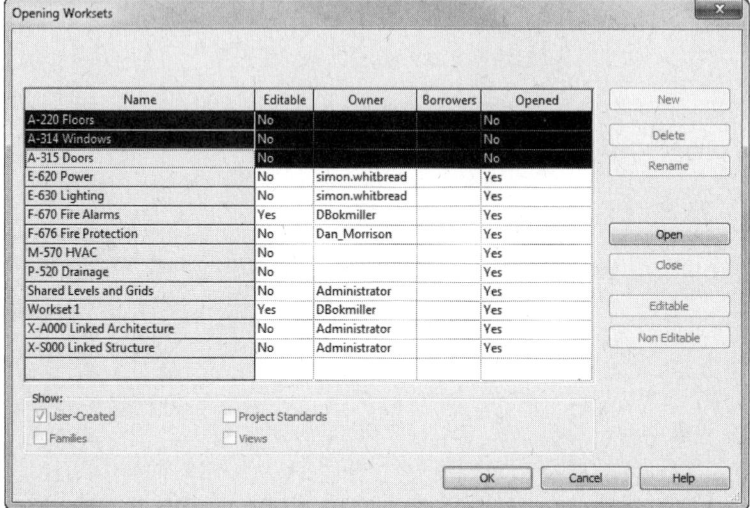

FIGURE 3.23 The Opening Worksets dialog box

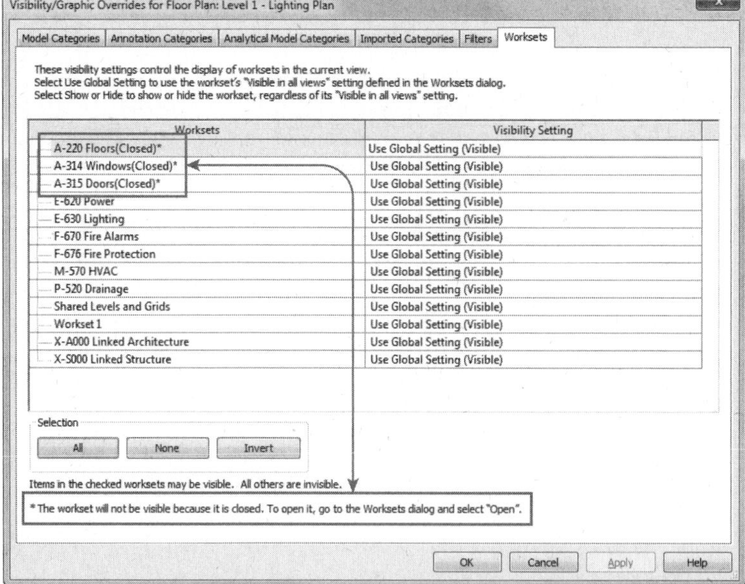

FIGURE 3.24 Visibility/Graphic Overrides dialog box

One way to utilize this functionality for improved performance is to create a workset for each Revit file that you will link into your project. This gives you the option of not opening the workset of a linked file without having to unload the linked file.

Enhancing Communication

In previous versions of Revit MEP, users actually had to *talk* to each other when someone wanted control of a workset or borrowed object—well, really! Seriously, though, this can and did lead to some strange work practices. Picture this: 10 people on a project team sitting at small desks in a small office, working on the same model…and the only mode of communication was email!

Users *can* stay in their comfort bubbles, and Revit now provides a "heads up" notification when an editing request has been made. In Figure 3.25, user DBokmiller wants ownership of a selection of objects but cannot have it until users Dan_Morrison and simon.whitbread relinquish control, so DBokmiller places a request.

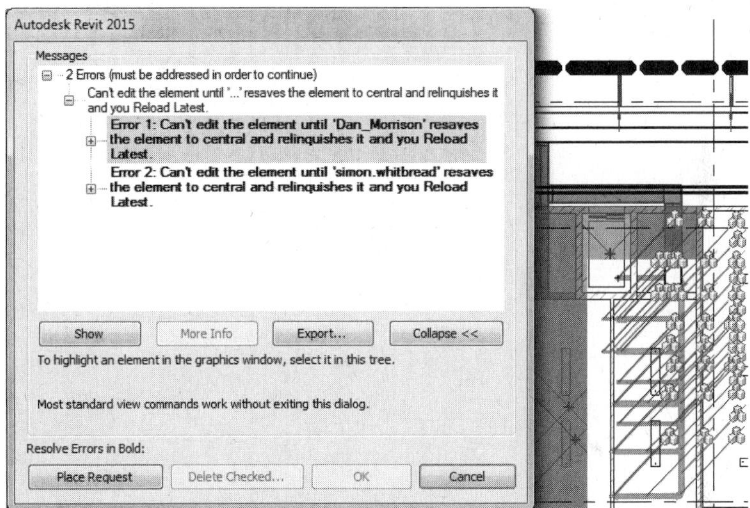

FIGURE 3.25 Workset place request

After the request has been made, a notification message, shown in Figure 3.26, pops up at both simon.whitbread's and Dan_Morrison's workstations.

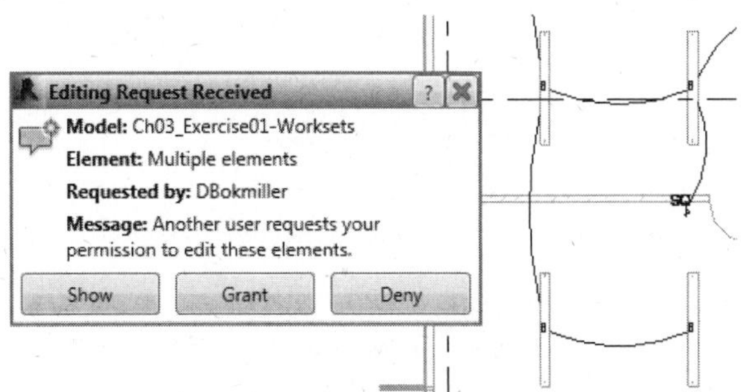

FIGURE 3.26 Editing Request Received messages

If the user ignores the notification, the status bar will show a highlighted request and indicate the number of requests (Figure 3.27).

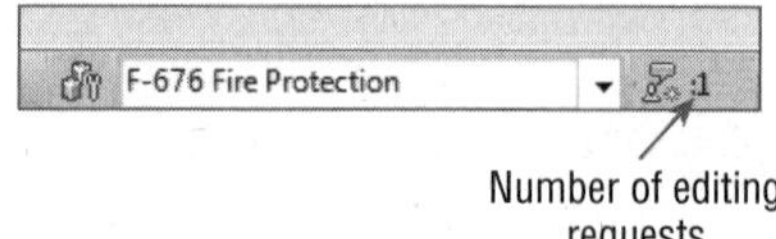

FIGURE 3.27 Status bar indicating requests

When the user clicks this message, the Editing Requests dialog box is displayed, as shown in Figure 3.28. This shows all the pending requests between you and other users, the objects involved, and, if necessary, whether synchronizing with the central file is required. This requirement may be due to objects being changed, edited, or deleted rather than only that the workset is owned.

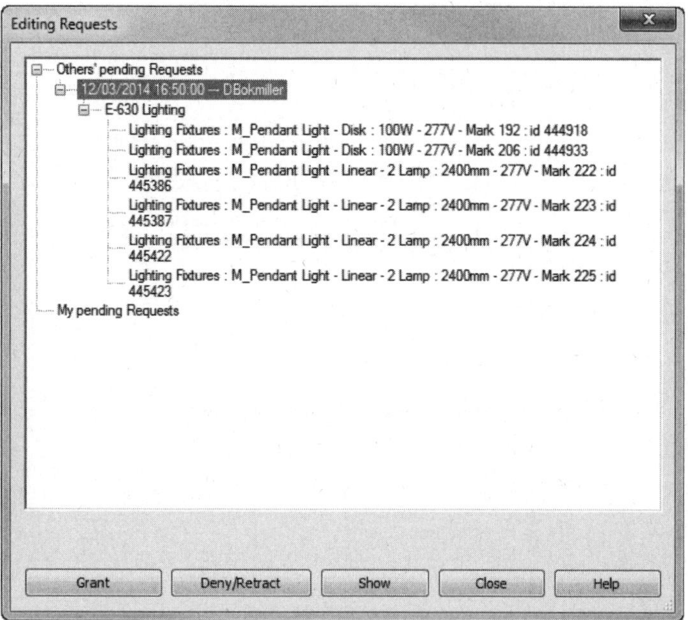

FIGURE 3.28 Editing Requests dialog box

And, of course, depending on the users' workflow, they can either grant or deny access to these objects. The varying results can be seen in Figure 3.29.

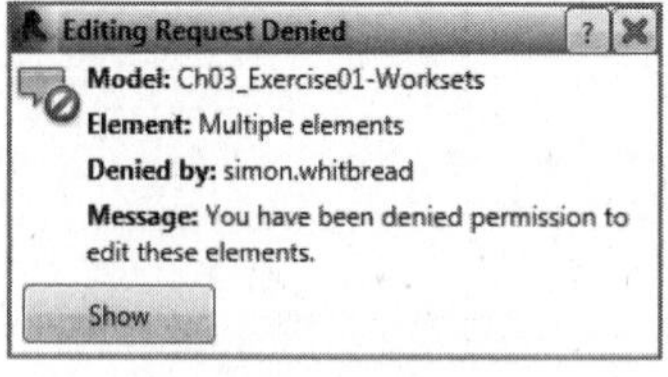

Editing request denied by user simon.whitbread

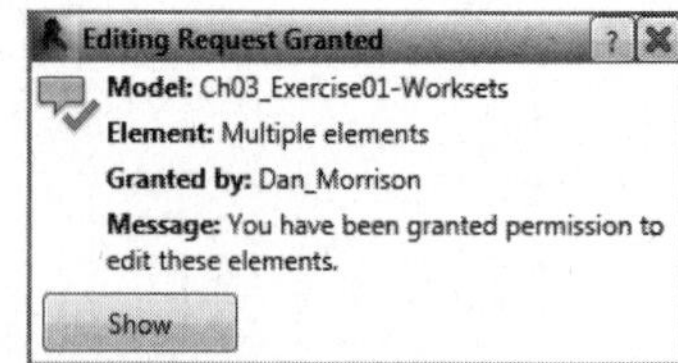

Editing request granted by user Dan_Morrison

FIGURE 3.29 Results of request actions

As described in Chapter 1, "Exploring the User Interface," you can turn on the worksharing display that allows you to see the owners and/or worksets of all the objects in the view in which you are working. This can be useful for general modeling or as an overview of the whole building model. Figure 3.30 shows the display.

FIGURE 3.30 Worksharing display

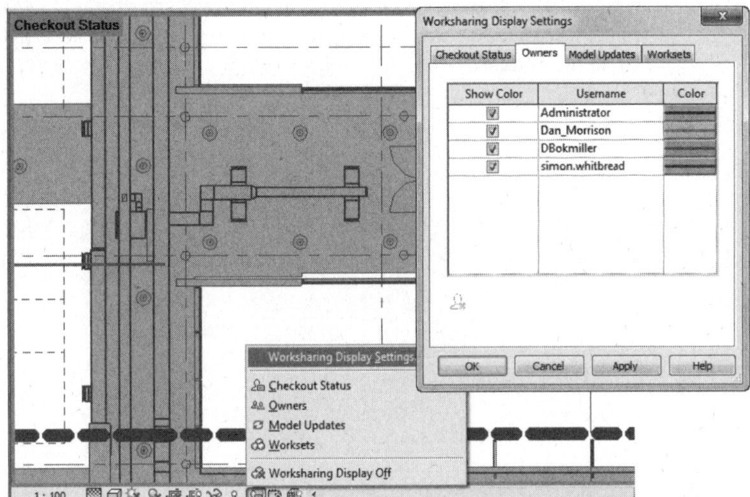

The Bottom Line

Create a central file by activating worksharing and dividing the model into worksets. Setting up your Revit project file correctly helps users easily visualize and coordinate their systems.

> **Master It** You are working on a project with a mechanical engineer, a plumbing designer, and an electrical engineer. Describe the types of worksets into which the model can be divided to accommodate the different systems for each discipline.

Allow multiple users to work on the same dataset utilizing local files. Revit MEP provides functionality to set up your project in a manner that allows users to edit and manage their systems without conflicting with other systems in the model.

> **Master It** Describe how to create a local file copy of a central file and how to coordinate changes in the local file with other users who are accessing the central file.

Work with and manage worksets. Working in a project with multiple users means that you likely will need to coordinate the availability of worksets.

> **Master It** Describe how you would isolate a system in the model so that no other user could make changes to that system. What is the best way to release a system so that others can work on it?

Control the visibility of worksets. Visualization is one of the most powerful features of a BIM project. Worksets give you the power to control the visibility of entire systems or groups of model components.

Master It You are facing a deadline and need to add some general notes to one of your plumbing sheets. Because of the intricate design of the HVAC system, your project file is very large and takes a long time to open. What can you do to quickly open the file to make your changes?

Chapter 4

Project Collaboration

Since engineers and architects started working together on building projects, an integrated project delivery has been the ultimate goal. The goal of consultants working together as seamlessly as possible is made more achievable by using a building information modeling (BIM) solution such as Autodesk® Revit® MEP 2015. Many are quick to believe that using a BIM solution automatically means coordination and integration, but the truth is that developing a building information model is only part of the process. You can build a 3D model and even put information into it, but it is how this information is shared and coordinated that defines an integrated project.

Revit MEP enables you to interact with the project model in a way that you can conceptualize the design as a whole, even if you are working on only pieces or parts. You do not have to work for a full-service design firm to participate in a project that results in a complete model. Architectural, structural, and MEP engineering systems can all come together regardless of company size, staff, or location. It is the sharing of computable data that makes for an integrated project delivery. Owners and contractors can also participate in the process. In fact, anyone who has any input into the design decisions should be included in and considered part of the project team.

Zooming in from the big picture a bit, you need to focus on your role as a project team member. You can be an effective player in the process by ensuring that the data you are sharing is usable, accurate, and timely. With a firm understanding of how Revit manages your information, you can develop some good practices and standards for collaborating with your project team.

In this chapter, you will learn to do the following:

- Prepare your project file for sharing with consultants
- Work with linked Revit files
- Coordinate elements within shared models
- Work with files from other applications
- Set up a system for quality control

Preparing Your Files for Sharing

In Chapter 3, "Worksets and Worksharing," you looked at ways to set up your project file to allow members of your design team to work collaboratively within their specific design disciplines. Although one goal is to make yourself more efficient and accurate, you must also recognize the importance of setting up and developing the project file in a way that you can easily share the design with your consultants. It is a good idea to consider whether the workflow or process you are setting up will have an adverse effect on other project team members.

Consulting In-House

The process for sharing information among consultants can be applied to your Revit project even if all the design team members work for the same company. Many full-service firms are finding it effective to treat the differing disciplines within their organization as "consultants" in order to achieve integrated coordination. Using this workflow helps reduce inaccurate assumptions that may occur and provides an atmosphere that encourages increased communication.

A Revit project file does not have to be set up as a central file in order to share it with others. If there is no need to establish worksets in your project, you can simply save your file as the design develops and share it when necessary. This is the simplest type of Revit project file to share, because there is no concern for receiving a local file by mistake or a file that is not updated with the most current design changes. As with all files that will be shared among team members, it is a good practice to name the Revit project file in a manner that clearly indicates the systems that it contains, such as `MEP Model.rvt` or `HVAC.rvt`. This makes linked files easy to manage and reload when updates occur.

If your Revit file has been set up with worksets, there are other considerations for sharing the file with your consultants. You should take care to realize that the decisions you make when setting up your worksets can affect those team members who need to visualize and coordinate with your design elements.

The first decision comes when you create your worksets. In the New Workset dialog box, you have the option of naming your workset, as shown in Figure 4.1. The name you choose should be descriptive so that others will know the types of items included in the workset. Using a descriptive name is also helpful to your consultants who have the ability to see what worksets are in your file. The other part of this dialog box offers you the option to make the newly created workset visible in all your model views. If you choose not to make the workset visible in all views, you will have to make it visible in each view that you want to see it in via Visibility/Graphic Overrides settings.

When you are creating your worksets, you may want to consider the Revit files that you will be linking into your project. It can be very useful to create a workset for each linked Revit file so that you can control not only each file's visibility but also whether a file is loaded into the project. Because you have the ability to choose which worksets to open when you open your file, you can determine which linked files will be present and visible when your file is opened. This can increase your productivity by improving file-opening and model-regeneration times. It also helps by not having to load and unload the links, which can cause problems with hosted elements. When you do not open a workset a linked file is a part of, the linked file is still part of your file; it's just not visible or "present" in your session.

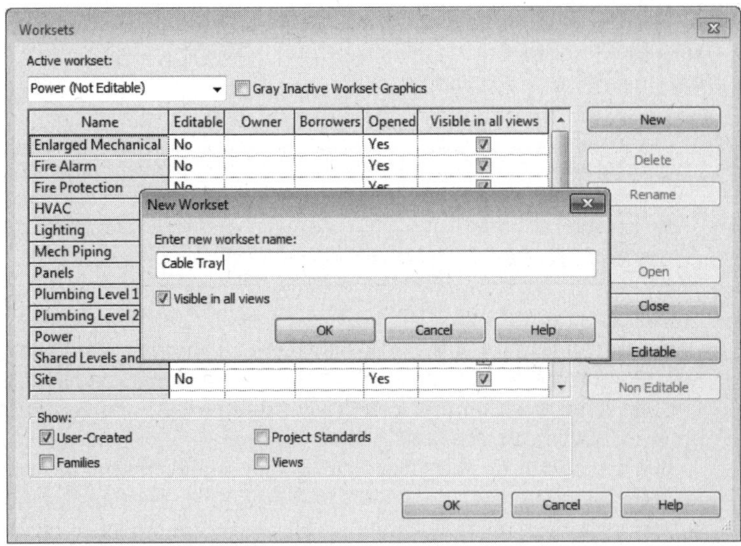

FIGURE 4.1 New Workset dialog box

LOADED LINKS

When you do not open the workset of a linked file, the link will show as Not Loaded in the Manage Links dialog box and in the Project Browser.

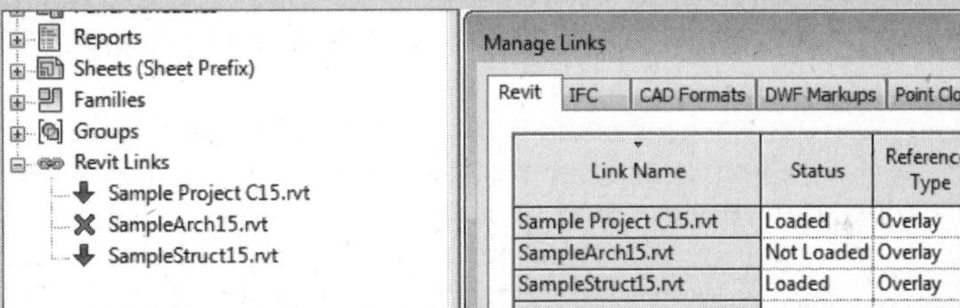

If you open the workset for the linked file, the link will be reloaded. If you close the workset of a linked file, the Project Browser will show it as unloaded, but the Manage Links dialog box will indicate that it is loaded.

The makeup of your Revit project template file has a lot to do with the preparation for sharing your file with others. Consider carefully the content that you put into your template. It is tempting to dump your whole family library into the template in order to have everything right at your fingertips, but this makes for large files that are not as easily shared. Once you have worked on a few projects, you will be able to determine what is really necessary to have in your template file.

There is no denying that Revit files can get to be very large. Purging any unused items from your files prior to sharing them is helpful in keeping file sizes to a minimum, but you should use this feature with caution.

PURGE WISELY!

Do not use the Purge Unused feature in Revit when you are working in a template file. After all, nearly everything in a template file is "unused."

Because of the size of the files, sharing them among consultants via email is not a recommended practice. Most people do not have the capacity to receive large files via email. Using an FTP site is the most common practice for file sharing. Also, certain third-party applications are designed specifically for project collaboration.

It is usually the primary design team that establishes the file sharing means and gives all teams access to upload and download files. Each consultant should have at least one designated person to manage the transfer of files for their team. This person should be responsible for making sure that the most current files have been shared. The frequency of updated files being posted to the site should be determined early on during a project kickoff meeting (you *are* having those, right?) and can be changed depending on the needs of the project. At a minimum, you should prepare to post your files once a week during active development. This will keep your consultants up to date with the progress of your design.

If you have enabled worksharing on your project, it is important that you send your *central file* to your consultants, not a local file. This ensures that they are receiving a file with updated information from all your team members. Consider a workflow that includes having all team members synchronize with the central file and then creating a new project file by using the Detach From Central option.

You also have the option in Revit MEP to remove worksets. Your consultants will, of course, be able to do this for themselves. But remember, if you have used worksets to control object visibility, the settings will be destroyed if worksets are removed. Of course, you gave the consultants *that* information at the project kickoff meeting, didn't you?

Working with Linked Revit Files

Revit MEP not only gives you the power to model and document your design but also enables you to coordinate with the designs of your consultants directly in your project file. This concept is not new to the world of digital documentation. It is the same workflow that occurs in 2D CAD: you receive a file from your consultant, overlay it into your file, and watch as it updates during the changes to the design.

The difference with Revit is in how much more you are able to coordinate by receiving a model that is not only a graphical representation but also a database with computable information. Some of the terminology is different when working with Revit. Instead of external references (*X-refs*), we call the files that are loaded into our project *linked files*. The following sections cover some best practices for loading, managing, and viewing links that are Revit RVT files.

Later in this chapter, and again in Chapter 5, "Multiplatform Interoperability: Working with 2D and 3D Data," you will learn about files of other CAD formats.

Linking Revit Files

When you are ready to bring a Revit file from a consultant into your file, you may want to first do some maintenance on that file. Copy the file you have received to your network. If the file you are receiving is a central file, you should open the file by using the Detach From Central option, as shown in Figure 4.2.

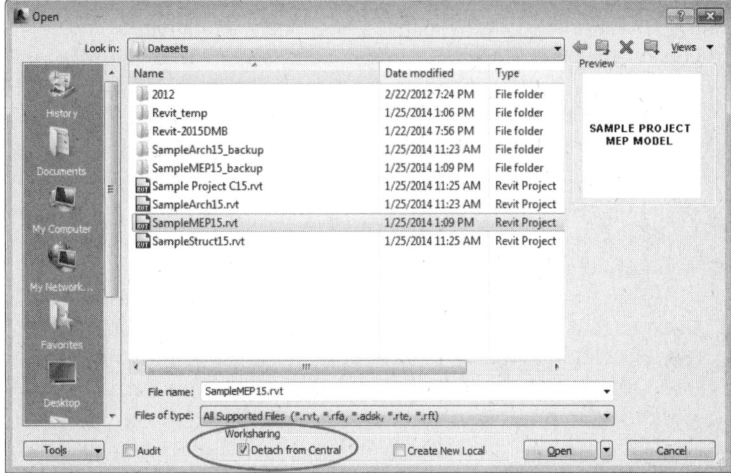

FIGURE 4.2 Using the Detach From Central option

As mentioned earlier, you have the ability to remove worksharing from a project file when using the Detach From Central option. The dialog box shown in Figure 4.3 provides options for preserving worksets or removing them from the file.

Detach Model from Central

Detaching this model will create an independent model. You will be unable to synchronize your changes with the original central model.
What do you want to do?

Detach and preserve worksets
You can later save the detached model as a new central model.

Detach and discard worksets
Discards the original workset information, including workset visibility. You can later create new worksets or save the detached model with no worksets.

Cancel

FIGURE 4.3 Detach Model From Central dialog box

Use caution when removing worksets from a file because this action affects the visibility and display of many types of elements. When you are using a consultant's model, this may be less important if you are concerned only with having that model linked into yours. Preserving the worksets, however, may make it easier for you to control the visibility of systems or specific components within the linked file. You may consider purging unused content and deleting views from a linked file to reduce file size; however, you will have to repeat the process each time you receive an updated version of the file.

When you open a file with the Detach From Central option selected, the file becomes a temporary project file stored in your computer's RAM. You are the owner of all the worksets in the file if you have chosen the option to preserve worksets. Once the file is open, you can save it to the location from which you will load it by using the Save As command. Using the same location as your project file will make it easier to manage all your linked files. If the filename does not suit your standards, you can give it any name you want. However, the location and the filename that you choose should remain the same throughout the life of the project. It is best to avoid overwriting a file with the same name by using Save As, so when you download the file and put it on your network, you may want to rename it prior to opening it. You should also avoid downloading it directly to the directory in which the working linked file resides, especially if you are not changing the filename. You do not want to overwrite the linked file before you get a chance to clean it up.

You then need to relinquish your ownership of all the worksets and save the file again. This ensures that the file you have received from your consultant is not attempting to coordinate with local files from another network. If the file you are linking is not a central file, you do not need to open it because there will be no worksets or local files associated with it, unless you are opening it to purge items and clean up views.

There is no need to keep an archive of all the files being sent to you. Revit files can be very large, so keeping an archive will quickly use up storage space. When worksharing has been enabled in a file, Revit keeps a backup log of the file. The Restore Backup button on the Collaborate tab allows you to roll back changes to the file. So if you require a previous version of your consultant's model, you could ask that consultant to save a rolled-back version of the file and send it to you. If you would like to keep archived versions of the project, it is best to use media such as a CD or DVD to save storage space on your network or hard drive.

Once the maintenance has been done on your consultant's file, you are ready to link it into your file. The first thing to do when bringing any type of file into your project is to make sure you have the appropriate workset active (if you have enabled worksharing). In a project file with multiple MEP disciplines, every discipline will need to use the architectural model for background and coordination, so you should place it on a workset that is common to all users. The Shared Levels and Grids workset is a good option if you have not created worksets specifically for linked files. This workset can be visible in all views without causing too much extra work to control the visibility of other elements within the workset. Let's first take a look at linking in the architectural model. Here are the steps:

1. With the appropriate workset active, click the Link Revit button on the Insert tab. Browse to the location of the file you saved after receiving it from your consultant. The position of the linked file is crucial to coordination, so before you click Open, you must determine the positioning of the file by using the Positioning drop-down menu at the bottom of the Import/Link RVT dialog box. Figure 4.4 shows the six options for placing the linked file into your project.

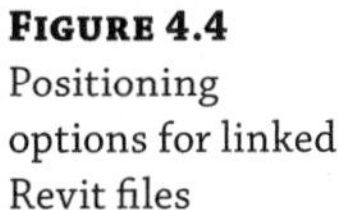

FIGURE 4.4
Positioning options for linked Revit files

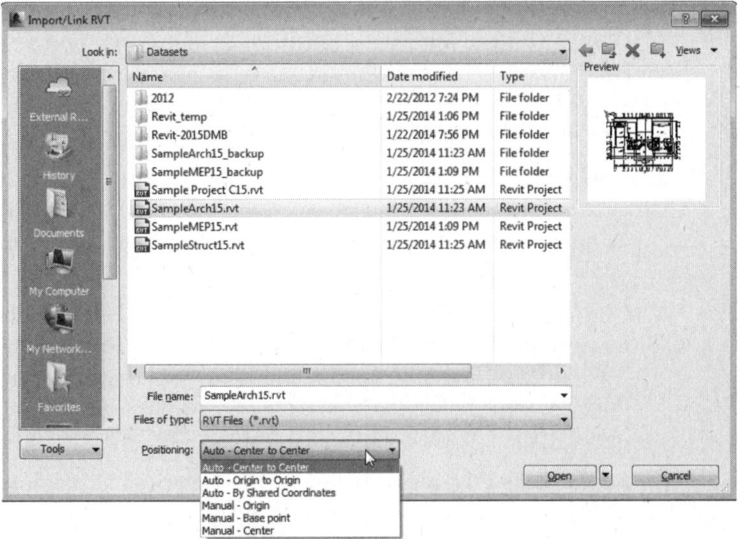

The three Manual options allow you to place the model into your file manually by using an insertion point from the origin, the center, or a specified base point of the file you are linking. These options are rarely used because they require you to locate the model manually, which can be difficult without a common reference point in both files.

The automatic options are more commonly used, and each has a specific function:

Auto – Center To Center This option links the file from its center point to the center point of your file. The center point is determined by the location of the model objects within the file. This option should be avoided unless you and your consultants have a coordinated center point and the makeup of the model will prevent that point from changing.

Auto – Origin To Origin This is the best option to use unless a shared coordinate system is required. The origin of the linked file will not change if the model changes size or shape, or even if building geometry is moved or rotated, so you will be able to stay coordinated with the building when major position changes occur.

Auto – By Shared Coordinates This option should be used when a project requires that common location coordinates be used. This is most commonly used on projects that have multiple buildings because it enables you to keep the relationship between buildings coordinated. If you link in a file that is using shared coordinates, you can use the same coordinates for your file.

Be careful when linking in a Revit file because the Auto – Center To Center option is the default. Forgetting to change the option could result in a serious headache further along in the project, because we know that architects *never* relocate the building, right? Make it a habit to use the Auto – Origin To Origin option, unless shared coordinates are required.

2. Once you have chosen a positioning option, you can choose options for loading worksets, similar to when you open a file that contains worksets. Just click the pull-down menu next to the Open button. You can open all the worksets or specify which ones you want. If you specify worksets to be open, they are the only ones whose components will be visible when the file is loaded.
3. Click the Open button to link the file into your project. The linked model file then appears in your file at the location determined by your Positioning option. If you selected a Manual option, you will need to click a position in the view window to place the linked model.
4. Once the linked model is in the proper position, you want it to stay there, so before you do anything with the linked model, it is a good idea to pin it in place. This will prevent users from accidentally moving the whole building when clicking and dragging items during design. Select the linked model, and click the Pin button that appears on the Modify panel of the Modify | RVT Links tab.
5. Repeat steps 1 through 4 for all the files you need to link into your project. Once you have all your Revit links in place, synchronize your file with the central file, or if your file is not using worksharing, simply save it.

Using Shared Coordinates

Using shared coordinates is a useful way to keep several linked files in the proper location and orientation within your project file. The key to using shared coordinates is establishing which file will determine the coordinate system. Every Revit project has two coordinate systems. One determines the project coordinates, while the other defines the real-world coordinates.

The Project Base Point of a project can be viewed by turning on its visibility, which is located under Site in the Model Categories tab of the Visibility/Graphic Overrides dialog box (see Figure 4.5). Site is an architectural category, so you must set the filter list to view Architectural categories.

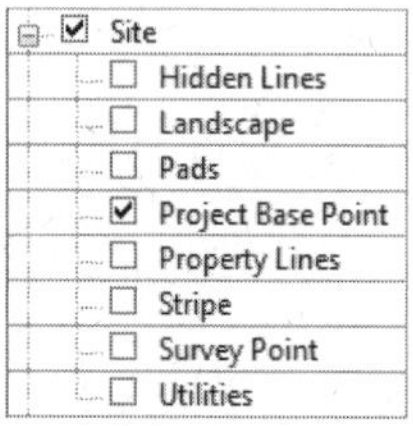

FIGURE 4.5 Project Base Point visibility settings

- ☑ Site
  - ☐ Hidden Lines
  - ☐ Landscape
  - ☐ Pads
  - ☑ Project Base Point
  - ☐ Property Lines
  - ☐ Stripe
  - ☐ Survey Point
  - ☐ Utilities

When you select the Project Base Point indicator in a view, you see the coordinates established for the Revit project. The N/S, E/W, and Elevation coordinates can all be set by selecting and editing the value along with the angle of the project relative to True North, as shown in Figure 4.6.

The paper clip icon allows you to move the entire project or to move only the Project Base Point location. When the Project Base Point is "clipped," moving it is the same as using the Relocate Project tool. This does not affect the model as it relates to the project coordinates, but if you are using shared coordinates to align with linked files, it will cause you to be out of alignment.

FIGURE 4.6
Editing a Project Base Point

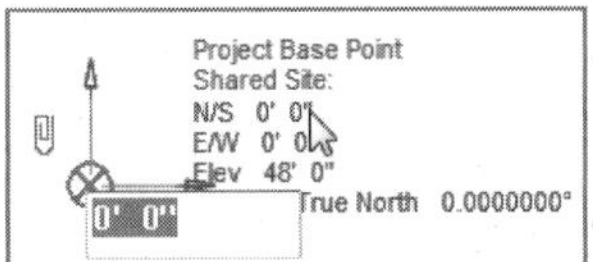

Moving the Project Base Point when it is "unclipped" causes the project coordinate system to move in relation to the model. This changes the shared coordinates of the Project Base Point. However, the shared coordinates of the model components do not change.

One way to use this tool for effective project coordination is to set the Project Base Point in your template to **0,0,0**, which is the default location in the project templates provided with the software. If all consultants utilize these settings, it will be easier to keep the models in alignment.

You also have the option to acquire the coordinates of a linked file. Use the Coordinates tool on the Project Location panel of the Manage tab, and select the Acquire Coordinates option. This allows you to select a linked file in the drawing area and sets your project coordinates to match those of the linked file. Figure 4.7 shows (left) the settings for a project prior to acquiring coordinates and (right) the settings after the coordinates of the linked model are acquired. This ensures that both files are working off of the same coordinate system. Notice that the Project Base Point is in the same location in relation to the building geometry.

FIGURE 4.7
Settings before acquiring coordinates (left) and after acquiring coordinates (right)

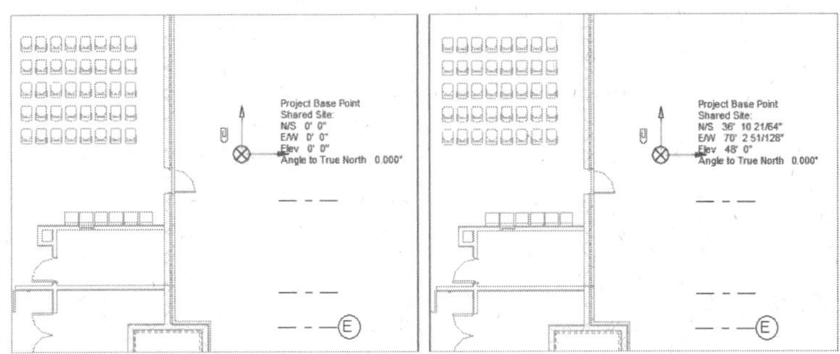

The *survey point* of a project can be used to define a real-world coordinate point within a project. The survey point can be made visible by using the Visibility/Graphic Overrides dialog box, as shown in Figure 4.8.

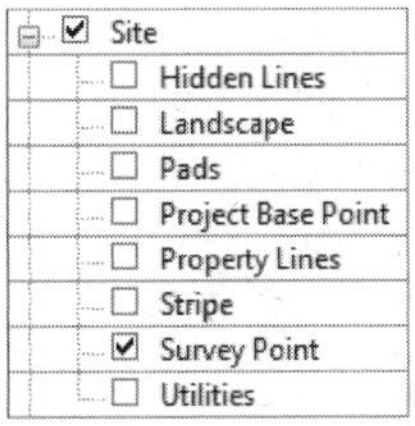

FIGURE 4.8
Survey Point visibility settings

- ☑ Site
  - ☐ Hidden Lines
  - ☐ Landscape
  - ☐ Pads
  - ☐ Project Base Point
  - ☐ Property Lines
  - ☐ Stripe
  - ☑ Survey Point
  - ☐ Utilities

The survey point shows as a triangle in the view. Moving a "clipped" survey point changes the position of the shared coordinate system in relation to the model and the project coordinate system. So, for example, if you have your survey point set to 0,0,0 and you move it, you are changing where 0,0,0 is located in your project. This will affect the location of your model components in relation to a linked file with which you are sharing coordinates.

Moving an "unclipped" survey point moves the point in relation to the shared coordinate and project coordinate systems. This does not change the shared or project coordinates of the model. It simply changes the location of the survey point. This allows you to move it to a location established by a linked file without changing the shared coordinates.

Managing Revit Links

Throughout the design process, you will want to keep up with the many changes occurring in the files you have linked into your project. Revit does not always automatically update your file with changes made in the linked files. The only time updates occur automatically is when you open your project file after the linked files have been updated. If you are in a working session of Revit and one of your linked files is updated, you will have to reload the link manually to see the update.

Updating files from your consultants requires the same process you used when you first received the files, except you do not have to insert them into your file again. Download the new file from your consultant, and apply the maintenance procedures discussed in the previous section. Be sure that you overwrite the existing file with the new one and avoid changing the name.

After you have updated the files in your project folder, you can open your project file. If you are working in a local file, you should synchronize it with the central file as soon as it is finished opening. This will ensure that the central file contains the updated linked file information.

Sometimes new versions of the files you are linking become available while you are working in your project file. If another user has updated the linked files and synchronized them with the central file, you will not see the updated links even when you synchronize with the central file. You will need to reload the links also. The same is not true for unloading links, however. If you unload a link and then synchronize with central, all other users will see the change when they synchronize.

COMMUNICATION

Working with Revit should increase the amount of communication between design team members. If you update a linked file, let your team members know. You can do this by creating a view in your project that is used by everyone, placing notices in that view, and then setting that view as the starting view for the project. This way, when someone opens the project, that person can immediately read what needs to happen next to be totally up-to-date.

To reload a linked Revit file, click the Manage Links button on the Manage tab. This opens the Manage Links dialog box, which enables you to manage the files you have loaded into your project (see Figure 4.9).

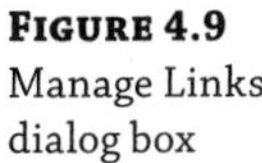

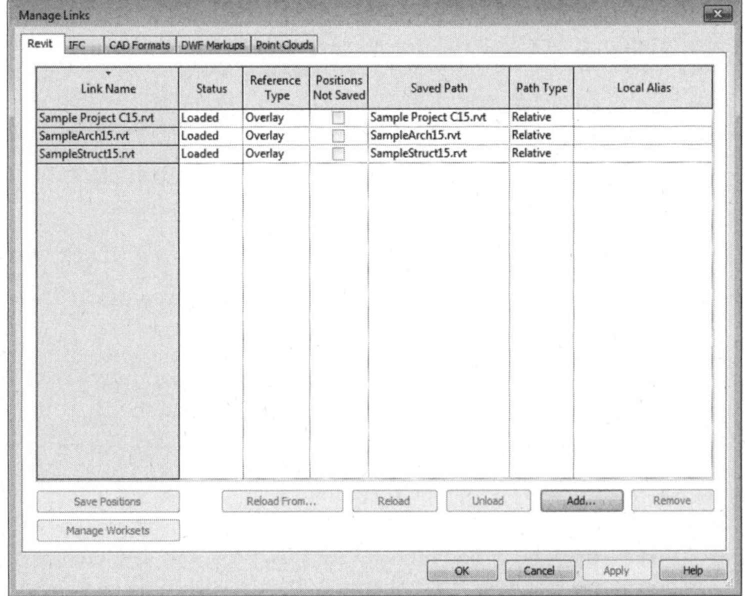

FIGURE 4.9
Manage Links dialog box

The Revit tab of the Manage Links dialog box lists all the Revit files linked into your file. Here, you can determine whether the file is an attachment or an overlay. This is the same behavior found in external references in the Autodesk® AutoCAD® platform. An *attachment* will need to travel with the file, while an *overlay* is only for the file to which it is linked. If a file you are linking in has other Revit files linked to it as overlays, you will see a dialog box indicating that the overlaid files will not link into your file when you load or reload the link. This allows you to have the architectural file linked into your file, and your file linked into the architectural file, without duplicating either model. In other words, your file does not come back to you when you link in the architectural file. The default setting for linking files is Overlay, because this is the best choice.

The Save Positions button in the lower-left corner of the dialog box is used when your project is using shared coordinates. If you move a link within your project, you will receive a warning dialog box with options for saving the new location, or you can use the Save Positions button.

Other buttons allow you to unload, reload, and remove links from your file. Once a link is removed, you cannot get it back by using the Undo feature; you will have to load the link back into your project. The Reload From button allows you to reload a link that may have moved to a new location on your network. You can even reload a different file altogether.

You can also use the Project Browser to manage the files linked into your project. All linked Revit files are listed at the bottom of the Project Browser. Right-clicking a link in the Project Browser provides a menu with quick access to link-management tools, as shown in Figure 4.10.

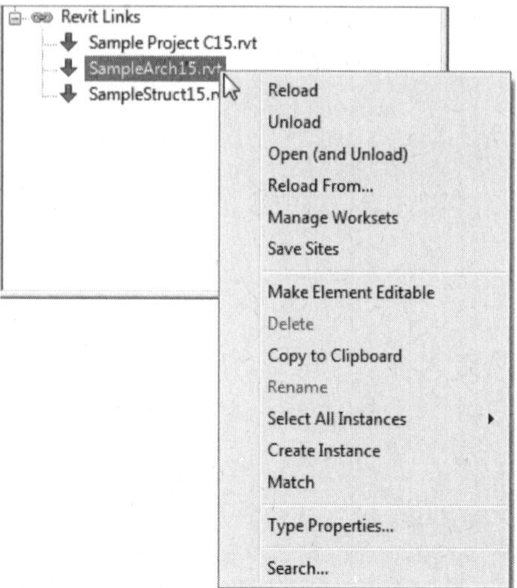

FIGURE 4.10 Quick access to link-management tools from the Project Browser

Notice that one option is Select All Instances. You can have multiple instances of a linked file in your project by selecting the link in the drawing area and copying it.

Controlling Visibility of Revit Links

When a Revit file is linked into your project, it is treated as one element—a linked model. Linking in the architectural model does not mean that you now have walls, doors, and windows in your project model. The model is seen as a single linked file. You do, however, have control over the visibility of the individual components that make up the linked model as well as the entire link itself.

When you link in a Revit file, a new tab appears in the Visibility/Graphic Overrides dialog box. This tab lists the linked Revit files and allows you to turn them on or off. If you have multiple copies of a link, they are listed beneath the name of the link, as seen when you click the + next to the link name. Each copy can be given a unique name for easy management. There is also a check box for setting the link to halftone. (This is not necessary for views set to mechanical, plumbing, or electrical disciplines because Revit automatically applies halftone to the architectural and structural elements in these discipline views.) This tab is useful for turning links on or off in views as needed during design, and the settings can even be applied to view templates. The Underlay column allows you to display the linked file as defined by the Halftone/Underlay settings established for the project.

You can also control the visibility of components within the linked Revit file. By default, the components in the Revit link will react to the settings for visibility that you apply to your view. So, if you were to turn off the Doors category in your view, the doors in the Revit link will also turn off in that view. The same is true for any overrides you may apply for line weight or color. Figure 4.11 shows that this behavior is indicated in the Visibility/Graphic Overrides dialog box as By Host View.

Clicking the By Host View button for a link opens the RVT Link Display Settings dialog box. This is similar to the Visibility/Graphic Overrides dialog box, but it is specific to the selected Revit link. The first tab of this dialog box allows you to set the visibility of the link. You can set the link to By Host View, By Linked View, or Custom.

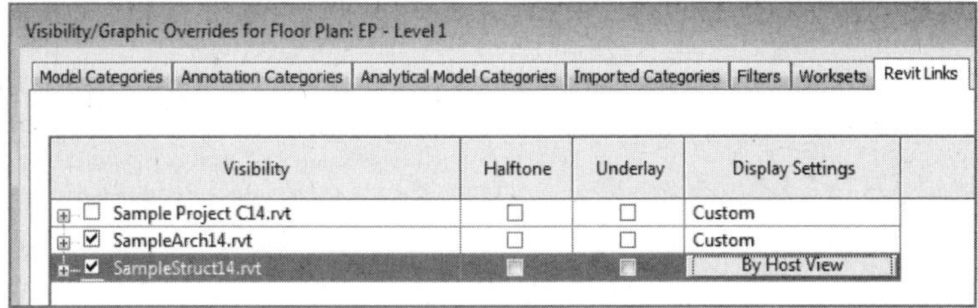

FIGURE 4.11 Linked Revit file Display Settings options

If you choose By Linked View, the option to select a view from the Revit link becomes active. Choosing a view from the linked project will set the link to be displayed in your view with all the settings from the view that resides in the linked file. You do not have access to the views contained in a linked file, but you can set the link to display in your file the same way as it appears in those views. This means that the link will display as set in that view despite any visibility settings in the host view. For example, in Figure 4.12, you see a view with the grids turned off in the host view, yet they are displayed because the linked file is set to display from a linked view where grids are displayed.

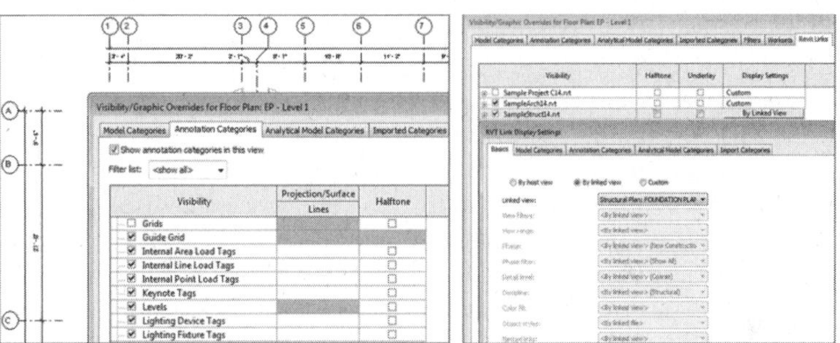

FIGURE 4.12 Example of linked file view settings showing the Grids category turned off in the host view (left) and By Linked View selected for the structural link (right)

It is not likely that your consultants will have set all of their views in a manner that matches your preferences for seeing the link, so you also have the Custom option for visibility. Selecting Custom activates all the setting options on the Basics tab of the RVT Link Display Settings dialog box. With this option, you not only can choose a linked view, you can also determine other behaviors for the display of the link. You do not have to choose a linked view if you want to control the visibility of only certain components. The Custom option is the same as accessing the Visibility/Graphic Overrides dialog box, but for the link only. Once you have selected Custom, you can use the other tabs in the dialog box to set the visibility of the components within the link. When you select a tab, the items are grayed out. You must set that specific category to Custom, as well, by using the pull-down at the top of the tab, as shown in Figure 4.13.

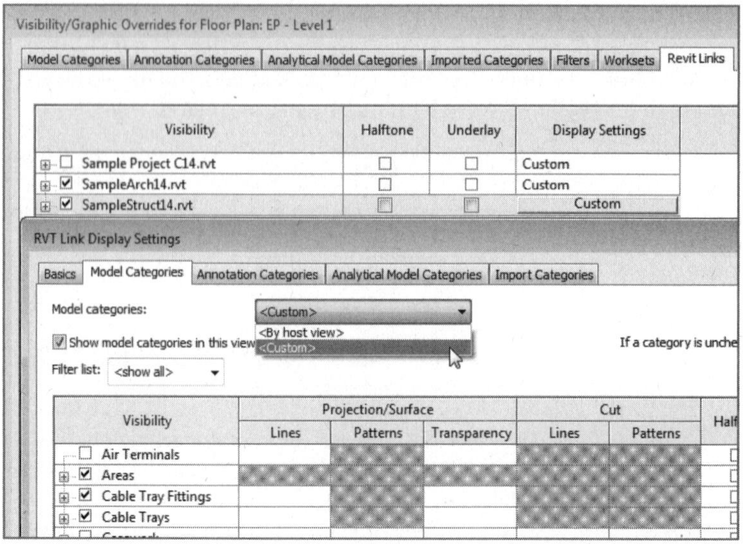

FIGURE 4.13
Setting a model category within a linked file to Custom

After setting a category to Custom, you can control the visibility of any Revit model category within the linked file. You can control elements in the Model categories as well as the Annotation categories and any Import items such as linked CAD files. Figure 4.14 (top) shows that the Grids category is displayed because the linked structural file is set to display by a linked view, even though the Grids category is turned off for the host view. A better solution might be to set the structural link to a Custom display and turn off all annotation categories except for Grids, as demonstrated in Figure 4.14 (bottom). Doing this will automatically keep the structural link as a halftone and will display only the items you want to see in your view.

In this example, the Custom option allows for the display of grids without displaying other structural annotations, such as dimensions.

You can also control the visibility of worksets within a linked Revit file. If you choose not to make your worksets visible in all views within your project, your consultants will have to turn on the visibility of the workset when your file is linked into their project file. The visibility of a workset can be turned on or off by accessing the linked Revit file in the Visibility/Graphic Overrides dialog box. Clicking the button in the Display Settings column for the linked file opens the RVT Link Display Settings dialog box. This dialog box has a tab for controlling the visibility of worksets, as shown in Figure 4.15. Setting the display to Custom allows you to turn on or off the visibility of any worksets within the linked file.

The output of Revit documents can vary depending on the type of printer you use. The most common issue is that the automatically halftone-linked files do not print darkly enough. Revit enables you to control how dark the linked files appear and print. You can find the Halftone/Underlay settings on the Additional Settings menu located on the Manage tab, as shown in Figure 4.16.

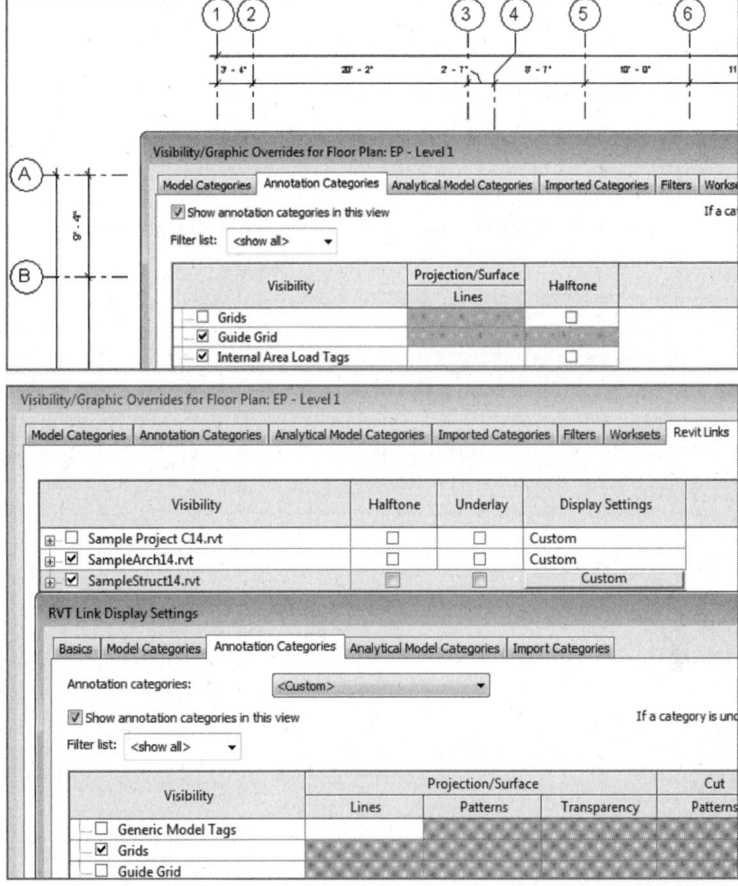

FIGURE 4.14 Grids turned off in the view (top); the structural link set to Custom and displaying only the Grids category (bottom)

FIGURE 4.15 Visibility control of worksets within a linked file

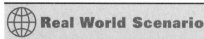

Linked Files for Project Templates

Mike has been tasked with creating his company project template. He works for an HVAC design firm and has to link the architectural and structural models whenever the company does a project. His various consultants do things differently, but there are some common settings he would like to add to his template to improve efficiency. Because every project is different, he cannot have linked models in his template file. Or can he?

Mike decides to link some dummy files into his template to act as placeholders for the actual models he will receive from his consultants. He creates a file called `Arch.rvt` and one called `Struct.rvt` and links them into his template. The files are empty, so they do not add a lot of bulk to his template, but they do give him the ability to create visibility settings for linked files in his view templates.

When Mike uses his template to start a project, he can overwrite his placeholder links with the actual models received from his consultants by using the Reload From option in the Manage Links dialog box, and all of his view settings will remain.

Figure 4.16
Halftone/
Underlay settings

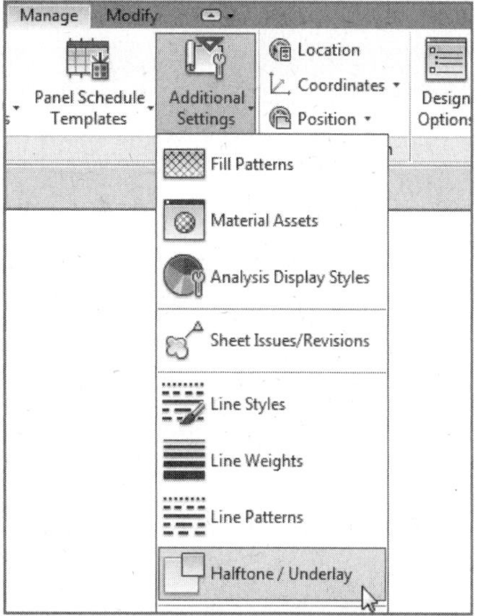

In the Halftone/Underlay dialog box, you can turn off the automatic halftone of linked architectural and structural files by deselecting the Apply Halftone check box. You can also override the line weight of a background Revit link. If you are using an underlay in your view, you can change the line pattern to any of the patterns you have loaded in your project. Figure 4.17 shows the Halftone/Underlay dialog box with sample settings applied.

The Brightness slider on the bottom half of the dialog box lets you manually adjust the percentage of halftone applied to all halftone items in the view, both linked items and those in your model. Notice that only the elements within the link that are halftone are affected. The plumbing fixtures are part of the linked architectural model, but because they are not an architectural or structural category, they are not affected by the adjustment. The settings that you use apply to the entire project, so you need to set them only once. This is a helpful tool for getting your documents to print properly.

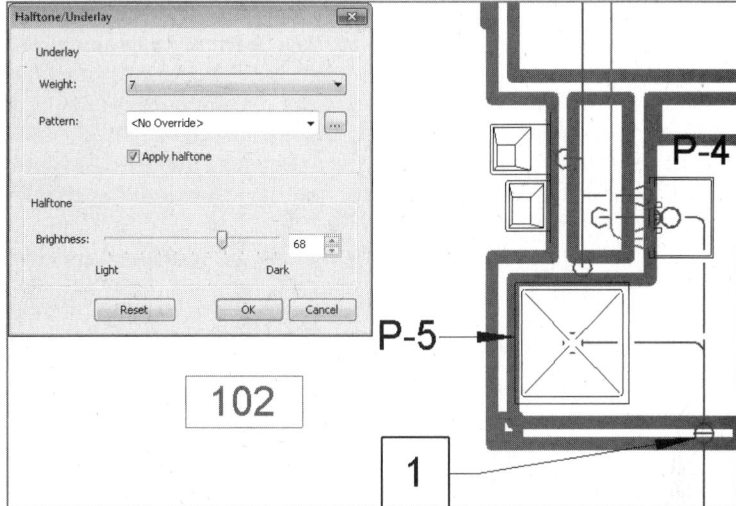

Figure 4.17 Halftone/Underlay sample settings applied

> **Printing Options for Halftone**
>
> You can use the Replace Halftone With Thin Lines option in the Print Settings dialog box if you choose not to adjust the halftone settings in your model but still want darker backgrounds.

Coordinating Elements within Shared Models

One of the key benefits of using a BIM solution such as Revit MEP is that you can see changes in the design more readily, because you see more of the other disciplines' work than you would in a traditional workflow. The ease of cutting section views and inspecting the model in 3D allows you to notice what is going on, not only with your design but also with the project as a whole. You may not have time to look over the model inch by inch, though, so there are some items that you can monitor to see whether the design changes in a way that affects your systems.

Monitoring Elements

Revit gives you the capability to monitor certain elements within a linked file in order to be made aware of any changes. This functionality is limited to a few categories because, after all, you wouldn't want to know every time the architect moved a chair or changed the color of a door. The types of components that can be monitored are items that, if changed, could have a major effect on your design, especially late in the game. The architectural categories that can be monitored for coordination are Levels, Grids, Columns, Walls, and Floors. These items are often hosts for components in your model, so being aware of changes to them provides you with a higher level of coordination.

The Copy/Monitor function in Revit not only lets you monitor an element of a linked file but also allows you to create a copy of that element within your file. The use of face-hosted elements eliminates the need to copy items just so that you can have something as a host. There are items, however, that are important to coordinate, such as levels and grids.

Your template file may contain levels in order to have preset views, but your levels will not likely be the same on every project. After pinning a linked file in place, the next thing you should get into the habit of doing is monitoring the levels. This mainly applies to the architectural link, because architects are the ones who will determine floor-to-floor heights. If your file has fewer levels than the linked file, you can copy the additional levels, and they will then be monitored automatically.

To coordinate with the levels in the linked file, follow these steps:

1. Open an elevation or section view of the model to see the level locations.
2. Align your levels to the levels in the linked file.
3. Set your levels to monitor the levels in the link by clicking the Copy/Monitor button on the Collaborate tab. Your two options for monitoring are selecting items in your file and selecting a link.
4. Click the Select Link option, and click the link in your view. The ribbon changes to display tools for Copy/Monitor.
5. There is no need to copy levels that already exist in your file, but you will want to modify them to match the name and elevation of the levels in the linked file. If you are prompted to rename corresponding views when changing a level's name, it is best to choose not to. Otherwise, the names of your views may not be correct according to your standards. If you do not change the level names, then your levels will monitor the linked levels relative to their location. Figure 4.18 shows an example of project levels and linked file levels.
6. Click the Monitor button on the Tools panel, and select the level you want to coordinate with the linked level.
7. Select the linked level that you want to monitor.
8. Repeat steps 5 and 6 for each level that you have in your file. If there is a level in the link that does not exist in your file, you can use the Copy button to create a monitored copy of the level.

It is not necessary to monitor all levels because your consultant's file may contain levels for use as coordination points rather than for view creation. Only monitor levels for which you need to create views or to which you need to associate your model components, as shown in Figure 4.19.

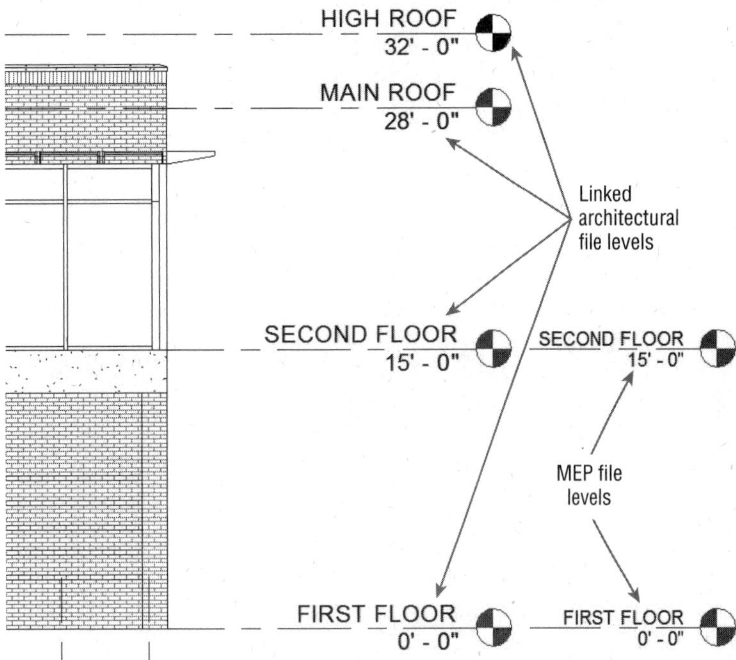

Figure 4.18 Project levels and linked file levels

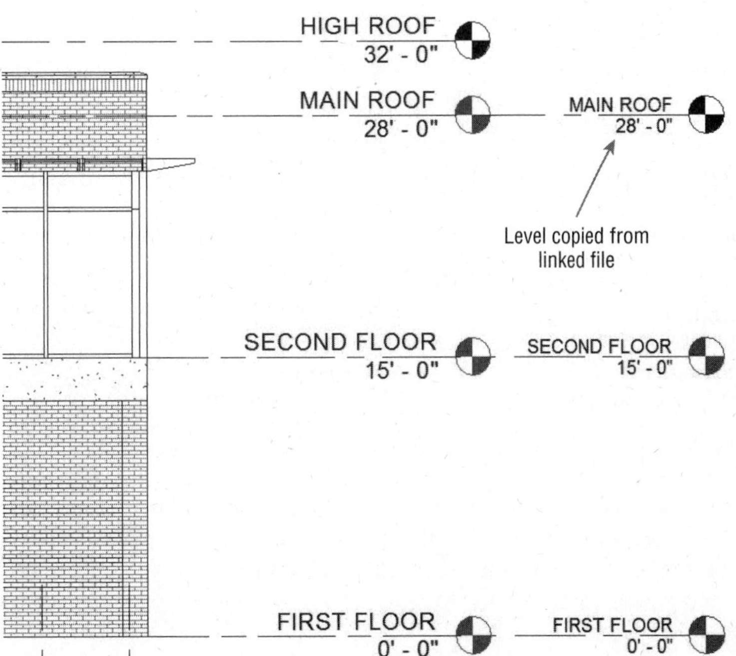

Figure 4.19 Using Copy/Monitor for levels

When you use the Copy button in the Copy/Monitor function, the copied element will automatically monitor the object from which it was copied, so there is no need to repeat the monitor process after copying an item.

9. After you have finished coordinating your levels to the levels within the linked file, click the Finish button on the Copy/Monitor tab. You can now create views for any additional levels you may have added.

You also have the ability to copy/monitor certain MEP elements within a linked file. Clicking the Coordination Settings button on the Coordinate panel of the Collaborate tab opens the dialog box for establishing how MEP elements will be copied from a linked file into your project. Figure 4.20 shows the dialog box. These settings are specific to the current project.

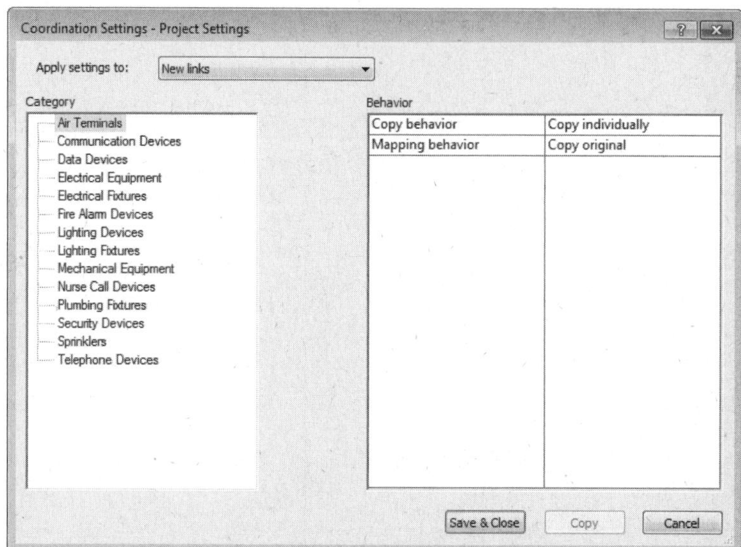

FIGURE 4.20 Coordination Settings dialog box

You can apply the settings to any of the linked files within your project by using the drop-down at the top of the dialog box, shown in Figure 4.21.

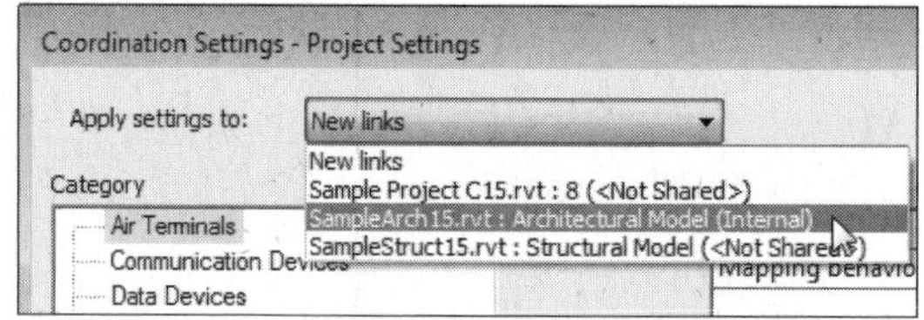

FIGURE 4.21 Apply Copy/Monitor settings

There are three choices for the Copy Behavior setting of each category, as shown in Figure 4.22. Items can be batch copied, which will allow for multiple elements of the category to be copied. Items can be copied individually, or you can choose to ignore a category.

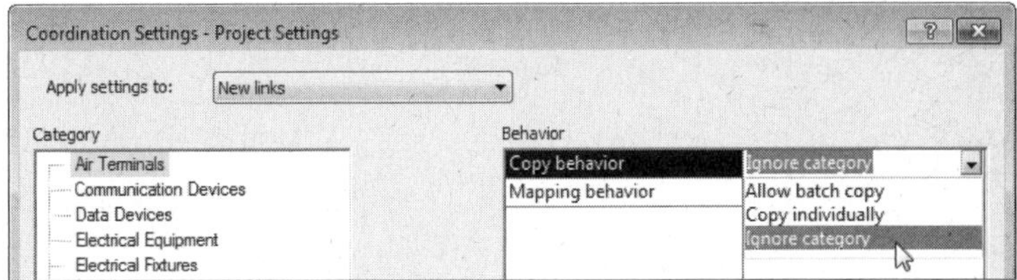

FIGURE 4.22 Copy/Monitor behavior settings

If you are applying settings for new links, the Mapping Behavior setting, shown in Figure 4.23, is set to copy the original components by default. If you have selected a specific linked file, you can set the mapping behavior for a category as long as the category is not set to be ignored.

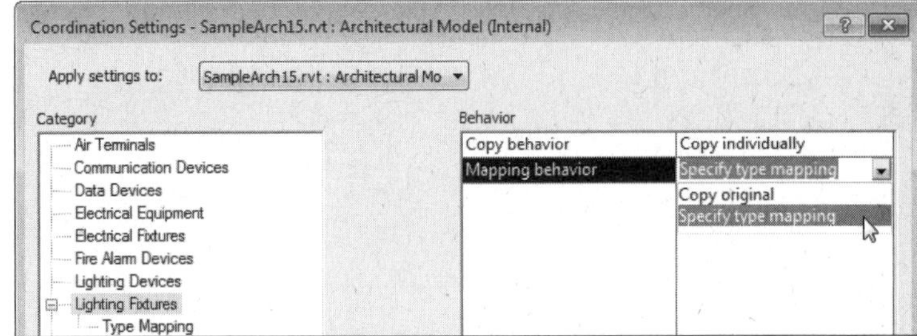

FIGURE 4.23 Copy/Monitor mapping options

When you choose the Specify Type Mapping option, the Type Mapping settings appear beneath the category in the list at the left of the dialog box. When you click the Type Mapping option below the category, the dialog box changes to show the items in that category that are in the linked file and a column for defining what family within your project to use, as shown in Figure 4.24. Be sure to map to a family that has the same insertion point and hosting option. Families with different insertion points will cause undesired results when mapped. You cannot map a ceiling-hosted family to a face-hosted family.

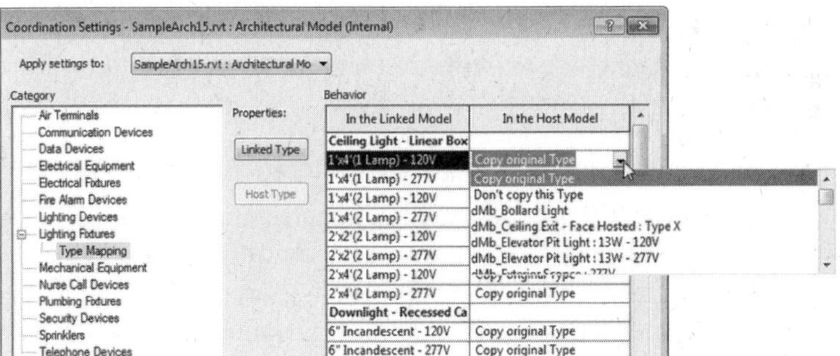

FIGURE 4.24 Type mapping options

The Linked Type and Host Type buttons allow you to view the Type Properties dialog box for the selected families. You cannot make changes to the properties, but you can see them in order to determine the right families to use, as shown in Figure 4.25.

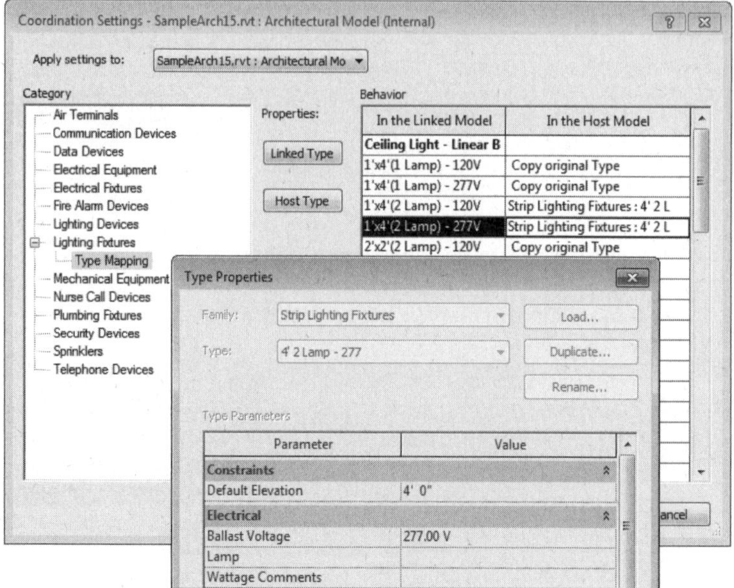

FIGURE 4.25 Type properties shown in the Coordination Settings dialog box

The main purpose for monitoring items is to be alerted when a change has been made to them. This is done by the Coordination Review feature within Revit. When you update your linked files, if there is a change to an item that you are monitoring, a warning will appear during the loading of the link. This warning lets you know that a Coordination Review needs to be executed. You can ignore this message, but just because you can, *should you*? Who will do the coordination review? This should be part of one team member's role in the project.

Responding to Change Alerts

To perform a coordination review, you can click the Coordination Review button on the Collaborate tab. The command is also on the Modify | RVT Links tab that appears when you select a link that has monitored elements in the view window. The dialog box that appears contains a list of the issues that require coordination, as shown in Figure 4.26. Expanding each issue will reveal the specific elements involved.

The Action column provides four options for dealing with the coordination issue:

Postpone If you choose to postpone the action, Revit will warn you of the issue each time your file is opened or the linked file is reloaded, until another action is taken.

Reject This option should be accompanied by a description in the Comment column to the right. If a change has been made that you must reject because of design constraints or for some other reason, you can select this option. When you send your file to your consultants, they will receive a notice that a coordination review is required and will see that you rejected the change. Most likely, a change that is rejected will generate communication between team members, but adding a comment is a good way to document the action choice. Comments will be visible to other team members only when the Create Report feature is used.

Accept Difference This choice can be used when the change does not affect your design and when the effort to coordinate outweighs the benefit. For example, you may be monitoring a wall in the architectural model to see whether it moves. On the day the project is due, you receive an alert that the wall has moved 1⁄32″. You could decide that the change is insignificant enough to allow for the difference.

Modify Your Element to Match the Item It Is Monitoring In Figure 4.27, you can see the result of using the Move Level option (shown earlier in Figure 4.26) so that the level is coordinated with the linked Revit model. When this option is chosen, the change is made automatically by Revit. Select the option, and click the Apply button to see the change occur. If you are not in a view that shows the items requiring coordination, you can select one of the items in the list and click the Show button in the lower-left corner. Revit will search for a view that shows the selected item and open that view.

FIGURE 4.26
Coordination Review dialog box

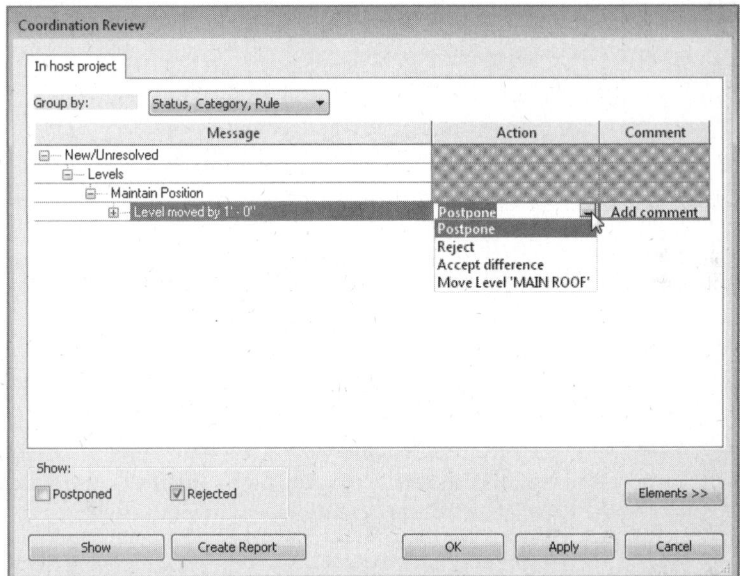

If the change made has too great of an effect on your model, you can simply undo the action and revisit the Coordination Review dialog box to select another action.

Reconciling Hosting

The use of face-hosted families allows you to attach your components to the 3D faces within a linked file. When the host of one of these types of families is deleted, the family will remain in the model, but it will no longer be associated with the linked file. This behavior can cause objects within your model to be floating in space when they should be attached to a surface. The most common reason for an element losing its host is that the host was deleted and redrawn instead of just being moved. For example, if you have some air terminals hosted by the face of a ceiling and the ceiling needs to move up, the architect may delete the ceiling and create a new one at the new elevation. This would cause your air terminals to be floating below the new ceiling.

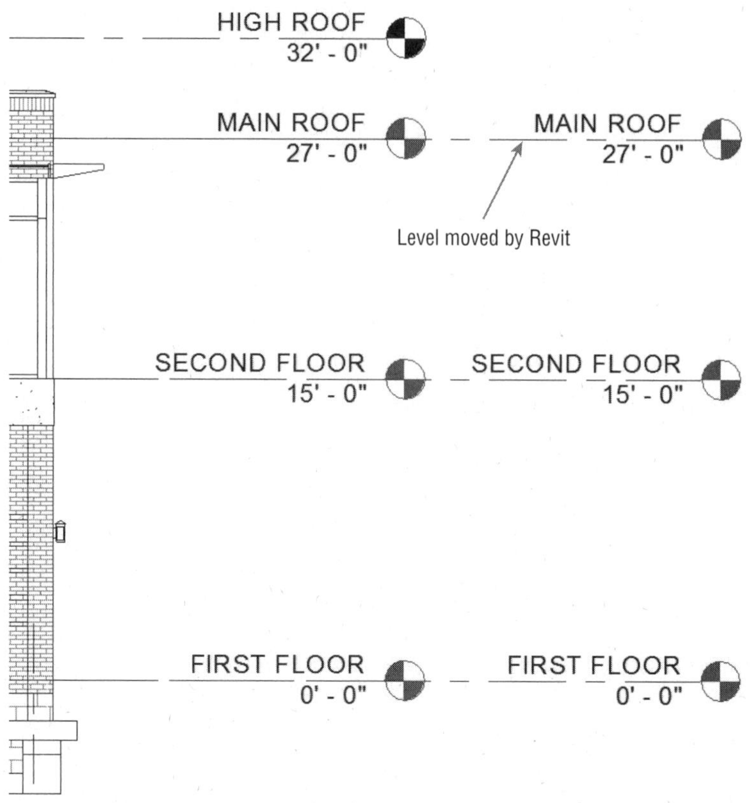

FIGURE 4.27 Level adjusted by coordination review

Revit MEP has a feature that allows you to identify and reconcile any families that have lost their host. Clicking the Reconcile Hosting button on the Coordinate panel of the Collaborate tab turns on the Reconcile Hosting palette, shown in Figure 4.28.

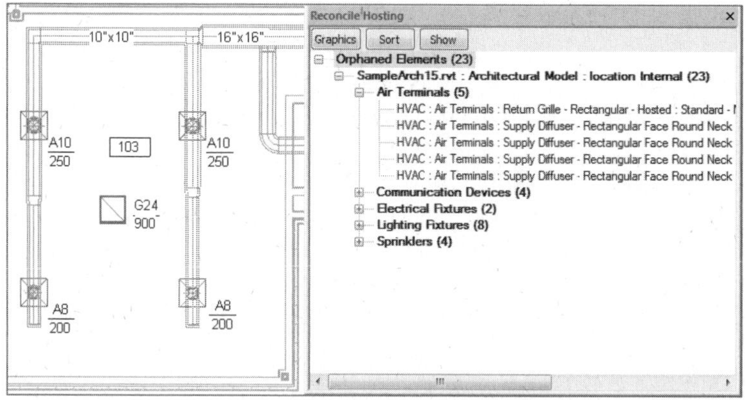

FIGURE 4.28 Reconcile Hosting palette

You can dock this palette to the interface or have it float. When the palette is active, any objects that are listed will be green in the model view. You can click the Graphics button on the palette to change the visual display of orphaned elements when the palette is active.

The Show button allows you to locate an item selected from the list if it is not readily visible in the current view. The Sort button lets you sort the list either by the linked file and then the categories or by the categories and then the linked file.

You can right-click an item listed in the palette and choose the option to delete it or choose the Pick Host option, which allows you to place the element on a new host.

Maintaining Project Coordination

Proper setup of your project file is essential for maintaining coordination throughout the life of the project. You can find an example of how to do this on this book's companion web page. Create a project file by following these steps:

1. Open the `Ch4Sample.rvt` file, which can be downloaded from `www.sybex.com/go/masteringrevitmep2015`. (Also download the `ArchModel.rvt` file.)
2. Open the MH - Level 1 floor plan view and click the Link Revit button on the Insert tab.
3. Select the `ArchModel.rvt` file, and choose the Auto – Origin To Origin positioning option. Click Open.
4. Select the linked model in the active view window, and click the Pin button on the Modify | RVT Links tab.
5. Open the North elevation view.
6. Click the Copy/Monitor button on the Collaborate tab. Click Select Link.
7. Click the linked model in the view window.
8. Click the Monitor button on the Copy/Monitor tab.
9. Click the First Floor level at the right, and then select the First Floor level of the linked model.
10. Repeat step 9 for the Roof level.
11. Click the Finish button on the Copy/Monitor tab.

Working with Files from Other Applications

Revit files are not the only type of files that you can link into your project. The Revit platform is compatible with many types of CAD formats as well. As you move into using a BIM solution for your projects, try to use CAD files as little as possible. A large number of linked CAD files in your project can cause the project file to perform poorly. Choose the files that will save you time overall on the project. The following CAD file formats can be linked into Revit:

- DWG
- DXF

- DGN
- ACIS SAT
- SketchUp

You can also insert image files and link Design Web Format (DWF) markups. There are two options for bringing non-Revit file types into your project: You can link them or import them. Linking is the preferred method, because a linked file will update as the file changes without you having to repeat the process of inserting the link. Linked CAD files will show up in the Manage Links dialog box with options for the pathing of files, reloading, and unloading. If you share your project that contains CAD links with a consultant and you do not give the consultant the CAD files, Revit will display the CAD link as it last appeared in your file.

LINKING VS. IMPORTING

Be careful when choosing to import a file rather than link it. When you import a file, the graphics are not the only thing brought into your project. All text styles, line styles, layers, dimensions, and so on are brought in as well. This can really clog up your project file and impede performance. Imported files will not update when changes are made. New versions of imported files must be put into your project manually as well.

Linking CAD Files

Because there is no Revit version for civil engineering, it is likely that you will receive the files from your civil engineering consultant in some type of CAD format. The process for linking these types of files is similar to linking a Revit file:

1. On the Insert tab, click the Link CAD button. The dialog box for linking a CAD file, shown in Figure 4.29, contains more options than the one for linking a Revit file.

   The check box in the lower-left corner provides the option for linking the file to the current view only. This will keep you from having to turn off the CAD link in any other view.

   The Colors drop-down list, shown in Figure 4.30, allows you to invert the colors of the CAD file, preserve them as they exist, or turn all the linework to black and white.

2. Determine which layers of the CAD file you want to load. This is similar to loading specific worksets of a linked Revit file. You can load all the layers within the file, you can load only those that are visible within the drawing (layers that are on and thawed), or you can specify which layers you would like to load, as shown in Figure 4.31.

   Choosing the Specify option will open a dialog box from which you can select the desired layers within the CAD file to load.

   Layers within the linked CAD file can be removed after the file is in your project by clicking the link in the view window and clicking the Delete Layers button in the Import Instance panel.

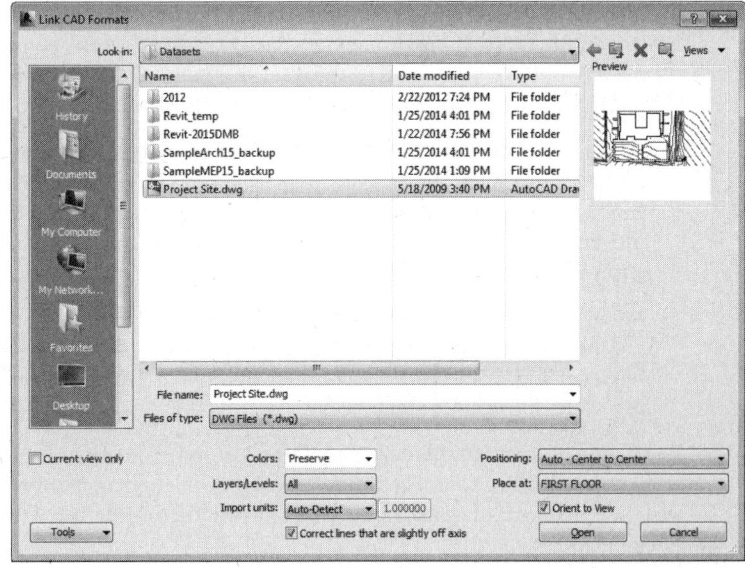

FIGURE 4.29 Link CAD Formats dialog box

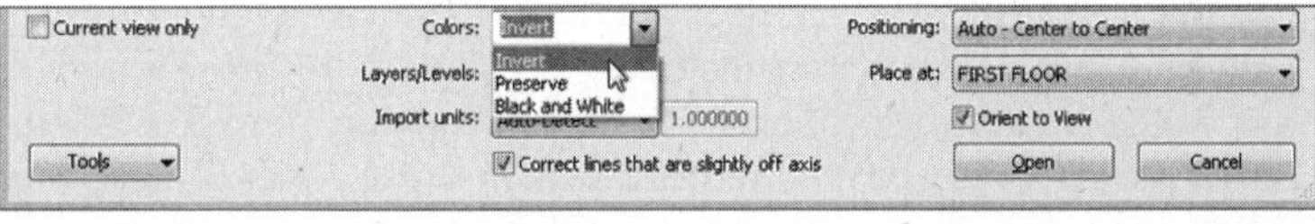

FIGURE 4.30 Color options for a linked CAD file

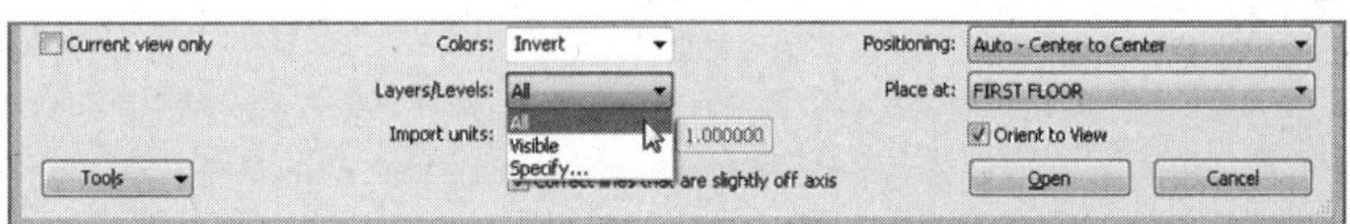

FIGURE 4.31 Layer options for a linked CAD file

3. Define the units for the file to be linked in. The Auto-Detect option, shown in Figure 4.32, causes Revit to use the unit setting that the CAD file is using. This can lead to inaccuracy if the units in the CAD file are not defined. The units can be modified in the properties of the linked CAD file after it is placed into the project.

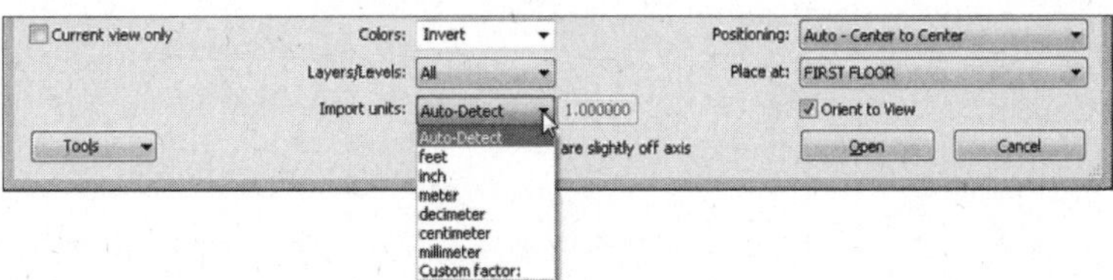

FIGURE 4.32 Import Units options for a linked CAD file

4. Position the CAD file. The positioning options for a linked CAD file are the same as for a linked Revit file. If you are using shared coordinates for your project, these coordinates need to be communicated to the civil engineering consultant in order for the site plan to align properly. If not, you can place the CAD file manually to line up the graphics.

   Typically, the architect will provide a building outline to the civil engineering consultant that will appear in the linked site plan and will handle the establishment of shared coordinates. Whatever method is chosen, be sure to pin the link in place to prevent accidental movement. The Orient To View check box in the lower-right corner will position the file appropriately, based on your view orientation, either Plan North or True North.

   If you choose to use the Import option instead of linking, the options for placing the file are the same except for the automatic orientation to your view. For the sake of good file hygiene, it is best to link CAD files instead of importing them, especially if you are bringing in the file only for temporary use.

The Correct Lines That Are Slightly Off Axis option helps reduce that pesky warning that informs you that a line is not completely straight by altering it automatically. This may not be a wise choice when linking a site plan due to the nature of the linework representing grading and other site features.

You can link any other type of CAD file needed in your project, such as files that contain details or diagrams. These types of drawings can be linked to a drafting view that can be placed on a sheet, or they can be linked directly onto a sheet. To remove a linked CAD file, you can simply select it in the view window and press the Delete key. This will remove it from the project completely.

You can view the properties of elements within a linked CAD file by selecting the link and clicking the Query button in the Import Instance panel that appears when the link is selected. When you click this, each element within the linked file can be selected, as shown in Figure 4.33.

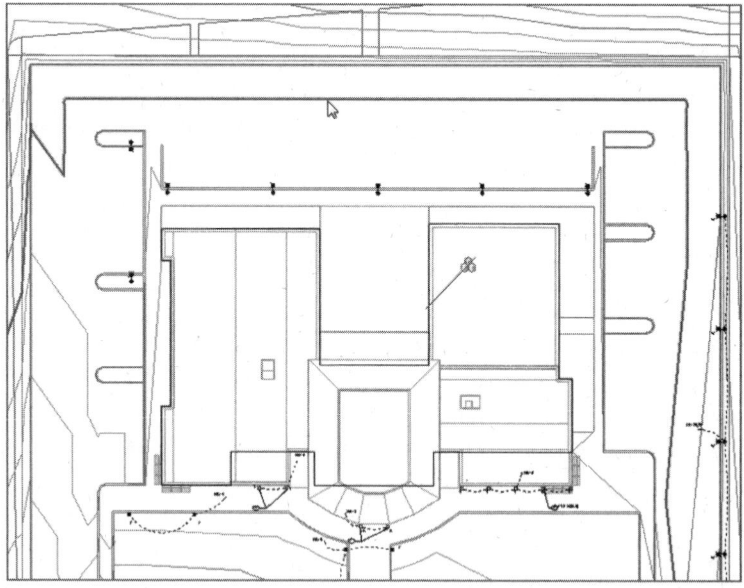

FIGURE 4.33 Selected item within a linked CAD file

Clicking an item will open the Import Instance Query dialog box, shown in Figure 4.34, with information about the selected item. The Delete and Hide In View buttons in this dialog box apply to the entire category of the selected item.

FIGURE 4.34
Import Instance Query dialog box

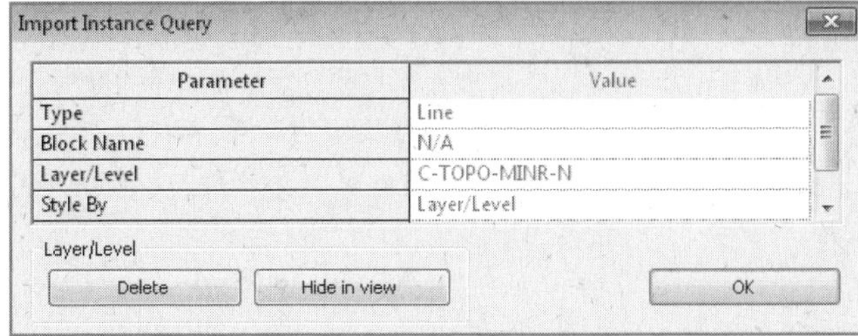

You can control the visibility of items in the linked CAD file from the Visibility/Graphic Overrides dialog box. Its Imported Categories tab contains a list of all linked and imported CAD graphics. The layers within the linked files are listed and can be turned on or off, and their color, line weight, and line pattern can be overridden.

A NOTE ABOUT NOTES

When you link a CAD file that contains text using an SHX font, the text will take on the font that your Revit project is using, as defined by the `SHXfontmap.txt` file (Arial by default). This may affect the formatting of some notes and callouts within the linked CAD file.

Exporting Your Revit File to a CAD Format

Sharing your project file with consultants who are not using Revit is as important as receiving their files. You can export your file to various CAD formats to be used by your consultants. The most important task is to establish the translation of model elements to CAD layers or levels. This is set up in the export options accessed by choosing Export ➢ Options from the application menu (see Figure 4.35).

When you select one of the file format export settings, the dialog box that appears contains a list of all the Revit model categories and their subcategories. You can assign a CAD layer or level and a color to each category and subcategory depending on whether the elements are displayed as cut or in projection. Figure 4.36 shows an example.

Once you have provided a layer and color for the elements that you need to translate to CAD along with setting the other export options, you can save the settings for future use. See Chapter 2, "Creating an Effective Project Template," for more information on establishing export settings.

With your export settings established, choose the appropriate CAD format from the Export tool on the application menu. The Export CAD Formats dialog box provides you with options for selecting multiple sheets or views to export and the properties of the exported files.

Click the Next button after you have chosen the views or sheets to export and a dialog box appears that will let you browse to the file export location. At this point, you can determine the software version to use for the export. If you are exporting a sheet view, you have the option to turn each view on the sheet into an external reference. If you are exporting a model view, selecting this option will cause any linked files in the view to be exported as separate CAD files to be used as external references. This option is the default if you choose the Manual option for file naming.

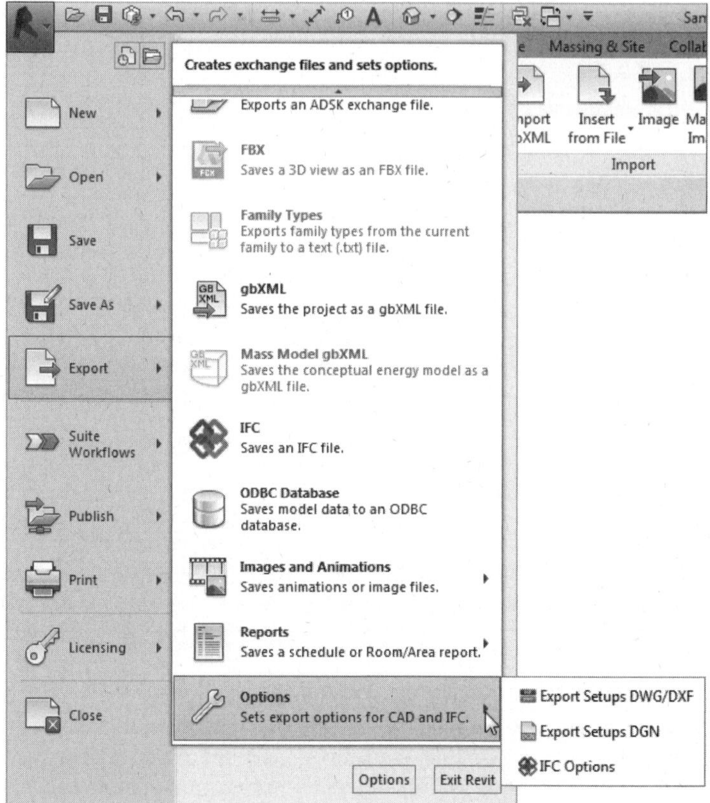

FIGURE 4.35
Export options

Figure 4.37 shows the resulting files from an export of a sheet that contains one model view and a schedule. The highlighted file is the complete sheet. The other files are external references that make up the sheet. The titleblock is a block entity in the DWG, and the schedule is linework and text in the sheet file.

Notice also that the logo in the titleblock was exported as an image file and a PCP file was created. This allows anyone you are sharing your files with to print them the same way you would.

Linking IFC Files

The process for bringing in IFC files has changed for the 2015 release of Revit MEP. In the past you would open the IFC file and then save it as a Revit file in order to link it into your project. The Link IFC button has been added to the Link panel of the Insert tab, and it allows you to bring in an IFC file without having to open the file.

When you click the Link IFC button, the dialog box that appears allows you to browse to the file location. The file types that can be linked are shown in Figure 4.38.

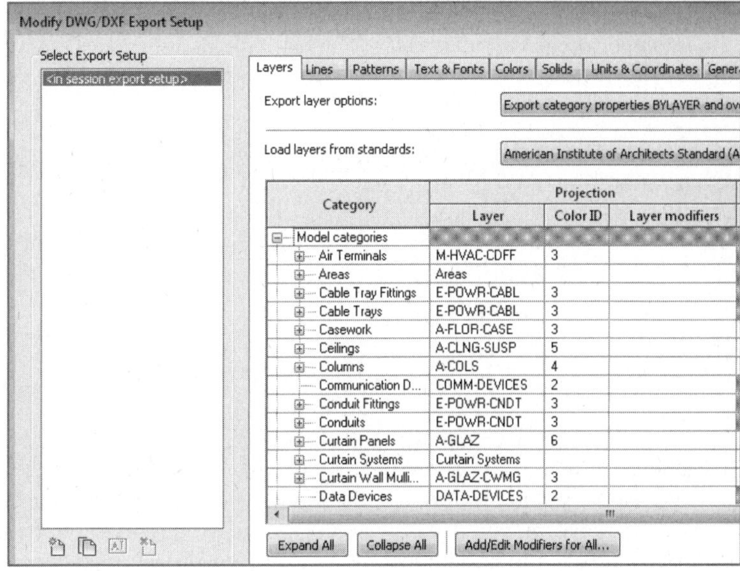

FIGURE 4.36
Layer export settings

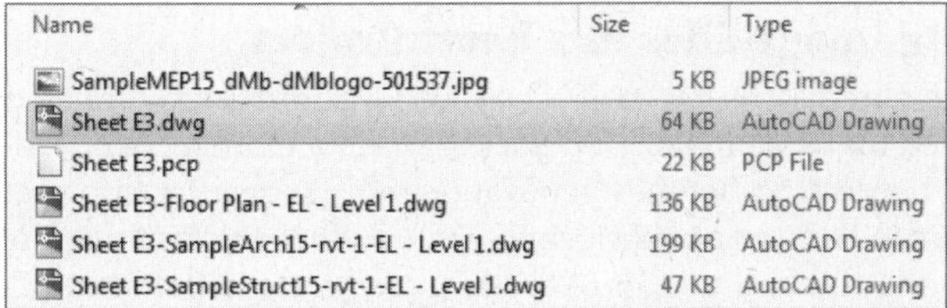

FIGURE 4.37
Files created from a Revit export

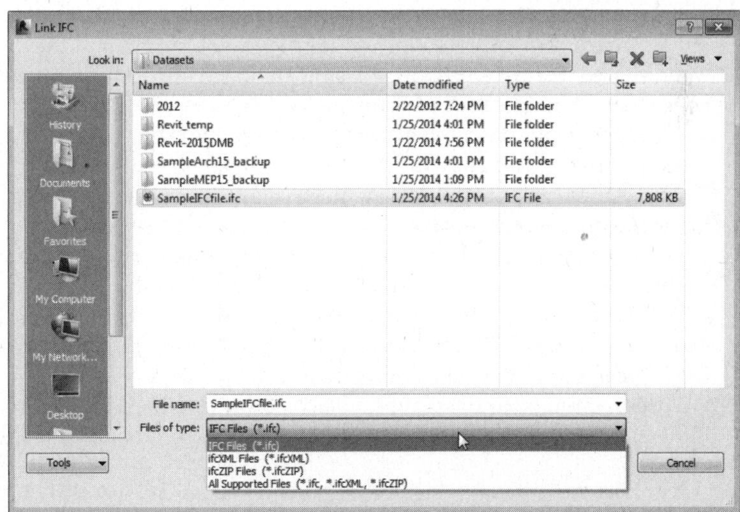

FIGURE 4.38
Link IFC dialog box

Once you select a file and click Open, Revit will read the file, convert it to a Revit file and link it into your project all in one step. The Revit file that it creates is saved in the same location as your project file. The link to the IFC file can be managed via the Manage Links dialog box, as shown in Figure 4.39.

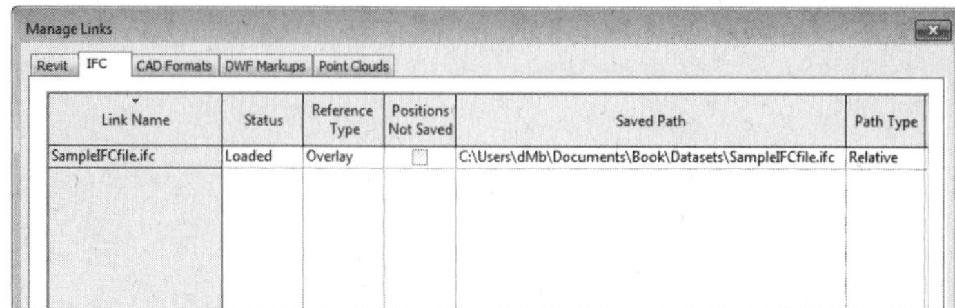

FIGURE 4.39 IFC file in the Manage Links dialog box

The file will be a part of the workset that is currently active when the file is linked in, and the visibility of the linked file can be managed the same way as any other linked Revit file.

When the IFC file is updated, the Revit file created by clicking the Link IFC button is updated; however, you need to use the Reload From option on the IFC tab of the Manage Links dialog box to update the link within your project. You cannot simply reload the linked Revit file.

Using Image Files in a Revit Project

Image files may be necessary for your Revit project to convey design information. They can also be used for presentation documents to add a more realistic look to the model and for logos on sheet borders. Sometimes, renovation projects require information from older documents that are not in Revit or a CAD format. You can save the time required to re-create this information by inserting scanned images of the documents. As with linking CAD files, be careful not to use too many images in your project for the sake of model performance.

You can insert an image file directly into any type of view except for 3D views (unless you are placing a decal). Click the Image button on the Insert tab, and browse to the location of the image. Images are imported into your project, not linked, and they will travel within the file when shared. Figure 4.40 shows placing an image into a sheet border. An outline of the image appears at your cursor for placement.

Once the image has been placed, you can resize it by clicking and dragging the grips at the corners of the image. The aspect ratio of the image is maintained when dragging a corner point. To access these grips after placement, just click the image. You can place text and linework on top of the image as necessary.

If you need to show an image in a 3D view for rendering, you can bring the image into your file by creating a decal. The Decal button is located on the Insert tab. Clicking the bottom half of this button allows you to place a loaded decal or access the Decal Types dialog box, shown in Figure 4.41. You will first need to create a decal type within your project by clicking the Create New Decal icon in the lower-left corner.

After naming your decal type, you can browse to the location of an image you want to use. If the image location changes, the decal will no longer display the image in the model. You will have to choose a new path for the decal type. This means that if you share your file with an owner or consultant, you need to also share any image files that are included.

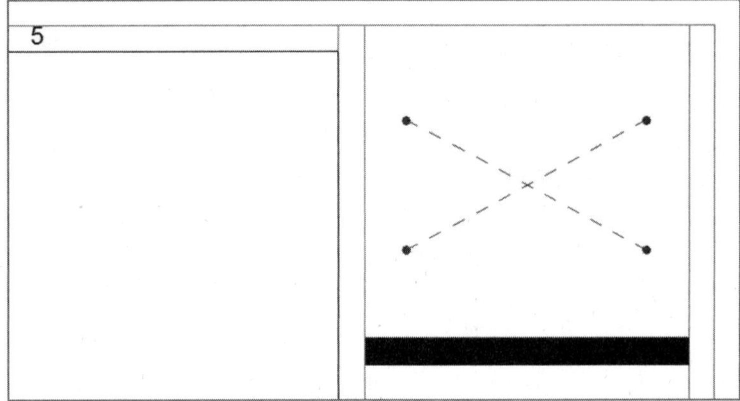

FIGURE 4.40 Placing an image into a view

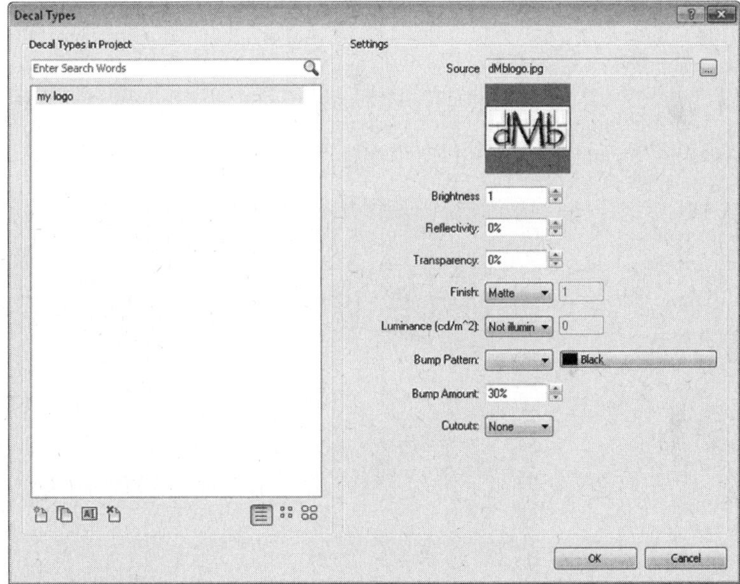

FIGURE 4.41 Decal Types dialog box

The dialog box offers other settings for the rendering appearance of the image. Once the decal type is created, you can use the Place Decal option on the Decal button to insert the image into a 3D view. Settings for the decal size appear on the Options Bar during placement. You can place the decal on any one-directional planar 3D face, such as a wall, curved, or straight. It will appear in the view as a box that defines the size of the image, as shown in Figure 4.42.

FIGURE 4.42 Placing a decal in a 3D view

The decal will display its associated image only in rendered views. This allows you to show things such as signs or logos without having to model them. Figure 4.43 shows an example. Valid image file types for decals are BMP, JPG, JPEG, PNG, and TIF.

FIGURE 4.43 Decal shown in a rendered view

Image files brought into your project will not appear in the Manage Links dialog box. You can use the Manage Images button on the Insert tab to see what images are used in your project. Decals will not appear in the Manage Images list. The Decal Types button also appears on the Manage Project panel of the Manage tab.

If you are working with a client or consultant who is not using Revit, you can still share your model by using the DWF export capabilities within Revit. You can export your model in either 2D or 3D format depending on your client's needs. DWF files are similar to PDF files in that they are meant to be viewed and commented on. The graphics and model geometry cannot be edited in a way that modifies the actual design model, but they contain more than just graphical information. This will help you include your clients or consultants in the BIM process of your project by providing them with the *I* in BIM—information.

To create a DWF file for sharing, choose the Export tool from the application menu. There you will see the DWF/DWFx option (see Figure 4.44).

FIGURE 4.44
DWF/DWFx Export tool

In the DWF Export Settings dialog box, you will see a preview of the current view and options for the output. If you want to create a 3D DWF, you need to have a 3D view open in the drawing area when you select the Export function. If your view discipline is set to Coordination, only the elements within your file will be exported; linked files will not be included in the DWF.

Setting Options for Quality Control

The topics in this chapter address how you can work with all the files in your project to better coordinate your design with your consultants. One of the best things you can do is to make sure that the file you are sharing is as complete and accurate as possible.

You can use some of the core functionality of Revit MEP to set up a system for quality control and project review. During visual inspection of the project, you may notice issues that require coordination. Unless you are the person responsible for modeling, there needs to be a workflow in place to document and manage the issues.

Consider creating an annotation family that acts as a comment tag for whoever may be reviewing the project. This tag can contain as little or as much information as you want. The sample shown in Figure 4.45 has parameters to assign a number, date, status, and owner of a comment along with space for a brief description. The project reviewer can place these tags throughout the project to point out areas that require modification or coordination. Comments can be made regarding issues within your file or issues about your consultant's files. When you share your file, your consultant can view the comments without the need for you to send additional information or files.

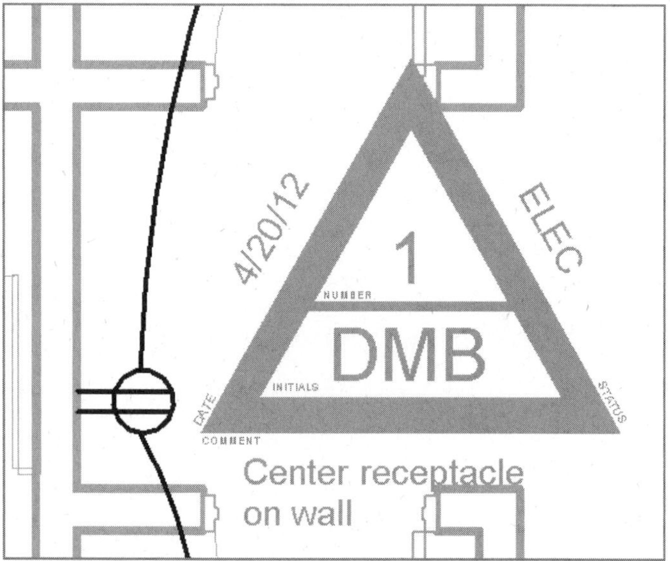

FIGURE 4.45 Sample review comment tag

These tags can be scheduled, and the schedule can be used as a means of tracking the comments. The schedule also allows users to easily locate the comment tags by using the Highlight In Model button on the Element panel of the contextual tab that appears on the ribbon. Figure 4.46 shows a sample schedule of a review comment tag used in a project.

As comments are addressed by users, the tags can be deleted from the views. An empty schedule would indicate that all comments have been addressed. Another option would be to add a parameter, such as a check box, to the comment tag to indicate when a comment has been addressed. Using this workflow can be an efficient and productive method for dealing with coordination issues during the design process.

FIGURE 4.46 Sample review comment schedule

<Review Comments>

A	B	C	D	E
Status	Number	Reviewer	Comment	Date
ELEC	1	DMB	Center receptacle on wall	4/20/12
ELEC	2	DMB	Are there enough lights in this room?	4/20/12
FIRE PROT	9	SAB	Move riser to avoid conflict with Struct framing	4/22/12
FIRE PROT	10	SAB	Sprinkler is in same tile as light fixture, relocate	4/22/12
HVAC	3	MAT	Raise air terminals in this space to match light fixtures	4/20/12
HVAC	4	RXB	Coordinate shaft opening with Structural	4/21/12
HVAC	5	DMB	Increase duct size for new calculated airflow	4/21/12
PLUMBING	6	RXB	Arch removed a fixture, reroute sanitary piping	4/21/12
PLUMBING	7	RXB	Arch removed a fixture, reroute sanitary piping	4/18/12
PLUMBING	8	RXB	Arch removed a fixture, reroute sanitary piping	4/18/12

Another option to consider for quality control is using DWF markups in lieu of the traditional "red line on paper" method. The benefit of using DWFs is not only in the reduction of printing but also that your markups, and how they are handled, can be documented and archived. You can generate a DWF file of multiple sheets, which can be digitally marked up using the free Autodesk Design Review software that can be installed with Revit or is available for download from `www.autodesk.com`. The marked-up DWF sheets can then be brought into Revit and overlaid on their corresponding sheet views by using the DWF Markup command on the Insert tab, as shown in Figure 4.47.

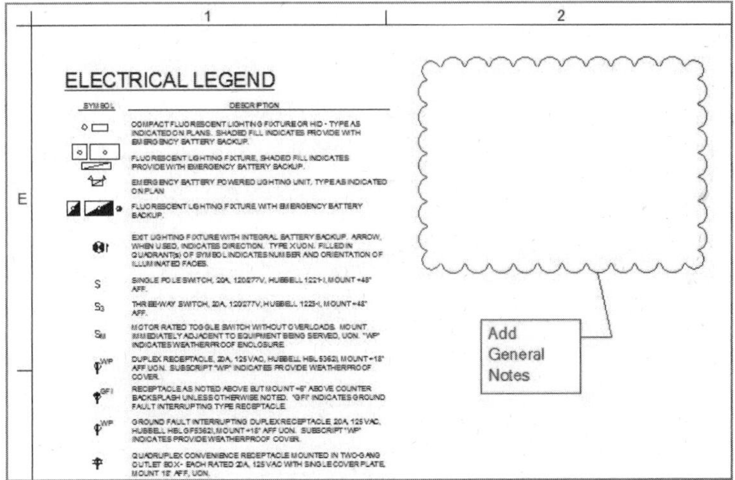

FIGURE 4.47 Revit sheet with DWF markup

As changes are made to your Revit file, you can edit the properties of the marks from the DWF, categorizing them as complete. The Revit file can then be exported to DWF again, and the new DWF file will show the marks as complete by highlighting them in yellow. The username and time of completion of the mark are also stored in the DWF file. This workflow enables you to keep track of who made changes and when those changes were made.

Using Autodesk Revit Server

Revit Server is an extension that you can use to work collaboratively on projects across a wide area network (WAN). This is a very useful application for projects that are being done by offices in different locations.

With Revit Server, you establish a master central file on a central server. This server must be accessible to all project team members.

Local servers house an Accelerator file, which is a copy of the central file. These servers must also be accessible to all users in each location of the project team. The Accelerator is an up-to-date version of the central file located on the central server.

Users work as they would normally, creating a local copy of the Accelerator file onto their workstation. As changes are made and the Synchronize With Central command is used, the local and central models are updated. The Accelerator on the local server is first updated, and then those changes are written to the file on the central server. This allows team members to be anywhere in the world and work on the same project file, as long as they have a local server that has access to the central server.

The Revit Server Administrator application is browser-based and can be accessed remotely. This application is used for managing the project files.

For more information on Revit Server, visit the following location:

```
http://help.autodesk.com/view/RVT/2014/ENU/?guid=GUID-5D844709-E6E9-4E3A-
9168-72CBB0F91F7C
```

Using Cloud-based Solutions

When working in an environment where not all involved parties are in the same location, using a cloud-based solution is an effective way to achieve coordination and collaboration.

Depending on what solution you use, a cloud-based project may allow access to project files in real time. This eliminates the need to wait for files to be uploaded or shared and ensures that all parties are using the same files. Users can access the files from anywhere with an Internet connection. Many cloud solutions offer mobile applications for field use. This means you do not need to have an installation of the software being used in order to work on the project files. All of these attributes further enhance a design and construction team's ability to coordinate efficiently.

There are many considerations for choosing a cloud-based solution for your projects. What type of hardware is required to run BIM software such as Revit MEP effectively? Will the hardware be internal to your network, allowing access from outside users, or will it be hosted by some third-party provider? What are the security risks? How is software licensing handled? Cloud computing is becoming popular in business and technology, and BIM projects can benefit greatly from it.

The Bottom Line

Prepare your project file for sharing with consultants. Taking care to provide a clean, accurate model will aid in achieving an integrated project delivery.

Master It Describe the importance of making worksets visible in all views when your file will be shared with consultants.

Work with linked Revit files. There are many advantages to using linked Revit files in your project. Revit provides many options for the visibility of consultants' files, allowing you to easily coordinate your design.

Master It How would you turn off a model category within a Revit link while allowing that category to remain visible in your model?

Coordinate elements within shared models. Revit can alert you to changes to certain model elements within linked files. Managing these changes when they occur can reduce errors and omissions later in the project and help keep the design team coordinated.

Master It MEP components within a linked file can be copied and/or monitored. True or false: You must have the same family loaded into your file in order to monitor it from a linked file.

Work with files from other applications. Not all of your consultants may use Revit. This does not mean that you cannot use their files to develop and coordinate your design. You can also share your design by exporting your file to a format they can use.

Master It Describe the difference between linking and importing a CAD file and why the linking option is preferred.

Set up a system for quality control. As a BIM solution, Revit provides functionality to keep your design coordinated with your consultants.

Master It What functionality exists in Revit that could allow a design reviewer to comment on coordination issues within a project?

Chapter 5

Multiplatform Interoperability: Working with 2D and 3D Data

This chapter introduces you to the best-practice techniques for importing data into your Autodesk® Revit® 2015 database, either directly into the project file or via a loadable family. The chapter also covers which data to use and when in the project life cycle to use it. Selecting a button that performs the import is easy—but, more important, why are you doing it? And for that matter, *should* you be doing it?

Not only can you import 2D information, but 3D solids contained in an import can now be exploded and manipulated within Revit. These two types of databases are different, so when you have to start working with other consultants who use other data types, you may experience issues such as the following:

Loss of Performance Typically, importing *any* other file format into Revit can be a bad idea. Yes, it is possible—but like eating too much candy, your file size can start to bloat and slow you down. Keep your project file lean, and minimize its intake of sweets whenever you can! But, keeping the food analogy going, cleaning that data—like washing your vegetables—can produce some excellent results. It's all in the preparation.

Difficulties Displaying and Printing Data Exactly the Same One of the most annoying problems is issues with fonts either not being installed or, in the case of legacy DWG data, not being fully supported and therefore never displaying in the same way as originally intended.

Data Loss Many issues can cause data loss in your final documentation. Issues include linked files being unloaded, workset visibility being incorrectly set, and printer driver problems.

We must ask, Is 2D *really* 2D? An Autodesk® AutoCAD® 2D DWG file can show up in a 3D view. Do you want it to?

In this chapter, you will learn to do the following:

- Decide which type of data you want to use on a project
- Link data consistently and in the correct location
- Prepare data prior to import

2D Data Types

Revit works reasonably well with file types other than native RVT project files. Many of the issues you will encounter are due to the differences between existing CAD technologies, which for the most part rely on *elements* (lines, arcs, and circles), while the newer BIM technologies are founded on *object-based* parametric databases.

The AutoCAD file format has differences even among drawings that are created in the same AutoCAD version. For example, virgin AutoCAD can sometimes produce an error when opening a DWG file that was created in any of the *vertical products* (AutoCAD® Civil 3D®, AutoCAD® Architecture, AutoCAD® MEP, and so on). When you import this file into Revit, the error shown in Figure 5.1 is displayed.

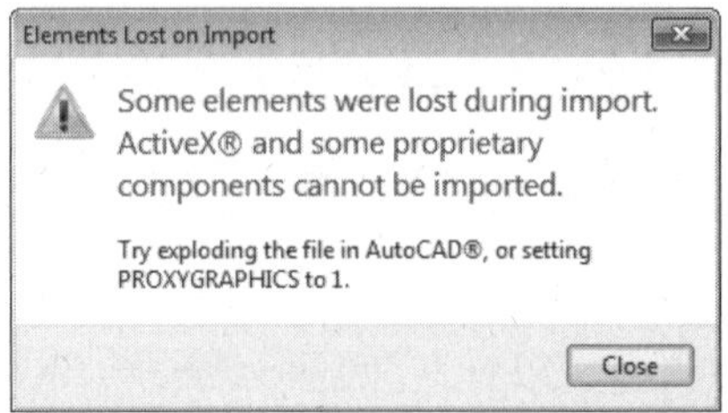

FIGURE 5.1
Elements Lost On Import warning

An additional message is the one displayed in Figure 5.2. Although not exactly an error message, it should make the user take notice—were you actually expecting objects to be in AutoCAD model space? If so, then there may be some fidelity issues with the drawing file that you are trying to link.

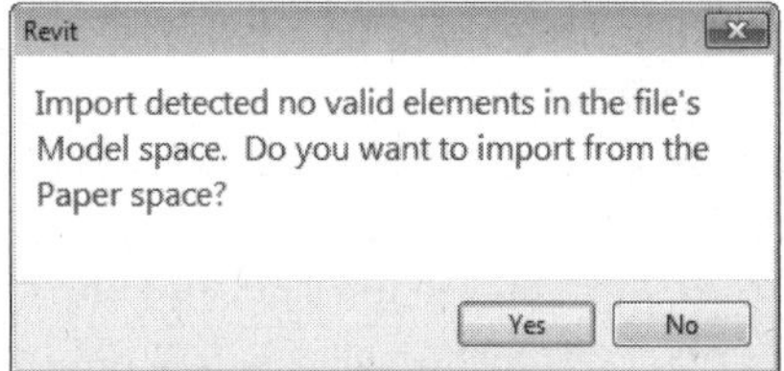

FIGURE 5.2
No valid elements

The issue you face here is whether the "intelligent" data in the AutoCAD file is important or, for the sake of the Revit project, can you explode (if possible) the objects to base elements that can be read in Revit?

You have other options if the data has been created in one of the vertical products. You'll learn about these options in the section "3D Data Types" later in this chapter.

MicroStation 2D DGN

Revit currently supports AutoCAD versions 2000 through 2015, and most MicroStation versions can be imported. The possible alternatives here include asking the originator to use their version of the Save As command to create an AutoCAD file format that MicroStation can handle, use a specially developed app to export to IFC, or export as a DXF file.

DXF

The Drawing Exchange Format (DXF) has been around for almost as long as DWG and DGN. It is a well-recognized and trusted translation medium between primarily 2D formats. The DXF file format also supports conversions to file formats 2000–2010, although care should be taken when using this format because it is generally regarded as offering the most basic compatibility with the likelihood of the worst fidelity.

MULTIPLE FILE FORMATS

The architect is using MicroStation for design, the structural engineer is using Revit Structure, the civil engineer is using AutoCAD Civil 3D, and the engineer is using Plant Design Management System (PDMS) to design a manufacturing plant. Does this sound like an unlikely scenario? No, this is a real-world example. How we as building services designers and engineers cope with and plan for this type of project will ultimately affect the project's outcome and profit.

2D Data for Standard Details

When importing 2D data for standard details, you may well be linking existing details from your company library. If you are using the same drafting standards in AutoCAD and Revit, this process is relatively easy. However, you might want to take a look at your existing company standards if you are planning on running two systems.

One of the important consideration points relates to the use of the legacy default AutoCAD SHX fonts, such as `romans.shx` or `isocp.shx`. The great thing about these fonts for AutoCAD users is that you can control the line weight of the text by utilizing different colors. However, although Revit displays these fonts, their appearance is governed by the `SHXFontMap` file, which can substitute a TrueType font; you cannot adequately control the line weight of text objects in Revit. In fact, the only way to edit the weight of the text is to make it bold. Again, this process involves editing the AutoCAD drawing. For example, Revit does not recognize all the codes CAD users have used for years, such as the degrees symbol (`%%d`), underline (`%%u`), and so on. In this respect, the developers of Revit felt that focusing on more-modern font technologies (TrueType fonts) was more appropriate in the long run than using the much older SHX font approach. Therefore, instead of using line weight, Revit favors a text output that is consistent with most other word processing software.

Thus, in order to use Revit *and* AutoCAD *and* have your output identical, you need to change your AutoCAD fonts to TrueType fonts. This has been a hot topic for many people implementing Revit. Once you get past the shock that this is required and that drafting standards need to change, the actual conversion process can be automated in AutoCAD.

When you import a file into Revit, you must ask yourself the following questions:

- Will this be used in more than one view?
- Is the file likely to be updated in other places (perhaps referenced by different projects, Revit and otherwise)?
- Can the drawing be exploded after it is imported? Note the term *imported*. If a drawing is linked, it cannot be exploded. Neither can it be *bound* like an X-ref or a linked Revit file. However, using the Import button in the Manage Links dialog box does create this bound condition available in AutoCAD.

Also worth noting is that when exploding an imported object, you have two options: Partial and Full. A partial explosion turns the result into the highest level of lines, circles, arcs, and text while respecting the existence of blocks, which can be partially exploded again. A full explosion reduces the imported drawing into its simplest representation of lines, arcs, circles, and text. Text becomes single lines of text rather than retaining any multiline settings, regardless of the explosion type. Entities not recognized by Revit—points, for example—are not translated and are lost in the explosion process.

When importing or linking into a plan, section, or elevation view, the drawing will show up in multiple views unless you select the Current View Only check box in the Import dialog box. See Figure 5.3.

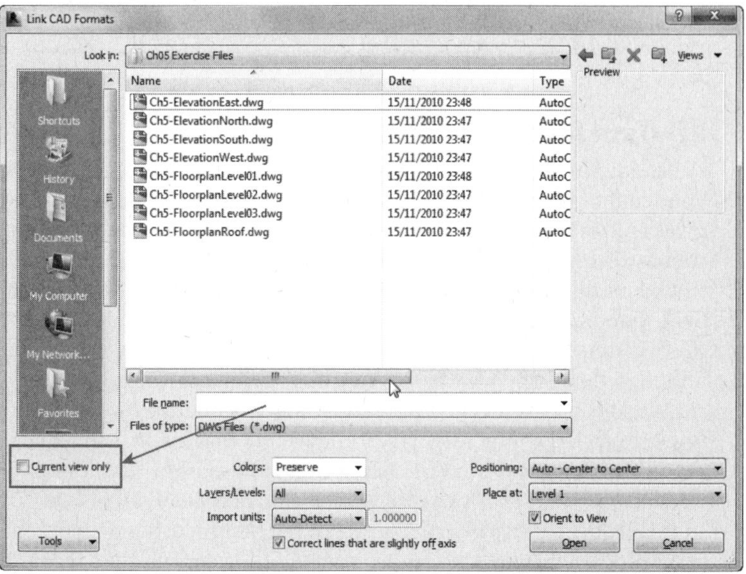

FIGURE 5.3
Current View Only option

If the view you are using is either a drafting or a legend view, the Current View Only check box is grayed out, because these views are only 2D.

When importing a file for use as a detail, positioning generally is not as important as when importing an overall plan. The Positioning options for importing are shown in Figure 5.4.

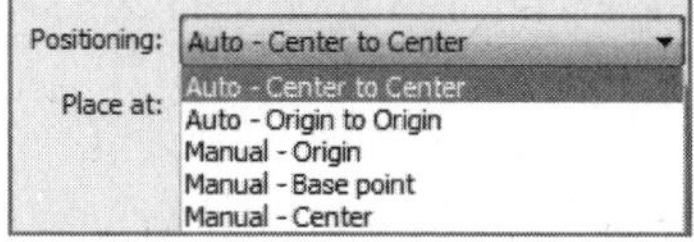

FIGURE 5.4
Positioning options

For details, you can generally use the manual options and place the details where required. Trying these options in a blank project file before you bring any file into your live project is always a good rule of thumb; it gives you a sense of where the objects are going to be and whether the scale is correct.

Figure 5.5 indicates the options available for import units. Although Auto-Detect is the default option and usually works, sometimes the originator of your imported data is not as rigorous as they should be and their units don't quite match their documentation. So specifying the units is preferable to letting Revit apply a default. Also, the scale used in the view should match the scale intended to display the detail in the original software used to make it. This ensures that geometry, hatching, and fonts will be as close to the same as possible. If this isn't set before importing the detail, then the poor fidelity can compound the issue of units being wrong.

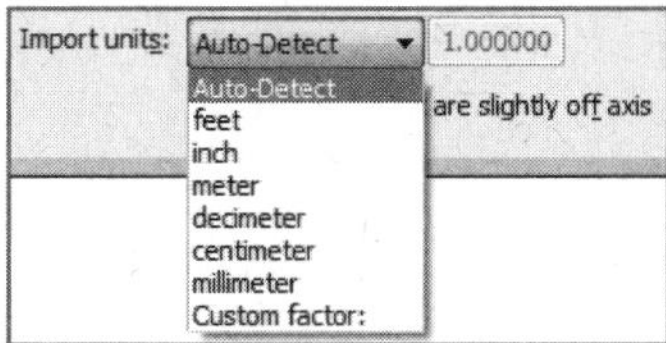

FIGURE 5.5
Import Units options

You have the option to correct lines that are slightly off axis, as shown in Figure 5.6.

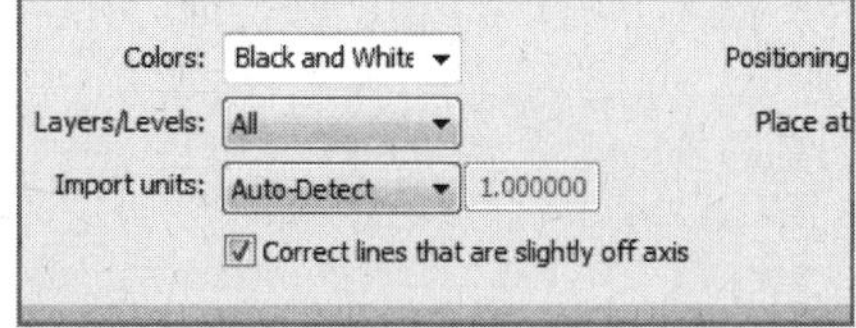

FIGURE 5.6
Correcting lines that are slightly off axis

This feature should be used with care, however, because those "slightly off-axis lines" may be part of the design intent!

2D Data for Plans, Sections, and Elevations

Let's say that you are using Autodesk Revit MEP and want your staff members to keep using that program, even though you have other projects in your office for which the architect is using traditional CAD-based drafting methods. Should you do these projects in AutoCAD or Revit? Once you have been using Revit for a while, using anything else feels like it takes far too long, and there's all that back-referencing, and checking sections tie up with the plans!

The following Revit workflow is tried and rigorously tested. Your staff members retain their knowledge, and the project design is still coordinated (albeit only with the other building services, not with the architecture—although the architect can provide you with sections as well as plans).

When going down this route, you need to consider how your project team generally works: either in one multiservice file or in multiple project files with only one service. If all services are in one model, linking the plans and sections into that file is probably the best way forward.

Our experience is working with multiple project files—Architecture, Structure, Electrical, HVAC, Fire, Plumbing, and Drainage. This is sometimes born of necessity because the project teams are in different geographic locations. Although a company might have technology to support distributed file servers and project teams on different continents, the reality is that managing this process can be more trouble than it is worth.

In this workflow, linking the 2D files into each project file is an option. The linked files appear only as linked overlays in the same way they do in AutoCAD. Managing the location of multiple linked files in multiple project files is a messy and time-consuming task. You have to rely on users not moving or deleting anything accidentally. Of course, this applies in any project, but the problem can become compounded under these circumstances. The best option here is to have one architectural file, one place to update and manage, and all your services files can be kept at the same stage for printing. This does require some setup at the start of the project, but once it's complete, it is almost as manageable as linking a model from the Revit Architecture software.

File Cleanup

Before you import anything into Revit, consider taking a few minutes to "sanitize" the file. This could be a simple task such as running an AutoLISP® routine in AutoCAD to purge unnecessary objects such as layers or blocks (named and unnamed). Change the Colors option to By Layer and delete anything that isn't necessary for your project, such as all those objects just outside the viewport that the architect was saving for a rainy day. Sometimes these objects can affect the positioning of an imported file: If an object is more than 20 miles (32.2 km) from the origin, inaccuracies and position issues can occur. In this case, it is necessary to open the file and delete those extraneous objects and resave.

If you do not have access to AutoCAD, an alternative is to start a new Revit project file, import the drawing, and fully explode it. Then export that view back to AutoCAD and import it into your Revit project. This is a bit circuitous, but it's a great way to clean a drawing as long as the fidelity of data such as line patterns, hatches, and text is maintained.

The following exercise will take you through linking plans and elevations into a new project file, creating levels and default views that any of the project engineers can use to obtain the prints they require for markup. Although this exercise uses a few of the more basic Revit commands, it is mainly designed to show a best-practice workflow, especially when linking this file into your services project files. At the end on the exercise, you will end up with a 3D wireframe model as shown in Figure 5.7.

Figure 5.7
3D wireframe model

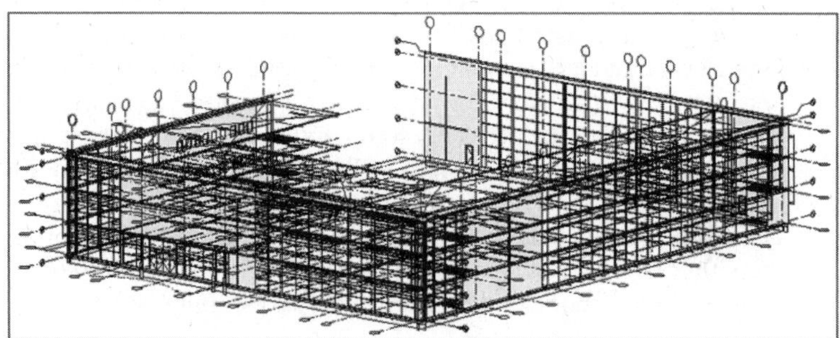

Follow these steps:

1. Create a new Revit MEP 2015 project file using the template `Ch5_Template.rte`. This file can be found at `www.sybex.com/go/masteringrevitmep2015`.
2. Open the Level 1 floor plan, and from the Insert tab, select Link CAD and select the drawing file `Ch5-FloorplanLevel01.dwg`. Use the following settings, shown in Figure 5.8:
   - Current View Only: Not selected
   - Colors: Black And White

- Layers/Levels: All
- Import Units: Auto-Detect
- Correct Lines That Are Slightly Off Axis: Not selected
- Positioning: Auto – Origin To Origin
- Place At: Level 1
- Orient To View: Selected

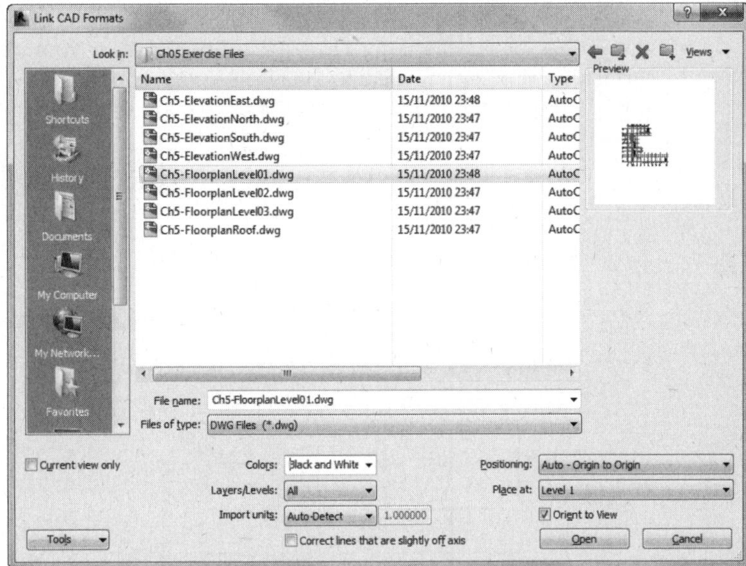

FIGURE 5.8 Import settings

3. The next step is to create building grids based on the architectural floor plan. From the Architect tab, select the Grid tool. With this active, use the Pick Lines option from the Draw panel. Although this is a quick method of creating grid lines, be sure to keep an eye on the grid head location. If the lines have been drawn in different directions, the result is that the grids are orientated differently. Clicking the grid head and selecting the adjacent check mark to swap the orientation will work—but only in this view. As long as you create these elements consistently, they will be displayed in a consistent manner through the rest of the project.

   Start with Grid 1 and select each subsequent grid, except the intermediate grids. You can come back and do those after creating Grid 10. Once the vertical grids are complete, do the horizontal ones. Starting at A, you will rename this first alphabetic grid and then follow with B, C, and so on. Once all the major grids are created, go back and create the intermediate ones. With this workflow, you have to rename only a few grids rather than every single one.

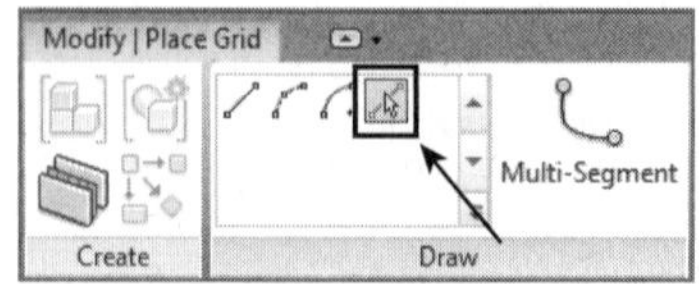

4. With the grids complete, open the North Elevation.
5. Navigate back to the Insert tab, select Link CAD, and select the file `Ch5-ElevationNorth.dwg`. Use the Auto – Center To Center positioning option, and ensure that Orient To View is checked.
6. Notice that the elevation drawing, while orientated in the correct plane, is not in the correct location with respect to the levels and grids. Use the Align tool to correct this, aligning Level 1 with 01-Entry Level and Grids 1, as shown in Figure 5.9.

FIGURE 5.9
Align Linked DWG

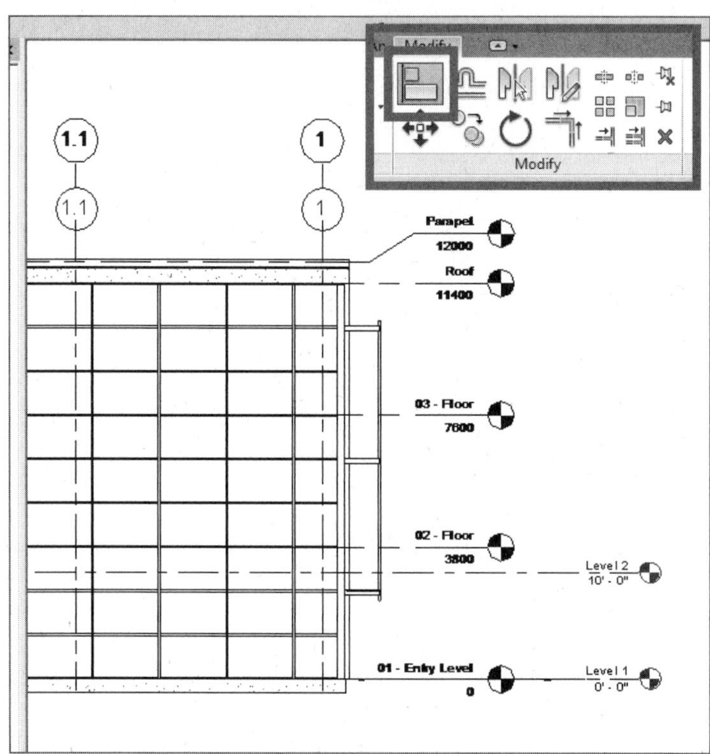

7. One other thing to notice is that the existing levels do not share the same name as the linked DWG. Select the Level 1 line and click the blue highlighted name of the level. Change this to match the DWG, and do the same for level 2. Revit then asks if you would like to rename corresponding views. Click Yes, as shown in Figure 5.10.

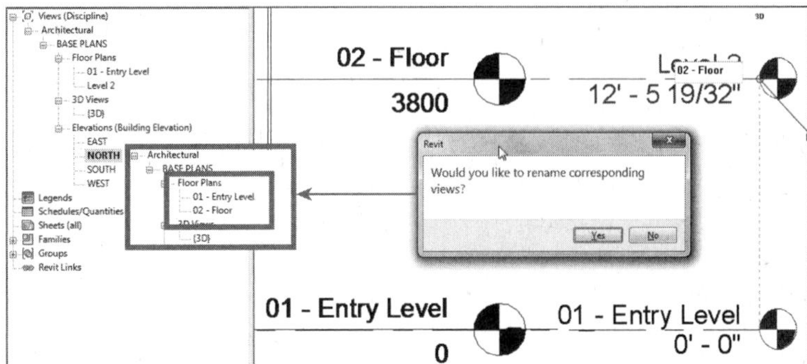

FIGURE 5.10 Renaming levels

NAMING NEW LEVELS

The newly created levels do not have the same names as the link file, so you need to edit them. When you are editing level names, Revit prompts you with a message, as shown here:

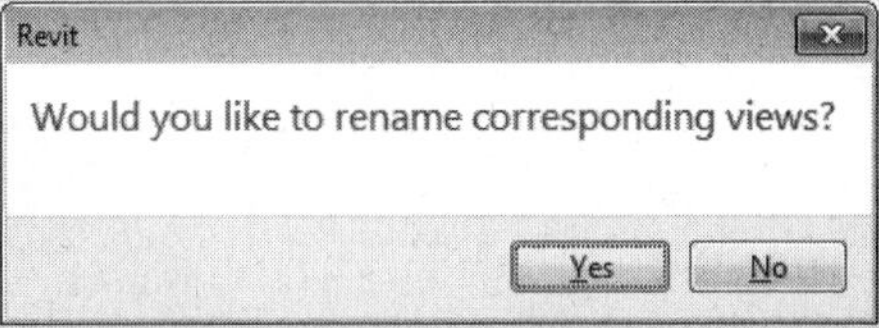

It is important to click Yes. At this point, you are trying to create a set of default views that match the architecture. Having a building level and a floor plan with matching names will save you and anyone else looking at the project file a lot of time.

8. Create additional levels for levels 03 - Floor, Roof, and Parapet, renaming each level to match the link file. You may find that the created levels do not show up in the Project Browser where you expect. In Figure 5.11, the levels created have ended up filed under Architectural / Power / Floor Plans. To place these views into Architectural / BASE PLANS / Floor Plans, select all three (A), right-click, and select Apply View Template (B). From the Apply View Template dialog, select Architectural Plan (C) and click Apply Properties (D). You will see the views move in the Project Browser (E).
9. Repeat step 2, opening each level (02 - Floor, 03 - Floor, and Roof) and linking the following DWG files:
   - `Ch5-FloorplanLevel02.dwg`
   - `Ch5-FloorplanLevel03.dwg`
   - `Ch5-FloorplanRoof.dwg`

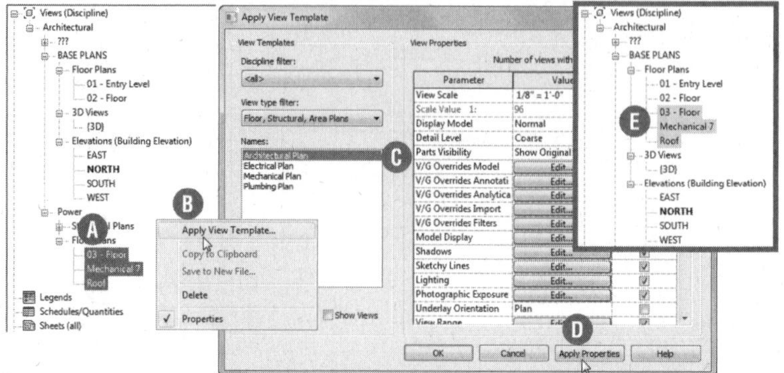

FIGURE 5.11
Applying the view template

10. With all the floor plans linked, we can turn our attention to the elevations. You already have the North elevation linked (step 5), and looking at the default 3D view, you can see in Figure 5.12 that although the file is aligned correctly in relation to levels and grid 1, it is in the middle of the building. Open 01 - Entry Level plan and use the Align tool to move the elevation to the north "face" of the floor plan.

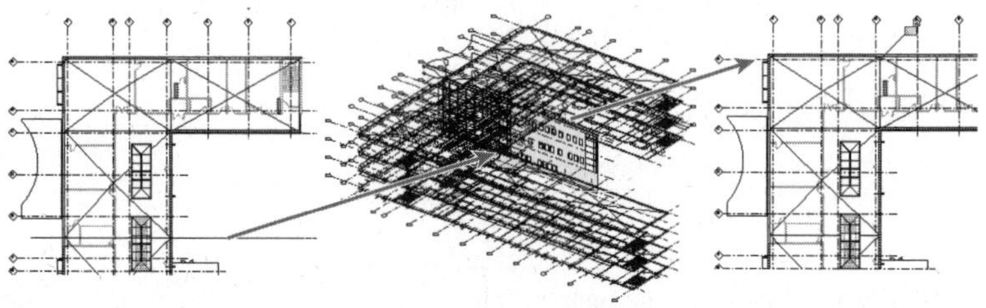

FIGURE 5.12
Aligning the elevation to the plan

11. Repeat steps 5 and 6, opening each of the remaining elevations in turn and linking the following files:
    - `Ch5-ElevationSouth.dwg`
    - `Ch5-ElevationWest.dwg`
    - `Ch5-ElevationEast.dwg`
12. Repeat step 10 for each elevation. It's a good idea to do this straight after linking each one; that way you don't end up aligning the incorrect one.
13. Open floor plan 01 - Entry Level and activate Visibility Graphics. Select the Imported Categories tab and uncheck all the linked DWG files except `Ch5-FloorplanLevel01.dwg`.

    Also, as indicated in Figure 5.13, click the plus sign to expand the layers in the link and turn off anything unwanted - like grids (S-GRIDIDM), for example.
14. Repeat step 13 for all the other floor plans and elevations, leaving only the link file appropriate to each view visible.

    When you have finished, open a 3D view. Your "building" should look similar to Figure 5.7.

15. Save the file. This can now act as the *architectural link file* for your entire project.

16. Using the same template file you used in step 1, create a new project file. This can be your HVAC documentation model.

17. Open the North elevation view and delete the two existing levels. The message that appears, displayed in Figure 5.13, informs you that views are being deleted. This is normal, so click OK.

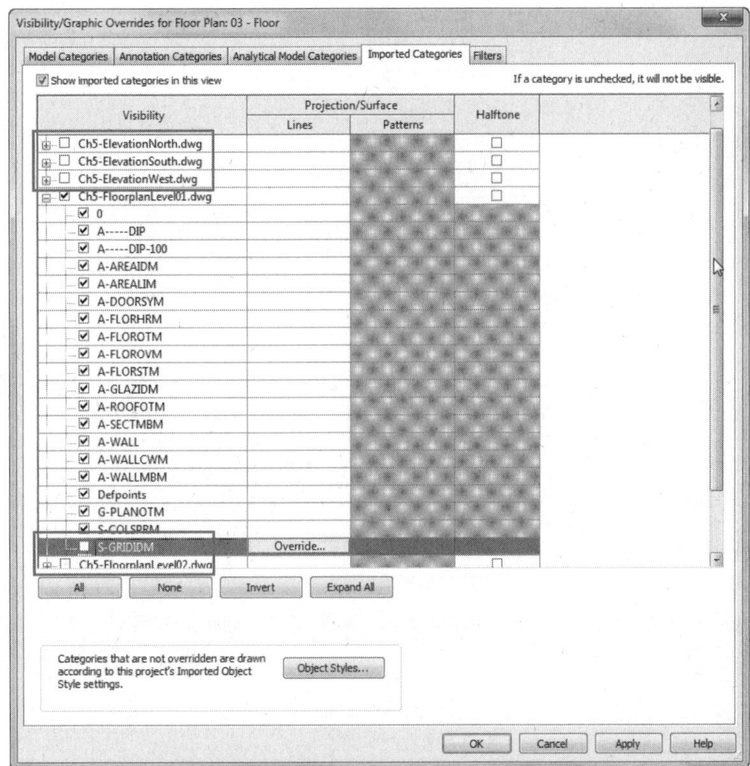

FIGURE 5.13 Applying visibility/graphic overrides for links

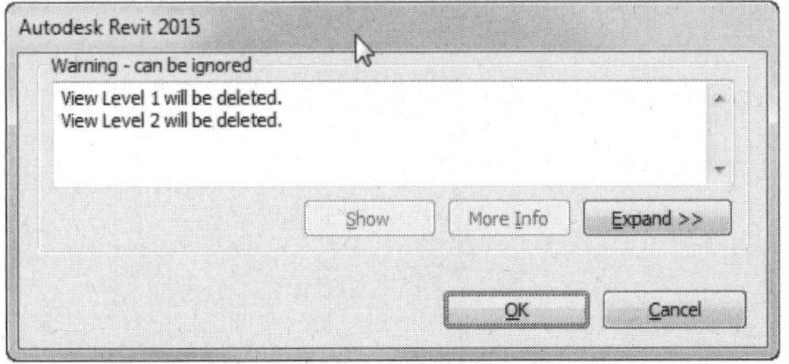

FIGURE 5.14 Viewing deletions

18. Link the file `Ch5_COMPLETE.rvt` by using the Origin To Origin method. Notice that none of the linked drawings are visible—you'll adjust that in step 20.

19. As with a standard Revit project, copy/monitor the levels and grids, and then create your plan views. Each of these views will display only the grids, not the linked drawing files.

20. In each of these views, adjust the visibility/graphics to override the view to the required settings, as shown in Figure 5.15.

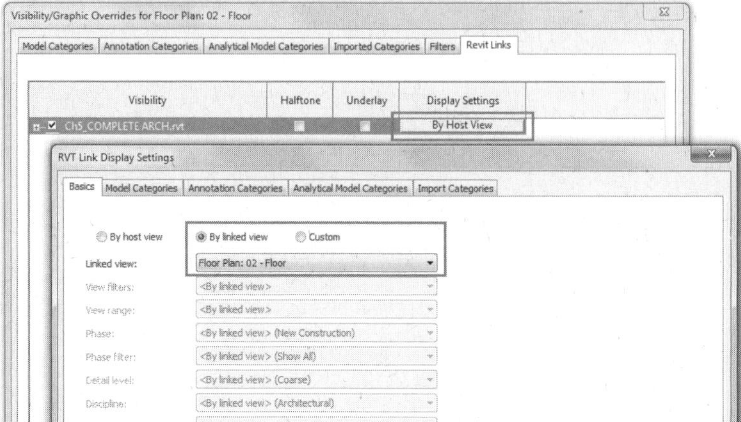

FIGURE 5.15
Visibility/Graphic Overrides

Whether you're linking or importing CAD data from other formats, although you can use the overrides to change what you see or how you see it, you can also, in fact, use the Import Line Weights option, as shown in Figure 5.16. This enables you to specify a DWG color number and associate it with a pen weight in Revit. This can range from using a series of default standards supplied with the software to loading your own (or partner's) standard, so the weights of lines are the same between CAD and Revit.

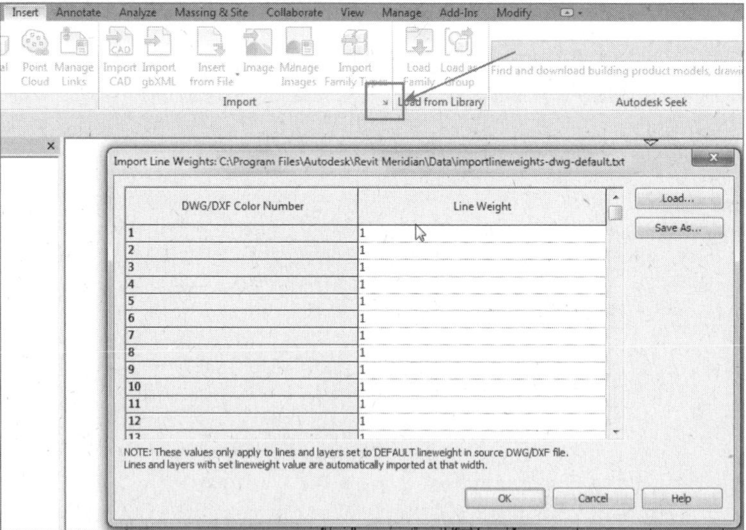

FIGURE 5.16
Import Line Weights option

In addition, you have the ability to select and query the layers in a linked/imported CAD file. Say, for example, you are unsure of the layering standard in the linked file; you can select that file and then use the Query command, as indicated in Figure 5.17. You can select lines and objects within the link file and choose the option to hide that selection in your current view.

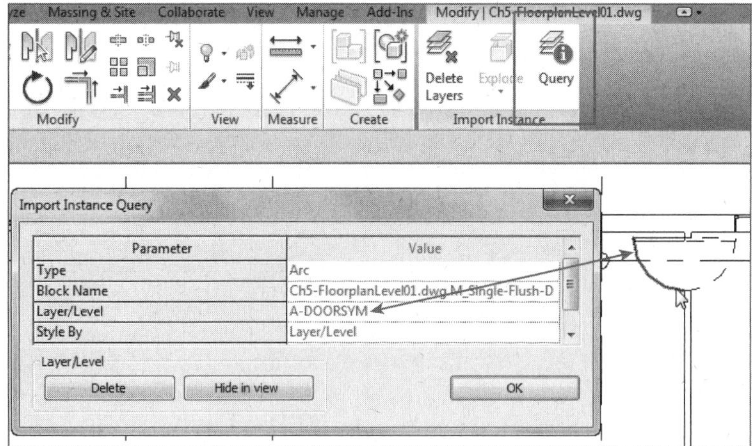

FIGURE 5.17 Querying imported layers

> **NON-REVIT LINKS**
>
> Although using linked AutoCAD DWG files in no way replaces a linked Revit architectural model, it does represent an efficient way to work with 2D data. There is now one place where architectural information is updated, including the building levels and grids. Because you created these as Revit objects, you can now use the Copy/Monitor option to place them in subsequent services files.

3D Data Types

This section is easy—well, it should be anyway. You are, after all, importing and manipulating 3D data in a 3D application. What could possibly go wrong?

It all depends on the type of data you want to import or link into your project. Let's start with the easiest—a Revit project file. Surely there cannot be anything difficult with that? What it boils down to, however, is the *other* users and how they have set up their projects. If you are lucky, they have a lot of experience and, most important, have communicated how the model is constructed to the entire project team.

Much also depends on what you, as an MEP user, want to get out of the project, so let's see.

Revit Project File

Working with external consultants can be very trying at the best of times. Think back to times when all you had to worry about was whether lines had been drawn on the correct layer and whether they were either by layer or by block. Yearning for the old days? Life did seem simpler then, but was it really?

Getting a set of drawings from the architect meant doing some preparation work such as running the odd AutoLISP routine to change layers, linetypes, and color. Then you had to make sure the plans all had the same User Coordinate System (UCS) settings and elevations and that sections matched floor and ceiling plans. Now we remember the pain!

However, now that we have swapped one system for another, there are a whole host of new problems. Worksets, especially ones that were off by default, did cause lots of problems. Since the release of Revit MEP 2011, however, you have been able to alter the default visibility status of worksets, and that particular issue has largely disappeared. With later releases, you can disable worksets when collaborating with others. When you open a workset-enabled file and click Detach From Central, a dialog box gives you the options shown in Figure 5.18.

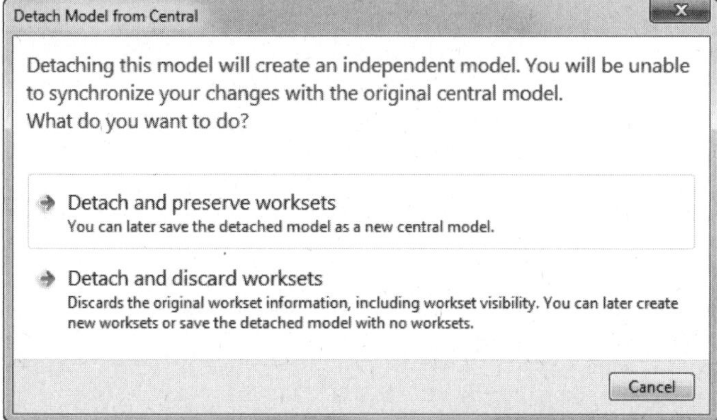

FIGURE 5.18 Detach Model From Central dialog box

Disabling worksets results, of course, in the loss of workset visibility. Unfortunately, some users utilize worksharing as a type of extended layer or visibility control. The trouble with this workflow is that the problem is exacerbated by the introduction of workset visibility control in view templates. Now there are six ways of turning off an object in a view in your project file:

- Visibility/Graphic Overrides
- Filters
- Design Options
- Phasing
- Worksets
- Hide Element

You can also control any linked file either in conjunction with your view settings or separately.

Project Phasing and Design Options

If an architect has an existing building and is developing new and future designs, that architect may have phases set up in the project file. You'll definitely need instruction from the architect on the particular phase of the project on which you are working, and what Phase filters were applied. Once you have a list of the phases in the architect's project and understand which ones apply to your contract, you can set up *phase mapping*.

Say the architect has Existing, New Build, and Interior phases. Your project has the phases First Fix and Second Fix. Select the linked Revit file, and from the Properties dialog box, select Edit Type. Then, in the Type Properties dialog box, select Phase Mapping, as shown in Figure 5.19.

FIGURE 5.19
Linked file type properties

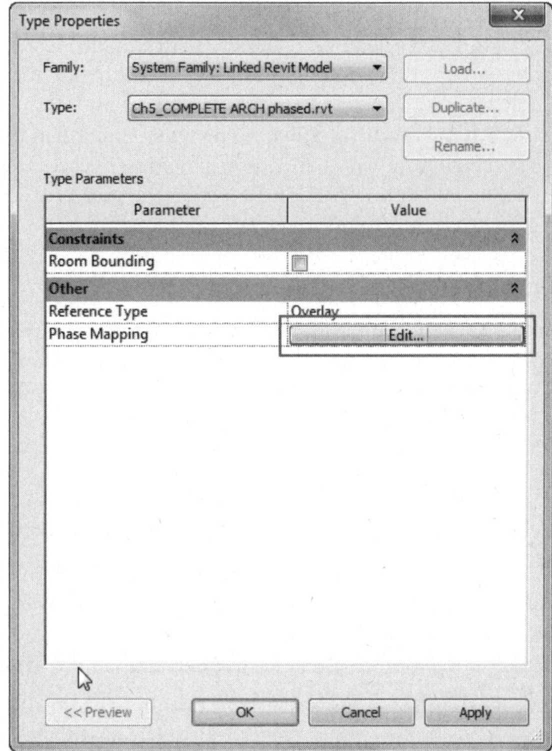

This is where you decide which phase in the architect's file corresponds to a phase in your project, as shown in Figure 5.20.

FIGURE 5.20
Phase mapping

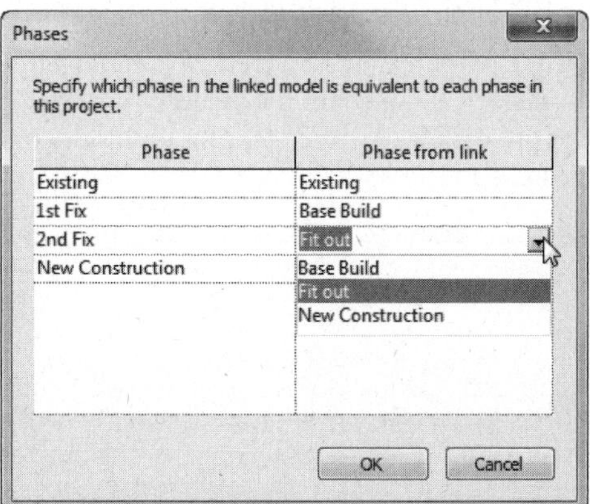

Once this mapping is finalized, any views set up in your project specifically for First Fix or Second Fix will also display the architectural model correctly. (Notice the term *model*. This has no effect on any linked DWG files because phasing applies only to model objects.)

Hopefully, by the time it comes to the MEP design, most major issues, such as whether the building is square or rectangular, will have been sorted out. However, if the architect is still in discussion with the client, you will need to be prepared to discuss the primary design option with the architect and, if are you being paid to, design for that option plus the other options that the architect thinks the client may like.

But we've jumped ahead here! What about the MEP concept and preliminary designs? How do we as modelers and designers fit in with what the architect is designing? What are our responsibilities, and how much are we modeling and designing in Revit?

If we are relying on the architect to provide a model at the concept stage so that we can run analysis calculations for a building's heating and cooling loads, we really need an airtight model. Chapter 17, "Solid Modeling," covers the merits of using the Mass Modeling tools in Revit to generate a building form.

Revit Family File

Revit families are the elements that bring any design to life. They hold data that, when created correctly, provides more than just a visible indication of an object's placement. Thus, team members should reach a consensus that Revit families are implemented to a certain standard:

- The appropriate family template file is used.
- Categories are set correctly.
- Subcategories are adequately and consistently named.

Within your company, you should have a standard for family creation. This standard could specify any of the techniques and best practices used in creating families that can be placed into your library.

Your standard should include items such as the following:

Common Orientation and Insertion Points If a family is exchanged with another, you really don't want it to jump 2 feet to the left and rotate 22.5 degrees.

Naming Conventions for Subcategories and Reference Planes This helps make the families perform as required in relation to visibility settings when loaded into the project. These conventions also aid users when familiarizing themselves with how best to create a family according to company standards.

A Standard, Companywide Shared Parameter File This ensures that families, even from different categories, can share the same type of data that can be reported, tagged, and scheduled in the project file. A great starting point for consistency is the Autodesk Revit Style Guide. It can be found at:

`http://seek.autodesk.com/MarketingSolutionsRevitStyleGuide.htm`

ADSK

The Autodesk Exchange File (ADSK) format covers multiple platforms. In its current format, which is XML based, ADSK allows the user to export from, say, the Autodesk® Inventor®

platform to an ADSK file, which can then be imported into Revit. There is functionality in Revit Architecture to export ADSK files for use with civil engineers, although this is not supported in MEP. This is a static form, but it does have the benefit that, if connectors have been placed in Inventor, their properties are taken through as Revit MEP connectors. You can open ADSK files from the Open command, and after you save them, they become loadable Revit families.

IFC

The Industry Foundation Classes (IFC) file format was introduced as a solution to the problems of multiple software vendors competing in 3D space. IFC is an XML file format that can be edited in text editors such as Windows Notepad. Although the IFC format is somewhat limited from within Revit itself, Autodesk has made the IFC import/export tools open source (freely available to programmers) and the Revit API has been expanded with each release to offer greater support for getting data to and from IFC.

Industry Foundation Classes

The current format for IFC is IFC4, although, at the time we were writing this book, Revit supported IFC 2×3. The format was developed by buildingSMART, formerly known as the International Alliance for Interoperability (IAI). More details can be found at `www.buildingsmartalliance.org`.

Using IFC can increase the number of consultants with whom you can interact. There is a potential downside, however. Unless you spend adequate time at the front end of the project discussing just how the data (format) is to be transferred with all parties, problems can arise from data that, when opened, is so inefficient as to be almost worthless. In some cases, it is preferable to use the import method as described in the previous exercise than it is to import an IFC file. On an average-size project, an IFC file can take literally hours to import, and then the objects that are imported might turn out to be in-place families.

Choosing the Right File Type

With a new project coming into the office, a meeting was set up between the architects, structural engineers, and MEP engineers. Both sets of engineers were using Revit as their base documentation software, while the architects were confirmed Bentley Architecture users. Although the architects had copies of Revit Architecture in the office, they continued to use the Bentley solution and had supplied an add-in for their current version of Revit to the engineers that allowed the export of `i.dgn`. Although this was fine for the architects, they in turn exported to IFC (using an appropriate plug-in). At around 50 MB, this file could routinely take 3 to 4 hours to process into Revit. At the same time, the internal fit-out was being done in 2D AutoCAD.

The engineers decided to do away with the IFC import altogether and create a wireframe model from the 2D drawings. This made the project much more efficient and manageable. Coordination did not lose out, however, because all consultants agreed to use Autodesk® Navisworks®. Each could discuss their issues at weekly project meetings in front of a large-format display monitor.

The case study "Choosing the Right File Type" highlights some of the issues that users face when using the IFC format. At the time of this writing, numerous companies are producing free as well as fee-based IFC viewers, which allow the user to view the building model and any properties that are attached to the building elements. Some of these software vendors also provide IFC cleaners that allow for the optimization of an IFC file prior to opening it in any other suitable software.

AutoCAD DWG

As described earlier in this chapter, native AutoCAD and MicroStation files are easily imported or linked into Revit. The purpose of doing so in the 2D environment is that it can be a good way of bringing together a project team with a wide range of skills.

The reasons for importing native 3D objects from AutoCAD can be a bit blurred. If you were modeling 3D building objects in AutoCAD, why wouldn't you do the same in Revit? It could be argued that a company already has a wide range of 3D library components that may or may not need to be parametric, so what would be the harm in importing those objects into a family template of the correct category that is then saved as a loadable Revit family? There are mixed opinions about this, especially when companies have to invest substantially in extra development work. With the bottom line speaking louder than it has for many years, a lot of companies are preserving or reusing as much as they can, in the hope that doing so will save them money. At the end of the day, it comes down to economics, but (and point this out to your employer) invest wisely and spend the necessary time on developing or purchasing your Revit library. The alternative is reusing the existing 3D data, but this often has detrimental effects on the project: file size, excessive complexity, and appearance all play their part in slowing down your production.

DWGs from Verticals

AutoCAD verticals (such as Architecture, MEP, and Civil 3D) and Bentley Architecture are object based, relying on additional object enablers to create more functionality. This can lead to proxy objects, discussed earlier in this chapter.

The way AutoCAD or MicroStation handles this intelligent information is to give the user the ability to export to IFC. Exporting `DWG/i.dgn` elements to IFC does work. Sometimes you even get real building elements when this data is opened in Revit. However, exporting isn't perfect. Many times the data is all there but can end up as in-place elements, which can be inefficient.

SketchUp

There! We said it!

Yes, you can.

Why?

OK. OK! Say that someone has modeled the entire city block and surrounding suburbs in Trimble SketchUp and you can import that model, enabling you to perform sun studies. Later in the book, you'll see how to do exactly the same thing in Revit and have something useful in your project file.

Other File Formats

So, while these 3D elements can be imported into Revit, the latest functionality introduced to Revit 2015, as mentioned at the start of this chapter, is the ability to import files (for example, ACIS solids in the form of SAT format files), explode them, and retain the 3D elements. This lets you directly manipulate the 3D object because it is now a free-form object within Revit that can be manipulated, stretched, and cut with voids just like any other Revit solid object. This function has the potential to greatly help in the transition from one file format to another.

However, this new feature has some limitations. Although rectilinear objects can be stretched and manipulated using shape handles, any radii remain static, even though they can be dimensioned. Figure 5.21 shows two examples. On the left, an ACIS solid created in AutoCAD and imported into a Revit mass can be seen. Notice the grips on each face but no controls on the arc. On the right, a similar model has been imported from SketchUp. The main difference is the way SketchUp uses triangulated surfaces to create arcs.

FIGURE 5.21
Imported ACIS solids

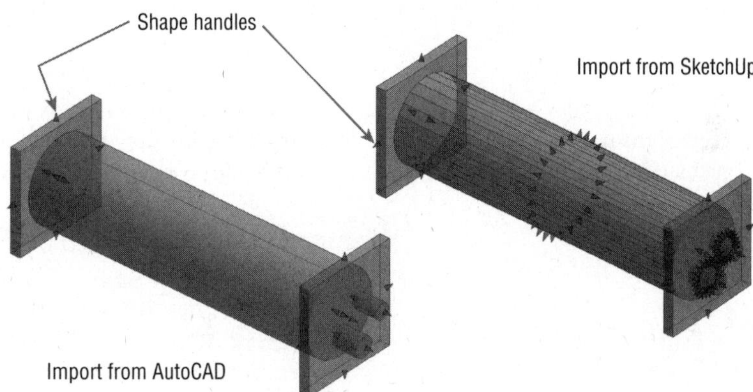

Point Clouds

Point clouds are beginning to be the new import for existing conditions. Obtain a laser scan of your building and it's a simple job to check design data against the As Built model. Revit supports a wide variety of formats (including PCG, which was the default file format in previous versions). In the 2014 release, the point cloud engine was changed to use RCP and RCS formats; the others must be processed on insertion into Revit. You can do this by selecting Raw Formats from the Files Of Type drop-down list, as shown in Figure 5.22.

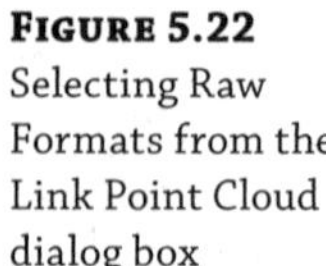

FIGURE 5.22
Selecting Raw Formats from the Link Point Cloud dialog box

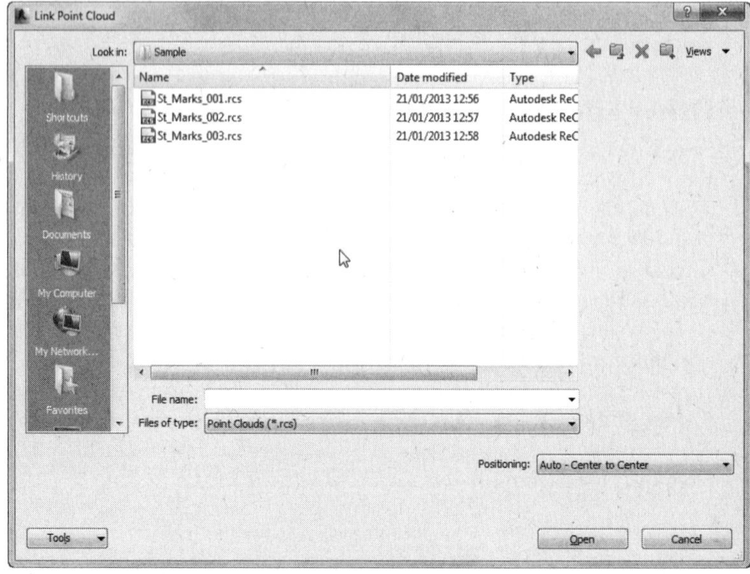

These raw files need to be *indexed*, as shown in the message box in Figure 5.23. This process creates the native (RCP) files. Although the conversion may take a while, this indexing is performed in the background, so you can continue to work on other things.

FIGURE 5.23
File Not Indexed message

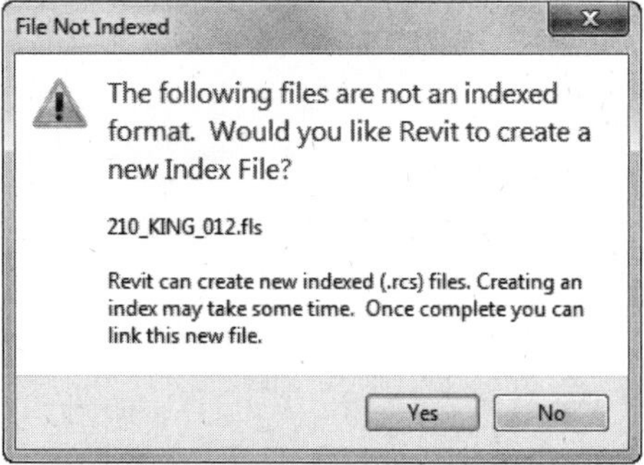

Once the RCP file is created, it can then be linked into your Revit project in the same way as any other linked file. This type of new format is a great way to start an as-built project. This type of data is going to take up resources, however, with files starting at around 200 MB. Nonetheless, the indexed file performs well after it is linked. With the point cloud data linked, you can view it in the same way as any other linked file. In Figure 5.24, you can see this cropped 3D view, which is displaying suspended luminaires.

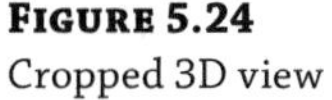

FIGURE 5.24
Cropped 3D view

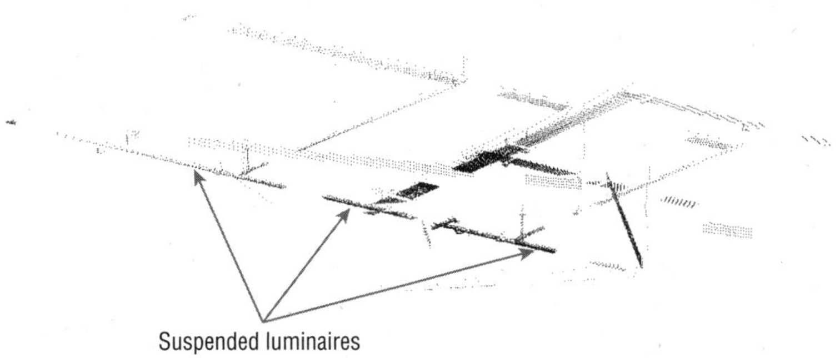

The Bottom Line

Decide which type of data you want to use on a project. Revit 2015 allows the user to import and reuse existing drawings from AutoCAD and other formats.

> **Master It** Having a good command of the tools available for importing other file formats will extend and enhance the integration of Revit with other CAD systems. When importing a 2D file format into Revit, what are the two best ways of ensuring that the data is shown in only one view?

Link data consistently and in the correct location. When bringing data into Revit, it is important to be able to define where an object is positioned.

> **Master It** An imported drawing has inaccurately placed or frozen layer objects that make the extents of that file greater than 20 miles (32.2 km). What should you do prior to the import?

Prepare data prior to import. Revit project files should be the easiest to link to your project. However, at times this process can become complicated.

> **Master It** After receiving a Revit Architecture model, you can see that some worksets are causing visibility issues when the file is linked to the Revit MEP model. How can this be solved?

Chapter 6

Parameters

The Autodesk® Revit® platform is sometimes referred to as a *parametric change engine*. Parameters are the very core of what makes Revit MEP such a powerful design and modeling tool. Parameters hold the computable data that defines the properties of not only model components but also everything that makes up a Revit project. They are the characteristics of all elements of a Revit project that ultimately determine behavior, appearance, performance, and information.

Parameters and properties are often considered synonymous, but it is the *parameters* that hold the information we store in elements; they determine the properties of a component. Properties may be static, but parameters allow for change to be propagated throughout the project.

When you realize the power of parameters in Revit and understand the types of things you can achieve with them, you will have a better understanding of why Revit can improve your workflow processes and the efficiency of your design projects.

In this chapter, you will learn to do the following:

- Manipulate the properties of parameters
- Work with type catalogs
- Work with shared parameters
- Use parameters in project files

Understanding Parameter Basics

Before you can understand how to use parameters to drive the properties of your objects, you need to understand the properties of parameters. When you create a parameter to hold some form of computable data, you want to define the way in which it will do so. Figure 6.1 shows the Parameter Properties dialog box accessed from within the Family Editor. Other versions of this dialog box that contain additional settings are discussed later in the chapter. This dialog box is the first place to go when adding a parameter to a family, a project, or a schedule.

There are four basic kinds of parameters in Revit MEP: system parameters, family parameters, project parameters, and shared parameters. Some parameters are hard-coded into the software. The values of these parameters can be edited as needed, but the parameters themselves cannot be removed or modified. In this chapter, these are referred to as *system parameters*.

Family parameters are used to build and define graphical structure and engineering data within component families. These parameters can be customized as needed to enhance the capabilities of component objects and to extract and analyze data.

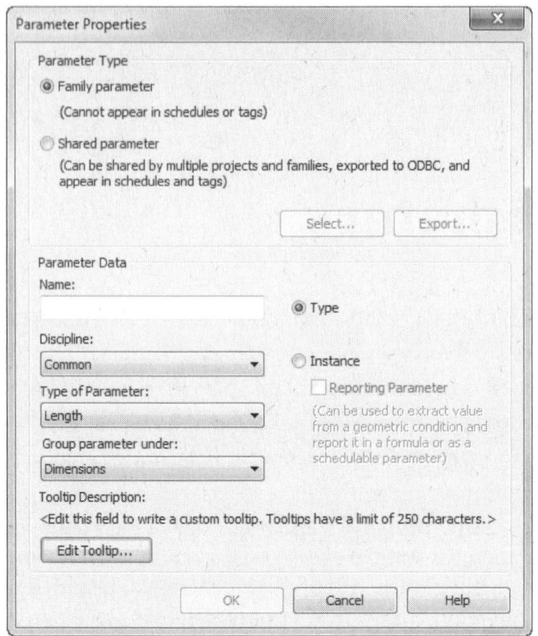

FIGURE 6.1 Parameter Properties dialog box

Shared parameters are useful to help maintain consistency within families and to coordinate information within a project. They are the most useful kind of parameter because they can be used in component families, schedules, tags, and annotations to report the same data in whichever format the user chooses.

Project parameters exist only in the project environment, as the name suggests. They can appear in schedules but not in tags. Their main advantage is that you can apply them to all families of a particular category or even multiple categories in a project instead of having to add the same parameter to every family. Project parameters can be created from the Project Parameters tool under the Manage tab.

Choosing the Correct Parameter

The first decision to make is what type of parameter to create. Family parameters can be created when working in the Family Editor, and they will be visible in a project when the family is selected. However, the information that they hold cannot be used in schedules or reported by a tag or annotation. Shared parameters can be used the same way that family parameters are used, but they are unique in that they can also be used in schedules and tags. However, this rule has its exceptions. For example, in a detail component family, you can't create shared parameters; you can create only family parameters. But family parameters created in a detail component family can appear in schedules yet still not in tags. Parameter types are discussed in further detail later in this chapter.

Naming Parameters

When you choose to add a parameter, it is likely that you have a specific purpose for it. That may sound like an obvious statement, but it is important to consider when you decide what to name the parameter. There is no harm in naming your parameters in a descriptive manner, especially when you are working with others who need to understand the purpose of a parameter. However, it is possible to be too verbose. Long parameter names can cause the annoyance of having to resize columns within dialog boxes in order to read the name.

Consistency is the key to good parameter naming. It can be frustrating to go from one family to another and see different names for parameters that provide the same information. Using descriptive words is also helpful, especially when you have similar parameters within the same object, such as a component that is made up of multiple shapes, each requiring a Width parameter. It can be difficult to work with parameter names such as W1, W2, W3, and so on, whereas using names such as Housing Width, Lens Width, and Bracket Width makes it easier to make adjustments or changes when working in the Properties palette or Type Properties dialog box of the object.

If you intend to abbreviate measurements such as length, height, or radius, be sure to use a consistent format. Will you use the abbreviation as a prefix or suffix to the descriptive portion of the name? Will punctuation such as dashes or parentheses be used? These symbols can have an effect on how those parameters perform in formulas.

Decide up front whether you will use height or depth to describe the third dimension of an object. The way you orient the families can also create inconsistency in parameter usage. What could be width for one family may be length for another. You can avoid this issue by considering the orientation of the family and where the parameters go.

There are two general systems for naming the parameters representing the three dimensions—either keep the parameter name meaningful to the family or always keep it consistent. So, if you were to use the first method (keep it meaningful), you would call the parameter's depth, height, or width based on what makes the most sense for the particular family. And if you were to go with the second method (always consistent), you would always call the three directions of the family the same—length, width, and height. In some cases, the length really may be width, and in others the width really may be depth. But if you are consistent and everyone at your company understands the concept, it all makes sense. In Figure 6.2, you can see a family that uses a consistent naming convention for the three main dimensions. From plan view, the horizontal parameter will always be called `LENGTH`, the vertical will always be called `WIDTH`, and the third parameter will always be called `HEIGHT`.

FIGURE 6.2
Choosing parameter names

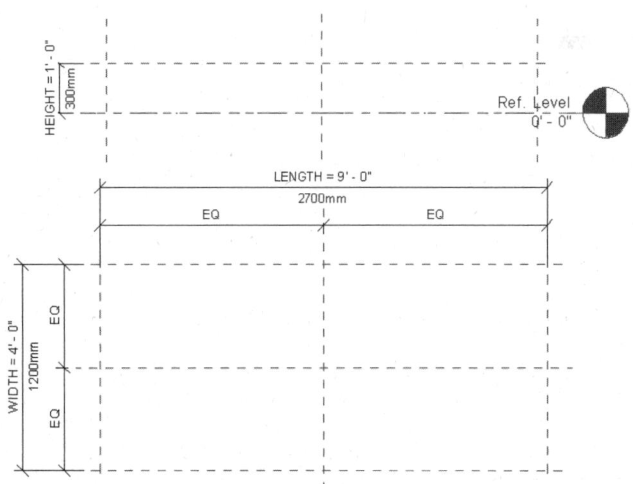

In addition, in this case all caps is used for the naming convention, which helps users to quickly spot any custom parameters in the Properties palette, although there are other ways to achieve this. For example, you can use an abbreviation of your company's name before or after the parameter name, such as MyCo_Length or Height_MyCo. Autodesk capitalizes the first letter of each word when developing parameters names (this is called title case or headline style), and this is the default for standards such as the Autodesk Revit Model Content Style Guide (`http://seek.autodesk.com/MarketingSolutionsRevitStyleGuide.htm`), Australian and New Zealand Revit Standards (`www.ANZRS.org`), and the bimstore Standards (`https://www.bimstore.co.uk/uploads/bim-types/bibles/bimstore-bible-revit-new.pdf`). Whichever you choose for your own standard, the key is to be consistent and stick to it.

Parameter naming is important because Revit is case sensitive and context sensitive when you refer to a parameter in a formula, calculated value, or filter. Spelling and capitalization accuracy are critical, so develop a naming convention that is as simple as possible while still being easily understood.

Using Type Parameters

Type parameters are the reason you can have multiple variations of a family within one file. Family types drive type parameters that are common to the host family, but potentially unique to each family variation - or 'type'. When you are creating a parameter, it is important to decide whether the parameter will be used to define a type within the family.

Type parameters can cause the most damage when misused because they enact changes to every instance of the family type to which they belong. For this reason, you will receive a warning when editing a type parameter in a schedule view, and accessing a type parameter in a model view requires an extra mouse click. However, you can customize the double-click function of the mouse to access the type properties. This can be done from Application ➤ Options ➤ User Interface.

ALWAYS DOUBLE-CHECK

Ethan needs to replace an existing 180 VA receptacle with a 360 VA one. Unfortunately, the Type Selector doesn't have this type of receptacle. When he takes a closer look at the family types, he notices the Volt type parameter but also realizes that if he is to change its value, the change will affect the entire project and all 180 VA receptacles will be changed to 360 VA. Instead, Ethan duplicates the existing 180 VA type to a new 360 VA type and then modifies the Volt type parameter. When editing a type parameter of a family in a project, always double-check that you do not need to create a new family type. It is a safer and better practice to create a new type if there is any doubt.

In some cases, you may choose to use instance parameters instead of type parameters, and we'll be discussing that shortly.

Type parameters do require that if you need to change just one or a few instances of an object, you will have to create a new family type. This can lead to having several types within a family, which causes your Type Selector to be cluttered and confusing. If you are creating a type parameter that will define a family type, it is best to name the family type as it relates to the value of the type parameter(s). A light fixture family, defined by its width and length parameters, would likely have family types with names such as 2′ × 4′ (600 mm × 1,200 mm) and 1′ × 4′ (300 mm × 1,200 mm), for example.

Type parameters also allow you to create type catalogs for families with extensive lists of parameter configurations. We will address type catalogs a little later.

Using Instance Parameters

Instance parameters provide the most flexibility for editing an object. They are easily accessed via the Properties palette when an object is selected. Create instance parameters for values that you want to be able to change for just the selected object. To use the example of a finish color, if the color is an instance parameter, then you could have one family type that could vary in color without having to create a separate family type for each color option. Another example is the Air Flow parameter for diffusers. You may use the same diffuser multiple times in your project, but the air flow they supply from one room to another most likely will vary.

The drawback to instance parameters is that they apply only to the selected objects. Thus, if you want to change an instance parameter value for all instances of an object, you will have to select each object and change it individually. Alternatively, you can select objects by using schedules or by right-clicking an object and choosing Select All Instances. Make sure you understand the difference between the options Visible In View and In Entire Project. Figure 6.3 shows the difference between these two options.

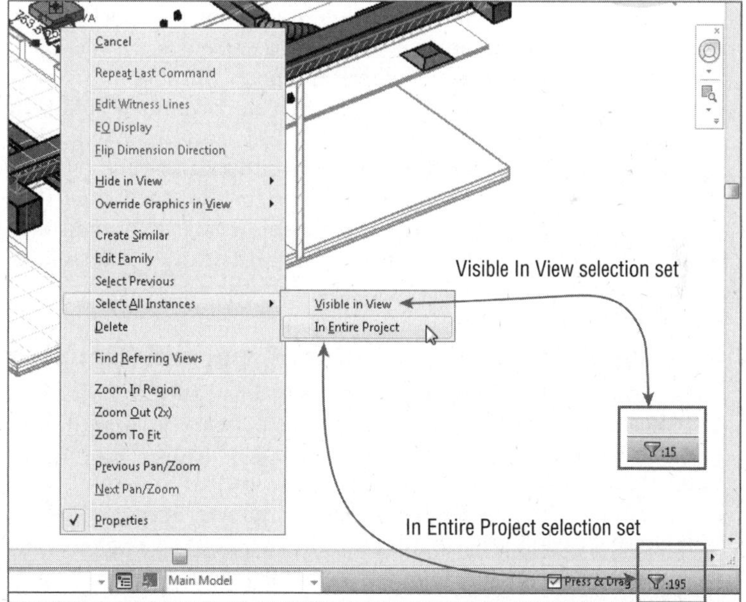

FIGURE 6.3 Selecting all instances

Real World Scenario

SELECTING ALL INSTANCES

Maria, an experienced Revit user in a hurry to issue drawings, is asked to remove circuit tags from the view in which she is currently working. She uses Select All Instances and mistakenly chooses the In Entire Project option. She doesn't notice the filter number indicating more than 2,000 objects selected. Maria proceeds to delete all tags and gets ready to issue the drawings. An hour later, she recognizes her error and wants to undo changes. Unfortunately, other people have been synchronizing work back to the central file, which includes some additional work to the lighting design in other parts of the building. Maria has no option but to go through the entire set to replace all tags. There is an option to tag all objects not already tagged (Tag All Not Tagged), which greatly reduces the amount of time required to re-annotate the output documentation (although she does have to repeat this in every view).

This experience doesn't put Maria off. She knows what happened and why, and the drawings go out on time. Now, in training sessions, she is able to demonstrate what not to do in a hurry (delete all tags in a project) and how to rectify the issue by using the Tag All Not Tagged option.

An instance parameter can be set to be a reporting parameter. A *reporting parameter* will hold a value that can be used in formulas for other parameters, or it can be used to drive the behavior of another parameter. These are most useful in wall- or ceiling-hosted families because, for example, you can use a reporting parameter to recognize the thickness of the host wall. Some portion of a dimensional reporting parameter must be associated to the host in order to be used in a formula. These parameters have a very narrow range of application, especially for the MEP disciplines. It may take a while until you find a purpose for them. In most cases, beginner Revit users create them by mistake and get even more confused about why the parameter doesn't work as expected.

Once you have defined a parameter as either instance or type, you can change it if required for the desired behavior. Just keep in mind that Revit will not let you change a type parameter to an instance parameter if that parameter is used in a formula of a type parameter. The rule of thumb is that instance parameters can't "drive" type parameters. Thus, it is best to know up front what kind of parameter to create.

Setting Parameter Discipline, Type, and Grouping

The Discipline drop-down list in the Parameter Properties dialog box contains the different disciplines that can be assigned to a parameter. Parameter discipline is important for defining the measurement units that the parameter value will have. Figure 6.4 shows the drop-down list of available disciplines.

The Type Of Parameter option in the Parameter Properties dialog box is directly related to the chosen discipline. Each discipline has a unique set of parameter types that relate to the various units of measurement for that discipline.

Figure 6.5 shows the Type Of Parameter options for the Common discipline. Notice that many of the types are the same as in the Project Units settings for the Common discipline of a project, such as Length, Area, and Volume.

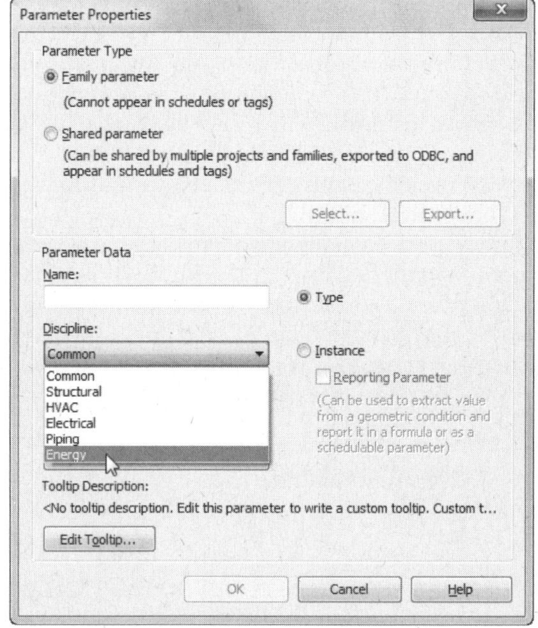

FIGURE 6.4 Parameter discipline options

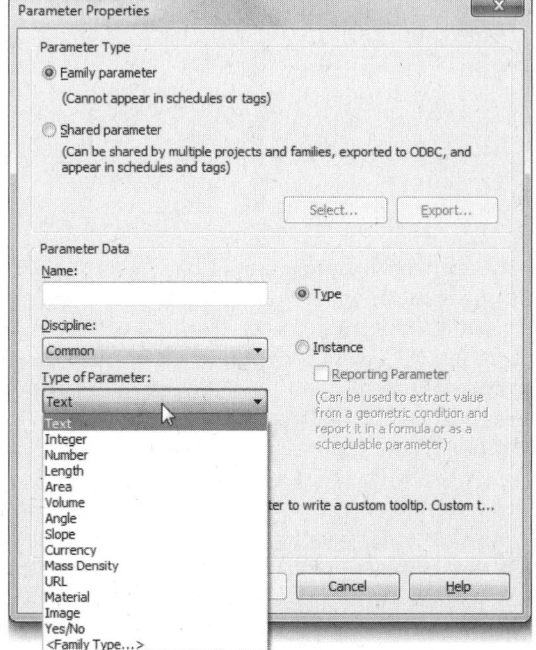

FIGURE 6.5 Type Of Parameter options for the Common discipline

There are additional options for parameter values that are not a unit of measurement. The Text option allows you to input anything for the value of the parameter. This is the most versatile option, but from an engineering standpoint, it offers the least amount of "intelligence" because a text string provides only information, not computable data. If the parameter value doesn't have specific units and will always be numbers, it is best to use Number instead of Text; this will allow you to use it in formulas if you ever need it. If you are creating a parameter that is scheduled and want the ability to input either numbers or text or a combination of characters, then the Text option is best.

The <Family Type...> option for a parameter is a useful tool when you have multiple nested families within a family. You can create a Family Type parameter to toggle between all the nested families. When the host family is loaded into a project, the parameter can be modified to display any of the nested families by selecting from the list in the Family Type parameter. Figure 6.6 shows an annotation family for graphic scales with several nested annotations loaded. A Family Type instance parameter has been created to allow the use of any of the nested families.

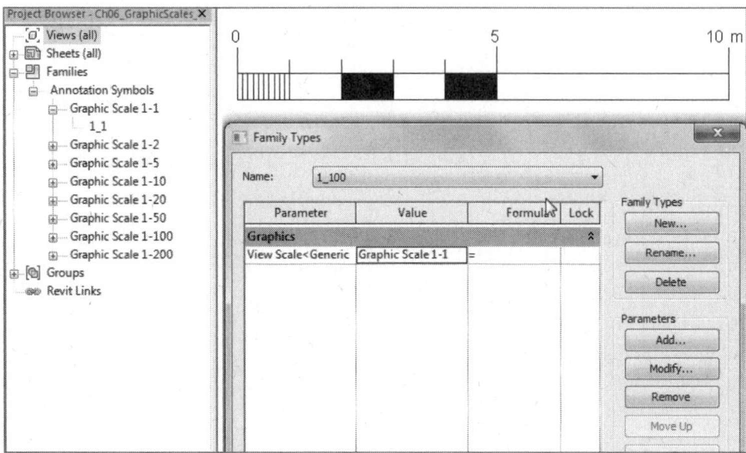

FIGURE 6.6 Family using Family Types parameter

You can use the Yes/No option if your parameter requires a simple yes or no value. The value for this type of parameter appears as a check box in the Properties palette, and it can be used to control the visibility of objects or to verify that a condition exists. In schedules, a Yes/No parameter appears as Yes, No, or a blank field. By default, Yes/No parameters are selected and grayed out in the Properties palette, which means it's in a limbo state that is neither yes nor no; this is when it will appear as a blank field on a schedule.

Other disciplines have options for Type Of Parameter that relate to units of measurement. When you select a specific Type Of Parameter setting, the value used for the parameter must be consistent with the unit of measurement. For example, if you choose the Air Flow option for the HVAC discipline, you could not input any value other than a number consistent with the unit of measurement you are using for airflow. This can cause problems with schedules when an object does not have a value for this parameter and you want to use something such as N/A or a dash to indicate that the value is not actually 0.

By default, the Type Of Parameter option is set to Length. This was introduced in Revit MEP 2011, whereas in older versions the default was Text. In older versions, it was easy to overlook this setting because of the versatility of the Text type, but with Length being the default now, Revit defaults to the most common parameter, but it is still important to set the proper type if Length is not what you need.

You can determine where the parameter will show up in the Properties palette or the Type Properties dialog box of an object, as shown in Figure 6.7. However, Revit will make a best guess, placing the HVAC/Airflow parameter into the Mechanical – Airflow group or the Electrical/Luminous Flux parameter into the Photometrics group, for example. The user can override this but should consider other users and content creators. If you are using shared parameters, it may well be a best practice to accept the defaults, unless the company documentation is very good. This will lead to less confusion because coworkers will know where to find similar data in families and projects.

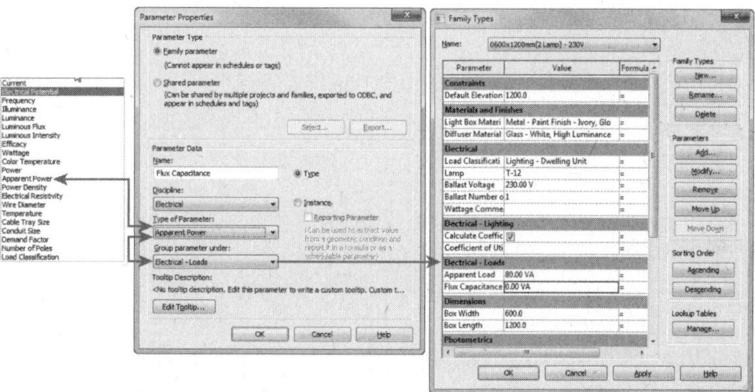

FIGURE 6.7
Parameter groups

The option for grouping parameters is sometimes confusing to people because they think that it is related to the Type Of Parameter setting. The Group Parameter Under setting does not have any bearing on the Type Of Parameter and Discipline settings, so you could have a Duct Size parameter that is placed in the Identity Data group. Parameter grouping is another area in which being consistent is important to improved workflow and efficiency. You want to be able to find your parameters in the same location for each family while editing in your model. If you are not going to use the default for Group Parameter Under all the time, it may be a good idea to take it a step further and create a company-standard document that outlines what Type Of Parameter setting goes in what Group Parameter Under setting. By finding the same parameters always in the same group, your users will be more efficient and comfortable with your company families.

New to Revit MEP 2015 is the ability to either sort parameters alphabetically (Ascending or Descending) or move them by using the additional buttons available in the Family Types dialog, as shown in Figure 6.8. When new parameters are added to a new family, they are automatically sorted alphabetically. If a family is upgraded from a previous version, the user then has the ability to sort the parameters with the Ascending or Descending buttons. Once the parameters are sorted, you can move each parameter up or down within each group. This means important parameters can be pushed to the top of a group, even though you may have sorted them alphabetically.

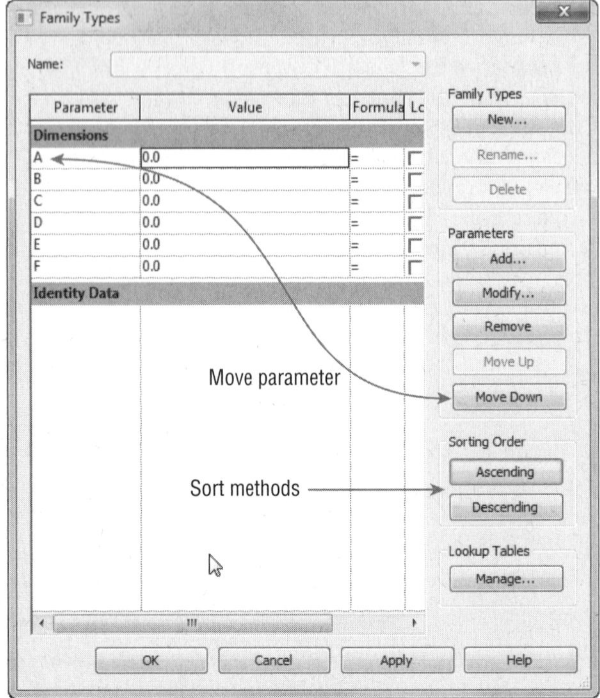

FIGURE 6.8 Parameter sorting

The current version of Revit does not allow users to customize any of these pull-downs. This creates challenges with various units that may need to exist at the same time in the project. A good example for that is the Power unit of measurement; it can be watts, BTU per second, horsepower, and a few more choices. But in a real project, chances are you will want to use horsepower for motors, watts or volt-amperes for electricity distribution, and maybe kilowatts for the entire building or major blocks of the building. In reality, you can't do that with Revit.

If you create a family that uses different units for certain parameters, the family units will be changed after it is loaded into the project. This is a significant roadblock for achieving true BIM because there are industry standards for the units (W, VA, KW, and so forth) that need to be used for a specific parameter. In most cases, the information (the *I* in BIM) becomes second in priority in order to complete the project in a biddable and readable fashion, which in many cases would involve using either numbers or text parameters instead of actual units. As a result of such workarounds, you may not be able to circuit certain devices or show their load on the panel schedules unless the chosen units are the same for the entire project.

Using Parameters in Families

Many parameters are created when working in the Family Editor. As content is planned, created, or edited, it becomes clear which type of data is needed for either analysis or reporting or to drive the geometry. When you're working with Revit families, you'll come across the term *flexing*, which essentially means changing dimensional parameter values to test whether a family is parametric (flexible) and can take various parameter values without being broken. Flexing a family can be done through the Family Types dialog box, by modifying a series of parameters and clicking OK. Another way to flex a family is to modify the parameter value directly in a plan view or any other view. All you need is to select the parameter and enter a different value for it. A third method of flexing a family is to select a reference plane and move it in order to flex the parameter value indirectly. This last method is further explained in the next section.

Dimensional Parameters Lock Function

You have the ability to lock *dimensional parameters* in the Family Editor so that they cannot be changed while working on the geometry of a family. There is a Lock column in the Family Types dialog box with a check box for each dimensional parameter. What is nice about this feature is that if you do not lock a parameter, you can change its value while working on the geometry, eliminating the need to stop and access the parameter to change its value manually. An object that is constrained by a dimension can be moved and the parameter's dimension value will adjust. This eliminates the pesky Constraints Are Not Satisfied warning dialog box that appeared in versions earlier than Revit MEP 2012. However, this warning will appear if a dimensional parameter is locked and an object is moved.

You can also edit the value of a dimensional parameter in the drawing area by clicking the text, just as you would edit a dimension object. This can be done whether the parameter is locked or not. Locking prevents only the accidental dragging of an object while you're working in the drawing area.

Parameter Types

When creating type parameters in a family, you set a specific value for each family type. When the family is inserted into a project, the values established in the family will remain until the family type is edited. Changing a type dimension, or any other type parameter in a project has to be carefully considered. Do you want to change a standard object, which could affect many instances of a family, or should you create a new family type? The answer to this may not always be as simple as it first seems.

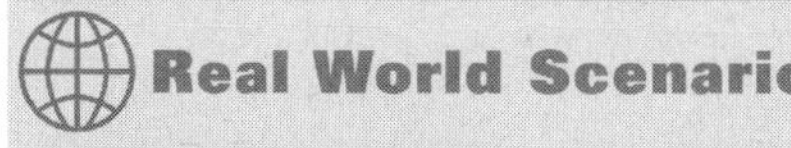

PARAMETER TYPES

While creating a lighting plan, Samir loads a family—Recessed Parabolic Luminaire, type 2′×4′—and places it in multiple locations. During the design process, the engineer indicates that she wants a different layout with 2′×2′ fixtures. Samir could change the type parameter for length to 2′ and have an immediate result. However, he knows that by doing so, he is not changing many of the other design criteria parameters, so he duplicates the family type, creates a new 2′×2′ type, and enters the design and dimensional parameters. He now needs to select and change the required existing luminaires from their current type to that new one. Although this process may take slightly longer than the first option, Samir is confident that any calculations will be correct and future changes will take even less time to make.

Instance parameters can be given a default value when created in a family. These parameters are easily identified in the Family Types dialog box via a suffix of *(default)*. This is the value the parameter is meant to have initially when it's placed into a project. The first attempt to place an instance of a family does not always have the default value defined in the family for an instance parameter. Subsequent placement of the same family uses the last input value. The value can be modified prior to placement of the family.

If you edit a family that exists in your project and then load it back into the project, the instance parameter values do not change from their existing states in the project. When you are loading a family into a project and a type parameter value in the family is different from those in the project, a dialog box that warns you that the object already exists in the project gives you the option to overwrite the family and its parameter values, which will change any type parameters to the value as it exists in the family. All instance parameter values will remain unchanged even if they are different in the family.

As mentioned earlier, Yes/No parameters are great for controlling the visibility of objects. After creating a Yes/No parameter, you can select the desired object and set its Visibility parameter to the value of the Yes/No parameter by using the small button at the far right of the Visibility parameter value in the Properties palette. Figure 6.9 shows the settings used to associate the visibility of the diagonal line with a Yes/No parameter.

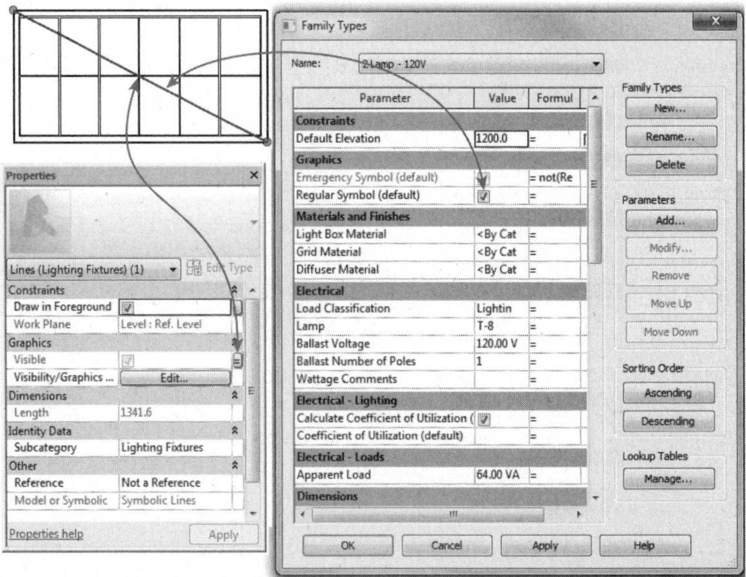

FIGURE 6.9
Yes/No parameter used in a family for visibility

YES/NO PARAMETERS IN NESTED ANNOTATION FAMILIES

To control the number of annotation families that are nested into a family, Yes/No parameters within an annotation are very useful. One example is for electrical receptacles. Many receptacles look essentially the same in the model, but the symbol used for each type may vary. Instead of creating a separate annotation symbol for each type of receptacle, consider using Yes/No parameters within one annotation to account for each symbol. The image shown here is an annotation family with all of the linework and regions required to represent each type of symbol used.

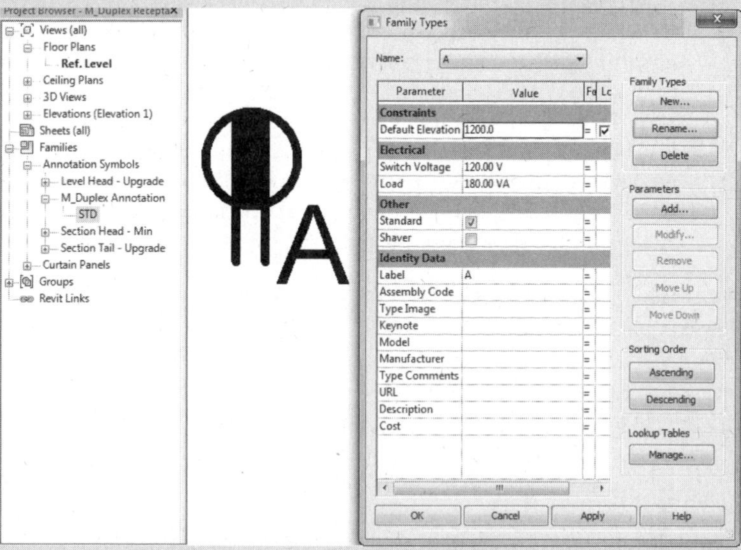

The visibility of the lines and regions is associated with Yes/No parameters so that when this annotation is nested into a family, the Yes/No parameters can be associated with parameters in the family. The result is a single receptacle family that can represent multiple types of receptacles, as shown here. Another way of accomplishing similar results is using the Family Type option mentioned previously.

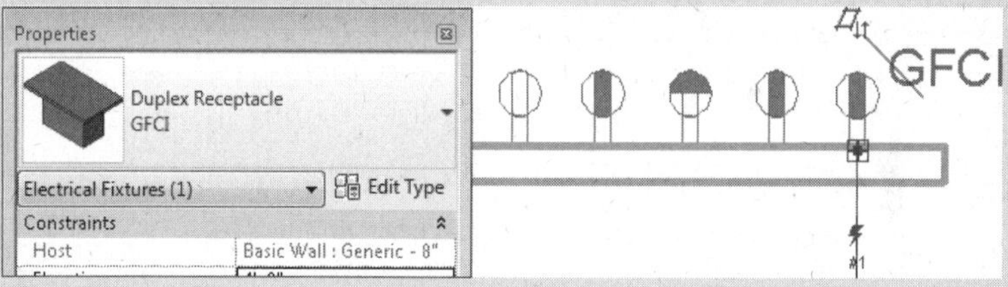

Type Catalogs

Families can sometimes become crowded with many types. The number of type parameters used to define a family type potentially increases the number of family types. When these families are loaded into a project, all of the family types are loaded. This can quickly cause your project to be overloaded with unused family types. One way to remedy this scenario is to create type catalogs for families that contain many types.

A *type catalog* is a TXT file that contains values for the type parameters of a family. Having a type catalog associated with a family allows you to select only the family types you want to load when you insert the family into a project. You can create a type catalog for a family by creating a TXT file that has the same name as the family and is located in the same folder as the family file. Because type catalogs are TXT files in comma-delimited format, it is easier to edit them using a spreadsheet program such as Microsoft Excel.

To create a type catalog from scratch, start a new spreadsheet file. Enter all the family types in the first column of the spreadsheet. Each column after that will be a type parameter within the family. The type parameters must exist in the family file and have some value in order to be used in the type catalog.

In the past, you couldn't have instance parameters as part of a type catalog, but now that is possible as well. If you leave a parameter value blank in the family, the type catalog will ignore the parameter when the family is loaded. So, even though the parameters in the family are essentially placeholders for the type catalog, they need to have something input for their value. Figure 6.10 shows an example of a type catalog for a motor connection family.

FIGURE 6.10 Sample type catalog

	A	B	C	D	E
1		Duct Width##Other##millimeters	Duct Height##Other##millimeters	Duct Diameter##Other##millimeters	Plenum Length##Other##millimeters
2	250x250-125	250	250	125	250
3	250x250-150	250	250	150	250
4	250x250-200	250	250	200	250
5	300x250-125	300	250	125	250
6	300x250-150	300	250	150	250
7	300x250-200	300	250	200	250
8	350x250-125	350	250	125	250
9	350x250-150	350	250	150	250
10	350x250-200	350	250	200	250
11	400x250-125	400	250	125	250
12	400x250-150	400	250	150	250
13	400x250-200	400	250	200	250
14	450x250-125	450	250	125	250
15	450x250-150	450	250	150	250
16	450x250-200	450	250	200	250
17	500x250-150	500	250	150	250

It is easy to see why a type catalog for this family is used; otherwise, all 15 family types would be loaded when this family is inserted into a project. Notice that the format for the type parameters is:

```
,parameter name##parameter type##units##
```

You can cheat with the parameter type a bit: Instead of remembering the proper formatting for all units, in most cases you can use Other.

Here are a few examples of proper formatting:

```
,Duct Width##HVAC_DUCT_SIZE##INCHES
```

```
,Power##ELECTRICAL_POWER##WATTS
```

```
,Air Flow##HVAC_AIR_FLOW##CUBIC_FEET_PER_MINUTE
```

```
,Width##LENGTH##FEET
```

At first the formatting can be confusing, and if you don't have a cheat sheet, it will be hard to remember it for the various parameters. However, if you look closely, you are probably noticing a pattern; you can make sense out of all this instead of just trying to remember it. Let's take a look at the Duct Width parameter, for example. When you are creating this parameter, you need to select options for Discipline (HVAC), Type Of Parameter (Duct Size), Group Parameter Under, and whether it will be Instance or Type, as shown in Figure 6.11. Now look at the formatting for the preceding Duct Width parameter again. You can see that the syntax is as follows:

<parameter name>##<Discipline_Type of Parameter>##units. OK, now this is a lot easier to understand and memorize than remembering about a 100 different configurations.

FIGURE 6.11
Parameter settings

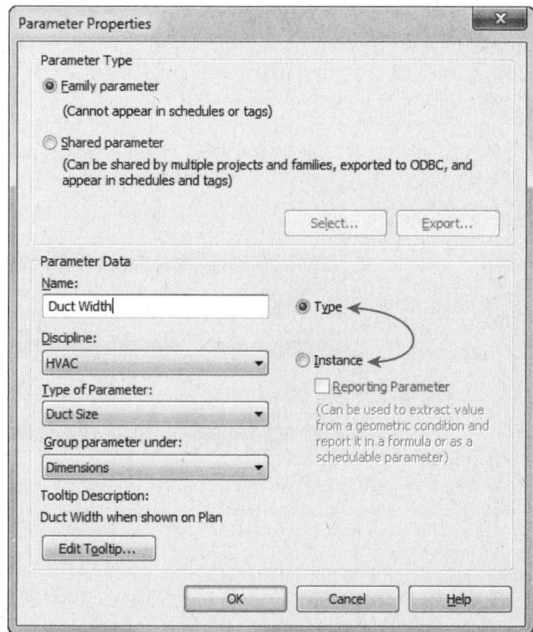

You can create a type catalog by exporting parameters from a family. Note that this method is not available in versions of Revit from 2011 and earlier, so the previous method should be used. In more complex families containing a lot of parameters that don't need to be controlled via a type catalog, the previous method would still be more efficient. To create a type catalog by exporting parameters from a family, do the following:

1. While in the family you want to create a type catalog for, choose Application ➤ Export ➤ Family Types. This exports the type parameters in a TXT file that you should save in the folder in which the family is located. This is the fastest way to create a type catalog; the downside is that it will contain all type parameters and in most cases you will need to clean it up a bit.

2. Create the spreadsheet and save it as a comma-separated values (CSV) file. If you receive a warning that some of the features of the file may not work when saved to CSV format, you can click Yes to save the file.

   Once the file is saved, you can browse to it and rename the file with a .txt extension to convert it. If you receive a warning that the file might become unusable when the filename extension is changed and asks if you want to proceed, click Yes.

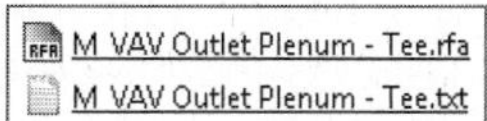

When a family with an associated type catalog is inserted into a project, a dialog box will appear that allows you to see the parameter values for each type and choose which family types you would like to load.

3. Choose family types by selecting them from the list. You can select multiple types, as shown in Figure 6.12. You can filter the Specify Types dialog box based on specific parameter values by using the drop-down list under the heading of each column.

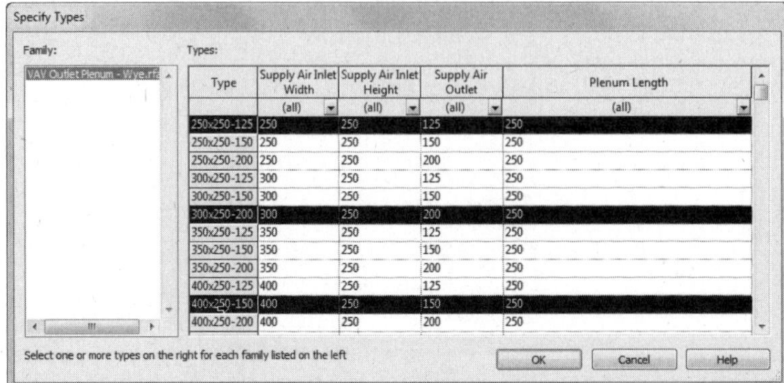

FIGURE 6.12 Specifying types from a type catalog

DRAG AND DROP FAMILIES WITH A TYPE CATALOG

The type catalog functionality of a family will work only if you use the Load Family option from the Insert tab of the ribbon. Dragging and dropping a family file that has a type catalog into your project will load only the default type. To access the type catalog after a family has been loaded into your project, you can locate the family in the Project Browser, right-click, and select Reload.

Formulas

Not all parameters in a family are used to drive the geometry directly; many are used to hold data that results from the creation of the geometry and that will be used for driving additional geometry or spatial relationships. This is done by creating a formula for a parameter. Formulas can vary in complexity and functionality, as shown in Figure 6.13. Pipe fittings are notorious for their complexity and the number of formulas they need in order to create the desired functionality.

One nice feature of formulas is that when you change a parameter name, it will be updated in all formulas where this parameter is used. Mathematical operators and Boolean functions can all be used. Placement of parentheses, proper units, case, parameter names, and context sensitivity are all important for your formulas to work properly. A warning will appear if the result of a formula does not match the units for a parameter or if a parameter name is misspelled.

Formulas can even be used for parameter types such as a Yes/No parameter. Figure 6.14 shows a Boolean formula used to determine when a check box should be selected for a Yes/No parameter. The formula indicates that the box is either deselected or selected when the conditions of the formula are true.

FIGURE 6.13 Formulas in fittings

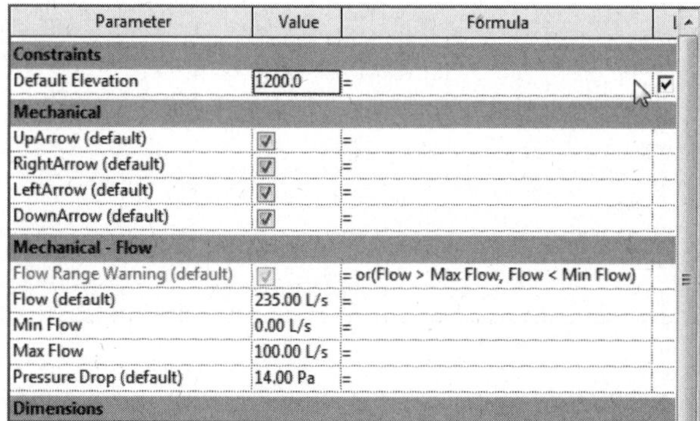

FIGURE 6.14 Boolean formula for a Yes/No parameter

Formulas using `if` statements are powerful for providing exact conditions and variations in parameter values based on other parameter values. The format for an `if` statement is as follows:

```
if(logical_test,value_if_true,value_if_false)
```

The *`value_if_false`* result is the value given to the parameter when the condition is not met. You can use other parameters to define the condition. For example, if you want a Width parameter to equal the Length parameter under certain conditions, you could write this formula:

```
if(Length>2' 0", Length, 1' 0")
if(Length>600mm, Length, 300mm)
```

This formula would cause the Width value to equal the Length value when the Length is greater than 2′-0″ (600 mm); otherwise, the Width value would be 1′-0″ (300 mm).

Crossing Parameter Types in Formulas

When referencing a parameter in a formula, it is important to know that you cannot use an instance parameter in a formula for a type parameter. You would need to either change the type parameter to an instance or change the instance parameter to a type parameter.

Real World Scenario

Parameter Use

Starting a new job in a consulting engineer's office, Brian finds that the drafting standard is to indicate duct type and construction by using textual information rather than doing so graphically. This means having 18 duct types defined in the project template, each with an identical Type Mark parameter. However, duplicate type marks produce an error message (which can be ignored). The way around this is for Brian to create his own shared parameter type mark, MyCo Type Mark. This method works well for Brian, allowing him to maintain his drafting standards and maximize his efficiency.

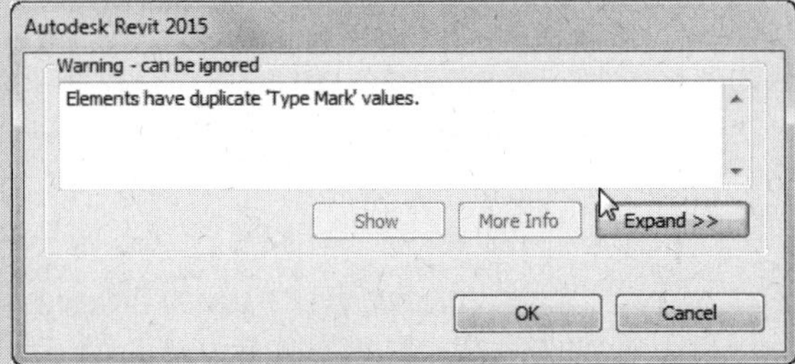

System Parameters

When you create a family, certain parameters exist by default. These parameters are hard-coded into the software and cannot be removed. You can use these parameters to avoid having to create custom parameters.

These parameters vary depending on the category you choose for the family. The system parameters under the Identity Data group are common to component families and are also included in system families within a project.

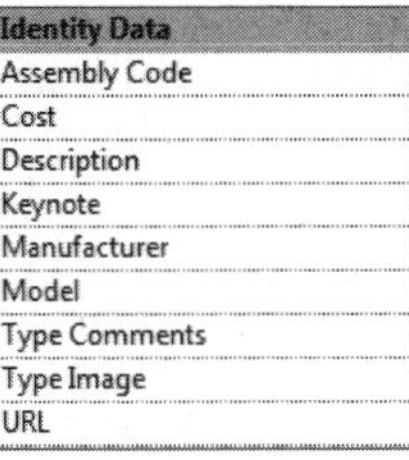

Identity Data
Assembly Code
Cost
Description
Keynote
Manufacturer
Model
Type Comments
Type Image
URL

There are, however, a few that do not appear in the Family Types dialog box when you're working in the Family Editor but do appear in the Type Properties dialog box or the Properties palette after the family has been loaded into a project. The most notable of these are the Type Mark, Offset, Level, Host, Mark, Phase Created, and Phase Demolished parameters. The Type Mark parameter is often used to identify a component with a tag or in a schedule. Because this parameter does not exist in the family file, you cannot use it in a type catalog. One way to avoid creating a custom parameter that does essentially the same job as the Type Mark parameter is to have your type catalog create family types named with the same value you would use for the Type Mark. Then you can tag or schedule that type parameter instead of the Type Mark parameter. To appear in a schedule or a tag, the parameter has to be a shared parameter.

Lookup Tables

Lookup tables are designed to drive instance parameter values via an external CSV file. They are similar to type catalogs in that they store parameter values. But type catalogs are meant for type parameters (even though in recent versions of Revit MEP you can control instance parameters with them as well). Perhaps the main difference between type catalogs and lookup tables is that type catalogs are accessed by Revit MEP when you are loading a family, while lookup tables are loaded when the software launches and Revit MEP uses all of their data all the time. In addition, type catalogs must reside in the same folder as the family; lookup tables are located in a different location than the family. Lookup tables are mostly used for pipe, duct, conduit, and cable tray fittings. But they can be used for anything else that requires constant referencing. When you install Revit MEP 2015, an extensive library of lookup tables is installed that can be referenced by families.

Lookup tables are CSV files that work like a type catalog. They provide values for dimensions based on other dimensions within the family. The data in lookup tables can be driven by design codes or manufacturing standards to ensure the graphical accuracy of your components. Pipe fittings, for example, have a nominal diameter that is used to identify the size, but the actual outside diameter is slightly different, especially for different pipe materials. A lookup table can provide the outside diameter dimension for each nominal diameter that exists in the table.

Since Revit 2014, content creators have had the ability to embed lookup tables directly into the family. In fact, the majority of families that are installed by default already have lookup tables embedded. This greatly reduces the issue of having to ensure that the table travels with the family (within a project) not only when being issued to external sources but also when your IT department is reluctant to place additional files into your lookup table folders on a protected network drive or into folders distributed to each computer on the network. With the lookup table embedded into the family, you will always get a correctly sized family regardless of where that family is loaded.

The Lookup Table Name parameter is used to identify which CSV file the family is referencing. The location of your lookup tables is defined in your `Revit.ini` file. When you type in the name of a lookup table, you do not need to include the full path to the file, only the name and filename extension. As with parameter names, referencing a lookup table name is case and context sensitive.

Once you have referenced the lookup table with the Lookup Table Name parameter, you can access the data in the table by using a formula for the value of a parameter. The formula using lookup table data is as follows:

```
text_file_lookup(Lookup Table Name, "Column Name", ↵
Value if not found in table, Value found in table)
```

The result of this formula will apply the value found in the table to the parameter, or it will apply the defined value given in the formula if none is found in the table. Figure 6.15 shows the formula used to determine the value of the Fitting Outside Diameter (FOD) parameter of a pipe-fitting family. The FOD column is searched for a value that coincides with the value given for the Nominal Diameter parameter, and that value is applied to the FOD parameter. If the Nominal Diameter value given in the family does not match one in the table, then Nominal Diameter + 1⁄8″ is used for the FOD.

FIGURE 6.15
Lookup tables in formulas

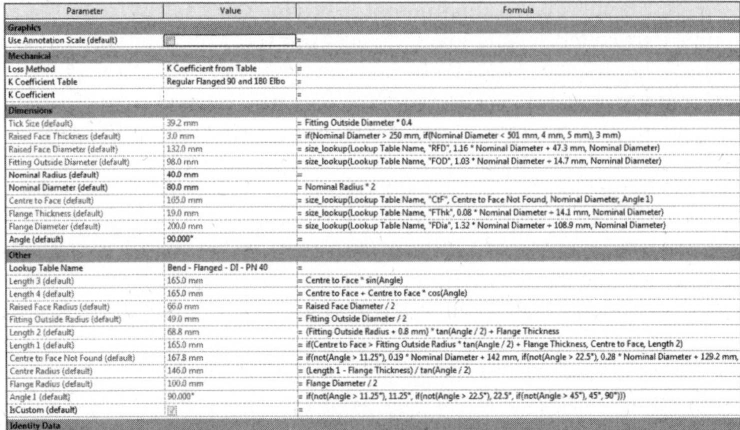

Parameter	Value	Formula
Graphics		
Use Annotation Scale (default)	☐	=
Mechanical		
Loss Method	K Coefficient from Table	=
K Coefficient Table	Regular Flanged 90 and 180 Elbo	=
K Coefficient		=
Dimensions		
Tick Size (default)	39.2 mm	= Fitting Outside Diameter * 0.4
Raised Face Thickness (default)	3.0 mm	= if(Nominal Diameter > 250 mm, if(Nominal Diameter < 501 mm, 4 mm, 5 mm), 3 mm)
Raised Face Diameter (default)	132.0 mm	= size_lookup(Lookup Table Name, "RFD", 1.16 * Nominal Diameter + 47.3 mm, Nominal Diameter)
Fitting Outside Diameter (default)	98.0 mm	= size_lookup(Lookup Table Name, "FOD", 1.03 * Nominal Diameter + 14.7 mm, Nominal Diameter)
Nominal Radius (default)	40.0 mm	=
Nominal Diameter (default)	80.0 mm	= Nominal Radius * 2
Centre to Face (default)	165.0 mm	= size_lookup(Lookup Table Name, "CtF", Centre to Face Not Found, Nominal Diameter, Angle 1)
Flange Thickness (default)	19.0 mm	= size_lookup(Lookup Table Name, "FThk", 0.08 * Nominal Diameter + 14.1 mm, Nominal Diameter)
Flange Diameter (default)	200.0 mm	= size_lookup(Lookup Table Name, "FDia", 1.32 * Nominal Diameter + 108.9 mm, Nominal Diameter)
Angle (default)	90.000°	=
Other		
Lookup Table Name	Bend - Flanged - DI - PN 40	=
Length 3 (default)	165.0 mm	= Centre to Face * sin(Angle)
Length 4 (default)	165.0 mm	= Centre to Face + Centre to Face * cos(Angle)
Raised Face Radius (default)	66.0 mm	= Raised Face Diameter / 2
Fitting Outside Radius (default)	49.0 mm	= Fitting Outside Diameter / 2
Length 2 (default)	68.8 mm	= (Fitting Outside Radius + 0.8 mm) * tan(Angle / 2) + Flange Thickness
Length 1 (default)	165.0 mm	= if(Centre to Face > Fitting Outside Radius * tan(Angle / 2) + Flange Thickness, Centre to Face, Length 2)
Centre to Face Not Found (default)	167.8 mm	= if(not(Angle > 11.25°), 0.19 * Nominal Diameter + 142 mm, if(not(Angle > 22.5°), 0.28 * Nominal Diameter + 129.2 mm,
Centre Radius (default)	146.0 mm	= (Length 1 - Flange Thickness) / tan(Angle / 2)
Flange Radius (default)	100.0 mm	= Flange Diameter / 2
Angle 1 (default)	90.000°	= if(not(Angle > 11.25°), 11.25°, if(not(Angle > 22.5°), 22.5°, if(not(Angle > 45°), 45°, 90°)))
IsCustom (default)	☑	=
Identity Data		

For additional information on working with parameters in family files, another good reference point is the Autodesk Families Guide, which can be accessed from the Autodesk Help site:

`http://help.autodesk.com/view/RVT/2015/ENU`

Help ➢ Revit Users ➢ Build the Model ➢ Revit Families.

Using Shared Parameters

Shared parameters are the most versatile parameters you can use, but they also require the most management. Used properly, shared parameters can help ensure that your schedules are coordinated and that your construction documents are reporting the correct information. Shared parameters can be type or instance parameters that are used in families or as project parameters. The main advantage to using shared parameters is that the data they hold can be exported or reported in tags and schedules.

Shared parameters are parameters that are created with their settings stored in a TXT file. It may help to think of this file as a library of parameters, similar to a library of model components.

SHARED PARAMETERS FILE

Do not attempt to edit your shared parameters' TXT files with a text editor. They should be edited through the Revit interface only.

When you need to add a parameter to a family or project, you can use one from your shared parameters file. This helps with the management of your content and project standards because you can be consistent in your use of parameters. It also helps with maintenance by allowing you to avoid duplication of parameters, which can cause coordination issues. Multiple parameters with the same name can show up as available for use in a schedule, and you will not be able to tell which one is the correct one to use.

You can create a shared parameter by doing the following:

1. Click the Shared Parameters button on the Manage tab. When you create a parameter in the Family Editor or add a project parameter, you have the option for it to be a shared parameter. Selecting this option activates the Select button in the Parameter Properties dialog box.
2. In the Edit Shared Parameters dialog box, you must first create a shared parameters file. Click the Create button to select a location for the file.

   You can have multiple shared parameter files, so it is a good idea to create a folder in a common location that you and others can access. But keep in mind that having multiple shared parameter files is possibly asking for trouble because you have to manage each file, ensuring that no duplicates exist.

   You can access these files by clicking the Browse button in the Edit Shared Parameters dialog box, which is shown in Figure 6.16.

FIGURE 6.16 Edit Shared Parameters dialog box

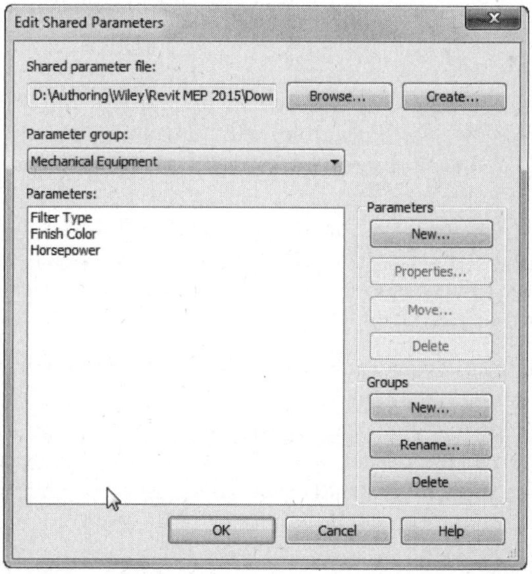

There are two components to a shared parameters file. The parameter group is a level of organization that you can establish to group parameters together. This is not the same group as shown in the Parameter Properties dialog box for defining where parameters will be listed. These groups are available so that you can keep your shared parameters organized. One common method of organization is to create groups based on family categories. Figure 6.17 shows an example of parameter groups created for parameters that apply to specific family categories. This method is intuitive and could help you find the parameters you need for the family you are creating much faster. But there are many parameters that will be used across multiple families (Length, Air Flow, and so forth), and it could be confusing.

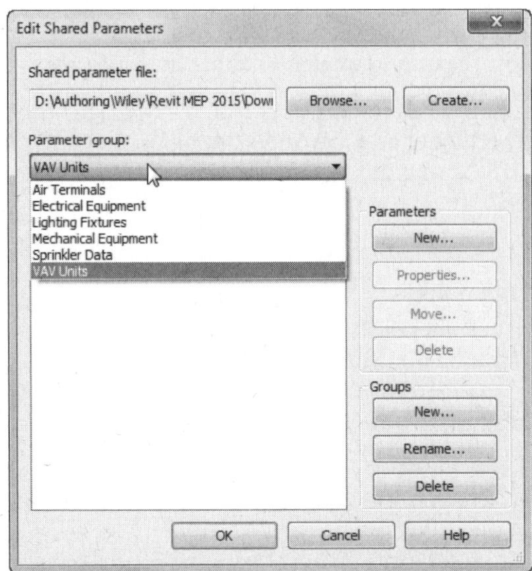

FIGURE 6.17 Method 1—using family categories

Notice that a group has been created for variable air volume (VAV) units. Although it is possible to create a group with any name, keep in mind that the parameters must be assigned to a category. In the case of these parameters, they will be applied to all mechanical equipment if they are used as project parameters, even though they are specifically designed for VAV units. The parameters in this group could be added to a lighting fixture family if chosen. Parameter groups can be renamed or deleted by using the buttons in the lower-right corner of the dialog box. You cannot delete a group until all parameters have been removed from it.

Another way to organize your shared parameter groups is to use the Group Parameter Under pull-down in the Parameter Properties dialog box. When you use this method, the position of the parameter grouping will be identical in both the shared parameters file and in the properties of the family, as shown in Figure 6.18. If you choose this method, don't hurry to create all of the groups exactly as they appear in the Parameter Properties dialog box. You will find that half of those groups are unnecessary, and you may never use them. So, create only what you need, and you can always add more as you find them necessary.

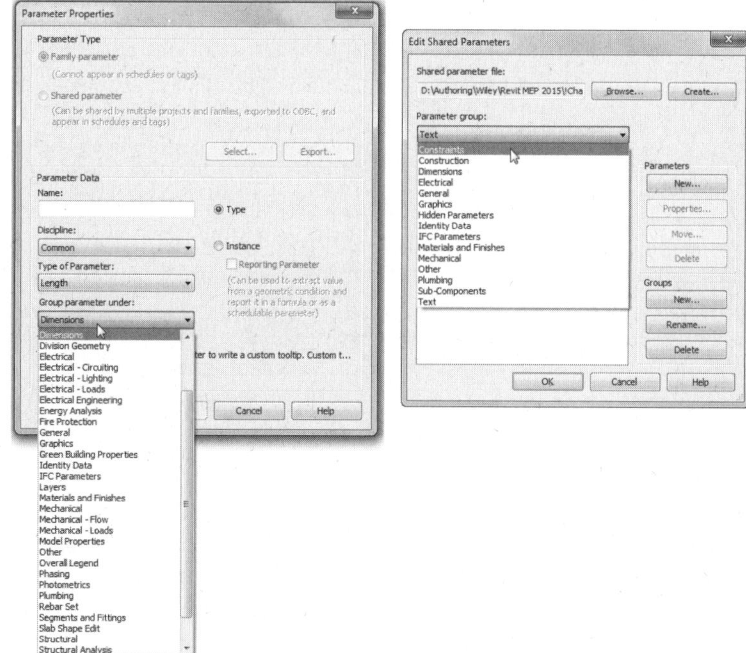

FIGURE 6.18
Method 2—using Group Parameter Under

3. After you have established a group in your shared parameters file, you can begin to create parameters. Click the New button in the Parameters section of the Edit Shared Parameters dialog box to open a Parameter Properties dialog box. This is not the same dialog box that you get when you create a parameter in the Family Editor or in a project. This is a simple dialog box, because all you need to define for a shared parameter are the Name, Discipline, and Type Of Parameter settings, as shown in Figure 6.19. The parameter that you create will be added to whatever group you have active when you click the New button.

   The Name, Discipline, and Type Of Parameter settings are the same options used for creating a family parameter.

4. Once a parameter has been created, you can select it and click the Properties button to view its settings. The settings cannot be changed after a parameter has been created. If you want to change a shared parameter, you have to delete it and re-create it with the new settings. If you do so, you will have to add the parameter back to any object that had the parameter you're replacing.

5. If you create the parameter in the wrong group, however, all is not lost. Simply select the parameter and click the Move button, which allows you to move the parameter to another group.

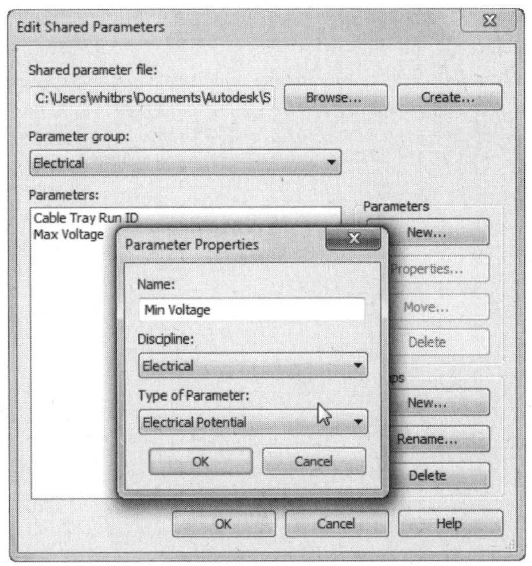

FIGURE 6.19 Parameter Properties dialog box for a shared parameter

Choose and establish shared parameter settings very carefully. A parameter that is deleted from your shared parameters file will remain in families or projects—you will not be able to add it to anything new. There is a get-out clause here if you have deleted a shared parameter that you later wish to keep. Open any family or project where you know the parameter exists. Select the parameter in the Type Properties dialog box and click Modify. Once you're in the Parameter Properties dialog box, click the Export button. This exports the shared parameter to a parameter group called Exported Parameters in the shared parameters file, and the parameter can be moved if necessary, as described earlier.

You can add a shared parameter to a family by doing the following:

1. Select the Shared Parameter option in the Parameter Properties dialog box. This activates the Select button, which opens the Shared Parameters dialog box.
2. Choose the group that contains the desired parameter, and then select the parameter from the list.
3. Once you click OK, you still need to define whether it will be a type or instance parameter and where it will be listed. These are the only two settings that can be modified after the parameter is added to the family.
4. Click the Edit button in the Shared Parameters dialog box to open the Edit Shared Parameters dialog box, where you can browse to another shared parameters file or make changes to the active file.
5. Once you exit this dialog box, you still need to select the parameter from the Shared Parameters dialog box to add it to the family. Once a shared parameter is added to a family, it can be used as a constraint or in formulas (just like any other parameter).

Managing shared parameters should be treated with the same importance as managing your content library. Because these parameters provide intelligence that carries through from a family all the way to your construction documents, it is important that they are maintained and used correctly. Preventing users from having full access to this file is one way of managing this, much in the same way as many libraries have restricted, read-only access.

One category for which shared parameters can become cumbersome is the Mechanical Equipment category. Typically, many characteristics of a mechanical unit are required to be scheduled, so shared parameters are necessary. Some of these characteristics are the same unit of measurement, but for a different component of the unit. Since you cannot add the same shared parameter to a family more than once, you may need to make multiple parameters of the same type. It is best to try to keep your shared parameters as simple as possible for this category. Naming parameters specifically for their use is helpful in keeping track of them. In addition, developing a standard for where these parameters are grouped in the families will help you avoid confusion when editing the properties of a family.

Even though it may initially require a bit of work, adding these parameters directly to your mechanical equipment families rather than as project parameters will go a long way in keeping your families from becoming overcrowded with unused parameters. Consider keeping a document such as a spreadsheet that lists all of your custom parameters and indicates whether they are family or project parameters, what parameter groups they exist in if they are shared parameters, where they are grouped in the properties of a family, and whether they are used as type or instance parameters. Having this document open will be helpful when creating new content, because you will know what parameters already exist and how to use them. As new parameters are created, the document can be updated. If you work in an environment with multiple users, it is best to keep only one copy of this document in a common location. You can organize the file and list the family in which the parameter is used or you can do it by schedule. Figure 6.20 demonstrates a sample Excel file that manages the shared parameters by schedules that they belong to.

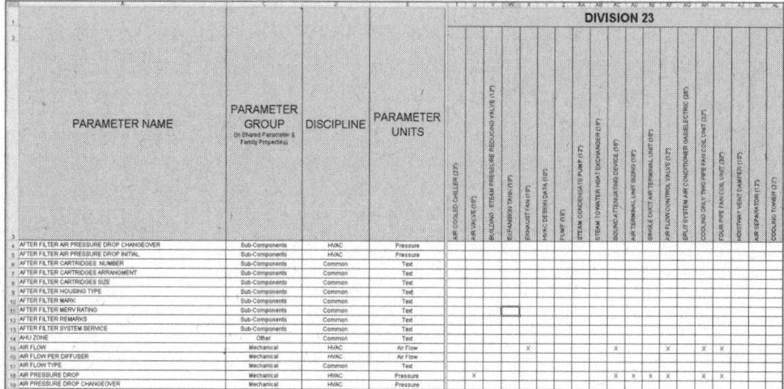

					DIVISION 23																		
	PARAMETER NAME	PARAMETER GROUP (In Shared Parameter & Family Properties)	DISCIPLINE	PARAMETER UNITS	AIR COOLED CHILLER (33")	AIR VALVE (18")	BUILDING - STEAM PRESSURE REDUCING VALVE (12")	EXPANSION TANK (18")	EXHAUST FAN (18")	HVAC DESIGN DATA (18")	PUMP (18")	STEAM CONDENSATE PUMP (17")	STEAM TO WATER HEAT EXCHANGER (19")	SOUND ATTENUATING DEVICE (18")	AIR TERMINAL UNIT SIZING (18")	SINGLE DUCT AIR TERMINAL UNIT (18")	AIR FLOW CONTROL VALVE (17")	SPLIT SYSTEM AIR CONDITIONER [illegible]	COOLING ONLY TWO PIPE FAN COIL UNIT (37")	FOUR PIPE FAN COIL UNIT (36")	HOISTWAY VENT DAMPER (18")	AIR SEPARATOR (17")	COOLING TOWER (27")
4	AFTER FILTER AIR PRESSURE DROP CHANGEOVER	Sub-Components	HVAC	Pressure																			
5	AFTER FILTER AIR PRESSURE DROP INITIAL	Sub-Components	HVAC	Pressure																			
6	AFTER FILTER CARTRIDGES NUMBER	Sub-Components	Common	Text																			
7	AFTER FILTER CARTRIDGES ARRANGMENT	Sub-Components	Common	Text																			
8	AFTER FILTER CARTRIDGES SIZE	Sub-Components	Common	Text																			
9	AFTER FILTER HOUSING TYPE	Sub-Components	Common	Text																			
10	AFTER FILTER MARK	Sub-Components	Common	Text																			
11	AFTER FILTER MERV RATING	Sub-Components	Common	Text																			
12	AFTER FILTER REMARKS	Sub-Components	Common	Text																			
13	AFTER FILTER SYSTEM SERVICE	Sub-Components	Common	Text																			
14	AHU ZONE	Other	Common	Text																			
15	AIR FLOW	Mechanical	HVAC	Air Flow					X					X			X		X	X			
16	AIR FLOW PER DIFFUSER	Mechanical	HVAC	Air Flow																			
17	AIR FLOW TYPE	Mechanical	Common	Text																			
18	AIR PRESSURE DROP	Mechanical	HVAC	Pressure		X								X	X	X	X		X	X			
19	AIR PRESSURE DROP CHANGEOVER	Mechanical	HVAC	Pressure																			

FIGURE 6.20 Sample Excel file organizing all shared parameters

Using Parameters in Projects

Parameters are typically handled at the component level for building objects, but there are also parameters for noncomponent objects such as views, sheets, and annotations. You may need to create custom parameters for system families that cannot be edited in the Family Editor. These parameters can be added to designated categories within your project so you can assign them to system families. Your projects themselves can have parameters that convey project-specific information. Understanding how to use parameters in a project is the key to getting the most benefit from constructing an intelligent model with computable data.

Project Parameters

The only way to add a parameter to a system family is to add it by creating a *project parameter*. This allows you to customize the information you want from elements within the model. Space objects can be given a lot of useful data to help make design decisions and to analyze the model performance. Project parameters make it possible to add this data to spaces and other elements that cannot be physically edited.

You can add a project parameter by clicking the Project Parameters button on the Manage tab. In the Project Parameters dialog box, you can see a list of any parameters that have been added to the project. Clicking the Add button opens the Parameter Properties dialog box, shown in Figure 6.21. This is the same dialog box as in the Family Editor but with additional settings to assign the parameter to an object category. The object category list includes all the component families, system families, in-place families, and even metadata that may not be physical geometry, such as views, sheets, project information, and so on.

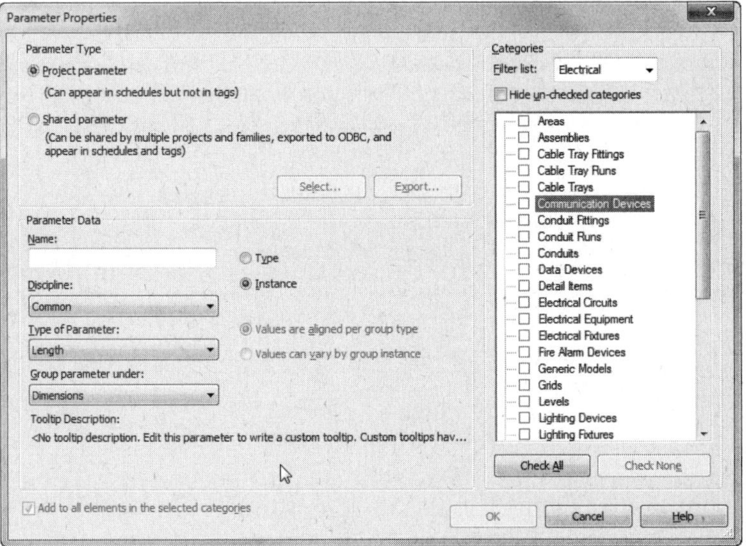

FIGURE 6.21 Parameter Properties dialog box for a project parameter

The settings for creating a parameter or adding a shared parameter are the same for project parameters. The only difference is the Categories section of the dialog box. This is where you can select the Revit category to which the project parameter you are creating or the shared parameter you are loading is applied in the project.

Project parameters are a great way to use shared parameters in families without having to edit each family individually. The check box in the lower-left corner indicates that the parameter will be added to all elements in the project that belong to the selected category. So, if there are parameters that you want to use on a particular category of elements, such as light fixtures, you can create the parameters as shared parameters and then load them as project parameters into your project template file. Then, whenever you load a family belonging to that category into your project, it will have the desired parameters, which can be used for scheduling or tagging.

Additionally in this dialog box are the radio buttons Values Are Aligned Per Group Type and Values Can Vary By Group Instance. They appear uneditable when Type Of Parameter is set to the default Length, but if you change it to Text, Area, Volume, Currency, or a few more, you will be able to switch between the two.

Values Are Aligned Per Group Type (Default) If an element with this instance parameter is part of multiple groups, the parameter value will be the same for corresponding elements in all group instances. While in Edit Group mode, you can select the element and modify the parameter on the Properties palette. Changing the parameter value for the element in one group will change the value for the corresponding element in all other instances of the same group type.

Values Can Vary By Group Instance If the element with this instance parameter is part of multiple groups, the parameter value can vary for corresponding elements in group instances. While in Edit Group mode, you can select the element and modify the parameter on the Properties palette. Changing the parameter value for the element in one group will not change the value for the corresponding element in other instances of the same group type.

If you change an existing parameter from Varies to Aligned, an error message appears, listing the elements with the parameter that will change. If you click Align Parameter Values, then all group instances will update to have the same parameter value. The value applied is the value that was assigned to the element in the first group instance.

DUPLICATE PARAMETERS

It is possible to create a project parameter with the same name and settings as a parameter that already exists in the elements to which it is being applied. This may not pose a problem for objects already loaded into your project, but keep in mind that a component may be loaded that already has a parameter equal to one of your project parameters. Managing project parameters is as essential as managing shared parameters and content.

When you add a parameter to your project and it is applied to elements in the chosen category, the parameter will not have a value. You can easily give the parameters values by creating a schedule of the elements and including the project parameters in the schedule.

Yes/No type parameters will be set to Yes (selected) by default and appear to be uneditable when they are viewed in a schedule or the properties of an element. You can click the grayed-out check box once to make it editable.

Parameters in Schedules

Family parameters and some system parameters cannot be used in schedules. If you do not want to use shared parameters in your families, you can create project parameters for scheduling information about components. In the Schedule Properties dialog box at the center of the Fields tab is an Add Parameter button, as shown in Figure 6.22. Clicking this button opens the Parameter Properties dialog box; this is the same dialog box that you get when you click Project Parameters. Essentially, you can create project parameters from the Project Parameters dialog box or from a schedule. All of them will appear in the Project Parameters list. However, there is a difference depending on whether you create them from the dialog box or from a schedule. When you create the parameters from a schedule, they will automatically be applied to the category of the schedule. For example, if you are scheduling mechanical equipment, creating a parameter in that schedule will automatically apply it to all mechanical equipment. But what if you want the same parameter to apply to other object categories as well? You can do this from the Project Parameters dialog box, where you will be given the opportunity to select any additional categories. As we mentioned in the beginning of this chapter, project parameters can appear in schedules but not in tags (see Figure 6.23).

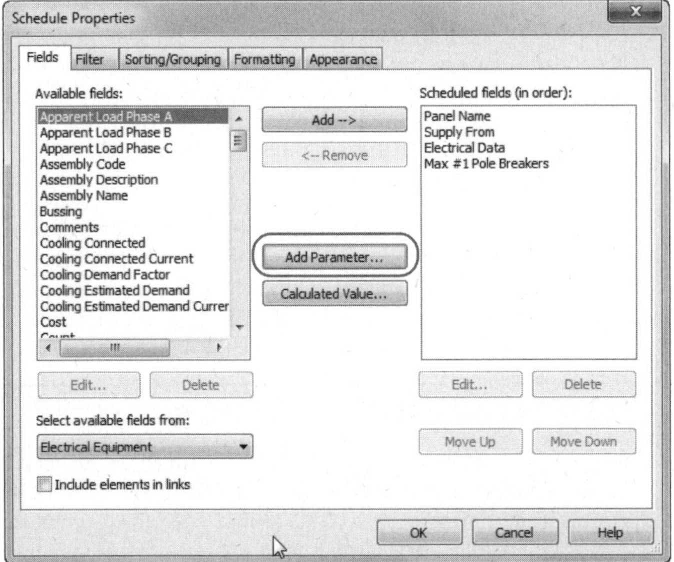

FIGURE 6.22 Schedule Properties dialog box for adding parameters

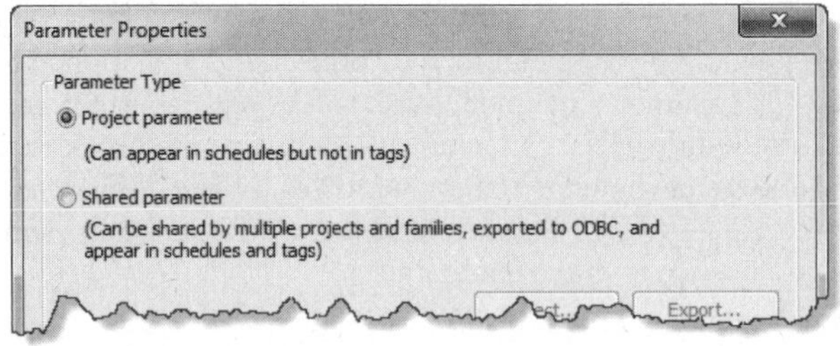

FIGURE 6.23 Parameter Properties dialog box

Using the Calculated Value feature of a Revit schedule will create a parameter to hold the value, but this parameter is not added to the properties of elements or the Project Parameters list. It appears only in the schedule where it was created and nowhere else.

Whether they are shared parameters or not, project parameters are required for scheduling system families such as duct, pipe, or cable tray. It is easiest to create these parameters when you are building the schedule for such elements. Once the parameter is created, you can access it from the Project Parameters button on the Manage tab to add it to other categories or make any necessary changes. Creating these parameters in schedules within your project template will ensure that they are consistently used from project to project.

One useful type of project parameter to create is for the schedule type of an element. This parameter can be applied to any category that is scheduled, and it is useful for filtering your schedules. Some people may prefer to create this parameter as a project parameter, which is easier and faster. We recommend creating it as a shared parameter and including it in all your families with a predefined value. This way, as you load boilers, chillers, AHUs, and so on, they will automatically be displayed on the appropriate schedules, assuming you have given them the appropriate value for the parameter and the schedule is using that as a filter.

Creating and Using Parameters in Families and Schedules

Understanding how to use parameters to get the information you require is the key to successfully reaping the benefits of Revit. Knowing where and when to use certain types of parameters will make it easy for you to manage the data within your Revit projects.

1. Download the `Ch6_Project.rvt` and `Ch6 Shared Parameters.txt` files found at `www.sybex.com/go/masteringrevitmep2015`.
2. Open the `Ch6_Project.rvt` file. Open the VAV Schedule view. Access the Fields tab of the Schedule Properties dialog box, and click the Add Parameter button.
3. Create a project parameter called **Schedule Type** with the following settings:
   - Instance
   - Discipline: Common
   - Type Of Parameter: Text
   - Group: Identity Data
4. Click OK to exit the Schedule Properties dialog box. For each VAV listed in the schedule, enter a value of **VAV** for the Schedule Type parameter.
5. Access the Filter tab of the Schedule Properties dialog box.

   Set Filter By to Schedule Type, Equals, and VAV, as shown in the following dialog box:

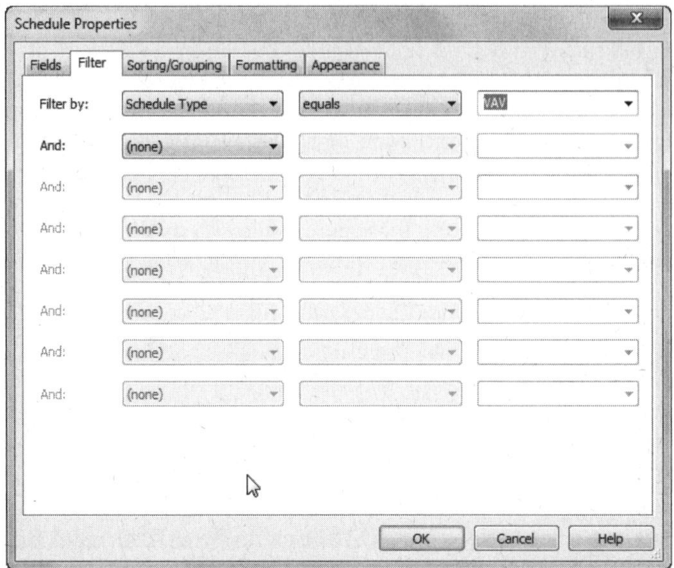

6. Click OK to exit the Schedule Properties dialog box. Notice that now only the VAVs are listed in the schedule. Click the Project Parameters button on the Manage tab of the ribbon. Notice that the Schedule Type parameter is now a project parameter that will be added to any mechanical equipment loaded into the project. Exit the Project Parameters dialog box.

7. Open the 1 – Lighting ceiling plan view. Click one of the light fixtures in the view, and click the Edit Type button in the Properties palette. Notice the Ballast Voltage parameter in the Electrical group. Click OK to exit the Type Properties dialog box.

8. Open the Lighting Fixture Schedule view. Access the Fields tab of the Schedule Properties dialog box. Notice that the Ballast Voltage parameter that exists in the lighting fixture family is not listed in the Available Fields list because it is a family parameter.

9. Click the Add Parameter button on the Fields tab of the Schedule Properties dialog box.

10. In the Parameter Properties dialog box, select the Shared Parameter option and click the Select button.

11. Click the Edit button in the Shared Parameters dialog box. Click the Browse button in the Edit Shared Parameters dialog box, and browse to the downloaded `Ch6 Shared Parameters.txt` file location. (Note that if you have never selected a shared parameters file, you will be asked to select one. Browse to the location of the downloaded file.)

12. Set Parameter Group to Lighting Fixtures. Click the New button under Parameters on the right side of the dialog box.

13. Create a new parameter named **Fixture Voltage**. Set Discipline to Electrical. Set Type Of Parameter to Electrical Potential. Click OK to exit the Parameter Properties dialog box. Click OK to exit the Edit Shared Parameters dialog box.

14. In the Shared Parameters dialog box, set the parameter group to Lighting Fixtures. Select the Fixture Voltage parameter from the list, and click OK to exit the Shared Parameters dialog box.

15. In the Parameter Properties dialog box, select the check box in the lower-left corner to add the parameter to all elements in the category. Set the parameter as a type parameter, and click OK to exit the dialog box.

16. Notice that the Fixture Voltage parameter is now in the Lighting Fixture schedule. You can now input values for voltage into the parameter.

VOLTAGE AND NUMBER OF POLE PARAMETERS—INSTANCE VS. TYPE

Revit MEP has a little-known feature that allows you to specify circuit information when the Voltage and Number Of Poles parameters are set to Instance when you create your circuits. The family lists the available voltage definitions for the project. If those parameters are set to Type, you will not have this choice. Refer to the following screenshot for an example.

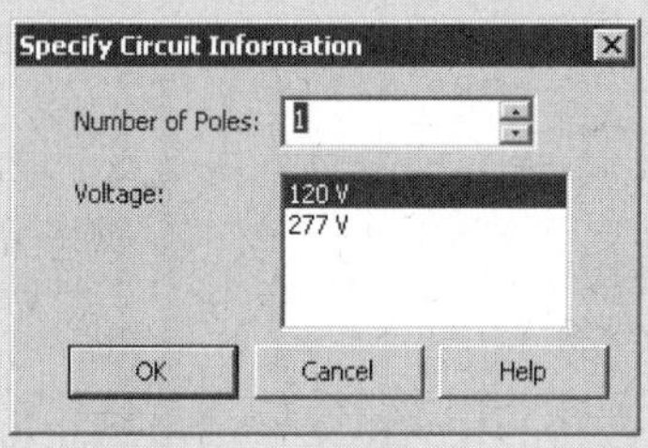

Specify Circuit Information

Number of Poles: 1

Voltage: 120 V 277 V

OK Cancel Help

View and Sheet Parameters

Views and sheets are system families, so you need to use project parameters to include additional information or functionality in them. This type of information may be necessary for construction documentation or simply for organizing your project for more efficient workflow. Depending on their use, these parameters may need to be shared parameters.

One of the more common parameters for views is the Sub-Discipline parameter. This parameter allows you to assign a subdiscipline value to the properties of any view to establish a secondary level of organization within the Project Browser. This parameter is already established in the default template files provided with Revit MEP 2015. For more information on using this parameter and other alternatives for Project Browser organization, refer to Chapter 2, "Creating an Effective Project Template." Much of the information that appears on a sheet border is common to every sheet. If the parameters that hold this information were unique to each sheet, it would be time-consuming to make certain changes. Project parameters that are applied to the Project Information category can be included in your titleblock so that the value can be changed in one location and globally updated to all sheets.

One example is for total sheet count. Including this information on a sheet as an editable parameter would require creating a shared parameter. A label of this parameter could then be placed within the titleblock family. The shared parameter could then be added as a project parameter applied to the Project Information category, as shown in Figure 6.24.

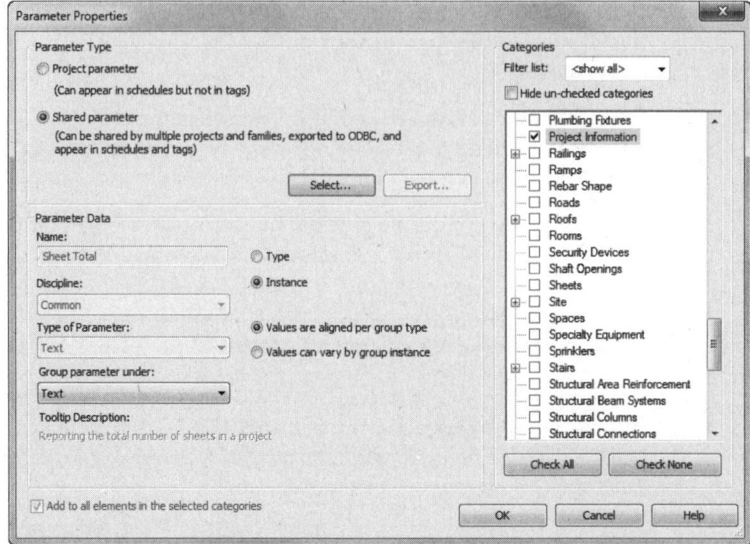

FIGURE 6.24
Project parameter for sheet total

Notice that the parameter is an instance parameter. You cannot create type parameters for the Project Information, Sheet, or View categories. However, since there is only one instance of Project Information in a project, essentially those instance parameters behave like type parameters. For example, say you create an instance project parameter called Building No. and apply it to Project Information. Even though it is an instance parameter, it is global for the project because there is only one instance of it. Instance parameters for views and sheets behave like normal instance parameters.

When the project information is edited, the value will be updated on every sheet in the project. Figure 6.25 shows this example on a titleblock in a sample project.

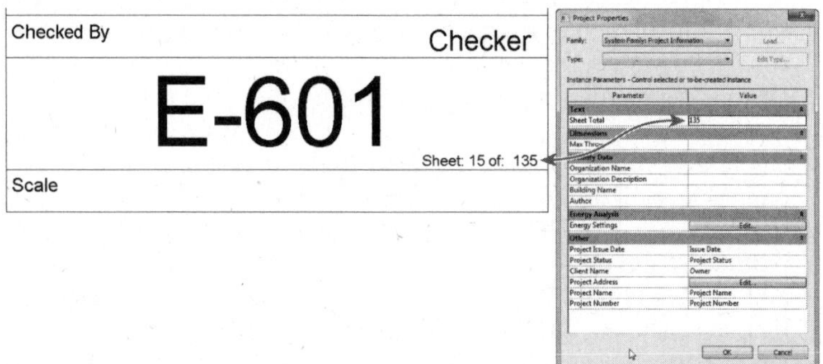

FIGURE 6.25
Shared parameter used on a sheet

Combining the power of shared and project parameters can give you the ability to report, tag, or schedule any data within your model or about your project in general. Once you understand how to use parameters effectively, the real work becomes managing them for consistency and accuracy within your projects.

Working with Formulas

Formulas let you create some truly intelligent families and in most cases can increase your designers' efficiency by automating certain tasks. Working with formulas in Revit has its own challenges that you need to be aware of. They are case sensitive, they are "aware" of units, and they won't work properly if your parameters use mathematical symbols (/ * – +) in their naming convention. Table 6.1 lists basic operators used in formulas. Table 6.2 gives a list of conditional statements used in formulas.

TABLE 6.1: Basic operators

+	Add: Length + Width	abs	Absolute Value: abs (–5) will return 5
-	Subtract: Length – Connector Protrusion	pi	Pi: pi() * (Radius ^ 2)—the circumference formula
*	Multiply: Width * Length	sin	Sine: sin (45)
/	Divide: Height/Length	cos	Cosine: cos (45)
^	Exponent: Length^3	tan	Tangent: tan (45)
log	Logarithm: log (100)	asin	Arcsine: asin (45)
sqrt	Square root: sqrt (49)	acos	Arccosine: acos (45)
exp(x)	E raised to an x power: exp (2)	atan	Arctangent: atan (45)
<	Less than		
>	Greater than		

TABLE 6.2: Conditional statements

if	if statement
and	Both statements are true
or	One of the statements is true
not	The statement is false

Sample Conditional Statements

Conditional statements are a very powerful way of controlling the behavior of your Revit families. For the most part, conditional statements work exactly the same way they do in Excel or any other program that supports them. Here are few examples for the most common conditional statements:

Simple `if` Statements `if(Neck Size<10",16",18")`

`if(Neck Size<250mm, 400mm, 450mm)`

Formula That Returns Strings `if(Neck Size>10","Neck Size is too Big "Neck Size is Correct")`

`if(Neck Size>250mm,"Neck Size is too Big "Neck Size is Correct")`

The next two types of statements (Logical and/or) are good for testing whether a diffuser has been sized correctly. Either of the following formulas could be used:

Using Logical `and` `If(and(Air Flow>Minimum Air Flow, Air Flow<Maximum Air Flow),"Correct", "Wrong Size")`

Using Logical `or` `If(or(Air Flow<Minimum Air Flow, Air Flow>Maximum Air Flow),"Wrong Size", "Correct")`

Both of the preceding statements give the result—a text string—stating whether a connection is correctly sized…or not.

Using Logical `not` `if(not(Top Alignment), 0", tan(15$) * b)`

Using Logical `not` for Yes/No Parameters `not(myCheckbox)`

Using `if` with Yes/No Condition `If (Length>10)`

(Note that both the condition and the results are implied.)

Embedded `if` Statement with Logical `and` `if(and(Maximum Air Flow < 391 CFM, Auto Size), 8", if(and(Maximum Air Flow < 641 CFM, Auto Size), 10", if(and(Maximum Air Flow < 1001 CFM, Auto Size), 12 1/2", if(and(Maximum Air Flow < 1651 CFM, Auto Size), 15", if(and(Maximum Air Flow < 2201 CFM, Auto Size), 17 1/2", if(and(Maximum Air Flow < 3001 CFM, Auto Size), 18", OVERRIDE HEIGHT)))))`

`if(and(Maximum Air Flow < 185 l/s, Auto Size), 200mm, if(and(Maximum Air Flow < 300 l/s, Auto Size), 250mm, if(and(Maximum Air Flow < 470 l/s, Auto Size), 350mm, if(and(Maximum Air Flow < 780 l/s, Auto Size), 400mm, if(and(Maximum Air Flow < 1000 l/s, Auto Size), 450mm, if(and(Maximum Air Flow < 1400 l/s, Auto Size), 450mm", OVERRIDE HEIGHT)))))`

Revit can be very picky about the units that you use in formulas. For example, you can't use the Number parameter in a CFM (l/s) parameter unless you do some sort of conversion. In most but not all cases, simply multiplying or dividing by 1 does the trick.

Rounding

Prior to Revit 2012, there were two options for rounding numbers: running them through an integer parameter (which automatically rounds them up) or adding 0.49 to the formula. In most formulas, the rounding needs to be to the next higher whole number, even if the number isn't higher than 0.5, such as for the occupancy of people. If the number is 2.4, it really needs to be 3. For example, 2.4 + 0.49 = 2.89, which will be rounded to 3.

As of Revit 2012, we have three additional functions to use: `Round(x)`, `Roundup(x)`, and `Rounddown(x)`. Note that `x` is unit-less (also known as a number, not CFM, not GPM, and so on). The `Round(x)` function rounds to the nearest whole number:

```
round (1.2) = 1
round (1.5) = 2
round (1.7) = 2

round (-1.2) = 1
round (-1.5) = 1
round (-1.7) = 2
```

The `Roundup(x)` function rounds to the largest whole number greater than or equal to `x`, such as in the following example:

```
round (1.0) = 1
round (1.4) = 2
round (1.6) = 2

round (-1.0) = -1
round (-1.4) = -1
round (-1.6) = -1
```

The `Rounddown(x)` function rounds to the smallest whole number less than or equal to `x`, as in this example:

```
round (1.0) = 1
round (1.4) = 1
round (1.6) = 1

round (-1.0) = -1
round (-1.4) = -2
round (-1.6) = -2
```

The Bottom Line

Manipulate the properties of parameters. The parameters used to define the properties of elements have properties of their own that define their behavior and how they can be used.

Master It It is important to know when and where parameters can be used for extracting data from a model or project. It is also important to understand how instance and type parameters are used. Describe how the use of instance and type parameters affects the way data is changed in a family.

Work with type catalogs. Type catalogs are powerful tools that allow you to load only what you need for a specific project.

Master It Certain families can have multiple family types. If a family has many types, all of them will be loaded into a project when the family is loaded. What can be done to limit the number of family types that are loaded when a family is inserted into a project?

Work with shared parameters. Shared parameters are useful because they can be used in schedules and in annotation tags. Shared parameters can be applied directly to families or added as project parameters.

Master It Managing shared parameters is as important as managing your component libraries. Explain the importance of keeping a common shared parameters file for multiuser environments.

Use parameters in project files. The use of parameters is not limited to component families. Parameters can be added to any element that makes up a Revit project.

Master It You can add parameters to system families only by creating project parameters. When you create a project parameter, it will be added to all the elements in the chosen category. Explain why managing project parameters is important to using them in schedules within a project.

Schedules

Schedules of a parametric model provide the most immediate return of information from the data inherent in the model. With the Autodesk® Revit® MEP 2015 platform, you can create schedules that are useful not only for construction documentation but also for data management, for object tracking, and even for making design decisions.

By building a model, you can look at it from many angles or viewpoints. Schedule views are simply another view of the model. Instead of looking at the physical elements that represent the design, a schedule allows you to view the data within the components in an organized and easy-to-manage format. Using schedules for data management is one way to increase efficiency, accuracy, and coordination within your Revit project. You can edit the properties of many objects quickly without having to locate the objects in the model.

Revit schedules can provide you with an accurate account of the objects that are being used in your project model. The ability to track and manage objects can help with cost estimation and material takeoff. With this information readily available, you have the power to make decisions that affect cost and constructability.

Harnessing the power of creating schedules in a Revit MEP 2015 project can help you reap the benefits that come with easy access to any model or project information.

In this chapter, you will learn to do the following:

- Use the tools in Revit MEP 2015 for defining schedules and their behavior
- Schedule building components
- Create schedules for design and analysis
- Schedule views and sheets for project management

Defining Schedules

Mastering the scheduling tools in Revit MEP 2015 will enable you to easily extract information from your projects. *Schedules* can be created and used on any of your Revit projects to establish consistency on construction documents and ease of data management for specified model objects.

Although there are different types of schedules, depending on their use and the items with which they are associated, the tools for creating them in Revit MEP 2015 are similar for whatever type of schedule you are creating. Because schedules are essentially a view of the model, the scheduling tools are located on the View tab of the ribbon, as shown in Figure 7.1.

Figure 7.2 shows the types of schedules that can be created by clicking the Schedules button. Note the filter list that allows you to narrow down the number of categories available in the list displayed.

FIGURE 7.1
View tab

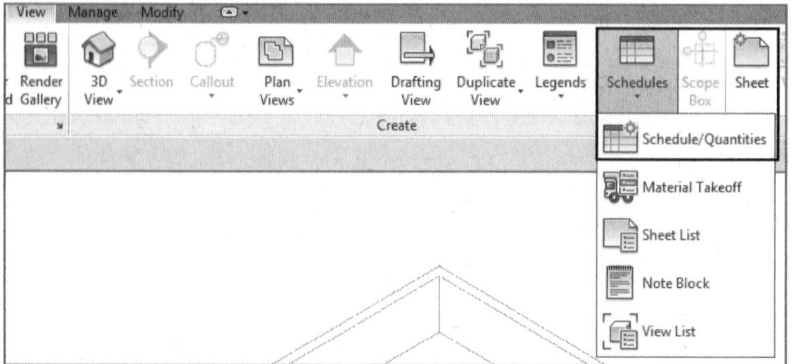

FIGURE 7.2
Schedule types

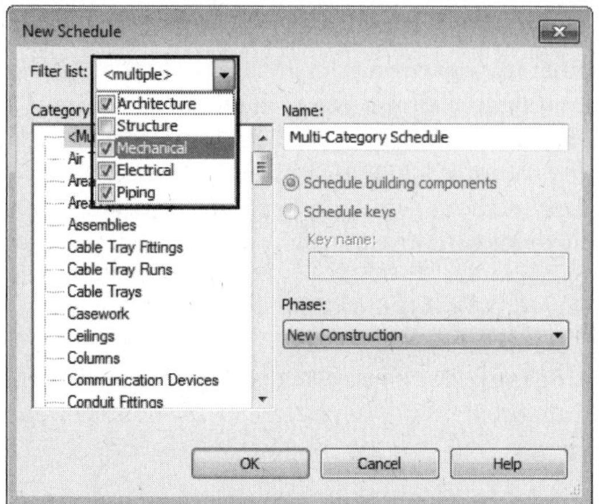

Clicking the View List or Sheet List option takes you directly to the View List or Sheet List Properties dialog box, where you can begin creating your schedule. Clicking the Schedule/Quantities or Material Takeoff option takes you first to a dialog box that allows you to select the Revit object category that you want to schedule. The Note Block option takes you to a dialog box where you can select the annotation family that you want to schedule.

In the New Schedule dialog box, you can define whether you are creating a schedule of building components or a schedule key. You can also set the project phase of the schedule view.

The *project phase* is an important property of schedules because only the objects in the model that belong to the same *phase* as a schedule appear in that schedule. The name that you give your schedule is what will appear in the main header of the schedule when it is placed on a drawing. If your drafting standards dictate that the text should be in all capital letters, you need to retype the name even if it is correct. From the Filter List pull-down, you can filter the object categories you can schedule. The pull-down is the same as the one in the Visibility/Graphic Overrides dialog box. This allows you to select items that are not MEP objects and may not even exist in your model. (In Revit 2012 and all prior releases, this filter option was a check box called Show Categories From All Disciplines.) Figure 7.3 shows a sample of the New Schedule dialog box with settings to build a Spaces schedule.

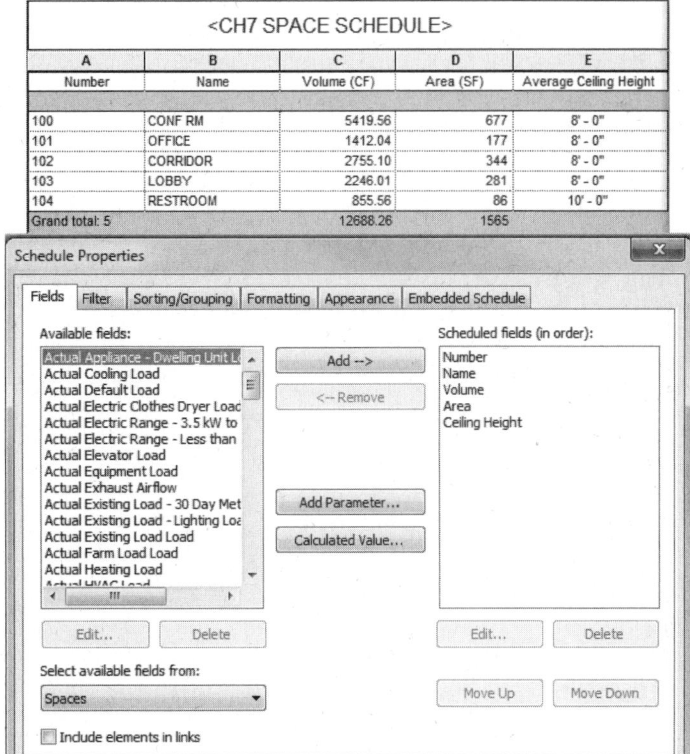

<CH7 SPACE SCHEDULE>

A	B	C	D	E
Number	Name	Volume (CF)	Area (SF)	Average Ceiling Height
100	CONF RM	5419.56	677	8' - 0"
101	OFFICE	1412.04	177	8' - 0"
102	CORRIDOR	2755.10	344	8' - 0"
103	LOBBY	2246.01	281	8' - 0"
104	RESTROOM	855.56	86	10' - 0"
Grand total: 5		12688.26	1565	

FIGURE 7.3 Sample schedule settings

Also note the angle brackets (< >) around the name of the schedule. This feature denotes a parameter value rather than user-entered text. You will learn of this and other new features of scheduling later in the chapter.

Another choice is to create a Multi-Category schedule. This type of schedule is for objects that are in different categories but have common parameters. Figure 7.4 shows an example of a Multi-Category schedule. Notice that the OmniClass Number parameter is used in the schedule even though not all objects have that parameter.

FIGURE 7.4 Sample Multi-Category schedule

<Multi-Category Schedule>

A	B	C	D	E
Family and Type	Type Mark	Description	Count	OmniClass Numbe
dMb_Round Neck Diffusers - Face Hosted: 2	A6	LAY-IN LOUVER FAC	4	
dMb_Round Neck Diffusers - Face Hosted: 2	A8	LAY-IN LOUVER FAC	2	
dMb_Round Neck Diffusers - Face Hosted: 2	A10	LAY-IN PERFORATED	1	
Exhaust Grill: 24 x 24 Face 12 x 12 Connecti	E12	LAY-IN LOUVER FAC	1	23.75.70.21.27.11
Rectangular Duct: Mitered Elbows / Tees			22	
Rectangular Elbow - Mitered: Standard			15	23.75.70.14
Rectangular Tee: Standard			3	23.75.70.14
Rectangular to Round Transition - Angle: 45			3	23.75.70.14
Return Diffuser: 24 x 24 Face 12 x 12 Conne	R12	LAY-IN PERFORATED	4	23.75.70.21.27.11
Wall Lamp - Bracket: 100W - 230V			3	23.80.70.11.11

Once you have chosen a category and established the initial settings from the new schedule dialog box, clicking OK opens the Schedule Properties dialog box. This dialog box has five tabs across the top that have settings to define the behavior and appearance of your schedule. When you're scheduling Space or Room objects as in Figure 7.3, there is an additional tab for building an embedded schedule within the schedule you are creating. A typical use for an embedded schedule might be a Space schedule that also references lighting fixture details, so quantities of luminaires per space or room can be created. An example of this is provided later in this chapter. It is good to move through the tabs sequentially, establishing the settings in each tab before moving to the next. The first two tabs let you determine what information will be scheduled, while the last three enable you to control how the data will be displayed and the graphical appearance of the schedule when placed on a drawing.

The Fields Tab

The Fields tab of the Schedule Properties dialog box contains many tools for choosing the information that will appear in a schedule. Figure 7.5 shows the Fields tab of a newly created Space schedule.

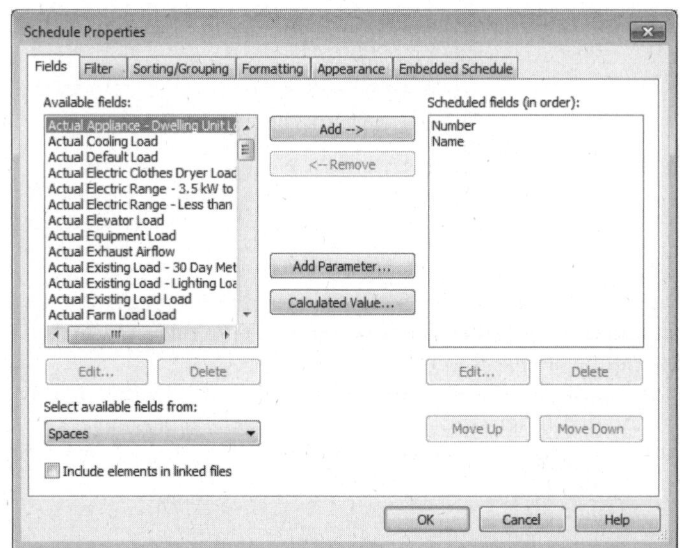

FIGURE 7.5
Fields tab of the Schedule Properties dialog box

The check box in the lower-left corner allows you to schedule items that are in any files that are linked into your project. The Available Fields list on the left side of the dialog box contains all the parameters that can be scheduled for the chosen category. The Edit and Delete buttons below the list become active only when you select a project or shared parameter that you have created. Only project parameters that are not shared parameters can be deleted.

Schedules and Parameters

Because of the relationship between objects, parameters, and schedules, the data within a Revit schedule is the same as the data assigned to the objects. This is known in Revit terms as *bidirectional associativity*. It is best to have a good understanding of how parameters work when you set out to build a schedule. For more information on the creation and management of parameters, see Chapter 6, "Parameters."

You can use the drop-down list in the lower-left corner to change the list of available fields to parameters from another category. This is primarily for Space and Room schedules because the two objects are essentially the same thing. You cannot select fields from Mechanical Equipment if you are creating a Lighting Fixture schedule, for example.

To establish the columns in your schedule, you simply select the parameter from the Available Fields list and click the Add button at the top center of the dialog box. This places the chosen parameter in the space on the right side of the dialog box. Another way is to double-click the parameter you want to add. Each parameter added to the schedule will be a new column, and the order in which they appear in the list determines the order of the columns in the schedule, from left to right. Once you have added a parameter to the schedule, you can use the Move Up and Move Down buttons to set the order. These buttons become active only when you select a parameter from the Scheduled Fields list on the right.

The Remove button at the top center allows you to remove a parameter from the schedule. This is not the same thing as deleting a parameter. Using either of the Delete buttons removes the selected parameter from your project and any objects in your project.

If you want to schedule information about the chosen category and a parameter does not exist that contains that information, you can click the Add Parameter button at the center of the dialog box. Clicking this button activates the Parameter Properties dialog box, where you can choose the type of parameter and its properties. The check box in the lower-left corner of the Parameter Properties dialog box (Labelled "Add to all elements in the category") is selected by default, and it is grayed out to ensure that the parameter you create is added to all the objects in the category you are scheduling. Once you have created a parameter, it is automatically added to the schedule.

Revit schedules have the ability to perform calculations on the data within the parameters that are included in a schedule. This information then appears as a unique column in the schedule. To create a calculated value column in your schedule, click the Calculated Value button at the center of the Fields Tab in the Schedule Properties dialog box. Give the value a descriptive name so that when it is seen in the list or schedule, its purpose will be clear. You can create a formula by including parameters in a mathematical equation, or you can calculate a percentage.

The percentage calculation returns the percentage of a specific parameter as it relates to the project as a whole. Figure 7.6 shows the settings for percentage calculation of the volume of Space objects and the resulting column in the schedule.

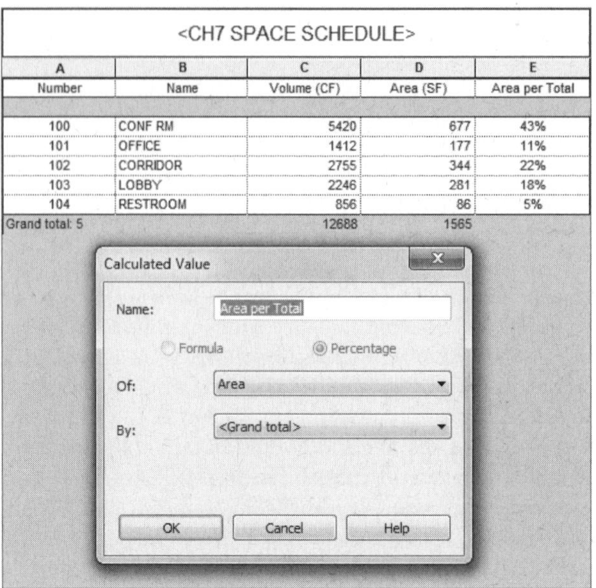

<CH7 SPACE SCHEDULE>

A	B	C	D	E
Number	Name	Volume (CF)	Area (SF)	Area per Total
100	CONF RM	5420	677	43%
101	OFFICE	1412	177	11%
102	CORRIDOR	2755	344	22%
103	LOBBY	2246	281	18%
104	RESTROOM	856	86	5%
Grand total: 5		12688	1565	

FIGURE 7.6
Percentage calculation in a schedule

When you're creating a calculated value based on a formula, it is important to use the proper Discipline and Type settings that coincide with the result of the equation. You will receive a warning stating that the units are inconsistent if the result does not match. Revit is case sensitive when it comes to typing in parameter names, so as you write your formula, it is crucial that you type the parameter name exactly. The small button next to the Formula field allows you to pick the parameter from a list and inserts it into your formula to ensure proper spelling and capitalization. A good rule of thumb is to be consistent with all your parameter names.

Once you have created a calculated value, it automatically appears in the Scheduled Fields list. If you use the Remove button to remove a calculated value from the schedule, it is deleted from the project. You can use multiple operators and multiple parameters to create complex formulas if necessary. One example of a simple formula for Space objects is to divide the volume by the area to determine the average ceiling height, as shown in Figure 7.7. This formula works only because the Space objects have an upper limit set to the level above and the ceiling objects are set to Room Bounding, thus defining the volume of the spaces.

CALCULATED VALUES LIMITATIONS

Calculated values appear only in the current schedule. They are not parameters that you would see in the properties of objects, and therefore they cannot be tagged or displayed anywhere outside the current schedule. In addition, calculated values can be somewhat hard to work with if you don't understand how to convert units in Revit. In most cases, conversion of units can be done by simply multiplying or dividing a parameter by 1. For example, Revit could give you an error if you try to divide volume by area. But if you "strip out the units" by multiplying both parameters by 1, you will get what you want: `Ceiling Height=(Volume*1)/(Area*1)`.

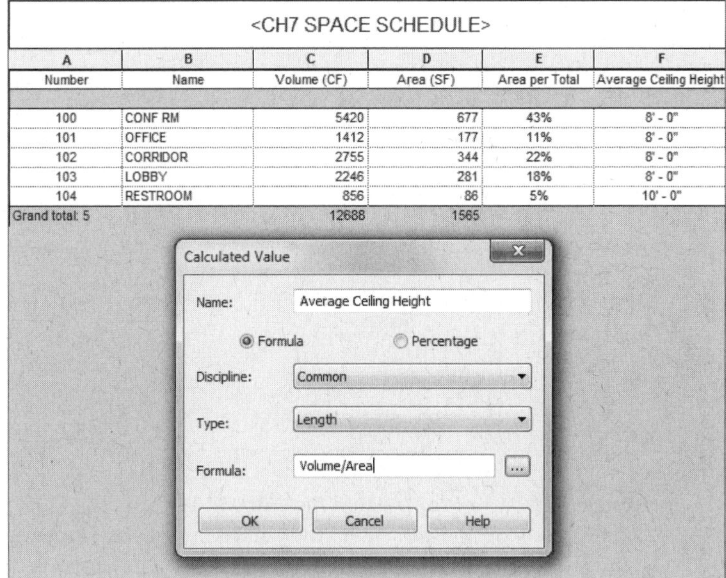

Figure 7.7
Space schedule with a calculated value for Average Ceiling Height

> **Visibility/Graphic Overrides for Schedules**
>
> A little-known trick for schedules is the ability to show objects from some linked files and not from all. This can be done from the Properties palette of the schedule by clicking Visibility/Graphic Overrides.

The Filter Tab

The next tab in the Schedule Properties dialog box is the Filter tab. The settings on this tab allow you to filter out unwanted items in your schedule. You can set certain criteria for parameter values that objects in the schedule category must meet in order to be included in the schedule. This is very useful when scheduling a category that has many unique types of items, such as the Mechanical Equipment category. For example, if you wanted to create a Pump schedule, you would have to schedule the Mechanical Equipment category. Without applying a filter to your schedule, all items categorized as Mechanical Equipment would show up in your schedule.

You can apply up to eight conditions that an object must meet to make it into the schedule. To set a condition for a parameter, that parameter must be included in your schedule. If you want to use a parameter for filtering but do not want it to show up in your schedule, you can use the options on the Formatting tab to hide the column of the unwanted parameter. There are some parameters (such as Cost, Family, and Type) to which you are not able to apply conditions.

Figure 7.8 shows a sample of a Mechanical Equipment schedule without any filter conditions applied to it.

FIGURE 7.8
Sample Mechanical Equipment schedule

<Mechanical Equipment Schedule>

A	B	C	D	E
Mark	Description	Level	Family	Type Mark
DOAS - 1		LOWER LEVEL	DOAS Supply to Return Connection	
VRF-12	Ceiling Recessed Units	GROUND FLOOR	PLFY-P-NCMU-E_4-way_24x24	
VRF-13	Ceiling Recessed Units	GROUND FLOOR	PLFY-P-NCMU-E_4-way_24x24	
VRF-23	Ceiling Concealed Ducted Low Profile	GROUND FLOOR	PEFY-P-NMSU-E_Low_Profile_Ducted	
VRF-24	Ceiling Concealed Ducted Low Profile	GROUND FLOOR	PEFY-P-NMSU-E_Low_Profile_Ducted	
VRF-22	Ceiling Concealed Ducted Low Profile	GROUND FLOOR	PEFY-P-NMSU-E_Low_Profile_Ducted	
HRU-16	Ceiling Recessed Units	GROUND FLOOR	PLFY-P-NCMU-E_4-way_24x24	
SP-1	BASE MOUNTED PUMP	GROUND FLOOR	M_Pump - Base Mounted	
SP-2	BASE MOUNTED PUMP	GROUND FLOOR	M_Pump - Base Mounted	
HRU-1	P-TKMU Outdoor unit	SECOND FLOOR	PURY-P72,96TKMU-A	
ERV-1	Energy Recovery with Cooling & Heating	SECOND FLOOR	Energy Recovery-ER_H	
VRF-10		SECOND FLOOR	PEFY-P-NMAU-E_Medium_Static_Ducted	
VRF-11	Ceiling Recessed Units	SECOND FLOOR	PLFY-P-NBMU-E_4-way_33x33	
HRU-2	P-YKMU Outdoor unit	SECOND FLOOR	PURY-P240,264,288YSKMU-A	
HRU-3		SECOND FLOOR	PURY-P168-288_YSJMU_Heat_Recovery_460V	
HRU-4	Ceiling Recessed Units	SECOND FLOOR	PLFY-P-NCMU-E_4-way_24x24	
HRU-5	Ceiling Recessed Units	SECOND FLOOR	PLFY-P-NCMU-E_4-way_24x24	
HRU-6	Ceiling Recessed Units	SECOND FLOOR	PLFY-P-NCMU-E_4-way_24x24	
HRU-7	Ceiling Recessed Units	SECOND FLOOR	PLFY-P-NCMU-E_4-way_24x24	
WH-1		SECOND FLOOR	Water Heater - Tankless	

To turn this into a Pump schedule, you would apply the Filter settings shown in Figure 7.9. Notice the many options for filter rules that can be used to narrow down the qualifying objects. Using these conditions in combination with certain parameters gives you a very powerful tool for scheduling exactly the objects you want.

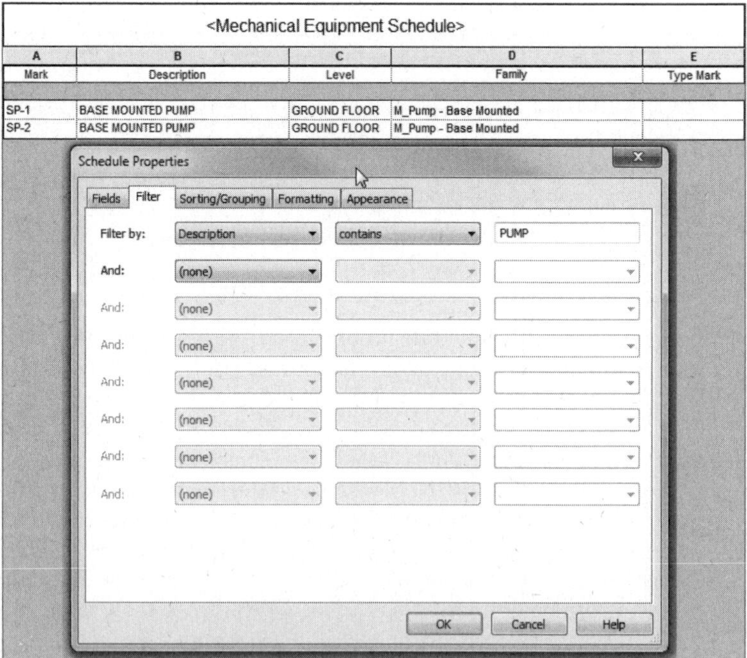

FIGURE 7.9
Filter settings for a Pump schedule

As items are brought into your model, they automatically appear in a schedule of their category as long as they meet the filter criteria. Remember that if you filter by a parameter, an object may not have a value assigned, so you should input data into the parameter when the object is brought into your project. This ensures that your schedule is showing all that it should. Additionally, you can use a working schedule, one that does not filter elements and is never placed on a sheet.

As mentioned earlier, another option for filtering a schedule is to set the schedule phase. The different options for the phase filter of a view can be applied to schedule views in the same way that they are applied to model views. So if you were to set the phase of a schedule view to New Construction and the phase filter to one that shows only New Construction, no items from any previous phase would appear in the schedule. You can select the phase from the New Schedule dialog box shown in Figure 7.2. There is no way to go back to that dialog box once you proceed, but you can change the phase of the schedule at a later time from the Properties palette.

The Sorting/Grouping Tab

In the Sorting/Grouping tab of the Schedule Properties dialog box, you can determine the order of the objects in a schedule and then group like items together. You can assign up to four group conditions and provide a header or footer for each group. Sorting can be done based on parameters that are used in the schedule. When you sort by a particular parameter, all the objects in the schedule that have the same value for that parameter are listed together.

Figure 7.10 shows a sample Luminaire schedule that has been sorted by the Type Mark parameter. Notice that each instance of the different fixture types is listed in the schedule and that the Count column (QTY) on the far right of the schedule confirms this.

FIGURE 7.10
Sample Luminaire schedule

<LUMINAIRE SCHEDULE>

A	B	C	D	E	F	G
TYPE	MANUFACTURER	MODEL	MOUNTING	VOLTAGE	WATTS	QTY
A	ACME	AC-12354	RECESSED IN CEILING	230 V	12 W	1
A	ACME	AC-12354	RECESSED IN CEILING	230 V	12 W	1
A	ACME	AC-12354	RECESSED IN CEILING	230 V	12 W	1
A	ACME	AC-12354	RECESSED IN CEILING	230 V	12 W	1
A	ACME	AC-12354	RECESSED IN CEILING	230 V	12 W	1
A	ACME	AC-12354	RECESSED IN CEILING	230 V	12 W	1
A	ACME	AC-12354	RECESSED IN CEILING	230 V	12 W	1
A	ACME	AC-12354	RECESSED IN CEILING	230 V	12 W	1
A	ACME	AC-12354	RECESSED IN CEILING	230 V	12 W	1
A	ACME	AC-12354	RECESSED IN CEILING	230 V	12 W	1
B	REALLY COOL LIGHTS	RCL 100-135	RECESSED IN CEILING	230 V	12 W	1
B	REALLY COOL LIGHTS	RCL 100-135	RECESSED IN CEILING	230 V	12 W	1
B	REALLY COOL LIGHTS	RCL 100-135	RECESSED IN CEILING	230 V	12 W	1
	REALLY COOL LIGHTS	RCL 100-135	RECESSED IN CEILING	230 V	12 W	1
		RCL 100-135	RECESSED IN CEILING	230 V	12 W	1
F			RECESSED IN CEILING	230 V	12 W	1
F	LIGHTER MAN		RECESSED IN CEILING	230 V	12 W	1
F	LIGHTER MAN			230 V	12 W	1
F	LIGHTER MAN	LM_23060		230 V	12 W	1
F	LIGHTER MAN	LM_23060	HAMMERED		12 W	1
F	LIGHTER MAN	LM_23060	HAMMERED INTO SURFACE			1
F	LIGHTER MAN	LM_23060	HAMMERED INTO SURFACE	230 V		
F	LIGHTER MAN	LM_23060	HAMMERED INTO SURFACE	230 V	60 W	
F	LIGHTER MAN	LM_23060	HAMMERED INTO SURFACE	230 V	60 W	1
F	LIGHTER MAN	LM_23060	HAMMERED INTO SURFACE	230 V	60 W	1
G	SPOTS	GS500TRFB	RECESSED IN CEILING	230 V	500 W	1
G	SPOTS	GS500TRFB	RECESSED IN CEILING	230 V	500 W	1
G	SPOTS	GS500TRFB	RECESSED IN CEILING	230 V	500 W	1
G	SPOTS	GS500TRFB	RECESSED IN CEILING	230 V	500 W	1
G	SPOTS	GS500TRFB	RECESSED IN CEILING	230 V	500 W	1

A schedule lists each instance of the objects by default. To group items together that have the same parameter values, you need to deselect the box in the lower-left corner of the Sorting/Grouping tab of the Schedule Properties dialog box. Figure 7.11 shows settings for the same

Luminaire schedule, where the Itemize Every Instance box has been deselected. Notice that each type of lighting fixture is listed only once; that's because the schedule is set to sort by fixture type. The Count column now indicates the total number of each type of fixture. The Grand Totals check box has also been selected to give a total number of lighting fixtures at the bottom of the schedule. You can also create a custom grand total title—a new feature to Revit 2015.

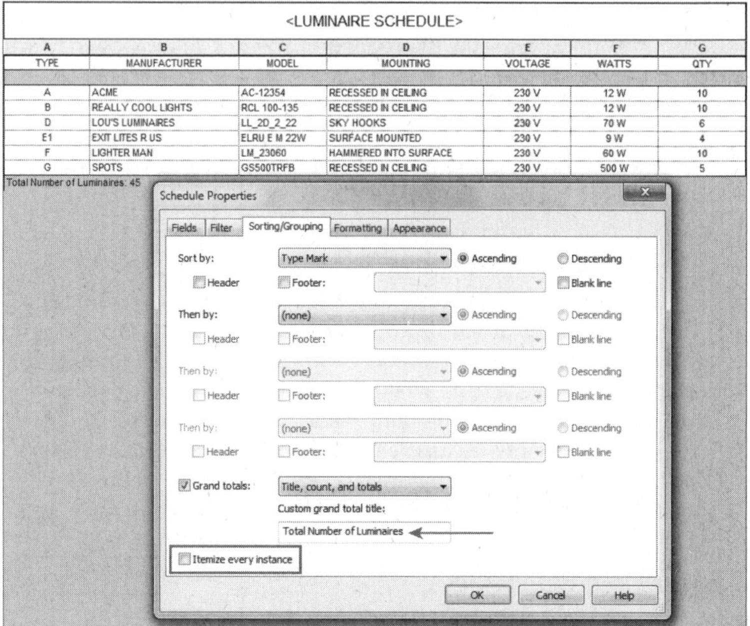

<LUMINAIRE SCHEDULE>

A	B	C	D	E	F	G
TYPE	MANUFACTURER	MODEL	MOUNTING	VOLTAGE	WATTS	QTY
A	ACME	AC-12354	RECESSED IN CEILING	230 V	12 W	10
B	REALLY COOL LIGHTS	RCL 100-135	RECESSED IN CEILING	230 V	12 W	10
D	LOU'S LUMINAIRES	LL_2D_2_22	SKY HOOKS	230 V	70 W	6
E1	EXIT LITES R US	ELRU E M 22W	SURFACE MOUNTED	230 V	9 W	4
F	LIGHTER MAN	LM_23060	HAMMERED INTO SURFACE	230 V	60 W	10
G	SPOTS	GS500TRFB	RECESSED IN CEILING	230 V	500 W	5

Total Number of Luminaires: 45

FIGURE 7.11 Luminaire schedule sorted and grouped by type

You can use the Sorting/Grouping settings with combinations of parameters to organize your schedules so that you can read the data within them easily. Figure 7.12 shows the Lighting Fixture schedule again, with settings to sort by the Type Mark parameter and a footer to indicate the total number of fixtures. The Ascending or Descending radio button can be used to determine the order of items within a sorted group. Notice that the fixture types are listed in alphabetical order because the Ascending option is used.

The Formatting Tab

The Formatting tab of the Schedule Properties dialog box has tools for setting how the data appears within a schedule. Each parameter used in the schedule is listed on the left side. When you select a parameter from the list, you can apply the settings available on the right side. You can also apply the settings to multiple parameters by holding down Ctrl or Shift.

The Heading setting establishes the name of the column in the schedule. The parameter name is used by default. Changing the column heading has no effect on the parameter itself, as shown in Figure 7.13, where the column headings have been changed to all caps. Even if the parameter name is what you want for your schedule column heading, you have to retype it if you want it in all capital letters. Figure 7.10, Figure 7.11, and Figure 7.12 are also good examples of this practice, where all the headings are in all caps (TYPE, MANUFACTURER, etc.).

FIGURE 7.12
Lighting Fixture schedule with two sorting options

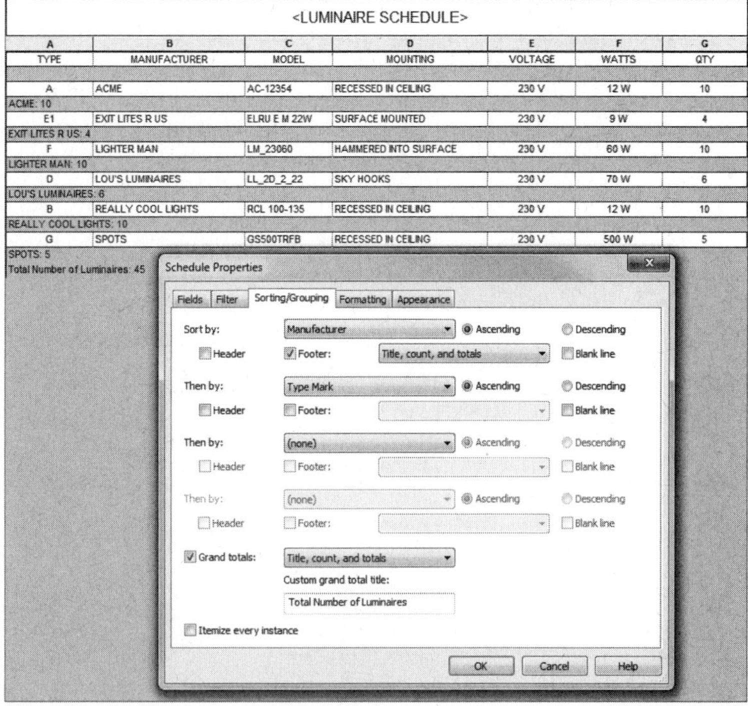

<LUMINAIRE SCHEDULE>

A	B	C	D	E	F	G
TYPE	MANUFACTURER	MODEL	MOUNTING	VOLTAGE	WATTS	QTY
A	ACME	AC-12354	RECESSED IN CEILING	230 V	12 W	10
ACME: 10						
E1	EXIT LITES R US	ELRU E M 22W	SURFACE MOUNTED	230 V	9 W	4
EXIT LITES R US: 4						
F	LIGHTER MAN	LM_23060	HAMMERED INTO SURFACE	230 V	60 W	10
LIGHTER MAN: 10						
D	LOU'S LUMINAIRES	LL_2D_2_22	SKY HOOKS	230 V	70 W	6
LOU'S LUMINAIRES: 6						
B	REALLY COOL LIGHTS	RCL 100-135	RECESSED IN CEILING	230 V	12 W	10
REALLY COOL LIGHTS: 10						
G	SPOTS	GS500TRFB	RECESSED IN CEILING	230 V	500 W	5
SPOTS: 5						
Total Number of Luminaires: 45						

FIGURE 7.13
Column heading settings

The Formatting tab also has settings for the orientation of the column headings and the alignment of the data within a column. Headings can be either vertical or horizontal, and the data can be aligned to the left, right, or center of a column.

Two additional types of formatting are available, depending on the type of parameter selected. The Field Format button becomes active when you select a parameter that is a measurement. In the Format dialog box that appears when you click the Field Format button, you can change the units and rounding accuracy of the data. You can also choose whether to show the unit symbol in the cell of the schedule. Whatever settings have been established for the project are used by default. You can deselect the box at the top of the Format dialog box to overwrite the settings within the schedule. Figure 7.14 shows format settings for the Area parameter used in a Space schedule. Unit Symbol has been set to None because the schedule column heading indicates the units.

FIGURE 7.14
Field format settings

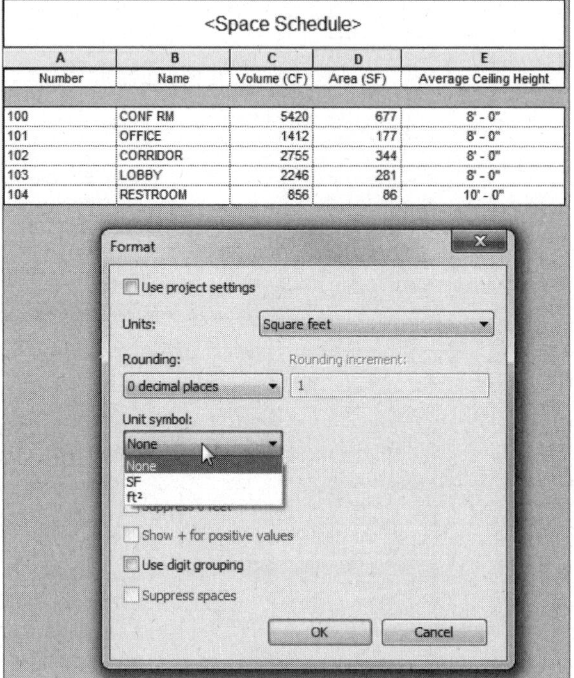

You can change the background color of a cell based on conditions that you apply by using the Conditional Format button. Clicking this button opens a dialog box where you can set a test condition for the value of a parameter and the background color of the schedule cell when the condition is met or not met. Additionally, since Revit 2014 you can display this conditional format on your output sheets. To do this, simply select the check box Show Conditional Format On Sheets. Figure 7.15 shows the Conditional Formatting dialog box for a calculated value in a schedule. The Background Color is set to turn red when the result of the calculation does not meet the test condition. The types of condition test options are shown in the Test drop-down list of the dialog box.

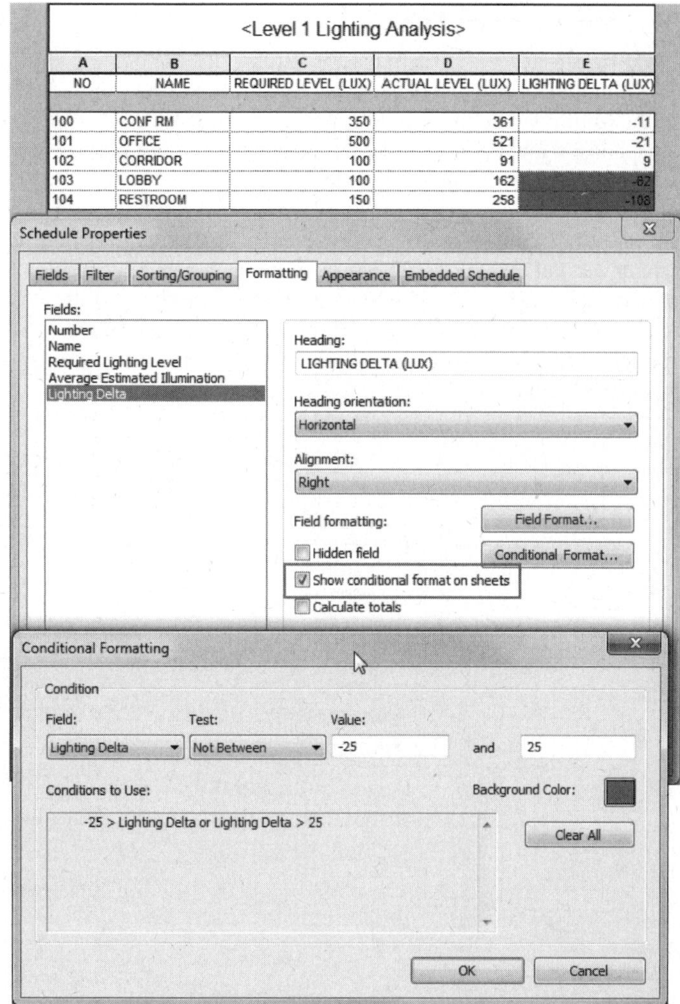

FIGURE 7.15
Sample Conditional Formatting dialog box

On the Sorting/Grouping tab is an option to display the totals for groups of objects. If you want to show the totals for an individual column, you can select the Calculate Totals box when you select a parameter on the Formatting tab. These totals will not appear if the Grand Totals option is not selected on the Sorting/Grouping tab.

Sometimes you need to include a parameter in a schedule for sorting purposes or for calculations but you do not want to display the column in your schedule. If this is the case, you can use the Hidden Field check box on the Formatting tab to hide a selected column. This can be very useful because it allows you to hide information without having to remove the information from your schedule. It also allows you to create a schedule with more information that is useful for calculations or design decisions but is more than would normally be shown on a drawing. When the time comes to put the schedule on a drawing, you can hide the unwanted columns.

The Appearance Tab

The Appearance tab of the Schedule Properties dialog box contains the settings that define how the schedule looks when placed on a sheet. Grid lines and an outline can be chosen from any of the line styles defined in your project. If you do not choose an option for the outline, the line style chosen for the grid lines will be used. The option to include grid lines within the headers, footers, or spacers is also available.

The check box to provide a blank row between the headings and schedule data is selected by default. If this is not how you normally display your schedules, you have to deselect this box whenever you create one. The Appearance tab also has settings for the text within a schedule, as shown in Figure 7.16. The font and text height that you choose for header text will be applied to all headings, subheadings, and the title of the schedule unless you opt to override these in the schedule itself. To do that, select the title or heading, and from the ribbon, select Font in the Appearance panel.

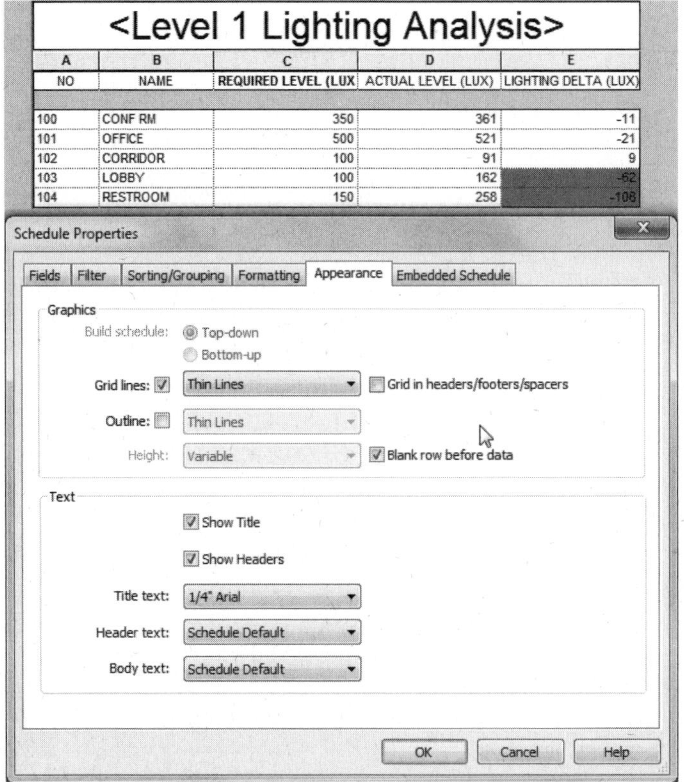

FIGURE 7.16 Appearance tab of the Schedule Properties dialog box

Editing a Schedule

Once you've created a schedule, you can edit it by using the same Schedule Properties dialog box. When you double-click a schedule in the Project Browser, the schedule is displayed in the drawing area. Using the persistent Properties box, you can access the tabs for the instance Properties list of a schedule view, as shown in Figure 7.17. Each tab has its own Edit button, but clicking any of these buttons takes you to the Schedule Properties dialog box. Whichever button you click from the list takes you to the corresponding tab within the dialog box.

FIGURE 7.17 Schedule view properties

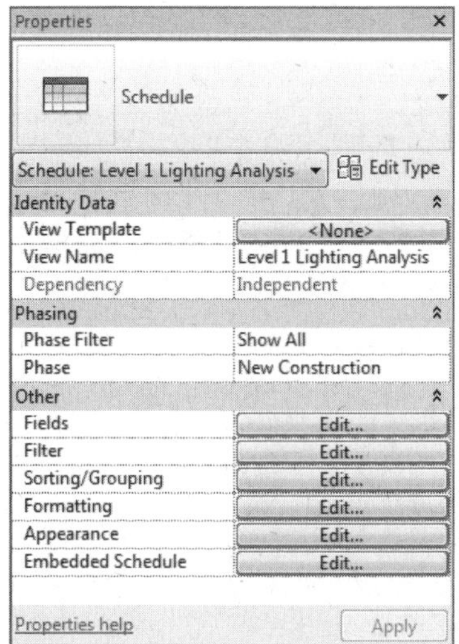

When you access the Schedule Properties dialog box, you can modify the schedule with any of the tools or settings that you would use to create a new schedule. One thing you cannot do is change what is being scheduled. For example, you cannot change a Lighting Fixture schedule to a Lighting Devices schedule because the Family category defines this.

Some of the formatting options that are defined can be modified in the schedule view, without having to access the Schedule Properties dialog box. In the schedule view, you can select anywhere within a column and use the Hide button on the ribbon to hide that column. There is also a Delete button on the ribbon to delete a row in the schedule. The majority of formatting tools have now also been added to the updated tab for modifying schedules and quantities.

To ensure consistency between all your schedules, use view templates. View templates allow you to quickly apply your company standards to a schedule or a group of schedules. To create a new schedule view template, simply right-click a schedule and select Create View Template From View.

Delete with Caution

It is important to understand what will happen if you click the Delete button on the ribbon when you select a row in a schedule. If your schedule is scheduling objects from your model and you delete a row, all the objects from that row will be deleted from the project. Depending on how your schedule is formatted, this could be one object or one thousand objects.

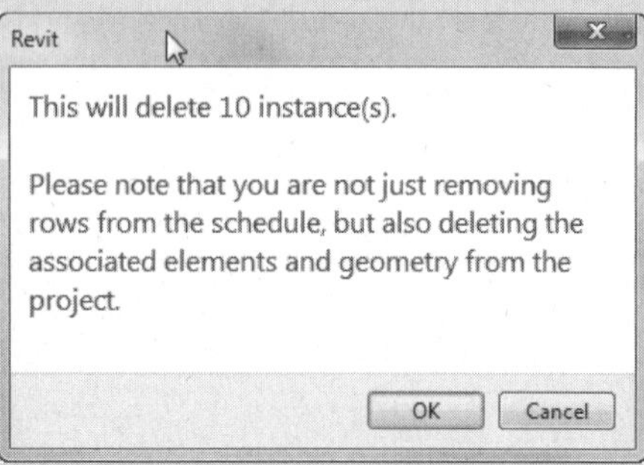

When you click in the cell of a column heading, you can change the text of the heading, eliminating the need to access the Formatting tab. You can change the title of the schedule with this method also, although this changes the name of your schedule in the Project Browser. Columns can be grouped together under a common heading by selecting the columns and clicking the Group button on the ribbon. Columns must be adjacent to each other to be grouped. The key to selecting columns for grouping is to hold down the left mouse button when you click the first column and then drag your cursor to highlight the columns to be included in the group. When you click the Group button, a new blank header appears above the columns, awaiting input. This is ideal for grouping similar data: locality details, measurements, and so forth (see Figure 7.18). Column groups can be removed by highlighting all the columns within a group and clicking the Ungroup button on the ribbon.

Figure 7.18
Schedule grouping

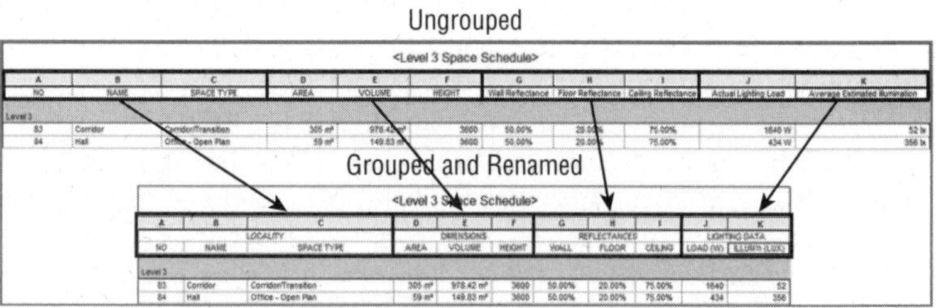

Another handy feature in Revit MEP 2015 is the ability to add new rows in the header of your schedule. This lets you use the schedule like a spreadsheet, so you can make it look similar to the data sheets you have been using for many years in other packages. In Figure 7.19, a row was added by using the Insert option from the Rows panel on the Modify Schedule/Quantities tab of the ribbon.

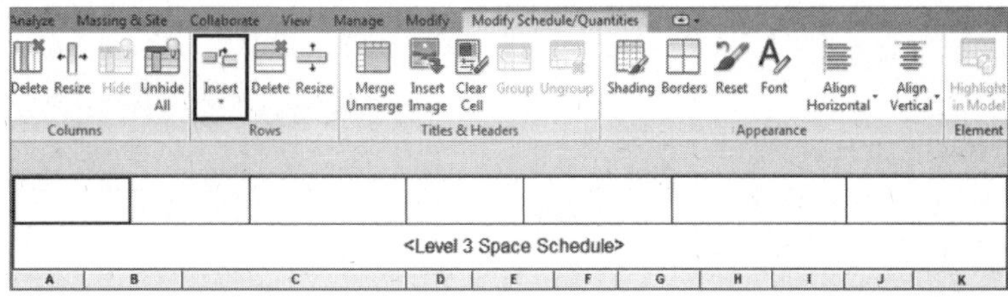

FIGURE 7.19
Schedule rows

Cells in this row can then be merged and parameters added to each merged cell as required. Figure 7.20 shows the schedule partially complete. Notice that fields can be added from the Parameters panel; text can be typed in; the size, font, and alignment of the values can be altered by using the Appearance panel; and an image—such as your company logo—can be added.

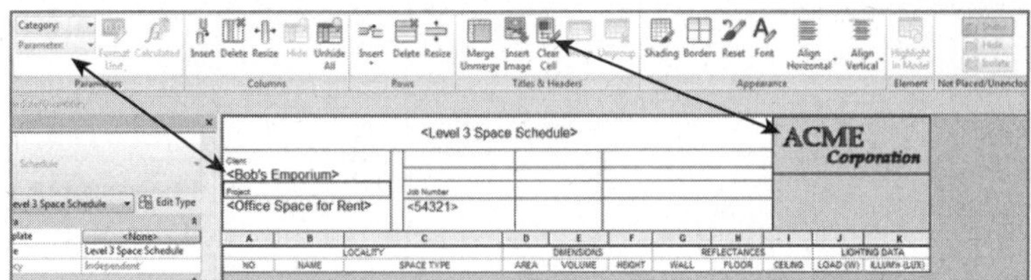

FIGURE 7.20
Schedule editing

This custom header can also have shading and borders applied either to individual cells or a selection, using the tools in the Appearance panel, as shown in Figure 7.21 and Figure 7.22. Click the appropriate button to change linetype, color, display, and so forth.

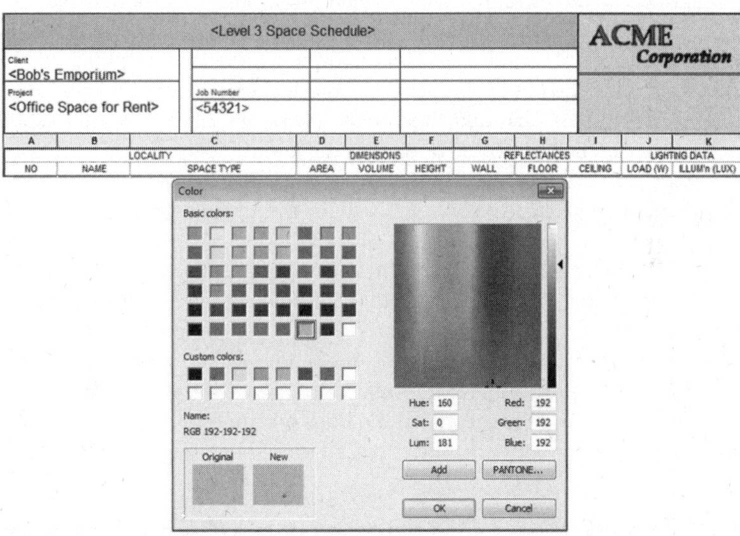

FIGURE 7.21
Schedule shading

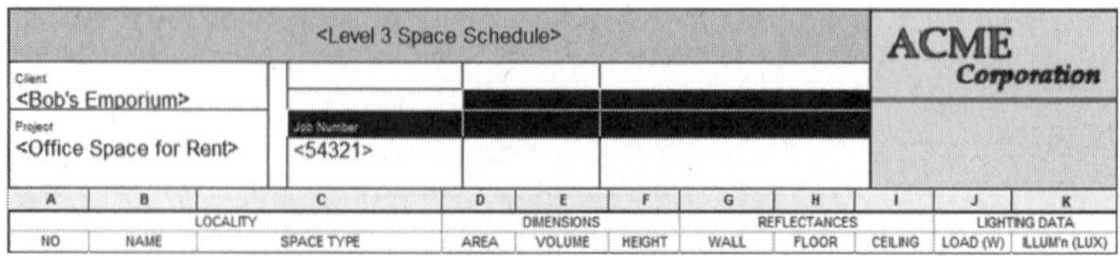

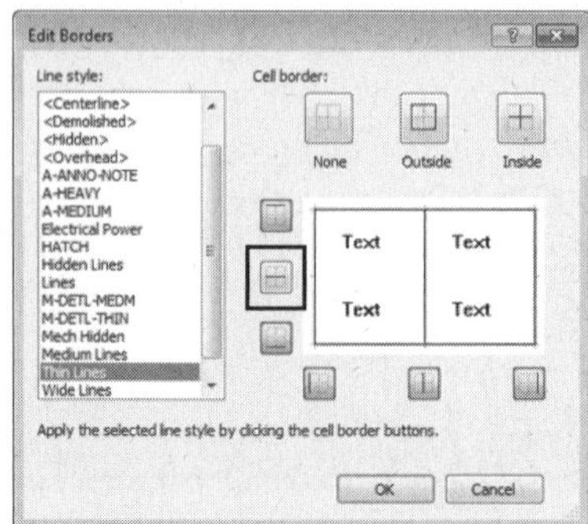

FIGURE 7.22
Schedule borders

One of the best features of using schedules in Revit is that you can edit parameter values of objects right in the schedule. If you are changing the value of a type parameter, you receive a warning letting you know that your change will be applied to all objects of that type when you finish editing the cell. Some cells turn into a drop-down list when you click them. This lets you select from previously inputted values for that parameter as long as those values are being used in the project. If you click a cell and you cannot edit it, that means that the parameter is a calculated value, it is a parameter of an object within a linked file, or the parameter does not exist in the object.

Because a schedule view is actually a view of the model, you can select a cell in a schedule and click the Highlight In Model button on the ribbon to see where the selected object exists in the model. This takes you to a view of the model, where the object can be seen. You can continue to click the Show button for different views. If you have grouped objects in your schedule and you are not itemizing every instance of the objects in it, then all the selected object types are shown. Used in conjunction with tiled views, this can aid in the selection and manipulation of objects.

Some schedules need multiple lines of input within one row, such as for comments or a description. This can be accomplished by pressing Ctrl+Enter when inputting information into a schedule cell or parameter value. Each time you press Ctrl+Enter, you create a hard return in the value, therefore starting a new line of text. When you are in the schedule view, you see only the first line of input in the cell. You do not see the other lines of input, so if you need to edit them, you have to retype all the lines within that cell or parameter value. The multiple lines appear when the schedule is placed on a sheet.

Scheduling Component and System Family Data

Almost any object type that is placed into a Revit model can be scheduled. This seems like a very generic concept, but if you consider the possibilities that exist, it is easy to see why using a parametric model can be a great benefit to your design processes. Having readily accessible information about the components that make up your design makes coordination and decision-making easier and more efficient.

It is important to know what kind of information about model objects can be scheduled, because the types of schedules that you can create for model objects depend on the data within those objects. Some data is inherent in the objects, based on how they are used in the model, such as elevation or location. Most of the data used in component object schedules comes from parameters that are added to the objects either as project parameters or directly in the component-family file as shared parameters. Family parameters cannot be scheduled.

Using the organizational and calculation tools within a Revit schedule can help you get the most from the data within the model components. The following sections cover some possibilities for scheduling building components.

Mechanical Equipment Schedules

The Mechanical Equipment model category covers a wide range of components. Chillers, water heaters, pumps, rooftop units, fans, and more all fall under the Mechanical Equipment category. As you have seen, using filters makes it possible to create specific schedules for different types of Mechanical Equipment components. The key to success with these schedules is developing a method that makes the filtering easy to use and manage.

When considering the information that is needed in your schedules, you can look at the parameters that already exist in every component and determine whether they can be used in lieu of creating a custom parameter. The Description parameter is one example of a parameter that is in every object. With the ability to change the heading in a schedule, you can use this parameter for any type of descriptive information that is scheduled about your components. You do not need to create a parameter for each type of information to be scheduled. For example, if your Mechanical Equipment schedule for pumps has a column for the mounting type, you could use the Description parameter to convey this information.

Every item that is placed into a model is given a Mark value. The Mark parameter is another useful parameter for scheduling mechanical equipment.

There are certain parameters (Family and Type, Type) that do not appear under the Filter tab as a choice and therefore cannot be used for filtering objects.

A Warning about Mark Values

When you manually change the Mark value of an object, the next object that you place that is in the same category will have a Mark value that is sequential to the value you input. For example, if you place a boiler and give it a Mark value of B-1, the next Mechanical Equipment object you place will be given a Mark value of B-2, even if it is not another boiler. Using Mark values to identify equipment requires you to manage the Mark value of an object when it is placed into your model. Assuming that boilers are numbered sequentially (B-1, -2, -3), as are pumps (P-1, -2, -3), and so forth, this field does require managing in the particular schedule for that equipment because this is considered to be unique data. The data type that requires management only from a project point of view is the Type Mark parameter. Rather than having a unique number, the Type Mark can describe something like a luminaire reference or power outlet, where there are many objects with the same reference.

The best reason for using the Mark parameter for Mechanical Equipment schedules is that it makes it easy to filter the schedule for specific items. Figure 7.23 shows a Mechanical Equipment schedule for pumps and the filter settings based on the Mark parameter. This setup allows for having unique Mark values for multiple instances of the same type of component.

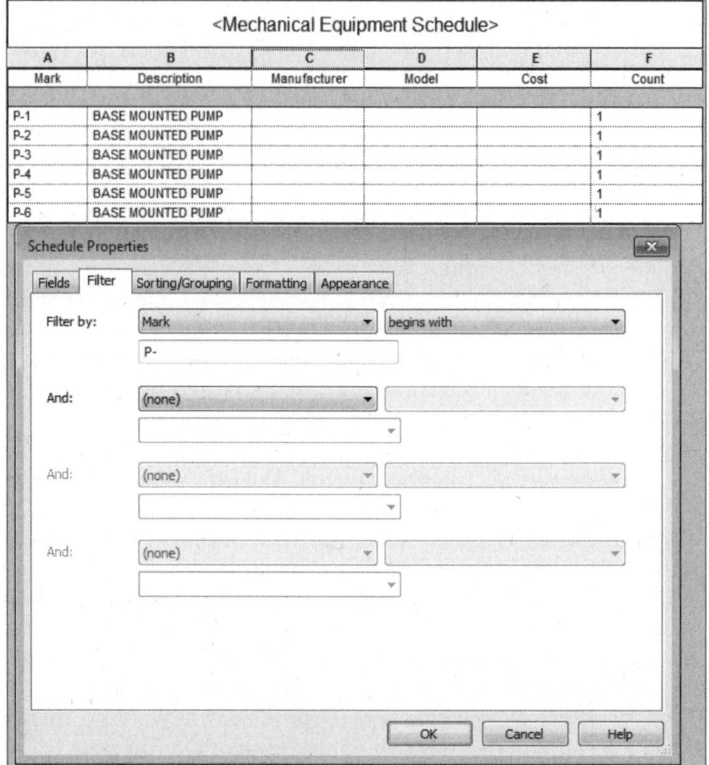

FIGURE 7.23 Pump schedule filtered by the Mark parameter

Another way to easily filter your Mechanical Equipment schedules is to create a project parameter called Schedule Type that is applied to the Mechanical Equipment category. You can then assign values for this parameter in order to create schedule filter rules. This may be the preferred method, because the Schedule Type parameter could be applied to all appropriate model categories and would give you a uniform method for filtering schedules.

If you have a schedule with a column for remarks or notes about an object, the Type Comments parameter can be a useful alternative to creating a custom parameter. The value of this parameter can refer to text notes associated with a schedule.

Lighting Fixture Schedules

The Type Mark parameter is useful for assigning a unique identifier to each fixture type within your project and eliminates the need for a custom parameter. If you use a standard set of fixtures for each design, you might consider naming each family type within your fixture families and using the type name to identify your fixtures in a schedule. The family type name shows up as Type in the Available Fields list, as shown in Figure 7.24.

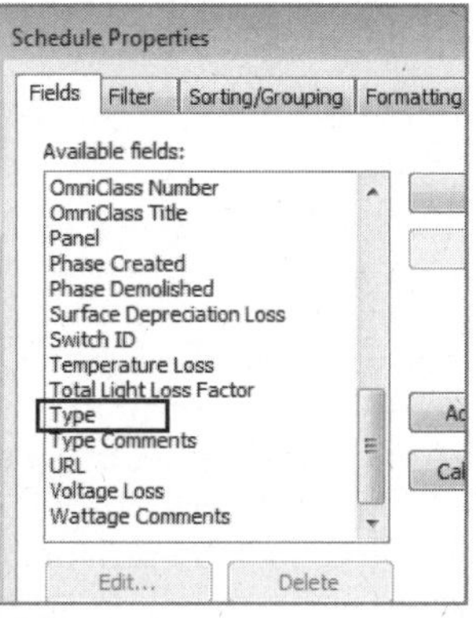

FIGURE 7.24
Family Type option in the Available Fields list

The URL parameter can be used for any component and is particularly useful for lighting fixtures. You can input a link to the cut sheet of a lighting fixture into its URL parameter for quick access to the additional information that a cut sheet provides. Figure 7.25 shows an example of a Lighting Fixture schedule with a URL column. When you click on the URL row, a small box at the right of the end of the URL cell shows up. The cut sheet file opens when you click that small box. Although this box is not initially visible, try clicking in the place where it *should* be. Notice how the URL responds, even though the box cannot be seen? Anywhere this type of box appears (URL, Material, Image, etc.), you can click this portion of the cell. That's a work-saving of 50 percent! Well, it's one fewer mouse click anyway, where there were two.

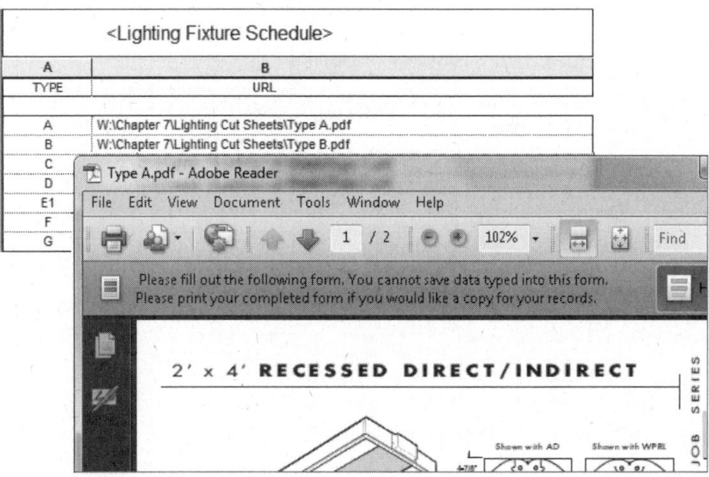

FIGURE 7.25
URL parameter used in a Lighting Fixture schedule

The paths you provide in URL parameters are not relative, so if you share or submit your Revit project file, the links are inactive unless you also share the cut sheets and you create new paths for the URL parameters.

System Family Schedules

Schedules are useful not only for component objects but for system families as well. Duct, Pipe, Cable Tray, and Conduit schedules can be created for use on construction documents or just for keeping track of quantities and materials.

Duct Schedules

A lot of information can be taken from a ductwork model. How you organize a Duct schedule depends on the type of information you are looking for and what you intend to do with it. Determining the amount of sheet metal for ductwork is one way to utilize the power of scheduling in Revit MEP 2015. Unfortunately, the Material Takeoff option of the Schedules tool on the View tab is restricted to component families. However, with some calculated fields and the right parameters, you can create a schedule that works as a material takeoff.

Figure 7.26 shows a sample Duct schedule with calculated values to determine the total area of material for both round and rectangular ducts. A duct material project parameter was created, and values were manually input for different duct types. The total area for each duct material is calculated at the bottom. This is just a small example of how you can get useful information from your model in schedule format. Keep in mind that because Revit is a parametric modeling tool, as ducts are removed, added, or changed, the schedule reflects those changes automatically.

Figure 7.26 Sample Duct schedule

<Duct Schedule>

A	B	C	D	E	F
Description	Width	Height	Width Area	Height Area	Area
PLAIN GALVANISED MILD STEEL					
PLAIN GALVANISED MILD STEEL	8"	8"	17 SF	17 SF	33 SF
PLAIN GALVANISED MILD STEEL	8"	8"	17 SF	17 SF	33 SF
PLAIN GALVANISED MILD STEEL	12"	8"	21 SF	14 SF	34 SF
PLAIN GALVANISED MILD STEEL	10"	12"	16 SF	20 SF	36 SF
PLAIN GALVANISED MILD STEEL	12"	12"	25 SF	25 SF	50 SF
PLAIN GALVANISED MILD STEEL	12"	12"	25 SF	25 SF	50 SF
PLAIN GALVANISED MILD STEEL	20"	20"	31 SF	31 SF	62 SF
					298 SF
STAINLESS STEEL					
STAINLESS STEEL	12"	12"	12 SF	12 SF	24 SF
STAINLESS STEEL	15"	12"	18 SF	14 SF	32 SF
STAINLESS STEEL	12"	12"	17 SF	17 SF	33 SF
STAINLESS STEEL	12"	12"	20 SF	20 SF	39 SF
STAINLESS STEEL	12"	12"	22 SF	22 SF	44 SF
STAINLESS STEEL	15"	12"	26 SF	21 SF	46 SF
STAINLESS STEEL	12"	12"	25 SF	25 SF	50 SF
STAINLESS STEEL	12"	12"	25 SF	25 SF	50 SF
					317 SF
Grand total: 15					616 SF

Another type of Duct schedule can help you keep track of what type of duct is used for different air systems. A schedule like this enables you to see whether any errors have occurred in the model based on design criteria. If all return-air ductwork is to be rectangular, for example, a schedule quickly reveals any duct that does not meet this requirement.

Pipe Schedules

Creating a custom Material Takeoff schedule for pipe is a little easier than for duct because pipe types can be assigned a material without creating a custom parameter. Figure 7.27 shows a sample Pipe schedule that is organized to show the total length of each pipe size per material.

Figure 7.27
Sample Pipe schedule for a material takeoff

<Pipe Schedule>

A	B	C
Material	Diameter	Length
Copper	1/2"	19' - 3 27/32"
Copper	3/4"	69' - 9 17/32"
Copper	1"	281' - 0 1/8"
Copper	1 1/4"	33' - 0"
Copper	1 1/2"	28' - 10 1/2"
Copper	2"	20' - 6 15/16"
Copper: 65		452' - 6 31/3
Plastic	2"	195' - 3 15/1
Plastic	3"	10' - 1 7/16"
Plastic	4"	100' - 7 23/3
Plastic: 35		306' - 1 3/32"
Stainless Steel	1/2"	372' - 4 13/3
Stainless Steel	1"	19' - 5 3/16"
Stainless Steel	1 1/4"	6' - 2 3/16"
Stainless Steel	2"	54' - 0 1/2"
Stainless Steel: 50		452' - 0 5/16"
Grand total: 150		1210' - 8 3/8"

Exporting Schedules

You can export Revit schedules by using the Export tool on the application menu. The exported TXT file can be imported into a spreadsheet for further computation or analysis. Although spreadsheets cannot be natively imported into Revit schedules, there are many third-party applications that allow the transfer of data between Revit and Excel; these can easily be found with a search on the Internet.

You can create Pipe schedules to input data quickly into the properties of pipes without having to locate each pipe in the model. One example where this may be useful is with pipe insulation. You can create a pipe insulation schedule like the one shown in Figure 7.28, which groups pipe insulations by their system types.

Figure 7.28
Sample Pipe Insulation schedule for parameter input

<Pipe Schedule>

A	B	C
System Type	Size	Insulation Thickness
Hydronic Return	100 mmø	25 mm
Hydronic Supply	20 mmø	25 mm
Hydronic Supply	20 mmø	25 mm
Hydronic Supply	20 mmø	25 mm
Hydronic Supply	20 mmø	25 mm
Hydronic Supply	20 mmø	25 mm

Insulation Thickness is an instance parameter of the Insulation Category. You can apply a value to several objects at once by grouping the insulation types and deselecting the Itemize Every Instance box on the Sorting/Grouping tab of the Schedule Properties dialog box. When you input a value for the Insulation Thickness parameter, it is applied to all pipes within that group. Just keep in mind that Insulation is considered a separate object, and pipes that don't have any insulation will not even appear on the Pipe Insulation schedule. For that reason, it is best to use two schedules, a Pipe schedule and a Pipe Insulation schedule. From the Pipe schedule, you can see and select the pipes that don't have insulation. While the pipes without insulation are still selected, you can apply Insulation from the plan view. Once all necessary pipes have insulation, you can manage them from the Pipe Insulation schedule.

Space Schedules

Spaces are typically scheduled to analyze their data to determine the performance of systems. However, creating a Space schedule can also help with model maintenance or quality control. A very simple Space schedule can be a useful tool for removing unwanted or misplaced spaces, reducing the risk of performing analysis of an incorrect model.

Spaces can be placed into a model manually or by using the Place Spaces Automatically tool on the Modify | Place Space contextual tab. The one drawback to the automated process is that Revit places a Space object in any enclosed area that is bounded by objects defined as Room Bounding and that is 0.25 square feet or larger. This often results in Space objects being placed in pipe and duct chases or in column wraps and other small enclosures. In a large model, it could be time-consuming to search for all the unwanted Space objects, making the automation of space placement seem unreasonable. When these spaces are found, deleting them removes them from the model only. They still exist in the project and could be inadvertently used again or have unnecessary analysis performed on them.

Consider creating a simple Space schedule that will quickly identify any unwanted spaces and allow you to delete them all completely from the project with a few clicks. When you link in an architectural model, one thing you need to do is set the Room Bounding parameter so that it defines the boundaries of your spaces. Placing a space within the same boundaries as a Room object will associate that space with the architectural Room object. So, unless your architect has placed Room objects in areas such as chases or column wraps, you can easily see which of your spaces match up with the rooms.

Figure 7.29 shows the settings for a Space schedule that can be used to eliminate unwanted spaces. The schedule is sorted and grouped by room number and level so that all spaces without an associated level (Not Placed) or room will be listed together at the top of the schedule. Not Placed spaces could have been created as a fast-track design method or as a result of architectural changes. Either way, it is up to the user to decide whether they are required.

The unwanted spaces can be highlighted in the schedule and then removed from the project by using the Delete button on the ribbon. You cannot use the Shift or Ctrl keys, but you can click and drag your cursor to select multiple rows within a Revit schedule.

The Schedule Properties dialog box for a Space schedule contains an additional tab for creating and managing an embedded schedule. This allows you to create an additional schedule that is set up within your Space schedule. On the Embedded Schedule tab, you can select the box to include an embedded schedule within your Space schedule and choose the model category you want to schedule. When you click the Embedded Schedule Properties button in the lower-left corner, a new Schedule Properties dialog box appears. You can then set up the embedded schedule in the same way you would set up a regular one. The Appearance tab is not available in an embedded schedule because the settings are controlled by the host schedule.

FIGURE 7.29
Settings for a Space schedule

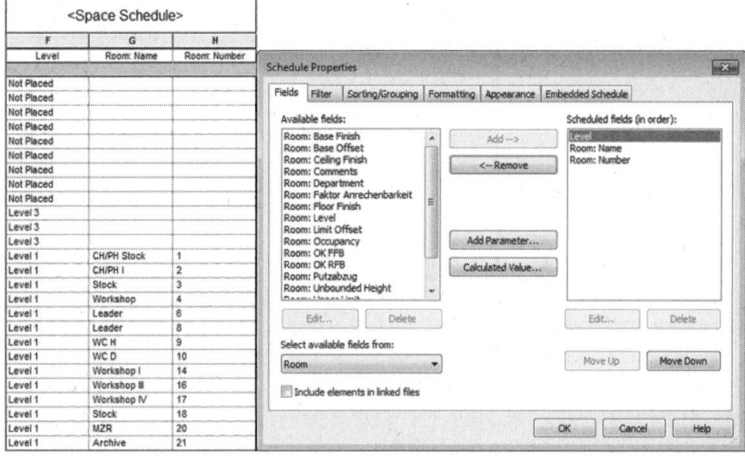

F	G	H
Level	Room: Name	Room: Number
Not Placed		
Not Placed		
Not Placed		
Not Placed		
Not Placed		
Not Placed		
Not Placed		
Not Placed		
Not Placed		
Level 3		
Level 3		
Level 3		
Level 1	CH/PH Stock	1
Level 1	CH/PH I	2
Level 1	Stock	3
Level 1	Workshop	4
Level 1	Leader	6
Level 1	Leader	8
Level 1	WC H	9
Level 1	WC D	10
Level 1	Workshop I	14
Level 1	Workshop II	16
Level 1	Workshop IV	17
Level 1	Stock	18
Level 1	MZR	20
Level 1	Archive	21

Figure 7.30 shows the Fields tab of a Lighting Fixture schedule that is embedded into a Space schedule. The fixtures in the embedded schedule are sorted and grouped by the Type Mark parameter, and grand totals are shown.

FIGURE 7.30
Embedded Lighting Fixture schedule settings

Schedule Properties
Fields | Filter | Sorting/Grouping | Formatting
Available fields:
Assembly Description
Assembly Name
Ballast Loss
Circuit Number
Coefficient of Utilization
Comments
Cost
Description
Efficacy
Electrical Data
Family
Family and Type
Add -->
<-- Remove
Add Parameter...
Calculated Value...
Scheduled fields (in order):
Type Mark
Count
Edit... Delete
Select available fields from:
Lighting Fixtures
Include elements in linked files
Move Up Move Down
OK Cancel Help

The information within the embedded schedule is included in the host Space schedule, as shown in Figure 7.31. By creating this type of schedule, you can see how many elements of a specific category are associated with each space.

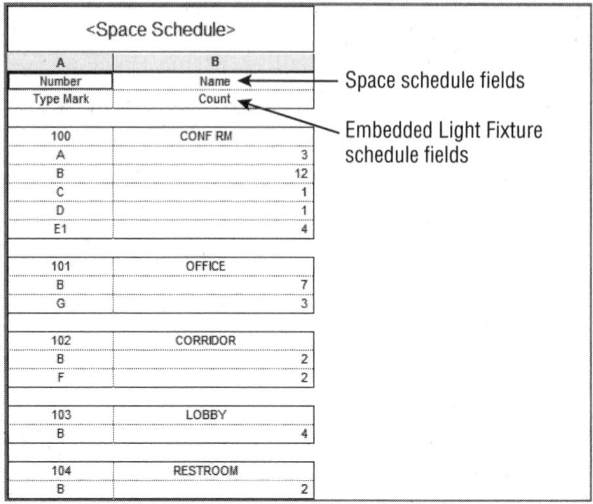

FIGURE 7.31 Space schedule with an embedded Light Fixture schedule

Model Component Schedules

Understanding the basic features of a component schedule will help you begin to develop your own methods for scheduling your Revit projects. Create a simple component schedule by doing the following:

1. Open the `Ch7_Schedules.rvt` file found at `www.sybex.com/go/masteringrevitmep2015`.
2. Click the Schedules button on the View tab and select Schedule/Quantities.
3. Select the Air Terminals category. Ensure that the Schedule Building Components option is selected and that Phase is set to New Construction, and then click OK.
4. On the Fields tab, select Type Mark from the Available Fields list and click the Add button. Repeat the process to add the System Type, Neck Size, CFM Range, Description, and Count parameters to the schedule.
5. On the Sorting/Grouping tab, select Type Mark in the Sort By drop-down. Deselect the Itemize Every Instance box in the lower-left corner.
6. On the Formatting tab, highlight all the parameters in the Fields list and set Alignment to Center.
7. On the Appearance tab, select the Outline box and change the line style to Wide Lines. Click OK to exit the Schedule Properties dialog box.

   In the second half of this exercise, we take a look at creating a space schedule that also contains an embedded schedule of air terminals.

8. Click the Schedules button on the View tab and select Schedule/Quantities.

9. Select the Spaces category. Ensure that the Schedule Building Components option is selected and that Phase is set to New Construction, and then click OK.
10. On the Fields tab, select Number from the Available Fields list and click the Add button. Repeat the process to add the Name parameter to the schedule.
11. On the Filter tab, select Number in the Filter By drop-down and set Begins With as the rule. Type **1** in the field below the Filter By drop-down.
12. On the Sorting/Grouping tab, select Number from the Sort By drop-down.
13. On the Formatting tab, select the Number and Name parameters and set Alignment to Center.
14. On the Embedded Schedule tab, select the Embedded Schedule box, select the Air Terminals category, and click the Embedded Schedule Properties button.
15. Add the Type Mark, System Type, and Count parameters from the Available Fields list.
16. On the Sorting/Grouping tab, select Type Mark in the Sort By drop-down. Select the Grand Totals box in the lower-left corner.
17. On the Formatting tab, select the Count parameter and select the Calculate Totals box. Click OK to exit the Embedded Schedule Properties dialog box.

Using Schedules for Design and Analysis

Scheduling building components to provide information on construction documents or to keep track of model components and materials is not the only use for schedules in Revit. Using schedules to analyze the performance of MEP systems in relation to the building model can help you make design decisions. The ability to see and manipulate the information directly in Revit can improve the efficiency of your design processes.

Traditionally, engineers use several tools to complete building analysis. Some are used "because we always have and we trust the results" even though these processes can be time-consuming. It is important to verify your design data so the results can be trusted without just relying on the output. So, it is a great idea to run some small tests—side by side, your trusted software with the newfangled one. Revit MEP not only provides a great conceptual level of analysis, it does it faster than many of the programs around. What's more, the data from Revit can be exported to a GBXML format that can then be imported into other programs, allowing verification, confirmation, and more-complex analysis without the time-consuming modeling or data input procedures required for those other packages.

When it comes to analysis, the focus is mainly on the Space objects in your model. Space objects hold a lot of information related to energy analysis, by direct input, input from third-party analysis, or as a result of the characteristics of components associated with the spaces. Understanding the type of information you can retrieve from spaces during the design process is the key to developing schedules that are most useful to your workflow.

Analysis can be as simple as checking to see whether the components you are using meet the engineering requirements or standards around which you are designing. This often requires that you manually set the requirement information property of your spaces. Selecting each space and accessing its properties to input this information is an inefficient practice.

Schedule Keys

A special type of schedule can be created to improve the process of adding information to your spaces. This is a *schedule key*, and it allows you to specify values for a parameter based on the value of a key parameter. One example is in lighting design, where a certain lighting level is required for specific types of rooms. A schedule key can be created to associate a specific lighting level value with each space key parameter value. The parameter associated with the key can be included in your Space schedule so that each space can be assigned a key and therefore a required lighting level. The required lighting level could be input manually into the parameter, but using a key ensures accuracy and consistency.

Click the Schedules button on the View tab and select Schedule/Quantities to create a schedule key. When you select the category you want to schedule, the option to create a schedule key becomes available on the right side of the dialog box. You can then choose a name for the key parameter in the Key Name field. A style-based name will automatically be placed in the Key Name field, but you can change it to whatever you want. After you create the schedule, a parameter with this name is added to all the objects in the category for which you are creating a schedule key. Figure 7.32 shows an example of the settings for a Space schedule key. Notice that the schedule has been named to identify it as a schedule key and not a component schedule.

FIGURE 7.32
Space schedule key setup

The Key Name parameter is automatically included in the Scheduled Fields area on the Fields tab of the Schedule Properties dialog box. Here, you can select parameters to which values are assigned based on the key value. In the case of a Space schedule key for lighting levels, the Required Lighting Level parameter is chosen, as shown in Figure 7.33.

The schedule key is sorted by the Key Name parameter by default. Unless you will be placing the schedule on a drawing, there is no need for any other settings within the Schedule Properties dialog box. The schedule key starts out blank. Click the New button on the Rows panel of the ribbon to add a row to the schedule. You can then edit the name of the key and assign a value to the associated parameter. Repeat the process to create additional rows and build your schedule key. Figure 7.34 shows an example of a Space schedule key for lighting levels.

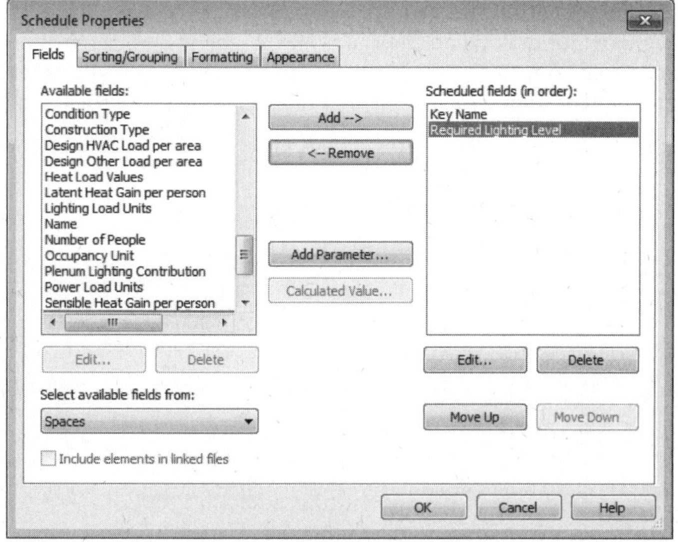

FIGURE 7.33
Space schedule key Fields tab

FIGURE 7.34
Sample schedule key

<Space Style Schedule>

A	B
Key Name	Required Lighting
Classroom	350 lx
Corridor	100 lx
Office	500 lx
Toilet	150 lx

Now that you have created the schedule key, each space has a Space Style parameter that can be assigned a value from the schedule key for the Required Lighting Level parameter. A schedule can be used to assign these values without having to access the properties of each space. When you are editing a key parameter value in a schedule, a drop-down list appears with all the key values, as shown in Figure 7.35.

A key parameter can be included in a schedule that is set up for analysis to increase the functionality of the schedule. Additional parameters were added to the schedule shown in Figure 7.35 to determine whether the lighting levels in each space meet the design requirements. A calculated value was added to show the difference between the required level and what is actually occurring in the space. This type of schedule allows you to quickly see the performance of the design components used, and you can adjust parameter values of the spaces to investigate options. Notice in Figure 7.36 that spaces, which have been assigned a Space Style value, have the corresponding Required Lighting Level parameter value from the key.

This same type of schedule can be created for airflow in spaces. The design airflow value can be checked against the actual airflow and the value calculated by a third-party analysis or directly from the Revit MEP 2015 Heating and Cooling Analysis tool.

The ability to see the performance-based data is essential to checking the quality of your design and for making appropriate changes to the design when necessary. Figure 7.37 shows an example of a duct airflow schedule that displays the properties related to the performance of the system rather than information about the physical properties of the ductwork.

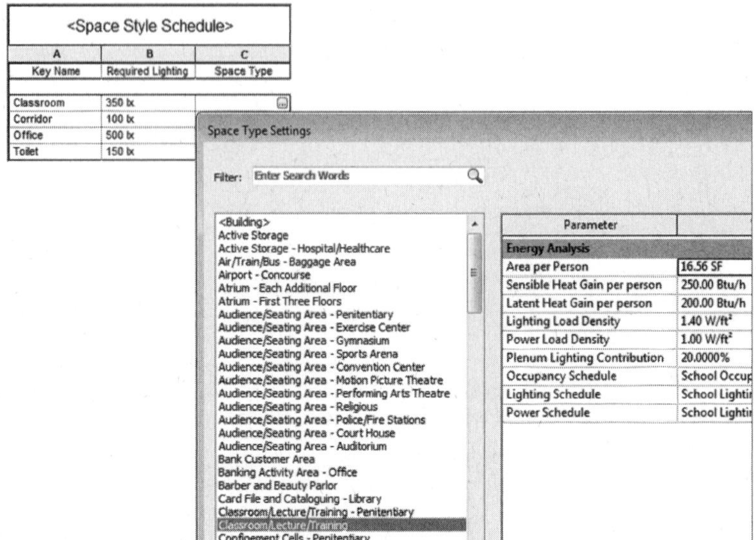

FIGURE 7.35 Editing a schedule key parameter

FIGURE 7.36 Space lighting level analysis schedule

<Level 1 Lighting Analysis>

A	B	C	D	E	F
NO	NAME	Space Style	REQUIRED LEVEL (LUX)	AVAERAGE EXSTIMATED (LUX)	Lighting Delta (LUX)
100	CONF RM	Classroom	350	374	24
101	OFFICE	Office	500	521	21
102	CORRIDOR	Corridor	100	101	1
103	LOBBY	Corridor	100	168	68
104	RESTROOM	Toilet	150	314	164

FIGURE 7.37 Duct Airflow schedule

<Duct Schedule>

A	B	C	D	E	F
System Name	Friction	Flow	Pressure Drop	Velocity	Velocity Pressure
Mechanical Supply Air 1	0.04 Pa/m	75.0 L/s	0.0 Pa	0.8 m/s	0.4 Pa
Mechanical Supply Air 1	0.04 Pa/m	75.0 L/s	0.0 Pa	0.8 m/s	0.4 Pa
Mechanical Supply Air 1	0.00 Pa/m	0.0 L/s	0.0 Pa	0.0 m/s	0.0 Pa
Mechanical Supply Air 1	0.07 Pa/m	100.0 L/s	0.0 Pa	1.1 m/s	0.7 Pa
Mechanical Supply Air 1	0.07 Pa/m	100.0 L/s	0.1 Pa	1.1 m/s	0.7 Pa
Mechanical Supply Air 1	0.07 Pa/m	100.0 L/s	0.0 Pa	1.1 m/s	0.7 Pa
Mechanical Supply Air 1	0.07 Pa/m	100.0 L/s	0.1 Pa	1.1 m/s	0.7 Pa

Real World Scenario

USING THIRD-PARTY DATA

Shelley uses a third-party application—IES—to analyze her HVAC designs. Because the software she uses is compatible with Revit MEP 2015, she can import the data generated from the third-party analysis into her Revit projects.

When this data is imported, she wants to be able to see the values as they pertain to each space in combination with the types of air terminals used in her design. Shelley has created a Space schedule with an embedded Air Terminal schedule that allows her to view the results from the third-party analysis in each space alongside the airflow properties of her air terminals. She has added this schedule to her project template so that it is available for each project on which she works, and now she has a consistent workflow for analyzing the results.

Panel Schedules

The ability to create custom Panel schedules was a long-awaited feature that was introduced into Revit MEP 2011. They are not created by using the scheduling tools but instead are generated by a predefined format residing in a panel-schedule template. There are tools to create a panel schedule template with settings for both the appearance of the schedule and the data that is reported.

Once you establish panel schedule templates within your project template, they are available for use on any project. If you want to create a custom Panel schedule, the first step is to create its template. You can find the Panel Schedule Templates tool on the Manage tab.

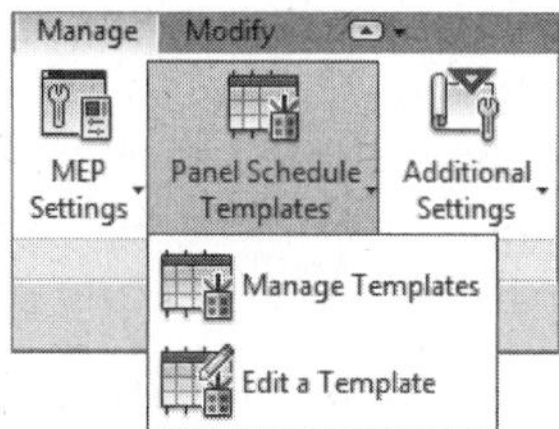

The Manage Templates option gives you access to your panel schedule templates for editing or duplication. Clicking this option activates the Manage Panel Schedule Templates dialog box. The first tab on the dialog box lists any templates in your file. The three types of panel templates that you can create are Branch Panel, Data Panel, and Switchboard. Once you have created a panel schedule template, the Make Default button enables you to establish a selected template as the default. Buttons at the bottom of the dialog box can be used to edit, duplicate, rename, or delete a template.

The second tab of the dialog box allows you to apply a panel schedule template to any panel in your project. When you make changes to your panel schedule templates, you can update the schedules for panels that are using the older version by selecting the panels from the list and clicking the Update Schedules button.

To build a custom template, start by clicking the default template in the list on the Manage Templates tab of the dialog box. Use the Duplicate button at the bottom of the dialog box to copy the default template. Select the newly created template in the list, and use the Edit button to begin customizing your Panel schedule.

DEFAULT TEMPLATES

To see a good example of how a panel schedule template can be formatted, check out the default templates in the `Electrical-defaults.rte` project template file. These defaults can be transferred to any file by using the Transfer Project Standards tool. If you want to start completely from scratch, you can use the default panel schedule templates from other project templates, which are totally blank.

All the tools for editing and formatting a panel schedule template are located on the Modify | Panel Schedule Template contextual tab that appears on the ribbon when you click to edit a template. Every panel schedule template has a header area, a circuit table, a load summary area, and a footer. That does not mean that you have to use all four of these areas. You can access the settings for the overall appearance and behavior of a panel schedule template by clicking the Set Template Options button on the contextual tab.

There are three main areas for the overall settings. Figure 7.38 shows the General Settings options. The Total Width setting determines the size of the schedule when placed on a sheet. The height is determined by the row height settings within the schedule. There is no longer a need to adjust column widths after placing a schedule onto a sheet because the widths are defined directly in the schedule template view. The number of slots shown is determined by the panel family used or defined here in the template options. You can deselect the boxes to remove the header, footer, or loads summary, but the circuit table cannot be removed.

The Circuit Table options allow you to define the format for the columns that display circuit loads. Single-phase panels can be created, and options for the third-phase loads column are available. These columns appear in the center of your schedule no matter what you do to format the other columns. The values in these columns cannot be edited, and you cannot replace them with another parameter. In Revit MEP 2015 you have the ability to show the phase values as either Load or Current.

The Loads Summary options let you set which load classifications will be listed when the loads summary is included in your schedule. All load classifications that exist in your project are shown on the left, and the ones that appear in the schedule are listed on the right. If you choose the option for displaying only those loads that are connected to the panel, all the classifications move to the Scheduled Loads list. When you create a Panel schedule, only the classifications that are connected appear; however, the loads summary has blank rows for the unused classifications, as shown in Figure 7.39.

The tools on the Modify | Panel Schedule Template contextual tab of the ribbon are the same kind of tools that you would find in a spreadsheet program. You can merge cells, add or delete columns and rows, set the borders and shading of cells, and set the alignment of column data. You can also adjust the font for a cell or group of cells. Many of these tools are also available on a menu that appears when you right-click a cell in the schedule view. You can adjust row and column heights and widths by clicking and dragging the borderlines in the schedule view.

The Parameters panel of this tab has a drop-down for selecting a category and a drop-down for selecting parameters within a chosen category to be placed in a column. You can place unique parameters in individual cells in any area of the schedule except for the circuit table. When you click a cell in the circuit table and select a parameter, that parameter populates all the cells in that column and the corresponding column on the other side of the table. When you click a cell in the Circuit Table area, the only category available in the drop-down is Electrical Circuits. In other areas of the schedule, you can choose parameters from the Electrical Equipment and Project Information categories.

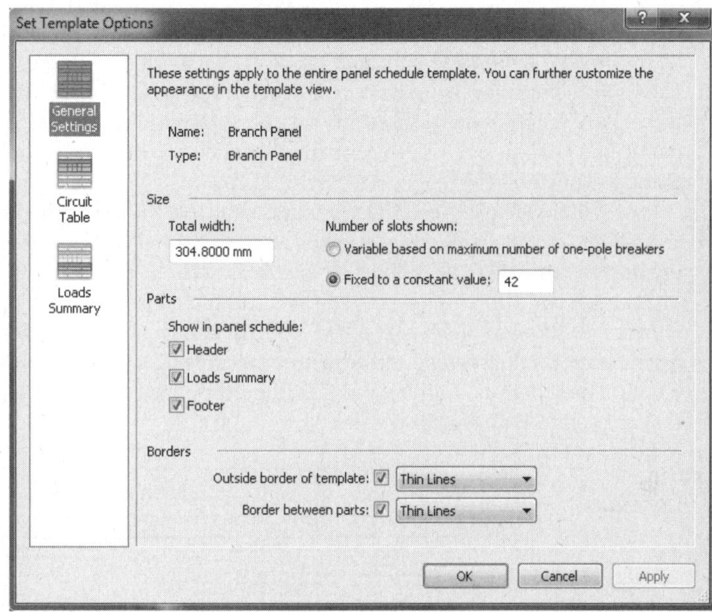

FIGURE 7.38
General Settings area for a panel schedule template

FIGURE 7.39
Loads summary

Load Classification	Connected Load	Demand Factor	Estimated Demand	Panel Totals	
HVAC	73502 VA	100.00%	73502 VA		
Lighting	9780 VA	125.00%	12225 VA		
Other	0 VA	0.00%	0 VA		
Receptacles	29520 VA	66.94%	19760 VA	Total Conn. Load:	112927 VA
Water Heater	125 VA	125.00%	156 VA	Total Est. Demand:	105643 VA
				Total Conn. Current:	136 A
				Total Est. Demand Current	127 A

You can set the units to be used in the circuit table with the Format Unit button on the Parameters panel. There is also a button for creating a calculated value in a cell. This tool works the same way as in a building component schedule. The Combine Parameters button allows you to put multiple parameters in a single cell. It is similar to the tool for building a label in an annotation or tag family. You choose the parameters for a cell, the options for a prefix or suffix, and how the parameters will be separated if necessary.

Using Schedules for Project Management

You can apply the scheduling capabilities of Revit to other areas of your project to facilitate project management and organize construction documents. You can even use schedules as a way to coordinate plan notes and ensure coordination between notes and their callouts.

Sheet List

Another type of schedule available on the Schedules button is a Sheet List schedule. A *Sheet List schedule* is built with the same tools as a model component schedule, but all the parameters are related to sheets. Creating a Sheet List schedule is useful for managing your project documentation because the schedule allows you to track what sheets have been created, revised, and checked. You can create custom parameters that apply to sheets for management by other means.

If you are required to submit a list of all the drawings in a submittal package, you can use a Sheet List schedule. Using a Sheet List schedule ensures that all the sheets created in your project are listed. Some submittals do not require all sheets to be submitted, so a custom parameter that allows you to control what sheets are included in a submittal is a good way to manage your sheet list.

As with most schedules that appear on construction documents, it is a good practice to have two Sheet List schedules in your project: one that has all the parameters that you need for tracking and making changes and another that is actually included in your construction documents. This keeps you from having to hide and unhide columns when working in the schedule view. Figure 7.40 shows a Sheet List schedule with a parameter for whether a sheet is submitted and, on the bottom, the corresponding Sheet List schedule that appears in the construction documents. The schedule on the bottom is filtered by the Submitted parameter so that only sheets that are selected appear in the list.

FIGURE 7.40
Sheet List schedules

<Sheet List>

A	B	C	D	E
Sheet Number	Sheet Name	Sheet Issue Date	Current Revision	Submitted
M201	1st Floor Plan_	03/06/13		☑
E601	Panel Schedule	03/06/13		☑
E301	North Level 1 -	03/06/13		☑
M601	Duct Sections	03/06/13		☐
M701	Mechanical Sc	03/06/13		☐
E201	Unnamed	03/06/13		☑
M202	1st Floor Plan_	03/06/13		☑
M203	1st Floor Plan_	03/06/13		☑
M100	MECHANICAL L	03/06/13		☐
E101	Electrical Powe	03/06/13		☑

<DRAWING LIST>

A	B	C	D
NUMBER	NAME	DATE	REV
M201	1st Floor Plan_A - HVAC	03/06/13	
E601	Panel Schedules	03/06/13	
E301	North Level 1 - Lighting Plan	03/06/13	
E201	Unnamed	03/06/13	
M202	1st Floor Plan_B - HVAC	03/06/13	
M203	1st Floor Plan_C - HVAC	03/06/13	
E101	Electrical Power Riser Diagram	03/06/13	

Even though you may have established how sheet views are organized in the Project Browser, it may not meet your requirements for listing the sheets included in a project submittal. You can use a custom parameter (Publish Order) to sort your Sheet List schedule in the order you require. You can use a numbering system in combination with the items being listed alphabetically to arrange the sheets in your schedule, as shown in Figure 7.41.

FIGURE 7.41
Sorting the Sheet List schedule

<Sheet List>

A	B	C	D	E	F
Sheet Number	Sheet Name	Sheet Issue Date	Current Revision	Submitted	Publish Order
M201	1st Floor Plan_	03/06/13		☑	1
E601	Panel Schedule	03/06/13		☑	5
E301	North Level 1 -	03/06/13		☑	10
M601	Duct Sections	03/06/13		☐	2
M701	Mechanical Sc	03/06/13		☐	3
E201	Unnamed	03/06/13		☑	4
M202	1st Floor Plan_	03/06/13		☑	7
M203	1st Floor Plan_	03/06/13		☑	8
M100	MECHANICAL L	03/06/13		☐	6
E101	Electrical Powe	03/06/13		☑	9

<DRAWING LIST>

A	B	C	D
NUMBER	NAME	DATE	REV
M201	1st Floor Plan_A - HVAC	03/06/13	
E201	Unnamed	03/06/13	
E601	Panel Schedules	03/06/13	
M202	1st Floor Plan_B - HVAC	03/06/13	
M203	1st Floor Plan_C - HVAC	03/06/13	
E101	Electrical Power Riser Diagram	03/06/13	
E301	North Level 1 - Lighting Plan	03/06/13	

Notice that different decade groups are used for each discipline so that sheets can be organized within a discipline. This allows the electrical site plan to be listed before the plan sheets, for example, without requiring a unique number to be provided for each sheet.

View List

A *View List schedule* is another type of schedule that can be created from the Schedules button on the View tab. Similar to a Sheet List schedule, a View List schedule can help you keep track of the views that exist in your project.

WHY NOT USE THE PROJECT BROWSER?

It may seem a bit redundant to create a View List schedule when all views are organized in the Project Browser, but a View List schedule enables you to view the properties of several views quickly and all at one time. It also allows for quick comparison and editing of multiple views.

When printing a set of construction documents, you want to be sure that all your views that should be on a sheet have been placed onto the appropriate sheet. Not only does this save you the time it would take to visually inspect each sheet, it can also save paper and wear and tear on your printer.

A View List schedule is constructed with the same tools as a Sheet List schedule, except only parameters that apply to views can be used in the schedule. Unfortunately, not all view parameters can be scheduled, but there are many that are useful for project management. When working in a project that includes phases, a View List schedule can be a useful tool for ensuring that views are set to the proper phase and have the proper phase filter applied.

To create a View List schedule that shows only views that are placed on sheets, you can use a filter. If you use the Sheet Number parameter as a filter with the Does Not Contain rule and leave the value blank, the expected result would be a schedule that shows only those views that are placed on a sheet.

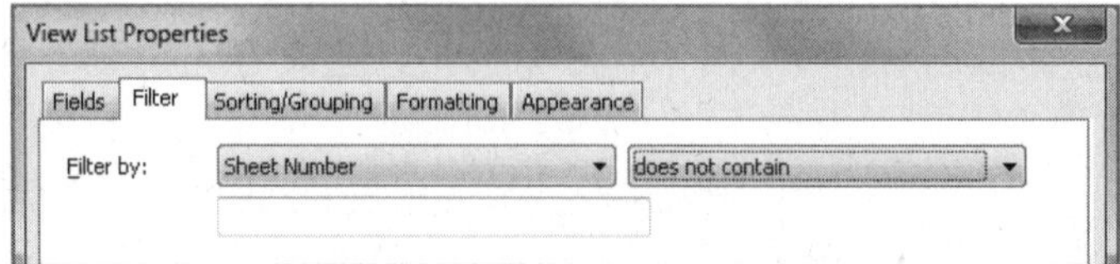

Normally, you would apply a filter to remove all the scheduled items that do not meet your filter requirements. However, using these settings actually removes all views that meet the requirements of the filter, causing your schedule to list all the views that have no value for the parameter.

Note Block

A *Note Block schedule* is part of an annotation family that is used in your project. Note Block schedules are very useful for managing plan notes on your construction documents as an alternative to keynoting. As note annotations are placed in a view, they can be given a description, and then a Note Block schedule can be created to list the descriptions of each instance of the annotation. Figure 7.42 shows the properties of a note annotation family used for plan notes.

FIGURE 7.42
Note annotation properties

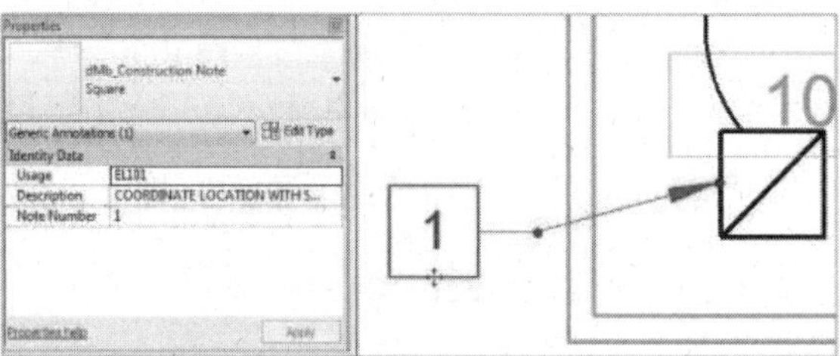

A Usage parameter has been created to determine to which sheet the note belongs. The Description parameter holds the contents of the note. Once a note annotation is placed in a view, it can be copied for each instance to create the next note in the list.

A Note Block schedule is created by choosing the Note Block option from the Schedules button on the View tab. The annotation family that is used for plan notes is selected to be scheduled. The title of the Note Block schedule should be a description of where the notes are located to make it easy to locate the Note Block schedule in the Project Browser. The Note Number, Description, and Usage parameters are added to the schedule. The schedule is then filtered by the Usage parameter so that only note annotations that appear on a specific sheet appear in the schedule, and the Usage parameter is hidden. The schedule is sorted by the Note Number parameter.

It is important to establish the Usage parameter value for the first note annotation placed into a view and then to copy that view whenever a new note is required. Copying the note annotation ensures that the Usage parameter value is the same for each note in the plan view. The Note Block view and its associated plan view can be tiled so that as you add note annotations to the plan view, you can see them appear in the schedule. The Properties palette gives you instant access to the Description parameter of the note annotation so changes can be made easily.

One benefit of using a Note Block schedule over static text for plan notes is that if you need to change what a note says, you can deselect the Itemize Every Instance option in the schedule to see each unique note; then, when you change the description of the note, it changes for all instances.

Another benefit is that if you need to delete a note, you can delete it from the Note Block schedule and all instances are removed from the associated plan view. This ensures that you do not have a note annotation in the plan view that references a note that does not exist in the plan notes. It also eliminates the need for having a note in the notes list with a value of Not Used because the notes can easily be renumbered in the Note Block schedule when a note is removed. Renumbering the notes in the schedule automatically updates the annotations in the plan view.

When you place the Note Block schedule onto a sheet with its associated plan view, you will want to adjust the Appearance settings so that the schedule title and headings are not shown, giving the schedule the appearance of a list rather than a schedule, as shown in Figure 7.43.

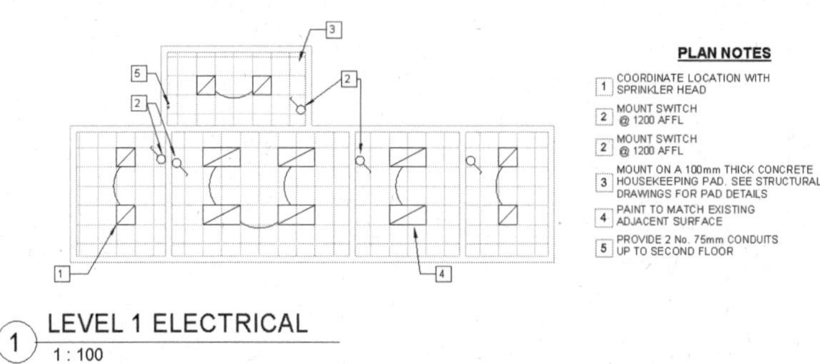

FIGURE 7.43 Note Block plan notes on a sheet

The symbolic representation for each note is provided by attaching a suitable image to the family, in the Type Image field, prior to loading the family into the project. This and the ability to link images into the project for scheduled objects (using the Image field) are both new to Revit MEP 2015. It is easy to get carried away when importing images and it is a good idea to review each one, to ensure project file performance isn't unduly affected by large files.

USING SCHEDULES ACROSS PROJECTS

One of the most popular ways to take a schedule from one project to another is to use the Insert Views From File command located under the Insert tab. Another, even easier way is to simply open the two projects in the same Revit session and use Ctrl+C/Ctrl+V to copy/paste.

The Bottom Line

Use the tools in Revit MEP 2015 for defining schedules and their behavior. The capabilities of schedules in Revit MEP 2015 can increase your project coordination and the efficiency of your workflow. The ability to track items within a model can help you better understand the makeup of your design.

> **Master It** The information in schedules comes from information stored within the objects of a Revit model. Explain why editing the data of an object in a schedule changes the properties of the object.

Schedule building components. Scheduling building components is the primary use of the scheduling tools in Revit. Schedules are used on construction documents to provide additional information about components so that drawings do not become too cluttered.

> **Master It** Understanding what information can be used in a schedule is important to setting up a specific component schedule within your Revit project. What types of parameters can be included in a schedule? What types cannot?

Create schedules for design and analysis. Scheduling can go beyond counting objects and tracking their information. You can also create schedules that assist in making design decisions by providing organized analytical information.

> **Master It** The information stored in Space objects often comes from their relationship with other objects. Some of the data for analysis needs to be input manually. Explain how using a schedule key can assist in adding data to a Space object.

Schedule views and sheets for project management. You can schedule not just the components that make up a model but also the views and sheets within your project. Specialized schedules for views and sheets are useful for project management.

> **Master It** A Note Block schedule enables you to list information about annotation families within your project. What are some of the benefits of using a Note Block schedule instead of static text for plan notes?

Part 2

Mechanical Design

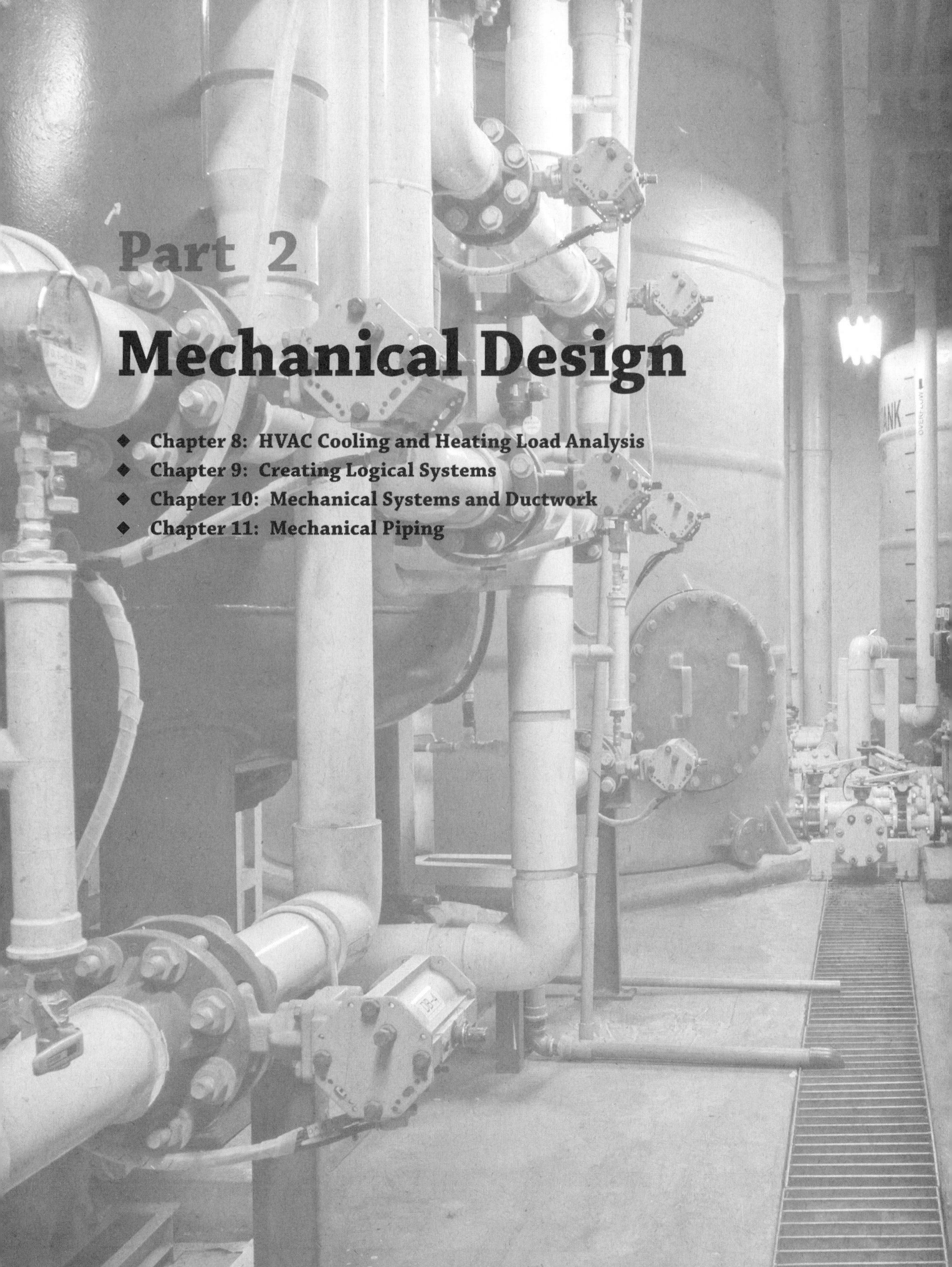

HVAC Cooling and Heating Load Analysis

Accurate modeling of a building is essential in designing and sizing an energy-efficient HVAC system for today's market. The majority of time during the mechanical design phase of a project can be spent on correctly modeling the building in a load-simulating program, such as Trane TRACE 700, DOE-2, or Carrier's Hourly Analysis Program (HAP).

Although these programs are essential to you, the mechanical designer, setting up the building accurately for equipment sizing within these programs often can be a tedious task. Each space is set up individually, and typically the physical layout and use of each space will be different. Alterations to the building design or space usage by the architect or building owner during this phase will cause you to return to any previously modeled spaces and coordinate the necessary changes. This is very time-consuming and can often be a point of contention between disciplines when changes occur later in the design phase.

Autodesk® Revit® MEP software enables you to model the building spaces accurately as well as quickly and efficiently track any building design and construction changes on the fly, all within the project file. Revit MEP also gives you the option either to model the HVAC loads within the program itself or to export the space load data via a Green Building XML (gbXML) schema file to an external simulation software program. An addition to this workflow is the ability to analyze the mass model (with a tool previously available only to subscription customers).

In this chapter, you will learn to do the following:

- Prepare your Revit MEP model for analysis
- Perform heating and cooling analysis with Revit MEP 2015
- Perform a conceptual energy analysis on your building
- Analyze duct and pipe system pressure with Revit MEP 2015
- Export gbXML data to load-simulating software

Modeling Spaces for Building Load Analysis

The key to any successful building load analysis, as well as energy analysis, lies with accurately modeling the spaces within the building. Components that need to be modeled for each space include, but are not limited to, building construction, such as walls, roofs, and floor slabs; external shading and windows; internal loads, such as the number of people, the activity within the space, the heat gain from lighting, and the equipment operated within the space; and external factors, such as solar heat gain to the space, weather and typical outdoor temperatures, and infiltration. These are but a handful of factors that need to be addressed for each space that is being created. Each of these factors has several significant inputs that can affect the reporting of heating and cooling loads within the space.

Creating Spaces

First things first—spaces need to be created in the project file. Why? It seems redundant to create spaces, seeing as how the architectural model already has rooms created and defined, right?

Not so.

In Revit MEP, *spaces* are created within room-bounding elements such as walls, floors, ceilings, roofs, and room separation lines that exist in a linked architectural model or from these types of elements within your MEP model. This means that the same elements that define a room in the architectural model define the spaces in your MEP model. Spaces carry the engineering data that is necessary for analysis, whereas rooms contain the information required by the architects. After loading your MEP project and linking in the appropriate architectural model, you want to make sure that the elements that make up a room—walls, doors, ceilings, and so on—will define your MEP space accurately. Figure 8.1 shows a sample building model with rooms.

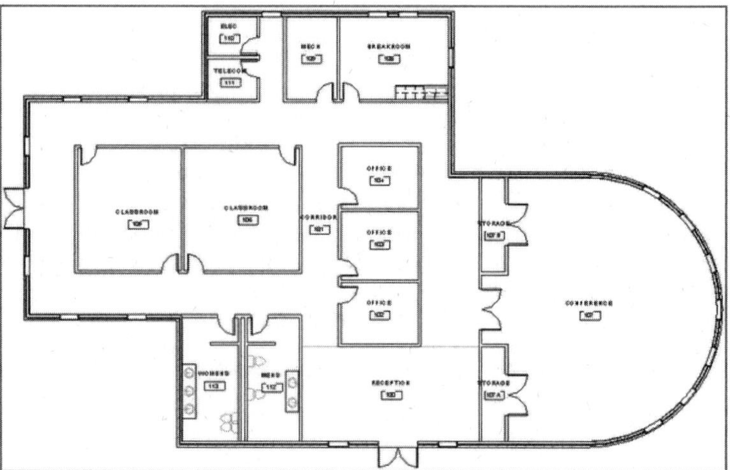

FIGURE 8.1 Sample building

Selecting the architectural link in your project activates the Edit Type button in the Properties palette. Clicking this button allows you to enable the selected link to be room bounding. This option forces the boundaries of the designed rooms to define the boundaries of the MEP spaces to be modeled. Figure 8.2 shows the Edit Type button and the Room Bounding type parameter.

When you're placing a space, if the link is not set to Room Bounding, you get a warning that the placed space is not in a properly enclosed region, and subsequently, if HVAC analysis is attempted, Revit will not be able to calculate load data for that space.

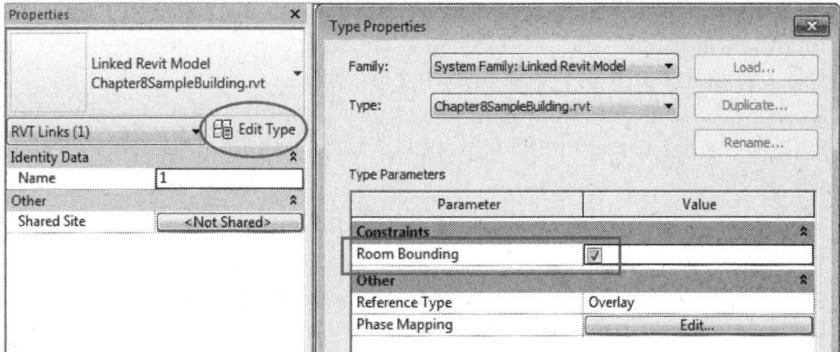

FIGURE 8.2 Defining boundaries of MEP spaces

Placing Spaces

Revit allows you to locate spaces within your model in two ways: by placing spaces manually or letting Revit locate boundaries and place spaces automatically. If your building has many rooms, allowing the program to place the spaces automatically for you can save time.

When using automatic placement, be sure that all the spaces created are the actual spaces that you intend to model. Check that areas such as utility chases, furrowed columns, and air spaces in wall constructions were not included when spaces were placed. To remove any unwanted spaces from the project file, open the System Browser, which is located on the View tab under User Interface (or you can press F9), and set the view to Zones by choosing Zones from the View drop-down menu at the top of the dialog box.

Select the desired spaces to remove by highlighting the space name, right-clicking, and selecting Delete, as shown in Figure 8.3. Click OK in the pop-up window to remove the spaces and any associated space tags permanently.

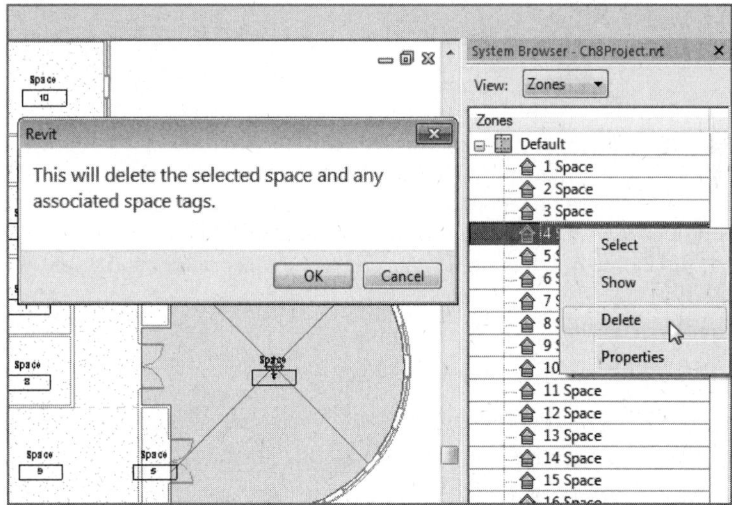

FIGURE 8.3 Deleting unwanted spaces from the project file

If you were just to select a space within an open view and delete it without using the System Browser, the space and its associated tag would be deleted from the model, but the space would still be present in your project. This has an effect on any building analysis performed as well as any HVAC systems that will be set up in the building. Systems are covered in depth in Chapter 9, "Creating Logical Systems," and Chapter 10, "Mechanical Systems and Ductwork."

Creating a Space Properties Schedule

When you're simulating the heating and cooling loads of a building, correctly modeling and accounting for space usage can be time-consuming. Often, design loads have to be revisited because of inaccurate space modeling or design changes, incomplete accounting of space usage, components, or internal loading. Creating a working schedule of the building space properties in Revit MEP will help you account for and coordinate these factors.

Typical of all schedules within Revit, the Space schedule provides a choice of several fields to display, to help track and modify data pertaining to each space. A working schedule such as this for space properties is an essential tool that enables you to track how changes in certain properties affect the loads within the spaces. Note that the schedule shown in Figure 8.4 is not intended to be provided to a client on a project sheet but rather to be used as a personal design tool within Revit to help you, the designer, organize the space data to better fit your personal workflow. Create this schedule as you see fit, using the many fields, sorting, and other formatting options available to organize the data you need readily.

FIGURE 8.4
Sample Space Properties schedule

Space Properties

Name	Number	Space Type	Number of People	Area	Construction Type	Condition Type	Occupiable	Zone
RECEPTION	100	Reception/Waiting - Hotel	10.334307	371 SF	<Building>	Heated and cooled	✓	Zone 04
CORRIDOR	101	Corridor/Transition	11.388886	1226 SF	<Building>	Heated and cooled	✓	Zone 01
OFFICE	102	Office - Enclosed	0.460825	104 SF	<Building>	Heated and cooled	✓	Zone 05
OFFICE	103	Office - Enclosed	0.543592	117 SF	<Building>	Heated and cooled	✓	Zone 06
OFFICE	104	Office - Enclosed	0.489737	105 SF	<Building>	Heated and cooled	✓	Zone 05
CLASSROOM	105	Classroom/Lecture/Training	0	Not Placed	<Building>	Heated and cooled		Zone 02
CLASSROOM	106	Classroom/Lecture/Training	18.896852	313 SF	<Building>	Heated and cooled	✓	Zone 03
CONFERENCE	107	Conference Meeting/Multipurpose	51.209407	1103 SF	<Building>	Heated and cooled	✓	Zone 08
STORAGE	107A	Inactive Storage	0.138972	50 SF	<Building>	Heated and cooled	✓	Zone 06
STORAGE	107B	Inactive Storage	0.138972	50 SF	<Building>	Heated and cooled	✓	Zone 08
BREAKROOM	108	Dining Area - Lounge/Leisure Dinin	12.84874	198 SF	<Building>	Heated and cooled	✓	Zone 10
MECH	109	Electrical/Mechanical	0.258269	93 SF	<Building>	Cooled		Zone 11
ELEC	110	Electrical/Mechanical	0.118043	42 SF	<Building>	Cooled		Zone 08
TELECOM	111	Electrical/Mechanical	0.122539	44 SF	<Building>	Cooled		Zone 09
MENS	112	Restrooms	1.282271	139 SF	<Building>	Heated and cooled	✓	Zone 07
WOMENS	113	Restrooms	1.413562	152 SF	<Building>	Heated and cooled	✓	Zone 07

In this schedule, you will also see any *not placed* spaces, (which are spaces that exist in the project but not in the model,) as well as any *redundant* and *not enclosed* spaces. They can also be deleted from the project by deleting them from this schedule. To do this, simply right-click the appropriate row in the schedule and select Delete Row.

During the initial Space Properties schedule creation, you might find the following fields useful:

Name Designate the space name.

Number Assign each space a number.

Space Type Describe how the space will be used.

Number of People Specify the space occupancy.

Area List the space area in square feet or meters.

Construction Type Describe the space's physical construction in this field. We go over the various construction options later in this chapter.

Condition Type Describe the type of space conditioning (such as Heated And Cooled, Heated, Cooled, or Unconditioned).

Occupiable This is a Yes/No check box that shows whether this space will be occupied.

Modifying Space Properties

You will notice that the program defaults to a generic space naming and numbering convention when placing spaces. It also sets the Space Type and Construction Type values as <Building>, indicating that the spaces will be modeled generically by relying on default building characteristics that are defined in the Building/Space Type Settings dialog box, shown in Figure 8.5, within the project file.

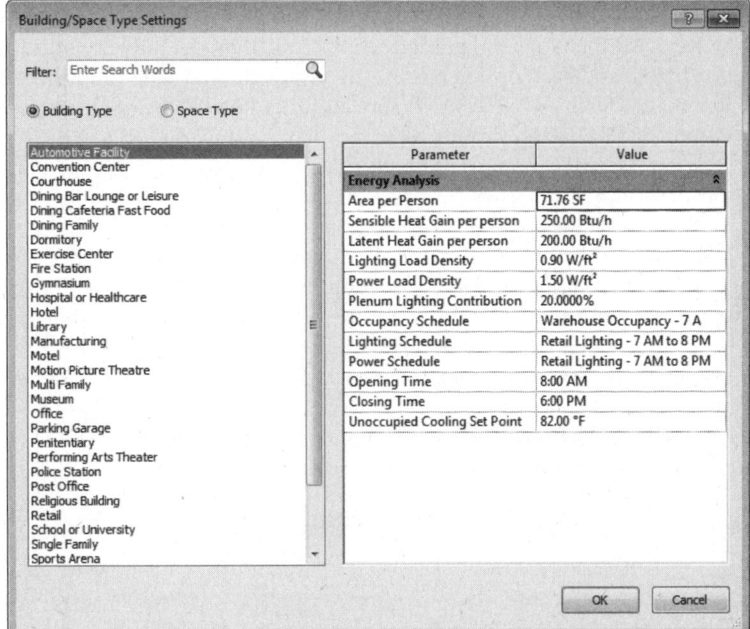

FIGURE 8.5 Building/Space Type Settings dialog box

SPACE NAMING

When creating spaces, Revit MEP assigns each one a generic space name and number. To reflect the linked architectural room names and numbers in your working schedule, add the fields Room: Name and Room: Number from the Rooms category in the Available Fields drop-down, located on the Fields tab in the Schedule Properties dialog box. Edit the space names and numbers to match the linked file. You can then hide the Room: Name and Room: Number columns to streamline your schedule and unhide them periodically to view any changes that may have occurred during the design. The Space Naming Utility add-in is another essential tool that, if installed, will name and number the spaces automatically per the architectural link. The Space Naming Utility is available for download from the Autodesk website for subscription customers.

How a space will be used is the overall factor driving the internal loads within a space. An enclosed office space is modeled differently from the conference room next door, and an office break room is modeled differently from a typical restaurant dining room. Lighting, population density, activity levels, equipment, and ventilation loads all vary with the space type.

If you open the Manage tab and then choose MEP Settings ➤ Building/Space Type Settings, you will be able to view and modify the space type options within Revit MEP as well as the global building types (see Figure 8.5).

In the Building/Space Type Settings dialog box, you can choose to define overall building types or individual space usage types. Defining an overall building type can be a good option if you want to do a quick takeoff of a typical building type for the overall model or when performing a preliminary energy analysis, which we touch on later in this chapter. You are given similar parameters to define how you model a building, as well as options to set building operating times (Opening Time and Closing Time) and an Unoccupied Cooling Set Point parameter.

Revit MEP has several predefined options to model how the building, as well as each space, is utilized, and each option has preset parameter and schedule values for the internal loads. Parameters such as Area Per Person, Lighting Load Density, Power Load Density, and Sensible Heat Gain Per Person should all be familiar to you. You can use the preset values within the program, or you can input more-accurate design load values based on typical code-driven or industry-standard values.

You can access the Space Type Settings dialog box from the Properties palette when a space is selected in your view. You can also access it from within your Space Properties schedule by locating the cell in the Space Type column (if used in your Space Properties schedule) for the space you would like to modify and then selecting the ellipsis that appears next to the current type name when you click in the field. If you click the People or Electrical Loads button in the Properties palette when a space object is selected, the default values within these windows are the values listed in the Space Type Settings dialog box. Figure 8.6 shows the dialog box for establishing the occupancy and heat gain values, while Figure 8.7 shows the schedule settings accessed from the Space Type Settings dialog box.

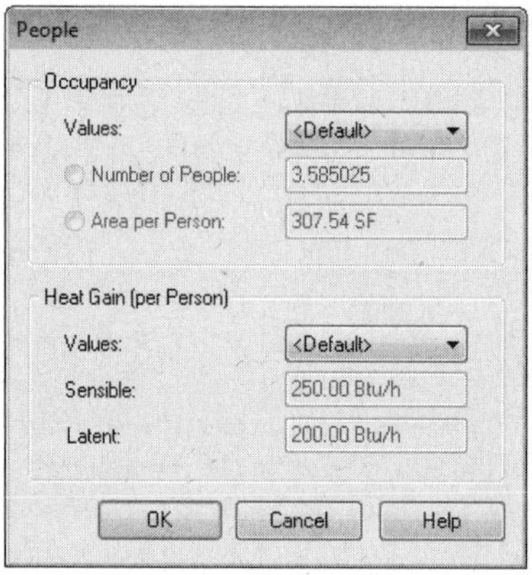

FIGURE 8.6
Default Occupancy and Heat Gain values

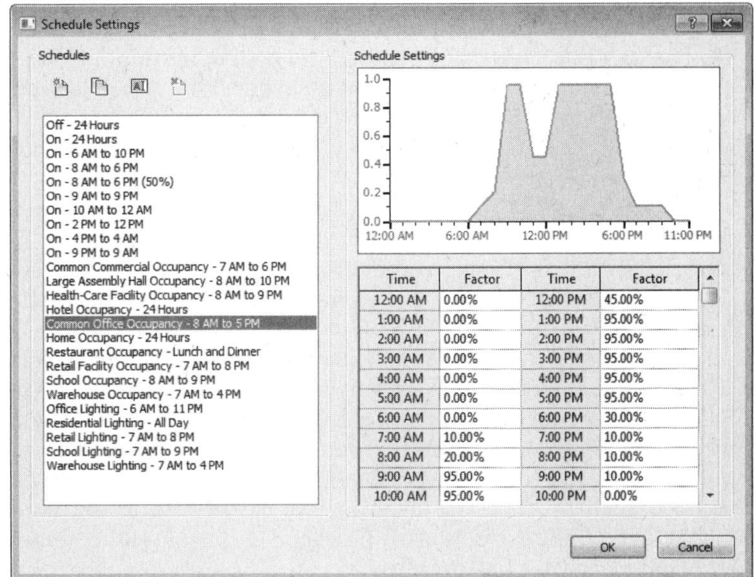

FIGURE 8.7 Schedule Settings dialog box

GOING ABOVE AND BEYOND

Doug has an issue. He has received the preliminary building model from the architect but has not been able to set up each space to get an accurate building load takeoff prior to the next project design meeting. Knowing that Revit MEP automatically defaults to a global building type, he adjusts the building type to Office, adjusts the required parameter values, and tells the program to lay out the spaces automatically.

Doug is able to quickly generate initial heating, cooling, and ventilation loads, and with that data, the mechanical design team will be able to analyze different system possibilities to condition the building and present options to the project team.

Revit MEP also has default Building and Space Properties schedule types that it uses to generate load data. You can modify the default schedules or create new schedules to fit your varying occupancy, power, and lighting needs. You can find the topics Schedules, People Heat Gain, and Building Type Data and Space Type Data in Revit MEP 2015 Help, under Analyze the Design ➢ Energy Analysis Building & Space Type Imperial Data.

Creating Zones

The next step in generating HVAC loads for your design building is to group similar spaces into *zones*. The main purpose of zoning spaces in an HVAC system is to provide common controllability of air quality or condition within the zone's spaces. A single point of control by a terminal unit, heat pump, or air-handling unit can set the temperature and air quality of the spaces within its defined zone.

Creating HVAC zones within your building allows you to control the airflow to given spaces, shut off airflow to areas that are not occupied, or increase airflow to spaces when the space load increases via a signal from a temperature sensor or other sensing device within the zone to a central control panel. Zoning also allows certain spaces to be controlled via a different system from that used in the rest of the building, such as having a dedicated server room constant volume system active 24 hours a day, while the rest of the building is controlled by a packaged variable air volume (VAV) rooftop system on a typical office's 8 a.m. to 5 p.m. schedule.

Zoning spaces in Revit MEP is easy. All spaces will be part of a zone called Default, until they are added to a specific one that you create. On the Analyze tab, click Zone. This activates the Zone tool, and you are automatically prompted to add the first space to the zone. Clicking a space adds it to the zone, and then you have the option of adding other spaces to that zone. Click the Finish Editing Zone button on the ribbon to end the editing session.

To edit a zone that has already been created, simply select the required zone in the open view by clicking on the border drawn around the zone, and the Modify | HVAC Zones contextual tab appears. Click the Edit Zone button, and the Edit Zone contextual tab appears. Here, you are able to modify the zone by adding or removing spaces. You can also select a zone by moving your cursor over the center of it until the zone highlights for preselection. This is indicated by a line that appears from the center of each space to the center of the zone.

A second way to create a zone is to select all the spaces you want to be in a zone, and then select the Zone tool on the Analyze tab. Creating a zone this way automatically groups the selected spaces without having to select each space individually with the tool active.

When selecting a zone displayed in an open view, the zone data appears in the Properties palette. From there, you are able to view the calculated heating and cooling loads and zone airflow (after heating and cooling analysis has been run), the physical data of the zone (area, volume, and perimeter), and its characteristic data, which include the following:

Service Type This drop-down allows you to select the type of system that will be serving the spaces within the zone. Revit MEP offers a variety of service type options based on four main groups of systems: Constant Volume, Variable Air Volume (VAV), Hydronic, and Other. Revit MEP automatically defaults to the service type that is selected in the Project Energy Settings window. See Chapter 2, "Creating an Effective Project Template," for information on how to establish project settings.

Coil Bypass This is where you input the manufacturer's coil bypass factor for the unit serving the zone. This value indicates the volume of air that passes through the coil, unaffected by the coil temperature.

Cooling Information This button allows you to set the zone cooling set point, coil-leaving air temperature, and zone humidity control.

Heating Information This button allows you to set the zone heating set point, coil-leaving air temperature, and zone humidity control during heating.

Outdoor Air Information This button allows you to input the ventilation loads for the zone: Outdoor Air Per Person, Outdoor Air Per Area, and Air Changes Per Hour. You may specify individual Outdoor Air options or enter a value in all three options. Revit MEP calculates heating and cooling loads with only the largest calculated outdoor airflow, not a combination of the three values. To obtain the required combined breathing-zone ventilation rate as defined in ASHRAE Standard 62.1, add the ventilation in cubic feet per minute (CFM) needed per occupant to the CFM required per area and divide the result by the zone area. Then enter this value in either of the first two options to force Revit into calculating the code-required ventilation rate.

A more accurate way to ensure that the correct ASHRAE Standard 62.1 (or other code) ventilation rate is modeled in the zone is to calculate the required outdoor air per the appropriate ventilation rate procedure and enter the result as shown previously.

OCCUPIABLE

When you are creating spaces to use for heating and cooling analysis, make sure that the Occupiable check box is selected in the space properties. This ensures that ventilation loads are computed as part of the space load.

Setting Building Construction Options

You are ready to investigate the physical properties of your building's exterior and interior constructions when all the spaces within your design building are placed, the internal data is identified, and the spaces have been grouped into zones, ready for the heating and cooling data to be analyzed. These elements control how heat leaves or enters your design spaces to or from the surrounding outdoor environment or adjacent spaces. Each element has a specific coefficient of heat transfer, or *U-value*, that is dependent on the element's material composition and assembly as well as its thickness.

But the architect who created the building elements has already defined the wall or roof construction. That data should already be loaded in with the link, right? Well, no. Although the architectural model will have accurate wall and roof constructions in the linked building, the U-values will not transfer from the link, unless the building has been modeled directly in the MEP project file. You have to define the building construction parameters. This will set U-values for the elements that bound your design spaces, allowing for heat transfer into and out of the spaces to be calculated and accounted for.

To set the building construction U-values, open the Manage tab and click Project Information, as shown in Figure 8.8.

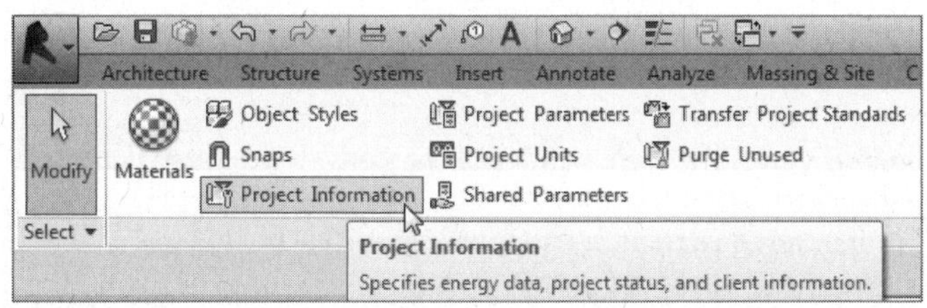

FIGURE 8.8 Project Information tab

From this window, click the Edit button for Energy Settings, and then click the ellipsis button next to <Building> in the Building Construction parameter. This brings you to the Building Construction dialog box (see Figure 8.9).

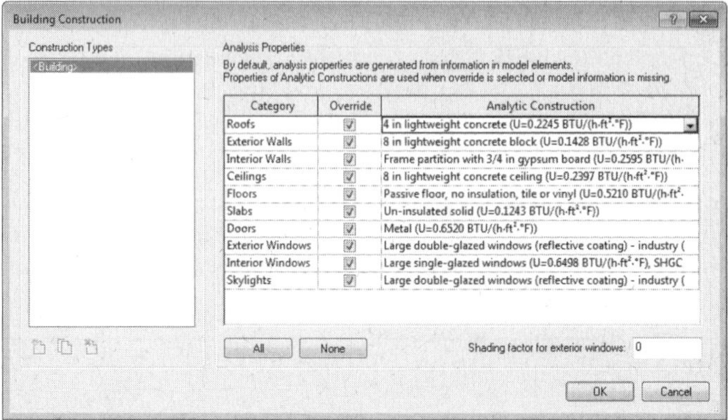

FIGURE 8.9 Building Construction dialog box

Here, you will be able to define the default construction characteristics for various building components. Clicking the drop-down arrow at each category exposes a wide array of common material constructions and assemblies from which you can choose to represent the walls, slabs, roof, and glazing, each with a unique U-value associated with it. Selecting the Override check box for a category forces the use of the Analytic Construction properties. These are defined when performing an energy simulation via the Energy Analysis tools on the Analyze tab or when information is missing. As stated earlier there really are no walls, roofs, or floors in your MEP model, so the Override boxes are selected by default.

The constructions for each category are customizable. The `Constructions.xml` file can be edited with any basic text editor, such as Notepad. The file is located here: `C:\Program Files\Autodesk\Revit2015\en-US`. This file is a combination of ASHRAE Standard 90.1, CIBSE, and manufacturer data for building envelope values. Unfortunately, the only way to determine which material comes from which location is to open the XML file, where a more comprehensive description of the material is found. Figure 8.10 shows the Revit representation and the same material properties in the XML file.

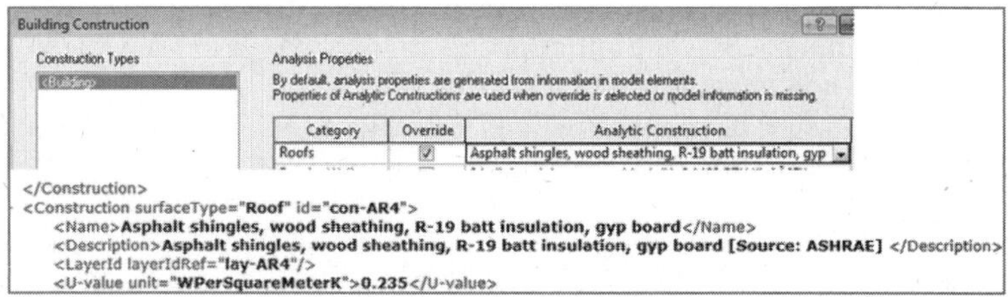

FIGURE 8.10 Example XML building data

If you look carefully, the U-values of each envelope construction are in W/M^2K rather than the IP value of Btu/(h × ft^2 × F). To utilize a custom construction, you must convert (if the project uses IP units) the construction U-value in Btu/(h × ft^2 × F) to W/M^2K by multiplying by the conversion factor 5.68.

As the designer, you can choose the construction option that is closest to the actual U-value that has been calculated through material thermal takeoffs of the architectural design, or you can create your own material in the XML file. Be aware, however, that this file cannot be located on a central server, so changes to this file that affect others would need careful management.

Just as all spaces are not going to be conditioned alike, some spaces have a physical construction that is different from that of the rest of the design building. For example, a utility space, such as a mechanical or electrical room, typically can be seen with exposed block wall construction, a bare floor slab, open-roof trusses or beams, and little or no insulation on the exterior walls. In Revit MEP, just as the individual space types can be defined differently from the overall building type, you have the option to have each individual space define its own construction U-values.

To alter the space construction, select a space in an open view, or if you have created a Space Properties schedule, select the ellipsis next to <Building> in the Construction Type column of the space that you want to edit. The Construction Type dialog box opens, and here you will be able to create individual space construction types as needed (see Figure 8.11).

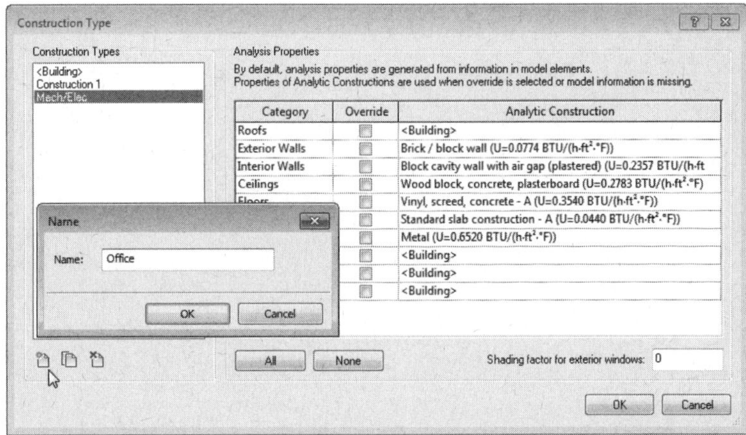

FIGURE 8.11 Construction Type dialog box

The same construction categories and options exist here that are available in the Building Construction dialog box. Create as many constructions as needed, and if there exist in your design several spaces that utilize a different construction from the main building, you will easily be able to select the appropriate construction from your created list. Note that you cannot alter the default <Building> construction type in this window. This is accessed from the Building Construction dialog box, mentioned earlier. Once you create a construction type, you cannot rename it. If you duplicate an existing type, it will automatically be given the same name with a sequential suffix number.

Performing Heating and Cooling Load Analysis

Once you have all your design spaces created and the respective parameters, conditioning systems, and space constructions defined, the next step is to pull all this data together into a heating and cooling load analysis report to tell you how this particular building will perform throughout the year. You will then use that data to refine your conditioning systems further as well as size the equipment you will assign to your HVAC zones.

You have already seen how the building and space construction can be modified to suit your building. But how do the different construction options affect the heat transfer into or out of the space? The engine that performs the heating and cooling load analysis in Revit MEP uses a Radiant Time Series (RTS) method to determine the building and space peak heating or cooling loads. This method takes into account the time-delay effect of heat transfer through building envelopes, from the outside, and into spaces. A brief explanation of this method follows, but the RTS method of calculation is defined in detail in Chapter 30 of the *2005 ASHRAE Handbook: Fundamentals*, as well as in the *Load Calculation Applications Manual*, also published by ASHRAE (visit `www.ashrae.org` for details).

The RTS calculation method determines cooling loads based on an assumption of steady periodic conditions, such as occupancy, design-day weather, and cyclical 24-hour heat gain conditions. Two time-delay effects are addressed during cooling load calculations:

- Delay of conductive heat gain through opaque massive exterior surfaces, such as exterior walls, the building roof, and floor slab on or below grade
- Delay of radiative heat gain conversion to cooling loads

Figure 8.12 shows a flowchart summarizing the RTS calculation method, also found in Revit MEP 2015 Help.

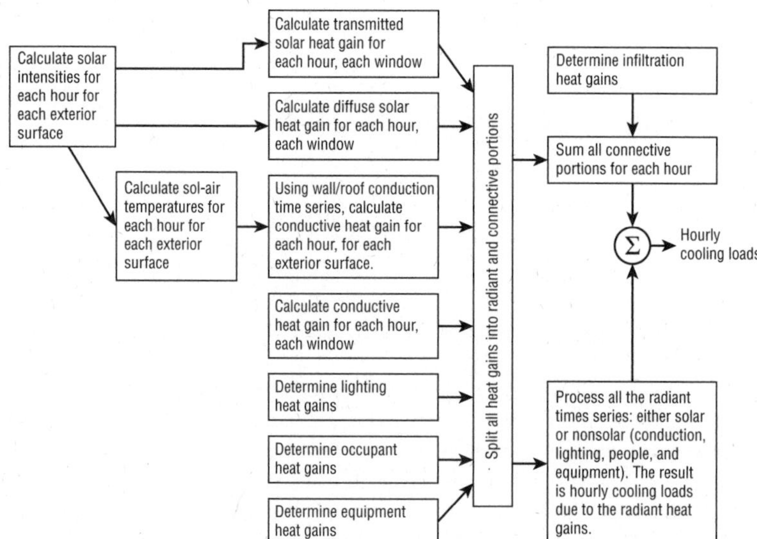

FIGURE 8.12 Radiant Time Series (RTS) calculation flowchart

Exterior building elements conduct heat because of a temperature differential between indoor and outdoor air; solar energy is absorbed by exterior surfaces as well. Because each surface has a mass and an associated thermal capacity of the materials that make up its construction, a time delay occurs from when the heat input of the outdoor and solar loads becomes heat gain to the interior space. The majority of energy that is transferred to a space as heat occurs through a combination of convection and radiation. The cooling load immediately picks up the convective part of the energy transfer, and any radiant heat is absorbed into the surrounding space constructions and interior room finishes.

The radiant heat is then transferred via convection from those surfaces to the space at a delayed time. Interior loads contribute to both the sensible heat gain of the space and a latent heat gain that is given off by people's activity within the space. The latent heat gain contributes to the instantaneous cooling load of the space, while the sensible heat gain from internals is absorbed and retransmitted by radiation to the space.

The engine sums up the calculated cooling loads to determine a total cooling load per each design hour, and it selects the highest load, or *peak*, for the design of the air-conditioning system. Note that Revit MEP uses, for the standard calculation, the hours of 6 a.m. to 6 p.m. for the design day, *not* the full 24 hours, and only the months of April through November (October through May for southern-hemisphere locations), *not* the full calendar year. The design day is derived from weather data for the location that you set during project establishment. Weather data is discussed later in this chapter.

Heating loads are calculated much the same way. The major differences are the obvious lower outdoor air temperatures in the heating design day, ignoring solar heat gains and internal heat gains, and the exclusion of the thermal storage effect of the building construction. Negative heat gains, or *heat losses*, are considered to be instantaneous; therefore, heat transfer is dealt with as conductive. Latent heat gains are treated as replacing any space humidity that has been lost to the outdoor environment.

The worst-case load, as determined by the Revit MEP engine, is based on the design interior and exterior conditions and loads due to infiltration or ventilation. Although solar effects are ignored, assuming night or cloudy winter day operation, Revit does recognize internal heat gain from people, lights, or miscellaneous equipment to offset the heating load needed. These additional factors can be edited for spaces, as shown in Figure 8.13. The Occupancy and Heat Gain settings and the Electrical Loads settings for lighting and power can either be specified as <Default> values or edited to suit a particular space.

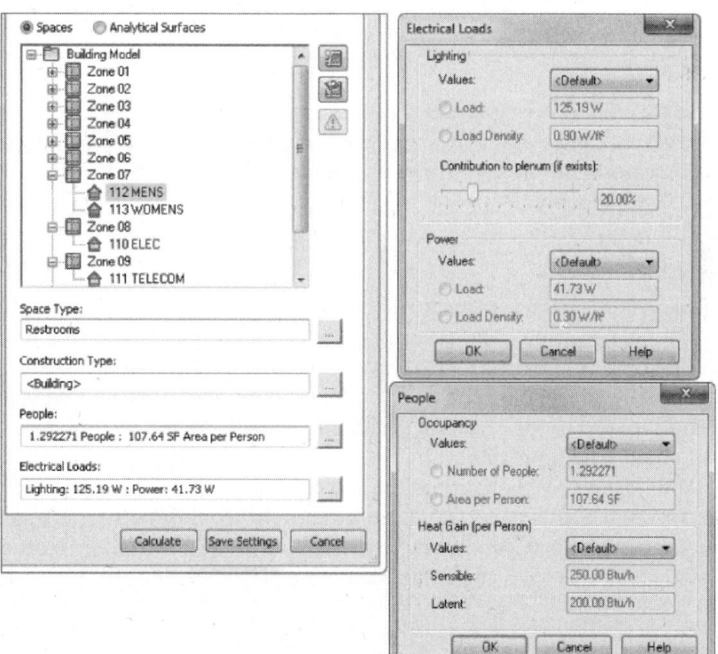

FIGURE 8.13
Additional loads

Load Analysis

Once you have a building model that is ready to analyze, the next step is to verify and specify, if needed, the building energy parameters by using the Heating And Cooling Loads tool, shown in Figure 8.14. On the Analyze tab, click the Heating And Cooling Loads button. The Heating And Cooling Loads dialog box appears, and on the General tab, you can view the building energy analysis project information that directly affects the heating and cooling analysis. You can also access these parameters through the Manage tab's Project Settings ➤ Project Information setting.

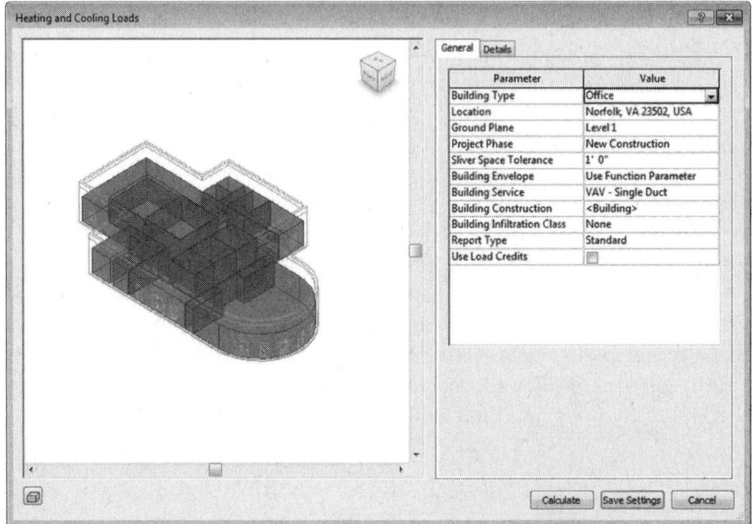

FIGURE 8.14
Heating And Cooling Loads dialog box

In this dialog box, you can set parameters such as the global building use type, building location, global conditioning system, overall building construction and ground plane, ground-level reference, and building infiltration. You can also define the level of detail you want to see in the load analysis report.

Weather Data

Earlier in the chapter, we discussed building type, service type, and building construction, but another major component of energy analysis is the physical location of the building. The location determines environmental conditions such as outdoor air temperature and humidity and also ASHRAE climate zone data. In the Heating And Cooling Loads dialog box, select the ellipsis button next to the Location parameter value to access the Location Weather And Site dialog box, shown in Figure 8.15.

You have two ways to input the project design city: select the location from the default city list, or use the Internet mapping service, as shown in Figure 8.15. If you are connected to the Internet, this option allows you to locate your project by using an interactive map through the Google Maps service. The default list contains major cities from which to select your location.

Select the city that is nearest to the project location, or if it is known, you can enter the exact address of your project building, if applicable, or the latitude and longitude GPS coordinates. Select Use Daylight Savings Time if it is appropriate for your project location.

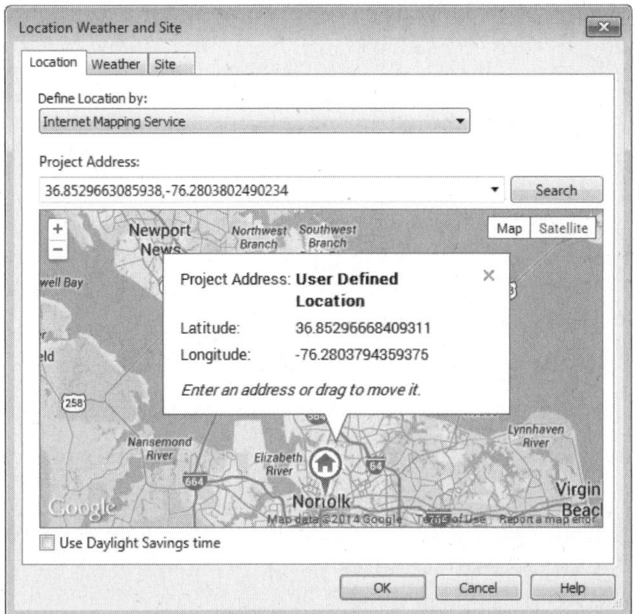

FIGURE 8.15
Location Weather And Site dialog box

The next step is to modify the cooling and heating design temperatures, if needed. You can use the default values that are associated with the weather station closest to your design city, or by deselecting that option, you can modify the Dry Bulb, Wet Bulb, and Mean Daily Range temperatures as needed to fit your design location. You may specify the Heating Design Temperature value and set the Clearness Number value, which ranges from 0 to 2, with 1.0 being an average clearness. Clearness is defined in section 33.4 of the *2007 ASHRAE Handbook: HVAC Applications* in the following way:

- Greater than 1.2: Clear and Dry
- 1.0: Average
- Less than 0.8: Hazy and Humid

Outdoor Air Infiltration

In the Heating And Cooling Loads dialog box, the Building Infiltration Class needs to be set next. When you click the drop-down at the right side of the Building Infiltration Class parameter value, you are given four choices to model the rate of outdoor air that enters the building, typically through leaks in the building envelope created at openings such as windows, doors, and locations where perpendicular building surfaces join. In Revit, infiltration is defined with the following categories:

- Loose: 0.076 CFM/ft^2 of outside air
- Medium: 0.038 CFM/ft^2 of outside air
- Tight: 0.019 CFM/ft^2 of outside air
- None: Infiltration air excluded from the load calculation

Sliver Spaces

The next parameter to define is Sliver Space Tolerance. *Sliver spaces* in Revit are narrow areas that are bounded by parallel interior room-bounding components (parallel interior walls). These spaces include, but are not limited to, pipe chases, HVAC shafts, furrowed columns, and wall cavities. A sliver space is included in the heating and cooling load analysis only if all three of the following requirements are met:

- Identical parallel room-bounding elements enclose the space.
- The width of the sliver space is equal to or less than the Sliver Space Tolerance parameter.
- A space component has been placed in the tangent spaces on either side of the sliver space.

If any one of these three requirements is not satisfied, Revit does not recognize any effects of the sliver space. If there are different geometries to the same sliver space, only the areas of the space that meet the previous criteria are counted in the load analysis. The sliver space volumes are added to the volume of the larger tangent analytical spaces.

You also need to define the detail level of the heating and cooling analysis report. Three report detail levels are available:

- Simple, which contains summary data for systems, zones, and spaces
- Standard, which expands the simple report to include psychrometric data as well as building-level summaries and load summary data for each space
- Detailed, which further expands the data displayed to include individual component contributions to zone and space loads

Before you finish, you must define the ground plane, the project phase, and whether to include heating or cooling load credits, which are negative load values that come from heat entering or leaving a space through a partition into another zone, for example.

Details

Before you run the analysis, you are given the opportunity to go through your created zones and spaces to make sure your desired settings have not been compromised and that there are no warnings that would produce undesired effects on your loads. Switching to the Details tab, you can view the space and zone data that directly affects the heating and cooling analysis, as shown in Figure 8.16.

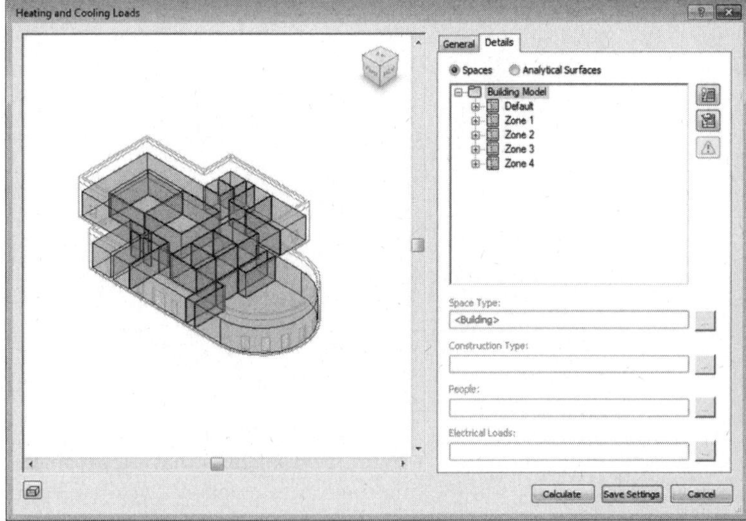

FIGURE 8.16
Building model details

After selecting a zone, you can expand the tree to view the associated spaces and verify or modify the zone service type, heating, cooling, and outdoor air information as needed. You can see whether a space is an occupied space, unoccupied space, or plenum space by the symbol preceding the space name in the tree, as shown in Figure 8.17.

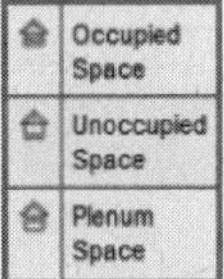

FIGURE 8.17
Space classification

The buttons at the right of the window allow you to highlight or isolate selected spaces or zones in the 3D view of the analytical model. There is also a button for reviewing any warnings associated with a space.

If a space is selected, you can set the space and construction type as well as internal load information. If, when you expand a zone, a warning symbol appears alongside a space, you can investigate by clicking the Show Related Warnings symbol and then correct or ignore the cause of the warning (see Figure 8.18). You can also zoom, pan, and orbit the 3D view for visual inspection of the spaces.

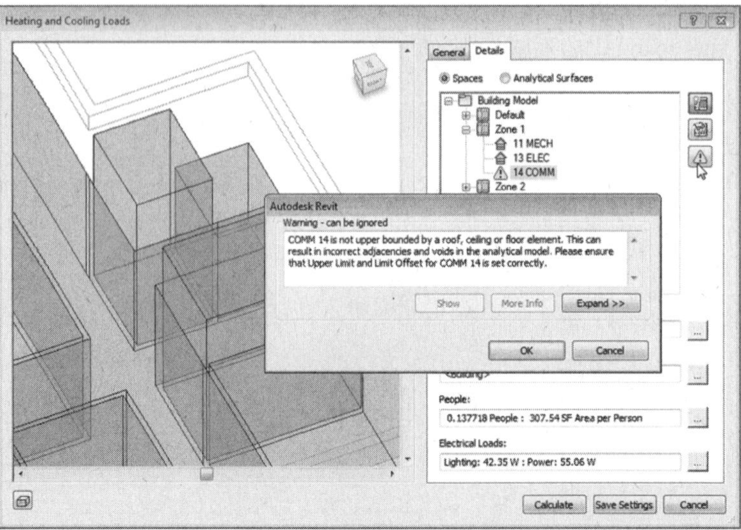

FIGURE 8.18
Warning

The space warning shown in Figure 8.18 suggests that a space exists without an upper bounding element. Click the Save Settings button, and you will be directed back to your model. Locate the space in question, and verify that the upper limit of the space is correct through the space's instance properties. You can also inspect the space visually by creating a section view through the space and verifying that the upper limit extends past a bounding element in the linked model.

Opening the Heating And Cooling Loads dialog box and selecting Analytical Surfaces allows you to view and isolate the physical elements that bound the spaces to be analyzed. You can isolate every individual bounding element that has been defined for the space—roofs, exterior and interior walls, ceilings, floors, and any air gaps or sliver spaces—and view them for any modeling errors before the simulation is performed. Figure 8.19 shows how a space can be isolated and the analytical surfaces displayed. This can help you identify where air gaps may exist or if surfaces are improperly categorized as interior or exterior.

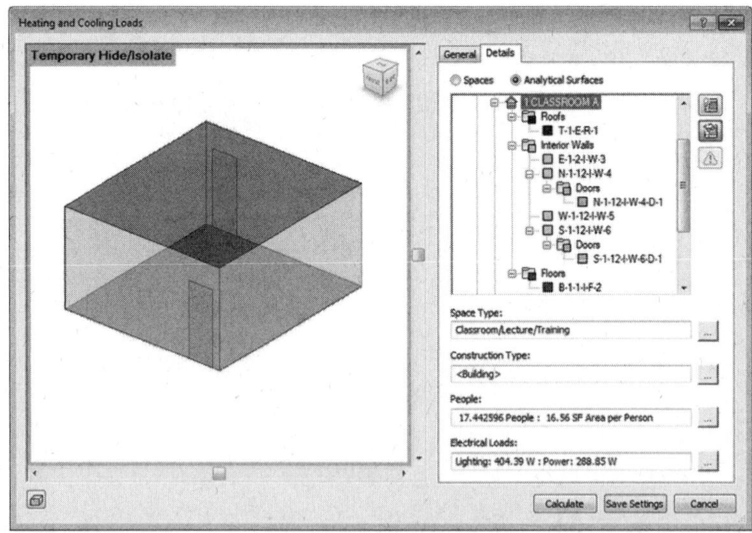

FIGURE 8.19
Analytical surfaces displayed in the Heating And Cooling Loads dialog box

Heating and Cooling Loads Report

Once all of the settings for spaces and zones meet your requirements, you can run an analysis by clicking the Calculate button.

After the simulation is completed, you are directed to the Heating And Cooling Loads report, shown in Figure 8.20. Depending on the level of report detail you selected prior to running the simulation, the tabulated results will be shown, broken into an overall project summary, a building summary, building-level summaries, individual zone data, and individual space data.

FIGURE 8.20 Sample Heating And Cooling Loads report showing the Project Summary and Building Summary areas

Project Summary

Location and Weather	
Project	Project Name
Address	
Calculation Time	Sunday, March 23, 2014 4:28 PM
Report Type	Standard
Latitude	42.21°
Longitude	-71.03°
Summer Dry Bulb	93 °F
Summer Wet Bulb	78 °F
Winter Dry Bulb	6 °F
Mean Daily Range	20 °F

Building Summary

Inputs	
Building Type	Office
Area (SF)	4,395
Volume (CF)	43,657.18
Calculated Results	
Peak Cooling Total Load (Btu/h)	**130,467.1**
Peak Cooling Month and Hour	July 2:00 PM
Peak Cooling Sensible Load (Btu/h)	127,752.1
Peak Cooling Latent Load (Btu/h)	2,715.0
Maximum Cooling Capacity (Btu/h)	130,505.8
Peak Cooling Airflow (CFM)	5,986
Peak Heating Load (Btu/h)	**101,844.8**
Peak Heating Airflow (CFM)	3,361
Checksums	
Cooling Load Density (Btu/(h·ft²))	29.69
Cooling Flow Density (CFM/SF)	1.36
Cooling Flow / Load (CFM/ton)	550.59
Cooling Area / Load (SF/ton)	404.20
Heating Load Density (Btu/(h·ft²))	23.18
Heating Flow Density (CFM/SF)	0.76

The Project Summary area lists the project information (name, address, location) as well as calculated design date and time, Summer Dry Bulb and Wet Bulb temperatures, Winter Dry Bulb temperature, and Mean Daily Range—values that should match the inputs you have entered with the weather data. The Building Summary area includes the global building type and its total analytical area and volume as well as the overall calculated performance of the building—peak cooling loads, peak heating loads, airflows, and building checksums.

The Level Summary area includes the analytical area and volume of each level of the design building, if applicable, as well as each level's individual performance values, similar to the Building Summary area. The Zone Summary area lists each analyzed zone along with its inputs, psychrometrics, and the calculated performance results. It also breaks down the various cooling and heating components and displays a list of the spaces that make up the zone along with a brief summary of the space performance. The Space Summary area displays the space analytical areas and space volume, load inputs, and space type as well as the calculated results for the space. It also contains a breakdown of the individual space components and how they contribute to the cooling and heating loads.

Revit MEP allows you to run a heating and cooling load analysis, make changes, and run a subsequent analysis all while retaining the reports run for each analysis. Load reports are individually time-stamped and can be accessed in the Project Browser under Reports. This enables you to easily flip to a previous report and quantify the changes in your design without resorting to printing out each report as it is generated. Each report can grow to several hundred pages, depending on the size of your job and the detail level selected.

Now is a good time to set up and run a sample HVAC load analysis in Revit. Here's how:

1. Open the file `Chapter 8 HVAC.rvt` available at `www.sybex.com/go/masteringrevitmep2015`.
2. Download and link in the Architectural model file `Chapter8SampleBuilding.rvt`, which can be found on the same web page. Use Origin To Origin placement when linking the file.
3. Set the property of the linked file to Room Bounding by selecting the link, editing its type parameters, and selecting the Room Bounding check box. Click OK.
4. Place your spaces. Click the Analyze tab, and select Spaces to begin placing your spaces in the view. Either select the rooms you want to model or click Place Spaces Automatically. Confirm the number of spaces created.
5. Create a working Space Properties schedule to manage space data. Click the Schedule/Quantities button.
6. Select Spaces as the category, and use New Construction as the phase. Click OK.
7. From the available fields, select the appropriate categories to match the Space Properties schedule shown earlier in Figure 8.4.
8. Adjust the Name and Number fields to match the architectural link, either by manually entering the values or by using a space-naming utility. Sort the rows in descending numerical order.
9. Notice that all the space types are set to <Building>, and the condition type is Heated And Cooled. If you examine the building type, you should see that it is set to Office. Choose Manage ➤ Project Information ➤ Energy Settings to confirm. Click OK twice.
10. In the Space Properties schedule, select the Space Type cell associated with Office 102. Open the Space Type Settings dialog box by clicking the ellipsis in that cell.
11. Set the Space Type parameter value to Office – Enclosed. Notice the changes in the space parameter values. Verify that Occupancy Schedule is set to Common Office Occupancy – 8 AM to 5 PM and that the lighting and power schedules are set to Office Lighting – 6 AM to 11 PM. Click OK.
12. Notice that the Number Of People value for Office 102 has changed. This reflects the different Area Per Person parameter value for Space Type – Office vs. Building Type – Office.
13. Set the remaining space type values appropriately.

14. Notice that the number of people in each space is taken out to six decimal places. Set the field format for this column to use fixed units with a rounding to 0 decimal places. Switch back to the 1 – Mech floor plan view.

15. Click the Heating And Cooling Loads button on the Analyze tab. Switch the view to Details, and expand the Default tree.

16. Each space has a warning symbol attached to it. Select a space. As you click the Warning button, you will see that the space is not upper-bounded by a roof, ceiling, or floor element. You need to set the upper limits of each space to ensure accurate building analysis. Click OK and then Cancel.

17. In the 1 – Mech floor plan, select all the spaces. In the Properties palette, set the upper limits of each space to Level 2 with a **0′-0″** (**0** for metric projects) offset.

18. Open the Heating And Cooling Loads dialog box, and verify that all the warnings have been cleared from the spaces.

19. Click Calculate.

20. View the building performance report that has been generated.

21. Switch back to the 1 – Mech floor plan and click the Zone button on the Analysis tab.

22. Create zones in the 1 – Mech floor plan. Group the spaces as shown in Figure 8.21, and name the zones per the sample schedule.

FIGURE 8.21 Grouping spaces in the floor plan

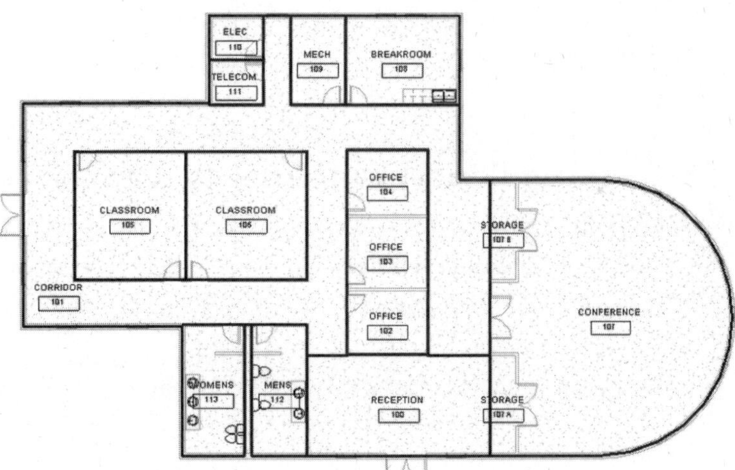

23. Select Zone 05 in the floor plan. Verify that the service type is VAV – Terminal Reheat and that the Cooling and Heating Information settings are both Default.

24. Click Edit for the Outdoor Air Information setting, and for this zone, enter **5 CFM** per person, and **0.06 CFM/SF** in the appropriate boxes. Set the space occupancies equal to **1** person.
25. Run another building analysis.
26. As you view the Zone Summary report for Zone 05, you should see that the Peak Ventilation Airflow value is 20 CFM. The Ventilation Density value equals 0.06 CFM/SF—the value you entered. The Ventilation/Person value, however, equals 7 CFM/person, which is not what was entered. Remember, Revit MEP takes the largest ventilation load, not the required combined ventilation load, when calculating the building performance.
27. To get the ASHRAE-required ventilation, do the following:
    a. Calculate the required ventilation from the measured area.
    b. Calculate the required ventilation from number of occupants.
    c. Add the two values, and divide by the total area.
    d. Enter this value in the Outdoor Air Information window for Zone 05.
28. Run the analysis again, and observe that the Zone 05 Ventilation Airflow value has changed to the airflow calculated in the previous step.
29. Using the Space Properties schedule, zone properties, and the Heating And Cooling Loads dialog box, adjust various parameters and rerun the heating and cooling analysis.
30. Use the different reports generated to compare the effects of your changes to the building.
31. Close the file.

Performing Conceptual Energy Analysis on Your Building

Revit MEP has the ability to perform a conceptual energy analysis on the project building directly within Revit. With the increasing requirement for projects to achieve Leadership in Energy and Environmental Design (LEED) certification from the U.S. Green Building Council (USGBC), it proves beneficial to analyze a simplified project building in the concept design phase. Knowing a building's possible energy performance will help you flesh out the design of the building systems. Having an idea of how the building will perform will also help your team with fleshing out the project's LEED checklist.

Setting Up the Model

First, before any energy analysis can be done, the feature has to be activated by clicking the Sign In link on the Information bar to log into the Autodesk® 360 platform, as shown in Figure 8.22. Go to `https://360.autodesk.com` for information about obtaining an Autodesk 360 account.

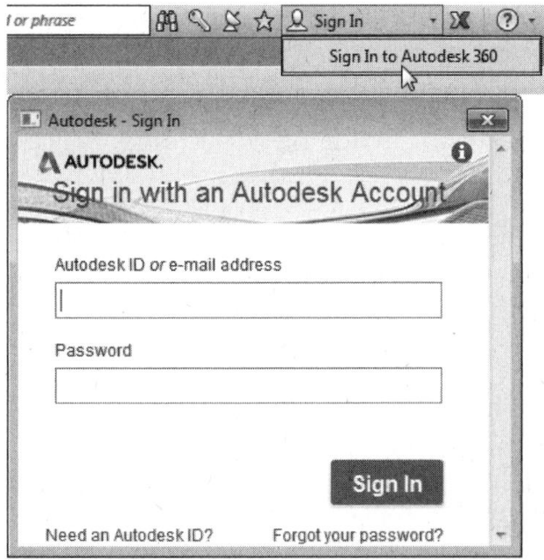

FIGURE 8.22 Logging in to Autodesk 360

On the Energy Analysis panel of the Analyze tab, you have tools for conceptual analysis, as shown in Figure 8.23. The two buttons at the left of the panel allow you to choose between using the actual building components for analysis or a mass model. The Use Building Element Mode tool (bottom button) establishes the model components as the basis for energy analysis. In this mode, an energy analytical model is automatically generated each time you use the Run Energy Simulation tool. The Use Conceptual Mass Model tool (top button) requires you to generate Mass objects in your project for analysis.

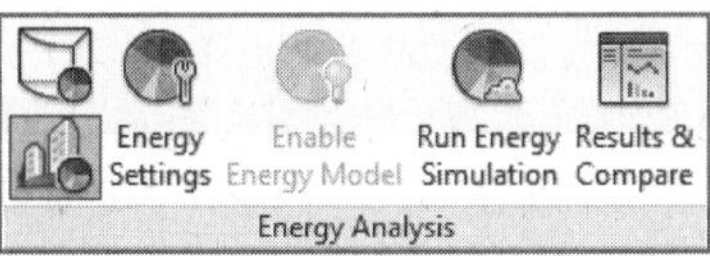

FIGURE 8.23 Energy Analysis tools

The Enable Energy Model tool is available only when using the Conceptual Mass Model mode. This tool toggles the analytical model on and off, so you can make changes without the analytical model updating in real time.

To begin using this mode, you need to set up a mass model; the mass model allows you to explore various building design ideas by conceptualizing the building through shapes. Under the Massing & Site tab, set the Show Mass button to Form And Floors via the pull-down menu. This will enable any mass form created to be visible, regardless of view settings.

Click the In-Place Mass button. Name the mass you want to model. Draw a closed sketch around the exterior envelope of the building. You can adjust the sketch to get the shape you need by moving the vertices to the desired location. Once the sketch is complete, click Create Form ➤ Solid Forms, and then click Finish Mass.

Next, create analytical floors. In a 3D view, select the mass, and adjust the height of the mass so that it encompasses all the building levels you wish to analyze. Under the Modify Mass tab, select Mass Floors. The levels that are intersected by the mass model appear in a pop-up window and are available to be selected for inclusion in the analysis.

Select Enable Energy Model and then click Energy Settings. Here the basic as well as optional energy settings can be defined, as shown in Figure 8.24.

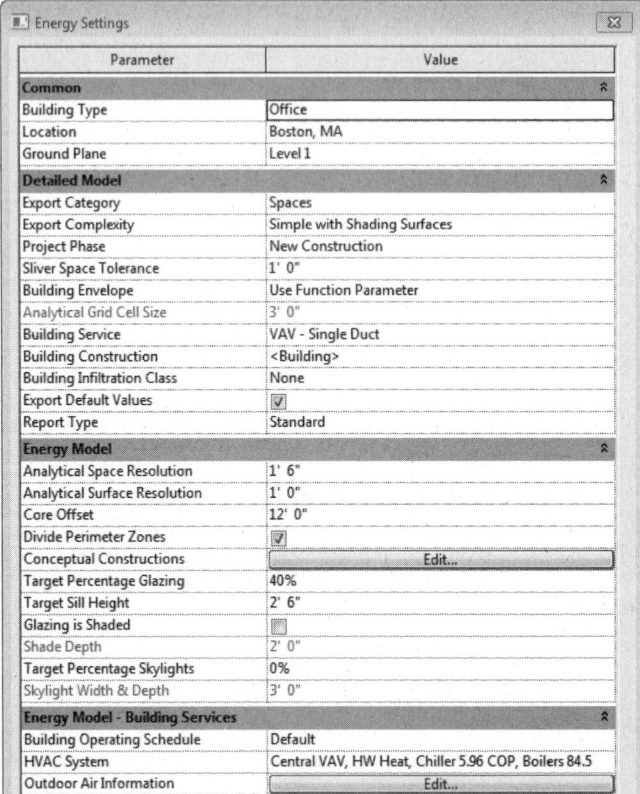

Energy Settings
Parameter
Value
Common
Building Type
Office
Location
Boston, MA
Ground Plane
Level 1
Detailed Model
Export Category
Spaces
Export Complexity
Simple with Shading Surfaces
Project Phase
New Construction
Sliver Space Tolerance
1' 0"
Building Envelope
Use Function Parameter
Analytical Grid Cell Size
3' 0"
Building Service
VAV - Single Duct
Building Construction
<Building>
Building Infiltration Class
None
Export Default Values
Report Type
Standard
Energy Model
Analytical Space Resolution
1' 6"
Analytical Surface Resolution
1' 0"
Core Offset
12' 0"
Divide Perimeter Zones
Conceptual Constructions
Edit...
Target Percentage Glazing
40%
Target Sill Height
2' 6"
Glazing is Shaded
Shade Depth
2' 0"
Target Percentage Skylights
0%
Skylight Width & Depth
3' 0"
Energy Model - Building Services
Building Operating Schedule
Default
HVAC System
Central VAV, HW Heat, Chiller 5.96 COP, Boilers 84.5
Outdoor Air Information
Edit...

FIGURE 8.24 Energy settings

The following settings are available:

Building Type Select the overall building type that will be simulated.

Location Set the geographic location of the building.

Ground Plane Verify that the ground level in your model is defined as the ground plane in the simulation; any levels below the ground plane will be treated as underground floors.

Core Offset If a building core is desired but currently not zoned or undefined, set the appropriate analysis distance from the perimeter of the building.

Divide Perimeter Zones If desired, activating this option will create four equal quadrant-based zones for each mass floor.

Conceptual Constructions Clicking the Edit button in this category enables you to set how the conceptual construction elements of the building will perform in the analysis. As shown in Figure 8.25, there are several categories to edit, and each category has several construction options to choose from.

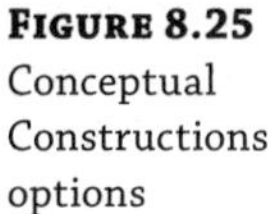

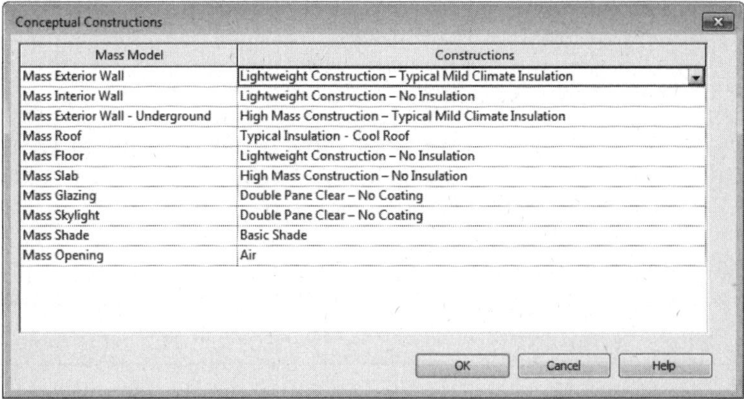

Conceptual Constructions

Mass Model	Constructions
Mass Exterior Wall	Lightweight Construction – Typical Mild Climate Insulation
Mass Interior Wall	Lightweight Construction – No Insulation
Mass Exterior Wall - Underground	High Mass Construction – Typical Mild Climate Insulation
Mass Roof	Typical Insulation - Cool Roof
Mass Floor	Lightweight Construction – No Insulation
Mass Slab	High Mass Construction – No Insulation
Mass Glazing	Double Pane Clear – No Coating
Mass Skylight	Double Pane Clear – No Coating
Mass Shade	Basic Shade
Mass Opening	Air

FIGURE 8.25 Conceptual Constructions options

A detailed explanation of each construction value, including R-value, Unit Density, Heat Capacity, SHGC, and Tvis (for glazing) can be found in Help under Revit Users ➤ Analyze The Design ➤ Autodesk 360 Energy Analysis ➤ Energy Settings ➤ Energy Model Settings.

Target Percentage Glazing This value approximates the preferred window percentage per mass zone (similar for Target Percentage Skylights).

Target Sill Height This value sets the bottom edge of the glazing.

You may then set a desired operating schedule for the building, approximate HVAC system performances, and any outdoor air information desired.

If you choose the Rooms option for the Export Category parameter, the settings options change slightly. The Include Thermal Properties setting becomes available, which enables you to use the thermal properties of the materials assigned to building components in the analysis. If no thermal properties are defined in an element, the analysis is done with the conceptual constructions.

Keeping It Simple

Remember that this is a *conceptual* energy analysis—not a full-blown LEED or EPACT energy analysis. You will use this tool to ensure that energy use and natural resources factor into the building layout, orientation, and system design. In Revit MEP, greater modeling complexity will not always result in greater analysis accuracy.

There are maximum limits that Revit can analyze to produce a successful conceptual energy report. For a complex building, you may have to disable the Divide Perimeter Zones option, reduce the Core Offset value to 0, and create custom zones to simplify the model. You need to model only major zones or spaces and combine smaller spaces into large zones. Spaces such as restrooms, closets, and stairwells do not need to be defined. If the model is kept complex, errors may be introduced in the simulation, and simulation performance may decrease without an appreciable increase in the accuracy of the results.

With a simplified mass model, Revit MEP allows for easy analysis and comparison of design options. Experiment with different mass forms, orientations, envelopes, schedules, occupancy, and zoning to determine which building changes will have the greatest impact on energy performance.

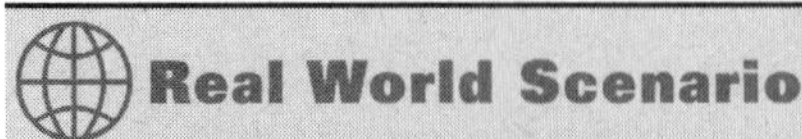

Conceptual Analysis

A new project RFP has come in, with a project goal of LEED Gold certification. Leslie has been given the task of investigating the best possible energy performance of three building concept options outlined in the RFP. Trouble is that there isn't time to accurately model the three building options in Revit.

By using the Conceptual Mass Model tool for energy simulation, Leslie is able to create generic mass models of each design and analyze several building and system configurations and orientations, enabling her to target the best-performing concept design to present to the team for consideration.

Performing Energy Simulation

When you are ready, switch to a 3D view of your project—Revit analyzes the mass displayed only in the 3D view. Click the Run Energy Simulation tool on the Energy Analysis panel of the Analyze tab. If you're logged in to Autodesk, you will see the dialog box shown in Figure 8.26. Use a unique name for each run so that you will be able to easily identify and compare designs. Click Continue to run the analysis.

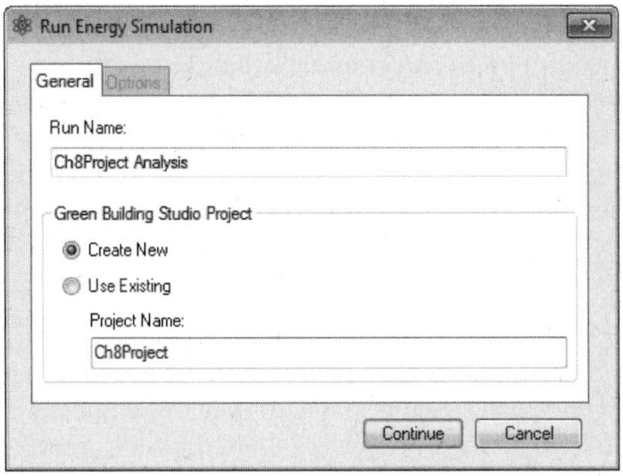

Figure 8.26 Run Energy Simulation dialog box

The analysis will occur "in the cloud," so you will be able to navigate through your project while the simulation runs. When the simulation ends, you will be prompted with an alert that the results are ready to view. Click the alert to view the results, or you can click the Results And Compare button on the Energy Analysis panel. Figure 8.27 shows a sample report dialog box.

Based on the inputs entered and how all the mass model variables were defined, the results displayed include conceptual Energy Use Intensity (EUI), Life Cycle Energy Use/Cost, and Renewable Energy Potential (PV and wind power) values and various graphs showing carbon emissions, heating and cooling loads, weather data, and fuel consumption and demand.

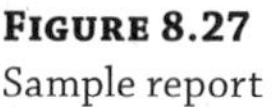

FIGURE 8.27
Sample report

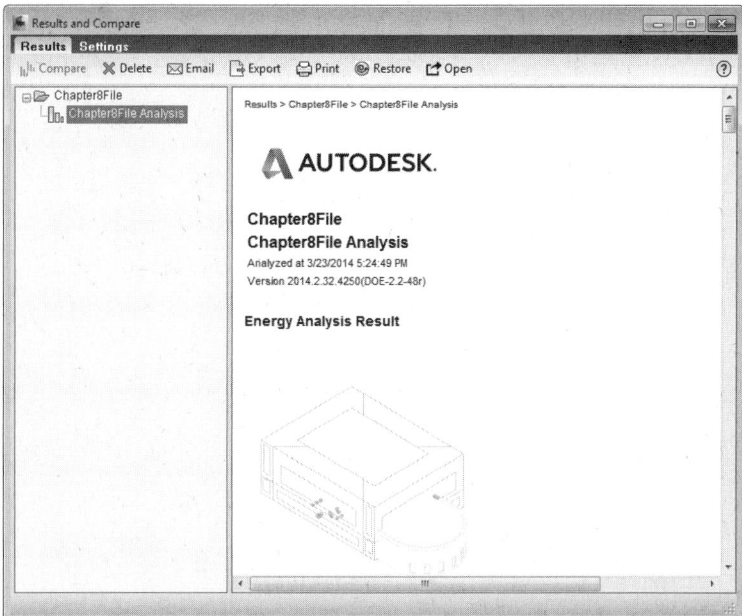

The Settings tab of the dialog box allows you to choose which results are to be displayed in the report. The report can be exported to PDF, XML, DOE-2 (`.inp`) or an EnergyPlus file (`.idf`). You can compare the results of multiple analyses by selecting the reports in the tree at the left of the dialog box and then clicking the Compare button. The reports will be shown side by side for easy comparison of each result category.

Analyzing Duct and Pipe System Pressure

Along with heating and cooling analysis and energy analysis, Revit MEP has the ability to generate pressure loss reports of correctly modeled duct and piping systems. Note that you must first have your duct or pipe systems routed and sized by using the duct and piping sizing tools. The procedures to do so are outlined in Chapters 10 and 11, respectively. We cover generating a duct pressure loss report in this chapter—the process is the same for piping systems.

To generate the duct loss report, use the Duct Pressure Loss Report tool found on the Reports & Schedules panel of the Analyze tab. You will see the Duct Pressure Loss Report – System Selector dialog box, which enables you to select the duct systems you want to include in the report from a list of available systems that have been correctly defined. You may also select the duct systems within the appropriate views and then click the Duct Pressure Loss Report button, or you may select the systems within the System Browser and then right-click and select Pressure Loss Report.

Note that pressure loss reports cannot be generated for fire protection or gravity flow (that is, sanitary) systems.

Click OK to generate the report. The Duct Pressure Loss Report Settings window appears and is where you will define the detail level of the report generated, as shown in Figure 8.28. The level of detail and the information reported is up to you. You can save the settings for the report in your project so that multiple types of reports can be generated.

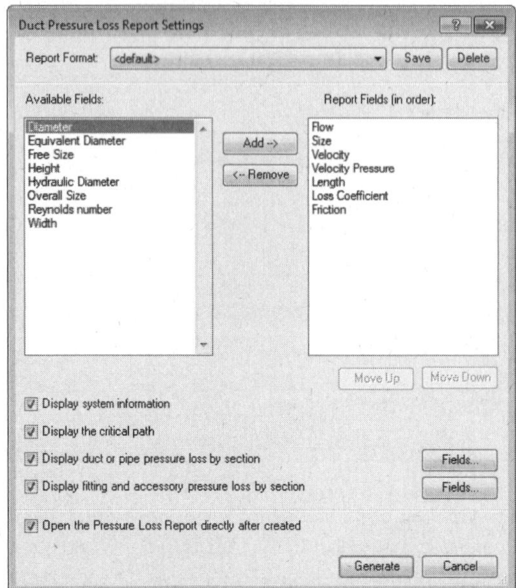

FIGURE 8.28 Duct Pressure Loss Report Settings dialog box

These generated reports, along with the System Inspector, provide a quick and useful way to double-check the designed systems with other third-party static pressure or flow calculations to ensure that the critical path and pressure loss in the Revit model match up to your intended design and equipment selections. The reports are also a way to break down complicated systems by components, identifying any sizing, flow, or friction anomalies that may be throwing off your design.

Exporting gbXML Data to Load-simulating Software

Now you've explored how to set up a building for heating and cooling load analysis and how to perform the analysis in Revit MEP. That's it, right? You're finished? You have an accurate energy analysis of every component in the building's heating and cooling systems?

The engine built into Revit MEP does not currently have the programming needed to perform a complete energy analysis of your building. Increasing LEED certification requirements means that you need an equally increasing level of detail in the building analysis, the comparison to the baseline building design, and the documentation to obtain the desired design certification. The solution to this dilemma is to export your Revit MEP model via Green Building XML (gbXML) format to a third-party simulation program, such as Trane TRACE 700 or Carrier's HAP.

gbXML was developed in the late 1990s to enable interoperability between building design models and engineering analysis tools. Its use by major CAD vendors and several major engineering simulation vendors helps to streamline time-consuming building takeoffs—helping to remove some of the cost associated with the design of energy-efficient buildings. Go to `http://gbxml.org` for more details on the purpose and origin of gbXML.

To export your Revit MEP model, click the Application Menu button and then choose Export ➤ gbXML. You will be directed to the Export gbXML dialog box, shown in Figure 8.29. Even though the architectural model is linked into your project, the geometry will be exported to your analysis program.

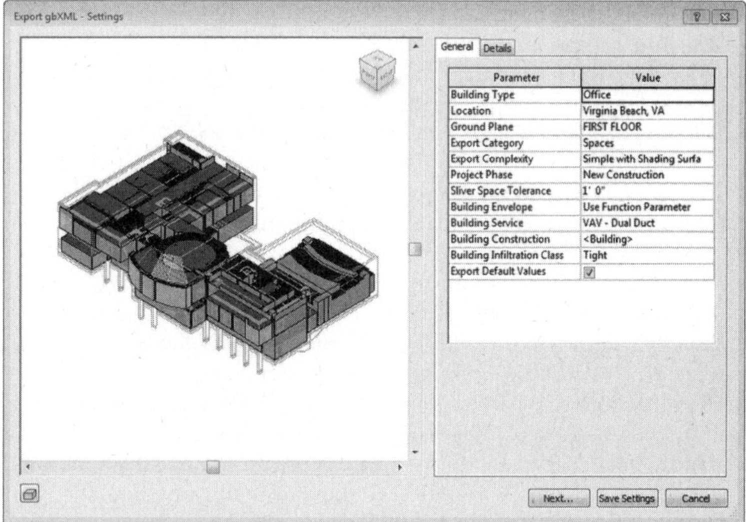

FIGURE 8.29 Export gbXML dialog box

This window looks nearly identical to the Heating And Cooling Loads dialog box (shown earlier in Figure 8.14). If a heating and cooling load analysis has already been performed, the majority of the parameters in the General tab should already be defined per your design requirements. If not, adjust the parameter values as needed; these parameters were discussed earlier in this chapter.

Two settings that exist in the export window, but not in the analysis window, are the Export Default Values and Export Complexity settings. If the Export Default Values box is selected, the default values for people, electrical loads, occupancy, lighting, schedules, and constructions will be exported, regardless of any user-overridden values. If this box is deselected, then only user-entered values will be exported.

Export Complexity is simply that: the level of complexity of the information contained within the exported gbXML file. Five levels of complexity exist and are described here:

Simple Curtain walls and curtain systems are exported as a single opening. Simple complexity is used for the heating and cooling analysis and is most suited for exporting.

Simple With Shading Surfaces This is the same as Simple but with shading surface information included.

Complex Curtain walls and panels are exported as multiple openings, with each panel as a separate opening.

Complex With Shading Surfaces This is the same as Complex but with shading surface information included; however, the shading surfaces (roof overhangs, free-standing walls, and so on) are not associated with any room/space.

Complex With Mullions And Shading Surfaces This is the same as Complex With Shading Surfaces but with mullions and curtain walls exported as simple analytical shading surfaces based on centerline, thickness, and offset.

The Details tab is identical to the analysis window, and as before, you are able to set or verify space energy parameters such as the building and space construction types, internal loads, and zone information such as the service type and temperature set points. You are able to view and verify that all the analytical surfaces are correct and address any construction or space modeling warnings that are present before exporting.

Click Next, and you are prompted to save the gbXML file. Browse to your project directory, and name the file accordingly. Your gbXML file is now ready to use.

Now you have complete model information set up to be read by a simulation program without issue and without any further manipulation, right? Unfortunately, that is not the case.

A major issue with the exported data deals with the building construction. Revit breaks larger elements, such as a floor slab in large or complex-shaped spaces, into smaller polygonal elements for computation. This means that a single floor element is broken into several individually tagged and defined floor elements in the same space. Revit MEP also has a tendency, depending on how the architectural link is modeled, to assign exterior wall values to interior walls that bound a space, or roof values to ceilings that bound a space.

If your design space has an unusual or atypical geometry, such as a curved wall, the number of individual elements within a single type can grow to the hundreds. This is a prevalent issue when trying to import your gbXML file into an outside simulation program. There simply is not enough capacity in the third-party programs to handle large numbers of building surfaces—sometimes stopping at the first eight surfaces and causing you, the designer, to have to examine each space individually to delete and remodel any surfaces in error.

Also, importing errors may occur when parameters such as the construction data U-values fall outside a common range predefined by your simulation software. Often it will prompt a warning message, but at other times the gbXML data will fail to import completely. Most of the time, the remedy, again, is to check each individual building element construction or assembly to make sure that the appropriate U-values are modeled. Otherwise, you are forced to create the assemblies manually from scratch. In addition to checking the construction, make sure your simulation program has properly read the internal load data—manually adjust or enter the data as required.

Do not be discouraged. Yes, you may experience some drawbacks when exporting and importing gbXML data from Revit. As a designer, any effort you make to reduce the time-consuming process of modeling each space of the building in your simulation program will be worth the effort. Although there are some shortcomings, with Revit MEP 2015 you have the ability to examine the model geometry and data within the space prior to analysis, which can save time on your projects and improve coordination.

The Bottom Line

Prepare your Revit MEP model for analysis. The key element to a successful building performance analysis is the proper accounting of all variables that will influence the results.

Master It Describe the relationship between rooms and spaces—are they the same element? Describe an essential tool that can be created to maintain and track space input data and building construction for a heating and cooling load analysis.

Perform heating and cooling analysis with Revit MEP 2015. Before a piece of equipment can be sized or duct systems designed, the building heating and cooling performance must be known in order to condition your spaces accurately.

Master It How does project location affect building heating and cooling loads? Describe methods to determine project location in Revit MEP 2015.

What is a sliver space, and how does it affect the building performance?

Perform a conceptual energy analysis on your building. Revit MEP 2015 gives you the ability to run an analysis on a project while it is in its conceptual design phase. This allows for quick testing of various options.

Master It What is the purpose of a conceptual energy analysis?

Will increasing the complexity of your concept building model produce the most accurate energy analysis?

Analyze duct and pipe system pressure with Revit MEP 2015. Pressure loss reports can be easily generated from your model. These can help with important design decisions and can show the differences between design variations.

Master It How is the pressure-loss report a useful addition to Revit MEP?

Export gbXML data to load-simulating software. Often, to complete the building analysis, the Revit MEP model has to be analyzed in greater detail by a third-party simulation program.

Master It What is gbXML? Why is it necessary to export your Revit MEP project?

Chapter 9

Creating Logical Systems

Creating and managing systems is the key to getting the Autodesk® Revit® MEP 2015 software to work for you. Systems represent the transfer of information between families. They are available for any ductwork or pipework system type you may have in your model. Electrical systems are also a part of Revit MEP and are discussed in Chapter 14, "Circuiting and Panels."

In this chapter, you will learn to do the following:

- Create and manage air systems
- Create and manage piping systems
- Configure duct connectors

Why Are Systems Important?

Systems are the logical connection between elements in the model. They are the link between the air terminal, the variable air volume (VAV) box, and the air handler, and they represent an additional layer of information above the physical connections made with ducts and pipes, the engineering information. Without systems, ducts and pipes act only as connections between two points. Systems are needed to generate the bigger picture and allow you to manage the elements on a building-wide level. Systems enable you to build more than just a three-dimensional model, they enable the engineering to be included in the model as well. You can create systems to represent supply, return, and exhaust air as well as plumbing, fire-protection, and hydronic piping. You can also create new system types to represent other uses of ducts and pipes outside the predefined types included in Revit MEP 2015.

Systems also aid in the documentation of a model. Because the systems link elements, and their engineering data, across the entire model, tags and other properties can be managed quickly and accurately. One example of this is using a pipe tag that includes not only the size but also the system abbreviation and, if needed, flow rate, velocity, or friction loss within the pipe. You can even set the temperature and fluid type for your system. Tagging any piece of pipe connected to the system, in any view, immediately generates a complete and accurate annotation.

Managing Systems

Managing systems is the easiest way to separate, say, a cold-water pipe from a hydronic pipe. If you can't separate the two, you will not be able to produce sheets showing certain systems and hiding others. As you draw a pipe or duct, Revit will automatically assign it to a system. If you are drawing pipe or ductwork from scratch, you can select the system type it will belong to from the Properties palette. If a duct system is created directly from the connectors of mechanical objects, the ducts assume the system of the host objects.

System Classification, System Type, and System Name

When first installed, the out-of-the-box project templates included with Revit will already have predefined system types that are based directly on its own system classifications. These default system types are shown in the following screenshot.

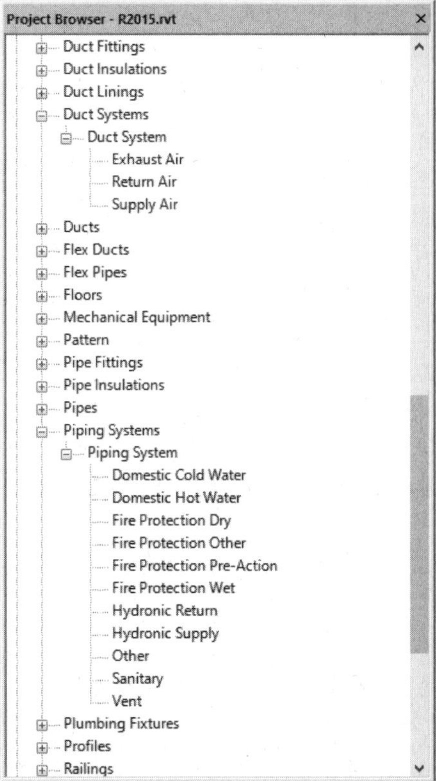

The system classifications are fixed. You can create new system types, but only by duplicating existing types. Thus you would create an Outside Air System type from Supply Air, Chilled Water Flow from Hydronic Flow, and so on. The choice of which original system type to duplicate is important because the connectors in each family can only be set to a system classification, so they will connect only to a system type that is also created from that system classification.

Even though the ducts are associated with a system, managing space air quantities has to be done externally. Entering all the information needed to accurately represent the mechanical systems in a building may seem like a daunting task at first, but the benefits of having all the information in one place and directly in front of the user can lead to more accurate designs. Instead of the user flipping between a building-load program and a duct-sizing chart (or wheel) and trying to keep track of which terminal box is serving which space, systems can handle all of that for the user. By feeding Revit MEP 2015 the load information, calculated internally or externally, and creating an air system for a space, the user can quickly determine the cubic feet per minute (CFM) required at each air terminal with a schedule or a custom space tag. The airflow will then be assigned to the terminal box, and the space that it is serving can appear in a schedule. One program can handle all of these tasks, which the user would have to do anyway.

Using connected systems can also improve performance for Revit. Even if systems are not being specifically set up, Revit is using systems behind the scenes to keep track of all the information in the model. You can enable or disable calculations per system type (Supply, Return, Exhaust, and so on), thus increasing the performance of the Revit model. To do this, select the Piping system from the Project Browser, right-click, and select Type Properties. All elements get assigned to their default system classification(s) (but not system types) based on the type of connector: supply air, return air, hydronic supply, and so on.

System Browser

The System Browser, shown in Figure 9.1, summarizes all the systems currently in the model. If that were all that it did, it would be a useful design tool. You could keep track of all the air and water in the building and see your system totals at a glance. But the System Browser in Revit MEP 2015 takes this idea a step further; it is a live link to the components in the system as well as their parameters. You have full control to modify the airflows, equipment types, and diffuser selection, all from a single window.

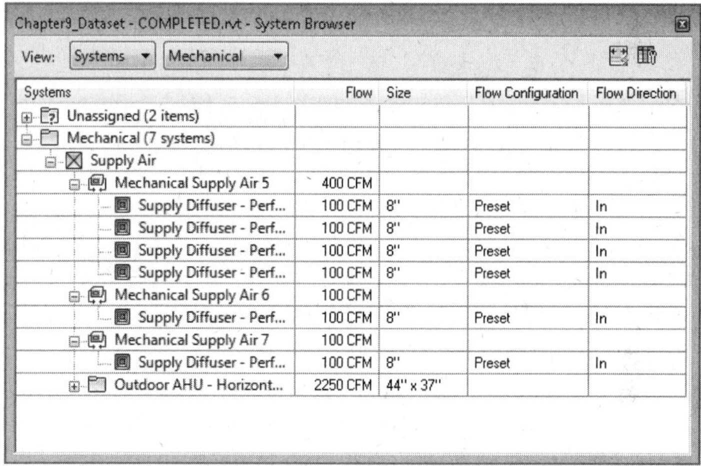

Systems	Flow	Size	Flow Configuration	Flow Direction
Unassigned (2 items)				
Mechanical (7 systems)				
Supply Air				
Mechanical Supply Air 5	400 CFM			
Supply Diffuser - Perf...	100 CFM	8"	Preset	In
Supply Diffuser - Perf...	100 CFM	8"	Preset	In
Supply Diffuser - Perf...	100 CFM	8"	Preset	In
Supply Diffuser - Perf...	100 CFM	8"	Preset	In
Mechanical Supply Air 6	100 CFM			
Supply Diffuser - Perf...	100 CFM	8"	Preset	In
Mechanical Supply Air 7	100 CFM			
Supply Diffuser - Perf...	100 CFM	8"	Preset	In
Outdoor AHU - Horizont...	2250 CFM	44" x 37"		

FIGURE 9.1
System Browser

You can access the System Browser from View ➤ User Interface ➤ System Browser or the F9 function key. The system browser is directly linked to the elements in the model. Elements that have yet to be assigned to a system will be shown as Unassigned. This can be seen in Figure 9.2.

In the System Browser, if you expand the system tree, you can see that when an object is selected, the corresponding item is highlighted in the drawing area. Conversely, selecting items in the System Browser highlights the objects in the drawing area, as long as the items are actually visible in that view. This is shown in Figure 9.3.

You can customize the system browser by setting up the columns it displays. The System Browser can get very large, so a second monitor is helpful. You can access the Column Settings dialog box by clicking the Column Settings button in the upper-right corner of the System

Browser, which gives you an expandable list of the information that can be referenced in the model (see Figure 9.4).

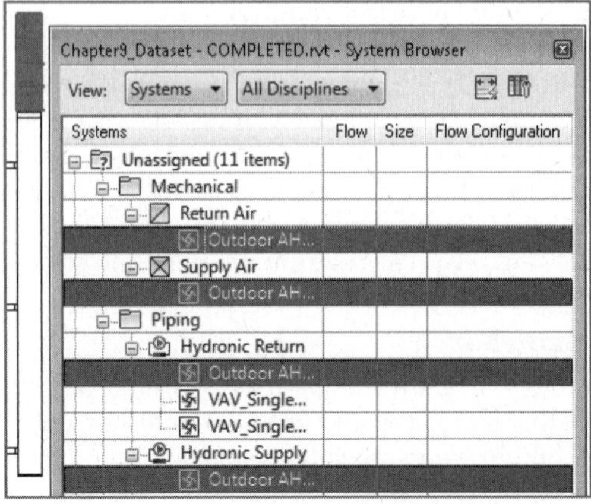

FIGURE 9.2
Examining unassigned systems and elements in the System Browser

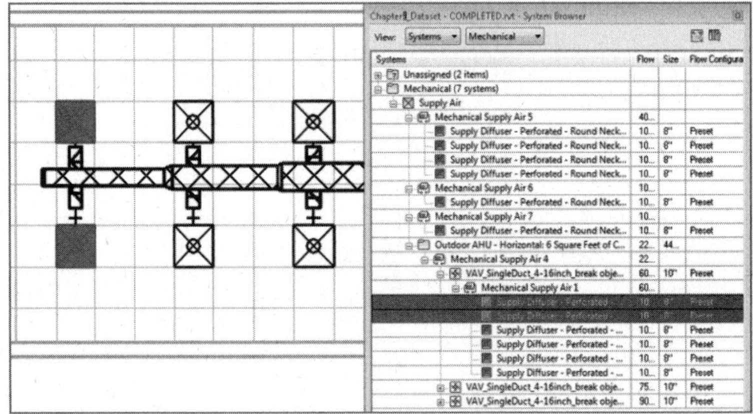

FIGURE 9.3
Selected elements in the drawing area highlighted in the System Browser

Obviously, not every parameter will be filled out for every part of the system, and some of the parameters will not be useful on a day-to-day basis. The columns you choose to display depend on your personal preferences and how you model your systems. For example, Space Number and Space Name populate only if the element and space touch. If spaces are bound by the ceiling, and terminal boxes exist above the ceiling, they will not be associated with a space. You have to use the Show command to find lost terminal boxes. To do this, right-click any element in the System Browser and select Show.

Ideally, every connection on every piece of equipment would be associated with a system, and the unassigned system category would be empty. This may not be realistic on a large job or where manufacturer content is being used. You may not need to model every condensate drain, but if the manufacturer has provided a connection point for it, there will be a listing in the System Browser. If your firm decides to use the System Browser to carefully monitor the systems and elements in the model, you may want to eliminate connectors that you will not be using to keep things clean.

To remove systems you must edit the family with the connector that is not being used. For more information on equipment families, see Chapter 19, "Creating Equipment."

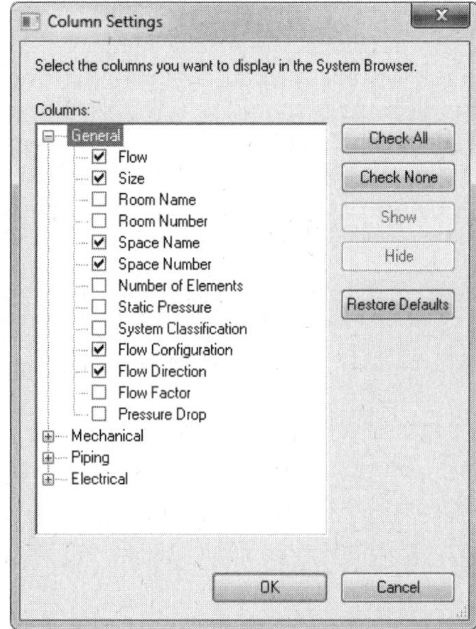

FIGURE 9.4 Column Settings dialog box

Real World Scenario

UNWANTED SYSTEMS

Steve has downloaded a fan coil unit from the manufacturer and has found that it has a condensate connector on each side. As Steve will only use one of these, he knew it would leave an unwanted, unassigned system in the project. To remedy this, Steve selected the offending family from the Project Browser, right-clicked, and selected Edit Family.

This opened the family in a new window and Steve was able to delete the connector he no longer required. Following this, he saved the family to his `Project Families` folder and loaded it back into the project.

He could then insert the fan coil unit family and connect the duct and pipework, leaving no unassigned systems.

Mechanical Settings

Before you can jump in and start creating systems, you need to set up several things to ensure that the systems work as they should. There is nothing wrong with the default settings, but every firm is different—each has its own standards, procedures, and design requirements. Most companies have developed their own standards and endeavor to adhere to various industry standards, and these are good guidelines to follow when using a new application such as Revit MEP 2015.

The Mechanical Settings dialog box, accessed from the Manage tab's MEP Settings panel, contains some of the most critical settings for using systems in Revit 2015. This dialog box, shown in Figure 9.5, was briefly covered in Chapter 2, "Creating an Effective Project Template." A more in-depth look is needed so you can understand how these settings affect systems in Revit 2015. All of these settings should be established in your company's project template. Changes to them should be discussed with the Revit team as well as the CAD manager, because data, visibility, and graphics can be dramatically affected by a minor change in this dialog box. Due to the specific nature of the information concerned, it is recommended that each discipline put an experienced person in charge of maintaining its own system settings.

FIGURE 9.5
Mechanical Settings dialog box

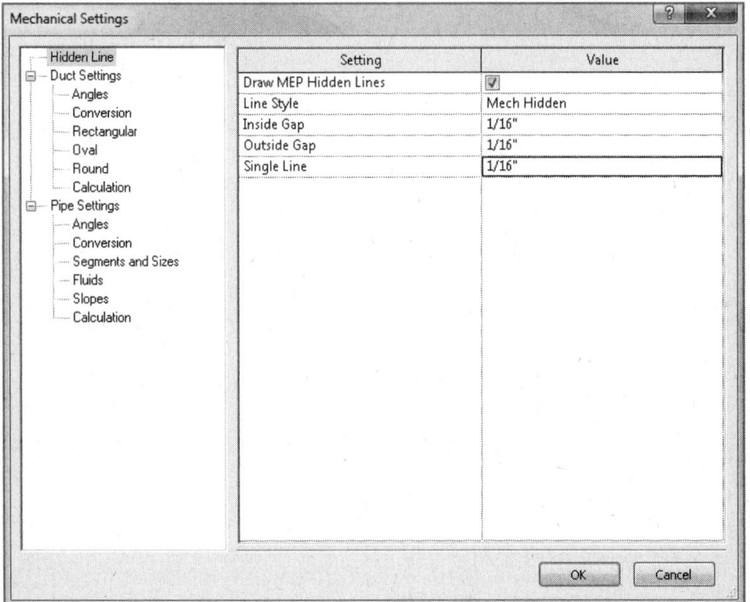

Several settings really affect systems graphically. For example, by choosing Hidden Line, you see Inside Gap, Outside Gap, and Single Line. By default, each one of these is set to 1/16" (1.5 mm). By changing the numeric size of each one of these parameters, you can get a different look that helps match your existing standards. We will look more closely at the Mechanical Settings dialog box separately for duct and pipe systems later in this chapter.

Setting Up Duct Systems

Before we can begin creating the system, we need to ensure that the duct and duct system settings are correct. Starting with the Mechanical Settings Dialog box we looked at earlier (Figure 9.5), expand Duct Settings and look at each section.

Duct Settings Duct Settings allows you to customize annotation sizes, suffixes, prefixes, and size separators.

Angles Here you can specify to use any angle, select an angle increment to be used, or select to confine the design to specific angles only.

Conversion This section is for setting the standard Duct Type and Offset parameters for both main and branch runs, as well as the flex duct type and maximum flex length allowed. These are the settings that will be applied when the Generate Layout feature of Revit MEP is used.

Rectangular, Oval, and Round In each of these you can specify the standard sizes for your ductwork, whether these sizes should appear in size lists, and whether they should be used by Revit when it is automatically sizing the ductwork.

Calculation Here you can see the calculation Revit uses for its duct sizing, velocity, and pressure drop calculation. New to Revit 2015, you can now select between the original calculations (The Darcy-Weisbach equation used in the ASHREA handbook of fundamentals) and the Haaland equation (based on guidelines from the Chartered Institution of Building Services Engineers [CIBSE]).

Now we can look at the duct type properties. You can access this from the families section of the Project Browser. Select Duct and choose any duct type, right-click, and choose Type Properties. You can create new duct types by duplicating existing ones.

In this dialog box, apart from parameters listed under the Identity Data group, there is only the Roughness value to be changed; however, from here you can also access the Routing Preferences dialog box (see Figure 9.6). With Routing Preferences, you can apply a list of each fitting you wish to be used and leave out those you do not. For example, you may wish to use flanged fittings only. You can also set the preferred junction type (Tap or Tee), although it is always a good idea to include at least one tap and one tee connection in the junction list because often you will need both. Defining the routing preferences correctly is essential to enable efficient modeling of duct systems. For standard duct types used regularly within the office, the routing preferences should be set up in the template file. See Chapter 2 for more information.

The Routing Preferences dialog box also gives you the Duct Size button to open the Mechanical Settings dialog. You can load additional duct fittings with the Load Family button.

Now let's look at the Duct Systems dialog box. Like ducts themselves, you can access the duct system type properties from the Families section of the Project Browser. You can also access them by right-clicking the system type in the System Browser. The Duct Systems dialog box (see Figure 9.7) is where you can create new systems by duplicating existing ones. You must be careful to use the correct existing system categories to begin with so you can then connect to the correct points in your families.

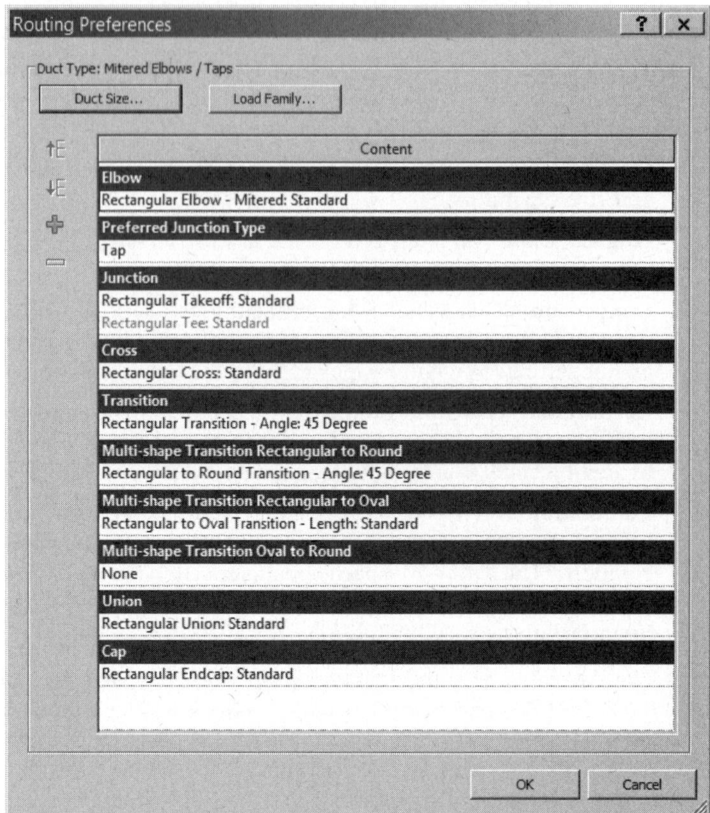

FIGURE 9.6
Routing preferences for ducts

Graphic Overrides This is where you can set the color, line weight, and line pattern of each system for display purposes.

Material Materials are primarily for rendering purposes, but they can be used for material takeoffs or as another method of filtering. However, applying a material to a system applies that material to the whole system, ducts, air terminals, and air handling equipment.

Calculations You can set the calculations to All, Flow Only, or None. The more calculations allowed, the more powerful Revit 2015 and specifically the systems in it can be; however, this comes at a cost to performance. Which setting is used here is dependent on the project itself and the level of in-model calculations required. Remember that this setting can be changed at any time and it is probably best that it be set to None or at least Flow Only except for the specific times that all calculations are needed.

System Classification The System Classification value is the original, or parent, system. This value, which is read-only, shows which type of connectors the system can connect into and is decided by the original system (Exhaust, Return, or Supply) that was duplicated to create the system you are working with.

Type Image New to families in Revit MEP 2015, this provides the ability to set an image file that can then be used in schedules. For duct systems, this should probably be an image of the parent equipment for the system, that is, the VAV or air handler.

Abbreviation This bit of data can be very useful because it can be tagged. Also, an abbreviation is neater on the drawing than using the entire system name.

Type Comments As with comments, type comments can be useful for filtering or tagging that may be different for different systems in the project.

URL Used to provide an external link for more information on the system.

Description Used for descriptive information about the system.

Rise / Drop Symbol Here you can specify which rise / drop symbol, from a fixed list of available symbols, to use for each system. Generally, supply air would be a cross and exhaust air would be a slash. Project or company standards will determine whether the symbols should be filled or if different symbols are to be used.

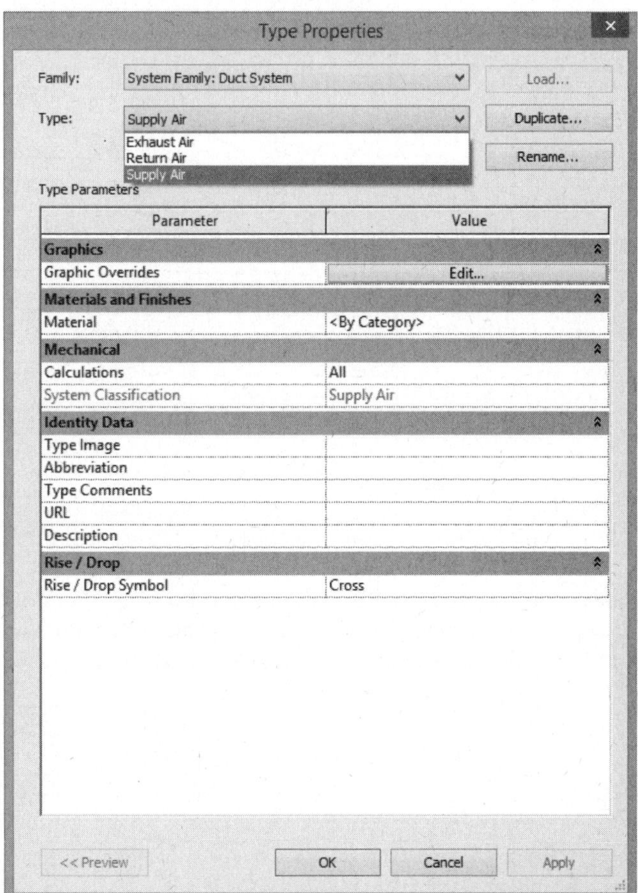

FIGURE 9.7 Duct Systems dialog box

Understanding Duct Connectors

Duct connectors in Revit MEP allow the user to connect ductwork to a family that may represent an air terminal, fan, VAV box, air handler, or chilled beam. Duct connections can also be used as a source for boiler combustion air and flues. There are many applications of duct connections beyond a simple supply air diffuser. In this section, you will learn how to set up many kinds of systems using duct connections.

You need a good understanding of the parameters besides height and width (or radius) needed in the connectors before you can set up air systems. There are 14 parameters associated with a duct connector when its system classification is not set to Fitting. Not all of the 14 are active all the time (see Figure 9.8). The standard Supply Diffuser that comes with the Revit install can be a good place to examine connectors.

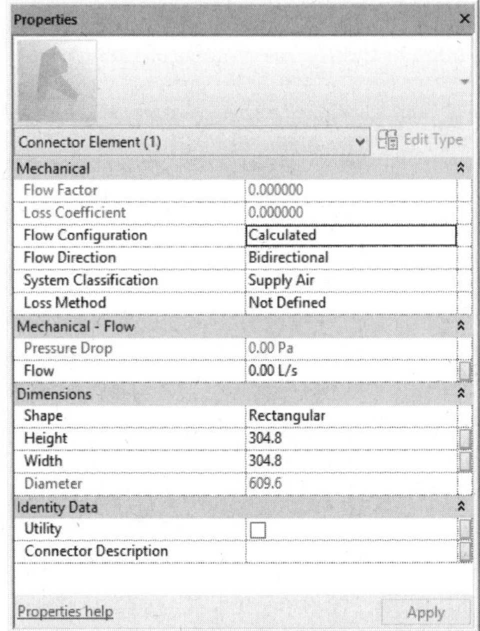

FIGURE 9.8
Parameters for duct connection

If the connector system classification is set to Fitting, the connector has only six parameters. Revit MEP has several system classifications available for duct connections that facilitate system creation and view filters within a project (see Figure 9.9).

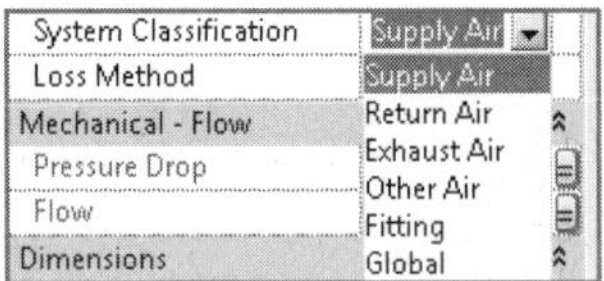

FIGURE 9.9
System classifications for duct connections

Starting at the top, here is an explanation of each duct connector parameter shown in Figure 9.8:

Flow Factor This parameter determines the percentage of the system flow that will be seen by the connector. It is available only when Flow Configuration is set to System. It is useful when using multiple devices, each of which is sized for part of the load.

Loss Coefficient Available only when Loss Method is set to Coefficient, this parameter is used in conjunction with the Flow parameter to determine the pressure drop.

Flow Configuration This parameter determines how the connector flow will be calculated.

Calculated This setting calculates airflow downstream of the connection and sets the Flow parameter to the sum of those flows. For example, a VAV Supply Air Outlet connector set to Calculated will add up all of the supply air requirements for connected supply air terminals that are using supply air connectors with a Preset flow configuration. In other words, child families using Preset will pass along their needs to the parent connector using a flow configuration of Calculated.

Preset No calculation is needed, and airflow is set to the Flow parameter. This can be used for the inlet connector of VAV boxes.

System This setting is similar to Calculated, but the flow factor comes into play. It is best used for splitting the total system airflow between air handlers.

Flow Direction Flow Direction can be set to In, Out, or Bidirectional. This setting refers to the direction that air is moving relative to the connector, not the direction in which the air is flowing. For example, a supply air diffuser should be set to In because the air is flowing from the connected duct *into* the connector of the diffuser. An exhaust grille would be set to Out because air is coming *out* of the connector and entering the system.

System Classification Here, the most appropriate system classification is chosen for the application. Supply Air, Return Air, and Exhaust Air are all pretty self-explanatory, but they also have other uses.

Supply Air Air that is to be supplied to a space can also be used to model outside air, which is also known as air to be delivered to a space or air handler. Supply air would usually also be used for outside air.

Return Air Air that is being returned from the space back into the system is called *return air.* It can also be used for relief air or transfer air, but exhaust can also make a good candidate.

Exhaust Air Air that is destined to leave the space as well as the system is called *exhaust air.* There can be different types of exhaust air that you may want different systems for, such as, for example, Kitchen Exhaust, Toilet Exhaust, General Exhaust, and Smoke Exhaust.

Other Air Other Air seems like a logical candidate for relief air or outside air; however, systems cannot be made with Other Air. In addition, if you want to utilize CFM calculations, you shouldn't use the Other Air system because it doesn't do those calculations.

Fitting The Fitting system type is merely a pass-through connection; there is no effect on the airflow or definition of the system. However, fittings do affect pressure-loss calculations.

Global Global connections can be either Supply Air, Return Air, or Exhaust Air. When you are creating the system in the project, you will be given the opportunity to select the type of system it should be. Fans are a good example of equipment that may use global connections because the same type of fan may be used in multiple system types.

Loss Method Not Defined, Coefficient, and Specific Loss are the options here, and Coefficient and Specific Loss each activate another parameter. Specific Loss should be used where the loss is known from a catalog or cut sheet. The pressure loss is taken literally as the entered value for Pressure Drop.

GLOBAL SYSTEMS

Global systems are perhaps the most flexible option under the System Classification parameter. However, they can also be the most dangerous for users not familiar with the way Revit airflow data works or those who are simply overlooking it. When System Classification is set to Global, users will be given the opportunity to choose the system type in the project. Remember that we can't create or delete any system classifications that Revit comes with. But we can create new system types (duct systems). Essentially, the System Type pull-down will list all duct systems from the project. Just keep in mind that you will not be able to change the Flow Direction setting, and therefore you must be aware of the flow orientation. For example, a fan that is being used for exhaust will need to face the opposite direction than if it is being used for supply.

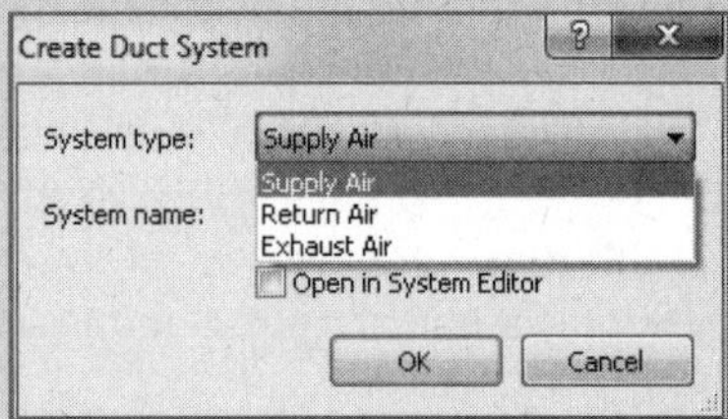

Pressure Drop This can be entered as a static value or linked to a family parameter. Units are handled in the Project Units dialog box (Manage ➤ Project Units). Pressure Drop becomes active when Loss Method is set to Specific Loss. It can be linked to a family or shared parameter.

Flow Values for the flow associated with the connector are dependent on flow configuration. It can be linked to a family or shared parameter.

Shape The Shape settings of Rectangular, Oval, and Round determine which dimension parameters are active and the shape of the duct that will connect to the connector.

Height Height is simply a dimension of the connector. It can be linked to a family or shared parameter.

Width Width is simply a dimension of the connector. It can be linked to a family or shared parameter.

Radius/Diameter Radius/Diameter is similar to Height and Width. Previous to Revit 2014, you could only use the radius and not the diameter when linking to a family or shared parameter; however, since Revit 2014, under Dimensions in the Family Properties tab, there is an option to use either Diameter or Radius for the round duct connector. Whichever of these options are chosen, it should be made standard across the project to avoid confusion.

Utility This indicates whether the connector is exported as a site utility connection or points to an Autodesk Exchange file (ADSK) for sharing with AutoCAD® Civil 3D®. It can be linked to a family or shared parameter.

Connector Description The option to assign a name to connectors shows up primarily when using the Connect To feature. It also appears when connection points are in the same vertical plane. It is a good practice to give your connectors a description so that they can be easily identified in families with multiple connectors. It can be linked to a family or shared parameter.

Creating Mechanical Systems

Now that you have reviewed the parameters of the mechanical systems that exist, you will learn how to apply them in a simple exercise:

1. Open the `Chapter9_Dataset.rvt` file found at `www.sybex.com/go/masteringrevitmep2015`.
2. Download the `Supply Diffuser - Perforated - Round Neck - Ceiling Mounted.rfa` family. Next, choose Insert ➢ Load Family, browse to where you have downloaded the family, and click Open (see Figure 9.10).

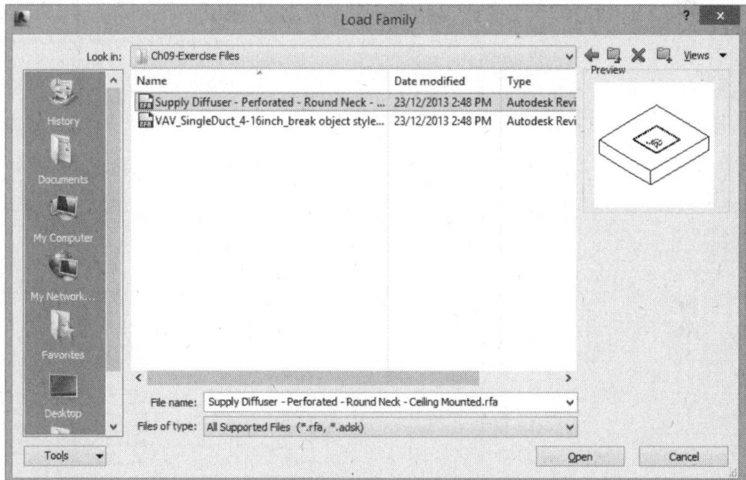

FIGURE 9.10
Selecting a supply diffuser

3. Now download `VAV_SingleDuct_4-16inch_break object styles.rfa` located at `www.sybex.com/go/masteringrevitmep2015`, and insert it into your model (see Figure 9.11).
4. After downloading all of your components, you will want to place some diffusers onto the ceiling shown in the 1 – Ceiling Mech view. Because this family is a face-based family, it will automatically attach to the ceiling surface. Make sure to select Place On Face located under Modify | Place Air Terminal. If you don't, the diffusers will try to attach to the wall, or any vertical surface for that matter (see Figure 9.12).

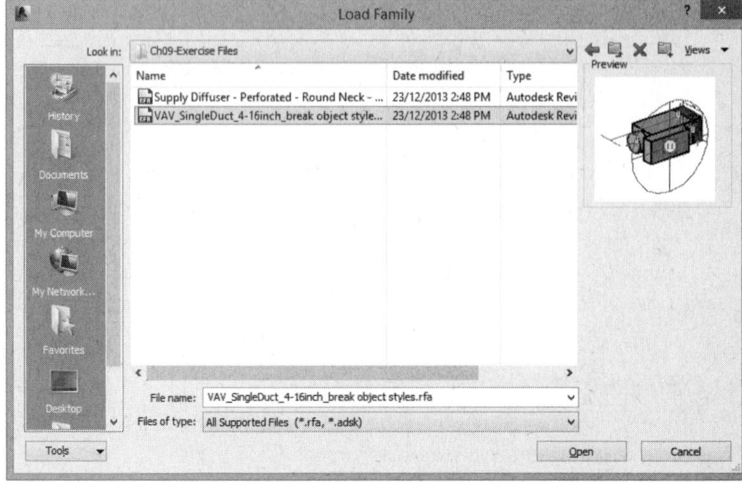

FIGURE 9.11 Loading a VAV single-duct family

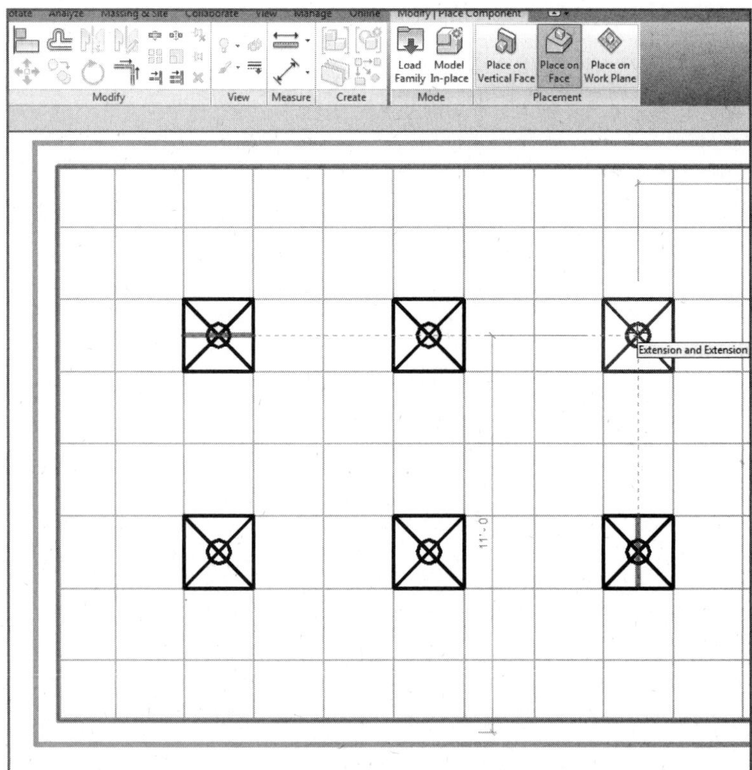

FIGURE 9.12 Placing the ceiling diffuser into the ceiling grid

5. Once you have placed the diffusers, use the Mechanical Equipment tool on the Home tab to place the downloaded VAV box above the ceiling at an elevation of 10′-0″ (3 m). You can adjust the elevation by changing the elevation offset in the properties (see Figure 9.13). Set the elevation prior to placement if you are in a reflected ceiling plan view or you may not see the VAV box when it is placed.

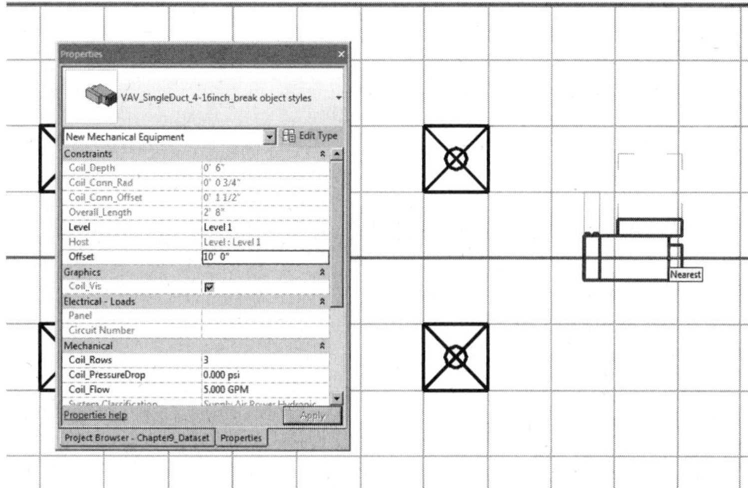

FIGURE 9.13
Changing the elevation offset for the correct elevation of equipment

6. Now that the VAV box and diffusers are in place, make them part of a system. Select any diffuser and click the Duct button on the Create Systems panel of the Modify | Air Terminals contextual tab (see Figure 9.14). This activates a dialog box, shown in Figure 9.15, that allows you to choose the system type and to assign a name to the system. You can assign a system name if you wish, or you can leave it as the default name that Revit supplies. Note that, as these are supply diffusers, you can choose only system types that are also of a supply system category.

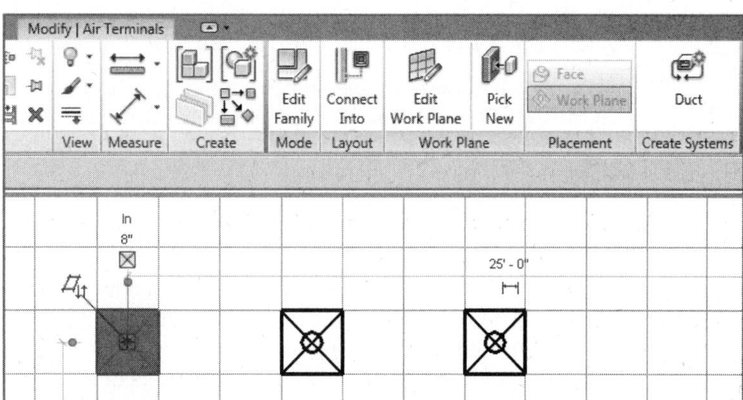

FIGURE 9.14
Creating a supply duct system

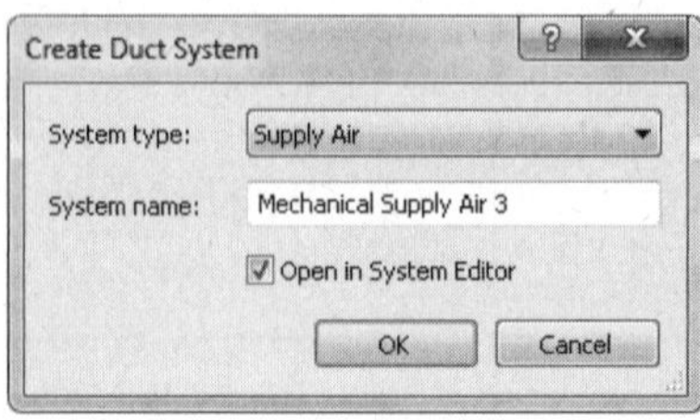

FIGURE 9.15
Create Duct System dialog box

7. Once you have made the system by clicking OK, the Modify | Duct Systems contextual tab is active on the ribbon. Click the Edit System button. Confirm that Add To System is selected, and select the other air terminals (see Figure 9.16).

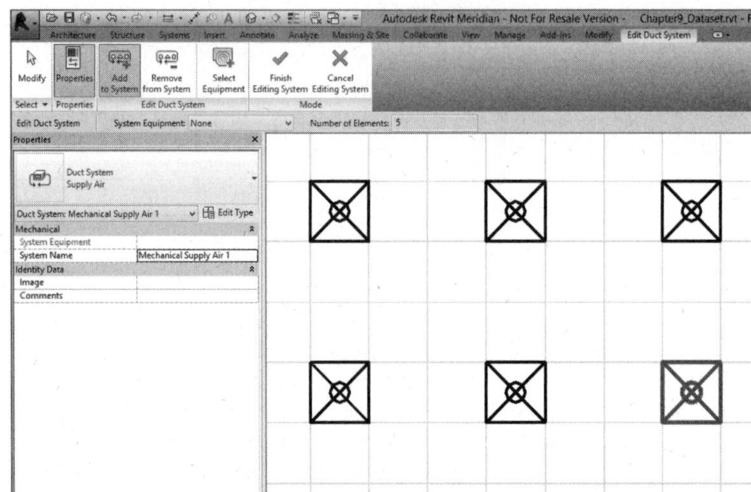

FIGURE 9.16
Editing supply duct systems

8. Now click the Select Equipment button, and select the VAV box to be the equipment for your system. Click the Finish Editing System button to complete the system.

9. With the system created, open the System Browser and select any of the diffusers. Notice that this selection also selects the appropriate diffuser in the drawing area. Now select the VAV as indicated in Figure 9.17. Notice that this also highlights Unassigned because the inlet to the VAV is not yet assigned to a system.

Now that you have created your system, you can route your ductwork and it will take on the characteristics of the system parameters you set up. Understanding how to make mechanical systems enables you to create any duct system you may need for your design. For further instruction on how to route ductwork, refer to Chapter 10, "Mechanical Systems and Ductwork."

You also have the ability to automatically create systems on the go as you route your ductwork/pipework. This means you don't need to create systems manually as in the previous exercise. Simply connect the supply duct to any diffuser and watch it become part of that system. But disconnecting the duct that "pushed" the system to the diffuser will not remove the diffuser from the system. Therefore, it will still be necessary to understand how to create and manage systems manually.

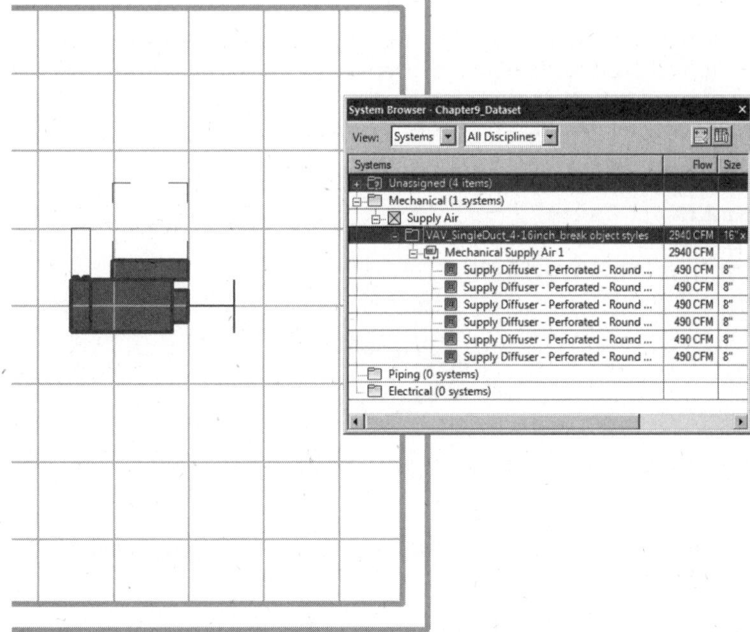

FIGURE 9.17
Selecting in the System Browser

You can remove elements from a system using the Remove From System button when editing the system. You can also do this by right-clicking the connector symbol and selecting Remove From System. You can use either method only if the element is not physically connected to any other piece of the system (including ductwork). Once all elements have been removed from the system, the system itself will be removed from the Revit file. You can also delete the system from the System Browser. This will reset all elements in the system to Unassigned and set the ductwork to Undefined.

Setting Up Piping Systems

Mechanical piping benefits greatly from systems in Revit MEP 2015. Graphics, annotations, flow, and pressure loss can all be handled with a small amount of setup in your project template. Pipe systems also allow filters to apply to all components in the system, including the fittings. Also, the System Browser acts as a graphical pointer to the designer with regard to how objects are connected in systems; it also provides benefits in terms of how the actual systems perform.

The first of these benefits is the ability to predefine the system in which pipes (and ducts) are created, allowing layouts to be designed without the need to set up systems in the first place. This allows the designer to create hot-water (HW) and cold-water (CW) pipe runs with graphical filters already in place to display the different systems being created.

Second, this allows for different systems to be interconnected. In order to do this, you just need to specify which system you wish to use before placing each piece of pipe.

Figure 9.18 displays sanitary and vent pipe systems with the system Sanitary 2 selected. When you are working with multiple systems that are connected, a fitting, an accessory, or equipment is needed between the two pipes or ducts for the separation of the systems to work. When the system change occurs at an elbow or tee, all is good. However, when you want to change the system but continue the pipe/duct in the same direction as the original one, you need to use the Split tool to insert a coupling fitting so you can have two systems. Even though everything seems to work visually when you have multiple systems connected in such a way, it is only for graphical purposes. The reality is that the ducts/pipes will lose all the calculations such as flow, pressure drop, and so forth.

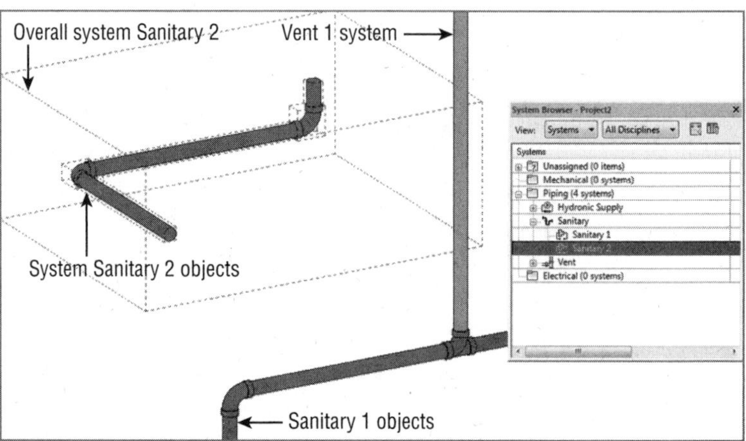

FIGURE 9.18
Dual-pipe systems

As the design progresses, systems may need to be merged with these new *systemless* systems. All the user has to do is connect the two systems. Figure 9.19 shows that after the two sanitary systems are joined, they effectively become one system with no further interaction required.

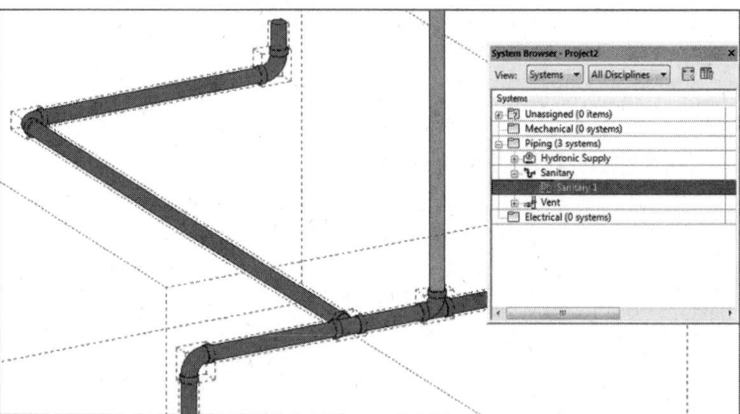

FIGURE 9.19
Merged systems

Understanding Pipe Connectors

Parameters required for piping connectors are similar to the parameters for air systems such as Flow Factor, Calculated, Preset, Flow Direction, and so on. The available pipe system types are as follows:

Hydronic Supply This pipe system can also be used for chilled-water supply, cold-water supply, steam, hot-water supply, and process-piping supply.

Hydronic Return This pipe system can also be used for chilled-water return, cold-water return, steam condensate, hot-water return, and process-piping return.

Sanitary This pipe system can also be used for grease waste, oil waste, storm drainage, acid waste, contamination drainage, and condensate drainage.

Vent This pipe system can be used for sanitary vent or any fume systems.

Domestic Hot Water This pipe system can also be used for hot-water systems such as 140-degree (60°C), 110-degree (43°C), and tempered water.

Domestic Cold Water This pipe system can also be used for filtered water, deionized water, and chilled water for remote drinking fountains.

Other This pipe system can be one of the most utilized if you have a large piping project. This can be used for medical gas piping, vent piping, liquid propane piping, natural gas piping, and air piping, as long as they don't require flow or pressure calculations.

Fire Protection This can be used for the building sprinkler piping, or it can be used for the utility fire protection coming into your building to connect the base of your fire-protection riser.

Wet Fire Protection This pipe system type normally is used for the layout of the piping from the riser to the sprinkler head.

Dry Fire Protection This pipe system is used for layout from the fire riser to the sprinkler head or standpipe to keep the system from freezing.

Pre-Action This pipe system can also be used for a deluge system.

Fire Protection Other This pipe system can be used for glycol antifreeze systems and for chemical suppression systems.

Creating Pipe Systems

There are several things to consider when setting up the components of a pipe system. You will need to define pipe types, load some fitting families, and create the necessary systems from the Project Browser by duplicating systems out of the box.

From the pipe type properties, you can assign routing preferences by size, as shown in Figure 9.20. For example, you may want to use a certain type of fitting only when routing pipes smaller than 6″ (150 mm) and another type of fitting for pipes larger than 6″ (150 mm). You may even want to choose different pipe segments (and therefore different materials) according to size, as shown in Figure 9.21. The pipe types should all reflect real-world values and the company standards and specifications. Even if you are not using Revit to size or lay out pipe automatically, not setting up the appropriate pipe types can cause headaches down the road because the Routing Preferences values still control which pipe fittings to use even if you are modeling the pipe manually. Pipe types should not be left at Standard and PVC. Those hardly cover the necessary piping systems that a building requires, and there will be fighting over what fittings should be standard and what materials should be used. Mechanical piping and plumbing piping should have their own pipe types. Even if exactly the same materials and fittings are being used, changes may arise, and splitting out pipe types late in a project will undoubtedly eat up a lot of time. This is one area of Revit MEP that enables you to have as many types as you want, so take advantage of it.

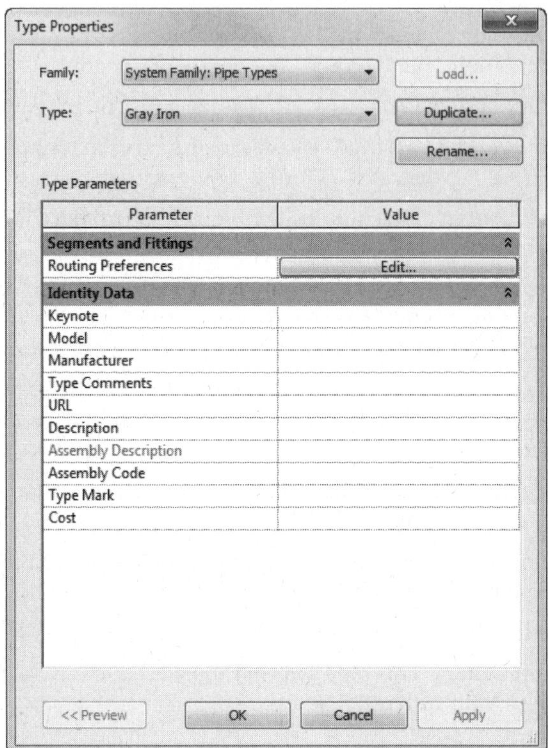

FIGURE 9.20 Pipe type properties

Pipe segments and sizes are set up in the Mechanical Settings dialog box, shown in Figure 9.22. All of these settings should also be determined by using company standards and specifications and created using industry standards. It may seem tedious to set up, but if the inside diameter of a 6″ (150 mm) hot-water pipe is not correct, and you are using a lot of it, your pipe volume calculations can be skewed.

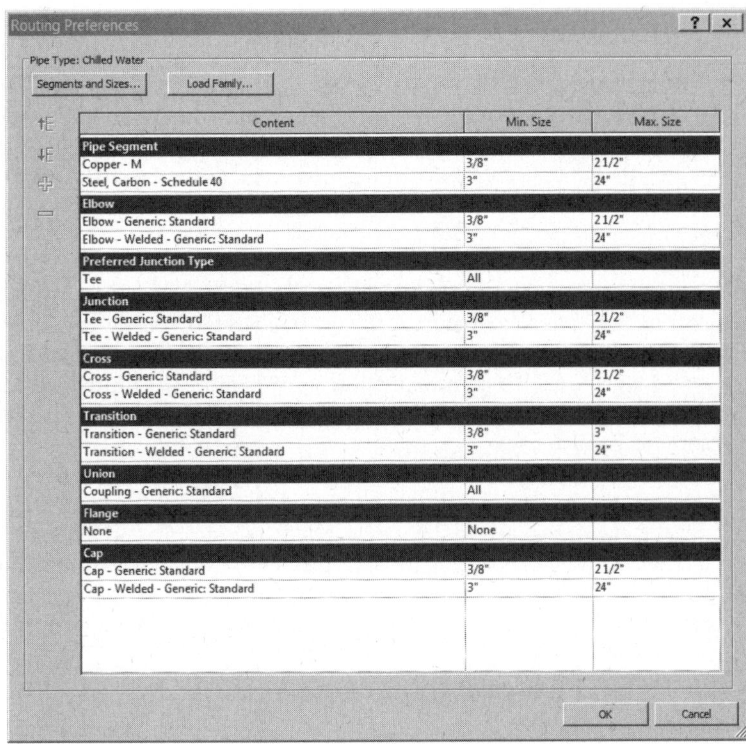

FIGURE 9.21 Routing preferences

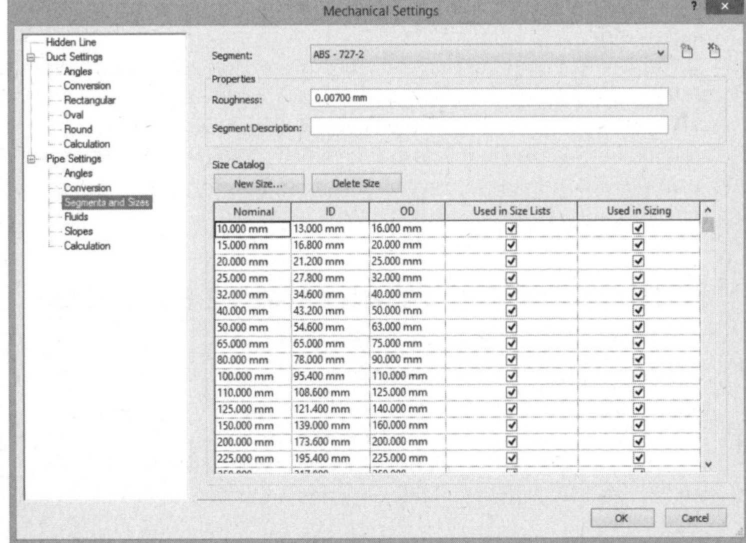

FIGURE 9.22 Pipe sizes

USED IN SIZE LISTS VS. USED IN SIZING

In the Mechanical Settings dialog box, Used In Size Lists means that the drop-down list for available sizes will contain this pipe size; this drop-down list can be easily accessed while routing or modifying pipe in the Generate Layout tool. Think of the Used In Sizing option as granting Revit permission to use a particular pipe size when using the duct- or pipe-sizing utility. If neither is selected, the size will not be available to the user.

Fittings should be assigned after sizes and materials for a couple of reasons. First, the connection type needs to match. A solvent-welded PVC fitting and a flanged steel fitting are vastly different. Second, the fittings need to be defined at all the available sizes for that type of pipe; if it goes down to 3⁄8″ (10 mm) or up to 36″ (900 mm), the fitting needs to accommodate. Fittings are specific to the type of system, which is another reason to separate pipe types for plumbing and mechanical uses.

Hydronic systems have value even if the equipment is not piped together. Terminal box reheat coils are a good example because details generally cover their final connections. By simply adding all the terminal boxes to a hydronic supply and hydronic return system, you can see the total flows for the entire model. You can use this flow summation to ensure that systems are adding up to what you expect and to compare flows between systems. That's just another way of using the benefits of systems during early design, when not everything is connected yet.

Creating Fire-protection Systems

Fire-protection systems in Revit MEP are a sort of hybrid between air systems and hydronic systems. Sprinklers, from a system standpoint, are similar to air terminals. Sprinklers are designed to distribute a fluid evenly over a given area, with pressure as the driving force of distribution. In the case of fire protection, water is the fluid, and the fire pump or city connection provides the pressure.

The key to a good, manageable fire-protection system is the families. Decide what type of system you will be using, and make sure appropriate families are developed before you or other users start laying out components. Revit does have the ability to load a family in the place of another, but that tends to cause issues with system connections, pipe connections, and hosting. Sprinklers, standpipes, hose cabinets, and fire pumps may have to be created for the systems to work properly.

Setting Display Properties of Systems

Pipe systems are similar to duct systems, but they do have more parameters. These can be found in the piping systems Type Properties dialog box, as shown in Figure 9.23, accessed from the Families section of the Project Browser under Piping Systems.

The parameters for pipe systems start the same as for duct systems: you have Graphic Overrides, Material, Calculations, and System Classification. Then we get some specialized values. Which values are available depends on the system category.

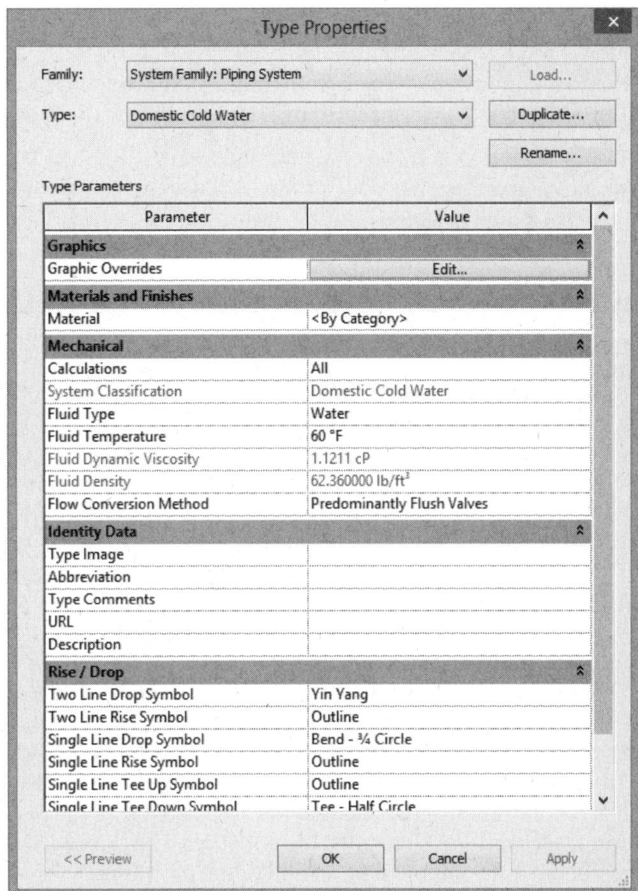

FIGURE 9.23
Piping Systems

Fluid Type, Fluid Temperature, Fluid Dynamic Viscosity, and Fluid Density are available only in Domestic Hot Water, Domestic Cold Water, Hydronic Flow, and Hydronic Return systems:

Fluid Type Most of the time this will be water, and Revit MEP 2015 provides choices for Propylene Glycol and Ethylene Glycol; however, you can create other fluid types in Mechanical Settings for refrigerant systems or medical gases or any other fluid type you require.

Fluid Temperature This is where you specify the temperature of the fluid.

Fluid Dynamic Viscosity This value is determined by the fluid type and temperature previously selected. It does require that the correct values are entered when setting up fluids other than water.

Fluid Density This value is determined by the fluid type and temperature previously selected. It does require that the correct values are entered when setting up fluids other than water.

Flow Conversion Method is available only in domestic cold and hot-water systems:

Flow Conversion Method Here you have a choice of Predominantly Flush Valves or Predominantly Tank Valves. Your choice here will determine how Revit converts a Fixture Unit value to a Flow Rate for pipe sizing and pressure calculations.

The identity data is the same as for duct systems and the Rise/Drop parameters are similar to the parameters for duct systems but include both single line and double line options and Tee Up and Tee Down options.

Understanding Child and Parent Relationships in Revit Systems

To fully understand systems, there is one more thing you should know about: the child-to-parent relationships they must form in order to work properly. This knowledge is especially critical when you are building families. Without understanding the child and parent and their purposes, you likely will have problems with system flow and any sort of calculations using Revit.

Figure 9.24 shows an example of a supply air system and its child and parent relationships that must be formed.

There is a pattern in the child and parent formation. The system should always start with a child (for example, an air terminal) and end with a parent (for example, an air handling unit). The child will be a connector whose flow configuration is set to Preset. A flow configuration set to Calculate will be a parent. A flow configuration set to System can be a parent or an intermediary. For example, a chilled water system with multiple chillers will need system connectors to be able to divide the flow between them, and they will still be the parent. Pumps and fans use system connectors because they will split the flow into two or more paths, each with a pump/fan, and then recombine it into the single path before it continues on to the parent.

It is not the families themselves that are the child or the parent but rather the connectors within those families. Generally, the outlet of a VAV box will be the parent to the diffusers it is supplying, but the inlet will be a child of the primary air system. A heat exchanger would have inlets and outlets of both child and parent type. This can be confusing for the user and is a good reason to make sure the Connector Description parameter is filled out.

Flow direction is also important to enable systems to function correctly. The Flow Direction parameter for the connector of a supply air diffuser should be set to In (as the air is flowing from the system into the connector), and as such the parent for that system needs to have Flow Direction set to Out. If these are not set this way, the system cannot calculate the airflows because there is not a definite direction of flow along the duct.

Using System Filters

Mechanical engineering documents describe complex systems and design intentions. It is easy to overwhelm the person trying to understand those intentions. Revit filters offer us additional control over the visibility of certain elements in views as well as the appearance those elements will have (if you chose filters to control color and linetype). Without filters, we wouldn't be able to create sheets for the various subdisciplines—separating medical gas systems from plumbing and mechanical, for example. Filters help us create high-quality documentation as well as provide a better way to examine our design and improve the coordination of our projects.

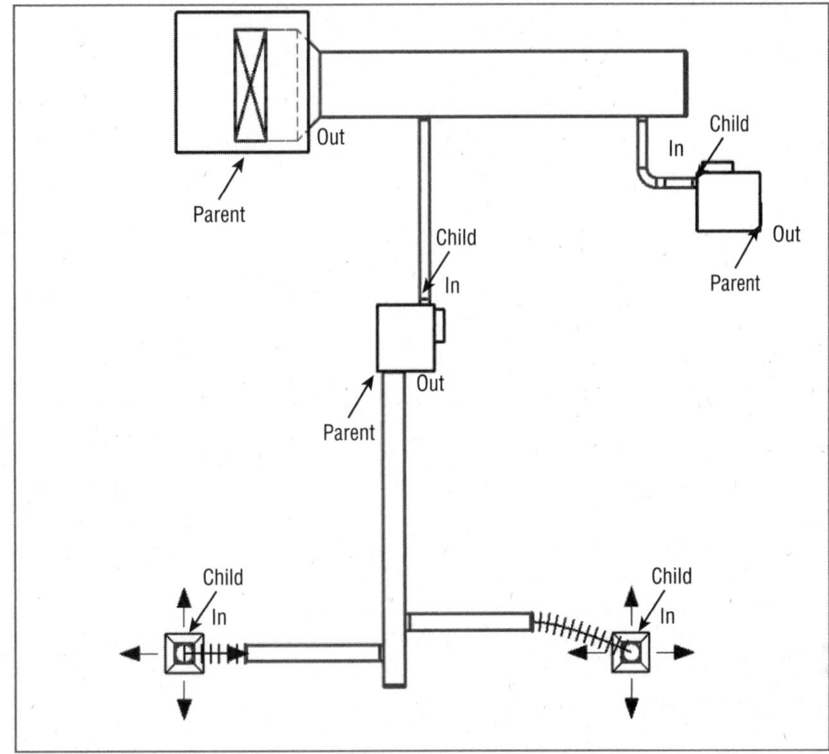

FIGURE 9.24 Children and parents in systems

To set up system filters, you can open any model view (plan, ceiling, elevation, section, and 3D are model views; nonmodel views are drafting views and legends) and type **VG** to access the Visibility/Graphic Overrides dialog box. Next, select the Filters tab and click Edit/New to open the Filters dialog box, shown in Figure 9.25. Notice that in this dialog box several filter names are in Revit by default. Remember that any changes made to filters after clicking Edit/New are global changes to the entire project, so adjusting filters should be left to the more experienced Revit users.

When you select any of the existing filters, certain categories have been selected. These are the categories for the items you want to have affected by the filter. Next, notice under Filter Rules that, by default, System Classification is selected. Because of the large number of filters typically created for a project, you should change the Filter By setting from System Classification to System Abbreviation. This helps identify and separate your systems properly.

If you try to use the default System Classification, soon you will find its limitations. The mechanical supply air system rule is set to System Classification to contain supply. This may not be a problem for small projects, but for larger ones that could have multiple supply systems, it won't work. This limitation is especially obvious when you have piping systems with numerous supply and return systems and distinguishing between all of them is critical. System Abbreviation has the necessary flexibility to allow for distinguishing hundreds of systems.

To create new system filters, the easiest method is to select an existing system filter and then click the Duplicate icon. After the system filter is duplicated, make sure the proper category elements are selected and then rename the filter rule to the name by which you want to filter.

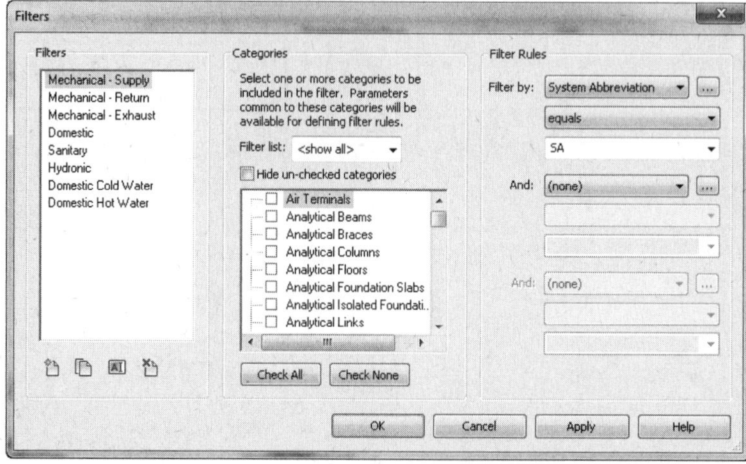

FIGURE 9.25
System filters

When you are finished creating new filters or modifying existing ones, click OK to get back to the Filters tab in the Visibility/Graphic Overrides dialog box. Click Add. This brings up the filters that you have created, so select those that are needed in the current view of your project. After the filters are loaded, you can turn the filters on and off and adjust line weights, colors, and patterns, as shown in Figure 9.26. You can apply those filters to other views by opening a view, clicking the View tab on the ribbon, and then selecting Visibility/Graphics. Next, select the Filters tab.

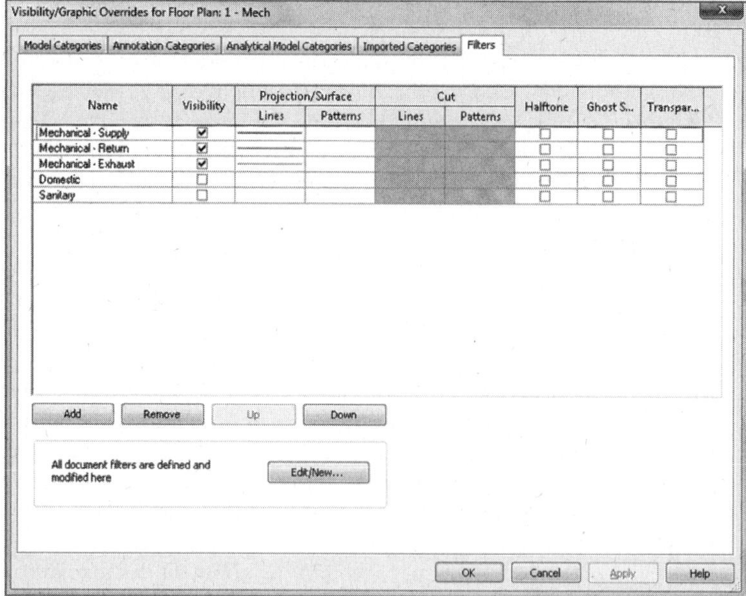

FIGURE 9.26
View filters

Mastering filter options enables you to create your models with the standards that your office has developed over years of producing CAD drawings.

Filters Save the Day

James has been working on a medical facility in Revit MEP 2015. When he completes the project, he submits it to the state review board to ensure that the plans meet the state requirements for standards of care for health facilities. The only comments from the reviewer are that she would like to have the different duct systems shown with different patterns to help differentiate the systems more clearly. To accomplish this, James uses system filters to distinguish the duct systems. The following steps show how he accomplishes his goal:

1. After using the shortcut VG to open the Visibility/Graphic Overrides dialog box, he chooses Filters ➤ New/Edit. Next, he duplicates Mechanical – Supply (twice) and renames the new filters **Mechanical Supply Air 1** and **Mechanical Supply Air 2**, as shown here.

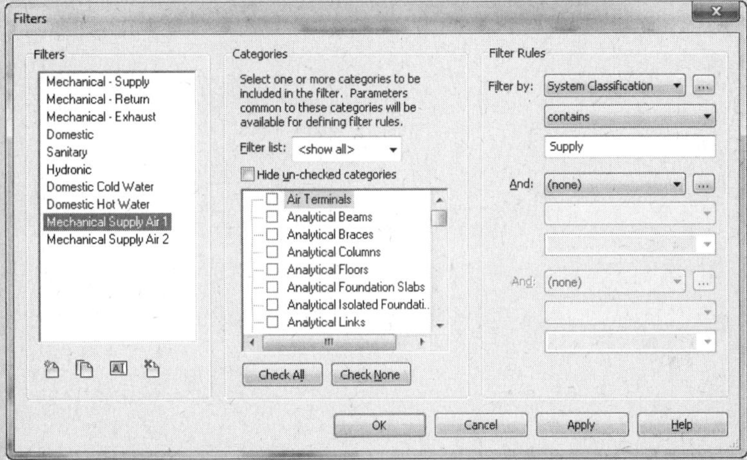

2. He changes the filter rules from System Classification to System Name and changes the Contains statement to **Mechanical Supply Air 1**. He repeats the process for Mechanical Supply Air 2.

continues

(continued)

Filters

Filters

Mechanical - Supply
Mechanical - Return
Mechanical - Exhaust
Domestic
Sanitary
Hydronic
Domestic Cold Water
Domestic Hot Water
Mechanical Supply Air 1
Mechanical Supply Air 2

Categories

Select one or more categories to be included in the filter. Parameters common to these categories will be available for defining filter rules.

Filter list: <show all>

Hide un-checked categories

Air Terminals
Analytical Beams
Analytical Braces
Analytical Columns
Analytical Floors
Analytical Foundation Slabs
Analytical Isolated Foundati...
Analytical Links

Check All
Check None

Filter Rules

Filter by: System Name
contains
Mechanical Supply Air 1
And: (none)
And: (none)

OK
Cancel
Apply
Help

3. After creating his filters, he adds them to his views and then alters the view overrides to help show the difference between the two supply systems.

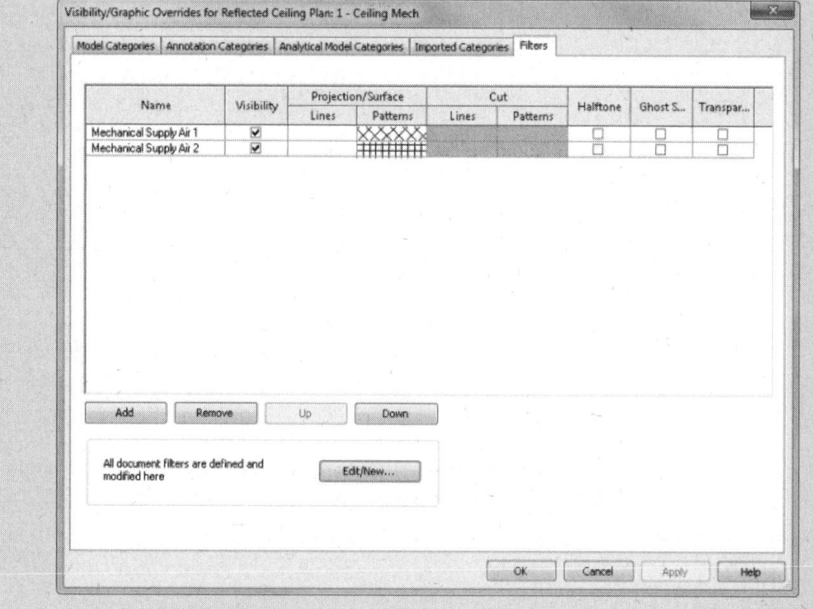

The Bottom Line

Create and manage air systems. Knowing how to manage air systems can help productivity by organizing systems so that items can be easily interrogated to verify that the systems are properly connected.

Master It True or false: Outside air cannot be modeled because there is no default system type from which to select.

Create and manage piping systems. By understanding how to change and manage piping systems, the user can create and maintain different systems effectively.

Master It A designer has been asked by an engineer to create a Grease Waste system to accommodate a new kitchen that has been added to a project. What would be the quickest way to accomplish this feat?

Configure duct connectors. Everyone who needs to create Revit MEP families should know how to properly configure pipe, duct, conduit, and cable tray connectors in the Family Editor.

Master It In order to proceed with the design, a mechanical engineer needs to create a custom air handling unit family that is not available from the manufacturer. One of the challenges is that he has to configure the duct connectors for supply, return, and outside air. What are the proper settings for those connectors?

Hint: We already mentioned the proper configuration of the supply and return air systems in this chapter. The only oddball here is the outside air. This is the same kind of decision that will have to be made when creating systems such as fuel, medical gas, and so on that do not exist as a system classification in Revit.

Chapter 10

Mechanical Systems and Ductwork

Ductwork, like pipework, is a system family through which the Autodesk® Revit® MEP platform can calculate airflow rates and pressure drops on any correctly defined system. Ductwork also provides the graphics for the traditional "drawn" documentation and the variety of ways this can be represented on a drawing sheet at different stages of a project, regardless of whether the duct is presented as a *single line* at concept design or as a fully coordinated *double line* for a construction issue.

The three main types of ducts are rectangular, round, and oval. They are the basis for your design and documentation. There are two ways of using ducts, either with the Duct tool or the Placeholder Duct tool. Placeholders allow the designer to rough in layouts in single-line mode.

Although at first glance this seems similar to a view that is set to a coarse level of detail, the placeholders display *only* a single line, regardless of the level of detail that is set. In addition, placeholders do not create fittings when a duct run is drawn, although they do show a symbolic representation where rises/drops occur. However, they still have the use of all the design tools that an engineer requires, allowing the duct to be sized based on airflow, elevation, and so on. All these duct types, whether placeholder or normal, connect to air terminals and a variety of mechanical equipment. They also host duct fittings and accessories. By using the fittings and accessories available with the standard installation, the user can create supply, return, and exhaust systems with very little additional thought.

During your implementation, however, you should also consider the benefits of creating additional duct types that suit the way you work and your company's standards.

In this chapter, you will learn to do the following:

- Distinguish between hosted and level-hosted components
- Convert placeholder ducts into ducts with fittings
- Use the various duct routing options
- Adjust duct fittings

Air Distribution Components

Air distribution components come in many shapes and sizes. Depending on the design, they can be mounted in a variety of ways:

- Diffusers in a ceiling
- Duct-mounted sidewall diffusers
- Wall mounted

- Floor diffusers
- Suspended

In each of these instances, the designer must decide whether to use hosted components (and if so, which type of hosting) or whether to just host to the active level/work plane. There are several ways of placing these objects, and some of these may be conflicting.

An example of this is an installation that has diffusers hosted in the ceiling as well as areas where the architect's design is for suspended fittings (see Figure 10.1). In this project, assume that there is an external architect and that the architectural model is being linked. This means straightaway that you cannot use ceiling-hosted air terminals. Although you can see the linked ceiling, Revit recognizes it only as a face. Because of this, the air terminals need to be created either as face-hosted families or families that are hosted to the level—that is, no physical hosting. Additionally, since Revit MEP 2014, there has been the ability to host an air terminal to a duct, regardless of how that particular family has been created. When placing a duct-hosted air terminal, click the Air Terminal On Duct button to access this feature.

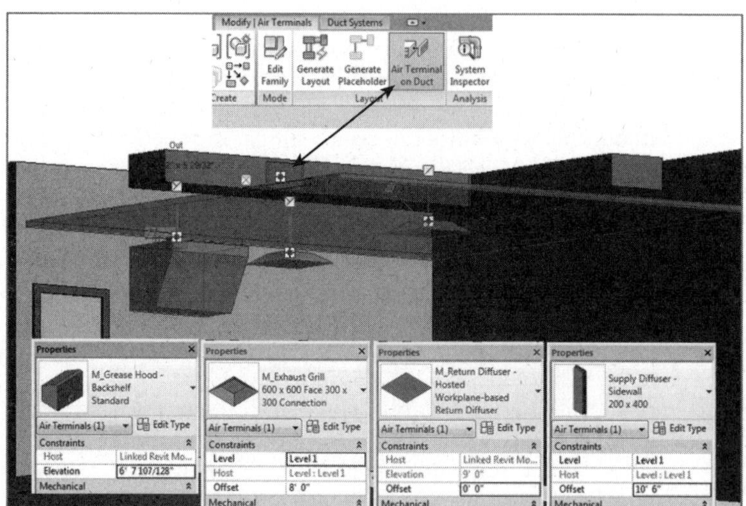

FIGURE 10.1 Diffuser hosting methods

The most important point here is that, after you commit to one type of family (hosted, level hosted, wall, and so on), you can exchange, for example, a ceiling-hosted air terminal only with a similarly hosted air terminal, not just those that are of the same category (see Figure 10.2).

FIGURE 10.2 Hosting error message

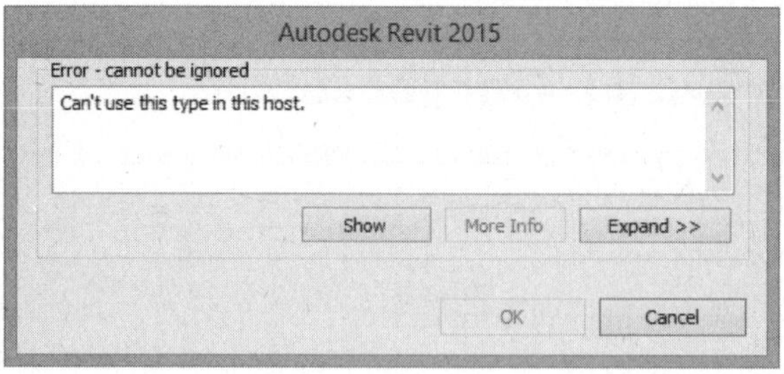

Autodesk Revit 2015

Error - cannot be ignored

Can't use this type in this host.

Show | More Info | Expand >>

OK | Cancel

The next problem is that the air terminals that are suspended are in fact the same type as those that are mounted within the ceiling tiles. The engineer wants to be able to schedule and filter them as one. How do you manage this?

The ability to copy/monitor air terminals (as well as lighting fixtures, mechanical equipment, and plumbing fixtures) means that the services engineers can monitor the locations of air terminals that the architect has placed because the architect is responsible for placing these objects. As with the other items that can be copied/monitored, the services designer can choose to copy the original family type from the linked file or "map" it to one of their own choosing. In Figure 10.3, you can see, however, that after the air terminals have been copied/monitored, regardless of the type of host association, this ceiling-hosted family has no host but is in the correct location specified by the architect.

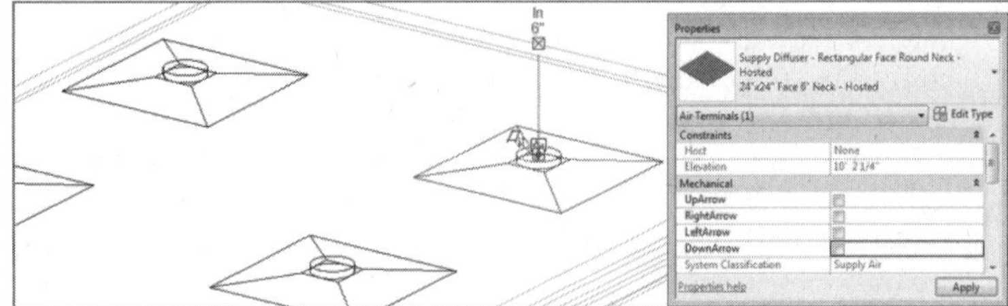

FIGURE 10.3
Copy/monitor level-hosting air terminals

CUSHION HEAD BOXES

A cushion head box is used as a connection to the air distribution components to assist in their performance and help in noise reduction. They can be built into the diffuser or can be supplied separately. So what is the best way to show them in the model? It may seem easier to create the diffuser family with the cushion head box included because then you won't have to add the cushion head box for each diffuser in the project. This is true. However, there are some variations to account for. Not every diffuser has a cushion head box; also, there could be multiple spigot connections to the box, and those connections—usually round for flexible duct connection—could be oval or rectangular, especially when low height is required or flexible ductwork not allowed.

The standard cushion head box may cover 90 percent or more of your project requirements, but having to create different diffuser families, or family types, for each cushion head type would be time consuming each time the diffuser family needs upgrading, and it would be confusing in the project both for selecting the correct family and when trying to create a diffuser schedule.

Whether as part of the diffuser family or separate, the spigot connection to the cushion head box can be sized automatically to your company standards or to manufacturer's requirements using an IF statement. For more information on using formulas and conditional statements, refer to Chapter 6, "Parameters." If the cushion head is built into the family, the connection will be sized as soon as you input the flow rate. If the cushion head is separate from the diffuser, then you must ensure that the diffuser is a part of a system and that the system calculations are set to Flow Only or All. Otherwise, the cushion head will not pick up the flow for the diffuser. Once your cushion heads are all in place and the sizes calculated, you can turn the calculations to None again.

Mechanical Equipment Components

Mechanical equipment comprises the components that make up the majority of large- to medium-size plant objects for the mechanical designer. From air conditioners (ACs) and air-handling units (AHUs) to air curtains and heat pumps, these all provide the geometry and parameters associated with HVAC design. As with all components, choosing the hosting type is important. A level-hosted object cannot be exchanged for a face-hosted or ceiling-hosted one.

Air Conditioning/Handling Units

The heart of the mechanical air system, the air-conditioning or air-handling units, can start life as generic "boxes" with intake and exhaust. Although basic in construction and with no manufacturer data attached, generic ACs/AHUs can have the same number of parameters as more detailed families. Similar in dimension and performance to generic ACs/AHUs, the concept box can be swapped out during the detail design period for a more detailed manufacturer or construction-issue family, or even for a set of families if the AC/AHU unit has been constructed from its manufacturer's component parts (see Figure 10.4). It is, however, entirely likely that the connectors in this generic unit will not be in the correct location when the more detailed manufacturer's family is loaded. This can mean some rework is necessary in order to produce a more accurate model.

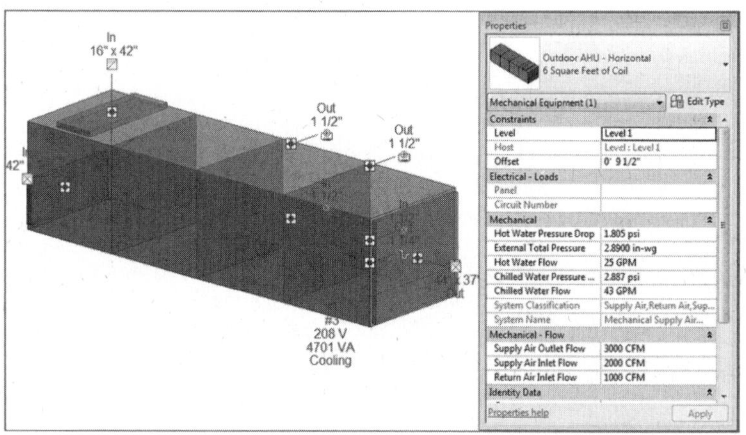

FIGURE 10.4 Basic AHU and parameters

The majority of large ACs/AHUs are generally placed on the level where they are inserted, while fan coil units (FCUs) or heat pumps are generally placed in a ceiling void, although they can also be in a plant room. The placement of these units can depend on whether the unit is mounted on rails, a plinth, or anti-vibration mounts and whether these mounting devices are part of the AC/AHU family (see Figure 10.5).

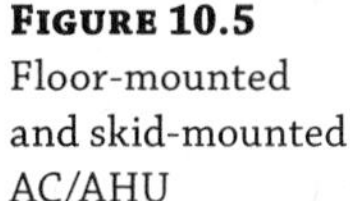

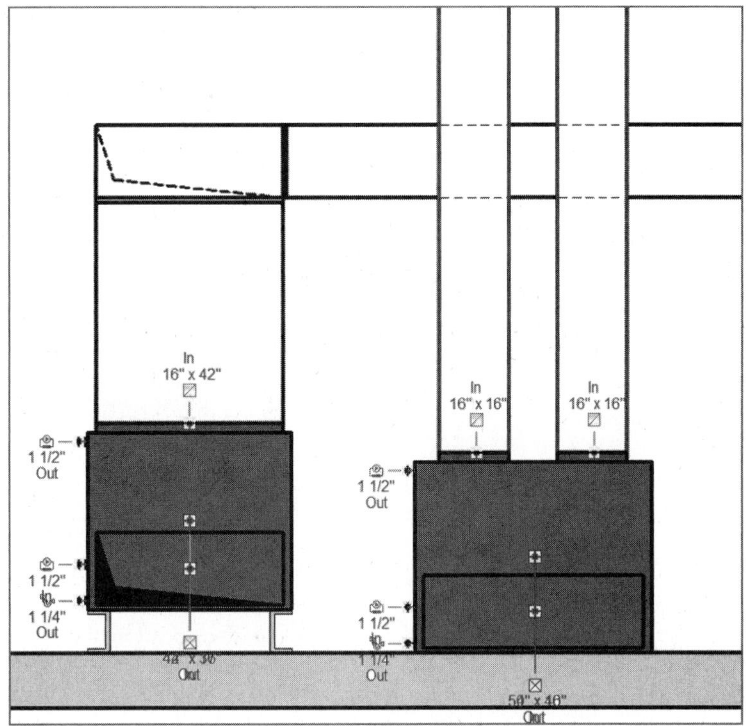

FIGURE 10.5 Floor-mounted and skid-mounted AC/AHU

MOUNTING OPTIONS FOR ACs/AHUs

There are two mounting options for ACs/AHUs.

FLOOR MOUNTED

In Figure 10.5, the mechanical plant on the right has been constructed to be mounted directly to the floor. The plant would probably be best created with a standard or generic template (in other words, level hosted). This way an offset could be applied to allow for a plinth, which may not be included in the model until a later time.

SKID MOUNTED

For the example on the left side of Figure 10.5, the family can be created in a couple of ways:

- The family can be created in the same manner as the previous example, which allows for an offset to be applied. This allows for the structural engineer to locate elements in their file. Then subsequent placement of the mechanical plant is done in the MEP file. This method could also be using units.
- Alternatively, the mechanical equipment family can have the structural elements built in, allowing the MEP designer to place the unit—including the rails—directly on the slab.

VAV Boxes

Generally created as level-hosted families, variable air volume (VAV) terminal boxes are usually mounted somewhere within the ceiling void, suspended from the underside of the slab above. In terms of placement, these are given an offset relative to the building level associated with the active view. Using the Properties palette, the offset can be predefined prior to the VAV being placed in this case. This makes for an easier workflow than in previous releases, in which most objects were placed on the reference level and then subsequently moved to the correct elevation (see Figure 10.6).

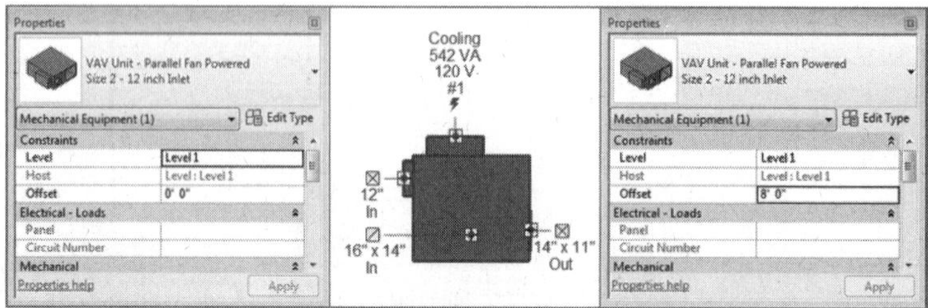

FIGURE 10.6 Changing the invert level

Connections to both AC units and VAV boxes can include heated- and chilled-water services and electrical for connecting to water and electrical systems (see Figure 10.7). Also note the connector labels in this view, which allow easier identification of connections and their flow direction, where applicable. These symbols also double as a shortcut to start creating ducts from the connector; just click the icon to start.

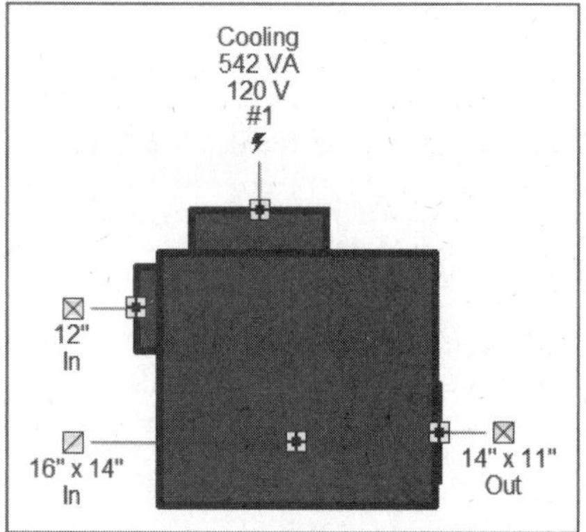

FIGURE 10.7 Typical mechanical and electrical connections to mechanical equipment

Heating and Cooling Elements

Heating coils, chilled-water coils, or reheat coils can be shown as part of the equipment or provided separately. They can also be duct mounted. Generally for FCUs, heat pumps, and most ACs/AHUs, the coil connections would be built into the equipment, but for a built-up AHU or for a VAV that may or may not include reheat, providing a coil separately can make it easier to swap out without changing the entire family. Duct-mounted coils need to be made adjustable to duct size and coil width (determined by the number of rows) and will need to have the pressure drop provided from the manufacturer's data.

Electric duct heaters can also be required. With these you need to ensure that you allow for the fire rating required., Building this into the family ensures that you are not relying on the users to remember it every time.

Ductwork

Ducts can be displayed in a variety of ways; they can be rectangular, round, oval, or as a placeholder, as shown in Figure 10.8.

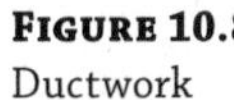

FIGURE 10.8
Ductwork

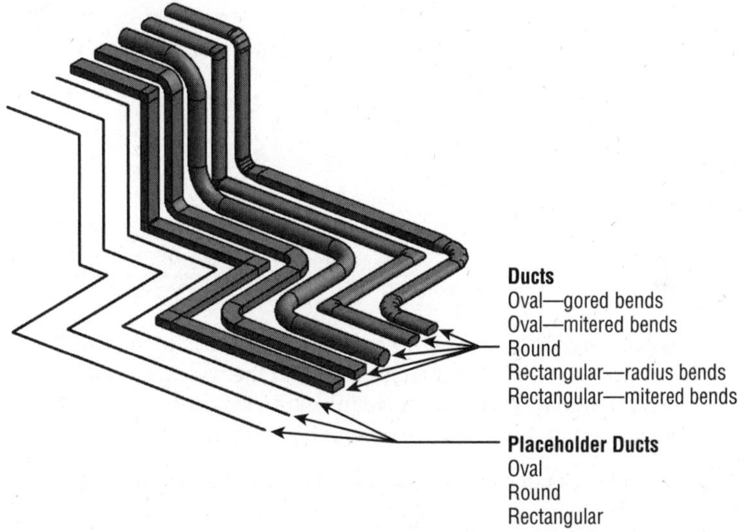

Placeholder ducts, as you can see in Figure 10.8, are shown only as a single line, although they retain nearly all the characteristics and properties of a regular duct. In Figure 10.9, you can see the differences. Placeholder ducts do not have values for Justification, Insulation, or Lining, because they are not needed at the conceptual stage of the project when placeholders are being used.

Within Revit ducts are system families, and they are the glue that hold systems together. However, it also relies on component or loadable families to create a duct type, as described in the next section. Although ducts hold a huge amount of information, for the user there are several important considerations to note, such as the type of bends, transitions, and other fittings that make up the duct run. Also take into consideration lining and insulation, which can be applied to runs or parts of runs after placement.

Since Revit MEP 2014, we have had the ability to specify the type of system that a duct is associated with (exhaust, return, or supply), without actually being connected to any equipment. You will be able to change the system type of a duct, even after it is connected to equipment, but not the classification. For example, if your duct is connected to a supply terminal, then you can change your system type to Outside Air, but not to return or exhaust air, as the Oustide Air System type should have been created from the Supply Air System Classification. If your duct is not connected to any equipment, you can change it to any system you like, as shown in Figure 10.10.

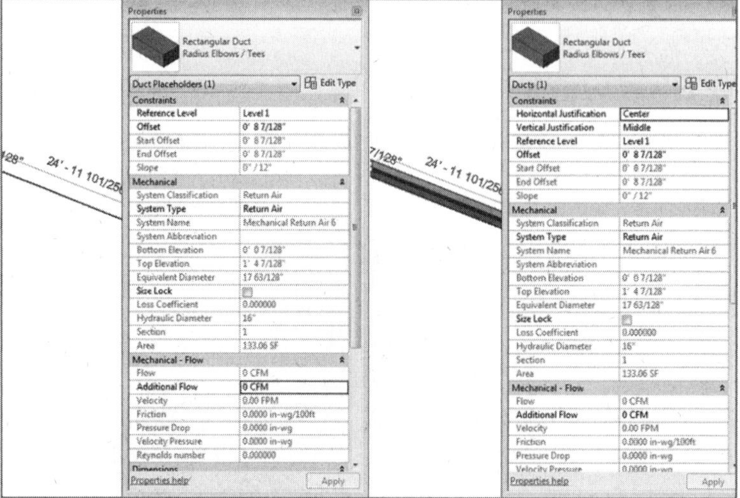

FIGURE 10.9
Design criteria for placeholder ducts

When highlighted in the System Browser, both ducts and placeholder ducts are highlighted in the drawing area. If a duct is created in the wrong system type, simply select one section of the run and change it to the required system. All the connected ducts and fittings will also change. This ability can have several benefits, including these:

- The user doesn't have to remember to select the appropriate system before creating a duct—its system type can be changed at *any* time.
- Differing systems can be connected together. An example of this for ducts could be a supply AHU with a redundant backup. Although the backup system is not included in the system calculations, it can connect to the main supply without affecting the calculations in that system.

In Revit MEP 2015, all systems are named. Even though they may be default names, it is easy to change them on the fly. You also have the ability to divide a system. This is dependent on elements within the system not being physically connected and could be used as a means for breaking up large systems that may be slowing down the design process. To achieve this, select an appropriate system, as shown in Figure 10.11. Notice that although it is physically not connected with a duct, it is a single system. Also, with the supply air system selected, you can see the new Divide System button on the ribbon.

FIGURE 10.10
Ducts associated with systems

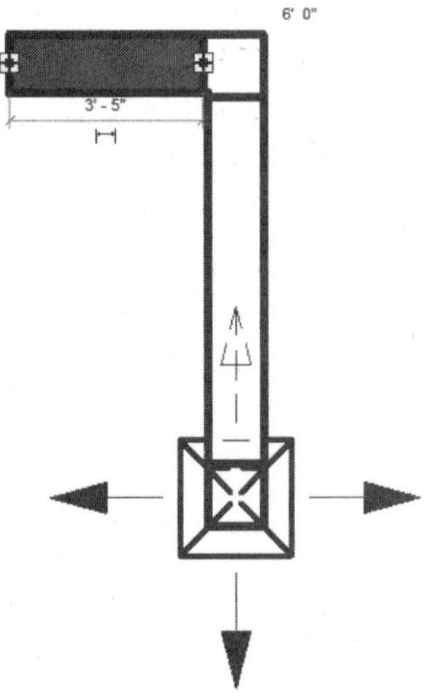

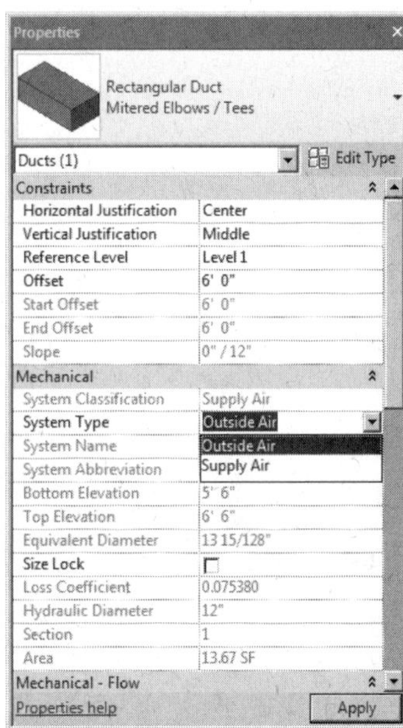

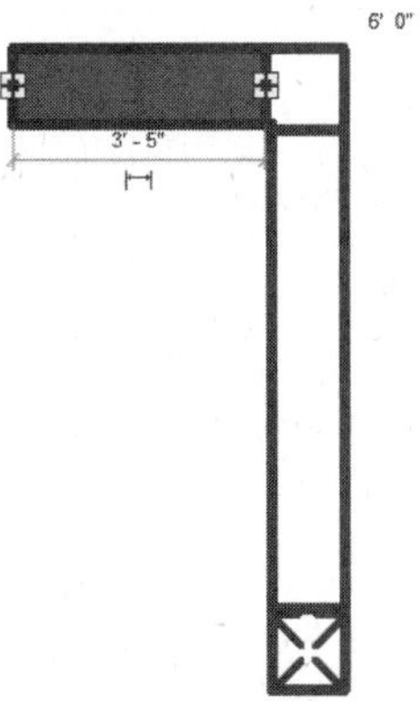

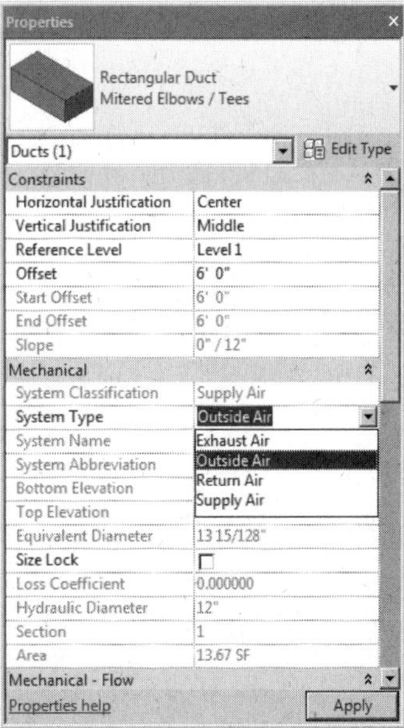

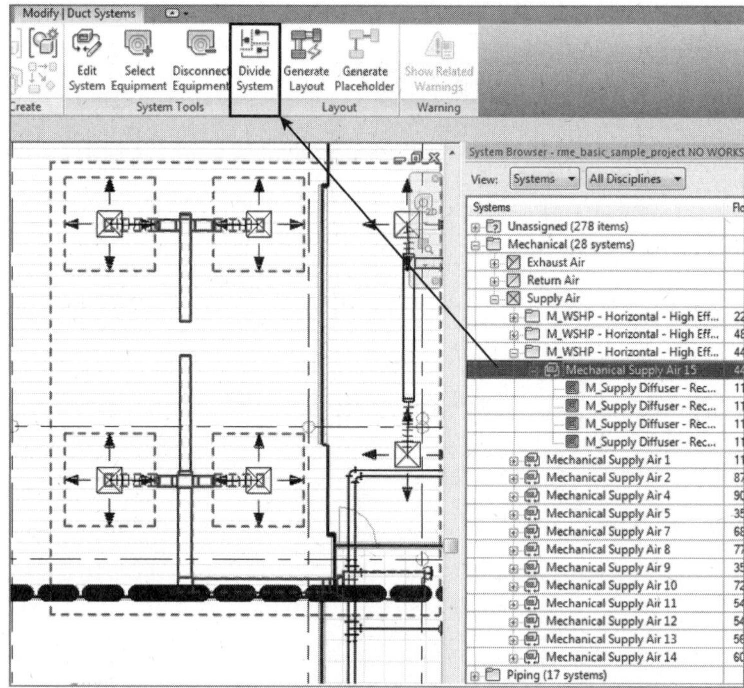

FIGURE 10.11
System Browser

Once you click the Divide System button, a message similar to the one in Figure 10.12 appears. The number of systems depends on the number of physical breaks in your original system.

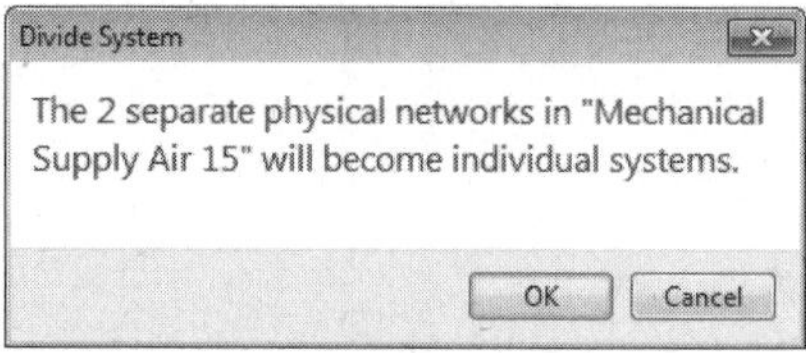

FIGURE 10.12
Divide System message

With the system now split, the original system and the new one (or however many have been created) are automatically sequentially numbered, as shown in Figure 10.13.

Interference checking in Revit 2015 is a comprehensive and accurate tool. Not only can you use the placeholder ducts (and pipes) in the interference check, but duct insulation can also be included as part of the process (see Figure 10.14).

Duct Types and Routing

Creating new duct types is a way of managing how your runs of ductwork and connect into each other, such as whether bends are mitered or radiused. Although you can change any of the fittings inserted retroactively, it is much easier to create a run in one go, using either the automatic or manual tools.

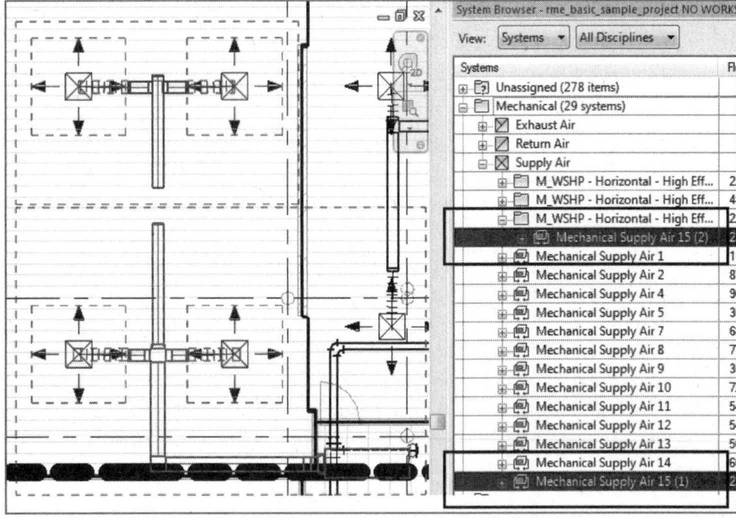

FIGURE 10.13 Systems shown separately

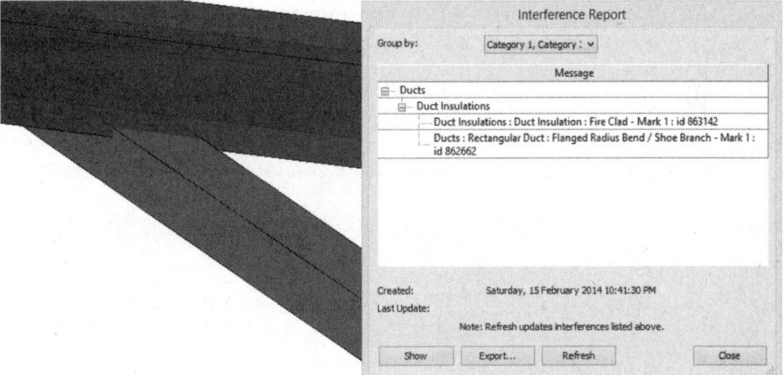

FIGURE 10.14 Interference check

Creating New Duct Types

Although it may be tempting to create types with names such as Exhaust and Supply, try to keep these names more specific, such as Stainless-2D Radius/Taps or Galvanized-Mitered/Tees. This way, the user only has to think about what material was used for the duct. Using a name that specifies Supply or Extract may be initially attractive, but doing so can lead to ambiguity and misunderstandings among the modeler, designer, engineer, and potentially the client. Another downside to this is the need to create multiple types of bends, tees, crosses, and so on for all the different material types *and* system types you are likely to use.

To create additional duct types or to edit existing types, right-click one of the existing types in the Project Browser (as is typical for all Revit system families). To create a new type, click Duplicate. This copies an existing duct type and appends the number 2 to the end of the name (for example, Mitered Elbows/Tees 2). Right-click again to access the type properties. At this point, you can choose to rename the duct type and supply the necessary fittings. These fittings need to be preloaded to use them, but you can also reuse those already in use in the project/template.

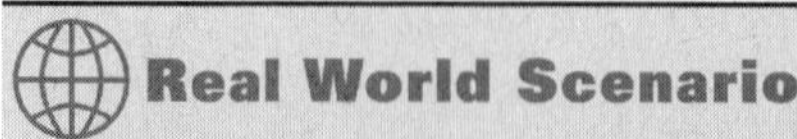

Schematic Layouts

Mike, the office drafter, has been given the task of preparing a schematic ductwork layout for mechanical engineer Carla. Because the design architect has yet to supply a building information model, Mike has some initial 2D AutoCAD plans and sections. Carla completes a rough design on paper along with calculations for duct sizes. When Mike starts the job, he links the AutoCAD section into a new section view. From here, he can create building levels based on the section. With this done, floor plans are created, and the AutoCAD plans are linked into the relevant levels. Mike can now create a single-line, schematic layout for the project. At this stage, floor offsets, beams, and coordination between services can almost be ignored because the duct is being shown only as a single line. The main benefit of this is that the bulk of modeling for the duct system can be achieved at an early stage of the project and retained or modified as the project progresses.

Using Automatic Duct Routing

When using the automatic routing tools, as a rule of thumb you should work on small sections—all the feeds to a VAV box is one good example. This means the computer has fewer objects to calculate and the routing suggestions have less room for error. Before even starting this process, check the options under Mechanical Settings (see Figure 10.15) for default Duct Type, Offset, and Maximum Flex Duct Length values because these are used during the routing process. Also note that these settings can be set for the different system types.

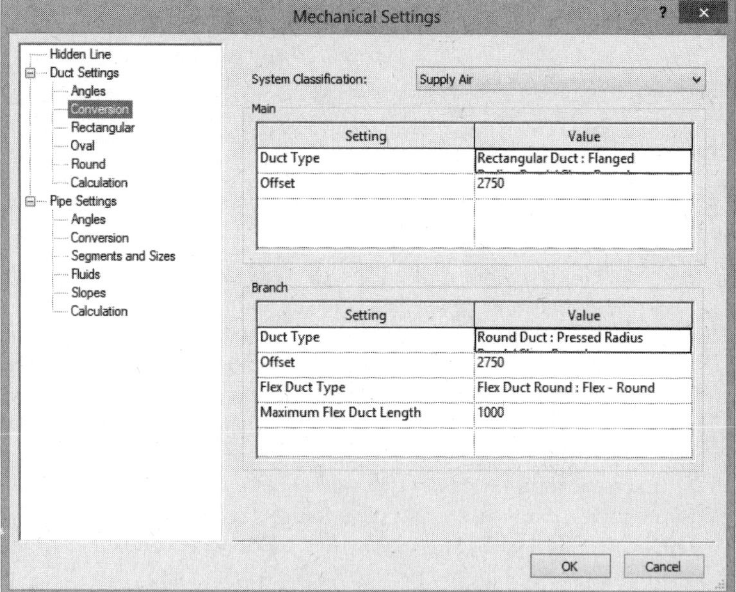

Figure 10.15
Mechanical settings

Now you're ready to use automatic duct routing. Here's how:

1. Place your VAV box, ensuring that it is located at the correct height. You can change it later if needed, but this may lead to you changing your duct route. Sometimes it is worthwhile to place the unit at the correct level and create a short run of duct from each connector. This gives you the correct levels of ducts (and pipes) from which you can then adjust the default height (Offset), as described in step 8.
2. Place your air terminals. At this point, it is a good idea to consider the following, not from a design point of view but from a Revit one:
   - What type are the ceilings (if any)?
   - If there are ceilings, should you use face-, ceiling-, or level-hosted families?
   - Are you going to create your own placeholder ceiling to host your families?
   - Should you use the ability to copy/monitor the air terminals already placed by the architect?
   - Choose the type of air terminal. Is it top, side, or even sidewall entry?
3. Once you've made all these decisions, it's time to start laying out the equipment. Figure 10.16 shows (1) a space where the upper limit has been defined as the level above; (2) that the Specified Supply Airflow value for the space has been entered manually; (3) Calculated Supply Airflow has been computed using the analysis tools; and (4) Actual Supply Airflow is calculated from the flow rates for the air terminals.

FIGURE 10.16
Space properties

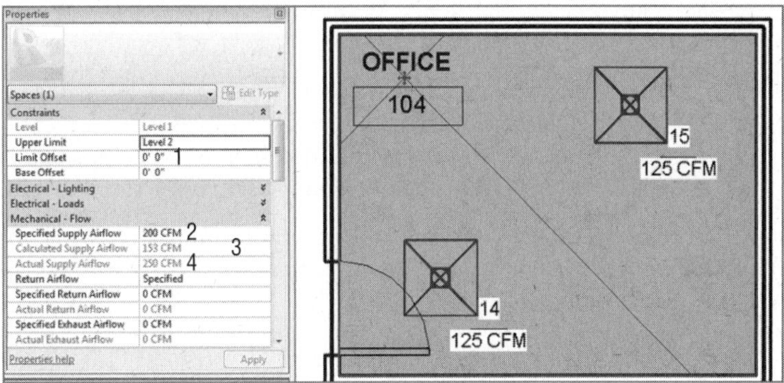

4. Creating a system is a relatively easy process in Revit MEP 2015. You can either select one air terminal, create the system, and then add others, or you can select all the air terminals you want to be in the system. On the ribbon, select the Duct option on the Create Systems panel (see Figure 10.17).

   After you click the Duct button, the Create Duct System dialog box appears (Figure 10.18).

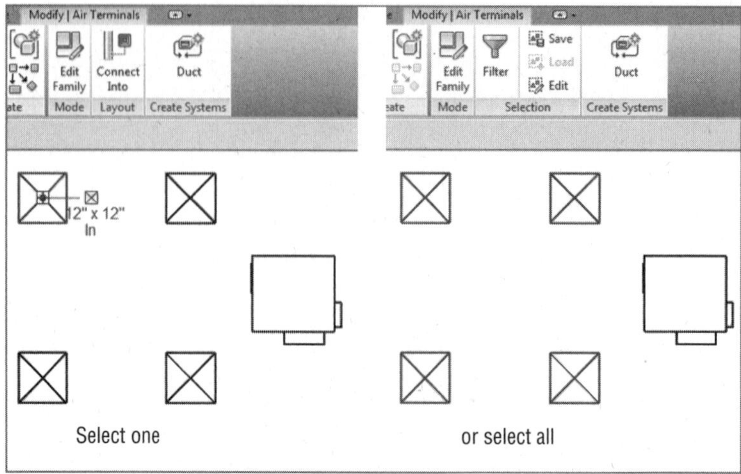

FIGURE 10.17
Create Systems panel

FIGURE 10.18
Create Duct System dialog box

This allows you to edit the system name and, if necessary, open the new system in the System Editor to add/remove objects and select equipment. Objects that are not part of the current system appear as halftone in the drawing area. When they are selected to be added to the system, their appearance changes to full weight (see Figure 10.19).

5. Once you have completed adding air terminals, click Select Equipment, and either select the equipment from the Options Bar drop-down or select the actual VAV box indicated on the plan, as in Figure 10.19.

6. Complete this task by clicking Finish Editing System. This is where the fun begins!

7. Hover over one of the items in the system (but do not select it) and press the Tab key. All the items in the system—air terminals and the VAV box—will now be enclosed in a dotted-line box. Without moving your cursor, left-click. This selects the system, as shown in Figure 10.20, and displays the system in the System Browser.

   With the system selected, you have several options; one of these is to create a layout. You can use either regular ducts or the placeholder option.

8. Select Generate Placeholder and, as shown in Figure 10.21, the sketch options for layout are displayed. For Solution Type, select Network, option 5. Remember that you can also edit the default settings for the duct offsets, as shown earlier in Figure 10.15, by clicking

the Settings button on the Options Bar. Most errors that occur using Layout are associated with either settings that fail to deal with elevations and duct types well, or duct or equipment that have not been placed at the correct elevations to allow the duct run to work at all.

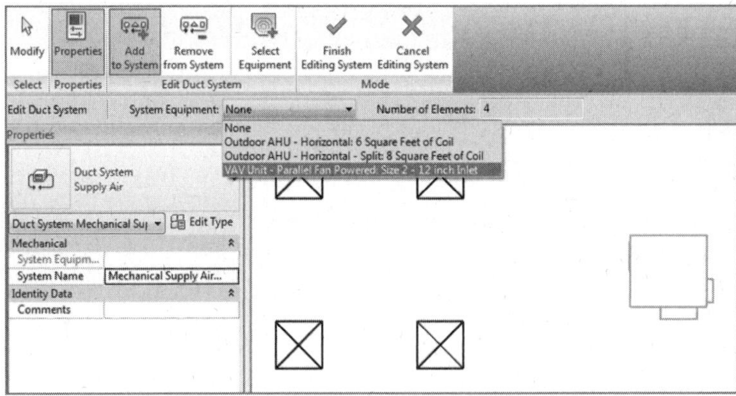

FIGURE 10.19
Add To System command

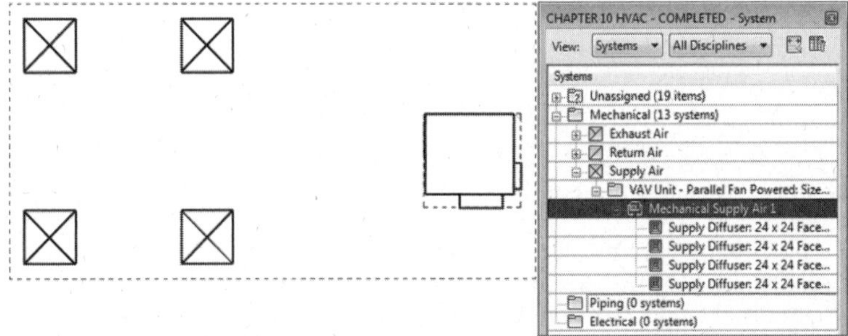

FIGURE 10.20
Tab-selecting the system

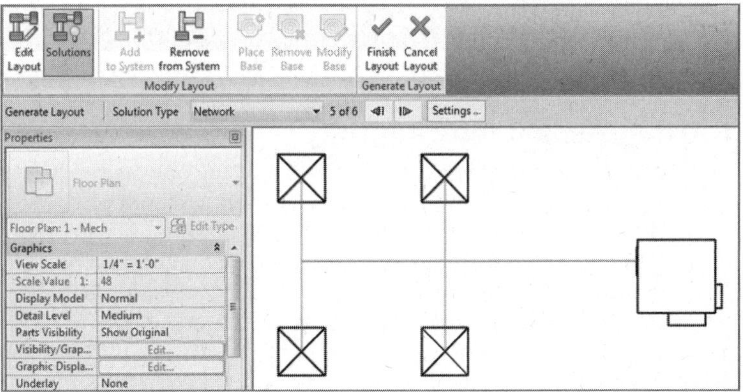

FIGURE 10.21
Generating a layout

You have several options for automatically generating your duct layout. These include Network, Perimeter, and Intersection options. Each can give you several solutions that can vary depending on the predefined settings for the duct layout, which can also be accessed from the Options Bar. Figure 10.22 shows that you can click the Edit Layout button, which allows you to select the layout lines in order to make changes to the layout. Using a plan and a 3D view side by side is a great way to ensure that a layout will work before clicking Finish Layout.

FIGURE 10.22 Ductwork routing solutions

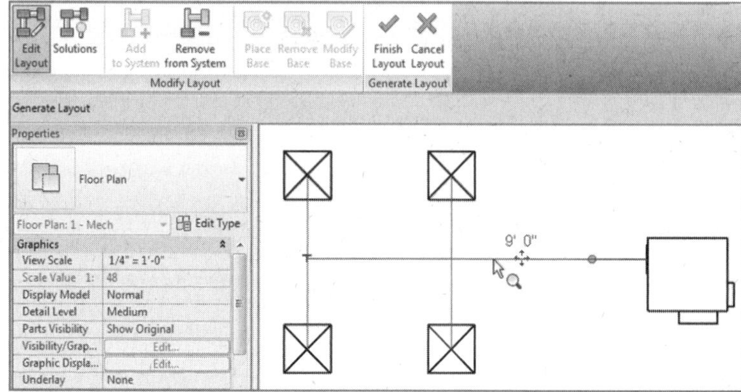

Main duct runs are shown in blue, while branch runs are shown in green.

9. Once you have settled on your preferred layout, click Finish Layout, and the duct layout is created (see Figure 10.23). Notice that the placeholder ducts are shown only as a single line.

It's worth pointing out here that the sizes used for this layout are based on the connection sizes and the settings for duct sizes located in the Mechanical Settings dialog box. There is another important consideration at this point. The designer/drafter must ensure that the default settings for the main and branch ducts are high enough above the air terminals and associated equipment to generate the layout; otherwise, the Layout tool cannot generate a layout, even if the layout is created with placeholder ducts. This can be achieved in two ways: either by selecting the Settings button on the Options Bar (shown earlier in Figure 10.21) or by selecting the actual sketch lines of the solution, which allows the user to manually choose the offset.

Using Manual Duct Routing

Using the automatic tools may seem too limiting or even pointless to an experienced design drafter who already knows the sizes and routing that must be used. These tools are great for a quick mock-up or presentation of a design that is more conceptual. However, with experience, most users eventually settle for a variety, sometimes for no better reason than "a change is as good as a rest." Sometimes, however, the manual tool is much more efficient, especially when connecting different areas into a system or laying out runs back to a rooftop AHU.

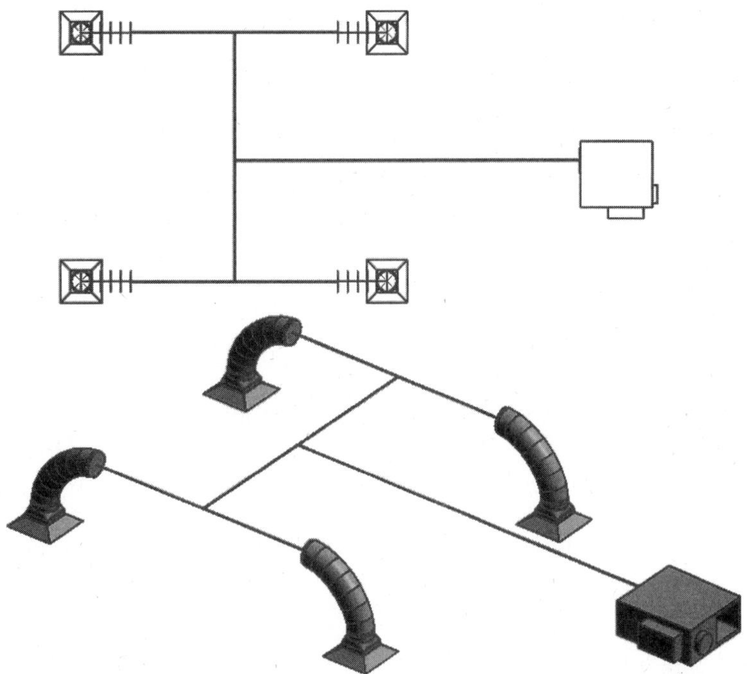

FIGURE 10.23
Completed duct layout

To begin manual duct routing, do the following:

1. Click the Duct tool on the Home tab on the ribbon, and then choose the type and its various options from the Properties palette, as shown in Figure 10.24.

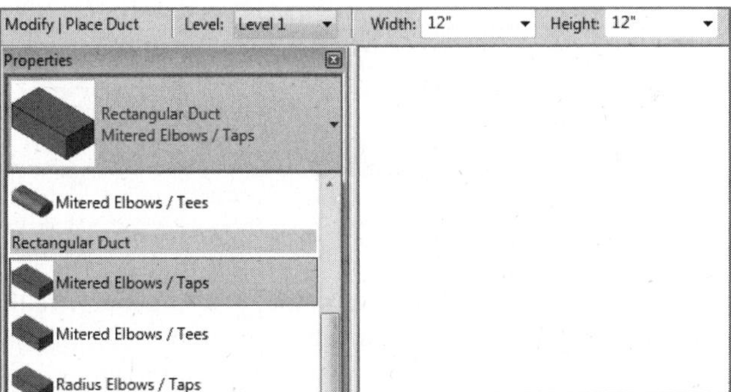

FIGURE 10.24
Duct types

Note the default settings in the Properties palette for constraints, including Justification, Reference Level, and Offset. The system type is undefined, and because the duct is unconnected, the airflow is 0.

You can adjust additional properties from the Options Bar and the Modify | Place Duct tab, shown in Figure 10.25.

FIGURE 10.25 Duct settings

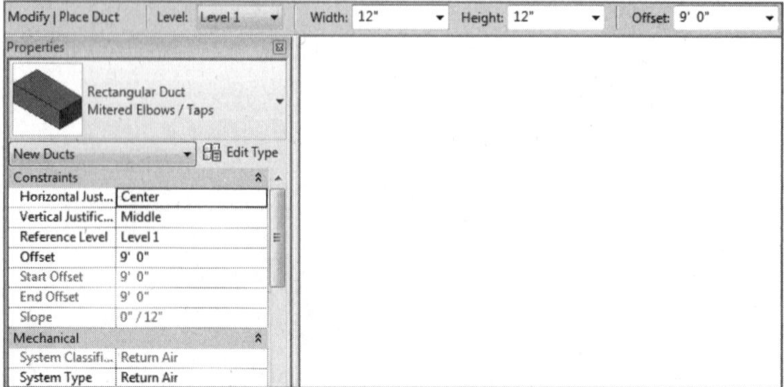

You can also inherit the elevation and size of existing connectors, whether from ducts or families, when connecting to them. For round or oval ducts, you can also choose the Ignore Slope To Connect option, meaning that the duct will connect regardless of slope, or you can use the specified angle.

2. The duct can then be created/drawn to whatever path you choose. For vertical offsets, type the new height into the offset box on the Options Bar. For an angled setup or set-down, it is best to work in an elevation or sectional view.

   In Figure 10.26, the duct has been split and a section created. To create a duct set-down, you would hover over one end of the duct, right-click the connector, and select Draw Duct. The duct would then be drawn along the preferred route.

FIGURE 10.26 Editing duct in sections

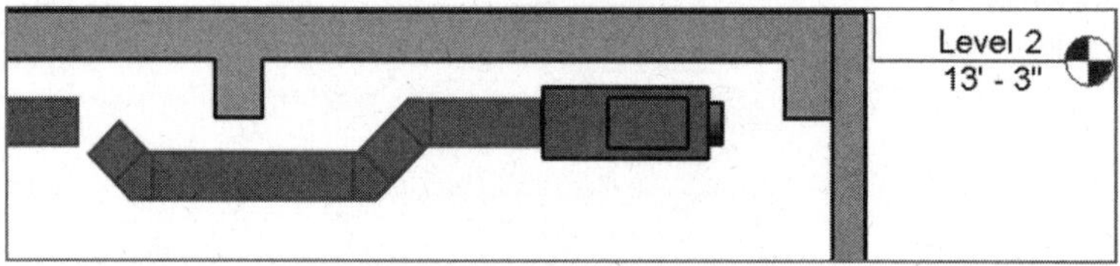

3. Using tools such as the Trim command, you can complete the run, as shown in Figure 10.27. Bear in mind, sketching a duct in sections or elevations must be done from connector to connector. Otherwise, the work plane of the view will be where the duct is placed. In section and elevation views, this is where the view's cut plane is. You see some strange duct runs if you don't pay attention to that.

FIGURE 10.27 Completing the set-down

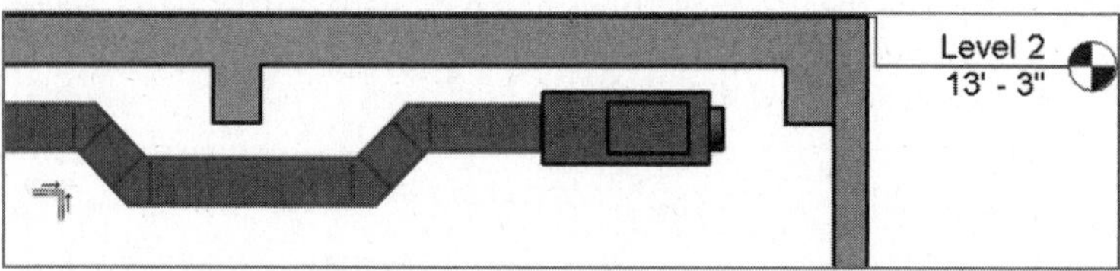

When creating ducts that set down/up or drop/rise, it can be much easier to model these in a section or elevation view, as shown in Figure 10.26 and Figure 10.27. To do this, first you need to create a suitable view. Quite often, individuals have a personal section that they move around the model. It can be opened when required, and then the duct (or whatever service is being worked on) is modified and the view is closed. This section, which should be named for the individual, can then be used to show a quick 3D view of the area using the Orient To View option.

Adjusting Fittings and Extending the Design

Changing the justification of ducts is a relatively easy task, but it can take practice to actually master. Selecting a duct or a run of ducts/fittings gives the user the option to change justification. Select your duct run, and from the Modify tab, select Justify.

This opens the Justification Editor, shown in Figure 10.28. Here, the control point can be displayed, and the alignment along the selected route can be selected by using the Alignment Line button. You can choose justification by using one of the nine Justification control buttons. This can have significant effects on your layout, so it is best to use this tool in small, easy-to-view sections or 3D views.

FIGURE 10.28
Duct Justification Editor

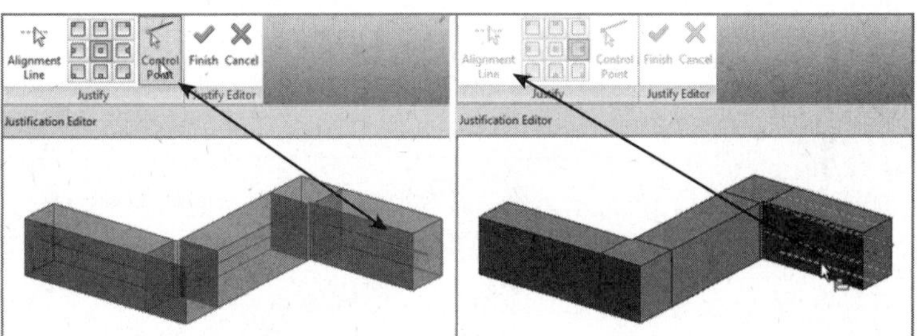

> **DUCTWORK JUSTIFICATION**
>
> When you're adjusting the justification of ductwork, some duct fittings (specifically duct transition fittings) have a tendency to move, shift, or even change length along the duct they are on. Therefore, you must allow for plenty of room along the duct run before and after any duct transition fittings for which you may want to change justification. When these objects have a slope applied, Revit is really re-creating that object completely, which is why objects can shift when using this tool.

You can also change an entire duct run from one type of duct to another. In previous versions, this involved multiple selections and filters. Now all the user has to do is select the duct run, as you can see in Figure 10.29. Here, the duct system has been selected, and the only proviso is that flexible ducts, air terminals, and mechanical equipment are not in the selection set.

This is a logical step, because the ducts and duct fittings in the selection set are usually also defined within the duct type. Therefore, when you select the objects and click the Change Type button, you are presented with a condensed Properties box that allows you to change the run type for others already in use in the project (see Figure 10.30).

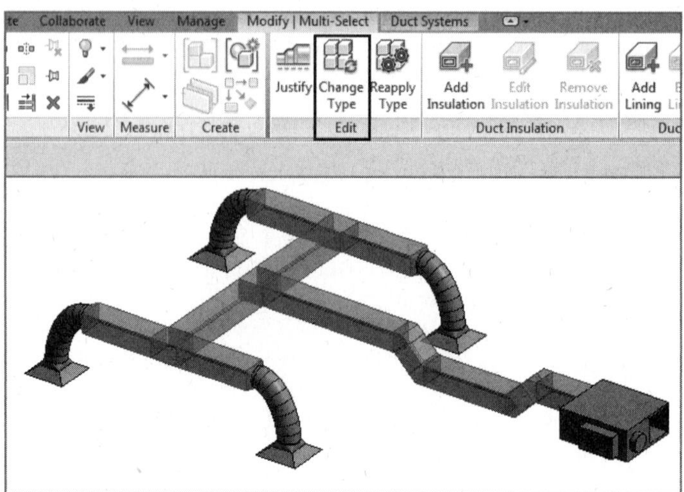

FIGURE 10.29 Changing the duct type

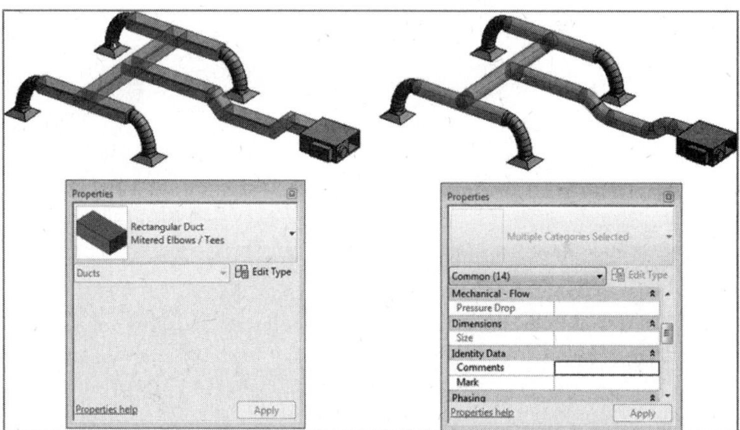

FIGURE 10.30 The changed duct type

In this next example, the design has gone through a few iterations, and changes have been made to various fittings and portions of the duct run. Since Revit MEP 2014, the Reapply Type option has been available. Selecting the entire run allows the user to reapply the original duct types to the objects selected, as shown in Figure 10.31.

FIGURE 10.31
Reapply duct type

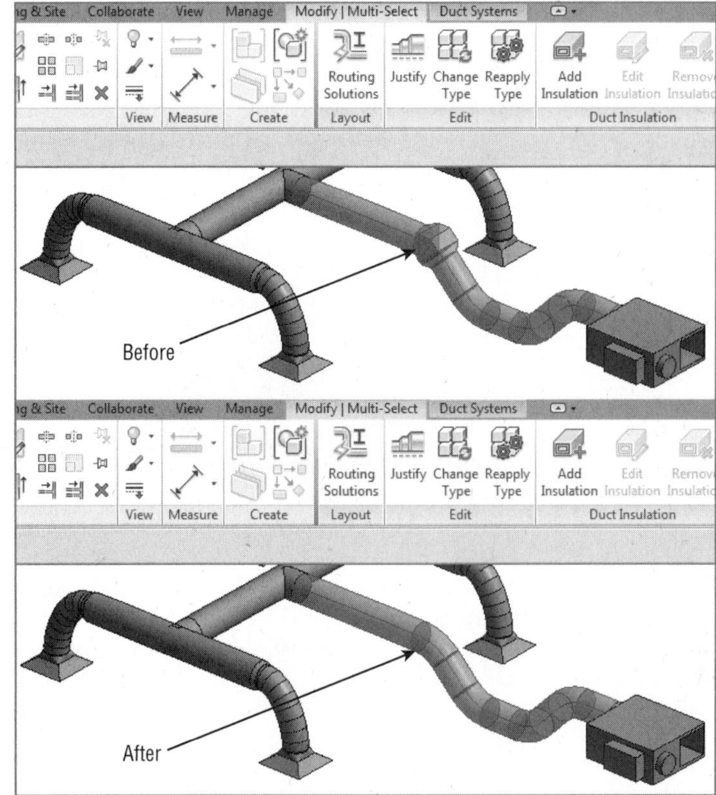

The direction of flow and graphical warnings are really helpful for the designer. The direction of flow is a temporary display when you select any object that has a mechanical or piping connection. This is a great benefit for designers and drafters because they can visualize which way air (or gas or water) is flowing through an object. As you can see in Figure 10.32, the selected VAV box has two supply ducts: one entering from the right and the other exiting from the left. There is also a return-air and electrical connection.

FIGURE 10.32
Flow connectors

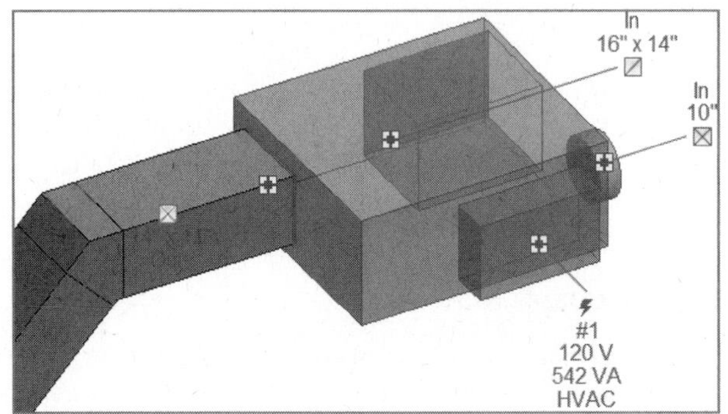

Warnings related to MEP connections can be displayed as graphical notifications when there is a disconnect in the system. You can change the warnings to suit your current task from the Analyze tab. Select the Show Disconnects button and then select the options you require, as shown in Figure 10.33.

FIGURE 10.33
Show Disconnects options

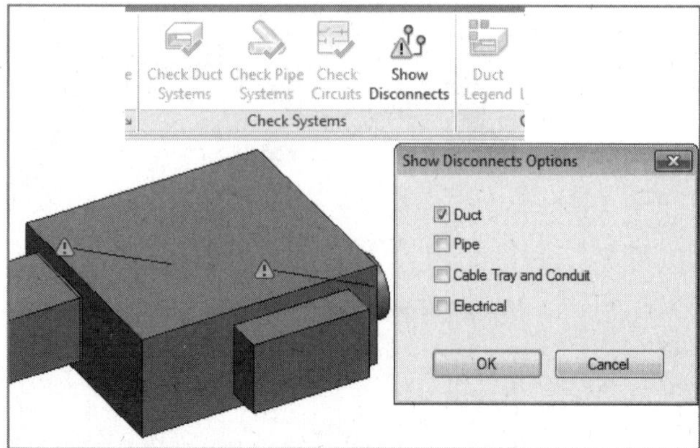

Since Revit MEP 2014 we have had the ability to cap open ends of a duct or pipe. The reason for doing this is that an open end in Revit (pipe or duct) results in incorrect calculations because Revit is expecting a contained system. To achieve this, either select a duct or create a selection set of ducts, and click the Cap Open Ends button displayed on the ribbon, as shown in Figure 10.34.

FIGURE 10.34
Cap Open Ends button

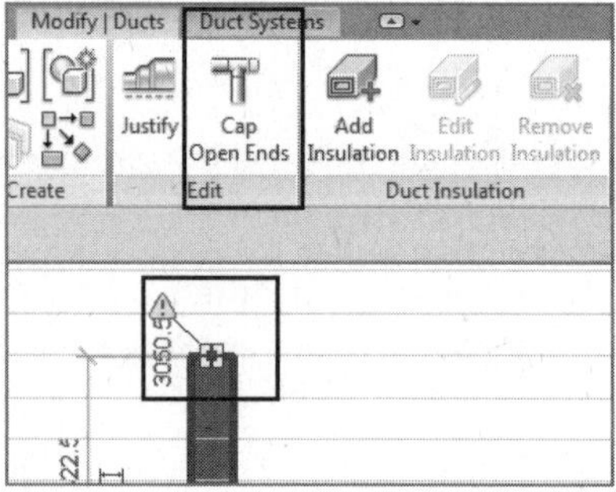

To extend an existing layout, as indicated in Figure 10.35, select one of the fittings (typically a bend or tee). Notice a small plus sign (+) adjacent to the side of the fitting that does not have a connector. Clicking this turns a bend into a tee and a tee into a cross, eliminating the need to delete a fitting and insert an appropriate one.

Duct Sizing

The most important factors to consider when using the Duct/Pipe Sizing tool is that the ducts form part of a system and that this system should have a name that suits your design (not a default), which is created at the same time as the system being created. The system must also have a valid airflow, so either you specify the airflow of the air terminals or that flow is specified from the space and volume calculations.

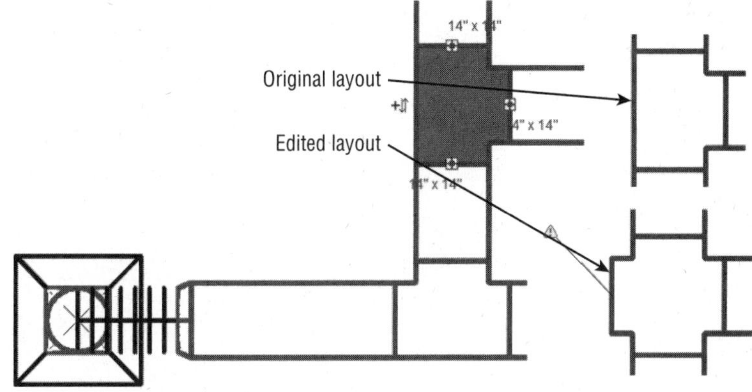

FIGURE 10.35
Extending the design

Use the Tab key to select your system, so all duct pieces in the system are highlighted (Figure 10.36).

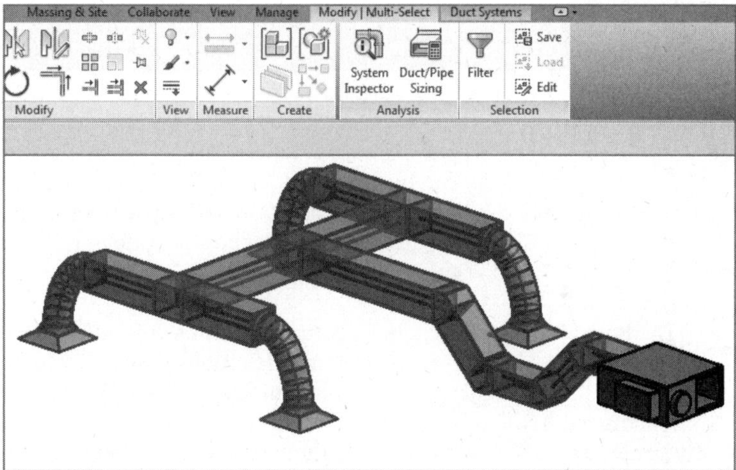

FIGURE 10.36
Tab-selecting the system and Duct Sizing tool

The Duct/Pipe Sizing tool is located on the Modify | Multi-Select tab of the ribbon. This button becomes active when you select a single duct or duct run that is part of a fully enclosed system, whose components are connected properly in regard to flow direction. Clicking the button opens the Duct Sizing dialog box. Figure 10.37 shows its available options.

Choosing a Duct Sizing Method

Although the sizing method you choose can be applied to an entire system, this is not necessarily the most efficient way to do things. If there are 5,257 objects in your system, it's probably not a great idea to ask your computer to process that amount of information—it may take a while! The logical choice is to split the task of duct sizing into manageable sections, such as a floor plan, a zone, or a group of air terminals fed from the same VAV box.

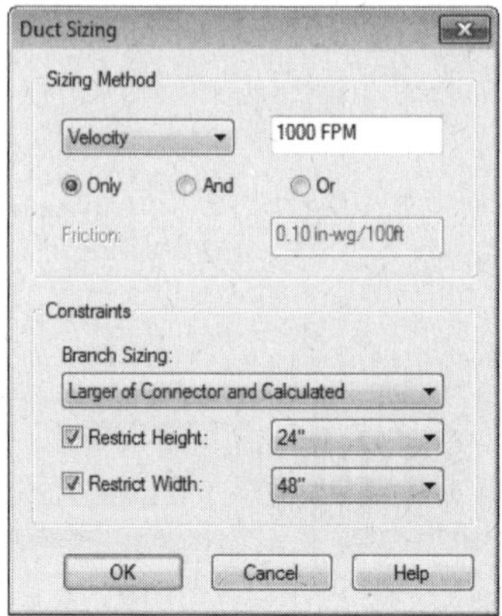

Figure 10.37
Duct Sizing dialog box

The various methods for sizing are as follows:

- Friction
- Velocity
- Equal Friction
- Static Regain

Friction and Velocity can be used independently of each other when using the Only option. Alternatively, they can be used in conjunction with each other with the And and Or functions.

These options allow the designer to force the sizing ducts to meet the parameters specified for both Velocity and Friction. With the Or method, the least restrictive of either of the parameters is used.

The Equal Friction and Static Regain methods use the ASHRAE duct fitting database.

Air properties are set in the Mechanical Settings dialog box, as are the available sizes of ducts used in the actual sizing calculations (see Figure 10.38 and Figure 10.39).

During the sizing process, you can also apply constraints to the branch parts of the run. These are defined as Calculated Size Only, Match Connector Size, and Larger Of Connector And Calculated (see Figure 10.40). Depending on the stage of the design or your actual role (such as consultant), you could choose Calculated Size Only, because the design is still in its early stages and the equipment is generic. These settings allow you to coordinate with other model components in areas where space is limited. For example, if you have only 2′-0″ (600 mm) of space above the ceiling, you could restrict the height of your duct to 20″ (500 mm).

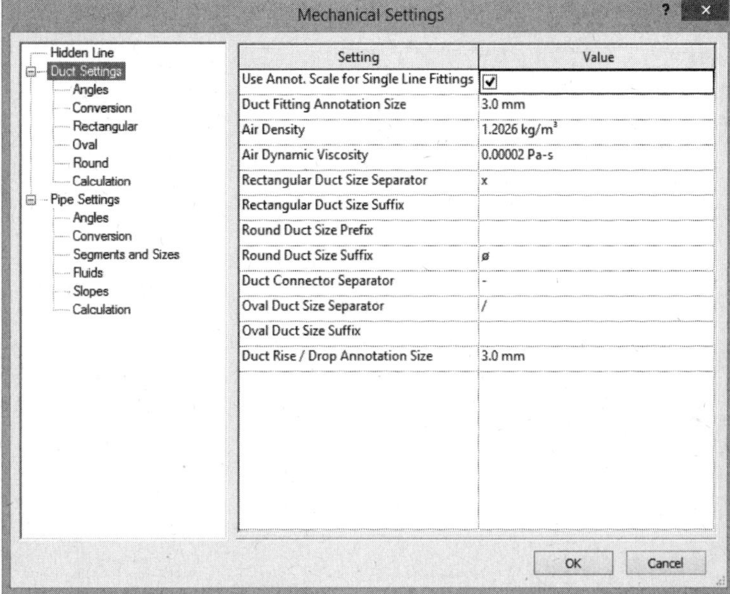

FIGURE 10.38 Mechanical Settings dialog box, Duct Settings

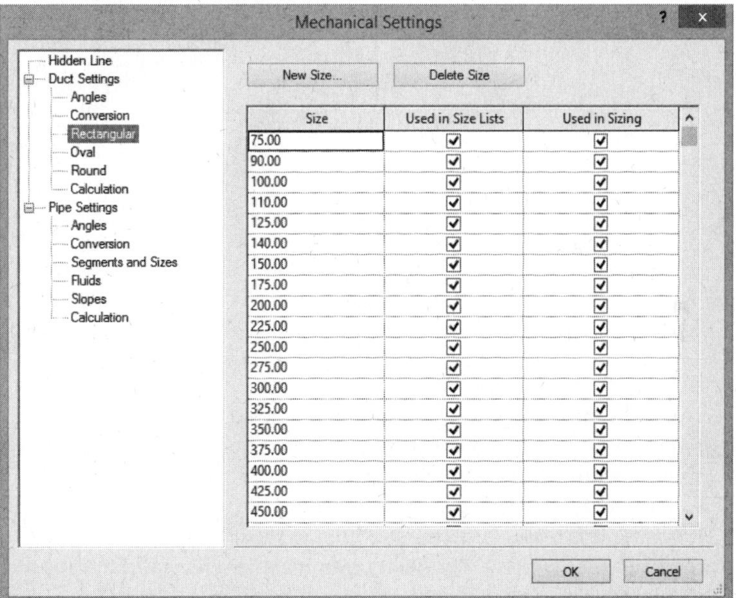

FIGURE 10.39 Mechanical Settings dialog box, duct sizes

However, later in the project when the equipment has been specified, as a contractor you may want to select Match Connector Size and Larger Of Connector And Calculated to reduce the number of duct sizes used on the project, thereby reducing your manufacturing costs.

FIGURE 10.40
Duct sizing constraints

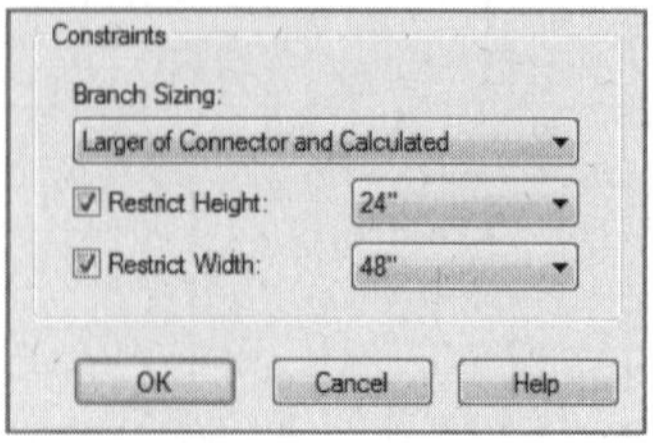

Constraints
Branch Sizing:
Larger of Connector and Calculated
Restrict Height: 24"
Restrict Width: 48"
OK Cancel Help

This dialog box also allows you to specify a limit on the size of the ducts, which can further reduce costs or give you the ability to specify, say, a continuous duct height in places where you know access is a potential issue.

To add insulation and lining to a selection set that contains both ducts and duct fittings, simply create your selection set and choose the appropriate option, as shown in Figure 10.41.

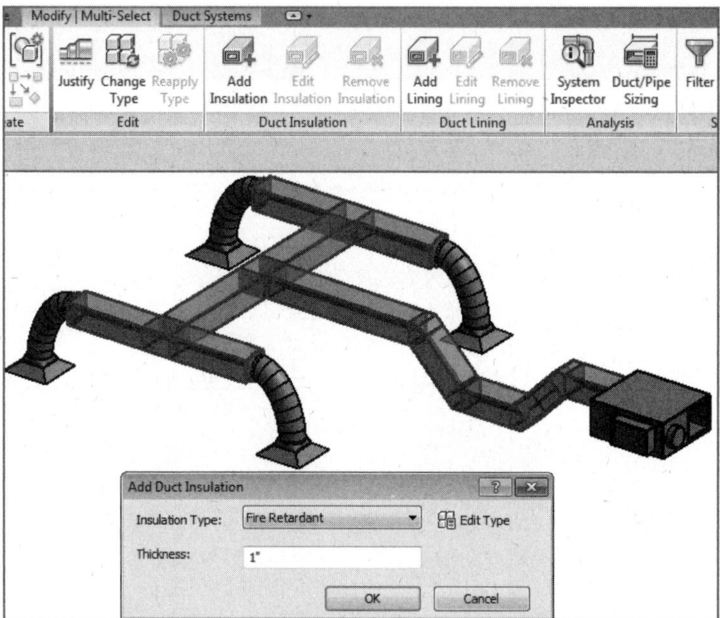

FIGURE 10.41
Insulation and Lining tools

Lining and insulation can have overrides or filters applied so that they display in the required manner, even to the extent of showing insulation as transparent with a hidden line style, as indicated in Figure 10.42.

Although lining and insulation can be added only as instance parameters, the workflow for using this tool is much easier than in most previous releases. Even so, if the entire system requires lined or insulated ducts, you have to select all ducts for the system and then specify the insulation or lining required.

Duct sizing works only where air terminals, ducts, duct fittings, and mechanical equipment are seamlessly connected with no gaps and where the equipment has a defined airflow. This airflow could be entered as part of the initial analysis or subsequent manipulation of the objects.

FIGURE 10.42
Insulation and lining graphic overrides

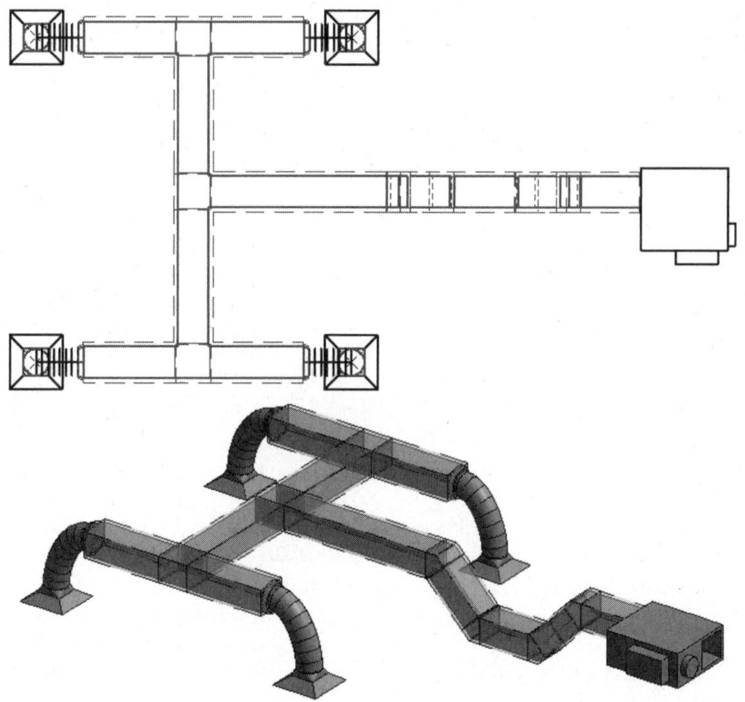

Once a system is created, you can use the analytical tools to inspect the duct system for airflow, pressure, and pressure loss. From the System Browser, select the system you want to analyze (as shown in Figure 10.43). Remember, you can also Tab-select the system. With the system selected, click System Inspector on the ribbon. If the Inspector tool isn't available, it's a clue that something is wrong.

FIGURE 10.43
Selecting a system

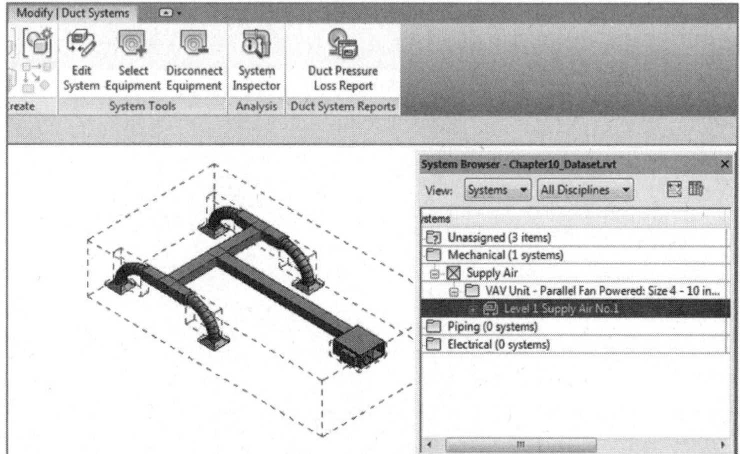

This activates the System Inspector tool, shown in Figure 10.44. Click System Inspector again and pass your cursor over the elements in the system; notice that airflow and pressure loss are defined.

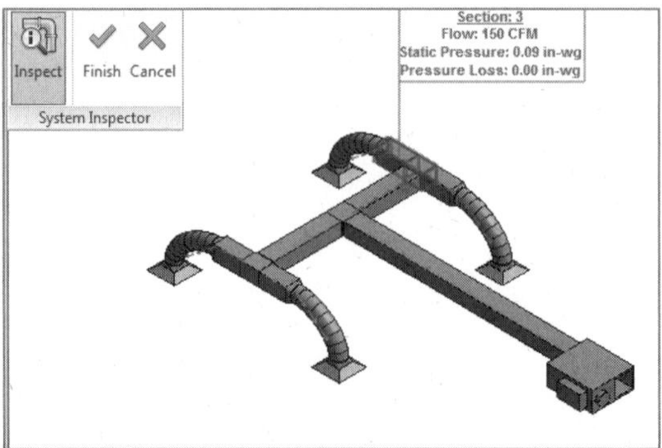

FIGURE 10.44
System Inspector

As with all calculations, you may want to keep a record of this analysis as part of your project documentation. Introduced in Revit MEP 2014 was the ability to create a duct (or pipe) pressure-loss report as discussed in Chapter 8, "HVAC Cooling and Heating Load Analysis." This tool is located on the Analyze tab or on the Modify | Duct Systems tab. Here you have a choice: either select the system first or specify the system you want to create the report on in the Analyze tab. Once the system is selected, the dialog box shown in Figure 10.45 is displayed. In this dialog, you can specify the fields to use and save the report format for later use. Clicking Generate creates an HTML web page of your results.

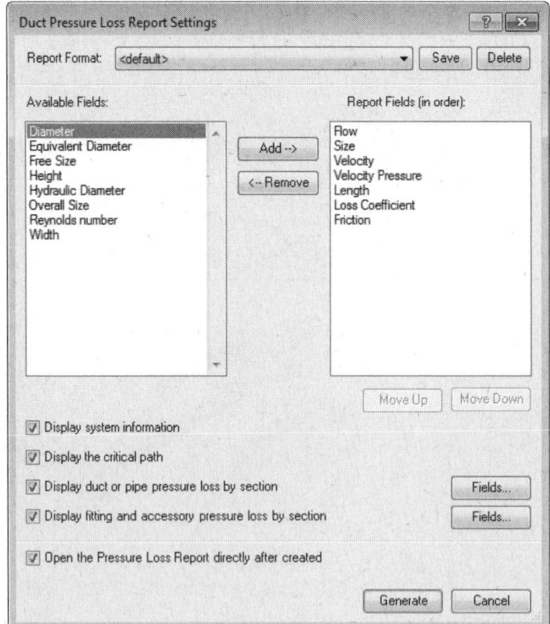

FIGURE 10.45
Duct Pressure Loss Report Settings dialog box

Using the Duct Routing Tools

Now that you have reviewed the process of using the duct routing tools, you will learn how to apply them in a simple exercise:

1. Open the `Chapter10_Dataset.rvt` file found at `www.sybex.com/go/masteringrevitmep2015`.
2. Open the floor plan view 1 – Mech, as shown in Figure 10.46. You can see that there are four air terminals (level hosted) mounted at 8′-0″ (2400 mm) above level and a VAV unit mounted at 11′-0″ (3300 mm). These have already been connected to a supply air system.

FIGURE 10.46
Plan view

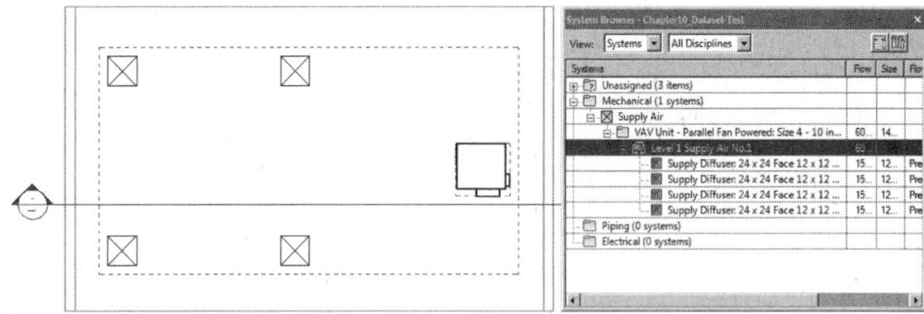

3. Hover your cursor over any one of the air terminals, and press the Tab key. This highlights the system, as indicated in Figure 10.46. Left-click, and the Modify | Duct Systems tab is activated. Click the Generate Placeholder button.
4. Click the Settings button on the Options Bar, and check that the Duct Conversion settings are as follows:
   - Main duct: Rectangular Duct: Mitered Elbows/Tees
   - Offset: 11′-0″ (3,300 mm)
   - Branch duct: Rectangular Duct: Mitered Elbows/Tees
   - Offset: 11′-0″ (3,300 mm)
   - Flexible duct: Flex Duct Round: Flex – Round with a maximum length of 6′-0″ (1,800 mm)
5. Use Solution Type: Network, 1 of 6, and click the Finish Layout button. Activate the default {3D} view and notice that, as shown in Figure 10.47, the main run of duct is shown as a single line. If the flexible duct is also shown as a single line, this is not by design; it indicates that the flexible duct is not connected correctly, which needs to be rectified.
6. If the flex duct is too short to be displayed properly, select one of the rectangular-to-round transitions and move it 2′-0″ (600 mm) toward the center of the duct run. This stretches both the placeholder duct and the flex duct, as shown in Figure 10.48. Repeat this process for each transition. You may find it easier to tile the open view windows and select the transition in the 3D view, but then actually move it in the plan view. Clicking the plan view should retain the selection, but if you lose it, just right-click and choose Select Previous.

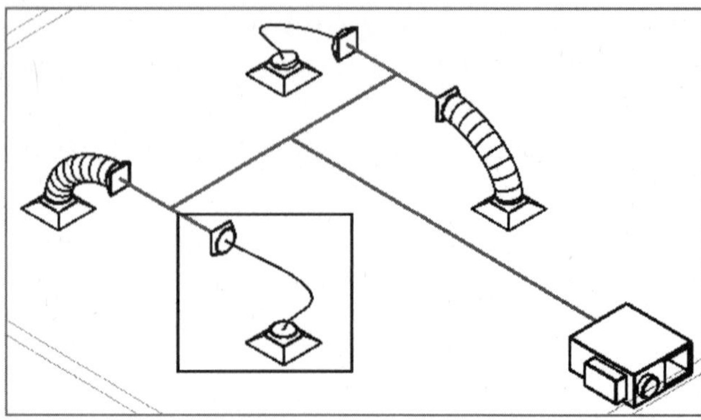

FIGURE 10.47
Default 3D view with flex errors

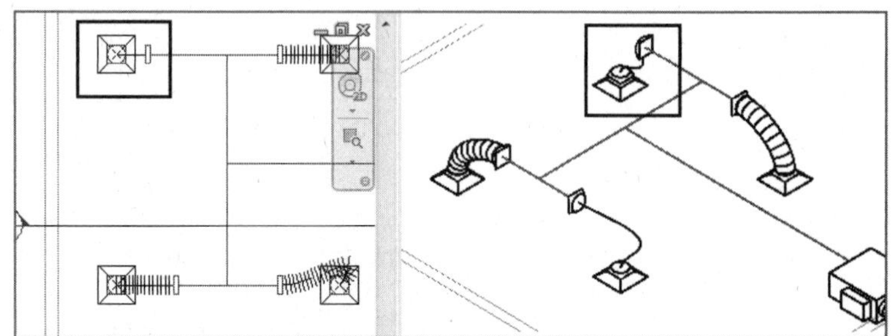

FIGURE 10.48
Moving transitions

7. The placeholder duct is ideal for concept and preliminary design, in which little detail is required for your drawings. Once this stage has passed, you can change the placeholder ducts to actual ducts with fittings. To do this, simply select the placeholder ducts in the 3D view, either by selecting them individually or selecting everything and using the Filter tool, as shown in Figure 10.49. Then click the Convert Placeholder button on the ribbon. Check to see that your results match Figure 10.50.

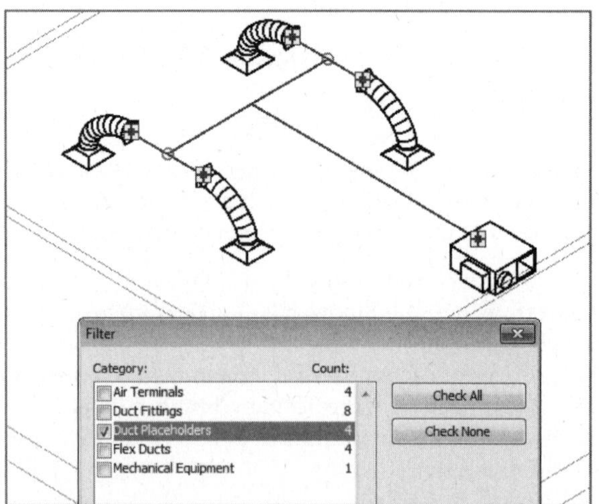

FIGURE 10.49
Duct placeholders

8. With the duct in place, open the Section 10.1 view. Here you can see there is a clash where you need to edit your duct to go under the beam. Using the Split tool, split the duct and delete the inner section and duct union fittings, as shown in Figure 10.51.
9. Complete the duct as required to avoid conflict with the beam.

Figure 10.50
Converted duct placeholders

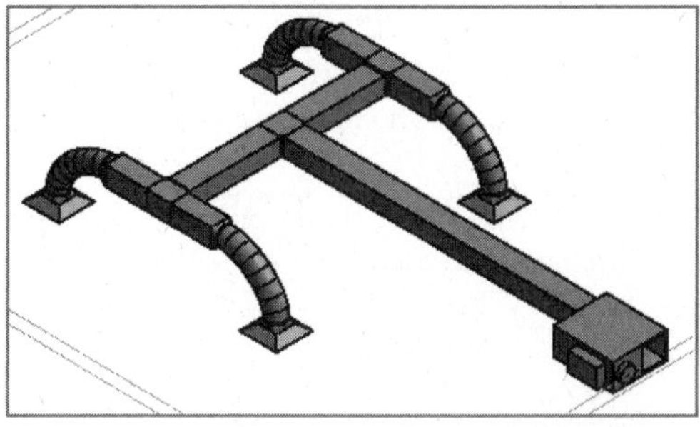

Figure 10.51
Split duct

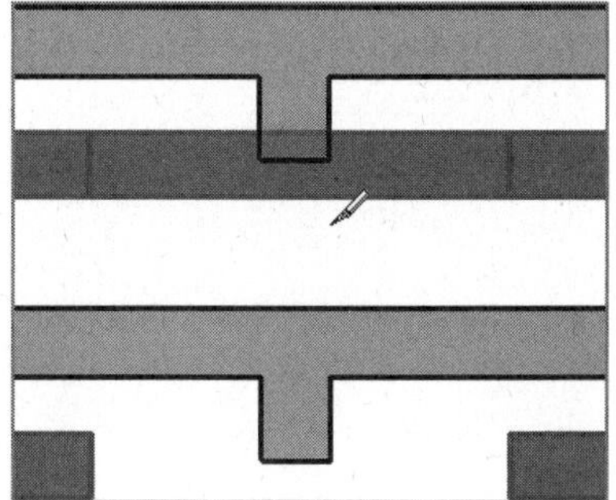

The Bottom Line

Distinguish between hosted and level-hosted components. Deciding whether hosted or level-hosted components are used is crucial for the success of your project. This decision will play a large factor in performance and coordination with other companies.

Master It Should you choose hosted or level-hosted components for your project?

Convert placeholder ducts into ducts with fittings. Using placeholders is a great way to "rough in" a duct layout without having to be too specific. Fittings are not used and the layout is extremely flexible.

Master It When progressing your conceptual design, at what point should you convert placeholder ducts into ducts with fittings?

Use the various duct routing options. When Revit MEP 2015 is used for duct layouts, the user must understand the functions of automatic duct routing and manual duct routing. Once these functions are mastered, the user can lay out any type of ductwork system.

Master It When asked to submit a design proposal for a multifloor office building, the HVAC designer needs to show a typical open-plan office that includes the supply and extract ductwork. How should the designer start this process?

Adjust duct fittings. Duct fittings are needed in systems to make the systems function properly and to produce documentation for construction. Being able to add or modify fittings can increase productivity.

Master It You have just finished your modeled layout and given it to your employer for review. Your boss asks you to remove a couple of elbows and replace them with tees for future expansion. What method would you use to accomplish this quickly?

Chapter 11

Mechanical Piping

Mechanical piping is the lifeblood of a heating and cooling system. Incorrect piping can lead to problems in the field, and locating the pipes may take months. There are simple two-pipe systems and more complex multipipe systems. When using the Autodesk® Revit® MEP 2015 software to lay out your systems, you can easily see your routing options and even calculate the total volume of fluid in your system.

In this chapter, you will learn to do the following:

- Adjust the mechanical pipe settings
- Select the best pipe routing options for your project
- Adjust pipe fittings
- Adjust the visibility of pipes

Mechanical Pipe Settings

When setting up the mechanical piping to route, apply the proper pipe material. This provides a more accurate layout by showing the correct pipe sizes and fittings for that system. You have to adjust several areas to set this up properly. Most important are the piping systems and pipe types settings. You can also adjust pipe segments and sizes as well as the fluids table as needed. Each is described here in more detail. After you set up these areas, you can concentrate on the autorouting or manual routing of pipes.

Piping Systems These are the pipe system types that are hard-coded into Revit projects and families. You have the options of creating new types, changing the names, and customizing the object styles for these system families within your project.

Pipe Types This is where choices can be made regarding the fittings, segment types, and material for each pipe type. As you model with a selected type, these fittings, segments, and parameters automatically populate the pipe system and the model. The pipe fittings must be loaded into the project in order for you to select them in the Type Properties dialog box.

Pipe Segments and Sizes These are set by choosing Mechanical Settings ➤ Segments And Sizes. You can select or duplicate a pipe segment, rename it, and apply the piping specifications for material, schedule/type, common sizes, and roughness of pipe walls.

Fluids Table You access the fluids table by choosing Mechanical Settings ➢ Fluids. You can duplicate, rename, and adjust the fluid type as well as its viscosity, temperature, and density.

Slopes Table From the slopes table, you can preset the pipe slopes that will be used for the project. You access the slopes table by choosing Mechanical Settings ➢ Slopes. The list of slopes will be available when you are a drawing pipe with a slope.

Angles From Mechanical Settings ➢ Pipe Settings ➢ Angles, you can choose whether the project can use any angles for pipe fittings or specific angles that are an industry standard.

Creating Piping Systems

Piping systems are an essential part of designing piping layouts in Revit MEP 2015. They allow you to separate pipes from one another based on the function they are serving, the color and line pattern they should be displayed with, the fluid type they carry, and so on. The Piping Systems properties can be accessed and customized from Families Browser ➢ Piping Systems (see Figure 11.1).

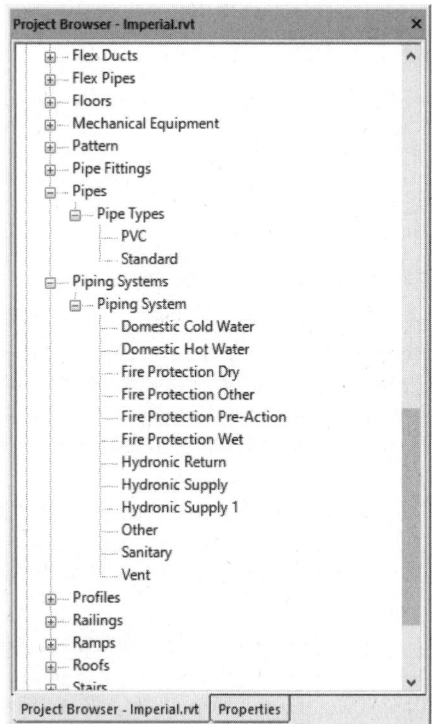

FIGURE 11.1 Accessing Piping Systems through the Project Browser

You can see the piping systems required in all projects in the Project Browser:

- Domestic piping systems (covered in other chapters):
  - Domestic Cold Water
  - Domestic Hot Water
  - Sanitary
  - Vent
- Fire-protection piping systems (covered in other chapters):
  - Fire Protection Dry
  - Fire Protection Other
  - Fire Protection Pre-Action
  - Fire Protection Wet
- Mechanical piping systems:
  - Hydronic Return
  - Hydronic Supply
- Other (You can't use any calculations for this option, so this option is appropriate only for systems that don't require calculations.)

Each of these items is what we call a *system classification*. System classifications are hard-coded in Revit, and you can't create new ones. However, you can create additional system types by right-clicking any of the existing piping systems in the Project Browser and selecting Duplicate. When duplicating piping systems, it is important to determine what the system classification should be and to select an existing piping system that is already assigned to that system classification. Once you create your piping system and realize that the system classification is incorrect, there is nothing you can do but delete it and start over with another one that has the correct system classification. In other words, system classifications have limitations: You are not allowed to change the system classification of piping systems or create or delete any system classifications. In addition, you must have at least one piping system for each of the 11 system classifications, and you cannot delete any of them even if you don't need them for your project.

Selecting the correct system classification can seem obvious for some system types—for example, chilled water is always going to be hydronic flow and return. However, lesser used systems can be more difficult—for example, medical gases and lab gases could fit into a number of different categories. It's essential to ensure that the system classification selected is then communicated to the entire team and used consistently throughout.

Each piping system can be assigned its own project-wide graphic override from within the system type properties (see Figure 11.2). This, combined with the ability to assign a segment of pipe to any of these piping systems without attaching it to a fixture or equipment, lets you improve the documentation produced earlier in the design process, when equipment families had not yet been built.

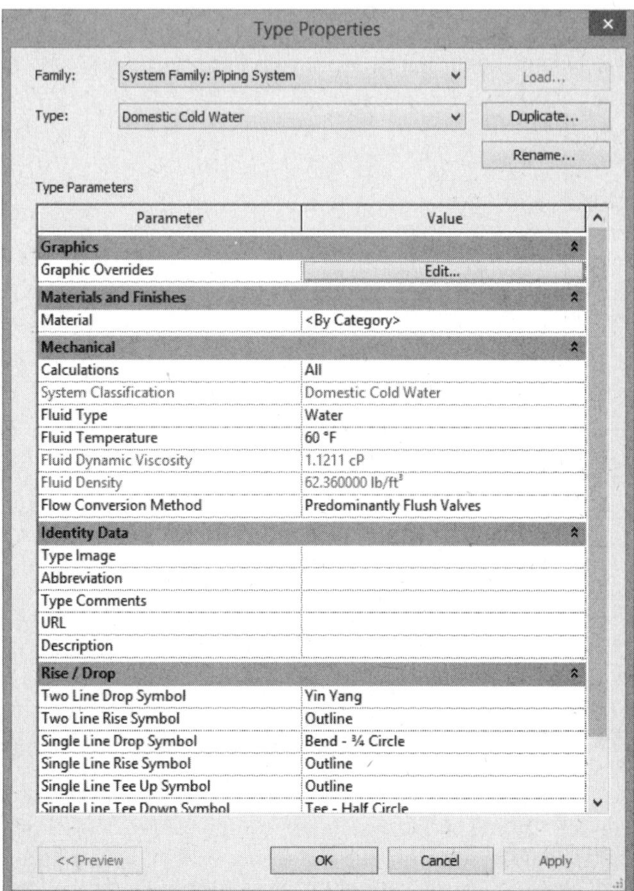

FIGURE 11.2
Properties for piping systems

Real World Scenario

BENEFIT OF PIPING SYSTEM GRAPHIC OVERRIDES

Ann is working on the early schematic of a mechanical piping design for a large convention center. The architect has already boxed out some space for the mechanical room containing chillers and pumps as well as the general location of the remote air-handling equipment. Now they need to begin coordinating piping chases throughout the structure.

Because the mechanical equipment has not yet been selected, Ann hasn't built the equipment families, but she still wants to be able to show both 2D and 3D plans of the proposed piping sizes and locations with the appropriate linetypes and colors. All that is required is for her to duplicate the existing piping system hydronic supply and create chilling water supply and heating water supply (CHWS, HHWS) piping systems as well as duplicate the hydronic return to make the chilled- and

continues

(continued)

hot-water return systems (CHWR, HHWR). Next, she right-clicks each and sets the graphic override for each system to match the office standard line weights, linetypes, and colors.

Now all that remains is to select the Pipe command and, before clicking to start a run, select the newly created system type in the Properties palette and model her pipe. The graphic overrides apply across the whole project, so every view will automatically show the mechanical pipe with the correct graphic settings.

One important drawback is that, because the linetype settings for piping systems are applied in all views, the common dashed-line patterns that are used with single-line pipe display (coarse or medium detail) will also dash the double-line pipe views (fine detail). For this reason, you can apply view filters to override any piping system graphic overrides. View filters are discussed in more detail later in this chapter in the section "Defining Systems Visibility through Filters."

Creating Pipe Types

Pipe types are typically set up in your company template. They represent the level of detail that your pipes and pipe fittings should display. There are many approaches to organizing your pipe types; in this section, you will examine the most common ones:

- Exact materials and fittings as they would be installed
- Generalized materials and fittings

The first approach is to think of pipe types from the perspective of the installer. The pipe type is related to the material and style of fitting used. For instance, both chilled- and hot-water mechanical pipes, 3' (900 mm) in diameter and under, are commonly constructed from copper with soldered or brazed sweat-joint fittings. This should be the basis of your pipe type. The benefit of this approach is a more detailed and accurate model. But the downsides can be overwhelming as well. Many systems could vary in materials and fittings, and the engineers may or may not know the material for the system at the time of modeling. And of course, in some cases, having too many material choices and fittings can overwhelm even the most knowledgeable modelers. This is a significant challenge when a company wants to target a high-detail level of the BIM model, but at the end of the day it would accomplish only what the person behind the computer is capable of. And in this case we are not talking about computer skills but engineering knowledge.

The second approach is to simplify things a bit and create pipe types that would cover more real-world systems under a single pipe type—for example, Gravity and Pressure. The gravity pipe type can be used for systems such as waste, grease waste, storm drain, and overflow leader. Pressure can be used for domestic hot water, domestic cold water, hydronic supply, hydronic return, and glycol. The limitations of this method are less-accurate models and volumes of the individual systems. Perhaps a combination of the two can be considered: generalization could be applied to most systems, except those for which volume calculations or the real size of fittings is of significant importance.

To modify and create new pipe types, in the Project Browser choose Families ➤ Pipes ➤ Pipe Types and then right-click the Standard type. Select Duplicate. This creates the additional pipe types you will need for your project. Next, right-click the duplicated pipe types and rename them to the pipe types you require. It is preferable to rename them to the pipe material type selected under Pipe Segment. You can find out or change the pipe material under the Pipe Segment selection by right-clicking the pipe type and choosing Type Properties ➤ Routing Preferences.

NAMING PIPE TYPES

Avoid naming your pipe types as system type names (such as *hot-water supply pipe*). Organizing your pipe types as the pipe systems may be logical to you, but it will make it harder if you use your model for an integrated project delivery for which you are partnered with a general contractor and mechanical subcontractors. The contractors will want to take the information and use as much of it for shop drawings as possible. This is where the *I* in BIM becomes more than a catchphrase. The more accurate the information about the material, fittings, and so on, the more accurate the material takeoffs will become for pricing and budgeting purposes.

Now that you have created your pipe types, you will want to change some of the parameter options. First, start the Pipe command and click Edit Type from the Properties palette. This opens the pipe type parameters. With regard to careful space planning, the accurate selection of fittings is the most important and most time-consuming task when setting up your pipe types.

Revit MEP 2014 introduced an improved pipe Type Properties dialog box with access to Routing Preferences settings (see Figure 11.3). In the past, you could assign only one elbow or tee family per pipe type; now you have the option to set different fittings based on the pipe size you are drawing (see Figure 11.4). You can also designate different pipe segments at different sizes. For example hydronic piping (whether chilled, condenser, or heating water) may be copper up to about a size of 4″ to 6″ (100 to 150 mm) and be carbon steel pipe above that size. If you are going to designate different pipe segments, you must also make sure you set the fittings accordingly at the same sizes.

Under the Identity Data parameters group in the Type Properties dialog box, the following parameters are available: Keynote, Model, Manufacturer, Type Comments, URL, Description, Assembly Description, Assembly Code, Type Mark, and Cost. If you have a certain manufacturer, model, or other special note that you want to denote on the plans, you can use these settings to describe your pipe type further.

Defining Fitting Angles

From Manage ➤ MEP Settings ➤ Mechanical Settings (see Figure 11.5), you can allow the user to use any angle, allow an angle increment to be used, or predefine the angles of pipe and duct fittings that Revit can use when you are laying out piping. When you are drawing pipes, Revit still displays all angles in their temporary dimensions, but once you click to finish the pipe, the created elbow is rounded to the closest angle you have allowed from the Angles settings. This can enforce the use of industry-standard angles, thus ensuring the use of cheaper fittings for the project instead of custom angle fittings, which usually come at a premium price.

Type Properties

Family: System Family: Pipe Types

Type: Gray Iron

Load... Duplicate... Rename...

Type Parameters

Parameter	Value
Segments and Fittings	
Routing Preferences	Edit...
Identity Data	
Keynote	
Model	
Manufacturer	
Type Comments	
URL	
Description	
Assembly Description	
Assembly Code	
Type Mark	
Cost	

<< Preview OK Cancel Apply

FIGURE 11.3 Type Properties dialog box

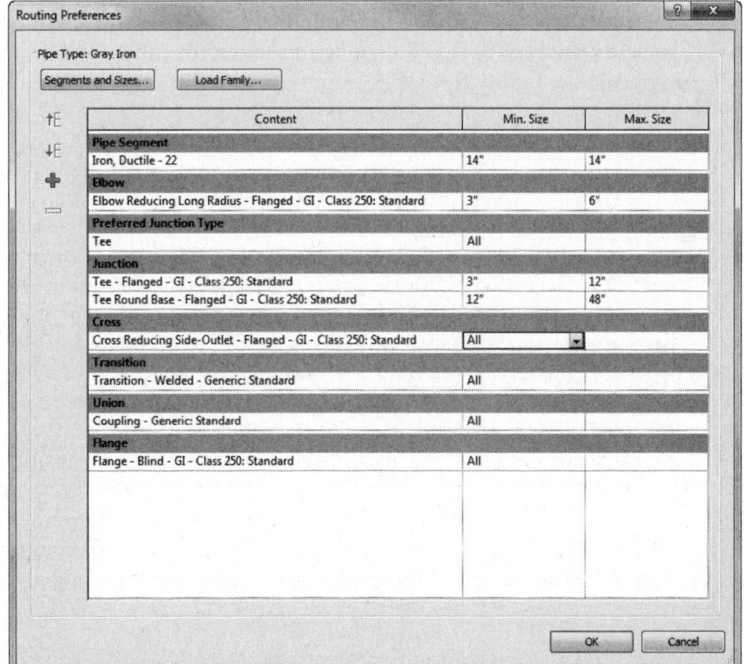

Content	Min. Size	Max. Size
Pipe Segment		
Iron, Ductile - 22	14"	14"
Elbow		
Elbow Reducing Long Radius - Flanged - GI - Class 250: Standard	3"	6"
Preferred Junction Type		
Tee	All	
Junction		
Tee - Flanged - GI - Class 250: Standard	3"	12"
Tee Round Base - Flanged - GI - Class 250: Standard	12"	48"
Cross		
Cross Reducing Side-Outlet - Flanged - GI - Class 250: Standard	All	
Transition		
Transition - Welded - Generic: Standard	All	
Union		
Coupling - Generic: Standard	All	
Flange		
Flange - Blind - GI - Class 250: Standard	All	

FIGURE 11.4 Routing Preferences dialog box

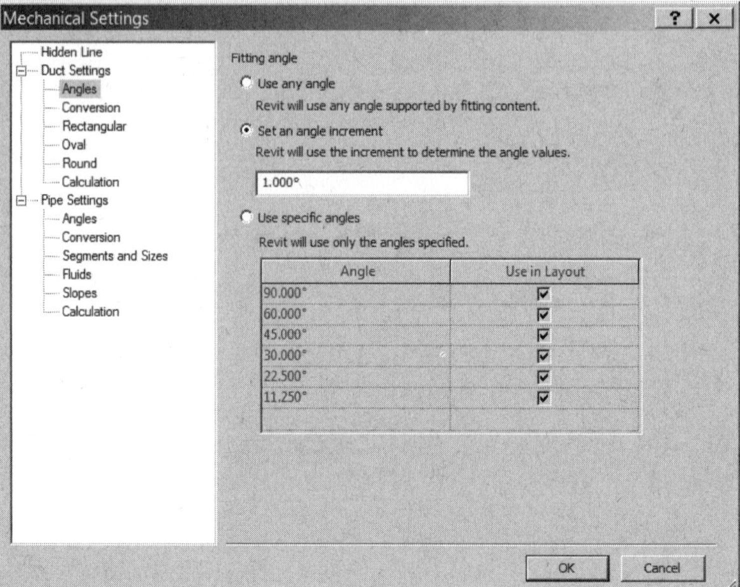

FIGURE 11.5 Pipe fitting angles

Selecting Fittings for Routing Preferences

Before you can adjust the routing preferences, you need to create the fittings that will go with your system pipe types. To accomplish this, open the Family Browser and choose Pipe Fittings. Then select the fittings that will be required for your Pipe Type parameters. You can either load the appropriate family from the Autodesk library or download manufacturer-specific fittings.

IMPORTANCE OF PIPE TYPE FITTINGS SELECTION

When possible, use fitting families that are true dimensions or that closely resemble the dimensions of the pipe fittings you have in your specifications. The physical dimensions are often very different because of the various methods of assembling the pipe. The perfect situation is to use fittings that have been properly modeled from the manufacturer. As more manufacturers adopt BIM, this information will become more accessible. It should be a regular task of every BIM manager to research what manufacturer's content is available. Perhaps this can be done annually in conjunction with each new Revit MEP release. Each time this task is undertaken, review what options are available for pipe fittings that come with Revit along with those available from other sources. You will have to take some time to familiarize yourself with the fittings directory located in the imperial library.

One noteworthy option that is missing from the fitting parameters is a pipe spud. To date, Autodesk has not included this pipe fitting family with its content. However, several pipe spud families can be downloaded from the Internet. If you would like to use one in your Steel-Welded pipe type, you first have to load the family into your project. Next, duplicate your pipe type and rename it **Steel-Welded-Tap**. It is *critical* that you have a separate pipe type because the Preferred Junction Type fitting parameter is set here. Change it to **Tap**, set Tee to None, and set the Tap parameter to **Pipe Spud** (the name of the family you have downloaded or created). Now you will be able to easily choose whether to model pipe with tee fittings by selecting the pipe type Steel-Welded or to model with spud-style tap fittings by selecting Steel-Welded-Tap.

Choosing Pipe Materials and Sizes

To access the pipe material settings, choose Systems ➢ Plumbing & Piping and then select the small arrow in the lower-right corner of the ribbon panel. This opens the Mechanical Settings dialog box. (Alternatively, choose Manage ➢ MEP Settings ➢ Mechanical Settings.) Next, choose Pipe Settings ➢ Segments And Sizes. If you want to create a new pipe segment, you can duplicate an existing pipe segment and rename it (see Figure 11.6). From here you can also change the Roughness setting and segment description or create a new pipe size.

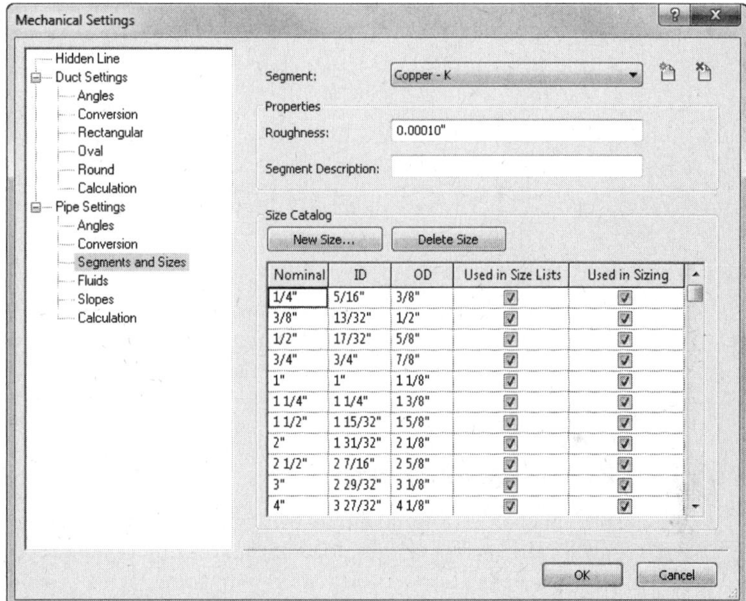

FIGURE 11.6 Creating new segments and sizes

Adjusting the Pipe Sizing Table

If you want to adjust the sizing table, choose Systems ➢ Plumbing & Piping, and select the small arrow in the lower-right corner of the panel to open the Mechanical Settings dialog box. Next, choose Pipe Settings ➢ Segments And Sizes. You can duplicate the schedule of pipe and apply the pipe wall thickness as required. You can also select and deselect the piping sizes to match your design standards (see Figure 11.6).

Using the Fluids Table

Revit MEP uses the fluids table when you are sizing your pipes or determining pressure drop. You can add information concerning temperature, viscosity, and density to the fluids table. To do this, choose Systems ➤ Plumbing & Piping, and select the small arrow in the lower-right corner of the panel to open the Mechanical Settings dialog box. Next, choose Pipe Settings ➤ Fluids. Then duplicate one of the fluid categories that is close to the one you need, and modify it as required (see Figure 11.7).

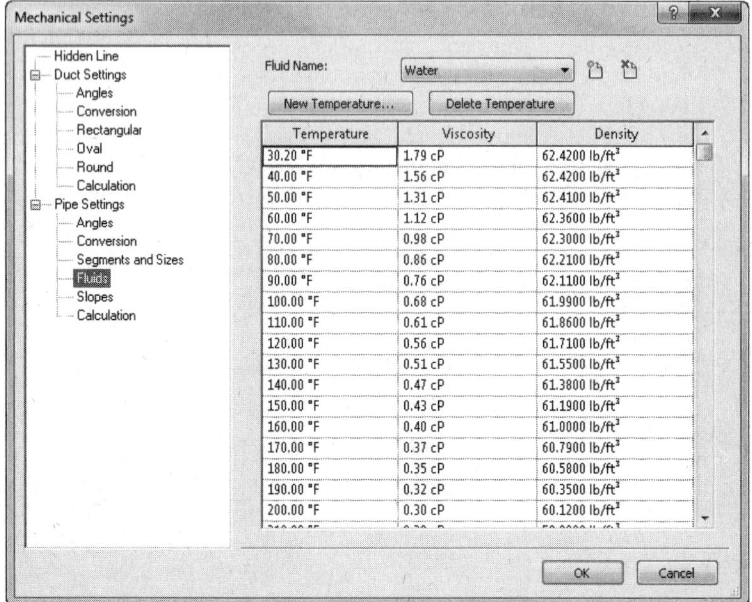

FIGURE 11.7 Fluids table settings

Pipe Routing Options

The size of a mechanical piping model can grow quite large because of the amount of fluids constantly transferred, so it is very important that routing is closely coordinated. Using Revit MEP 2015, you can improve visual coordination with color-coded systems and use interference checking to monitor conflicts with cable trays or sprinkler piping. Two routing options are available when you set out to design your piping model: the autoroute option and the manual routing option. Both are described in this section.

In smaller systems, the autoroute feature may be beneficial. However, in most circumstances, manual routing will be of greater benefit. This is because a good design engineer can optimize a system with regard to construction of pipe and coordination with other trades, especially structure.

Automatic Pipe Routing

Ideally, you have everything set up in your pipe types before you begin routing piping. To start automatic pipe routing, first assign your equipment to a piping system. Select two or more pieces of mechanical equipment, and from the Modify | Mechanical Equipment tab, click Create Systems ➤ Piping (see Figure 11.8a) and then name your piping system (see Figure 11.8b).

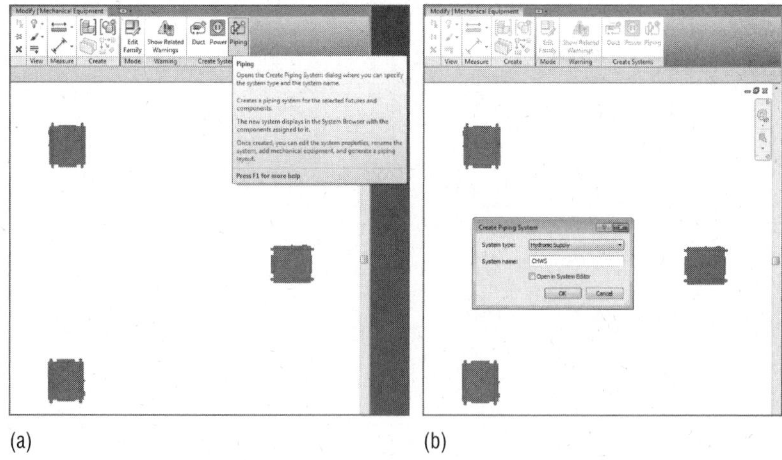

FIGURE 11.8 Creating your piping system

Next, select any piece of equipment assigned to the system and click the Generate Layout button. You have four options for generating the layout: Network, Perimeter, Intersections, and Custom. Each one has several routing solutions from which you can choose, consisting of a main pipe route (blue) and branches (green):

Network This solution creates a bounding box around the components selected for the piping system and then bases several solutions on a main segment along the centerline of the bounding box with branches coming from the main segment.

Perimeter This solution creates a bounding box around the components selected for the system and proposes several potential routing solutions. You can specify the Inset value that determines the offset between the bounding box and the components. Inset is available only when the Perimeter option is selected.

Intersections This solution bases the potential routing on a pair of imaginary, perpendicular lines extending from each connector for the components in the system. There are potential junctions in the proposed solutions along the shortest paths, where the lines from the components intersect.

Custom This solution becomes available after you begin to modify any of the other solutions.

The autoroute feature is most useful in small, simple layouts. Usually, the greatest benefit comes from using the autoroute pipe as a starting point and finishing with the additional manual layout. You can set the mounting height by clicking the Settings button from the Options Bar and inputting a new offset. Make sure to define the offset for both Main and Branch, as shown in Figure 11.9. When you're working with the autorouting command, several factors can affect the outcome—incorrect configuration of connectors, settings conflicting with the proximity of the equipment, elevation of the main pipe route and the branches, selecting flex duct type to be used, and so forth. For optimal results, have a plan view and a 3D view tiled to provide the most feedback about the final layout.

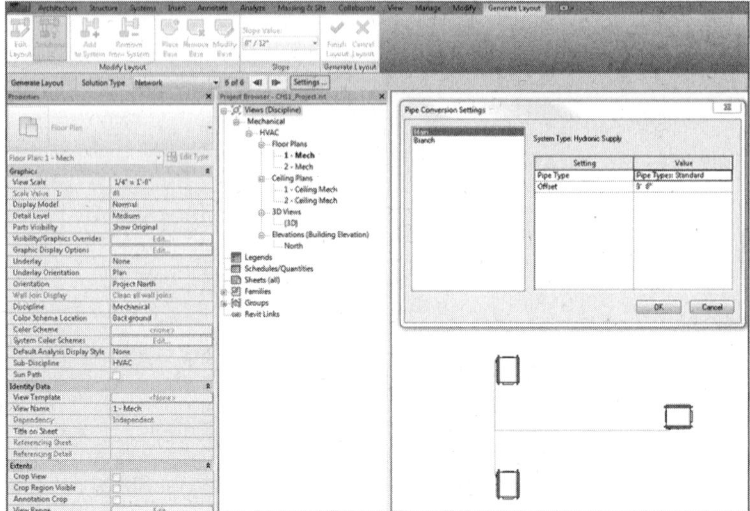

FIGURE 11.9 Autoroute piping layout

Manual Pipe Routing

When you are modeling pipes in Revit, develop good habits at configuring all the necessary settings while in the Pipe command. This is especially valid for inexperienced Revit users. Developing good modeling habits will serve you in the long run. Don't rush yourself. Take your time to confirm that all the settings are properly configured before you even draw the pipe. Some of the settings to pay attention to are Diameter and Offset from the Options Bar; System Type from the Properties palette; and Justification, Automatically Connect, Inherit Elevation And Size, Slope Off, Slope Up, Slope Down, Slope Value, and Tag On Placement, all available from the ribbon. You see that there are lots of settings to control, and they will certainly affect the outcome. So take your time to develop good habits when you are just starting with Revit.

When routing, manually start the piping run at the elevation that you know will most likely be out of the way of other disciplines. Use the following steps to set up and place mechanical equipment, create a hydronic supply and return, and manually route pipe to all pieces of equipment:

1. Open the `Ch11_Project.rvt` file found at `www.sybex.com/go/masteringrevitmep2015`.
2. One of the best practices is for the architectural model to be linked into the mechanical model. Download the model `C11_base.rvt` file found at `www.sybex.com/go/masteringrevitmep2015`.
3. Choose Insert ➢ Link Revit, select the directory into which you downloaded the Revit base, select Auto – Origin To Origin from the Positioning drop-down, and then select Open. By selecting Origin To Origin, you are assured that the model will be properly located (see Figure 11.10). Open the default 3D view {3D}, to review the architectural model.

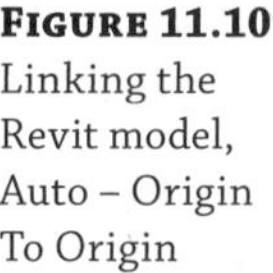

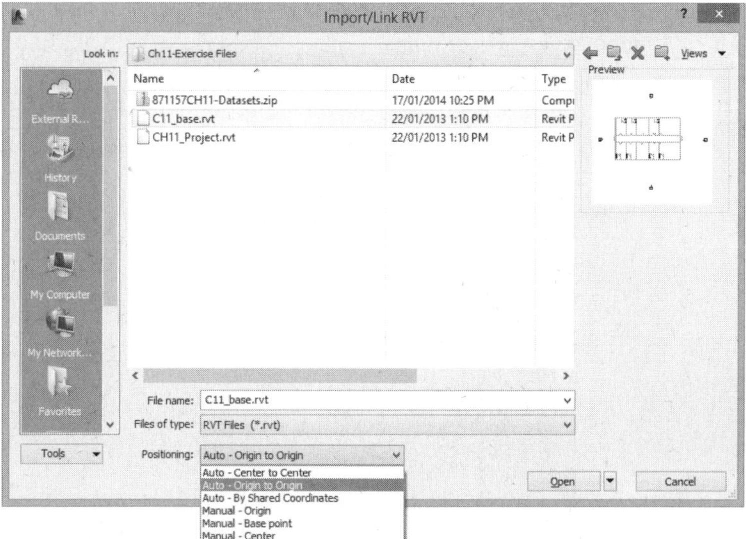

FIGURE 11.10 Linking the Revit model, Auto – Origin To Origin

IMPORTANCE OF TEMPLATES

To improve productivity in piping layouts, make sure to create and maintain project templates that contain your company standards. Properly created project templates ensure that everyone in your firm is on the same page when creating mechanical piping systems. For more information on how to create project templates from existing projects, refer to Chapter 2, "Creating an Effective Project Template."

4. Open the North Elevation and, from the Collaborate tab, click Copy/Monitor, pull down and click the Select Link choice, and then move the mouse over any architectural element to select the linked file and enter Copy/Monitor mode.
5. Click the Options button. For Reuse Matching Levels, choose Reuse If Within Offset and click OK. This ensures that your existing levels and floor plans will be reused instead of creating duplicates.
6. While still in the Copy/Monitor tool, select the Copy command to copy Level 1 and Level 2, and then click Finish.
7. Open view 1 – Mech. Download the file `WSHP - Horizontal.rfa` from `www.sybex.com/go/masteringrevitmep2015`. Choose Insert ➢ Load Family. Select `WSHP - Horizontal.rfa` from where you saved it and then click Open (see Figure 11.11).

   Note that this is a standard Revit file that is included within the U.S. Imperial Content library, and as long as U.S. Imperial Content has been loaded with Revit, the file can also be found at Insert ➤ Load Family ➤ Imperial Library ➤ Mechanical ➤ MEP ➤ Air-Side Components ➤ Heat Pumps.

FIGURE 11.11 Water source heat pumps

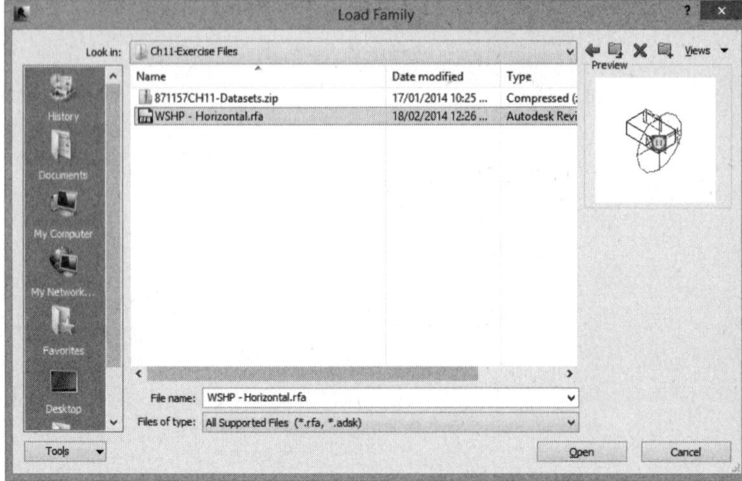

8. Choose Systems ➤ Mechanical Equipment, and start placing the water source heat pumps (type 006) into each room. If needed, you can use the spacebar before placing the equipment to rotate it 90 degrees. After you have placed all the heat pumps into the model, right-click the water source heat pump you first placed and choose All Instances ➤ Visible In View. Then, in the Properties palette, change the Offset parameter to 9′-0″ (2,750 mm). This will allow you to set the correct elevation of equipment (see Figure 11.12).

FIGURE 11.12 Verifying the offset for the correct elevation

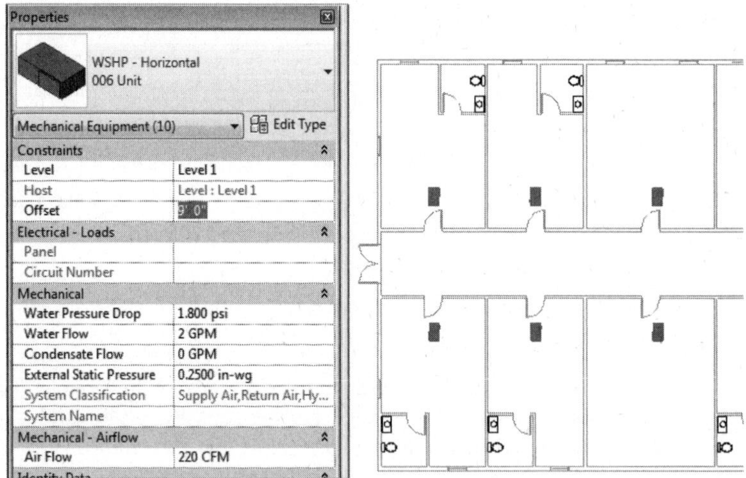

9. Your system will require a fan coil unit and a closed-circuit cooling tower. Both families are already loaded into your project. Place them into the appropriate locations, as shown in Figure 11.13.

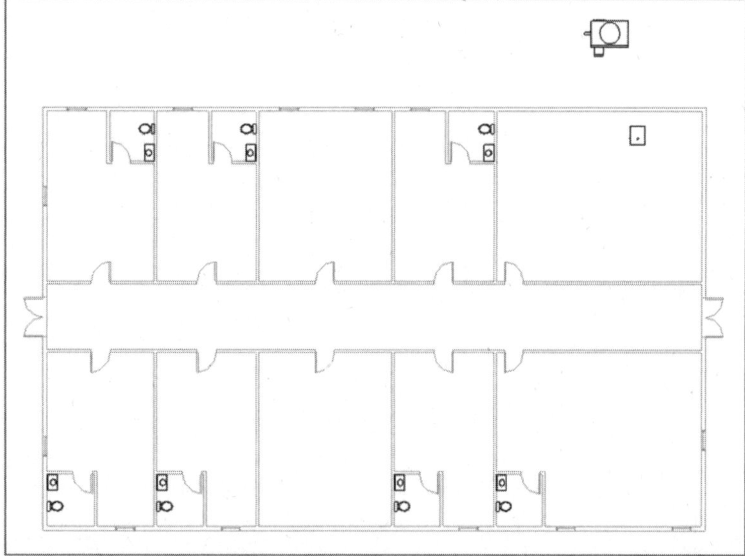

FIGURE 11.13 Placing mechanical equipment

10. Next you need a centrifugal pump. Choose Insert ➢ Load Family ➢ Imperial Library ➢ Mechanical ➢ MEP ➢ Water-Side Components ➢ Pumps. Select `Centrifugal Pump - Horizontal.rfa` and then click Open. Place the pump where you want it to be located in the mechanical room (see Figure 11.14).

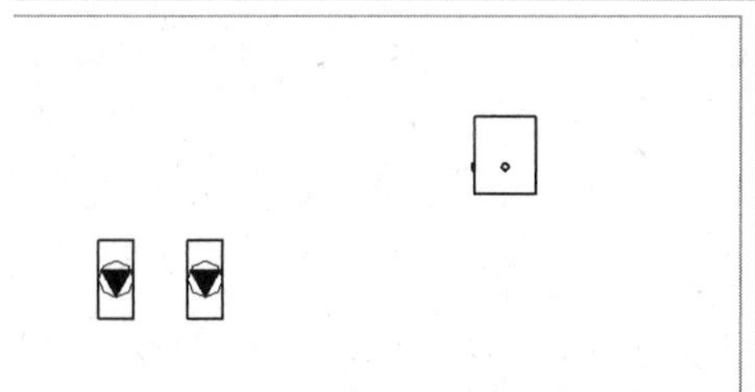

FIGURE 11.14 Placing the pump in the mechanical room

11. You are now in a position to start routing piping. Route your mains first so you can make sure that most of the piping will fit before connecting all the branches to the mains. Select the proper piping material before starting your layout. This will help if you need to do a quantity takeoff for budgeting purposes. To route your pipe, choose Systems ➢ Pipe. Change the Offset parameter to 8′-6″ (2,600 mm) and Pipe Size to 2″ (50 mm); also make

sure to select the pipe system type and route piping mains in the corridors and into the mechanical room (see Figure 11.15).

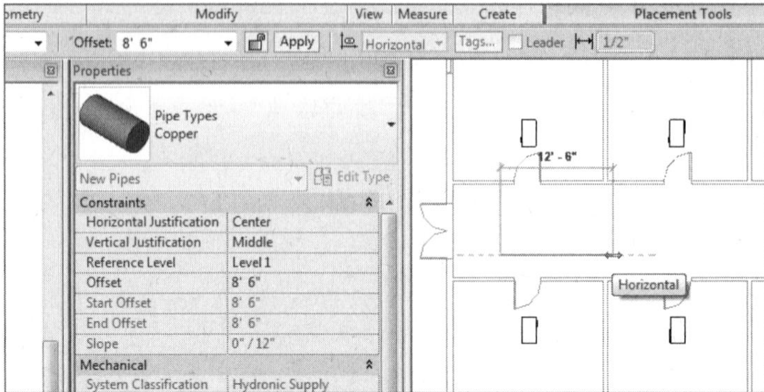

FIGURE 11.15
Routing pipe mains

12. Before you start connecting piping, you will need to make sure that your mechanical equipment is set up for both hydronic supply and return systems. To do this, select one of the pieces of mechanical equipment, and then choose Modify | Mechanical Equipment ➢ Piping. In the System Type list box, select Hydronic Return, as shown in Figure 11.16.

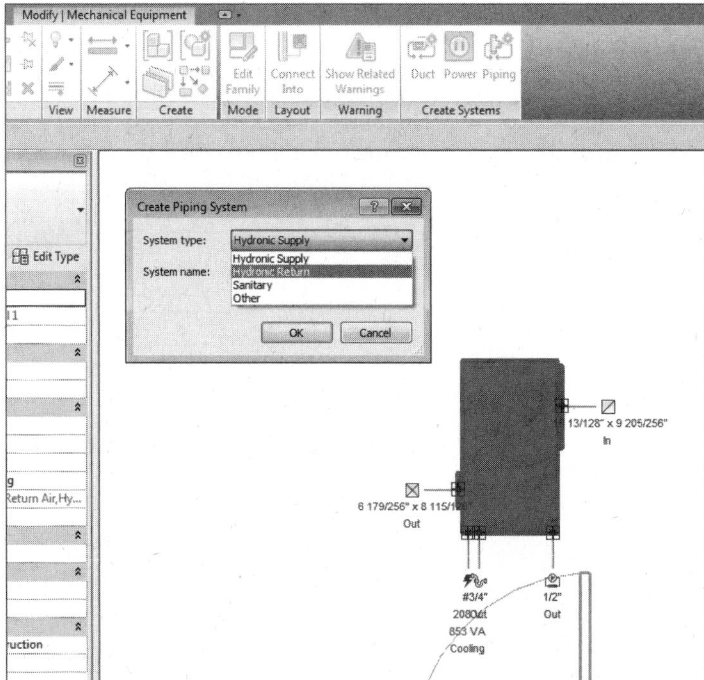

FIGURE 11.16
Creating mechanical piping systems

13. After you have selected the hydronic return, go to the Edit Piping System tab, select Edit System, and edit the Hydronic Return system name. Then select Add To System (see Figure 11.17), and select all mechanical equipment that contains Hydronic Return connections. Repeat with Hydronic Supply.

FIGURE 11.17 Adding equipment to systems

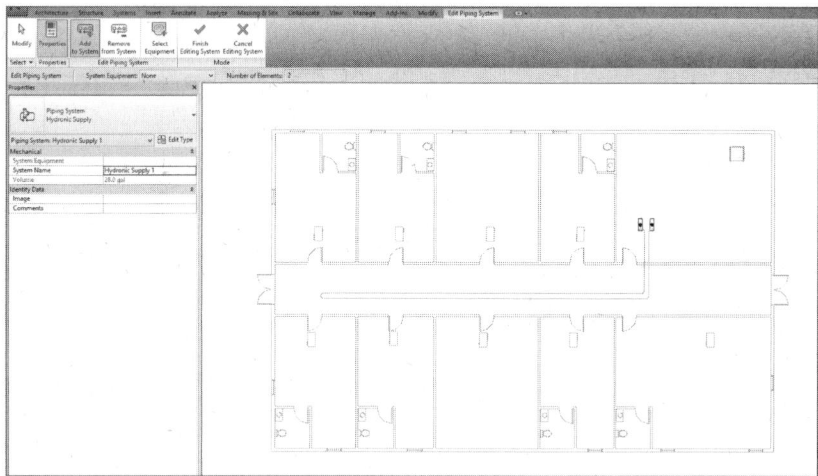

14. Cutting sections when routing piping can really improve the coordination success of your Revit model. If you want to automate things a bit, instead of drawing all the pipes yourself, you can select any equipment with pipe connectors, select Connect Into from the Modify | Mechanical Equipment tab, shown in Figure 11.18, and then select the equipment connector you want to connect to an existing pipe (see Figure 11.19).

FIGURE 11.18 Selecting Connect Into

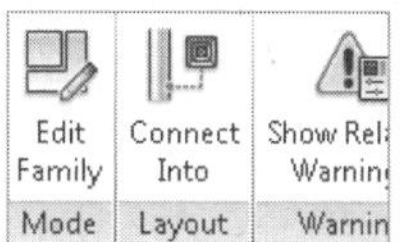

15. Repeat steps 6 through 13 for all your piping systems. Taking a few minutes to review any clashes between the structure, mechanical, and architectural models can really cut down on potential field conflicts. After you have coordinated with other services/structures and verified your layout, the layout will be complete.

Pipe Fittings

Without fittings, piping would not be worth a whole lot. Fittings help shut off the flow, help regulate temperature, and help save lives. In Revit, most fitting families have the following functions:

End Cap These can be placed only at the end of pipes.

Tee, Tap, Wye, or Cross These can be placed anywhere along pipe runs.

Transitions, Couplings, or Unions These can be placed only at the end of pipes. They are used to join a smaller, larger, or same-sized pipe.

Flange These can be placed at the end of pipes or face to face with another flange.

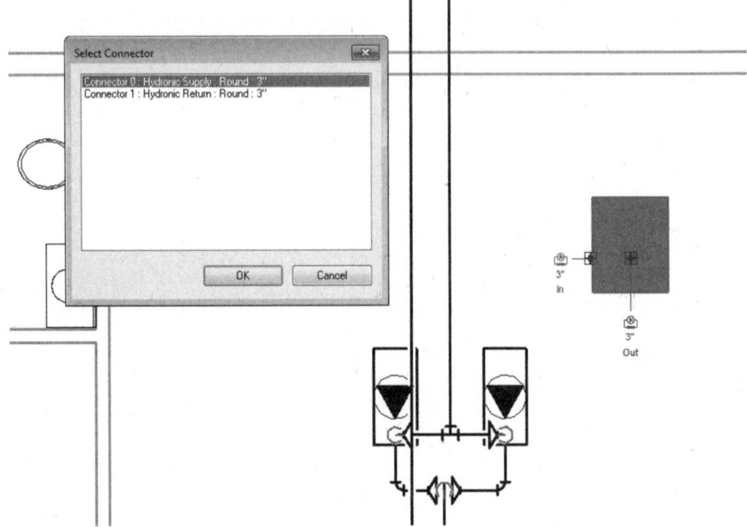

Figure 11.19
Using Connect Into

Using Pipe Fitting Controls

Understanding pipe fitting controls can really make life easier if you are routing a lot of piping. When you are laying out your piping, turn 90 degrees to create an elbow. If you click the elbow, you will notice a plus (+) sign. If you click that sign, it will change from an elbow to a tee, allowing you to add more piping and continue your pipe routing. If you click the minus (–) sign, it will downgrade the fitting. When you see the symbol on a fitting, it allows you to rotate the fitting, and the symbol allows you to flip the fitting.

The display of both fittings and valves can be challenging as you rotate the elements to represent the actual needed position. In some cases, they may become invisible. For example, when you place a valve in plan view at either coarse or medium detail level, you will see its symbolic representation, but if you go to a section, you won't see the valve at all. However, if you change it to fine detail level, you can see the geometry of the valve. This is because the valve is displayed as a symbol when showing single-line pipes, and with all of its 3D modeled geometry when in double-line pipe views. Currently the symbol can be displayed in only two opposite views (two sections, or floor plan and ceiling—in all other views it will be invisible). This is a known limitation with Revit, and to avoid it you should consider developing a standard for displaying valves and fittings, and at a certain level of detail.

Placing Valves

When you need to add valves to your piping, select the System tab and then select Pipe Accessory. Use the Type Selector to select the type of valve you want to use. Most valves are *break into* types, so you can place them into a pipe run and they will break into the piping, maintaining connections at either end (see Figure 11.20). This behavior works even when you remove the valve: The pipes automatically fill in the gap where the valve used to be.

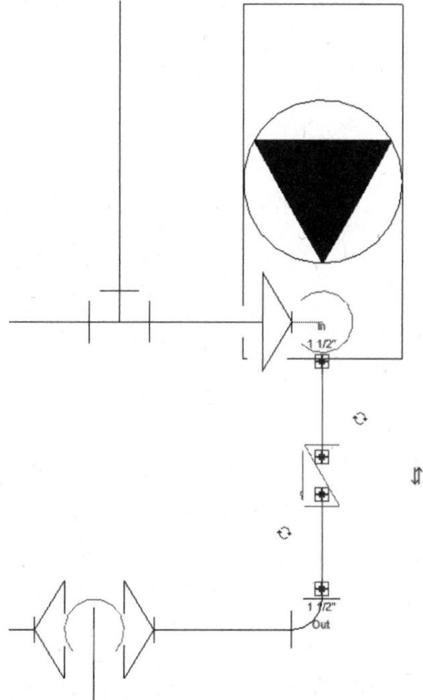

Figure 11.20
Valve breaks into a piping system

For some logical family categories, you can set this *break into* functionality in the Family Editor; choose Create ➤ Properties ➤ Family Category And Parameters (see Figure 11.21).

Adding Piping Insulation

Certain pipes require insulation. In some cases, this may be accomplished by simply annotating the insulated pipe, but in other cases you may need to model and display the pipe insulation. Pipe insulation in most cases is required when pipes are displayed as double lines. Currently, in order to place pipe insulation in Revit, the pipes need to be laid out already. You can do that by selecting individual pipes or entire runs of pipes and fittings and using the Add Insulation command under Modify | Pipes (see Figure 11.22). Pipe insulation visibility can further be controlled from the Visibility/Graphic Overrides dialog box and Object Styles, like any other Revit category. Once insulation has been added, it cannot be selected straight from the model. Rather, select the duct pieces and then click the Edit Insulation button.

Defining Systems Visibility through Filters

Revit MEP 2015 automatically creates logical piping systems for you when you lay out pipes, even when pipes are not connected to equipment. When drawing pipes, you need to specify the system type they belong to. The system type can define the line weight, linetype, color, and system abbreviation. The system abbreviation can be used to define what system will appear on what sheet via filters. This helps you hide the mechanical pipes in the plumbing views, and vice versa.

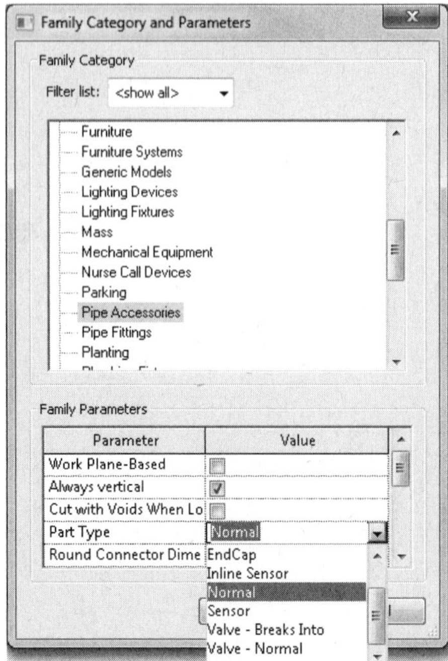

FIGURE 11.21 Defining *Breaks Into* behavior

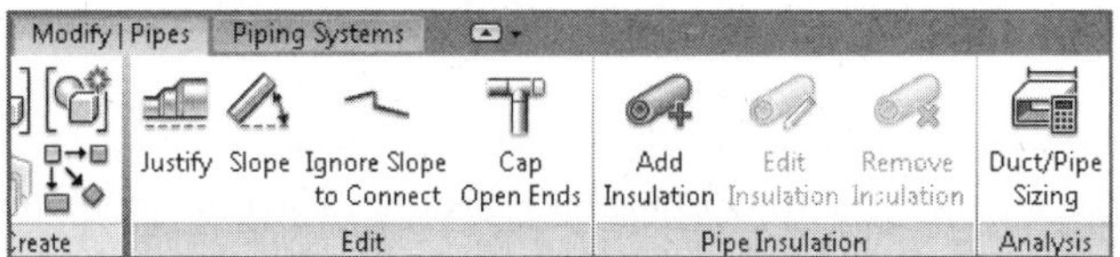

FIGURE 11.22 Adding pipe insulation

Establishing a good naming convention for the filters is important, because that would be the order in which you see them in your Properties palette when drawing pipes. The default examples of filters and their settings are not going to get you too far with your projects. We recommend that you take your time and come up with a complete list of systems that your company uses and create them as system types and filters in Revit MEP. Organizing all of them in Microsoft Excel can be very beneficial! Notice that the Filter By setting is set to System Abbreviation Equals AV, as shown in Figure 11.23. Bear in mind that the parameter System Abbreviation was not available prior to Revit MEP 2012, and the settings would be different for those projects and templates. To create new filters, simply click the New button in the lower-left corner.

Once the filters have been created, go into each view where you want the different disciplines to show up and type **VG** to bring up the Visibility/Graphic Overrides dialog box. Click the Filters tab, and add the newly created filters. If the view is controlled by a view template, then you must do this through View ➤ View Templates ➤ Manage View Templates. Using the Visibility check boxes on the Filters tab, you can define the systems to be visible in that view. In the past, filters were used to also define color, line patterns, and in some cases line weights.

Since Revit MEP 2012, the recommended place to control those is in the System Type settings for the pipe. This way, those settings will be global rather than per view. However, the filters would still be managed and would control what system is visible in what view (see Figure 11.24), and they would still control line patterns, color, and line weights for specific cases. An example of this would be when you are using a 3D view. When you control the colors and line patterns of your systems in the 3D views, it will color the contour of the pipe, making the pipes hard to see. You could then override those in the filters with a solid pattern; this way, your 3D views would be a lot easier to view and understand (see Figure 11.25 and Figure 11.26).

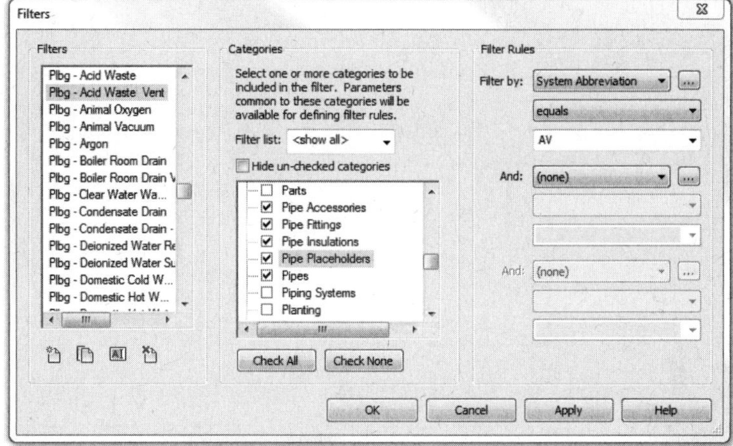

FIGURE 11.23 Sample filters and their settings

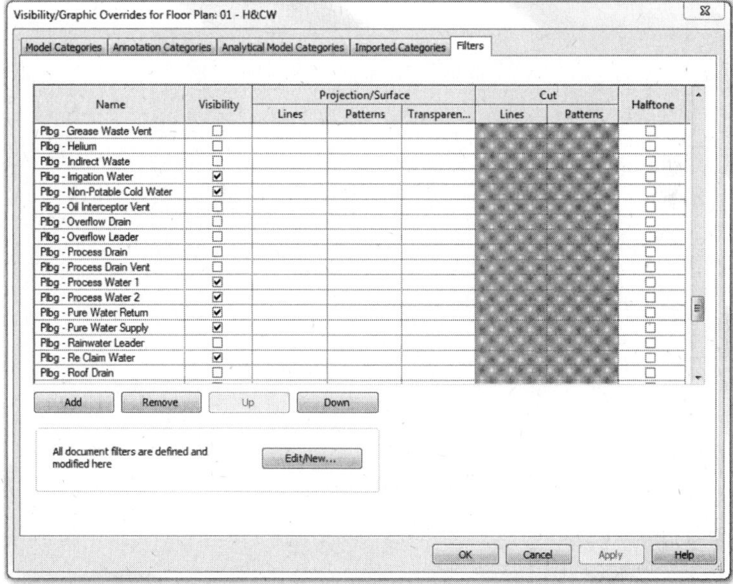

FIGURE 11.24 Adjusting visibility of pipe and duct systems through filters

Now that your plans are coordinated and are displayed the way you require, you are well on your way to completing your documentation.

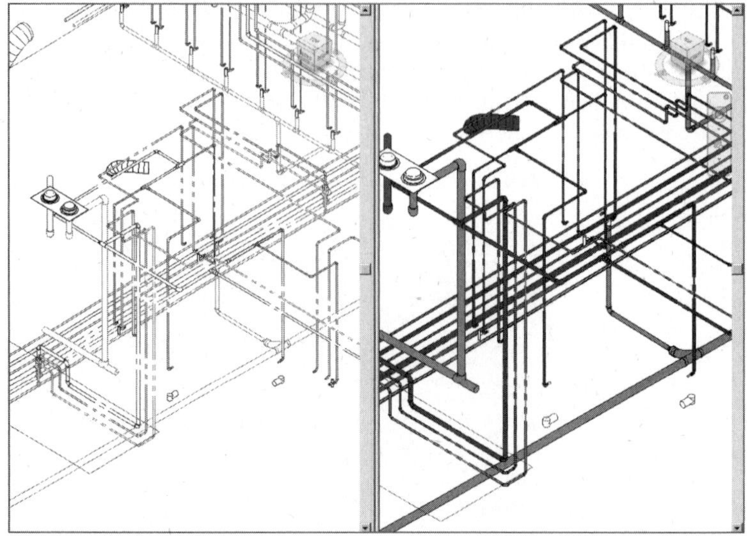

FIGURE 11.25 The same model displayed without filter overrides (left) and with overrides (right)

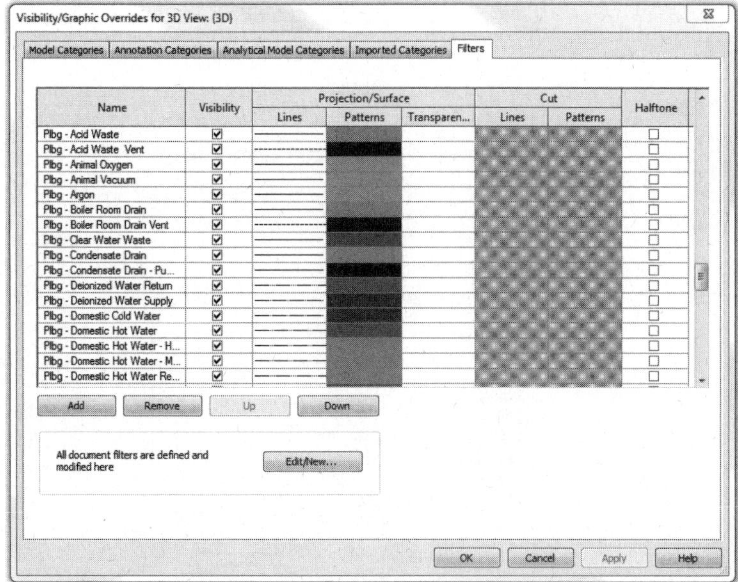

FIGURE 11.26 Applying filter overrides for 3D views

The Bottom Line

Adjust the mechanical pipe settings. Making sure the mechanical piping settings are properly set up is crucial to the beginning of any project.

Master It A designer has just been asked to model a mechanical piping layout, and the engineer wants to make sure the designer will be able to account for the piping material used in the layout. What steps must the designer take to complete this request?

Select the best pipe routing options for your project. When using Revit MEP 2015 for your mechanical layouts, you must understand the functions of automatic pipe routing and manual pipe routing. After mastering these functions, you can lay out any type of piping system.

Master It The engineer has just come back from a meeting with the owner and architect, and it has been decided that there will be a heated-water system and a chilled-water system rather than a two-pipe hydronic system. How would you modify your hydronic layout to accommodate the change?

Adjust pipe fittings. Pipe fittings are needed in systems to make the systems function properly and to produce documentation for construction. Being able to add or modify fittings can increase productivity.

Master It You have printed a check set for review and have noticed that there are no shutoff valves. Now you need to load the shutoff family. In what directory should you look for pipe fittings?

Adjust the visibility of pipes. Being able to adjust the visibility of pipes gives the mechanical designer or user the ability to set up multiple views and control the graphics for documentation.

Master It The engineer has just come back from a meeting with the owner and architect, and it has been decided that there will be a heated-water system and a chilled-water system. You have just modified your hydronic layout to accommodate the change. Now the owner wants the pipes to be color-coded so it's easier to visualize the changes. Describe how this would be done.

Part 3

Electrical Design

Lighting

It may be difficult at first to see a good reason for making the effort to include lighting systems in a 3D building model. After all, lighting can be represented by drafting symbols, can't it? Although that is true, a BIM project is much more than just creating a 3D model. The data from an intelligent lighting model can be used for analysis and can aid in design decisions.

Including light fixtures and their associated devices in an Autodesk® Revit® model will allow you to coordinate your complete electrical design by providing electrical load information. They can also be used to develop presentation imagery by generating realistic light in renderings.

Creating a lighting model with Revit MEP enables you to develop your design while generating the necessary construction documents to convey the design intent.

In this chapter, you will learn to do the following:

- Prepare your project for lighting design
- Use Revit MEP for lighting analysis
- Compare and evaluate hosting options for lighting fixtures and devices
- Develop site lighting plans

Efficient Lighting Design

Let's face it, ceiling plans are one of the biggest coordination pain points for a design team. Nearly every MEP discipline has some type of element that resides in the ceiling. Using intelligent lighting families will help you, the electrical designer, stake your claim to that precious real estate. Using 3D geometry to represent light fixtures means that you can detect interference with other model elements. This does not mean that your lighting fixture families will have to be modeled to show every trim ring, reflector, tombstone, or lens. The basic geometry is usually enough to satisfy the requirements for model coordination.

The intelligence put into your families is what will benefit you the most from an electrical standpoint. Photometric data, manufacturer, model, voltage, and number of lamps are just a few examples of the types of properties that can reside in your fixture families. An in-depth look at creating lighting fixture families takes place later in Chapter 20, "Creating Lighting Fixtures."

Spaces and Lighting

For the spaces in your model to report the correct lighting level, they must be modeled accurately. If the height of the space is short of the ceiling, the lighting fixtures will not be in the space and thus no lighting data will be seen or be detectable by Revit for that space. The room calculation point feature available in lighting fixture families allows you to associate a fixture with a space even though the fixture is not within the bounds of the space. See Chapter 20 for more information on this feature.

A ceiling can be defined as a room-bounding element, which means that it can define the upper boundary of a space. If you model your spaces so that their upper limit is higher than the ceiling heights, you can be sure that you are getting accurate volume information for the spaces. When you are placing spaces into the model, set the upper limit to the level above the current level on which you are working to ensure proper volumes. If you have a space that spans multiple ceiling heights, make sure you set the upper limit appropriately, as shown in Figure 12.1.

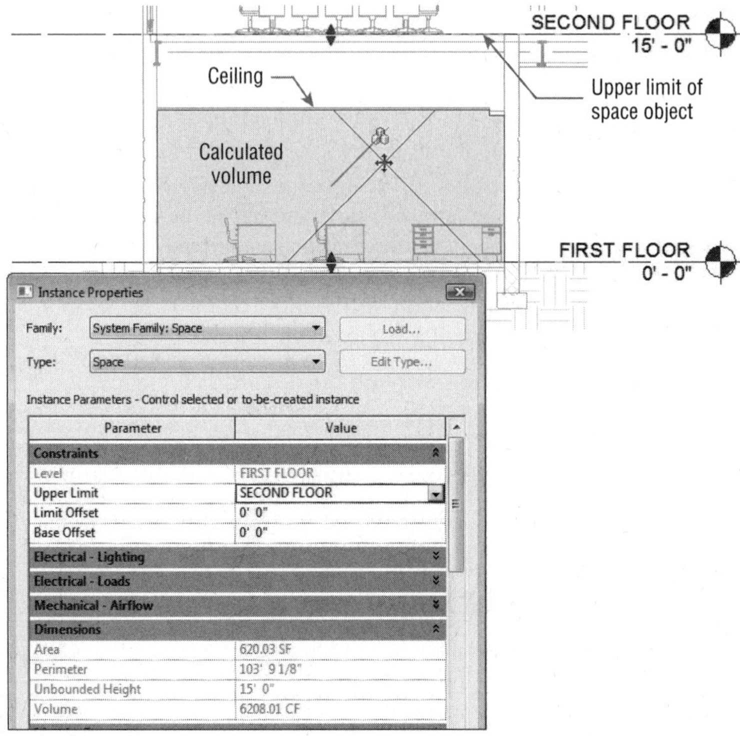

FIGURE 12.1
Space volume and ceiling relationship

Real World Scenario

KNOW YOUR LIMITS

Phil is getting some strange numbers from his lighting calculations. He checks his spaces and finds that the volumes of the rooms at the perimeter of the building are being calculated not to the ceiling but all the way up to the next level. A quick phone call to his architect reveals that the mechanical designer has requested that the ceilings in these rooms be set so they are not room bounding. This is necessary for accurate heating and cooling load calculations.

Phil is glad that his file is separate from the mechanical file because all he has to do is set the upper limit of his exterior spaces to match the ceiling heights, thus allowing for accurate lighting calculations.

Space volume is important to the proper calculation of average estimated illumination within a room. The ability to calculate the volume of a space can be turned on or off to help with file performance. If you intend to use Revit MEP to analyze your lighting design, you need to ensure that this setting is turned on. Do this by clicking the Room & Area panel drop-down on the Architecture tab, shown in Figure 12.2.

FIGURE 12.2
Room & Area panel

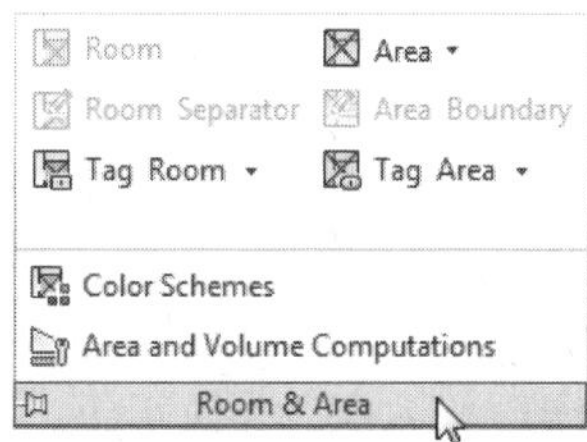

Select the Area And Volume Computations tool to access the settings for space volume computations. Choose the setting shown in Figure 12.3 when using Revit MEP for lighting analysis.

FIGURE 12.3
Areas And Volumes setting

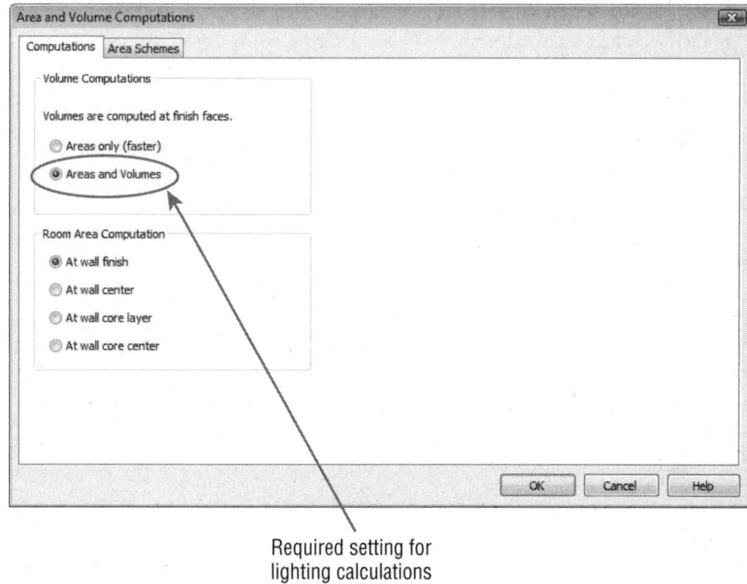

You can practice placing and manipulating spaces by doing the following:

1. Open the `Ch12 Exercise.rvt` file, which can be downloaded from `www.sybex.com/go/masteringrevitmep2015`.
2. Open the 1 – Lighting plan view and link in the architectural model file `Ch12 ArchModel.rvt`, which can also be downloaded from the book's website. Use the Auto – Origin To Origin positioning option for placement.
3. Set the property of the linked file to Room Bounding by selecting the link, clicking the Edit Type button in the Properties palette, and selecting the Room Bounding box.

4. Click the Space tool on the Analyze tab.
5. On the Options Bar, set Offset to **8′-0″** (**2440** mm), and place a space in the large curved room at the right side of the building.
6. Create a Building Section view looking north through the large room.
7. Open the section view, and select the Space object. (You may have to hover your mouse pointer on the room edges.) Notice that the upper limit is below the Ceiling object in the room.
8. Check the instance properties of the space, and verify that the volume is computed under the Dimensions group. If not, go back and set your model to compute volume by adjusting the Area And Volume Computations settings on the Room & Area panel of the Architecture tab.
9. Once again, with the Properties palette showing the properties of the space, change the Limit Offset parameter value to **10′-0″** (**3050** mm) and examine the Volume parameter value of the space. You may need to click the Apply button on the Properties palette for the change to take place.
10. Change the Limit Offset parameter value to **12′-0″** (**3660** mm), and note that the Volume parameter value stays the same. This confirms that the ceiling is acting as a room boundary.
11. Open the 1 – Lighting plan view, and click the Space button on the Analyze tab to place another space in the room located in the upper-right corner of the building. Before placing the space, on the Options Bar, set the upper limit of the space to Level 2, and set the Offset to **0′-0″** (**0** mm). Then click in the room to create the space.
12. Create a section view of this room, and select the Space object. Notice that the space extends beyond the ceiling. This confirms that the ceiling is not set to be room bounding.
13. In the section view, select the Space object, and use the grip arrow to stretch the top of the space beyond the roof. Notice that the space fills the entire volume up to the roof.
14. Continue placing spaces in the model, and examine their properties based on the settings you choose on the Options Bar for placement.

The Reflected Ceiling Plan

The first step in creating a well-coordinated lighting plan is to ensure that your reflected ceiling plan is properly set up to display the model in a way that allows you to see all the items necessary to coordinate as you design. Adjust the view range settings of your view so that all ceilings are clearly visible, and turn on any worksets or component categories from other disciplines that may contain items in the ceiling. You can set the categories from other disciplines to halftone to see your lighting layout more clearly. If you are linking in files from MEP consultants, use the visibility control options for linked files to achieve the desired result.

If you intend to display the ceiling grids on your lighting construction documents, you have to make visibility adjustments to ensure that the building model is displayed correctly.

Remember that with a reflected ceiling plan, you are looking up at the model, so certain elements, such as plumbing fixtures or windows, may not appear as desired until you adjust the view range and the Visibility/Graphic Overrides. Stairs also display differently in reflected ceiling views than they do in normal plan views. Also, consider that the order of objects is different than in a plan view. A fixture shown below an object in a plan view appears to be above the object in a reflected ceiling plan view. This may have an adverse effect on your construction documents.

Another method for displaying ceiling grids on the construction documents of your project is to create a reflected ceiling plan view that shows only the ceiling objects. This view can be placed on a sheet in the same location as the lighting floor plan view. When placed onto a sheet, the view can be snapped to the same location as the floor plan view so you can be sure of the alignment. This allows you to display the model correctly as a plan view and still be able to see the ceiling grids or surfaces. For best results, you should place the ceiling plan view on the sheet first and then the lighting plan view on top of it.

There is often debate between architects and electrical designers as to whose model should contain the ceilings. Ceilings are not always required in early project submittals, so the architect may not get around to modeling them when the electrical designer needs them. This may prompt the electrical designer to create ceilings in their model in order to begin the lighting design, which can cause coordination issues after the architect begins designing the ceilings in the architectural model. Having duplicate information in multiple models can be a recipe for error. The electrical designer would have to keep the ceilings in the electrical model coordinated with the architect's ceilings and would have to ensure that all model views were displaying the proper ceilings. This extra effort defeats the purpose of using a BIM solution such as Revit MEP and hampers the effort to achieve a coordinated project delivery because it adds another level of manual coordination that creates more opportunities for error.

You may use the option of creating reference planes in your model to host your lighting fixtures temporarily. When the ceilings are placed in the architectural model, you could then re-host your fixtures to them. Another option is to use nonhosted families in your project. Because you cannot replace a nonhosted family with a hosted one, you have to make the decision to use hosted or nonhosted.

Lighting fixtures that are modeled in the architectural model are another thing to consider. Many architects like to create lighting layouts for their design to get a feel for how the rooms will look with lighting fixtures in the ceiling or to create renderings. If the architect uses 3D families to represent the lighting fixtures, this can cause problems for the electrical designer when it comes to using the linked model for hosting. Lighting fixtures in the architectural model will most likely cut a hole in the ceiling where they are placed. An electrical designer who attempts to put a light fixture in the same location as the fixture in the linked file may not be able to do so because there won't actually be a ceiling there. There is also the chance that a face of the fixture in the link hosts the fixture in the MEP file. So if the architect deletes the fixture in their file, the fixture in the MEP file will not have a host and will not respond to changes.

Early in the project, the architect and electrical designer should agree on who will model the ceilings and in which model they will reside. They should also coordinate which types of families will be used if the architect intends to place lighting fixtures in the architectural model. If they need to be modeled in one file initially, they can be copied and pasted into another file if necessary. Another option is to use the Copy/Monitor tool to copy the lighting fixtures from the architectural model. The ultimate goal is to have one ceiling design that all disciplines can use for layout and coordination.

Lighting Worksets

When working in a model file with other MEP disciplines, it is best to create a lighting workset to distinguish model elements that would belong to that design system. It may even be necessary to create multiple worksets for lighting systems. Doing so will allow you to divide your lighting design into separate systems (such as interior and exterior) or by floor levels.

This can aid you in controlling the visibility of groups of model elements and can also help multiple users work on different sections of the lighting model at the same time without interfering with each other's designs.

Lighting Analysis

Because you are placing light fixtures for the purpose of a layout that is coordinated with other disciplines, you can also get design information that will help you make decisions on the types of lights to use. You can use the power of the scheduling capabilities of Revit MEP to create a schedule of the spaces in your model that shows the lighting fixtures used and the lighting criteria in which you are interested. You can review this schedule as you place lights into the model to see whether you are making the right choices for lighting fixtures.

Figure 12.4 shows a simple version of this type of schedule. The last column is a calculated value that shows the difference between the required lighting level and the actual level. A difference greater than 5 foot-candles causes the cell to turn red. Because there are no lights in the model yet, none of the spaces has the required lighting level, so every cell in the column is red. Your goal as a designer is to achieve a schedule with no red cells in the final column.

FIGURE 12.4 Sample lighting analysis schedule

Space Lighting Schedule - Analysis

ROOM NO.	ROOM NAME	REQ LTG LEVEL	AVG EST ILLUMINATION	LOAD PER ARE	DIFF BETWEEN AVG AND REQ
100	lobby	20 fc	0 fc	0.00 W/ft²	-20 fc
100A	reception	30 fc	0 fc	0.00 W/ft²	-30 fc
101	corridor	20 fc	0 fc	0.00 W/ft²	-20 fc
102	corridor	20 fc	0 fc	0.00 W/ft²	-20 fc
103	training 1	50 fc	0 fc	0.00 W/ft²	-50 fc
104	training 2	50 fc	0 fc	0.00 W/ft²	-50 fc
105	training 3	50 fc	0 fc	0.00 W/ft²	-50 fc
106	training 4	50 fc	0 fc	0.00 W/ft²	-50 fc
107	break room	30 fc	0 fc	0.00 W/ft²	-30 fc
107A	stor	20 fc	0 fc	0.00 W/ft²	-20 fc
108	comm - MDF	20 fc	0 fc	0.00 W/ft²	-20 fc
109	main electrical	20 fc	0 fc	0.00 W/ft²	-20 fc
110	elev mech	20 fc	0 fc	0.00 W/ft²	-20 fc
111	recept stor/files	20 fc	0 fc	0.00 W/ft²	-20 fc
112	public toilet men	10 fc	0 fc	0.00 W/ft²	-10 fc
113	public toilet women	10 fc	0 fc	0.00 W/ft²	-10 fc
114	auditorium / theatre	30 fc	0 fc	0.00 W/ft²	-30 fc

Prior to using this schedule, you should assign a target lighting level for all the spaces that you will analyze. Create a project parameter to be used for your targeted lighting level. This should be an instance parameter so that it can vary from space to space. Set the discipline of the parameter to Electrical and the type to Illuminance. Group the parameter in the

Electrical-Lighting group so that it can be easily located. Give the parameter a name such as **Required Lighting Level** so that the intended use of the parameter is clear. You can create this project parameter in your project template file for use on every project if desired. Remember that you can use project parameters in schedules, but you cannot create an annotation tag for them, so if you want to use the parameter in a tag, use a shared parameter. For more information on creating parameters, see Chapter 6, "Parameters."

Once you have established a parameter for the target lighting level of a space, you can create another type of schedule to associate standard lighting levels with certain types of spaces. This is not a schedule of building components but rather a key that will assign a target lighting level to a space based on the type of space. This is known as a *schedule key*.

To create a schedule key, you use the same tool that you would use to create a regular schedule and do the following:

1. In the New Schedule dialog box, select Spaces as the category to be scheduled.
2. At the right side of the dialog box, name your schedule to indicate its use, and select the Schedule Keys option rather than the default Schedule Building Components option.
3. The key name that you choose becomes an instance parameter of all the spaces in the model. The parameter is located in the Identity Data group of parameters. Choose a name that clearly identifies the purpose of the parameter, as shown in Figure 12.5.

FIGURE 12.5
Creating a new schedule key for spaces

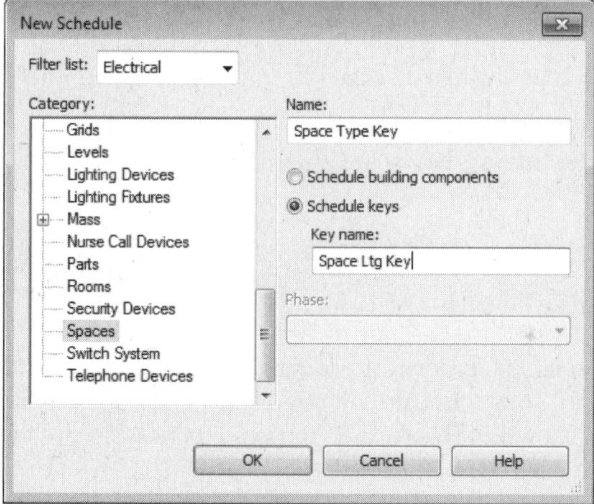

4. Click OK in the New Schedule dialog box to access the Schedule Properties dialog box. Key Name is added as a scheduled field by default, as shown in Figure 12.6.
5. On the left side of the dialog box, select the parameter that you created as the target lighting level for your spaces and click the Add button to include it in the schedule. These are the only two fields required for this schedule, and there is no need to format them or adjust the appearance of the schedule because it is used only for analysis.
6. Click OK to create the schedule.

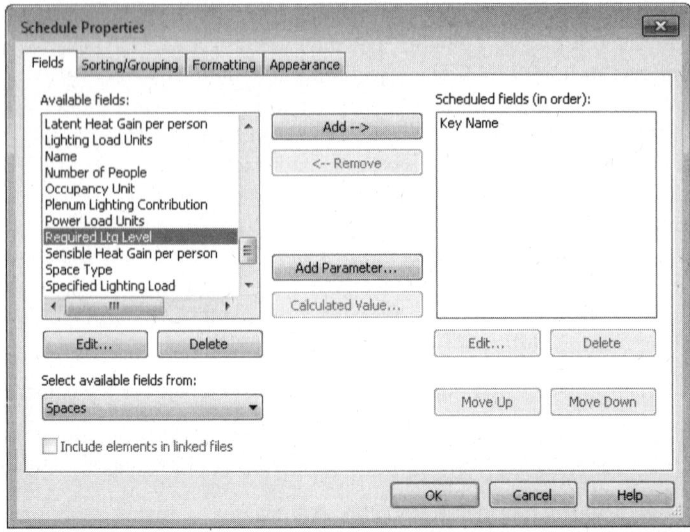

FIGURE 12.6 Schedule Properties dialog box

7. The schedule does not contain any data rows. At this point, you need to build your key for lighting requirements. Click the Insert button on the Rows panel of the Modify Schedule/Quantities tab and select the Data Row option to create a row in your schedule.
8. Change the name of the key in the schedule to that of a common type of building space.
9. Add the appropriate lighting level for that type of space in the second column of the schedule, as shown in Figure 12.7.

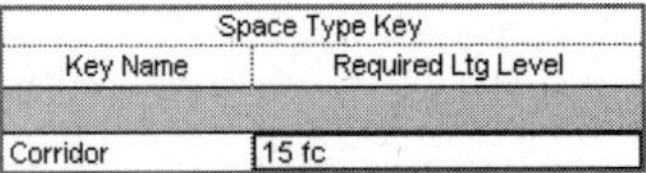

Space Type Key	
Key Name	Required Ltg Level
Corridor	15 fc

FIGURE 12.7 Schedule key data input

10. Repeat the process of adding rows, creating space types, and assigning lighting levels until your schedule contains all the space types you require for analysis of your project, as shown in Figure 12.8. You can create a comprehensive list in your project template file for use on future projects.

FIGURE 12.8 Schedule keys with required lighting levels

Space Type Key	
Key Name	Required Ltg Level
Auditorium	30 fc
Conference	30 fc
Corridor	15 fc
Janitor	15 fc
Kitchen	30 fc
Lobby	20 fc
Mech/Elec	20 fc
Office	50 fc
Storage	15 fc
Toilet	10 fc
Training/Classroom	50 fc
Waiting/Lounge	30 fc

The purpose of creating the schedule key is to maintain consistency throughout the model and to assign target lighting levels to spaces easily. You can now include the parameter created by the schedule key in your lighting analysis schedule and assign space types to all your spaces without having to select them in the model and edit their properties. Use the drop-down list in the parameter value to select an appropriate type for the space. When you select a space type, the lighting level associated with that type is input into the parameter for the target lighting level of that space, as shown in Figure 12.9. The value for the change calculated by the Lighting Delta conditional format automatically appears in the schedule when a key is assigned to a space.

FIGURE 12.9 Space lighting keys applied in a schedule

Space Ltg Analysis							
Room: Numb	Room: Name	Space Ltg Key	Required Ltg Level	Average Estimated Illumina	Ceiling Refle	Lighting Calculation Work	Lighting Delta
100	lobby	Lobby	20 fc	10 fc	0.75	2' - 6"	-10 fc
100A	reception	Lobby	20 fc	26 fc	0.75	2' - 6"	6 fc
101	corridor	Corridor	15 fc	13 fc	0.75	2' - 6"	-2 fc
102	corridor	Corridor	15 fc	21 fc	0.75	2' - 6"	6 fc
103	training 1	(none)		0 fc	0.75	2' - 6"	
104	training 2	Auditorium		41 fc	0.75	2' - 6"	
105	training 3	Conference		41 fc	0.75	2' - 6"	
106	training 4	Corridor		41 fc	0.75	2' - 6"	
107	break room	Janitor		32 fc	0.75	2' - 6"	
107A	stor	Kitchen Lobby		46 fc	0.75	2' - 6"	
108	comm - MDF	(none)		21 fc	0.75	2' - 6"	
109	main electrical	(none)		20 fc	0.75	2' - 6"	
110	elev mech	(none)		32 fc	0.75	2' - 6"	

You do not need to assign a type to a space in order to input a value for its targeted lighting level. Simply input a value into the schedule cell for the target lighting level. Notice in Figure 12.10 that room 100A has not been assigned a space type, yet a value has been given for the target lighting level.

FIGURE 12.10 Calculated values in a lighting analysis schedule

Space Ltg Analysis							
Room: Numb	Room: Name	Space Ltg Key	Required Ltg Level	Average Estimated Illumina	Ceiling Refle	Lighting Calculation Work	Lighting Delta
100	lobby	Lobby	20 fc	10 fc	0.75	2' - 6"	-10 fc
100A	reception	(none)	30 fc	26 fc	0.75	2' - 6"	-4 fc
101	corridor	Corridor	15 fc	13 fc	0.75	2' - 6"	-2 fc
102	corridor	Corridor	15 fc	21 fc	0.75	2' - 6"	6 fc
103	training 1	Training/Clas	50 fc	0 fc	0.75	2' - 6"	-50 fc
104	training 2	Training/Clas	50 fc	41 fc	0.75	2' - 6"	-9 fc
105	training 3	Training/Clas	50 fc	41 fc	0.75	2' - 6"	-9 fc
106	training 4	Training/Clas	50 fc	41 fc	0.75	2' - 6"	-9 fc
107	break room	Waiting/Loun	30 fc	32 fc	0.75	2' - 6"	2 fc
107A	stor	Storage	15 fc	46 fc	0.75	2' - 6"	31 fc
108	comm - MDF	Mech/Elec	20 fc	21 fc	0.75	2' - 6"	1 fc
109	main electrical	Mech/Elec	20 fc	20 fc	0.75	2' - 6"	0 fc
110	elev mech	Mech/Elec	20 fc	32 fc	0.75	2' - 6"	12 fc

With a target lighting level assigned to each space, you can now determine how well the fixtures you have chosen are lighting the spaces. You can use the Space Lighting Analysis schedule to quickly see the types of adjustments required to meet the target levels. You can even include space parameters such as finishes and make adjustments to them for more accurate results.

CALCULATION CAUTION

Revit MEP uses basic lighting calculation methods to provide an average estimated illumination for spaces. These values can be very useful in spaces where all lighting fixtures are at the same elevation. However, the values will be incorrect for spaces with light fixtures at varying elevations.

For example, if you have a space with four lighting fixtures at 10′-0″ and another two at 8′-0″ above the floor, the average estimated illumination result is given as if all fixtures are at 8′-0″. So regardless of the properties of the fixtures, Revit calculates from the elevation of the lowest fixture. This is true even if the lowest fixture has no photometric properties (no light source).

Hosting Options for Lighting Fixtures and Devices

Hosting fixtures and devices is important for coordination with other model elements and also reduces the time spent modifying layouts to match design changes. There are a few options for hosting, and you should choose the one that works best for the type of fixtures you are using and the file setup of your project. Face-hosted families are most commonly used because they work in many scenarios, but at times you may need to use an alternative hosting method.

Lighting Fixtures in a Ceiling

Face-hosted lighting fixture families are most commonly used because they can be attached to ceilings in your model or ceilings within a linked file in your model. You can use face-hosted fixtures to represent recessed, surface-mounted, and pendant lights.

CUTTING HOLES IN THE CEILING

Lighting fixture families can be made to cut the ceiling when they are placed. If you are attaching them to a ceiling that is in a linked file, the fixture does not cut the ceiling. This has no effect on lighting calculations and affects only the appearance of the model. If your architect is using your lighting model for a reflected ceiling plan, ceiling grid lines will be visible through lighting fixtures that cross them.

The default hosting for a face-hosted family is to a vertical face. To place lighting fixtures onto a ceiling, you need to select the Place On Face option, located on the Placement panel of the contextual tab that appears when placing a lighting fixture family. Lighting fixture families for ceiling-mounted lights should have an insertion point at one corner of the fixture. This lets you align the fixture to the ceiling grid on placement. If the family you are using does not have an insertion point at a corner, place the fixture on the ceiling and use the Move or Align tool to line it up with the grid.

Using the Align tool is great for lining up your fixtures with ceiling grid lines, but it is important that you do not lock the alignment. Face-hosted families do not move with the grid lines when changes are made to the ceiling. Locking the alignment causes constraint errors when the link is updated after the grid has moved. Either way, the lighting fixture stays attached to the ceiling if its elevation changes.

Once you have placed lighting fixtures onto a ceiling, you can copy them where needed. It is important to copy only the fixtures within the ceiling by which they are hosted. If you attempt to copy a face-hosted fixture from one ceiling to another that has a different elevation, you may receive a warning that the new instance of the fixture lies outside its host or that the fixture will remain at the elevation of the original. This will cause the fixture to be in the model without a host or to be above or below the ceiling, which can result in an inaccurate model. If the fixture is not hosted by the ceiling, it will not react to any changes in the ceiling elevation. If the fixture is above the ceiling, lighting calculations will be inaccurate because it will not be inside the space.

The Create Similar command is an easy way to use the same type of fixture family from one ceiling to another. Use this command instead of Copy to duplicate a fixture family in another location. When you use this method, you have to set the hosting option to Place On Face before picking the location of the new fixture. Use the Pick New tool on the Work Plane panel of the Modify | Lighting Fixtures contextual tab to move a lighting fixture from one ceiling to another.

Face-hosted lighting fixture families can be used in areas where a ceiling does not exist. Another choice for placement is to use the Place On Work Plane option. This associates your fixture to a defined plane in the model. Because of the mounting behavior of face-hosted families, it is important to draw your reference planes in the correct direction. Drawing a reference plane from right to left orients the plane properly for overhead lighting fixtures. Drawing from left to right causes your lighting fixture families to be upside down in the model, as shown in Figure 12.11.

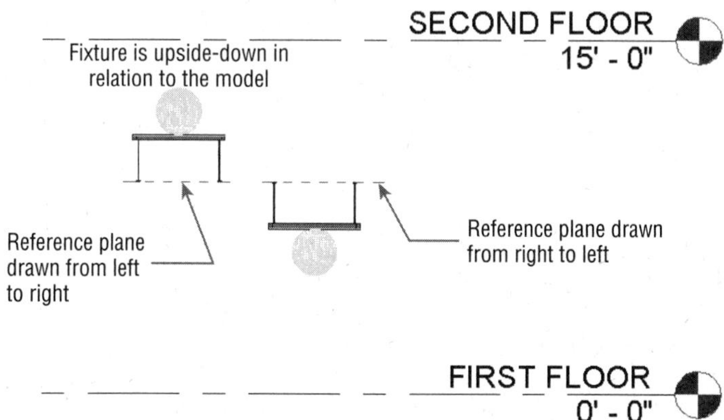

FIGURE 12.11 Lighting fixtures hosted by reference planes

Lighting Fixtures in Sloped Ceilings

Sloped ceilings can host lighting fixtures. Although this is an improvement to previous versions of Revit MEP, there are some consequences. When the fixture is sloped, its symbolic line representation is no longer visible in a plan view. Figure 12.12 shows the same lighting fixture hosted by a sloped ceiling and a flat reference plane. The section view indicates that the fixture is hosted properly, but the plan view displays the fixture differently.

The fixture that is attached to the sloped ceiling displays the actual fixture geometry at an angle, while the fixture on the flat reference plane shows the symbolic lines used to represent the fixture. Because symbolic lines can be displayed only in a view that is parallel to the plane in which they are created, there is no way to display these lines when the fixture is sloped. You would need to either add a note to your documents that identifies the sloped fixtures or add the sloped-fixture representation to your symbol legend.

Another option is to use model lines in your lighting fixture family instead of symbolic lines. Model lines display in plan views if the fixture is in a sloped ceiling. When using this method, consider defining subcategories in the lighting family for a luminaire body and sloping symbol. This gives you greater control over the look of your family. You wouldn't, after all, want the symbolic model lines showing up in any sections.

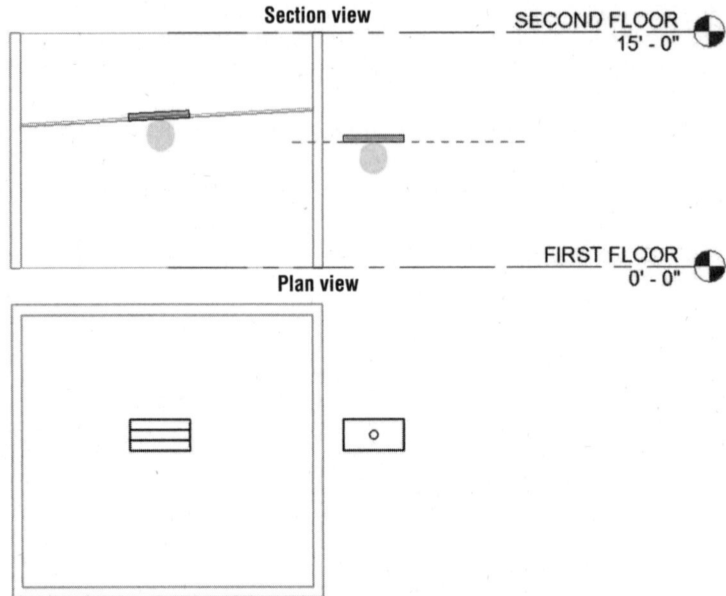

FIGURE 12.12 Lighting fixture in a sloped ceiling and on a flat reference plane

Ceiling Changes

Changes to ceilings may require some management of the lighting fixtures in your model. Face-hosted lighting fixtures maintain their association with the ceiling when there is a change in elevation, but you should also be concerned with any lateral movement, especially with grid ceilings.

Lateral movement can have different effects on your lighting fixtures depending on how the grid was placed into the model. Grids that are placed by automatically locating the boundaries of a room do not affect your light fixtures when they are moved laterally. This is true as long as the movement does not cause your fixtures (which won't move laterally with the ceiling) to be located outside the boundaries of the ceiling. If the architect deletes a ceiling and then replaces it, your fixtures will become orphaned when you get the updated architectural file, and they will remain at the elevation of the original ceiling and will no longer respond to changes in the elevation of the new ceiling. You will have to use the Pick New tool to associate the fixtures with the new ceiling.

Ceilings that are created by sketching the shape of the ceiling have a different effect on your fixtures when moved laterally. If the entire ceiling is moved, your light fixtures will remain in their location relative to the ceiling. If a boundary of the ceiling is edited by dragging it to a new location while in sketch mode, your fixtures will remain where they are located; however, any attempts to place new fixtures into the ceiling may cause them to appear outside the host, and you will receive a warning indicating that the fixture has no host. You can use the Pick New tool then to place the fixture into the ceiling.

Because ceilings tend to move around quite a bit in the early stages of a design, you may want to consider hosting your lighting fixtures to a reference plane until the major changes have settled down. At that point, you could move your fixtures into the ceilings by using the Pick

New tool. In the meantime, encourage the architects you work with to avoid deleting ceilings and simply alter the ones that exist, when possible.

Overhead Fixtures in Spaces with No Ceiling

Not every building area for which you need to provide lighting will have a ceiling. Having a space with no ceiling does not mean that you cannot use a face-hosted fixture family. Pendant fixtures can be face-hosted to the floor or structure above, as shown in Figure 12.13.

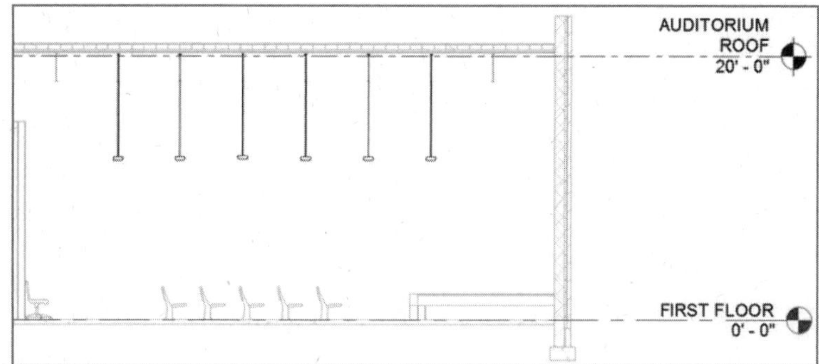

FIGURE 12.13 Pendant fixtures hosted by structural framing members

Another option for using hosted fixtures in a space with no ceiling is to use a reference plane that defines the elevation of the fixtures. This is an effective method for lighting large spaces in which one or two reference planes can handle all the lighting fixtures. It is not recommended that you use this method for multiple spaces, because having many reference planes hosting items in your model can negatively affect your file performance.

You can also use lighting fixture families that do not require a host object. You have to set and manage their elevations manually. These types of fixtures should have a parameter that lets you define the mounting height, or you can use the Offset parameter.

Wall-mounted Lights

Lighting fixtures can be mounted to walls as well as ceilings. In fact, you can place a face-hosted lighting fixture family on any vertical surface. However, you should note that any model element categorized as a lighting fixture does not have the ability to maintain its annotation orientation. This means that you cannot use an annotation symbol nested directly in the family to represent the lighting fixture in a plan view when the fixture is mounted to a vertical face. See Chapter 20 for information on nesting an annotation into lighting fixture families that are mounted on vertical surfaces.

One option to work around this shortcoming is to categorize your wall-mounted lighting fixture families as lighting devices instead of lighting fixtures. This gives you the ability to use a symbol, but it could also result in additional effort to control visibility and to schedule these devices along with all your other lighting fixtures.

Your best option, if you absolutely must use face-hosted families and represent wall-mounted lights with symbols, is to create linework in the family that represents the fixture. Then set the visibility of the linework so that it appears only in front and back views. This is necessary because, with the face-hosted family placed on a vertical face, the fixture is seen from within the plan view from the back. The linework must be done with model lines; therefore, they do not react to changes in view scale. This technique is discussed in further detail in Chapter 20, but as shown in Figure 12.14, it is quite achievable.

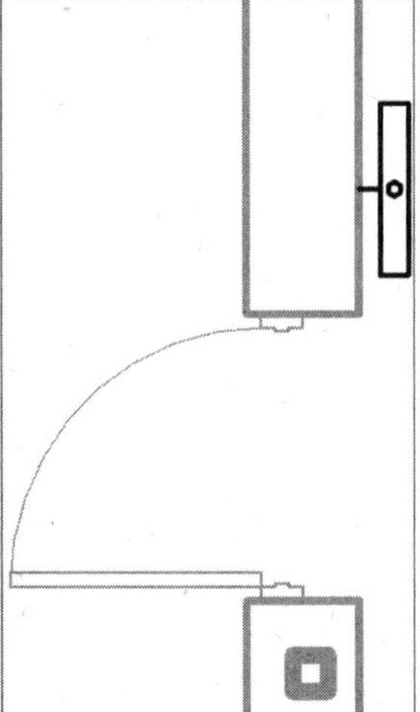

FIGURE 12.14 Face-hosted fixture mounted on a vertical wall with model lines to represent the fixture

The use of nonhosted families for wall lighting is perfectly acceptable. This requires that you manually maintain the association of the fixtures with the walls because you cannot lock the family to the linked wall. With a nonhosted family, you can use an annotation symbol to represent the lighting fixture in a plan view. This works well for exit lights because the actual fixture is typically not shown; rather, a symbol is shown.

Switches

Using face-hosted lighting switch families keeps your switches coordinated with the locations of their host walls. This does not mean that the movement of doors does not affect the hosting of your switches. Because you cannot constrain your switches to a distance from a door in a linked file, if the door moves so that the switch is in the door opening, you will see the warning shown in Figure 12.15 that the switch has lost its association with the host.

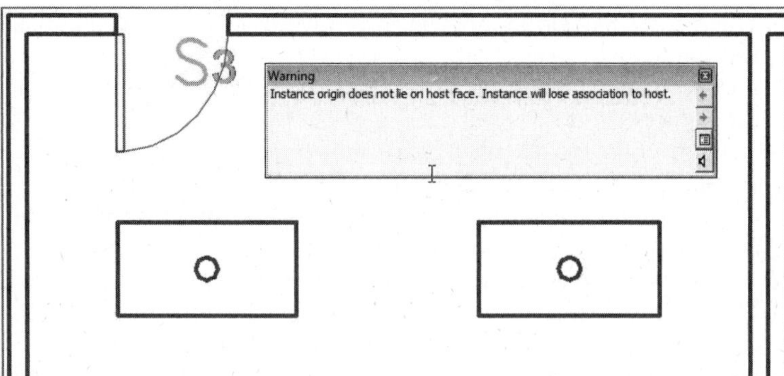

FIGURE 12.15 Warning that a switch has lost association with its host

You can associate your switches with the lighting fixtures that they operate, provided that the switch family Part Type parameter is set to Switch, as shown in Figure 12.16.

FIGURE 12.16
Part Type settings of a switch family

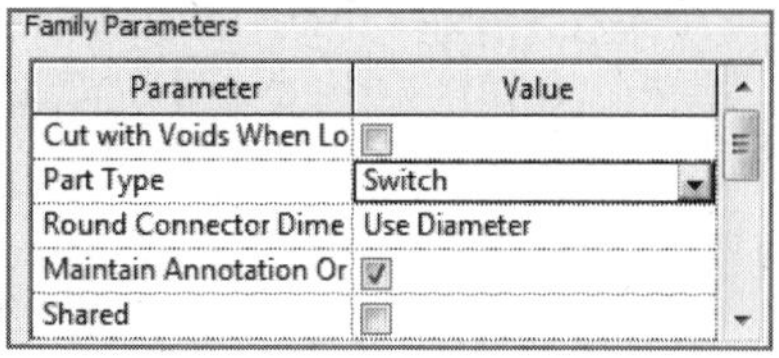

Family Parameters

Parameter	Value
Cut with Voids When Lo	☐
Part Type	Switch
Round Connector Dime	Use Diameter
Maintain Annotation Or	☑
Shared	☐

To create a switch system, do the following:

1. Select a lighting fixture, and click the Switch button on the Create Systems panel of the Modify | Lighting Fixtures contextual tab. This changes the ribbon to the Modify | Switch System contextual tab.

   On the System Tools panel of this tab, you have options to select the switch to be used for the system and to edit the system. Editing the system allows you to add or remove elements and view the properties of the switch system. Click the Select Switch button, and select the desired switch in the drawing area.

2. After selecting a switch, you can select additional lighting fixtures to be included in the system by clicking the Edit Switch System button. Click the Finish Editing System button once you have selected all of the fixtures for the system.

3. To view the system, place your mouse pointer over any item that is part of the system and press the Tab key until dashed lines are shown connecting the fixture(s) back to the switch. This highlights the system elements and indicates their connectivity.

4. With the dashed lines highlighted, click to select the system.

A switch system can contain only one switch, so for lighting fixtures controlled by multiple switches, such as three-way switches, you can select only one switch for the system. In the example shown in Figure 12.17, the three-way switch at the lower end of the room would also control the lighting fixtures but cannot be added as part of the switch system highlighted and indicated with dashed lines.

Switches can be assigned an ID by using the Switch ID parameter, which helps identify their relationship with lighting fixtures. This parameter exists in families that are categorized as lighting devices. When you select a lighting fixture and access the Switch Systems tab, you see the ID of the switch associated with that light fixture in parentheses, in the System Selector drop-down on the System Tools panel of the tab.

Creating switch systems is independent of any circuiting of the lighting fixtures and switches. You still need to include the switches in the power circuit for the lighting fixtures if you want to remove them from the Unassigned category in the System Browser. Having as many elements as possible assigned to systems helps improve the overall performance of your model.

FIGURE 12.17
Switch system

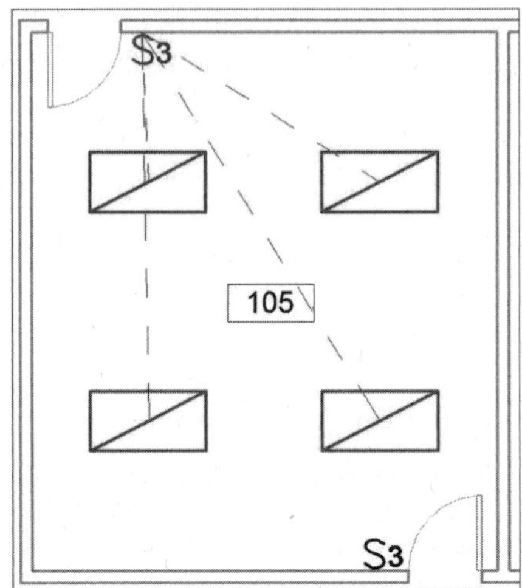

Site Lighting

Although you cannot do lighting analysis on site lighting within Revit MEP, a site lighting design can be useful to coordinate loads within panels and create a realistic view of the model from the exterior. Locations of poles, bollards, and other site lighting fixtures can be coordinated with other utilities within the project site. You can also create renderings to get an idea of the coverage of your lighting fixtures on the site.

The Site Plan

If you are working with a civil engineering consultant, it is likely that the engineer is developing the site plan with some sort of CAD software. When the engineer uses a BIM solution, the 3D information (such as elevation points and contours) can be shared with Revit. This is necessary only if you are interested in creating topography within Revit to match the information in the site file. Otherwise, what you require from your civil engineering consultant is just linework that represents the layout of the site. Knowing the layout of parking lots, sidewalks, and major site elements should be enough for you to generate a site lighting design. In one sense, you are working with the site plan in the same manner that you would if you were using a typical 2D CAD system for your design. The difference is that, with Revit MEP, you can use the data within your design to help make decisions and to coordinate with other disciplines and project systems. Ask your consultant for a flat CAD file that you can use throughout the project—in other words, a file that the consultant will update as changes are made to the project site.

The civil engineering and architectural consultants on your project may be sharing files also. At a minimum, the architect would share the building model so that the civil consultant could properly locate the building on the site. Your architect may choose to use the 3D data from the site file to generate a site plan within Revit. If so, you can use this information to create your site lighting layout. Although the architectural site model would give you topographical information, it also is only as up to date and accurate as the architect keeps it.

To get started, do the following:

1. Create a view associated with the ground level of your project. Because this is a site plan, the view does not have to contain only lighting system elements, so categorize your view in a manner that makes the most sense for your Project Browser organization. It may be best to create a subdiscipline under Electrical called **Site** to keep all your site-related views properly organized.

2. Set the View Range settings to display the building model properly—that is, as it would appear in a site plan. You can set the Top setting of your view and the Cut Plane setting to an elevation higher than the building so that it appears as seen from high above.

   It should not be necessary to use a plan region unless you require the cut plane to be lower in a specific area of the site. If the building is represented in the linked site file, you may choose to not show the linked building model in your view. However, this workflow would mean that you are relying on the civil engineering consultant for an accurate representation of the building outline instead of getting that information from the architectural model.

3. Link the CAD file from your consultant into this view. Consider the option for linking the file into this view only, if it is the only place that the site CAD file needs to appear. You could also create a workset for the linked site file so that you can easily control whether it is loaded when your file is opened.

   Whatever you decide, be sure to link the file; do not import it. An imported site file can wreak havoc on your model, and you will not be able to update the file automatically when it changes.

4. Depending on the origin of the site file and your Revit file, you may have to place the site drawing manually into your view. The site file should contain an outline of the building, so you can align it with your linked Revit architectural model. If not, it may be necessary to open the site CAD file and create an alignment-point indicator used to match up with your file.

OPENING THE SITE FILE PRIOR TO LINKING

Opening the site file prior to linking is not uncommon. Many people do this to clean up the file prior to bringing it into their project. Unused layers and linework can be deleted to make the file easier to manage after it is linked into your project. Keep in mind that using this practice means that you will have to do it every time your consultant gives you an updated version of the file. If you manually position the site plan into your view, you will have to use the Pin tool to pin it in place and prevent accidental movement. CAD files that are linked in by using the automatic positioning options are pinned in place by default.

Site Lighting Layout

With your site plan in place and a view that represents the building in relation to the site, you can now begin to place site lighting fixtures in your model. If you have enabled worksharing in your project, it is best to create a workset for the site lighting plan, or at least for site elements in general. Lighting fixtures that are mounted to the exterior of the building should be included in this workset if they are to be displayed in the site plan view.

A limited number of site lighting fixtures come with Revit MEP, so you likely will have to get your site lighting families from manufacturers' websites or create them yourself. The chapters on content creation in Part 5 of this book will equip you with the skills necessary to create any lighting fixture that your project requires.

The topographic surface from a linked Revit site model does not provide you with a face on which to host your fixtures. You can use the option to place your fixtures on a work plane and associate them with the ground level defined by the building. This works fine for a 2D plan view representation of the site, but if you need to show the site plan in section, elevation, or 3D, you have to adjust your lighting fixtures to match the topographic elevation of their location. You cannot adjust the Elevation parameter of your lighting fixture families that are hosted by a work plane or level, so it may be best to use nonhosted families for site lighting. Notice in Figure 12.18 that the elevation of the lighting fixtures is not set to match the topography. Face-hosted fixture families were used in this example, since the 3D view is used only for reference.

Site Lighting Analysis

Revit MEP can calculate the average estimated illumination of a Space object by using the data from the photometric web file associated with a lighting fixture, but only because the Space object has a volume. Exterior lighting levels cannot be calculated. Most exterior lighting calculation applications are able to import CAD data, so you could export your model to CAD and use the file in your analysis software.

You can, however, use Revit MEP for visual analysis of your site lighting layout. Lighting fixtures that contain photometric web files can display the pattern of light emitted from the fixture in renderings. Creating exterior renderings of your project will give you an idea of the coverage of your lighting fixtures on the site. This can help you determine whether you are using the right type of fixture or whether you need to adjust the number of fixtures used or the spacing of fixtures.

To see the exterior lighting in a rendered 3D view, you need two things. You need to have a surface upon which the light shines, and you need fixtures that contain a light source. If you are using a 2D CAD file for your site plan, you can place a dummy surface at ground level to act as your site surface. Your 3D view should be set with a nighttime sun position so that the sun does not interfere with your lighting. You can display the sun position by using the Sun Settings options on the View Control Bar, as shown in Figure 12.19.

FIGURE 12.18
Site lighting fixtures in 2D (top) and 3D (bottom) views

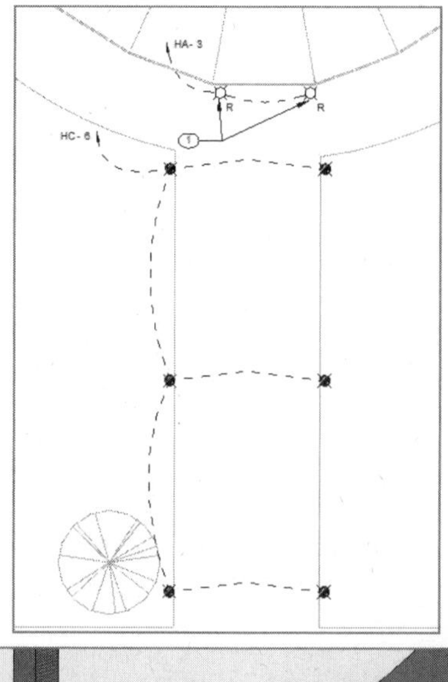

FIGURE 12.19
Sun Settings tool

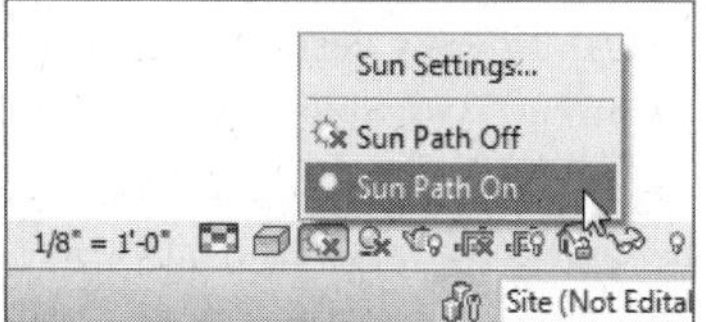

When you turn on the sun path, you may see a dialog box with options for displaying the sun path based on the sun settings defined in the Graphic Display Options settings of the view, as shown in Figure 12.20.

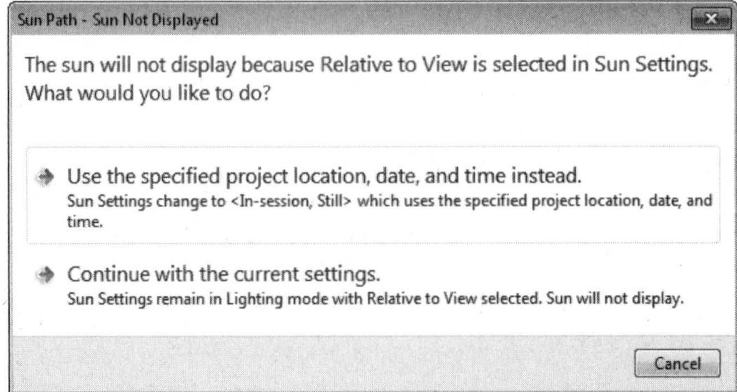

FIGURE 12.20
Options for sun path display

If you choose the option of using project location and date, the sun path appears in the view, as shown in Figure 12.21. You can adjust the position of the sun by dragging it along the path, or you can click the time shown and edit it manually. The date can also be edited by clicking the text.

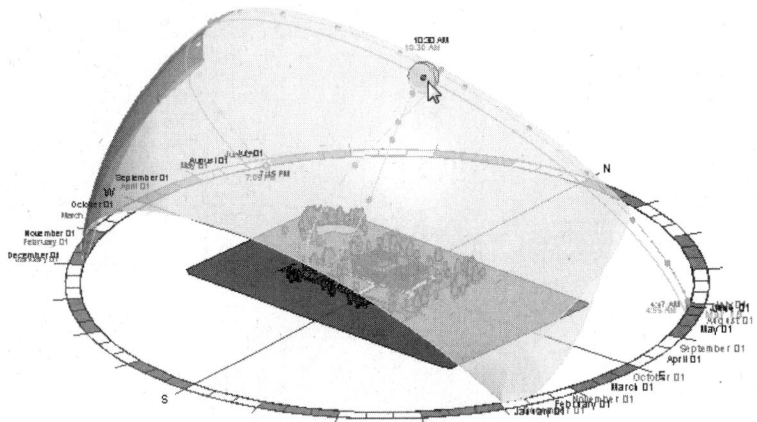

FIGURE 12.21
Sun path shown in a 3D view

To render your site lighting, do the following:

1. Click the Show Rendering Dialog button on the View Control Bar of your 3D view, and set the lighting scheme as shown in Figure 12.22. It is best to do your renderings in draft mode when you are testing your design because of the amount of time it takes to render a view. Choose the Exterior: Artificial Only lighting scheme.
2. You can group lights together and choose which groups to render. This decreases your rendering times because Revit takes into account only the lights within the selected group. To create a light group, simply select a fixture and use the Light Group tool on the Options Bar, as shown in Figure 12.23.

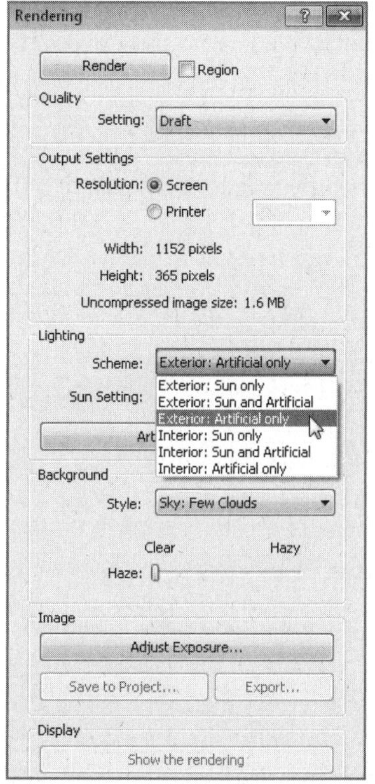

FIGURE 12.22 Rendering settings for a draft mode view

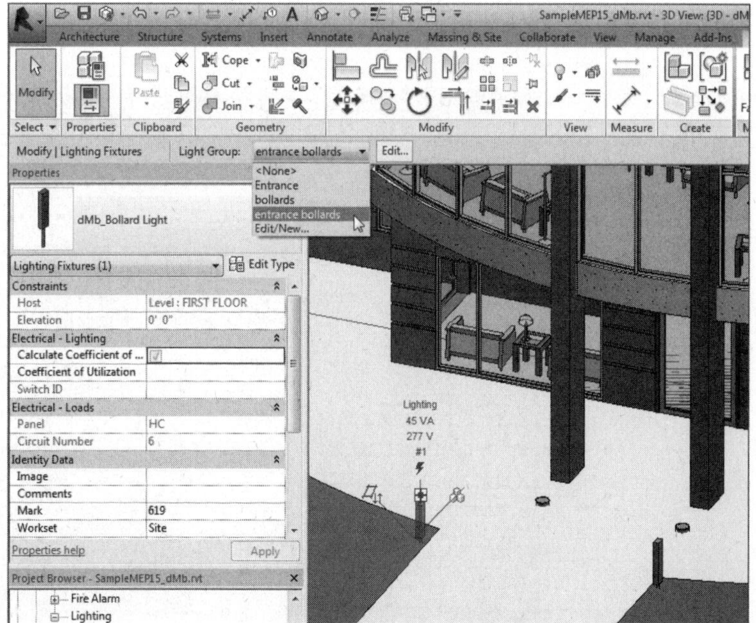

FIGURE 12.23 Selecting a light group

3. Click the Artificial Lights button in the Rendering dialog box to determine which groups of lights will be rendered (see Figure 12.24). You can turn on or turn off entire groups of lights or individual fixtures to decrease rendering times.

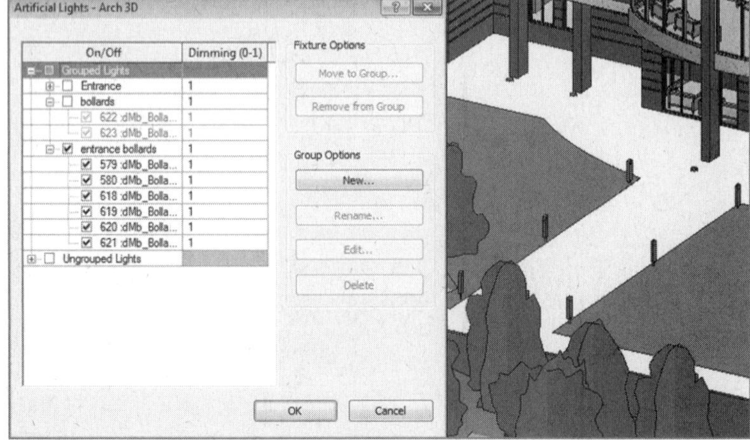

FIGURE 12.24
Choosing which groups of lights to render

4. Click the Render button at the top of the Rendering dialog box to generate a rendering of the view.

Once the rendering is finished, you will be able to see the lighting from your fixtures and how the light appears on the site. You can click the Adjust Exposure button to lighten or darken the image for more detail. The rendered view is a useful tool for the visual analysis of your lighting model. If you want to use the rendered view for presentation purposes, you can render the view at a higher level of detail. Figure 12.25 is an example of a draft-level rendering showing bollard lighting on a sidewalk.

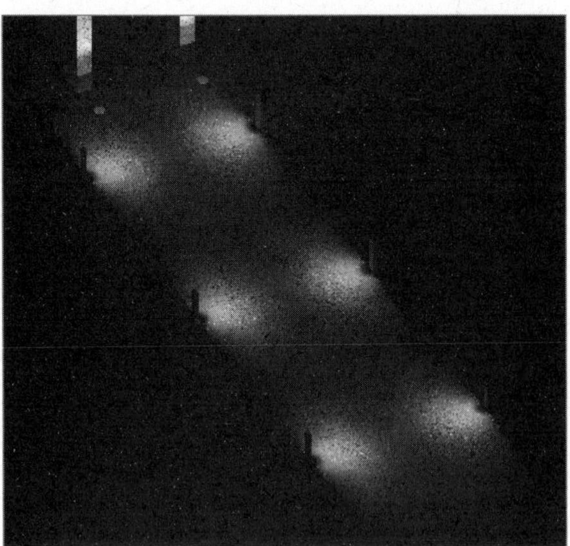

FIGURE 12.25
Sample rendering of site lighting

The Bottom Line

Prepare your project for lighting design. The greatest benefit you can receive from a lighting model is coordination with other systems. Properly setting up the project file is key to achieving this coordination.

Master It Describe the relationship between ceilings and engineering spaces. How can you be sure that your engineering spaces are reporting the correct geometry?

Use Revit MEP for lighting analysis. Although the design of electrical systems is usually represented schematically on construction documents, you can use the intelligence within the model to create a design tool that analyzes lighting levels.

Master It What model elements contain the data required to determine proper lighting layout?

Compare and evaluate hosting options for lighting fixtures and devices. As a BIM solution, Revit MEP offers multiple options for placing your lighting model elements into your project. These options are in place to accommodate several workflow scenarios.

Master It What is the default hosting option for face-hosted families? Describe the limitations of representing wall-mounted lights with symbols and how they can be shown in a plan view.

Develop site lighting plans. Creating a site lighting plan allows you to coordinate with civil engineering consultants as well as with your architect. These plans are also useful for presentation documents and visual inspection of lighting coverage on the site.

Master It What is the benefit of using nonhosted lighting fixture families for site lighting?

Chapter 13

Power and Communications

Modeling power systems with a building information modeling (BIM) solution such as the Autodesk® Revit® MEP 2015 program is just as important to project coordination as modeling systems that contain large amounts of physical data, such as HVAC systems. As with a lighting model, the key component to a power systems model is the data within the model elements. This information determines how systems can be put together. It can be extracted from the model for use in analysis and to aid in design decisions.

There is something to be said for the physical model of a power system as well. Receptacles and junction boxes are relatively small compared to other system components, but with a large number of them in a project, the potential for interference is increased.

Building communication systems have become more complex with advances in modern technology. Voice and data networks and devices, along with security and fire alarm systems, are major design elements of new construction as well as renovation of existing buildings. Revit MEP 2015 has the tools necessary for you to communicate your design in a 3D model that contains the important data needed to ensure an efficient and effective workflow. Electrical equipment can be large and a clearance space is usually required around the equipment for service. Large conduit and cable tray runs are important coordination considerations as well.

In this chapter, you will learn to do the following:

- Place power and systems devices into your model
- Place equipment and connections
- Create distribution systems
- Model conduits and cable tray

Modeling Methods for Power and Systems Devices

Power and systems plans can easily be created in your Revit model to show the locations of outlets and other types of electrical devices. You can use symbols, model elements, or a combination of the two to represent the design layout. The choice you make depends on the level of coordination you want to achieve and the amount of information you intend to extract from the design.

Revit MEP 2015 comes with basic device components for creating electrical layouts. Because you do not need to go into great detail to model these small elements, it is easy to create your own device families that match your company standards for electrical symbols. We cover creating electrical devices in Chapter 21, "Creating Devices," and we cover creating symbols in Chapter 18, "Creating Symbols and Annotations."

The Device button on the Systems tab is used for placing a device into your model. This is a split tool with two parts. Clicking the top half of the button invokes the command to insert an electrical device. Clicking the bottom half of the button reveals a drop-down menu of specific categories of devices, as shown in Figure 13.1. When you select a specific type of device from the drop-down menu, the top half of the Device button changes to match the category you have chosen. You can then click the top half of the button to invoke the command to insert that type of device. Selecting a device from a specific category causes the Type Selector to populate only with devices in that category.

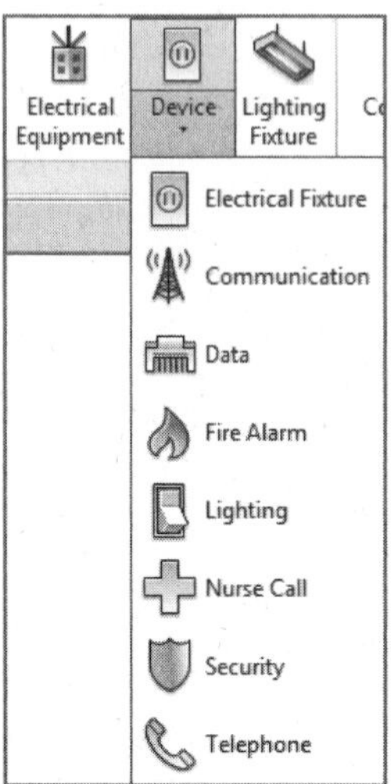

FIGURE 13.1 Drop-down menu from the Device button

Select the Electrical Fixture category to insert power receptacles into your model. It is a good practice to go directly to the Type Selector after choosing a device category to insert. The Type Selector drop-down list contains all the families in the selected category that are loaded into your project. The list is organized by the family names highlighted in gray, with the family type names listed beneath each one. At the bottom of the list is a section with the most recently used families in that category. With tooltip assistance turned on, placing your mouse pointer over a family in the list reveals a thumbnail view of the family. Figure 13.2 shows an example of the Type Selector drop-down list for the electrical fixtures loaded in the project.

If there is no family loaded into your project that matches the category you selected from the Device drop-down button, you are prompted to load one. The default library contains an `Electrical` folder with architectural and MEP families in subfolders. The architectural families do not contain any electrical connection data and are there for modeling device locations. The receptacle families located in the `Terminals` subfolder of the `Electric Power` folder under MEP are the ones to use for modeling your electrical systems. The `Information and Communication` folder contains families to be used for communications systems, including the `Fire Alarm` folder that has families for fire alarm design. All of these types of devices can easily be created because the level of model detail is not as important as the connector data. One family can be duplicated several times and given a different connector type so a library of power and communications families can be built.

It is a good idea to take some time to familiarize yourself with where families are located in the Revit MEP 2015 library structure.

FIGURE 13.2
Type Selector drop-down menu

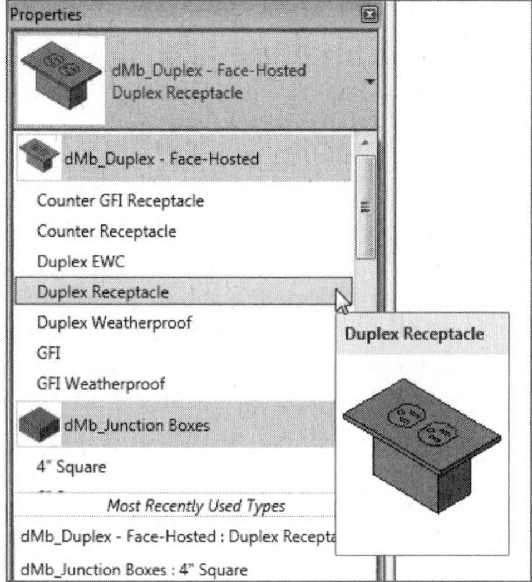

Using Annotation Symbols

Power and communications plans are typically shown schematically by using symbols to represent the various devices and outlets. Therefore, annotation symbols are another key element of the families used to represent the design. Different symbols can be used within the same family to represent the different types of that family. This helps reduce the number of families required to maintain a complete library for design as well as the number of families loaded into your project. Using multiple annotations within a family makes for easy modification of your design. Figure 13.3 shows a single communications family with three types utilizing different symbols.

FIGURE 13.3
Multiple symbols in a device family

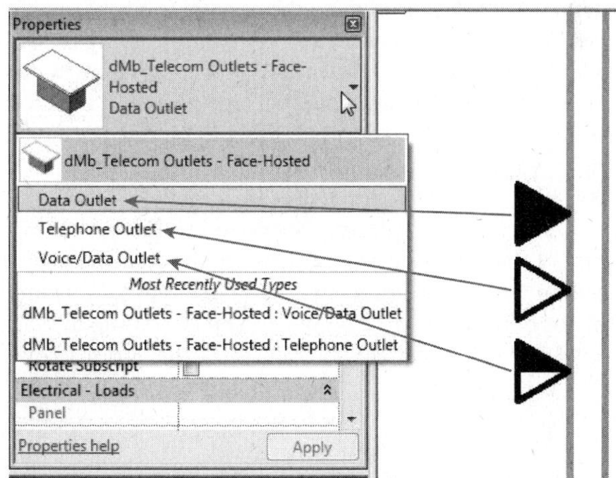

Using Face-hosted Families

It is best to use face-hosted families to model your receptacle and communications layouts, because these types of elements are typically hosted by walls and casework that you want to keep track of. Unless otherwise noted, the examples discussed in this chapter refer to face-hosted family types. This gives you the freedom to place the devices on any face within the building model. These types of components move with their hosts, so you spend less time moving your devices around to keep up with changes to the building model. If a device host is deleted from the model, the device remains in place. This gives you the opportunity to relocate or remove the device manually and adjust any associated circuitry.

When you select a face-hosted device type to place in the model, the default placement is to a vertical surface. When you place your mouse pointer near a vertical surface such as a wall, the symbol used to represent the device appears. You can press the spacebar to flip the orientation of the device to either side of the face upon which you are placing it. Figure 13.4 shows a receptacle hosted on each side of the face of a wall. As you can see, this affects not only the symbol orientation but also the model component.

FIGURE 13.4
Orientation of receptacles on a vertical surface

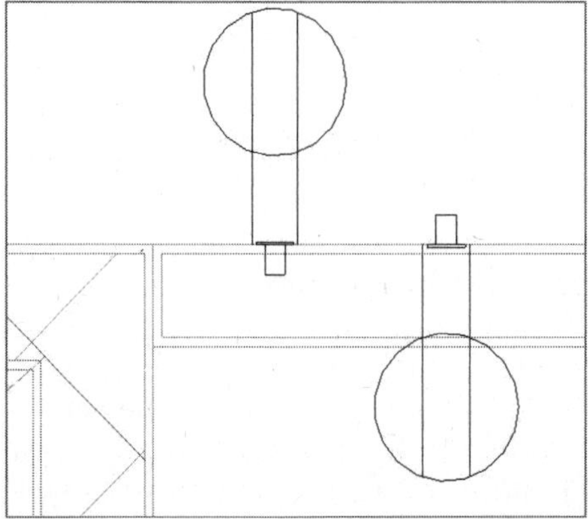

If the device family you are using is not face hosted, pressing the spacebar will rotate the device in 90-degree increments parallel to the plane of the current view. After a face-hosted device has been placed, selecting it and pressing the spacebar rotates the device 90 degrees parallel to the host face. This causes your annotation symbol to "disappear," because annotations are visible only in views parallel to the view in which they are placed. Figure 13.5 shows two systems outlets hosted by a wall. Both outlets were placed the same way, but the outlet on the right was rotated using the spacebar after placement. Notice that the annotation symbol of the outlet on the right is not visible in plan view.

Take care when placing devices on walls that contain multiple layers. Because of the structure of these types of walls, there can be several vertical faces on which to host the device, as shown with a power receptacle in Figure 13.6. You can use the Tab key to cycle through the hosting options for the face on which you are trying to place the device. Setting a view to a higher level of detail may help you recognize the various layers within a wall.

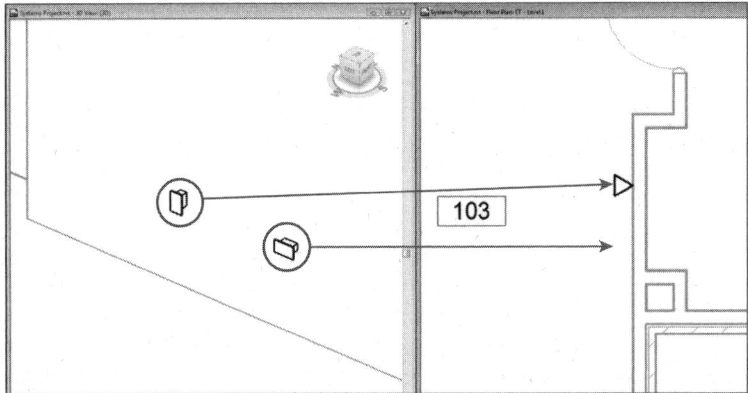
103

FIGURE 13.5
Outlet placement and rotation

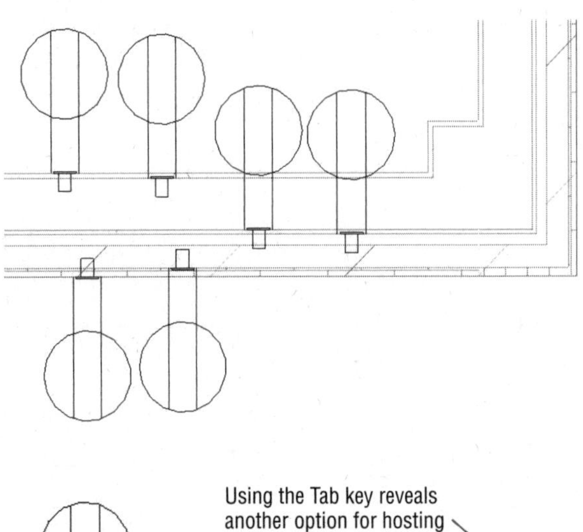

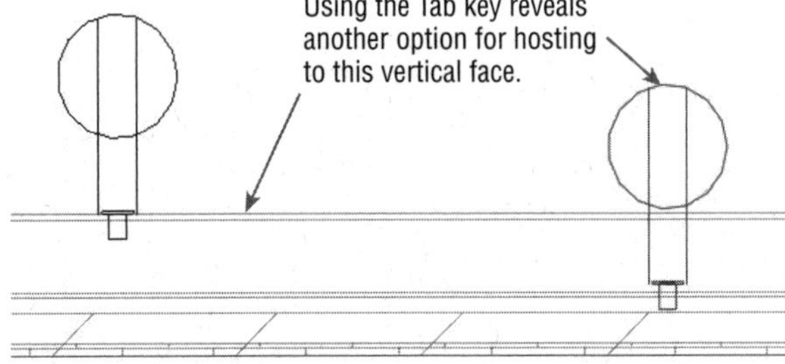
Using the Tab key reveals another option for hosting to this vertical face.

FIGURE 13.6
Multiple hosting options in a compound wall (top); using the Tab key for hosting options (bottom)

Because any 3D surface can be used as a host, you can place devices on curved walls and the component and symbol will follow the curve as you move your mouse pointer along the surface.

There is no need to rotate the symbol or component after placement, saving time in laying out your design.

Real World Scenario

ON THE FLOOR

Johan is working with an architect on a facility that will be used as a data-management center. The main portion of the building is open office space on a raised floor. Because of the open nature of the floor plan, many floor boxes are needed for power and communications distribution. He is able to accommodate the design requirements by using face-hosted components that are hosted by the floor system. His plan views show the locations of the boxes with a standard symbol, and he is able to coordinate the locations with the office furniture layout.

Devices or outlets can be placed in floors or ceilings as well. To do so, you need to select the Place On Face option from the Placement panel of the contextual tab after you have chosen your device. This enables you to place devices such as speakers onto the ceilings within your model, as shown in Figure 13.7.

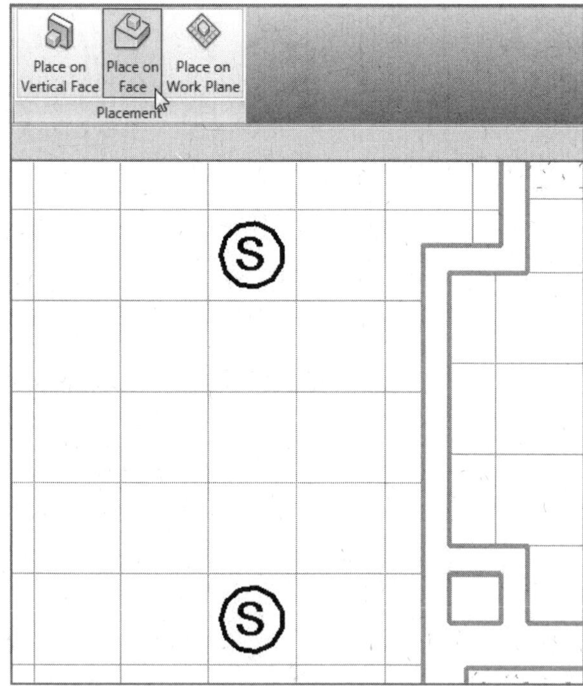

FIGURE 13.7 Devices placed onto a ceiling face

When you place devices or outlets onto floor objects, be sure that you are selecting the appropriate floor as a host. Often in projects, the architect models a floor object to act as a placeholder to show a floor in section or elevation views while the actual floor is being modeled in the structural project file. Use the Visibility/Graphic Overrides settings to turn on the appropriate floor object for hosting. This ensures that, if the floor object is removed from the architectural model, your devices or outlets remain hosted. Use the cursor tooltip or status bar to confirm that the correct floor is displayed in your view, as shown in Figure 13.8.

FIGURE 13.8 Floor-hosted device in appropriate host

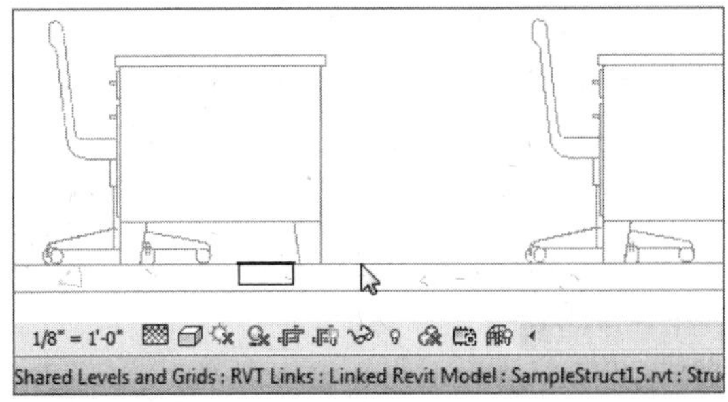

Avoiding Interference of Symbols

Because of the schematic nature of construction documents for electrical designs, it can sometimes be difficult to place components without causing interference between the symbols used to represent them. Figure 13.9 shows two power receptacles placed in a model at the correct location for the intended design, but the symbols used for construction documentation are interfering with each other.

FIGURE 13.9 Receptacles with interfering symbols

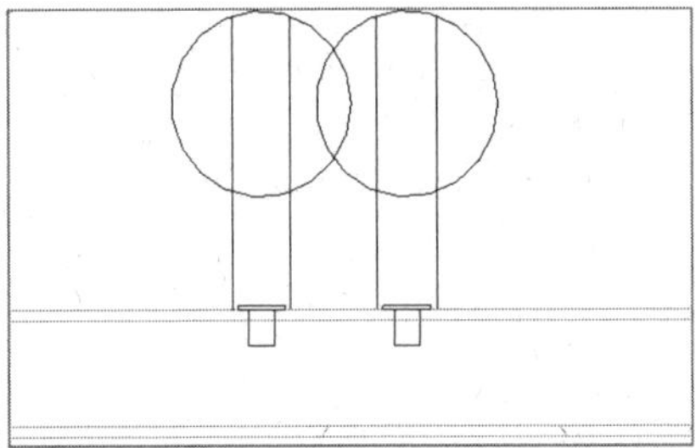

This scenario raises the question of whether it is more important to build the model accurately or to show the schematic symbols correctly for construction documentation. Using the functionality of families and nested annotations, Revit MEP gives you the ability to do both. Parameters within your component families can be used to offset the annotation symbols nested within them from the actual model components. In Figure 13.10, you can see how an offset parameter is used to shift the receptacle annotation of a family, allowing for both accurate placement of the receptacles and correct symbolic representation.

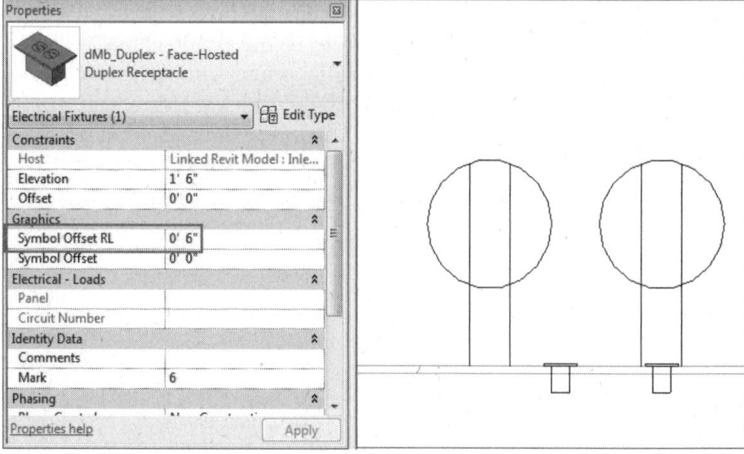

FIGURE 13.10 Receptacle annotation offset

This functionality can also be used for devices that are vertically aligned in the model. In a floor plan view, these devices would appear to occupy the same space. A standard practice is to show one receptacle symbol at the location on the wall and another symbol offset from the wall at the same location. By using an offset parameter, you can achieve the same result. Figure 13.11 shows an instance parameter used to offset the symbol of a receptacle that is above another (left) and a section view and plan view of the receptacles (right). Using this functionality maintains both the model integrity and the schematic plan.

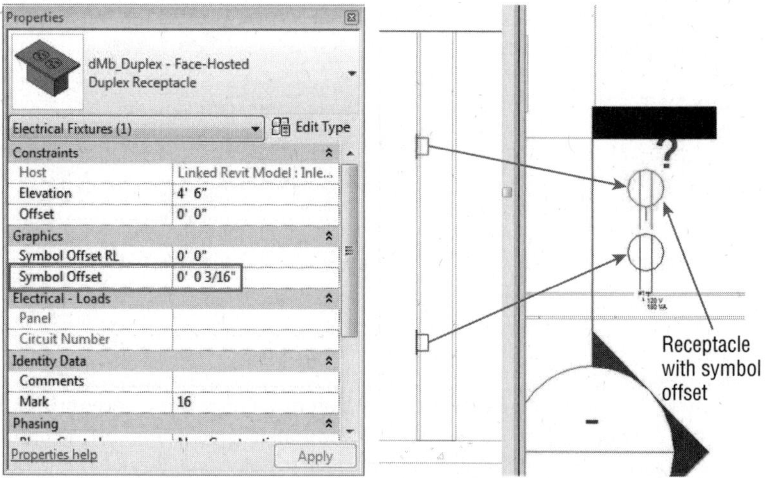

FIGURE 13.11 Instance parameter settings for a symbol offset (left); section and plan views of the receptacles (right)

Other devices, such as junction boxes, can be placed in the model in the same manner as receptacles or communication outlets. Creating different types within a junction box family is a good way to keep track of specific loads. Junction boxes for systems furniture can be hosted by the floor to show location, if the furniture is not modeled in 3D. Boxes that are located above the ceiling can be hosted by the ceiling object and given an offset to maintain their distance from the ceiling if the ceiling height should change. When you place a junction box in a reflected ceiling plan and give it an offset, the box offsets from the front face of the ceiling. This means the box will move toward the floor, so if you need the box to be above the ceiling, you have to give it a negative offset, as shown in Figure 13.12.

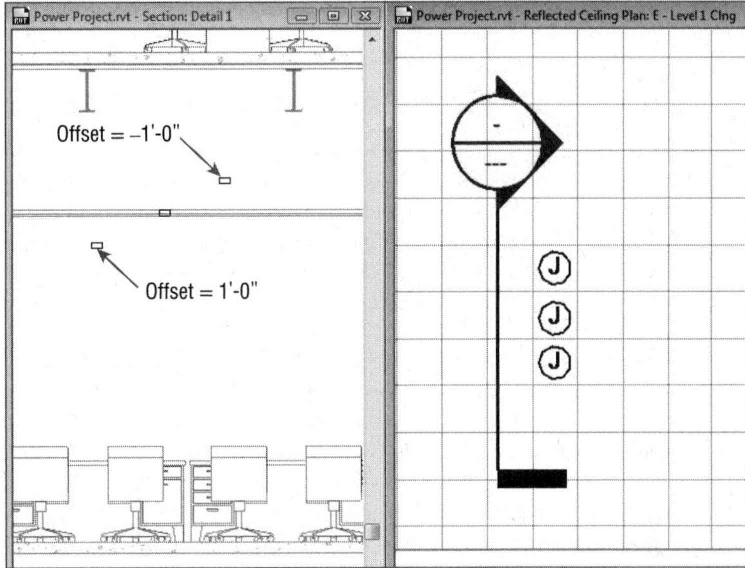

FIGURE 13.12 Ceiling junction boxes with offsets

Creating Circuits

When you place devices or outlets into your project, you can assign them to a system by creating a circuit for them. The connector in the family determines the type of circuit you can create. When you select a device in the model that contains a connector, the Create Systems panel appears on the contextual tab for that type of device. Clicking the button creates a circuit for that device. At this point, it is not necessary to select a panel for the circuit because you may not have placed the equipment yet, but having your devices on circuits improves file performance. Figure 13.13 shows the available circuit types for a device that contains both a data connector and a telephone connector. A circuit can be created for each type of connector in the family.

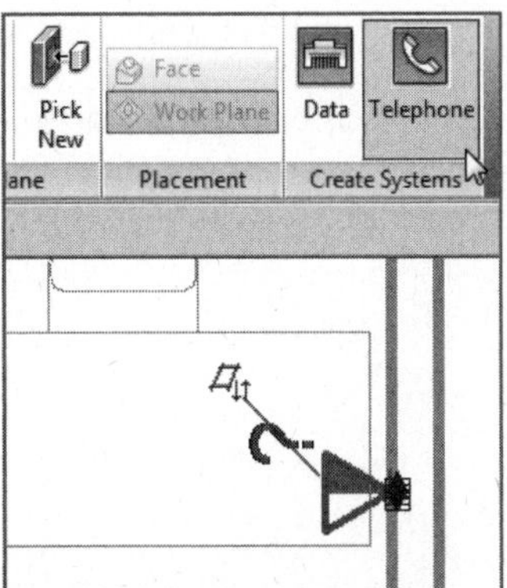

FIGURE 13.13 Circuit options for a multiconnector device

Some of your devices may require multiple connectors for different systems, such as a floor box with both power and data outlets. If your project contains several of these devices, it is best to have the nested symbolic families on different subcategories within the multiconnector device family. This way, their visibility can be easily controlled in both power and communications views.

Placing Devices and Equipment Connections

Certain elements within a power design do not require a physical component in the building model, such as the points of connection to the electrical system. You use a symbol to represent these points and indicate the locations of the connections to the electrical contractor. With Revit MEP 2015, you can represent these connection points with schematic symbols while building "intelligence" into the electrical model. Because the electrical information of a component is defined by its electrical connector, you can use symbols that contain connectors to account for the connections in your electrical model.

Equipment connections are the most common of these types of components. If you are linking an HVAC model into your project, you can use equipment connections that contain electrical information that matches the electrical specifications for the component within the HVAC model. In this case, you would need to use an equipment connection family that contains an electrical connector. If you are working in a model that also contains the HVAC equipment, you can use an equipment connection symbol without an electrical connector (as long as the mechanical equipment family has an electrical connector) and use the data from the HVAC equipment for your design.

You also have the option of using the Copy/Monitor tool to copy and monitor mechanical equipment families from a linked file. This is a good way to coordinate the location of equipment. However, you are relying on the mechanical model to be using the appropriate family with the correct electrical data. If the equipment in the mechanical model does not contain an electrical connector, you need to monitor it with one that does. This means that you have to load a similar mechanical equipment family that has an electrical connector into your project to be used for monitoring. Although this functionality is a step in the right direction toward coordinating mechanical and electrical components, it requires careful management of components used in the models and increased communication between consultants.

Figure 13.14 shows an equipment connection family used for an elevator. The elevator equipment has not been modeled, so an equipment connection family with an electrical connector is used. Because the equipment connection family is used for many types of equipment, the load is an instance parameter. This allows for adjustments to the load for each connection without having to create a new type within the family.

The mechanical equipment shown in Figure 13.15 is in the same model as the electrical components and has an electrical connector. In this case, a symbol without any electrical data is sufficient to represent the equipment connection.

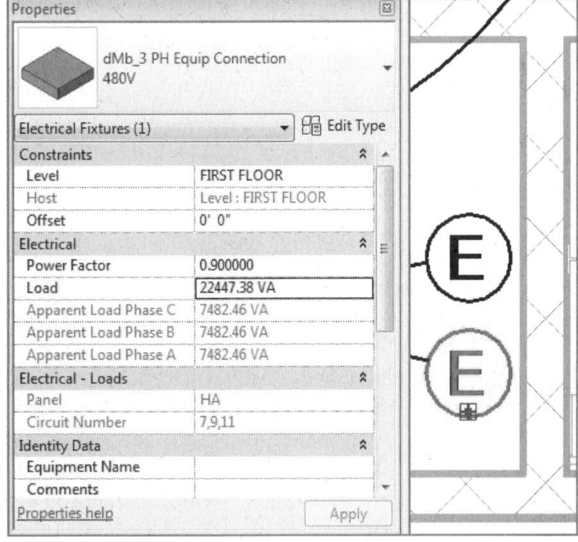

FIGURE 13.14 Equipment connection with a connector

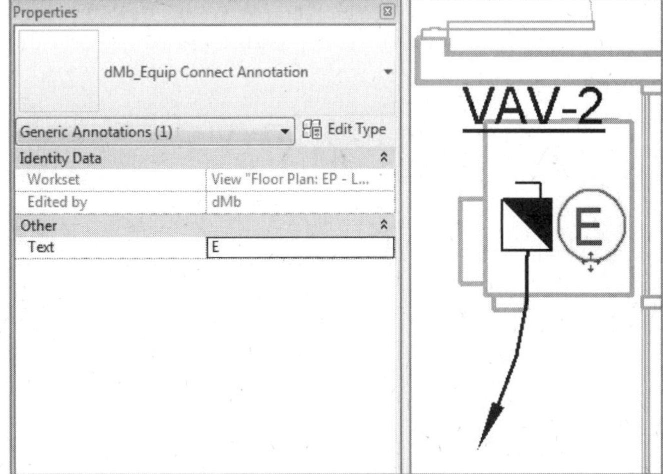

FIGURE 13.15 Equipment connection symbol

In either case, the equipment connection can be attached to its associated model component by using face-hosted families. Constraints, such as locked alignment, can also be used, but only if both constrained elements are in the same model. Aligning and locking a component to a linked component causes a constraint error if the linked component moves and the linked file is reloaded.

Another example of an electrical design component that does not have any physical geometry is a motor connection. A motor connection can be represented in the electrical model in the same way an equipment connection can be represented. The electrical data for the motor can come from either the equipment family or the symbol family used to represent the equipment.

Disconnect Switches

Disconnect switches may not require model components, depending on their use and who is to provide them for construction. Certain types of equipment come with a means of disconnect built into them, while others require that a disconnect switch be provided in addition to the equipment.

A disconnect switch that the electrical contractor is required to provide should be included as a model component in order to coordinate location and space requirements. Face-hosted families should be used, because these types of disconnect switches may be mounted on walls or directly to the equipment that they serve. The disconnect switch family that comes with Revit MEP 2015 has several types based on voltage and rating. This family is found in the `Electrical/MEP/Electric Power/Terminals` folder of the library that installs with the software. The family is categorized as electrical equipment; therefore, using a symbol to represent this family is difficult because face-hosted electrical equipment does not contain the parameter to maintain annotation orientation. Therefore, each disconnect switch displays at its actual size based on the type chosen, as shown in Figure 13.16.

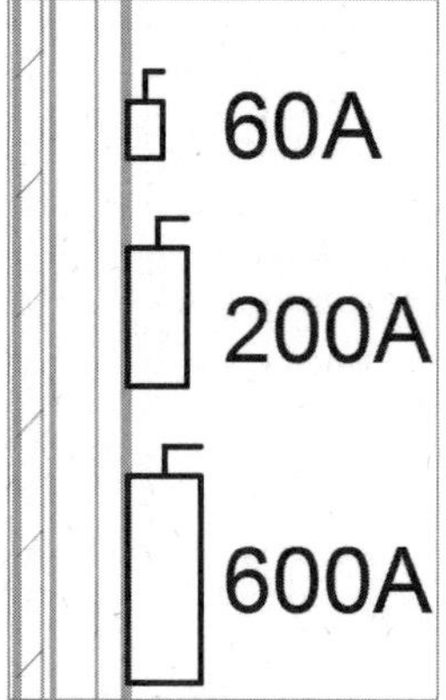

FIGURE 13.16 Disconnect switches in the building model

When a point of disconnect is required to be shown on the electrical plan but no equipment needs to be provided, a symbol can be used similar to the equipment connection symbol. There is no need for an electrical connector in your disconnect symbol family because a disconnect switch carries no load. However, wiring home runs for equipment are typically shown from the disconnect point, so you may want to include a connector point in your disconnect family for attaching wiring, or the wiring can be connected to the load source but drawn from the disconnect switch symbol.

CONNECTORS

Families that have connectors can be assigned to engineering systems. Having many components in your model that have not been assigned to systems may lead to poor file performance.

Figure 13.17 shows a point of disconnect for a variable air volume (VAV) box. The electrical connector is in the VAV family, so the point of disconnect is represented as a symbol. As with the equipment connection, the disconnect symbol can be constrained to the equipment to provide coordination with changes to the model as long as the equipment family is in the same file.

FIGURE 13.17
Disconnect symbol for equipment

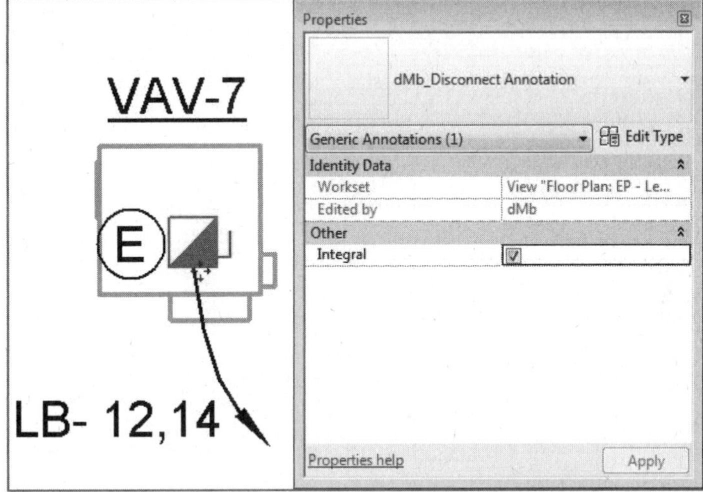

Distribution Equipment and Transformers

Distribution equipment not only plays an important role in the function of a building, it's also an important element of a building model. These types of components require space for accessibility. Using accurately sized model components for distribution equipment allows you to coordinate early on with the architectural model for space requirements.

Transformers can be modeled at various sizes depending on their ratings and voltages. This works well if you want to show the actual size of the transformers on your power plans. If you choose to represent your transformers with a symbol, one can be added to your transformer family. It is not necessary to use face-hosted families for transformers because they are typically located on the floor. An offset can be applied to wall-mounted transformers for placement at the proper height.

To place a transformer, do the following:

1. Click the Electrical Equipment button on the Systems tab and select the appropriate family type from the Type Selector to place a transformer in your model. The Options Bar

allows you to rotate the transformer after placement, or you can use the spacebar to rotate the transformer prior to placing it in the model.

2. When you have placed the transformer in the desired location, it is best to assign distribution systems for the primary and secondary sides. It is a good practice to do this at the time of placement so that the transformer will be available as an option for service when you establish your distribution model. Selecting a transformer after it has been placed activates the Distribution System drop-down list on the Options Bar. This drop-down contains a list of all the distribution systems defined in the electrical settings of your project. Only distribution systems that match the connector voltage of your transformer appear in the list, as shown in Figure 13.18.

FIGURE 13.18
Distribution System drop-down for a transformer

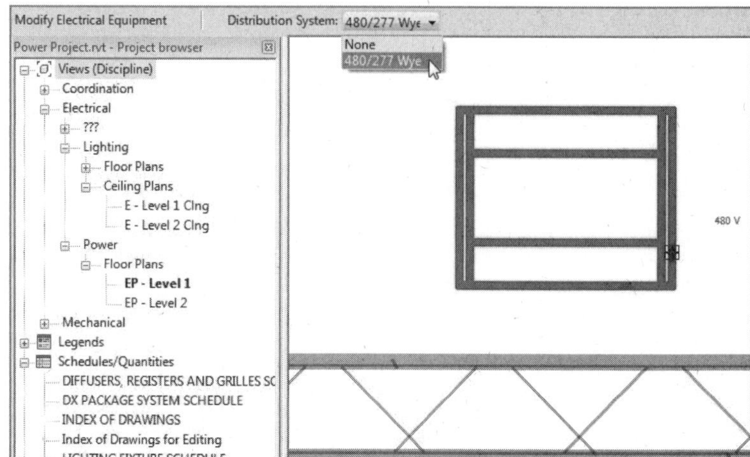

3. To set the distribution type for the secondary side of the transformer, you need to access the element properties of the component. The Secondary Distribution System parameter is an instance parameter that contains a list of the distribution system types defined in the electrical settings of your project. There is no connector in the transformer family for the secondary side, but it is important to establish the distribution system for connectivity of components in your distribution model. Figure 13.19 shows the option for selecting a secondary distribution system for a transformer.

HOUSEKEEPING

The pads for your electrical equipment can be either added to the equipment families or created as separate components. If they are to be created as separate components, you should coordinate with your structural consultant about who will create them. See Chapter 19, "Creating Equipment," for information on creating pads within equipment families.

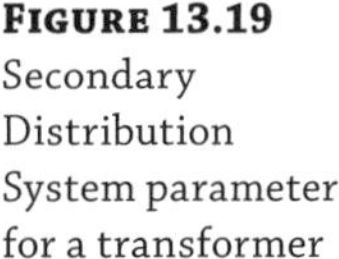

FIGURE 13.19 Secondary Distribution System parameter for a transformer

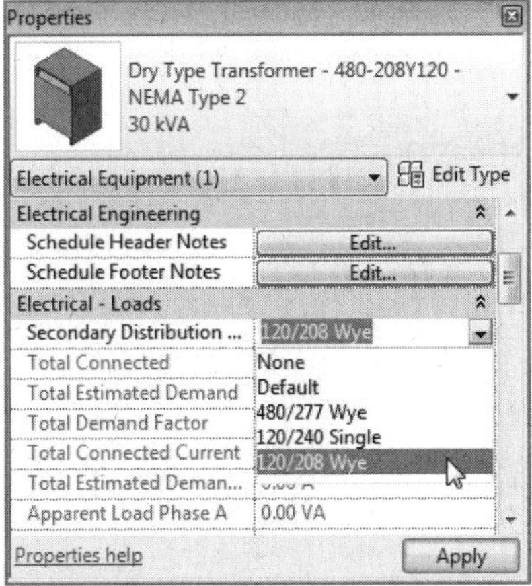

Switchboards

The various components that make up a switchboard are available in the `Distribution` folder within your library. Utility, metering, transformer, and circuit breaker sections are all available. Family types can be created within the families to meet the requirements of your design. If you do not know the exact equipment that will be used for your project, these families can act as placeholders until the equipment is chosen. Symbols can be used for various levels of model detail. The layout of switchboard sections can be used in elevation details if required.

To place a switchboard component, do the following:

1. Click the Electrical Equipment button on the Systems tab. Select the component from the Type Selector drop-down list, or load the family if necessary.
2. Use the spacebar to rotate the equipment prior to placement.

   Figure 13.20 shows the use of the spacebar to rotate objects adjacent to an angled wall or other objects. Begin by placing the object as usual (top), and then hover your mouse pointer over the desired host object until it highlights (middle), and press the spacebar (bottom). The object you are placing rotates in line with the chosen host.

   Components of the switchboard can be constrained together to move them as a whole unit if necessary.

3. Make sure that each component contains a connector that will define it as part of a distribution system.

Figure 13.21 shows an example of a switchboard layout in plan view (top) and section view (bottom).

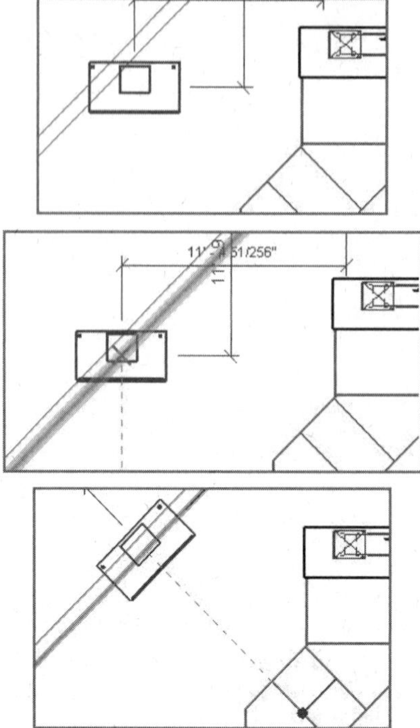

Figure 13.20
Using the spacebar to rotate objects

The distribution system of a switchboard component can be defined after placement by selecting the element and using the Distribution System drop-down on the Options Bar or by editing the instance properties in the Properties palette.

Panels

Electrical distribution panels are called many things by different users, such as *panels, panelboards,* or *breaker boxes.* In this book, we refer to them as *panels* and *panelboards.* The process for placing panels into your model is similar to placing other types of electrical equipment. The panel families that come with Revit MEP 2015 are useful because they are easily customized to meet your company's standards for panel representation on construction documents. These families are face hosted, so if you want to use nonhosted families for your panels, you will have to create them from scratch.

Many companies use specific symbols to represent panels based on their voltage. The panel families that come with the software simply represent the size of a panel by displaying the box. You can add a detail component to them that contains a filled region and that represents your standard. If you want to use a scalable annotation symbol, it must first be nested into a shared, face-hosted family that is then nested into your panel family. See the sidebar "Scalable Symbols for Wall Lights" in Chapter 20, "Creating Lighting Fixtures," for information on how to get a scalable annotation family into a face-hosted family that does not have the Maintain Annotation Orientation parameter.

If you decide to use a detail component, it must be placed in the Front or Back elevation view of the family in order to be displayed when the panel is mounted to a vertical surface.

FIGURE 13.21
Switchboard layout

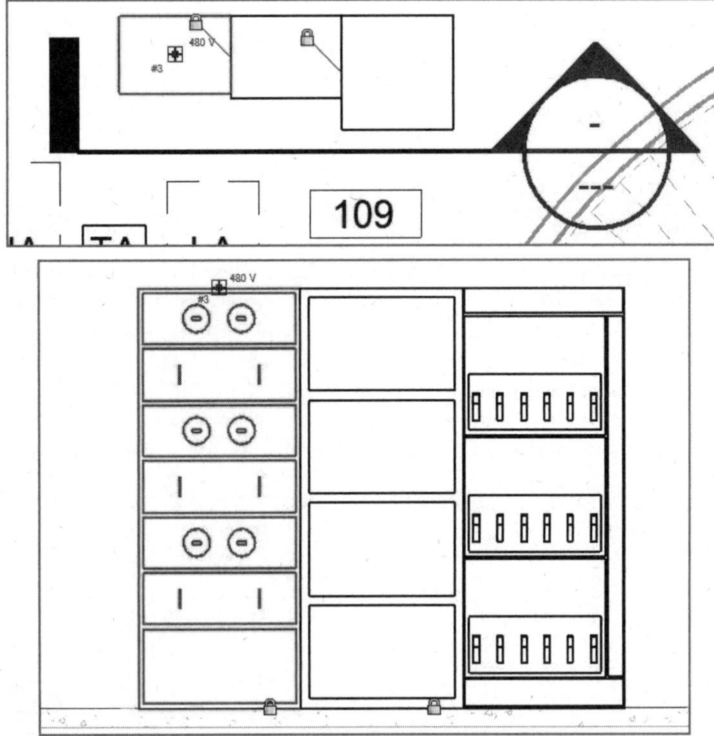

> **NESTED ANNOTATIONS**
>
> Annotation symbols cannot be placed in section or elevation views of families.

Figure 13.22 shows a panel family with a nested detail component family that is a filled region representing a 208-volt panel. This detail component is constrained to the parameters in the panel family and changes size with the panel.

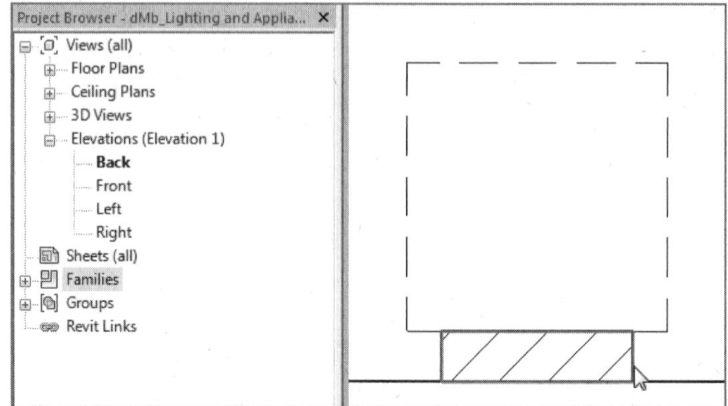

FIGURE 13.22 Detail component in a panel family

Clearance space is an important issue when placing panels into your model. You could draw detail lines, or even model lines directly in your project view to represent the clearance spaces, but that would be difficult to manage when changes occur. Elements can be added to your panel families to represent clearances, not only for 2D plan views but also for the 3D model. This lets you check for interferences with objects that infiltrate the clearance space. In Figure 13.23, you can see a panel family that has linework to represent the clearance area in front of the panel for plan views and solid extrusions that represent the 3D clearance areas.

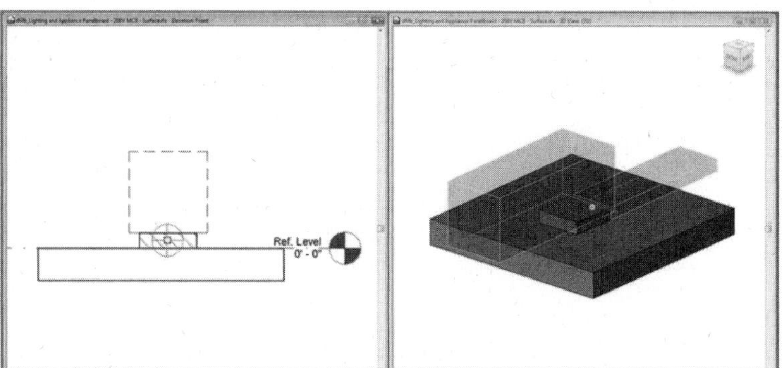

FIGURE 13.23 Panel family with clearance elements

Using subcategories for the clearance elements gives you the ability to control their visibility in your model views. The 3D clearance space does not have to be visible in your model in order for Revit to detect that an object is interfering with it.

Customizing your Revit families to meet your company's standards makes them easier to use and can help utilize the model information for design decisions. To customize a panel with clearance space lines, do the following:

1. Open the `Ch13Panel.rfa` file found at `www.sybex.com/go/masteringrevitmep2015`.
2. Click the Object Styles button on the Settings panel of the Manage tab. Create a new subcategory under Electrical Equipment called **Clearance Lines** for the 2D lines that will

show the clearance area in plan view. Choose a line weight of 4, blue line color, and hidden line pattern for this subcategory. Click OK to close the Object Styles dialog box.

3. Open the Front elevation view.
4. Click the Symbolic Line button on the Annotate tab. Select Clearance Lines from the drop-down list on the Subcategory panel of the Modify | Place Symbolic Lines contextual tab.
5. Draw a line from the upper-left corner of the panel object 4″ (100 mm) to the left. Draw a perpendicular line 3′-0″ (1 m) up from the panel. Draw a line 2′-4″ (0.7 m) to the right. Draw a line down, perpendicular to the front of the panel. Draw a line to the upper-right corner of the panel to complete the clearance area. (You can use different dimensions according to your standards. The point is to draw the space in front of the panel.)
6. Click the Aligned button on the Dimensions panel of the Annotate tab to draw a dimension from the left reference plane to the clearance line parallel to it. Click the lock grip to constrain the clearance line to the reference plane. Repeat the process for the reference plane and parallel clearance line on the right side of the panel.

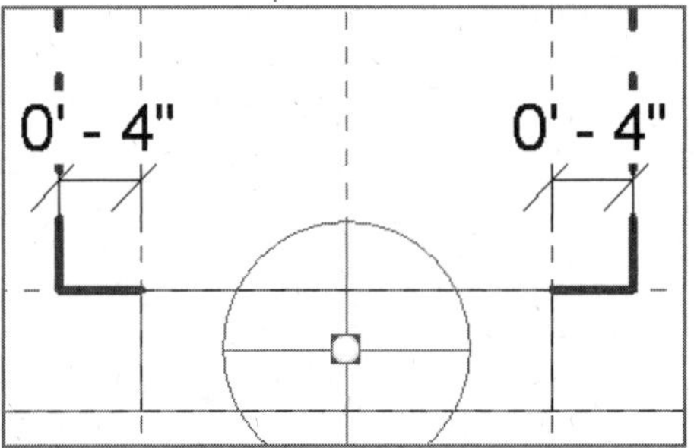

7. Dimension from the reference plane that defines the depth of the panel to the clearance line parallel to it in front of the panel. Lock the dimension.

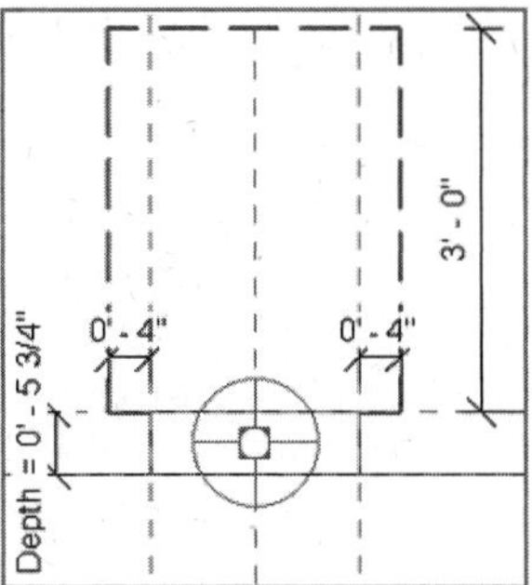

8. Use the Save As command to save the panel family to a location of your choice.

9. Create a new project file, and click the Wall button on the Architecture tab to create a wall in plan view.

10. Load the new panel family into your project. Use the Electrical Equipment button on the Systems tab to place an instance of the family onto the wall.

11. Use the View tab, and click the Visibility/Graphics button. Once you're in the dialog box, expand the Electrical Equipment category. Notice that the Clearance Lines subcategory now exists in the project. Turn on the display of electrical equipment, and click OK to close. You should now see your family and clearance linework.

Assigning a distribution system to your panels is crucial to the intelligence in your electrical model. This lets you create circuits for devices and lighting fixtures as well as model the distribution system. The Distribution System drop-down is available on the Options Bar when you place a panel into your model.

Creating Similar Panels

If you use the Create Similar command to place a new panel in your model that is just like another one, you still need to select a distribution system for the new panel.

Panels can be named using your naming standard by editing the Panel Name parameter. When using the panel families provided in your library or customized versions of them, you can control the size of a panel by establishing the number of poles. The Max #1 Pole Breakers parameter allows you to establish the number of poles available in the panel. An examination of the type parameters of one of these families reveals that the height of the panel is determined by the number of poles. The other parameters, such as Mains, Enclosure, Modifications, and Short Circuit Rating, which appear in the Electrical – Circuiting group of instance parameters are for information that will appear in the panel schedule. These parameters do not factor into the electrical characteristics of the panel or distribution system. They exist for reporting purposes only and have to be edited manually.

The Circuit Naming, Circuit Prefix Separator, and Circuit Prefix parameters allow you to control the naming of circuits that are fed from the panel. Because these are instance parameters, you can name circuits differently for each panel if necessary. You do not need to use these parameters to tag your circuits.

Other Equipment

Component families can be used to represent any type of electrical equipment required in your Revit project. Items such as generators, automatic transfer switches, starters, and variable frequency drives are available in the library. Figure 13.24 shows a diesel generator on the site plan of a project. The generator family is displayed differently depending on the Detail Level setting of the view. In Coarse detail, the generator appears as a simple box, while in Fine detail the shape of the equipment is visible.

FIGURE 13.24
Generator in a Revit model

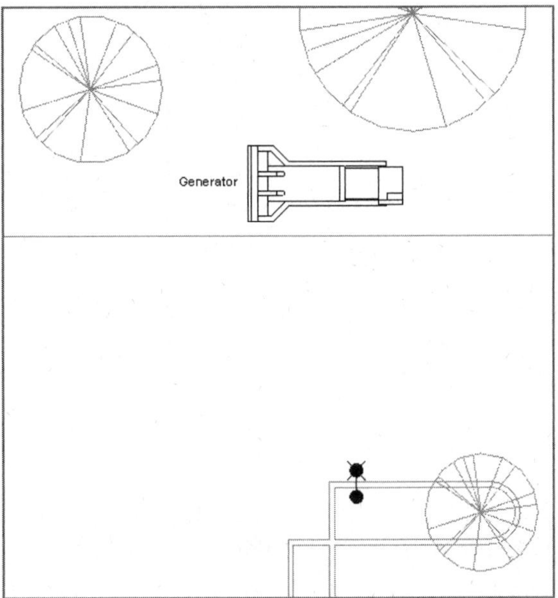

For telephone device systems, you can use a family to represent the punch-down blocks that act as the termination point for the telephone wiring within the building. This enables you to keep track of your telephone devices in different areas of the building. It is best to use a face-hosted family for this type of equipment because it is typically wall mounted. If your equipment family behavior is set to Other Panel, the Create Panel Schedules button appears on the Modify | Electrical Equipment contextual tab. You can create a panel schedule template that can be used for communications equipment to show connected devices. See Chapter 7, "Schedules," for information on creating panel schedules.

Server racks or audio equipment racks can be either wall-mounted or free-standing equipment, so nonhosted families can be used to accommodate either condition. A server rack family can be used as the equipment for your devices with data connections, and an audio equipment rack family can be used for devices with communications connectors. Be aware that many families provided by manufacturers to be used for data distribution are assigned to the Specialty Equipment category. In Revit MEP, that is an architectural category and will appear as halftone (gray or lighter) automatically. To make them appear as other MEP families, you'll need to change their category to Electrical Equipment or Data Devices. Figure 13.25 shows server racks placed in the center of a room to allow for the required clearances for the equipment.

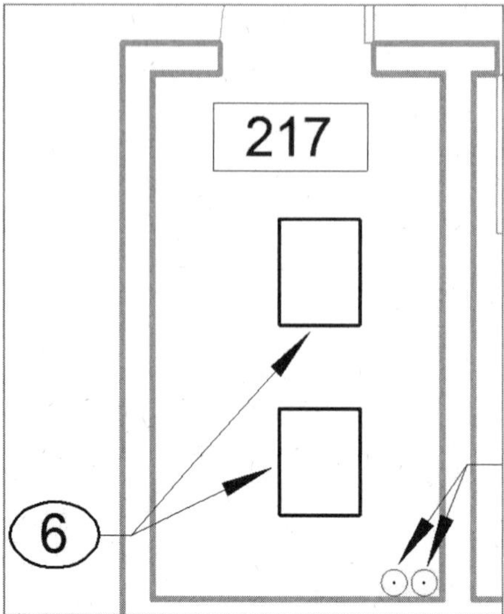

FIGURE 13.25
Server racks

> **ELECTRICAL COMPONENT FAMILIES**
>
> Detailed electrical equipment can be modeled using the Autodesk® Inventor® software and the model can be exported as an ADSK file. This file format can be used directly in your Revit project or in component families that you create. Electrical connection points transfer from the Inventor file to Revit during the export process.

Creating Power Distribution Systems

Having electrical equipment components in your Revit project enables you to coordinate space requirements and interferences with other building systems, but it also allows you to build intelligence into the model by establishing distribution systems. Establishing the distributive relationship between electrical components gives you the ability to keep track of loads from the branch circuit panels all the way to the main electrical equipment.

This is where the importance of assigning a distribution system to your electrical power equipment as it is placed comes into play. With the equipment in place, you can easily create the relationship from component to component. You can start at any component and connect to related equipment upstream. You are able to work upstream only when building distribution systems in Revit MEP. Because you will be assigning the equipment that feeds a component, it is best to start at the branch circuit panels and work your way upstream through the system. No wiring or conduit needs to be modeled to establish the electrical connection between two distribution components.

To create a distribution system, follow this general process:

1. Start by selecting one of your low-voltage branch circuit panels. If you have not already done so, assign a distribution system to the panel from the drop-down on the Options Bar. The Modify | Electrical Equipment contextual tab appears on the ribbon. Because the connector in the panel family is a power connection, a Power button appears in the Create Systems panel of the tab. Click this button to create a power circuit for the selected element. The active tab on the ribbon changes to the Modify | Electrical Circuits contextual tab. Click the Select Panel button to choose the equipment that feeds the selected component.

2. There are two ways you can select a panel: either by clicking the panel in the drawing area or by selecting it by name from the Panel drop-down list on the Options Bar. The drop-down makes it easy when the panel you need is not shown in the current view. The only components that show up in the drop-down or are available for selection in the drawing area are those that have connectors that match the distribution system of the selected component. This includes any panel or equipment in your project, not just in the current view.

   In Figure 13.26, a power circuit is created for panel LA. Notice that transformer TA is the only equipment available to feed the selected panel, because the connector properties of panel LA match up with the settings of the distribution system for the secondary side of the transformer.

FIGURE 13.26 Selecting a panel for a distribution system

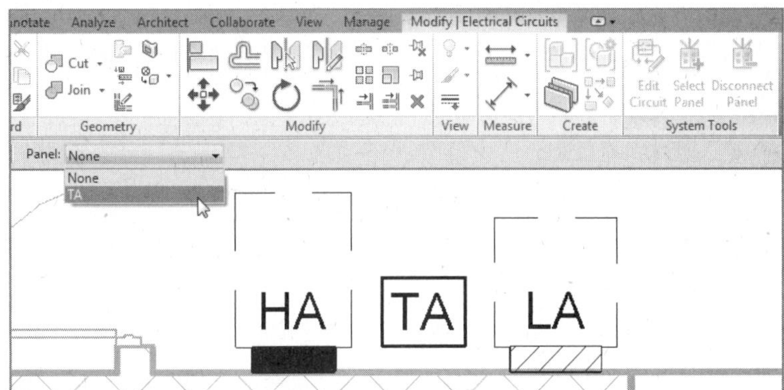

   When the panel is selected and the Electrical Circuits tab is active, a dashed box is displayed around all elements that are part of the circuit. An arrow is also shown pointing from the item for which the circuit was created to the panel or equipment chosen to feed it. By placing your mouse pointer over an electrical component and pressing the Tab key, you can see whether a circuit has been created for it and the components of that circuit, as shown in Figure 13.27.

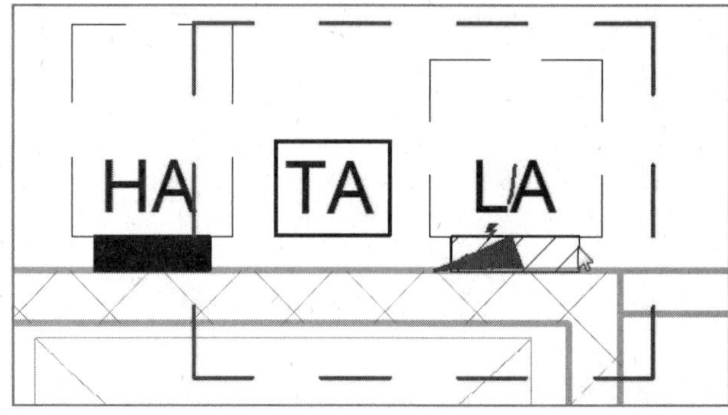

FIGURE 13.27 Using the Tab key to identify a circuit

3. Moving upstream from this point, you now need a circuit and panel for the transformer. In Figure 13.28, you can see that the steps for creating a circuit have been repeated for transformer TA. The list of available panels for the circuit is longer because there are more distribution components in the model that match the connector properties of the primary side of transformer TA. In this example, panel HA is the equipment chosen.

   Also, notice in Figure 13.28 that naming your panels and equipment is important prior to creating distribution systems. The metering section of the switchboard was not given a name and shows up in the list as its type name along with its electrical characteristics.

You can repeat this process for equipment as far upstream as you want to keep track of load information. Obviously, you aren't going to model the utility company's equipment or the local power plant, so when you get to the last component, you will not have any panel or equipment to select for its circuit. It is still recommended that you create a circuit for this equipment, because you cannot access the properties of the circuit and establish feeder information.

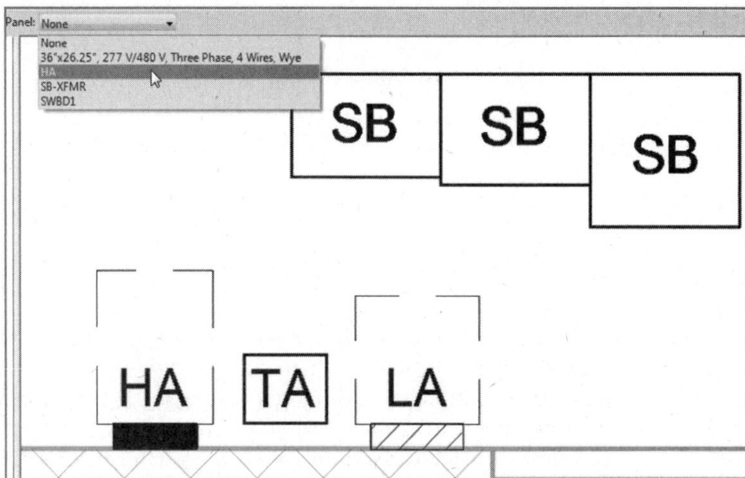

FIGURE 13.28 Selecting a panel for a distribution system

Power Diagrams

The most common way to communicate a distribution system is by a riser or one-line diagram. This schematic representation displays the connection relationships between electrical distribution equipment in a clear and easily readable manner (unless the project is large and complicated, in which case readability becomes debatable).

One of the first questions that comes up about using Revit MEP for electrical design is whether it can automatically create a power riser diagram from the components within the model. Unfortunately, at this point, it does not have that capability. This does not mean that you cannot create a diagram directly in your project. The drafting tools within Revit MEP 2015 provide you with all you need to create your diagrams, or if you are more comfortable using a CAD application for drafting tasks, you can link a CAD-generated diagram into your project.

Tips for Creating Power Diagrams

It is best to have a library of commonly used symbols to facilitate quick and easy creation of your power diagram. Symbols for items such as panels, transformers, grounding components, and generators can easily be created and stored for future projects. These symbols can contain parameters that make it easy for you to schedule and manage changes to the component data.

Consider creating a detail section view of your switchboard equipment or main distribution panel as the starting point for your diagram. In this view, you can turn off any linked files and worksets that do not need to be shown, leaving you with an elevation view of your equipment and the project levels, which are typically shown on riser diagrams.

Symbols can then be placed into this detail view to represent the electrical distribution equipment. Detail lines can be drawn in the view to represent the connection between elements. You can use the power of Revit to create linetypes specific to your needs for electrical diagrams to increase your efficiency when drafting. Although the symbols and linework are not tied to the model elements that they represent, you are able to coordinate data required in both places without having to switch between applications. Figure 13.29 shows an example of a power diagram created by using an elevation view of the switchboard, symbols, text, and detail lines.

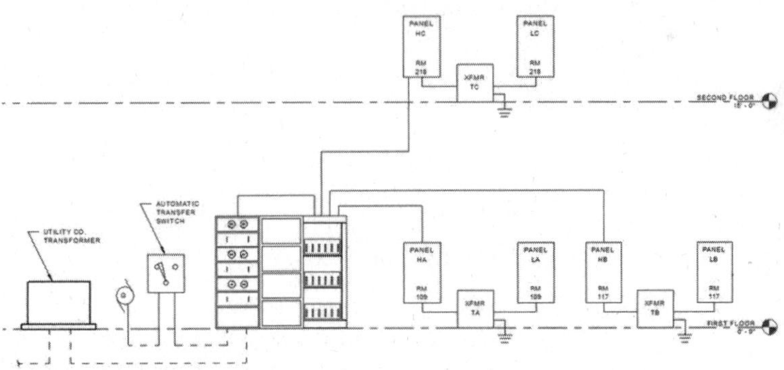

FIGURE 13.29 Power diagram created in Revit

Temporary dimensions and alignment lines make drafting and editing diagrams in Revit MEP easy, and with a little practice, you can become proficient with the available tools. We are all looking forward to the day when power diagrams will be generated automatically from the model, but until then, you have the tools necessary to create them.

Creating a Fire Alarm System Model

Fire alarm systems are often shown with the electrical construction documents, although on occasion they are handled separately. The same tools that allow you to model other electrical systems can be used for fire alarms. As with any unique system, it is recommended that you create a workset for the fire alarm system to allow for multiple-user access to the model. If a consultant uses Revit MEP to create the fire alarm system for your project, you can link in their model for coordination.

The number of fire alarm device families that are included with the installation of Revit MEP has increased over the years, but you may need to create devices that match your company standards. Fire alarm construction documents are usually schematic in nature, so the annotation symbols are the important part of your fire alarm system families. The `Manual Pull Station.rfa` family provided with Revit MEP 2015 can be copied and modified with the appropriate annotations to build your library of fire alarm devices. For more information on creating symbols and devices, see Chapter 18 and Chapter 21. Because fire alarm devices are typically mounted to walls and ceilings, face-hosted families are the best option.

Placing fire alarm devices into your model follows the same workflow as placing power or communications devices:

1. Click the Device button drop-down on the Systems tab, and select the Fire Alarm category. If no fire alarm devices are loaded into your project, you will be prompted to load one.

> **No Devices Loaded**
>
> You can increase productivity by having the devices that you use most often loaded into your project template, avoiding the need to interrupt your workflow by loading them as needed. On the other hand, it is possible to overload your template, so choose only those devices that you know will be used regularly.

2. Choose the desired device from the Type Selector, and choose a placement option for the host of your device. You can place pull stations, horns, strobes, and smoke detectors on any 3D surface in the model.
3. Use a reflected ceiling plan view to place devices on the ceiling. Be sure to turn on the visibility of other devices such as lighting fixtures, air terminals, and sprinklers to coordinate the location of your fire alarm devices in the ceiling. These other devices will be on other categories not necessarily visible in your view. They may also be on nonvisible

worksets or linked files, so you have to control the visibility of the individual element categories.

Fire Alarm Riser Diagram

Because wiring is typically not shown on fire alarm drawings for the connectivity of the system, a fire alarm riser diagram is an important piece of the project. Although Revit cannot automatically generate a riser diagram from the devices placed into your model, you can use your model as a diagram, depending on the size and shape of the building. Figure 13.30 shows a floor plan with fire alarm devices placed throughout the building.

FIGURE 13.30
Sample fire alarm plan

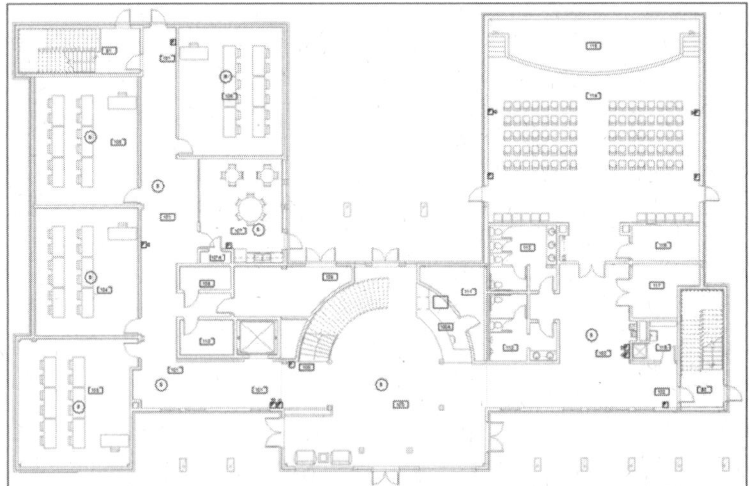

With the devices in place, the view can be duplicated and used as a diagram. Right-clicking the view in the Project Browser and selecting the Duplicate With Detailing option gives you an exact copy of the view, including any annotation and detail lines. Using the Visibility/Graphic Overrides settings to turn off the linked models leaves just the fire alarm devices and room numbers shown. Room numbers and other items that do not need to be shown can be hidden in the view. Detail lines can then be added to the view to show the connectivity of the system, as shown in Figure 13.31. Using this method creates a diagram that is showing the actual locations of the devices, so as changes are made to the design, you need to edit only the detail lines in this view to update your diagram.

This method has its drawbacks; the process would need to be repeated for every floor of a multistory building, resulting in several diagrams, so it is not a riser diagram in the true meaning of the term. It may also be difficult to use on a single-story building that is very large, where the devices are spread out, causing the diagram to be too large to justify the use of document space. However, if your project is the right size and shape, this method is a way to have your diagram tied directly to the model.

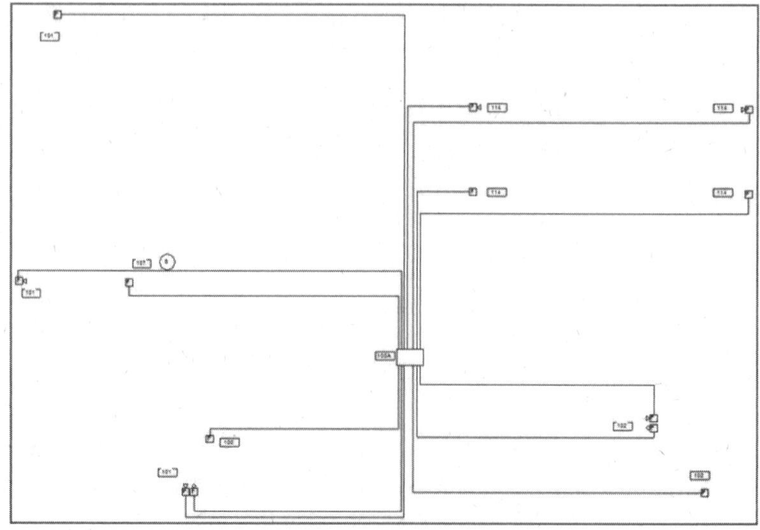

FIGURE 13.31 Fire alarm view with detail lines to be used as a riser diagram

Fire Alarm Diagram Using Drafting Tools and Symbols

A more traditional approach is to generate a diagram by using drafting tools and symbols. This can be done while still utilizing some of the model information, such as levels and an elevation of the fire alarm control panel or equipment. You can create a detail section of your control panel and then add symbols and detail lines to generate the riser diagram. In this section view, you can show the building levels and use constraints to maintain the relationship of your symbols to the levels so that, if changes are made, your diagram updates appropriately. The same symbol families that are nested into your fire alarm device families can be loaded into your project file for use in your diagram.

By utilizing the drafting tools available along with annotations and families, you can generate a fire alarm riser diagram without having to link in a CAD file and switch between applications to make changes. Figure 13.32 shows a simple example of how Revit MEP 2015 can be used for fire alarm diagrams.

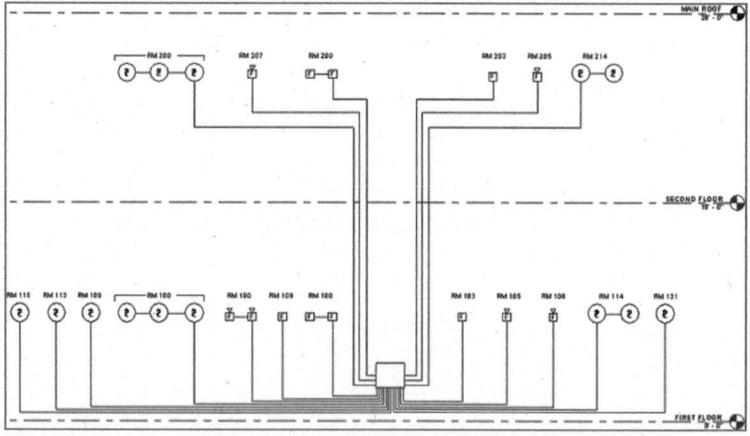

FIGURE 13.32 Sample fire alarm riser diagram using detail lines, text, and symbols

Modeling Conduit and Cable Tray

The tools for modeling conduit and cable tray were introduced in Revit MEP 2011. With them, you can create conduit and cable tray runs within your project model for coordination with other system components. Conduit and cable tray are system families for which you can define different types. Parameters can be used for tagging and scheduling these families to keep track of quantities and materials if desired. The techniques for modeling conduit and cable tray are similar to those for placing ductwork or pipe. You likely will not model all the conduit required for your project, so the size limit for conduit that will be modeled should be made clear early in the project.

Generally, you model conduit only when it may present a coordination issue with other building components. Some clients provide expectations for what is to be modeled and will often define the level of detail required for a model, including minimum conduit sizes. However, you may need to model smaller conduits if they are run grouped together, which can be a significant coordination issue.

There are two styles of system families for conduit and cable tray. You can create runs that utilize fittings or runs that do not. If you want to model a run of conduit that will be bent to change direction, use the style without fittings. This allows you to determine the length of the run and does not add components to the model that would not exist in the construction.

Because there are two styles for conduit and cable tray, there are also two schedule types that can be created. The Cable Tray Runs category in the New Schedule dialog box is for the cable tray style without fittings. This schedule style contains parameters for reporting the total length of a run, including any change in direction. The Cable Trays or Cable Tray Fittings schedule style is used for the cable tray style that utilizes fittings. This type of schedule can be used to report data about the individual pieces that make up a run of cable tray. The same schedule types are available for conduit, as shown in Figure 13.33.

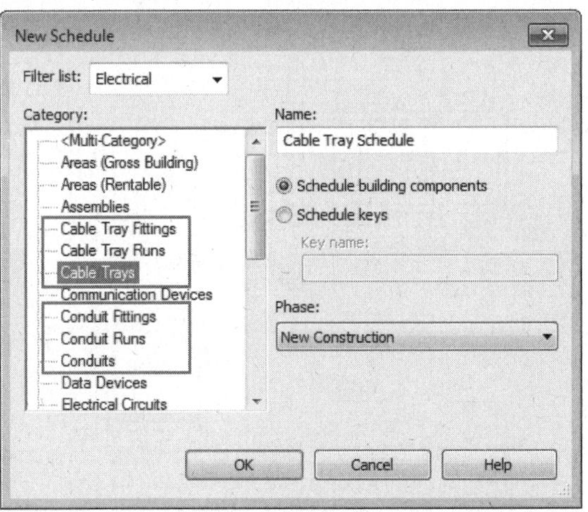

FIGURE 13.33 Conduit and cable tray schedule categories

When you model a run of cable tray or conduit by using the style without fittings, it does not mean that no fittings exist in the run. You still have to define what fittings will be used to transition or change direction, but the length of the fittings will be included in the total length of the run. Figure 13.34 shows the fittings assigned to a cable tray style without fittings.

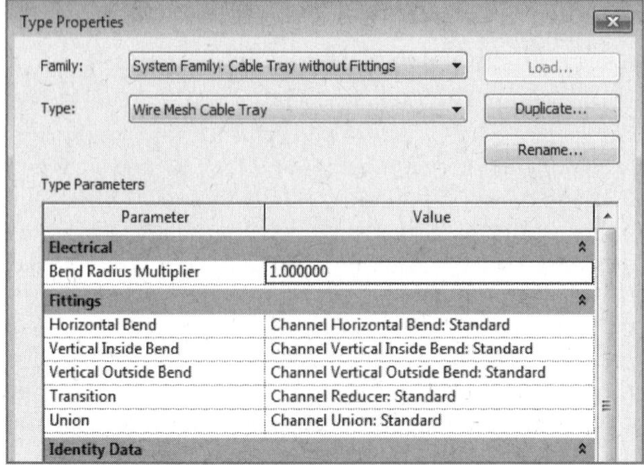

FIGURE 13.34
Fittings assigned to a cable tray family

A fitting family must be assigned to each parameter in order to model a run of conduit or cable tray. Even if you are not modeling a condition that requires a tee, you still must have a fitting family assigned for tees. It may seem counterintuitive to assign fittings to a system family without fittings, but it is necessary in order for the runs to be modeled. When you model a run without fittings, the fittings used have a value of Bend for their Bend Or Fitting parameter. For runs modeled using fittings, the parameter value is Fitting. This can be useful information when scheduling conduit or cable tray.

The bend radius for cable tray elbows is set to the width of the cable tray by default. The Bend Radius Multiplier parameter can be used to define a bend radius for different types within the system family. The bend radius of an elbow can be modified directly in the model by selecting the fitting and editing the temporary radius dimension that appears, as shown in Figure 13.35. The bend radius for conduit elbows is determined by a lookup table defined in the fitting family.

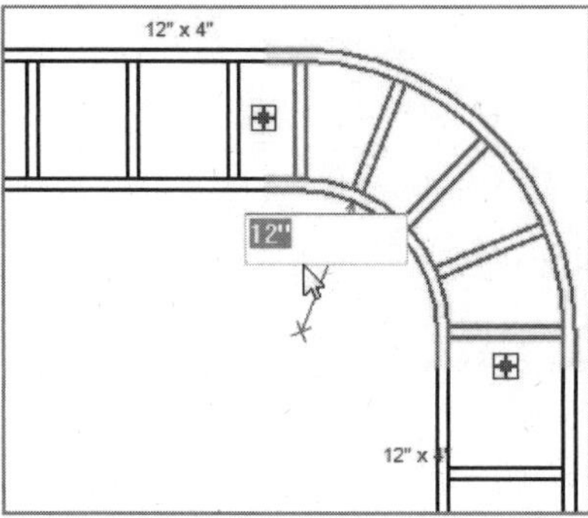

FIGURE 13.35
Editing a cable tray bend radius

Conduit is displayed as a single line in views set to Coarse or Medium detail level. Cable tray is displayed as a single line in views set to Coarse detail level. In views set to Medium detail level, cable tray is displayed as two-line geometry. Ladder-type cable tray is displayed as a ladder in views set to Fine detail level.

Defining Electrical Settings

Conduit and cable tray settings and sizes can be defined in the Electrical Settings dialog box, which is accessed via the MEP Settings button on the Manage tab. The general settings are used to define the visibility behavior of conduit or cable tray when shown as single-line graphics, as shown in Figure 13.36. A suffix and separator can be defined for tagging.

FIGURE 13.36
Cable tray general settings

Electrical Settings

Hidden Line
General
Wiring
Wire Sizes
Correction Factor
Ground Conductors
Wiring Types
Voltage Definitions
Distribution Systems
Cable Tray Settings

Setting	Value
Use Annot. Scale for Single Line Fittings	☐
Cable Tray Fitting Annotation Size	0' 0 1/8"
Cable Tray Size Separator	x
Cable Tray Size Suffix	ø
Cable Tray Connector Separator	-

Rise/Drop graphics can be defined for both cable tray and conduit. Clicking the Value cell activates the Select Symbol dialog box, which allows you to choose a graphic representation for a conduit or cable tray rise or drop, as shown in Figure 13.37. Graphics can be defined for both single-line and two-line representations. You cannot create your own symbols to use for this representation.

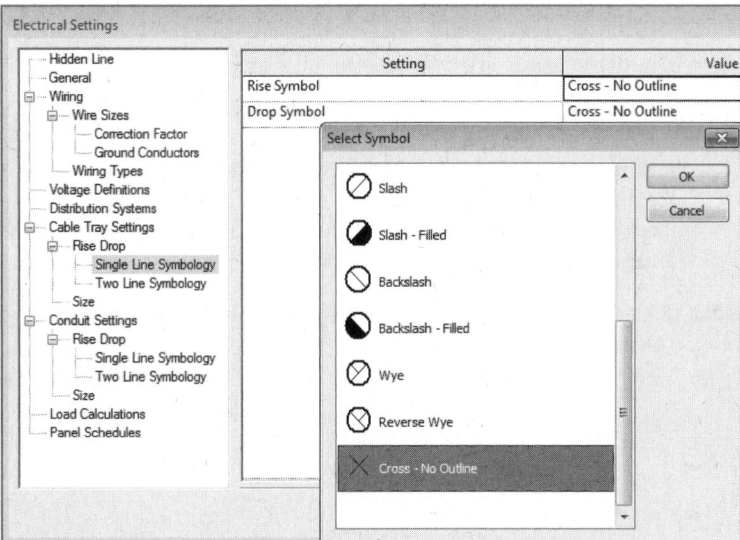

FIGURE 13.37
Rise/drop symbol options

The Size settings for cable tray are very simple. You can input sizes available for cable tray and also choose whether certain sizes are available for your project by selecting the box in the Used In Size Lists column, as shown in Figure 13.38.

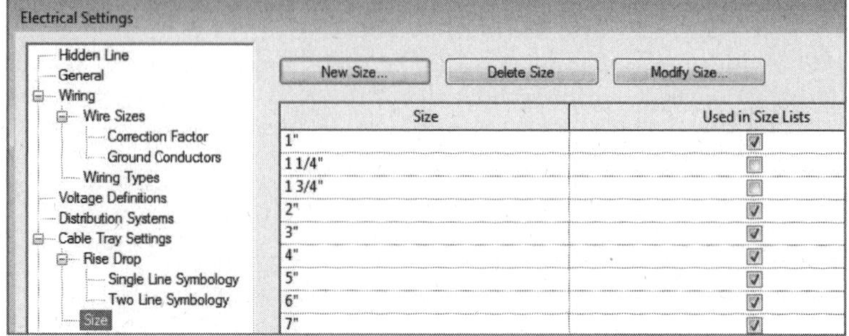

FIGURE 13.38 Cable tray Size settings

The Size settings for conduit are more detailed because of the difference in dimensions for various conduit materials. Sizes and a minimum bend radius can be defined for each conduit material type, as shown in Figure 13.39.

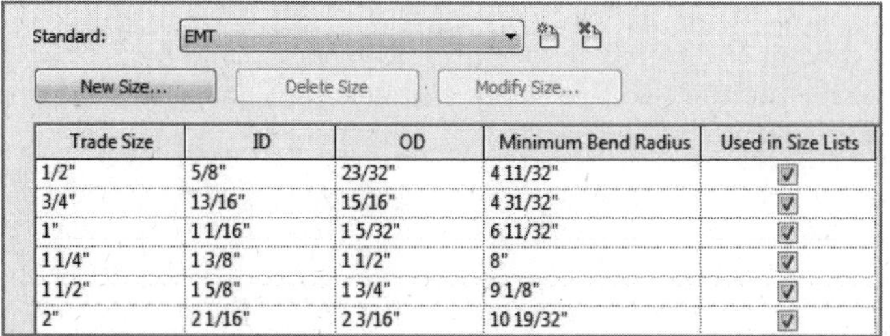

FIGURE 13.39 Conduit Size settings

You can create additional settings for materials by clicking the Add Standard button next to the drop-down at the top of the dialog box. A few standards are predefined, and you can use them as the base settings for creating custom standards. Figure 13.40 shows the predefined conduit standards provided with Revit MEP 2015.

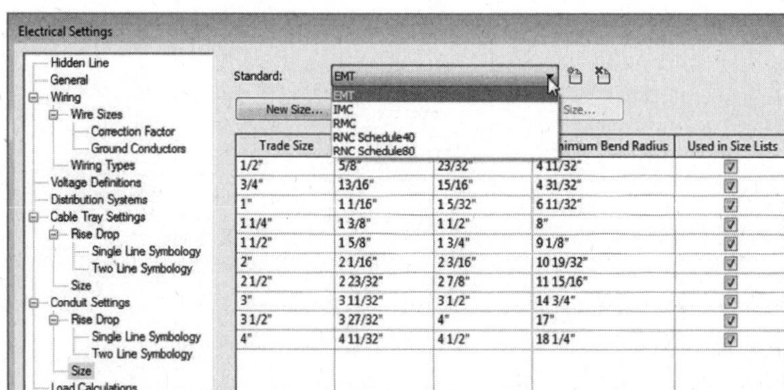

FIGURE 13.40 Conduit standards for Size settings

Whether or not a conduit size is available for your project is determined by selecting or deselecting the check box in the Used In Size Lists column. Be sure to set your Project Units settings to coincide with the available sizes. For example, if you set the Rounding value of the Conduit Size units to the nearest 1/2", then even if the 1 1/4" conduit size in the Electrical Settings dialog box is set to be available in size lists, it does not appear in the list. If you are using metric units, the Rounding setting must match the number of decimal places of the conduit or cable tray sizes in order for a conduit or cable tray size to appear in the available sizes list.

The settings for conduit and cable tray that you use most often should be established in your project templates so that you can begin modeling right away. The settings can be modified to meet any unique requirements of a project after the project file has been created.

Placing Conduit in a Model

Once you have defined the desired settings for conduit and cable tray, you can begin modeling in your projects. To model a run of conduit, click the Conduit button on the Systems tab. Choose the desired style (with or without fittings) from the Type Selector in the Properties palette. The Diameter drop-down on the Options Bar displays the list of available sizes based on the settings defined in the Electrical Settings and Project Units dialog boxes. The Offset drop-down on the Options Bar determines the elevation of the conduit above the level of the currently active view. Click in the drawing area to start the run of conduit. Move your mouse pointer in the desired direction, and click to finish the run or change direction.

The Modify | Place Conduit contextual tab also contains tools for placement. The Justification button allows you to define the point along the conduit that determines its elevation. If you choose to draw conduit with a vertical justification at the middle and the horizontal justification at the center, then the value given for the offset of the conduit is directly in the center of the conduit. These settings allow you to draw conduit from the top, middle, or bottom to coordinate elevations with other model elements. The elevation of a conduit can be changed after it is drawn by selecting the conduit and editing the value in the Offset drop-down on the Options Bar or the Offset parameter in the Properties palette.

The Automatically Connect button on the contextual tab is set by default. This setting means that a fitting is automatically placed when one conduit touches another in the model. The Tag On Placement button can be selected to tag conduit automatically as it is drawn. A conduit tag must be loaded into the project, and settings for the tag placement are available on the Options Bar.

The Inherit Elevation button allows you to set the elevation of the conduit you are modeling to match that of an object to which you are connecting. The Inherit Size button sets your conduit size to match that of an object to which you are connecting. You can use the spacebar to inherit both the elevation and size of an object to which you are connecting.

You can change the elevation in the midst of modeling a run by changing the Offset value in the drop-down and then continuing the run. Revit automatically inserts the proper fittings and vertical conduit to transition to the new elevation. The Offset Connections panel, shown in Figure 13.41, allows you to connect conduits at different elevations either by using a vertical riser conduit or by applying a slope to connect directly. When you start drawing conduit at an elevation, you can apply either of these settings and connect to conduit at a different elevation. The run of conduit is modeled directly to the point of connection, with a vertical riser or whatever slope is required to make the connection.

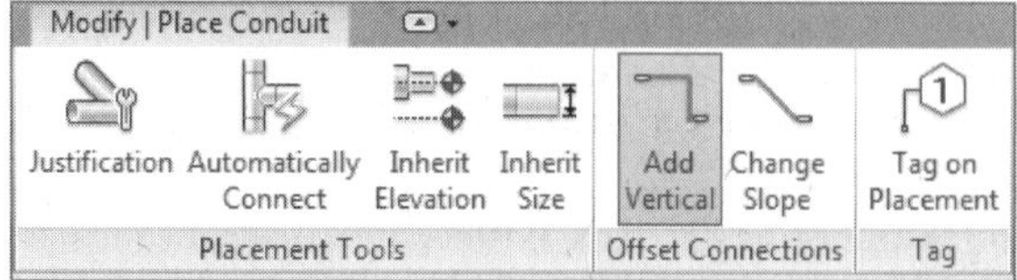

FIGURE 13.41 Conduit placement options

To connect conduit to equipment or a device, the object must have a conduit connector. When you select the object, you can right-click the conduit connector grip and choose the option to draw conduit from the connector, as shown in Figure 13.42. This connector is defined as a *face connector*, which means that conduit can be connected anywhere on the face of the equipment. It also means that multiple conduits can be connected to the face.

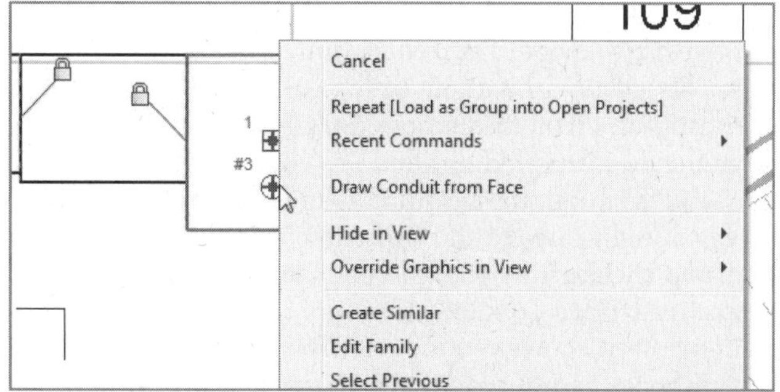

FIGURE 13.42 Drawing conduit from a connector

Selecting this type of connector allows you to choose the position of the connection prior to drawing the conduit. The connection point can be dragged to any location on the face, or you can edit the temporary dimensions to locate the connection point. Once you have determined the location, click the Finish Connection button on the Surface Connection contextual tab. You can now draw the conduit from the connector. Be sure to assign an appropriate Offset value prior to drawing. Once the conduit has been drawn, you must disconnect it from the connector point on the equipment if you want to move the location of the connection. Figure 13.43 shows plan and section views of conduit drawn from the top of an electrical equipment object.

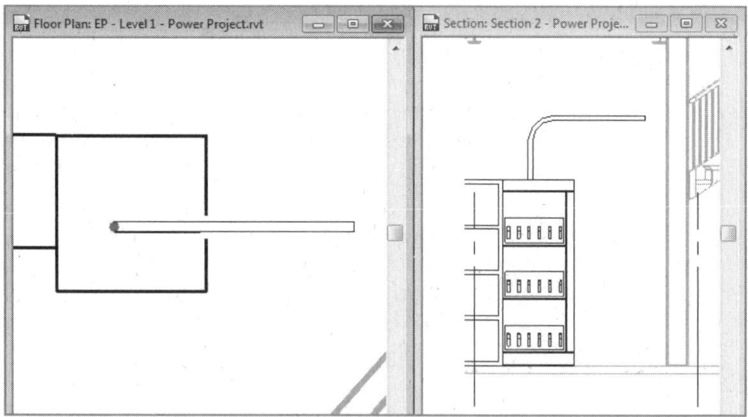

FIGURE 13.43 Conduit drawn in a model

Individual connectors have a static location that can be modified only by editing the family. Only one conduit can be drawn from this type of connector. These are useful when the point of connection is clearly defined on a piece of equipment.

Revit MEP 2015 has tools that allow you to model parallel runs of conduit. This is very useful for modeling banks of conduit runs quickly, without having to model several runs or make copies.

To model parallel runs of conduit, you need to start with a single run. Once the run is complete, you can click the Parallel Conduits button on the Electrical panel of the Systems tab. This activates the Parallel Conduits contextual tab, which contains settings for the parallel runs, as shown in Figure 13.44.

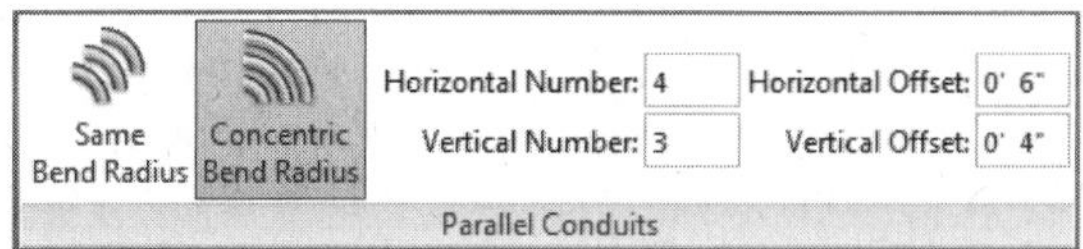

FIGURE 13.44 Options for parallel conduits

You can choose for the conduits to all have the same bend radius or to use concentric bends, which take up less space and provide a more uniform layout. The Offset fields allow you to assign the spacing both horizontally and vertically between the runs. A positive value for the vertical offset places runs above the original, while a negative value places them below.

After you establish the desired settings, place your cursor over one of the conduits or fittings in the original run. You will see a reference line or lines indicating the side to which the parallel runs will be placed. You can move your cursor slightly to change sides. Press the Tab key to highlight the entire run, and then click to create the parallel runs. Figure 13.45 shows a simple example of parallel runs that were created by using the Parallel Conduits tool.

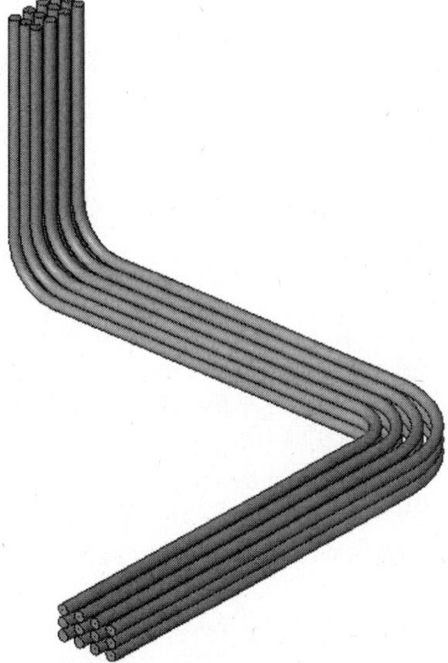

FIGURE 13.45 Parallel conduit runs

MINIMUM BEND RADIUS

When you're creating parallel conduit runs and using the Concentric Bend Radius setting, the bend created for a parallel run might be smaller than the minimum bend radius allowed for the fittings used. In this case, you will be given the option, via a dialog box, to use the minimum or cancel the operation.

Placing Cable Tray in a Model

The process for modeling cable tray is the same as for conduit. There is a drop-down on the Options Bar for the Width and Height settings of the cable tray, as defined in the Electrical Settings dialog box. Cable tray can be connected to equipment or devices that have cable tray connectors. Cable tray connectors have a static location and cannot be moved along the face of the family without editing the family.

You can connect conduit to cable tray by snapping your mouse pointer from the cable tray edge when drawing the conduit. The conduit connects to the center of the cable tray so, if you are using the Fine detail level setting, the centerline of the conduit appears beyond the connected edge of the cable tray, as shown in Figure 13.46.

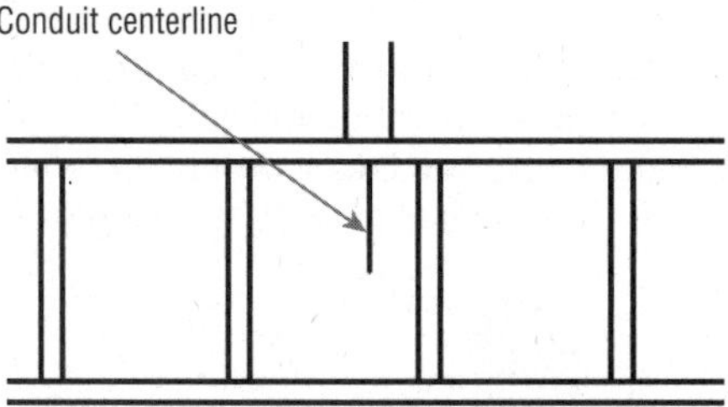

FIGURE 13.46 Conduit connected to cable tray

You can remedy this by turning off the centerline of conduit in the Visibility/Graphic Overrides settings of the view.

Creating Family Types

You can create unique family types for conduit and cable tray system families. Select a conduit or cable tray in the model, and click the Edit Type button in the Properties palette. Or you can double-click a conduit or cable tray family in the Project Browser to access the Type Properties dialog box for that family. Click the Duplicate button in the dialog box to create a new family type. Give the new family type a descriptive name that defines the type. You can then assign fittings or parameter values that make the type unique from other types within the family. The newly created family type will be available in the Type Selector when you're placing conduit or cable tray.

The types of conduit and cable tray that you most commonly use should be defined in your project templates for easy access. Additional fittings can be loaded to create unique family types if the project requires them.

The Bottom Line

Place power and systems devices into your model. Creating electrical plans that are correct not only in the model but also on construction documents can be achieved with Revit MEP 2015.

Master It Having flexibility in the relationship between model components and the symbols that represent them is important to create an accurate model and construction documents. Is it possible to show a receptacle and its associated symbol in slightly different locations to convey the design intent properly on construction documents? If so, how?

Place equipment and connections. Electrical equipment often requires clearance space for access and maintenance. Modeling equipment in your Revit project allows you to coordinate clearance space requirements.

Master It Interference between model components can be detected by finding components that occupy the same space. Explain how you can determine whether an object interferes with the clearance space of an electrical equipment component.

Create distribution systems. Proper set up of distribution systems is the backbone of the intelligence of your electrical design. It helps you track the computable data within your project.

Master It Because your project may contain multiple distribution system types, explain the importance of assigning distribution systems to your electrical equipment and naming your equipment.

True or false: You cannot create a power riser diagram with Revit MEP 2015.

Model conduit and cable tray. Large conduit and cable tray runs are a serious coordination issue in building designs. Revit MEP 2015 has tools that allow you to model conduit and cable tray to coordinate with other model components.

Master It Conduit and cable tray can be modeled with two styles. One style uses fittings, and one does not. Does this mean that no fittings need to be assigned to the style that does not use fittings? Explain how this affects the scheduling of the components.

Circuiting and Panels

You put information into the components that you use to build your Autodesk® Revit® MEP models so you can use that data to confirm the integrity of your design and improve coordination. The computable data in a model is dependent on the systems that you establish. Revit MEP recognizes many types of systems for airflow and piping. For electrical projects, the systems are the types of circuits you create to establish the relationship between a fixture or device and its associated equipment. This relationship is typically conveyed on construction documents by schematic lines representing the wiring. Circuit types that can be created include power, data, communications, security, and others.

With the parametric and connective nature of model components, you have the ability to maintain the relationship between your model elements and the schematic wiring associated with them. Wires can be used to display information with tags and extract, or offer, data in schedules. Even if you do not choose to show wiring on your construction documents, you can still take full advantage of the Revit process by creating and managing electrical circuits.

The electrical settings established for your projects are the backbone of creating circuits and wiring. When properly set up in your project template, they can make creating and managing circuits easy and efficient.

In this chapter, you will learn to do the following:

- Establish settings for circuits and wiring
- Create circuits and wiring for devices and fixtures
- Manage circuits and panels
- Use schedules for sharing circuit information

Establishing Electrical Settings

The electrical settings for your project determine your ability to connect devices and equipment and also define how wiring and electrical information is displayed. You can define the types of voltages available and also the distribution system characteristics. This allows you to connect devices properly and prevents you from accidentally wiring objects to the wrong panel. You can set the visibility behavior of tick marks to show wire counts and how wire tags display the electrical information. All of these settings are project specific, so you can create a standard setup in your project template based on company or project-type requirements.

You can access the electrical settings at any time by typing **ES** or by clicking the MEP Settings button on the Manage tab.

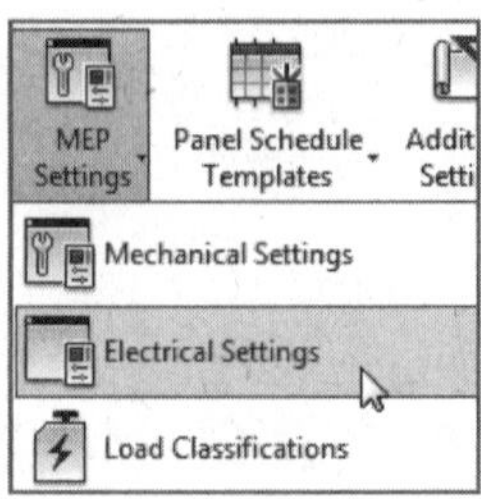

The Hidden Line settings in the Electrical Settings dialog box allow you to establish the size of the gap that is shown when a conduit and cable tray cross over each other. The gap size is relative to the scale of the views. These gaps appear only when a view is set to Hidden Line mode.

The General settings determine how the electrical data is displayed for devices and the format for describing the electrical characteristics. These settings do not affect the behavior of electrical devices or circuits; they affect only how information is displayed in the Electrical Data parameter of devices. There are also settings for circuit naming if you name your circuits by phase.

This section is also where you can define how load names are capitalized in panel schedules. You can choose from the preset options provided. Changing these settings after panel schedules have been generated does not affect the existing load names in a schedule.

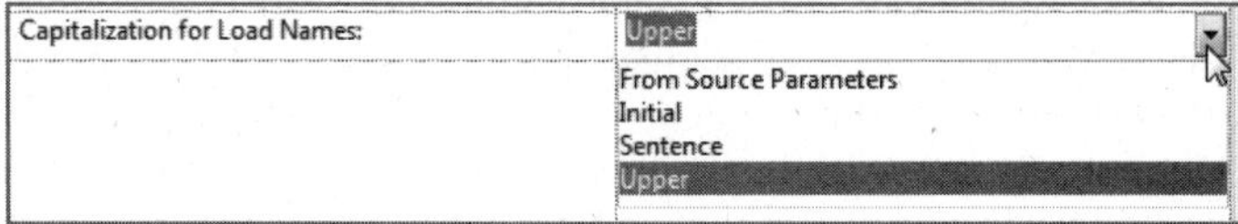

Wiring Settings

In the Wiring settings section of the Electrical Settings dialog box, you can define the ambient temperature to be used in order to apply a correction factor to the load of a circuit. The default setting is 86°F (30°C), which applies a correction factor of 1 for any of the three wire temperature ratings. In this section, you can also define the size of the gap that is displayed when wires cross. The value you input into this setting indicates the print size of the gap on a full-size print.

Tick marks for wiring are also defined in the Wiring section of the Electrical Settings dialog box. You can create an annotation family to use as a tick mark if the defaults do not comply with your standards. The family must be loaded into your project in order for it to be assigned to represent hot, neutral, or ground wires. You can choose to show a slanted line across the tick marks to represent the ground conductor no matter what families you use. There are three options for displaying tick marks, as shown in Figure 14.1. Changing the display setting for tick marks affects all wires in your project.

The three tick mark settings are as follows:

Always With this setting, tick marks are displayed on any wire when it is drawn.

Never With this setting, tick marks are not displayed on any wire when it is drawn.

Home Runs With this setting, tick marks are displayed only on wiring home runs and not on wires between devices on the same circuit.

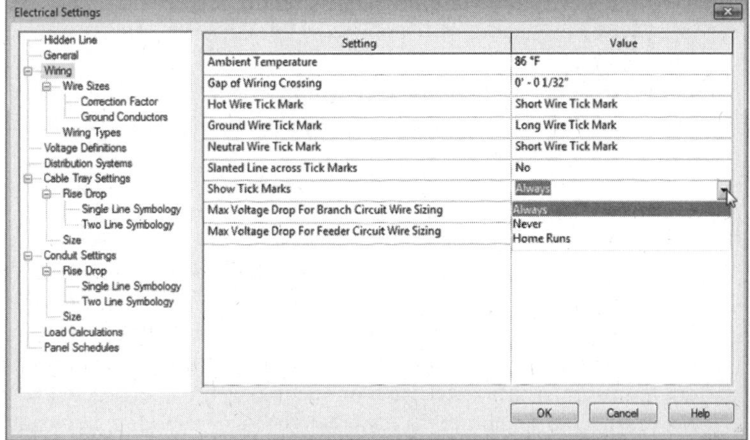

FIGURE 14.1
Wiring section of Electrical Settings dialog box

In this section, you can also define the maximum voltage drop percentage for branch circuits and feeders.

The Wire Sizes section of the Electrical Settings dialog box allows you to define the sizes of wires you want to use for different circuit ampacities. You can set the wire sizes for aluminum and copper wire. You can even create a different wire material, temperature rating, or insulation type if your project requires it. You can vary the wire sizes for the three standard wire-temperature ratings and for different types of insulation. This gives you the ability to control the types of wires used for different circuits because you can remove ampacity ratings for different wire temperature and insulation combinations.

The Used By Sizing column allows you to establish which wire sizes are available to be used when the wire size of a circuit is calculated. You can assign only one wire size per ampacity, so if, for example, you want to use #12 wire for 15-amp and 20-amp circuits, you would have to delete the 15 A ampacity and set the size for the 20 A ampacity to #12 wire. This does not mean you cannot use a 15-amp circuit in your project. The smallest wire size available in your list is for an ampacity smaller than the smallest in your list. Figure 14.2 shows an example of wire sizes for a project. Any circuits smaller than 20 amps in the project have to use #12 wire.

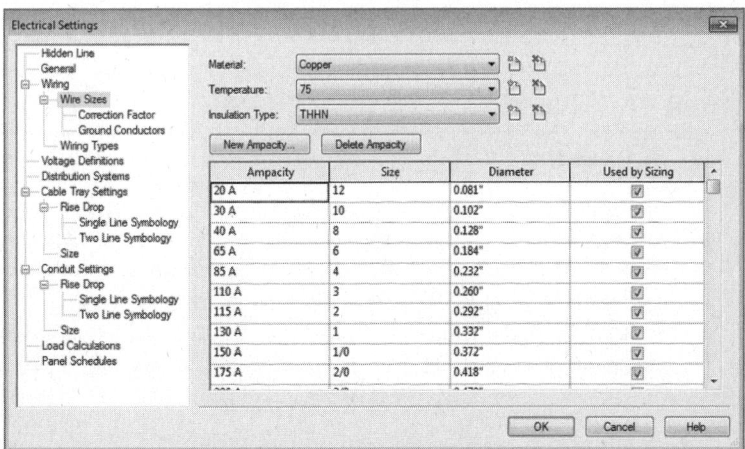

FIGURE 14.2
Wire size settings

The Correction Factor section of the Electrical Settings dialog box is for setting a correction factor based on temperature to be used in load calculations. You can set correction factors for different wire temperature ratings and materials. The Ground Conductors section allows you to set the equipment grounding conductor size for different ampacities of different wire materials. So, you have the ability to control several factors that determine the wire sizes that are calculated for your circuits.

In the Wiring Types section of the Electrical Settings dialog box, you can create different types of wires for different uses. By creating different wire types, you have the ability to assign all the desired settings to a type, and as with component families, you can switch between wire types in the model. Creating wire types also provides you with an easy way to control the visibility of certain wires by using a view filter. You can give your wire types unique names that define their use or some characteristic about them. You can set the material, temperature rating, and insulation used by a wire type. You can also set the maximum wire size for a type. If a circuit requires a larger wire size than the maximum, parallel sets of wires that do not exceed the maximum size are automatically created to accommodate the load. You can establish whether your wire type requires a neutral conductor and, if so, set the neutral size equal to the hot conductor size or set it as an unbalanced circuit. After the neutral conductor is sized, the value you input for the neutral multiplier is assigned. Although there are conduit tools for modeling, there is no connection between the conduit or cable tray and circuits yet. It is necessary to use these settings to establish the conduit material for your wire type so that these can be passed through the system and used for voltage drop calculations. Figure 14.3 shows some examples of wire types created for a project.

FIGURE 14.3
Wire types

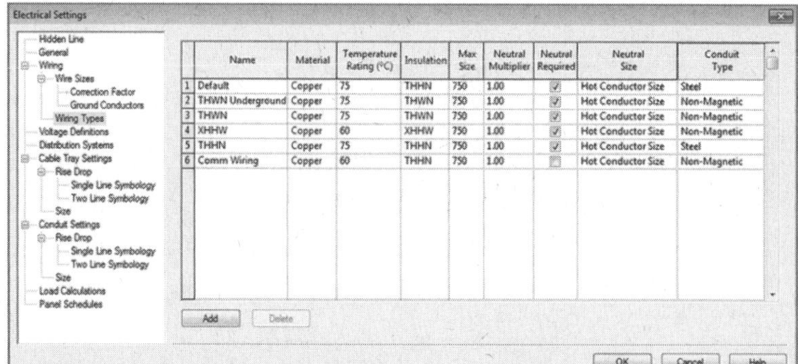

BY DEFAULT

The `default.rte` project template contains a wire type named Default. If you do not create any wire types, the Default wire type is used for all circuits. This wire type is aluminum, which may result in unexpected wire sizes. In addition, you must set a few parameters in a particular order for the electrical systems to work. These are as follows:

Voltage Definitions These describe the full range of electrical conditions a project will face, whether it is a 12-volt circuit for a nurse call system; 110 volts for mains electrical power and lighting; or 400-volt, three-phase power. Each voltage definition needs to be set before distribution systems are created.

Distribution Systems These cannot be created until the voltage definition exists.

Assigning Electrical Equipment Electrical equipment must be assigned to a distribution system so that the final devices can connect into an electrical system.

Voltage Definitions

In the Electrical Settings dialog box, the Voltage Definitions section is for establishing the minimum and maximum values for the voltages used in your project. This allows for different ratings on devices or equipment. These voltages are used to establish different distribution-system definitions. You can add voltages to your project by clicking the Add button at the bottom of the dialog box and giving the voltage name and minimum and maximum values. To remove a voltage from your project, select the voltage and then click the Delete button at the bottom of the dialog box. You cannot delete a voltage if it is used by a distribution system definition in your project. You must delete the distribution system first, and then the voltage can be deleted. Setting up standard voltage definitions in your project template saves you time when setting up a project. Figure 14.4 shows some standard voltage definitions.

FIGURE 14.4
Voltage definitions for a project

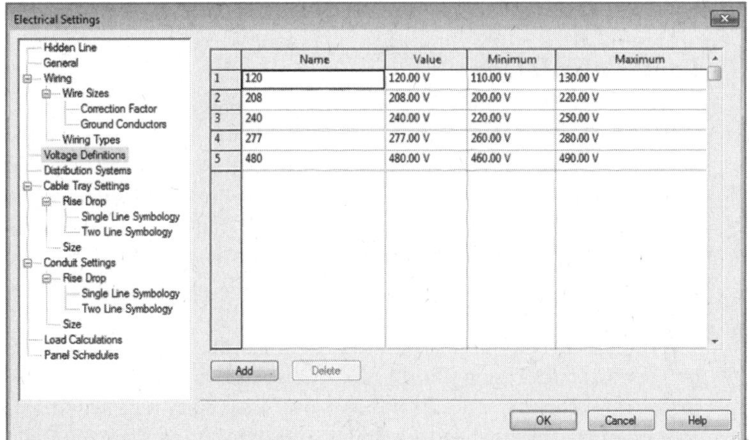

Distribution Systems

You can define the distribution systems for your project in the Distribution Systems section of the Electrical Settings dialog box. The connectors in your electrical families need to coincide with the systems you define so that you can assign devices and equipment objects to a system. You can create single-phase or three-phase systems in delta or wye configurations and establish the number of wires for the system. The line-to-line and line-to-ground voltages for a system can also be defined. It is important to note that it is possible to create systems that do not actually exist in the industry. For example, you could create a three-phase system and set the line-to-line voltage to 120 volts and the line-to-ground voltage to 277 volts. Use caution when creating distribution systems because they are very important for creating circuits for devices and equipment. Voltages can be assigned only as line-to-line or line-to-ground if they have been defined in the Voltage Definitions section. Figure 14.5 shows some examples of distribution systems created for a project.

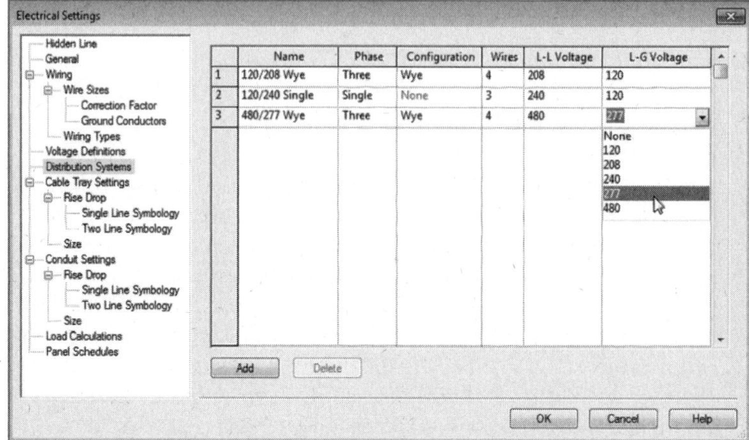

FIGURE 14.5
Distribution systems for a project

Load Calculations

In the Load Calculations section, you can establish demand factors and load classifications applied to the circuits in your project. The load classifications of the connectors in your electrical families determine which demand factor they will take on in your project. In this section, you can deselect the check box so that calculations for loads in spaces will not be done, which can improve the performance of your project. However, if you are scheduling spaces to view the engineering data they hold, you will not see any values derived from the model. You can use preset values if desired. To see the actual values based on the data within your model components, this setting must be turned on.

When you click the Load Classifications button in this section, the Load Classifications dialog box opens. In this dialog box, you can create new load classifications and define the demand factor used for them and a lighting or power load class for use with spaces. The available demand factors appear in the drop-down list, and the Demand Factors dialog box can be accessed by clicking the button next to the Demand Factor drop-down, as shown in Figure 14.6.

It is best to keep your load classification names simple and descriptive because you will have to assign them to the connectors in your electrical families. When working in the Family Editor, you can use the Transfer Project Standards tool on the Manage tab to transfer load classification settings from your project or template file into the family to ensure coordination.

FIGURE 14.6
Load Classifications dialog box

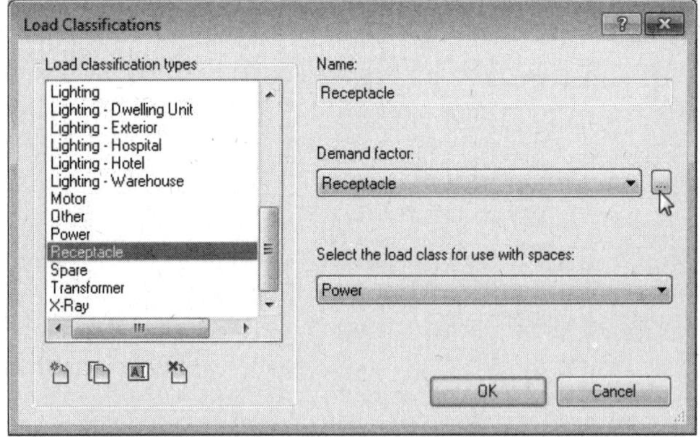

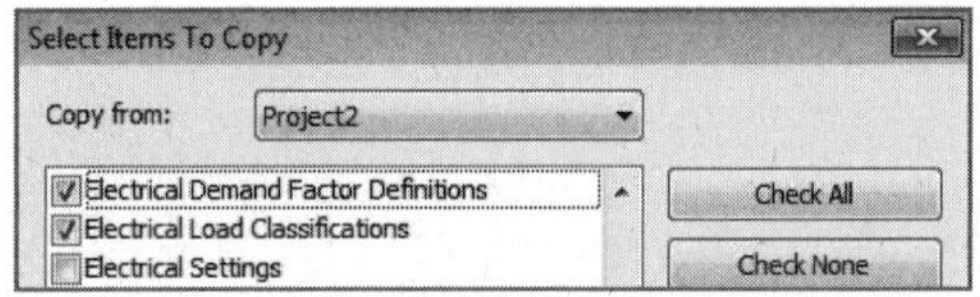

There are many load classifications that come with the default electrical templates. You can create your own by using the buttons below the list, in the lower-left corner of the dialog box. The Spare classification cannot be assigned a demand factor and cannot be transferred to family files for use on connectors. It exists so that spares can be accounted for in your panel schedules.

In the Demand Factors dialog box, you can define the demand factors that are assigned to load classifications. The default electrical templates come with an extensive list of demand factors, and you can create your own by using the buttons in the lower-left corner of the dialog box. Figure 14.7 shows the Demand Factors dialog box. The Calculation Method section is where you determine how the demand will be calculated. Additional load can be added to the calculated result by selecting the check box at the bottom of the dialog box.

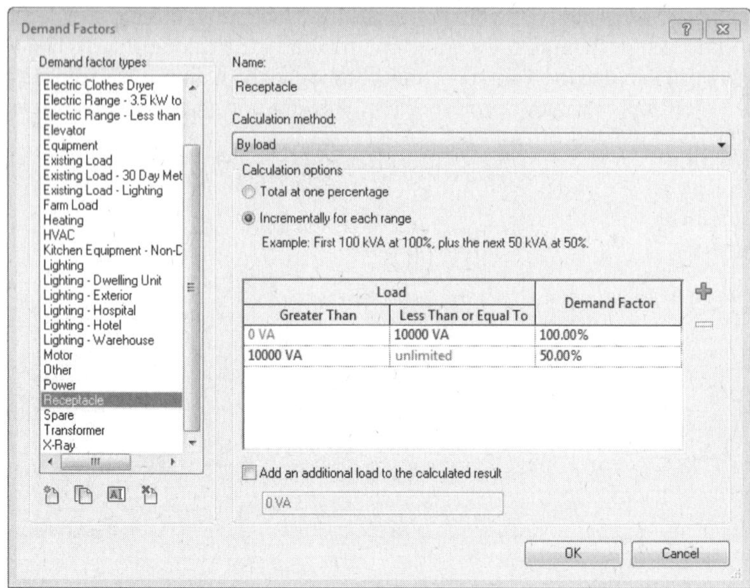

FIGURE 14.7
Demand Factors dialog box

There are three methods that can be used for calculation:

Constant You use the Constant method to set a demand factor for all objects that use the load classification to which the demand factor is assigned.

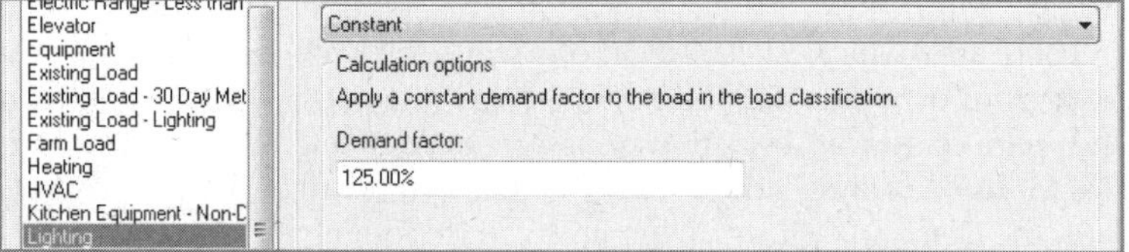

By Quantity You use the By Quantity method to assign a demand factor to multiple items. You can assign different factors to ranges of items or the same factor to items, depending on how many there are. Figure 14.8 shows this method used for a motor load classification. The calculation option is set to calculate incrementally for each range. The ranges defined, result in the first motor load being calculated at 125 percent and any other motors at 100 percent. Figure 14.9 shows this option used for clothes-dryer load classification. The option is set to assign the demand factor to all objects within a range that defines the quantity of objects. These settings will calculate the first four dryers at 100 percent, the next dryer at 85 percent, the next at 75 percent, and so on.

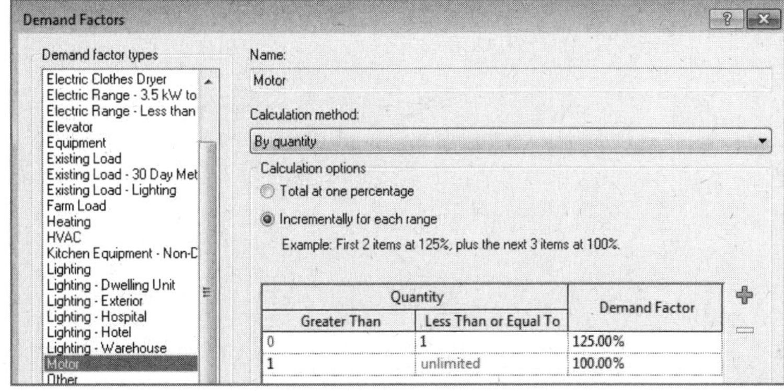

FIGURE 14.8 Incremental demand factor settings using the By Quantity method

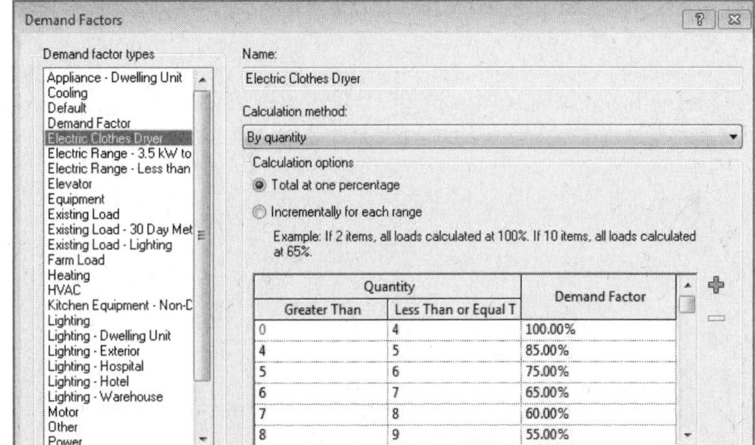

FIGURE 14.9 Total demand factor settings using the By Quantity method

By Load You use the By Load method to assign a demand factor to different ranges of loads. You can assign different factors to ranges of loads or the same factor to the total load connected to a panel. Figure 14.10 shows the settings using this method incrementally for each range defined. These settings will calculate the first 10,000 VA at 100 percent and anything greater at 50 percent. The option to calculate the total at one percentage would be used if you wanted to set the demand factor for a total load range. For example, you could set the factor at 100 percent for 10,000 VA, meaning that if the total load on the panel were 10,000 VA, then all loads would be calculated at 100 percent.

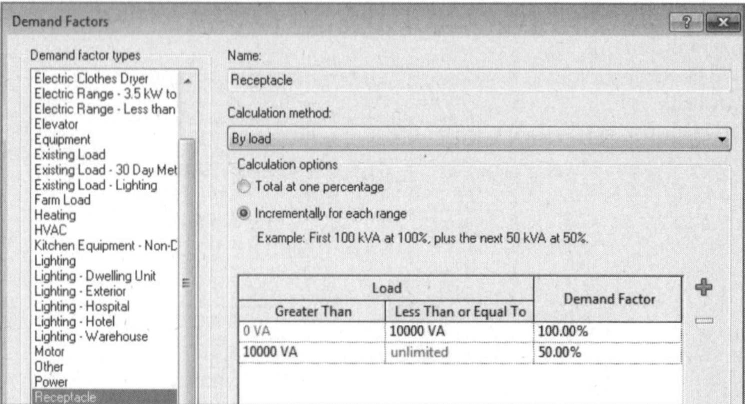

FIGURE 14.10 Incremental demand factor settings using the By Load method

The Panel Schedules settings in the Electrical Settings dialog box allow you to assign a name for all spares and spaces in your panel schedules. You can choose to include spares in your panel totals and also merge multipole circuits into a single cell. Changing the Merge setting immediately affects your panel schedules. If you change the default name for spares or spaces, that name is applied only to new spares or spaces added to panels.

CKT	Circuit Description	Trip
1	SPARE	20 A
3	Lighting training 1 103	20 A
5	POWER ELEV MECH 110	20 A
7		
9		

Real World Scenario

SETTINGS FOR TEMPLATES

Duncan and Abbey Engineering recently broadened its range of project types. Making the transition to Revit opened up opportunities to pursue projects that the company normally would not do. The company recognized the power of having a Revit template for its projects and quickly set up templates with electrical settings for the different project types. Duncan and Abbey Engineering is now doing work in different countries that require unique settings for voltage and distribution systems. Having templates with preset electrical settings for each of its client's unique standards saves the company time and reduces the possibility for error.

Creating Circuits and Wiring for Devices and Fixtures

With Revit MEP 2015, you can create circuits for devices or equipment to keep track of the loads within your panels. Circuits are the "systems" that are recognized for electrical design. You can create a circuit for devices or fixtures without selecting a panel so that, at a minimum, you have removed them from the default system and therefore your project file performance will not suffer.

When you are working in Revit MEP 2015, circuits and wires are not the same thing. *Circuits* are the logical connection between elements, similar in terms to HVAC, piping, and plumbing systems. Electrical circuits and systems are unique in Revit in that they do not require physical connections as the other disciplines do. Wires are a schematic, annotative representation of the means to make the connection only, meant to help the contractor understand what approach was intended for wiring in certain conditions.

The type of circuit that you can create for a device depends on the properties of the connector in the device family. The most important property is System Type, which defines the kind of circuit that can be created for the device. Figure 14.11 shows the properties of a connector in a receptacle family and the various types of systems that can be assigned to the connector. Other properties of the connector also define the type of circuit that can be created for the family, such as voltage and number of poles.

FIGURE 14.11
Device connector properties

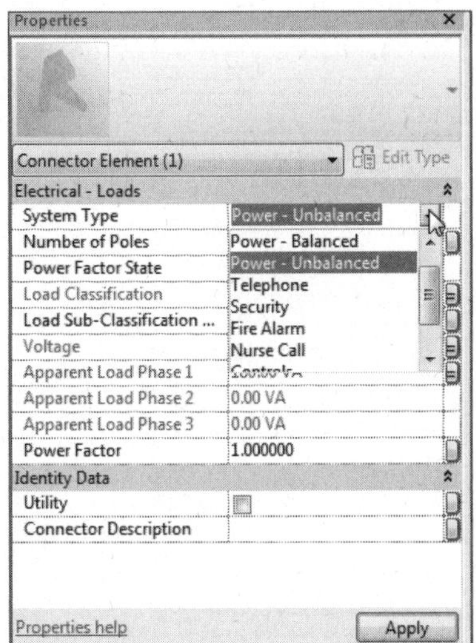

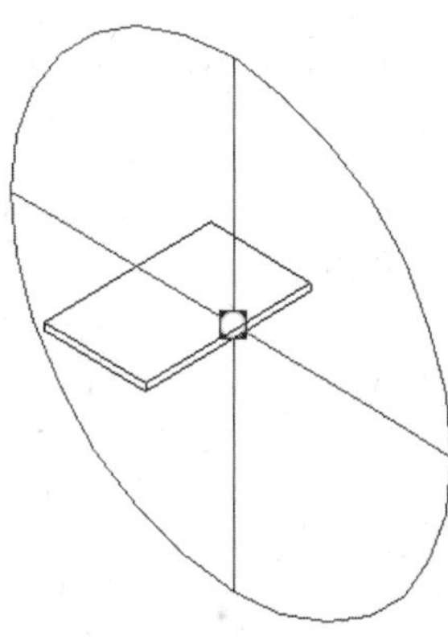

When you select a device in your model, the Create Systems panel of the contextual tab displays a button to create the type of circuit that matches the properties of the connector in the selected family. If there are multiple connectors in the selected device, a button is available for each type of connector. In Figure 14.12, a floor box containing a power and data connector is selected.

FIGURE 14.12
Create Systems panel of the contextual tab for a selected device

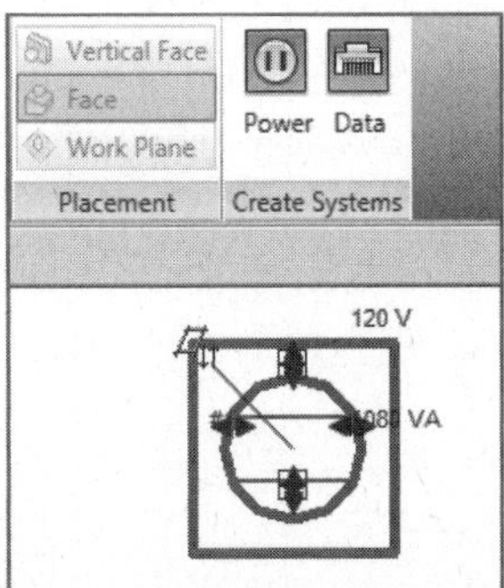

Clicking a button on the Create Systems tab creates a circuit for the selected device and changes the ribbon to the Modify | Electrical Circuits contextual tab. On this tab, there are tools to edit the circuit or to select a panel for the circuit. The properties of the circuit can be seen in the Properties palette when this tab is active. Click the Select Panel tool on the System Tools panel of the tab to choose a panel for the circuit. You can select the panel by clicking it in the drawing area, or you can use the drop-down on the Options Bar and select the panel by name. Only panels with a distribution system that matches the connector properties of your family will be available in the drop-down list. That includes the secondary side of transformers, so it is important to name your equipment and panels so that they are easily identified, as shown in Figure 14.13.

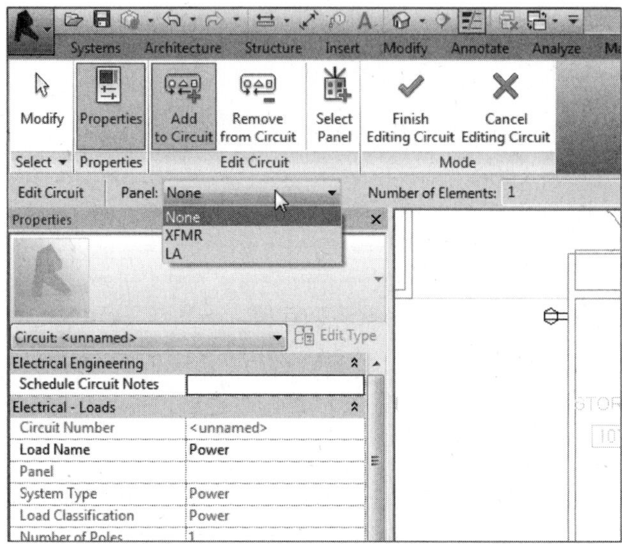

FIGURE 14.13
Panel drop-down list on the Options Bar when selecting a panel for a circuit

DISTRIBUTION SYSTEMS

Many users forget to assign the secondary distribution system to their transformers. Get in the habit of assigning the secondary system as soon as you assign the primary distribution system in the Properties palette.

When you select a panel for the circuit, a dashed box appears in the drawing area that encompasses the components of the circuit, and a dashed line with an arrow indicates the home run to the panel. Clicking one of the buttons on the Convert To Wire panel of the contextual tab converts the indicated home run to wire. You have two choices for the graphical type of wire: Arc Wire or

Chamfered Wire. Arc wiring can be used for straight lines between components if that is your standard. Figure 14.14 shows the indicated home run (top) and the result of clicking the Arc Wire button on the Convert To Wire panel (bottom).

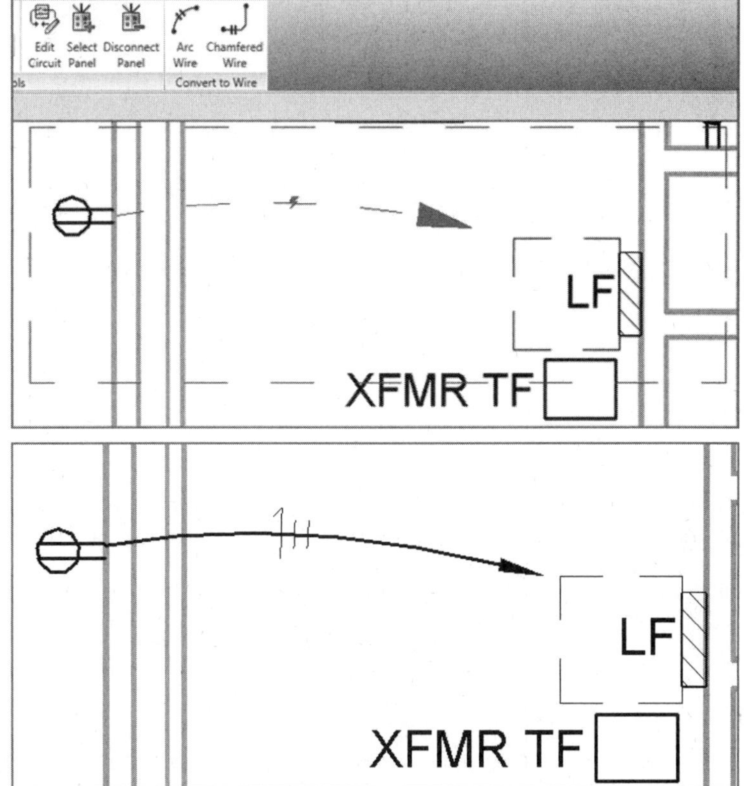

FIGURE 14.14 Indicated home run for a circuit (top); wire automatically generated by clicking the Arc Wire button on the Convert To Wire panel (bottom)

When you select multiple devices or fixtures with the same connector type, the button to create a circuit is available on the contextual tab. This allows you to select all the elements for a circuit and create the circuit in one step. An icon appears in the drawing area to convert the indicated wire to arc- or chamfer-type wiring, as shown in Figure 14.15. This keeps your cursor in the drawing area for improved efficiency.

Some of your elements may have more than one connector of the same type. When you select an element with multiple connectors and click the button to create a circuit, a dialog box appears that allows you to select the connector for which you are creating the circuit. Figure 14.16 shows this dialog box for a receptacle with two power connectors. Once you have chosen a connector, you can complete the process of creating a circuit. When you select the device again, you still have the option to create a circuit for the remaining connector.

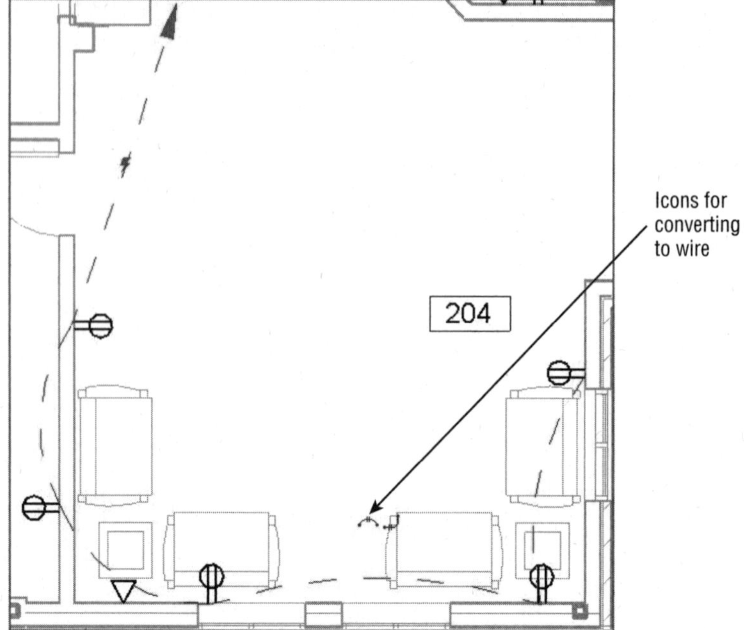

FIGURE 14.15
Multiple items selected for a circuit

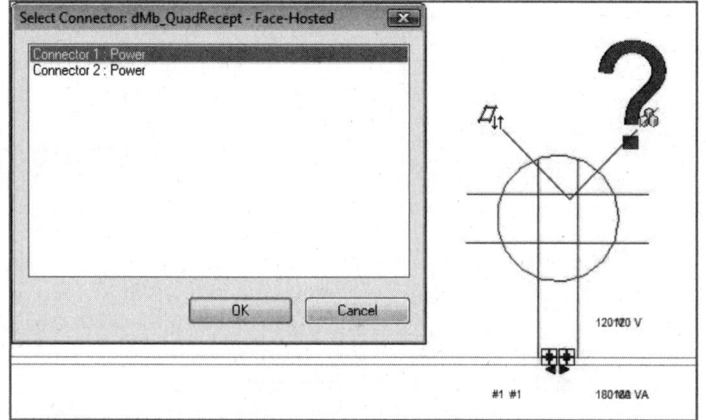

FIGURE 14.16
Select Connector dialog box

When you are creating circuits for lighting fixtures, it is important that the properties of the connector in the switch family match those of the connector in the lighting fixture family, except for load. If you use a Controls system type for the connector in your switch families, you cannot add it to the circuit for the light fixtures, but you can still draw the wiring from the lights to the switch. If your switch does not have a connector, you have to use detail or model lines to represent the wiring from a fixture to the switch. If you use the Wire tool to draw from a fixture to the switch or from the switch to a fixture, a home run is created when you connect to the fixture.

Editing Wiring

If the wiring that is automatically generated is not drawn exactly as you would like, it can be edited. When you select a wire, grips enable you to change the wire's arc and location. Right-clicking the wire also gives you the ability to add vertices to or remove them from the wire, giving you even more control over its final appearance.

> **WHAT IS WIRE?**
>
> In Revit MEP 2015, wire is a special type of symbolic line. Wires are not model components, and they are visible only in the view in which they are drawn.

The small blue circles that appear near the ends of the wire are grips for changing the end points of the line that represents the wire. These Change End Offset grips do not represent the point where the wire is connected; they are only the graphical representation of the wire. The actual point of connection is indicated by the connector symbol ⊞. The Change End Offset grips allow you to show the wire from any point on the device or fixture regardless of the location of the connector. Occasionally, the connection point grip and the Change End Offset grip are in the same place. You can use the Tab key to toggle between them for selection.

The larger blue circle with two lines tangent to the end points of the wire is for changing the arc of the wire. The + and – grips that appear near the wire are for adding or removing hot conductors, respectively. These are discussed later in this chapter. Figure 14.17 shows the editing grips for a wire.

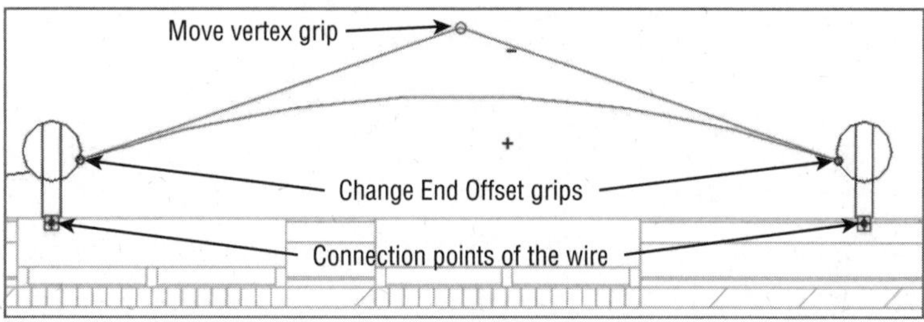

FIGURE 14.17 Wire-editing grips

> **GET A GRIP**
>
> Thick symbolic lines can sometimes make it difficult to see the wire-editing grips. Setting your view to Thin Lines makes it easy to locate the grips.

The wire shown in Figure 14.18 (top) can be edited with the grips so that it is drawn from the symbols correctly and does not interfere with other devices that are not part of the circuit.

Figure 14.18 (bottom) shows the edited wire. The end offsets are changed, and the arc of the wire is reversed for a cleaner-looking drawing.

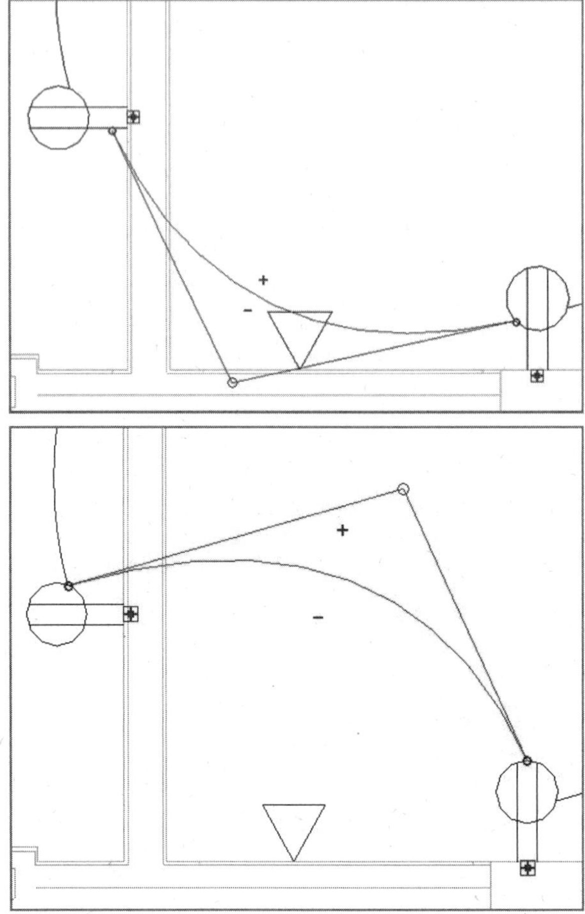

FIGURE 14.18
Wire that needs to be edited (top); the results of using the grips to change the appearance of the wire (bottom)

You can use the connection point grip to change the object to which a wire is connected. Click and drag the grip to a new object to connect the wire to it. If you click the connector grip and drag it off an object, the wire is displayed as a home run. When changing the connection point of a wire, it is a good practice to make sure you snap to the connection point of the object to which you are connecting. This ensures that you do not have any erroneous home runs in your project. Figure 14.19 shows a wire moved from between two fixtures (top) and the wire connected to another fixture by dragging the connection point grip (bottom).

The type of wire that is created by using the Convert To Wire button is the last type of wire that was drawn in your project, or the default wire type is used if none has been manually drawn. You can change a wire type by selecting it and choosing a new type from the Type

Selector in the Properties palette. You can change all the wires for a circuit by editing the properties of that circuit.

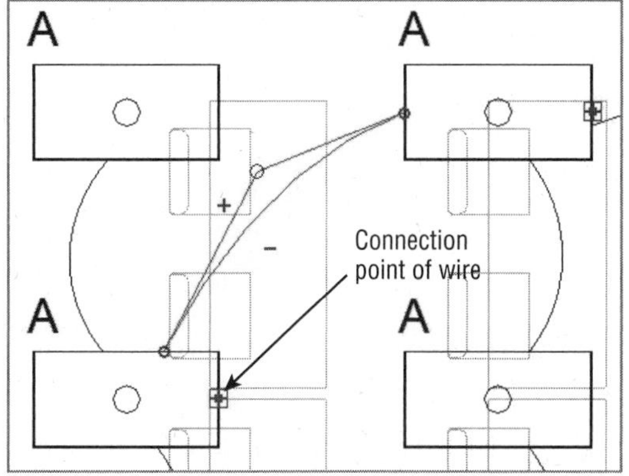

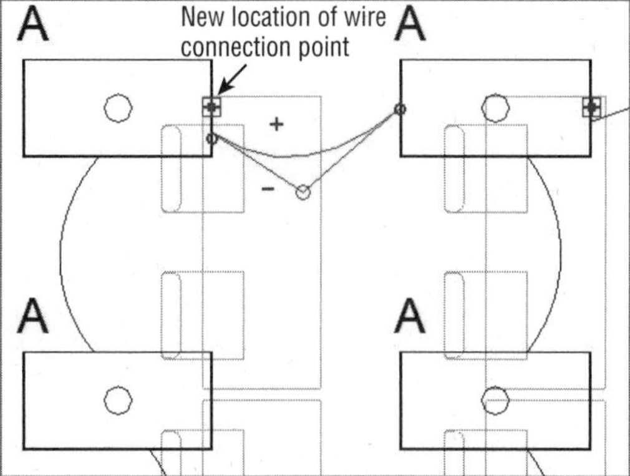

FIGURE 14.19 Wire connected between two fixtures (top); the result of dragging the connection point to another fixture (bottom)

Editing Circuits

When you select a device or fixture that has a circuit, the Electrical Circuits contextual tab appears with tools for editing and managing the circuit. If the device you have selected contains multiple connectors and circuits, the System Selector drop-down allows you to choose which circuit you would like to edit.

Click the Edit Circuit button to add or remove elements from the circuit. When you click the Edit Circuit button, the Edit Circuit contextual tab appears. All items that are not part of the circuit turn to halftone in the drawing area, including annotation and wiring, while elements of the circuit remain as normally displayed. The Add To Circuit button is automatically selected when you click the Edit Circuit button. You can click any device or fixture in your view to add it to the circuit. You can also select devices or fixtures from other locations if you have multiple views of the model open. If you select an element that does not have a connector that matches the distribution system of your circuit, you receive a warning dialog box, and the element is not added to the circuit. Figure 14.20 shows a warning displayed as a 120-volt receptacle is selected to be added to a 277-volt lighting circuit.

FIGURE 14.20
Circuit warning

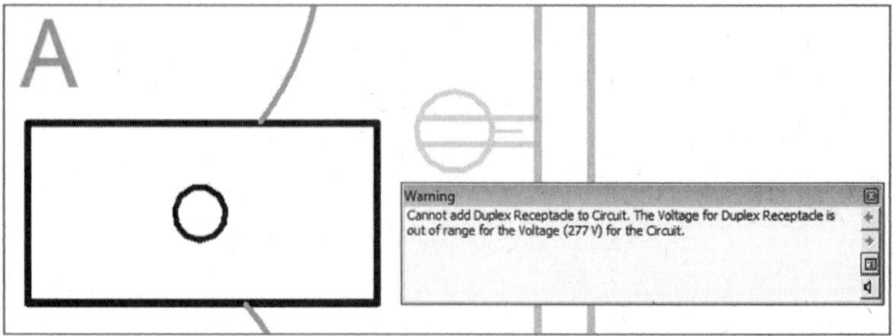

When you select a device or fixture that has a connector matching the distribution system of the circuit to which you are adding an item, the display of the device or fixture changes from halftone to normal. You can click the Remove From Circuit button on the Edit Circuit contextual tab to remove items from the circuit. Once you have finished adding or removing items from a circuit, click the Finish Editing Circuit button to complete your changes. If you have wiring drawn to show items on a circuit and you remove some of the items, the wiring will not be removed from the view.

Another method for adding or removing objects to a circuit is to select the object and right-click its connector grip. If you do not have your cursor over the connector grip when you right-click, you will get a menu with tools for visibility control. Right-clicking the connector will give you the same menu, but with additional tools for circuiting. Select the Add To Circuit option from the menu, and click any device or fixture that is part of the circuit that you want to connect to. You also have the option to create a new circuit from the context menu.

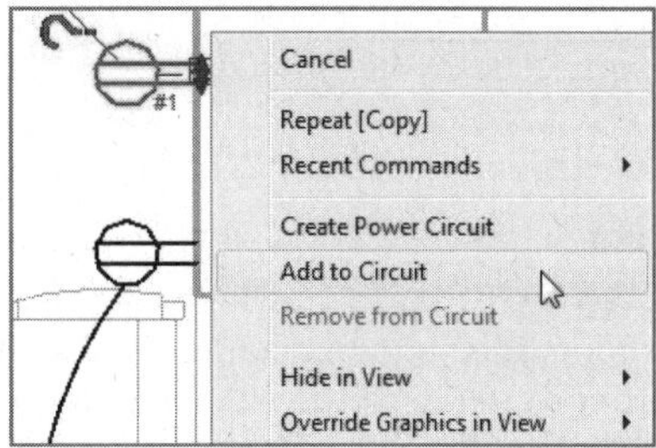

When you select an element on the circuit to which you want to add your device or fixture, you are given the option to automatically generate wiring that shows the added device as part of the circuit.

Selecting a device that is already part of a circuit and right-clicking its connector gives you a menu with the option to remove the element from the circuit. Removing a fixture or device from a circuit does not delete any wiring connected to it, but the wiring may change depending on the location of the removed element in the circuit. Figure 14.21 shows how wiring can be affected when a device is removed from a circuit. The receptacle in the lower-right corner was removed from the circuit. The receptacle in the upper-right corner is still part of the circuit, so the wiring has changed to a home run. Also, the wire from the unconnected receptacle to the one on the left has changed to a home run because it is not part of the circuit but has a device downstream that is part of the circuit. In any case, removing elements from a circuit usually requires some cleanup of the wiring.

FIGURE 14.21
Wire changed by removing a device from a circuit

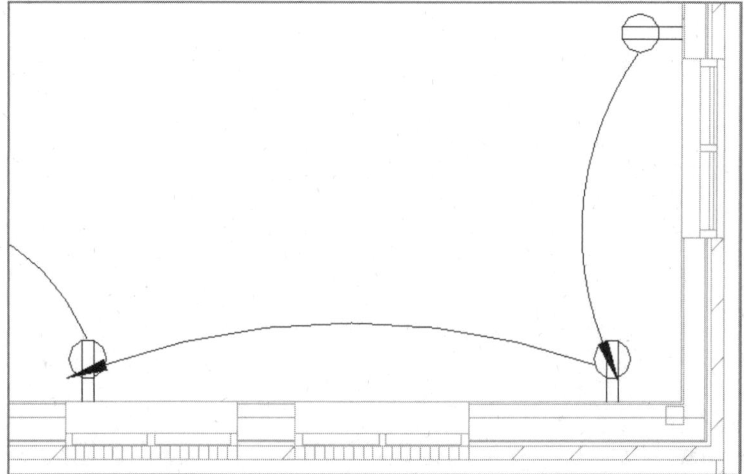

The workflow for creating circuits can be easily learned and can become second nature to your design and modeling processes. Practice creating circuits by doing the following:

1. Open the `Ch14_Circuits.rvt` file from `www.sybex.com/go/masteringrevitmep2015`.
2. Open the EP – Level 1 floor plan view. Select the four receptacles in Office 104. Click the Power button on the Create Systems panel of the Modify | Electrical Fixtures tab.
3. Click the Select Panel button on the System Tools panel of the tab. In the Panel drop-down on the Options Bar, select panel LA.
4. Click the Arc Wire button on the Convert To Wire panel of the Electrical Circuits tab.
5. Click the Tag By Category button located on the Tag panel of the Annotate tab. Deselect the Leader box on the Options Bar, and select the home run created for the circuit. Click the Modify button on the ribbon to exit the Tag command.
6. Repeat steps 1–5 for the three duplex receptacles in Office 103.
7. Select the quadruplex receptacle in Office 103. Right-click one of the connector grips. Select the Add To Circuit option from the menu. Click one of the duplex receptacles in Office 103. Click the arc-type wiring grip that appears. Select the quadruplex receptacle again, and right-click the other connector. Select the Add To Circuit option from the menu. Click one of the duplex receptacles in Office 103. Press the Esc key to finish.

8. Open the EL – Level 1 view. Figure 14.22 shows how the wiring and tags should appear.

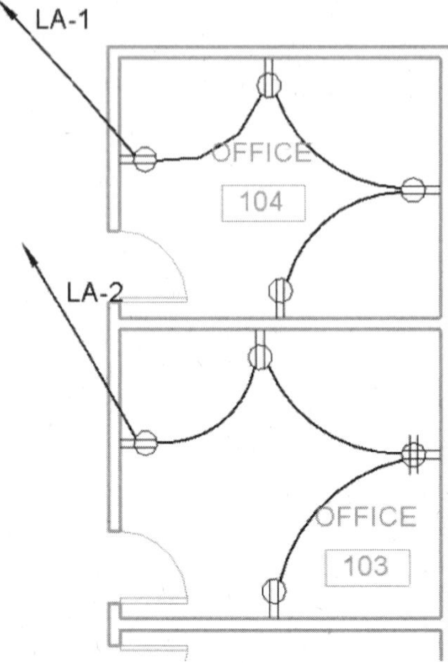

FIGURE 14.22 Receptacle wiring and tags

9. Create a power circuit for the lights in Office 104 by selecting the two luminaires in the plan. Select panel HA from the Panel drop-down on the Options Bar, and click on the temporary arc to generate the wiring.
10. Click the Tag By Category button located on the Tag panel of the Annotate tab. Ensure that the leader option is not selected on the Options Bar, and select the home run created for the circuit. Click the Modify button on the ribbon to exit the Tag command.
11. Repeat steps 9 and 10 for the lights in Offices 103 and 102.
12. Select the home run for the Office 102 circuit, and using the vertex grip, drag the wire up until it connects with the left light fixture in Office 103.
13. Select the double home run from the light fixture in Office 103, and use the vertex grip to drag the wire up to the left light fixture in Office 104. Notice that a multicircuit run of wiring has been created.
14. Select the switch in Office 102, and right-click its connector. Select the Add To Circuit option from the menu, and select one of the light fixtures in the room. Click the arc-type wiring grip to create the wire. Use the wire-editing grips to adjust the display of the wire.
15. Repeat step 14 for Offices 103 and 104. Figure 14.23 indicates the linked wiring and tag appearance.

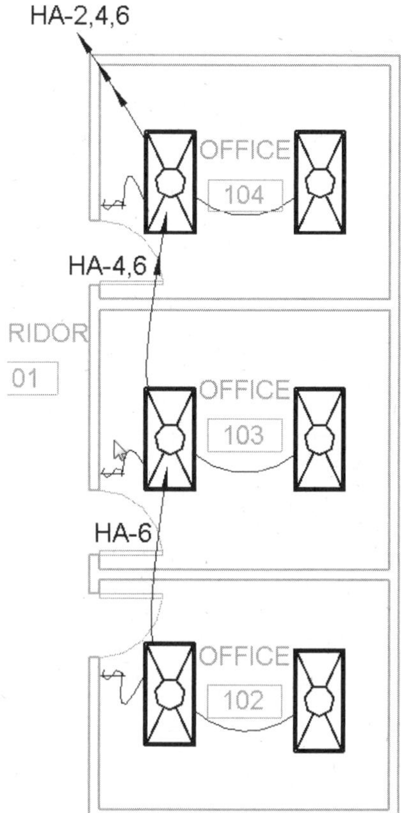

FIGURE 14.23 Wiring to Luminaires

Drawing Wires Manually

To create the wiring for your circuits, you don't have to use the automatic wiring capability of Revit MEP 2015. You can quickly and easily draw wires manually. In some cases, it may be easier to draw the wire than to make adjustments to automatically generated wiring; for example, some offices show wire only on home runs, which would mean deleting a lot of extraneous wiring if they used the automatic feature.

To draw wiring, click the Wire button on the Home tab. The bottom half of the button is a drop-down list with options for the style of wire you can draw. You can draw arc or chamfer wires automatically and spline wires manually. These options indicate only how the wire is drawn and have nothing to do with wire types or the electrical properties of the circuit or devices. Once you have selected a wiring style, you can choose a wire type from the Type Selector in the Properties palette. You can use the Tag On Placement button on the contextual tab to place a tag on the wire as you draw it.

You can draw wire anywhere in your plan views, so it is important that you snap to the component geometry of the elements for which you are showing the wire. If you draw a wire between two symbols, it may appear that the wire connects them, but if the wire is not "attached" to the devices, the wire does not move when the devices move. To ensure that your wire is connected to an element, you need to snap to a point on the component geometry, not the symbol that represents the component. As long as your cursor is over some part of the component when you start your wire, the wire connects to the component at the electrical connector. Figure 14.24 shows a wire being drawn from a mechanical unit by clicking the edge of the unit (top), and the wire attaching to the electrical connector of the unit (bottom).

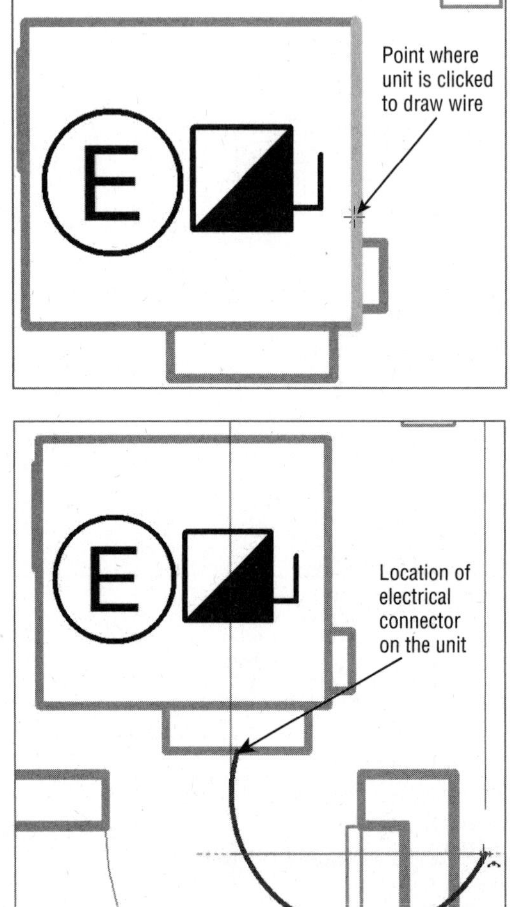

FIGURE 14.24 Drawing a wire from a unit (top); the wire connected to the unit at the electrical connector (bottom)

The mechanical unit shown in Figure 14.24 has an electrical connector, so the equipment connection and disconnect switch symbols on the electrical drawing do not require a connector or any electrical properties. The wiring to this unit can be modified to be shown from the disconnect switch symbol while maintaining its connection to the unit, as shown in Figure 14.25.

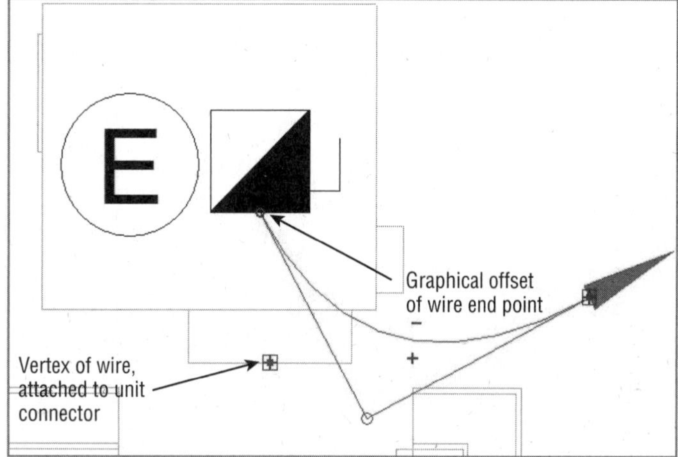

FIGURE 14.25 Modified wire graphics

Arc- and chamfer-style wires are drawn by clicking a start point for the wire, a middle point, and an end point. To draw wire between two components, start your wire at one component, click somewhere between the two items, and click the second component to end the wire. Spline-style wires allow you to click several times between elements.

To draw a wire home run, you simply start a wire at the connector of a device or fixture and leave the other end of the wire unconnected. If the component from which you draw is assigned to a circuit, the wire shows an arrowhead indicating a home run. If the component is not assigned to a circuit, the wire appears without an arrowhead until the element has been assigned to a circuit.

Drawing a wire between components does not mean that they are on the same circuit. If you draw a wire from a component that is on a circuit to another component that is not on a circuit, the second component is not added to the circuit. You can draw wire between components that are not on the same circuit, creating a multicircuit run of wiring. A home run wire is displayed between components that are on different circuits, as shown in Figure 14.26.

You can show multiple home runs from a single component that has multiple connectors. If you use the automatic wire option, it works only for the first circuit that you create. You have to draw the second home run manually by following these steps:

1. Select the component and click the button on the Create Systems panel to create a circuit.
2. Choose a connector from the dialog box that appears, select a panel for the circuit, and choose a wire style from the Convert To Wire panel on the contextual tab.
3. Select the component again to create a circuit for the next connector.
4. Select a panel for the circuit, but do not choose a wire style to be drawn. Instead, select the wire that was automatically created for the first circuit, and make note of the location of the connector.

5. Click the Wire button on the Systems tab, and manually draw a wire from the component, starting the wire at the connector not occupied by the existing home run.

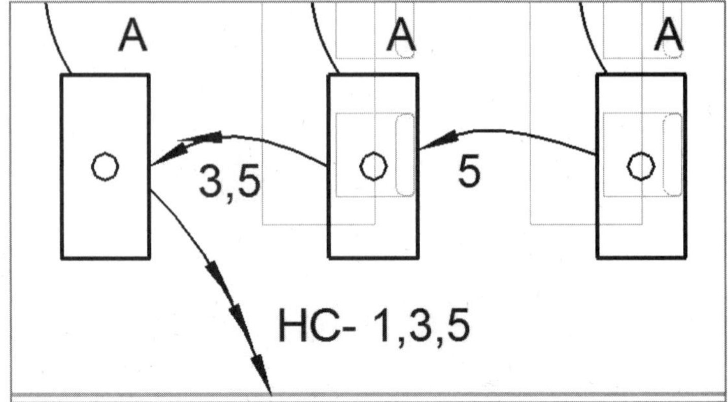

FIGURE 14.26 Multicircuit run of wiring

You can use a wire tag to confirm that the home runs are not connected to the same connector, as shown in Figure 14.27.

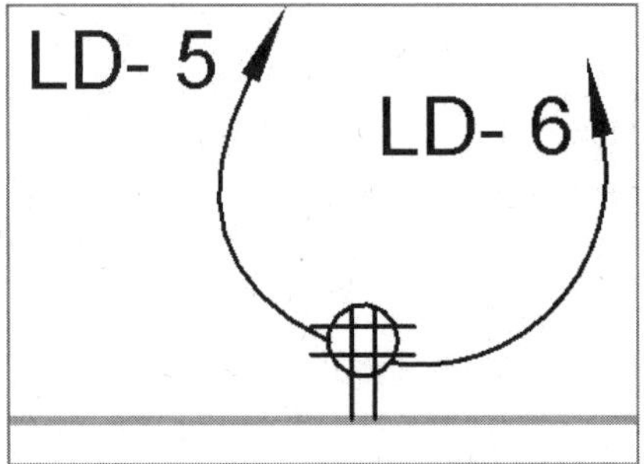

FIGURE 14.27 Multiple home runs from a single device

Controlling Wire Display

Using a filter to control the display of wires in your project is an effective method for distinguishing between different wire types. As mentioned earlier, creating wire types in the electrical settings of your project makes it easy to isolate specific wires for visibility control. This allows you to show wire such as underground, overhead, or low-voltage wire in the same view and be able to visually identify the different types.

To create a filter for wires, click the Filters button located on the Graphics panel of the View tab. In the Filters dialog box, select the New button in the upper-left corner. Give the filter a name that clearly identifies its purpose or the types of elements to which it applies. You can use the Select option and select a wire in the view to create a filter for the selected items only. Use the Define Criteria option to create a filter for all of the instances of the desired type that you want to display. In the Categories section of the dialog box, select the Wires check box to apply the filter to wires. In the Filter Rules section of the dialog box, choose the Type Name parameter from the Filter By drop-down list. Set the condition to Equals in the second drop-down list, and choose the name of the wire type to which you want to apply the filter in the third drop-down list. This creates a filter that affects only wires with the type name chosen, as shown in Figure 14.28.

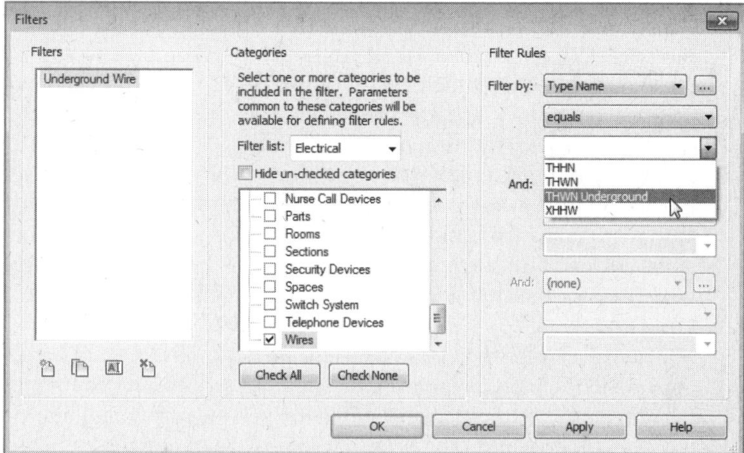

FIGURE 14.28
Filter settings for a wire-type filter

To apply the filter to your view, access the Visibility/Graphic Overrides settings for the view and select the Filters tab. Click the Add button in the lower-left corner, and choose the filter you created for the wires from the Add Filters dialog box. Click the Override button in the Lines column for the filter. Set the Weight, Color, or Pattern overrides for the filter to display the wire as desired. Figure 14.29 shows floor boxes with underground wire in the same view as receptacles with wire as it is normally displayed.

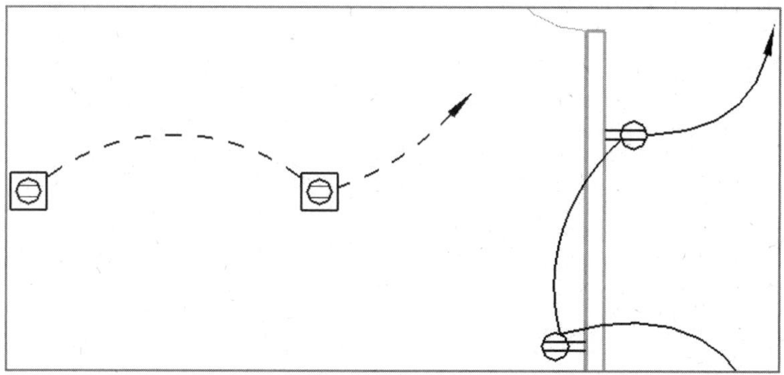

FIGURE 14.29
Using a filter to display different wire types in the same view

Managing Circuits and Panels

By creating circuits for your devices, fixtures, and equipment, you have the ability to manage the properties of those circuits and the panels to which they are connected. You can also manage the location of circuits within your panels to balance loads and track the total electrical load for your project. The electrical connectors in your families determine some of the properties of the circuit to which they are connected.

Circuit Properties

To access the properties of a circuit, select an element connected to it and then select the Electrical Circuits contextual tab. If the selected component has multiple circuited connectors, you can choose which circuit properties to access by selecting the circuit from the System Selector drop-down list. The properties of the circuit are displayed in the Properties palette. Click the Properties button on the ribbon to access the Properties palette if it is not already active. Because most of the data comes from the electrical characteristics of the connector and the distribution system, many of the parameters of the circuit are grayed out and are not editable. Revit takes the load information from the components on the circuit and calculates the apparent load and current as well as the voltage drop and wire size. You can change the type of wire used for the circuit by editing the Wire Type parameter. This defines the type of wire used for calculations.

You can change the Load Name parameter to give the circuit a more descriptive name that appears in the panel. When you are creating a circuit for components and the load exceeds 80 percent of the circuit-breaker rating, you get a warning. It does not prevent you from overloading a circuit, however. The default breaker size for circuits is 20 amps. The Rating parameter indicates the circuit-breaker size for the circuit and can be changed to meet the requirements of your circuit. Choosing the size of circuit breakers is the realm of the engineer; it's your decision. Revit is meant to help you resolve circuits that are overloaded or could become overloaded by being designed too close to ideal tolerances. People express anxiety about computers making too many decisions or replacing them. Revit helps keep track of information and provides us with results that help us make informed choices about equipment and circuit design.

Wire Properties

When you select a wire in a model, you can access that wire's properties in the Properties palette. Clicking the Edit Type button in the Properties palette opens the Type Properties dialog box, which displays the parameters for the wire as defined in the electrical settings for the project. You can add information such as a description or type mark to the wire type.

The instance properties of the wire control the display of tick marks and the number of conductors for the circuit. There are three options for the Tick Marks parameter:

Calculated This is the default value for wires, and it indicates that the number of conductors is determined by the circuit and distribution system properties, regardless of whether the tick marks are displayed.

On Selecting On displays tick marks on the selected wire.

Off Selecting Off turns off the display of tick marks on the selected wire.

The number of conductors can be increased or decreased by editing the values of the Hot, Neutral, and Ground Conductors parameters. You can change the number of hot conductors by using the + and – editing grips that appear in the drawing area when you select a wire. The location of the tick marks on a wire can be changed by clicking the solid blue dot that appears at the center of the tick marks when a wire is selected.

Panel Properties

In the instance properties of a panel, you can provide information about it that appears in the panel schedule. You can add notes to the header or footer of a panel schedule by clicking the Edit button in the Schedule Header Notes and Schedule Footer Notes parameters, respectively. The Mains parameter is for indicating the size of the main circuit breaker and does not affect any load calculations. The Max #1 Pole Breakers parameter allows you to assign the number of poles in the panel. You can also indicate the short-circuit rating, enclosure type, and any modifications by editing the respective parameters.

You can define how the circuit tags will appear in your drawings by editing the Circuit Naming, Circuit Prefix, and Circuit Prefix Separator parameters. The standard wire tag is a label that displays the circuit number. There are four options for circuit naming:

Panel Name This option places the name of the panel in front of the circuit number when a wire or device is tagged. You can use a separator such as a dash between the panel name and circuit number by using the Circuit Prefix Separator parameter.

Prefixed This option places the prefix defined in the Circuit Prefix parameter in front of the circuit number when a wire or device is tagged.

Standard This option does not add any additional information to tags that display the circuit number of a selected wire or device.

By Phase This option displays the Circuit Naming By Phase label defined in the Electrical Settings in front of the circuit number listed in the panel schedule.

Figure 14.30 shows three circuits to panels that use different naming conventions. The panel for the circuit in the lower left uses the Panel Name option with a hyphen as a separator. The panel for the receptacle on circuit 2 uses the Standard circuit-naming option, and the panel for the circuit on the right uses a prefix *PWR* and a slash as a separator.

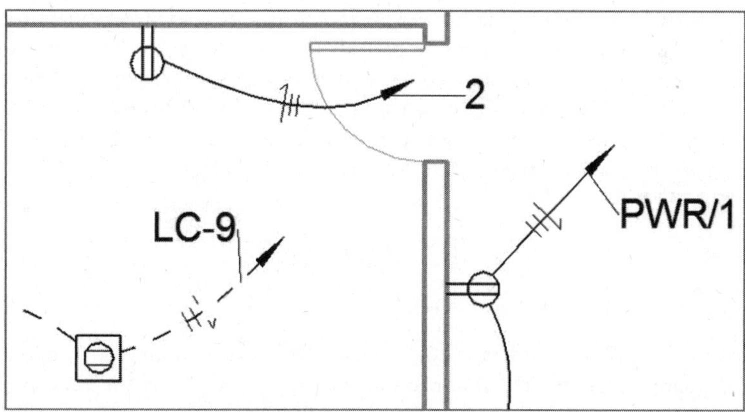

FIGURE 14.30 Wire tags using different circuit-naming options

When you select a panel, the Modify | Electrical Equipment contextual tab appears. The Edit Panel Schedule button, available when a panel schedule has been created for the panel, allows you to change the location of circuit connections within the panel. In this view of the panel, you can change the fonts used in the cells to match your standards. Select a cell or multiple cells, and right-click to change the font. In the Edit Font dialog box, you can set the font, font size, font style, and font color (see Figure 14.31).

FIGURE 14.31
Edit Font dialog box for a panel schedule

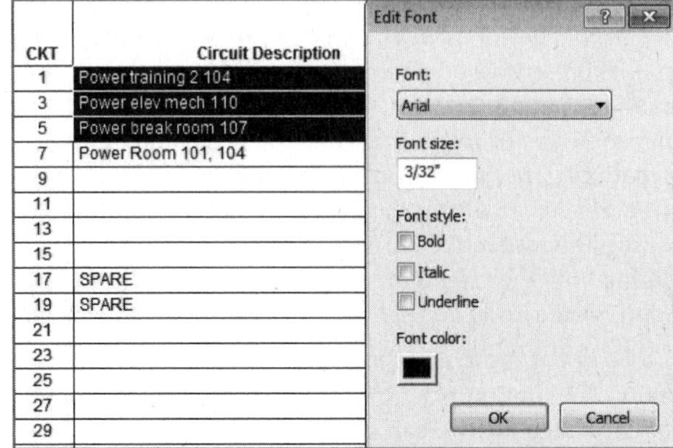

You can change the name of a circuit by simply editing the value in the cell. This updates the value of the Load Name parameter of the circuit. Once you have made changes to circuit names, and you select a cell that has been edited, the Update Names button on the ribbon becomes active. Clicking this button returns the circuit name to the default, which includes the load-classification name and the location of the object.

You can change the size of the circuit breaker for a circuit by editing the cell in the panel schedule. This updates the value of the Rating parameter of the circuit. If you edit the breaker to a size that causes the circuit to be overloaded, you receive a warning dialog box.

To balance the loads in a panel, you can click the Rebalance Loads button on the ribbon. This moves circuits around in the panel to achieve the most balanced configuration possible across the phases. This may cause unwanted results, so use caution with this feature. For example, you may have a multicircuit wiring run that occupies circuits 1, 3, and 5, but after rebalancing the loads, the circuits end up as 1, 4, and 18. It may also move multipole circuits to locations where they normally would not be placed. To avoid this scenario, you can use the Group/Ungroup button that becomes active when you select multiple circuits. This maintains the order of the circuits and moves them as a single unit. Grouped circuits are indicated with a blue, dashed box around them. Selecting any cell within a group of circuits and clicking the Group/Ungroup button removes all the circuits from the group, not just the selected cell or cells.

CKT	Circuit Description	Trip	Poles
1	Power training 2 104	20 A	1
3	Power elev mech 110	20 A	1
5	Receptacle-Rm 107	15 A	1
7	Power Room 101, 104	20 A	1

You do have the option to relocate circuits manually. To change the position of a circuit in a panel, click the circuit number. This activates the move buttons on the Circuits panel of the tab. You can move the circuit up or down the side of the panel it is on. When you move a circuit up or down to a space that already contains a circuit, the two circuits change places. Circuits can also be moved from one side of the panel to the other. As with moving up or down, moving a circuit to an occupied space on the other side of the panel causes the two circuits to swap locations.

When you select a panel for a circuit, the first available circuit in the panel is found and the circuit is placed there. Spares and spaces can be added to occupy circuits in the panel. Because you cannot choose the circuit number for a circuit when it is created, when you add a circuit to the panel, the circuits occupied by spaces or spares are not used.

To insert a spare or space, select an unoccupied circuit number, and click the Assign Spare or Assign Space button on the Circuits panel of the tab. A light brown background is applied to the cells for the circuit number. This background is a visual indication that the circuit is locked. A locked circuit cannot be moved in the panel. You can edit the name of a locked circuit and also change its breaker size. Any occupied circuit in the panel can be locked by using the Lock/Unlock button on the Circuits panel of the tab. The only way to remove a spare or space is to select it and click the Remove Spare/Space button on the Circuits panel of the tab.

The ability to lock circuits in a panel comes in handy when you are relocating circuits. You can lock circuits so that when others are moved, the locked circuits remain in place and are not swapped with the circuit you are moving.

PARTIALLY FILLED PANELS

Your panel schedule templates define the number of slots that are shown for the panel, based on either the number of one-pole breakers or a fixed value. Consider creating panel schedule templates for various sizes of panels based on the number of slots available.

Other Panels and Circuits

Circuits can be created for any of the categories of electrical systems. Wire types can be created to distinguish these systems visually if wiring is shown. The panels for these systems can be used to manage the circuit locations. You can create panel schedule templates for the various types of panel schedules that you use in your projects. Figure 14.32 shows the Edit Circuits dialog box for a telephone terminal block used as the panel for the telephone circuits in a project.

FIGURE 14.32 Telephone circuits

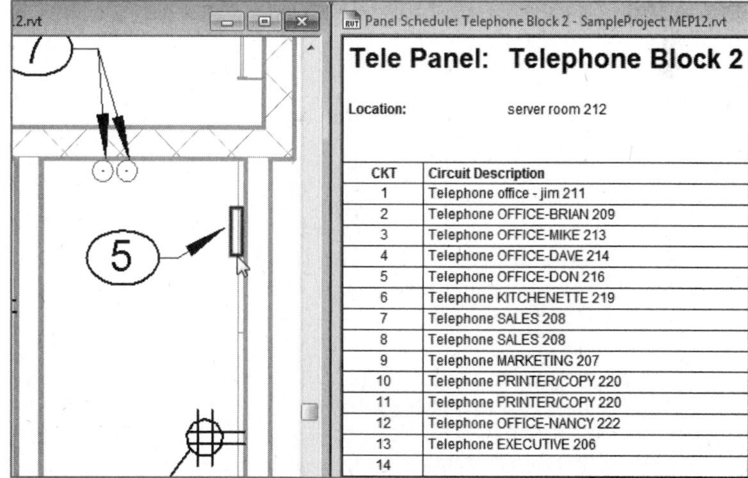

CKT	Circuit Description
1	Telephone office - jim 211
2	Telephone OFFICE-BRIAN 209
3	Telephone OFFICE-MIKE 213
4	Telephone OFFICE-DAVE 214
5	Telephone OFFICE-DON 216
6	Telephone KITCHENETTE 219
7	Telephone SALES 208
8	Telephone SALES 208
9	Telephone MARKETING 207
10	Telephone PRINTER/COPY 220
11	Telephone PRINTER/COPY 220
12	Telephone OFFICE-NANCY 222
13	Telephone EXECUTIVE 206
14	

Although telephone wiring is not normally shown on a typical set of construction documents, creating these systems provides you with information that can help in making design decisions. This type of information could later be modified to represent the as-built conditions of your project, which could then be useful for facilities maintenance. It is about putting the *I* in your BIM project.

Using Schedules for Sharing Circuit Information

A *Panel schedule* is a special type of schedule that is automatically generated from the data within the panel objects. When you select a panel, the Create Panel Schedules button appears on the Modify | Electrical Equipment contextual tab. Clicking this button allows you to select a template to be used for the Panel schedule.

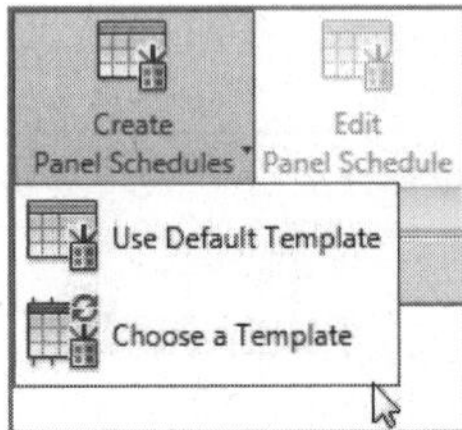

Once you have chosen a panel schedule template, the Panel schedule appears in the Project Browser, as shown in Figure 14.33.

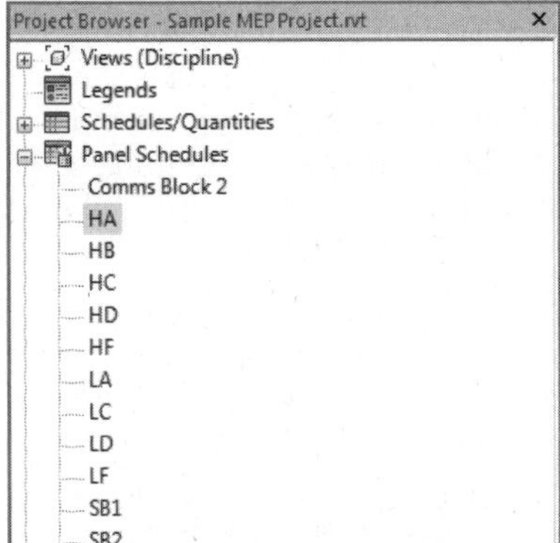

FIGURE 14.33
Panel schedules shown in the Project Browser

You can access the panel schedules by double-clicking them in the Project Browser or by selecting the panel in a view and clicking the Edit Panel Schedule button. You can change the template used for a Panel schedule by right-clicking it in the Project Browser and choosing the Change Template option.

PANEL SCHEDULE TEMPLATES

See Chapter 7, "Schedules," for information on creating and managing panel schedule templates.

You can place Panel schedules on your sheets by dragging and dropping them from the Project Browser. When you place a Panel schedule onto a sheet, it is formatted according to the settings defined in the panel template. Changes made to the circuits in your model or in the Edit Circuits dialog box of the panel automatically show up in the Panel schedule. Changes made to the panel schedule template that define the size and appearance of the schedule are automatically applied to the schedule on a sheet. You can snap to the border of a panel schedule to align your schedules on a sheet.

You can create schedules for panels and circuits that can be used to extract information about your project. Organizing the data contained in your project regarding electrical loads can help you make design decisions and keep your design coordinated with other disciplines. Schedules can also be created to supplement the Panel schedules that are generated.

Circuits hold a host of useful data that can be scheduled for project coordination and design. Figure 14.34 shows a schedule of electrical circuits that displays information that can be used to verify circuit locations as well as length, voltage, breaker size, and wire size. This type of schedule may be useful because you can display and manage information about the circuits that may not appear in your Panel schedules. Having this information in a schedule makes it easy to check your design and make any necessary changes.

FIGURE 14.34
Electrical circuit schedule

Electrical Circuit Schedule

Circuit Number	Load Name	Voltage	Length	Voltage Drop	Breaker Size	Apparent Current	Wire Size
HA							
1	Lighting Room 103, 104, 105	277 V	288' - 5 3/4"	5 V	20 A	10 A	1-#8, 1-#8, 1-#8
2	Exterior Lighting - Entrance	277 V	311' - 3 5/32"	2 V	20 A	2 A	1-#12, 1-#12, 1-#12
3	Site Lighting	277 V	78' - 3 1/2"	0 V	20 A	1 A	1-#12, 1-#12, 1-#12
4	Site Lighting	277 V	57' - 8 5/8"	0 V	20 A	0 A	1-#12, 1-#12, 1-#12
5	SPARE	277 V	0' - 0"	0 V	20 A	0 A	1-#12, 1-#12, 1-#12
6	SPARE	277 V	0' - 0"	0 V	20 A	0 A	1-#12, 1-#12, 1-#12
7,9,11	ELEVATOR	480 V	28' - 11 1/16"	1 V	50 A	27 A	3-#6, 1-#6, 1-#10
8,10,12	TA	480 V	7' - 0 17/32"	0 V	50 A	14 A	3-#6, 1-#6, 1-#10
HB							
1	Lighting STAIR 3 S3	277 V	82' - 2 23/32"	0 V	20 A	1 A	1-#12, 1-#12, 1-#12
2	Lighting STAGE 115	277 V	103' - 1 7/32"	1 V	20 A	1 A	1-#12, 1-#12, 1-#12
3	Lighting AUDITORIUM/THEAT	277 V	232' - 9 3/16"	4 V	20 A	5 A	1-#12, 1-#12, 1-#12
4	Exterior Lighting	277 V	76' - 6 25/32"	0 V	20 A	0 A	1-#12, 1-#12, 1-#12
5	Lighting Room 102, 100, S3, 1	277 V	279' - 3 3/16"	5 V	20 A	5 A	1-#12, 1-#12, 1-#12
6	Site Lighting	277 V	101' - 3 27/32"	0 V	20 A	0 A	1-#12, 1-#12, 1-#12
7	Lighting Room 112, 113, 102,	277 V	131' - 6 7/16"	1 V	20 A	2 A	1-#12, 1-#12, 1-#12
8	Lighting Room 118, 117, 116	277 V	57' - 7 17/32"	0 V	20 A	2 A	1-#12, 1-#12, 1-#12
15	SPARE	277 V	0' - 0"	0 V	20 A	0 A	
17	SPARE	277 V	0' - 0"	0 V	20 A	0 A	
19,21,23	TB	480 V	6' - 6 1/8"	0 V	50 A	11 A	3-#6, 1-#6, 1-#10
20	SPARE	277 V	0' - 0"	0 V	20 A	0 A	

The Bottom Line

Establish settings for circuits and wiring. Proper setup of a project's electrical characteristics is an important part of the workflow when you're creating circuits and wiring. Settings can be stored in your project template and modified on an as-needed basis.

Master It The distribution systems defined in a project make it possible to connect devices and equipment of like voltages. Do you need to have voltage definitions in order to create distribution systems? Why or why not?

Create circuits and wiring for devices and fixtures. Circuits are the systems for electrical design. Wiring can be used to show the connection of devices and fixtures in a schematic fashion.

Master It Circuits can be created for devices or equipment even if they are not assigned to a panel. Circuits can then be represented by wiring shown on construction documents. Give two examples of how you can add a device to a circuit that has already been created.

Manage circuits and panels. With the relationship between components and panels established, you can manage the properties of circuits and panels to improve your design performance and efficiency.

Master It While checking the circuits on a panel, you notice that there are only 14 circuits connected, but the panel has 42 poles. How can you reduce the amount of unused space in the panel?

Use schedules for sharing circuit information. Panel schedules can be used on construction documents to convey the load information. Schedules can also be created for use as design tools to help track electrical data.

Master It The information in Revit panel schedules may not meet the requirements of your document or design standards. Describe how you can use the data within your Revit model to provide the required information.

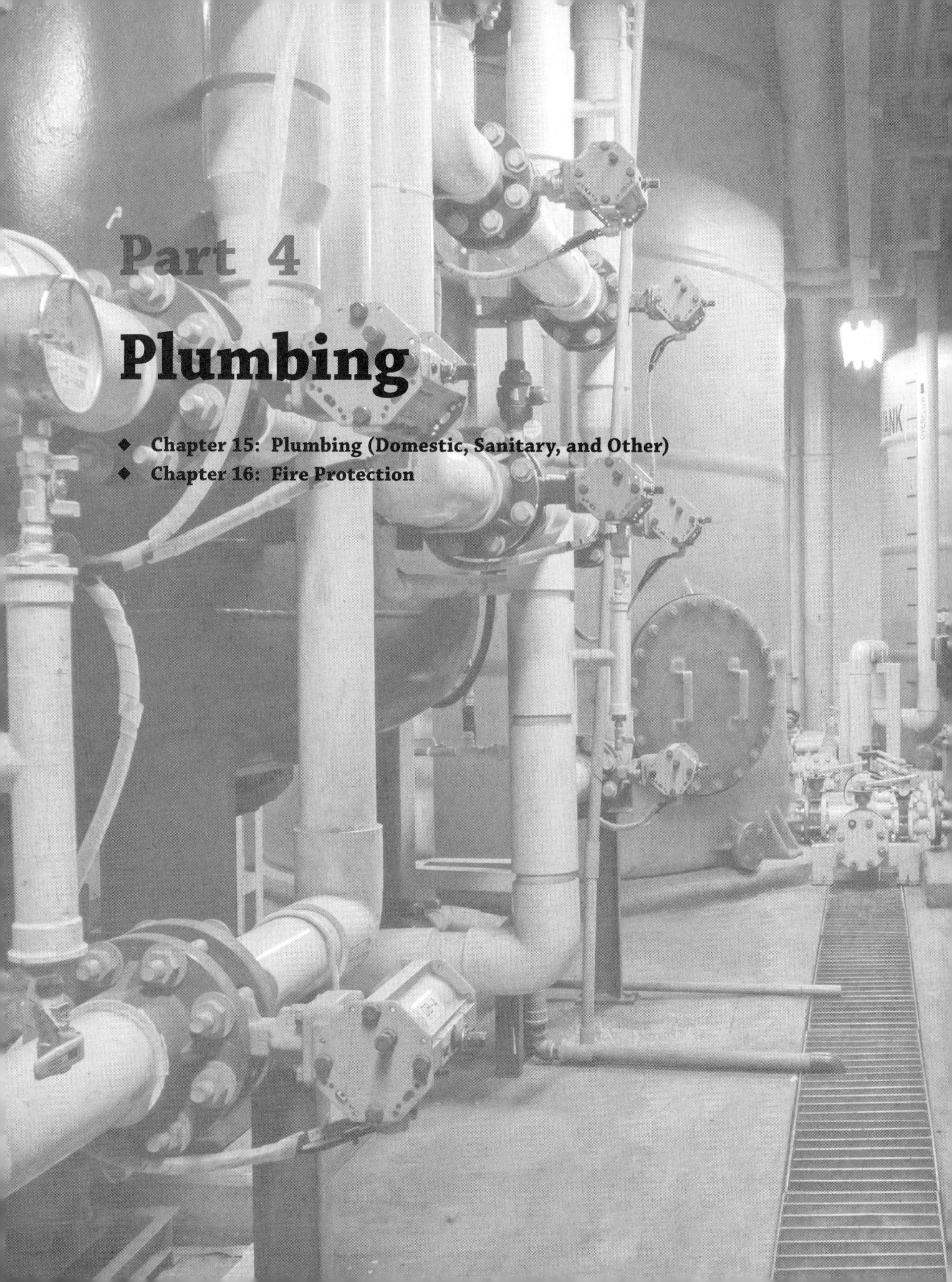

Part 4

Plumbing

Chapter 15

Plumbing (Domestic, Sanitary, and Other)

The process we used to route plumbing piping has come a long way from drawing circles and lines on paper. Over the past 30 years, tools such as the straight edge, 30/60 triangles, and the Timely template have been replaced by CAD systems. With more owners requiring BIM, a plumbing designer has to become a virtual pipe installer. Instead of just drawing circles and lines, you have to understand more about how fittings go together to construct your piping design. This is where the Autodesk® Revit® MEP 2015 software excels; it can help you create your designs more accurately and efficiently. But make no mistake—now more than ever before, you need to plan in advance for your plumbing projects. What are the BIM goals for the project? What is the level of detail you are targeting? Develop and document new workflows between you and the architect; create custom content; be much more dependent on accuracy and any changes made by the architect. Those are just a few of the challenges you face, and if you take the time to open the conversation with the architect and internally in your company, you will have accomplished the biggest challenge that people ignore when starting their first plumbing project—planning and setting the expectations!

In this chapter, you will learn to do the following:

- Configure plumbing views
- Customize out-of-the-box Revit plumbing fixtures for scheduling purposes
- Adjust the plumbing pipe settings
- Select the best pipe routing options for your project
- Adjust pipe fittings

Configuring the Plumbing Views

One of the most important parts of a successful plumbing project is configuring the view settings. Many companies tried the plumbing portion of Revit in their early stage of the Revit implementation, and most of them walked away from it saying, "It's not ready yet." Without the proper configuration, it will never be ready for your company either.

Global Settings and View-specific Settings

You need to adjust several settings so your pipes are properly displayed. The following list is certainly not comprehensive, but it should point you in the right direction and show what to pay attention to when setting up your plumbing sheets:

- All plotted views should be set to Hidden Line.
- Detail Level should be set to Coarse, because most regulatory authorities still require single-line plumbing drawings.
- View range should be adjusted to display necessary pipe systems.
- Visibility Graphics categories should be set to display the appropriate object categories. If worksharing is enabled, it is more efficient to turn off other disciplines' objects by using worksets instead of managing every single object. However, good worksharing practices must be in place, and all objects must be associated with the appropriate workset.
- Pipes going under plumbing fixtures will be completely hidden. To resolve this, plumbing fixtures should be set to Transparent for your model and any linked Revit models containing plumbing fixtures. Note, however, that plumbing fixtures with a high level of detail may start displaying unnecessary lines.
- Wall cut patterns should be turned off. For example, architects often assign cut patterns for their walls to display the fire rating. While this is not important for the mechanical or electrical plans, it is crucial for the plumbing plans, where most objects are in the wall (see Figure 15.1).

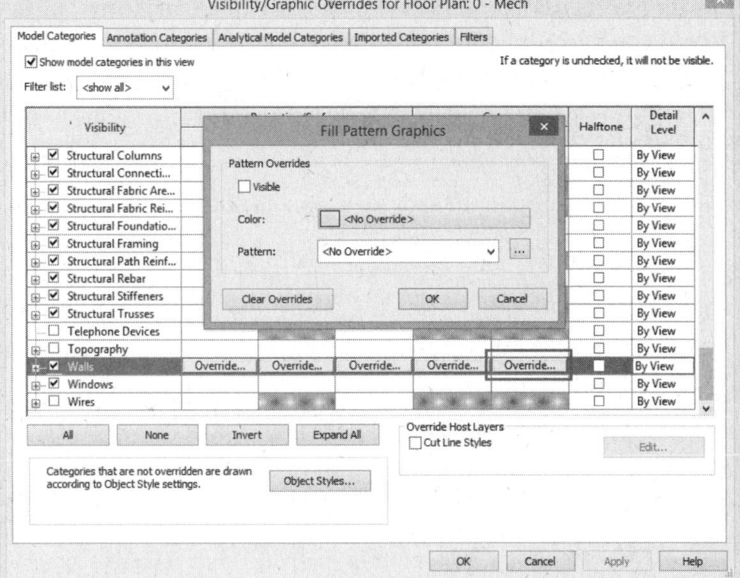

FIGURE 15.1 Turning off wall cut patterns

- Pipe Rise/Drop Annotation Size under Mechanical Settings should be changed to suit. If you're not sure what you will need, 7/128″ (1. 5 mm) is a good starting point.
- For buildings that are not orthogonally oriented, scope boxes should be set up and associated with the views. Another, simpler method is to rotate the crop region so you can lay out your pipes orthogonally to your screen.
- Configure the Single Line gap under Mechanical Settings to match your company standard. If you do not have one, 3/128″ (0.6 mm) is a good starting point.

Defining Systems Visibility Through Filters

Revit MEP 2015 automatically creates the piping systems for you when you lay out pipes, even when pipes are not connected to plumbing fixtures. When drawing pipes, you need to specify the system type they belong to. The system type can be used to define the line weight, linetype, color, and system abbreviation. The system abbreviation can be used to define what system will appear on what sheet via filters. This helps you hide the mechanical pipes in the plumbing views, as well as separate your sheets between domestic and sanitary pipe layouts.

Establishing a good naming convention for the filters is important, because that defines the order in which you see them in your Properties palette when drawing pipes. The default examples of filters and their settings are not going to get you too far with your projects. We recommend that you take your time and come up with a complete list of systems that your company uses and create them as system types and filters in Revit MEP. Organizing all of them in Excel can be beneficial. Notice that the Filter By setting is set to Equals under the System Abbreviation, as shown in Figure 15.2.

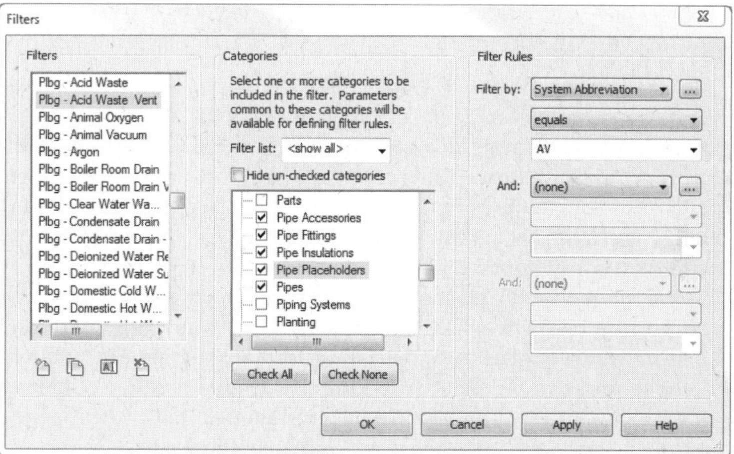

FIGURE 15.2 Sample filters and their settings

Once the filters have been created, go into a view where you want the different disciplines to show up and type **VG** to bring up the Visibility/Graphic Overrides dialog box. Click the Filters tab, and add the newly created filters. Using the Visibility check boxes, you can define the systems that would be visible in that view. You can then use this view to create a view template that can be applied to all views that require these settings. Filters can also be used to define color, line patterns, and in some cases, line weights. There are times when you will need filters to do this; however, the recommended place to control these is in the system type. This way, those settings will be global rather than per view. However, the filters will still be managed and they will control what system is visible in what view (see Figure 15.3).

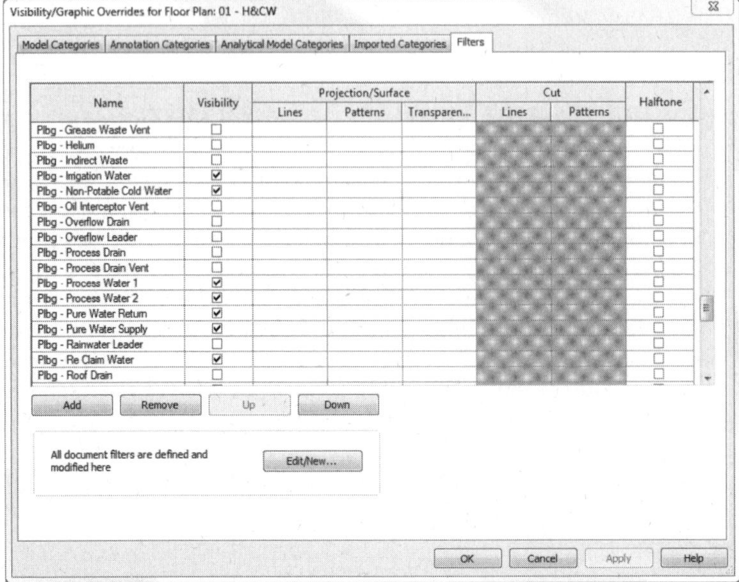

FIGURE 15.3
Adjusting the visibility of pipe and duct systems through filters

Now that your plans are coordinated and displayed the way you require, you are well on your way to completing your documentation. Consider using the same filters to display 3D views that can enhance the design, making it easier to understand and further reducing errors.

Every rule has its exception, and here is a great example for it. Controlling the colors and line patterns of your systems in the 3D views would color the contour of the pipes, making the pipes hard to see. Instead of going that route, we suggest you override those in the filters with a solid pattern; this way, your 3D views will be a lot easier to see and understand (see Figure 15.4).

One common drafting standard is to show all piping serving a given floor in the same view. For instance, on the sheet showing the restroom located on the second floor of a three-story building, you would expect to see all the sanitary piping below the second floor and the vent piping in the second-floor attic serving that restroom. You would not want to see the sanitary pipe serving the third-floor restroom, even though it also occupies the second-floor attic, and you would not want to see the vent piping serving the first floor.

One way to accomplish this selective visibility in projects with overlapping view ranges is with workset visibility. You can assign all the piping serving the first, second, and third floors to specific first-, second-, and third-floor worksets. This will allow you to turn off the first- and third-floor worksets, cleaning up your second-floor view. See Chapter 3, "Worksets and Worksharing," for more information.

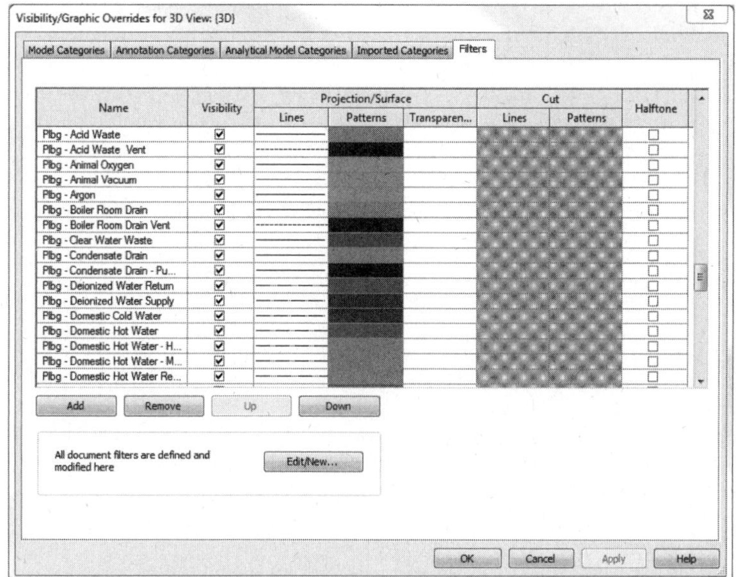

FIGURE 15.4 Applying filter overrides for 3D views

Working with Plumbing Fixtures

Plumbing fixtures are as important to the look of an architectural design as granite countertops or marble tile. Plumbing fixtures, when properly selected, not only enhance the visual design but also promote cleanliness and hygiene. Plumbing fixtures normally are placed by the architect during schematic design to coordinate usability and meet the requirements of governing codes. For this reason it is essential to have good communication between architects and engineers. The power that Revit gives you in collaboration does not reduce the need for a good working relationship with other consultants but rather increases it.

From a plumbing design point of view, different criteria must be examined. What are the water conservation guidelines? Are the plumbing fixtures required to meet LEED standards? Other questions should be asked during design: Will you, as the designer, want to use the same plumbing fixtures that the architect's model uses to connect to your piping, or will you substitute your company's standard fixtures? If so, do you need to apply shared parameters that reflect the design standards required? For example, in the United States there are two major plumbing codes: the Uniform Plumbing Code and the International Plumbing Code. To complicate matters further, some states adopt one of these two codes and then add their own amendments, creating their own state code.

With Revit MEP 2015, you can apply this information through the use of parameters. This can be done in a couple of ways. First, you can edit the information in the family itself by selecting a plumbing fixture family and editing the information through the Type Properties dialog box, shown in Figure 15.5.

FIGURE 15.5
Editing the Type Properties

Type Properties

Family: 16-Water Closet - Flush Tank1 — Load...

Type: Zurn — Duplicate...

Rename...

Type Parameters

Parameter	Value
Dimensions	
Sanitary Radius	2"
Sanitary Diameter	4"
Cold Water Radius	1/4"
Cold Water Diameter	1/2"
Identity Data	
URL	HTTP://WWW.ZURN.COM
Type Comments	18" ADA
Model	201100.11
Manufacturer	ZURN
Keynote	12" ROUGH-IN
Description	PROVIDE W/ENLONGATED OPEN
Cost	200.00
Assembly Code	
Assembly Description	
Type Mark	P-4
OmniClass Number	23.45.05.21.11.11
OmniClass Title	Water Operated Water Closets

<< Preview OK Cancel Apply

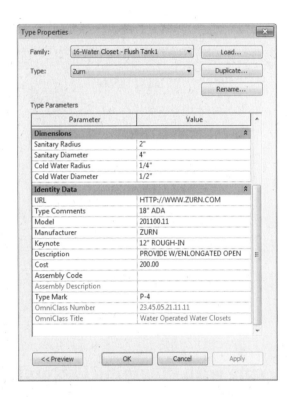

The second way to edit the information is to create a *type catalog*. Using type catalogs enables the user to easily produce more information about different types or models of the same family. For example, most bathroom manufacturers use model numbers to show the differences in finishes, rough-in locations, handle locations, and handicap accessibility information. Also, type catalogs allow the plumbing design to be easily changed from one manufacturer to another.

The easiest way to create a type catalog is to first open a family and then choose Application Menu ➤ Export ➤ Family Types. This creates a TXT file with all the parameters that are already in that family. The advantage of this method is that it quickly formats the type catalog the way it should be; the disadvantage is that it exports all parameters within the family, and you may need to clean up the type catalog if you don't want all parameters included.

Another method is to create a TXT file manually that will populate the information. To create this TXT file, do the following:

1. Open Microsoft Excel. (If you do not have Excel, you can use Notepad or Apache OpenOffice to achieve the same goal. OpenOffice can be downloaded from `www.OpenOffice.org`.) Save the spreadsheet as a comma-separated values (CSV) file, making sure to name it by using the plumbing fixture's family name.

2. Leave cell A1 blank. This is necessary for the type name of the family, such as Kohler or American Standard, to be listed in column A properly.

3. Next, you will add the parameter name followed by the parameter unit in row 1. For this example, you will be using the following system parameters from the identity data located in the plumbing fixture family:

Keynote	Keynote##other##
Model	Model##other##
Manufacturer	Manufacturer##other##
Type Comments	Type Comments##other##
URL	URL##other##
Description	Description##other##

4. Add the information for each row that you want to be able to schedule (see Figure 15.6).

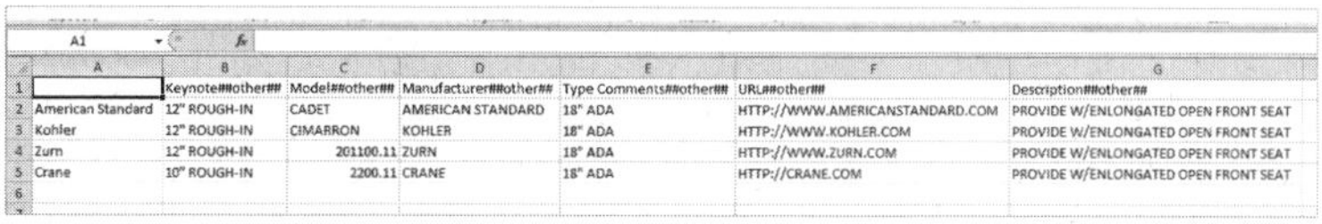

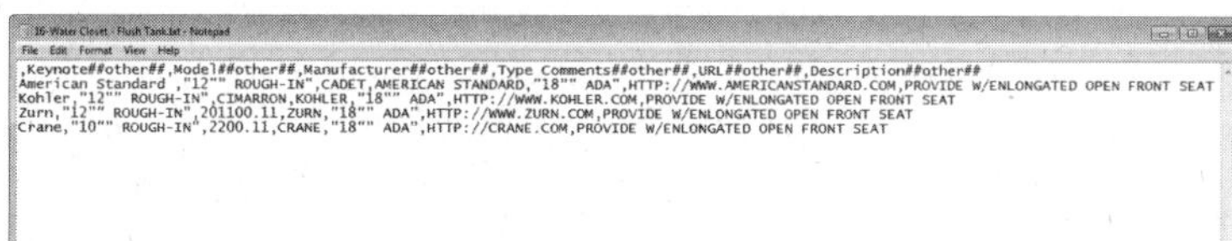

	A	B	C	D	E	F	G
1		Keynote##other##	Model##other##	Manufacturer##other##	Type Comments##other##	URL##other##	Description##other##
2	American Standard	12" ROUGH-IN	CADET	AMERICAN STANDARD	18" ADA	HTTP://WWW.AMERICANSTANDARD.COM	PROVIDE W/ENLONGATED OPEN FRONT SEAT
3	Kohler	12" ROUGH-IN	CIMARRON	KOHLER	18" ADA	HTTP://WWW.KOHLER.COM	PROVIDE W/ENLONGATED OPEN FRONT SEAT
4	Zurn	12" ROUGH-IN	201100.11	ZURN	18" ADA	HTTP://WWW.ZURN.COM	PROVIDE W/ENLONGATED OPEN FRONT SEAT
5	Crane	10" ROUGH-IN	2200.11	CRANE	18" ADA	HTTP://CRANE.COM	PROVIDE W/ENLONGATED OPEN FRONT SEAT
6							

FIGURE 15.6 Creating a CSV file for type catalogs

5. Once everything has been input, save the file. Make sure that when the file is created, it is located in the same directory as the family it references.

6. Go to the directory where you saved your file, and rename the extension from `.csv` to **`.txt`**. To review what the TXT file looks like or to make quick edits without converting back to a CSV file, you can open this file with Notepad (see Figure 15.7).

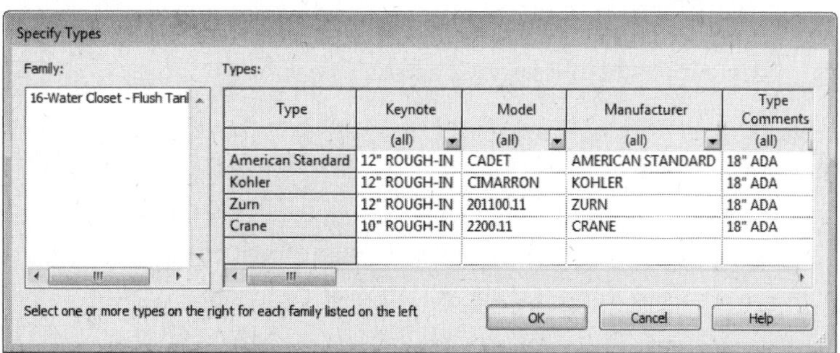

```
,Keynote##other##,Model##other##,Manufacturer##other##,Type Comments##other##,URL##other##,Description##other##
American Standard ,"12"" ROUGH-IN",CADET,AMERICAN STANDARD,"18"" ADA",HTTP://WWW.AMERICANSTANDARD.COM,PROVIDE W/ENLONGATED OPEN FRONT SEAT
Kohler,"12"" ROUGH-IN",CIMARRON,KOHLER,"18"" ADA",HTTP://WWW.KOHLER.COM,PROVIDE W/ENLONGATED OPEN FRONT SEAT
Zurn,"12"" ROUGH-IN",201100.11,ZURN,"18"" ADA",HTTP://WWW.ZURN.COM,PROVIDE W/ENLONGATED OPEN FRONT SEAT
Crane,"10"" ROUGH-IN",2200.11,CRANE,"18"" ADA",HTTP://CRANE.COM,PROVIDE W/ENLONGATED OPEN FRONT SEAT
```

FIGURE 15.7 Opening the TXT file in Notepad

If you created your file properly, you should see a catalog of information when inserting the family (see Figure 15.8). For more information on type catalogs and their uses, see Chapter 6, "Parameters" and Chapter 19, "Creating Equipment."

Specify Types

Family: 16-Water Closet - Flush Tanl

Types:

Type	Keynote	Model	Manufacturer	Type Comments
	(all)	(all)	(all)	(all)
American Standard	12" ROUGH-IN	CADET	AMERICAN STANDARD	18" ADA
Kohler	12" ROUGH-IN	CIMARRON	KOHLER	18" ADA
Zurn	12" ROUGH-IN	201100.11	ZURN	18" ADA
Crane	10" ROUGH-IN	2200.11	CRANE	18" ADA

Select one or more types on the right for each family listed on the left

OK Cancel Help

FIGURE 15.8 Type catalog

Now that you have information added to your plumbing fixture family and you have placed the plumbing fixtures into the plan, you will want to schedule that information.

To accomplish this, go to the Analyze or View tab on the ribbon, and then select Schedule/Quantities. This opens the Schedule dialog box, shown in Figure 15.9. Select Plumbing Fixtures from the Category group, and then click OK.

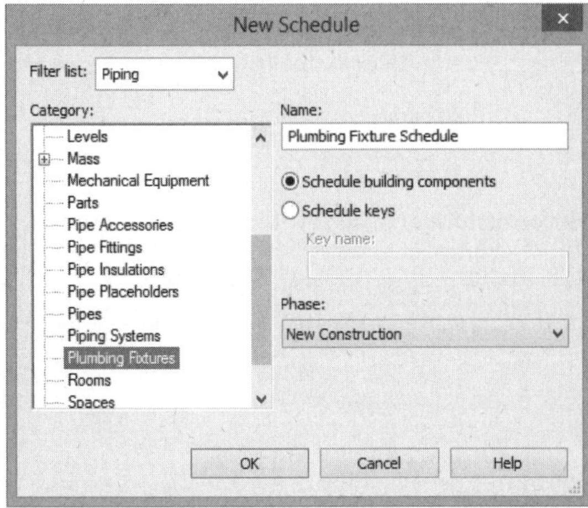

FIGURE 15.9 Select Plumbing Fixtures from the Category group.

Next, select the information from the Available Fields dialog box and add it to the Schedule Fields (In Order) dialog box. Then click OK, which will create your schedule (see Figure 15.10).

FIGURE 15.10 Plumbing fixture schedule

Plumbing Fixture Schedule

Type Mark	Description	Type Comme	Manufacturer	Model	Keynote	Count
P-1	PROVIDE W/ENLONGATED OPEN FRONT SEAT	18" ADA	AMERICAN STANDARD	CADET	12" ROUGH-IN	1
P-2	PROVIDE W/ENLONGATED OPEN FRONT SEAT	18" ADA	KOHLER	CIMARRON	12" ROUGH-IN	1
P-3	PROVIDE W/ENLONGATED OPEN FRONT SEAT	18" ADA	CRANE	2200.11	10" ROUGH-IN	1
P-4	PROVIDE W/ENLONGATED OPEN FRONT SEAT	18" ADA	ZURN	201100.11	12" ROUGH-IN	1
P-4	PROVIDE W/ENLONGATED OPEN FRONT SEAT	18" ADA	ZURN	201100.11	12" ROUGH-IN	1
P-4	PROVIDE W/ENLONGATED OPEN FRONT SEAT	18" ADA	ZURN	201100.11	12" ROUGH-IN	1
P-4	PROVIDE W/ENLONGATED OPEN FRONT SEAT	18" ADA	ZURN	201100.11	12" ROUGH-IN	1
P-4	PROVIDE W/ENLONGATED OPEN FRONT SEAT	18" ADA	ZURN	201100.11	12" ROUGH-IN	1

Now that you have created the Plumbing Fixture Schedule, you may not want to see duplicate information or blank lines, so you will need to sort the data. To do this, go to the Properties palette, select Sorting/Grouping, change the Sort By option to Type Mark, and then deselect the Itemize Every Instance check box. Now your schedule will show only the items that have unique information (see Figure 15.11). For more information on customizing the appearance and content of schedules, see Chapter 7, "Schedules."

FIGURE 15.11 Sorted schedule

Plumbing Fixture Schedule

Type Mark	Description	Type Comme	Manufacturer	Model	Keynote	Count
P-1	PROVIDE W/ENLONGATED OPEN FRONT SEAT	18" ADA	AMERICAN STANDARD	CADET	12" ROUGH-IN	1
P-2	PROVIDE W/ENLONGATED OPEN FRONT SEAT	18" ADA	KOHLER	CIMARRON	12" ROUGH-IN	1
P-3	PROVIDE W/ENLONGATED OPEN FRONT SEAT	18" ADA	CRANE	2200.11	10" ROUGH-IN	1
P-4	PROVIDE W/ENLONGATED OPEN FRONT SEAT	18" ADA	ZURN	201100.11	12" ROUGH-IN	5

Working with Architectural Linked-in Plumbing Models

When using Revit MEP for plumbing, you have two main options for coordinating plumbing fixtures between architectural linked-in models and plumbing models. The first option is to manually place the plumbing designer's edited plumbing fixtures over the architectural plumbing fixtures. The second option is to use the Copy/Monitor feature.

Using the Copy/Monitor feature either places an exact copy of the architect's fixture family or allows you to select your family. You can use a family that has already been edited with proper connectors and scheduling information. When you are placing fully modeled plumbing fixtures with connectors, you will need to turn off the architectural plumbing fixtures. Otherwise, any slight difference in graphical representation or location between your plumbing fixtures and the architectural plumbing fixtures will be a disaster for your final plot sheets. Using plumbing fixture assemblies or connector placeholders is more forgiving. In this case, the architect is in control of the graphical representation of the plumbing fixtures, and you are in control of the plumbing fixture information and specifications. By fixture assemblies or connector placeholders, we mean placing your own families, which could be as simple as cylinders that are hosting the necessary connectors and all parameters for scheduling purposes. When you place those, you can decide where to put them and how to orient them, whereas with the Copy/Monitor tool as mentioned earlier, you are dependent on the architect's family building skills.

With either method, you have to take care that your fixtures remain coordinated with any architectural plan changes. If you place your families manually, you have to check locations visually. If you use the Copy/Monitor function, Revit will notify you that there has been a change via the Collaborate ribbon tab ➤ Coordination Review. Also, the Copy/Monitor feature does not automatically update to show any new fixtures that the architect may have added.

You should also consider how the architectural families and your families are made. The two major points of consideration are the orientation and the insertion point of the architectural families and your families. If they don't match, Copy/Monitor most likely will create more work for you because you will have to move and rotate every instance of a family that doesn't match orientation and position. But by doing that, you would also produce a Copy/Monitor alert. So, the bottom line is that if the orientation and insertion point don't match, it is easier to place the families manually, and if you like the benefits of Copy/Monitor alerting you when the architect moves those elements, you can still monitor your manually placed fixtures against the architectural fixtures. We'll talk more about this later in the chapter.

Instead of duplicating the fixtures in the architectural and plumbing files, another scenario you could consider is to have the engineering company take them over and let the architect display the plumbing fixtures from the plumbing model. This will certainly eliminate inconsistency between the two models, but it could be hard to achieve for some companies based on their culture and workflows.

With either of the options, you can use plumbing fixture families that represent only the piping portion of each fixture. These custom pipe assemblies are fittings preassembled or modeled to line up in the locations of the linked architectural plumbing fixtures. These are created as plumbing fixture families.

Creating Custom Pipe Assemblies

Many piping conditions are not worth modeling piece by piece, such as piping beneath counters for p-traps and supply lines or complicated pipe and valve assemblies. If a plumber can preassemble these off site or perhaps prefabricate them as an assembly on site and then just move them into place; it may be logical to emulate this by building custom families that represent a complete assembly instead of using individual families that must be connected to one another repeatedly in the model.

Custom pipe assemblies can be represented in one of two ways in the Family Editor. First, you can use sweeps to represent the p-trap, wye, and associated piping, as shown in Figure 15.12. This method creates a smaller file size and reduces the size of the overall plumbing model. Assemblies representing fittings with sweeps and extrusions would not allow you to schedule the fittings directly. However, if quantity takeoffs are important to you, they can be achieved by creating shared parameters that store the number and type of fittings that are used in the assembly.

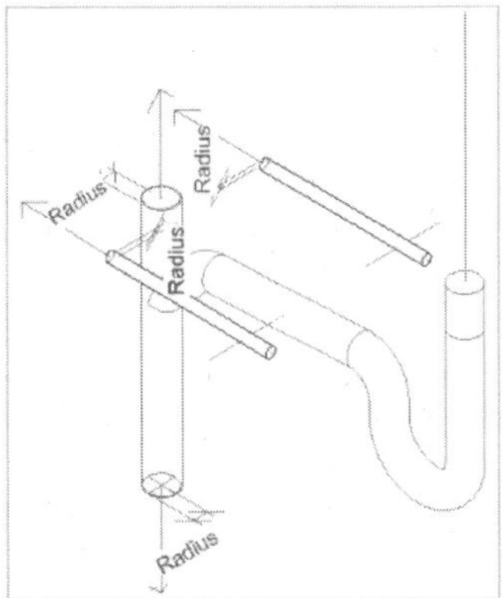

FIGURE 15.12 Representation of a pipe assembly created with sweeps

The second method is to assemble nested families, which can allow for better quantity takeoffs for all the fittings, create more-accurate dimensional information when supplied by manufacturers, and be easier for the plumbing designer to create. The downside is that it produces a larger family file. This second option will help you achieve more of the building information modeling (BIM) status as well as a more accurate visual representation of the plumbing systems in addition to taking advantage of already existing content, hopefully reducing modeling efforts (see Figure 15.13).

Now let's examine how nested piping assemblies are put together and some key areas to be mindful of:

1. Open the `PR-Sinks and Lavs.rfa` file found at `www.sybex.com/go/masteringrevitmep2015`.

2. Several modified pipe-fitting families are nested into this family that make up the assembly. They are `Trap P - PVC-DWV.rfa`, `Tee Sanitary-PVC-DWV.rfa`, `PVC-DWV Pipe Section.rfa`, `Plug-PVC-DWV.rfa`, `Elbow -Copper Type L.rfa`, and `Copper Type L Pipe Section.rfa`. These can all be found at `www.sybex.com/go/masteringrevit-mep2015`, or you can get the originals from the `Pipe Fitting` directory located in the Imperial library.

3. When placing the fittings together, make sure to align, lock, and dimension each one, as shown in Figure 15.14. If not, the fittings will pull apart.

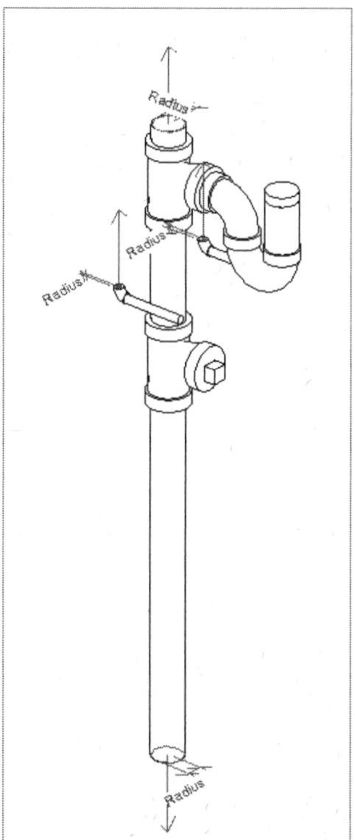

FIGURE 15.13
Nested pipe assembly

4. When creating your pipe assembly, make sure that the Center Front/Back reference plane is placed at the wall's finish face in the project. When you do this, the family will easily snap into place.

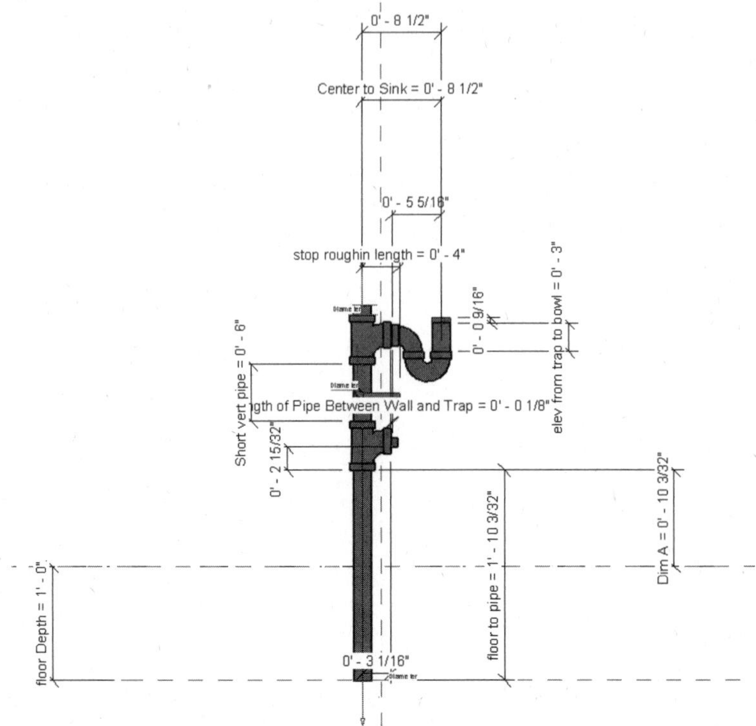

FIGURE 15.14 Aligning, locking, and dimensioning nested families

PLUMBING FIXTURE FAMILIES ARE NOT CREATED EQUAL

Plumbing fixture families are not always created equal. Rather than starting the family by modeling the front of the fixture oriented appropriately in the front view, some modelers will just model in whichever view is available. This has always been a problem in Revit, and as more families become available, the issue will increase. This can cause a few problems when aligning your fixture family to the architect's or when replacing one fixture with another. For additional information on hosting behaviors of families, please refer to the section "Hosting Options" in Chapter 19.

As your skills grow and you start creating your own content, please remember simple modeling etiquette. The family should be modeled in the proper orientation. The Front, Back, Top, Bottom, Left, and Right views should match the orientation of the product being modeled. This will increase productivity when aligning other items such as pipe assemblies under plumbing fixtures as well as avoid issues with Copy/Monitor.

Various examples of both simple and complex plumbing fixture families can be downloaded from Autodesk User Group International (`www.augi.com`) and the Autodesk University website (`http://au.autodesk.com`).

5. You can add parameters to flex your piping to align it under a sink or lavatory or to give a certain depth to account for a floor slab. You can make these parameters as complex or as simple as you want (see Figure 15.15).

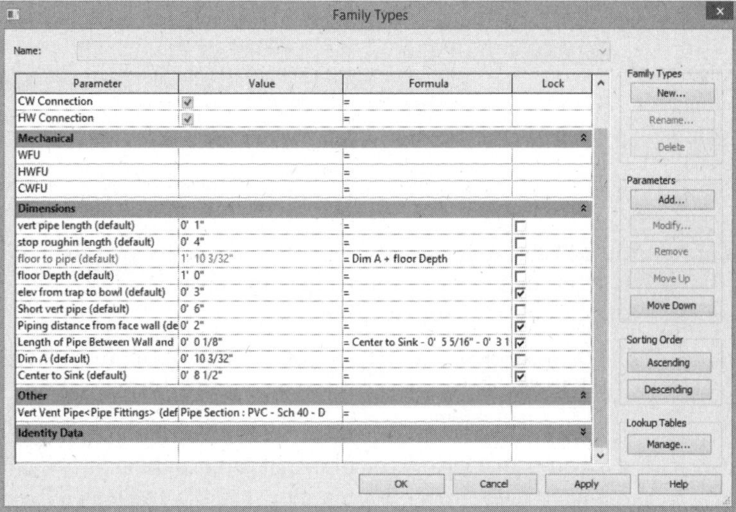

FIGURE 15.15 Using parameters to flex the piping assembly

6. Make sure that when adding a water piping connection to a rough-in pipe, you add an elbow pointing in the direction of the pipe routing (for example, from the floor or from the ceiling). This will help with autorouting and manual routing (see Figure 15.16).

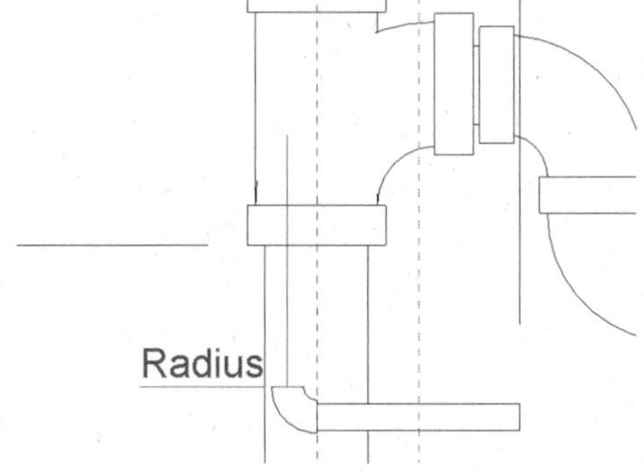

FIGURE 15.16 Adding a simple elbow pointed in the direction of flow

Now that you have reviewed some of the items that make up a pipe assembly, you can place the pipe assembly family in your plumbing model and align it with the architectural plumbing fixtures without having to turn them off. If the architect adds a plumbing fixture, you now have the capability to view it. By following this workflow, you can both tag and schedule the pipe assembly family while the graphic representation needs are satisfied by the family in the architectural linked file.

Copying/Monitoring Plumbing Fixtures

Now let's take it a step further. If the plumbing fixtures that the architects are using match the same orientation and insertion point of your pipe assemblies, you can copy/monitor the pipe assemblies directly behind the plumbing fixtures. Then, when the architect moves a plumbing fixture, you will receive a warning that you need to coordinate your view (see Figure 15.17).

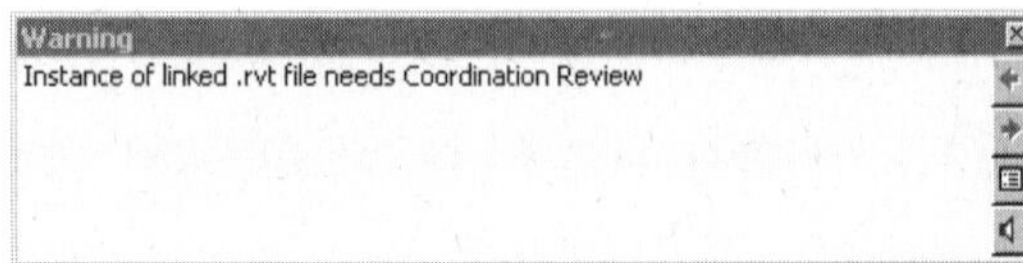

FIGURE 15.17 Coordination Review warning

You will also have the capability to copy and change all of the plumbing fixtures on multiple levels at one time. This can be a huge time-saver.

To use Copy/Monitor, do the following:

1. Choose Collaborate ➢ Copy/Monitor ➢ Select Link, and then select the architectural background.

   When you click the architectural file, the ribbon should change to Copy/Monitor. If it doesn't, that means you didn't click the architectural file. Trying to select objects by clicking on their surface is a common mistake. In Revit, all selection is done by clicking the contour of the object, not on the surface. If that happens to you, you will need to start over with the Copy/Monitor command.

2. In the Copy/Monitor panel, select Batch Copy. Click Specify Type Mapping Behavior & Copy Fixtures.
3. A Coordination panel opens, displaying Category and Behavior selection tables. Select Type Mapping, and replace the plumbing fixtures from the architect with the ones you created (see Figure 15.18).
4. Click Copy and then select the plumbing fixtures you want to copy (see Figure 15.19).
5. If you are working on multiple floors, you can select the plumbing fixtures from all levels while in an elevation view, and then you can use the Filter command to isolate only the plumbing fixtures.

   If you highlight the assembly, you should see the monitoring symbol on the assembly, as shown in Figure 15.20.

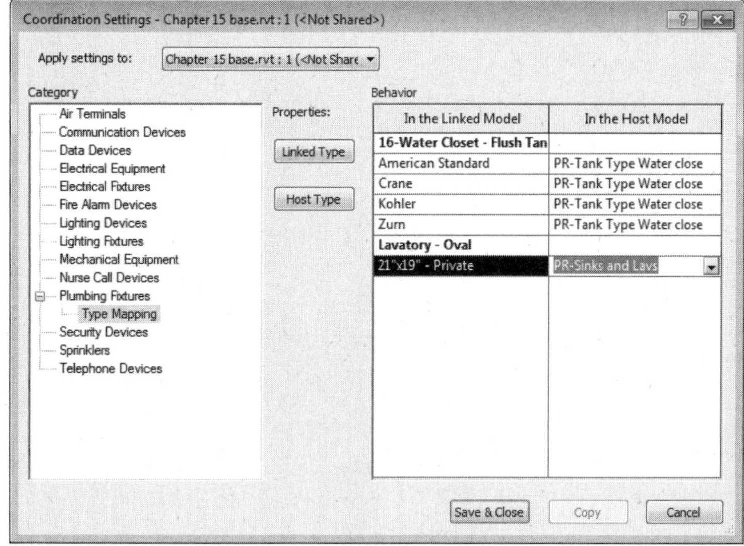

FIGURE 15.18
Type Mapping option

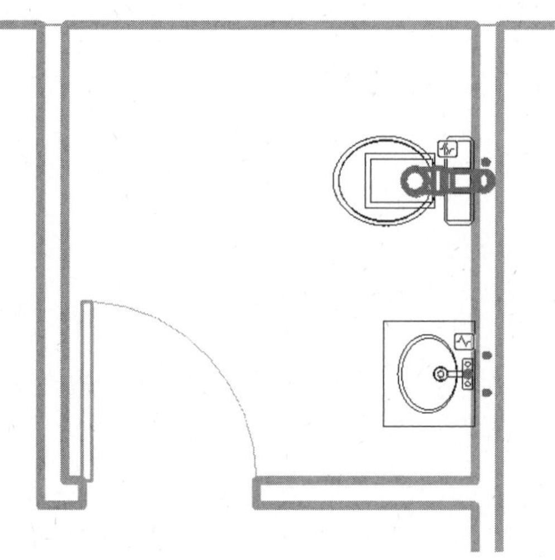

FIGURE 15.19
Copying and replacing fixture types

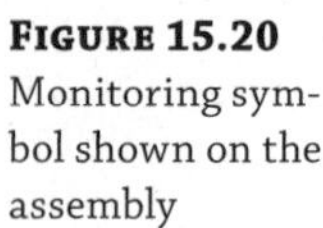

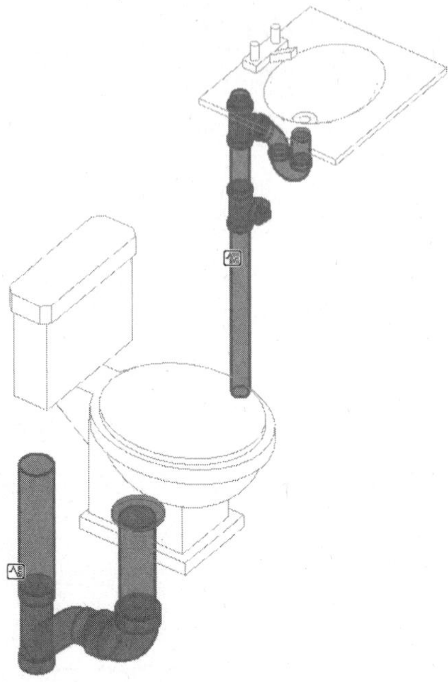

FIGURE 15.20
Monitoring symbol shown on the assembly

To take full advantage of the Copy/Monitor feature, you will need to coordinate all of your plumbing fixtures with your pipe assemblies, but you will find it is time well spent.

PLANNING AHEAD FOR CHANGE

Whether they are copy/monitored or just manually adjusted in the MEP model, moving plumbing fixtures that are connected to piping systems can often cause these systems to break. This then requires remodeling by the plumbing consultant to reconnect the piping system to the plumbing fixture.

When Revit tries to maintain the connection—particularly with sloped pipework—the results can be unpredictable. Avoid the extra work by disconnecting the pipework yourself before moving the fixture.

Each remodeled pipe adds cost to the MEP project, and over the entire project this added cost can be substantial. It is recommended, therefore, to avoid making the final connection to the plumbing fixture until you are more certain that any future architectural changes will be minimal.

Another option is to use flexible pipework so the system can stay connected for all of your engineering calculations. You can wait until the end of the design phase and replace these flexible pieces with your final connections then.

A less traditional way of using the Copy/Monitor tool, especially when the insertion point and orientation between the architectural fixtures and yours don't match, is to batch-copy all of the architectural plumbing fixtures and place a little dot or a cylinder. The idea is to create a relationship between your model and the architectural model that will provide you with alerts whenever the architect moves or deletes plumbing fixtures. Remember, you will not be notified when the architect places new fixtures, but the workaround for that is to batch-copy/monitor all fixtures with every update of the architectural background. This way, you will be able to see the number of newly copied/monitored elements (that is, new plumbing fixtures) in the architectural model. You will still need to manually place your own plumbing fixtures or pipe assemblies, but knowing what changes the architect made to the plumbing fixtures will be a huge time-saver.

Choosing Pipe Settings and Pipe Routing Options

When setting up piping to route, you should apply the proper pipe material so that quantity takeoffs can be easily scheduled. Another reason to apply the appropriate pipe material and pipe fittings is to get the invert elevation for sloping systems. If the pipe material and fittings are incorrect, the invert elevation value will not be reliable.

There are several areas you have to adjust to set this up properly. Most important are the Piping Systems and Pipe Types settings. These and other piping parameters are discussed at length in Chapter 11, "Mechanical Piping." Also covered in that chapter are the two routing options, autoroute and manual. Here, you will examine the options available for sloped piping. One thing to note is that currently Revit doesn't come with no-hub fittings. Some manufacturers are making them, but be aware that they can be over-detailed and you may experience performance issues with your projects. As a start, using the PVC fittings that come with Revit MEP 2015 should produce reasonable graphical results.

Sloping Pipe

When modeling pipe, you can use either the autoroute or the manual routing feature. You are more likely to have success with a manual layout when using sloped pipe. Before you lay out your pipes, it is a good idea to check the Slopes settings located under Manage ➤ MEP Settings ➤ Mechanical Settings ➤ Pipe Settings ➤ Slopes. From here you will be able to add or delete slopes that would be available for you to use when drawing pipes.

For sloping pipe to work properly, it needs to have start and end points. To set up sloping pipe, open `Ch15_plumbing.rvt` and `Ch15_base.rvt`. This file is found at `www.sybex.com/go/masteringrevitmep2015`. Next, do the following:

1. Open the Sanitary view and make sure that you have your view range set correctly because you are going to be routing pipes below 0′-0″ (0 mm). Select View Range from the Properties palette, and change Bottom and View Depth to Unlimited for your lowest-floor views, as shown in Figure 15.21. A good starting point for upper-floor view ranges is –3′-0″ (–1 m). (This setting will vary according to your project.)
2. Look at your routing choices for your main. Then locate your end run fixture, floor clean-out, or wall clean-out.
3. Locate your sanitary point of connection (POC) outside the building. Locate the sanitary piping at –4′-0″ (–1.2 m), below the finished floor.

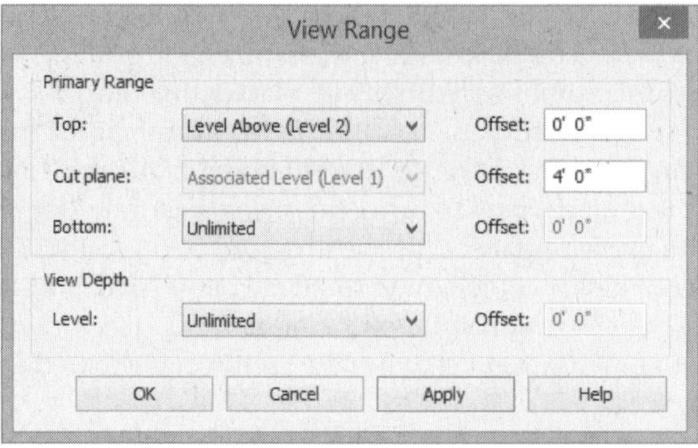

FIGURE 15.21 View Range settings

4. Select the Pipe toolbar located on the Systems tab of the ribbon. Before you start routing your pipe, be sure to select Slope Up, as shown in Figure 15.22, and set the Slope Value to 1/8″ / 12″ [25 degrees]. Make sure you have the justification set to your preference. You can also enable the Show Slope tooltip, which would display Start Offset, Current Offset, and Slope right next to your cursor as you draw your pipes.

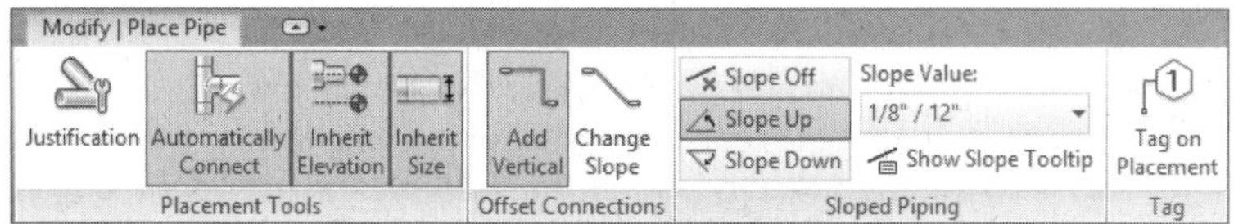

FIGURE 15.22 Recommended settings for drawing nonsloping pipe layouts

5. Start your run from the sanitary point of connection, and route into your last fixture or clean-out. You now have a main trunk off of which you can build your system.

SLOPED PIPE SYSTEMS ARE LIKE TREES

When you are routing sloped pipe systems, think about sketching a tree—starting from the base of the tree, working from the base to the branches, and then from the branches to the leaves or, in this case, a water closet. The secret to successfully modeling sloped pipe is to draw your piping from the main first.

6. Select the Pipe toolbar, and then select the point on the main from which you want to route. After starting your pipe run, you can select the Inherit Elevation and Inherit Size buttons from the toolbar, as shown in Figure 15.23, or you can press the spacebar one time. This makes the new piping connect at the same elevation and size as the pipe main you selected to start the run. Then route out to the water closets or any other components that take a 1/8″ [25 degree] slope.

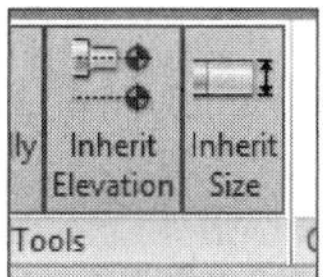

FIGURE 15.23 The Inherit Elevation and Inherit Size options

7. Route all of your sloped pipe that contains the same degree of slope first. Then route all of the next matching slope. Having a redundant pattern will add to your efficiency and productivity. Now you should have a sloped system (see Figure 15.24).

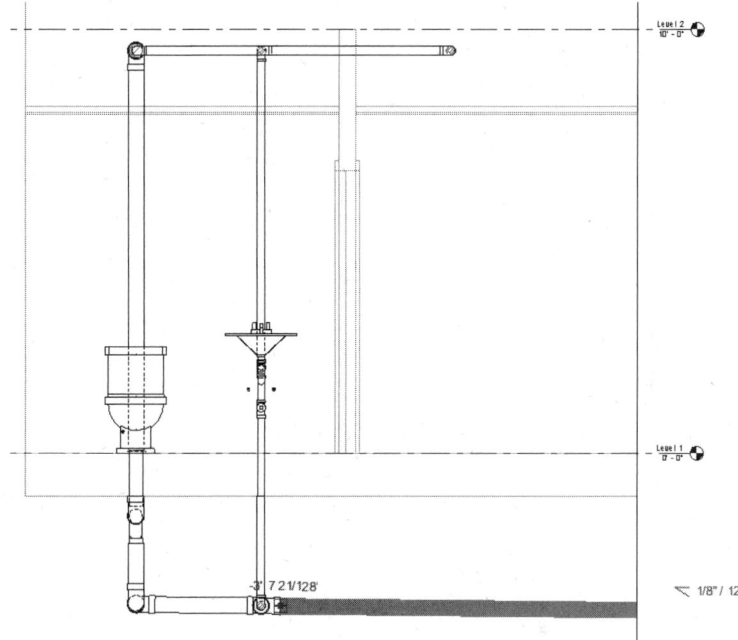

FIGURE 15.24 Sanitary layout with sloped piping

8. New to Revit MEP 2015 is the ability to choose whether you want to use Add Vertical or Change Slope when connecting from A to B (see Figure 15.25). This replaces the Ignore Slope To Connect option found in previous versions of Revit.

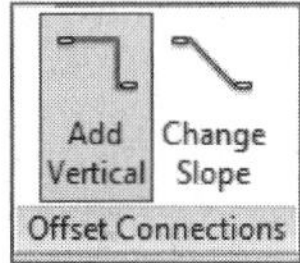

FIGURE 15.25 Add Vertical and Change Slope options

Annotating Invert Elevation and Slope

Once your piping model is at the desired slope and elevation, you can easily apply parametric elevation and slope annotations. Choose Annotate ➢ Dimension ➢ Spot Slope or Spot Elevation. The slope tag is very simple; it can be placed at any point along a pipe run while you're viewing single- or double-line pipe.

The elevation tag is more complicated. The Spot Elevation tag can show only the top and/or bottom elevation of the pipe selected. You must be able to see double-line pipe (Fine Detail) in order to place the Spot Elevation tag. This tag exists only within the project. It is a system family, and it cannot be edited in the Family Editor. This means that all changes are done in the Properties and Type Properties palettes within the project interface. In the Options Bar, you will want to make sure to set the elevation to reference the correct level. Also in the Options Bar, you should set the Display Elevations option to either Bottom Elevation or Top And Bottom Elevation. In the Type Properties dialog box, you will likely want to change the Units Format value and the Display Elevations format to match your standard for labeling pipe elevation—for example, B.O.P. = bottom of pipe (see Figure 15.26).

If you prefer to annotate the elevation of the pipe centerline, you will have to use a pipe tag. This is the same type of annotation family as the common pipe diameter tag. You can duplicate and edit that family to change the label to include the parameters Start Offset and End Offset. Note that these parameters can display the elevations of only the two endpoints of each pipe segment. Like the Spot Elevation tag, they cannot display the elevation at any point along the pipe segment.

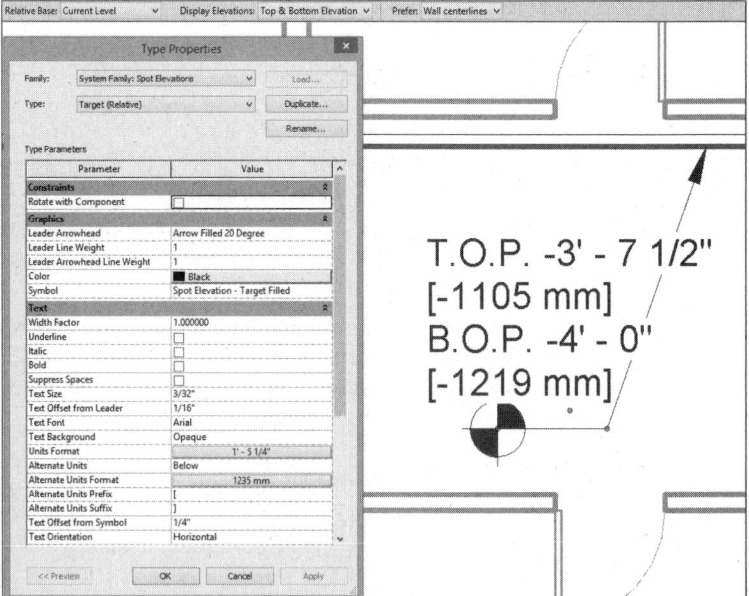

FIGURE 15.26
Customizing the Spot Elevation tag

Using Fittings

Without fittings, piping would not be worth a whole lot. Fittings help shut off, regulate, and open up flow of fluid in systems—and, most important, save lives. In Revit, most fitting families have the following functions:

End Cap These can be placed only at the end of pipe.

Tee, Tap, Wye, and Cross These can be placed anywhere along pipe runs.

Transitions, Couplings, and Unions These can be placed only at the end of pipe. They are used to join a smaller, larger, or same-size pipe.

Flange These can be placed at the end of pipe or face to face with another flange.

Using Pipe Fitting Controls

Understanding pipe fitting controls can really make life easier if you are routing a lot of piping. When you are laying out your piping, turn 90 degrees to create an elbow. If you click the elbow, you will notice a plus (+) sign. If you click that sign, it will change from an elbow to a tee, allowing you to add more piping and to continue your pipe routing. If you select the minus (–) sign, it will downgrade the fitting. When you see the symbol on a fitting, it allows you to rotate the fitting, and the symbol allows you to flip the fitting.

Placing Valves

When you need to add valves to your piping, select the Home tab and click Pipe Accessories. Use the Type Selector to select the type and size of valve you want to use. Most valves will *break into* the piping and connect as you simply select a piece of pipe (see Figure 15.27).

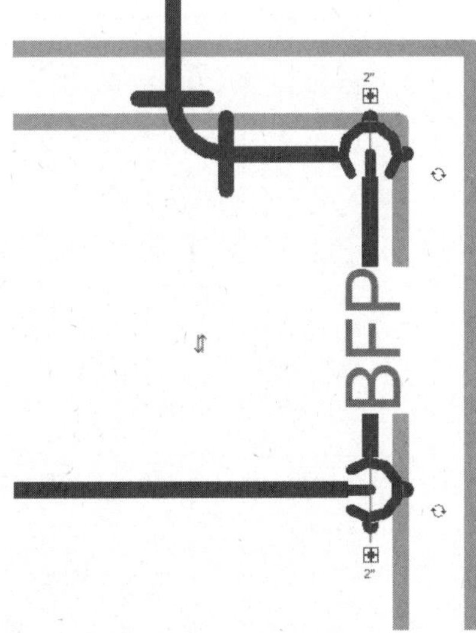

FIGURE 15.27
A fitting breaks into the piping system.

Real World Scenario

A Fitting End

In early 2008, an AEC firm from Knoxville, Tennessee, was working on a hotel project in Pigeon Forge, Tennessee. It was the first hotel produced in Revit for this firm. This work for a 90-room hotel had already gone over the estimated projected design hours because of constant changes of field conditions.

The building used conventional sanitary plumbing with traditional multiple-vent stacks. The project went out for bid, and when the bids came back, the building was slightly over the estimated budget. The design team was asked to figure a way to reduce the costs back to the budgeted amount. After carefully reviewing the project, the plumbing designer and engineer decided to use a PVC version of a Sovent plumbing system. Only two families would have to be created for Revit: an aerator and a de-aerator fitting. The cast-iron version of the system has been successfully used in northern parts of the United States in high-rise design for years.

The problem the plumbing designer faced with using such a system was that no one had installed one in eastern Tennessee. Plumbing code officials had never seen the system installed, and they stated it did not meet traditional methods of vent design. By using a section under codes that allowed for the use of engineered plumbing systems, the design team proceeded to design the system. Because the existing layout was already in Revit, using it to redesign the system was the logical choice.

Within two working days, the model and contract documents were revised with the new layout, which was then rebid. The cost of the vent system was reduced by one-third, which led to fewer holes being cut, fewer man-hours, and reduced fire-stopping costs. Because the plumbing contractor had never before installed a Sovent system, being able to use printouts of the 3D model helped speed up the installation of the system and ensure that it was installed properly.

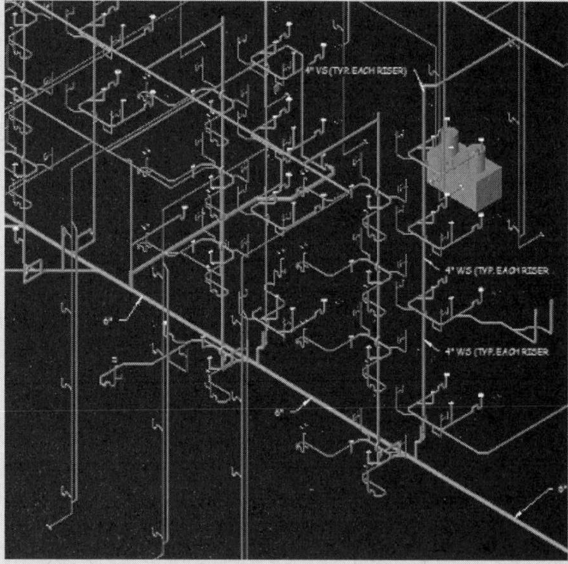

Although the project may have lost money for the firm, the hotel owner was happy knowing that his construction costs were within budget and that his hotel could open on time.

The Bottom Line

Configure plumbing views. Learning the proper way to set up your template will ensure a consistent graphical representation across projects and improve efficiency.

Master It When you are setting up your project/template views, where would you control the linetypes and colors of pipe systems?

Customize out-of-the-box Revit plumbing fixtures for scheduling purposes. Out-of-the-box plumbing fixtures (or any other equipment for that matter) do not have all the necessary parameters to complete a typical plumbing schedule.

Master It What would you need to do in order to create a plumbing fixture schedule?

Adjust the plumbing pipe settings. Pipe settings are crucial to the ability to have Revit MEP model your plumbing layout, the way it will look, and the way it will perform.

Master It Do fitting parameters have to be set up in the system pipe types?

Select the best pipe routing options for your project. When using Revit MEP 2015 for your plumbing layouts, you must understand the functions of automatic pipe routing, manual pipe routing, and sloping pipe. Once you master these functions, you can lay out any type of piping system.

Master It A plumbing designer has just been asked to lay out a sloped plumbing system and has only a day to pipe up a clubhouse. Where should the designer start the pipe route?

Adjust pipe fittings. Pipe fittings are needed in systems to make the systems function properly and to produce documentation for construction. Being able to add or modify fittings can increase productivity.

Master It You have just finished your modeled layout and have given it to your employer for review. Your boss asks you to remove a couple of elbows and replace them with tees for future expansion. What would be your method to accomplish this quickly?

Chapter 16

Fire Protection

Fire-protection designers use a variety of methods and software programs to lay out fire-protection systems. In the Autodesk® Revit® MEP 2015 software, fire protection is probably one of the least mentioned features. However, there are considerable benefits to performing this process in Revit MEP, including coordination and clash detection with other services and building elements.

In this chapter, you will learn to do the following:

- Place fire-protection equipment
- Create fire-protection systems
- Route fire-protection piping

Understanding the Essentials of Placing Fire-Protection Equipment

Proper planning in placing fire-protection equipment is essential when trying to create a productive layout with Revit MEP 2015. You should plan to have most of your equipment roughly located during the schematic design phase of the project, which helps with productivity and coordination with other disciplines. You need to use proper design methods to verify whether a fire pump is required on a project.

Although pump manufacturers are starting to provide Revit content, they are still few and far between. If you look under Imperial Library ➤ Fire Protection, you will find several components that can be used out of the box for fire protection. Others can be found as mechanical or piping components. For example, the backflow preventer is located under Imperial Library ➤ Pipe ➤ Valves ➤ Backflow Preventers.

Point of Connection

You should start your model by understanding where your water supply starts. Normally, a civil engineer provides location details. There is no special need for a model element to represent this *point of connection (POC)*. You can simply begin drawing pipe at the appropriate location. However, you may want something to help identify this POC. You can display this information in your design model by either creating a water meter family or modifying an end cap family. To modify an existing family to indicate the water inlet point, do the following:

1. Open the `Ch16_Dataset.rvt` file found at `www.sybex.com/go/masteringrevitmep2015`.
2. In the Project Browser, scroll down to the Families section, expand the Pipe Fittings category, and select Cap – Generic.

3. Right-click the family and select Edit. This opens the Family Editor.
4. Click the Revit Home button and choose Save As ➤ Family. Save this family as **`Fire Protection Point of Connection.rfa`** in your office's custom family folder.
5. Edit the newly created family by changing the family type from Pipe Fitting to Mechanical Equipment, located under Modify ➤ Properties ➤ Family Categories And Parameters.
6. This family may also be a convenient tool for tracking pressure and flow. To do this, select Family Types and add three new parameters: **Static Pressure**, **Residual Pressure**, and **Gallons Per Minute**.

   When creating these new parameters, be sure to use the piping discipline and appropriate units. Also, because you will want to either tag or schedule the data contained in these parameters, you need to use shared parameters. (See Chapter 6, "Parameters," for more information.) You can leave the end cap the way it is modeled, or you can use model lines with an ellipse to create a break line symbol that shows up in single-line piping, as shown in Figure 16.1. After drawing the model lines, select them and change the Family Element Visibility Settings options to not show the lines in fine detail (usually reserved for double-line piping). To do this, choose Properties ➤ Graphics ➤ Visibility/Graphic Overrides, and then in the dialog box that opens, click the Edit button. In the next dialog box, deselect the Fine check box.

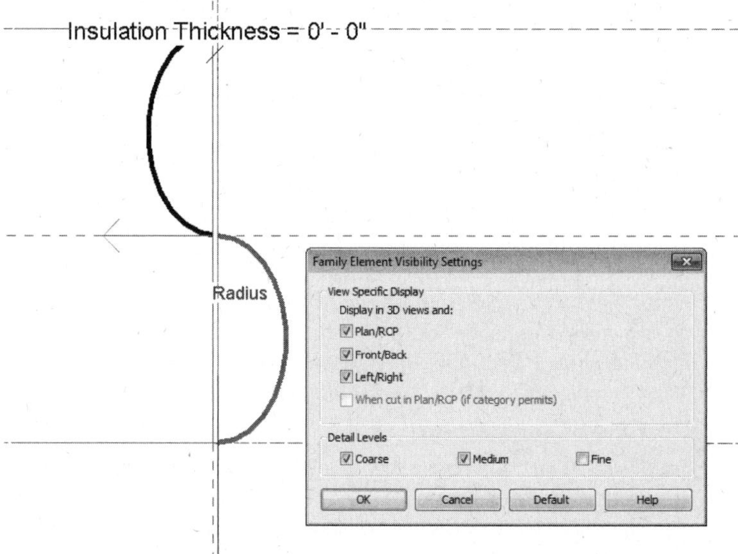

FIGURE 16.1 Fire-protection point of connection

7. Select the pipe connector, and change its system classification from Fitting to Fire Protection Wet and change the flow direction to Out. Map the flow to the Gallons per Minute parameter you created.
8. Delete any undesired existing linework.

FLOW DIRECTION

In our POC family, the pipe connector flow direction is set to Out because water flows *out* of the water meter/POC and *in* to the pipe. Conversely, water flows *out* of the pipe and *in* to each fire sprinkler, so the flow direction for the pipe connector in a sprinkler family should be set to In.

Fire Pump Assembly

You should try to preassemble as many of the fire-protection components as possible to help reduce production time. Figure 16.2 shows a fire pump preassembled so that you would have to change out only certain components—for example, changing the pump for a smaller or larger pump, depending on what is called for by the calculated fire flow demand.

FIGURE 16.2 Preassembled fire pump

To create a preassembled fire pump, do the following:

1. Save a Revit file named **`pump assembly model.rvt`**.
2. Connect as much of the pump assembly as possible, taking into account where most of the components will likely be placed. You can use a split-case pump that comes with Revit MEP as your base fire pump. This normally gives a large enough footprint after every piece has been assembled, but always verify the size of the equipment with the manufacturer's cut sheets to keep from making a costly mistake.

   You can use an inline pump to represent a jockey pump because it matches closely in size. The inline pump is located under Imperial Library ➢ Mechanical Components ➢ Water Side Components ➢ Pumps.

   It may be hard to find Revit families to represent the control panels. For these, you can create a family by using an electrical equipment family type. Another option for showing the control panel is to model it temporarily as an in-place component to help with space planning (see Figure 16.3).

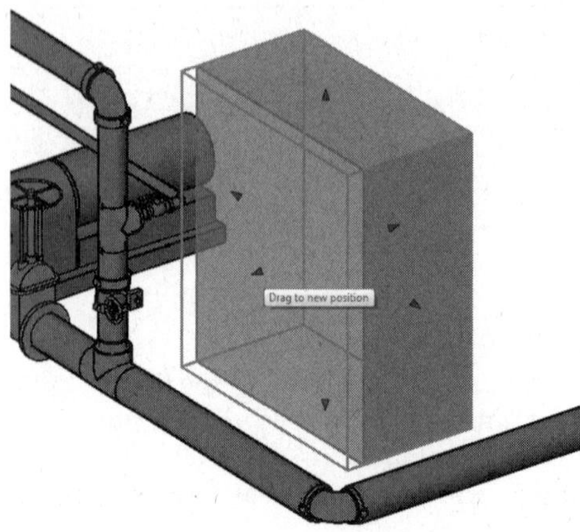

Figure 16.3
In-place component

This component would be used as a placeholder to ensure that the control panel is accounted for. Usually, the electrical engineer documents the detailed panel information apart from your fire-protection model.

3. Once you have your layout the way you want it, save the model for future use by selecting the elements required and clicking Create Group. When prompted for a name, be sure to give it a suitable one—for example, **Fire Alarm Pump Set**, not Group 130.

4. Modify the group insertion point and then save the group as a library group. This assembly can then be loaded as a model group, be linked and then bound, or even simply copied and pasted.

   Using the link method gives far more flexibility when positioning this object—as long as it is subsequently bound to allow access to the connections. Be aware that any hosted families used in this process lose their associated host.

   The copy-and-paste method gives you a warning for any hosted elements because of the lost association. Even though the individual elements' hosting association is lost, they retain their location properties correctly.

   The two preceding example methods—either creating a group of a standard layout or copying and pasting—provide the most effective way to apply common layouts across projects. Similar results may be achieved with a single complex family, but perhaps it won't provide the necessary flexibility to accommodate the project specifics.

Fire Riser Assembly

Fire risers for most small projects are assembled from the same basic parts. The ideal way to handle assemblies like this is to create them as a mechanical equipment family. This lets you place a single family quickly during schematic design. The placement of the fire riser is crucial for understanding where the fire line needs to be routed and for space planning within the building. This family can be constructed from nested valve and fitting families along with extruded solids to indicate pipes (see Figure 16.4).

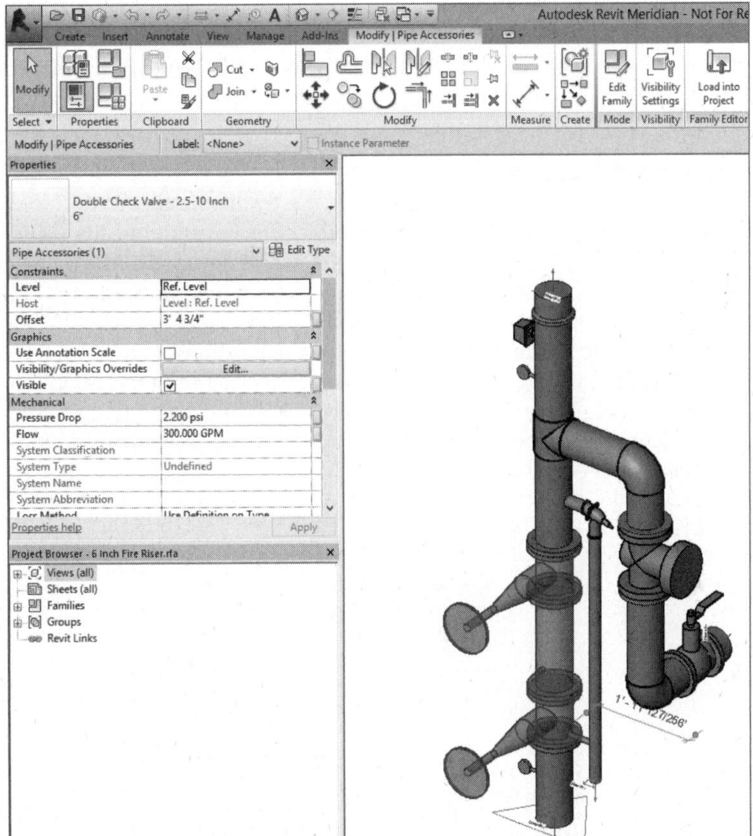

FIGURE 16.4
Fire riser assembly

To review what components make up this family, do the following:

1. Open `6 Inch Fire Riser.rfa` located at `www.sybex.com/go/masteringrevitmep2015`.
2. Several pipe fitting and pipe accessory families are nested into this family and make up the riser. They are as follows: `Pipe Elbow.rfa`, `Pipe Tee.rfa`, `Alarm Pressure Switch.rfa`, `Ball Valve - 2.5-6 Inch.rfa`, `Check Valve - 2-12 Inch - Flanged .rfa`, `Double Check Valve - 2.5-10 Inch.rfa`, `Multi-Purpose Valve - Angle - 1.5-2.5 Inch - Threaded.rfa`, and `Plug Valve - 0.5-2 Inch.rfa`. You can insert these from the `Pipe Fitting and Pipe Accessories` directory located in the imperial library.
3. Because system piping cannot be routed in the Family Editor, you need to create extrusions for the piping sections and then add the fire-protection connectors. When adding

the connectors, make sure the arrows point in the direction of the pipe to be connected and that the flow direction is set correctly.

By assembling the riser as a single family, you can coordinate the location in which it is being installed and then start planning how to route your piping. This family does not need to be parametrically flexible. The assembly will still speed your production for future projects even if it needs to be edited manually for different sizes and configurations.

Sprinkler Heads

Now that you know about fire pump assemblies and how to create a standard fire riser, you can start planning for the type of fire-protection sprinkler heads you need to use for your model. Revit MEP 2015 has several types of sprinkler heads from which you can choose. The different family types of sprinkler heads are hosted and nonhosted.

Hosted sprinkler heads are normally face-based families. When using these types of families, you need to locate them on a surface. The locations depend on the installation and the type of sprinklers, which could be wall, ceiling, slab, or soffit mounted. The surfaces can be part of the linked architectural model or reference planes defined within your fire-protection model.

Nonhosted sprinkler families must have the Offset height parameter set to locate the heads at the proper elevation (see Figure 16.5).

FIGURE 16.5 Nonhosted sprinkler heads

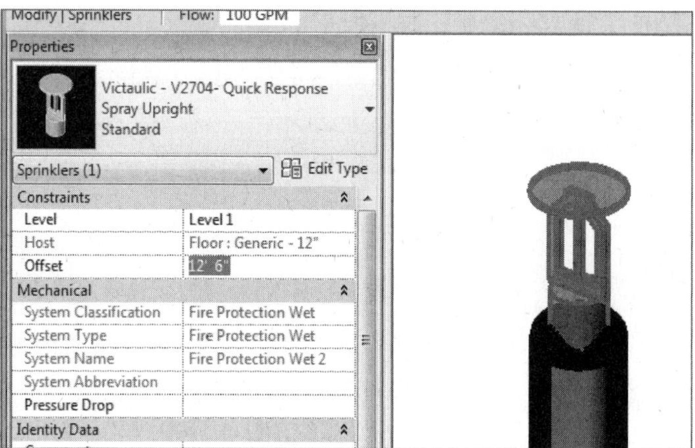

Upright sprinkler heads are normally nonhosted because they are located in spaces that do not have ceilings, such as storage rooms or mechanical closets. If you do not set the offset height, the heads will come in at a default of 0″ (0 mm), which could locate the heads on or below the floor level. This is easily fixed by clicking the button to place a sprinkler and changing the Offset setting in the Properties palette before placing the family.

Creating Fire-Protection Systems

You can create several types of fire-protection systems. They are as follows:

Fire Protection This can be used for the building's sprinkler piping, or it can be used for the utility fire protection coming into your building to connect the base of your fire-protection riser.

Wet Fire Protection This pipe system type is normally used for the layout of the piping from the riser to the sprinkler head when freezing is not expected.

Dry Fire Protection This pipe system type is normally used for the layout of the piping from the riser to the sprinkler head when there is potential for damage from freezing.

Preaction This pipe system can also be used for a deluge system.

Fire Protection Other This pipe system can be used for a glycol antifreeze system, and it can also be used for a chemical suppression system.

You can also refer to piping systems in Chapter 11, "Mechanical Piping," for more information. When creating a fire-protection system, one thing to remember is that the system does not calculate and autosize as it does for domestic water systems. The main reason is that fire-protection systems have no true way of selecting and calculating which heads are in the highest demand.

Real World Scenario

STRENGTH IN NUMBERS

John's employer has just come back from a meeting with a high-profile client who is seeking a fire-protection model in BIM. The client wants to see the total flow for the highest demand on the system so their building can pass fire-inspection requirements as mandated by the local fire marshal. John has already calculated the system load, so he knows where the highest demand will be located. He decides that the easiest way to accomplish this is to set the Comments parameter to calc-gpm for the sprinkler heads and then filter these heads through a schedule with a grand total of gallons per minute (GPM). After reviewing John's work, the inspector approved the client's building, and the client was satisfied.

To replicate what John did, you can do the following:

1. Select the sprinkler heads that need to be modified, and set the Comments parameter to calc-gpm.

Continues

Continued

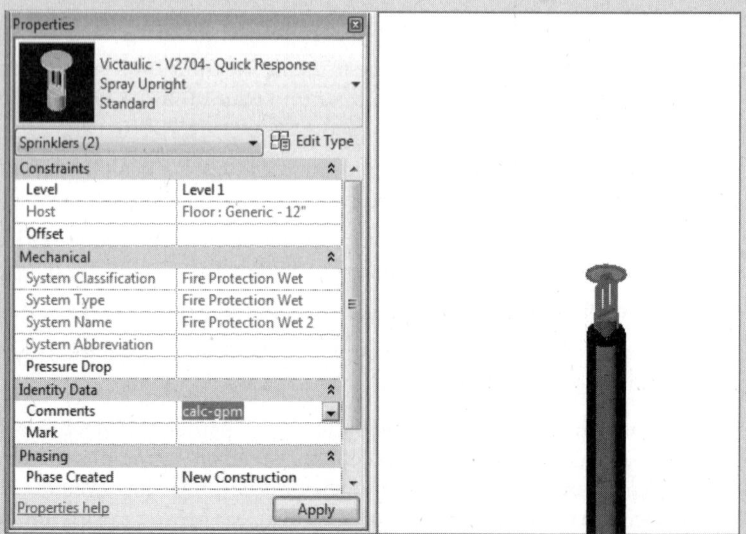

2. Go to the View or Analyze tab on the ribbon, and then select Schedule/Quantities. The New Schedule dialog box opens. Select Sprinklers from the Category group, and then click OK.

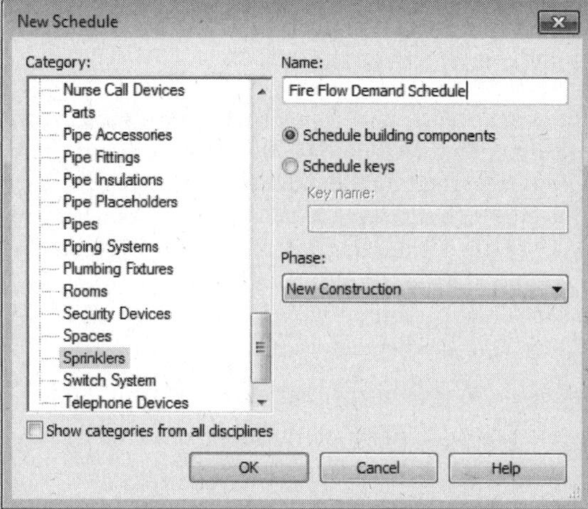

3. From the Available Fields dialog box, select the parameters Flow and Comments, and add them to the Schedule Fields (In Order) dialog box. Then click OK, which creates your schedule.

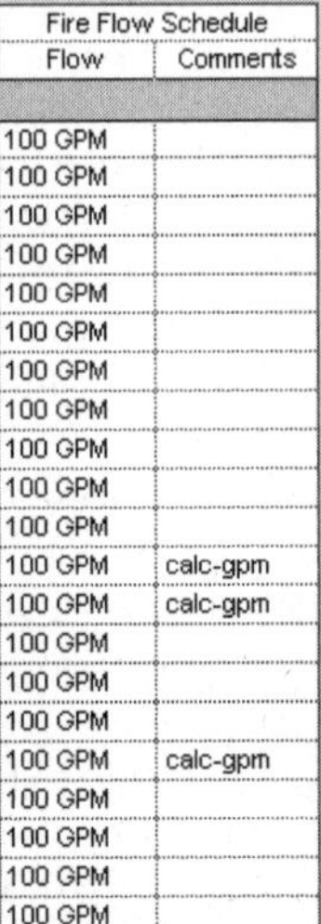

Fire Flow Schedule	
Flow	Comments
100 GPM	
100 GPM	
100 GPM	
100 GPM	
100 GPM	
100 GPM	
100 GPM	
100 GPM	
100 GPM	
100 GPM	
100 GPM	
100 GPM	calc-gpm
100 GPM	calc-gpm
100 GPM	
100 GPM	
100 GPM	
100 GPM	calc-gpm
100 GPM	
100 GPM	
100 GPM	
100 GPM	

4. Now that you have the sprinkler schedule, you want to total only the sprinklers with comments. To do this, you have to set several parameters:
   a. From the Properties Browser, select the Filter tab and then change the filter to Comments.
   b. Set the Equals parameter to calc-gpm.
   c. Select Sorting/Grouping, and change the Sort By pull-down menu to Comments.
   d. Select Itemize Every Instance.
   e. Select the check box Grand Totals and change the drop-down menu to Totals Only.
   f. Select the Formatting tab, highlight Flow, and select the Calculate Totals check box. Next, highlight Comments, and select Hidden Fields.

Now your schedule will show only the items you want to appear, including the total GPM flow.

100 GPM
100 GPM
100 GPM
300 GPM

If the system were to try to calculate by GPM, it would account for every sprinkler head on the system, which would grossly oversize the system. Also, the fire-protection system at this time has no effective way of calculating the water pressure as it goes higher in elevation.

Creating a Fire-Protection Wet System

When creating a fire-protection wet system or one of the systems previously mentioned, you would first select all the components that are going to be associated with that system. Selecting these items may be easier if you use the Temporary Hide/Isolate command to hide the model categories that you do not want to include. Select Hide Category to do this (see Figure 16.6). You can also use the feature Selection Sets to remember the selected items for future usage. After you have selected all components that you want, simply click the Save button from the Selection panel located under the Modify | Multi-Select tab. When nothing is selected, you can find the tool under the Manage tab.

In case a system has already been started, you can add to it by selecting a component on the system. Click Piping Systems ➢ Edit System ➢ Add To System, and then window all the items you want to add to the system. If this is done correctly, you should see all the items in the System Browser under the system you created (see Figure 16.7). As of Revit MEP 2014, the sprinkler heads can also be added to the system automatically as they are connected by the pipework. This can be an easier way to create the systems because you don't have to organize the systems manually before you start drawing the pipework. However, it also means you need to act with extra caution because systems can disappear without warning if connected in the wrong way.

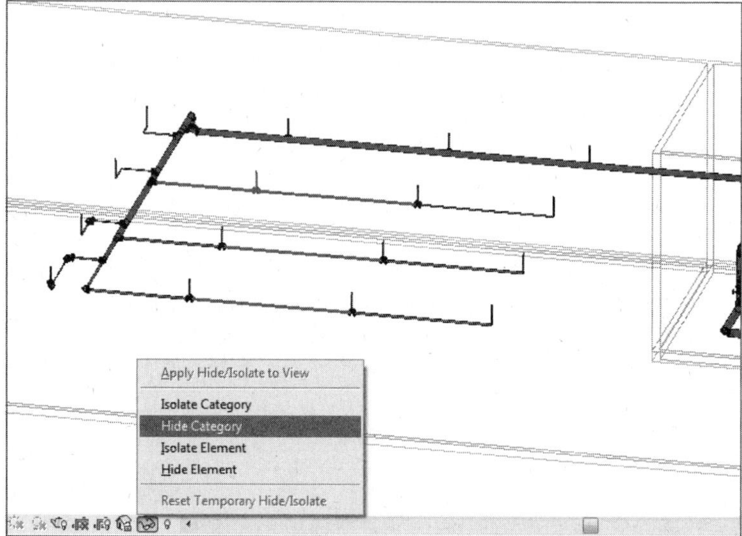

FIGURE 16.6
Adding sprinkler heads to a system

Filtering Fire-Protection Systems

Once your fire-protection system is created, you need to make sure the piping will filter correctly. You can use filters to separate the fire-protection pipes from all other pipes in your Revit model. This assists you with turning off all other pipes from the fire-protection views and sheets.

For controlling the linetypes and line colors of your systems, you should use piping systems, located in the Project Browser under Families. From the piping systems properties, you can assign the color, linetype, and system abbreviation for your systems. From the same dialog box, you can also disable the flow calculations for your fire systems if they are not required. This increases your Revit project performance and does not waste system resources on computing systems' flow data that may not be important to you.

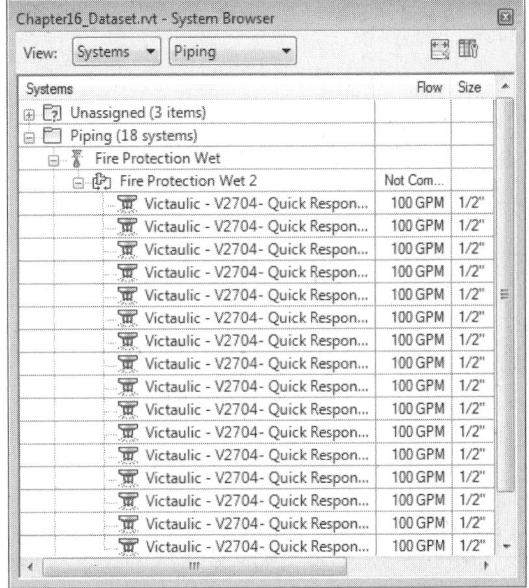

FIGURE 16.7
Fire-protection system in the System Browser

The main benefit of using this relatively new method of controlling your colors and linetypes vs. using the old method of filters is that the settings are global and apply to all views. You still need to manage filters in order to control what systems are visible in what views. But at least when you cut a section or go to a 3D view, all of your components that are already connected to a system will be displaying the appropriate colors and linetypes, without the need to apply a view template.

To create a fire-protection filter, do the following:

1. On the View tab, choose Graphics ➤ Filters. The default keyboard shortcut VG takes you to the same location.

2. Click Edit/New. The Filter Settings dialog box opens. You should notice that several filters are already created. Select the Domestic Hot Water filter, right-click, and select Duplicate. Right-click again, and rename the filter to the type of piping system you are filtering. In the right corner, you will see a section named Filter Rules.

    a. If you want all fire-protection systems in your project to be displayed the same, keep the Filter By parameter set to System Classification. The filter rule should be set to Contains, and the data required is **Fire Protection**. Make sure that you correctly capitalize all words in the text field.

    b. If you want to have the option to change the display of various types of fire-protection systems within your project, change the rule from System Classification to System

Abbreviation. The System Abbreviation rule must be unique to every system and therefore can be used for creating your filters and separating one system from another. The filter rule should be set to Equals, and the text field must match the System Abbreviation exactly (see Figure 16.8).

FIGURE 16.8 Filtering by system abbreviation

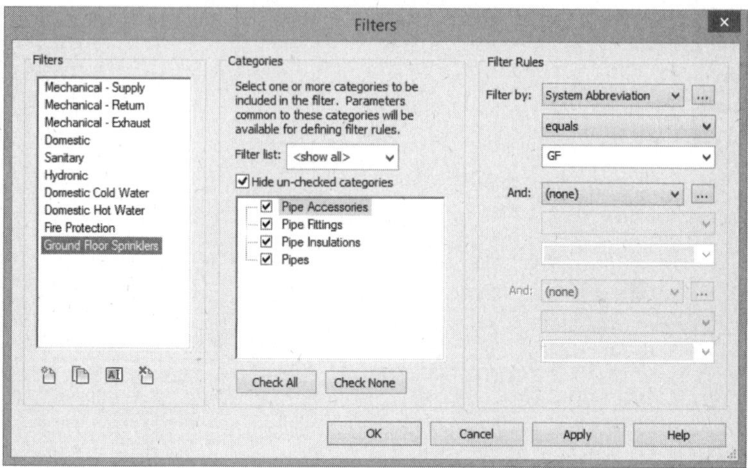

Now you will see the Visibility/Graphic Overrides dialog box open to the Filters tab. Click Add, and you should see the newly created filter (see Figure 16.9).

FIGURE 16.9 Using filters to override the graphic display

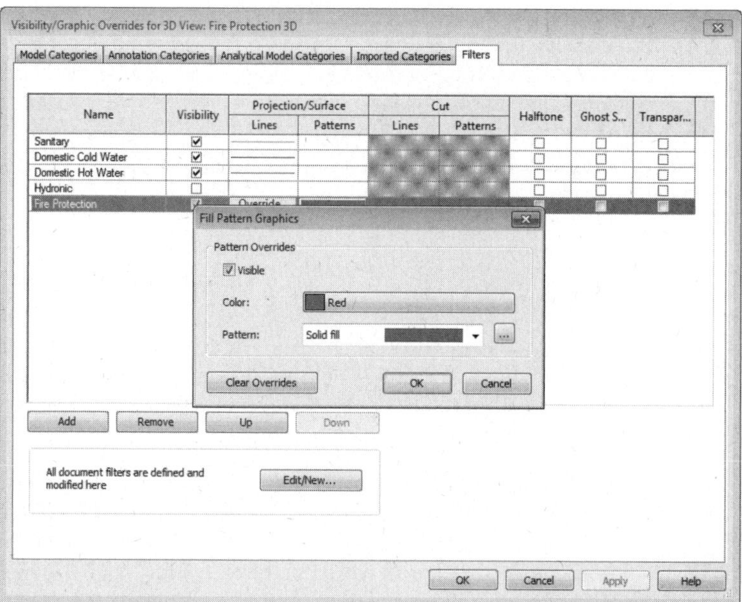

Using Mechanical Joint Fittings

So what do you do if you require special fittings? It's quite common to see mechanical joints required on fire-protection systems. Because they do not exist in the out-of-box content of Revit MEP 2015, you are stuck with three choices:

- You can use regular fittings and then copy and rename them to the type of fittings you need, as was demonstrated for the fire pump. Then you can use schedules to count the number and make of the fittings.
- You can create your own custom fittings. This requires that you have enough time and money to create every fitting you need. If you can afford it, this option is worth the investment in the long haul.
- You can find a manufacturer that has already developed their content. Victaulic has most, if not all, of their products in Revit on its website at `www.victaulic.com`. You can download them and load the fittings you need for your layout. No matter the source of your content, always take the time to test it to ensure that it works the way it should. Manufacturers that are starting to produce Revit content are looking to the industry for guidance. If you find something that doesn't work, let the manufacturer know.

COPYING THE LOOKUP TABLES

When downloading or developing your own fittings, be sure to copy the lookup tables into the lookup table folder called for by the `revit.ini` file. If you don't do this, the automatic adjustment of fittings may not work properly. You can also then embed these files into your family to enable them to be used without the lookup table being present.

Routing Piping and Adjusting Settings

Now you are nearly ready to route piping. There are still a number of pipe settings that will help you. Pipe systems and pipe types settings are important to adjust. Pipe material, the pipe sizing table, and the fluids table can also be altered as needed. These were explained previously in Chapter 11.

The various options for automatic and manual pipe routing were also discussed in Chapter 11. Unlike for mechanical piping or domestic and sanitary piping, automatic pipe routing is more likely to be a productive option. Fire-protection piping is often much more symmetrical than piping in other disciplines, making autorouting easier to manage. Refer to Chapter 11 to review both auto and manual pipe routing.

The Bottom Line

Place fire-protection equipment. When starting a fire-protection model, placing the equipment can make or break your design. The ability of Revit to verify your layouts early through the coordination of this equipment with other disciplines can set the pace for a successful project.

Master It What method can be used to help speed up production when using a standard fire riser on multiple buildings?

Create fire-protection systems. Content is one of the most critical aspects when taking on a Revit project. Fittings are the hardest families of all to make; finding some fittings that satisfy your company needs before starting a project is critical!

Master It What are your options for fire-protection fittings?

Route fire-protection piping. Fire-protection piping can be routed by a couple of methods. It can be set up with different materials to help with takeoffs and specifications. Once piping has been routed, it can be coordinated with other disciplines to reduce errors and omissions.

Master It What are some of the methods to deal with fittings that may not be supplied with Revit MEP 2015?

Part 5

Managing Content

Chapter 17

Solid Modeling

It may seem like being able to create solid models efficiently and effectively would be more appropriate for disciplines such as architecture and structural engineering. However, with these skills, you can create the types of components needed to convey your design accurately. MEP families such as pumps, condensers, valves, and even lighting fixtures can have very complex shapes or structures, and knowing how to create these objects with a minimum amount of effort is key to being productive while remaining accurate with your design.

Although MEP components are often complex, it is important to keep your families as simple as possible while still making them recognizable and useful. This does not mean that all of your objects should be boxes and cylinders, but it also does not mean that you should be modeling the rivets, screws, handles, and hinges either. As a general rule of thumb, if you can see something at a scale of 1⁄8″ = 1′-0″ (1:100), then model it; treat anything else as detailing. Of course, this is not a hard-and-fast rule, but as you become more proficient with the software, you will find a balance that works best for your workflow.

Knowing how to create solid model objects that are accurate to the specified components is as important as making them recognizable. Allowing for parametric changes will make your families universally applicable to your projects and design standards.

In this chapter, you will learn to do the following:

- Model solids and voids
- Orient geometry by using reference planes and lines
- Ensure the parametric change capability of models
- Determine optimal visibility settings for solids
- Create in-place Mass objects for analysis and documentation

Solids and Voids

The first step to success in creating solid model objects is to be able to think in 3D and to visualize the object you are attempting to create. It may be helpful to first sketch out the basic shapes needed to build the solids and voids that will make up a family. This will help you determine where to start and what the relationships between multiple solids will be. It can also help you understand how the object needs to be modeled in order for it to be used properly in your projects.

How you approach building a solid model may depend on the type of family you are creating. Face-hosted families are commonly used for MEP components, and when creating solids or voids in a face-hosted family, you need to consider their relationship to the host extrusion. The same is true for element-hosted families such as wall- or ceiling-mounted equipment. Building solid geometry in level-based families is similar when considering how the family will be placed into a project. Because the tools are the same in any type of family, a level-based environment will be used for most of the examples in this chapter, except when discussing relationships to hosts. Much of the work described in this chapter is done in the Family Editor environment.

IN-PLACE FAMILIES

Although the Autodesk® Revit® platform gives you the ability to create an in-place family directly in your projects, this feature should be used with care and, as a rule of thumb, only where unique objects are required. An example in the building services world is a custom duct transition, for which a standard, loadable family would not fit the bill. A complex plant area is one good example of where this could occur. Another would be loading a 3D DWG into an in-place family. This would give you the ability for interference-checking of the external data that would not exist if you just loaded that DWG file into Revit without the aid of the family container.

The availability of this feature can lead to display and feature anomalies if you happen to be collaborating with an architect or structural engineer. For example, if the architect models a wall in place, it cannot be copied/monitored in the MEP file and can have detrimental effects on the performance of all models. If possible, talk to the project architect and try to figure out a better solution for the project.

MEP families are usually distinct in their form and function, and component families can easily be found or created to represent equipment or fixtures, so the need to model in place can be reduced for MEP disciplines.

Extrusions

While you're working in the Family Editor, the Home tab of the ribbon contains the tools necessary for creating component families. The Forms panel of the Home tab holds the tools for building solid model geometry. In essence, all the tools are for creating extrusions; they just vary in their functionality. The Extrusion tool is the most commonly used because it is the most basic method for generating a solid. The idea behind creating a solid with the Extrusion tool is that you are going to sketch a profile and then extrude that profile to a defined depth.

When you click the Extrusion button on the Forms panel, the Modify | Create Extrusion contextual tab appears on the ribbon. This tab contains the tools needed to create the shape of the extrusion. The same drafting tools that are available for any common drafting task are available when you're sketching the shape for solid geometry. When you're working in sketch mode, the reference planes and any other graphics in the view will be displayed as a halftone, and the sketched linework will be magenta as a visual indicator that you are working in sketch mode.

The sketch you draw for the shape of an extrusion can be as simple as a circle or as complex as you can imagine. The most important thing is to create a closed loop with no intersecting lines. You will receive an error message if you attempt to finish a sketch that does not form a closed loop. The Error dialog box allows you to continue sketching so that you do not have to start over, or you can quit the sketch, which will discard the work done while in sketch mode and return you to the Family Editor.

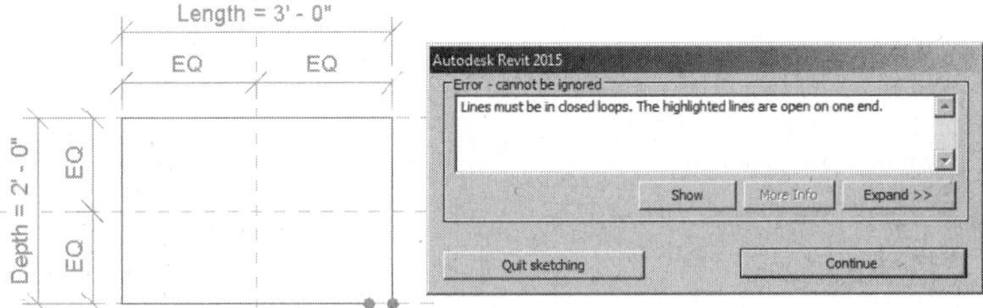

The sketch for an extrusion does not have to be a single, continuous set of lines. You can draw several shapes for a single extrusion as long as each shape is drawn in a closed loop. You cannot draw shapes that intersect each other. When you draw one shape inside another, Revit will extrude the area between the two shapes, as you can see in Figure 17.1, which shows one rectangle drawn inside another. This is a useful method for reducing the need for void geometry in a family. Autodesk recommends avoiding the use of too many voids in a family because this can adversely affect file performance.

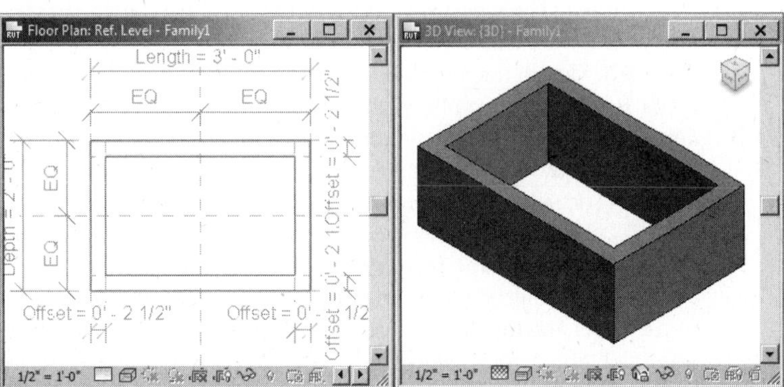

FIGURE 17.1
Multishape extrusion

As you are working in sketch mode, you can define the properties of the extrusion prior to completing the sketch. Your sketch will define the shape of the extrusion, but you also need to determine the distance of the third dimension for your solid geometry. The Depth setting on the Options Bar allows you to set the distance for the extrusion. Alternatively, you can use the Extrusion End and Extrusion Start parameters visible in the Properties palette while sketching, keeping in mind that these both reference the workplane of the extrusion. These values can be changed after the sketch is completed and the extrusion is made, but it is helpful to know the value prior to completing the sketch. The default value is 1′-0″ (300 mm), but if you change it, the value that you input will be used for the next extrusion, until you exit the Family Editor.

When you have completed the sketch for an extrusion, you must click the green check mark button on the Mode panel of the contextual tab in order to exit sketch mode and return to the Family Editor. If you want to cancel the creation of the extrusion, you can click the red X button on the Mode tab. If, during the process of sketching, you change the ribbon while in sketch mode, the contextual ribbon tab may disappear from view, which can lead to some confusion at first because the FinishEdit Mode button is not visible. Just remember (and this applies in all instances) that the active tab of the ribbon is always highlighted, so take a look back at the ribbon and simply select the correct tab.

You can edit the shape of an extrusion by clicking it and dragging the grips that appear at each shape handle of the solid geometry. This includes changing the depth of the extrusion, which can be done by editing it in a view perpendicular to the view in which the extrusion was sketched. Using grips for editing is an easy but inaccurate method for changing the shape of an extrusion. To apply specific dimensions, you can edit the sketch by clicking the Edit Extrusion button on the contextual Modify | Extrusion tab that appears when you select the extrusion in the drawing area. Clicking this button activates sketch mode and allows you to make changes to the shape handles of the geometry by using dimensional input.

Blends

A *blend* is solid geometry that comprises two profile sketches that can be different shapes, positions, and sizes. The approach to creating a blend is the same as for an extrusion, with an extra step for creating the shape for each end. When you click the Blend button on the Forms tab, sketch mode will be activated, and you can begin creating the shape for the base of the blend.

The base of the blend is the face of the solid geometry that is drawn on the reference plane with which the blend is associated. This is also referred to as First End in the properties of the blend. The sketch for the base geometry of a blend can contain only one closed loop.

Once you have completed the sketch for the base, you must click the Edit Top button on the Mode panel of the contextual tab. This will keep you in sketch mode, and the base geometry will be grayed out. You can sketch the geometry for the top of the blend anywhere in the drawing area. The solid geometry will be extruded to connect the base to the top along the depth distance and any distances in the X or Y direction. Figure 17.2 shows the result of a top sketch that is a different shape from that of the base geometry.

When you select a blend, the Modify | Blend contextual tab contains buttons that allow you to edit either the top or the base sketch by clicking the applicable button on the Mode panel. When you enter into sketch mode, you have the option to edit the other sketch if necessary by clicking the button on the Mode panel. You can also edit the vertices that are formed by the transition from the base shape to the top by clicking the Edit Vertices button.

The tools on the Edit Vertices tab of the ribbon, as shown in Figure 17.3, can be used to change how the transition occurs from the base shape to the top shape.

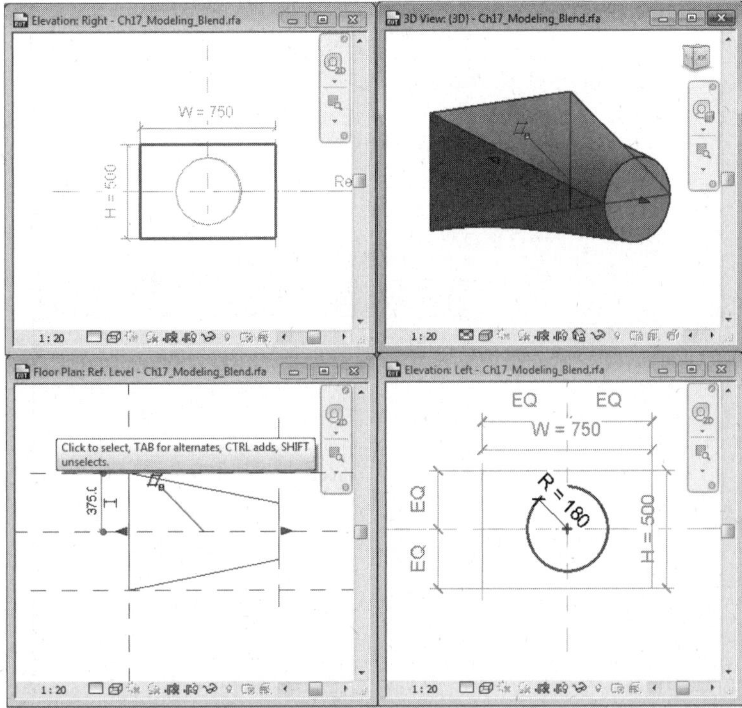

FIGURE 17.2
Blend with different sketches

Depending on the shapes you have drawn, there will be different options for the vertices that define the transition. When editing the vertices of a blend, you can twist the vertices left or right. It is possible to twist too far, but you will not be warned until you exit sketch mode. Grips appear on the blend that allow you to edit vertices manually. The open circle grip is for adding a vertex, while you can click the solid grip to remove the vertex on which it exists (see Figure 17.4). It is helpful to work in a 3D view when editing vertices because you can more clearly see the effect on the solid geometry. The Reset button on the Edit Vertices tab will return the orientation of the vertices to their original format.

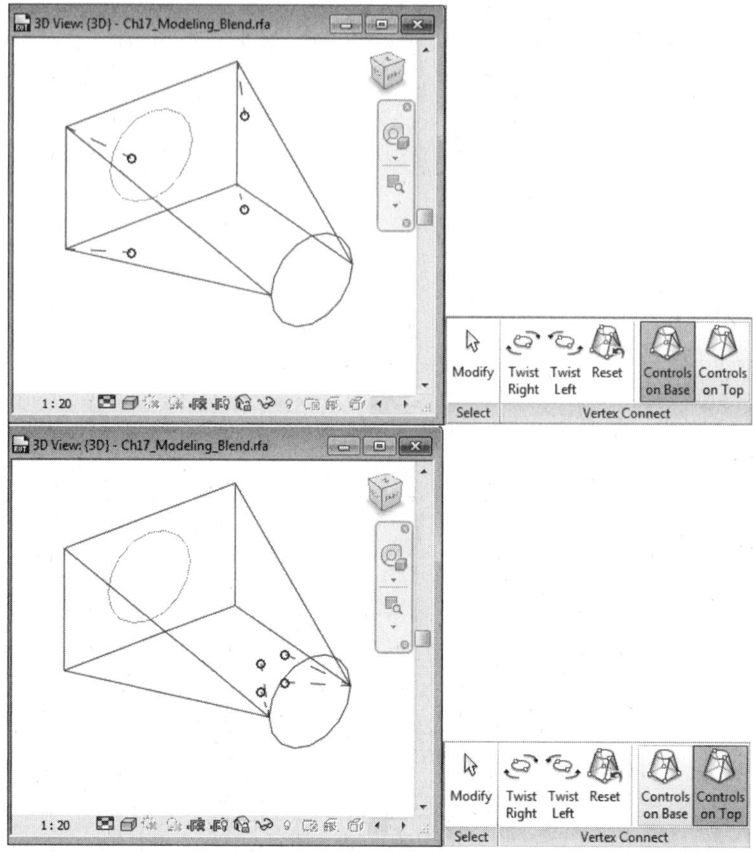

FIGURE 17.3
Editing vertices

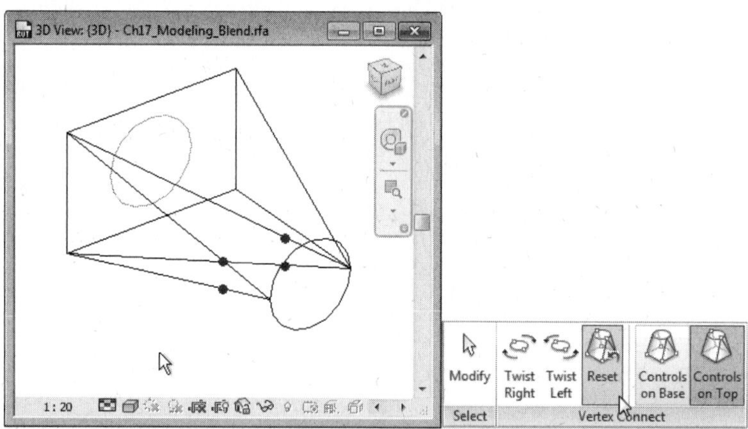

FIGURE 17.4
Vertex editing grips

Once you have finished editing the vertices of a blend, you must click the Modify button on the Edit Vertices tab to return to the sketch mode tab. As always, you must then click the green check mark button to exit sketch mode. The file Ch17_Modeling_Blend.rfa is provided as an example and can be found at www.sybex.com/go/masteringrevitmep2015.

Revolves

A *revolve* is a profile that spins around a specified axis. Using the Revolve tool allows you to create spherical solid geometry. You can start creating a revolve by clicking the Revolve button on the Home tab in the Family Editor. You can begin either by sketching the shape of the revolve or by selecting or creating the axis of rotation around which the shape will revolve. However, the profile must not cross over the axis. If it does, Revit will provide a warning indicating that it cannot make the form when the Finish Edit Mode button is selected.

The axis of rotation will always be perpendicular to the shape that you create, so it helps to first determine the orientation within the family of the shape you are creating. Once that has been determined, you will know where the axis needs to be and can switch to the appropriate view. For example, if you wanted to create a hemispherical solid that would lie flat when placed into a plan view, you would draw the axis perpendicular to the plan view. Switching to an elevation view in the Family Editor would allow you to draw the axis perpendicular to the plan. To do this, first define or select a workplane to host the axis line; this ensures that the profile is oriented correctly.

Clicking the Axis Line button on the Modify | Create Revolve contextual tab activates sketch mode with two drawing tools available in the Draw panel of the tab. You can either draw the axis or pick an existing line. The reference planes that determine the insertion point of a family are good choices for an axis line. Once you have drawn or selected an axis, you will remain in sketch mode, but the Draw panel will populate with the usual drawing tools for creating the shape of the revolve.

The shape of the revolve can be drawn anywhere in the view in which the axis is drawn. When you are sketching the shape of the revolve, you must create a closed loop or multiple closed loops. You can sketch shapes away from the axis to create an interior circular space within the solid geometry, as shown in Figure 17.5.

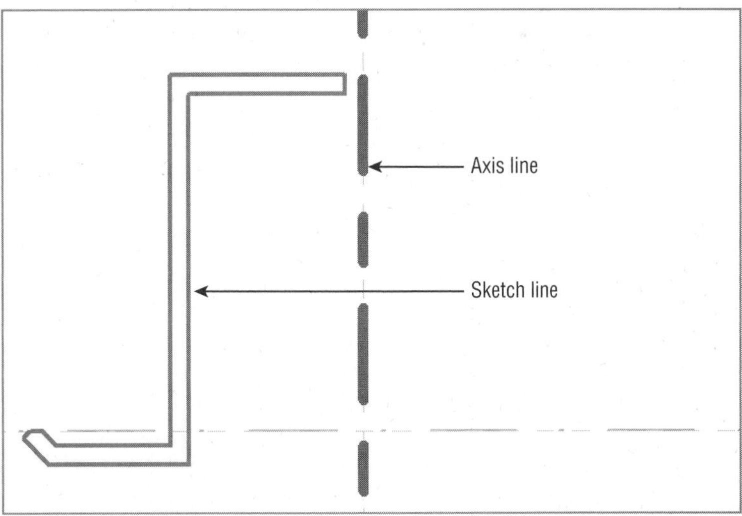

FIGURE 17.5
Revolve shape drawn away from the axis

When you have completed the shape, you can click the green check mark button to exit sketch mode. The shape will be extruded in a circular path around the axis, forming the solid geometry. Figure 17.6 shows the resulting solid geometry formed by the shape and axis shown in the previous figure.

FIGURE 17.6
Revolve solid geometry

To create a spherical shape with a revolve, draw an arc shape adjacent to the axis line. Because the shape must be a closed loop, you will have a shape line at the axis, but this line will not be seen because it will be in the interior of the solid geometry. Figure 17.7 shows the sketch of a simple hemisphere solid.

FIGURE 17.7
Hemisphere revolve sketch

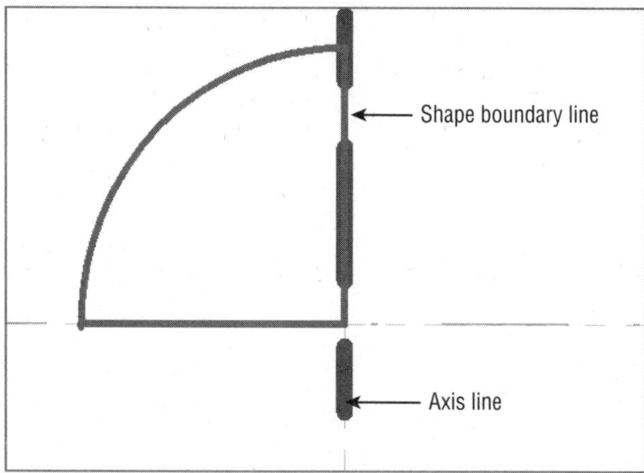

Unlike extrusions and blends, a revolve solid does not have a depth parameter. The depth or height of a revolve is determined by the sketch dimensions. A solid revolve has parameters that allow you to control how far around the axis the solid geometry is extruded.

Adjusting the Start Angle and End Angle parameters adds further complexity to a solid revolve shape. Figure 17.8 shows the effects of values used in the parameters on a solid hemispherical revolve. Once you edit the parameters in the Properties palette, you can use the grips to pull the faces of the geometry around the axis. You can also select the temporary dimension that appears and input a value.

FIGURE 17.8
Revolve parameters

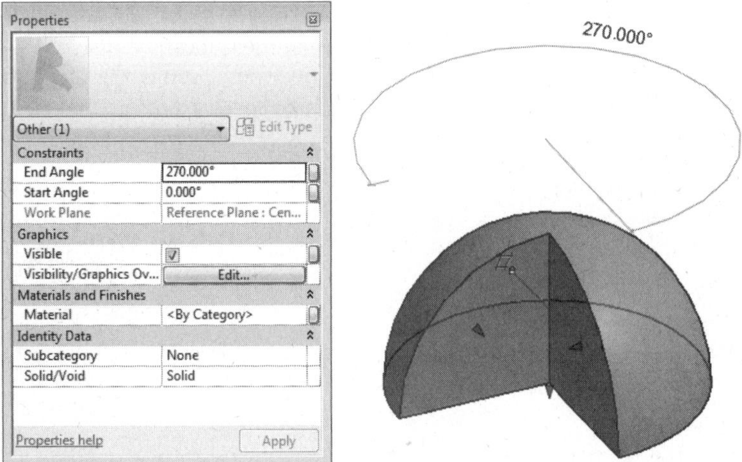

The files `Ch17_Modeling_Revolve1.rfa` and `Ch17_Modeling_Revolve2.rfa` are provided as examples and can be found at `www.sybex.com/go/masteringrevitmep2015`.

Sweeps

A *sweep* is an extrusion that follows a specified path. As with any solid geometry, it is important to first decide the orientation of the solid geometry within a family so that you can determine the location of the path for a sweep. When you click the Sweep button on the Home tab in the Family Editor, sketch mode is activated, and the contextual Modify | Sweep tab appears on the ribbon.

The first step in creating a solid sweep is to define the path of the extrusion. You can either sketch the path by using the standard drawing tools or pick existing lines in the family. You cannot pick reference planes as a path for a sweep. However, you can pick reference lines, because they have a set length. You can also use existing geometry, either solid or void form, as a host for the pick lines. This gives you much more flexibility, especially if the host is parametrically driven.

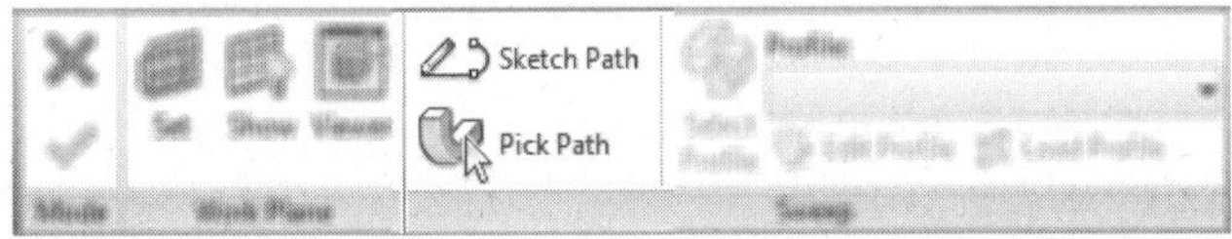

After creating the path for the sweep, you must click the green check mark button to exit sketch mode for the path. This returns you to sketch mode for the sweep geometry. With the path drawn, an origin and workplane indicator for the sketch profile location is shown on the path, as seen in Figure 17.9. The profile location indicator can be moved anywhere along the path while you're sketching the path by selecting the indicator and dragging it to the required location. This allows you to locate the profile parallel to a view plane, this will make sketching the profile easier. This is especially useful when creating paths that contain arcs because the profile may end up in the middle of an arc, at an angle that would be difficult to draw. The location of the profile plane will not have any effect on predefined profile families. For curved sweeps that do not display the profile in a regular view, it can be easier to sketch a small, straight segment prior to the curve. This will then give you a profile origin that does conform to a standard view. Once the profile is created, you can go back and delete the straight section of the path.

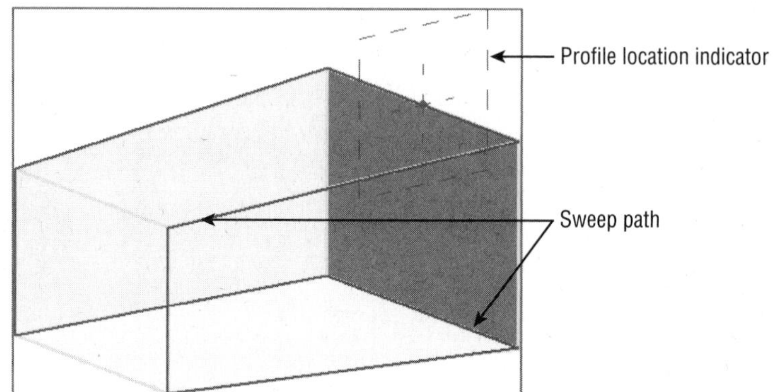

FIGURE 17.9
Sweep path and profile location

You can create the profile for the sweep by sketching, or you can select a predefined profile by clicking the Select Profile button on the Sweep panel of the Modify | Sweep contextual tab. When you click this button, any loaded profiles will be available in the drop-down list on the Sweep panel. If no profiles are available in the file in which you are working, you can click the Load Profile button on the Sweep panel. The content library that is loaded when you install Revit MEP 2015 contains a `Profiles` folder. From this folder, you can choose a predefined shape for use in your sweep geometry.

PROFILE FAMILIES

You can build a library of profiles that can be used when generating family geometry. This will allow you to maintain consistency in the way sweep geometry is generated. You can use the `Profile.rft` family template to create a profile family.

The profile for a sweep can be drawn in a view that is parallel to the profile location plane or in a 3D view where the path is visible. You can draw the profile in a plane that is perpendicular to the path but not parallel to the profile plane. This will cause an error when you attempt to complete the sweep by exiting sketch mode. The best option is to draw the profile in a plane that is both perpendicular to the path plane and parallel to the profile plane. When you select a predefined profile, it will automatically be placed in the profile plane.

Once you have chosen or created a profile for the sweep, you can click the green check mark button to exit sketch mode and complete the solid geometry. To make changes to a sweep, select the solid geometry and click the Edit Sweep button. You can modify the path by clicking the Sketch Path button, or you can modify the profile by clicking the Select Profile button and then the Edit Profile button, as shown in Figure 17.10.

FIGURE 17.10
Editing the profile

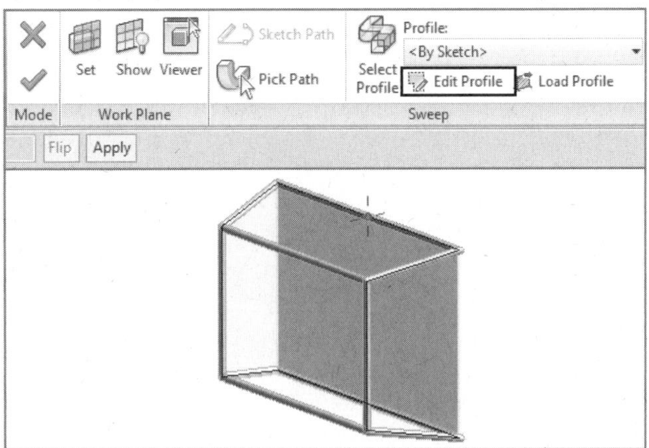

You cannot change the location of the profile plane after the profile has been created, so it is best to determine its location when creating the path for the sweep. This can be done by carefully planning the path because the location of the profile plane by default is the midpoint of the first line created in the path. Once the path has been created, the profile plane can be moved to the start, midpoint, or end of any segment of the path as long as this is done before the profile is sketched or selected; it cannot be changed afterward. The file `Ch17_Modeling_Sweep.rfa` is provided as an example and can be found at `www.sybex.com/go/masteringrevitmep2015`.

Swept Blends

A *swept blend* is a combination of a sweep solid and a blend solid. This tool allows you to create a sweep that has two profiles, one at each end of a single segment path. The solid geometry will transform from the shape of the first profile to the shape of the second profile along the path.

The process for creating a swept blend is similar to that of creating a sweep, with an extra step for defining the shape of the second profile. When you click the Swept Blend button on the Home tab in the Family Editor, sketch mode is activated, and you can draw or pick a path for the extrusion to follow. When you draw a path line, the first profile location will be at the start of the line, and a second profile location will be placed at the end of the line.

You cannot use multiple lines to create a path for a swept blend because the profile plane for the second profile occurs at the end of the first line drawn and any additional lines drawn afterward cannot be included in the path; you will receive an error, as indicated in Figure 17.11. This is also true if you use the Pick Path option. You can select only one line for the path.

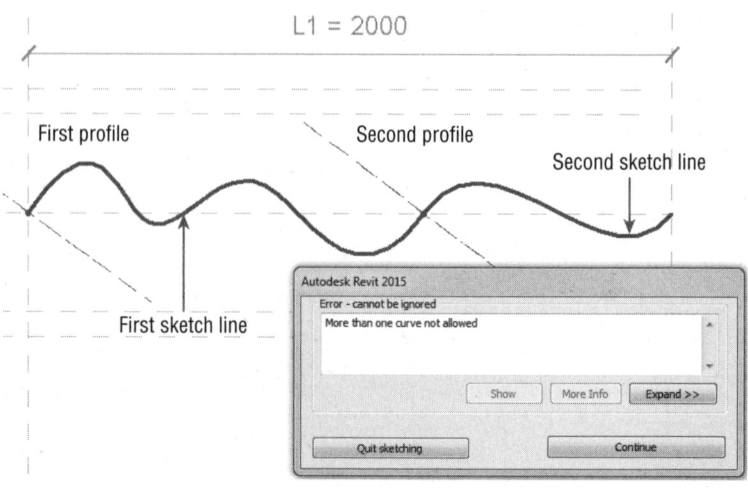

FIGURE 17.11
Multiple lines for a swept blend path

Instead of using multiple lines, you can use the Spline drawing tool for creating a complex path with a single entity. Figure 17.12 shows how a spline can be drawn to represent the same shape shown in the previous figure.

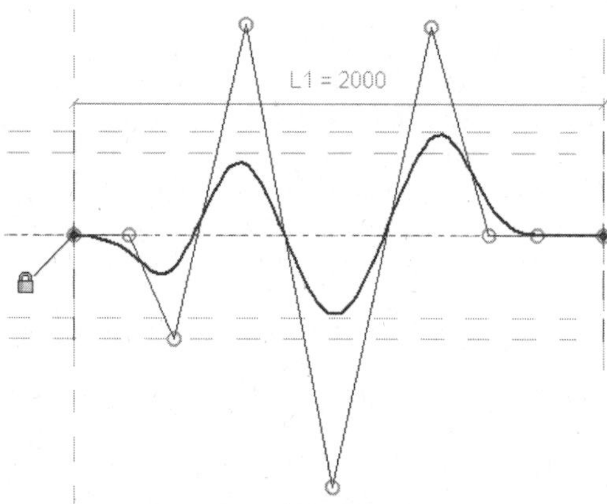

FIGURE 17.12
Spline path for a swept blend

When you click the green check mark button to exit sketch mode for the path, the Swept Blend panel provides tools for defining each of the profiles. Each profile can be drawn, or a predefined profile family can be used. After you click one of the profile buttons, you must click the Edit Profile button to draw the shape. The Go To View dialog box will appear so that you can choose a view where the profile sketch can be drawn. Once you have finished the profile shape, you can exit sketch mode by clicking the green check mark button. You can then create the second profile by clicking the Select Profile 2 button and then the Edit Profile button.

Because you are defining each end of a swept blend solid with a profile shape, you can create a twist in the solid geometry by locating the profile sketches at different elevations from the plane of the path. Figure 17.13 shows an example of a swept blend in which the profiles are drawn above and below the plane of the path, creating a solid that not only changes shape from one end to the other but also changes elevation.

FIGURE 17.13
Swept blend with profiles offset from the path plane

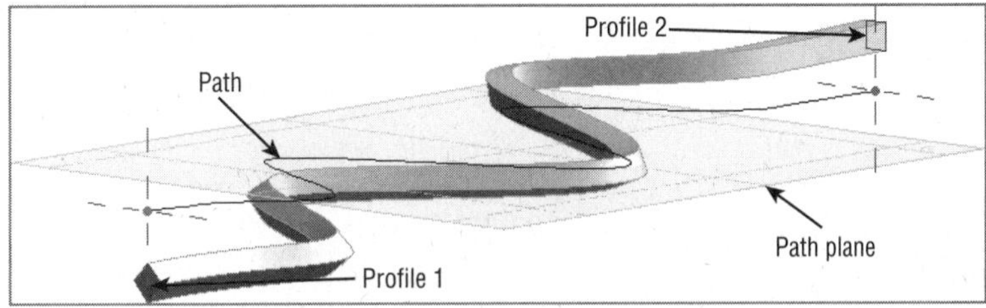

The file `Ch17_Modeling_SweptBlend.rfa` is provided as an example and can be found at `www.sybex.com/go/masteringrevitmep2015`.

Joining Geometry

In some cases, it may be easiest to create a solid form by creating multiple individual solids and then combining them. When you select an extrusion in the Family Editor, the Geometry panel on the contextual tab contains tools for joining geometry.

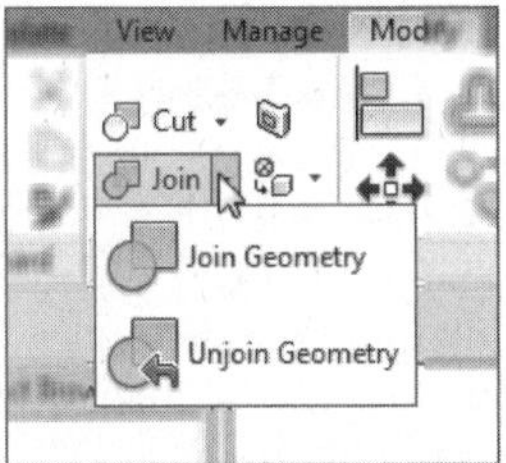

When you join geometry in the Family Editor, you create a union between the selected solids; although they appear to be one, they are still separate, editable forms. When geometry is joined, you can select all the forms by placing your mouse pointer over one of the forms and using the Tab key to select any forms joined to it. This makes for easier editing in the Family Editor, and the joined geometry can be assigned a material property, or the visibility of the joined multiple objects can be controlled with one setting.

Each individual form within a set of joined geometry can be edited normally. Solid forms do not even need to be touching each other to be joined. If you want to break the relationship of forms that are joined, you can select one of the solid forms and click the Unjoin Geometry option on the Join button. You will then be directed to select the solid geometry that you want to be unjoined from other geometry.

Voids

To this point, all the discussion on modeling tools has been for creating solid geometry, but sometimes it is necessary to create a void form. *Voids* can be used to cut shapes out of solid geometry, and in the case of hosted families, voids can be used to cut the host. Additionally, the void form can be utilized as a framework for hosting solid geometry. Some solids are easier to create by modeling a form and then using a void form to remove a portion of the solid geometry.

The same tools for creating solid geometry are used for creating void geometry. The Void Forms button on the Home panel of the Family Editor contains a drop-down list of the tools for creating a void.

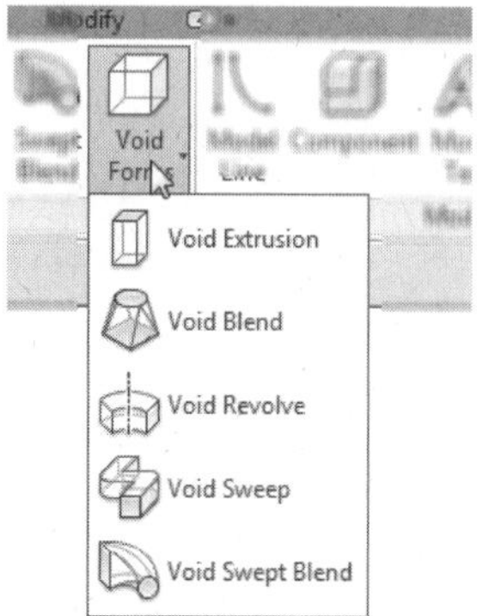

Because the form tools are so similar, you can even create solid geometry and then change it to a void by editing the Solid/Void parameter in the properties of a solid form. Voids can also be changed to solid geometry by editing the same parameter. This will work in both instances as long as those elements are not involved in a join or cut relationship with another solid or void. If they are, that relationship must be broken before you can change their nature.

In an earlier example, you saw a multishape extrusion drawn as one rectangle inside another to create a solid with its center hollowed out all the way through (see Figure 17.1). If you did not want the open space in the center to pass all the way through the solid, you could create multiple solids that result in the desired form, or you could use a void form to cut out the desired space in the solid, as shown in Figure 17.14.

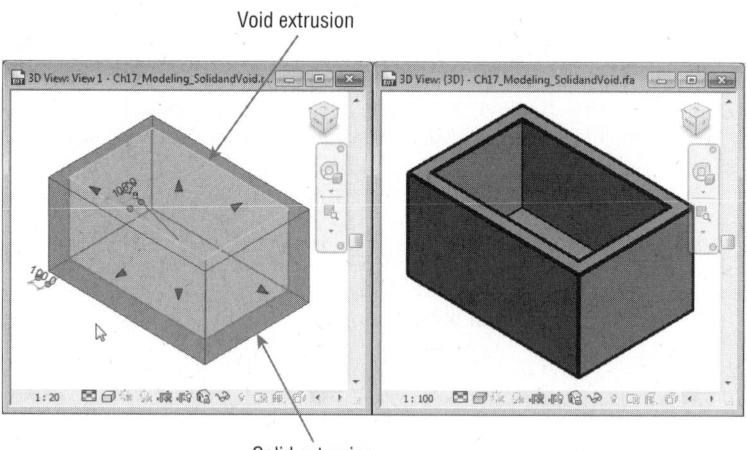

FIGURE 17.14 Void geometry in a solid form

The file `Ch17_Modeling_SolidandVoid.rfa` is provided as an example and can be found at `www.sybex.com/go/masteringrevitmep2015`.

When you create a void form while in the Family Editor, it will appear in the 3D views as a transparent form and as orange lines in plan and elevation views as long as it is not cutting any solid geometry. The void will not automatically cut any solid geometry unless it is drawn overlapping the solid geometry. So, if you were to draw a void form independent from any other geometry in the view and then move the void so that it overlaps solid geometry, the solid would not be cut.

You can tell the void form which solid geometry to cut by selecting it and then clicking the Cut button on the Geometry panel of the contextual tab. You can select the void or the solid geometry first and then select the other to establish the cut relationship.

STATUS BAR

The status bar at the bottom of the user interface will guide you through the steps for cutting or joining geometry when you are using the tools on the Geometry panel. To select an invisible void, first select the solid. The void appears, and you can select it.

You can establish the cut relationship with a void and a solid before they are overlapping. After you use the Cut tool and create the relationship, the void will cut the solid when it is moved to overlap the solid. You can create a cut relationship between one void and multiple solid objects, as shown in Figure 17.15. The void form has been highlighted in this image to illustrate that it is a single void cutting multiple solid objects. A void will remember its cut relationships; this allows us to create cut and not-cut conditions or to show different cutting shapes parametrically.

FIGURE 17.15 Void cutting multiple solids

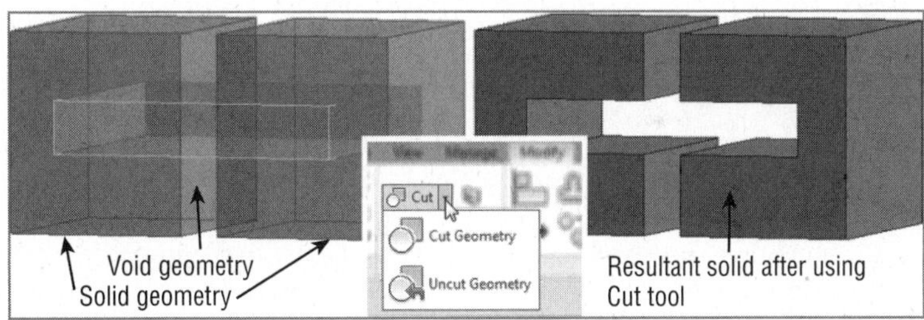

The file `Ch17_Modeling_MultipleSolidandVoid.rfa` is provided as an example and can be found at `www.sybex.com/go/masteringrevitmep2015`.

In the case of a hosted family, you can use the Cut tool to create a cut relationship between a void and the host geometry. This is useful for lighting fixture and air terminal families when you want to show that the component requires an opening in its host. This type of relationship can be established within face-hosted or with model-hosted families. However, when you're using face-hosted families in a project, the void will not cut a linked host face.

While voids are an important modeling feature, consideration should be given to all the other solid modeling tools to create forms before resorting to using voids. As stated earlier in the chapter, having many voids in families, or having overly detailed families, can negatively affect file performance.

For some families, it may be tempting to use void forms to define the required clearance space around mechanical and electrical equipment. There are other methods to define these spaces without burdening your projects with void geometry. For more information on creating clearance spaces within families, see Chapter 19, "Creating Equipment."

Reference Planes and Lines

When you begin to create a solid, it is important to understand how the current view will affect the orientation of that solid. When you click one of the buttons on the Forms panel of the Home tab, you will be taken into sketch mode for the solid. A contextual tab appears on the ribbon with tools for generating the sketch, or shape, of the solid. The view you are in determines the plane for the sketch, and the depth of the solid will be perpendicular to the sketch plane. If you are working in a file that contains multiple planes that are parallel to the current view, you can select a plane to which you can associate the extrusion by clicking the Set button on the Work Plane panel of the contextual tab. From the Work Plane dialog box that appears, you can choose the desired plane from the drop-down list that shows only named reference planes, as shown in Figure 17.16.

FIGURE 17.16
Work Plane dialog box

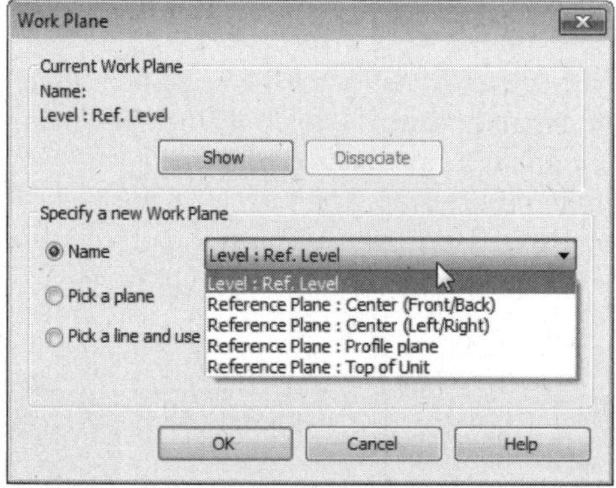

If you choose a reference plane that is not parallel to the current view, the Go To View dialog box will appear after you click OK in the Work Plane dialog box. The Go To View dialog box, shown in Figure 17.17, offers views that exist in the family file that are parallel to the selected reference plane. You can also choose a 3D view in which to work if you are more comfortable working in 3D to generate solid geometry. You can click the Show button on the contextual tab for a visible reference of the plane chosen for the sketch. This is especially helpful when creating a sketch in a 3D view.

You do not have to set the reference plane to begin sketching the shape of the solid. Sketching it directly in the view associates the solid geometry with the plane of that view, such as the reference level of a family. However, it does make sense to pay close attention to the active workplane, especially before starting this process, as Revit can be finicky about changing a workplane in the middle of a procedure.

When you are using reference planes to build solid geometry, it is a good idea to give any custom planes a name so that they can be easily identified and selected from the list in the Work Plane dialog box. This can be especially helpful when creating families with multiple solids; giving reference planes names such as *Top of Unit* or *Face of Device* aids in associating other geometry within the family to the plane, as shown in Figure 17.18.

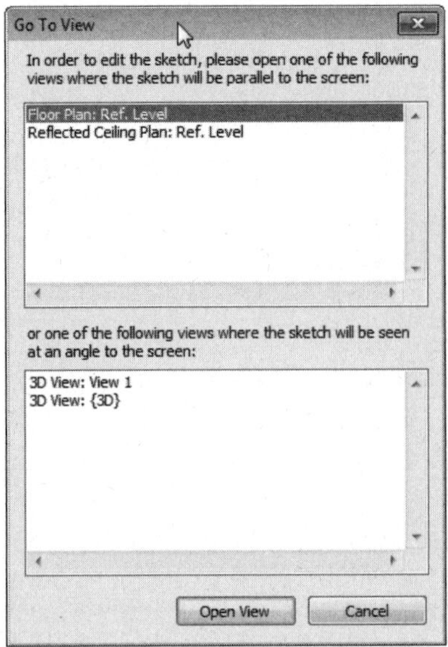

FIGURE 17.17 Go To View dialog box

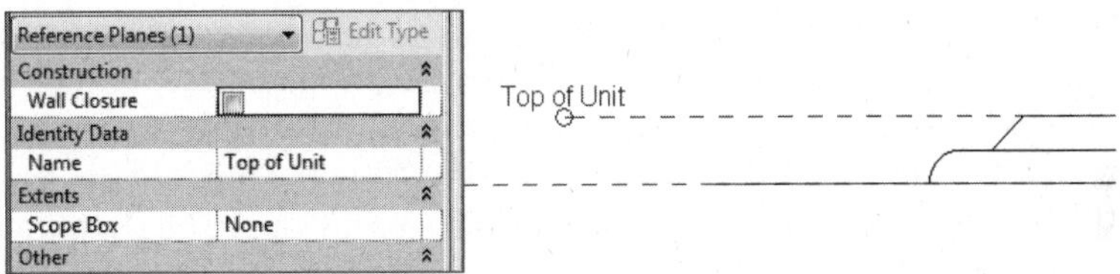

FIGURE 17.18 Named reference planes

You can control how a reference plane in a family is accessed when the family is loaded into a project by editing the Is Reference parameter, as shown in Figure 17.19. You can set the parameter to associate the plane with the orientation of the family by choosing any of the directional choices, such as Front, Back, Bottom, Center (Left/Right), and others. You can also choose whether the reference plane is used for dimensioning when the family is loaded into a project.

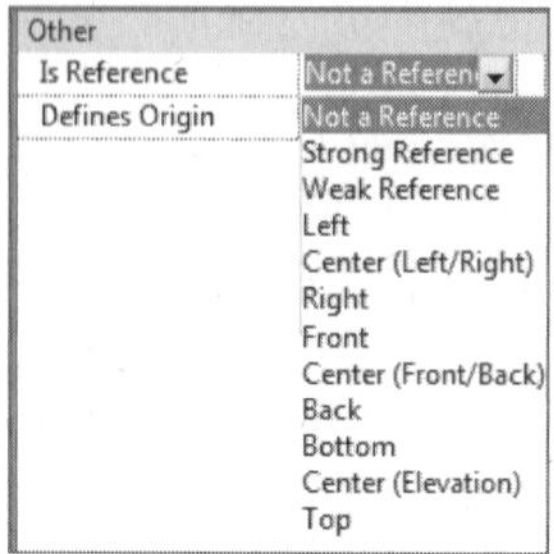

FIGURE 17.19
Is Reference parameter

There are directional and non-directional parameter options, firstly the non-directional:

Not A Reference When placed into a project, the plane will not be available for dimensioning or alignment. This is a good setting for planes created in a family that are used only for association within the family. It will prevent unwanted selection or highlighting of a family when your mouse pointer passes over the plane.

Strong Reference When the family is placed into a project, the plane will be the first choice for temporary dimensions. This setting is best used for planes in a family that define the portions of a family to which you would dimension or align when using the family in a project.

Weak Reference You use this setting when you want to be able to dimension or align to the plane but do not want temporary dimensions applied to the plane when placing the family in a project.

For example, if you have a family that you want to place at its edges but also want to dimension or align to its center, you would define reference planes at its edges as strong references and a reference plane at the center as a weak reference. This is typical for families such as lighting fixtures or air terminals.

Then the directional parameters:

Left, Right, Front, Back, Top and Bottom When viewed from the Ref. Level plan view, front is nearest the bottom of the screen. These give the user the ability to correctly position an object, and when named correctly, can also give an indication within the project if the family has been incorrectly mirrored rather than rotated.

Center (Left/Right), Center (Front/Back) and Center (Elevation) These are, in most cases, the best options when choosing the origin point of the family, which can be used in conjunction with the Defines Origin parameter, this allows you to set a reference plane as one of the planes of the origin of a family. Two planes must be set as defining the origin, and the planes must intersect. The intersection of the planes in plan view will determine the insertion point of the family.

Reference lines are useful in creating solid geometry when you do not want to create an infinite plane of reference. Unlike reference planes, reference lines have a start point and an end point. When you draw a straight reference line, two planes are formed at the line. One plane is parallel to the plane in which the line is drawn, and the other is perpendicular to that plane. This allows you to use the reference line in views parallel and perpendicular to where it is drawn. Figure 17.20 shows a reference line that has been selected to show the four workplanes that can be used, one at each end, one horizontal, and one vertical. Arced reference lines can be used for reference but will not create planes.

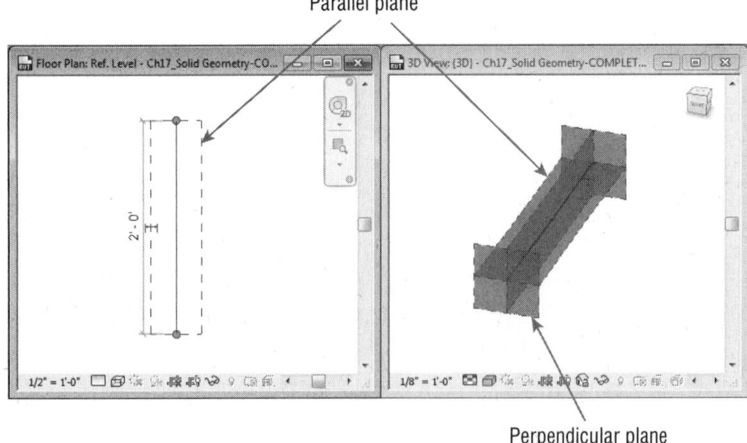

FIGURE 17.20
Reference line and its planes

Reference lines can be dimensioned when a family is placed into a project, and they also have a parameter that allows you to set them as a strong or weak reference or not as a reference at all. You cannot use reference lines to define the origin of a family.

Solid geometry can be aligned to reference lines in the same way they are aligned to reference planes. Using reference lines and planes is the most effective way to create parametric behavior of solid geometry within a family.

Mastering the tools for creating solid geometry will make content creation an efficient part of your Revit MEP 2015 implementation. Practice creating different types of solids by completing the following exercise:

1. Open the `Ch17_Solid Geometry.rfa` file found at `www.sybex.com/go/masteringrevitmep2015`.
2. Click the Extrusion button on the Forms panel of the Home tab. Select the Circumscribed Polygon drawing tool from the Draw panel. See Figure 17.21.

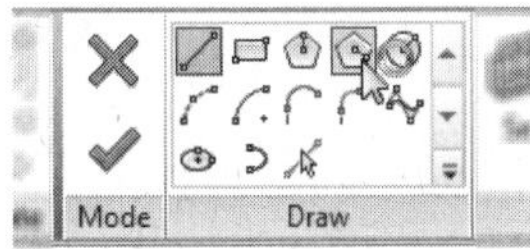

FIGURE 17.21
Draw panel

3. On the Options Bar, set the depth of the extrusion to **0′-1/2″** (**12** mm) and the number of sides to **4**.
4. Click at the intersection of the reference planes to start the extrusion. Drag your cursor to the right along the horizontal plane until the radius is **1′-0″** (**300** mm), and then click to complete the sketch. See Figure 17.22.

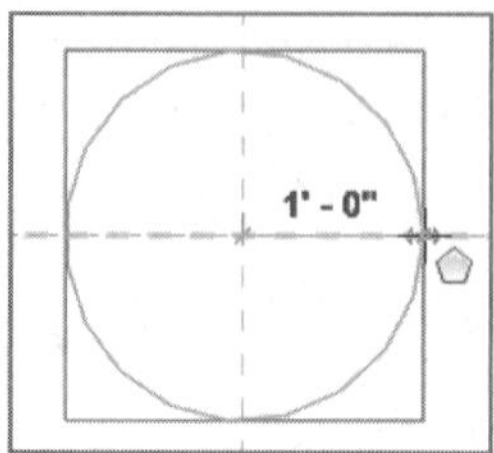

FIGURE 17.22
Sketch

5. Click the green check mark button on the Mode panel of the Modify | Create Extrusion contextual tab to finish creating the extrusion.

   Now we will create a blend that will be mounted on top of this extrusion.

6. Click the Blend button on the Forms panel of the Home tab. Select the Rectangle drawing tool from the Draw panel.

7. In the Properties box, set the First End constraint to **0′-1/2″** (**12** mm) and the Second End constraint to **0′-1″** (**25** mm), and from the Options Bar, change the Offset value to **0′-1/2″** (**12** mm). Select the upper-left corner of the extrusion drawn in the previous steps and drag your cursor to the lower-right corner, snapping to the end point at the corner. If the sketch rectangle is on the outside of the first extrusion, press the spacebar, which will flip the sketch orientation so that the offset is to the inside (see Figure 17.23).

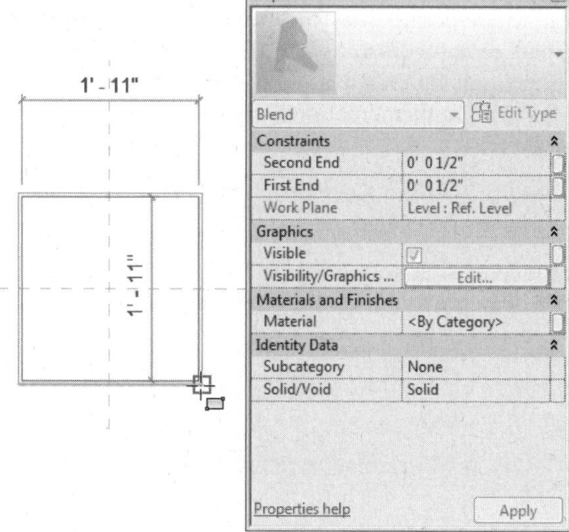

FIGURE 17.23
Creating the bottom sketch of the blend

8. To create the top portion of the blend, click the Edit Top button on the Modify tab, shown in Figure 17.24. Then draw a rectangle as in step 7, but with the offset inside the first extrusion. Remember, pressing the spacebar flips the orientation (see Figure 17.25).

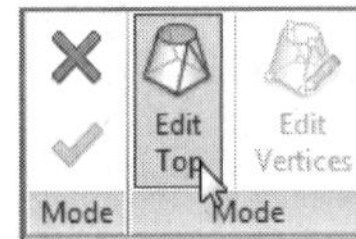

FIGURE 17.24
Edit Top button

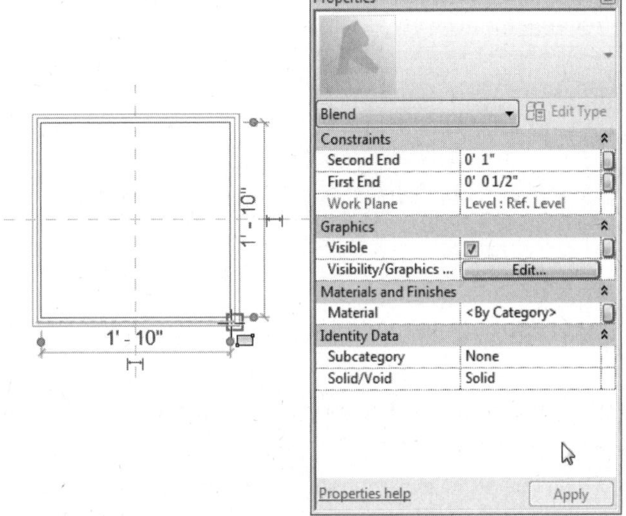

FIGURE 17.25
Creating the top sketch of the blend

9. Click the green check mark button on the Mode panel of the Modify | Create Blend contextual tab to finish creating the blend. Open the default 3D view to verify that the two solids sit one on top of the other, as shown in Figure 17.26.

   Now, let's add a form that follows the base of our previously created extrusion.

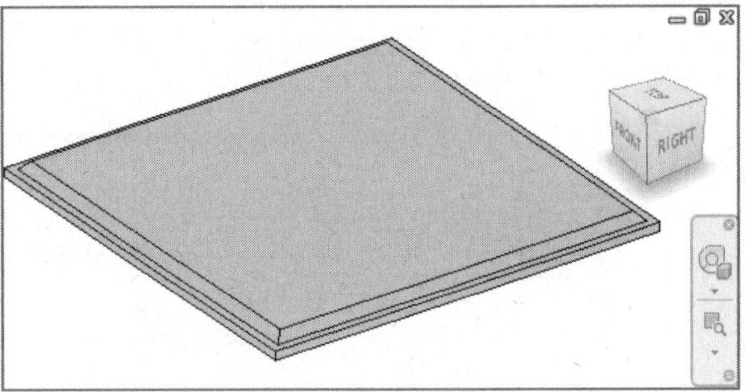

FIGURE 17.26
Default 3D view

10. Click the Sweep button on the Forms panel of the Home tab. Select the Pick Path drawing tool from the Sweep panel on the ribbon, shown in Figure 17.27.

FIGURE 17.27
Pick Path tool

11. Select the four lines, as shown in Figure 17.28, that form the base of the bottom solid, rotating the 3D view as necessary.

FIGURE 17.28
Selecting the path of the sweep

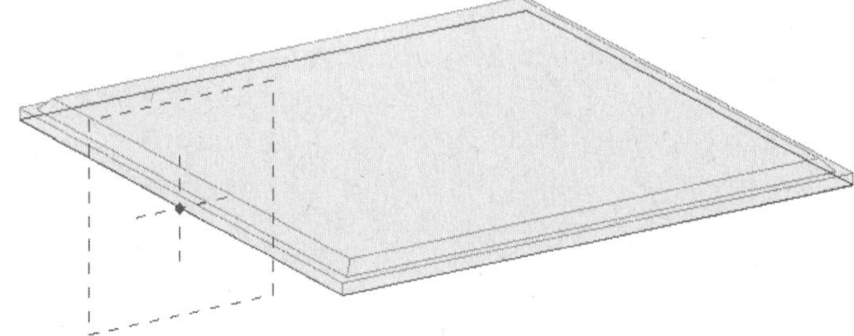

12. Click the green check mark button on the Mode panel of the Modify | Sweep ➤ Pick Path contextual tab to finish creating the sweep path.
13. Open one of the elevation views so you are able to view the green crosshairs of the origin of the profile, as indicated in Figure 17.29. Click the Edit Profile button, shown in Figure 17.30, on the Sweep panel. Depending on which line you selected first, you may be prompted to open a view in which the profile can be drawn.

FIGURE 17.29
Sketching the sweep

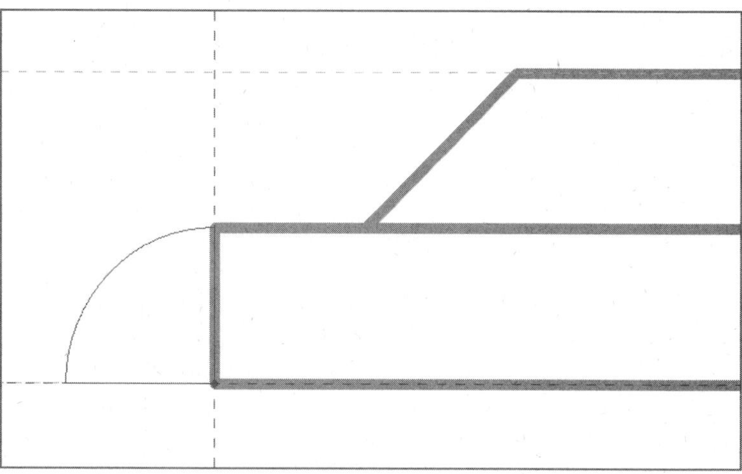

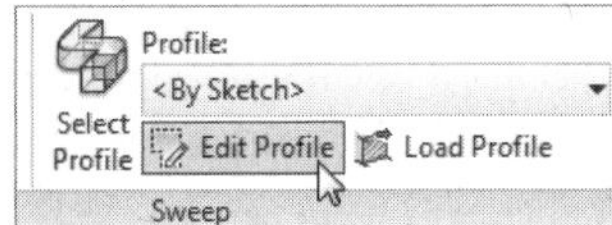

FIGURE 17.30
Edit Profile button

14. From the Draw panel, select the Center-Ends Arc drawing tool and use the origin point of the path for the center of the arc. Using the top end point of the base extrusion as the radius length, draw the arc through 90 degrees. Complete the profile with two straight lines.

15. Click the green check mark button on the Mode panel twice to complete the creation of the sweep. Open the default {3D} view to display the completed form, as shown in Figure 17.31.

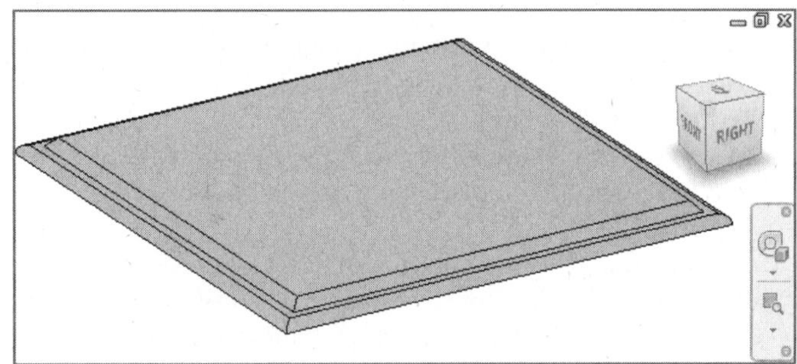

FIGURE 17.31
Completed form

Constraints and Dimensions

Making the solid geometry in your families parametric gives you the ability to create multiple types within a single family and offers a higher level of management and control of the properties of components. The key to making your solid geometry parametric is to constrain the geometry to reference planes and lines. This enables you to apply the parametric behavior to the planes and lines, which allows for multiple solid forms to react to changes to the parameters. Although you do have the ability to assign parametric constraints directly to the solid geometry, it is recommended that you assign it to reference planes or lines so that changes to a solid that affect other solids within the family are more easily achieved and managed.

Geometry can easily be constrained to a reference plane by using the Align tool on the Modify tab, or you can simply drag the edge of a solid to a reference plane or line and it will snap into alignment. Once the solid is aligned, the padlock grip appears, allowing you to lock the alignment.

Some solid forms do not need a reference plane or line to be parametrically managed. Whenever you are sketching a circle and want to control the radius with a parameter, you can apply the parameter directly to the sketch. This is done by activating the temporary dimension that indicates the radius when sketching the circle. Clicking the dimension grip will change the temporary dimension to a permanent one, which can then be assigned to a parameter. Alternatively, you can create a diameter dimension, as shown in Figure 17.32.

FIGURE 17.32
Radial and diameter dimensions

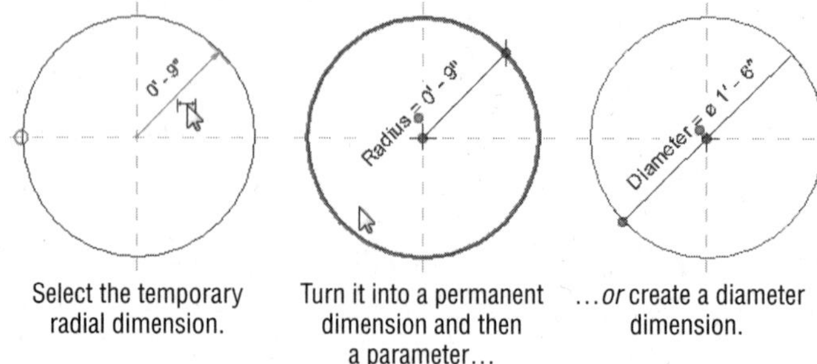

When you complete a sketch that contains dimensions within the sketch, the dimensions will not show unless you are in sketch mode. You can constrain sketch lines to reference planes while working in sketch mode, but if you are using dimensional constraints, it is best to put the dimensions directly in the family so that they will be visible while you are working on the family. It can be frustrating to place a dimension only to find that one already exists in the sketch of a solid.

Creating angular constraints is often necessary for solid geometry. When you need to create angular parametric behavior for a family, it is best to use reference lines instead of reference planes. The location of the end point of a reference line can be constrained so that the line can be rotated with the end point serving as the axis of rotation. An angular dimension can be used to create the parametric behavior of the reference line, as shown in Figure 17.33. The padlock grip indicates that the reference line has been locked to the horizontal reference plane, although it is not necessary to lock the end point to the reference plane if the reference line is drawn connected to the plane.

FIGURE 17.33
Reference line with angular parametric behavior

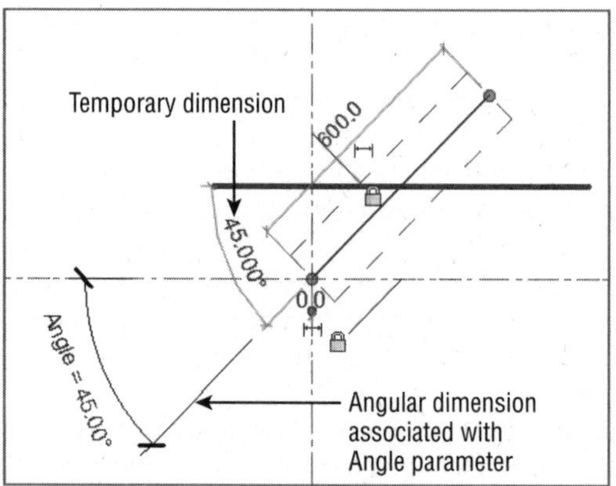

This type of angular constraint is useful for rotating solid geometry within a family. Figure 17.34 shows an extrusion that was modeled in the vertical plane of the reference line.

Because the plane of the line was used, the extrusion is associated with the line so that, when the angle of the line changes, the solid will stay with it. The dashed lines indicate the original location of the line prior to changing the angle parameter to 120 degrees.

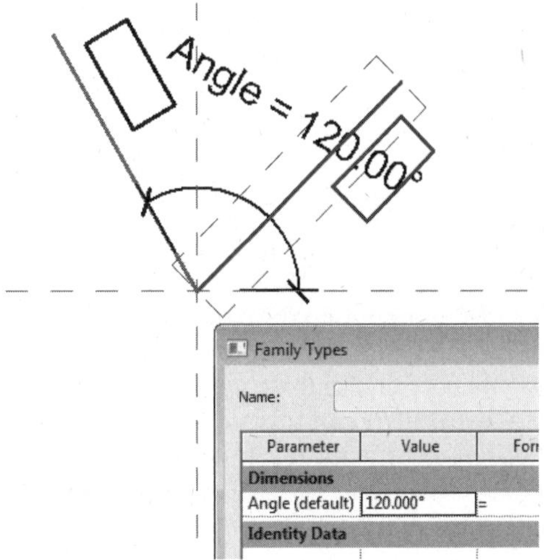

FIGURE 17.34 Extrusion constrained to the reference line

Although reference lines work well for this type of constraint and parametric behavior, they can cause undesired results when the angle of solid geometry is supposed to change while the geometry remains in a fixed location. The solid geometry shown in Figure 17.35 is a sweep with a rectangular profile. The path of the sweep is an arc that is locked to the reference line and to the reference plane. As the Angle parameter is modified, the length of the sweep increases. A Radius parameter has also been applied for the sweep path.

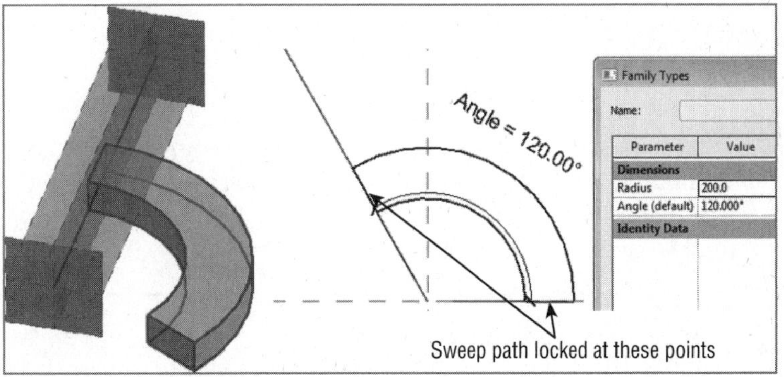

FIGURE 17.35 Sweep constrained to the reference line

This type of parametric relationship will behave as expected—up to a certain point. Flexing the family reveals that, at larger angles, the geometry may not stay associated to the reference line, which could cause an incorrect representation of the solid, as shown in Figure 17.36. Notice that the solid geometry could change orientation across the horizontal reference line and appear to be mirrored instead of swept through 240 degrees.

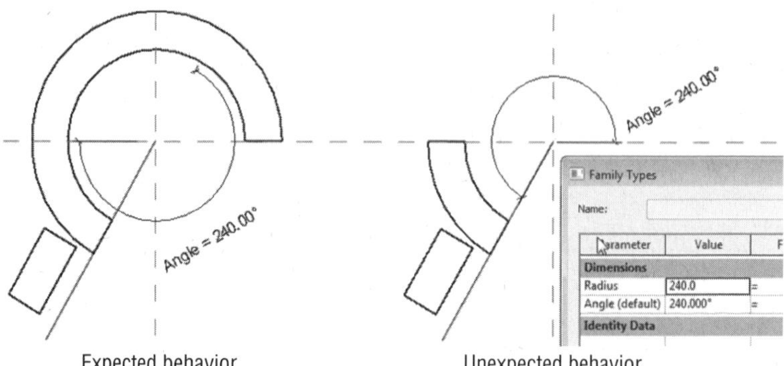

FIGURE 17.36 Undesired sweep geometry from the angular constraint

Different angles input into the parameter result in a different undesired behavior of the solid geometry. The purpose of this example is not to point out shortcomings of the software but to demonstrate that one choice for creating an angular constraint may not work for all situations.

An alternative solution for this scenario would be to use an angular dimension of the sweep path itself instead of constraining to a reference line. Figure 17.37 shows the dimension parameters applied to the path of a sweep. The angular dimension was created by selecting the path and then activating the temporary dimension, which was then associated with the Angle parameter.

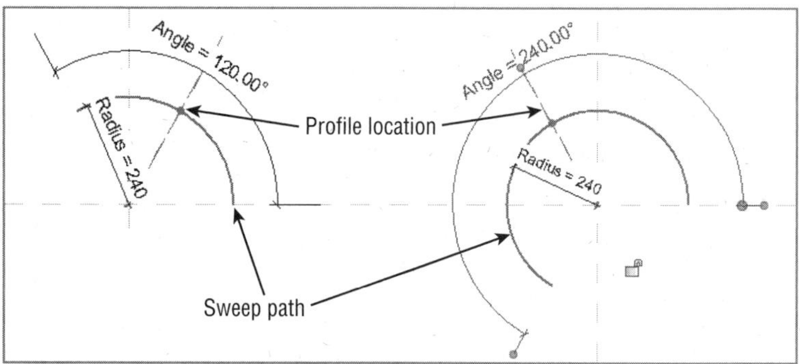

FIGURE 17.37 Sweep path with parametric constraints

With the path of the sweep being defined by the angle instead of its association to a reference line, the desired results for the solid geometry can be achieved.

The file `Ch17_Modeling_ReferenceLINES.rfa` is provided as an example and can be found at `www.sybex.com/go/masteringrevitmep2015`.

Real World Scenario

CIRCLE OF LIGHT

Catherine is working on a project that has a rotunda and requires lighting that follows the curve of the walls. Knowing that many changes will occur before the final decision is made on this high-profile area, she creates a lighting fixture that represents a custom linear LED strip. She creates a sweep with an arced path, provides a parameter to control the length of the arc by adjusting its angle, and provides a parameter for the length of its radius. As her architect works with the client to finalize the design, Catherine can easily keep up with the changes by editing parameters instead of having to re-create the fixture each time the model changes.

Visibility Control

The visibility parameters of solid geometry provide useful means for controlling the behavior of solids in a family that is used in a project. For many MEP discipline families, the actual solid geometry is not shown in plan views, but instead a symbol is used. This is especially true for electrical devices and even some light fixtures.

If you are concerned about file performance, it is a good practice to limit the visibility of solid geometry to only the types of views in which it needs to be seen. Symbolic or model lines can be used to represent the geometry in views where the solid does not have to be shown, such as plan views or reflected ceiling plans. Setting the visibility of solid geometry to appear in 3D views, sections, and elevations is important because it helps keep your project coordinated by allowing you to locate items when a section or elevation view is created, without having to draw additional linework in the section or elevation view.

In some cases, you may also want to control the visibility of solid geometry based on the detail-level setting of a view. For example, you may set the visibility of the solid geometry in a power receptacle family so that the geometry shows only in views set to Fine detail. This enables you to see the actual location of the receptacles quickly by switching the view detail level for instances where you are trying to coordinate exact locations. It also benefits other disciplines, such as architectural, that may want to see the receptacle geometry in a section or elevation.

To set the visibility of solid geometry in the Family Editor, select the geometry and click the Visibility Settings button located on the Mode panel of the contextual tab that appears on the ribbon.

In the Family Element Visibility Settings dialog box, you have options for setting where the solid geometry will be visible when the family is used in a project. Figure 17.38 shows the dialog box and the available options.

FIGURE 17.38
Family Element Visibility Settings dialog box

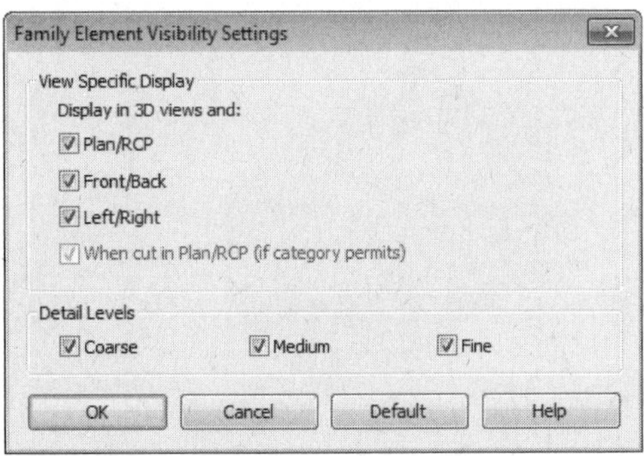

All solid geometry is visible in 3D views when the category of the family is visible. The View Specific Display options allow you to select other types of views where the solid geometry will be visible. Keep in mind that, for face-hosted families, the Front/Back setting will display the geometry in a plan view when the geometry is hosted by a vertical surface. The Left/Right setting is for section and elevation views taken from the side of the geometry. One of the options is to display the geometry when the cut plane of a view intersects the geometry. This option is not available for all categories of families and is typically used for architectural and structural types of families such as doors or windows.

In the Detail Levels section of the dialog box, you can select the detail levels in which the geometry will be visible. When using symbolic or model lines to represent the geometry in plan and Reflected Ceiling Plan (RCP) views, consider what detail level will be used for section, elevation, and 3D views so that the geometry will be displayed when desired. When creating duct and pipe fitting and accessory families, be sure to set the Detail Levels settings within the Family Element Visibility Settings dialog box to match the behavior of duct and pipe system families so that the solid geometry will be displayed in Medium detail for duct and Fine detail for pipe-related families. Any model lines used to represent the objects should appear only in Coarse detail for duct and Coarse and Medium for pipe.

In some cases, you may want to represent an object with a very simple shape for plans using Coarse detail and a more realistic shape in smaller-scale views using Fine detail. The box shown in Figure 17.39 is set to appear at Coarse detail, while the more detailed solid geometry appears at Medium and Fine detail levels.

The visibility settings you apply will not affect the geometry while you are working in the Family Editor; that is, its behavior does not match its behavior in a project. Solid geometry will remain visible in the Family Editor so that you can work on the family. In all views within the Family Editor, solid geometry will appear halftone if the visibility settings of the geometry cause the object to be not visible in the same type of project view. In other words, if you set an object to appear only in Fine detail and your 3D view in the Family Editor is set to Medium detail, the solid will be halftone in the Family Editor 3D view. This is a helpful visual aid when you're working in a family because it helps you understand the visibility behavior of the geometry.

The visibility of solid geometry can also be controlled by the Visible parameter in the properties of the geometry. This is a Yes/No parameter that simply determines whether the geometry is visible. This parameter can be associated with another parameter defined in the family for control of the solid visibility when the family is used in a project.

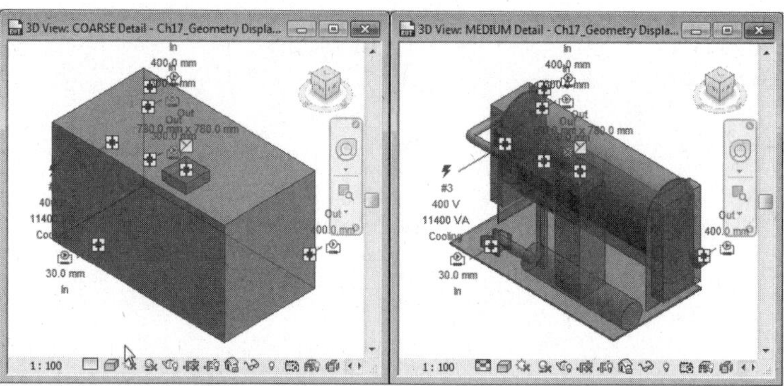

FIGURE 17.39
Geometry display at different detail levels

Another option for the visibility of solid geometry is to assign a material to it by using the Material parameter. You can create a custom material type with settings that are desired for use in your projects. One example is to create geometry in a family that represents the required clearance space for equipment. Along with visibility control settings, a material can be applied to the solid geometry to make it semitransparent when viewed in a 3D project view. See Chapter 20, "Creating Lighting Fixtures," for more details.

When you are considering the visibility of solid geometry in a family, keep in mind that the visibility of the entire family is controlled by its category. In some cases, you may want to control individual components independently from the family category. You can create subcategories within a family by clicking the Object Styles button on the Manage tab in the Family Editor. Once you have created a subcategory, you can assign solid geometry to the category by using the Subcategory parameter in the properties of the geometry.

The file `Ch17_Geometry Display_Chiller.rvt` is provided as an example and can be found at `www.sybex.com/go/masteringrevitmep2015`.

In-Place Massing

The tools in this chapter have been aimed at the Family Editor, but they can also be used in the project environment to create a building form. Although this task may traditionally be the preserve of the design architect, especially during the concept stage, the building services design engineer could also use these tools to create a building object that can be used for analysis from the early stages. This may occur if the architectural models are too inaccurate to use for analysis or, as mentioned in Chapter 5, "Multiplatform Interoperability: Working with 2D and 3D Data," are not available at all.

The exercise in Chapter 5 took you through the process of creating a wireframe building model. The following exercise takes this a step further as you generate an in-place mass from which very basic analysis can be achieved:

1. Open the `Ch17_HVAC_Massing.rvt` file found at `www.sybex.com/go/masteringrevitmep2015`. (You will need to download the file `Ch17_COMPLETE.rvt` at the same time because it is a Revit link file required for this exercise.)

2. Open the 01 – Entry Level view, and from the Massing And Site tab, select the In-Place Mass tool. A dialog box might open, indicating that Revit has enabled the Show Mass mode, as shown in Figure 17.40. This may occur because the Mass category is typically turned off by default.

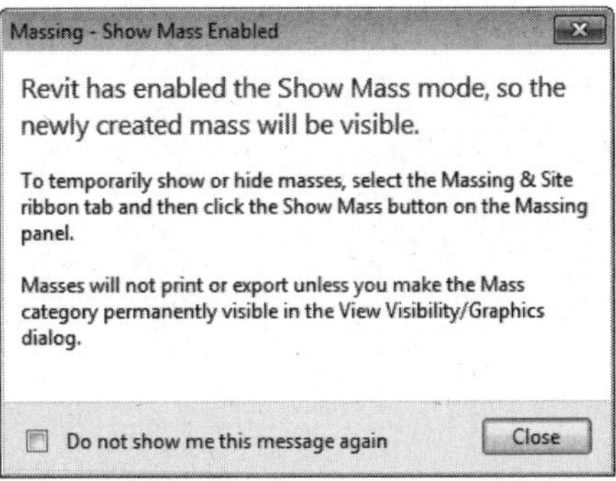

FIGURE 17.40
Show Mass enabled

3. Give the mass a suitable name. From the Draw panel, shown in Figure 17.41, select the Line tool and trace over the building outline. At this point, the tracing does not have to be super accurate; you can come back to this later to make it more suitable.

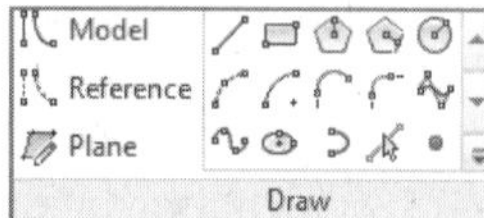

FIGURE 17.41
Draw panel

4. When you have completed a closed path, click the Modify button on the ribbon and then open a 3D view and select the completed path. From the ribbon, select the Create Form button (see Figure 17.42).
5. If the Mass object is higher than you intended, as indicated in Figure 17.43, use the grip tools to push the top of the mass to the correct height. If you change the 3D view to Front, you will see that as you stretch the mass, it snaps to other objects.
6. Click the Finish Mass button (which has a green check mark).

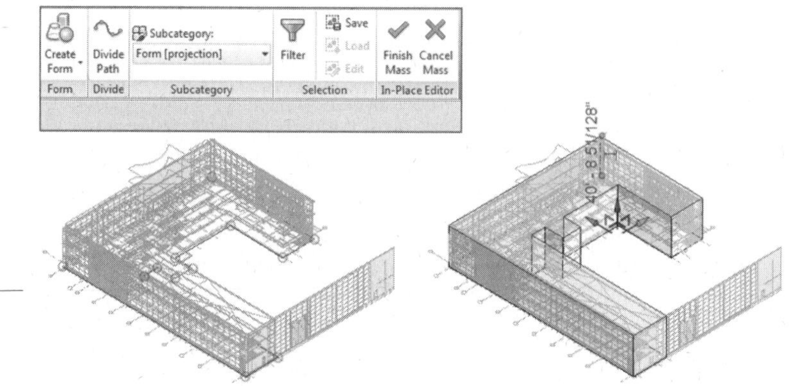

FIGURE 17.42
The Create Form button

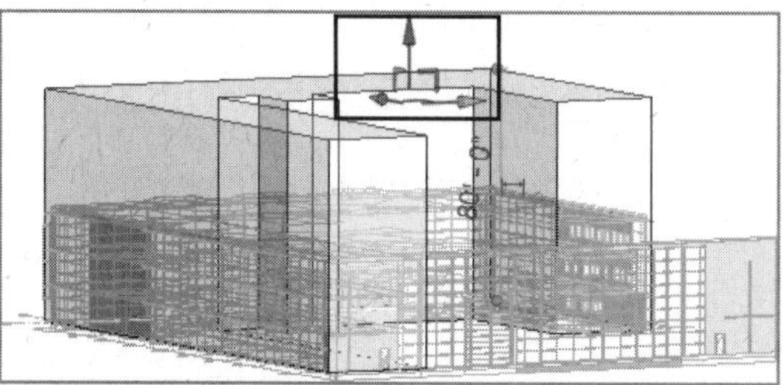

FIGURE 17.43
Stretching the Mass object

7. For clarity, the linked file can now be turned off in the 3D view. Select the Mass object, and from the Modify tab, select the Mass Floors button. In the dialog box that opens, place a check mark next to the levels in which you want to create a Mass floor, as shown in Figure 17.44.

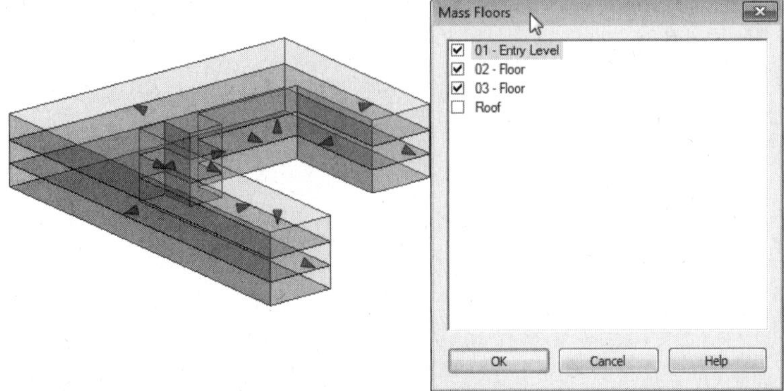

FIGURE 17.44
Mass Floors dialog box

8. From the Project Browser, open the Mass Floor schedule. Although no building elements have been created, there is already an accurate total for floor areas for the entire building. This can be seen in Figure 17.45.

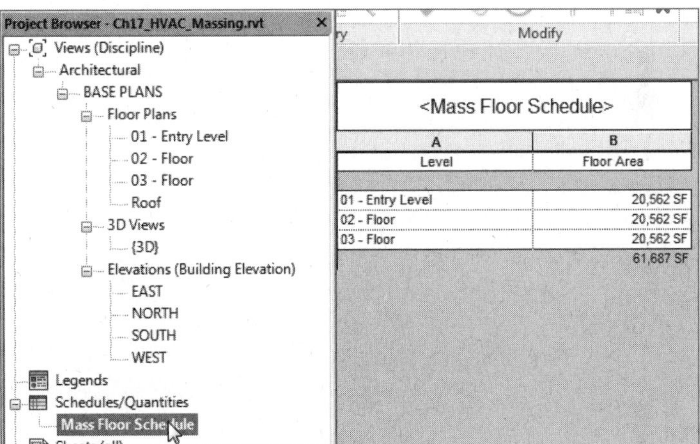

FIGURE 17.45
Mass Floor schedule

9. Using the tools on the Architect tab's Model By Face panel, shown in Figure 17.46, start by creating the floors and roofs. Select the Floor By Face tool, and select the Mass floors. (You can select them individually or use a crossing selection box. The method isn't really important because you are selecting only Mass floors.)

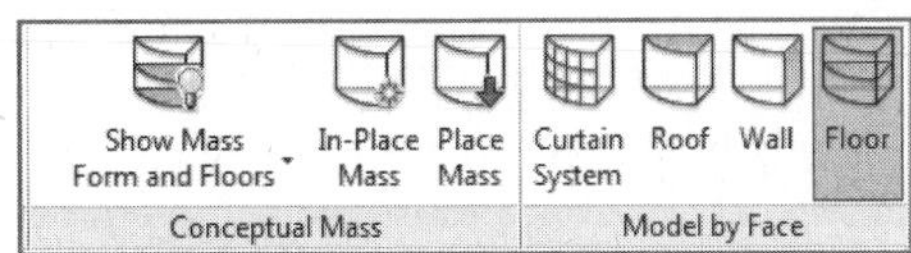

FIGURE 17.46
Model By Face panel

10. Click the Create Floor button. Floors are added to the model, as shown in Figure 17.47.

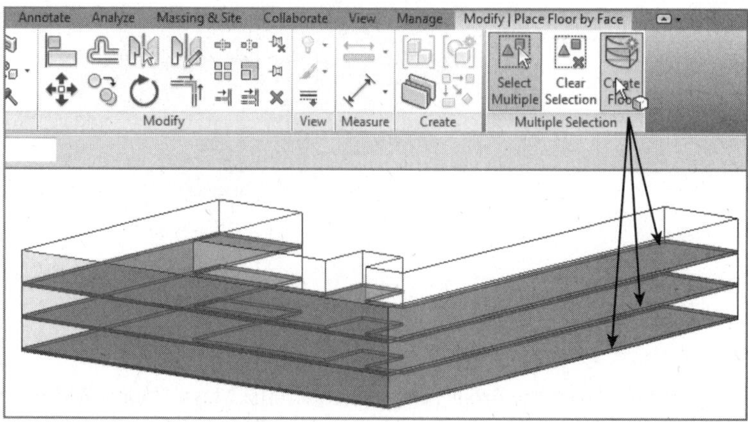

FIGURE 17.47 Creating floors

11. Repeat steps 9 and 10 for the roof—except use the Roof By Face tool.

 The walls are going to be treated in three separate stages: normal solid walls, curtain walls, and curtain walls being used as windows.

12. In Figure 17.48, you can see the placement for normal walls; select the Wall button from the Model By Face panel of the Architect tab. Note that the level and height of the wall are set to Automatic on the Options Bar.

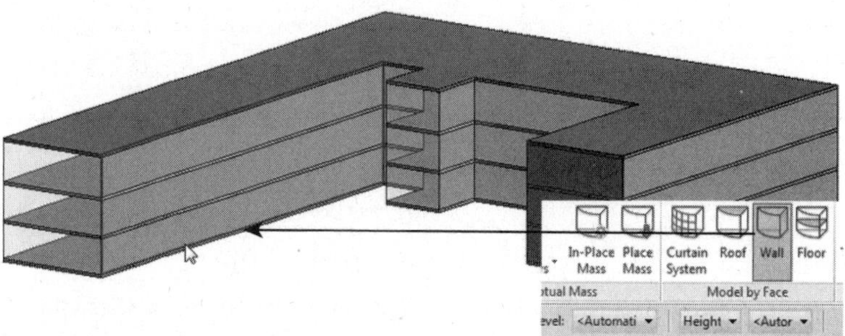

FIGURE 17.48 Creating walls

13. Make sure you have selected the correct wall type. Then select each face of the mass, in turn, where you want a solid wall to appear. (The wall type isn't extremely important because the analysis data for this particular exercise is taken from user input, not the actual wall material. However, glass will appear as an opening, as shown in Figure 17.49.)

Figure 17.49
Creating curtain walls

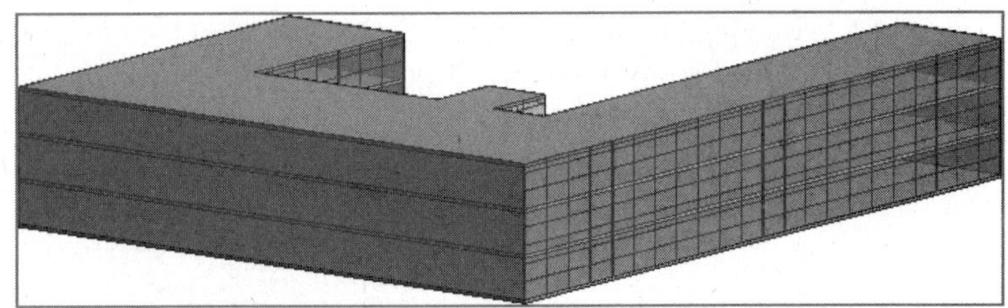

14. Repeat step 12, this time selecting the Curtain System option from the Model By Face panel. You have the option to pick several faces of the mass at the same time, just as for the floors. Do not be tempted to do this, because the result will be *one* curtain wall, covering several faces. If the mass changes substantially, you may have to delete the walls and start again.
15. Large window openings can be created by using curtain walls in conjunction with the Cut Geometry tool. This hosts the curtain wall within a host wall, effectively creating windows without having to resort to window families, which could take more time and effort. From the Architect tab, select the Wall tool. Figure 17.50 shows that in this instance, the Options Bar indicates the Level and Height settings of the wall you are going to create.

Figure 17.50
Options Bar

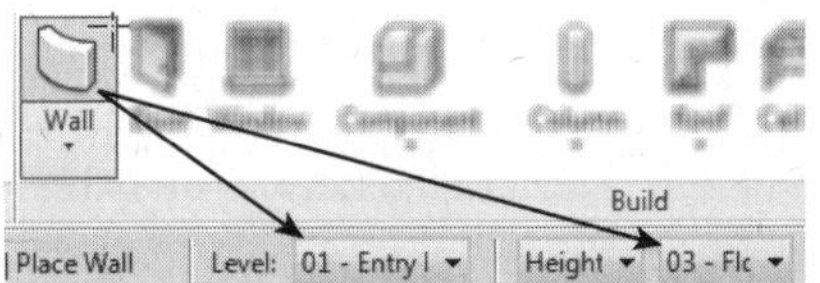

16. Select the wall type Curtain Wall: Exterior Glazing. Set the start level to Level 1 and the height to Level 3, and draw a curtain wall, as shown in Figure 17.51. Note the message stating that the highlighted walls are overlapping.

Figure 17.51
Walls overlapping

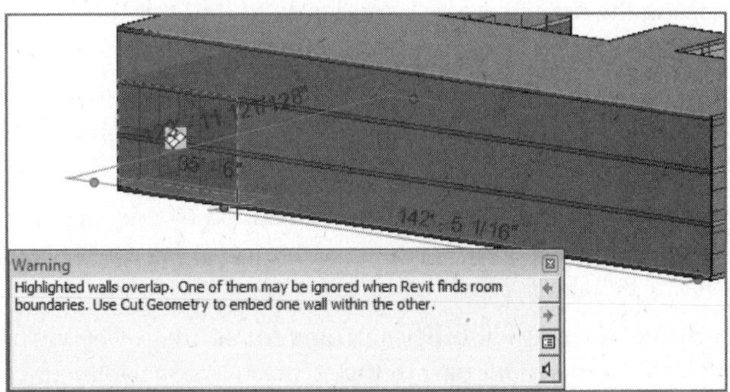

17. From the Modify tab, select the Cut tool. Start by selecting the solid wall and then select the curtain wall. The result can be seen in Figure 17.52.

FIGURE 17.52
Walls cut

The more you populate this model, the more data that can be derived from it. Starting from the in-place mass gives you the added benefit of having an airtight model that will work for all stages of your analysis. It's up to you how much detail you wish to go into.

The Bottom Line

Model solids and voids. Being able to model efficiently will decrease the time you spend creating content and give you more time to spend on design decisions. Solid geometry is crucial for the physical coordination of components to achieve a design that will result in fewer changes during construction—when changes are the most expensive.

Master It Several tools are available to create the shapes needed to represent MEP discipline components. Each tool generates an extrusion in a unique way. Describe the difference between a swept blend and a regular sweep.

Orient geometry by using reference planes and lines. Reference planes and lines are the most effective way to define the orientation of solid geometry within a family. Reference planes define how an object will be inserted into a project.

Master It Knowing the resulting orientation of an extrusion prior to creating it will save lots of time by not having to duplicate modeling efforts. Nothing is more frustrating than taking the time to create a solid only to find out that it is in the wrong plane. Describe the process for creating an extrusion that is associated with a custom reference plane.

Ensure the parametric change capability of models. Building solid geometry to represent MEP discipline components is good. Building the geometry with parametric change capabilities is even better.

Master It Solid geometry can be defined by parameters that can change the size or shape of the geometry. Reference planes and lines are an important part of creating parametric behavior. Why?

Determine optimal visibility settings for solids. The visibility behavior of solid geometry plays an important part in the creation of consistent and coordinated construction documents.

Master It It is important to know how a family will be used in a project to determine the visibility settings required for the solid geometry in the family. Why is it important to set the Detail Level visibility settings for pipe- and duct-related families?

Create in-place Mass objects for analysis and documentation. In-place Mass objects allow the designer to quickly produce a building form at a time when the project architect may not be able to provide a model that is suitable for early analysis purposes.

Master It Using massing tools can speed up the design process. What tools would you use to quickly model glass and windows?

Chapter 18

Creating Symbols and Annotations

Many of the components of an MEP design are represented on drawings as symbols. Having a well-stocked library of symbols can improve your efficiency in creating device families and reduce the time spent on drafting tasks. Symbols can also be used to create project legends that can be utilized on different project types when required.

Companies have spent many hours and significant funds to develop and maintain their drafting standards. Many think it is important to create construction documents that are recognizable as their work. To make the transition to the Autodesk® Revit® MEP 2015 software without losing the signature look of your company construction documents, you can create annotation styles and symbols in Revit format.

Having a good understanding of how annotation objects can be used in Revit MEP 2015 will enable you to easily optimize content and create documents that align with your company standards.

In this chapter, you will learn to do the following:

- Create symbolic lines and filled regions
- Use symbols within families for representation on drawings
- Work with constraints and parameters for visibility control
- Use labels to create tags

Using Drafting Tools in Revit

It is easy to assume that because Revit MEP 2015 is a BIM solution, it does not have very good tools for drafting tasks. The truth is that the drafting tools available in Revit MEP are very useful for creating symbolic linework, hatch patterns, and annotation objects. Becoming proficient with these tools will greatly reduce your need to rely on a CAD application for drafting tasks. The more work you can do in Revit MEP, the less work you'll need to do in multiple applications, which will increase your efficiency and make managing standards and content easier.

The drafting tools available when drawing in a project view are the same as those available in the Family Editor. These tools appear on the Draw panel of the contextual tab when you click the Detail Line button, Symbolic Line button, or Model Line button, depending on the type of file in which you are working. Figure 18.1 shows the Draw and Line Style panels as they appear on the Modify | Place Detail Lines contextual tab when the Detail Line button on the Annotate tab is clicked. The Line Style panel allows you to choose the style of line that will be drawn. Only line styles defined in your project will be available.

FIGURE 18.1
Available shapes and line styles for lines

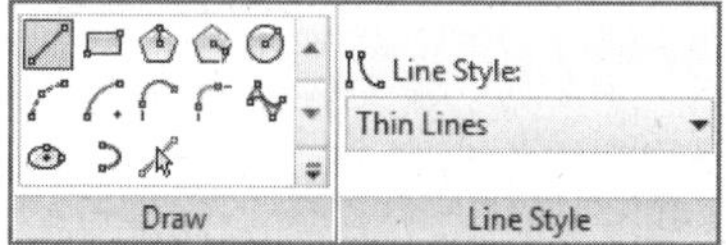

You can use the buttons in this panel to draw lines or shapes. Clicking a button activates various options on the Options Bar that enable you to set conditions for the linework.

When you click the Line button on the Draw panel, for example, the option to draw a chain of lines appears on the Options Bar. This option continues the Line command from the last point you click to end a line. This can save extra clicks because you do not need to click the start point for each new line you draw. If you draw a series of lines, they are joined at their end points. If you deselect the Chain check box on the Options Bar, you need to click in the drawing area to establish the start point of each new line you draw.

By holding down the Shift key while you are drawing a line, you force it to snap to the orthogonal axis. The temporary dimensions allow you to see the length and angle of the line you are drawing. You can type in a number to automatically set the length of a line. You can change the angle of a line by selecting it after it is drawn and editing the temporary angle dimension. You can also use the Drag Line End grips that appear when you select a line to change its length and/or angle.

When lines are drawn with Revit and they are connected at their end points, the end points remain connected when either of the lines is moved. There is no "stretch" command in Revit because lines maintain their connections at end points. You can select the Rectangle button on the panel to click a start point and opposite corner for an end point of a rectangle. Once drawn, the rectangle is treated as four separate lines, not a single entity. When you select any one of the lines and move it, the adjacent lines adjust to maintain the shape of a rectangle.

The panel has two buttons for drawing polygons: one for a polygon inscribed in a circle and one for a polygon circumscribed around a circle. Either one gives you choices on the Options Bar for the number of sides and also to draw at an offset. You can select the Radius box on the Options Bar to set the radius of the imaginary circle that determines the size of the polygon.

To move or edit a shape as a whole, you must select all the lines that make up the shape. This is easily done by using a selection/crossing window or by placing your mouse pointer over one of the lines and then pressing the Tab key until all the lines are highlighted. Once you have selected a shape, you can use the grips at the end points to edit the shape without breaking the connection of the lines.

Figure 18.2 shows two rectangles that have been edited. The rectangle on the left was edited by selecting the line on the right side and dragging the line's end point. The one on the right was edited by selecting the entire shape and dragging the end point in the upper-right corner.

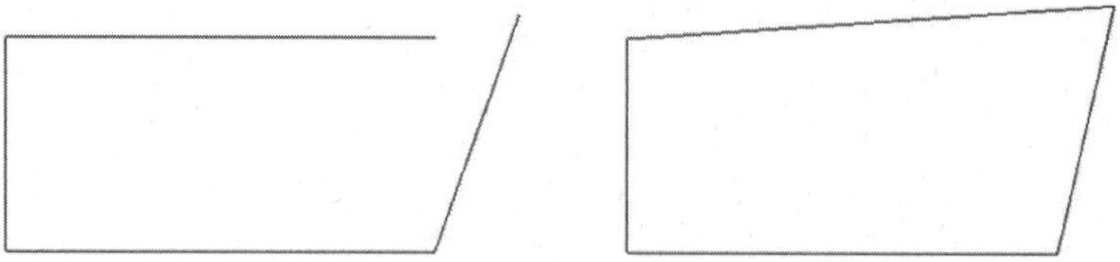

FIGURE 18.2
Editing options for linework

The Circle button allows you to draw a circle by selecting the center point and then dragging your cursor to set the radius. You can type in a length for the radius after you click to set the center point, and the circle is drawn automatically with a radius of your chosen length. The temporary dimension for the radius remains on the screen after you click to set the radius. You can then click the temporary radius dimension to edit it. When you click a circle that has been drawn, the Drag Line End grip that appears can be dragged to set the size of the circle. The Options Bar also has a radius option to set the size of the circle prior to selecting a center point.

TEMPORARY DIMENSIONS

Temporary dimensions are useful for more than just modifying items as you draw. You can click a temporary dimension and click the icon that appears to change the dimension from temporary to an actual annotation dimension in the view. You may accidentally click this icon from time to time. The dimension created can be deleted if unwanted.

Drawing Arcs

The Draw panel contains four buttons for drawing arcs. The first two are for drawing arcs whether or not they are connected to any other type of linework, while the other two are for drawing specific types of arcs that relate to lines:

Start-End-Radius Arc Ideal for sketching an arc when its center isn't known, this button is used for drawing an arc by selecting a start point and an end point and then dragging your mouse pointer to define the radius. You can preset the radius on the Options Bar. When you set the radius prior to drawing, you need to click to set the start and end points. The third click determines the direction of the arc instead of the radius. You can input a length for the temporary dimension while drawing to establish the distance between the start and end points and then again to establish the radius. The grips that appear when you select an arc are for changing the radius or the arc length.

Center-Ends Arc Ideal for sketching an arc when its center is known, this button is used for drawing an arc by first clicking to establish the center point and then clicking to set the first end point. From this end point, an arc is drawn with a radius that is the distance from the center to the selected end point when you click to establish the second end point. You can draw an arc to a maximum 180-degree angle by using this tool. When you drag your mouse pointer to establish the end point and move it past 180 degrees from the start point of the arc, the direction of the arc changes. Once the center and radius have been defined, you can type in the angle.

Tangent-End Arc This button can be used to draw an arc from the end point of an existing line or arc. Once you click the end point to begin drawing the arc, you drag your mouse pointer and an arc appears, with the existing line or arc remaining tangent to it. This tool is useful for transitioning from a straight line (or another arc) to a curve without having to draw separate items and then adjust tangency. You can edit the radius of the arc after it is drawn by editing its temporary dimension. Because the line is tangent to the arc, the larger you make the radius, the shorter the line becomes. This tool is useful when sketching geometry, because it provides a clean transition from the curved surface to the flat surface.

Fillet Arc This button is for drawing an arc that creates a filleted corner between two lines. Unlike other CAD applications that apply a fillet by using an editing command, Revit considers this creating an arc where there was none. Clicking the button prompts you to select the lines for the fillet. Dragging your mouse pointer reveals the arc to be created between the two lines. You cannot type a radius length while dragging the arc, but you can edit the temporary dimension that appears after the fillet arc is drawn. Alternatively, you can preset the radius on the Options Bar.

Using Other Drawing Tools

These additional buttons are also useful:

Spline This button is used for drawing free-form lines. Each click point creates a vertex that can be edited to change the curve of the line at that point. The Drag Line End grips that appear at the end points of a spline lengthen or shorten the entire spline when they are dragged to new locations. You cannot type any lengths while drawing a spline, and there are no temporary dimensions to edit after the spline is complete. You can add and delete control points to a spline after you sketch it if necessary. The more points you use, the more accurately you can adjust the shape. Splines cannot be trimmed to other lines, and the Split tool doesn't work on them either. The start and end points affect the whole spline if you adjust their location.

Ellipse This button can be used to draw an ellipse by first selecting the center point and then defining the length of each axis. Once you have drawn the ellipse, you can use the grips that appear at each quadrant to edit the size and shape of the ellipse. You can also edit the temporary dimensions that appear, to adjust the distance from the center to the quadrant (half of the axis length).

Partial Ellipse This button is used for drawing half an ellipse. Unlike the arc tools, the Partial Ellipse button creates a parabola instead of an arc that has a uniform radius. When using this button, you click to establish the start and end points and then drag your mouse pointer to define the height of the parabola. You can enter dimensions while drawing, or you can use grips and temporary dimensions for editing after the partial ellipse is drawn.

Pick Lines This button is used to create Revit linework by selecting lines that already exist in the view. You can select lines from a linked or imported CAD file, and a Revit line will be drawn in the same location. This tool is very useful for duplicating CAD details or symbols. You cannot use window selection to pick multiple lines, but you can use the Tab key to select multiple lines that are connected. The Offset option on the Options Bar allows you to create lines that are offset by a specified distance from the lines you select.

Create Similar

The Create Similar tool in Revit MEP 2015 is useful for duplicating a model component. However, when this tool is used on linework, it activates the Line command with the selected line style only, not the specific tool for the shape selected. For exxample, if you click a circle and use the Create Similar tool, you still need to click the Circle button on the Draw panel.

Creating Filled Regions

Filled regions are useful in the symbols that represent model components. By controlling the visibility of filled regions, you can use them to represent different types of an object. There are two types of patterns that filled regions can use: Model and Drafting. Model patterns represent real-world dimensional values (for example, for tile shapes or ceiling grids), while Drafting patterns represent printed dimensions (such as parallel vertical lines that are a set distance apart). Drafting patterns will be the same regardless of view scale, whereas Model patterns are affected by the scale of a view and look more realistic in perspective (camera) 3D views. The Drafting pattern types should be used when creating filled regions for symbols.

To create a filled region within an annotation family, click the Filled Region button located on the Detail panel of the Create tab. Filled regions cannot be created in component families. When you click the Filled Region button, a contextual tab appears, containing the Draw panel. Unlike with hatch patterns in other software, Revit needs us to define the boundary of regions. This might seem like more work, but it does allow for more control over the appearance of each boundary segment; it is quite powerful. The same tools discussed earlier can be used to define the boundary of the region. The type of line used for the region boundary can be chosen from the drop-down on the Subcategory panel. You can use invisible lines for the region boundary in order to avoid duplication of linework. The boundary lines of a region can eliminate the need for some lines as well since there is no point in drawing detail lines in the same place as the boundary of a region.

Figure 18.3 shows two symbols with filled regions. The boundary lines of the symbol on the left are thicker than the linework of the symbol, causing the region to appear to be too large. The region on the right has invisible lines for its boundary, so only the pattern is displayed.

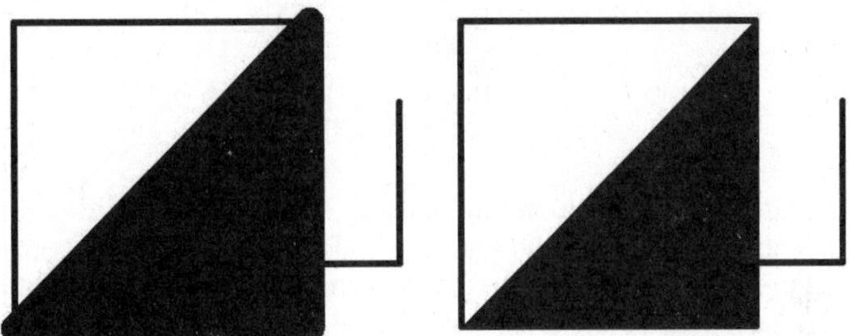

FIGURE 18.3 Filled region boundaries in a symbol

Building a Symbol Library

As with most CAD systems, it is helpful to have a library of symbols that are used repeatedly on projects and in details, diagrams, and families. You can create a library of Revit symbols that matches your CAD library and thereby reduce your dependence on importing CAD data into your projects. These symbols can be nested into component families in order to create construction documents that show your design as you normally would, but also with the benefit of 3D model information.

Generic Annotations

Annotation families are typically tags, but one type can be used to create symbols that can be nested into component families or used directly in your project. The `Generic Annotation.rft` template can be used to create an annotation family that is not categorized as a tag. To create a new generic annotation, click the New link in the Families section of the Recent Files screen and browse to the `Annotations` folder. You can also click New ➤ Annotation Symbol from the application menu, as shown in Figure 18.4.

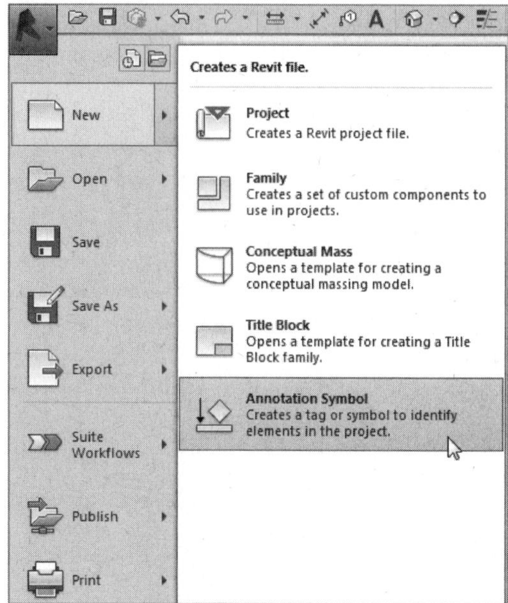

FIGURE 18.4
Creating a new annotation symbol from the application menu

The generic annotation family contains horizontal and vertical reference planes that intersect to define the insertion point of the family. There is also a text object that serves as a reminder to assign the family to a category. When creating a symbol for use in a component family, there is no need to change the category of the annotation family. Delete the text object immediately so as not to forget to do so later. Annotation families are created at a scale of 1:1, so it is important to draw your symbol at its printed size. When used in a project or nested into a component family, the annotation scales according to the view scale of the project or family.

If you already have a library of CAD symbols, you can use them to create your Revit symbols by importing them into the annotation family and then duplicating the linework with Revit lines. CAD files cannot be linked into families, so you must use the Import CAD button on the Insert tab when working in the Family Editor.

When you're importing a CAD file, the layers are imported as subcategories, so if you subsequently explode the imported CAD file, any linetypes defined are added with a prefix of `IMPORT-`. These subcategories are unnecessary and only add extra weight to your files. Both the line patterns and subcategories remain in your file even if you delete the imported CAD file.

There is a workflow that lets you convert your existing CAD symbols to Revit without creating unwanted baggage within the Revit family. Linework that is created in an annotation family can be copied and pasted to another annotation family. You can start by creating a generic annotation family into which you will import your CAD symbols. Once you have created the linework in Revit, you can delete the imported CAD linework and copy the Revit linework to your Clipboard. You can then create a new generic annotation family and paste the Revit linework into it. By doing so, you will have an annotation family that does not contain any of the imported subcategories or line patterns.

Subcategories

There is a single annotation category for all generic annotations in a project. To control the visibility and appearance of your symbol lines, you need to create subcategories for them. Otherwise, all symbols for all families will have the same appearance throughout your project. Make subcategories that are specific to the kind of symbol you are creating so that you can control those specific symbols independently from other generic annotations.

Be as specific as you like with the names of subcategories to avoid any confusion. One example of organizing your object styles in your families is to follow the line styles in your project. For example, a line style named 01 – Continuous – Black gives you all the information you need for a line, and you can assign it to a specific symbol or a portion of the symbol. If you decide that the line weight thickness is not appropriate, you can switch it from 01 – Continuous – Black to 02 – Continuous – Black. Using this method, your families will have a consistent look. One limitation to using such a generic method of naming the object styles is that when you are controlling visibility graphics in your project, you will be controlling them for all annotation symbols assigned to 01 – Continuous – Black.

You may wish to name your subcategories to aid in the visibility control of nested annotations within your component families. For example, you may choose to create a subcategory for disconnect symbol lines that you draw in an annotation family that is to be nested into a disconnect switch component family. By naming the subcategory clearly, you can easily determine the subcategory for which you need to adjust the visibility.

To create a subcategory, access the Object Styles settings in the family file from the Object Styles button on the Manage tab. Click the New button in the Object Styles dialog box, and give the subcategory a name. You can set the line weight, line color, and line pattern for the subcategory. These settings will carry through when the annotation family is loaded into a project or component family file. You can choose to use the default settings for the subcategory and override them in the project or family file into which the annotation is loaded. When you draw linework or a filled region in the annotation family, set the line style to the newly created subcategory in the drop-down list on the Subcategory panel. Figure 18.5 shows a subcategory created in an annotation family (top) and how the subcategory appears when the annotation family is loaded into a project (bottom).

With a CAD file from your symbol library imported into a new annotation family file, you can use the Pick Lines button on the Draw panel to duplicate the CAD linework. If you have defined line styles with colors, it may be helpful to invert the colors of the CAD file during import so that it is clear which lines are CAD and which are Revit. As stated earlier, the CAD file should be deleted when all the linework has been duplicated. Save the annotation to your own Revit MEP 2015 library in the appropriate discipline folder within the `Annotations` folder. It is a best practice to separate your custom families from the Autodesk ones, making it easier to upgrade your families the next time you upgrade your software. You can now use the annotation family in a project file by loading it into your project and clicking the Symbol button on the Annotate tab.

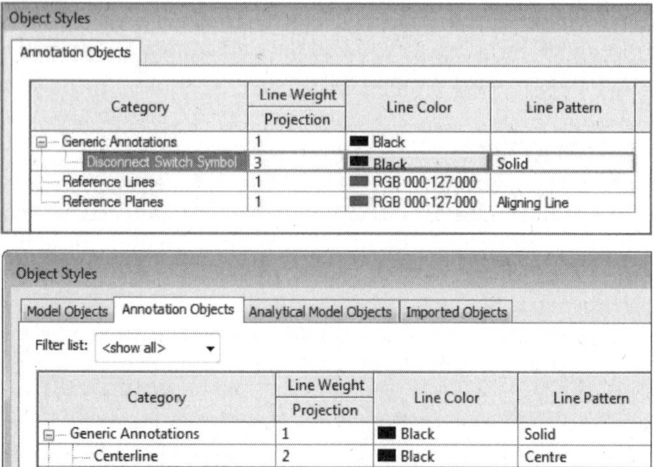

Object Styles

Annotation Objects

Category	Line Weight Projection	Line Color	Line Pattern
Generic Annotations	1	Black	
Disconnect Switch Symbol	3	Black	Solid
Reference Lines	1	RGB 000-127-000	
Reference Planes	1	RGB 000-127-000	Aligning Line

Object Styles

Model Objects | Annotation Objects | Analytical Model Objects | Imported Objects

Filter list: <show all>

Category	Line Weight Projection	Line Color	Line Pattern
Generic Annotations	1	Black	Solid
Centerline	2	Black	Centre
Disconnect Switch Symbol	3	Black	Solid
Generic Model Tags	1	Black	Solid
Grid Heads	1	Black	Solid
Guide Grid	1	PANTONE Process	Solid
Internal Area Load Tags	1	Black	
Internal Line Load Tags	1	Black	
Internal Point Load Tags	1	Black	

FIGURE 18.5 Subcategory settings displayed in an annotation family (top) and a project file (bottom)

FAMILIES VERSION

When you create families in Revit MEP 2015, you can use those families only in Revit MEP 2015. Therefore, it may be a good idea to create your families in an earlier version of Revit, allowing you to use the same families for projects that are still in older versions!

Your annotation family can also be loaded into a component family for use as a schematic symbol representation of the component. Open the component family, and click the Load Family button on the Insert tab. Browse to the annotation family that you want and click Open. On the Annotate tab, click the Symbol button to place the loaded annotation family into the view. You can place an annotation symbol into a family only in floor plan or ceiling plan views, not elevations or 3D views. Place the symbol so that its insertion point matches the insertion point of the component family. When one family is loaded into another, the loaded family is considered to be *nested*. Figure 18.6 shows a thermostat annotation nested into a thermostat component family.

Based on the purpose and functionality of your component family, the nested annotation may need to show all the time. The symbol for a thermostat family shows all the time, but a symbol for a valve family shows only when the pipe is displayed in a single line. In order to achieve this behavior, select the nested family and click the Visibility Settings button from the Modify | Generic Annotations tab. From the newly opened Family Element Visibility Settings dialog box, you can control the detail level of the nested symbol's display. Pipes display as a single line in Coarse and Medium detail levels, so those two check boxes should remain selected for a valve family, and the Fine check box should be deselected.

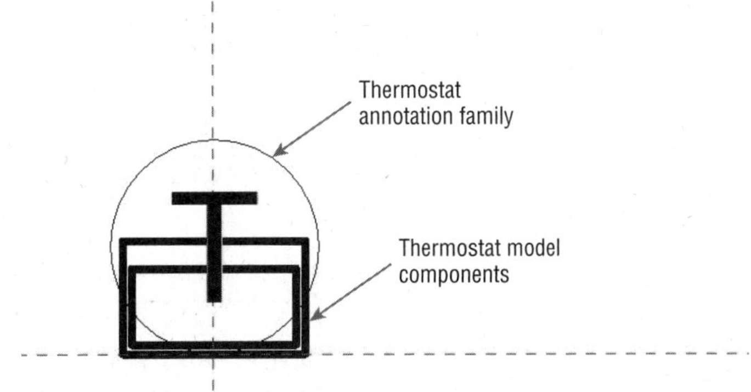

FIGURE 18.6 Annotation family loaded into a component family

Text and Labels

You can use text or labels in your symbols along with linework and filled regions. Text is simply text within your symbol that does not change. For example, if your thermostat symbol always contains only the letter *T*, you can use text in the annotation family. The only way to change the text is to modify it directly in the family by clicking it to change its value. If you want to be able to change the value of a text object in the family through the family's properties, you need to use a label. Labels act in a similar manner to attributes in an Autodesk® AutoCAD® block, and they display the value of the parameter to which they are assigned.

To place text into your annotation family, click the Text button on the Create tab within the Family Editor. Select the desired text style from the Type Selector in the Properties palette. If the text style you want to use does not exist, you can create it. When you create a text style in a family and load the family into another family or a project file, the text style does not carry over into the file into which you are loading. This means that if you want to use the text style in the project, you also need to create it within the project. It is possible to have a text style in a family with the same name as a text style in your project but different settings, such as font or text height. This can be particularly confusing when it comes to fonts. Your default font and default text heights are important considerations for your implementation. If you want to use anything other than the default font (Arial), you need to not only set up your project template with all the necessary styles but also create your own family templates.

In previous versions of Revit, you could rename the RFT files by changing the `.rft` filename extension to `.rfa`, modify and save them, and then rename them back to RFT files in order to create custom family templates. With Revit 2015, you cannot open an RFA file that is a renamed RFT file. If you really need a library of custom family templates, you can create RFA files that have all the settings for each family category you need, and then use those files by copying and renaming them.

When you place a text object into your family, it is important to consider the orientation of the text when the family is used in your project. Text objects have an instance parameter called Keep Text Readable that allows you to set the orientation of the text so that it can be read from left to right or from bottom to top. Annotation families also have a family parameter called Keep Text Readable that applies to any text within the family. You can find this parameter by clicking the Family Category And Parameters button on the Properties panel of the ribbon, as shown in Figure 18.7. It is not necessary to set both parameters to Keep Text Readable in order for the text to remain readable when the family is inserted into a project. When you are working in the Family Editor, the Family Category And Parameters setting governs.

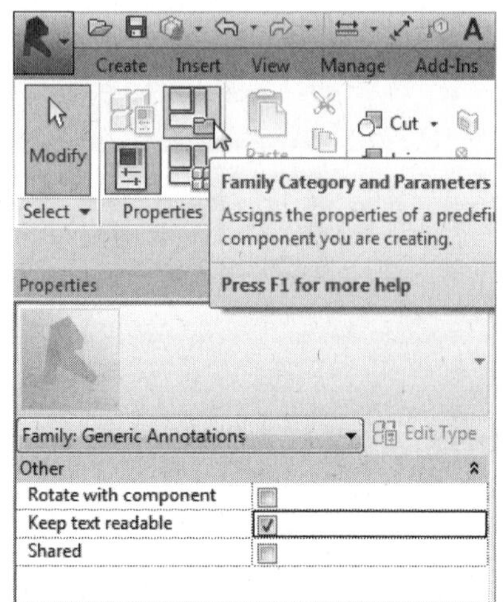

FIGURE 18.7 Keep Text Readable parameter of an annotation family

Detail Components

Although you cannot place an annotation family in any view other than a plan view while working in the Family Editor, you can use a detail component family in lieu of an annotation family. This is useful for adding symbol lines or regions to a face-hosted family that does not have the Maintain Annotation Orientation parameter, such as a light fixture or electrical equipment.

A filled region is often used for electrical panels, to represent panels with different voltages or for declaring emergency use. You cannot create a filled region directly in the component family, and creating one in an annotation family does not work because it needs to be displayed in the panel's Front or Back elevation view. The Back elevation view is what is displayed when a face-hosted family is hosted to a vertical surface. To show a filled region in the front or back elevation of a face-hosted family, you must create a filled region within a detail component and nest the detail component into the face-hosted family. The nested detail component can be placed in either the Front or Back elevation view to be displayed in a project plan view.

To create a detail component, click the New link in the Families section of the Recent Files screen, or choose New ➢ Family from the application menu. Select the `Detail Item.rft` template and click Open.

Detail items are meant to represent real objects, but with only a 2D representation instead of 3D. This means that the size and parameters you use should be created with actual dimensions in mind. You may want your detail component to change size with the component family that it represents, so you need to create parameters for its size. In the example of a filled region for an electrical panel, you need to make the length and width of the region parametric so that it can change size with the panel model component.

Figure 18.8 shows a filled region created in a detail component that has instance parameters that define its length and width. The boundary lines for the filled region are invisible lines. If you find that invisible lines negatively affect the display of the family, you can use a line style that matches the family category and display the border instead of the geometry.

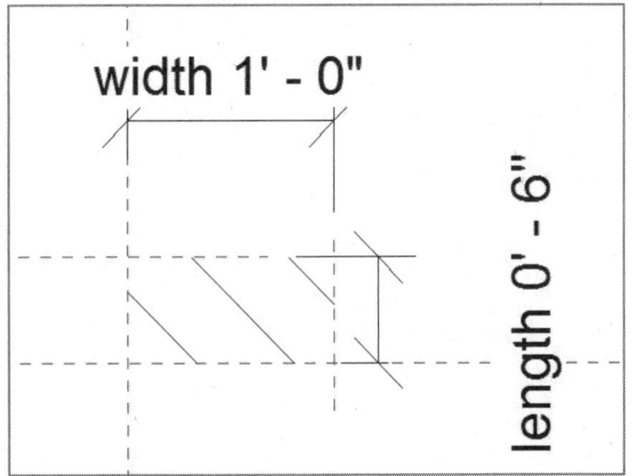

FIGURE 18.8 Filled region in a detail component family

The detail component family can then be loaded into the panel family, and the boundaries of the filled region can be constrained to the geometry of the panel object, as shown in Figure 18.9. The boundaries of the filled region can be stretched and locked to the reference planes in the panel family because of the length and width instance parameters in the detail component family.

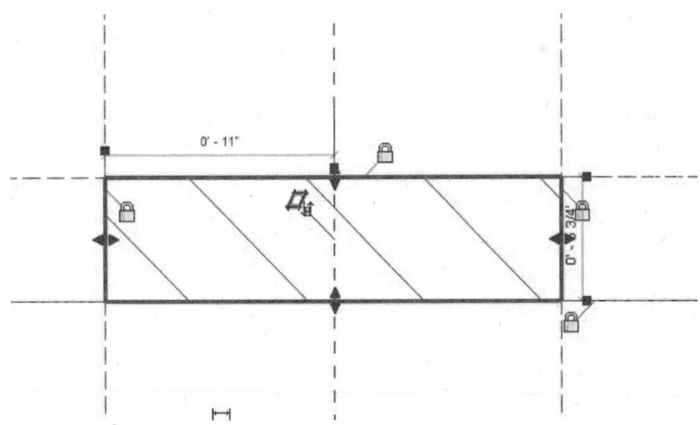

FIGURE 18.9 Detail component filled region in a panel family

When the panel family is used in a project, the filled region adjusts to the different sizes of the panel, creating the desired representation for the panel in a plan view, as shown in Figure 18.10.

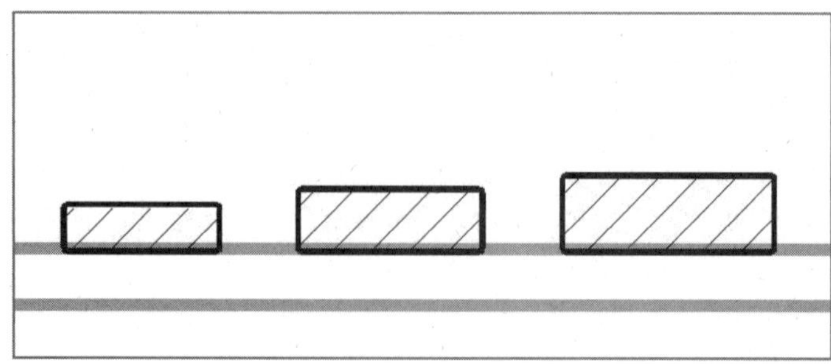

FIGURE 18.10
Various sizes of the same panel family

Unlike annotation families, detail components are not drawn at their print size. When you create a detail component family for use as a symbol, such as for a wall-mounted light fixture, you must draw the symbol to scale. The detail component will not adjust to changes in the view scale.

 **Real World Scenario**

MAKING THE TRANSITION

It can be difficult to adopt an entirely new software solution when you have so much reusable content in your current drafting application. Using a new application does not mean that you cannot create your construction documents to look the same as they do in your current drafting application.

The ability to create the symbols that you use for documentation and to place them in the model components can improve the quality of your projects. Consider taking the time to create a library of annotation families that matches what you currently have. You will be surprised at how quickly your library grows!

Controlling Visibility of Lines, Regions, and Annotations

Elements in a family have unique visibility-control options. You can also use parameters to control what lines, regions, or text are visible for the various types within your family. This functionality allows you to have multiple symbols drawn within the same annotation family that can be nested into a component family containing multiple types. By doing so, you can avoid having numerous separate families for the same kind of component.

Using Visibility Parameters

Lines, regions, and text have a parameter called Visible that allows you to designate whether the item can be seen. It is not likely that you will create linework in your family only to turn off its visibility permanently, but you can turn it on or off, in a project where it matters, by associating its Visible parameter with a Yes/No type parameter in the family. This allows you to show certain lines, regions, or text for one family type and then turn them off to show others for another type.

The receptacle annotation in Figure 18.11 has two filled regions. The vertical region is displayed to represent a GFI receptacle, while the half-circle horizontal region is for a countertop receptacle.

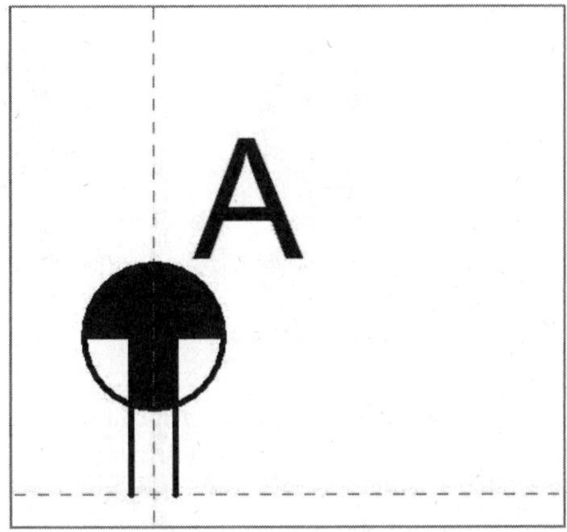

FIGURE 18.11 Annotation family with multiple filled regions

The visibility of each region can be set to the Yes or No (selected or deselected) value of a parameter defined in the family. This is done by associating the value of the parameter with another by clicking the small button at the far right of the parameter value field. When the annotation family is loaded into a component family, its parameters can be associated with parameters in the component family that define the type of component and therefore which region to display. Figure 18.12 shows that the visibility of the vertical region is associated to a parameter in the annotation family called GFI.

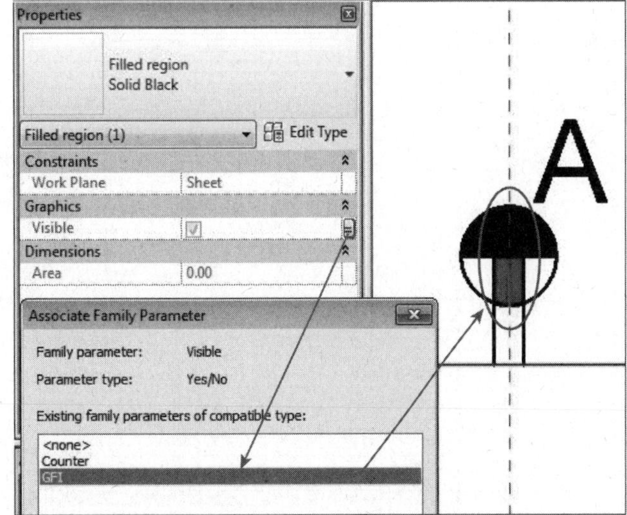

FIGURE 18.12 Visibility of a region associated to a parameter

Figure 18.13 shows that when the annotation is used in a component family, the visibility of the regions depends on the family type used in a project. The process of nesting annotation families into component families is described in more detail in Chapter 21, "Creating Devices."

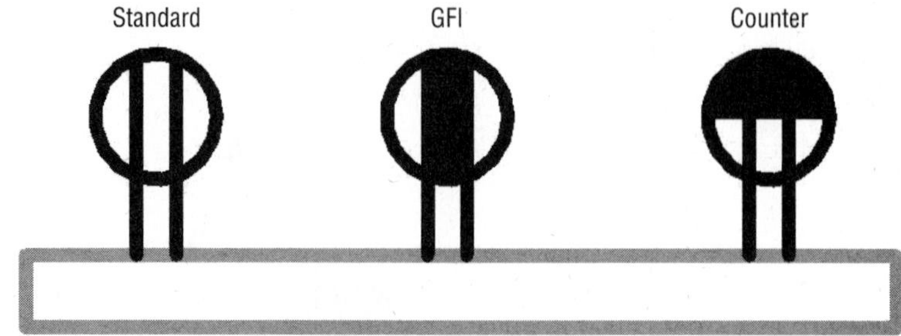

FIGURE 18.13 Display of an annotation family based on component type

Another visibility control option for annotation families is the orientation of the symbol. As stated earlier, the orientation of text within an annotation family can be controlled with the Keep Text Readable parameter. However, it may be your standard or preference to keep the text reading from left to right regardless of the symbol position. This can be achieved with a combination of text objects and visibility parameters.

You can copy a label or text in your annotation family and rotate it so that when the family is rotated, the label or text reads from left to right. The visibility of each label or text object can be set to an instance parameter, allowing you to control which label or text to display at each instance of the component. Figure 18.14 shows a thermostat annotation family with two instances of a label. One has been rotated, and its visibility has been associated to a parameter in the family.

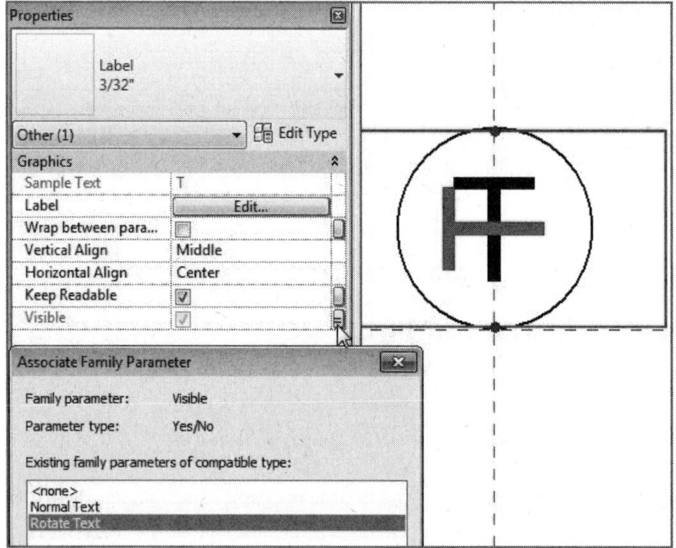

FIGURE 18.14 Annotation family with multiple instances of the same label

When used in a component family, the parameter controlling the visibility of each label can be associated with a Yes/No type parameter of the component. The result is that when the component is used in your model, you can control the visibility of the label to display the annotation symbol in the desired orientation. In Figure 18.15, the topmost thermostat has been modified to display the rotated label in the annotation family, while the thermostat on the bottom is displayed as normal.

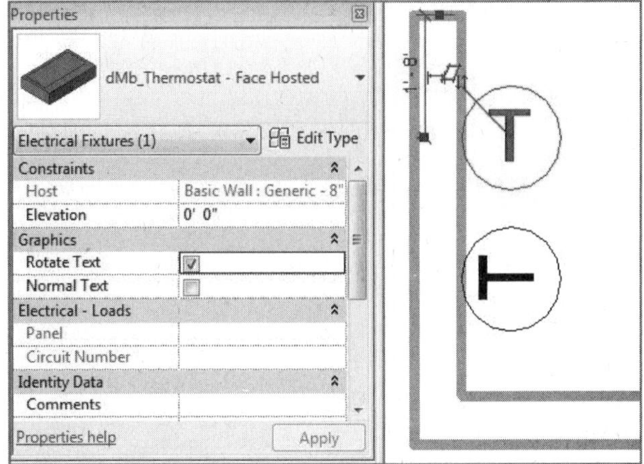

FIGURE 18.15 Multiple display options for a label within a family

This functionality can also be applied to the linework in your annotation family. It may be necessary to create a separate annotation family for the symbol that is to be rotated so that when you insert the families into a component family, the insertion point will be the same. Figure 18.16 shows an annotation family for a light switch (top) and an annotation family for a light switch symbol that is to be rotated when inserted into a component family (bottom).

The two annotation families can be placed into a light switch component family with the normal switch annotation placed into the family at the appropriate insertion point and the switch annotation for the rotated symbol placed into the family and rotated 180 degrees. Yes/No parameters are used to control the visibility of each nested annotation. The result is a switch family that can be displayed as desired depending on its orientation in your model. Figure 18.17 shows the switch family mounted to a wall; the switch on the right has been modified to show the rotated (or "flipped") symbol.

Using Constraints

You can create reference lines in your annotation families to which you can constrain the linework. This allows you to make the annotation family parametric, giving you the freedom to move the annotation symbol independently from the component when using nested annotations in component families. This is most useful when working with face-hosted families.

As stated in Chapter 13, "Power and Communications," it is sometimes necessary to offset the symbol for a component so that it does not interfere with other symbols. For face-hosted items, an offset to the left or right can be created in the component family after the annotation is nested. The offset to show the symbol away from its host needs to be created directly in the annotation family.

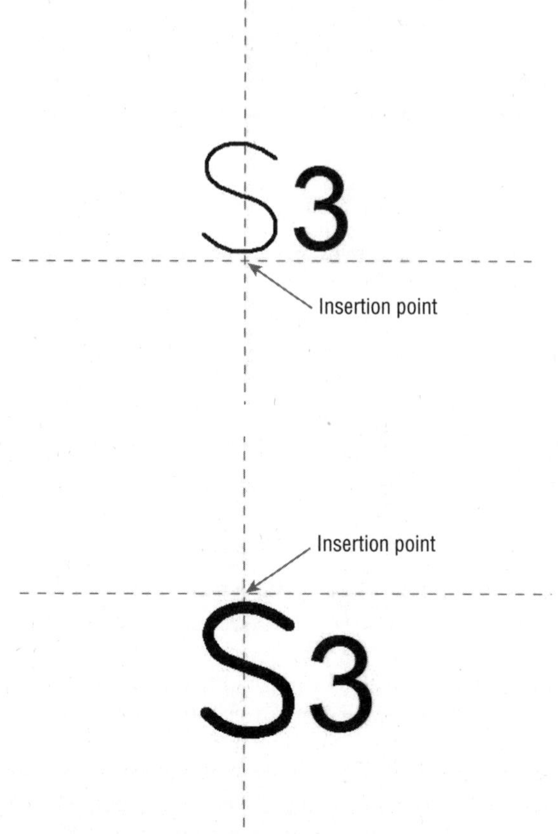

FIGURE 18.16
Light switch annotation (top); light switch annotation to be rotated (bottom)

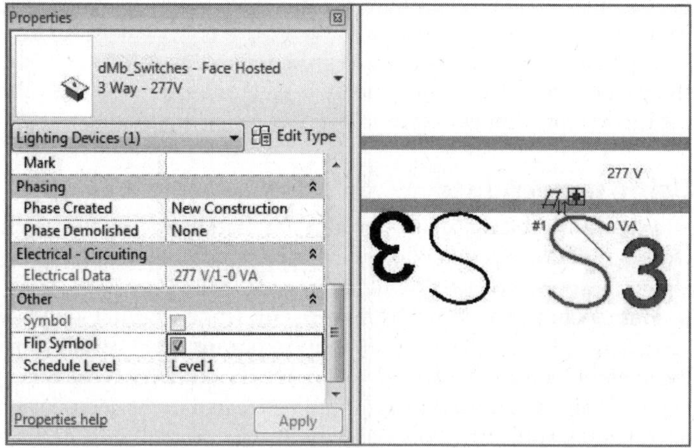

FIGURE 18.17
Display options for a light switch symbol

To create an offset for a symbol that will show the symbol offset from its host, do the following:

1. Open the `Ch18_Duplex Annotation.rfa` family found at `www.sybex.com/go/masteringrevitmep2015`.
2. On the Family Editor's Create tab, click the Reference Line button on the Datum panel.
3. Draw a horizontal reference line above the horizontal reference plane that defines the insertion point. The reference line needs to be only long enough that you can dimension to it.
4. Dimension from the horizontal reference plane to the reference line by clicking the Aligned button on the Dimension panel of the Create tab.
5. Select the dimension, and select the Add Parameter option from the Label drop-down on the Options Bar, as shown in Figure 18.18.

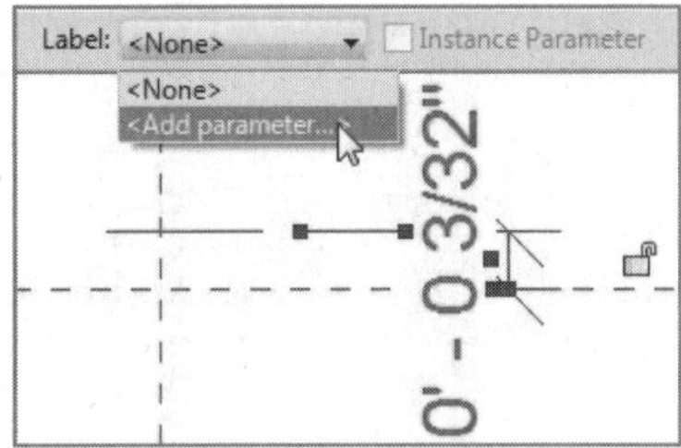

FIGURE 18.18 Assigning a parameter to dimension

6. In the Parameter Properties dialog box, name the parameter **Symbol Offset**, choose Graphics for the group, and make it an instance parameter. Click OK.
7. Select the symbol linework and label. Do not select the reference planes or reference line. Group the selected items by clicking the Create Group button on the Create panel of the contextual tab, shown in Figure 18.19. Name the group **Duplex**, and click OK to continue.

FIGURE 18.19 Creating a group

8. Click the Align button on the Modify tab, and align the group to the reference line by selecting the reference line and then an end point of one of the vertical lines in the receptacle symbol. Lock the alignment by clicking the padlock icon, shown in Figure 18.20.
9. Click the Family Types button on the Properties panel of the ribbon. Input **0** for the value of the Symbol Offset parameter. Click OK.
10. Open the `Ch18_Duplex Receptacle.rfa` file found at `www.sybex.com/go/masteringrevitmep2015`.

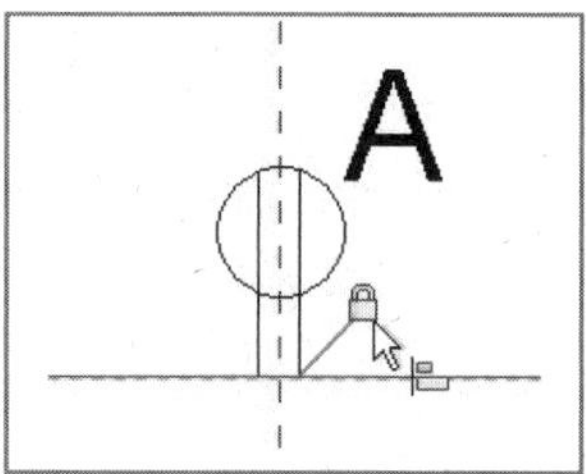

FIGURE 18.20
Aligning and locking the group

11. Switch windows back to the annotation family. Click the Load Into Project button on the Family Editor panel of the ribbon.
12. Place the annotation symbol at the intersection of the reference planes in the receptacle family; see Figure 18.21.

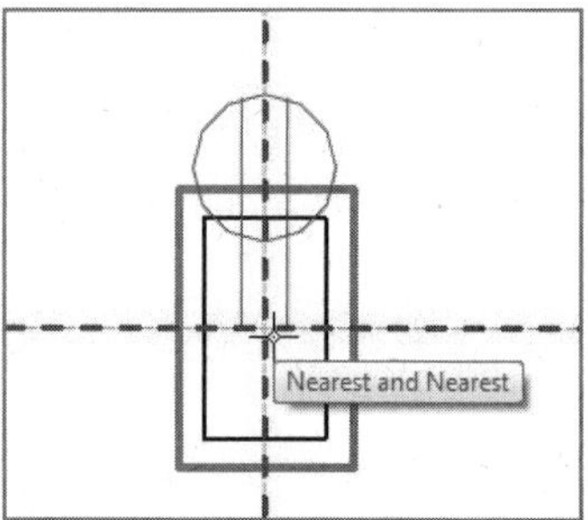

FIGURE 18.21
Placing the annotation symbol

13. Select the annotation symbol, and click the small box to the far right of the Symbol Offset parameter in the Properties palette. (Click the Properties button to turn on the palette if needed.) In the Associate Family Parameter dialog box, select the Symbol Offset From Wall parameter, as shown in Figure 18.22. This lets you control the nested symbol parameter values from within the main family, without the need to edit the family. Click OK. Save the family.

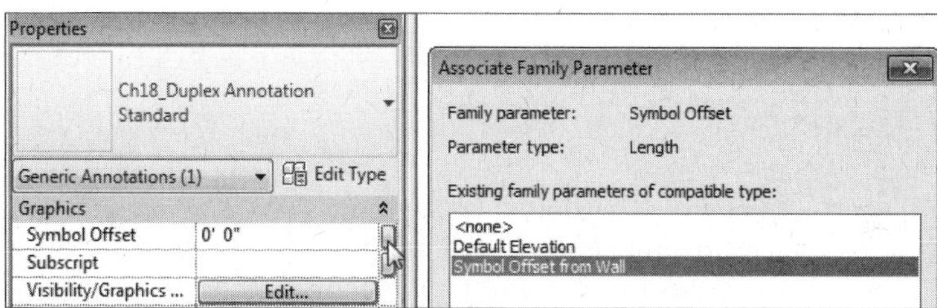

FIGURE 18.22
Controlling the nested annotation symbol parameters via parameters from the main family

14. Load the receptacle family into a project file. Place a receptacle on a vertical host. Select the receptacle, and input a value of **1/4″** (**6** mm) for the Symbol Offset From Wall parameter. Set the Detail Level setting of your view to Fine. Notice that the symbol is offset from the wall while the component remains hosted inside the wall.

Note that you must use a value for the offset that relates to the actual size of the symbol, because the symbol size in the view is determined by the view scale.

Using Labels and Tags

The most common type of annotation family is a tag. Tags can be created for any category of Revit model element to report information about the element on your sheet views. A tag family can contain a combination of labels and linework. The `Generic Tag.rft` family template can be used to create a tag, which can then be categorized for a specific element category. There are also category-specific tag templates that can be used, and you can even use the `Generic Annotation.rft` template and change its category to a tag. Tags are much more useful than plain text because they update automatically when the parameters of an element are changed. Using labels in your tag families does this. Using tags in lieu of text objects saves you editing time and improves coordination.

You can place a label into your annotation family by clicking the Label button on the Text panel of the Create tab. When you click in the drawing area to place the label, the Edit Label dialog box appears. When you use the generic annotation template, any parameters that exist in the family are listed in the box on the left side. If none exist, you can create one by clicking the Add Parameter button in the lower-left corner of the dialog box. After you give the parameter a name and define its type and whether it is an instance or type parameter, it appears in the list.

When you use the generic tag family template, the parameters that are available in the Edit Label dialog box (see Figure 18.23) are parameters that apply to the Generic Models category. The drop-down list above the list of parameters allows you to switch between the category parameters and dimension parameters.

FIGURE 18.23
Parameters available in a generic tag

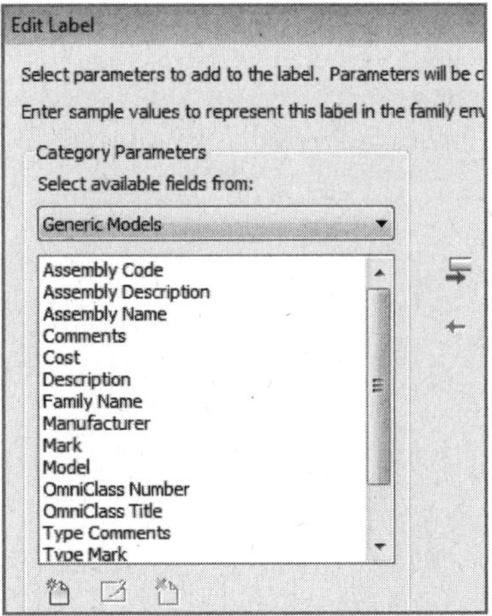

If you categorize your annotation family as a tag for a specific element category, the parameters for that element category appear in the Edit Label dialog box. Figure 18.24 shows a list of parameters for an electrical equipment tag, including the common parameters. Any shared parameters that you have created for the element category can also be added. See Chapter 6, "Parameters," for more information about shared parameters.

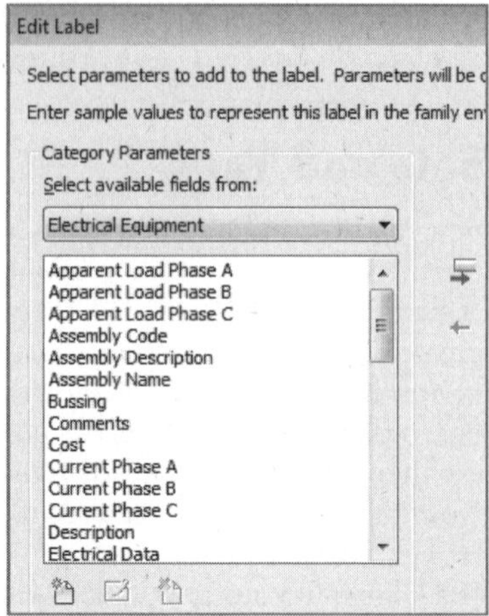

FIGURE 18.24 Parameters for an electrical equipment tag

Label Format Options

You can assign a parameter to your label by selecting it from the list and clicking the Add Parameter(s) To Label button (with the green arrow).

You can apply a prefix or suffix to the label. These appear at every location of the tag in your project. The Sample Value column allows you to input a value that will be seen when you are editing the tag family. If a value is given for the parameter while you are editing the tag family, the sample value will be overwritten.

It is possible to add multiple parameters to a single label. Doing so will list the parameter values in the same label object. Selecting the check box in the Break column of the Edit Label dialog box creates a hard return after the value of the parameter when it is displayed in the label. This enables you to have a label with multiple lines of text, as shown in Figure 18.25.

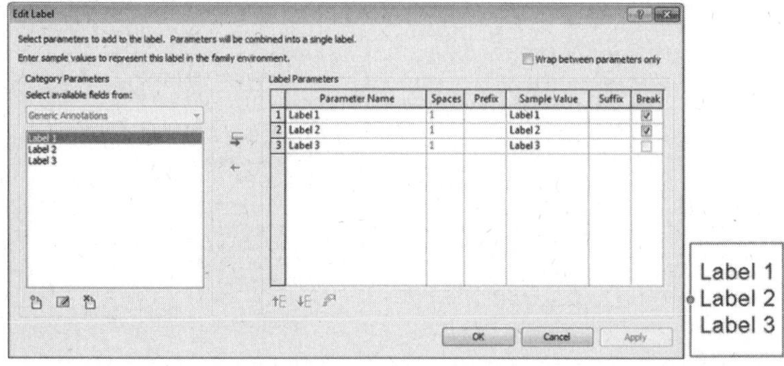

FIGURE 18.25 Single label with multiple parameters

If you do not use the Break option, the parameter values will be displayed on a single line. If the single line of parameter values exceeds the bounding box of the label, the values wrap in the same manner as a text object. You can select the box in the upper-right corner of the Edit Label dialog box to wrap the values between parameters only. This prevents values of a single parameter from ending up on multiple lines. Figure 18.26 shows a multi-parameter label on a single line and the same label with its bounding box shortened and the Wrap Between Parameters Only option selected. Notice that the value for the Description parameter did not wrap.

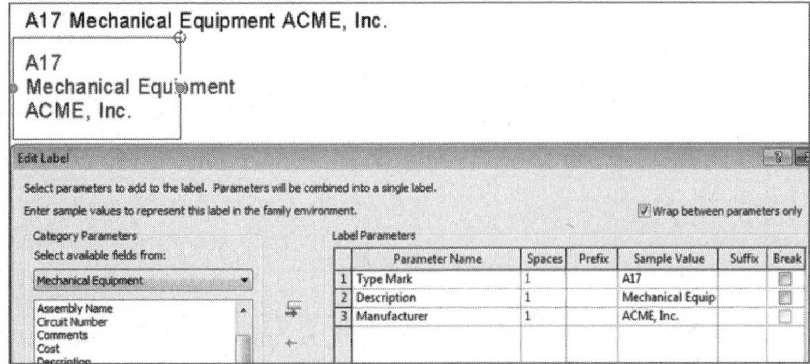

FIGURE 18.26
Multi-parameter label

When you click OK to close the Edit Label dialog box, the label appears displaying the sample values. The label properties can be edited to display the parameter values as desired. Select the label, and access the Properties palette to edit the alignment of the text and its readability instance properties. The type properties of the label define the text used to display the parameter values. You can assign a color and line weight to the text and define whether the background is transparent or opaque. A tag with a label that has an opaque background masks out any elements that it is placed over in your project views.

In the Text group of a label's type properties, you can assign a font and text size. You can also make the text bold, italicized, or underlined. You can apply a width factor to the text as well.

FOLLOW THE LEADER

You cannot define the type of arrowhead for a tag family leader when you are editing the family. The leader arrowhead definition is a type property of a tag family after it is placed into a project. It is a good idea to add all your commonly used tags to your project template file and then define the arrowhead. This lets users concentrate on using the software instead of having to change properties with each new tag type used.

Labels and Linework

Your tag families can be a combination of labels, text, and linework. It is important to position these items around the family's insertion point. Improper placement of items in a tag family causes inaccuracies in the location of leader lines when the tag is placed into a project. The same drafting tools used to create an annotation family can be used in tag families.

Figure 18.27 shows a duct tag that contains labels and linework. There are two labels, so they can be positioned independently. A suffix was added to each label. The linework is positioned at the intersection of the reference planes for proper leader orientation when the tag is used in a project.

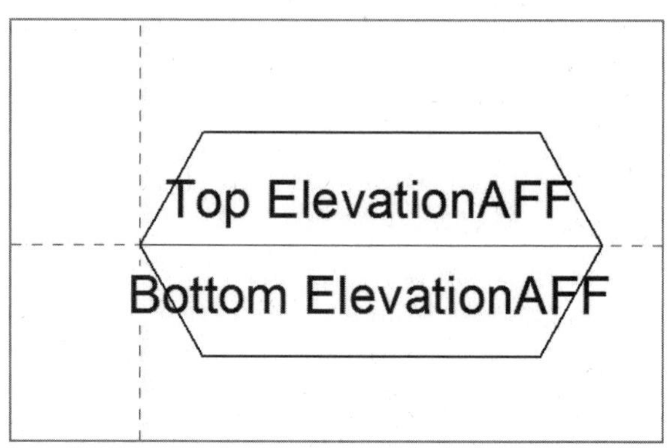

FIGURE 18.27
Sample duct tag family with linework and labels

> **OH, SNAP!**
>
> You cannot snap to text objects or labels, so you have to position them manually. However, text objects and labels align with other text and labels in the drawing area.

When you properly locate the graphics in your tag families, their leaders maintain connection with the tag graphics regardless of which direction the leader is pointing, as shown in Figure 18.28.

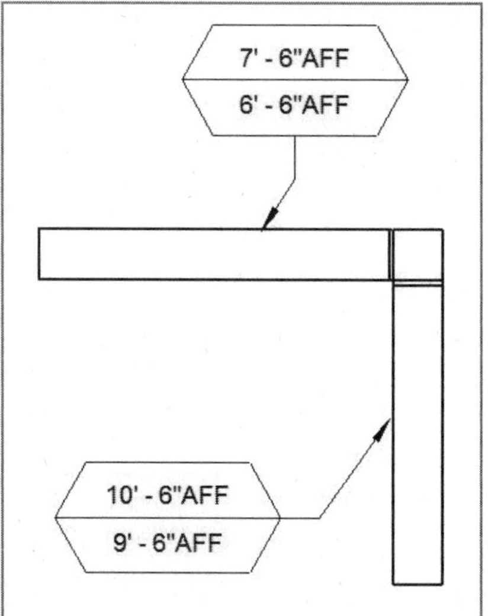

FIGURE 18.28
Tags with leaders

When you place a tag family into your project view, there is an option on the Options Bar to orient the tag vertically or horizontally. If you want your tag to align with its associated item, you can select the box in the Rotate With Component parameter. You can find this by clicking the Family Category And Parameters button on the Properties panel of the ribbon when editing the family. Setting your tag family to rotate with its associated component disables the option to set the tag to horizontal or vertical because the tag aligns with the component, as shown in Figure 18.29.

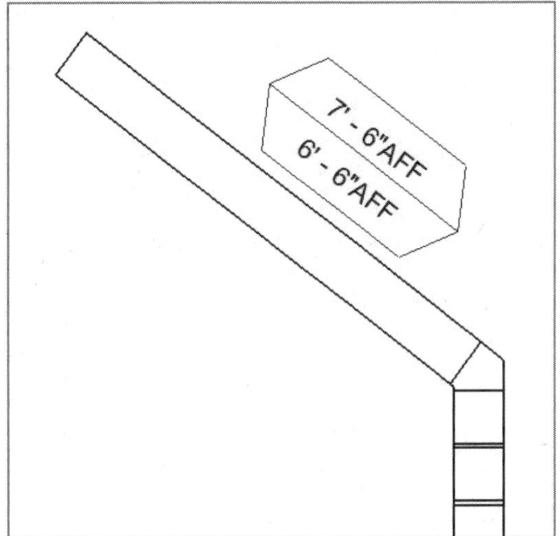

Figure 18.29
Tag aligned with angled duct

The Bottom Line

Create symbolic lines and filled regions. Not only is Revit MEP 2015 a modeling application, it also contains the tools necessary to accomplish drafting tasks.

Master It Having a good command of the tools available for creating symbols helps you create families that represent your design elements exactly the way you want to see them. What line tool is best suited for duplicating the linework of an imported CAD symbol?

Use symbols within families for representation on drawings. Given the schematic nature of MEP plans, symbols and annotation objects are important parts of your Revit MEP 2015 workflow, allowing you to represent your model components according to your company standards.

Master It By having annotation symbols nested into your component families, you can create an accurate 3D model that is displayed schematically on your construction documents. Explain the importance of creating subcategories for the graphics in your annotation families.

Work with constraints and parameters for visibility control. The parametric modeling capabilities of Revit 2015 make it a powerful BIM solution. These capabilities can be used in annotation families as well.

Master It A common scenario for a Revit project is to link consultant files into your project file. Because of this, face-hosted families are often used. Face-hosted components can be attached to either a vertical or horizontal host, so the ability to separate the annotation symbol from the host needs to be created in the annotation family.

When using a length parameter to define the offset of a symbol from its host, what value should be input for the parameter when the component family is in a project?

Use labels to create tags. Tags are the most commonly used annotation families in a project. They are used to report information about objects in a Revit model.

Master It The use of labels is much more effective than using text objects for keeping documents coordinated.

If your project requires that you show AFF after each pipe elevation tag on your construction documents, how can you accomplish this globally, throughout your project?

Chapter 19

Creating Equipment

The equipment families used for the design of your MEP engineering systems are important—not only for coordinating the physical model but also for establishing the components that serve as the equipment for your engineering systems. The properties you assign to your equipment families will define how they can be used in relation to other components within a system.

Many mechanical and electrical equipment items require clearance space for maintenance and installation. With the Autodesk® Revit® MEP 2015 software, you can define the required clearances for equipment families either directly in the family files or as a separate component. This gives you the ability to coordinate your model fully to avoid costly conflicts during construction.

Creating equipment families that are generic enough for use early in the design process, yet parametrically changeable, will help you transition through design phases and changes to systems smoothly and efficiently. The physical properties of MEP equipment are similar enough in most cases to use simple geometry that can be sized according to specified equipment.

Whether you are creating equipment for mechanical, plumbing, or electrical systems, knowing how the equipment will be used from an engineering standpoint as well as a modeling standpoint will help you create the types of families that fit your workflow and processes best.

In this chapter, you will learn to do the following:

- Create MEP equipment families
- Add connectors to equipment for systems
- Create clearance spaces for equipment
- Add parameters to equipment

Modeling MEP Equipment

With the rising popularity of building information modeling (BIM), more and more manufacturers are providing their products for use in a virtual model environment. This can be very useful when you get to the stage in your design where you can specify the exact equipment to be used. Early in the design, however, you may not know what equipment will be used. Furthermore, you may not yet have done calculations that would determine the size of the equipment needed.

All of this boils down to a need for MEP equipment families that are realistic in size and function but also parametrically editable to compensate for changes in the design of both the project and the systems used. These families need to be flexible enough to handle the seemingly constant change that occurs early in the design process, but they also need to have the functionality to represent their intended purpose accurately.

Some of the resistance to adopting a BIM approach for designing a project stems from the fact that too much information is required early on that is not known in a typical project environment. Having usable equipment families can alleviate some of that concern and allow you to move forward with your design processes.

Hosting Options

When planning for a family, there are plenty of things to consider. One of the first is how the family will be placed into a project model. Is the equipment inline with duct or pipe? Does the equipment require a building element to which it will be attached? Knowing the answers to these types of questions will help you start with the right family template so that the equipment you create can be used properly in your projects.

Generally speaking, there are three hosting family behaviors: generic, face based, and object based. The generic families are the most common families, and they are not constrained to any adjacent geometry; instead, they are constrained to the level they are placed on. Face-based families are commonly used as grills, diffusers, plumbing fixtures, and so on. In order to place those families, you need to have a present host (wall, floor, counter, and so on). The host can be either in your MEP model or in any Revit-linked files. Object-based families are almost never used in Revit MEP. This is because they require the physical presence of the host in your model and they can't be placed on hosts that exist in any of the linked Revit models. In other words, you can't place any object-based diffusers on the architectural ceiling unless you have ceiling objects modeled in your own MEP model (not through the link).

To make the right decision about what hosting behavior you should choose, you need to know the pros and cons of those behaviors.

Generic (nonhosted) families behave pretty much like any other object in Revit—they change location only if you move them.

Object-based families behave like face-based families for the most part, except that they need the host to exist in the model and not be part of a linked Revit file.

Face-hosted families have one major advantage: they follow the plane of the host. Anytime the architect adjusts the ceiling location, your diffusers will adjust accordingly. Cool, right? Ceiling diffusers follow the elevation of the ceiling, and the water closet follows the plane of the wall (not the elevation, but the actual plane of the wall finish). Ironically, this advantage is its biggest disadvantage. It is important to understand that as your objects move with the hosted element, any connected pipes or ducts will adjust to fit and can potentially disconnect and break the integrity of the system. When you receive the new architectural background and try to open your MEP model, you will get the message shown in Figure 19.1.

FIGURE 19.1 Message that appears when you're using face-hosted families

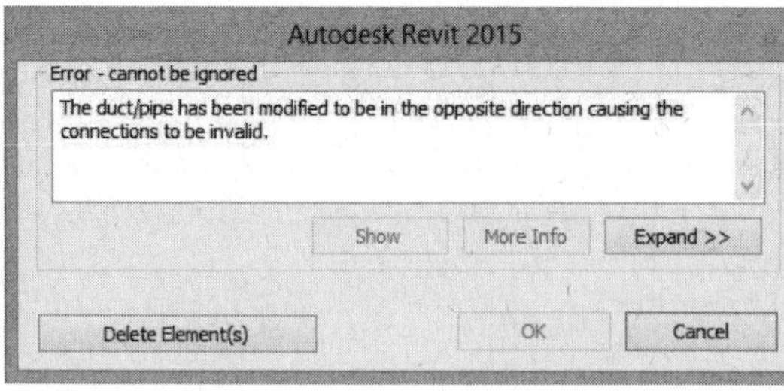

This message, as you can see, has only two options: Delete Element(s) will delete some pipes, pipe fittings, ducts, and duct fittings; Cancel will cancel the process of opening your project. The bottom line is that in order to open your project, you must delete certain elements. It is good practice when you are designing with Revit MEP to have all pipes and ducts connected, and as you move a main piece of pipe, any branches that exist should extend or shorten. Knowing that fundamental behavior of Revit, let's translate it to a face-hosted family that is following the host. Let's say you have placed a plumbing fixture on top of the architectural plumbing fixture; the only difference is that your plumbing fixture has a connection point where you can connect your pipes, as shown in Figure 19.2.

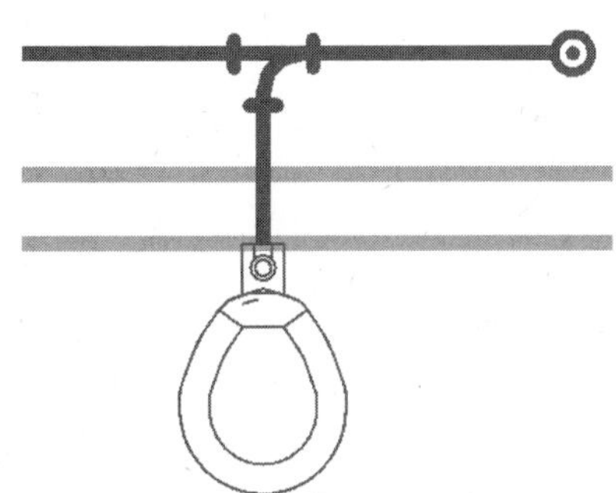

FIGURE 19.2 Connected plumbing fixture

When the architect relocates the hosting wall (toward or away from the main), your plumbing fixture will follow. Revit will do its best to maintain the integrity of any connected pipes. Therefore, the short pipe coming off the main will either extend or shorten. If this pipe is shortened so far that the elements can't remain connected, Revit will not know how to reconfigure the whole system and will simply try to delete the short pipe. This is why you'll get the message that certain elements need to be deleted.

Once you accept the message and open your model, the only way to find which pieces have been deleted is to inspect the entire model visually. This can be a time-consuming and frustrating process.

Face-based families are powerful and at the same time dangerous. As a rule of thumb, you should consider creating face-based families for any objects that require following the host but don't have any connected elements (receptacles, thermostats, switches, and so on). When you have elements connected to the object, proceed with caution because those connections may break.

Equipment that sits on the floor of a room or at the exterior of a building does not need to be created as a hosted family. When you place a generic (nonhosted) family into your project, it will be associated with the level of the view in which it is placed. However, if the equipment requires a pad for housekeeping or structural support, you may want to make the family face hosted so it can be attached to the face of the pad. This will allow for coordination with changes to the pad, assuming that the structural engineer or architect provides the pad. If the equipment you are creating always requires a pad, you can build it directly in the equipment family—that's assuming that you are responsible for placing and sizing the pad. When the structural engineer is responsible for the equipment pad, you can use the Offset parameter of your mechanical equipment to elevate it on top of the pad.

You can also use the Align tool to align your equipment to the architectural wall, floor, or ceiling; however, your equipment will not move with the architectural element if that model is adjusted.

Once you have determined the hosting behavior of an equipment family, you can build the solid geometry of the equipment in relation to the host object or reference plane that represents how the family will be placed into a model.

Family Categories

There are essentially two choices for categorizing your equipment families: Mechanical or Electrical Equipment. This may seem limiting, but keep in mind that you can make any subcategories you choose. It may be necessary to categorize an equipment family as some other model category, depending on how it is used in your projects. This is typically done for visibility control or scheduling purposes, although for scheduling the most common way is to use a parameter for filtering out just the equipment you want to display in your schedule. Variable air volume (VAV) boxes need to be in a different schedule than boilers, although both of them are mechanical equipment. By creating a parameter such as Schedule Filter and assigning the value in the VAV box family to, say, VAV, you will be able to schedule (filter out) VAV boxes separately from the other equipment in the project. Alternatively, if you use a rigid naming structure in your family names or type marks, these can be used to separate out the different equipment elements in schedules.

Systems Equipment

If you were to build an equipment family and categorize it as something other than Mechanical or Electrical Equipment, you would not be able to assign it as the equipment for a system when you create MEP systems in your project.

You can set the category of a family by clicking the Family Category And Parameters button on the Create tab in the Family Editor, as shown in Figure 19.3.

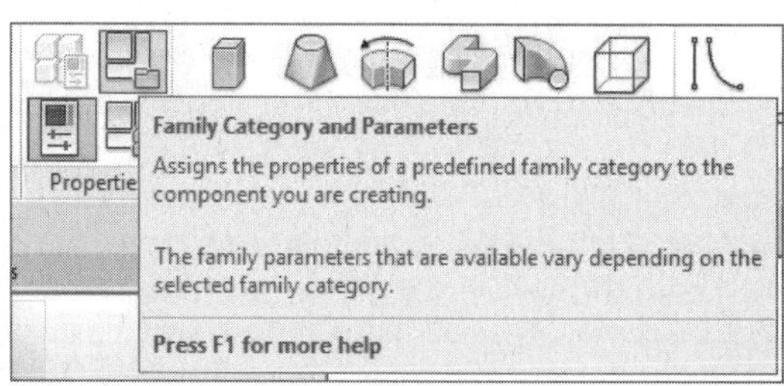

Figure 19.3 Family Category And Parameters button

When you categorize a family as Mechanical Equipment, you can set its behavior with the Part Type parameter, as shown in Figure 19.4. The Normal option is for equipment that is simply placed into the model and stands on its own, while the Breaks Into option is for equipment that is inline with ductwork or pipe. The Breaks Into option allows you to insert the family directly into a run of duct or pipe without having to first create an opening for the equipment.

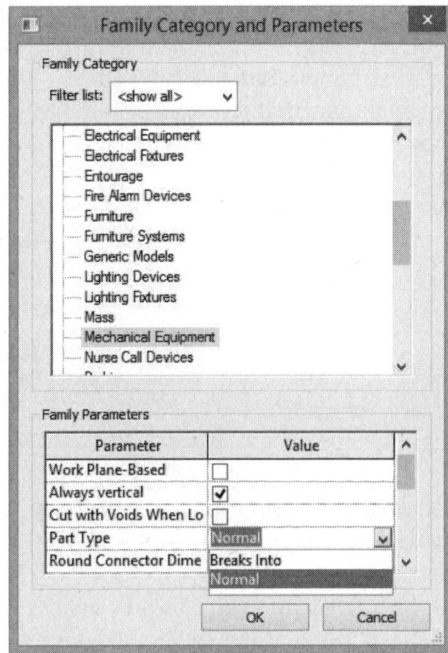

FIGURE 19.4 Part Type options for Mechanical Equipment families

The Part Type parameter for Electrical Equipment families also has options for defining the equipment behavior, as shown in Figure 19.5. These options let you define how the equipment is used in an electrical system.

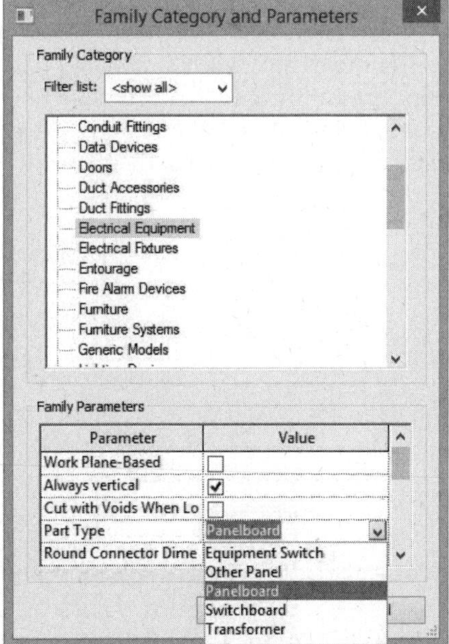

FIGURE 19.5 Part Type options for Electrical Equipment families

If you choose the Panelboard option, you can set the configuration of the breakers and circuit numbering in the panel. This corresponds to the template used for panel schedules, as shown in Figure 19.6. Panel Configuration, along with Part Type parameters, define the relationships between panels in the project schedules. Therefore, careful consideration is advised.

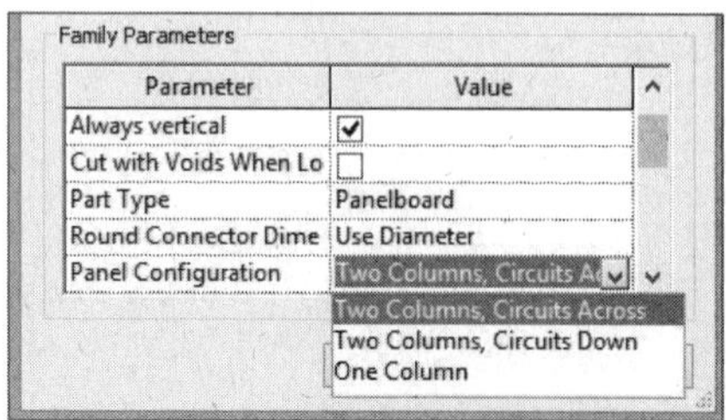

FIGURE 19.6 Panel configuration for electrical equipment

Since Revit MEP 2014 there has been an option for Round Connector Dimension. It is here that you can select whether you wish to use Radius or Diameter to dimension your round connectors, be they ducts, pipes, or conduits.

Another family parameter that you should consider is the Always Vertical option. Selecting this option causes the equipment family to always appear vertical at 90 degrees, no matter how the host is sloped. This setting is used for nonhosted families. If you are creating a nonhosted family and you want to be able to place the family in any orientation, you can set the Work Plane-Based option. This allows you to place a nonhosted family onto any workplane defined in your project. Otherwise, if you place a nonhosted family into a project and it is associated with the level of the view placed, you will not be able to rotate the family in section or elevation views.

Setting the family to Work Plane-Based does not mean that you can rotate the family in section or elevation, but you can create a reference plane that is at the desired rotation in the project and associate the family with that plane, as shown in the section view in Figure 19.7. When you place a Work Plane-Based family into a project, the option to place the family onto a face is available on the Placement panel of the contextual tab.

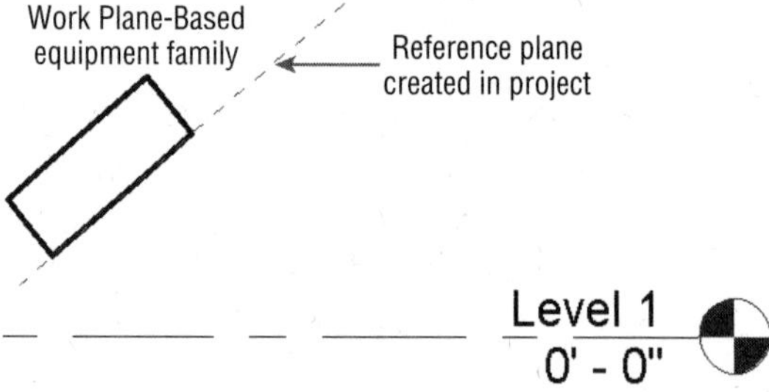

FIGURE 19.7 Work Plane-Based equipment in a project

This functionality is useful because it allows you to use nonhosted families in a face-hosted fashion.

FACE-BASED AND GENERIC CHOICES

Generic families are sometimes called nonhosted families, but that's untrue because they are actually hosted (or based) on the level into which they are inserted. Some companies create generic and face-based versions of the same families for use in different project scenarios. When placing generic families in your projects, consider using the Place On Work Plane option wherever possible to eliminate the need for duplicate family versions. Generic families are the better choice for anything that is connected to pipes, ducts, conduit, and cable tray. And face-based families are the better choice for objects that do not have hard connections—light fixtures, receptacles, switches, and so on. Generally, mechanical and plumbing designers should consider using mainly generic families and electrical designers should consider using mainly face-based families, but there will always be exceptions to the rules.

Detail Level

When you are modeling your equipment families, consider the amount of detail required to represent the equipment. Mechanical components can be complicated structures that include many intricate parts. It is not necessary to model your equipment families to a high level of detail for them to function properly in your projects. If you need to show equipment with a lot of detail, you can use model lines or symbolic lines to represent the equipment in views where the high level of detail is needed while keeping the family geometry simple.

Most equipment families can be modeled using simple geometric forms such as cubes and cylinders. If the equipment family you are creating requires more complex geometry, you will need to use the other modeling tools available in the Family Editor, such as the Sweep, Blend, and Revolve tools.

For instances where you need to show only the amount of space required for equipment, you can model it as a box that is visible in Coarse detail views. More-detailed geometry can be modeled to show in views with a finer level of detail. The important thing to remember when using this technique is that the connection points for ductwork or pipe should be located on the outer edges of the box geometry. Otherwise, you might end up with pipes and ducts that appear disconnected, as shown in Figure 19.8.

Geometry for Connection Points

MEP discipline equipment families can include connectors for ducts, pipes, conduit, and even cable tray if necessary. These connectors are added to define the function of the equipment from an engineering standpoint. Connectors are added by one of two methods: either by placing them on a face of the solid geometry or by associating them with a workplane within the family. When you associate a connector with a workplane, it can be located anywhere in that plane. Connectors placed with the Face option on the Placement panel of the contextual tab will automatically attach to the center of the face.

Using the Face option is useful when you know that the connection point is always at the center of the geometry—because if the geometry changes size, the location of the connector will adjust, or if the geometry changes location within the family, the connector will move with it. This method requires less constraint within the family for the location of the connector, but it may be necessary to model extra geometry to provide a correctly located face for a connector.

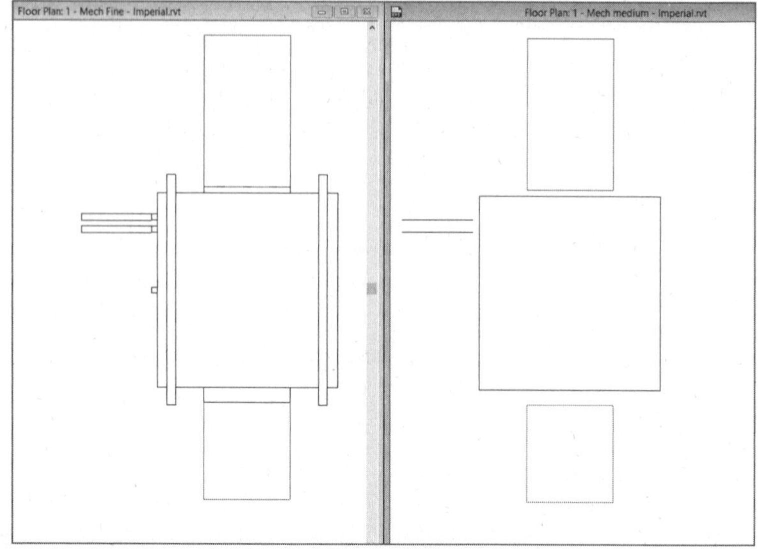

FIGURE 19.8
Pipes and ducts that appear disconnected when in Medium detail level

Creating geometry for the location of connectors is an easy way to manage not only connector locations but also connector sizes. The size of a connector can be associated with the size of its geometry host face. This allows for accurate modeling of connection points of different family types within a family.

Geometry used for connection points may be more easily dimensioned than connectors themselves because you can dimension to the edges of geometry, whereas connectors can be dimensioned only to their center points. For example, if you have a rectangular duct connection that varies in size yet needs to maintain a certain distance from the edge of the unit, you can model geometry that is constrained to the dimensional requirements and then host the connector to that face. Figure 19.9 shows an example of an extrusion used in this manner. The 0′-6″ (150 mm) and 0′-4″ (100 mm) dimensions are locked to hold the extrusion in place when the Unit Height and Unit Width parameters are changed and when the SupplyHeight and SupplyWidth parameters change.

Using extrusions for connection points can make it easier to identify where to connect pipes, duct, or conduit to your equipment when working with the family in a project. More information on connector geometry is provided in the section "Adding Connectors to Equipment Families," later in this chapter.

Equipment Pads

When you are creating an equipment family that needs to be mounted on a pad, it may be best to include the pad geometry directly in the equipment family. This enables you to ensure that the appropriate dimensions are used for the pad without having to make any changes in another file, such as a structural or architectural link. If the equipment does not always require a pad, you can use parameters to control the display of the pad. Family types can be created for easy selection of pad-mounted versions of the equipment.

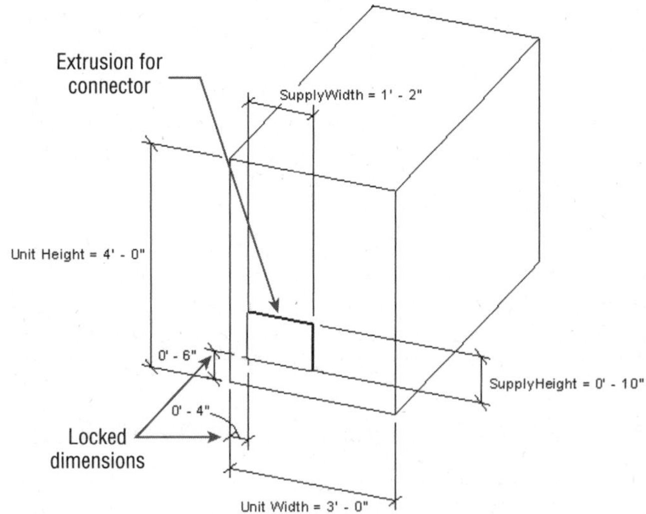

Figure 19.9
Extrusion used for connector host

The key to creating pad geometry in an equipment family is to provide a reference for the top of the pad so that the equipment geometry can be modeled in the correct location and maintain a proper relationship with the pad. If you are creating a face-hosted family, the pad should be modeled so that it is associated with the host extrusion, as shown in Figure 19.10. Keep in mind that pads don't always have a parallel top and bottom. If the roof is sloping, obviously the pad needs to follow the slope, but it still needs to create a level top surface for the equipment. In those cases, the pads can be a bit more complicated. A common approach is to create multiple extrusions within the same pad family and control which one is visible and when (through visibility parameters) based on the sloping conditions in the project.

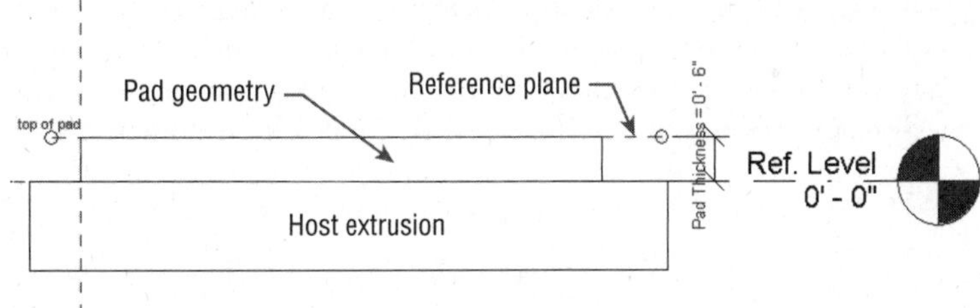

Figure 19.10
Pad modeled in equipment family

Pad Coordination

If you work in the same company with a structural engineer or perhaps have a close working relationship with a structural consultant, you have an opportunity to utilize the power of BIM by collaborating on the design and use of equipment pads.

Most MEP engineers know the basic size and shape of the pads that their equipment requires, but in cases of heavy equipment and unique design requirements, a structural engineer is often used to design an equipment pad that meets the applicable codes for construction.

A foundation family can be created that can be nested into an equipment family. This family can contain all of the parameters and data that a structural engineer might use to represent the pad in their design model, and the size parameters can be associated to parameters in the equipment family. Formulas can even be applied to adjust the properties of the nested pad when changes in size are made to the equipment.

Of course, not everyone has the luxury of having other engineers design portions of their equipment families. However, this example is just another one of the many ways that Revit and BIM are changing how things can be done in the design industry to improve project quality.

Adding Connectors to Equipment Families

The connectors that you add to an equipment family will ultimately determine the types of systems for which that family will be available in your Revit projects. Connectors can be added for the completion of air, fluid, and electrical systems when the family is selected as the system's equipment in your project.

In most cases, the location of connectors on equipment families is easily handled by geometry modeled specifically for the connector. However, it is not always necessary to have connector geometry. Some equipment families are simply used for equipment location and do not need to be modeled to any level of detail. Early in the design of a project, you may want to use placeholder equipment families until specified equipment can be chosen based on calculations. It is still helpful for these types of families to have connectors so that duct, pipe, and conduit can be connected and system analysis can be performed.

If you place the connectors by reference planes, you can dimension directly to a connector by selecting it and then activating the temporary dimension to the center of the connector. Once it is activated, you can associate the dimension to a parameter. This can be done only if you use the Work Plane option for placing the connector. Using the Face option constrains the connector to the center of the face so its location cannot be changed without changing the host face. Figure 19.11 shows how a connector placed on a Work Plane can be dimensioned and parametrically managed.

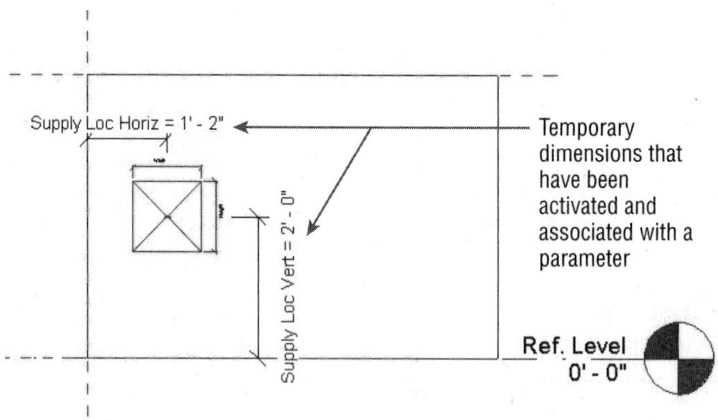

FIGURE 19.11
Connector location dimensions

In this example, if you want to keep the right and bottom edges of the connector static when the connector changes size, you would need to write a formula for the connector dimension parameter. For example, with a parameter that defines the connector width, such as SupplyWidth, the left edge of the connector can be made to stay at 0′-8″ (200 mm) from the left edge of the equipment by using a formula for the Supply Loc Horiz parameter, as shown in Figure 19.12.

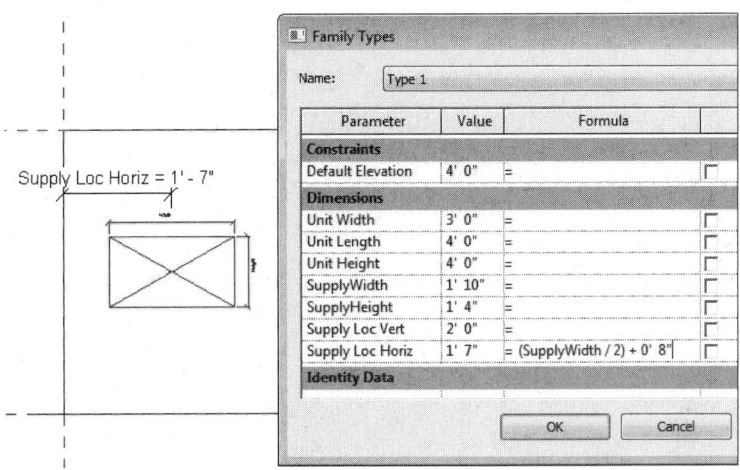

FIGURE 19.12 Connector location using formula

When you have equipment that has several pipe connectors, it is helpful to create geometry for the connectors. Otherwise, you would have to define a reference plane for each connector unless they all connect at the same plane. With geometry used to indicate a point of connection, you can dimension and constrain the geometry and then use the Face option for connector placement. This does not eliminate the need for dimensions or constraints; it only takes them off the connector object itself.

When you sketch a circle to create a cylinder, the point at which you draw the center can be dimensioned while you are in sketch mode. This dimension can be used for the location of the connector, as shown in Figure 19.13. The radius of the sketch can also be dimensioned and associated with a parameter for easy size adjustment. Remember, when creating circular connectors, use a circle for the sketch, not an arc that is copied/mirrored. This is because the center point of the pipe connector will snap to the centroid of one of the arcs, not that arc's center point.

Revit MEP 2013 was the first version to introduce the Diameter dimension. This allows you to control round extrusions and connectors with one parameter, and without the additional formulas that were required in the past.

Reference planes or lines can also be used to determine the location of the connection point geometry. This is easily done for pipe connections by activating the Center Mark Visible parameter of the circle you are sketching, as shown in Figure 19.14.

While you're in sketch mode, the center mark allows you to align and lock the sketch to reference planes or lines used to control the geometry location, as shown in Figure 19.15.

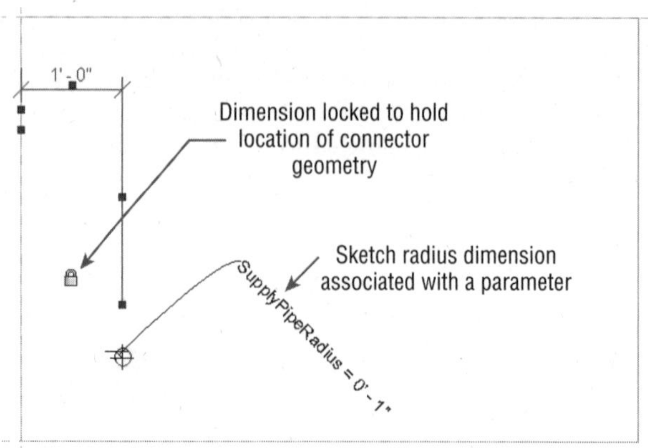

FIGURE 19.13 Geometry for cylindrical connector

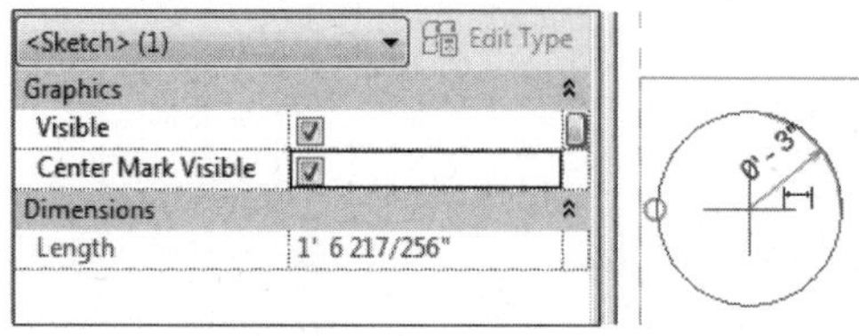

FIGURE 19.14 Using the parameter Center Mark Visible

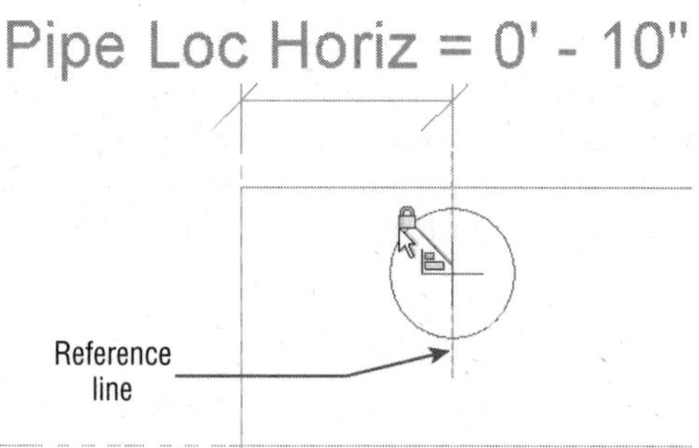

FIGURE 19.15 Sketch center mark aligned to reference line

> **PIN IT**
>
> To hold the location of connector geometry, you can pin it in place instead of using dimensional constraints. Connectors themselves can be pinned if no geometry is used for their location. Pinning a connector will have no effect on its ability to change size parametrically.

With the geometry in place, a connector can be added by using the Face option for placement.

You can adjust the connector properties to associate the size of the connector with the parameter created for the geometry diameter, as shown in Figure 19.16. Associating the values to parameters in this way is known as *parameter mapping*. Parameter mapping allows you to make connector parameters visible and accessible in project environments.

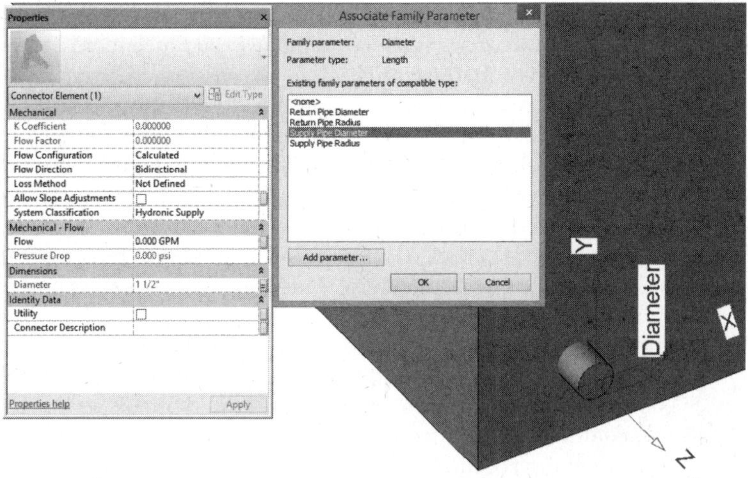

FIGURE 19.16 Associating a parameter with the connector diameter

The Diameter parameter has been available only since Revit 2014. As mentioned earlier, you can switch between radius and diameter by using the Round Connector Dimension parameter in the Family Category And Parameters section. Alternatively, you could also do this via the Properties palette (see Figure 19.17).

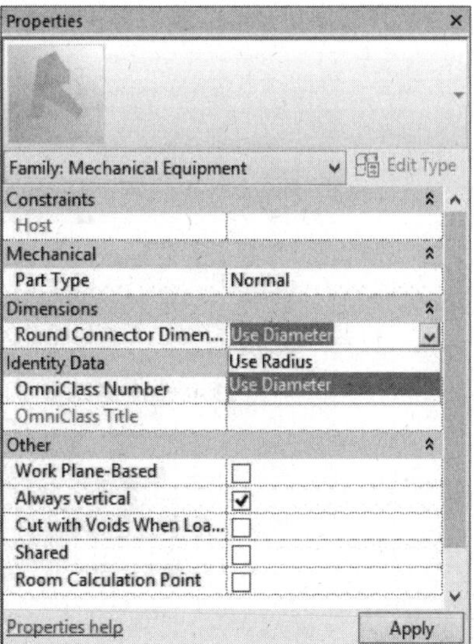

FIGURE 19.17 Changing between radius and diameter

Using the Face option is the easiest way to place connectors into a family. The direction of the connector can be easily flipped by using the blue arrows grip ⇅ that appears when you select the connector. The direction arrow of a connector indicates the direction that pipe, duct, conduit, or cable tray will be drawn from the connector.

When using the Face option to manage the location of a connector parametrically, you will need to create additional geometry that gives you much more accurate control over the location of the connector within the family.

When you place connectors by using the Work Plane option shown in Figure 19.18, they may not be facing in the right direction. If you placed the connector by using a named reference plane and selecting it from the list, as shown in Figure 19.19, the blue arrows grip will not work to flip the direction. Instead, you will have to rotate the plane with which the connector is associated or redraw the plane in the opposite direction. If you are going to place connectors by named reference planes, it is probably a good idea to remember that you should be drawing your reference planes clockwise. This way, the orientation of the connectors will be always defaulted appropriately.

The benefit of using the Work Plane option is that you can locate a connector anywhere on the plane. In case you created your reference plane in the wrong direction, and rotating it is not an option at this point because this would break the constrained geometry, you can still work around this limitation. Drag the reference plane grip past the other end, which will flip the orientation of the reference plane and the connector. Another option is to use named reference planes, choose the Pick A Plane option, and select the hosting plane from the drafting area.

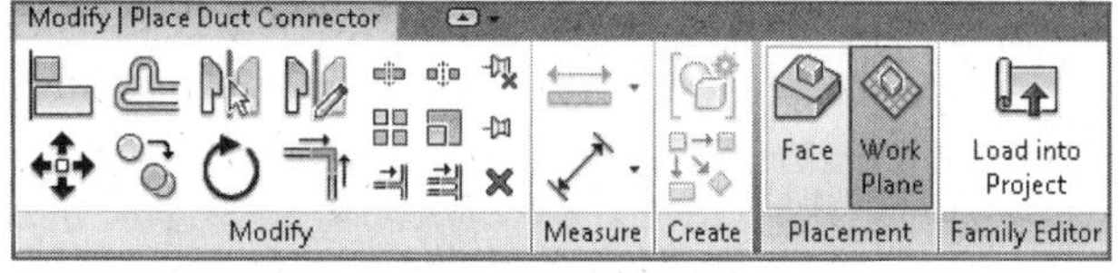

FIGURE 19.18 Placing a connector by work plane

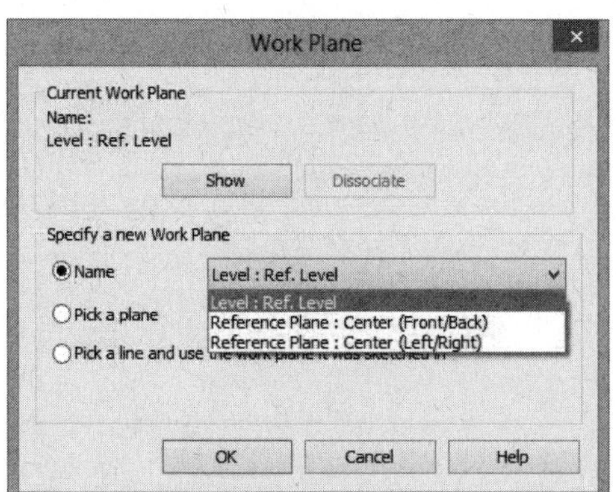

FIGURE 19.19 Placing a connector by work plane using the Name pull-down

PLANE DIRECTION

If you draw a reference plane from left to right in a plan view, connectors attached to it will point up. A reference plane drawn from right to left will cause the connectors to point down. In other words, always draw your reference planes clockwise to ensure the proper default location for your connectors.

The decision of whether to use the Face or Work Plane option for connectors depends on how you want to control the location of the connector. Whatever method you choose, once a connector is placed, you can adjust its properties so that the equipment family will behave as desired in your projects.

Duct Connectors

You can select the system type of a duct connector from the Options Bar, as shown in Figure 19.20, when you click the Duct Connector button on the Create tab in the Family Editor.

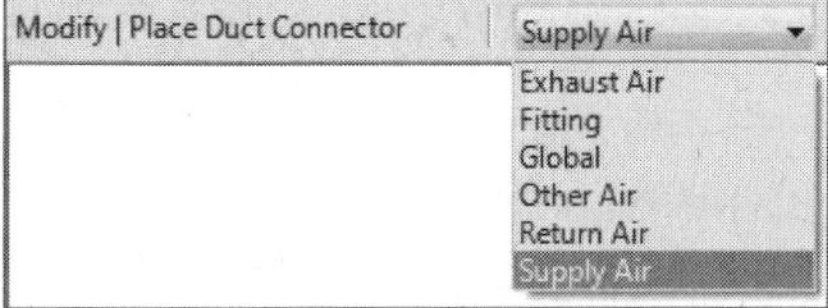

FIGURE 19.20 Defining the system type for duct connectors

The Global option enables the air system to be based on the system the equipment is connected to when the family is used in a project. A good use of the Global option is for fans, where the same fan family could be used for any system type. Fitting connectors do not have parameters to define air system behavior, and they are typically used on duct-fitting families to establish connectivity.

For air systems equipment, your duct connectors should be set with the properties that coincide with the behavior of the equipment that the family represents. Figure 19.21 shows the properties of a duct connector that has just been added to a family.

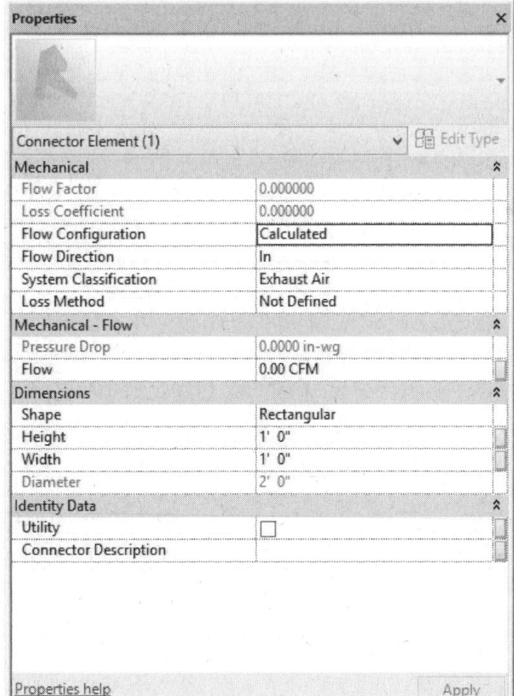

FIGURE 19.21 Duct connector properties

Flow Configuration The Flow Configuration parameter sets how the flow is determined at the connector point, as shown in Figure 19.22.

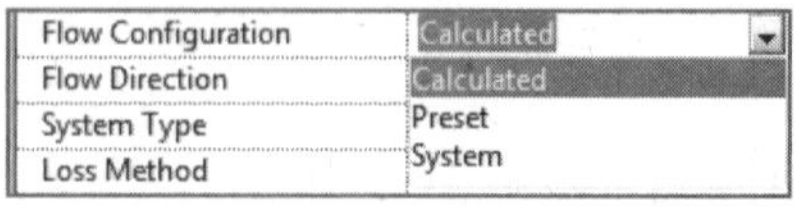

FIGURE 19.22
Flow Configuration parameter in duct connector properties

Flow Configuration	Calculated
Flow Direction	Calculated
System Type	Preset
Loss Method	System

Calculated This option adds up all the flow values from objects downstream in the system.

Preset This option is for direct input of the flow value at the connector point.

System This option can be used if the flow at the connector point is a percentage of the entire flow for a system. With the System option, you will have to provide a value for the Flow Factor parameter. For example, if the equipment you are creating is used in a system with other equipment in your project and it provides 30 percent of the flow, Flow Configuration would be set to System and Flow Factor would be set to 0.33.

Flow Direction The Flow Direction parameter defines the direction of the air at the connector point.

IN OR OUT?

Do not confuse Flow Direction with the direction of the arrow shown on the connector itself. You may have a connector with an arrow that points away from the equipment, indicating the direction of duct from that point, while the direction of the air is into the equipment. Flow direction is important because when you use the equipment in a project, the flow direction must coincide with the objects to which the equipment is connected. If your connector flow direction is *in*, the object to which it is connected should have a flow direction of *out*. Making a connection between connectors with the same flow direction will produce analysis errors in your projects.

System Classification System Classification determines which system type can be connected to the connector. For duct connectors, the choices are Supply Air, Return Air, Exhaust Air, or Other Air, or you can choose Fitting or Global.

Selecting Supply, Return, or Exhaust Air will mean you can connect to (or create) those types of systems, remembering that if you set up an outside air system type in your project using supply air, then you can only use a supply air connector for this system. Other Air is used for purely graphical representations of ductwork that will not create an intelligent system.

By selecting Fitting, you will remove all parameters other than angle, shape, and size, and the connector will act as a fitting, not able to calculate or preset a flow rate but instead just pass it through the family.

Global is used for families such as fans with connectors that can be used for more than one system category.

Loss Method The Loss Method parameter allows you to assign either a coefficient, by placing a value in the Loss Coefficient parameter, or a specific loss, by placing a value in the Pressure Drop parameter. Keep in mind that these values are for the selected connector. If you have additional connectors in the family, you can also assign unique values to them.

Shape Use the Shape parameter to define the connector as round, rectangular, or oval. The dimensions of a connector can then be assigned in the connector properties. Placing values for the Height, Width, or Radius parameters of a connector sets the size of duct drawn from that connector. If you want to change the size of the connector in the family properties, you can associate its dimensions with parameters created in the family, as shown in Figure 19.23.

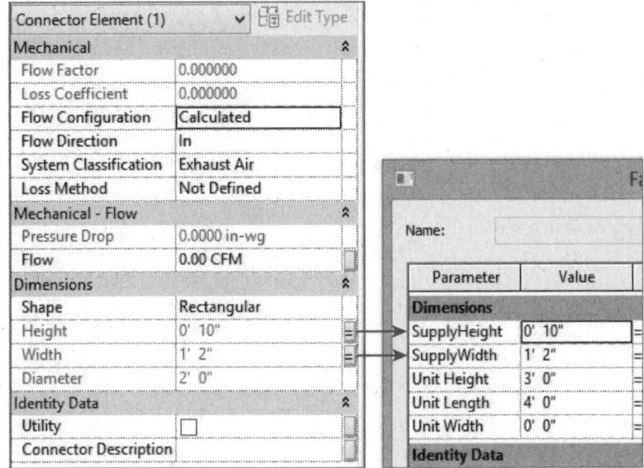

FIGURE 19.23 Connector dimensions associated to family parameters

Utility The Utility parameter for a connector is used to define whether the connector indicates a utility connection. This allows for coordination when your project is exported for use in AutoCAD® Civil 3D® software. The connection points defined as utilities will be available in the exported file for coordination of things such as service entrance locations and invert elevations.

The dimensions of a connector can be associated with a parameter by clicking the + sign grip that appears near the connector label when the connector is selected in a view, as shown in Figure 19.24.

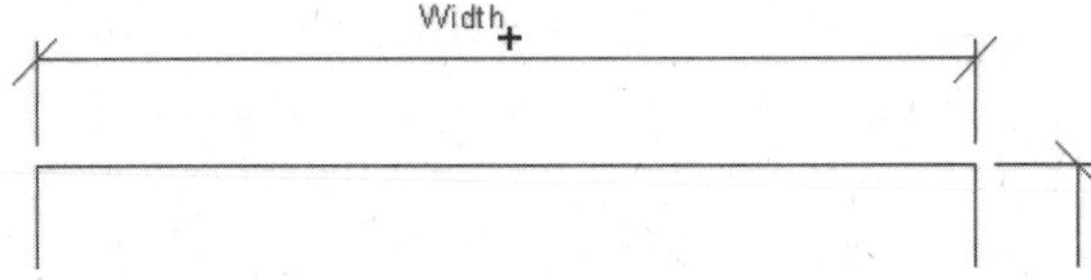

FIGURE 19.24 Associating parameters with a dimension using the + sign grip

It is important to establish the orientation of the Width and Height dimensions of a connector on your equipment. Otherwise, duct or duct fittings that are connected to the connection point may not be oriented properly. Connectors located on the side of the equipment should be easy to orient and configure. The height of the connector is the Z axis (up). However, connectors on the top or bottom surface of families can be a little tricky because there is no clear *up* direction. In those cases, testing the family in the project environment is best in order to see what makes the most sense.

The most common way to identify the "correct" orientation is to draw a duct and make sure that you are not getting any transitions. If you are getting transitions, you need to rotate the connector and change the mapped parameters for duct height and duct width. You can rotate a connector placed with the Face option by clicking and dragging it; however, this is an inaccurate method of rotation. Using the Rotate tool allows you to set a specific angle of rotation. If you use the Pin tool to lock the location of a connector, you will also not be able to rotate it. This can be useful if you find that you are accidentally clicking and dragging the rotation of your connectors when working in the Family Editor.

Pipe Connectors

Connectors for pipes can be placed on your equipment families in the same manner as duct connectors. You can find options for setting the system type on the Options Bar, as shown in Figure 19.25, when you click the Pipe Connector button on the Create tab in the Family Editor.

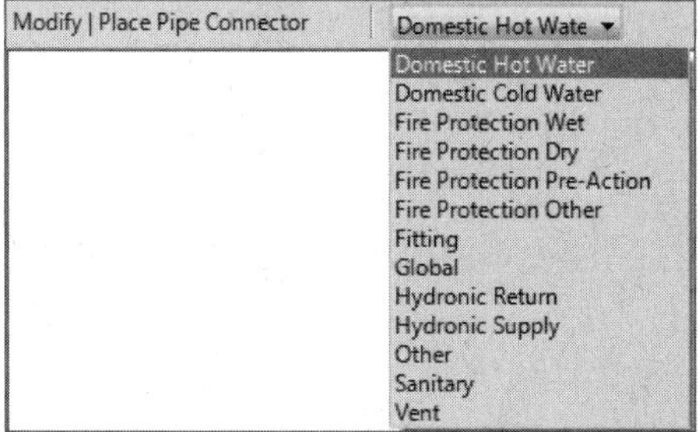

FIGURE 19.25 Defining the system type for a pipe connector

The properties for a pipe connector are similar to those of a duct connector, except that they deal with the flow of liquid instead of air. Because liquid flows differently, there are some different choices for the same parameters you would find in a duct connector:

Flow Configuration The Flow Configuration setting for a pipe connector has options depending on the system type. Systems related to plumbing pipes have an additional Flow Configuration option called Fixture Units. This establishes that the flow at the connector is based on the value given to the Fixture Units parameter, as shown in Figure 19.26. Notice that the Flow parameter is not active when using the Fixture Units option for Flow Configuration.

Radius/ Diameter The size of the connector is determined by the Radius or Diameter parameter depending on which is selected for the Round Connector Dimension parameter. If you are using the radius, then unless the connector does not need to change size with different family types, you should associate the Radius parameter with a family parameter for easy editing, as shown in Figure 19.27. Since pipe sizes are usually given as the nominal diameter of the pipe, you can also create a parameter for pipe size and use a formula to derive the radius from the size given. That way, your input is consistent with industry standards.

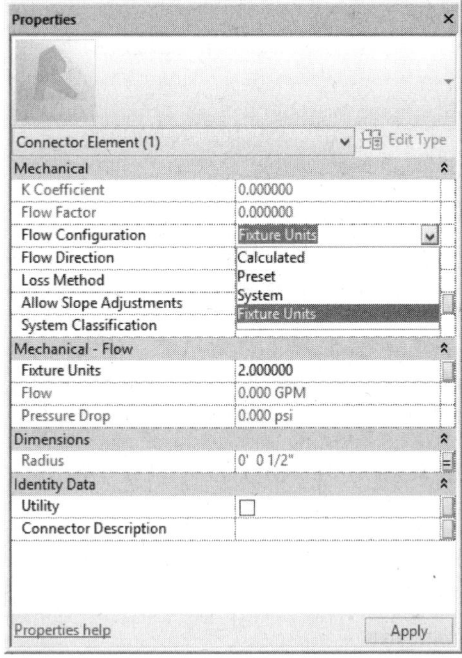

FIGURE 19.26 Properties of a pipe connector for plumbing pipe

PipeRadius	0' 0 1/4"	= Pipe Size / 2
Pipe Size	0' 0 1/2"	=

FIGURE 19.27 Pipe radius formula

Allow Slope Adjustments The Allow Slope Adjustments parameter lets you establish whether the pipe attached to the connector can be sloped. If you do not select the box, then when you apply a slope to pipe that is connected to the connector, you will receive an error message that the angle between the elements is too great and the pipe will become disconnected from the equipment.

If you draw a sloped pipe from a connector that allows for slope adjustment, the Pipe Connector Tolerance angle defined in the MEP settings of your project will determine the maximum angle that a sloped pipe can enter a connector. If the angle is exceeded, a straight run of pipe and an elbow fitting will be drawn from the connector prior to the sloped pipe.

Electrical Connectors

There are three kinds of connectors for electrical systems—conduit connectors, cable tray connectors, and electrical connectors:

Conduit Connectors These can be added by clicking the Conduit Connector button on the Create tab in the Family Editor. The Options Bar provides two choices for conduit connectors, as shown in Figure 19.28.

Figure 19.28 Selecting an individual or surface connector from the Options Bar

Individual Connector This option is for placing a single connection point in a specific location on the equipment. These connectors have properties for adjusting the angle and setting the radius of the connector.

Surface Connector Surface Connector is a unique and powerful option because it allows you to establish an entire surface of the equipment geometry as a connection point for conduit. Figure 19.29 shows a conduit surface connector that has been added to the top of an electrical panel family. This allows for the connection of multiple conduits at any location on the top of the panel. The Angle parameter can be set to allow for adjustments in the angle of the surface to which the connector is attached. This parameter is typically used in fitting families, but it may also have an application in an equipment family.

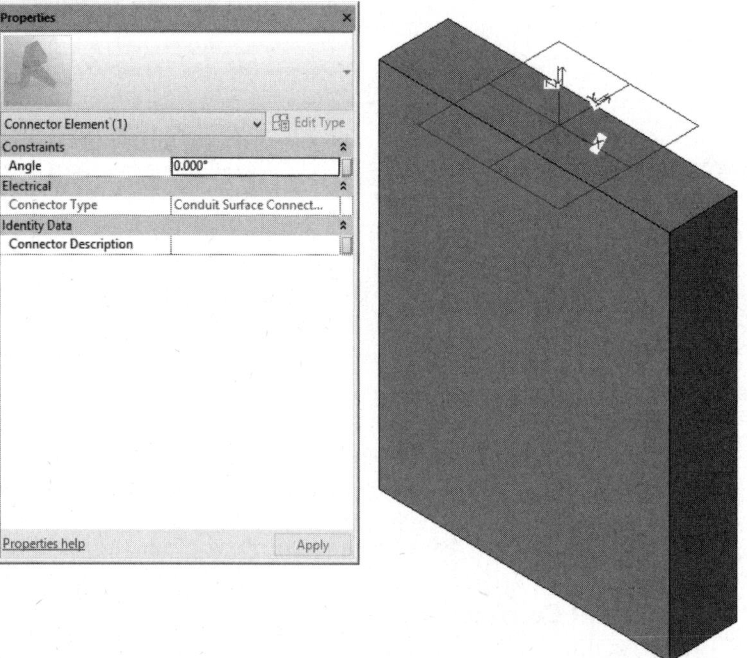

Figure 19.29 Conduit surface connector on the top surface of a panel family

When an equipment family with a surface connector is used in a project, conduit can be drawn to or from the surface by using the Conduit tool on the Systems tab. The surface containing the connector will highlight when you place your cursor over it. Selecting the surface will activate the Surface Connection mode, which allows you to drag the connector location to any point on the surface. This process can be repeated several times for the same surface connector, allowing you to model multiple conduits from your equipment, as shown in Figure 19.30. See Chapter 13, "Power and Communications," for more information on modeling conduit.

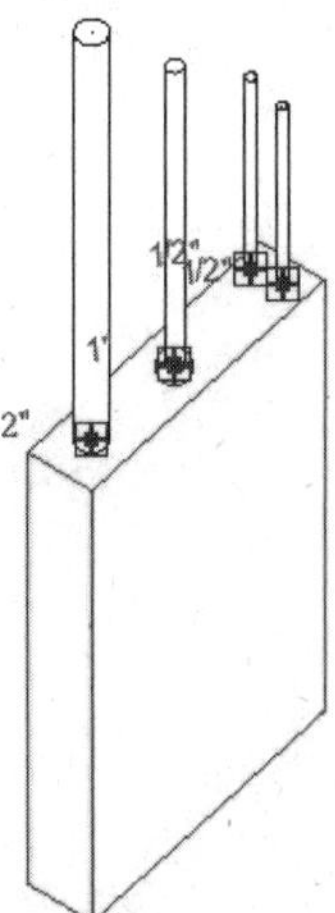

FIGURE 19.30 Multiple conduits from a surface connector

Cable Tray Connector The Cable Tray Connector button on the Create tab in the Family Editor allows you to place a point of connection for cable tray. These connectors are similar to the individual conduit connector, having properties for the angle and for setting the height and width of the connector.

Electrical Connector Clicking the Electrical Connector button on the Create tab in the Family Editor allows you to place a point of connection for wiring, which will also define the type of system in which the equipment can be used. The Options Bar allows you to define the system of the connector prior to placement.

FACE OPTION

When you're placing electrical connectors on equipment families, the Face option for placement is usually best. Electrical connectors do not have a direction property, and the wiring can be drawn to any point on the equipment. You would need to use the Work Plane placement option if you had to move the connector for easier access or because it interfered with another connector. Just be sure not to place multiple connectors on the same face when using the Face option or they will be difficult to select when you're working in a project.

When placing an electrical connector, you need to specify what electrical system type it is going to serve, as shown in Figure 19.31. Many properties of an electrical connector can be associated with family parameters for easy management and creation of family types.

The Voltage parameter determines the distribution systems in your project where the equipment can be used. This must be coordinated with the value of the Number Of Poles parameter.

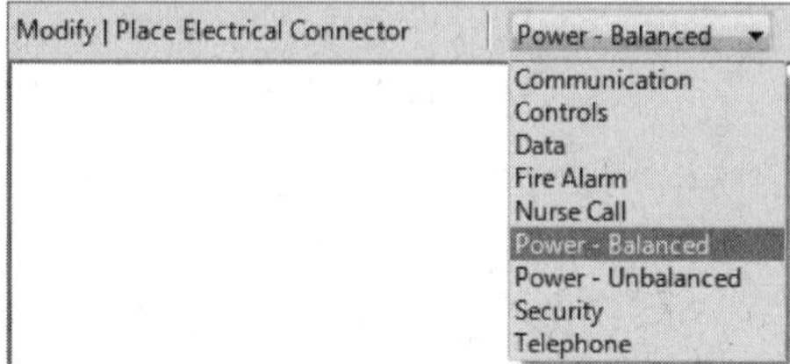

FIGURE 19.31 Defining the system type for the electrical connector

The Load Classification parameter enables you to assign a load classification to the connector that will determine the demand factor when the connector is used in a project. Even though you can create a new load classification in the family, and it will be available in the project when the family is loaded, it is not recommended to do it that way. You should map the Load Classification connector parameter to a Load Classification shared parameter. This way, you would be able to select the load classification from the project. Managing your load classifications from one place (in the project) is much more efficient than managing them in every family with an electrical connector. If you create custom load classifications in your families, they will be available in your project; however, you will not be able to delete them from the project!

FACE OPTION

If you create, for instance, the Voltage and the Number Of Poles parameters when circuiting those families in the project environment, Revit will produce a dialog box that allows you to assign the values for Voltage and Numbers Of Poles. This adds greater flexibility to the family application and reduces the family types needed.

Multiple Connectors in Families

Many MEP equipment families have multiple types of connectors. Your work environment may determine the connectors that you add to equipment families. For example, if your projects contain all MEP systems in one model, you may want to have electrical connectors in your HVAC equipment families that require electricity. If you have a separate model for each discipline, there is no need to have an electrical connector on any of the mechanical equipment families because the connection cannot be made through a linked file.

It is possible to link connectors in a family. This is useful when you want the system behavior to pass through from one connector to the other—for example, when you have a pipe fitting. Linking the connectors propagates system information through the fitting, so fluid flow in is related to fluid flow out of the fitting. You don't need to use the Link function for most families that contain parameters storing the fluid or air flow. However, the Link functionality is needed for fittings because they don't have those parameters and that's the only way to pass the flow through the fitting. You can link connectors by selecting one of the connectors and clicking the Link Connectors button on the Connector Links panel, as shown in Figure 19.32.

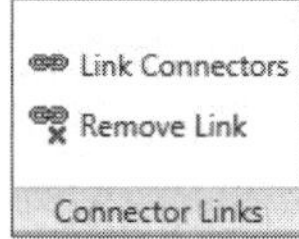

FIGURE 19.32 Linking connectors

Linked connectors will take on the Flow Configuration value of the primary connector. So even if you have a connector in the family that has a Flow Configuration set to Preset, if it is linked to a primary connector set to Calculated, the behavior of the connector in a project will be as if the connector is set to Calculated. You can tell whether connectors are linked in a family by selecting one of the connectors in the Family Editor. Red arrows will appear between linked connectors, as shown in Figure 19.33.

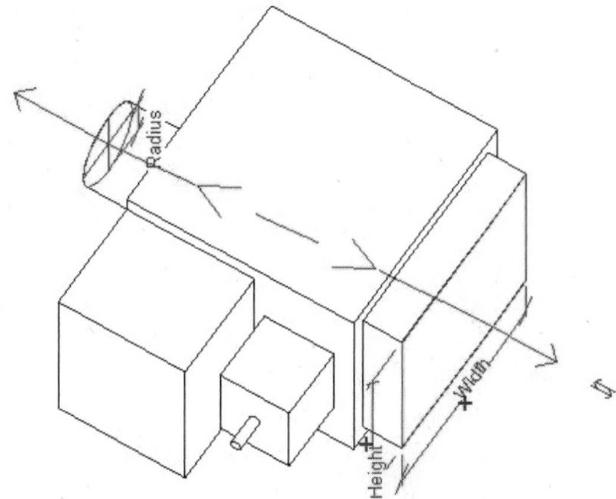

FIGURE 19.33 Linked connectors in an equipment family

The *primary connector* in a family is the first connector of each type added to the family and is indicated by crosshairs in the connector graphics. Figure 19.34 shows an equipment family with multiple types of connectors. You can change which connectors are the primary ones by clicking the Re-assign Primary button that appears on the Primary Connector panel of the contextual tab when you select a connector. Clicking the button allows you to select another connector, which will become the primary for that type.

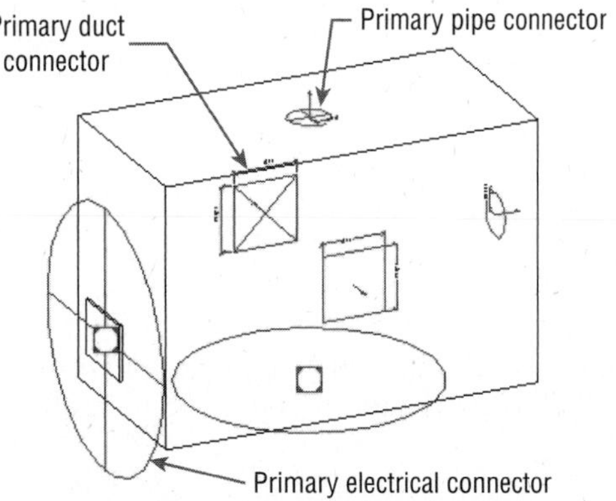

FIGURE 19.34 Equipment family with primary and secondary connectors

Naming connectors in a family makes it easier to understand which one you are connecting to when working in a project. You can name a connector in the Connector Description parameter in the connector's properties. When you use the Connect Into tool in a project on a family with multiple connectors, the connectors will appear in a list with their names so you can choose the correct one.

Now that you have learned about creating an equipment family, practice some of the basic skills by completing the following exercise. No matter what your discipline of expertise, these steps will help you become more familiar with the process of creating equipment families:

1. Open the `Ch19_equipment.rfa` file found at `www.sybex.com/go/masteringrevitmep2015`.
2. In the Ref. Level view, a corner of the equipment pad is at the intersection of the reference planes. Create a vertical reference line to the right of the vertical plane and a horizontal reference line above the horizontal plane, as shown in Figure 19.35. These lines will be used to define the length and width of the pad. Reference lines are mostly used if you need to control an angle parameter for geometry, such as a door swing.

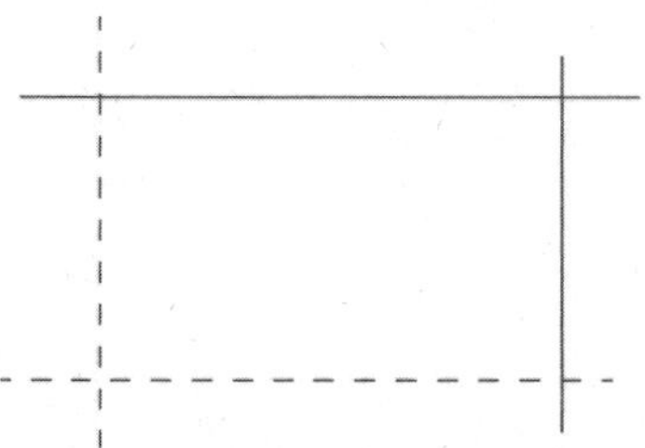

FIGURE 19.35 Creating reference planes for the pad

3. Create a dimension from the vertical reference plane to the vertical reference line. Select the dimension, and click the Label drop-down on the Options Bar. Select the Add Parameter option. In the Parameter Properties dialog box, name the parameter **PadLength**. Set the parameter to an instance parameter and click OK. Repeat the process for the horizontal reference line, using **PadWidth** for the parameter name, as shown in Figure 19.36.

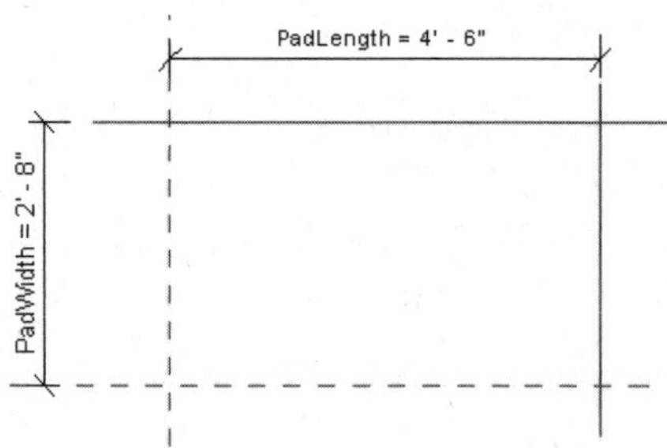

FIGURE 19.36 Creating dimensions and parameters for the equipment in plan orientation

4. Open the Front elevation view. Draw a horizontal reference plane above the Ref. Level. Select the plane, and name it **TopOfPad** in its element properties. Create a dimension

from the Ref. Level to the horizontal plane. Create an instance parameter for the dimension called **PadDepth**; see Figure 19.37.

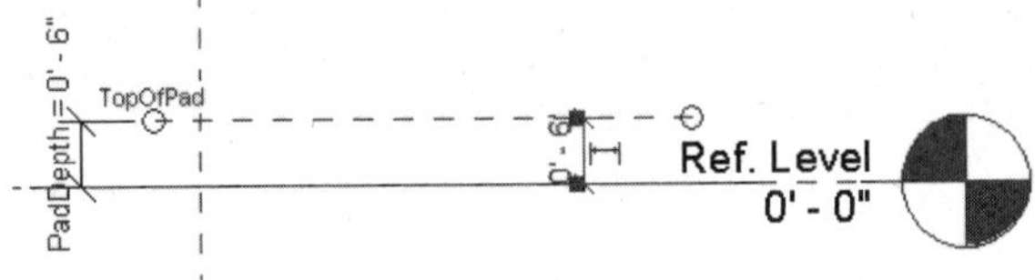

FIGURE 19.37 Creating dimensions and parameters for the equipment in elevation orientation

5. Open the Ref. Level view. Click the Extrusion button on the Create tab and sketch a rectangle. Align and lock the sketch lines to the reference lines and planes. Click the green check mark button to complete the sketch. Open the Front elevation view. Align and lock the top of the extrusion to the TopOfPad reference plane drawn in step 4.
6. Click the Family Types button on the Properties panel of the Create tab. Create a Yes/No instance parameter called **Pad**, grouped under Construction, as shown in Figure 19.38.

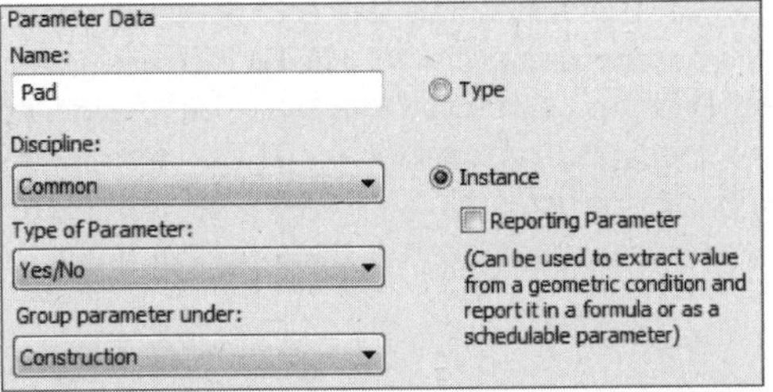

FIGURE 19.38 Creating a Yes/No visibility parameter

7. Select the extrusion created for the pad. In the Properties palette, click the small box at the far right of the Visible parameter and associate the parameter to the Pad parameter created in step 6; see Figure 19.39. Click OK.

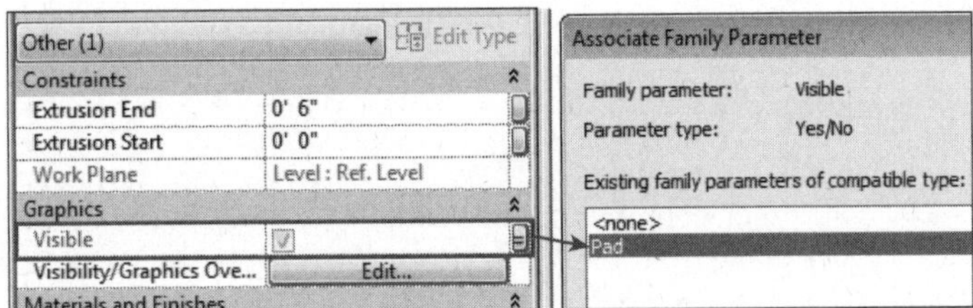

FIGURE 19.39 Associating the Yes/No visibility parameter with the Pad

8. Open the Ref. Level view. Create a vertical reference plane 4″ (100 mm) to the right of the Center (Left/Right) vertical plane. Create another vertical plane 4″ (100 mm) to the left of the vertical reference line drawn in step 2. Create a horizontal reference plane 4″ (100 mm) above the Center (Front/Back) horizontal plane and another one 4″ (100 mm) below the horizontal reference line drawn in step 2, as shown in Figure 19.40.

You'll notice that in this step we broke a few rules. However, those rules will be more important from a consistency standpoint and for families that are having connectors that are hosted on the reference planes. If you are making such a family, you should consider keeping the Center (Left/Right) reference plane as is and creating two reference planes (one to the left and one to the right) for the UnitLength. This way, the name Center (Left/Right) will actually represent the reality.

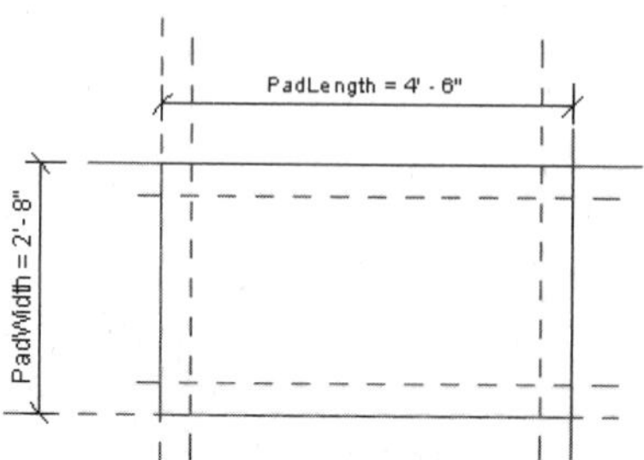

FIGURE 19.40 Creating reference planes for the equipment

9. Dimension between the two vertical planes drawn in step 8, and create an instance parameter for the dimension called **UnitLength**. Repeat the process for the two horizontal planes drawn in step 8, with **UnitWidth** as the parameter name. Add a dimension for the 4" (100 mm) distance from the initial vertical plane and the vertical plane drawn in step 8. Repeat the process for the 4" (100 mm) distance between the initial horizontal plane and the one drawn in step 8, as shown in Figure 19.41. Be sure to lock the dimensions by using the padlock grip that appears when the dimension is placed.

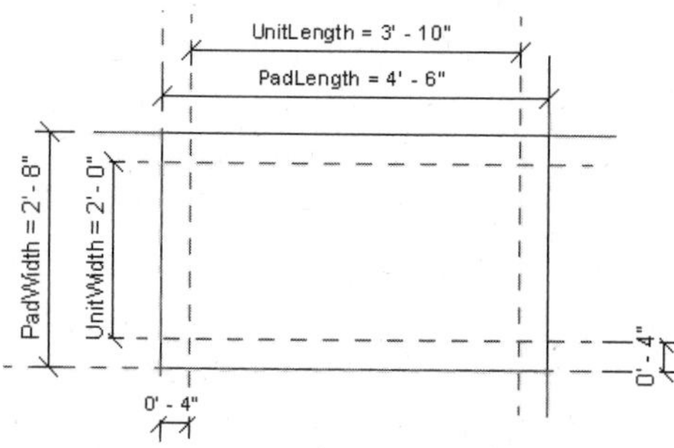

FIGURE 19.41 Creating dimensions and parameters for the equipment in plan orientation

10. Click the Set button on the Work Plane panel of the Create tab. Select the TopOfPad reference plane from the Name drop-down list in the Work Plane dialog box. Click OK.
11. Click the Extrusion button and sketch a rectangle. Align and lock the sketch lines to the reference planes drawn in step 8. Click the green check mark button on the Mode panel to finish the sketch.
12. Open the Front elevation view. Draw a reference plane from left to right above the extrusion created in step 11. Name the reference plane **TopOfUnit**. Add a dimension between

the TopOfPad reference plane and the TopOfUnit plane. Create an instance parameter for the dimension called **UnitHeight**. Align and lock the top of the extrusion created in step 11 to the TopOfUnit plane. Refer to Figure 19.42.

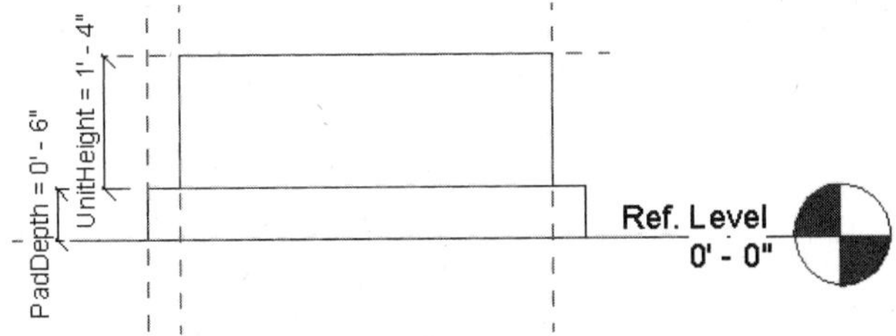

FIGURE 19.42 Creating dimensions and parameters for the equipment in elevation orientation

13. Click the Family Types button on the Properties panel on the Create tab. Create an instance parameter called **SupplyHeight** and one called **SupplyWidth** using the settings shown in Figure 19.43. Give each of the parameters a value of **10″** (**250** mm).

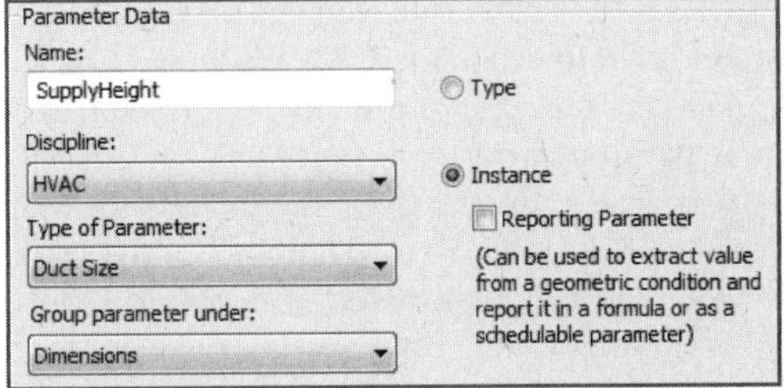

FIGURE 19.43 Configuring settings for a parameter

14. Repeat step 13, creating parameters called **ReturnHeight** and **ReturnWidth**. Click OK to exit the Family Types dialog box.

15. Open the default 3D view. Click the Duct Connector button on the Create tab. From the drop-down on the Options Bar, select Supply Air for the system. Place your cursor at an edge of the top extrusion to highlight the end face. You can use the Tab key if the desired face will not highlight when your cursor is on one of its edges. Click to select the face, and place the connector as shown in Figure 19.44.

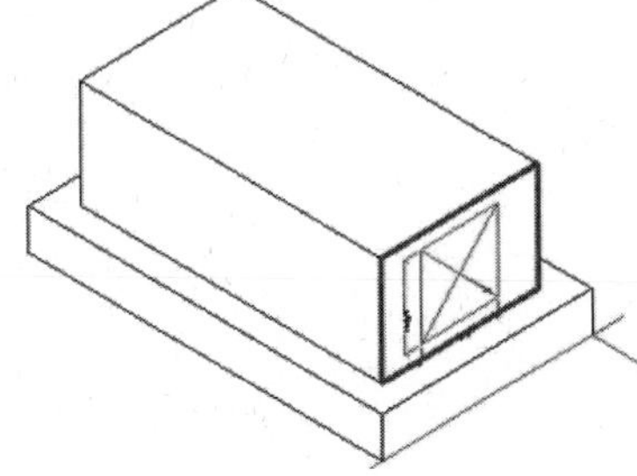

FIGURE 19.44 Placing the supply duct connector in 3D view

16. Rotate the view to show the opposite end of the extrusion. From the drop-down on the Options Bar, set the system type to Return Air. Select the face opposite from the Supply Air connector, and click to place the connector; see Figure 19.45.

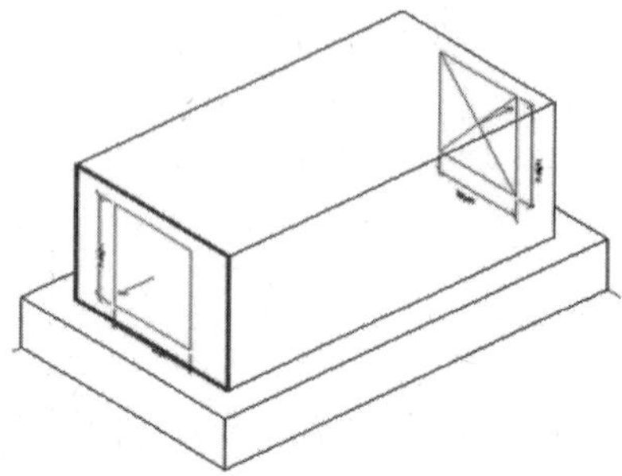

FIGURE 19.45 Placing the return duct connector in 3D view

17. Click the Modify button or use the Esc key to finish placing connectors. Select the Supply Air connector, and access its element properties. Confirm that the Flow Configuration parameter is set to Calculated. Set the Flow Direction parameter to Out. Click the small rectangle to the far right of the Flow parameter, and then click Add Parameter to create a new parameter called SupplyAirFlow. Make it an Instance parameter and click OK twice to finish. Repeat the same process for the height and width of the connector. Click the small rectangle to the far right of the Height parameter to associate it with the SupplyHeight family parameter, as shown in Figure 19.46. Click OK to close the Associate Family Parameter dialog box.

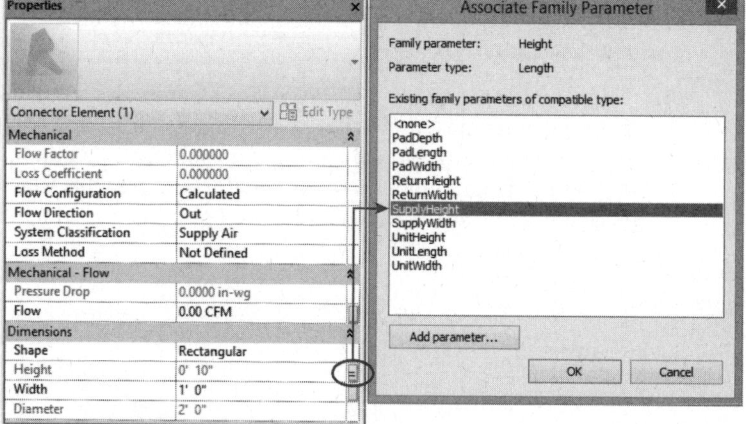

FIGURE 19.46 Associating a connector parameter to a family parameter

18. Associate the Width parameter of the Supply Air connector to the SupplyWidth family parameter. Click OK.

19. Select the Return Air connector in the view, and access its element properties. Set the Flow Configuration parameter to Calculated. Set the Flow Direction parameter to In. Click the small rectangle to the far right of the Flow parameter and click the Add Parameter button to create a new parameter called ReturnAirFlow. Make the parameter an instance parameter; fluid and air flow parameters should always be instance parameters because they should be adjustable values in the project environment. Associate the Height and Width parameters to the ReturnHeight and ReturnWidth family parameters.

20. Click the Electrical Connector button on the Create tab. From the drop-down list on the Options Bar, set the system type to Power – Balanced. Place the connector on one of the side faces of the equipment extrusion. Click the Modify button or use the Esc key to finish placing connectors.

21. Select the electrical connector and access its element properties. Set the Number Of Poles parameter to **3**. Set the Load Classification parameter to HVAC by clicking the small box that appears in the value cell, as shown in Figure 19.47, and choosing HVAC from the Load Classifications dialog box.

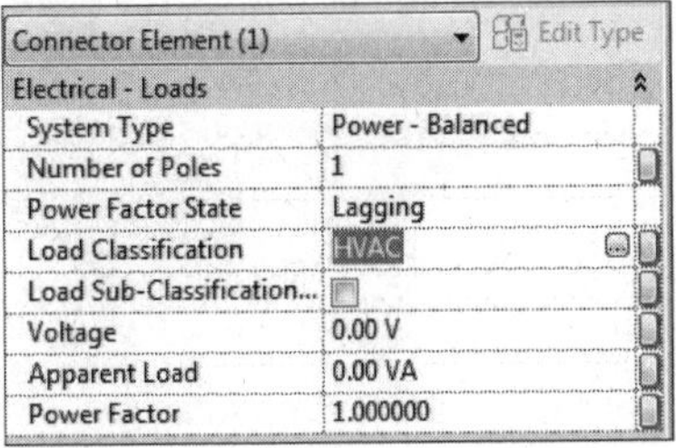

FIGURE 19.47 Configuring the properties of an electrical connector

22. Click the small rectangle at the far right of the electrical connector's Voltage parameter to associate it with a family parameter. Because no family parameter is available, click the Add Parameter button at the bottom of the Associate Family Parameter dialog box. Create an instance parameter named **UnitVoltage**. Because the Voltage parameter was selected, the other properties of the parameter are already selected. Click OK to close the Parameter Properties dialog box. With the UnitVoltage parameter highlighted in the list, click OK to close the Associate Family Parameter dialog box.

23. Repeat step 22 for the Apparent Load parameter of the connector. Name the family parameter **UnitLoad**.

24. Click the Family Types button on the Properties panel of the Create tab. Set the value of the UnitVoltage parameter to **480**. Set the value of the UnitLoad parameter to **5000**. Click OK to close the dialog box. Select the electrical connector in the view, and access its element properties. Confirm that the values have been associated with the connector parameters.

You can save this family and use it to practice techniques for creating equipment. Load the family into a test project to test its behavior and usability.

Creating Clearance Spaces

Most MEP equipment requires some sort of clearance space for safety or maintenance reasons. Modeling the clearance spaces directly in your equipment families is useful for model coordination. Because the space is part of the family, any objects encroaching on the space will show up when you run an interference check of your model. You can choose to keep the spaces visible during modeling for visual reference to avoid such interferences. Even if you choose to turn off the visibility of the spaces, any interferences will still be detected.

Figure 19.48 shows an electrical panel family with clearance spaces modeled for the front of the panel and the space above the panel.

FIGURE 19.48
Clearance spaces in an equipment family

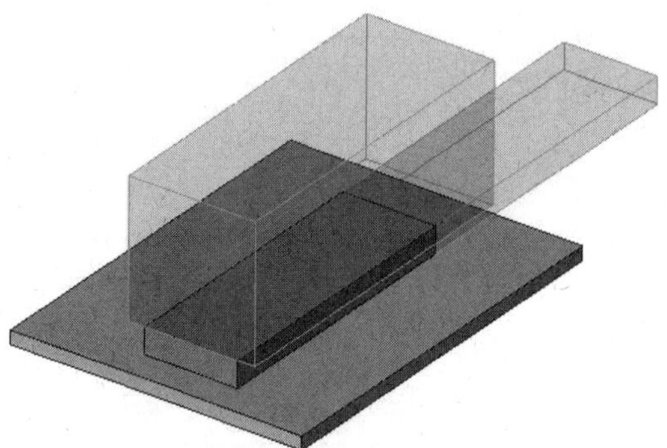

You can create clearance spaces by modeling an extrusion in the family that is associated with a reference plane at the appropriate face of the equipment. You can use other reference planes to control the size of the clearance space and constrain it to the equipment. In the example of the electrical panel, reference planes were created to constrain the top of the panel so that the front clearance space will always be 6″ (150 mm) above the top of the panel. The dimension for the space height was done in the extrusion sketch, as illustrated in Figure 19.49, which shows the plan view of the face-hosted family.

Once you have modeled a clearance space extrusion, there are properties that you can apply to it for visibility, as shown in Figure 19.50. In the panel example, a unique material type was created and applied to the extrusions for their semitransparent display. This keeps them from blocking out the actual equipment when shown in a model view.

A subcategory was created for the clearance space extrusions so they can be turned off in model views without turning off the equipment category. The subcategory is given a color for the edge lines of the clearance space extrusions to stand out from other solid geometry, as shown in Figure 19.51.

You should always ask yourself the following question: "Just because I can do it, does that mean I really should do it?" In the preceding example showing you how to create a subcategory to control the visibility of the clearance separately from the rest of the geometry, it may seem like a great way to achieve what you need at the time. But as your library grows, you will find it hard to manage those custom subcategories in individual families. Having a standard for when to create them and what to name them can help. In addition, you should consider other available options. In this case, you could assign the clearance to the Hidden Lines subcategory, which comes with most 3D-based Revit family templates. You could also use the Visibility parameter to control when it is turned on or off. Essentially, you can achieve similar functionality by taking a different route.

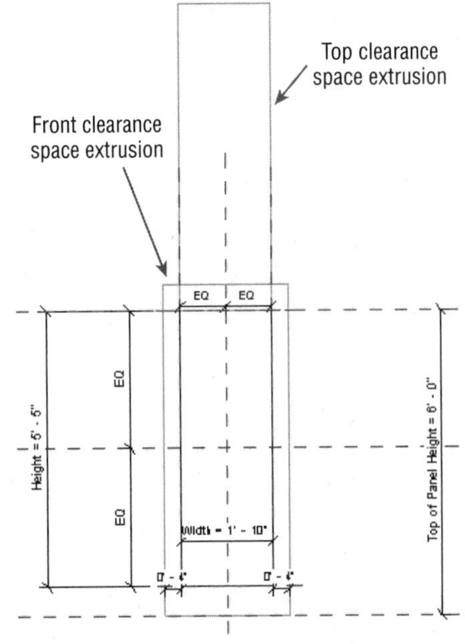

FIGURE 19.49 Clearance space reference planes in an equipment family

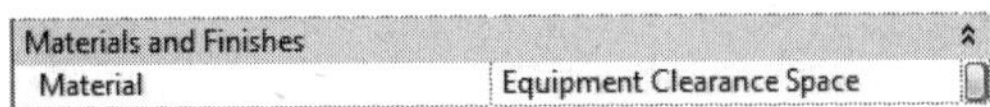

FIGURE 19.50 Associating material for the clearance

FIGURE 19.51 Display of the clearance extrusion in Visibility Graphics

Object Styles

Model Objects | Annotation Objects | Imported Objects

Category	Line Weight		Line Color	Line Pattern
	Projection	Cut		
Electrical Equipment	1		Black	
Clearance Area Lines	1		Black	Hidden
Clearance Space	1		RGB 255-128-064	Solid
Hidden Lines	1		Black	Dash

Although having solid geometry in an equipment family to represent clearance spaces is useful for interference coordination, you may not want to have the solid geometry displayed in plan views. Model or symbolic lines can be used to represent the clearance space for plan views. The visibility of these lines can be controlled by a Yes/No type parameter or by a subcategory. Figure 19.52 shows clearance space lines in the Front elevation view of the panel family. The lines exist in the Front elevation view so that they will be visible in plan views when the panel is attached to a vertical host.

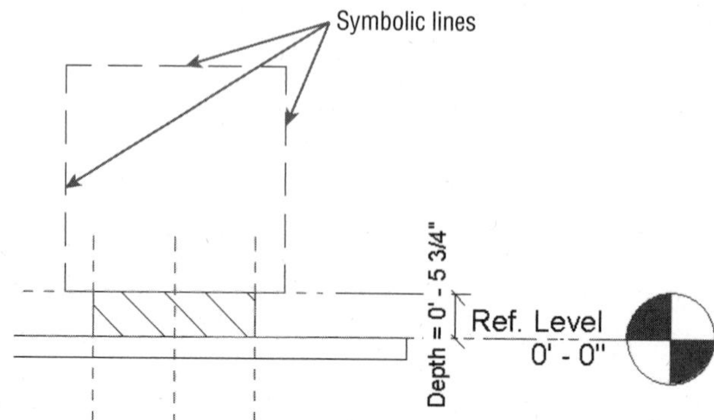

FIGURE 19.52 Lines representing clearance space in a family

Another option for adding clearance spaces to your equipment is to create unique clearance-space families. These families should be categorized as mechanical or electrical equipment families, but you could categorize them as any of the available subcategories, depending on how you want to control their visibility. In a project file with worksharing enabled, a workset could be created for equipment clearance spaces, as an option for making it easier to control the visibility of all equipment in a view. There is a downside to relying on worksets for visibility control, however, because you may also be using worksets as an option to load selected parts of the project. This can lead to confusion, not just within your company's project team but also for those working collaboratively with you.

Clearance space families can be face-hosted families for easy attachment to the solid geometry of your equipment families. Consider making individual families with the dimensions for each unique type of clearance or for specific types of equipment.

The example of displaying solid geometry (the clearance) with linework can be applied to most families' solid geometry. Displaying lines instead of geometry will improve your overall project performance with your families because Revit will need to regenerate lines instead of surfaces. This can be especially noticeable for round objects such as pipe connectors and their extrusions, because the software will try to simplify those round surfaces by breaking them down to multiple flat surfaces.

Adding Parameters and Constraints

The key to having equipment families that are usable in the early stages of your designs is to have families that are easily modified to meet the demands of frequent changes to your project model. Using parameters gives you the flexibility to change not only the size of equipment but also the values of connectors.

Three simple dimensions can define most equipment: length, width, and height. By using these parametrically, you can be confident that your equipment families occupy the space required for them in the model, even if they do not look exactly like the object they represent. Be consistent with your use of these parameters and particularly the naming convention you use. They do not need to be shared parameters unless the information is to be included in schedules. However, you could create them as shared parameters for consistent naming. Because there may be other dimensions in your families, it is best to give these parameters a descriptive name, such as Unit Length or Equipment Width, to distinguish them as the overall size. Of course, having these parameters in your families is not enough; you need to have the family geometry associated with them.

MEP equipment schedules vary in size and information, not only from one company to another but even in the same company, depending on the project standards or client demands. Mechanical equipment schedules are particularly difficult to manage without the proper use of parameters in your equipment families. The use of shared parameters is necessary for scheduling the systems information required from equipment schedules. The problem is that all mechanical equipment families are in one category.

To avoid having families with unnecessary parameters, it may be best to apply your shared parameters directly in the equipment families instead of using project parameters. That way, you can be sure that you have only the parameters required for the scheduling of the specific families in your mechanical equipment schedules.

Connectors have parameters that you may need to change based on the performance of your engineering systems. Creating parameters in your families with which the connector parameters can be associated allows you to change the connector values without having to open, edit, and reload your families. The main thing to remember when creating these parameters is that they must match the units of the connector parameter in order for them to be associated. For example, you cannot associate a connector's Voltage parameter with a number or integer parameter.

When you are creating equipment, you will often find yourself creating many types of the same equipment at different sizes, such as, for example different sizes of a terminal box based on inlet sizes. This is where type catalogs can be helpful. Each parameter in the type catalog must be a valid Type and use a valid unit selection. Also each parameter must actually be present in the family before the type catalog can insert the desired values. See Chapter 6, "Parameters," for more information on how to set up type catalogs.

Type Catalog References

Type catalogs can be referenced by using system parameters and shared parameters. The format for the type parameter must be*##parameter name##parameter type##units*; these parameter types and units must exactly match the format required by Revit.

Here are a few examples of proper formatting:

```
Duct Width##HVAC_DUCT_SIZE##INCHES
Power##ELECTRICAL_POWER##WATTS
Air Flow##HVAC_AIR_FLOW##CUBIC_FEET_PER_MINUTE
Width##LENGTH##FEET
```

The following list contains some of the parameter types and their units that can be used in creating a type catalog TXT file:

Common Types Note: For Unit Types of Text, Integer, Number, URL, Material, Yes/No, and <Family Type>, the Unit Type is Other and there are no specific units.

Length feet, inches, millimeters, centimeters, meters

Area square_feet, square_inches, square_meters, square_centimeters, square_millimeters, acres, hectares

Volume cubic_yards, cubic_feet, cubic_inches, cubic_meters, cubic_centimeters, cubic _millimeters, liters, gallons

Angle degrees

HVAC Types

HVAC_duct_size feet, inches, millimeters, centimeters, meters

HVAC_pressure inches_of_water, pascals, kilopascals, megapascals, pounds_force_per _square_inch, inches_of_mercury, millimeters_of_mercury, atmospheres, bars

HVAC_friction inches_of_water_per_100ft, pascals_per_meter

HVAC_velocity feet_per_minute, meters_per_second, centimeters_per_minute

HVAC_air_flow cubic_feet_per_minute, liters_per_second, cubic_meters_per_second, cubic_meters_per_hour, gallons_us_per_minute, gallons_us_per_hour

Piping Types

pipe_size feet, inches, meters, centimeters, millimeters

piping_pressure pascals, kilopascals, megapascals, pounds_force_per_square_inch, inches_of_mercury, millimeters_of_mercury, atmospheres, bars, feet_of_water

piping_temperature fahrenheit, celsius, kelvin, rankine

piping_velocity meters_per_second, feet_per_second

piping_flow liters_per_second, cubic_meters_per_second, cubic_meters_per_hour, gallons_us_per_minute, gallons_us_per_hour

Electrical Types

electrical_power watts, kilowatts, British_thermal_units_per_second, British_thermal _units_per_hour, calories_per_second, kilocalories_per_second, volt_amperes, kilovolt _amperes, horsepower

electrical_apparent_power watts, kilowatts, British_thermal_units_per_second, British_thermal_units_per_hour, calories_per_second, kilocalories_per_second, volt_amperes, kilovolt_amperes, horsepower

electrical_current amperes, kiloamperes, milliamperes

electrical_potential volts, kilovolts, millivolts

electrical_frequency hertz, cycles_per_second

electrical_illuminance lux, footcandles, footlamberts, candelas_per_square_meter

electrical_luminous_intensity candelas, lumens

For more information on parameters, see Chapter 6, and for more information on schedules, see Chapter 7, "Schedules."

The Bottom Line

Create MEP equipment families. The ability to create the types of equipment families needed for accurate modeling of components and systems is a major factor in the success of your Revit projects.

Master It MEP equipment can be quite complex in its structure. Complex geometry can have an adverse effect on model performance. What are some ways to model equipment in its simplest form yet still convey the proper information on construction documents?

Add connectors to equipment for systems. Adding connectors to equipment families will make them functional for use in the design of engineering systems.

Master It It is important to know how your equipment families will be used in your projects from an engineering standpoint as well as for model coordination. Explain how connectors determine the behavior of an equipment family.

Create clearance spaces for equipment. Space for safety and service of equipment is crucial to building design. The ability to coordinate clearances around equipment improves project quality and can reduce construction and design cost.

Master It Equipment families with built-in clearance spaces allow you to determine quickly and easily whether the equipment will fit into your project model. Describe some options for controlling the visibility of clearance spaces so that they are not shown when not needed.

Add parameters to equipment. Parameters in your equipment families can be useful for creating schedules in your Revit projects that report data directly from the equipment used in the design. Family parameters can enable you to make equipment families that are changeable without having to create new families.

Master It Shared parameters must be used in your equipment families if you want to schedule the data they provide. If you are creating parameters for parametric behavior of the solid geometry, do they also need to be shared parameters?

Chapter 20

Creating Lighting Fixtures

Lighting fixtures can be located anywhere in a building. They hang from ceilings and structures; they are mounted in floors, walls, and stairs; and they even stand on their own. With the Autodesk® Revit® MEP 2015 software, you can make any shape or form into a lighting fixture family so that, if your project requires it, you can create a unique fixture. However, the majority of lighting fixtures used in building design consist of a few basic shapes. Unless your project requires it for visualization, there is no need to go into great detail when creating the geometry of your lighting fixture families. Keeping their design simple will enable you to focus more on the computable data within your fixture families.

Lighting fixtures are unique Revit MEP families because they can be used not only to create a coordinated 3D model but also as a design tool. They can display the output of light for a specific fixture type by referring to separate IES files. The photometric data for a specific lighting fixture can be applied to a lighting fixture family regardless of the geometry of the family. This gives you the freedom to build families for the basic size, shape, and mounting options of lighting fixtures and then apply manufacturer-specific data to them for an accurate lighting design. Lighting fixture families can also contain electrical data, which allows for connection to distribution systems.

There are many options for the level of detail and data you can put into your lighting fixture families.

In this chapter, you will learn to do the following:

- Create different types of lighting fixture families
- Use a light source in your lighting fixture families
- Create and manage fixture types and parameters
- Use lines and symbols to represent lighting fixtures

Understanding Types of Lighting Fixture Families

Prior to creating a lighting fixture family, it is important to know how it will be used in your projects. The first thing to consider is how the fixture will be hosted in your model. Lighting fixture families can be hosted by specific building elements such as walls or ceilings or by any three-dimensional face within your model. You can also create lighting fixture families that do not require a host. Each hosting option determines how the geometry of the fixture is to be oriented in the family file. It is also important to realize that a family created with one type of hosting template cannot be exchanged for another, even though they may be of the same category. For this reason, planning, naming conventions, and training for staff are all important.

There are family template files (`.rft`) for different types of hosted lights. You can also use one of the generic family templates and later categorize the family as a lighting fixture. When you use a lighting fixture template, a reference plane for the elevation of the light source is already included. Using a generic template will require you to add a reference plane for the light source if needed.

Nonhosted Lighting Fixtures

Nonhosted lighting fixture families are useful in areas that do not have a ceiling or for free-standing lights. They can be given an offset to the level at which they are inserted to show them above the floor. They are also useful for wall-mounted lights, when you need to show a symbol on your drawings instead of the actual fixture. The symbol can be nested into your fixture family without concern for the annotation orientation because the fixture will always be vertical. One example of this use is a wall-mounted exit light. Figure 20.1 shows an exit light family that has a nested annotation. The geometry of the fixture is modeled to appear correctly when placed adjacent to a wall, while the annotation is nested to display in plan views.

The drawback to this scenario is that, although you show the fixture adjacent to a wall, if the wall moves, the fixture does not move with it. This can cause inaccuracies on your drawings and therefore requires manual editing of the fixture locations. Thus, you must carefully consider the types of light fixture families used with this method.

As with any family you create, the insertion point is an important consideration when building the geometry of a lighting fixture. When you create a lighting fixture with the `Generic Model.rft` family template, Revit opens four views automatically, with the floor plan view as the active view.

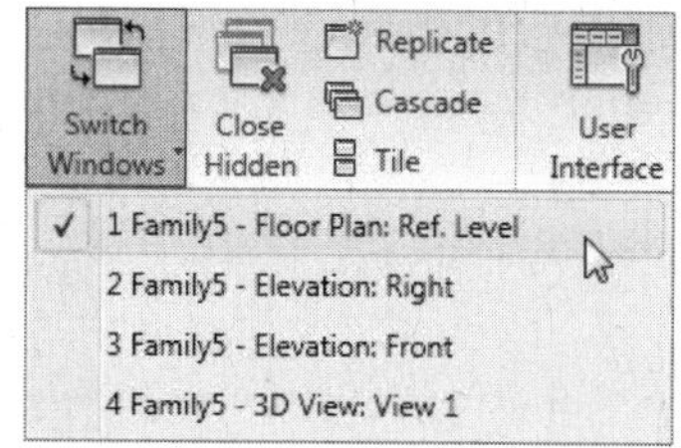

The intersection of the reference planes in the Floor Plan: Ref. Level view defines the insertion point of the family. Be sure to build the fixture geometry around the insertion point in a manner that makes it easy to place the fixture into your models. Fixtures that need to be adjacent to elements are easier to insert when their geometry is properly oriented with the insertion point. Also, take into consideration how the fixture may be rotated in your model.

Because of the potential complexities of creating a new family and maintaining company standards and consistency, it can be useful to have a standard "family-planning" sketchpad, where design, parameters, and reference planes can all be drawn out before committing yourself to an actual family. Figure 20.2 shows an example of a form used for planning the construction of a Revit family.

Creating geometry in the Ref. Level view places it at the reference level. The reference level in a family is a placeholder for the project level when you insert the family into a project. That is how a light fixture inserted on the second level of your project is associated with the second level. Therefore, the elevation or offset that you apply to the fixture is relative to the level at which it is placed. If you are creating a nonhosted lighting fixture that you want at a specific elevation when you insert the family, you can build the geometry at the desired elevation. This has the potential to cause confusion when using the Offset parameter, so a best practice is to use the reference level.

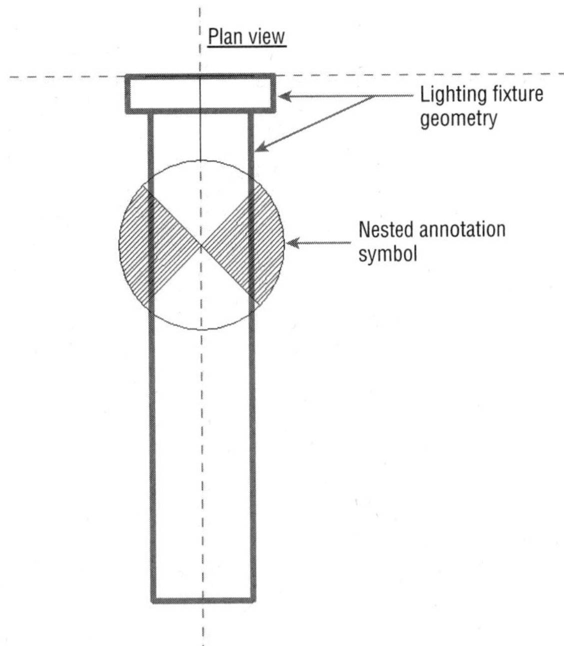

FIGURE 20.1
Nonhosted exit light family

Real World Scenario

OFFSET VS. ELEVATION

Grant has created a lighting fixture modeled at 8′-0″ (2440 mm) above the reference level in the family file. When he inserts the family into his project, it has an Offset value of 0′-0″ (0 mm). In the lounge on the first floor of the project, the lights need to be at an elevation of 10′-0″ (3050 mm), so he changes the Offset parameter value to 2′-0″ (610 mm) for each instance of the fixture in the lounge.

Later that day, Grant's project manager, Lucy, is reviewing the Revit file and selects one of the light fixtures to view its properties. She notices the offset of 2′-0″ (610 mm) and, assuming that this is supposed to represent the elevation of the lighting fixture, she changes the value to 10′-0″ (3050 mm). Concerned with quality control, she checks and changes the properties of all of the fixtures in the break room area. It is not long afterward that she receives an email from Grant wondering why the lighting fixtures in the room are 18′-0″ (5490 mm) above the first-floor level.

Of course, this is also a case where using multiple views such as sections, elevations, or 3D views to examine the model would be helpful.

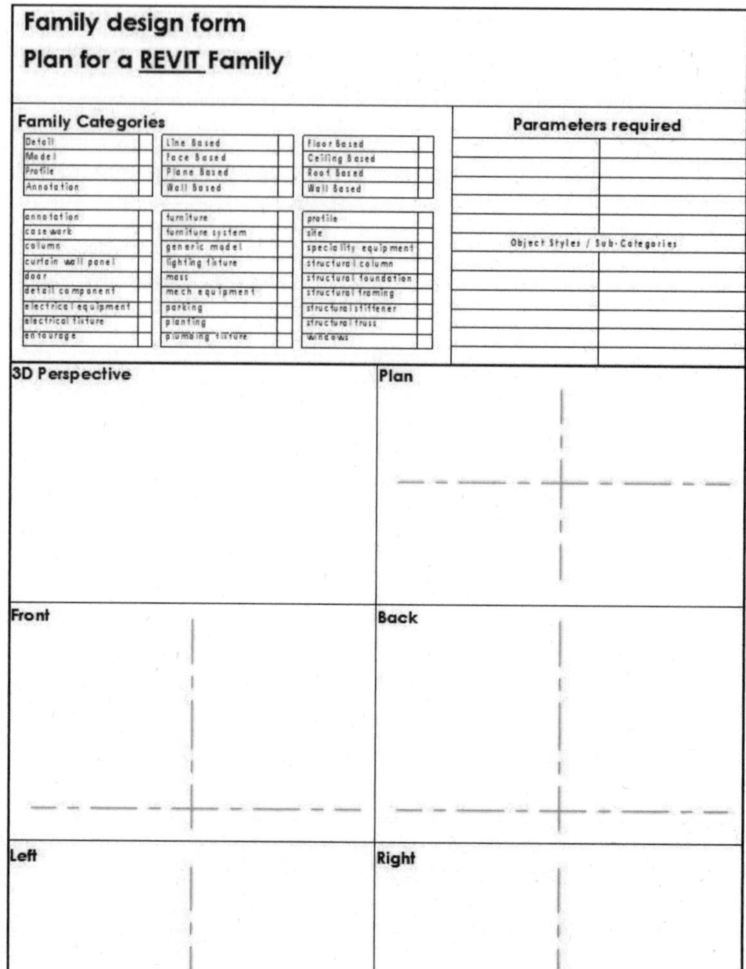

FIGURE 20.2
Sample family-planning design form

If you do not want to use the Offset parameter of an instance when working in a project file, you can control the elevation of a fixture by placing a reference plane in the family. The plane can be dimensioned and associated with an instance parameter to edit and manage the elevation of the fixture easily. Draw a reference plane in an elevation view when working in the Family Editor. Be sure to give the plane a name so that you can select it later as the host for your fixture geometry.

You can set the reference plane as the current plane for modeling by using the Set button on the Work Plane panel of the Create tab on the ribbon. This lets you choose a plane, such as the one you just created, to model your geometry on. If you have already created the geometry for your lighting fixture, you can select it and click the Edit Work Plane button on the Work Plane panel of the contextual tab. In the Work Plane dialog box, click the Name radio button and choose the plane you created for the fixture elevation from the drop-down list (see Figure 20.3).

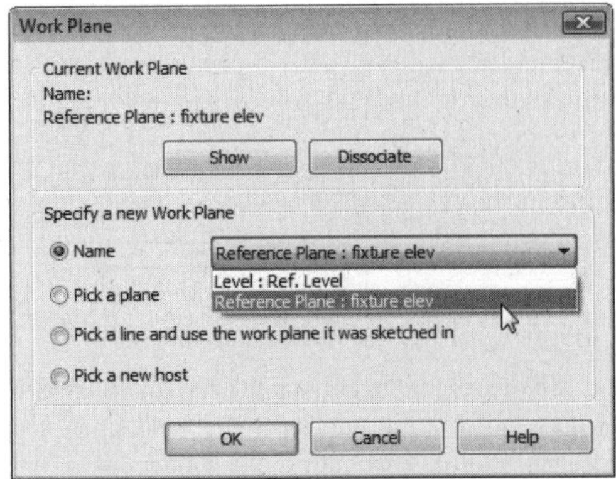

FIGURE 20.3
Choosing a new work plane for family geometry

Depending on the type of forms you use for the geometry, you may have to select them independently to change the plane they are associated with. You can select and change the work plane of different form types (extrusions, revolves, or blends) only if they are on parallel planes.

Because you can change the work plane of an item only to a parallel plane, select those items that have been created on the same plane or a parallel plane. If an extrusion is created while in an elevation view, it is associated with a vertical plane and cannot be moved to a horizontal plane. However, you can align and lock it to a horizontal plane.

Figure 20.4 shows an elevation view of a nonhosted fixture family. A reference plane has been created to define the fixture elevation. The rectangular solid extrusion was created in the plan view, and its work plane was changed to the elevation plane. The arced void extrusion was created in the left elevation view and aligned and locked to the fixture elevation plane. The dimension has been associated to an instance parameter for fixture elevation.

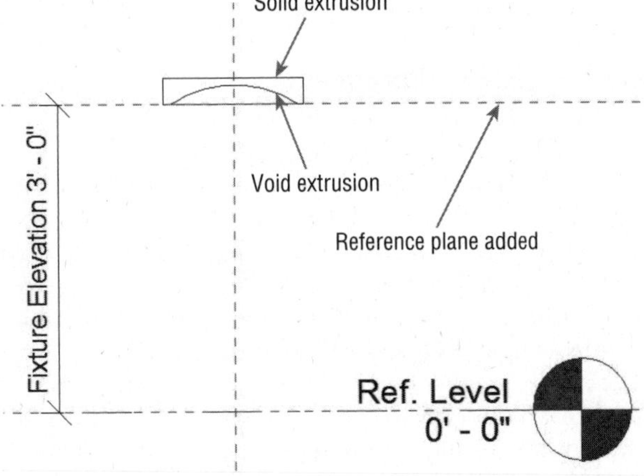

FIGURE 20.4
Nonhosted family with an elevation plane

Creating a fixture with an elevation parameter does not disable the functionality of the Offset parameter, so be sure that you and your users understand the difference. When your family is placed into a project, the offset is applied to the entire family, while the elevation is applied to the geometry within the family.

If you want your lighting fixture families to follow the slope of a surface such as a sloped ceiling, you need to deselect the Always Vertical parameter. This setting is found in the Family Categories And Parameters dialog box that you can access from the Create or Modify tab.

Family Parameters

Parameter	
Work Plane-Based	☐
Always vertical	☐
Cut with Voids When Loaded	☐
Light Source	☑

Setting the family to Always Vertical causes the fixture to attach to its associated work plane in its normal orientation even if the plane is sloped. Deselecting the parameter causes your fixture family to follow the slope of its associated plane or level.

Any annotation symbols nested within the fixture family are displayed only in plan views that are parallel to the view they are created in, so they are not displayed if the fixture is mounted to a sloped plane.

Another useful setting for nonhosted families is the Work Plane-Based option found in the Family Category And Parameters dialog box. This setting allows you to create a family that does not require host geometry yet can be associated with a plane in a model.

Using this option gives you the ability to associate a family with a named reference plane in your model, in the same way that a face-hosted family attaches to a 3D face. You can change the host plane of the family at any time after placement in the model.

When placing a family of this type into your model, you have to choose the Place On Work Plane option from the placement panel on the ribbon. The Place On Face option is set by default but will not work for this type of family. You can choose any named reference plane, even sloped planes, or any level in the project.

When used with the Always Vertical setting, the family attaches to a sloped plane; however, the geometry of the family remains vertical and does not follow the slope of the plane.

Face-hosted Lighting Fixtures

Creating face-hosted fixture families adds another level of coordination to your projects because the families move with their associated hosts. This keeps your fixtures at the correct elevations when ceiling heights change. Fixtures mounted to vertical host faces, such as walls, also move with changes to the vertical host locations. Face-hosted families can also be hosted by reference planes within the project. In an area with no ceiling, a reference plane or level can be created to host lighting fixtures at a specific elevation.

To create a lighting fixture family that is face-hosted, you can use the `Generic Model face based.rft` family template. Once you've opened it, you can change the category of the family by clicking the Category And Parameters button on the Family Properties panel of the Create tab. When you change the category to Lighting Fixtures, the Light Source parameter becomes available. Select the box if your fixture will have a light source to be used for rendering or lighting calculations (see Figure 20.5).

The face-based template contains a generic extrusion that is used as a reference for the host when the family is placed into a model. You can change the size of the extrusion, but you cannot delete it. The extrusion is necessary in order for your family geometry to know how to attach to its model host. It also allows you to indicate how void extrusions cut their host.

FIGURE 20.5
Family Category And Parameters dialog box

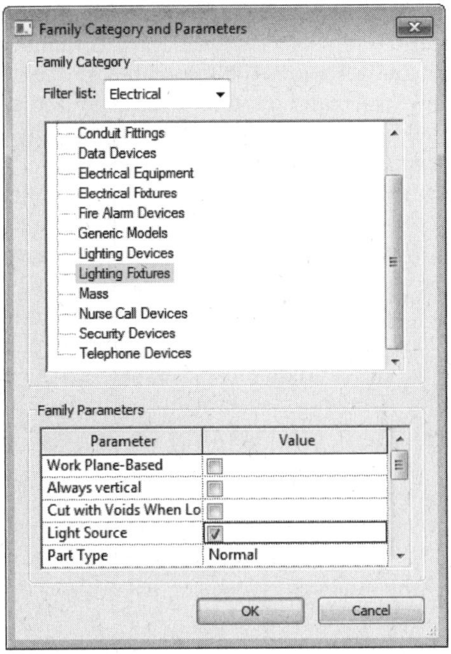

CUT THROUGH A LINK?

Families with a void designed to cut the host do not cut the face of an object in a linked file. This does not affect light output when you're using families with a light source as long as the light source is not inside solid geometry within the fixture.

Face-hosted families also contain a reference-level plane at the face of the placeholder extrusion. This face represents the face of a ceiling or wall host when the family is placed into a model. The placeholder extrusion face is locked to this reference plane and cannot be unlocked, so although you *can* associate the extrusion to another plane, it is not a good idea. Doing so will change only the thickness of the extrusion, which is not important.

To build a recessed lighting fixture, you want your extrusions to be inside the placeholder extrusion. Although the fixture looks upside down in the family file, it will have the correct orientation when hosted by a ceiling or reference plane in your project file, because the placeholder extrusion represents the host object when the family is used in a project. Surface- or pendant-mounted lights should be modeled adjacent to the face of the placeholder extrusion.

Face-hosted Families for Wall-mounted Lights

When creating a face-hosted family for a wall-mounted light fixture, you need to treat the placeholder extrusion as though it were a wall. When working in the Ref. Level plan view of the family, it is as though the wall has been laid flat on the ground and you are looking down at it. It is easy to assume that the distance from the edge of the placeholder extrusion to your geometry will be the mounting height of the fixture. That is not the case (see Figure 20.6).

Face-hosted families have a Default Elevation parameter used when the family is placed on a vertical face. When they are placed into a model on a vertical face, the Elevation Instance Parameter becomes active and is used to set the mounting height. The Default Elevation parameter is simply a starting point until an elevation is assigned after the placement of the family. You can set the Default Elevation within the family file to any value that you want for the mounting height when the fixture is first placed into your project, but because of the functionality of the Properties palette, you may need to input a value during initial placement. It is a type parameter, so you can use it to define different family types if desired. In the project environment, the Elevation parameter is active only when the family is placed on a vertical host. When a face-hosted family is placed on a horizontal host, the Elevation parameter is inactive and cannot be edited. Figure 20.7 shows a wall-mounted light that was placed into the model at an elevation of 4′-0″ (Default Elevation) and then given a mounting height of 7′-6″ (Elevation) after placement.

When you create an extrusion to represent the body of a light fixture that is to be hosted by a vertical face, it is often easier to create it in a left or right elevation view instead of the Ref. Level plan view. By doing so, the extrusion you create will be associated with the Center Left/Right reference plane. Additional reference planes can be added to create constraints for fixture length, depth, and width.

FIGURE 20.6
Face-hosted family for a wall-mounted light

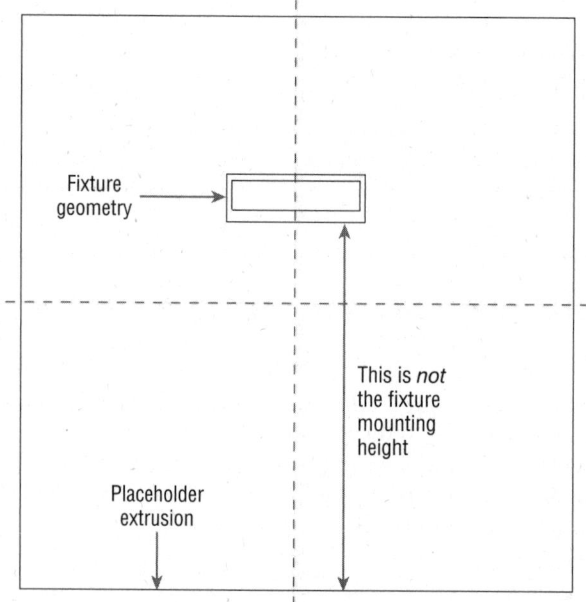

FIGURE 20.7 Wall-mounted fixture with an elevation

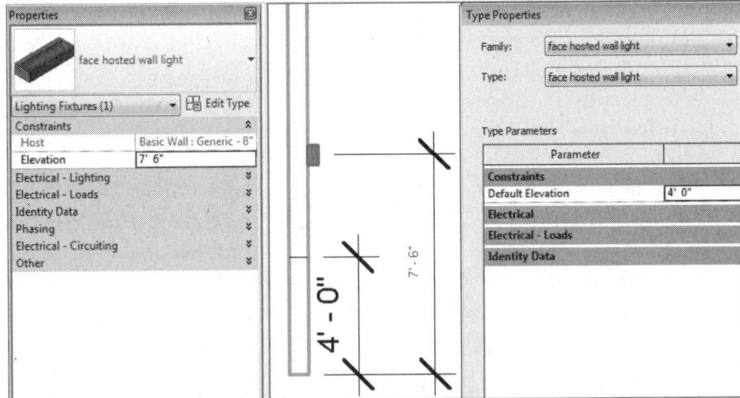

Fixture Types Based on Dimensions

When you are creating lighting fixtures, you first need to decide what type parameters are going to be used to determine the different types within the family. One common practice is to create fixtures based on their dimensions. This is a good starting point for developing a fixture library, and additional parameters can be added later to create more types within the family for more-specific purposes.

For example, you can start by creating a recessed fluorescent troffer. Then, creating parameters for the length and width of the fixture allows you to make types in the family such as 2×4, 2×2, or 1×4. This is a very generic method for creating fixtures, but it is useful for general modeling when lighting analysis or circuiting is not required. The depth of the fixture should also be considered because it is an important dimension for coordination of the space above the ceilings within a model.

This can be done for any kind of fixture you may use in a project, such as downlights, surface-mounted fixtures, and pendant fixtures. A library of generic (or "placeholder") fixtures is useful in the preliminary design stages of a project. Early on you may not know exactly what fixtures will be used, but you can use these generic fixture families to represent the basic layout and design intent. Because they are categorized as lighting fixtures, you can easily replace them with the actual fixtures to be used when the decision is made. Just remember that you cannot replace face-hosted families with nonhosted ones by using the Type Selector. You have to place one type and remove the other manually.

Fixture Types Based on Fixture Performance and Lighting Characteristics

Having fixture families based on size and shape is a good start, but you also need fixtures that are defined by their specific uses and performance. This is especially true if you intend to use your Revit model for lighting analysis. It is a good practice to develop lighting fixture families that meet the design requirements of your Revit projects so you don't have to create a separate fixture family for every light fixture you use.

You can create families based on their performance and appearance. Not only does a parabolic fixture perform differently than a lensed fixture, it also looks different, so creating separate families for each type may be necessary. Appearance is important only if you are concerned with modeling to a level of detail that requires a visible difference between the two fixtures, but it may be easier to manage separate families than one family with several types.

With these fixtures, the dimensions are important for defining different types, but they do not need to define the family itself. You can create a parabolic troffer family with types such as 2×2 and 2×4, but you also want parameters to define the voltage, load, or number of lamps. Each type parameter that you add to a fixture family can determine a fixture type within that family. This allows you to use a unique IES file for each type.

There are many lighting manufacturers from which to choose when specifying your fixtures in a project. It is not necessary to have a library that contains each and every option. You can make a set of lighting fixture families that cover the basic fixture types and then modify them to manufacturer specifications as needed. Choose an IES file that meets the basic requirements for the fixture type as the baseline for that type of fixture. When you use the fixture in a project, you can get an idea of its performance prior to deciding which specific manufacturer and model number to use. Some people have resisted using a BIM solution such as Revit MEP for their projects because they think they have to make too many decisions early on in the project that they are unable to make. Using a baseline fixture type will allow you to move forward with the project and make the more specific decisions when necessary.

Figure 20.8 shows the types within a parabolic 2×4 light fixture family; the No. Of Lamps and Ballast Voltage parameters were used to determine the family types. A unique file is required for the Photometric Web File parameter for each variation in the number of lamps, but it is not required for each voltage.

There is no right or wrong answer to how many light fixture families you should have. How you use the software and your design standards will help determine the types of fixture families you require. A minimum number of families that can be readily adjusted to the specifics of your project will be easiest to manage and maintain.

However you decide to create a fixture, it is important to build your fixture family so that when it is placed in a model, it can be associated with a Space object in order to provide the desired engineering data from calculations. A light fixture that is not inside or touching a Space object does not generate an average estimated illumination for that Space object. Figure 20.9 shows a group of fixtures placed higher than the upper limit of an engineering Space object; therefore, there is no illumination calculated for the Space object.

One way to remedy this is to use the Room Calculation Point that can be added to families such as light fixtures. This point allows you to associate a light fixture with a space even though the fixture is not within the bounds of the space. To add a Room Calculation Point to a light fixture family, select the box in the Family Category And Parameters dialog box.

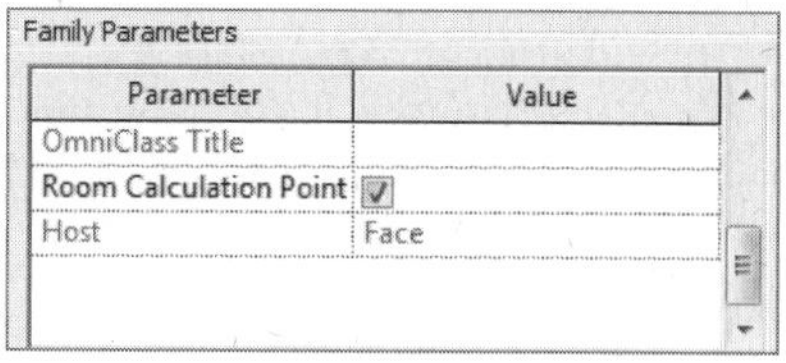

Family Parameters

Parameter	Value
OmniClass Title	
Room Calculation Point	☑
Host	Face

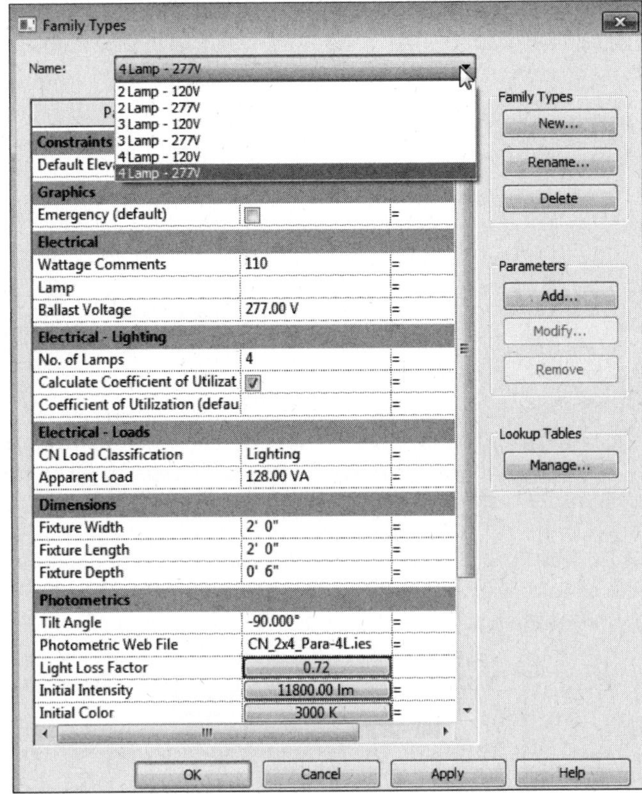

FIGURE 20.8
Lighting fixture family types

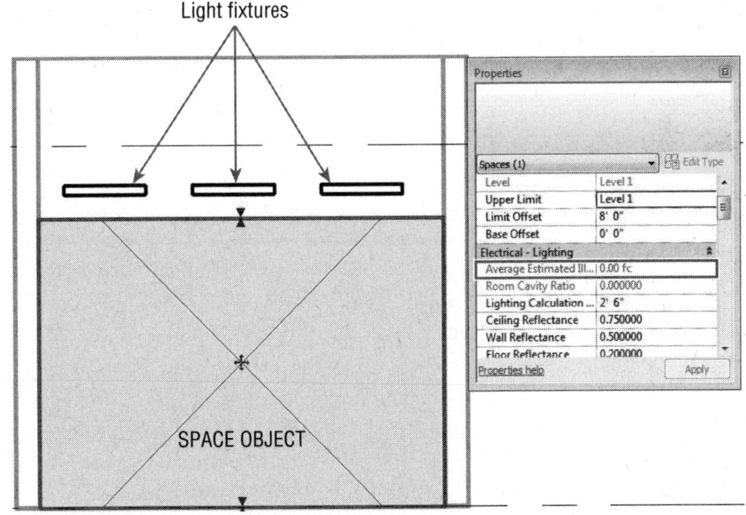

FIGURE 20.9
Fixtures outside the limits of a Space object

The point can be located anywhere in the family by dragging it along either axis, as shown in Figure 20.10. The location is set in the family and cannot be modified in the project.

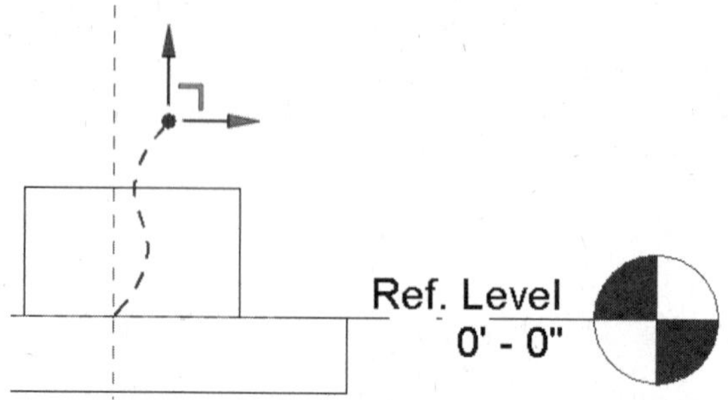

FIGURE 20.10 Room Calculation Point in a light fixture family

This feature should be used with caution. It can result in incorrect lighting calculations because, while the fixtures can be associated with a space, the volume of the space may not be correct. Figure 20.11 shows light fixtures that are associated with a space because of the Room Calculation Point.

Another drawback to this feature is that the location of the Room Calculation Point cannot be modified in the project environment. You have to edit the family and reload it into the project in order to make a change.

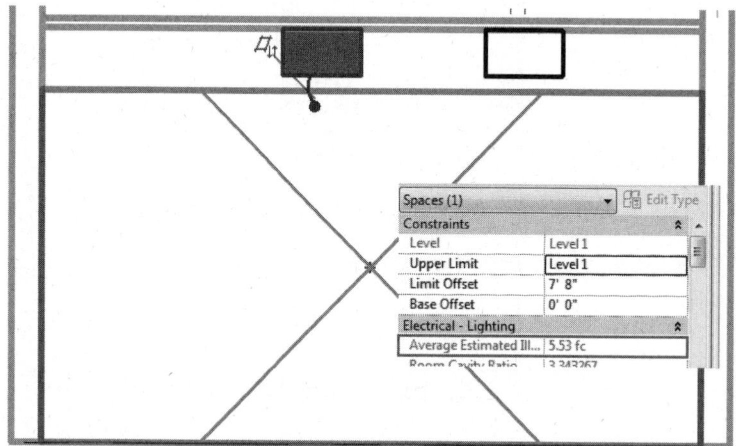

FIGURE 20.11 Light fixtures using the Room Calculation Point to associate with a space in a project

Naming Conventions

A standard naming convention goes a long way in helping you maintain and manage your lighting fixture families. When you create a lighting fixture or modify an existing family, it is best to distinguish it from families that come installed with Revit MEP. This prevents the files from being overwritten if you update your library at the installation of a new release of the software.

A common practice is to prefix the family name with your initials or your company's acronym. This not only distinguishes the families as unique to you or your company, it also keeps them organized because they will all be listed together alphabetically.

The naming of IES files is also important to file management and organization. Most IES files that are provided by manufacturers are named with a convention that is unique to whoever is providing them. It can be difficult to determine the type of fixture that an IES file is associated with if the fixture is not named in a manner that indicates its type or performance. When you acquire an IES file, consider renaming it to indicate its characteristics so that those using the file can easily see what type of fixture it represents.

Figure 20.12 shows that the IES file used in the Photometric Web File parameter has been named so that it clearly indicates that it should be used for a parabolic 2×4 fixture.

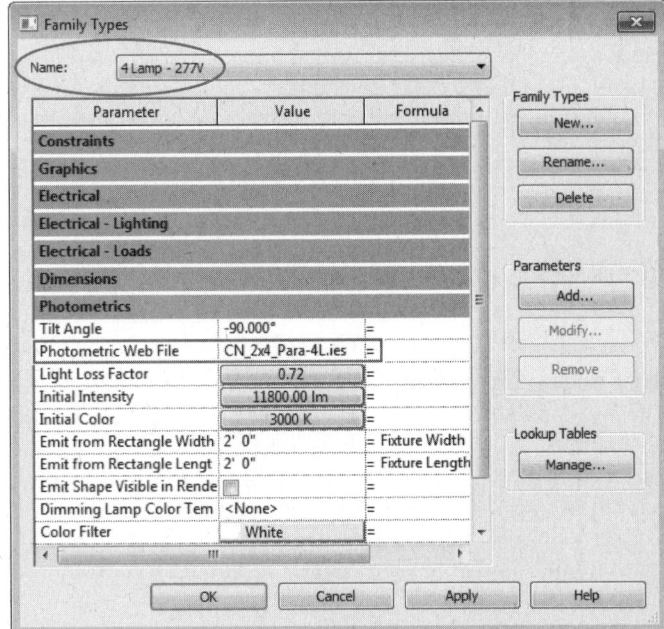

FIGURE 20.12 Photometric Web File parameter named to match fixture type

Performing a Lighting Analysis

Your lighting fixture families require a light source if they are to be used for rendering or lighting calculations. A light source is a unique feature of a lighting fixture family that acts as the part that emits light. This does not necessarily mean a lightbulb, because you can define the shape of the light source according to how light is seen coming from the fixture. When you look at a light fixture that has a lens, the light appears to come from the shape of the lens.

> **GARDEN OF LIGHT**
>
> In lighting design circles, it is often said that a *bulb* is something you plant in your garden; light fixtures have *lamps*.

You can also define the light distribution from the light source. Setting how the light is thrown from a fixture gives you a more accurate representation of the behavior of the fixture for lighting calculations and rendering. To give your family the exact photometric characteristics of a specified fixture, you can designate a photometric web file for the light source and also define settings such as color and intensity.

Lighting fixture families created from a light fixture template have one light source by default. It is possible to have a fixture family with multiple light sources, such as track lights or a chandelier. This requires creating a separate family that defines the light source, and then nesting it into your fixture family. The nested family must be shared in order to act as a light source. Shared nested families are actually loaded as individual families into the project as well as being seen as part of their host family. This means shared nested track lighting heads could be placed separately if desired as well as appear in a schedule separately as individual light fixtures or as part of the whole track and head lighting family. You can set a family to be shared by selecting the Shared box in the Family Category And Parameters dialog box.

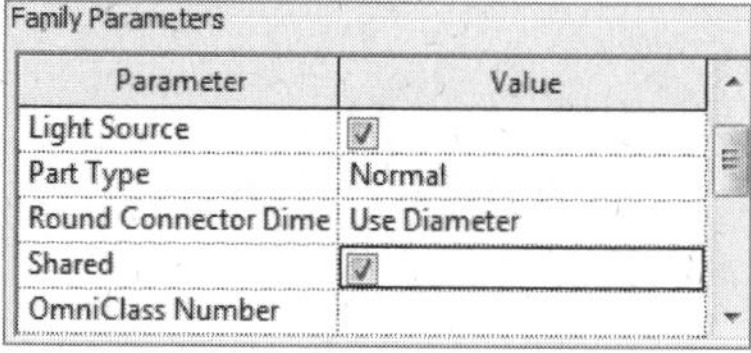

Light Source Location

When starting with the `Generic Model.rft` template and categorizing the family as a light fixture with a light source, you will see the light source as a yellow object in the drawing area. Yellow can be a difficult color to work with on a white background, so you may want to change the color by accessing the Object Styles settings within the family file. The light source appears at the insertion point on the reference plane. You can move the light source to anywhere in 3D space within the family file. Figure 20.13 shows a light source for a site light pole that has been moved to the face of the fixture.

Depending on the light source definition settings you chose, you can change the size of the light source by editing the Light Source Symbol Size and Emit From Line Length parameters within the family. Click the Family Types button on the Properties panel of the ribbon in the Family Editor to access these parameters (see Figure 20.14). These parameters are not available if you are specifying a photometric web file.

Light source objects have axes that allow you to align and lock them to the fixture geometry or to a reference plane. If you place the light source inside solid geometry, you receive a warning that no light will be emitted when the family is in a rendered view. The light source can be located on the face of your fixture geometry, or it can be located within a void inside the geometry for a more realistic representation of the fixture. Figure 20.15 shows a downlight family with a light source located inside the geometry of the fixture. The light distribution that appears to pass through the sides of the fixture will be blocked by the solid geometry when shown in a rendering. A material can be applied to the geometry to affect how the light will be reflected inside the fixture.

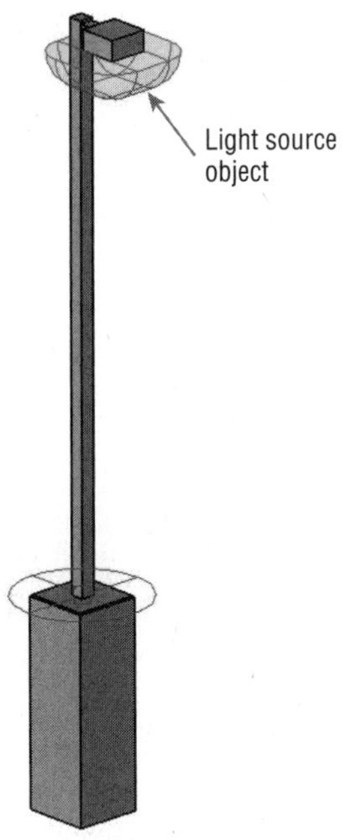

FIGURE 20.13
Light source of a pole light family

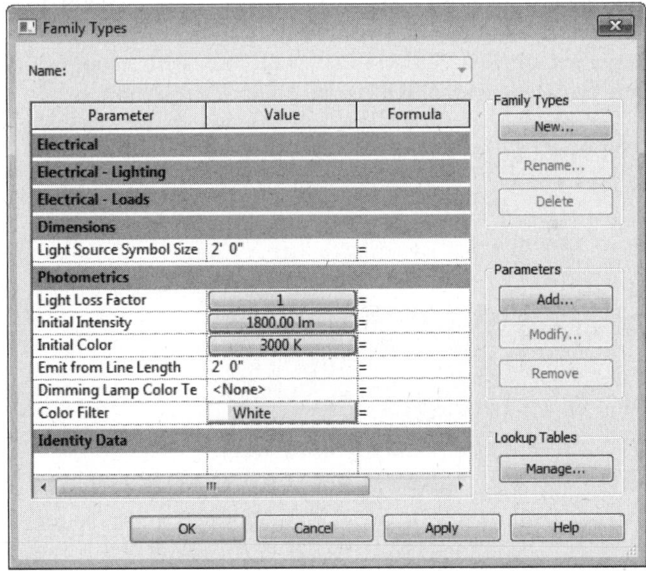

FIGURE 20.14
Light source size parameters

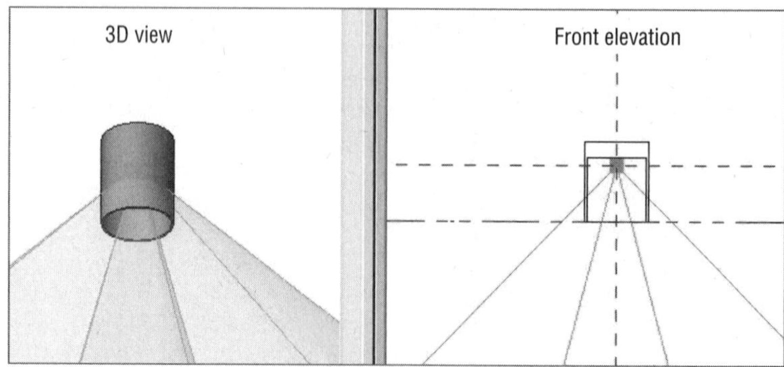

FIGURE 20.15 Light source inside fixture geometry

If you use the `Lighting Fixture.rft` template to create a family, you see an additional reference plane that defines the location of the light source. The light source object is locked to this plane and cannot be unlocked. The reference plane cannot be removed from the family. The location of this plane can be controlled parametrically to adjust the location of the light source if needed.

Light Source Definitions

You can define the shape of the light source and its distribution pattern by clicking the Light Source Definition button on the Lighting panel of the contextual tab that appears when you select the light source. You can choose from four shapes: point, line, rectangle, and circle. You can combine any of these shapes with one of the four light distribution patterns located at the bottom of the Light Source Definition dialog box. Pattern options are spherical, hemispherical, spot, and photometric web (see Figure 20.16).

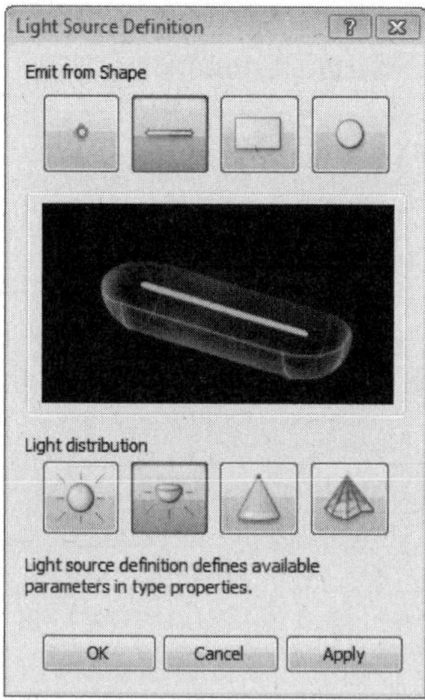

FIGURE 20.16 Light Source Definition dialog box

The light distribution patterns have different properties. The spherical and hemispherical distributions have the basic settings for size and photometric data, while the spot distribution has additional settings for the tilt angle and beam spread. The photometric web distribution has a parameter for tilt angle and one to define the light source by a photometric (IES) file. The properties of the light source distribution are all associated with type parameters of the fixture family. Figure 20.17 shows the properties of a light source with a spot distribution. Notice that the parameter values are mapped to family parameters (indicated by the = to the right side of the parameter value).

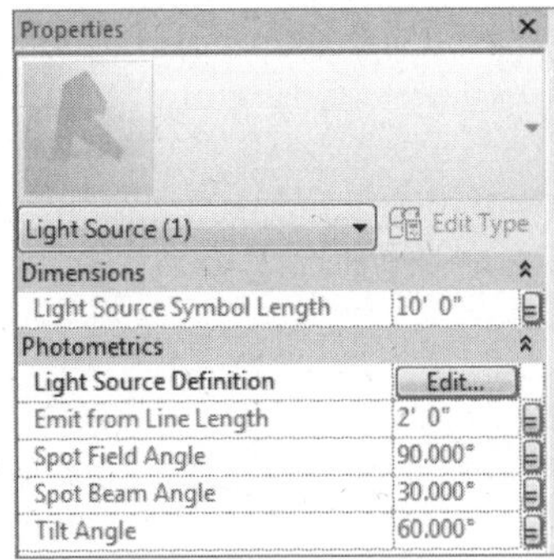

FIGURE 20.17 Light source properties

Light Source Parameters

The family parameters that control the properties of the light source are type parameters in the Photometrics parameter group. The parameters vary depending on the light distribution style chosen. These parameters have more to do with rendering appearances than with lighting calculations, because the IES file associated with a fixture drives the calculation values.

You can apply a light loss factor to the fixture family by clicking the button in the Light Loss Factor parameter cell. This opens a dialog box for choosing one of the two methods for applying a light loss factor. The Simple method allows you to use the slider in the dialog box to assign a total light loss factor to the family, while the Advanced method provides more-specific options. You can input values for losses and depreciation manually or use the sliders. The combination of settings in the Advanced method generates a total, as shown in Figure 20.18.

You can set the Initial Intensity parameter by any of the four values shown in the dialog box that appears when you click the button in the parameter cell. You can choose any of the value options to input. This information is often found in a lamp catalog or may be stored in the IES file associated with a fixture. You do not need to know the value for each option. When you input a value, the other options populate according to your input. Figure 20.19 shows an example in which an input was given for Luminous Flux and the other values populated accordingly.

VIEWING THE INFORMATION IN A PHOTOMETRIC WEB FILE

Many lighting manufacturers that provide photometric files of their products also offer viewers that allow you to see the information contained within the file. These are useful tools for helping you to input the correct engineering data into your Revit lighting fixture families.

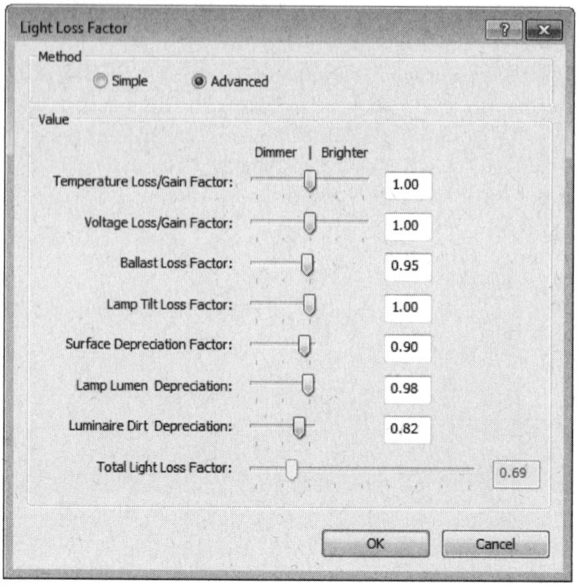

FIGURE 20.18
Advanced light loss factor settings

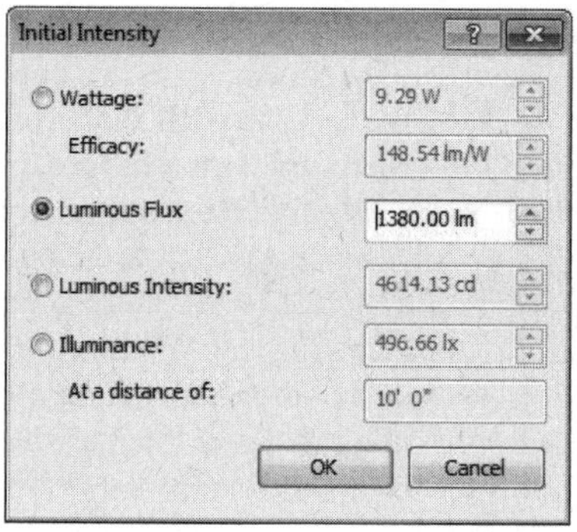

FIGURE 20.19
Initial Intensity dialog box values

Clicking the button in the Initial Color parameter cell opens a dialog box that lets you choose the color temperature of the light. The Color Preset drop-down offers settings based on various common lamp types and also offers the option to input a custom color temperature value, as shown in Figure 20.20.

The Dimming Lamp Color Temperature Shift and Color Filter parameters are also for the appearance of the light from the fixture in renderings. You can apply a predefined lamp curve to affect the color and intensity of lights when they are dimmed. You can also apply a color filter to change how the light appears coming from the fixture.

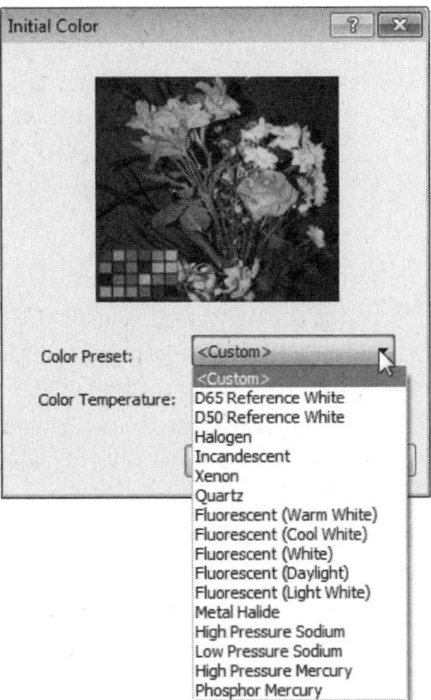

FIGURE 20.20 Initial Color dialog box

Using Fixture Families as Intelligent Objects

Fixture families can do more than represent the geometry of the light fixtures used in your projects. You can add intelligence to your fixture families to make them useful for engineering and design decisions.

Using Parameters

As with any kind of family you create, the parameters you use provide the intelligence within your lighting fixture families, making them easily modifiable and useful for calculations.

Use family parameters to constrain the geometry of a fixture or to add data to it. Family parameters cannot be included in a schedule or tagged in views, so be sure to use them only for data that is not necessary to show on your construction documents.

As mentioned previously in this chapter, dimensions are good parameters to have in your fixture families. They allow you to customize a family to the exact dimensions of fixtures specified for your project without having to create an entirely new family. These dimension constraints are also useful for controlling the symbolic representation of fixtures, which is discussed later in this chapter.

Another useful parameter is one for electrical load. This gives you a parameter with which to associate the connector parameter so that when fixtures from different manufacturers are chosen, you can edit the family parameter and update the load of the connector.

Some types of lighting fixtures, such as site lighting fixtures, are available in different voltages that require a different number of poles for connection to a circuit. Having a parameter that defines the number of poles enables you to easily modify the connector by using parameter association. A fixture family with this parameter can have a type for 208V single-phase (two poles), 208V three-phase (three poles), or 277V single-phase, for example.

Adding Connectors

One feature of your lighting fixture families that makes them useful for the design of your projects is an electrical connector. Adding connectors to your families lets you connect them to electrical circuits in order to manage your panel loads and also lets you use wiring objects that maintain a connection to the fixtures when they are moved in the model.

The location of a connector in a lighting fixture family is not as important as on other types of electrical objects because the graphical representation of the wiring stops at the edge of the fixture. The easiest placement method for adding a connector is to choose the Face option. This places the connector in the center of whichever 3D face you select. Click the Electrical Connector button on the Connectors panel of the Create tab, and then choose the Face option on the Placement panel of the contextual tab that appears.

Next, choose the type of connector from the drop-down list on the Options Bar. You can change the type later by accessing the properties of the connector if needed. If you are using the connector to circuit your lights to a power panel, choose one of the power type connectors.

As you place your cursor over the fixture geometry, the 3D faces become highlighted, indicating where the connector can be placed. You can use the Tab key to cycle through available faces that have a common edge. Once you have highlighted the desired face, click to place the connector. There is no need to dimension or constrain the connector because it is always in the center of the selected 3D face.

If you want to control the location of a connector, you can use the Work Plane method of placement. This method requires that you select a plane on which to place the connector. You can use any named reference plane within the fixture family. Choosing the Work Plane option opens a dialog box with options for specifying the desired plane. You can pick the plane from a list or choose to select the plane manually. Figure 20.21 shows the dialog box and the various planes available in a sample lighting fixture family.

Once you have selected a plane for placement, the connector appears at the insertion point of the family. You can then move the connector by selecting it and using the Move command on the Modify | Connector Element contextual tab. It is important to use the Move command because attempting to click and drag the connector only rotates the orientation of the Connector object.

After you have moved the connector to the desired location, you can convert the temporary dimensions to actual dimensions to constrain the location of the connector if necessary.

The properties of a connector determine how the fixture family behaves electrically. The parameters of a connector can be associated with parameters of the fixture family so that they can be changed parametrically in a project or be given different values for different types within the family. For example, you can have a fixture family with multiple voltage options. The Voltage parameter of the connector can be associated with the Voltage parameter of the family by clicking the small square to the far right of the connector's Voltage parameter. This opens a dialog box that allows you to choose the family parameter to which you can associate the connector parameter. Only family parameters that match the discipline and type are available, so you cannot associate a Voltage parameter with something that is not a voltage.

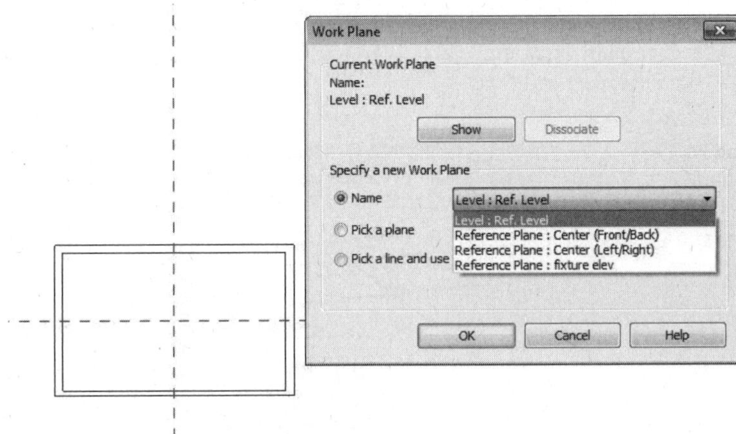

FIGURE 20.21 Work Plane connector placement dialog box

It can be helpful to associate the Load Classification parameter of a connector to a family parameter for load classification. This lets you easily change the classification and demand factor of a fixture family to suit the specific needs of a project, without having to edit the fixture family.

Representing Light Fixtures on Construction Documents

As with most parts of an electrical design, a lighting plan can be represented symbolically. There is no real need to show the actual fixtures in the model on construction documents. Using symbolic lines and symbols to show lighting fixture locations enables you to represent fixtures that are alike with a common symbol. This reduces the number of symbols required, simplifying your construction documents. For example, although your project may have several types of 2×4 recessed fixtures, they can all be represented with the same symbol in your plan views.

Using symbolic lines and symbols also helps improve the performance of your Revit model. 2D graphics can be more easily processed and regenerated than 3D graphics. Although it is recommended that you model your light fixtures in the simplest form possible, you may receive fixture families from manufacturers or other sources that are modeled at a more complex level. Having many light fixtures in a project and showing their 3D graphics can significantly affect how well your model performs.

Another reason for using symbolic lines or nested annotation symbols in your lighting fixture families is that it gives you another level of visibility control for your fixtures. Through your use of parameters, a light fixture can display different configurations of symbolic lines based on variations within the fixture without you having to create another family or family type.

A good example of a light fixture using a nested annotation symbol is an exit light. These fixtures are commonly shown on construction documents as a symbol, instead of the actual light fixture showing. However, the symbol may be shown in different configurations, depending on the number of faces or direction arrows that are on the fixture. Figure 20.22 shows an exit light family in both plan and 3D views. Notice that a symbol is used to represent the fixture in ceiling plan view and that a filled region within the symbol indicates the location of the face of the fixture.

FIGURE 20.22
Exit lighting fixture in plan and 3D views

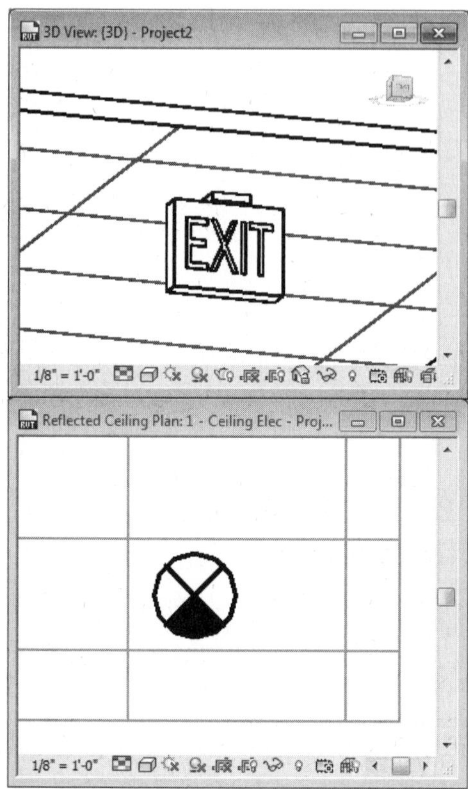

Creating this type of functionality is easily achieved by using a nested annotation family in the lighting fixture family. The annotation family contains lines and filled regions whose visibility is controlled by Yes/No parameters.

To create an exit light family with multiple display options, do the following:

1. Open the `Ch20_Exit Light Annotation.rfa` family found at `www.sybex.com/go/masteringrevitmep2015`.
2. Draw a circle with the center point at the intersection of the reference planes. The radius of the circle should be small (approximately 3⁄32″ or 2.5 mm) so that the annotation is the correct size at different view scales.

3. Draw a line from one quadrant of the circle to the opposite quadrant. Rotate the line 45 degrees, using the center of the circle as the axis, and mirror the line by using one of the reference planes as the axis, creating four equal quadrants within the circle.

4. Create a filled region by tracing over the top quadrant. Use invisible lines for the border of the filled region and Solid Fill for the pattern. Click the green check mark button on the contextual tab to finish creating the filled region.

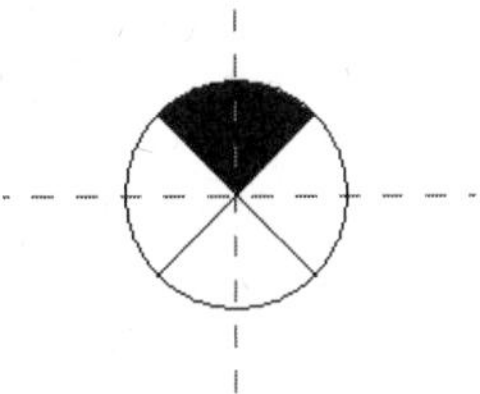

5. Mirror the filled region by using the reference plane perpendicular to the region as the axis, to create another filled region directly opposite the first region.

6. Click the Family Types button on the Properties panel of the Create tab. Create a new parameter by clicking the Add button to the right of the dialog box. Name the parameter **FACE1**. Set the parameter as an instance parameter, and set Type Of Parameter to Yes/No. Click OK.

7. Repeat step 6 to create another parameter named **FACE2**. Click OK to exit the Family Types dialog box.

8. Select one of the filled regions. Click the small box to the far right of the Visible parameter in the Properties palette. Select FACE1 from the list and click OK. Select the other filled region and repeat, choosing FACE2 from the list. Save and exit the family.

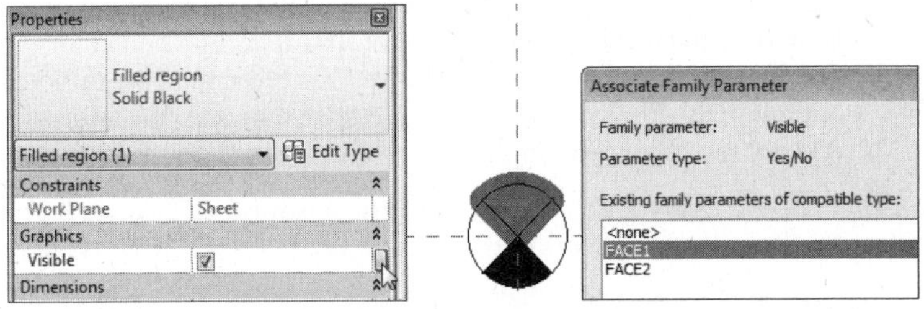

9. Open the `Ch20_Ceiling Exit Light.rfa` family found at `www.sybex.com/go/masteringrevitmep2015`.

10. Create a 4″ (100 mm) square extrusion centered at the intersection of the reference planes. Set the depth of the extrusion to 1″ (25 mm). Create another extrusion that is 2 1/2″ (63 mm) wide and 12″ (300 mm) long. In the Properties palette, set Extrusion Start to 1″ (25 mm) and Extrusion End to 11″ (275 mm). Center the extrusion at the intersection of the reference planes.

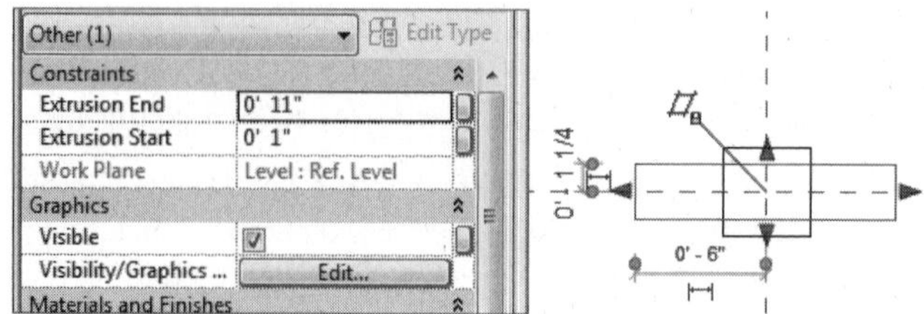

11. Select both extrusions, and click the Visibility Settings button on the Mode panel of the contextual tab. Remove the check mark from the box next to Plan/RCP and click OK. This keeps the extrusions from being visible in plan views or reflected ceiling plans.
12. Click the Family Types button on the Properties panel of the Create tab. Create a new parameter by clicking the Add button at the right of the dialog box. Name the parameter **Show Face 1**. Set the parameter as an instance parameter, and set Type Of Parameter to Yes/No. Group the parameter under Graphics. Click OK.
13. Repeat step 12 to create another parameter named **Show Face 2**. Click OK to exit the Family Types dialog box.
14. Click the Load Family button on the Insert tab. Browse to the annotation family you created and click Open. Click the Symbol button on the Annotate tab, and place the annotation symbol at the intersection of the reference planes.
15. Select the annotation symbol, and click the small box to the far right of the FACE1 parameter in the Properties palette. Choose Show Face 1 from the list and click OK. Repeat for the FACE2 parameter, choosing Show Face 2 from the list. Save and exit the family.
16. Open the `Ch20_SampleProject.rvt` file found at `www.sybex.com/go/masteringrevitmep2015`.
17. Open the 1 – Ceiling Elec view, and click the Load Family button on the Insert tab. Browse to the newly created exit light fixture family and click Open. Click the Lighting Fixture button on the Create tab. Select the Place On Face option from the contextual tab, and place the fixture on the ceiling. Notice that only the annotation symbol is displayed and not the extrusion graphics.
18. Click the light fixture, and deselect the box for the Show Face 2 parameter in the Properties palette. Notice that the filled region for FACE2 is no longer displayed.

Not all light fixtures are represented by an annotation symbol. Some fixtures need to be shown at their actual size for coordination purposes. If a nested annotation is used for these types of fixtures, the annotation changes size with the scale of the view, which would be an inaccurate representation. Symbolic lines can be used in a fixture family to represent the outline of a fixture without having to show the model graphics within the family.

Symbolic lines appear in any view that is parallel to the view in which they are created. When you're adding symbolic lines to a lighting fixture family, they need to be drawn in the Ref. Level Floor Plan view or Ref. Level Ceiling Plan view for ceiling-mounted fixtures. If the fixture you are creating is wall mounted, draw the symbolic lines in either the Front or Back elevation view.

Symbolic lines do not change size in different scale views, so they can be drawn to match the size of the fixture. You can constrain symbolic lines to reference planes or model graphics so that they move when the fixture is changed.

When working in a lighting fixture family, any symbolic lines belong to the Lighting Fixtures subcategory by default. You can create a unique subcategory for the lines to allow for greater visibility control within the model.

If your lighting family is to be placed on a sloped ceiling and you are using symbolic representation, you need to create them as model lines with their own subcategory. Figure 20.23 shows two light fixture types, A and B, placed on level and sloped ceilings. Type A has model lines, while type B uses symbolic lines to reflect the symbolic representation. In planning a type of family like type B, consider that the symbolic representation requires a subcategory such as Lighting Fixture – Symbol.

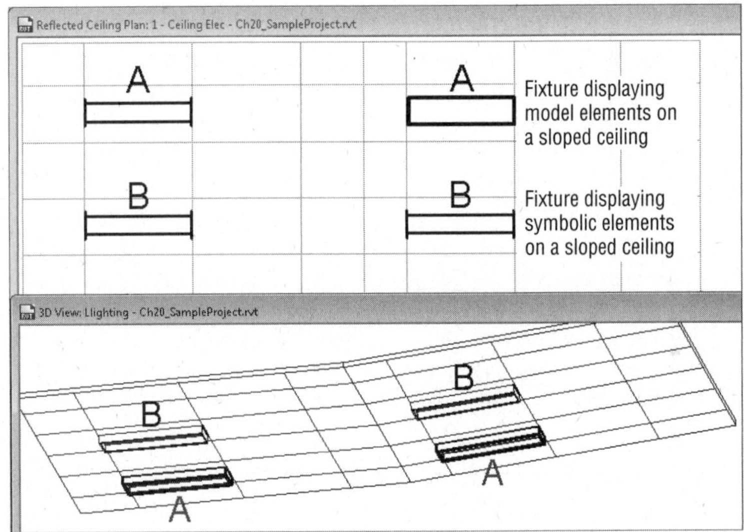

FIGURE 20.23 Light fixtures with symbolic/model lines

Although this does mean that view templates have to be adjusted carefully to take into account the symbolic and model elements of the family, you can use the same light family in both level and sloped ceilings and retain your graphical standards.

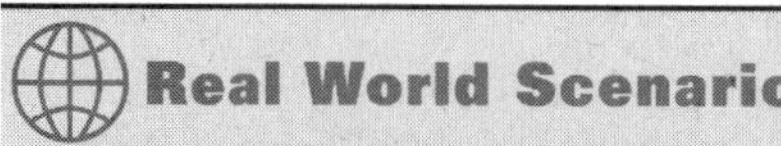

Scalable Symbols for Wall Lights

The Lighting Fixture family category in Revit is missing an important parameter. The Maintain Annotation Orientation parameter is not available for this category. This means that you cannot nest an annotation family into a face-hosted light fixture family and have the annotation show up when the fixture family is hosted by a vertical surface. This has left many users frustrated and looking for ways to work around this shortcoming. The key is that whatever symbology is put into the family must react to changes in view scale within a project.

Jose Fandos discovered one such workaround that achieves this goal quite well. He decided to create a face-hosted family that contained nothing but a nested annotation family of the symbol he wanted for the fixture family. By making this a shared family, he was able to nest it into his light fixture family in an elevation view and have it appear when used in his projects.

As with any workaround, some important factors have to be considered for it to work properly. The first is that you cannot see the nested annotation of the intermediate family when placing it in the fixture family in the Family Editor. You can draw temporary model lines in the intermediate family to use as placement guides and then delete them by editing and reloading the family.

The second is that the face-hosted family must have its Shared property activated in order for the symbol to appear in a project.

You need to be careful with how you name this family. Because it is shared, it gets loaded into a project when its host family gets loaded. So if you have multiple fixture families with intermediate families that have the same name, the intermediate family will be overwritten in the project if you are not careful.

For example, you can have an exit light family with an intermediate family named NestedAnnotation. That intermediate family would look like an exit light. You might also have a wall sconce family with an intermediate family named NestedAnnotation. If you were to load the wall sconce family into a project after having the exit light loaded, you would be prompted to overwrite the nested intermediate family, which would change all of the exit lights to look like the sconce. The other option is to not overwrite the nested family, which would cause all of the sconces to look like exit lights. This can all be avoided by taking care with your naming conventions.

Another thing to consider is how you categorize the intermediate family. Because it is shared, it will show up in any schedules of its category.

When used properly, this workaround is a viable solution to having scalable annotations for wall-mounted light fixtures. For more information on the process, see Jose's blog at:

`www.andekan.com/blog/2012/11/06/annotationsymbols-for-lighting-fixtures-showing-in-plan/`

Although you can draw symbolic lines in a lighting fixture family, you cannot create a filled region. Filled regions are useful for showing a portion of the fixture filled in to denote an emergency lighting fixture. If you create a filled region in an annotation family and then nest that annotation into a fixture family, the annotation cannot be resized to match the fixture if its dimensions change. However, you can use a detail component family instead.

You can create a detail component family with parameters for length and width. A filled region can be drawn in the detail component family that is constrained to the parameters. When nested into a lighting fixture family, the parameters of the detail component can be associated with the parameters within the fixture family so that the detail component will match the size of the fixture. Figure 20.24 shows a detail component family designed to indicate when a lighting fixture is an emergency type.

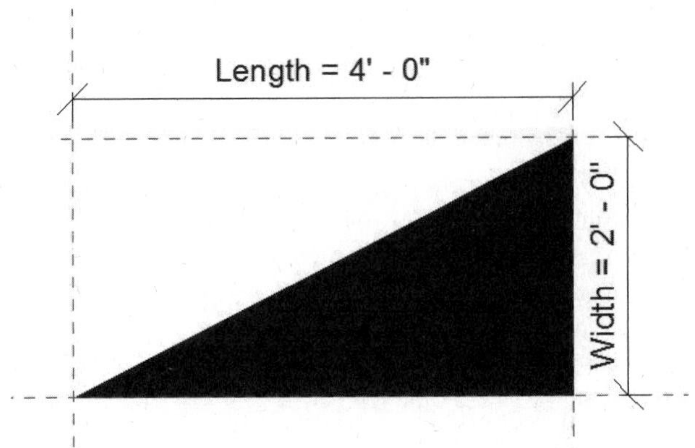

FIGURE 20.24 Detail component family for an emergency lighting fixture

With the detail component nested into the fixture family, its visibility can be associated with a Yes/No parameter so that it can be turned on or off as desired. This should be an instance parameter so that the same fixture type can be shown as normal or as emergency. Figure 20.25 shows two instances of a light fixture, one of which has been set to an emergency light.

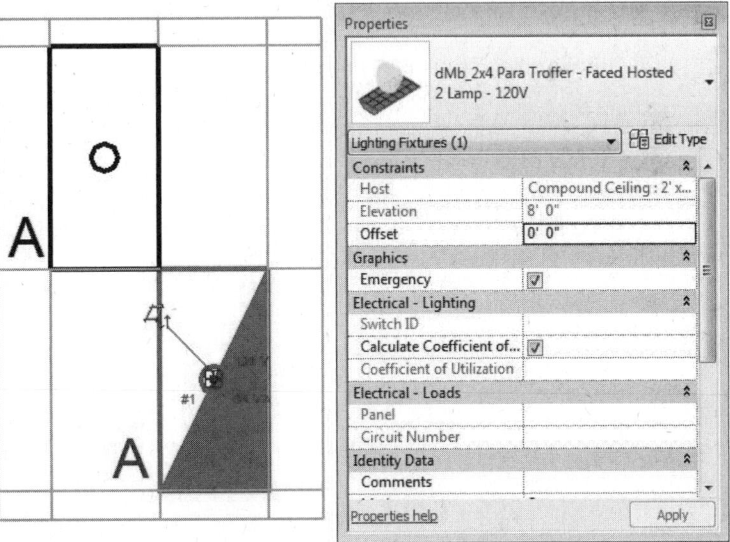

FIGURE 20.25 Lighting fixture family with a detail component for emergency lighting display

Detail components can be more useful than annotation symbols because they can be placed easily into an elevation view within a fixture family, whereas annotation symbols require extra steps and management. When you create a wall-mounted fixture that is face hosted, the Front or Back elevation view is what you will see when the fixture is hosted by a vertical face, so any symbolic representation must be placed in the Front or Back elevation view of the family.

The Bottom Line

Create different types of lighting fixture families. Many types of lighting fixtures are required for various applications within a building. With Revit MEP, you can create any type of lighting fixture and include any data associated with that fixture.

> **Master It** Knowing how a lighting fixture will be used in a Revit model is important for determining the kind of fixture family to create. True or false: A nonhosted light fixture family cannot be associated to a work plane.

Use a light source in your lighting fixture families. Lighting fixtures can be used in making design decisions because they not only represent the fixture as a model, they also contain photometric data from real-world lighting fixtures for use in lighting analysis.

> **Master It** Photometric web files can be obtained from lighting fixture manufacturers. These files provide the lighting distribution characteristics of a fixture when added to a family. How can you be sure that the IES file you are using is appropriate for the type of fixture in which it is being used?

Create and manage fixture types and parameters. The parameters of a lighting fixture family are what make it an intelligent object. They can be used to create multiple types within the same family or to manage the electrical characteristics of a fixture.

> **Master It** Connectors are what determine the electrical properties of a lighting fixture family. Describe the process of ensuring that a connector has the same load and voltage values that have been assigned to the fixture.

Use lines and symbols to represent lighting fixtures. Some lighting fixtures are shown on construction documents as symbols, while others are shown as their actual size. Symbolic lines or annotation symbols can be used to eliminate the need to display model graphics.

> **Master It** Annotation symbols nested into lighting fixture families can represent the fixture without having to show the model graphics. Is it possible to use a nested annotation family to represent a wall-mounted fixture in a face-hosted lighting fixture family? Explain.

Chapter 21

Creating Devices

Device families can be used by any MEP discipline to represent the types of components that are crucial to engineering systems but do not necessarily play a major part in the physical model of the systems. Components such as thermostats, switches, and receptacles are all important to how engineering systems are used, yet their size is generally not an issue when it comes to interference with other model components.

Although devices do not require very detailed modeling, it is useful to have solid geometry that represents the devices in your projects. This enables you to coordinate their locations when it is important to collaborate with other disciplines. It may seem unnecessary to model receptacles or switches, but because these types of items are shown in a set of construction documents anyway, you might as well show them correctly in the model for further coordination. With a good library of device families, no additional effort is required to add model devices as opposed to adding symbols that hold no system information or model "intelligence."

Device families can be given connectors that enable them to be included in the engineering systems that you create in your projects. This adds another level of intelligence to the systems and allows you to keep track of things such as circuits and device-component relationships.

Because no single standard for devices is used by all engineers and designers, it is important that you develop the device families to work the way you design. Of course, it is also important that these components look the way you want them to on your construction documents and that they meet the requirements of the CAD standards to which you adhere.

In this chapter, you will learn to do the following:

- Select a family template
- Model device geometry
- Use annotations to represent devices
- Add parameters and connectors

Modeling Device Geometry

Creating solid geometry for device families is similar to modeling equipment families, only on a smaller scale. The level of detail for devices can be kept very simple to represent the components. In most cases, the geometry does not need to be parametrically controlled, but in some families, parametric geometry is useful. Junction boxes are a good example. You can create one junction box family with parametric geometry so that multiple types can be created by editing the dimensions of the geometry. This eliminates the need for separate families for each junction box size.

Category and Parameters

As with any family you are about to create, you should first decide how the family will be used in your projects. For the most part, device families should be face-hosted families because they will likely be placed in walls, floors, and ceiling surfaces. Of course, there are some exceptions, such as junction boxes, which you may want to put into the model without a host. The hosting option you choose determines the family template that will be used. The generic family templates can be used because you can categorize the family after you have started.

Although face-hosted families are preferred, using them has some drawbacks. When the host of a device is deleted in the model, the device becomes orphaned. This means that the device maintains its location but is no longer associated with the model. This can be frustrating when hosts are deleted and redrawn instead of the original host being moved. This scenario will require you to pick a new host for the devices in order to maintain coordination with the model.

If you choose to create device families that do not require a host, keep in mind that you will have to manually coordinate their locations in the model with the walls, floors, and ceilings that they are associated with when changes are made.

Once you decide whether your family will be hosted or not hosted, you should select the family template you start with. You start creating a new family by choosing Application Menu ➤ New ➤ Family. This opens the New Family – Select Template File dialog box. For the creation of devices, you need just a few templates: `Generic Model.rft`, `Generic Model face based .rft`, `Generic Annotation.rft`, and `Detail Item.rft`. Those four family templates will cover nearly all of your needs. This is because the generic family templates can be assigned to various family categories. Once you start a family, you can see the full list of categories you can use for a given family template by clicking the Family Category And Parameters button located under the Create tab.

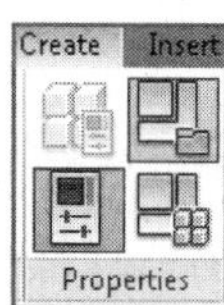

The four family templates are described in the following list:

`Generic Model/ Generic Model face based.rft` The only difference between these two templates is the hosting method. The template can become a lighting fixture, fire alarm device, electrical equipment, security device, and more. As soon as you select a category, the Autodesk® Revit® MEP 2015 assigns the appropriate parameters to the new category you selected.

`Generic Annotation.rft` This file can be used for all symbols that need to be nested into the model geometry of any device families. Generic annotation families behave like text and dimensions in the project environment—they maintain their size so they print at the correct size regardless of the scale of the view. For example, if you create an annotation with a text note 3/32″, that would be the print size no matter the scale of the view.

`Detail Items.rft` This is meant to represent real-world objects but in one 2D orientation, such as top, side, or section. In some cases, detail items may be used when the host-family template has certain limitations. For example, you can't create a filled region in a generic family, but you could insert a detail item that contains a filled region. Detail items would also be used to display the faceplate detail on a variety of devices that would otherwise be the same. To do this using the generic model would be time-consuming and use far more memory in the model. The dimensional parameters in detail items can be mapped to parameters in the host family so the host family drives the size of the nested detail item. This is not possible with the Generic Annotation template, which is mostly used for symbolic representations not meant to represent the real size of the 3D object (the host). In other words, if you need to hatch a portion of your light fixture to display it as an emergency light, use the Detail Items template. But if you need to display the receptacle symbol, use the Generic Annotation template.

A family such as a receptacle is usually created from two separate families: a model family that contains the model geometry, connector, and all necessary parameters and a symbol family (made from `Generic Annotation.rft`) that is inserted—or, as we say in Revit terminology, *nested*—into the model family.

There are a few more templates that you may end up using here and there, but these four templates will cover the majority of your family creation needs. Spend some time to customize them and incorporate your standard line styles, filled regions, materials, and so forth.

All of the device categories have the same parameters, but the options for the Part Type parameter vary depending on the category. Figure 21.1 shows the available part types for the Lighting Devices category. These are the same options for the Nurse Call and Security Devices categories. The other device categories do not have the Switch option. Using the Switch option allows you to specify the device as the switch for a system in your model.

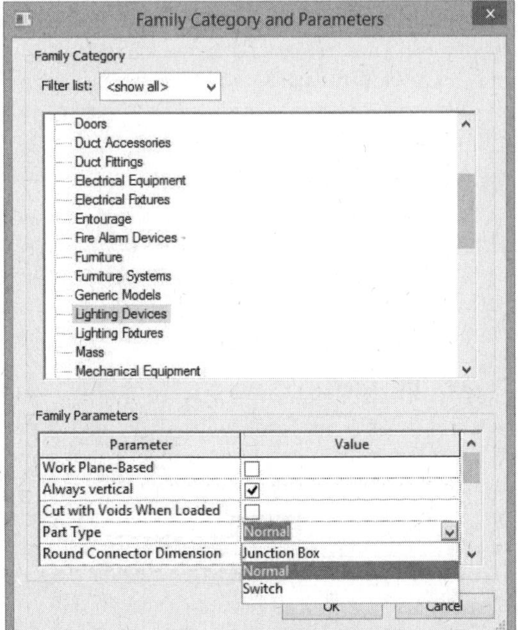

FIGURE 21.1 Part types available for a Lighting Devices family

The Maintain Annotation Orientation parameter is important for device families that use a nested annotation symbol to represent the object in your model views. This parameter allows the annotation to be displayed regardless of the hosting of the device. This means that the annotation symbol is displayed whether the device is mounted to a vertical or horizontal surface. If the device is placed on a sloped surface, the annotation does not appear.

Select the box in the parameter called Shared if you want to load your device family into another family and be able to schedule the device individually when the host family is used in a project. With this functionality, you can create a family such as a typical systems furniture layout and have the outlets included by nesting them into the furniture family, for example. Unfortunately, the connectors of nested families are not detected when the host family is placed in a project. Because of this limitation, it is recommended to avoid nesting families that contain connectors because you will not be able to use any of the electrical Revit features—circuiting, wiring, panel schedule loads, connect conduit, and so forth. You can still schedule the data of the connector. One exception to this could be bedhead panels for a hospital, where you know the number of connectors required but they may be in a different order for different bedheads. In this case the connectors can be included in the host family and even flexed to be able to move to the correct position (important for medical gas outlets) after the individual devices have been arranged.

The OmniClass parameters are for classifying a family for sharing on websites such as Autodesk Seek. If you share a family, it can be identified or filtered based on its classification. This is also a way to associate the family with a specification class. You do not need to assign an OmniClass number to your families in order to share them. But if you do, that would be another way you could filter elements in your schedule. The assembly code (which uses Uniformat code, but an out-of-date version) can also do this—and can be changed on a family type basis rather than all types of the family needing to be the same. The OmniClass parameter is found under Family Category and Parameters and can be changed only in the Family Editor. The assembly code is found under Family Types and can be edited in the project by editing the Family Type properties.

Geometry and Reference Planes

With the family category and parameters established, you can begin modeling the geometry of your device family. It is a good idea to establish the category right away because this activates device-specific parameters, if applicable, and also because, once you start working, it is easy to forget until you attempt to use the family in a project. It can be frustrating to work on a family and load it into a project only to find that it is not available when you click the button to place it in your model.

The amount of solid geometry that you include in a device family depends not only on the object you are creating but also on how it will be used in your projects. If your intent is to use devices only so their symbols are shown on your plans and you are not concerned with 3D visualization, you can use a simple box with the actual size. This at least lets you see the location of the device in section and elevation views for coordination with things such as casework, openings, and any other elements from all disciplines. If you do require more detail, it can be more efficient to use detail items or symbolic lines rather than more solid geometry.

Solid geometry is not required in order to place connectors into the family, but it gives you a good reference point for the connectors. The default reference planes in the generic family templates define the insertion point of the family. The vertical plane is the center point between the left and right side, while the horizontal plane defines the front and back of the family. The insertion point will be at the intersection of these two planes. You can change the properties of a reference plane so that it establishes the insertion point by editing the Is Reference and Defines Origin parameters.

For face-hosted families, these planes define the insertion point only as it relates to the face of the host extrusion. If you place a device family into a model and attach it to a vertical face, you have to give it an elevation. A default elevation is assigned in the type parameters of the family.

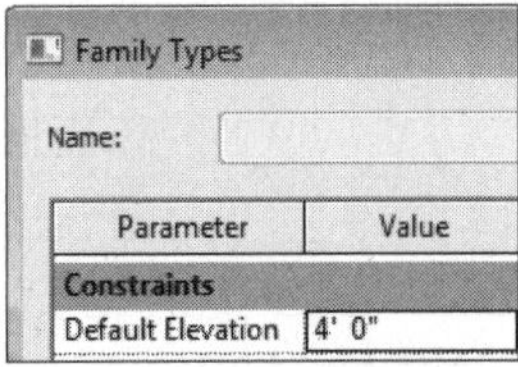

When you're placing a device in your project, the Elevation parameter in the Properties palette can be used to adjust the mounting elevation of the device. When you use the Device tool on the Electrical panel of the Systems tab, subsequent placement of devices in the same category will use the last elevation value input during placement, regardless of the value in the Default Elevation parameter. If you select a device and use the Create Similar tool, the default elevation, as defined in the family, is used (unless modified prior to placement). Either way, it is best to apply the most commonly used value for the type of device to the Default Elevation parameter so that if users do not manually apply an elevation, the device is placed correctly for most instances.

If you determine that your device family should be parametric, it is best to use reference lines or planes to establish the dimensions that are to be editable. For the most part, the length, width, and depth dimensions should give you enough flexibility to create the various family types within your device family that meet your modeling needs.

When using a reference line or plane to create a dimension, consider how you want the geometry to change upon data input. Should the geometry grow or shrink in one direction? Does it need to grow an equal distance on each side of the center? These types of questions will help you determine the amount and placement of references. The order in which you draw reference planes determines the direction that a parametric dimension between them moves. This behavior applies only to reference planes. In Figure 21.2, the vertical reference plane on the left was drawn first. When the Length parameter is updated, the reference plane on the right will be the one that moves.

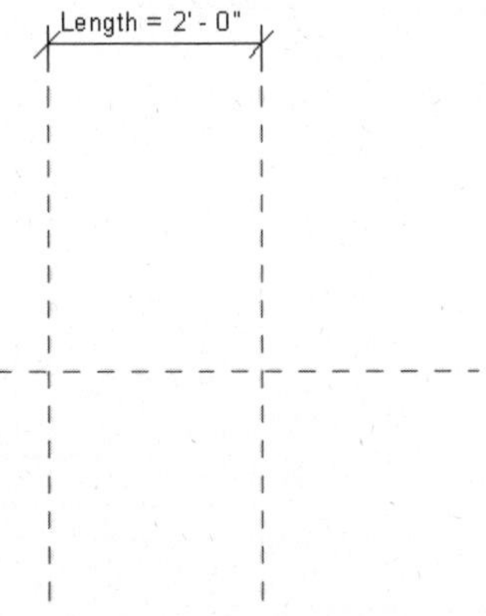

FIGURE 21.2 Reference planes with parametric dimension

Because the two default reference planes are already in the family when you begin, any reference planes dimensioned to them will move when parameters are updated. You can use the Pin button on the Modify | Reference Planes tab to lock the position of a reference plane. This will keep it from moving when a parametric dimension is updated. So, it is possible to move one of the default planes with a parametric dimension by pinning a new plane and unpinning the default. Although possible, it is not recommended that you move the planes that define the insertion point of the device. Obviously, you cannot pin both reference planes that have a parametric dimension between them; otherwise, you will get an error when the parameter value is changed.

Pinning Reference Lines

Reference lines always move when parametrically dimensioned to a reference plane. Even if you pin a reference line in place, it moves when pushed by a parametric dimension.

The majority of your device families can be modeled as simple boxes. It is important to create the solid geometry in the correct orientation, in the same way that it will be used in your projects. Face-hosted devices should be modeled so that the geometry is inside the host, or lying on the surface of the host where applicable. For families that are not parametric, you can simply create the solid geometry at the appropriate size and position it relative to where you want the insertion point.

Set the visibility of your device geometry as desired by clicking the Visibility Settings button on the Mode panel when you select a solid form. Even though you will not likely show this geometry in your plan views, allowing the geometry to be visible at some level of detail can be helpful so that you can determine the exact location of the device when needed. The geometry should be kept visible in Front/Back and Left/Right views so that your devices can be seen in section and elevation. This will allow for coordination with architectural and structural features as well as give you the ability to edit the device location when working in section or elevation views. Figure 21.3 shows the visibility settings for device geometry that work well for standard model views while allowing for a view of the geometry in Fine detail views. Your results may vary depending on the level of detail used for your plan views at certain scales.

Figure 21.3
Visibility settings for device geometry

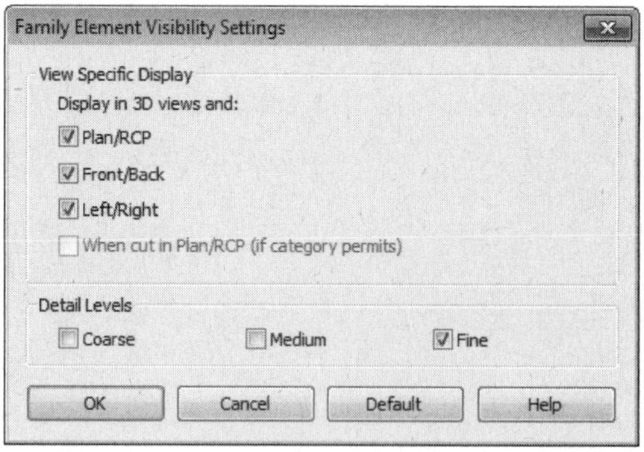

FACE-HOSTED VISIBILITY

When you are creating a face-hosted device family, remember that the Ref. Level view in the Family Editor is parallel to the front face of the host extrusion. If you want to set the visibility of device geometry so that it does not appear in model plan views when hosted by a vertical face, you must deselect the Front/Back visibility of the geometry. This rule changes based on the mounting orientation of the device—floor, wall, ceiling. What is front for one device may be elevation for another. When you're placing devices on a sloped surface, the 3D geometry will have to represent the device because symbols are not visible on sloped surfaces and in 3D views.

Another option for viewing device family geometry is to create a Yes/No parameter that controls the visibility of the solid forms in the family. The Visible parameter of a solid form can be associated with the Yes/No parameter. This enables you to turn on the geometry when needed for coordination in plan views. However, using this type of visibility control will turn on or turn off the geometry everywhere that it can be seen, so section and elevation views will also be affected.

When creating geometry in a face-hosted family, be aware that, if you model a solid form so that it is inside the host, the device will not be visible when the family is hosted by a floor unless the view range of the view includes the floor. Figure 21.4 shows a device family hosted by a floor in a project. The device is not visible in the plan view because the bottom of the view range is at the face of the floor. Technically the device is not within the view range and is therefore not visible.

FIGURE 21.4 Device family hosted by a floor

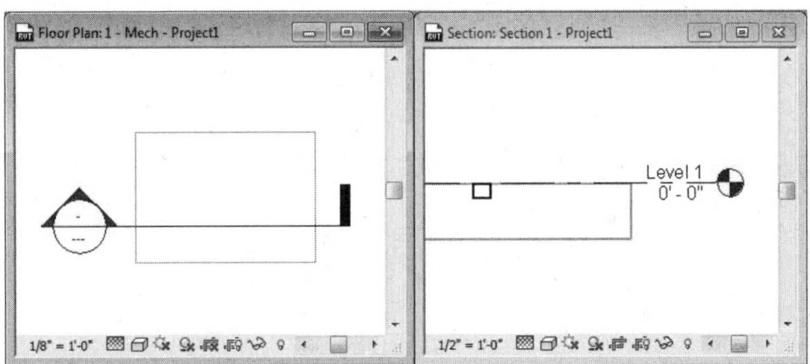

One way to avoid this scenario is to adjust the view range of your plan views so that the bottom of the view is slightly below the top face of the floor geometry. This could have an adverse effect on the overall look of your floor plan, depending on how the building is designed. Another option is to create the solid geometry in the family so that it protrudes from the host. This may not be a completely accurate representation of the device, but the protrusion can be minimal. Extending past the face of the host just 1/256" (0.1 mm) is enough to cause the device to appear.

If you are creating a device family for an object that requires a face plate, the plate geometry should be modeled to the surface of the host for a face-hosted family. This eliminates the need to extend the device geometry past the face of the host because the plate geometry will make the family visible when it's floor hosted. Figure 21.5 shows how adding face-plate geometry to the family in the previous example causes it to be displayed properly in the project plan view when hosted by a floor.

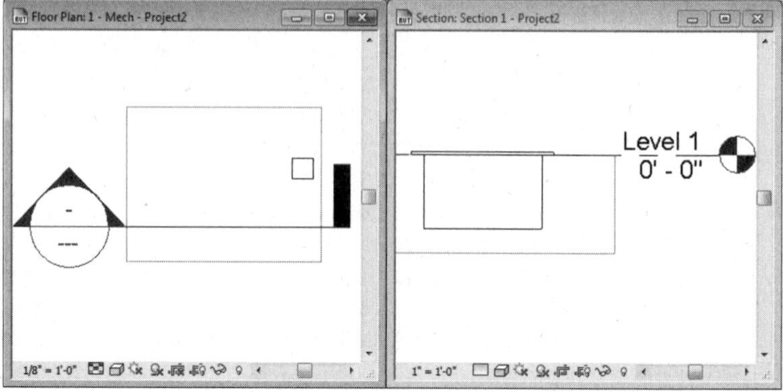

FIGURE 21.5 Device family with face-plate geometry

Symbolic lines are useful for adding detail to a device family without adding a lot of complexity to the family. Symbolic lines drawn on the face plate of a device are useful for identifying the device when viewed in section or elevation views. These lines are visible only in views parallel to the plane in which they are drawn, so they appear in plan views only when the device is mounted horizontally. Vertically hosted devices shown in plan views do not display the symbolic lines; however, the lines show in section and elevation views. This is useful for interior elevations when devices need to be coordinated with casework or furniture. Can you tell which device is a power receptacle, which is a switch, and which is a telephone outlet in Figure 21.6?

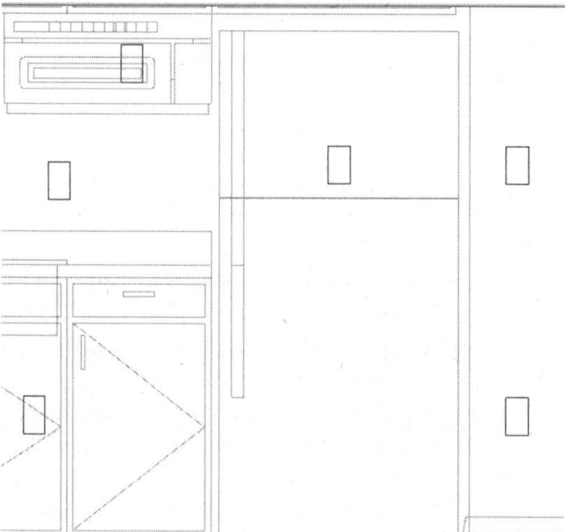

FIGURE 21.6 Devices shown in a section view

Without symbolic lines to identify the devices, additional information might have to be added to the view for the construction documents. Also, while working in the project, you would have to select the device to see what it is. With symbolic lines added to the families, it is much easier to determine what the devices are in section or elevation views. This can enhance coordination of your construction documents and improve productivity during design. Figure 21.7 shows the same devices with symbolic lines added to identify them.

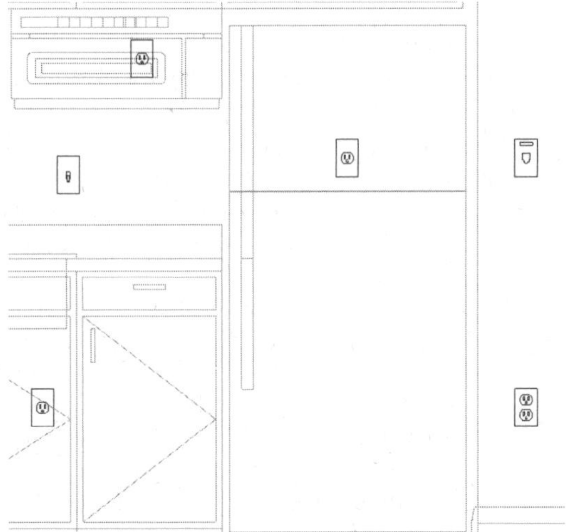

FIGURE 21.7 Devices with symbolic lines for identification

Using Annotations for Devices

Although the use of symbolic lines is helpful for identifying devices in section and elevation views, these objects are typically represented in plan views by symbols. Annotation families can be added to your device families to represent them in the same manner you would add them for a traditional 2D CAD project. Nested annotations can be parametric as well, allowing you to control their orientation and visibility so that they can be shown on your construction documents in an appropriate manner. These same annotation families can be used as your legend symbols to ensure that they match what you are showing in plan view.

An annotation family is loaded into another family in the same way a family is loaded into a project. Click the Load Family button on the Insert tab of the Family Editor to load an annotation family.

ANNOTATION LIBRARY

Having a well-stocked library of annotation families is useful for creating devices. You can build a library of symbols that matches your library of CAD blocks. You can even use your CAD blocks to develop your Revit symbols by importing them and duplicating their linework, but be sure to remove the imported CAD data after you have created a Revit version of the symbol. See Chapter 18, "Creating Symbols and Annotations," for more information on creating annotation families.

As mentioned earlier, the Maintain Annotation Orientation parameter is important for face-hosted families. When you place an annotation family into your device family, it appears only in model views that are parallel to the view in which it is placed in the family. With the parameter selected, you can place the annotation in the Ref. Level view of the family and it appears even when the device is hosted vertically. Currently, the Maintain Annotation Orientation parameter is not available to all families, which could be a significant limitation when creating families. Annotation families cannot be placed into an elevation view when you're working in the Family Editor.

Once you load an annotation family into your device family, you can place it in the Ref. Level view by dragging it from the Project Browser to the drawing area or by using the Symbol button on the Annotate tab within the Family Editor. While placing the annotation, you can snap to reference planes or reference lines within the device family. The snap point within the annotation is its insertion point defined by the reference planes in the annotation family. You cannot snap linework or geometry to the linework within a nested annotation. Once the annotation is placed, you can use the Move tool to locate the annotation, or you can click and drag it to the desired location.

The annotation family that you use in a device family should be located in the proper relationship to the geometry of the family so that, when the device is placed into a project on a vertical face, the annotation symbol is aligned with the device host. The insertion point of the annotation family is important to establish a proper relationship to the device geometry as well as the host of the device family. Figure 21.8 shows the location of a junction box annotation family nested into a device family. The insertion point of the annotation is the center of the circle. When the family is used in a project, the annotation does not correctly align to the device family host.

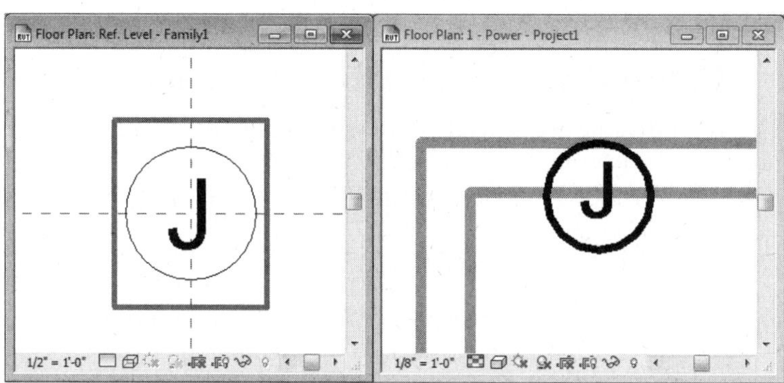

FIGURE 21.8
Annotation family location in a device family, and display behavior when used in a project

The alignment of the annotation with the vertical reference plane is correct, but regardless of where the annotation is located along that vertical plane, it is displayed in the project incorrectly. The solution is to have the insertion point of the annotation at the bottom quadrant of the circle. That way, when the annotation orientation is "maintained," it is displayed properly, as shown in Figure 21.9.

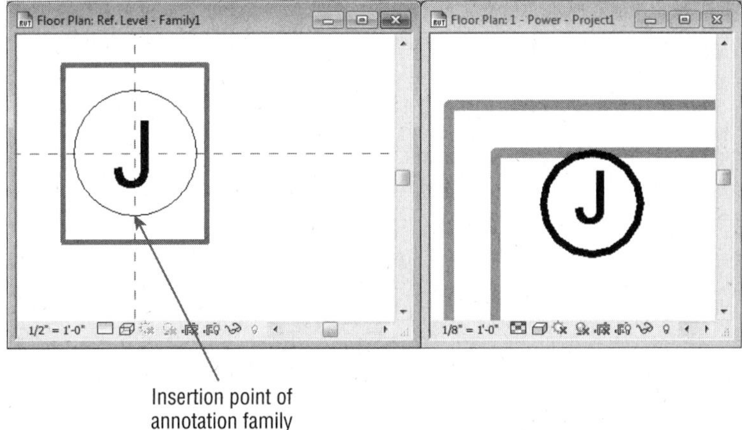

FIGURE 21.9 Annotation family with proper insertion point for use in a vertical host

The orientation of an annotation symbol may not be correct for every instance in your projects. In some cases, the annotation may need to be rotated to appear as desired.

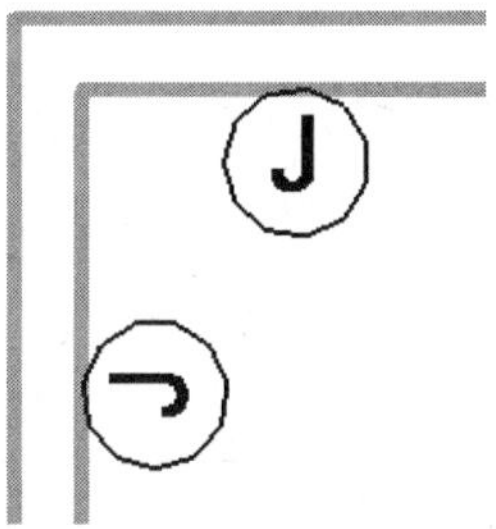

You cannot rotate the annotation separately from the device family after the device is placed into a project. If you edit the device family, rotate the annotation, and then load it back into the project, all instances of the device will have a rotated annotation.

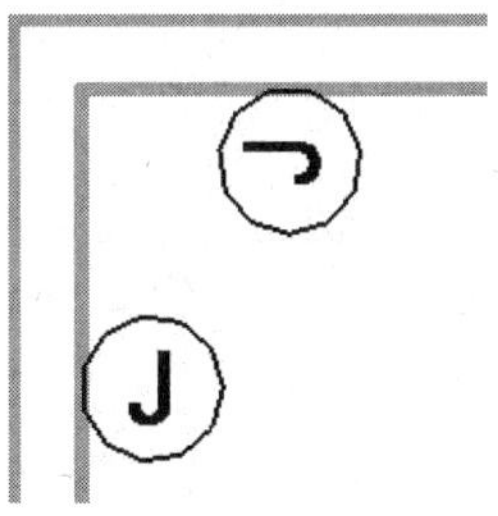

Consider using multiple annotations within a device family to allow for displaying a rotated annotation symbol when required. Yes/No parameters can be used to control the visibility of the individual nested annotations, giving you the ability to toggle between annotations when using the device family in a project. Figure 21.10 shows a device family with multiple nested annotations.

FIGURE 21.10 Device family with multiple nested annotations

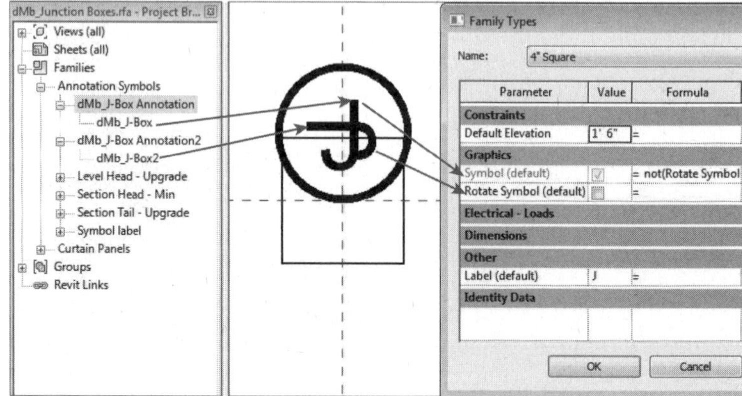

The Symbol parameter controls the visibility of the annotation for normal orientation, and the Rotate Symbol parameter controls the visibility of the rotated annotation. A formula was used so that, when you're working in a project, you can select only one of the boxes for each instance, preventing both annotations from being accidentally displayed. With this type of behavior built into your device families, you can display devices in your projects as desired.

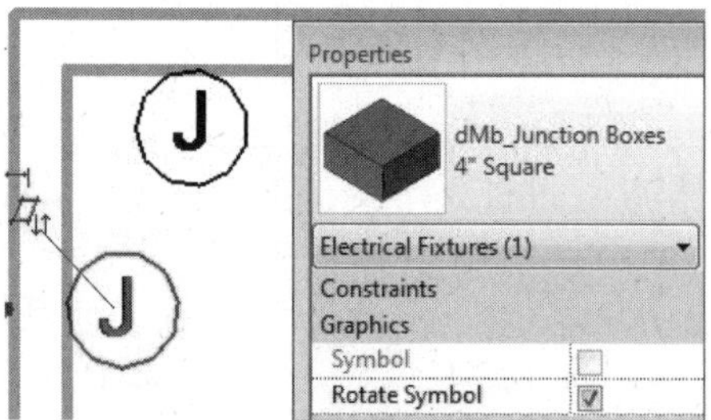

Another method for controlling annotation behavior is to apply an offset parameter so that the annotation symbol can be offset from the actual location of the device. This is useful when two devices are next to each other and their annotation symbols interfere. This can be done directly in the device family by creating a reference plane parallel to the plane that defines the left and right sides of the device. You can place this reference plane a set distance from the origin plane of the device and pin it in place. This will give you the ability to move the annotation symbol to the right or left of the device. You can lock the annotation symbol to another reference plane that's parallel to the offset plane.

A dimension between the two planes can be associated with an instance parameter that defines the offset distance, as shown in Figure 21.11. The annotation family is aligned and locked to the reference plane so that it moves when the dimension is edited. The Is Reference parameter for both the reference plane and reference line should be set to Not A Reference.

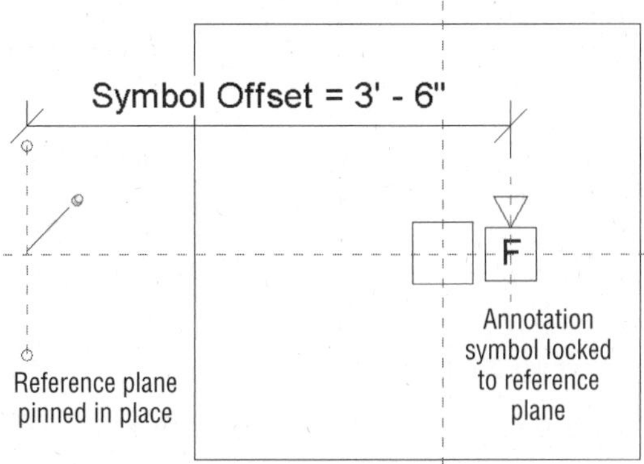

FIGURE 21.11 Reference plane used for annotation symbol offset

You can also use a reference line instead of a reference plane to lock the symbol in place. Enabling grips in families allows you to modify dimensional parameters without entering values in the properties of the dimensional parameters. Grips can be handy when you don't know, or care, what the exact dimension is; instead, you can pull a grip handle and see your family stretch to fit a certain space. To enable grips, two things need to happen: First, the Is Reference parameter for the reference plane (or reference line if you used that) needs to be set to anything but Not A Reference. And second, the dimensional parameter to that reference plane has to be an instance. When those two conditions are true, your family will display grips in the project environment. Keep in mind that, in many cases, you may want a grip only on one end of the dimensional parameter. In those cases, you can set the Is Reference parameter to Not A Reference for the reference plane where you don't want a grip.

A default value can be used for the offset distance to allow for the normal display of the annotation. This value depends on the location of the reference plane used to define the offset. Using this type of parametric behavior gives you the freedom to orient the annotation symbol with the device geometry without affecting the device geometry location. Figure 21.12 shows how an offset parameter is used to achieve the desired display of the annotations. The items on the left have interfering symbols because of the locations of the device geometry. The items on the right are displayed properly without affecting the device locations. (The device geometry is visible only to show the offset.)

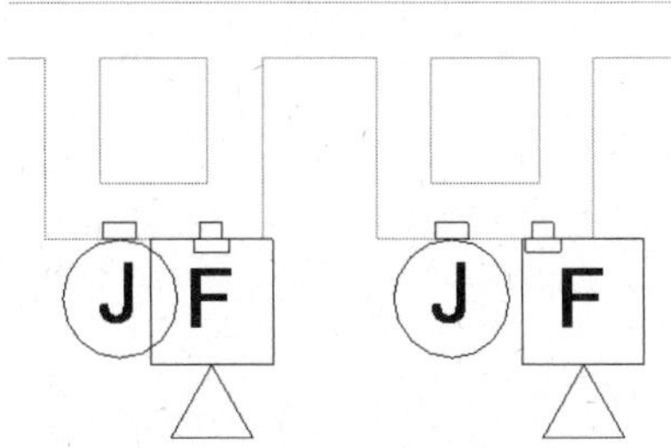

FIGURE 21.12 Symbol offset parameter used for proper device display

You can use this same functionality to create an offset that pulls the annotation away from the device geometry or use both to create both horizontal and vertical flexibility of the symbol. The offset plane or line can be created directly in the device family only if the family is a non-hosted type. For a face-hosted family, you need to have an offset defined in the annotation family. The parameter that defines the offset can be associated with a parameter in the device family for controlling the offset. See Chapter 18 for information on how to create an offset within an annotation family.

Having device families that are functional for both your 3D model and your construction documents enable you to be more efficient with your design and project coordination. Now that you have learned about creating a device family with a nested annotation, practice the techniques to make a device family usable in a project by completing the following exercise:

1. Open the `Ch21_Device Family.rfa` file found at `www.sybex.com/go/masteringrevitmep2015`.
2. Click the Family Category And Parameters button located on the Properties panel of the Create tab.
3. In the Family Category And Parameters dialog box, set the category to Electrical Fixtures. Set the Part Type parameter to Junction Box, and select the box for the Maintain Annotation Orientation parameter. Click OK.
4. Select the extrusion located at the intersection of the reference planes. Click the Visibility Settings button located on the Mode panel of the Modify | Extrusion contextual tab. Remove the check mark from the Front/Back box in the Family Element Visibility Settings dialog box. Also remove the check mark from the Coarse and Medium boxes. Click OK.
5. Click the Symbol button on the Detail panel of the Annotate tab. Confirm that the Ch21_J-Box annotation is shown in the Type Selector, and click to place the annotation symbol in the drawing area near the extrusion.
6. Click the Reference Plane button on the Datum panel of the Create tab, and draw a vertical reference plane to the right of the vertical reference plane that defines the origin.

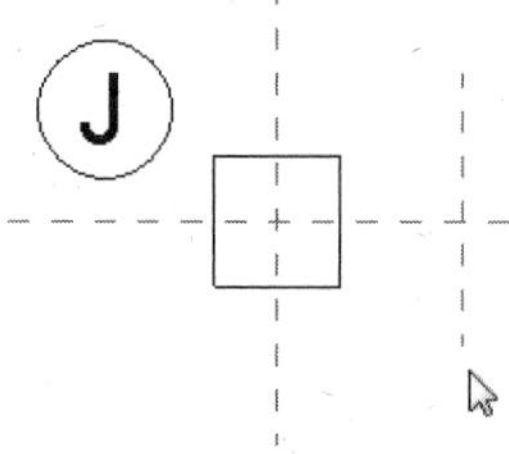

7. Click the Align button on the Modify panel of the Modify tab. Select the vertical reference plane drawn in step 6, and then move your mouse pointer over the center of the

annotation symbol, highlighting the vertical reference within the annotation. Then click to align the symbol to the reference plane. Click the padlock grip to lock the alignment.

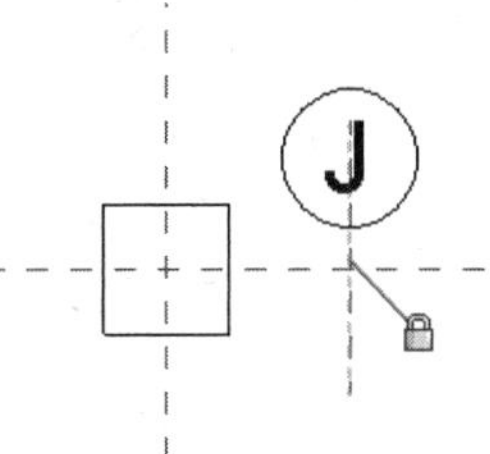

8. With the Align tool still active, click the horizontal reference plane, and then move your mouse pointer near the bottom quadrant of the annotation symbol, highlighting the horizontal reference within the annotation, and click to align the symbol to the reference plane. It is not necessary to lock this alignment.

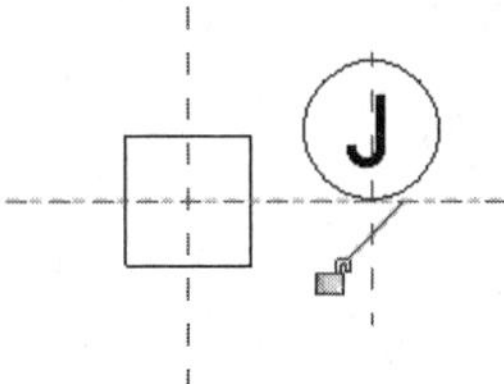

9. Draw another vertical reference plane 2′-0″ (600 mm) to the left of the extrusion. Click the Pin button on the Modify tab to pin the plane in place.

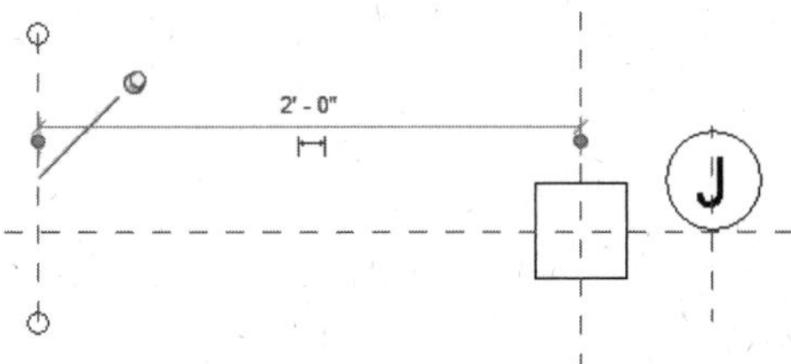

10. Click the Aligned button on the Annotate tab, and create a dimension between the planes drawn in steps 6 and 9.

11. Select the dimension created in step 10. Choose the <Add Parameter> option from the Label drop-down on the Options Bar.

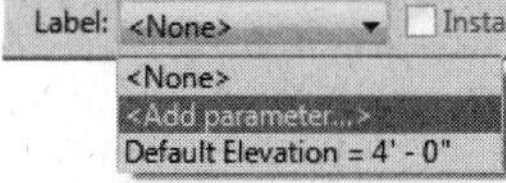

12. Create an instance parameter with the following settings:

Parameter Type: Family parameter

Name: SymbolOffset

Group Parameter Under: Graphics

Instance check box: Selected

Click OK to exit the Parameter Properties dialog box.

13. Click the Family Types button on the Properties panel of the Create tab.

14. In the Family Types dialog box, set the Symbol Offset parameter value to **2′-0″** (**600** mm) and click OK.

15. Save the family to a location that you can access to test its usability in a project.

Adding Parameters and Connectors

The device families you create can do more than just indicate device locations on your drawings. Connectors can be added to device families for use with systems. Connectors are the true *I* in *building information modeling* (*BIM*) when it comes to electrical design in Revit. Without connectors, we would have 2D symbols with 3D geometry representing an electrical design. With connectors, we can connect conduits and cable trays, assign devices to circuit numbers, generate panel loads, assign home runs to wires, and much more. The parameters you add to a device family can hold the engineering data required to connect devices to the appropriate system and account for their effect on the entire system. Adding connectors also allows you to use the wiring tools available in Revit MEP 2015. Revit wire objects that are attached to devices will move and stretch with edits to the device location, reducing the amount of work required to make a simple change.

Using Parameters for Labels

Using labels in device families seems like the logical solution to provide the information sometimes shown with devices. Although adding text labels to the annotation families that are used in your device families works well, at times the text needs to be moved for an instance of the device within a project. The best way to have the freedom to move text associated with a device is to create a parameter that holds the value and to use a tag in your project that reads that parameter. This places the information directly in your project, not embedded in the device family, allowing you to place the tag wherever you want.

To use a project tag for device labels, you can use one of the coded parameters that exist for the family type. The Description parameter is a good candidate if you are not using it for other information. Keep in mind that this is a type parameter, so whatever value you use will apply to all instances of that type. This can result in having to create unique family types for each unique label. Using a shared parameter allows you to make it an instance parameter that can be a unique value for each instance of the device in your project. If you want to use a custom parameter for the tag, it must be a shared parameter. (See Chapter 6, "Parameters," for more information on shared parameters.) Figure 21.13 shows that a shared parameter has been added to a device family for its candela rating. There is no label in the device family for this parameter; it is simply there to give a value when the device is tagged in a project.

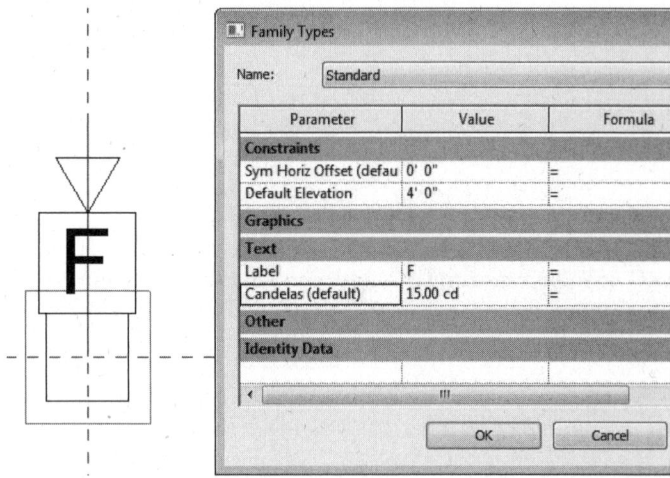

FIGURE 21.13
Shared parameter added to a device family for tagging

This type of functionality in your device families allows you to place the text associated with the device anywhere in the project view to avoid conflict with other graphics. A tag family must be created that reads the parameter used. When creating the tag, be sure to categorize it as a tag for the appropriate type of device. Another benefit of using a tag for a device label is that you can use a leader on the tag when necessary. Figure 21.14 shows how the device with a custom parameter and a tag can be used in a project. The text shown is a Fire Alarm Device tag that was created to read the custom instance parameter called Candelas.

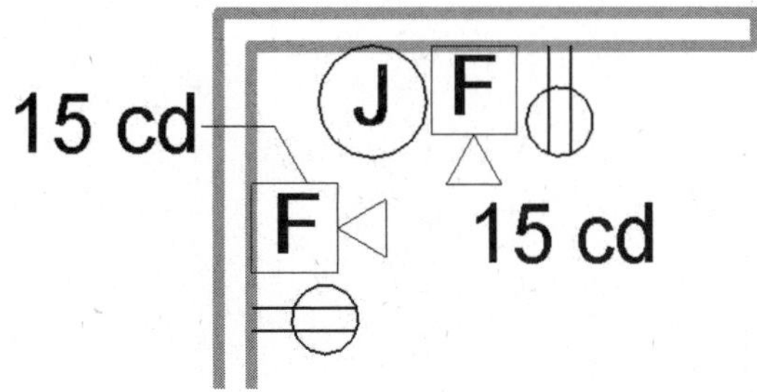

FIGURE 21.14
Sample device family with a tag for a label in a project

Adding Connectors

The connectors that you add to device families will most likely be electrical connectors because these families are the types of building components for controlling systems or power distribution. There are several types of electrical connectors from which to choose. The type you add should coincide with the function of the device in your projects.

When you click the Electrical Connector button on the Create tab in the Family Editor, you can choose the connector type from the drop-down on the Options Bar.

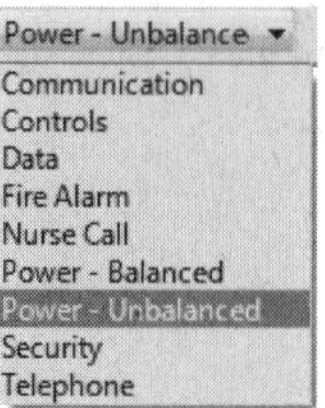

The connector can be placed on the face of any 3D geometry that exists in the device family. If you are creating a family without any 3D geometry, you can use the Work Plane placement option for the connector. You can find this option on the Placement panel of the Modify | Place Electrical Connector contextual tab.

An equipment connection and a motor connection are examples of device families that might not warrant having any 3D geometry yet still require a connector for use in the electrical systems defined in your projects. The properties of the connector are what define the system behavior of the device family. Most of the electrical connector system types do not have any parameters for defining electrical behavior. These connectors are simply used for keeping track of connectivity between the devices and their equipment, so their properties are very simple.

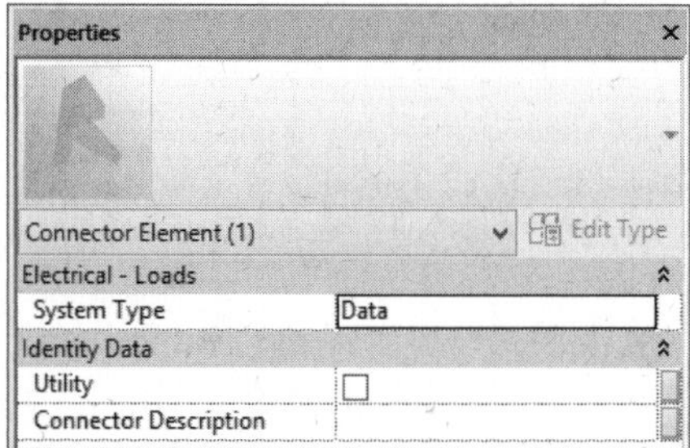

The Power – Balanced and the Power – Unbalanced system options for a connector contain more properties that are specific to the system behavior. These properties define the electrical characteristics of the device, which then determine the distribution system that the device is using within your projects.

Because you cannot change the properties of a connector when working in a project without editing the family in which it resides, it is best to associate the connector parameters to parameters defined in the device family. This allows you to control the electrical characteristics of the device through the Properties palette. A connector parameter can be associated with a family parameter by clicking the small button at the far right of each of these parameters. This opens a dialog box that lets you select the family parameter with which to associate the connector parameter. Only family parameters of the same type will appear in the list. Figure 21.15 shows how the Apparent Load parameter of a connector is associated with a family parameter. Notice that only one parameter is available in the list, because it is the only family parameter that is an Apparent Power type.

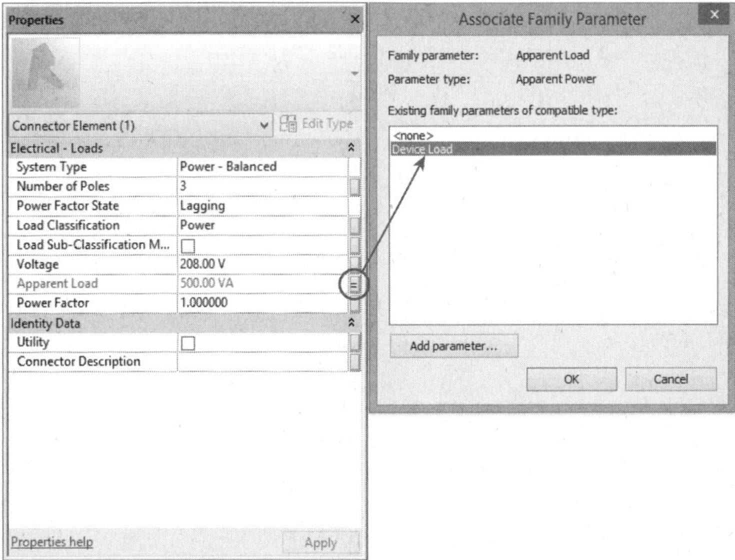

FIGURE 21.15 Associating a connector parameter to a family parameter

Although the Apparent Load parameter can be an instance parameter, the parameters that you use to define the device's voltage or number of poles should be type parameters. In the case of a motor connection device family in which specific loads are used for each voltage, you could use a type parameter for the apparent load. With these settings in place, you can use a type catalog to create the various types of motor connections. Figure 21.16 shows a sample type catalog for a three-phase motor connection device family. The values for the parameters are taken from a code table. This ensures that the proper load values will be used when the devices are connected to systems in a project. This family is a good way of going around the limitation that Revit doesn't "see" connectors through linked files. For example, when you link the mechanical model into your electrical model, even though the mechanical equipment may contain electrical connectors and data, you won't be able to use it for circuiting, panel schedules, and so on. Instead, you can place your own symbol containing the necessary connectors and data. This limitation is not an issue when mechanical and electrical equipment are working within the same Revit file.

FIGURE 21.16 Sample type catalog for a device family

Specify Types

Family: dMb_3PH Motor Connection

Types:

Type	Horsepower	Device Voltage	Device Load
	(all)	(all)	(all)
208V - 50HP	50	208	51962
208V - 60HP	60	208	61315
208V - 75HP	75	208	76557
208V - 100HP	100	208	98727
208V - 125HP	125	208	124361
208V - 150HP	150	208	143414
208V - 200HP	200	208	191218
480V - 1/2HP	0.5	480	876
480V - 3/4HP	0.75	480	1275
480V - 1HP	1	480	1673
480V - 1 1/2HP	1.5	480	2390

Even though the motor connection family has no 3D geometry, the connector is available when the device is used in a project. Although the location of an electrical connector is not that important in a family that contains 3D geometry, it is very important for a family without geometry. Be sure to locate the connector at the insertion point of the family. Otherwise, you can end up with undesired results in your project, as shown in Figure 21.17.

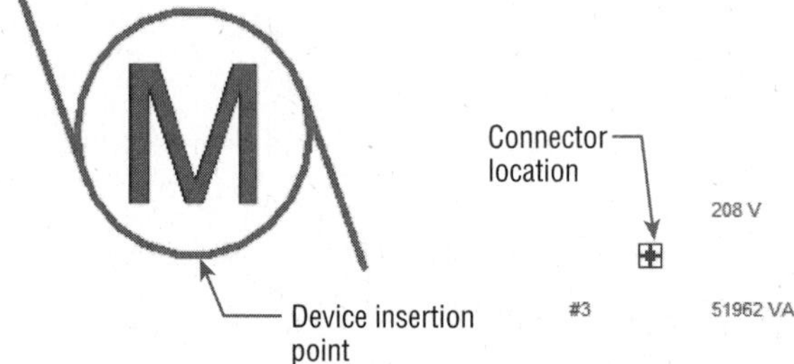

FIGURE 21.17 Device family with improper connector location

For some device families, you may need multiple connectors. This may be due to different systems within the device or because the device has multiple connection points.

A floor box device family, for example, can be created that allows for the connection of all the types of systems within the box. With all the connectors added to the device family, the device can be connected to the appropriate systems when used in a project. Figure 21.18 shows a floor box family with multiple connectors in a project. The systems associated with the connectors can be created for the device in the project.

A junction box is another example of a device family that may require multiple connectors. In this case, the connectors are the same type. Their properties can be associated with the same family parameters or unique ones. Having multiple connectors of the same type within a device family allows you to connect the device to multiple circuits. Figure 21.19 shows how having two connectors in a junction box device family allows the device to be connected to multiple circuits in a project.

When using multiple connectors in a device family, it is a good idea to use the Connector Description parameter to identify the connectors. This will help with creating systems when working in a project. When a device has multiple connectors and you are creating a system for the device, a dialog box lists the available connectors.

FIGURE 21.18
Device with multiple connectors in a project

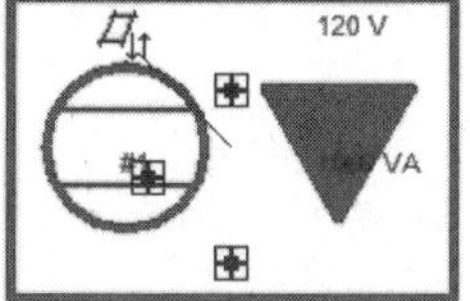

FIGURE 21.19
Junction box with multiple connectors

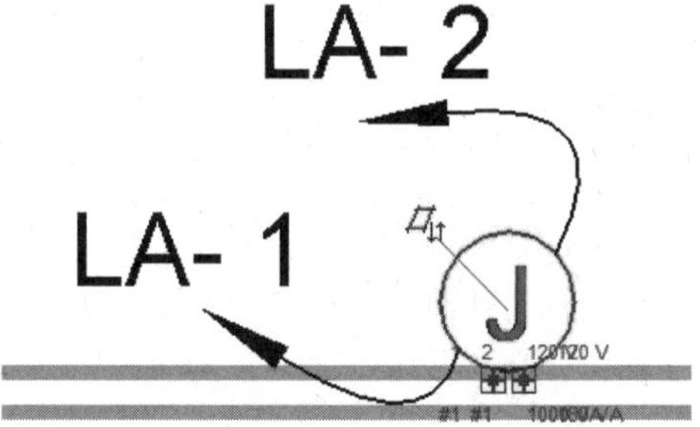

The current version of Revit MEP has a limitation with switches. You cannot assign a switch family to multiple systems even when the family contains multiple connectors.

Real World Scenario

POWER FOR SYSTEMS FURNITURE

Wendy is working on a large office building project. The open floor plan requires systems furniture to be used. She is required to provide a junction box for each group of furniture, but each cubicle within the group needs its own power source. By adding connectors to her junction box family, she is able to show that multiple circuits are provided to each junction box location.

In another area of the building, she is using quad receptacles. To limit the load on each circuit, she needs a unique circuit for each pair of outlets within a quad receptacle. She creates a quad receptacle device family that has two connectors. The connector voltages are associated with the device family voltage, and she creates two load parameters, one for each connector. Keep in mind that there is only one Circuit Number parameter in the Properties palette when you're selecting a device. However, she can access all information for each circuit (Circuit Number, Wire Number, Panel Name, Length, and so on) within a family by selecting it and going to the Electrical Circuits tab.

The Bottom Line

Select a family template. An important step when creating a device (or any family, for that matter) is the selection of the family template.

> **Master It** Stephanie has been assigned to create a new line of receptacles that matches her company display standards and takes their functionality to the next level. What family template would be most appropriate for receptacles?

Model device geometry. The 3D geometry of a device family may not be its most important component, but there are things you can do to make the geometry useful for project coordination and accuracy.

> **Master It** Device families are commonly face hosted because of the way they are used in a project model. Describe why a device family that is hosted by a floor in a project may not appear correctly in a plan view.

Use annotations to represent devices. Because of their size and simple shapes, device families are not typically shown on construction documents. Instead, a symbol is used to represent the device. Annotation families can be nested into device families for display in project views.

> **Master It** The orientation of an annotation family nested into a device family is important for proper display in project views. What is the device family parameter that allows for the display of the annotation in plan and section views? What hosting options in a project allow this parameter to work?

Add parameters and connectors. The connectors used in device families provide the engineering characteristics of the device so that it can be incorporated into systems within a project.

> **Master It** You cannot edit the parameters of a connector while working in a project file. Describe how you can change the properties of a connector without having to edit the device family.

Chapter 22

Details

With all the emphasis on using Autodesk® Revit® MEP 2015 as a design tool, it is easy to assume that it is weak when it comes to traditional drafting. Your projects do not need to be modeled to the smallest level of detail just because they can be. Many of the details that are used to convey design intent with a traditional 2D drafting method can also be used on a Revit project. In fact, it is best to keep your model as simple as possible and handle the more detailed information with, well, details.

The transition to Revit can be difficult, because it may seem that you will have to abandon all the details you have accumulated over the years. However, you can use the CAD details you have in their native format directly in your Revit projects, or you can easily convert them to Revit format and begin to re-create your library. Actually, Revit provides you with an opportunity to update and organize your library of details.

Using the tools available in Revit MEP 2015 for details and diagrams will enable you to create a complete set of construction documents.

In this chapter, you will learn to do the following:

- Use Revit drafting and detailing tools efficiently
- Use CAD details in Revit projects
- Build a Revit detail library
- Create detail views of your Revit model

Drafting and Detailing Tools

Whether you are embellishing a model view or creating a detail or diagram on a drafting view, the Annotate tab provides the necessary drafting tools to generate linework, patterns, and symbols. The Detail Line button enables you to draw linework that is specific to the view in which it is created.

When you click the Detail Line button, the Modify | Place Detail Lines contextual tab appears on the ribbon. This tab is very much like the Modify tab, but it also contains the Draw panel, which allows you to select from an assortment of line tools to create either lines or shapes.

The Line Style panel lets you choose the type of line that will be used.

Line Styles

Line styles are an important part of your Revit projects because you can create styles that match the line patterns used for model components and other CAD applications. This allows you to maintain a consistent look throughout your construction documents without having to override the graphic representation of each line. For example, you can create a style to be used for lines that represent domestic cold-water pipes with the same line pattern used in a view filter that applies to the actual domestic cold-water pipes or that matches the Graphic Overrides settings for a Domestic Cold Water system, as shown in Figure 22.1.

Figure 22.1
Line style matching model display

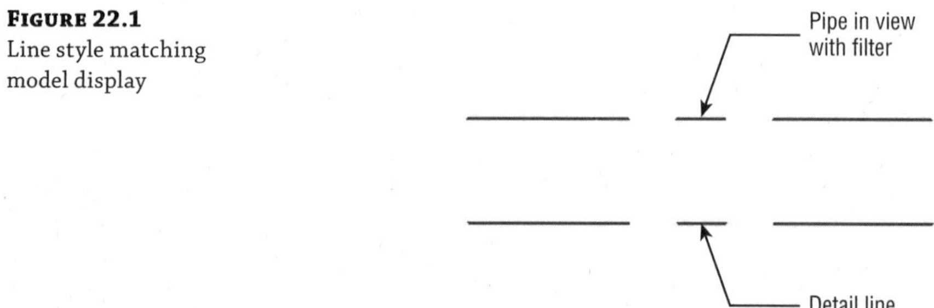

It may be helpful to think of line styles as family types for lines. You can draw a line with any line style and switch it to another style by using the selector drop-down on the Line Style panel of the contextual tab that appears when a line is selected. This gives you the freedom to draw a detail or diagram with one line style, focusing on the content of what is being drawn. You can then go back and change selected lines to more appropriate line styles if necessary.

Regions

Filled regions are areas with a chosen pattern that can be used to represent a material or designated area of a detail. When you create a filled region, you can choose a line style for the border of the region. When you are drawing a detail that requires a filled region, determine how its boundaries will interact with the rest of the detail and choose appropriate border lines. Using the borders of a filled region requires less linework because you don't have to draw a line over the border of a filled region.

Figure 22.2 shows a detail of a concrete floor penetration. A filled region is used to represent the concrete floor. The border lines of the region where the electrical box penetrates the floor are thicker than the rest. This is done so that additional lines do not have to be drawn to represent the box.

Notice that at the outer edges of the filled region, no border lines are shown. You can use the Invisible Lines line style for borders of a filled region that you do not want to show. This is also useful when you have two filled regions that are adjacent. One region can define the line of the detail, while the overlapping region border can be set to invisible. This is necessary only if the overlapping lines cause the detail to look incorrect.

Invisible Lines

Invisible Lines is one of the line styles that comes with Revit MEP 2015, but it's available only for use in sketch mode. To use an invisible line anywhere in your project, you can create your own invisible line style by setting the color of a line style to white.

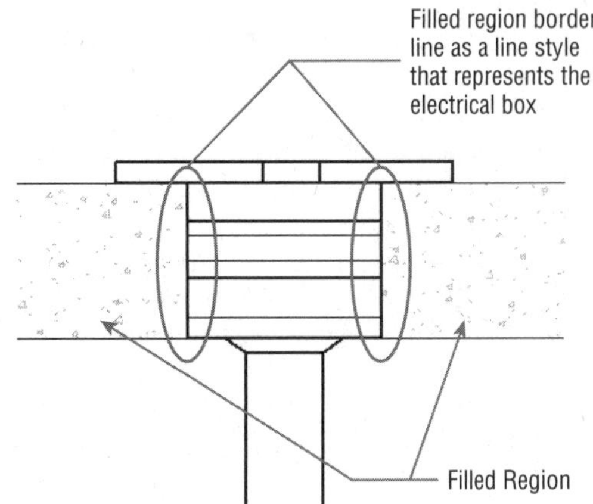

FIGURE 22.2
Filled region in a detail

To draw a filled region, do the following:

1. On the Annotate tab, click the Region button and then select the Filled Region option. This changes the ribbon to a contextual tab for drawing the region. All visible elements in the drawing area become halftone because drawing a region is done in sketch mode. The same tools for drawing detail lines are available when sketching a region.
2. Choose a line style for the borders of the region, and draw lines to define the region's shape. Lines must form a closed loop to create a region.
3. Choose a pattern for the region from the Type Selector in the Properties palette prior to completing the sketch. (The pattern can be changed after completion by selecting the region and choosing a pattern from the Type Selector.)
4. When you have finished sketching the region shape, click the green check mark button on the Mode panel of the contextual tab to finish and exit sketch mode. (If you want to abandon the creation of the region, you can click the red X button on the Mode panel.)
5. Select the filled region to activate grips that allow you to push and pull the edges to change the region's shape. Edges can be aligned with other items in the view. An edge can be modified only to the point where it does not cause another edge to be too small or disappear.
6. To make changes to the borders of a filled region, you can click the Edit Boundary button on the Mode panel of the contextual tab that appears when the region is selected. This returns you to sketch mode for making changes to the region's shape or to redefine the border line styles.

When you have a filled region that overlaps other detail lines, you can select the region and use the Bring To Front or Send To Back button on the Arrange panel of the contextual tab to change the draw order. If the region is defined as having an opaque background, it masks out any linework behind it as long as the view is set to the Hidden Line model graphics style. Annotation objects are not masked by a filled region unless the region is a solid fill that is the same color as the text or annotation and the text style is set to Transparent. A wireframe view causes any linework behind a region to be displayed unless the region is a solid fill.

You can use two types of patterns for filled regions. *Drafting patterns* change with the scale of the view in order to appear the same when the view is placed on a sheet. *Model patterns* are sized based on the dimensions of what the pattern is used to represent (ceiling tile, floor tile, brick, and so forth) in the model and look different in views of a different scale on a sheet.

To create a filled region pattern, click the Additional Settings button on the Manage tab and select Fill Patterns. Choose whether you want to create a drafting or model pattern at the bottom of the Fill Patterns dialog box based on whether you are representing a real-world pattern such as tile or simply a pattern used to fill space. Click the New button to create a pattern. You can choose between parallel lines or crosshatched lines, setting the angle and spacing of the lines for a simple pattern. If you choose the Custom option in the New Pattern dialog box, you can import a PAT file, as shown in Figure 22.3.

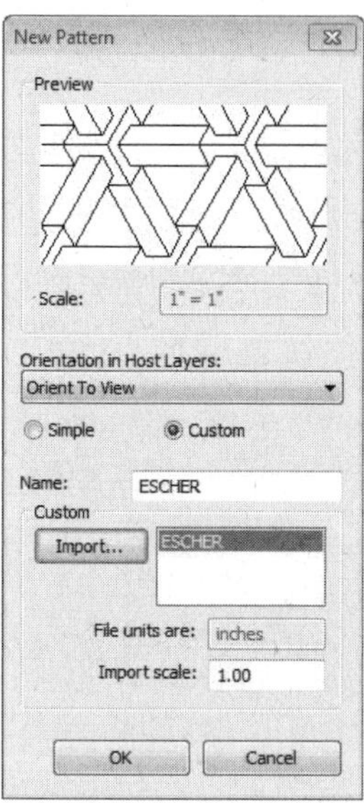

FIGURE 22.3
Custom pattern for filled region

Once you create a custom pattern, the scale option cannot be modified. You must reimport the pattern to change the scale. You can set the Orientation In Host Layers setting for a drafting pattern when it is used as a cut pattern for objects such as walls, floors, and roofs. You can choose to keep the pattern aligned with the element, orient the pattern to the view, or keep it readable. The settings for drafting patterns are described here:

Aligned With Element This option causes the pattern to maintain its relationship to the host.

Orient To View This option causes all patterns to have the same alignment.

Keep Readable This option causes the pattern to behave in the same manner as text. The pattern maintains its alignment until it is rotated past 90 degrees, where it flips to keep its intended alignment.

These settings do not have any effect on filled regions that are drawn manually.

Once you have a pattern, you can assign it to a filled region style. Select a filled region, and click the Edit Type button in the Properties palette to edit a style or create a new one. Click the Duplicate button to create a new style, giving it a name that clearly defines what it is. It is usually best to name a filled region style with the same name as the pattern it uses. Click the Fill Pattern parameter to select a pattern used for the style. Other parameters allow you to set the transparency of the background, the line weight, and the color of the lines. These settings are for the pattern used by the style, not for the lines that define the border, as shown in Figure 22.4.

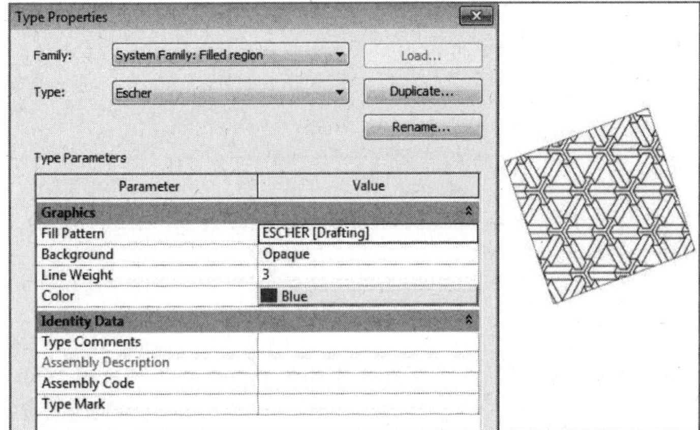

FIGURE 22.4 Filled region style settings

Another type of region you can use in details is a masking region. A *masking region* is a shape that masks out any linework behind it. It is essentially a blank filled region. Masking regions block out any model elements, detail lines, or filled regions in a detail view that is set to the Hidden Line visual style. The tools for creating a masking region are exactly the same as for a filled region. These regions are useful when creating a detail displaying model elements that may contain components that you do not want to be seen in the detail. You can use the border lines of a masking region to define portions of a detail in the same manner as with filled regions.

Similar to filled regions, masking regions mask out items only when the view is set to Hidden Line. Annotation objects are not masked by masking regions.

Detail Components

Many items within details are used repeatedly from one detail to the next. It can be tedious and time-consuming to locate a detail that contains a specific item that you know you have drawn previously so that you can use it in a detail you are currently drawing. *Detail components* are special families that can be used to represent objects commonly used in details, saving you repetitive drawing time. When you install Revit 2015 and its content, a `Detail Items` folder is included in the content library. The families in this folder are sorted by their construction-specification categories. Each folder contains families that you can use in your details to save the time it would take to draw them repeatedly. Many of the families have multiple versions, each of which is drawn from a different viewpoint so that they can be used in section detail views.

Detail item families are different from annotation families because their size is not dependent on the scale of the view in which they are drawn and they are intended to be used as a 2D representation of model geometry. They are representations of building components drawn at their actual size. These items can be used when the building model has not been modeled to a level of detail to include the actual items. Certain architectural and structural elements do not need to be included in their respective models in order for these disciplines to achieve their project goals. When you create a section or callout of the model for a detail, you need to include detail components for a true representation of the design.

Don't Get Confused

Although they are referred to as *detail components*, these families are actually under the Detail Items category.

It is a common practice to use generic styles for elements such as walls, floors, or roofs so as not to weigh down the model with unnecessary detail that can be handled with detail views. For example, although an exterior wall may have an outer layer of brick, the wall can be modeled generically, and detail components can be used in a detail view to show the brick layer. Detail components are useful for MEP discipline details as well. Many structural member components are available in the library. Items such as angles, beams, and channels can be quickly and accurately represented when creating a detail. Figure 22.5 shows an example of detail components used to create a detail.

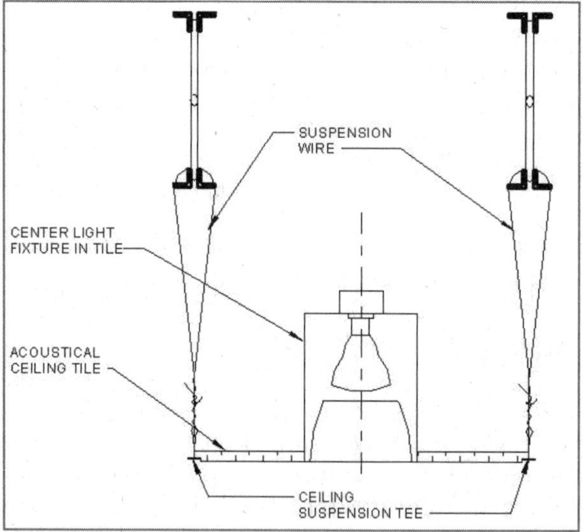

Figure 22.5
Sample detail using detail components

Even though the lighting fixture shown in the detail was included in the model, a detail component of a section view of a light fixture was used in the detail because the actual model component used was a simple cylinder. Every item shown in Figure 22.5 is a detail component family except for the centerline and annotations.

You can use detail component families to create repeating detail component styles. Repeating detail components allow you to quickly represent repetitive instances of components such as brick, glass block, or roof decking. They can also be used for MEP items such as pipe or conduit, as shown in Figure 22.6. In this example, the repeating detail was drawn horizontally to represent the rows of conduit.

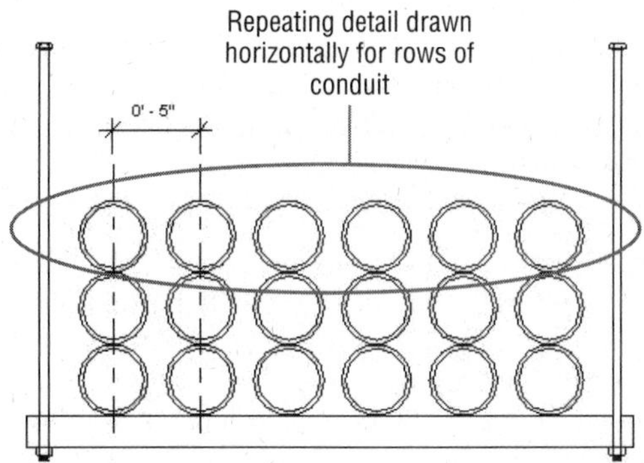

FIGURE 22.6 Repeating detail for conduit rack

To create a repeating detail component style, click the Component button on the Annotate tab and select the Repeating Detail Component option. Click the Edit Type button in the Properties palette, and click the Duplicate button in the Type Properties dialog box. Name your style so that it can be easily identified for its use. Figure 22.7 shows the Type Properties dialog box for a repeating detail.

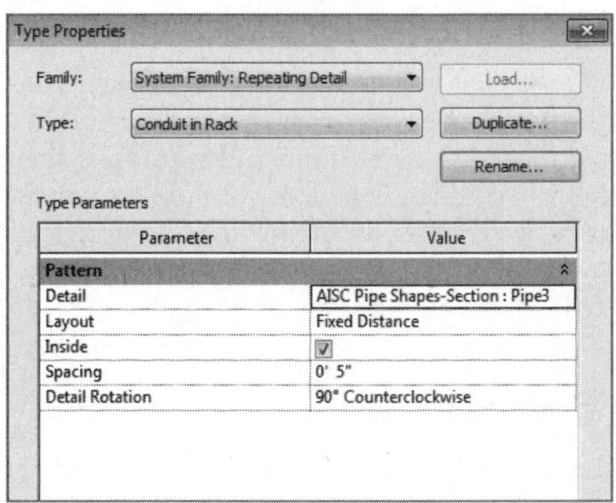

FIGURE 22.7 Repeating detail properties

The Detail parameter allows you to select a detail component family that is loaded into your project for the repeating detail.

The Layout parameter has four settings:

Fill Available Space This option places as many instances of the detail component that fit within the length of the path drawn for the repeating detail without overlapping the graphics.

Fixed Distance This option can be used with the Spacing parameter, which defines the distance between each instance of the detail component. The number of detail components with the spacing that completely fit within the length of the path will be displayed.

Fixed Number This option equally spaces the detail component along the length of the path drawn.

Maximum Spacing This option allows you to set the maximum distance between instances of the detail component. When the Maximum Spacing option is used, the space between instances may be less than specified, depending on the length of the path. This ensures that a complete instance will occur at each end of the path. Additional instances are added as changes to the path length cause the maximum spacing to be reached.

The Inside parameter determines whether the first and last instance of the detail fits within the length of the path drawn. The insertion point of the detail component determines the placement of the first and last instances. Figure 22.8 shows two repeating details with the same settings except that the top row's Inside parameter is set to No and the bottom row's is set to Yes. Notice that the bottom row has fewer instances of the detail component even though the path distance is the same.

FIGURE 22.8
Repeating details

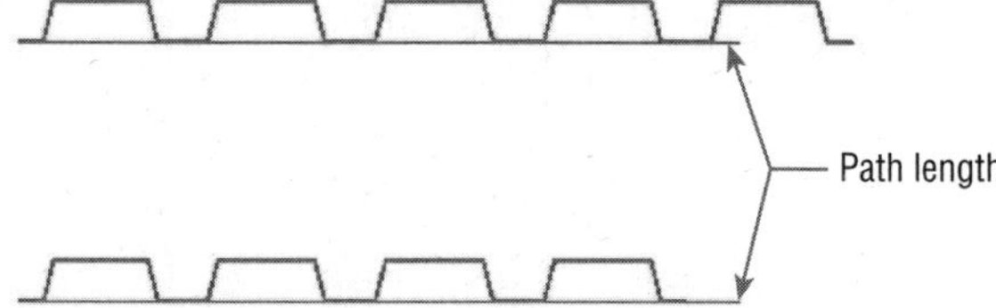

You can use the Detail Rotation parameter to rotate the detail component family so that it follows the path in the proper manner.

Because repeating detail components are system families, you cannot store them in your library, but you can create them in your project template for use on every project. Another alternative is to create a project file with all the styles you use and then transfer them into your projects as needed. The detail component families used in the repeating detail styles will be transferred along with the styles.

CAD Details

One of the primary benefits of a CAD application is the ability to save and reuse drawings. Because of this, most companies have spent years accumulating a vast array of CAD details. Making the transition to Revit does not mean that you can no longer use your library of CAD details. You can use CAD details and diagrams in your Revit projects, or you can re-create them in Revit format to build a new library of details for use on your projects. Converting your details to Revit reduces the number of CAD files you have to link into your projects, which helps improve file performance.

The key to success when using CAD details in a Revit project is to link the CAD file. If you have any concern for standards and for file performance, do not import CAD files into your project. It can be tempting to import a CAD file, explode it, and then clean it up for use in your project. Although this might provide immediate results, it can have an overall negative effect on your project. When you explode an imported CAD file, text and line styles are created for each unique text style and layer within the CAD file. The more of these unnecessary styles that you bring into your project, the poorer your file performance will be. It also opens the door for deviation from standards, because nonstandard text styles and line patterns will be available for use in other areas of the project.

If your project contains line patterns that have come from imported CAD files, you can remove them to avoid improper use. The line patterns show up as IMPORT- patterns in the Line Patterns dialog box, as shown in Figure 22.9.

FIGURE 22.9 Imported line patterns

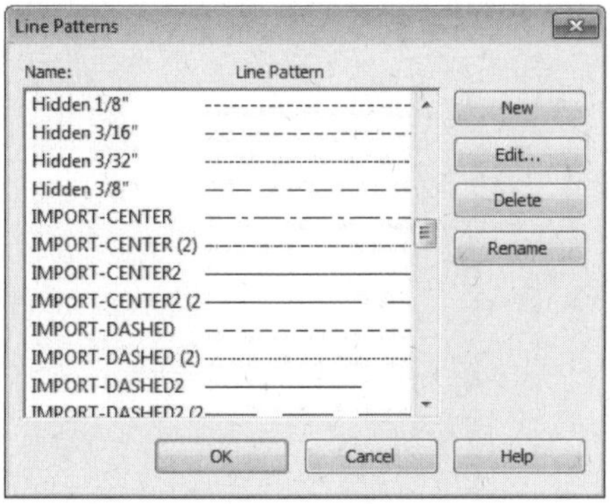

You cannot remove them using the Purge Unused tool, but you can remove them manually from the project in the Line Patterns dialog box.

When you link a CAD detail into your project, it may not look exactly as it does in CAD. Variations in text styles from CAD to Revit can cause an undesired display of text notes and leaders. CAD details can be easily converted to Revit format, which enables you to display the detail correctly. Prior to linking a CAD file, it is best to open the file with its native application and set the text styles to match the text settings in your Revit project. Having the text defined the same way in both files ensures proper formatting.

Using Drafting Views

CAD details or diagrams can be linked directly onto a sheet in your Revit projects. If you intend to convert a detail to Revit format, however, it is best to link it into a drafting view instead of onto a sheet. This allows you to save the view as a file for use on future projects.

Even if you are going to use CAD details in your project without converting them, linking them into drafting views helps keep your project organized. Drafting views can be organized in the Project Browser, which helps you keep track of what details exist in your project. This also enables you to create detail references to their location on sheets. You can specify the properties of drafting views to group them into their appropriate locations within the Project Browser for easy access and management.

It is best to set the scale of a drafting view that is used for linked CAD details to the same scale in which the details are drawn. This ensures accurate display of annotative objects within the CAD details.

Converting Details

When you link a CAD detail into a drafting view by clicking the Link CAD button on the Insert tab, you have some options for its display. One of the choices is for the colors of the CAD lines. Many people use colors in CAD to indicate the line weight of printed lines. Choosing the Preserve option in the Link CAD Formats dialog box, as shown in Figure 22.10, maintains the colors of the linework when inserted into Revit. This helps you to determine which Revit line styles to use when converting the detail.

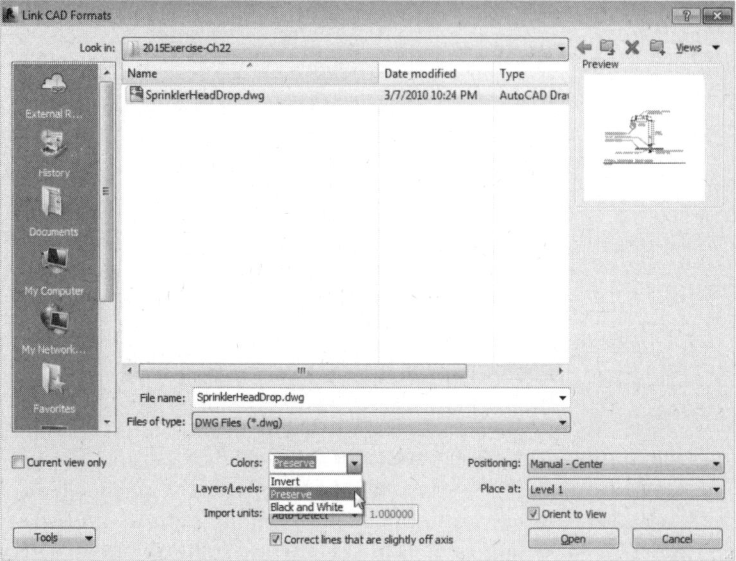

FIGURE 22.10 Color options for a linked CAD file

There are a few ways to convert a CAD detail into Revit format. The most time-consuming and least desirable method is to import the CAD file, explode it, and convert the line and text styles to Revit lines and text. This should not be done directly in your project but rather in a separate file in order to keep the imported styles from populating your project. The file should then be purged of all unused styles, and line patterns should be removed before the file is saved to a library or used in projects.

The easiest method for converting CAD details to Revit format is to link the file into a drafting view and trace the linework. Although tracing seems like a tedious task, there is a drafting tool that expedites the process. With a file linked into a drafting view, click the Detail Line button on the Annotate tab. On the Draw panel, select the Pick Lines tool, as shown in Figure 22.11.

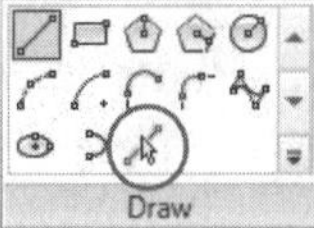

FIGURE 22.11
The Pick Lines drafting tool

The Pick Lines tool allows you to select lines within the CAD file, and it places a Revit line in the same location that matches the selected line. With this tool, you can pick the lines of a CAD detail and have a Revit version of the detail within a short period of time.

You cannot use the window-selection feature to select the lines. Each line must be selected individually. However, when you combine this tool with the Tab selection functionality of Revit, you save time and reduce the number of clicks. Placing your cursor over a desired line and pressing the Tab key highlights any lines connected to the line under your cursor, as shown in Figure 22.12. With the multiple lines highlighted, you can click to select them, which places a Revit line at each location.

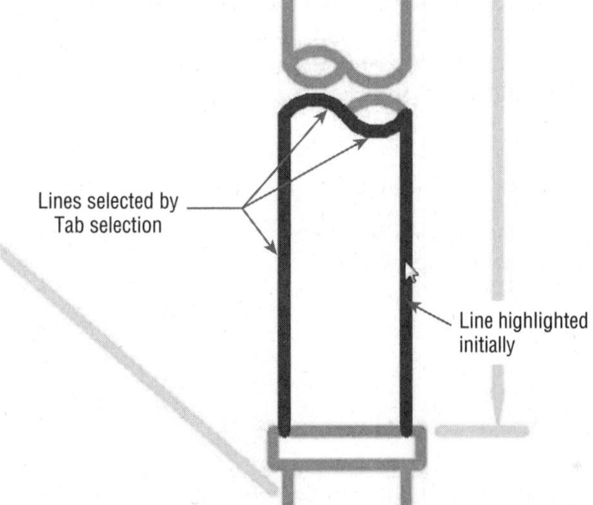

FIGURE 22.12
Tab selection of multiple lines

SHORT LINES

Revit cannot draw a line that is shorter than 1/32" (0.8 mm). When you are converting a CAD detail, you may come across lines that are too short to be drawn. Even though lines may highlight when you use Tab selection, they will not be drawn when clicked, and any lines connected to them will not be drawn. When you place your cursor over a line in a CAD detail, the cursor indicates whether the line can or cannot be drawn. You may need to make adjustments to your details to accommodate this limitation.

In some cases, you may need to create a very small circle. You can use the Scale feature on the Modify tab to shrink a circle to a smaller size than you can create when drawing it initially.

When you are using the Pick Lines tool to convert a CAD detail, you may want to choose a line style that is thicker than the lines being copied. This helps you keep track of which lines have already been converted, especially if your CAD detail is drawn with black lines. As you click to draw Revit lines, a padlock icon displays and allows you to lock the line to the CAD detail line. This is unnecessary, because the CAD detail will be removed after you are finished. Once you have completed the line conversion, you can select the Revit lines and change their style to match the intent of the detail. Using this process is more efficient than constantly switching between line styles during the process of converting the detail.

You cannot use the Pick Lines tool to copy the text within a CAD detail, so you have to place notes and dimensions manually. Use the ability to override dimension text when necessary for details that are not drawn to scale. You have to create any required filled regions manually as well.

Once a CAD detail has been converted to Revit format, you can use the Manage Links tool to remove the linked CAD file or simply select the linked CAD graphics and delete them, leaving you with a native Revit detail that can be saved to a detail library for future use.

Reducing your reliance on linked CAD files is an important step toward reducing project load times, view regeneration, and other causes of poor file performance. Because details are such an important part of any project, having Revit details available for use is crucial to the success of a project. Now that you have learned some options for converting a CAD detail, practice by completing the following exercise:

1. Open the `Ch22_Details.rvt` file found at `www.sybex.com/go/masteringrevitmep2015`.
2. Click the Drafting View button on the View tab.
3. Name the view **Sprinkler Head Drop Detail**. Set Scale to Custom and Scale Value to **1**, as shown in Figure 22.13.

FIGURE 22.13 New Drafting View dialog box

4. Download the `SprinklerHeadDrop.dwg` file found at `www.sybex.com/go/masteringrevitmep2015`. Save the file in a location that you can access during this exercise.
5. With the newly created drafting view open, click the Link CAD button on the Insert tab.
6. Browse to the location of the downloaded CAD file. Select the file, and set the Colors option to Preserve. Choose Manual – Center for the Positioning option, as shown in Figure 22.14, and click Open.

FIGURE 22.14 Linked CAD file options

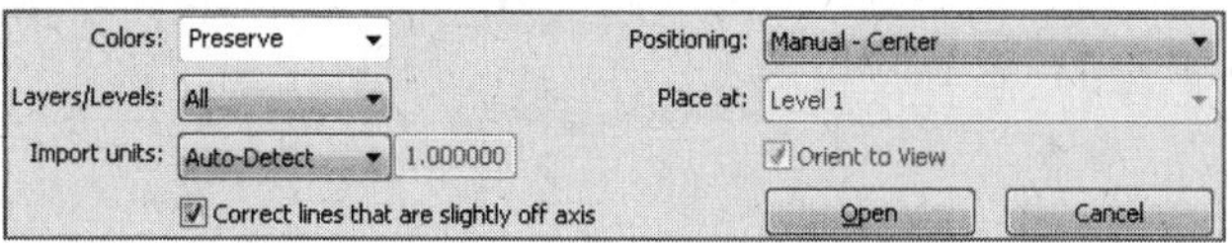

7. Click in the drawing area to place the CAD detail in the drafting view. Zoom to where you can comfortably see the entire detail.
8. Click the Detail Line button on the Annotate tab. Choose the Pick Lines tool from the Draw panel, and set Line Style to Wide Lines on the Line Style panel of the ribbon, as shown in Figure 22.15.

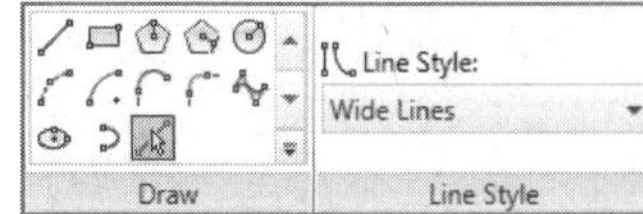

FIGURE 22.15
Line Style ribbon panel

9. Place your cursor over the circle called out as the SPRINKLER BRANCH LINE in the detail. With the circle highlighted, click to place a Revit line.
10. Place your cursor over the vertical line at the top-left side of the circle. Press the Tab key to highlight all three lines at the top of the circle, and then click to draw Revit lines; see Figure 22.16.

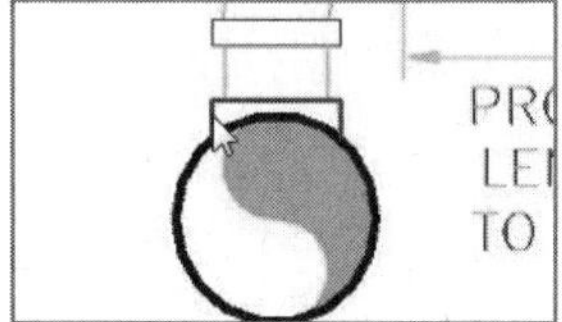

FIGURE 22.16
Tab selection of multiple lines using the Pick Lines tool

11. Continue placing lines by clicking the CAD detail lines, using the Tab key when applicable, until you have completely duplicated the detail linework, including the detail title text line. Do not use the padlock icon to lock the Revit lines to the CAD detail.
12. Click the Region button on the Annotate tab and select Filled Region. Select the Pick Lines tool from the Draw panel, and set the line style to Thin Lines in the Line Style panel.
13. Place your cursor over the lower arc inside the circle that is called out as SPRINKLER BRANCH LINE in order to highlight the line, as shown in Figure 22.17.

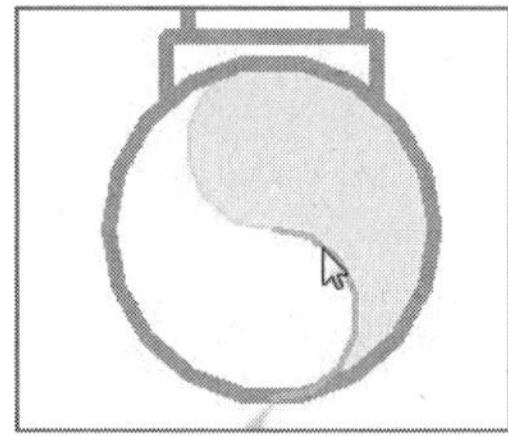

FIGURE 22.17
Arc selection

14. Press the Tab key twice to highlight the connected linework, and click to draw the region border. (Be careful not to move the cursor off the line while pressing the Tab key.) Click the green check mark on the Mode panel of the ribbon to exit the region's sketch mode.

15. Select the linked CAD file and move it off to the side, away from the newly created Revit linework. It is easiest to select the CAD file by clicking the text because the linework has been covered by Revit lines. You may also choose to select the CAD file and temporarily hide it in the view.
16. The CAD file is drawn with standards that set the line weight based on the color of the line. In this example, Red = Thin Lines, Green = Medium Lines, and Blue = Thick Lines. Convert the Revit lines to their appropriate line style by using the Line Style drop-down on the contextual tab that appears on the ribbon when you select a line. You can select multiple connected lines by using the Tab key. You can also hold down the Ctrl key and use the window-selection feature to select multiple lines that are not connected.
17. With the linework completed, place text and leaders to match those shown in the CAD detail. It may be helpful to move the CAD detail back into alignment with the Revit linework for placement of text notes and leaders.
18. Click the Aligned button on the Dimension panel of the Annotate tab to create a dimension in the same location as the horizontal LENGTH AS REQD dimension of the CAD detail. Click the dimension text to modify it. In the Dimension Text dialog box, choose the Replace With Text option and enter **AS REQD**. In the Text Fields section, enter **LENGTH** in the Above field; see Figure 22.18.

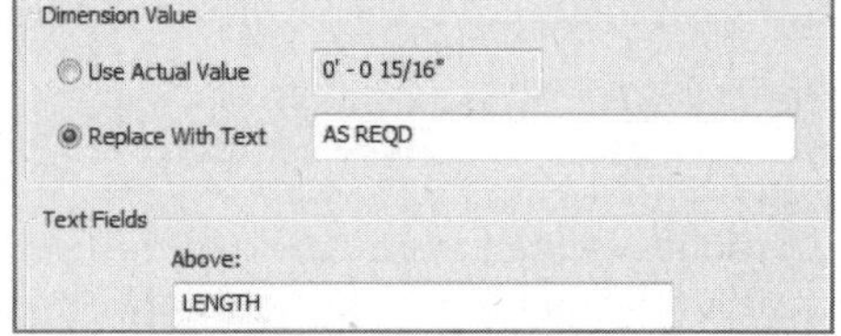

FIGURE 22.18 Dimension text override

19. Repeat step 18 for the vertical dimension in the detail.
20. With the detail complete, use the Manage Links tool to remove the CAD file.
21. Locate the drafting view in the Project Browser. Right-click the view, and select the Save To New File option. Browse to a location to save the file.

Strategies for Creating a Detail Library

When you right-click a drafting view in the Project Browser, one of the menu options is Save To New File, as shown in Figure 22.19.

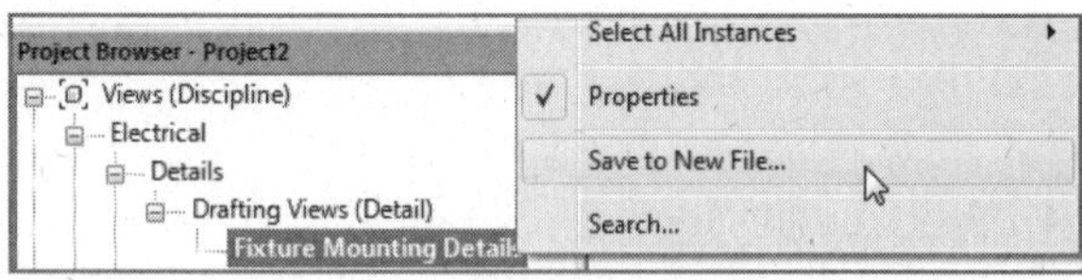

FIGURE 22.19 Drafting view context menu

Saving a drafting view as a file allows you to put it in a location where you can build a library of details and diagrams that can be accessed for use on other projects. You can organize your detail library in any manner that suits your workflow or processes. One option is to create a drafting view that has several common details on it. The view can then be saved as a file and the file can be opened for editing. Within this new file, the drafting view can be duplicated and a new drafting view for each detail created, leaving you with a single file containing multiple drafting views, each with its own unique detail. This makes it easy to locate specific details or to place an entire group of details into your project. Figure 22.20 shows an example of a detail file containing multiple drafting views for individual details.

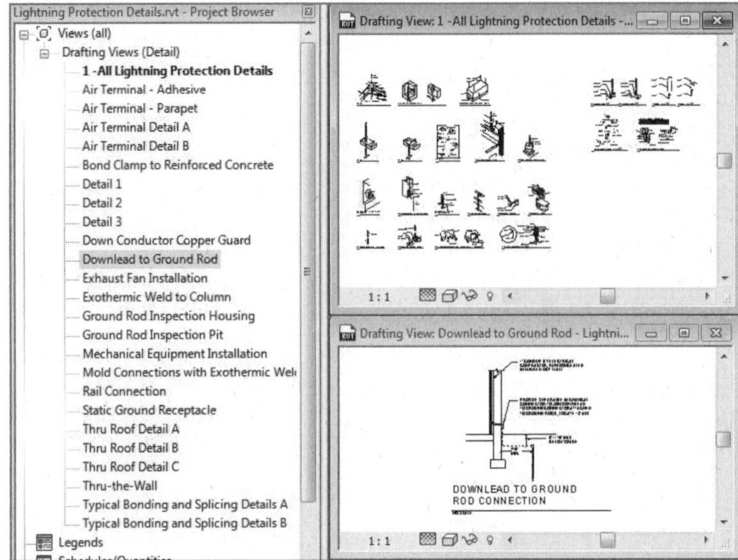

FIGURE 22.20
Sample detail file organization

When you create a drafting view for each detail, you can easily bring the detail into your project, without having to load a drafting view or an entire set of details. This reduces the number of views in your project, making the Project Browser more navigable and keeping your project file size minimized. Figure 22.21 shows a sample Project Browser organization for detail views.

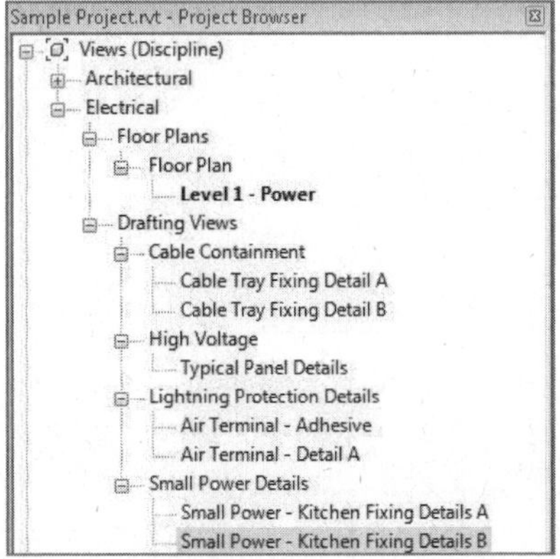

FIGURE 22.21
Sample detail view organization

When inserting details with the Insert From File button on the Insert tab, you have two choices: Insert Views From File and Insert 2D Elements From File, as shown in Figure 22.22. Each option is explained in the following sections.

Figure 22.22
Insert From File options

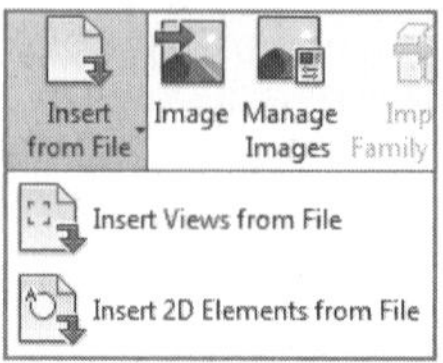

Inserting 2D Elements

The Insert 2D Elements From File option allows you to bring in a detail without having to load the drafting view into your project. This is the preferred method if you have created a separate drafting view for each detail. It is also possible to bring in the annotation and detail lines from a model view such as a floor plan, section, or elevation. When you choose this option, a dialog box appears for you to browse to the file containing the detail. When you open the file, the Insert 2D Elements dialog box appears; see Figure 22.23.

Figure 22.23
Insert 2D Elements dialog box

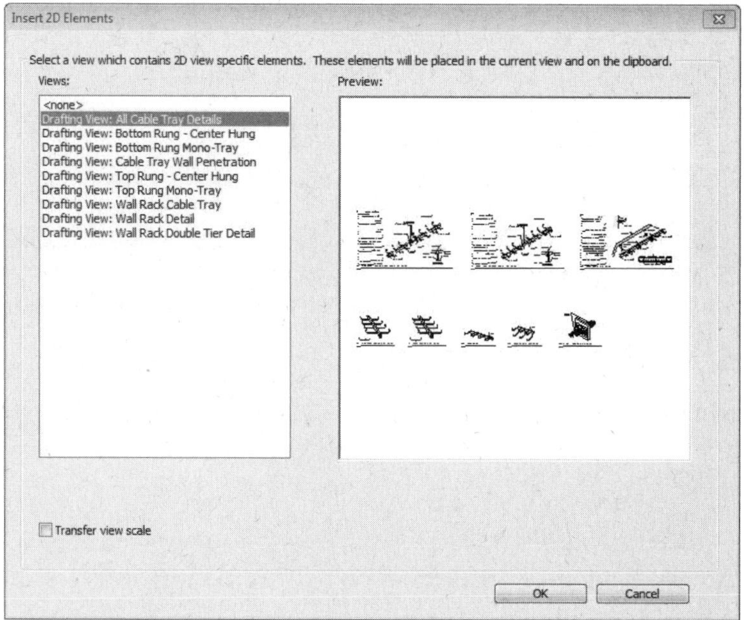

In this dialog box, you can select the view that contains the detail (or any view that has 2D annotation) you want to place into your project. When you click OK to load the detail, you may get a dialog box alerting you to duplicate types within the detail file and your project file.

The types defined in your project will be used. When you click OK, the detail is ready for placement in the current view of your project.

You should begin this process with a drafting view open in your drawing area. Because the detail is coming from a drafting view, you cannot place it directly onto a sheet by using this process. To get the detail onto a sheet, the detail must first be placed onto a drafting view, and then the view can be placed onto a sheet.

These elements can also be pasted into a callout view of a plan or section so that the detail relates directly to the model. In the properties of the view, the Display Model parameter can be set to Do Not Display, as shown in Figure 22.24.

FIGURE 22.24
Display Model parameter setting

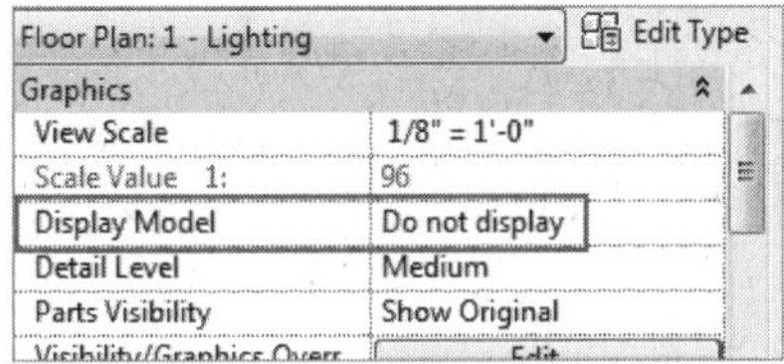

> **ORGANIZING DETAILS ON A DRAFTING VIEW**
>
> You can limit the number of drafting views required in your project by grouping details that will appear on the same sheet into drafting views. However, it may require some planning of sheet layouts prior to sheet creation. It also means you cannot use reference bubbles for individual detail titles, so this should be done only for sheets showing typical details that are not referenced in the model views or where details are referenced by their title.

When the detail is placed into your drafting view, it is just as if you drew the detail manually in the view. You can edit the lines and text if necessary to modify the detail for your specific project. If you change the detail significantly enough that you want to keep it as a new detail, you can copy and paste it into a new drafting view in the detail file where it came from.

Inserting Views

The Insert Views From File option loads selected views from a chosen file. You should use this method if you want to have the drafting view in your project. Choosing this option brings up a dialog box where you can browse to the file containing the view you want to load. This does not have to be a file located in your detail library. For example, if you know of a drafting view in another project that has details on it that you want for your project, you can browse to that project file and choose the drafting view from it.

The Insert Views dialog box that appears when you open a file shows any views available for loading into your project. You can select multiple views, including drafting views, schedules, and reports to be added to your project. You can also insert entire sheets of details by selecting a sheet from the list instead. Revit will create the sheet, load all the drafting views, and put them on the sheet in your project. The Preview Selection option in the lower-left corner enables you to see the entire contents of the view prior to loading it. When you click OK in this dialog box, you may get another dialog box indicating that there are duplicate types between the file and your project and that your project types will be used. When you click OK, the selected views are added to your project. The views appear in the Project Browser based on their properties and your browser organization, so it is a good idea to give your detail library files the same view properties that you use in your projects. This makes the views easy to locate when they are inserted and saves you time in organizing your Project Browser.

You can also insert entire sheets of details by selecting a sheet from the list instead. Revit will create the sheet, load all the drafting views, and put them on the sheet in your project. Use caution as Revit will also load and use the titleblock from the file that you are taking details from.

 **Real World Scenario**

IDEAS FOR DOWNTIME

Steve works for an MEP firm that is implementing Revit 2015. The firm has determined that the best course of action is to train its personnel immediately prior to the kickoff of their first Revit project.

The training has taken place. However, the project's schedule has been changed. Work on the project will not begin for a month, and Steve is worried that he will lose the knowledge he acquired during training.

One way he can maintain his familiarity with Revit 2015 is to begin converting his vast library of CAD details into Revit format, because his company intends to use Revit for MEP exclusively in the future.

By setting up a detail library, Steve has been able to work with Revit 2015 on a daily basis, keeping himself familiar with the interface and some of the functionality so that when the project begins, he will not have forgotten all of his training. An additional benefit is that he will not need to rely heavily on CAD details for his projects.

Model Detail Views

Many project details are independent drawings that represent the construction of a component, but some details are taken from the design to further enhance the level of information given in plan, section, or elevation views. Details are often used to convey the installation of components rather than just to provide information about them. It is important to a coordinated design to be able to convey the intent of placement of building objects and their relationship with other components.

You can use detail views in your projects to provide additional information about the model that is not part of the model as a whole. For example, you may have a pipe being run in the space of a column wrap at several locations throughout the model. You may choose to show this one time in a detail view and then denote where it occurs in each floor plan, instead of modeling it at each occurrence. Unlike drafting views, detail views allow you to show model elements. Using detail views can help you provide the necessary level of information for the project without weighing down the model and spending time on repetitive modeling tasks. For example, a typical detail explaining how a roof drain pipe should usually be anchored to a column is perfect for a drafting view and 2D detailing, while a detail view may be necessary to show how a roof drain on the second floor must offset near the column at a specific grid intersection because it is for specific elements and locations and shows how the contractor should deal with it.

Plan Callouts

The Callout tool on the View tab is one way to create a detail view from an area of your model. When you click the Callout button, you can choose what type of callout to create from the Type Selector in the Properties palette: either a Floor Plan callout that is used for enlarged plans or, to isolate a specific area of a plan, a Detail callout that creates a detail view.

Detail views are unique types of views in Revit. They have properties similar to plan, section, and elevation views, but they also have settings specific to the area of the model being shown. Detail views take on the discipline of the view in which they are drawn. The Show In Parameter option allows you to display the callout in the parent view only, which is the view where the callout is initially drawn, or in any intersecting views, which means the callout will be displayed in any views that show the area of the plan from which the callout is taken. Unlike a regular floor plan view, you cannot adjust the View Range settings of a detail view.

A detail view shows the portion of the model within the boundaries of the callout box. This box determines the crop region within the detail view, as shown in Figure 22.25.

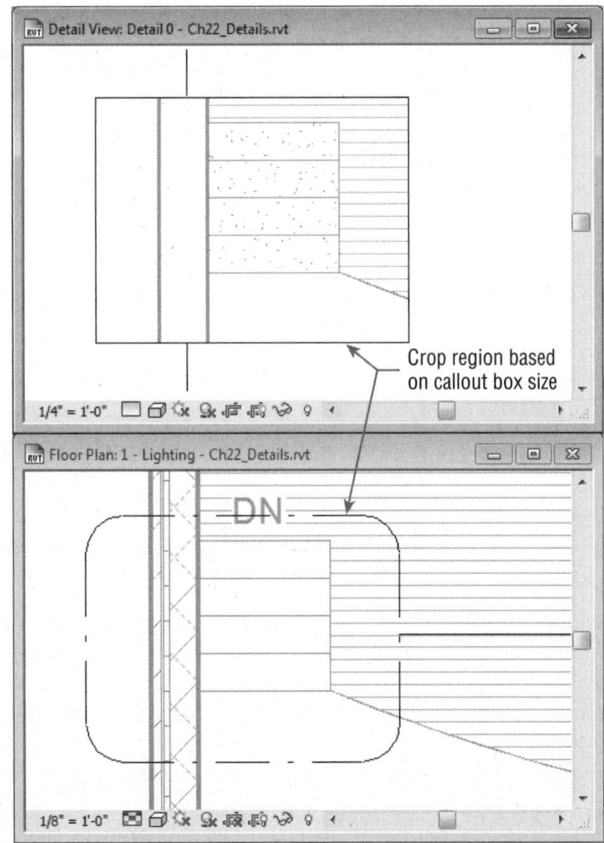

FIGURE 22.25
Callout box and crop region

A detail view taken from the plan, elevation, or section shows any grid lines or levels whose 3D extents cross within the boundaries of the callout to help with location information. These datum annotation elements can be turned off if necessary, but you cannot edit them in a detail view. They move to maintain their relationship to the crop region when the crop region is adjusted.

Revit MEP 2015 can create a nonrectangular crop region. This works for both floor plan and detail view callouts. Figure 22.26 shows a nonrectangular callout and the associated detail view. Notice that the nested annotation symbols for the receptacles do not display in the detail view. The actual model graphics of the receptacle family are displayed because the detail level of the detail view is set to Fine and the receptacle family is created to display the outlet box at Fine detail.

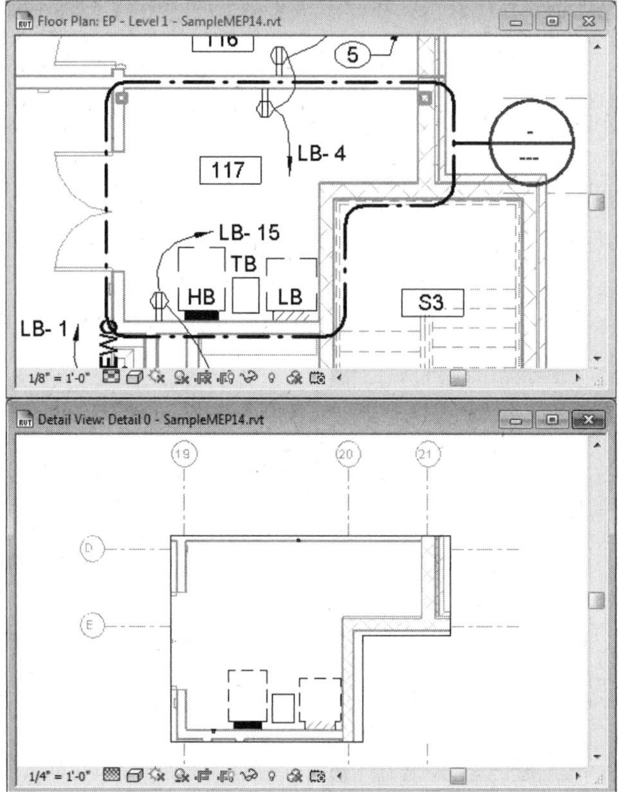

FIGURE 22.26 Nonrectangular callout and detail view

The main purpose of a detail view is to see a specific portion of the model and then add detail lines, regions, and other annotation objects to provide additional information about the design. Once a detail view has been created, you can use the same drafting tools as used in a drafting view to embellish the model information shown in the view. Filled regions can be added to show materials that may not be shown on the actual model objects. Masking regions can be used to block out items that you do not want to show in the detail. Figure 22.27 shows how you can add to the detail view of an electrical floor box in order to provide more information about the object and its location.

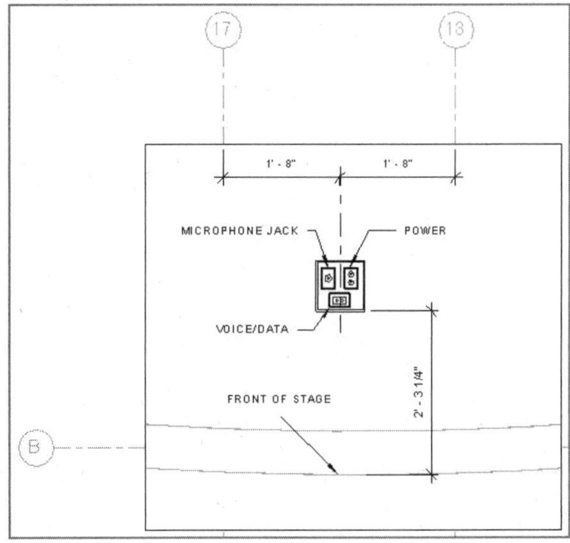

FIGURE 22.27 Detail view of a floor plan with added information

If you already have a detail drawn and you want to call out an object or an area of your model and reference that detail, you can use the option to reference another view. This option appears on the Options Bar when you click the Callout button on the View tab, as shown in Figure 22.28.

FIGURE 22.28 Options Bar setting for referencing another view

This associates the callout with the view selected in the drop-down list next to the Reference Other View option instead of creating a new detail view. This option is useful for details that occur in multiple locations throughout a project. Instead of creating a new detail view for each occurrence, you can create one and then reference that view in every location required on your plans using a callout. When you delete a callout that references another view from a model view, the referenced view remains in your project. With this functionality, you can combine your library of drafting details and callouts to convey design intent in a manner that is easily managed and coordinated.

Section Callouts

Another method for creating a detail view is to create a section view of an area of the model. One of the types of section views that can be created is a detail view, as shown in Figure 22.29.

This type of section is created in the same way as a building section, but the view created is a detail view instead of a model section view.

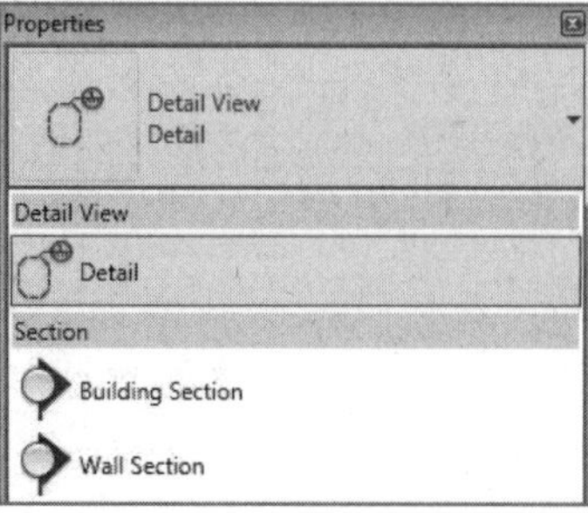

FIGURE 22.29 Section view types

Creating section detail views allows you to show project information without having to model elements that you ordinarily would not model to show in plan views. The same drafting tools used in drafting views can be used to provide additional information to the view in order to convey design conditions without having to add model components.

Section detail views can reference other views in the same way as plan callout detail views. This allows you to create the detail drawing once and reference it as many times as needed in your project.

In some cases, you may be able to use a building section to convey more of the design intent without having to embellish the section with detail annotations. You can create section tags to differentiate between model section and detail section marks in your views. Figure 22.30 shows how section tags can be used for different types of sections. This helps you know what a section mark is used for when you come across it in a plan view. You can find the settings for section tags by clicking the Additional Settings button on the Manage tab.

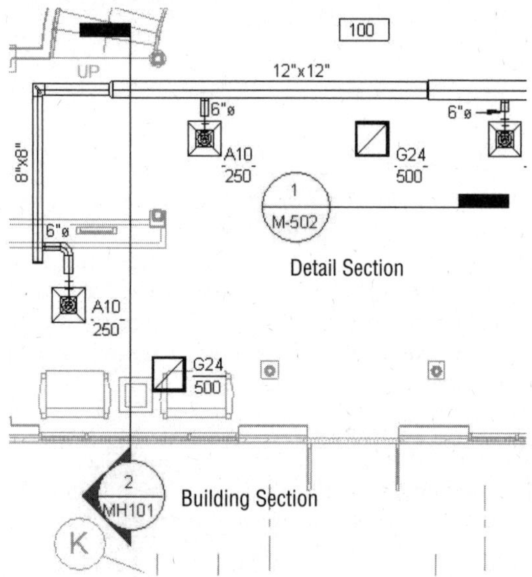

FIGURE 22.30 Section marks for different types of views

The Bottom Line

Use Revit drafting and detailing tools efficiently. Revit MEP 2015 has many tools for creating the details and diagrams needed to enhance your model and provide the necessary level of information for your projects.

> **Master It** Although the drafting tools in Revit MEP 2015 may be unfamiliar at first, learning to use them efficiently and effectively helps you spend more time focusing on design decisions instead of drafting efforts. Describe how filled regions can be used not only to display a pattern but also to provide line information in a detail.

Use CAD details in Revit projects. Much of the detail information used in your projects may already exist in another format. When you transition to Revit, you can still use your CAD details.

> **Master It** Using CAD details in a Revit project can be a quick way to complete your construction documents in a timely manner. However, using many CAD files for details can have a negative effect on file performance, so it is important to link CAD files whenever they are used. Explain why importing and exploding CAD files can adversely affect your project.

Build a Revit detail library. Having a library of details saves time on projects because you don't have to draw details that have already been created.

> **Master It** Drafting views can be saved as individual files for use on projects as needed. True or false: A drafting view will be added to your project when you use the Insert 2D Graphics From View option of the Insert From File tool. Explain.

Create detail views of your Revit model. Some details require the model to be shown in order to show installation or placement of objects.

> **Master It** Callout views can be created from plan, section, and elevation views. Explain how detail views are different from drafting views.

Chapter 23

Sheets

At first, it can be easy to view Autodesk® Revit® MEP 2015 as nothing more than a modeling tool. Some argue about whether Revit can produce construction documents of the same quality that we have grown accustomed to in traditional CAD systems. Construction documents are extremely important because, until we reach the day when clients and contractors require virtual models as the official deliverables for project construction, drawing sheets will continue to be the documentation standard.

Revit 2015 has features that allow you to create construction documents from your model. You can include the schedules, details, and diagrams that you would normally provide for a coordinated and detailed set of drawings.

Many people view their construction documents as their product. They want their product to be unique so that when others see it, they will know where it came from. You can develop standards for your construction documents that allow you to provide a unique and consistent look for your product.

Working with sheets in a Revit project is similar to traditional CAD practices. The main difference is that the plan, section, and elevation information comes from views of your model, which allows for better coordination. Changes to the model are propagated throughout the project, so any sheets containing a view of the changed area are automatically updated. Actually, the sheet itself is not updated; it is just that the view resides on the sheet. It may be best not to think of your sheets as separate from your project. They are simply the place where all the view information extracted from the model is coordinated.

Once you learn how to use the tools available for generating a set of construction documents from your Revit model, you will see the benefits of using coordinated, computable data and 3D modeling to design your projects.

In this chapter, you will learn to do the following:

- Create a titleblock
- Establish sheets in your project
- Place views on sheets
- Print and export sheets

Creating a Titleblock

Whether you refer to it as a sheet border, drawing border, or some other name, a *titleblock* consists of the graphics that define the boundaries of a sheet. Some of your clients may have specific requirements for the size, shape, and information provided in the titleblock used for their projects. You may have already developed these for use in CAD projects as well as a company titleblock for use when the client does not specify one. These CAD titleblocks can be used to develop titleblock families for your Revit projects. This ensures a consistent look between your Revit sheets and CAD sheets, especially if the need should arise to combine CAD and Revit drawings in a document set.

Titleblocks are a unique family type within Revit. To create a new titleblock, you can choose one of the presized templates available in your template library. When you choose to create a new family, you can browse to the location of your titleblock family templates. Depending on which templates you choose to install with Revit 2015, you will see templates available for standard sizes or one for creating your own unique size. Clicking New ➤ Title Block on the application menu takes you to the location of your titleblock templates, as shown in Figure 23.1.

FIGURE 23.1 Titleblock templates

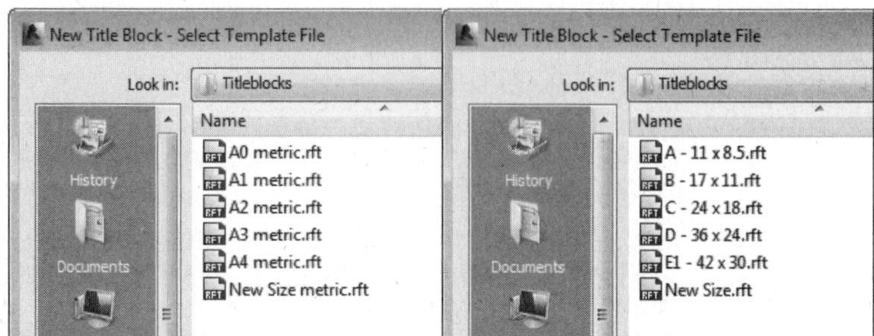

The templates for creating a titleblock contain a rectangle for defining the limits of the sheet size. If you are using the New Size template, the rectangle can be modified by dragging its lines to the appropriate size. You can also select one of the lines and edit its dimensions so that you can input the precise size for the limits of the titleblock. If you are using a template with a preset size, the rectangle is already dimensioned to the appropriate size.

Using Existing CAD Graphics

Once you have chosen a template and the size has been determined, you can import a CAD titleblock for reference. When working in the Family Editor, you cannot link a CAD file. The styles in the CAD file will become Revit styles within your titleblock family, so you may want to do the work in a file and then copy the Revit linework to another blank file when finished. This keeps your titleblock family free from unwanted styles. Chances are there will be many unnecessary styles from the CAD file and they do not conform to your naming standards. This excess information will be carried through to every project that uses the titleblock. The idea here is to create a titleblock family that is in clean, native Revit format.

Click the Import CAD button on the Insert tab of the Family Editor to import your CAD titleblock. You may want to use the Preserve option for the colors in the CAD file so that you can draw an appropriate Revit line to match the line weight based on the CAD color. Align the imported CAD file with the rectangle in the family so the titleblock fits properly, and pin it in place to avoid any accidental movement.

The Line button on the Create tab of the Family Editor allows you to draw the lines necessary to trace the imported CAD graphics. You can use the Pick Lines tool on the Draw panel of the Modify | Place Lines contextual tab to generate Revit lines quickly in the same location as the CAD graphics.

> **OBJECT STYLES**
>
> The templates for creating a titleblock have some predefined object styles that determine the lines used in the titleblock. You can create line styles, but they will not be available for use in the family. You must use object styles for the linework in a titleblock family. This distinguishes the lines from the line styles in your projects so that changes to project line styles do not affect your titleblock. You can create any object styles you need for your titleblock family by clicking the Object Styles button on the Manage tab in the Family Editor.

Using Text and Labels

When you finish creating Revit lines that match those of your CAD titleblock, you also need the annotation objects that provide sheet and project information. Determine which annotation objects in the CAD file can be Revit text objects and which need to be labels. Any text that is constant from sheet to sheet and does not need to change during the course of a project can be a text object in your titleblock family. For example, if your titleblock provides information about who designed, drafted, and checked a drawing, you can place text in the titleblock as the titles for this information. Figure 23.2 shows imported CAD graphics in a titleblock family with a text object placed in the same location as text in the CAD file.

FIGURE 23.2
Revit text object used in a titleblock family

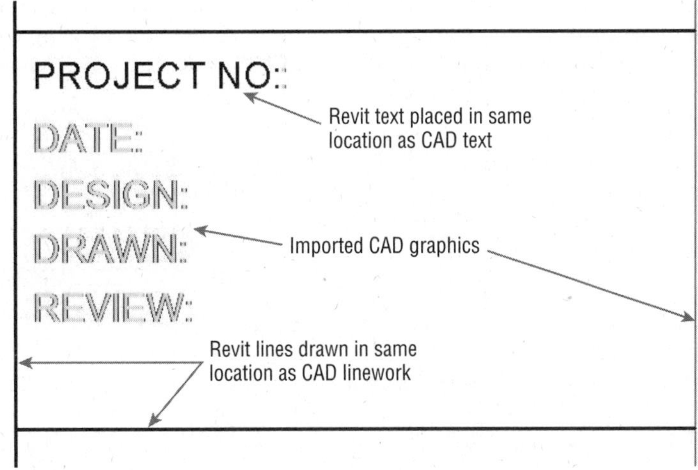

For more information about using the drafting tools available in Revit 2015 and using CAD graphics, see Chapter 22, "Details."

You can create text styles within the titleblock family to match those used in the CAD version of the titleblock. You create different styles by duplicating the standard text style available when the family is created.

A titleblock typically contains information about the project in general along with information specific to the items shown on the sheet. The key to coordinating the information that appears on your sheets is to coordinate from where the information is taken.

The most effective way to provide information on a titleblock is by using parameters. The use of parameters lets you make changes in a single location that updates all of your sheets in the project. Labels are used to show the information in a titleblock. Label styles should be created to match the text used in your CAD titleblock.

Labels should be used in your titleblocks in the same way that attributes are used in CAD. Click the Label button on the Create tab to create a label. You can edit the default label style by clicking the Edit Type button in the Properties palette and then the Duplicate button in the Type Properties dialog box.

Time for a Change?

When you transition to doing projects in Revit, you may find that it is easier and more efficient to use some of the default settings. This is especially true with fonts. The default font used by Revit is Arial, and although this may not be in line with your CAD standards, using it saves you time in re-creating annotations and managing them in families and projects.

When you click in the view to place the label, the Edit Label dialog box appears with a list of available parameters for the label. These are all built-in parameters that exist for either sheet objects or project information. If one of the parameters matches the kind of information you are trying to include in your titleblock, select it from the list and click the green arrow button to add it to the label, as shown in Figure 23.3. These parameters are available in the properties of your project sheets or in the project information on the Manage tab. When their values are input or modified, the label in the titleblock family updates.

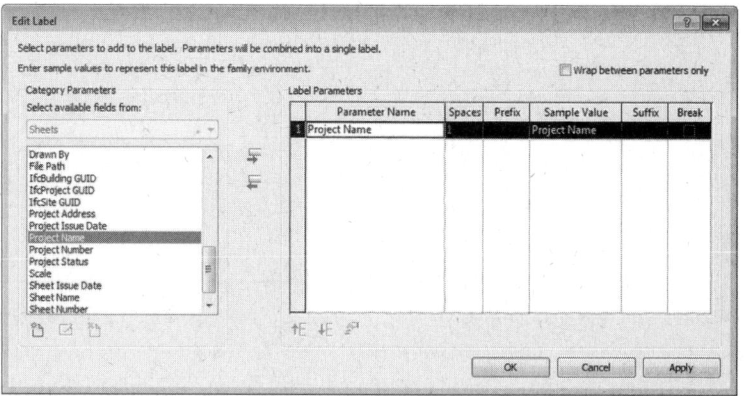

FIGURE 23.3
Adding a parameter to a label

When you exit the Edit Label dialog box, the label is added to the view. You can edit the label in the view in the same way as you would a text object. Clicking the label activates grips for editing the location, rotation, and limits of the label.

If your titleblock requires a label that is not one of the built-in parameters in the list in the Edit Label dialog box, you can click the Add Parameter icon in the lower-left corner of the dialog box. In titleblock families, only shared parameters can be used for custom labels. Click the Select button in the Parameter Properties dialog box to choose a parameter from your shared parameters file. If the parameter does not exist in your file, you can create one. Figure 23.4 shows an example of shared parameters used in titleblock families. See Chapter 6, "Parameters," for more information on creating and using shared parameters.

FIGURE 23.4 Shared parameters sample for a titleblock

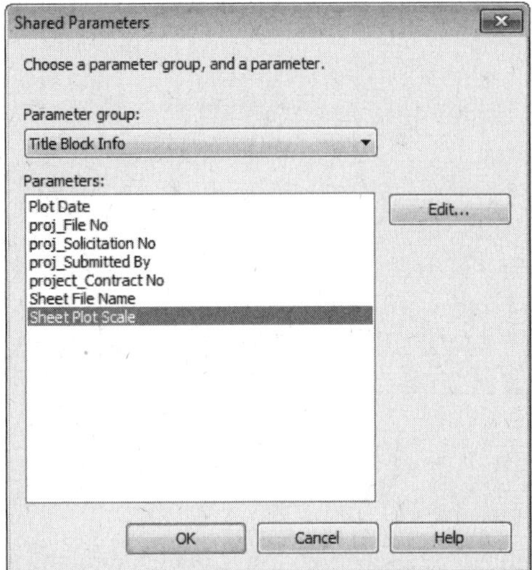

If your titleblock contains an area for a sheet revision schedule, you can create a schedule within the titleblock family that uses the parameters for revisions. On the Family Editor's View tab, you click the Revision Schedule button on the Create panel.

The Revision Properties dialog box looks the same as a regular schedule properties dialog box, with parameters for revisions. The schedule will automatically be populated with parameters, but you can use whichever parameters you choose. You cannot create additional parameters for a revision schedule. Figure 23.5 shows the default settings for a revision schedule.

On the Appearance tab of the Revision Properties dialog box, you can establish whether the schedule is built from the top down or the bottom up. You can also set the schedule height to a specific value to keep it from growing outside of the bounds defined by the titleblock, or you can allow it to have a variable height.

Once you have set the schedule properties, you can insert the schedule into the titleblock graphics by dragging and dropping it from the Project Browser. After placing the schedule in the view, you can select it and choose a rotation option from the Rotation On Sheet drop-down list on the Options Bar. This allows you to orient your revision schedule vertically if necessary.

Take some time to explore the titleblock families that are provided with the software to see how the revision schedule is configured.

FIGURE 23.5
Revision schedule properties

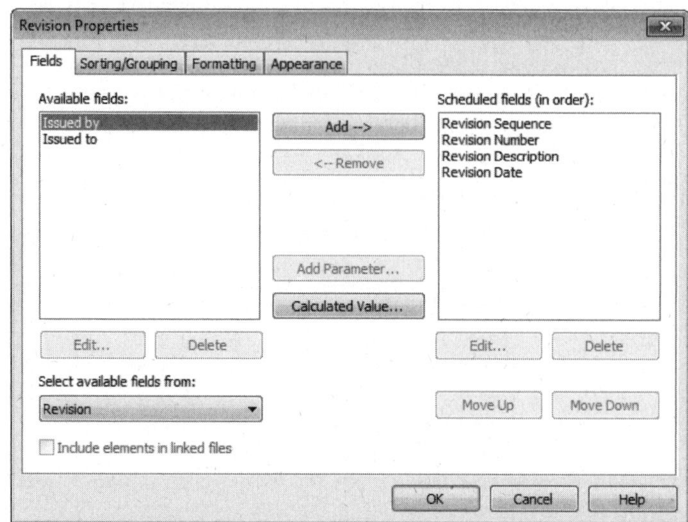

Using Logos and Images

If your titleblock contains a company logo, you can include it in your Revit titleblock family as either an image or linework. Linework used to represent a logo can be made into an annotation family that can be loaded into the titleblock family. This reduces the number of lines in the titleblock family, because many logos tend to contain numerous small lines. This also allows you to make changes to the logo without having to edit the titleblock family, except to reload the logo.

If you have an image file for your logo, you can load it into the titleblock family by clicking the Image button on the Insert tab in the Family Editor. You can resize the image to fit the titleblock graphics as necessary. Test the quality of the logo image by printing a sample sheet to ensure that the image used provides the expected results.

It may be best to have whoever is responsible for generating your company logo create one specifically for your Revit titleblocks. The image file should be a high-quality image that is appropriately sized for the titleblock.

MULTIPLE COMPANY LOGOS

Jo works for a company with offices in several cities. Her company titleblock looks the same for each office location, except for the company logo.

Instead of having a separate titleblock family for each office location, she decides to import each location's logo into one titleblock. She quickly discovers that she cannot control the visibility of imported images with parameters.

Her solution is to create a generic annotation family for each office location and import the desired logo into it. Then she loads the generic annotation families into her titleblock family. The visibility of the generic annotation families can be controlled with Yes/No parameters, so she creates a different family type for each office location and a corresponding Yes/No type parameter to display the appropriate logo.

Now when she loads the titleblock family into her projects, she can choose which type to use based on her office location, and the correct logo is displayed.

Working with Sheets in a Project

A Revit project is much more than a virtual 3D model with intelligent objects. All the documents that would be created for a building design in a traditional CAD environment can also be created in a Revit project. The nice thing is that these documents, or *sheets*, are contained in the same file with the model and its views. This allows for coordination directly with the building model and allows you to manage all the construction documents for a project in a single location.

Creating sheets in your Revit projects is a simple process of right-clicking the Sheets heading in the Project Browser and selecting the New Sheet option. You can also use the Sheet button on the Sheet Composition panel of the View tab. The New Sheet dialog box, shown in Figure 23.6, lists any titleblock families that are loaded into your project. You can select which titleblock to use for the sheet and click the OK button. If your titleblock has not been loaded into your project, you can click the Load button to browse for the appropriate titleblock.

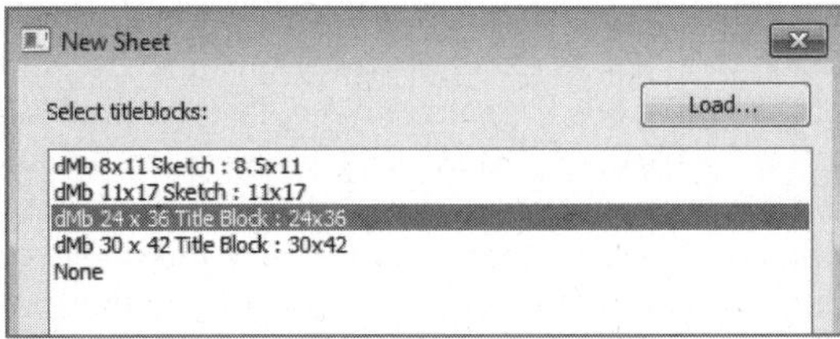

FIGURE 23.6 Titleblock families in the New Sheet dialog box

The bottom half of the dialog box, which is not shown in Figure 23.6, allows you to select any placeholder sheets that you may have created. Creating placeholder sheets is discussed later in this chapter.

> **AVAILABLE TITLEBLOCKS**
>
> It is a good idea to have your titleblock family loaded into your project template so that it is immediately available when sheets are created. If you have several titleblock families for various project types or clients, you can load them into your project template, and when sheets are created, the appropriate one can be selected. Be sure to delete the unused titleblock families from a project after the titleblock style has been established to avoid accidental misuse of an incorrect titleblock during sheet setup. Titleblock families are located under Families ➤ Annotation Symbols in the Project Browser.

Once you have chosen a titleblock and clicked OK, the sheet will be created and active in the drawing area. Depending on the parameters you have in your titleblock family and the data you may have already entered into the project, some of the information may already be filled out in the sheet. Revit automatically applies a sheet number to the sheet, starting with A101. When you change the sheet number, the next number in the sequence will be applied to the next sheet. For example, if you give a sheet a number of M-1, the next sheet you create will automatically be numbered M-2.

You can change the values of the labels in the titleblock either by selecting the titleblock and editing them in the drawing area or by selecting the titleblock and changing the parameter values in the Properties palette. As with all parameters, if the label turns red when selected, that means it is a type parameter and must be edited in the type properties of the selected object. Some of the labels may be properties of the project information and may not appear in the properties of the sheet. Edits to Project Information parameters are applied to all sheets where labels are reporting the information. You can access the Project Information parameters by clicking the Project Information button on the Manage tab.

As you give your sheets names and numbers, they begin to appear in the Project Browser based on your sheet organization settings.

Organizing Project Browser Sheets

You can organize the sheets that you create in your projects in the Project Browser for easy access and coordination. Right-click the Sheets heading in the Project Browser, and select Browser Organization to establish the organizational structure for sheets in your project. The Browser Organization dialog box appears and displays the Sheets tab, as shown in Figure 23.7. A few preset options can be used, or you can create new types for custom organization.

To create a new type of organization, click the New button on the right side of the dialog box. Give the organization type a name that describes how the sheets will be organized. This opens the Browser Organization Properties dialog box, similar to the one that appears for organizing views. The first tab allows you to apply a filter rule to the sheet organization. You can filter by parameters that apply to sheets. On the Grouping And Sorting tab, your sheets can be grouped by parameters that apply to sheets, as shown in the example in Figure 23.8. You can apply up to six levels of grouping to organize your sheets.

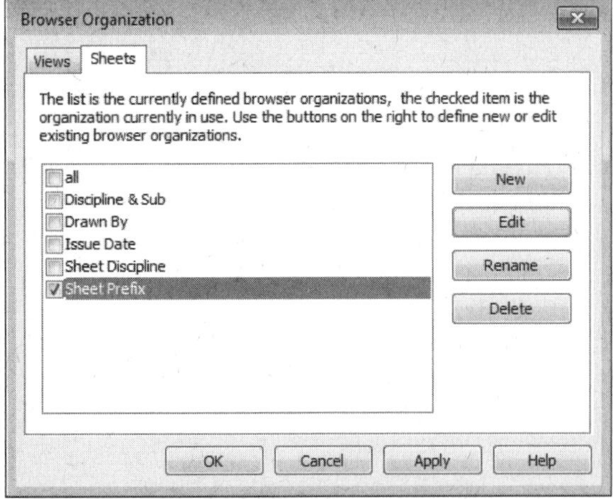

FIGURE 23.7 Preset types for browser organization of sheets

Once you have chosen a parameter for grouping, you can specify the use of all the characters or a specific number for display in the Project Browser. Figure 23.9 shows how sheets appear in the Project Browser based on the settings for organizing by sheet number using one leading character. The sheet groups are listed alphabetically by default.

You can add other parameters to sheets so that they can be listed in the Project Browser as desired. Figure 23.10 shows that a project parameter called Sheet Discipline has been created to organize the order of sheets in the Project Browser.

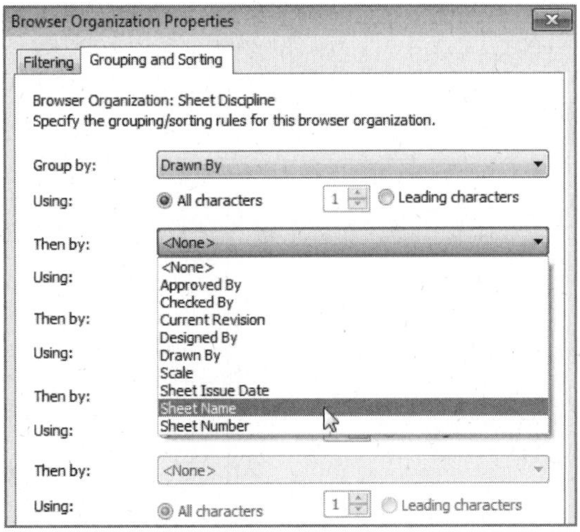

FIGURE 23.8 Parameters available for sheet organization

Additional levels of grouping are useful when you have a large number of sheets. Figure 23.11 shows a parameter called Sub-Discipline being used as a secondary level of organization. This makes it easier to find specific sheets after the sheet list becomes very large. Only one of the sub-disciplines has been expanded in the Project Browser for image clarity.

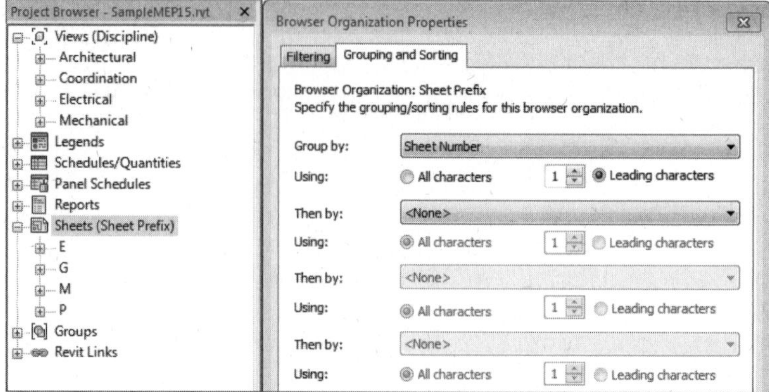

FIGURE 23.9 Sample sheet organization by sheet number

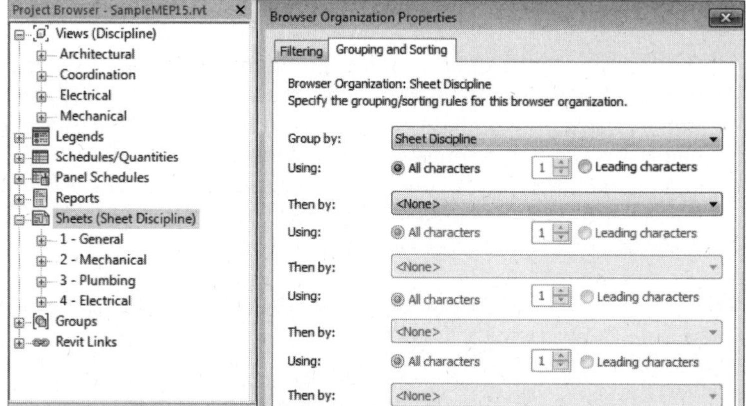

FIGURE 23.10 Custom parameter used for sheet organization

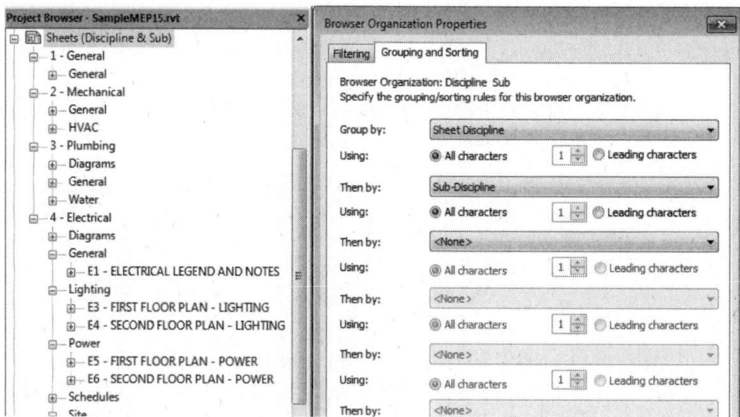

FIGURE 23.11 Parameter used for two levels of sheet organization

You can search the list of sheets for specific words by right-clicking the Sheets heading in the Project Browser and selecting the Search option. This feature can be useful for locating specific sheets or sheet types in a large project. The search results will even be applied to the names of views that are located on sheets.

Placing Views on Sheets

In a Revit project, the model is developed to prove the design and constructability of the building, and views are created to display the model in a way that communicates the design. Annotations, dimensions, and detail lines are added to views to enhance them further so that the design intent is clear. These views eventually need to be put onto construction documents for official submittal of the project. You can place views onto sheets by simply dragging them from the Project Browser onto a sheet that is open in the drawing area and clicking to place them. You can even drag and drop a view onto a sheet name in the Project Browser. This opens the sheet for placement of the view.

A *guide grid,* which is a set of lines that appear overlaid on a sheet, can be used for placing a view in a specific location on a sheet. Whether or not a sheet contains a guide grid is determined by the sheet properties. You can choose the grid style by using the Guide Grid parameter of the sheet properties, as shown in Figure 23.12.

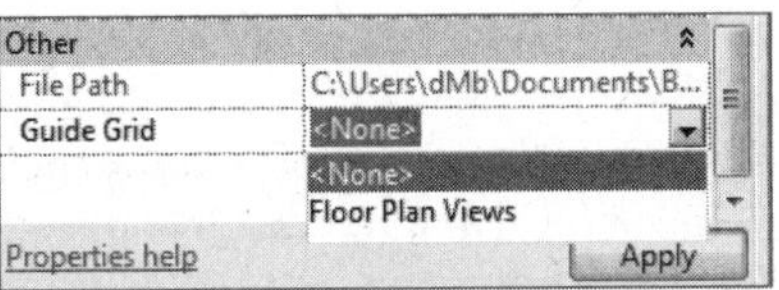

FIGURE 23.12 Guide Grid parameter

To establish the settings for a guide grid, you must have a sheet open in the drawing area. When you click the Guide Grid button on the Sheet Composition panel of the View tab, you are prompted to give the grid style a name. Consider using names based on the types of views placed onto the sheets or based on a unique feature of the building, such as its shape, that determines what portion of the building is shown when dependent views are used.

A standard grid of blue lines appears over the sheet after you have given it a name. The size of the default grid is determined by the extents of your titleblock. You can select the grid by clicking one of the lines at the outer edge. This activates grips that allow you to size the grid manually, as shown in Figure 23.13. You can move the entire grid by selecting the grid, placing your cursor over an outer edge line, and dragging it. If you move a guide grid, its location changes on any of the sheets in which it is used. You can also use the Move tool for more accurate movement of the grid. You may want to consider pinning your guide grids in place once you have established their location and settings.

When you select a guide grid, you can modify the spacing of the lines by accessing its properties. The Guide Spacing parameter, shown in Figure 23.14, enables you to set the distance between both the vertical and horizontal lines of the grid.

Unfortunately, you cannot snap or align to the grid lines when establishing the grid's location on the sheet, and the grid does not snap to the graphics of your titleblock. However, you can zoom in very close and drag the edges to the desired locations. There really should be no need to move the entire grid. Establish the spacing first, and if the grid must be moved, use the Move tool for accuracy. The key is that after you establish a grid style, it appears in the same location on each sheet to which you apply it. You can apply only one Guide Grid style to a sheet at a time.

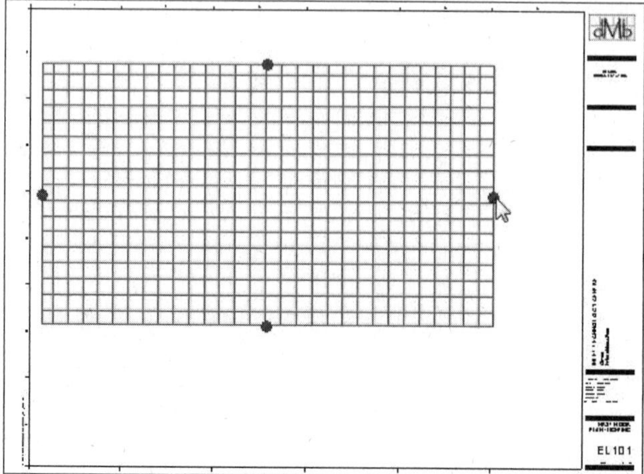

FIGURE 23.13 Grips for editing the size of a guide grid

When you drag a view from the Project Browser onto a sheet, you click to place it on the sheet. It does not snap to the guide grid at this time. You can then select the view and use the Move tool to align it to the grid by selecting a point on a datum object such as a column grid line, reference line, reference plane, or level and moving it to one of the guide grid lines. The view snaps to the guide grid line when a point on a datum object is selected.

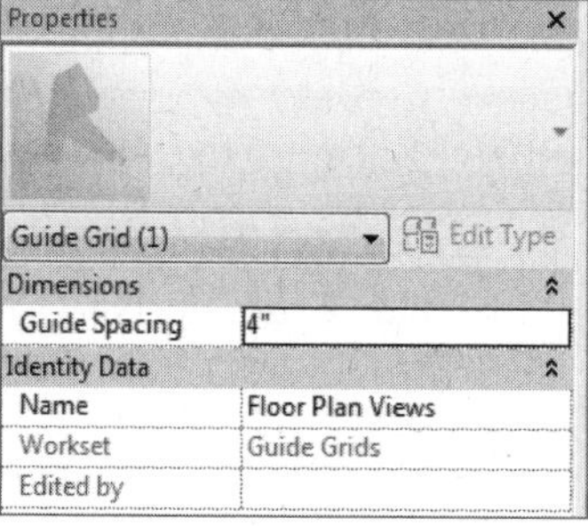

FIGURE 23.14 Guide Spacing parameter

DATUM OBJECTS

Datum objects are annotation objects that can help determine the size and shape of the building and can be associated with model elements. Grid lines, reference planes, and levels are datum elements. If you are linking in architectural and structural models and using their grid lines or levels, you cannot snap them to your guide grid lines. You must have datum elements in your view to align to the guide grid.

Figure 23.15 shows how a view would be moved from a point on a column grid line in order to line up with a guide grid line.

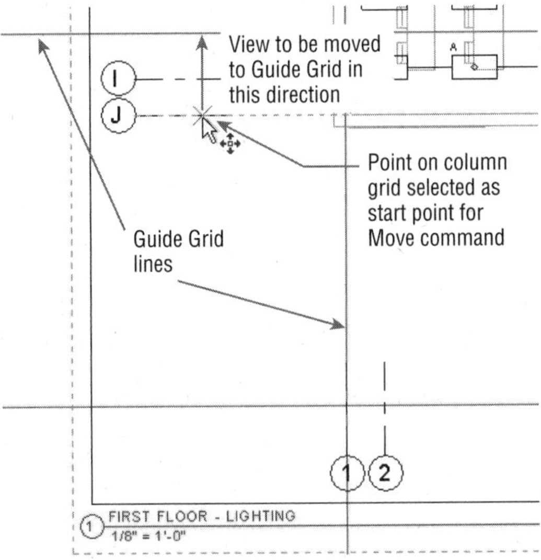

FIGURE 23.15
Moving a view to a guide grid line

Guide grid lines do not print when they are visible in a sheet. You can control their visibility either by using the parameter in the sheet properties or by turning off the category in the Visibility/Graphic Overrides settings for the sheet. The Guide Grids category is located on the Annotations tab of the Visibility/Graphic Overrides dialog box.

When you place a view onto a sheet, you have the option to rotate it by selecting a rotation direction from the drop-down that appears on the Options Bar during placement, as shown in Figure 23.16. You can change the rotation of a view after the view has been placed by using the same drop-down.

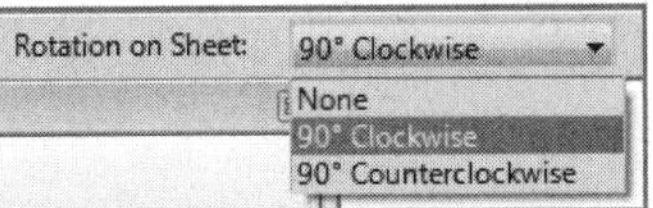

FIGURE 23.16
View rotation options

This does not allow you to continue rotating the view in the chosen direction. The settings on the drop-down are in relation to the normal orientation of the view. Thus, you can display the view normally, rotated 90 degrees clockwise, or rotated 90 degrees counterclockwise.

Working with Viewports

Rotating a view causes the view title to be rotated as well. The style of a view title is determined by the viewport type. Viewport types can be created so that the same kind of views are represented with different title styles. For example, an enlarged plan is a floor plan view, but you may want to use a callout bubble for the location of the view, whereas a normal floor plan does not require a callout bubble. Drafting views of details do not need a title if the detail title is included in the detail itself, so a viewport type without a title would be used.

When you select a viewport on a sheet, the properties that appear in the Properties palette are for the view. Clicking the Edit Type button displays the type properties for the viewport, shown in Figure 23.17.

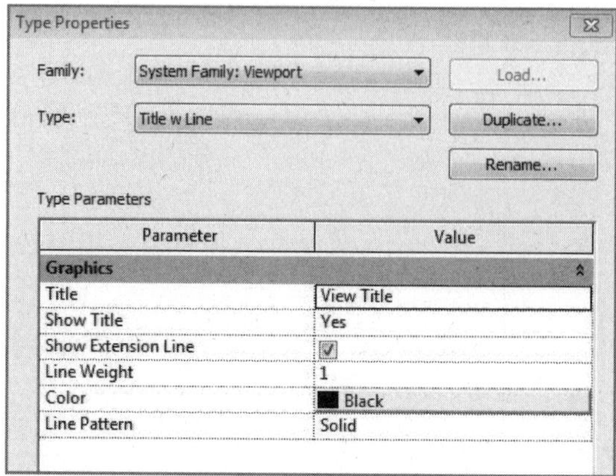

FIGURE 23.17
Type properties of a viewport

You use the Title parameter to define the annotation family used for the viewport title. Different view title families can be loaded into your projects for different viewport types. The Show Title parameter can be used to create a viewport type without a title for views that do not require one. In those cases, the sheet name is usually sufficient to describe what is visible on the sheet, so a view title is a bit redundant. Another choice is to show the title only when a sheet has multiple viewports.

TITLE FAMILIES

You can create view title families with any of the graphics you require for a view title. You do not need to include the title line in the family because it is generated by placement of the view. Labels used in a view title family can reference parameters for sheets, but you cannot create custom parameters. You should adjust the limits of the label text to allow for long titles, unless you intend for the title text to wrap, forming a multiline title. It may be necessary to create multiple family types for titles that need to wrap.

To change the location of a viewport title on a sheet, you can click the title line and drag the title to the desired location. To change the length of the title line, you must select the viewport. This activates grips at the ends of the title line that can be dragged to change the line length.

By default, the title of a viewport is the same as the name of the view in the Project Browser. Project views have a parameter called Title On Sheet that enables you to use a title that is different from the view name. This helps you keep your views organized as desired in the Project Browser while using the desired titles for views on your sheets, as shown in Figure 23.18.

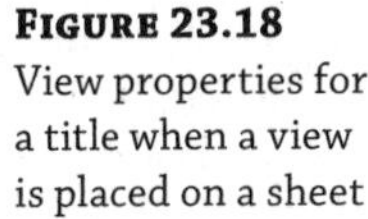

FIGURE 23.18
View properties for a title when a view is placed on a sheet

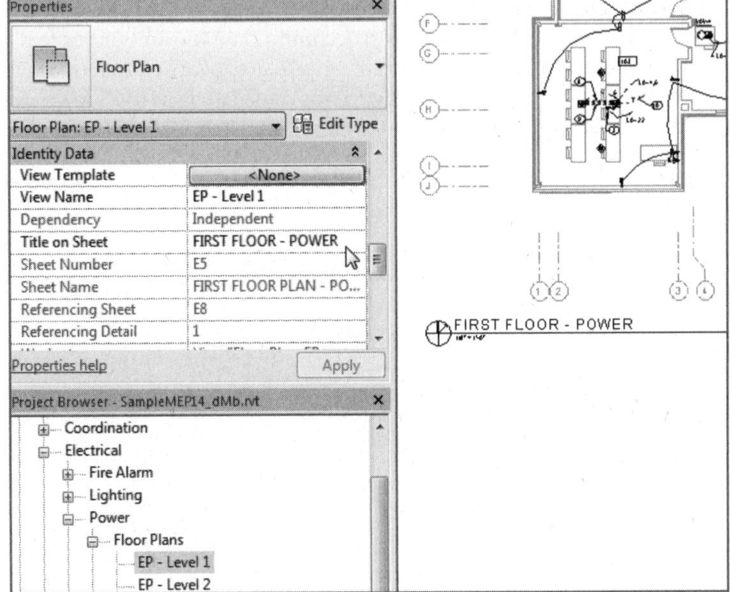

Adding Annotations

Annotation objects can be added directly to sheet views. You can place items such as north arrows, graphic scales, and other symbols directly on sheets in conjunction with viewports, title lines, or titleblock graphics. To place these items onto sheets, you use the Symbol button on the Annotate tab. Annotation objects on a sheet snap to titleblock geometry, but you cannot snap to title lines or schedule graphics other than the outline of a schedule. If you have an annotation, such as a north arrow symbol, that needs to be part of your view titles, it can be nested into your view title annotation family.

You can also add text directly to a sheet by using the Text tool on the Annotate tab. Plan notes or general notes can be typed directly on a sheet, or if you have a set of notes that is used on every project, you may want to put those notes in a drafting view so that they can be saved as a separate file or included in your project template. Another option is to put the notes in a legend view, which allows you to place the same notes on more than one sheet.

> **VIEWS ON MULTIPLE SHEETS**
>
> Plan, section, and elevation views can be placed on only one sheet. This is also true for drafting and detail views. Schedules and legend views can be placed on multiple sheets.

Placing Schedules

Schedules are placed on sheets in the same way as views, by dragging and dropping them from the Project Browser. When you place a schedule onto a sheet, it may not look the same as it does when the schedule view is open in the drawing area. The columns of a schedule can be resized on a sheet by using the triangular grips that appear at the top of each column-separation line. The height of each row adjusts to accommodate the amount of text within a cell when the column width is modified. The small grip that appears at the right side of a schedule allows you to split the schedule if it is too long to fit on a sheet. Figure 23.19 shows that when you split a schedule, the headings are applied to each section.

FIGURE 23.19
Splitting a schedule

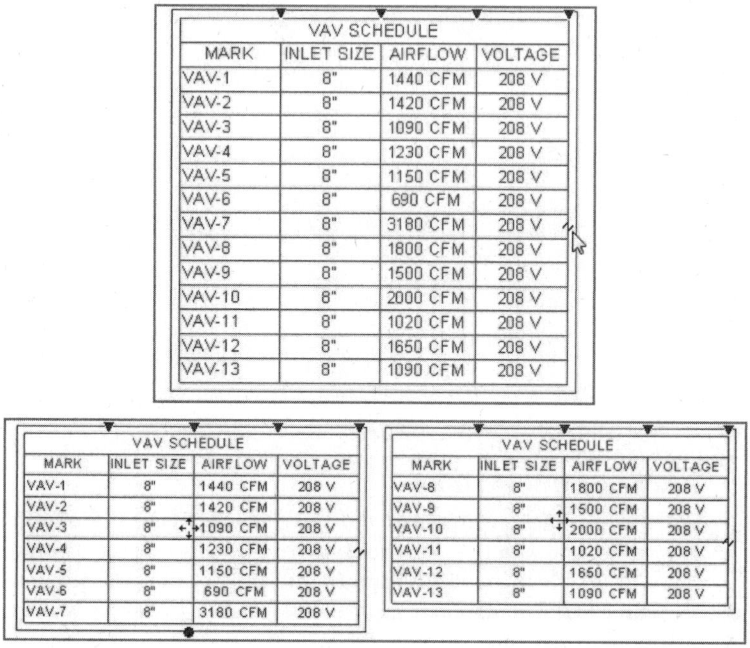

VAV SCHEDULE			
MARK	INLET SIZE	AIRFLOW	VOLTAGE
VAV-1	8"	1440 CFM	208 V
VAV-2	8"	1420 CFM	208 V
VAV-3	8"	1090 CFM	208 V
VAV-4	8"	1230 CFM	208 V
VAV-5	8"	1150 CFM	208 V
VAV-6	8"	690 CFM	208 V
VAV-7	8"	3180 CFM	208 V
VAV-8	8"	1800 CFM	208 V
VAV-9	8"	1500 CFM	208 V
VAV-10	8"	2000 CFM	208 V
VAV-11	8"	1020 CFM	208 V
VAV-12	8"	1650 CFM	208 V
VAV-13	8"	1090 CFM	208 V

VAV SCHEDULE			
MARK	INLET SIZE	AIRFLOW	VOLTAGE
VAV-1	8"	1440 CFM	208 V
VAV-2	8"	1420 CFM	208 V
VAV-3	8"	1090 CFM	208 V
VAV-4	8"	1230 CFM	208 V
VAV-5	8"	1150 CFM	208 V
VAV-6	8"	690 CFM	208 V
VAV-7	8"	3180 CFM	208 V

VAV SCHEDULE			
MARK	INLET SIZE	AIRFLOW	VOLTAGE
VAV-8	8"	1800 CFM	208 V
VAV-9	8"	1500 CFM	208 V
VAV-10	8"	2000 CFM	208 V
VAV-11	8"	1020 CFM	208 V
VAV-12	8"	1650 CFM	208 V
VAV-13	8"	1090 CFM	208 V

A schedule can be split multiple times if necessary. The dot grip at the bottom of the first section of the schedule can be dragged up or down to control at which row the split occurs. To put a split schedule back together, click and drag one of the blue arrow grips that appears in the center of a section onto another section of the schedule.

Schedules can be snapped to guide grid lines on a sheet by using the Move tool and snapping to the outline graphics of the schedule as the starting point. This can be useful for schedules that appear on multiple sheets, such as a Room schedule.

Using Sheet Lists

A *sheet list* is a special kind of schedule that can be used to display project sheet information on a title sheet or anywhere within your project. You create sheet lists in the same way as other schedules, and the parameters that are available apply to sheet views. You can also use a sheet list to keep track of the information that is required on your sheets.

When you begin a project, you can create a sheet list and input projected sheets to estimate the contents of your construction document set. This is done by creating placeholder sheets in the sheet list. A placeholder sheet can be created by adding a new row to a sheet list schedule. With the sheet list open in the drawing area, click the Insert button on the Rows panel and select

Data Row to add a row. If you have a filter applied to your sheet list, the new rows may not appear if they do not meet the filter requirements. Creating a "working" sheet list that shows all sheets and information is a useful tool for sheet management. Another sheet list can be created to be placed on a title sheet for your construction documents.

The new row added to your sheet list has a sheet number that is the next in sequence with the last sheet that was created. Adding a row to the schedule does not create an actual sheet view, so the placeholder sheet does not appear in the Project Browser. Any of the parameters used in your sheet list can be given values for the placeholder sheet.

When the time comes to create the actual sheet that the placeholder represents, you can choose the placeholder sheet from the New Sheet dialog box, as shown in Figure 23.20. You must also choose a titleblock option for the sheet to be created.

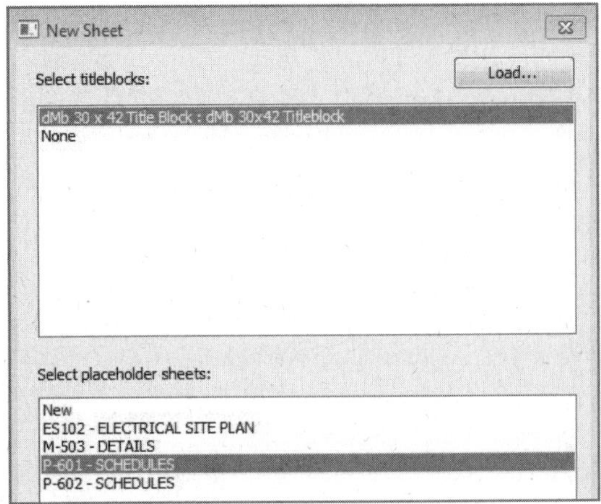

FIGURE 23.20 Choosing placeholder sheets in the New Sheet dialog box

When you have chosen the titleblock and placeholder sheet, clicking OK in the New Sheet dialog box creates the sheet. All the information that was entered into the sheet list for the placeholder sheet populates the appropriate labels in the titleblock of the sheet. The sheet now also appears in the Project Browser.

Using placeholder sheets is a good way to keep track of consultant sheets that are not part of your project file. For example, if you are working with a civil engineering consultant who is not creating a Revit file, you can represent their drawings with placeholder sheets in your project to keep an accurate sheet count and sheet list.

Being able to create your project documents directly in the file that contains your model is one of the benefits of using Revit MEP 2015. Now that you have learned some of the skills required to create sheets, practice by completing the following exercise:

1. Open the `Ch23_Project.rvt` file found at `www.sybex.com/go/masteringrevitmep2015`.
2. Right-click Sheets in the Project Browser. Select the New Sheet option.
3. Choose the D 22 × 34 Horizontal titleblock in the New Sheet dialog box and click OK.
4. Select the titleblock in the drawing area, and in the Properties palette, change Sheet Name to **FIRST FLOOR PLAN – HVAC**. Change Sheet Number to **M-101**. Click the Apply button in the Properties palette. Notice that the titleblock information is updated.

5. Right-click Sheets in the Project Browser, and select the New Sheet option. Choose the D 22 × 34 Horizontal titleblock and click OK.
6. Repeat step 4, naming the sheet **SECOND FLOOR PLAN – HVAC**. Notice that the sheet name you entered in step 4 is available in the drop-down of the parameter. Each time you type in a name, it is stored in this list. You can pick a name from the list and modify it as needed for a new sheet. This helps keep names consistent and avoids typing errors. You do not have to edit the Sheet Number option because it was created automatically in sequence with the previous sheet.
7. Open the M-101 sheet again. Click the Guide Grid button on the Sheet Composition panel of the View tab. Name the guide grid **Floor Plans** and click OK.
8. Select the guide grid by clicking one of its outer edges. In the Properties palette, change the Guide Spacing parameter value to **4″**.
9. In the Project Browser, drag the 1 – Mech floor plan view to the drawing area. Click to place the view anywhere on the sheet.
10. Select the view, and click the Move button on the Modify | Viewports contextual tab. Click the horizontal C grid line to start the move, and click the first horizontal guide grid line near the bottom of the titleblock. Click the Move button again, and select a point on vertical grid line 1 to start the move. Click the first vertical guide grid line at the left of the titleblock within the bounds of the titleblock. Be sure to move horizontally so that the C grid line stays aligned with its guide grid line, as shown in Figure 23.21. (Note that you can also snap to the intersection of a datum element and the Guide Grid.)

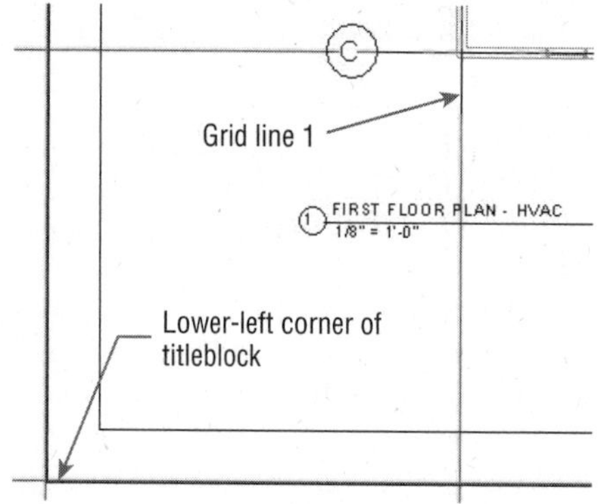

FIGURE 23.21 Alignment of grid lines to the guide grid

11. Open the M-102 sheet, and drag the 2 – Mech floor plan view onto the sheet. Click the Guide Grid button on the View tab, choose the existing Floor Plans guide grid, and click OK, as shown in Figure 23.22. Repeat step 10 to align the view to the guide grid.
12. Open the Sheet List schedule by double-clicking it in the Project Browser. Click the Insert button on the Rows panel of the ribbon and select the Data Row option. In the schedule, change Sheet Number to **M-501** and Sheet Name to **SECTIONS AND DETAILS** for the new row.

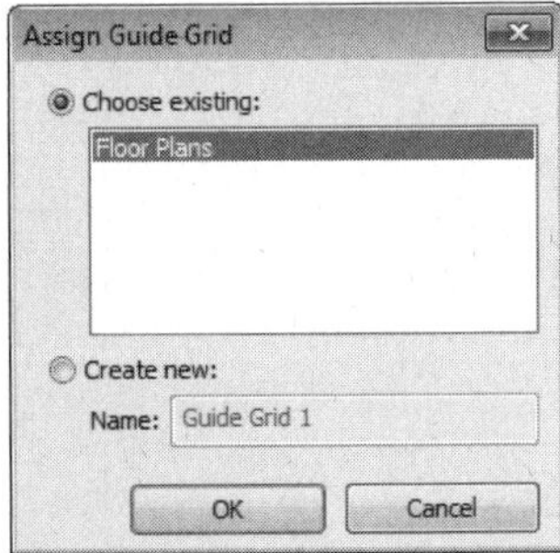

FIGURE 23.22
Assign Guide Grid dialog box

13. Right-click Sheets in the Project Browser and select the New Sheet option. In the New Sheet dialog box, select the M-501 SECTIONS AND DETAILS placeholder sheet and click OK.
14. Drag the Section 1 view from the Project Browser onto the sheet. Drag the DUCT DETAILS drafting view onto the sheet from the Project Browser.
15. Select the detail view on the sheet. In the Properties palette, click the Edit Type button. In the Type Properties dialog box for the Viewport family, click the Duplicate button. Name the new family type **No Title** and click OK. In the Type Properties dialog box, change the Show Title parameter to No, as shown in Figure 23.23. Click OK in the Type Properties dialog box, and confirm that the detail viewport on the sheet has no title or line.

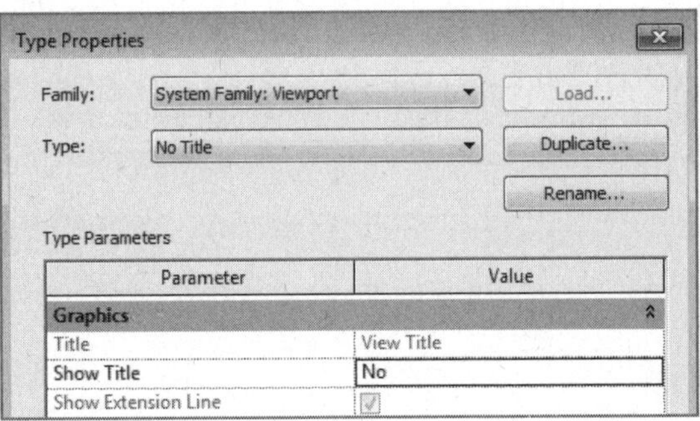

FIGURE 23.23
Viewport properties

16. Right-click Sheets in the Project Browser and select the Browser Organization option. Select the check box next to the Sheet Prefix option. Click the Edit button. On the Grouping And Sorting tab, set the first Group By drop-down list to Sheet Number using one leading character, as shown in Figure 23.24.
17. Click OK to close all dialog boxes. Notice how the sheets are organized in the Project Browser.

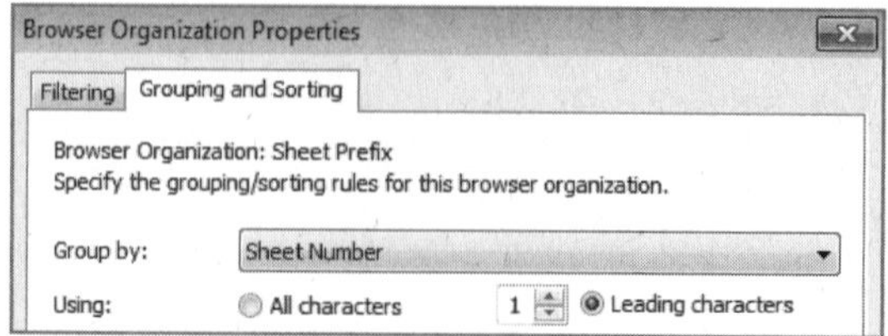

FIGURE 23.24 Browser organization setting

Making Sheet Revisions

Revisions are part of nearly every project. You can keep track of revisions to a Revit project by using a revision schedule in your titleblock families and managing the revisions with Revit.

When you make a change to your model and you want to issue it as a revision, you can draw a revision cloud directly in the view, or the cloud can be drawn on the sheet displaying the view. Either way, you should first establish the properties of the revision. To create a revision in your project, click the Revisions button on the Sheet Composition panel of the View tab, shown in Figure 23.25. This tool can also be found on the Additional Settings button of the Manage tab, under Sheet Issues/Revisions.

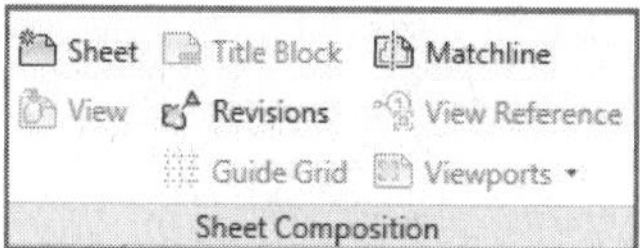

FIGURE 23.25 Sheet Composition ribbon panel

Do not confuse this with the Revision Cloud button on the Annotate tab, which is used to draw the actual cloud graphics. The Revisions button activates the Sheet Issues/Revisions dialog box, where you can define the revision and establish the behavior of the revision schedule and graphics. Figure 23.26 shows the dialog box. Notice the available settings for the numbering, which are Numeric, Alphabetic, or None if you do not want numbered revisions.

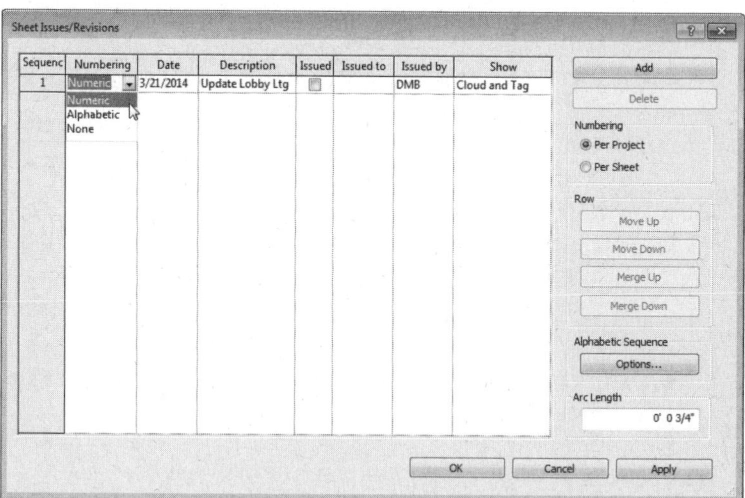

FIGURE 23.26 Sheet Issues/Revisions dialog box

The settings on the right side of the dialog box allow you to number your revisions by sheet or by the entire project. Clicking the Add button in the upper-right corner creates a new revision sequence. The move buttons in the Row section enable you to move a revision up or down the list to change the order in which revisions appear in the schedule. The merge buttons allow you to combine the contents of one revision with another. Once you have created a revision sequence, it cannot be deleted. You must merge it with another revision. The Alphabetic Sequence setting can be defined to eliminate unwanted letters or establish a custom numbering system.

When you use the Per Sheet revision sequence setting, the revisions are listed as they occur on each sheet. So you could, for example, have a revision number 2 in your revision sequence that is the first revision to occur on a sheet. Therefore, it will be listed as number 1 in the revision schedule on the sheet and in its tag.

If you use the Per Project revision sequence setting, you can have a revision number 2 in your sequence, and if it is the only revision on a sheet, it will show up as number 2 in the schedule and its tag.

New to Revit 2015 is the Arc Length setting, which allows you to define the size of the arcs used to draw your revision clouds. The value you use for this setting will apply to all revision clouds, including those that have already been drawn. Use caution because this may affect existing revision clouds in an undesirable manner.

With the settings established for a revision, you can use the Revision Cloud button on the Detail panel of the Annotate tab to draw a cloud around the modified area. When you click the Revision Cloud button, it activates the Modify | Create Revision Cloud Sketch contextual tab. The Draw panel is available on this contextual tab and allows you to choose from various drafting tools to sketch a revision cloud. Press the spacebar to flip the orientation of the cloud bubble when drawing clouds. Be sure to select the green check mark on the Mode panel to finish creating the revision cloud and exit sketch mode. The properties of the cloud can be used to determine the revision sequence of which the cloud is a part. Figure 23.27 shows a revision cloud that was drawn in a floor plan view and the resulting revision schedule on the sheet where the view resides. Notice that the cloud has been tagged using a revision tag that reports the revision number.

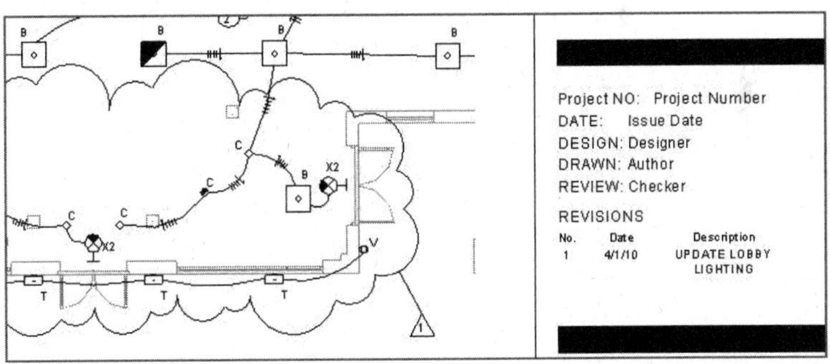

FIGURE 23.27
Revision cloud in a view

You can use the Issued parameter in the Sheet Issues/Revisions dialog box to establish that a revision has been issued. When a revision sequence has been marked as issued, you cannot add revision clouds to it. Sorting your revision schedule by sequence is a good way to organize your revisions. This allows you to use a custom numbering system without having to sort by it.

The visibility of revision clouds and their tags can be controlled via the Visibility/Graphic Overrides dialog box. Their categories are located on the Annotation Categories tab of the dialog box.

If you want to show a revision in the schedule of a sheet but that sheet does not contain a view with the revision, or the revision is not drawn on that sheet, you can do so by using the Revisions On Sheet parameter found in the Instance properties of the sheet. Click the Edit button and choose which revisions are to be shown in the revision schedule.

Printing Sheets

Although Revit 2015 has many features that allow you to visually verify the coordination of your design and documents, printing is still a necessary part of a Revit project workflow. There are so many types of printers and print drivers that it would be difficult, if not impossible, to describe print settings that would work for everyone on every project. The best thing that you can do to make your printing tasks easier and more efficient is to take a sample project and experiment with different print settings until the desired results are achieved.

Any of the views in your project can be printed, except for schedules. A schedule would have to be placed on a sheet so that the sheet could be printed. Schedules can be exported to TXT files for use in and for printing by other software.

Printing options are located on the application menu, and clicking Print activates the Print dialog box shown in Figure 23.28. This dialog box allows you to establish the printer to be used, define the name and location when printing to a file, and define which views or sheets are to be printed.

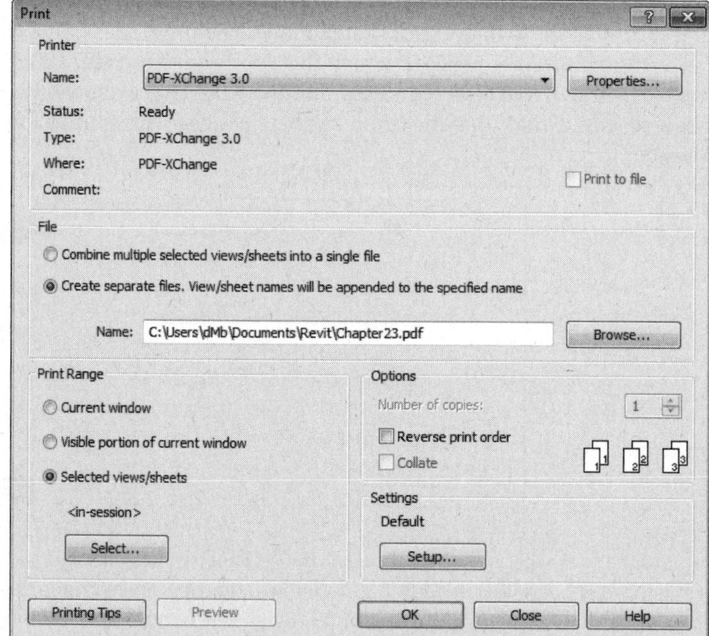

FIGURE 23.28
Print dialog box

Clicking the Setup button located in the Settings section activates the Print Setup dialog box shown in Figure 23.29, which can also be accessed via the application menu. This dialog box contains settings for how the print appears on the paper or in the file.

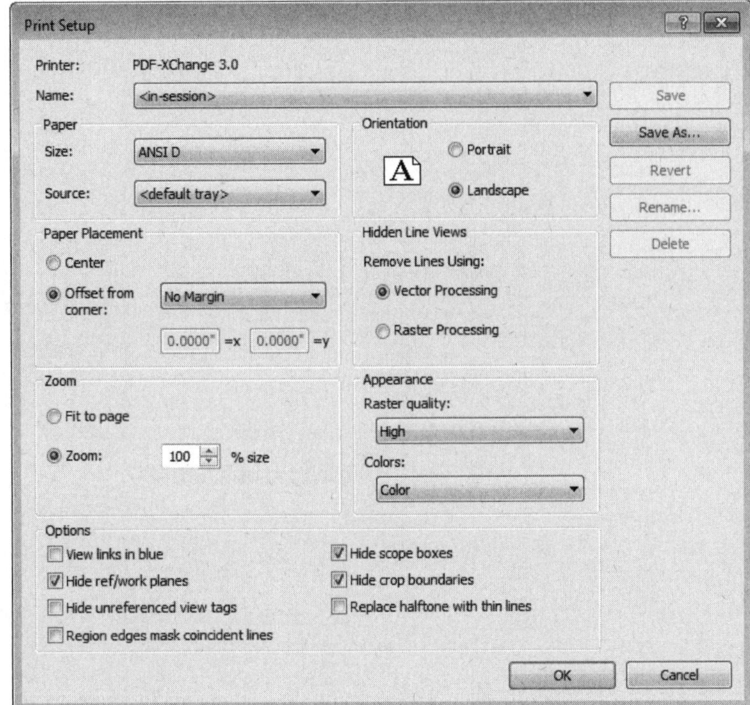

FIGURE 23.29
Print Setup dialog box

The Name drop-down list at the top is for saved print setups. Once you have established the settings that produce the desired print quality, you can save the setup for future use by clicking the Save button in the upper-right corner.

Vector or raster processing can be used for views set to Hidden Line. You may get varying degrees of quality depending on your printer drivers, so it is best to experiment with each option to determine the best one. For the Raster Processing option, you can choose the quality in the drop-down list in the Appearance section. The Colors drop-down in this section allows you to choose an option for color prints or black lines. The Grayscale option in this drop-down converts any color lines to their grayscale equivalent when printing to a black-and-white printer.

In the Options section at the bottom of the dialog box, you can hide certain types of objects, such as reference planes and view crop regions. There are also settings to hide section, callout, or elevation marks that reference views that are not placed on a sheet. This is useful because it eliminates the need to hide those objects individually in the views prior to printing. The option to replace any halftone lines with thin ones is a useful setting if your printer driver causes halftone lines to be too faint when printed.

With the settings established, clicking OK returns you to the Print dialog box (if that is where you accessed the Print Setup dialog box), where you can determine what is to be printed. In the

Print Range section, you can choose to print what is currently visible in the drawing area or the currently open view, or you can select views and sheets to be printed. Clicking the Select button in this area activates the View/Sheet Set dialog box, which lists all the printable views and sheets, as shown in Figure 23.30.

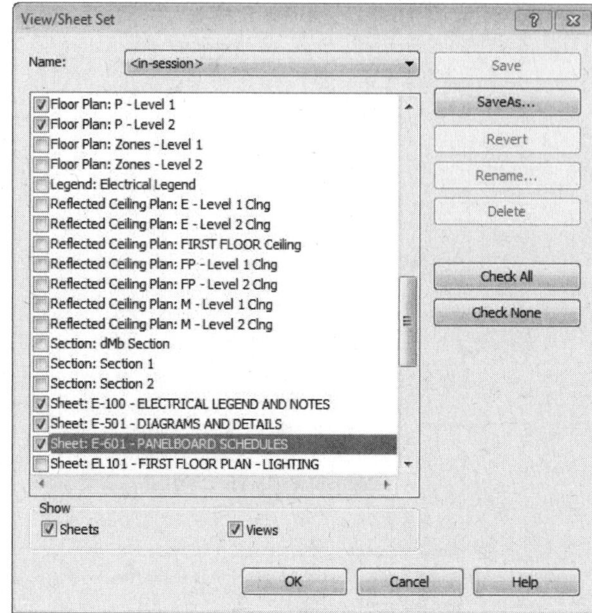

FIGURE 23.30
View/Sheet Set dialog box for printing

In this dialog box, you can select the desired sheets or views to be printed. You can filter the list of available views and sheets to show only views or only sheets by using the check boxes at the bottom of the dialog box. Once you have chosen a set of views or sheets, you can save the selection set for future use. The Name drop-down at the top of the dialog box lists all the saved selection sets.

Exporting Sheets

You can export your sheets to CAD or DWF format as an alternative to printing directly from Revit or to collaborate with clients and consultants who may not have the ability to view Revit files. You can find the Export options on the application menu. There are many options for export, but for sharing sheets, the two that we will focus on are exporting to CAD and exporting to DWF. Selecting CAD Formats from the Export options and choosing a file format activates the Export CAD Formats – Views/Settings dialog box. Figure 23.31 shows this dialog box for the DWG file format.

EXPORT SETTINGS

It is important to establish the settings for exporting to CAD formats so that your files will be accurate when translated to the chosen CAD file format. See Chapter 2, "Creating an Effective Project Template," for more information on establishing settings for exporting to CAD.

The Select Export Setup drop-down list at the top of the dialog box allows you to choose the export settings that you have established and saved.

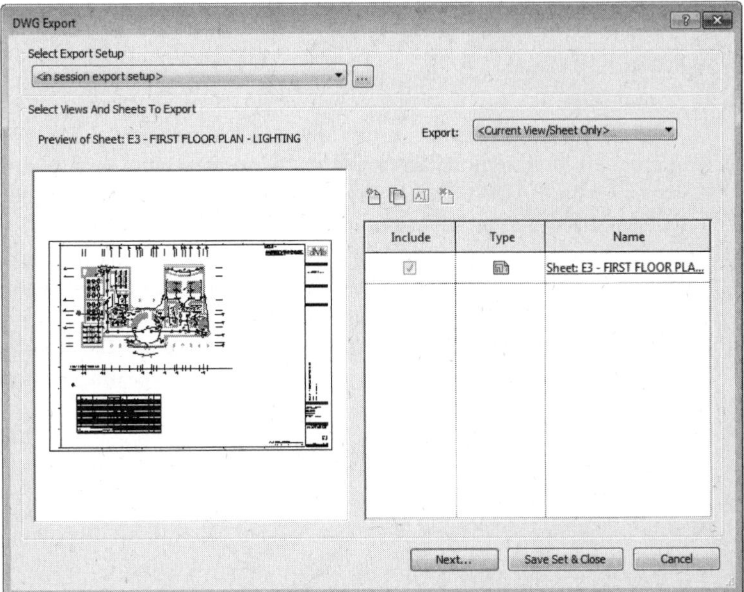

FIGURE 23.31
DWG Export dialog box

The preview area of the dialog box shows the current view open in the drawing area. The right side of the dialog box is for establishing which sheets or views are to be exported. You can create a set of views and/or sheets by clicking the New Set icon. Once you give the set a name, all the printable views and sheets appear in the list. The drop-down at the top of the right side, shown in Figure 23.32, enables you to filter the list for specific types of views or sheets.

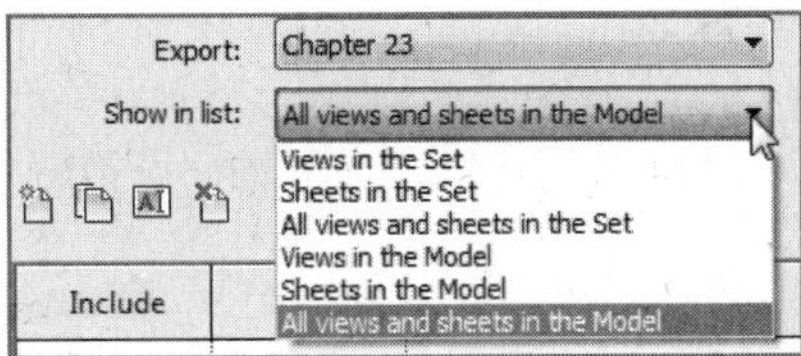

FIGURE 23.32
Export filter list

You can use the check boxes in the Include column of the list to determine which sheets or views will be exported. Once the list is established, you can click the Save Set & Close button so that the next time you access the dialog box, it returns to the saved settings.

Once you have established the settings for export, clicking the Next button allows you to browse to the location for the exported CAD file(s). The check box at the bottom of the window creates separate DWG files for each view that is on a sheet when you're exporting Revit sheets. You can specify a prefix to the names of the files and also the file type, as shown in Figure 23.33.

FIGURE 23.33
Export file naming options

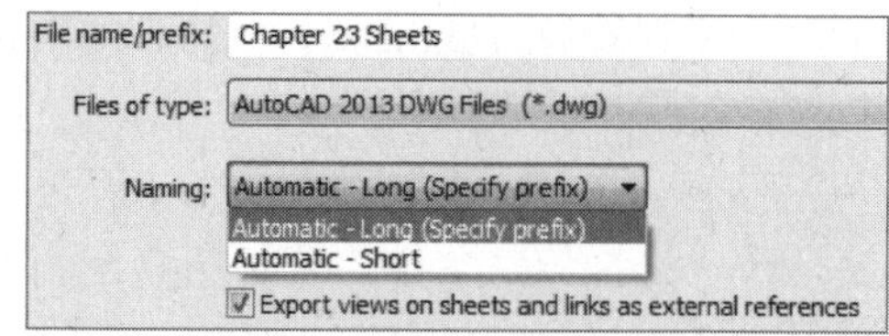

The option to export sheets or views to DWF works in the same way as exporting to CAD, except additional options are available because of the capabilities of a DWF file to report element properties. In the DWF Export Settings dialog box, the DWF Properties tab allows you to export the properties of your Revit model elements and to access print settings prior to export. The Project Information tab gives you direct access to the project information contained in your Revit project. You can edit the parameters in this dialog box to update any project information, such as issue date, prior to export.

When you click the Next button, you can browse to a location for the DWF file. There is an option in the browse window to combine all the views and/or sheets to be exported into a single DWF file.

If you are sharing your sheets or views with someone who is unable to open a DWF file, you can export to DWFx format, which can be viewed by using the free XPS Viewer, available for download from Microsoft. The viewer is not able to view files containing 3D graphics, so it should be used only for 2D files.

The Bottom Line

Create a titleblock. A titleblock can be the signature for your projects. Its design and layout can be an immediate indicator of who has created the construction documents. A titleblock is also important for conveying general project and specific sheet information.

Master It To ensure that your Revit projects look the same as, or similar to, your other projects, it is necessary to have a titleblock family that looks the same as other file format titleblocks you use. Describe the process for creating a Revit titleblock family from an existing CAD format titleblock.

Establish sheets in your project. The sheets that make up your construction documents can be organized in your Revit projects for easy access and for management of project information.

Master It A Sheet List schedule is a useful tool for managing the information shown on your construction documents as well as for organizing the order of sheets for your project. Is it possible to create parameters for sheets that can be used in the sheet list? Explain.

Place views on sheets. For a Revit project, the construction documents are created as a result of the model, whereas in traditional CAD environments, the sheets are the main focus. You can put your construction documents together by placing the views you have created onto your sheets.

Master It Uniformity among sheets in a document set is important not only to the look of a project but also for ease in document navigation. Explain how guide grids can be used to place model views in the same location on individual sheets.

Print and export sheets. Although we live in a digital age, the need to print sheets and views is still part of our daily workflow. With the ability to work with consultants from all over the world, the need to share digital information is crucial. Exporting sheets and views to a file format that can be easily shared increases our ability to collaborate with consultants.

Master It Printing sheets is often necessary for quality control of a project. How can you keep section and elevation marks of views that are not used on your sheets from printing?

Appendix

The Bottom Line

Each of The Bottom Line sections in the chapters suggests exercises to deepen skills and understanding. Sometimes there is only one possible solution, but often you are encouraged to use your skills and creativity to create something that builds on what you know and lets you explore one of many possibilities.

Chapter 1: Exploring the User Interface

Navigate the ribbon interface. The ribbon is an efficient user interface style that works well in Revit. The ability to house numerous tools in a single area of the interface allows for maximum screen real estate for the drawing area.

Master It Along with the standard tabs available on the ribbon interface, contextual tabs are available while you're working on a project. Explain what a contextual tab is and how it may differ throughout your workflow.

Solution A contextual tab is an additional tab that appears when an object is selected. It is an extension of the Modify tab that contains tools specific to the editing of the selected object.

Utilize user interface features. Many features are available in the Revit MEP 2015 user interface that allow for quick access to tools and settings. The use of keyboard shortcuts can also improve workflow efficiency.

Master It To enhance workflow efficiency, it is important to know how to access features of the user interface. What tool can be used to activate or remove user interface features?

Solution The User Interface tool on the View tab can be used to turn on or turn off user interface features.

Use settings and menus. Establishing settings for your user interface is another way to create a working environment that is the most efficient and effective for your use of Revit MEP 2015.

Master It The use of keyboard shortcuts has been part of design and drafting software for a long time. The ability to customize the shortcuts to best suit your workflow is key to improved efficiency. How can the settings for keyboard shortcuts be accessed? How can modified keyboard settings be reset?

Solution The Keyboard Shortcuts dialog box can be accessed from the User Interface tab of the Options dialog box, from the User Interface button on the View tab, or by using the KS keyboard shortcut. To reset keyboard shortcuts for Revit MEP 2015 to default settings, delete the file `%APPDATA%\Roaming\Autodesk\Revit\Autodesk Revit 2015\KeyboardShortcuts.xml`.

Chapter 2: Creating an Effective Project Template

Set up views and visibility. The settings for views are crucial to being able to visualize the design and model being created and edited in a project. Establishing the default behavior for views and visibility of objects can increase not only the efficiency of working on a project but also the accuracy of design.

Master It The properties of a view determine how objects and the model will appear in the view. Along with Visibility/Graphics Overrides, what other view property determines whether items are visible in that view? For a floor plan view, describe all components of this property.

Solution The view range determines what elements can be seen in a view based on their elevation. The View Range dialog box consists of Primary Range and View Depth settings. Primary Range is further broken down into Top, Bottom, and Cut Plane.

For a floor plan, Top defines the elevation from which the model is being viewed. Bottom is the extent to which the model is being viewed from the Top setting. In other words, it is how far you are looking. The cut plane is an imaginary line cutting through Architectural and Structural elements at a set elevation. The view depth is used to view items below the Bottom setting; however, these will be set to halftone and cannot be selected or adjusted.

Establish project settings. Many project settings can be established in a Revit template to determine the display of objects in views and on construction documents. There are also settings that define the makeup of the project itself.

Master It Phase settings for a project are very important for defining what portions of a building design occur in certain phases. Explain why having phases established in a template might require a separate template file for phased projects.

Solution When phases are established in a project, it is important to assign a phase to each view so that objects modeled in a view will belong to the phase of the view. If you are creating a template with phases and preset views, you will want to have a view type for each phase. If you use this template for a project that does not require phasing, you will have many unnecessary views already established in your project.

Define preloaded content and its behavior. The more items you have available for immediate use when a project begins, the more your focus can be on design decisions and less on loading required items. In a multiuser environment, preloaded content ensures that improper variations, which can cause inconsistencies in the project documentation, do not occur.

Master It Having system family types defined in your template is just as important as having the appropriate components loaded. Explain why certain component families are required in order to create and define MEP system family types.

Solution To create and define duct, pipe, cable tray, and conduit system family types, you need fitting component families loaded. The system families cannot be modeled without their fittings defined.

Create sheet standards. As with other template elements, standards for sheets are a useful component to have established.

Master It Having a predefined organization for drawing sheets in your template will ensure consistency from one project to the next. True or false: You must have all the required sheets for any project built into your template in order for them to be organized properly. Explain.

Solution False. You need to establish only the organization settings. As new sheets are created in a project, they are organized according to the settings, assuming the criteria are filled in. Most criteria have to be filled in and managed manually for the organization to take place.

Chapter 3: Worksets and Worksharing

Create a central file by activating worksharing and dividing the model into worksets. Setting up your Revit project file correctly helps users easily visualize and coordinate their systems.

Master It You are working on a project with a mechanical engineer, a plumbing designer, and an electrical engineer. Describe the types of worksets into which the model can be divided to accommodate the different systems for each discipline.

Solution The model can be divided into: HVAC and mechanical piping worksets for mechanical systems; domestic and sanitary water piping worksets for plumbing systems; and lighting and power worksets for electrical systems.

Allow multiple users to work on the same dataset utilizing local files. Revit MEP provides functionality to set up your project in a manner that allows users to edit and manage their systems without conflicting with other systems in the model.

Master It Describe how to create a local file copy of a central file and how to coordinate changes in the local file with other users who are accessing the central file.

Solution Browse to the central file in the Open dialog box and select the Create New Local check box. Alternatively, copy/paste the central file to a new folder, open the pasted file, and click Save.

Use the Synchronize With Central command to coordinate changes made in the local file with the central file.

Work with and manage worksets. Working in a project with multiple users means that you likely will need to coordinate the availability of worksets.

Master It Describe how you would isolate a system in the model so that no other user could make changes to that system. What is the best way to release a system so that others can work on it?

Solution Create a workset for that system, and and place any model elements you have created on that workset. Take ownership of the workset to prevent changes from other users. Use the Relinquish All Mine command to release ownership of the workset, allowing others to have access to the components on that workset.

Control the visibility of worksets. Visualization is one of the most powerful features of a BIM project. Worksets give you the power to control the visibility of entire systems or groups of model components.

Master It You are facing a deadline and need to add some general notes to one of your plumbing sheets. Because of the intricate design of the HVAC system, your project file is very large and takes a long time to open. What can you do to quickly open the file to make your changes?

Solution From the Open dialog box, select the Open drop-down and choose Specify to open only the worksets required to complete the task.

Chapter 4: Project Collaboration

Prepare your project file for sharing with consultants. Taking care to provide a clean, accurate model will aid in achieving an integrated project delivery.

Master It Describe the importance of making worksets visible in all views when your file will be shared with consultants.

Solution If you do not make a workset visible in all views, the model elements on that workset will not be visible to consultants when they link in your file.

Work with linked Revit files. There are many advantages to using linked Revit files in your project. Revit provides many options for the visibility of consultants' files, allowing you to easily coordinate your design.

Master It How would you turn off a model category within a Revit link while allowing that category to remain visible in your model?

Solution Select the Revit Links tab in the Visibility/Graphic Overrides dialog box. Click the By Host View button in the Display Settings column next to the appropriate linked file. Change the display to Custom. Select the appropriate tab within the RVT Link Display Settings dialog box, and turn off the desired category.

Coordinate elements within shared models. Revit can alert you to changes to certain model elements within linked files. Managing these changes when they occur can reduce errors and omissions later in the project and help keep the design team coordinated.

Master It MEP components within a linked file can be copied and/or monitored. True or false: You must have the same family loaded into your file in order to monitor it from a linked file.

Solution False. You can use type mapping to monitor a component with another type that is loaded into your project, as long as they share the same hosting behavior.

Work with files from other applications. Not all of your consultants may use Revit. This does not mean that you cannot use their files to develop and coordinate your design. You can also share your design by exporting your file to a format they can use.

Master It Describe the difference between linking and importing a CAD file and why the linking option is preferred.

Solution When a file is linked, it can be updated by reloading the link. An imported file will not update when the original CAD file is updated. Importing causes unnecessary information from the CAD file to be brought into Revit, which can increase file size and greatly impede file performance.

Set up a system for quality control. As a BIM solution, Revit provides functionality to keep your design coordinated with your consultants.

Master It What functionality exists in Revit that could allow a design reviewer to comment on coordination issues within a project?

Solution Annotation symbols can be created and used throughout the model to comment on design issues. The annotations can be scheduled to organize and manage issues that need to be addressed.

Chapter 5: Multiplatform Interoperability: Working with 2D and 3D Data

Decide which type of data you want to use on a project. Revit 2015 allows the user to import and reuse existing drawings from AutoCAD and other formats.

Master It Having a good command of the tools available for importing other file formats will extend and enhance the integration of Revit with other CAD systems. When importing a 2D file format into Revit, what are the two best ways of ensuring that the data is shown in only one view?

Solution During the import process, ensure that the Current View Only check box is selected, or import the file directly into a legend or drafting view.

Link data consistently and in the correct location. When bringing data into Revit, it is important to be able to define where an object is positioned.

Master It An imported drawing has inaccurately placed or frozen layer objects that make the extents of that file greater than 20 miles (32.2 km). What should you do prior to the import?

Solution Open the file in its native program, and then clean the file before importing to Revit.

Prepare data prior to import. Revit project files should be the easiest to link to your project. However, at times this process can become complicated.

Master It After receiving a Revit Architecture model, you can see that some worksets are causing visibility issues when the file is linked to the Revit MEP model. How can this be solved?

Solution Open the file and click Detach From Central. The next dialog box gives you the option Detach And Discard Worksets. When you choose this option and save this file, it then has no worksets. This option should be used only if you are working remotely, away from the other team members, or if you are working on a frozen model.

Chapter 6: Parameters

Manipulate the properties of parameters. The parameters used to define the properties of elements have properties of their own that define their behavior and how they can be used.

Master It It is important to know when and where parameters can be used for extracting data from a model or project. It is also important to understand how instance and type parameters are used. Describe how the use of instance and type parameters affects the way data is changed in a family.

Solution Type parameters are used to define different family types within a family. Changes to a type parameter affect every instance of the type it's defining. Instance parameters are unique to each instance of an element as it exists in the project. Changes to an instance parameter occur only at the selected instance of a family.

Work with type catalogs. Type catalogs are powerful tools that allow you to load only what you need for a specific project.

Master It Certain families can have multiple family types. If a family has many types, all of them will be loaded into a project when the family is loaded. What can be done to limit the number of family types that are loaded when a family is inserted into a project?

Solution A type catalog can be created to allow for the selection of specific family types when a family is loaded into a project.

Work with shared parameters. Shared parameters are useful because they can be used in schedules and in annotation tags. Shared parameters can be applied directly to families or added as project parameters.

Master It Managing shared parameters is as important as managing your component libraries. Explain the importance of keeping a common shared parameters file for multiuser environments.

Solution Because a shared parameters file is a library of parameters, you want to keep it in just one location to be shared by multiple users. This will prevent the unnecessary duplication of parameters that contain the same type of data.

Use parameters in project files. The use of parameters is not limited to component families. Parameters can be added to any element that makes up a Revit project.

Master It You can add parameters to system families only by creating project parameters. When you create a project parameter, it will be added to all the elements in the chosen category. Explain why managing project parameters is important to using them in schedules within a project.

Solution It is possible to create a project parameter that has the same settings as a parameter that already exists in some of the families being scheduled. This would create confusion as to which parameter should hold the data for the schedule.

Chapter 7: Schedules

Use the tools in Revit MEP 2015 for defining schedules and their behavior. The capabilities of schedules in Revit MEP 2015 can increase your project coordination and the efficiency of your workflow. The ability to track items within a model can help you better understand the makeup of your design.

Master It The information in schedules comes from information stored within the objects of a Revit model. Explain why editing the data of an object in a schedule changes the properties of the object.

Solution Schedule views are just another view of the model objects. So, when you edit an object in a schedule, you are actually editing the properties of that object.

Schedule building components. Scheduling building components is the primary use of the scheduling tools in Revit. Schedules are used on construction documents to provide additional information about components so that drawings do not become too cluttered.

Master It Understanding what information can be used in a schedule is important to setting up a specific component schedule within your Revit project. What types of parameters can be included in a schedule? What types cannot?

Solution Project parameters and shared parameters can be included in a schedule as well as some of those that are inherent in objects. Family parameters cannot be included in schedules.

Create schedules for design and analysis. Scheduling can go beyond counting objects and tracking their information. You can also create schedules that assist in making design decisions by providing organized analytical information.

Master It The information stored in Space objects often comes from their relationship with other objects. Some of the data for analysis needs to be input manually. Explain how using a schedule key can assist in adding data to a Space object.

Solution A schedule key allows you to assign a value to a parameter based on the key value, which ensures consistency throughout the project. Key values can be added to objects via a schedule without having to access the properties of each individual Space object.

Schedule views and sheets for project management. You can schedule not just the components that make up a model but also the views and sheets within your project. Specialized schedules for views and sheets are useful for project management.

Master It A Note Block schedule enables you to list information about annotation families within your project. What are some of the benefits of using a Note Block schedule instead of static text for plan notes?

Solution When a note is removed from the list in a Note Block schedule, all the associated annotation instances are removed from the plan. Notes can easily be renumbered in the Note Block schedule.

Chapter 8: HVAC Cooling and Heating Load Analysis

Prepare your Revit MEP model for analysis. The key element to a successful building performance analysis is the proper accounting of all variables that will influence the results.

Master It Describe the relationship between rooms and spaces—are they the same element? Describe an essential tool that can be created to maintain and track space input data and building construction for a heating and cooling load analysis.

Solution A room is a region that can be occupied within the architectural building model. A space is the design region, based on an architectural room, within the MEP model. Be sure to select the Room Bounding option on your link to ensure that the same elements that define the room boundaries also define the respective space boundaries.

Developing a working Space Properties schedule, either by creating a custom schedule or by modifying an existing one, will enable you to track and modify space properties as needed to account properly for critical properties that affect the space loads.

Perform heating and cooling analysis with Revit MEP 2015. Before a piece of equipment can be sized or duct systems designed, the building heating and cooling performance must be known in order to condition your spaces accurately.

Master It How does project location affect building heating and cooling loads? Describe methods to determine project location in Revit MEP 2015.

What is a sliver space, and how does it affect the building performance?

Solution The location of the project building determines the environmental conditions surrounding the building. Information such as ASHRAE climate zone data determines minimum design conditions to which the building construction must perform. Two methods exist in Revit to determine project location: selecting the design city from a list of default cities within Revit or using an Internet-mapping service and locating the exact coordinates of your design building.

A sliver space is a narrow space in the building bounded on two sides by occupiable interior spaces—pipe chases, HVAC shafts, wall cavities, and so on. The volume of the sliver space is added to the larger of the two adjacent interior spaces when the building's performance is analyzed.

Perform a conceptual energy analysis on your building. Revit MEP 2015 gives you the ability to run an analysis on a project while it is in its conceptual design phase. This allows for quick testing of various options.

Master It What is the purpose of a conceptual energy analysis?

Will increasing the complexity of your concept building model produce the most accurate energy analysis?

Solution A conceptual energy analysis performed in Revit MEP 2015 will allow for a variety of design options to be tested quickly, showing the impact on the energy performance of the building with each change.

Increasing the concept model complexity prior to performing the energy analysis is not always the best practice because a more complex model creates more room for analysis errors and can affect simulation performance. Keeping the concept model as simple as possible will allow the program to run efficiently.

Analyze duct and pipe system pressure with Revit MEP 2015. Pressure loss reports can be easily generated from your model. These can help with important design decisions and can show the differences between design variations.

Master It How is the pressure-loss report a useful addition to Revit MEP?

Solution The pressure-loss reports generated within Revit MEP 2015 will show the pressure loss of each component in a completely modeled and sized duct or pipe system. This enables the user to check the modeled critical path in Revit vs. outside calculations to verify the design, and subsequent reports can be generated to show how a change in the duct system affects the overall critical path pressure.

Export gbXML data to load-simulating software. Often, to complete the building analysis, the Revit MEP model has to be analyzed in greater detail by a third-party simulation program.

Master It What is gbXML? Why is it necessary to export your Revit MEP project?

Solution gbXML is an Extensible Markup Language file that can be written and read by multiple programs. It allows interoperability between building modeling programs and energy-simulating programs.

It is necessary to export the Revit MEP model via the gbXML data format to a third-party simulation program because Revit does not offer the user extensive customization of the spaces, zones, building constructions, or even the heating and cooling systems requirements. It also does not have the capability for energy analysis of the building as required by LEED and other energy-conscious organizations.

Chapter 9: Creating Logical Systems

Create and manage air systems. Knowing how to manage air systems can help productivity by organizing systems so that items can be easily interrogated to verify that the systems are properly connected.

Master It True or false: Outside air cannot be modeled because there is no default system type from which to select.

Solution False. Although there is no default Outside Air system, the system can be created by using Supply Air and renaming the system to Outside Air.

Create and manage piping systems. By understanding how to change and manage piping systems, the user can create and maintain different systems effectively.

Master It A designer has been asked by an engineer to create a Grease Waste system to accommodate a new kitchen that has been added to a project. What would be the quickest way to accomplish this feat?

Solution The designer can easily create a new system called Grease Waste from the Project Browser by duplicating the Sanitary system, applying an abbreviation of GW, creating the necessary filter for the system, and adding all the plumbing components that are required to be on the system.

Configure duct connectors. Everyone who needs to create Revit MEP families should know how to properly configure pipe, duct, conduit, and cable tray connectors in the Family Editor.

Master It In order to proceed with the design, a mechanical engineer needs to create a custom air handling unit family that is not available from the manufacturer. One of the challenges is that he has to configure the duct connectors for supply, return, and outside air. What are the proper settings for those connectors?

Hint: We already mentioned the proper configuration of the supply and return air systems in this chapter. The only oddball here is the outside air. This is the same kind of decision that will have to be made when creating systems such as fuel, medical gas, and so on that do not exist as a system classification in Revit.

Solution Looking at the air handling equipment, the engineer has decided that this equipment is at the very top of the systems for supply air and return air; therefore, these connectors should act as parents. He also understands that the air handling unit itself is not a parent or a child, therefore it is possible for other connectors to act as a child (hydronic return is child to the boiler or any other equipment that may be prior to the boiler in the system tree; outside air is also a child and the outside air fan will be the parent).

Knowing how systems and airflow work in Revit, he configures the connectors the following way:

Supply Air Connector:

Flow Configuration – Calculated
Flow Direction – Out
System Classification – Supply Air

Return Air Connector:

Flow Configuration – Calculated
Flow Direction – In
System Classification – Return Air

Outside Air Connector:

Flow Configuration – Preset
Flow Direction – In
System Classification – Supply Air

Note: Since he is not allowed to create Outside Air System Classification, he should use a System Classification that has similar behavior (Flow Configuration and Flow Direction).

Chapter 10: Mechanical Systems and Ductwork

Distinguish between hosted and level-hosted components. Deciding whether hosted or level-hosted components are used is crucial for the success of your project. This decision will play a large factor in performance and coordination with other companies.

Master It Should you choose hosted or level-hosted components for your project?

Solution A mixture may well be the best solution, but whichever you choose, consistency is the key. If you start with level hosted, stick with that type of component during the life of the project because you will find it difficult to change between hosted and level hosted.

Convert placeholder ducts into ducts with fittings. Using placeholders is a great way to "rough in" a duct layout without having to be too specific. Fittings are not used and the layout is extremely flexible.

Master It When progressing your conceptual design, at what point should you convert placeholder ducts into ducts with fittings?

Solution It is often best to wait to do this for as long as possible. There will always be areas where coordination is crucial in a confined space and 3D objects are the only way forward, but on a project where there are several common or typical layouts, the conversion can be left until later. As a designer, you could also consider discussing with the HVAC contractor whether a single-line model is adequate to produce construction drawings. If the placeholders are based on intended dimensions (and updated when necessary), they can still provide inference checking, even into later design stages.

Use the various duct routing options. When Revit MEP 2015 is used for duct layouts, the user must understand the functions of automatic duct routing and manual duct routing. Once these functions are mastered, the user can lay out any type of ductwork system.

Master It When asked to submit a design proposal for a multifloor office building, the HVAC designer needs to show a typical open-plan office that includes the supply and extract ductwork. How should the designer start this process?

Solution The designer should start by laying out air terminals and, if required, VAV units. Then, the designer should use the Layout Tool to generate an initial duct design.

Adjust duct fittings. Duct fittings are needed in systems to make the systems function properly and to produce documentation for construction. Being able to add or modify fittings can increase productivity.

Master It You have just finished your modeled layout and given it to your employer for review. Your boss asks you to remove a couple of elbows and replace them with tees for future expansion. What method would you use to accomplish this quickly?

Solution Select the elbow and click the + sign; this changes the elbow to a tee.

Chapter 11: Mechanical Piping

Adjust the mechanical pipe settings. Making sure the mechanical piping settings are properly set up is crucial to the beginning of any project.

Master It A designer has just been asked to model a mechanical piping layout, and the engineer wants to make sure the designer will be able to account for the piping material used in the layout. What steps must the designer take to complete this request?

Solution First, the designer must figure out what piping materials are needed. Next, the designer duplicates the piping and associated fittings. Once the piping and fittings have been duplicated and renamed to the piping material as needed, the designer assigns the fittings to the proper pipe types. This ensures that all of the fittings and piping can be accounted for when the piping is routed. In addition, the designer can create schedules (Chapter 7) and produce a list of all pipes and pipe fittings being used for the design.

Select the best pipe routing options for your project. When using Revit MEP 2015 for your mechanical layouts, you must understand the functions of automatic pipe routing and manual pipe routing. After mastering these functions, you can lay out any type of piping system.

Master It The engineer has just come back from a meeting with the owner and architect, and it has been decided that there will be a heated-water system and a chilled-water system rather than a two-pipe hydronic system. How would you modify your hydronic layout to accommodate the change?

Solution First, duplicate your mains. Rather than a two-pipe system (one supply, one return), you will have a four-pipe system (one heated-water supply, one heated-water return, one chilled-water supply, one chilled-water return). The designer will also have to change out the mechanical equipment to add chilled-water coils. Additional chillers and pumps may also be required. Once you have all your equipment added and modified, add the mechanical equipment to the proper systems by changing the hydronic supply systems to heated-water supply, heated-water return, chilled-water supply, and chilled-water return. This will allow the pipes to be filtered properly.

Adjust pipe fittings. Pipe fittings are needed in systems to make the systems function properly and to produce documentation for construction. Being able to add or modify fittings can increase productivity.

Master It You have printed a check set for review and have noticed that there are no shutoff valves. Now you need to load the shutoff family. In what directory should you look for pipe fittings?

Solution You should first look in the imperial library for pipe and then valves. If you have a manufacturer that is creating proper Revit content, its fittings would be the preferred choice. Also, you can refer to Autodesk Seek at `www.seek.autodesk.com`. Check other sites, such as Autodesk User Group International at `http://forums.augi.com/showthread.php?t=99663`, for additional content.

Adjust the visibility of pipes. Being able to adjust the visibility of pipes gives the mechanical designer or user the ability to set up multiple views and control the graphics for documentation.

Master It The engineer has just come back from a meeting with the owner and architect, and it has been decided that there will be a heated-water system and a chilled-water system. You have just modified your hydronic layout to accommodate the change. Now the owner wants the pipes to be color-coded so it's easier to visualize the changes. Describe how this would be done.

Solution First, you will modify your system types' colors and assign the appropriate system abbreviation values; then create filters that match the system abbreviations (remember that the text is case sensitive), and apply the filters to each view. Remember that system types control how systems appear; filters control whether the system appears for a particular view.

Chapter 12: Lighting

Prepare your project for lighting design. The greatest benefit you can receive from a lighting model is coordination with other systems. Properly setting up the project file is key to achieving this coordination.

Master It Describe the relationship between ceilings and engineering spaces. How can you be sure that your engineering spaces are reporting the correct geometry?

Solution Ceilings can be set to define the upper boundaries of Room and Space objects.

The upper limit of a space should be set to the level above the level of the current view to ensure that room-bounding ceilings define the actual height of the space.

Use Revit MEP for lighting analysis. Although the design of electrical systems is usually represented schematically on construction documents, you can use the intelligence within the model to create a design tool that analyzes lighting levels.

Master It What model elements contain the data required to determine proper lighting layout?

Solution Spaces contain data that determines the average estimated illumination within them. Lighting fixtures can use photometric web file information to provide accurate light output from the fixture family.

Compare and evaluate hosting options for lighting fixtures and devices. As a BIM solution, Revit MEP offers multiple options for placing your lighting model elements into your project. These options are in place to accommodate several workflow scenarios.

Master It What is the default hosting option for face-hosted families? Describe the limitations of representing wall-mounted lights with symbols and how they can be shown in a plan view.

Solution The default hosting option for face-hosted families is to place them on a vertical face.

Lighting fixtures cannot maintain the orientation of annotations within the family. In a plan view, wall-mounted fixtures can be represented by the actual graphics of the fixture or by model lines drawn in the fixture family.

Develop site lighting plans. Creating a site lighting plan allows you to coordinate with civil engineering consultants as well as with your architect. These plans are also useful for presentation documents and visual inspection of lighting coverage on the site.

Master It What is the benefit of using nonhosted lighting fixture families for site lighting?

Solution Nonhosted fixture families can be adjusted to match the elevation of the topographic surface, if necessary. Hosted elements do not offer as much control when trying to coordinate with topography.

Chapter 13: Power and Communications

Place power and systems devices into your model. Creating electrical plans that are correct not only in the model but also on construction documents can be achieved with Revit MEP 2015.

Master It Having flexibility in the relationship between model components and the symbols that represent them is important to create an accurate model and construction documents. Is it possible to show a receptacle and its associated symbol in slightly different locations to convey the design intent properly on construction documents? If so, how?

Solution Yes. You can add parameters within the family that allow for an offset of the symbols that represent the model components in a plan view.

Place equipment and connections. Electrical equipment often requires clearance space for access and maintenance. Modeling equipment in your Revit project allows you to coordinate clearance space requirements.

Master It Interference between model components can be detected by finding components that occupy the same space. Explain how you can determine whether an object interferes with the clearance space of an electrical equipment component.

Solution You can build the required clearance spaces into your equipment families or build a separate family to be used for clearance space. You can use interference-checking capabilities in Revit to find interferences with the clearance spaces.

Create distribution systems. Proper set up of distribution systems is the backbone of the intelligence of your electrical design. It helps you track the computable data within your project.

Master It Because your project may contain multiple distribution system types, explain the importance of assigning distribution systems to your electrical equipment and naming your equipment.

True or false: You cannot create a power riser diagram with Revit MEP 2015.

Solution Assigning a distribution system to electrical equipment allows for other items of the same distribution type to be connected to the equipment. Naming equipment makes it easy to locate when connecting elements.

False. A riser diagram can be created using a drafting view with detail lines and annotation symbol families.

Model conduit and cable tray. Large conduit and cable tray runs are a serious coordination issue in building designs. Revit MEP 2015 has tools that allow you to model conduit and cable tray to coordinate with other model components.

Master It Conduit and cable tray can be modeled with two styles. One style uses fittings, and one does not. Does this mean that no fittings need to be assigned to the style that does not use fittings? Explain how this affects the scheduling of the components.

Solution You must assign fitting families to be used by the style without fittings. The fittings must exist in order for the conduit or cable tray to be modeled. Scheduling styles without fittings enables you to report the total length of a run. Scheduling styles with fittings is done to report data about the components that make up a run.

Chapter 14: Circuiting and Panels

Establish settings for circuits and wiring. Proper setup of a project's electrical characteristics is an important part of the workflow when you're creating circuits and wiring. Settings can be stored in your project template and modified on an as-needed basis.

Master It The distribution systems defined in a project make it possible to connect devices and equipment of like voltages. Do you need to have voltage definitions in order to create distribution systems? Why or why not?

Solution Yes, voltages must be defined first to create distribution systems because they are used to establish the line-to-line and line-to-ground values for the system.

Create circuits and wiring for devices and fixtures. Circuits are the systems for electrical design. Wiring can be used to show the connection of devices and fixtures in a schematic fashion.

Master It Circuits can be created for devices or equipment even if they are not assigned to a panel. Circuits can then be represented by wiring shown on construction documents. Give two examples of how you can add a device to a circuit that has already been created.

Solution You can right-click the device connector, select the Add To Circuit option, and then click a device that is on the circuit to which you want to connect.

You can select a device that is part of the circuit and then click the Edit Circuit button on the Electrical Circuits contextual tab. You then click the Add To Circuit button and select the device to be added.

Manage circuits and panels. With the relationship between components and panels established, you can manage the properties of circuits and panels to improve your design performance and efficiency.

Master It While checking the circuits on a panel, you notice that there are only 14 circuits connected, but the panel has 42 poles. How can you reduce the amount of unused space in the panel?

Solution Click the panel and access its instance properties. Change the Max #1 Pole Breakers parameter to a smaller value, or right-click the panel in the Project Browser and select a template that utilizes fewer circuits.

Use schedules for sharing circuit information. Panel schedules can be used on construction documents to convey the load information. Schedules can also be created for use as design tools to help track electrical data.

Master It The information in Revit panel schedules may not meet the requirements of your document or design standards. Describe how you can use the data within your Revit model to provide the required information.

Solution There is much more data contained in electrical circuits and panels than what may be shown in the panel schedules. You can create a schedule of electrical circuits that shows the information you need.

Chapter 15: Plumbing (Domestic, Sanitary, and Other)

Configure plumbing views. Learning the proper way to set up your template will ensure a consistent graphical representation across projects and improve efficiency.

Master It When you are setting up your project/template views, where would you control the linetypes and colors of pipe systems?

Solution You would control them from the system type. The pipe type can be modified by expanding Families ➤ Piping Systems ➤ Piping System. Select the system you need to modify, right-click, and select Type Properties.

Customize out-of-the-box Revit plumbing fixtures for scheduling purposes. Out-of-the-box plumbing fixtures (or any other equipment for that matter) do not have all the necessary parameters to complete a typical plumbing schedule.

Master It What would you need to do in order to create a plumbing fixture schedule?

Solution First, you would add the necessary shared parameters to all plumbing fixture families and then load them in the project and create a schedule. The schedule will be populated from the data in the shared parameters as soon as you start placing plumbing fixtures in the model. If there is no data in the shared parameters, you will be able to enter it in the schedule or from the family's properties.

Adjust the plumbing pipe settings. Pipe settings are crucial to the ability to have Revit MEP model your plumbing layout, the way it will look, and the way it will perform.

Master It Do fitting parameters have to be set up in the system pipe types?

Solution Yes. If you do not set up the fitting parameters properly, you will have mixed materials or fittings that may not be placed automatically when routing piping in your model.

Select the best pipe routing options for your project. When using Revit MEP 2015 for your plumbing layouts, you must understand the functions of automatic pipe routing, manual pipe routing, and sloping pipe. Once you master these functions, you can lay out any type of piping system.

Master It A plumbing designer has just been asked to lay out a sloped plumbing system and has only a day to pipe up a clubhouse. Where should the designer start the pipe route?

Solution The plumbing designer should start from a point of connection outside the building and work inward, from main to branch to fixture.

Adjust pipe fittings. Pipe fittings are needed in systems to make the systems function properly and to produce documentation for construction. Being able to add or modify fittings can increase productivity.

Master It You have just finished your modeled layout and have given it to your employer for review. Your boss asks you to remove a couple of elbows and replace them with tees for future expansion. What would be your method to accomplish this quickly?

Solution Select the elbow and then click the + sign. This will change the elbow to a tee.

Chapter 16: Fire Protection

Place fire-protection equipment. When starting a fire-protection model, placing the equipment can make or break your design. The ability of Revit to verify your layouts early through the coordination of this equipment with other disciplines can set the pace for a successful project.

Master It What method can be used to help speed up production when using a standard fire riser on multiple buildings?

Solution Create a nested family with all the components required on the fire riser.

Create fire-protection systems. Content is one of the most critical aspects when taking on a Revit project. Fittings are the hardest families of all to make; finding some fittings that satisfy your company needs before starting a project is critical!

Master It What are your options for fire-protection fittings?

Solution Revit MEP 2015 comes with some generic fittings that may satisfy your needs. In addition, some manufacturers, such as Victaulic, have produced extensive libraries of fire-protection fittings. And finally, you can create your own or modify those from the library or from a manufacturer.

Route fire-protection piping. Fire-protection piping can be routed by a couple of methods. It can be set up with different materials to help with takeoffs and specifications. Once piping has been routed, it can be coordinated with other disciplines to reduce errors and omissions.

Master It What are some of the methods to deal with fittings that may not be supplied with Revit MEP 2015?

Solution Use existing fittings for spatial restraints and visual coordination only, create your own fitting families, or use manufacturer-supplied content.

Chapter 17: Solid Modeling

Model solids and voids. Being able to model efficiently will decrease the time you spend creating content and give you more time to spend on design decisions. Solid geometry is crucial for the physical coordination of components to achieve a design that will result in fewer changes during construction—when changes are the most expensive.

Master It Several tools are available to create the shapes needed to represent MEP discipline components. Each tool generates an extrusion in a unique way. Describe the difference between a swept blend and a regular sweep.

Solution A swept blend is used when the shape of the extrusion changes from one end to the other. A sweep is an extrusion of a consistent shape along a path.

Orient geometry by using reference planes and lines. Reference planes and lines are the most effective way to define the orientation of solid geometry within a family. Reference planes define how an object will be inserted into a project.

Master It Knowing the resulting orientation of an extrusion prior to creating it will save lots of time by not having to duplicate modeling efforts. Nothing is more frustrating than taking the time to create a solid only to find out that it is in the wrong plane. Describe the process for creating an extrusion that is associated with a custom reference plane.

Solution You first must create a reference plane and give it a unique name. Then, when you choose a form tool, you can set the reference plane that the form will be associated with by using the Set button on the Work Plane panel of the Home tab in the Family Editor.

Ensure the parametric change capability of models. Building solid geometry to represent MEP discipline components is good. Building the geometry with parametric change capabilities is even better.

Master It Solid geometry can be defined by parameters that can change the size or shape of the geometry. Reference planes and lines are an important part of creating parametric behavior. Why?

Solution The dimensional parameters used to define geometry should be assigned to the dimensions associated with reference planes and lines to which the geometry is locked. This allows you to maintain the relationships of multiple solids when parameter values change.

Determine optimal visibility settings for solids. The visibility behavior of solid geometry plays an important part in the creation of consistent and coordinated construction documents.

Master It It is important to know how a family will be used in a project to determine the visibility settings required for the solid geometry in the family. Why is it important to set the Detail Level visibility settings for pipe- and duct-related families?

Solution The pipe and duct system families have specific visibility behavior to show as a single or double line. Your pipe and duct component families should be set with the same visibility settings for consistency on construction documents.

Create in-place Mass objects for analysis and documentation. In-place Mass objects allow the designer to quickly produce a building form at a time when the project architect may not be able to provide a model that is suitable for early analysis purposes.

Master It Using massing tools can speed up the design process. What tools would you use to quickly model glass and windows?

Solution Glazing can be quickly added to the model by using either face-based curtain systems or curtain walls cut into a host wall.

Chapter 18: Creating Symbols and Annotations

Create symbolic lines and filled regions. Not only is Revit MEP 2015 a modeling application, it also contains the tools necessary to accomplish drafting tasks.

Master It Having a good command of the tools available for creating symbols helps you create families that represent your design elements exactly the way you want to see them. What line tool is best suited for duplicating the linework of an imported CAD symbol?

Solution The Pick Lines tool allows you to select the linework of an imported file and create a Revit line to match.

Use symbols within families for representation on drawings. Given the schematic nature of MEP plans, symbols and annotation objects are important parts of your Revit MEP 2015 workflow, allowing you to represent your model components according to your company standards.

Master It By having annotation symbols nested into your component families, you can create an accurate 3D model that is displayed schematically on your construction documents. Explain the importance of creating subcategories for the graphics in your annotation families.

Solution Symbols are created as generic annotations, which is a single category within Revit. A subcategory must be created to control the visibility of a specific symbol independently from the Generic Annotations category.

Work with constraints and parameters for visibility control. The parametric modeling capabilities of Revit 2015 make it a powerful BIM solution. These capabilities can be used in annotation families as well.

Master It A common scenario for a Revit project is to link consultant files into your project file. Because of this, face-hosted families are often used. Face-hosted components can be attached to either a vertical or horizontal host, so the ability to separate the annotation symbol from the host needs to be created in the annotation family.

When using a length parameter to define the offset of a symbol from its host, what value should be input for the parameter when the component family is in a project?

Solution You need to input a length that relates to the actual size of the symbol, because the symbol size in a view is determined by the view scale.

Use labels to create tags. Tags are the most commonly used annotation families in a project. They are used to report information about objects in a Revit model.

Master It The use of labels is much more effective than using text objects for keeping documents coordinated.

If your project requires that you show AFF after each pipe elevation tag on your construction documents, how can you accomplish this globally, throughout your project?

Solution When defining the label in your pipe elevation tag, you can add AFF as a suffix for the label.

Chapter 19: Creating Equipment

Create MEP equipment families. The ability to create the types of equipment families needed for accurate modeling of components and systems is a major factor in the success of your Revit projects.

Master It MEP equipment can be quite complex in its structure. Complex geometry can have an adverse effect on model performance. What are some ways to model equipment in its simplest form yet still convey the proper information on construction documents?

Solution The basic shapes of equipment can be modeled, and symbolic or model lines can be used to represent the actual geometry in plan views. The solid forms used to create the geometry can be set to show only in 3D views. Simple forms can be set to show at lower levels of detail, while more-complex geometry can be reserved for finer detail.

Add connectors to equipment for systems. Adding connectors to equipment families will make them functional for use in the design of engineering systems.

Master It It is important to know how your equipment families will be used in your projects from an engineering standpoint as well as for model coordination. Explain how connectors determine the behavior of an equipment family.

Solution Connectors have properties that define the behavior of the family, depending on the system type of the connector. Duct and pipe connectors determine the direction of flow that may affect how the equipment can be connected in project systems. Electrical connectors determine the distribution systems for which the equipment is used.

Create clearance spaces for equipment. Space for safety and service of equipment is crucial to building design. The ability to coordinate clearances around equipment improves project quality and can reduce construction and design cost.

Master It Equipment families with built-in clearance spaces allow you to determine quickly and easily whether the equipment will fit into your project model. Describe some options for controlling the visibility of clearance spaces so that they are not shown when not needed.

Solution The visibility of clearance space geometry can be controlled by creating a unique subcategory for the geometry or by using Yes/No type parameters to toggle the visibility.

Add parameters to equipment. Parameters in your equipment families can be useful for creating schedules in your Revit projects that report data directly from the equipment used in the design. Family parameters can enable you to make equipment families that are changeable without having to create new families.

Master It Shared parameters must be used in your equipment families if you want to schedule the data they provide. If you are creating parameters for parametric behavior of the solid geometry, do they also need to be shared parameters?

Solution They need to be shared parameters only if they are to be used in a schedule. Family parameters cannot be scheduled.

Chapter 20: Creating Lighting Fixtures

Create different types of lighting fixture families. Many types of lighting fixtures are required for various applications within a building. With Revit MEP, you can create any type of lighting fixture and include any data associated with that fixture.

Master It Knowing how a lighting fixture will be used in a Revit model is important for determining the kind of fixture family to create. True or false: A nonhosted light fixture family cannot be associated to a work plane.

Solution False. You can set the Work Plane-Based option to allow the family to be associated to a plane.

Use a light source in your lighting fixture families. Lighting fixtures can be used in making design decisions because they not only represent the fixture as a model, they also contain photometric data from real-world lighting fixtures for use in lighting analysis.

Master It Photometric web files can be obtained from lighting fixture manufacturers. These files provide the lighting distribution characteristics of a fixture when added to a family. How can you be sure that the IES file you are using is appropriate for the type of fixture in which it is being used?

Solution The information in an IES file obtained from a manufacturer can be viewed using third-party software. Files should be renamed to indicate the type of fixture for which they are used.

Create and manage fixture types and parameters. The parameters of a lighting fixture family are what make it an intelligent object. They can be used to create multiple types within the same family or to manage the electrical characteristics of a fixture.

Master It Connectors are what determine the electrical properties of a lighting fixture family. Describe the process of ensuring that a connector has the same load and voltage values that have been assigned to the fixture.

Solution The load and voltage values of a connector can be associated with the load and voltage of a fixture by accessing the instance properties of the connector and using the box in each parameter value to associate it with the appropriate family parameter.

Use lines and symbols to represent lighting fixtures. Some lighting fixtures are shown on construction documents as symbols, while others are shown as their actual size. Symbolic lines or annotation symbols can be used to eliminate the need to display model graphics.

Master It Annotation symbols nested into lighting fixture families can represent the fixture without having to show the model graphics. Is it possible to use a nested annotation family to represent a wall-mounted fixture in a face-hosted lighting fixture family? Explain.

Solution Yes. An annotation family can be nested into an intermediate, shared, face-hosted family that can be nested into a fixture family.

Chapter 21: Creating Devices

Select a family template. An important step when creating a device (or any family, for that matter) is the selection of the family template.

Master It Stephanie has been assigned to create a new line of receptacles that matches her company display standards and takes their functionality to the next level. What family template would be most appropriate for receptacles?

Solution The most appropriate selection would be the generic, face-based family template. This template allows Stephanie to predefine default placement of elevation; in addition, the receptacles will follow the plane of the host (wall, ceiling, floor) when the architect moves those hosting elements, and it will be versatile in that it can be placed on any surface within the MEP model, including Revit linked files.

Model device geometry. The 3D geometry of a device family may not be its most important component, but there are things you can do to make the geometry useful for project coordination and accuracy.

Master It Device families are commonly face hosted because of the way they are used in a project model. Describe why a device family that is hosted by a floor in a project may not appear correctly in a plan view.

Solution If the geometry of the device family is flush with the host extrusion and the bottom of the view range is set to the face of the floor, the device family will not appear in a plan view when hosted by a floor.

Use annotations to represent devices. Because of their size and simple shapes, device families are not typically shown on construction documents. Instead, a symbol is used to represent the device. Annotation families can be nested into device families for display in project views.

Master It The orientation of an annotation family nested into a device family is important for proper display in project views. What is the device family parameter that allows for the display of the annotation in plan and section views? What hosting options in a project allow this parameter to work?

Solution The Maintain Annotation Orientation parameter allows nested annotation families to be visible in plan and section views. The parameter displays the annotation when the device family is hosted to a vertical or horizontal surface.

Add parameters and connectors. The connectors used in device families provide the engineering characteristics of the device so that it can be incorporated into systems within a project.

Master It You cannot edit the parameters of a connector while working in a project file. Describe how you can change the properties of a connector without having to edit the device family.

Solution The parameters of a connector in a device family can be associated with the device family parameters. The properties of a device can be modified directly in a project, thereby updating the connector properties.

Chapter 22: Details

Use Revit drafting and detailing tools efficiently. Revit MEP 2015 has many tools for creating the details and diagrams needed to enhance your model and provide the necessary level of information for your projects.

Master It Although the drafting tools in Revit MEP 2015 may be unfamiliar at first, learning to use them efficiently and effectively helps you spend more time focusing on design decisions instead of drafting efforts. Describe how filled regions can be used not only to display a pattern but also to provide line information in a detail.

Solution The line styles used for the borders of a filled region can convey information about the detail while enabling you to avoid overlapping other lines and regions.

Use CAD details in Revit projects. Much of the detail information used in your projects may already exist in another format. When you transition to Revit, you can still use your CAD details.

Master It Using CAD details in a Revit project can be a quick way to complete your construction documents in a timely manner. However, using many CAD files for details can have a negative effect on file performance, so it is important to link CAD files whenever they are used. Explain why importing and exploding CAD files can adversely affect your project.

Solution Exploded CAD files cause many text and line styles to be created, among other things like object styles, rendering materials, line patterns, and dimension and text styles. These styles are unnecessary and could be used by mistake instead of the standard styles developed specifically for Revit projects.

Build a Revit detail library. Having a library of details saves time on projects because you don't have to draw details that have already been created.

Master It Drafting views can be saved as individual files for use on projects as needed. True or false: A drafting view will be added to your project when you use the Insert 2D Graphics From View option of the Insert From File tool. Explain.

Solution False. When you use this option, only the graphics drawn in the selected view are placed into a view in your project.

Create detail views of your Revit model. Some details require the model to be shown in order to show installation or placement of objects.

Master It Callout views can be created from plan, section, and elevation views. Explain how detail views are different from drafting views.

Solution Detail views show a portion of the actual model within the callout border. You cannot show or see the actual model graphics in a drafting view.

Chapter 23: Sheets

Create a titleblock. A titleblock can be the signature for your projects. Its design and layout can be an immediate indicator of who has created the construction documents. A titleblock is also important for conveying general project and specific sheet information.

Master It To ensure that your Revit projects look the same as, or similar to, your other projects, it is necessary to have a titleblock family that looks the same as other file format titleblocks you use. Describe the process for creating a Revit titleblock family from an existing CAD format titleblock.

Solution The CAD titleblock can be imported into a new Revit titleblock family. The drafting tools can be used to create Revit lines that match the CAD lines. Labels and text can be placed in the same locations as CAD text and attributes.

Establish sheets in your project. The sheets that make up your construction documents can be organized in your Revit projects for easy access and for management of project information.

Master It A Sheet List schedule is a useful tool for managing the information shown on your construction documents as well as for organizing the order of sheets for your project. Is it possible to create parameters for sheets that can be used in the sheet list? Explain.

Solution Yes, custom parameters can be created for use in a sheet list. These parameters can be shared parameters or project parameters.

Place views on sheets. For a Revit project, the construction documents are created as a result of the model, whereas in traditional CAD environments, the sheets are the main focus. You can put your construction documents together by placing the views you have created onto your sheets.

Master It Uniformity among sheets in a document set is important not only to the look of a project but also for ease in document navigation. Explain how guide grids can be used to place model views in the same location on individual sheets.

Solution Guide grids can be established so that column grids in the model views can be snapped to the same location on each sheet.

Print and export sheets. Although we live in a digital age, the need to print sheets and views is still part of our daily workflow. With the ability to work with consultants from all over the world, the need to share digital information is crucial. Exporting sheets and views to a file format that can be easily shared increases our ability to collaborate with consultants.

Master It Printing sheets is often necessary for quality control of a project. How can you keep section and elevation marks of views that are not used on your sheets from printing?

Solution The Options area of the Print dialog box has check boxes for hiding unwanted graphics and view tags.

Index

Note to the Reader: Throughout this index **boldfaced** page numbers indicate primary discussions of a topic. *Italicized* page numbers indicate illustrations.

B

C

D

E

H

I

M

N

O

P

Q

R

S

U

V

X

Y

Z